Canadian

Business

and the Law

Third Edition

Canadian
Business
and the Law

Dorothy DuPlessis
University of New Brunswick

Steven Enman
Acadia University

Shannon O'Byrne
University of Alberta

Sally Gunz
University of Waterloo

THOMSON
NELSON

Australia   Canada   Mexico   Singapore   Spain   United Kingdom   United States

**Canadian Business and the Law,
Third Edition**

by Dorothy DuPlessis, Steven Enman,
Shannon O'Byrne, and Sally Gunz

**Associate Vice President,
Editorial Director:**
Evelyn Veitch

Publisher:
Veronica Visentin

Acquisitions Editor:
Shannon White

Marketing Manager:
Kathaleen McCormick

Developmental Editor:
Tracy Yan

**Photo Researcher/Permissions
Coordinator:**
Donna Dudinsky

Production Service:
GEX Publishing Services

Copy Editor:
Karen Rolfe

Proofreader:
GEX Publishing Services

Indexer:
GEX Publishing Services

Manufacturing Coordinator:
Ferial Suleman

Design Director:
Ken Phipps

Interior Design:
Sarah Battersby

Cover Design:
Will Bache

Cover Image:
Stephen Swintek/Stone/Getty
Images

Compositor:
GEX Publishing Services

Printer:
RR Donnelley

Library and Archives Canada
Cataloguing in Publication

Canadian business and the law /
Dorothy DuPlessis ... [et al.]. -
3rd ed.

First ed. published under title:
Canadian business & the law.
Includes bibliographical references
and index.
ISBN 978-0-17-625267-0

1. Commercial law—Canada.

KE919.C36 2007   346.7107
C2007-900807-0
KF889.C36 2007

This book provides legal information of interest to those studying business law. It neither offers nor
contains legal advice of any kind. If you have a personal legal question that requires legal advice, please
consult a lawyer.

About the Authors

Dorothy Roberta Ruth DuPlessis, B. Com. (Dalhousie University), LL.B. (Dalhousie University), M.B.A. (Dalhousie University), LL.M. (University of London), is a professor in the Faculty of Business Administration, University of New Brunswick (Fredericton). She is also a member of the Nova Scotia Barristers' Society. Professor DuPlessis has taught courses in business law, administrative law, international law, and Internet law at both the undergraduate and graduate levels. She has also lectured at the Czech Management School and at the Institute of Professional Management. Professor DuPlessis has published articles on auditor's and director's liability, copyright, and university administration. She is also the law examiner for the Certified General Accountants Association of Canada.

Steven Enman, B.B.A. (Acadia University), LL.B. (Dalhousie University), LL.M. (Bristol University), is an associate professor in the Fred C. Manning School of Business Administration, Acadia University, and a former director of the school. He has taught Business Law at Acadia since 1979. He was admitted to the bar of Nova Scotia in 1978 and is a member of the Nova Scotia Barristers' Society and the Canadian Bar Association. Professor Enman is a member of the Academy of Legal Studies in Business. He is the editor of two editions of *Canadian Business Law Cases*. He has presented papers at conferences dealing with privacy, unconscionable contracts, and commercial morality.

Shannon Kathleen O'Byrne, B.A. (University of Regina), M.A., LL.B., LL.M. (University of Alberta), is a professor in the Faculty of Law, University of Alberta, and a former Associate Dean of Graduate Studies and Research. She was admitted to the Law Society of Alberta in 1987 and is a past member of the Board of Directors of the Edmonton Bar Association. She is the recipient of the University of Alberta's highest teaching honour, the Rutherford Award for Excellence in Undergraduate Teaching, as well as the Faculty of Law's Teaching Excellence Award, named after the Hon. Mr. Justice Tevie Miller.

Professor O'Byrne's articles have been cited with approval by courts across the country, including the Supreme Court of Canada. She has delivered papers at academic conferences in Canada, Japan, Ireland, and the United States. Professor O'Byrne has also had the honour of presenting at National Judicial Institute conferences as well as to numerous professional organizations including the Canadian Bar Association.

Contents

Preface xv
Table of Cases xx
Table of Statutes xxix

Part 1 The Legal Environment of Business 1

Chapter 1 Knowledge of Law as a Business Asset 2

Business Law in Practice 3
Law in the Business Environment 4
   Rules and Principles 4
How and Why the Law Works 9
   Knowledge of the Law as a Business Asset . . . 11
Law and Business Ethics 11
Business Law in Practice Revisited 14
Chapter Summary 15
   Key Terms and Concepts 16
   Questions for Review 16
   Questions for Critical Thinking 16
   Situations for Discussion 17

Chapter 2 The Canadian Legal System 19

Business Law in Practice 20
Introduction 21
The Canadian Constitution 22
The Legislative Branch of Government 23
   Statute Law and Jurisdiction 23
The Executive Branch of Government 28
The Judicial Branch of Government 29
   The System of Courts 29
   The *Canadian Charter of Rights and Freedoms* . . 30
Sources of Law 36
Classifications of Law 37
   Domestic versus International Law 37
   Substantive versus Procedural Law 37
   Public versus Private Law 38
   Common Law versus Civil Law 38

Administrative Law and Business 39
Business Law in Practice Revisited 41
Chapter Summary 42
   Key Terms and Concepts 44
   Questions for Review 44
   Questions for Critical Thinking 45
   Situations for Discussion 46

Chapter 3 Managing Legal Risks 48

Business Law in Practice 49
Assessing the Legal Environment 49
   Legal Risk Management Plan 50
Applying the Four-Step Process 50
   Identify the Legal Risks 50
   Assess Functional Areas 51
   Review Business Decisions 51
   Examine Business Relationships 52
   Evaluate the Risks 52
   Devise a Risk Management Plan 54
   Implement the Plan 57
Interacting with the Legal Environment 62
   Reacting When Prevention Fails 62
   Managing Legal Services 63
Business Law in Practice Revisited 65
Chapter Summary 66
   Key Terms and Concepts 67
   Questions for Review 67
   Questions for Critical Thinking 68
   Situations for Discussion 68

Chapter 4 Dispute Resolution 70

Business Law in Practice 71
Introduction 71
Business Activities and Legal Disputes 72
   The "Slip and Fall" 72
   The Bylaw Change 72
   The Delinquent Customer 73
   The Dissatisfied Customer 73

The Damaged Goods 73
The Problem Employee 74
The Motor Vehicle Accident 74
Resolving Disputes through Negotiation 74
Clarification of the Situation 74
The Negotiation Process 75
The Dissatisfied Customer 75
The Damaged Goods 76
The Problem Employee 76
When Negotiations Fail 76
Alternative Dispute Resolution 78
How ADR Works 78
ADR Sources 80
The Litigation Process 82
Stages of a Lawsuit 84
Enforcement 88
Appeals 88
Business Law in Practice Revisited 91
Chapter Summary 92
Key Terms and Concepts 93
Questions for Review 93
Questions for Critical Thinking 94
Situations for Discussion 95

Part 2 Contracts   97

**Chapter 5 An Introduction to
                Contracts   98**
Business Law in Practice 99
Introduction to Contract Law 99
Legal Factors in Their Business Context:
Creating the Contract 102
Communication 102
Bargaining Power 104
Legal Factors in Their Business Context:
Performing or Enforcing the Contract 105
Business Relationships 105
Economic Reality 106
Reputation Management 106
Business Law in Practice Revisited 107
Chapter Summary 108
Key Terms and Concepts 109
Questions for Review 109
Questions for Critical Thinking 109
Situations for Discussion 109

**Chapter 6 Forming Contractual
                Relationships   111**
Business Law in Practice 112
The Contract 112
An Agreement 113

Offer 113
Definition of Offer 113
Certainty of Offer 113
Invitation to Treat 113
Termination of Offer 116
Acceptance 120
Definition of Acceptance 120
Communication of Acceptance 120
Formalization 127
Consideration 127
The Nature of Consideration 127
Pre-existing Legal Duty 128
Variation of Contracts 129
Promises Enforceable without Consideration . . 129
Promise under Seal 129
Promissory Estoppel 130
Partial Payment of a Debt 131
Intention to Contract 132
Business Agreements 132
Family Agreements 133
Managing the Risks in Contract Formation . . . 133
Business Law in Practice Revisited 133
Chapter Summary 134
Key Terms and Concepts 135
Questions for Review 135
Questions for Critical Thinking 136
Situations for Discussion 136

Chapter 7 The Terms of a Contract   139
Business Law in Practice 140
The Content of a Contract 141
Terms 141
The Parol Evidence Rule 147
Using Contractual Terms to Manage Risk 150
Changed Circumstances 150
Conditional Agreements 151
Limitation of Liability Clause 153
Exemption Clause (or Exclusion Clause) . . . 154
Liquidated Damages Clause 158
Business Law in Practice Revisited 158
Chapter Summary 160
Key Terms and Concepts 161
Questions for Review 161
Questions for Critical Thinking 162
Situations for Discussion 162

**Chapter 8 Non-enforcement
                of Contracts   165**
Business Law in Practice 166
The Importance of Enforcing Contracts 167
Contracts Based on Unequal Relationships 168

Legal Capacity. 168
   Minors 168
   Mental Incapacity 169
   Duress. 170
   Undue Influence. 170
   Unconscionability 172
Misrepresentations and Important Mistakes. . . . 175
   Misrepresentation of Relevant Facts 175
   Mistake. 178
Contracts Based on Defects 181
   Illegality 181
   Writing as a Requirement 183
Managing the Risks of Unenforceability. 187
Business Law in Practice Revisited. 187
Chapter Summary. 188
   Key Terms and Concepts 189
   Questions for Review 189
   Questions for Critical Thinking 190
   Situations for Discussion 190

Chapter 9   Termination and Enforcement of Contracts   193

Business Law in Practice 194
Termination of Contracts: An Overview. 195
Termination through Performance 195
   Performance by Others 196
Termination by Agreement 196
   By Agreement between Parties. 196
   Transfer of Contractual Rights. 197
Termination by Frustration 198
Enforcement of Contracts 200
   Privity of Contract 201
   Statutory Modifications of the Doctrine. . . . 202
   Breach of Contract 203
Managing Risk 212
Business Law in Practice Revisited. 212
Chapter Summary. 213
   Key Terms and Concepts 215
   Questions for Review 215
   Questions for Critical Thinking 216
   Situations for Discussion 216

Part 3   Business Torts   219

Chapter 10 Introduction to Tort Law   220

Business Law in Practice 221
Defining Tort Law 221
How Torts Are Categorized 224
Tort Law and Criminal Law. 225
   Purposes of the Actions 225
   Commencing the Actions 225
   Proving the Actions 226

Liability in Tort 227
   Primary and Vicarious Liability 227
   Liability and Joint Tort-Feasors 229
   Liability and Contributory Negligence. 230
Damages in Tort 231
   The Purpose of Damages. 231
   Pecuniary and Nonpecuniary Damages 231
   Punitive or Exemplary Damages. 233
   Aggravated Damages 233
Tort Law and Contract 234
Managing Tort Risk. 234
Business Law in Practice Revisited. 235
Chapter Summary. 235
   Key Terms and Concepts 237
   Questions for Review 237
   Questions for Critical Thinking 238
   Situations for Discussion 238

Chapter 11 The Tort of Negligence   240

Business Law in Practice 241
The Law of Negligence. 241
   What Is Negligence? 241
Defences to a Negligence Action 248
   Contributory Negligence. 248
   Voluntary Assumption of Risk 248
Negligent Misstatement (or Negligent
   Misrepresentation) 249
   Negligence and Product Liability 251
   Negligence and the Service of Alcohol. . . . 252
The Negligence Standard versus
   Strict Liability 256
Business Law in Practice Revisited. 257
Chapter Summary. 258
   Key Terms and Concepts 260
   Questions for Review 260
   Questions for Critical Thinking 261
   Situations for Discussion 262

Chapter 12 Other Torts   265

Business Law in Practice 266
Introduction 266
Torts and Property Use 267
   Occupiers' Liability 267
   The Tort of Nuisance 271
   Trespass to Property. 273
Torts from Business Operations 274
   Torts Involving Customers. 274
   Business to Business Torts. 276
Managing the Risk of Diverse
   Commercial Torts 282
Business Law in Practice Revisited 283

Chapter Summary. 284
   Key Terms and Concepts 285
   Questions for Review 285
   Questions for Critical Thinking 286
   Situations for Discussion 287

Part 4 Structuring Business Activity   289

Chapter 13 The Agency Relationship   290

Business Law in Practice 291
The Nature of Agency. 291
   Agency Defined 292
Creation of Agency 293
   Agency by Agreement 293
   The Concept of Authority 294
   Agency by Estoppel. 297
   Agency by Ratification 300
Duties in the Agency Relationship 301
   Duties of the Agent 301
   Duties of the Principal. 305
Contract Liability in the Agency Relationship. . 305
   Liability of the Principal to the Outsider . . . 305
   Liability of the Agent to the Outsider. 306
   Liability of an Undisclosed Principal 306
   Liability of the Agent to the Principal 307
Tort Liability in the Agency Relationship 307
Termination of Agency Agreements 309
Business Law in Practice Revisited 310
Chapter Summary. 310
   Key Terms and Concepts 312
   Questions for Review 312
   Questions for Critical Thinking 313
   Situations for Discussion 313

Chapter 14 Business Forms and Arrangements   316

Business Law in Practice 317
Forms of Business Organization 317
   The Sole Proprietorship. 317
   The Partnership. 320
   Partnership Variations. 330
   The Corporation. 332
   Business Arrangements. 336
   The Franchise 336
   Joint Venture 340
   Strategic Alliance 340
   Distributorship or Dealership. 341
   Sales Agency 341
   Product Licensing 341

Business Law in Practice Revisited. 342
Chapter Summary. 342
   Key Terms and Concepts 344
   Questions for Review 344
   Questions for Critical Thinking 345
   Situations for Discussion 345

Chapter 15 The Corporate Form: Organizational Matters   348

Business Law in Practice 349
The Corporation Defined 349
Stakeholders in the Corporation. 351
   Pre-Incorporation Issues 351
   Provincial and Federal Incorporation 352
   Shares and Shareholders. 352
   A Corporate Name 356
The Process of Incorporation 358
Organizing the Corporation. 358
Financing the Corporation. 360
   Debt Financing. 360
   Equity Financing. 360
   Securities Legislation 362
Business Law in Practice Revisited 366
Chapter Summary. 367
   Key Terms and Concepts 368
   Questions for Review 368
   Questions for Critical Thinking 369
   Situations for Discussion 369

Chapter 16 The Corporate Form: Operational Matters   372

Business Law in Practice 373
Corporate Liability 373
   Liability in Tort 374
   Liability in Contract 374
   Criminal and Regulatory Liability 375
Directors and Officers 378
   Duties of Directors and Officers. 378
   Liabilities of Directors and Officers 384
   Avoiding Liability 387
Shareholders and Creditors 388
   Shareholders 388
   Creditor Protection 397
Termination of the Corporation. 398
Business Law in Practice Revisited 398
Chapter Summary. 399
   Key Terms and Concepts 400
   Questions for Review 400
   Questions for Critical Thinking 400
   Situations for Discussion 401

Part 5 Property   403

Chapter 17 Personal Property   404

Business Law in Practice 405
The Context of Personal Property 405
   Description 405
   Acquisition of Ownership 406
   Possession without Ownership 406
   Obligations Arising from Ownership
      and Possession 407
   Rights Arising from Ownership
      and Possession 407
   Personal Property Issues 408
Principles of Bailment 409
   Overview 409
   The Contract of Bailment 411
   Liability of Bailees 412
   Liability of Bailors 413
   Remedies 414
Types of Bailment for Reward 416
   The Lease 416
   Storage 417
   Repairs 418
   Transportation 419
   Lodging 419
Risk Management 421
Business Law in Practice Revisited 421
Chapter Summary 422
   Key Terms and Concepts 423
   Questions for Review 423
   Questions for Critical Thinking 424
   Situations for Discussion 424

Chapter 18 Intellectual Property   426

Business Law in Practice 427
Introduction 427
Creation of Intellectual Property Rights 428
   Patents 428
   Industrial Designs 434
   Trademarks 435
   Copyright 441
   Confidential Business Information 446
Acquisition and Protection of Intellectual
     Property 450
   Assignments and Licences 450
   Protection of Intellectual Property 451
Business Law in Practice Revisited 453
Chapter Summary 454
   Key Terms and Concepts 455
   Questions for Review 455

   Questions for Critical Thinking 456
   Situations for Discussion 456

Chapter 19 Real Property   458

Business Law in Practice 459
Ownership 459
   Interests in Land 460
   Limits on Ownership 461
   Registration of Ownership 462
Acquisition of Ownership 464
   The Purchasing Transaction 464
   Participants in the Transaction 465
   Stages in the Transaction 466
   Incomplete Transactions 471
The Real Estate Mortgage 472
   How a Mortgage Works 472
   Terms of the Mortgage 473
   Life of a Mortgage 474
   Mortgagee's Remedies 475
The Real Estate Lease 476
   The Landlord–Tenant Relationship 476
   Terms of the Lease 477
   Rights and Obligations 478
   Termination of the Lease 480
Disposition of Property 480
Risk Management 481
Business Law in Practice Revisited 481
Chapter Summary 482
   Key Terms and Concepts 483
   Questions for Review 483
   Questions for Critical Thinking 484
   Situations for Discussion 484

Part 6 Employment and
Professional Relationships   487

Chapter 20 The Employment
Relationship   488

Business Law in Practice 489
Employment Law 489
The Employment Relationship 490
   Employee versus Independent Contractor . . . 490
   Implications of an Employment
      Relationship 491
Risks in Hiring 492
   Vicarious Liability 492
   Negligent Hiring 493
The Hiring Process 493
   Human Rights Requirements 493
   Employment Equity 498

Formation of the Employment Contract...... 498
   Offer of Employment 499
The Employment Contract 501
   Express and Implied Terms............ 501
   Content of the Contract 501
Terms and Conditions 502
   Employee Welfare Issues............. 502
   Workplace Discrimination 505
   Workplace Privacy.................. 509
The Union Context 512
Business Law in Practice Revisited......... 512
Chapter Summary..................... 513
   Key Terms and Concepts 514
   Questions for Review 514
   Questions for Critical Thinking 515
   Situations for Discussion 516

Chapter 21 Terminating the Employment Relationship   518

Business Law in Practice 519
Ending the Relationship 519
Dismissals for Just Cause 520
   Serious Misconduct................. 521
   Habitual Neglect of Duty 522
   Incompetence..................... 522
   Conduct Incompatible................ 522
   Willful Disobedience................ 522
   Other Causes 523
   Non-Cause and Near Cause 524
   Risks in Just Cause Dismissals 524
Dismissal with Notice 525
   Reasonable Notice Periods 525
   Developments in Notice 526
   Risks in Dismissal with Notice 527
Constructive Dismissal................. 527
   Fundamental Changes 528
   "Bad" Behaviour................... 529
   Risks in Constructive Dismissal 529
Wrongful Dismissal Suit................ 530
   Manner of Dismissal 532
   Wrongful Dismissal Damages.......... 532
Termination Settlements 535
   Negotiation of the Settlement 536
   The Release 536
The Union Context 536
   Grievance and Arbitration 536
   Seniority........................ 537
   Discipline and Discharge 537
Business Law in Practice Revisited......... 537

Chapter Summary 538
   Key Terms and Concepts 539
   Questions for Review 539
   Questions for Critical Thinking 540
   Situations for Discussion 540

Chapter 22 Professional Services   543

Business Law in Practice 544
Businesses and Professional Services 544
   Relationships and Obligations 545
   Ethical Obligations 545
   Hiring Professionals In-House 545
Responsibilities of Professionals to Clients
   and Others Who Rely on Their Work 546
   Responsibilities in Contract............ 546
   Fiduciary Responsibilities 547
   Responsibilities in Tort 550
Professionals' Risk Management Practices..... 554
   Professional Service Contracts 554
   Incorporation and Limited Liability
     Partnerships 554
   Insurance 554
Governance Structures of Professions 555
   Legislation 555
   Professional Practice 555
   Disciplining Professionals............. 556
Business Law in Practice Revisited......... 558
Chapter Summary..................... 559
   Key Terms and Concepts 560
   Questions for Review 560
   Questions for Critical Thinking 561
   Situations for Discussion 562

Part 7 Sales and Marketing   565

Chapter 23 Sales and Marketing: The Contract, Product, and Promotion   566

Business Law in Practice 567
What Is Marketing Law? 567
Contract of Sale 568
   Terms Relating to the Product.......... 568
   Sale of Goods Legislation in Canada....... 568
   Consumer Protection Legislation 571
   Transfer of Title.................. 574
   Delivery of Goods................. 577
The Product 578
   Basic Principles................... 578
   Design and Manufacture 579

Packaging and Labelling. 580
Product Warnings 581
Promotion. 582
Industry Standards and Legislation 582
Misleading Advertising 582
Performance Claims 585
Tests and Testimonials 586
Promotion through Selling Practices. 587
Business Law in Practice Revisited. 587
Chapter Summary. 588
Key Terms and Concepts 590
Questions for Review 590
Questions for Critical Thinking 591
Situations for Discussion 591

Chapter 24 Sales and Marketing: Price, Distribution, and Risk Management   594

Business Law in Practice 595
Price. 595
Pricing Practices between Producer and
Commercial Purchaser. 596
Pricing Practices between Seller and
Consumer. 600
Distribution (Place) 603
Organizational Structure 603
Discriminatory Distribution Practices 604
Direct Marketing. 605
Risk Management in Marketing. 608
Business Law in Practice Revisited. 611
Chapter Summary. 611
Key Terms and Concepts 613
Questions for Review 613
Questions for Critical Thinking 614
Situations for Discussion 614

Part 8 Financing the Business   617

Chapter 25 Business and Banking   618

Business Law in Practice 619
The Banking Relationship. 620
Regulation of Banks 620
The Bank–Customer Agreement 620
Duties of the Bank and the Customer 621
The Bank–Customer Relationship. 622
Negotiable Instruments 623
Implications of Creating a Cheque. 625
Implications of Accepting a Cheque. 627
Electronic Banking 629
Methods of Payment 633

Business Law in Practice Revisited. 633
Chapter Summary. 634
Key Terms and Concepts 635
Questions for Review 635
Questions for Critical Thinking 636
Situations for Discussion 636

Chapter 26 The Legal Aspects of Credit   639

Business Law in Practice 640
Overview of Credit. 640
Regulation of Credit 642
The Credit Agreement. 646
Security 647
Priority among Creditors. 649
Remedies 650
Lenders' Remedies 650
Limits on Lenders' Remedies. 651
Borrowers' Remedies. 652
Personal Guarantees. 653
The Guarantee Agreement. 654
Avoiding Guarantor Obligations. 655
Business Law in Practice Revisited. 657
Chapter Summary. 658
Key Terms and Concepts 659
Questions for Review 659
Questions for Critical Thinking 660
Situations for Discussion 660

Chapter 27 Bankruptcy and Insolvency   663

Business Law in Practice 664
Business Failure 664
Debtor Options 665
Informal Steps. 665
Proceedings before Bankruptcy 665
Bankruptcy. 668
Creditor Options 668
Action Taken by Secured Creditors against
Specific Assets 669
Petitioning the Debtor into Bankruptcy. . . . 669
Bankruptcy 670
Administration of Bankruptcy 670
Identification of Debts. 673
Distribution to Creditors 674
Discharge 676
Personal Bankruptcy 676
Bankruptcy Offences 677
Managing Legal Risks in Financing a Business . 678
Business Law in Practice Revisited. 678
Chapter Summary. 679
Key Terms and Concepts 680

Questions for Review 680
Questions for Critical Thinking 681
Situations for Discussion 681

Part 9 Transference of Risk   685

Chapter 28 Insurance   686

Business Law in Practice 687
Introduction 687
The Insurance Contract 688
  Duty to Disclose 688
  Insurable Interest 691
  Indemnity 692
  Subrogation 692
The Policy 693
Insurance Products 694
  Auto Insurance 695
  Occupiers' Liability Insurance 699
  Comprehensive General Liability Insurance . 699

Errors and Omissions Insurance 700
Property Insurance 701
Business Interruption Loss Insurance 702
Environmental Impairment Insurance 703
Key-Person Life Insurance 703
Remedies of the Insured 703
  Against the Broker 703
  Against the Insurance Company 704
Business Law in Practice Revisited 706
Chapter Summary 706
  Key Terms and Concepts 708
  Questions for Review 708
  Questions for Critical Thinking 709
  Situations for Discussion 709

Glossary 712
Copyright Acknowledgments 722
Index 723

Preface

In *Canadian Business and the Law*, Third Edition, legal knowledge is regarded as a business asset that builds competitive advantage for the individual and the organization alike. This text demonstrates how the law can protect persons and their property as well as resolve disputes. The text also shows that the law facilitates personal and commercial interactions. In short, the law provides both opportunities to be capitalized on and risks to be managed.

Canadian Business and the Law is written from the perspective that the law plays an integral role in all business decisions. Furthermore, it systematically advocates a risk management approach as the optimum way of dealing with legal considerations in the business world. A risk management model is introduced in Part 1 and applied in every subsequent part of the book. Topical coverage is organized as follows:

- Part 1 establishes the rationale for students' study of business law. It accounts for what the law is, where it comes from, and how the law regulates business. It also establishes risk management as the recurring theme of the book and the study of business law.

- Parts 2 and 3 recognize that the legal issues a businessperson is most likely to face are in the areas of contract law and tort law. Part 2, Contracts, and Part 3, Business Torts, provide a practical and contextualized analysis of these important areas. Here students acquire not only an essential legal grounding in contract and tort principles, but also the basic background for the specialized topics discussed later in the book. These two essential parts of the book are carefully written so that Contracts and Torts can be read and taught in whichever sequence is preferable to the user.

The fundamentals of contract law are examined in depth in Part 2 to allow for application in context in later parts, which deal with topics such as agency, partnership, employment, and insurance. By applying the law to particular relationships, students gain insight into the kinds of contracts that will figure prominently in their professional lives.

In our experience, students best understand the law when it is related to core subject areas in the business curriculum, including finance, human resources, sales, and marketing. For this reason, the remaining parts of the book look at the functional areas of business and consider legal issues in relation to those activities:

- Part 4 concerns the selection and use of the form of business.
- Part 5 examines the creation, acquisition, use, and protection of property.
- Part 6 analyzes the acquisition and use of human resources.
- Part 7 focuses on the selling and marketing of goods and services.

- Part 8 addresses financing the business activity.
- Part 9 explores the transference of risk through the use of insurance.

Our work in *Canadian Business and the Law* focuses on meeting a number of objectives:

- Our most important aim is to explain the basic legal principles and concepts in a business context that is engaging and relevant for all readers.
- A second objective is to reinforce that all aspects of the legal environment necessitate active management. We offer a model for identifying, evaluating, and managing legal risk in Chapter 3. Examples of the model's application to business enterprises and a risk management orientation are reflected in the treatment of legal subjects throughout the text.
- A third objective is to convey legal information in contexts geared to the practical application of knowledge. A **Business Law in Practice** scenario opens each chapter with a business situation containing both legal and managerial implications. Questions posed by the opening scenario give students direction and purpose and encourage critical thinking as they read the chapter. As a means of testing the students' comprehension and analytical skills, the scenario is revisited later in the chapter with suggested responses to the opening questions.

The practical application of legal knowledge is reinforced through boxes provided throughout the text entitled **Business Application of the Law.** These provide examples of the impact of the law on business enterprises. By illustrating how legal issues arise in the business environment and how these issues are managed, this feature helps students develop a concrete understanding of why the law matters in a business context.

- A fourth goal of the text is to recognize that the important legal considerations inherent in the emergence of new technologies, internationalization and globalization of the economy, and environmental concerns cut across traditional legal subjects. These topics are integrated throughout the body of the text and through features entitled **Technology and the Law, International Perspective**, and **Environmental Perspective.**
- A fifth goal is to provide a pedagogically effective framework for the presentation of judicial decisions. Our special Case format begins with a description of the business context surrounding the legal dispute in question, followed by a concise statement of the relevant facts that led to the legal conflict. Next, a statement of the legal issues is provided as a summary of how the court resolved the conflict. The feature concludes with several questions that students are asked to consider to deepen their understanding of the case under study. This feature focuses on context and relevance. Judicial rulings are summarized and supplemented with brief excerpts of judicial language.

The **Landmark Case** and **Business and Legislation** features provide an account of pivotal case law and historical legislative initiatives, which can be essential to grasping contemporary law.

Finally, an **Ethical Considerations** feature assists the student in assessing the sometimes uncomfortable compromises that the law forges between competing interests.

What's New in This Edition

We introduce overall improvements that more accurately reflect the role of the law in today's business world. We have included updates where significant changes in the law have occurred. We have also replaced many of the feature boxes with more recent and relevant examples. Some of the specific changes and additions we have made to the second edition include:

- A more fully integrated discussion of risk management throughout the book. In particular, risk management is expanded in Parts 5, 7, and 8.

- New **Business Law in Practice** scenarios. Nine of the 28 chapters feature new or substantially revised situations around which chapter content is organized.

- The feature, **Business and Legislation,** which highlights legislation that affects business, has been expanded to include such developments as franchising (Chapter 14) and incorporation (Chapter 15).

- A discussion of the legal implications of technology has been expanded and integrated throughout the text. Examples include the controversy around music swapping (Chapter 18) and the Y2K aftermath (Chapter 28).

- New cases. At least 20 cases have been added or substituted, including 10 from the Supreme Court of Canada. Examples include duty of care related to alcohol (Chapter 11); directors' liability (Chapter 16); and the patentability of genetically modified plants (Chapter 18).

- More real-world business examples in new **Business Applications of the Law** boxed features. Examples include Lord Black's legal difficulties (Chapter 15); liability of accounting firms (Chapter 22); unjustified product performance claims (Chapter 23); and bankruptcy protection (Chapter 27).

- New **International Perspective** boxes. Examples include the anti-smoking treaty (Chapter 2) and the BlackBerry litigation (Chapter 18).

- New **Ethical Considerations** boxes. Examples include protection for whistle blowers (Chapter 21) and regulation of payday loans (Chapter 26).

- New end-of-chapter material. Most chapters now feature 18 **Questions for Review** and eight **Situations for Discussion.** Many of the Situations are based on judicial decisions. All of them relate the law to business situations and the decisions that managers must make.

Canadian Business and the Law, Third Edition, is offered as a modern resource for learning the fundamentals of business law from a business perspective. Rather than simply providing a summary of the law, it presents traditional business law topics in a manner that resonates with commercial reality. If you have any suggestions for improvements, additions, or clarifications, please let us know:

Dorothy DuPlessis   ddupless@unb.ca
Steve Enman   enman@acadiau.ca
Shannon O'Byrne   sobyrne@law.ualberta.ca

The Teaching and Learning Package

Instructor's Guide—IRCD (ISBN 0-17-644227-8)

The Instructor's Guide is designed to assist the instructor in preparing lectures and to offer lecture-tested ideas and strategies. The guide also provides suggested answers and explanations for all of the questions and problems presented in the text. Further, it gives ideas for projects, research activities, and class preparation plans.

Test Bank (Included on IRCD)

The Third Edition Test Bank offers instructors a rich resource of test items that have been developed specifically for the text. Questions represent a range of difficulty from recall through analysis. Multiple choice, short answer, and essay questions are provided.

Computerized Test Bank (Included on IRCD)

The Computerized Test Bank provides instructors with the enhanced functionality of an electronic format, including the ability to add, modify, or delete questions; scramble multiple choice answers; and set parameters for the range and type of questions desired in the test generated.

PowerPoint® Slides (Included on IRCD)

More than 400 slides are provided with *Canadian Business and the Law*, Third Edition, to support lecture preparation and presentation.

Video (ISBN 0-17-644219-7)

The video **component** is composed of "lecture-launchers" that highlight key aspects of the course. The video is supported by a video guide that provides a topical overview, suggested introductions to each segment, and suggested questions to encourage in-class discussion.

Website
www.businesslaw3e.nelson.com

Instructors and students alike will find this site a useful resource. Instructors will be able to download instructor resources, access case summaries, and obtain key case updates. Students will be able to check their understanding of material covered in the course with interactive chapter quizzes, link to Internet resources referenced in the book, and view relevant federal and provincial legislation.

Student Study Guide (Online Only)

The Study Guide is designed to support mastery of the course content through reinforcement of the learning objectives and core concepts. It provides a variety of self-test opportunities with explanations for the suggested answers.

Acknowledgments

Canadian Business and the Law, Third Edition, was a team effort, and credit for the text must be widely shared. We would like to thank our student research assistant Meredith Hagel of the University of Alberta.

In addition to the valued educators noted below, we extend our appreciation to our colleagues who made an important contribution by commenting on draft chapters in this or earlier editions. They include: James McGinnis of Parlee McLaws; Ronald Hopp, Wayne Renke, David Percy, Gerald Gall, Lewis Klar, Moe Litman, Linda Reif, Barbara Billingsley, Erin Nelson, and Kathryn Arbuckle, of the Faculty of Law, University of Alberta; James Gaa of the School of Business, University of Alberta; Michael Pratt of the Faculty of Law, Queen's University; Dion Legge of Macleod Dixon; Darren Charters of the University of Waterloo; and Warren Griffin.

We thank Bill Goss, Tom Kaufman, Don McCurdy, Michael H. Rayner, and Marcella Szel for their assistance in providing practical materials.

We would like to acknowledge research and administrative support from the Faculty of Law at the University of Alberta, the Faculty of Administration at the University of New Brunswick, the Fred C. Manning School of Business Administration at Acadia University, and the School of Accountancy and the Faculty of Arts at the University of Waterloo

We are grateful to Thomson Nelson's editorial, sales, and marketing team, including Veronica Visentin, Shannon White, Tracy Yan, Kathaleen McCormick, and Evelyn Veitch for their insights and support throughout the development of this project.

Finally, our deep appreciation goes to those who were instrumental in the preparation of this text by providing direction through their insightful reviews provided for the second edition. They include:

Peter Bowal,
Haskayne School of Business

Darren Charters,
University of Waterloo

Vincent Durant,
St. Lawrence College

Mary Gibbons,
George Brown College

Robert F. Morrison
Acadia University

Don Valeri,
Douglas College

By dedication of this book we thank our families for their sacrifice and support.

Dorothy's dedication is to Neil, Andrea, and Charles.
Steve's dedication is to Jennie, Michael, and Edward.
Shannon's dedication is to Jamie, Kerry, and Sean.

Table of Cases

The boldface page locators below denote pages on which the cases are developed in the text.

3464920 Canada Inc. v. Strother, (2005) 38 B.C.L.R. (4th) 159 (C.A.) (pages **327–28, 346**)

447927 Ontario Inc. v. Pizza Pizza Ltd. (1987), 62 O.R. (2d) 114 (H.C.) aff'd by (1990), 72 O.R. (2d) 704 (C.A.) (page 346n)

671122 Ontario Ltd. v. Sagaz Industries Canada, Inc., [2001] S.C.C. 159 (page **491**)

A & BB Rice Inc. v. Wigmore Farms Ltd. (2005), 141 A.C.W.S. (3d) 559 (Ont. S.C.J.) (page 217n)

Abramowich v. Azima Developments Ltd. (1993), 86 B.C.L.R. (2d) 129 (B.C.C.A.) (page **146**)

Abrams v. Sprott Securities Ltd. (2003), 67 O.R. (3d) 368 (C.A.) (page **155**)

Action Travail des Femmes v. C.N.R. Co. (1987), 40 D.L.R. (4th) 193 (S.C.C.) sub nom. *Canadian National Railway Co. v. Canada (Canadian Human Rights Commission),* (1985), 20 D.L.R. (4th) 668 (F.C.A.) (page 495n)

Adams v. Confederation Life Insurance, [1994] 6 W.W.R. 662 (Alta Q.B.) (page 704n)

ADGA Systems International Ltd. v. Valcom Ltd. (1999), 43 O.R. (3d) 101 (C.A.), leave to appeal to S.C.C. refused [1999] S.C.C.A. No. 124 (pages 385n, 402n)

A.E. LePage Ltd. v. Kamex Developments Ltd. (1977), 78 D.L.R. (3d) 223 (Ont. C.A.), aff'd (1979), 105 D.L.R. (3d) 84n (page 323n)

A.E. LePage Real Estate Services Ltd. v. Rattray Publications (1994), 21 O.R. (3d) 164 (C.A.) (page 637n)

Alberta Wheat Pool v. Northwest Pile Driving Ltd. (1998), 80 A.C.W.S. (3d) 692 (B.C. S.C.), reversed in part (2000), 80 B.C.L.R. (3d) 153 (C.A.) (pages 230–31)

American Home Assurance C. v. Canadian Pacific Railway, [2004] 44 Alta. L.R. (4th) 389 (page 700n)

Andrews v. Grand & Toy Alberta Ltd., [1978] 2 S.C.R. 299 (page 232n)

Anns v. Merton London Borough Council, [1977] 2 All E.R. 492 (H.L.) (page **243**)

Armada Lines Ltd. v. Chaleur Fertilizers Ltd. (1994), 170 N.R. 372 (F.C.A.) rev'd [1997] 2 S.C.R. 617 (page 217n)

Arnold v. Teno, [1978] 2 S.C.R. 287 (page 232n)

Atlas Supply v. Yarmouth Equipment (1991), 103 N.S.R. (2d) 1 (N.S.C.A), leave to appeal to the S.C.C. refused, [1991] e S.C.R. ix (pages **173–74**)

Azar v. Fancy Pastry Shop Ltd. (1984), 63 N.S.R. (2d) 124 (S.C.T.D.) (page 162n)

Bank of Montreal v. Duguid (2000), 47 O.R. (3d) 737 (C.A.) (page **171–72**)

Bank of Montreal v. Wilder (1986), 32 D.L.R. (4th) 9 (S.C.C.) (page 661n)

Bank of Nova Scotia v. Fraser (2002) NSSC 197 (page 638n)

Bardal v. Globe & Mail Ltd. (1960), 24 D.L.R. (2d) 140 (Ont. H.C.) (pages **525, 526**)

Barrick v. Clark, [1951] S.C.R. 177 (page 137n)

Bayshore Trust Company v. Assam, [1992] O.J. No. 715 (Gen. Div.) (page 485n)

Bay Tower Homes v. St. Andrew's Land Corp. (1990), 10 R.P.R. (2d) 193, Ont. H.C.J. (page 191n)

B.C. Rail Ltd. v. Canadian Forest Products Ltd. (B.C.C.A., 7 July 2005) (31159) (page 425n)

B.G. Preeco I (Pac. Coast) Ltd. v. Bon Street Hldg Ltd. (1989), 37 B.C.L.R. (2d) 258 (C.A.) (page **402**)

Big Bend Hotel Ltd. v. Security Mutual Casualty Co. (1980), 19 B.C.L.R. 102 (S.C.) (page **389**)

Bigg v. Boyd Gibbins Ltd. [1971], 2 All E.R. 183 (C.A.) (page **117**)

Blackwater v. Plint, [2005] 3 S.C.R. 3 at para. 20, per McLachlin C.J. (page **227**)

BMG Canada v. Doe [2005] 4 F.C.R. 81 (C.A.) (page **446**)

Bogle v. McDonald's Restaurants Ltd., [2002] EWHC 490 (Q.B.) (pages **233–34**)

Boma Manufacturing Ltd. v. CIBC (1996), 203 N.R. 321 (S.C.C.) (page 636n)

Bresson v. Ward (1987), 79 N.S.R. (2d) 156 (Cty. Ct.) (page 485n)

Brinkibon Ltd. v. Stahag Stahl Und Stahlwaren-handelsgesellschaft mbH, [1983] 2 A.C. 34 (page 123n)

British Columbia Ferry Corp. v. Invicta Security Corp. (1998), 167 D.L.R. (4th) 193, (B.C.C.A.) (page 239n)

British Columbia (Public Service Employee Relations Commission) v. BCGSEU, [1999] 3 S.C.R. 3 (pages **496, 474**)

British Columbia (Superintendent of Motor Vehicles) v. British Columbia (Council of Human Rights), [1999] 3 S.C.R. 868 (page 496n)

British Railways Board v. Herrington, [1972] A.C. 877 (H.L) (page 268n)

CAE Industries Ltd. v. R. (1985), 20 D.L.R. (4th) 347 (C.A.), leave to appeal to S.C.C. refused (1985), 20 D.L.R. (4th) 347n (page 113n)

Campbell v. Wellfund Audio-Visual Ltd. (1995), 14 C.C.E.L. (2d) 240 (B.C.S.C.) (page 541n)

Canada (Commissioner of Competition) v. Sears Canada Inc. [2005] C.C.T.D. No. 1 (Trib. Dec. No. CT2002/004/158b) (page **601**)

Canada (Human Rights Commission) v. Canadian Airlines International Ltd., 2006 SCC 1 (page 507n)

Canadian Aero Service Ltd. v. O'Malley, [1974] S.C.R. 592 (pages **381–82,** 500n)

Canadian Indemnity Co. v. Canadian Johns-Mansville Co., [1990] 2 S.C.R. 549 (page 709n)

Canadian Pacific Hotels Ltd. v. Bank of Montreal (1987), 40 D.L.R. (4th) 385 (S.C.C.) (page **628–29**)

Canadian Private Copying Collective v. Canadian Storage Media Alliance [2005] 2 F.C.R. 654, leave to appeal refused [2005] S.C.C.A. No. 70 and [2005] S.C.C.A. No. 74 (page **446**)

The Canadian Real Estate Association v. Sutton Real Estate Services Inc. [2003] J.Q. No. 3606 (Que. C.S.) (QL) (page **157**)

Canadian Shredded Wheat Co. Ltd. v. Kellogg Co. of Canada Ltd. (1938), 55 R.P.C. 125 (P.C.) (page 439n)

Carlill v. Carbolic Smoke Ball Co., [1893] 1 Q.B. 256 (C.A.) (page **122**)

Carling O'Keefe Breweries of Canada Ltd. v. CN Marine Inc. (1989), 104 N.R. 166 (F.C.A) (pages **420, 385, 389**)

Castle v. Wilkinson (1870), 5 L.R. Ch. App. 534 (page 210n)

CCH Canadian Ltd. v. Law Society of Upper Canada, [2002] F.C.A. 187 (page 444n)

Ceccol v. Ontario Gymnastic Federation (2001), 204 D.L.R. (4th) 688 (Ont. C.A.) (page 525n)

Chantiam v. Packall Packaging Inc. et al. (1998), 159 D.L.R. (4th) 517 (Ont. C.A.) (page 710n)

Cherniwchan v. Two Hills No. 21 (1982), 21 Alta. L.R. (2d) 353 (Q.B.) (page 522n)

Chet's Transport Inc. v. Seaway Distributors Ltd. (1987), 81 N.S.R. (2d) 299 (N.S.S.C.) (page 425n)

Childs v. Desormeaux (2006), 266 D.L.R. (4th) 257 (S.C.C.) (pages **254–55**)

Ciba-Geigy Canada Ltd. v. Apotex Inc., [1992] 3 S.C.R. 120 (pages **276–77**)

Citadel General Assurance Co. v. Iaboni (2004), 241 D.L.R. (4th) 128 (Ont. C.A.) (page 475n)

Compagnie mutuelle d'assurances Wawanesa v. GMAC location ltée. [2005] R.R.A. 25 (Que. C.A.) (page 711n)

Cooper v. Hobart (2001), 206 D.L.R. (4th) 193 (S.C.C.) (page 243n)

Co-operatives Insurance Association v. Kearney (1964), 48 D.L.R. (2d) 1 (S.C.C.) (page 490n)

Corey Developments Inc. v. Eastbridge Developments (Waterloo) Ltd. (1997), 34 O.R. (3d) 73, aff'd (1999) 44 O.R. (3d) 95 (C.A.) (page **148**)

Cosco Inc. v. Cambridge Recreation Products Inc. [1995] OJ. No. 717 (Gen. Div.) (OL. OJ) (page 217n)

Costello v. Blakeson, [1993] 2 W.W.R. 562 (B.C.S.C.) (page 247n)

Craig Agency of Ontario v. Bennett (1977), 14 O.R. (2d) 740 (H.C.J.) (page 191n)

Craig Estate v. Higgins (1993), 86 B.C.L.R. (2d) 64 (S.C.) (pages **179–80**)

Crocker v. Sundance Northwest Resorts Ltd., [1988] 1 S.C.R. 1186 (pages **249, 255**)

Cronk v. Canadian General Insurance (1995), 25 O.R. (3d) 505 (C.A.) (pages **526**)

David Polowin Real Estate Ltd. v. Dominion of Canada General Ins. Co. (2005), 76 O.R. (3d) 161 (Ont. C.A.), leave to appeal to S.C.C. dismissed 26 January 2006 (pages **697–98**)

Dey v. Forest Products Ltd. (1995), 162 N.B.R. (2d) 207 (C.A.) (page 527n)

Dickinson v. Dodds, [1876] 2 Ch.D. 463 (C.A.) (page **118, 119**)

Doiron v. Devon Capital Corp. (2003), 339 A.R. 371 (Alta. C.A.) (pages **296–97**)

Donoghue v. Stevenson, [1932] A.C. 562 (H.L.) (pages **242, 243, 258, 260, 268, 269, 552**)

Donovan v. N.B. Publishing (1996), 184 N.B.R. (2d) 40 (N.B.C.A.) (page 527n)

Dowling v. Halifax (City of), [1998] 1 S.C.R. 22 (page **524**)

Dubé v. Labar, [1986] 1 S.C.R. 649 (page 248n)

Dunne v. Gauthier, [2000] B.C.J. No. 2404 (S.C.) (QL) (page 247n)

Eastern Power Ltd. v. Azienda Communale Energia (1999), 178 D.L.R. (4th) 409 (Ont. C.A.) application for leave dismissed, [1999] S.C.C.A. No. 542 (page 124n)

Eastmond v. Canadian Pacific Railway (2004), 254 F.T.R. 169 (Fed. Ct.) (pages **510–11**)

Edwards v. Boulderwood Development (1984), 64 N.S.R. (2d) 395 (C.A.) (page 485n)

Ellis v. Friedland, [2001] 2 W.W.R. 130 (Alta. Q.B.) affirmed (2003), 277 A.R. 126 (C.A.) (page 172n)

Elsley v. J.G. Collins Insurance Agencies Limited, [1978] 2 S.C.R. 916 (page **183**)

Entrop v. Imperial Oil Limited (2000), 189 D.L.R. (4th) 14 (Ont. C.A.) (pages **508–09**)

Ernst & Young v. Stuart (1997), 144 D.L.R. (4th) 328 (B.C.C.A.) (page **278**)

Farber v. Royal Trust Co., [1997] 1 S.C.R. 846 (pages **528–29**)

Farquhar v. Butler Bros. Supplies Ltd. (1988), 23 B.C.L.R. (2d) 89 (C.A.) (page 534n)

Financial Collection Services Ltd. v. Carlsen (1995), 166 A.R. 78 (Q.B.) (page 190n)

Fine's Flowers Ltd v. General Accident Assurance Co. of Canada (1977) 81 DLR (3d) 139 (Ont. C.A.) (pages **301–02**)

Fobasco Ltd. v. Cogan (1990), 72 O.R. (2d) 254 (H.C.J.) (page 137n)

Ford v. Quebec (A.G.), [1988] 2 S.C.R. 712 (pages 32n, **33**)

Fp Bourgault Ind. Cultivator Division Ltd. v. Nichols Tillage Tools Inc. (1988), 63 Sask. R. 204 (Q.B.) (page 123n)

Frame v. The Fort Garry Hotel (2002), 162 Man. R. (2d) 267 (Q.B.) (pages **269–70**)

Fraser Jewellers (1982) Ltd. v. Dominion Electric Protection Co. et al. (1997), 34 O.R. (3d) 1 (C.A.) (pages 155n, 415n)

Free World Trust v. Electio Santé Inc., [2000] 2 S.C.R. 1024 (page 433n)

Gallen v. Allstate Grain Ltd. (1984), 9 D.L.R. (4th) 496 (B.C.C.A.) (page **149**)

Gateway v. Arton Holdings Ltd. (1991), 106 N.S.R. (2d) 180 (S.C.), aff'd (1992), 112 N.S.R. (2d) 180 (C.A.) (pages **143–44**)

Gilbert Steel Ltd. v. University Construction Ltd. (1976), 12 O.R. (2d) 19 (C.A.) (page **128–29**)

Gilford Motors Co. v. Horne, [1933] Ch. 935 (C.A.) (page 402n)

Glenko Enterprises Ltd. v. Ernie Keller Contractors Ltd., [1994] 10 W.W.R. 641 (Man. Q.B.), aff'd [1996] 5 W.W.R. 135 (Man. C.A.) (page **144**)

Goodman Rosen Inc. v. Sobeys Groups Inc., 2003 N.S.C.A. 87 (page **479**)

Grabka v. Regina Motor Products (1970) Ltd., [1997] S.J. No. 770 (Prov. Ct.) (page **573**)

Grant Bros. Contracting Ltd. v. Grant, 2005 NSSC 358 (page **683**)

Gregorio v. Intrans-Corp. (1994), 18 O.R. (3d) 527 (C.A.) (page 389n)

Hadley v. Baxendale (1854), 9 Exch. 341 (pages 153n, **206, 207**)

Hagerman v. City of Niagara Falls (1980), 29 O.R. (2d) 609 (H. Ct. Jus.) (page **271**)

Haig v. Bamford (1976), 72 D.L.R. (3d) 68 (S.C.C.) (pages **551, 552, 553**)

Haldane Products Inc. v. United Parcel Service (1999), 103 O.T.C. 306 (Sup. Ct. Just.) (page 202n)

Hall v. Hebert [1993], S.C.R. 159 at para. 58 (per Cory J.) (page 221n)

Hartson v. Hunter, [2006] NLTD 59 (S.C. T.D.) (page 239n)

Hayward v. Mellick (1984), 26 B.L.R. 156 (Ont. C.A.) (page **467**)

Hedley Byrne & Co. v. Heller & Partners, [1964] A.C. 465 (H.L.) (page 551n)

Henry Browne & Sons Ltd. v. Smith, [1964] 2 Lloyd's Rep. 477 (Q.B.) (page 370n)

Hercules Managements Ltd. v. Ernst & Young, [1997] 2 S.C.R. 165 (pages 243n, **229, 249–51, 260, 552, 553**)

Highway Properties Ltd. v. Kelly, Douglas & Co. Ltd. (1971), 17 D.L.R. (3d) 710 (S.C.C.) (page **485**)

Hodgkinson v. Simms, [1994] 3 S.C.R. 377 (pages 304n, 547n, **548–49**)

Hollinsworth v. BCTV, [1996] 6 W.W.R. 54 (B.C.C.A.) (page **282**)

Houghton Graphic Ltd. v. Zivot (1986), 33 B.L.R. 125 (Ont. H.C.), aff'd (1998), 38 B.L.R. xxxii (Ont. C.A.); leave to appeal refused (1988), 38 B.L.R. xxxii (S.C.C.) (page 346n)

Howell v. Coupland (1876), 1 Q.B.D. 258 (C.A.) (page 199n)

Hubbert v. Dell Corp. 359 Ill. App. 3d 976 (2005) (page 157n)

Hunt v. Sutton Group Incentive Realty Inc. (2001), 52 O.R. (3d) 425 (Sup. Ct. Jus.); rev'd on other grounds (2002), 215 D.L.R. (4th) 193 (C.A.) (pages **252–53**)

Hunter v. Southam (1984), 2 S.C.R. 145 (page **33**)

Hunter Engineering Co. v. Syncrude Canada Ltd. (1989), 57 D.L.R. (4th) 321 (S.C.C.) (pages **204–05, 384**)

IBI Leaseholds Ltd. v. Evergreen Building Ltd. (BCCA, Nov. 29, 2005), leave to appeal to S.C.C. granted 22 June 2006 (page 486n)

Imperial Brass Ltd. v. Jacob Electric Systems Ltd. (1989), 72 O.R. (2d) 17 (H.C.J.) (page 218n)

Imperial Oil Ltd. v. Quebec (Minister of the Environment), [2003] 2 S.C.R. 624 (page 470n)

Indermaur v. Dames (1867), L.R. 2 C.P. 311 (page 268n)

ING Insurance Co. of Canada v. Sportsco International L.P., [2004] O.J. No. 2254 (Ont. Sup. Ct.) (page 710n)

Insurance Corp. of British Columbia v. Hoang, (2002), 42 C.C.L.I. (3d) 235 (B.C.S.C.) (page 709n)

Irwin Toy v. Quebec, [1989] 1 S.C.R. 927 (pages 25n, **33**)

Jen-Den Investments Ltd. v. Northwest Farms Ltd., [1978] 1 W.W.R. 290 (Man. C.A.) (page 185n)

Jirna Limited v. Mister Donut of Canada Ltd., [1975] 1 S.C.R. 2 (page 338n)

Jones v. Shafer Estate, [1948] S.C.R. 166 (pages **223–24**)

Jorian Properties Ltd. v. Zellenrath (1984), 26 B.L.R. 276 (Ont. C.A.) (page 217n)

J.T.I. Macdonald Corp. c. Canada (Procureuer générale) [2002] 2 J.Q. No. 5550 (page 31n)

Jung v. Ip, [1988] O.J. No. 1038 (D.C.) (page **465**)

Kamloops (City) v. Nielsen, [1984] 2 S.C.R. 2 (page 243n)

Kanitz v. Rogers Cable Inc., [2002] O.J. No. 665 (S.C.) (page **164**)

Kauffman v. Toronto Transit Commission, [1960] S.C.R. 251 (page **246**)

Kavcar Investments v. Aetna Financial Services (1989), 62 D.L.R. (4th) 277 (Ont. C.A.) (page 661n)

Keays v. Honda Canada Inc., 2006 CanLII 33191 (Ont. C.A.) (page **533**)

Kelly v. Linamar Corporation, [2005] O.J. No. 4899 (page 542n)

Kosmopoulos v. Constitution Insurance Co. of Canada, [1987] 1 S.C.R. 2 (page 710n)

Kupchak v. Dayson Holdings Ltd. (1965), 53 W.W.R. 65 (B.C.C.A.) (page 176n)

Ky Zur Investments Ltd. v. David Friesen Holdings Ltd. (1994), 160 A.R. 378 (Q.B., Master in Chambers) (page **101**)

LAC Minerals Ltd. v. International Corona Resources Ltd. (1989), 61 D.L.R. (4th) 14 (S.C.C.) (page **448**)

Lampert Plumbing (Danforth) Ltd. v. Agathos, [1972] 3 O.R. 11 (Ont. Co. Ct.) (page 347n)

Landmark Inns of Canada Ltd. v. Horeak (1982), 18 Sask. R. 30 (Q.B.) (page 375n)

Lansing Building Supply (Ontario) Ltd. v. Ierullo (1990), 71 O.R. (2d) 173 (Dist. Ct.) (page 324n)

LeBlanc v. Marson Canada Inc. (1995), 139 N.S.R. (2d) 309 at paras. 17–18, aff'd (1995) 146 N.S.R. (2d) 392 (C.A.) (pages 241n, 245n)

LeCar GmbH v. Dusty Roads Holding Ltd. (2004), 222 N.S.R. (2d) 279 (N.S.S.C.) (pages **389–90**)

Lefkowitz v. Great Minneapolis Surplus Store, Inc., 251 Minn. 188, 86 N.W. 2d. 689 (1957) (page 114n)

Lennard's Carrying Co. v. Asiatic Petroleum Co., [1915] A.C. 705 (page 374n)

Little Sisters Book v. Canada, [2000] 2 S.C.R. 1120 (page **33**)

Lloyds Bank v. Bundy, [1975] Q.B. 326 (C.A.) (pages 167n, 172n)

London Drugs Limited v. Kuehne & Nagel International Ltd. (1992), 97 D.L.R. (4th) 261 (S.C.C.) (pages **201–02,** 411n, **384**)

Lovelace v. Ontario, [2000] 1 S.C.R. 950 (page 498n)

Lowe (D.J.) (1980) Ltd. v. Roach (1994), 131 N.S.R. (2d) 268 (S.C.), aff'd (1995) 138 N.S.R. (2d) 79 (C.A.) (page 425n)

Lowe (D.J.) (1980) Ltd. v. Upper Clements Family Theme Park Ltd. (1990), 95 N.S.R. (2d) 397 (S.C.T.D.) (pages **121–22,** 416n, 394n)

Lucena v. Craufurd (1806), 2 B. & P. (N.R) 269 at 301 (H.L.) (page 691n)

MacDonald v. Klein, [1998] O.J. No. 4922 (Ont. Gen. Div.) (page 516n)

MacDonald v. Schmidt, [1992] B.C.J. No. 230, (S.C.) B.C.J. No. 230 (S.C.) (page 346n)

Machtinger v. HOJ Industries Ltd., [1992] 1 S.C.R. 986 (page 525n)

Mandrake Management Consultants Ltd. et al. v. Toronto Transit Commission, [1993] 102 D.L.R. (4th) 12 (Ont. C.A.) (pages 273n, 288n)

Manulife Bank of Canada v. Conlin (1996), 203 N.R. 81 (S.C.C.) (page **656**)

Maracle v. Travellers Indemnity Co. of Canada, [1991] 2 S.C.R. 50 (page 130n)

Marche v. Halifax Insurance Co., [2005] 1 S.C.R. 47 (page **690**)

Marshall v. Canada Permanent Trust Co. (1968), 69 D.L.R. (2d) 260 (Alta. S.C.) (page 192n).

Martin v. International Maple Leaf Springs Water Corp. (1998), 38 C.C.E.L. (2d) 128 (B.C.S.C.) (page 541n)

Matheson v. Watt (1956), 19 W.W.R. (N.S.) 425 (B.C.C.A.) (page 413n)

Mattel v. 3894207 Canada Inc. 2006 SCC 22 (pages **439–40**)

McErlean v. Sarel (1987), 61 O.R. (2d) 396 (C.A.), leave to appeal to S.C.C. refused (1988), 63 O.R. (2d) x (note) (page 268n)

McFadden v. 481782 Ontario Ltd. (1984), 47 O.R. (2d) 134 (H.C.) (page 385n)

McKinley v. BC Tel, [2001] 2 S.C.R. 161 (pages 521n, **523–24**)

McKinney v. University of Guelph, [1990] 3 S.C.R. 229 (page **33**)

McNaughton Automotive Ltd. v. Co-Operators General Insurance Co. (2001), 54 O.R. (3d) 704 (Ont. C.A.), leave to appeal to S.C.C. dismissed March 7, 2002 (pages **697–98**)

Mead Johnson Canada v. Ross Pediatrics (1997), 31 O.R. (3d) 237 (Gen. Div.) (pages **281, 547**)

Megill-Stephenson Co. Ltd. v. Woo (1989), 59 D.L.R. (4th) 146 (Man. C.A.) (page 185n)

Merchant Commercial Real Estate Services Inc. v. Alberta (Registrar of Corporations) (1997), 199 A.R. 12 (Q.B.) (page 370n)

Merchant Retail Services Ltd. v. Mustoe (1990), 115 A.R. 210 (Prov. Ct) (page 168n)

Merk v. International Assn. of Bridge, Structural, Ornamental and Reinforcing Iron Workers, Local 771, [2005] 3 S.C.R. 425 (page **430**)

Mitchell v. C.N.R. Co. (1974), 46 D.L.R. (3d) 363 (S.C.C.) (page 268n)

Mitchell v. Westburne Supply Alberta, [2000] 2 C.C.E.L. (3d) 87 (Alta. Q.B.) (page **532**)

Montreal (City of) v. Montreal Locomotive Works Ltd., [1947] 1 D.L.R. 161 (P.C.) (page 490n)

Morrison v. Coast Finance Ltd. (1965), 54 W.W.R. 257 (B.C.C.A.) (page 167n)

Murano v. Bank of Montreal (1995), 20 B.L.R. (2d) 61 (Ont. Gen. Div.), varied (1998), 41 B.L.R. (2d) 10 (Ont. C.A.) (page **652**)

Nethery v. Lindsey Morden Claim Services Ltd. (1999), 127 B.C.A.C. 237 (B.C.C.A.) (page 529n)

Newell v. Canadian Pacific Airlines Ltd. (1976), 14 O.R. (2d) 752 (Co. Ct.) (page 218n)

Newfoundland (Human Rights Commission) v. Newfoundland (Minister of Employment and Labour Relations) (1995), 127 D.L.R. (4th) 694 (Nfld. S.C.T.D.) (page 494n)

Norberg v. Wynrib (1992), 12 C.C.L.T. (2d) 1 (S.C.C) (pages 172n, 224n)

North American Systemshops Ltd. v. King, (1989), 68 Alta. L.R. (2d) 145 (Q.B.) (page **156**)

North Ocean Shipping Co. Ltd. v. Hyundai Construction Co. Ltd., [1978] 3 All E.R. 1170 (Q.B.) (page 170n)

North York Branson Hospital v. Praxair Canada Inc. (1998), 84 C.P.R. (3d) 12 (Ont. Ct. (Gen. Div.)) (page 597n)

Nova Scotia v. Weymouth Sea Products Ltd. (1983), 4 D.L.R. (4th) 314 (N.S. C.A.) (page 123n)

Ocean City Realty Ltd. v. A & M Holdings Ltd. et al. (1987), 36 D.L.R. (4th) 94 (B.C.C.A.) (page 314n)

O'Keefe v. Loewen (1995) (page 96n)

Ontario (Human Rights Commission) v. Simpson-Sears Ltd. (1985), 23 D.L.R. (4th) 321 (S.C.C.) (page 495n)

Ortega v. 1005640 Ontario Inc. (C.O.B. Calypso Hut 3), [2004] O.J. No. 2478 (C.A.), leave to appeal refused, [2004] S.C.C.A. No. 377 (page 262n)

Ottenbreit v. Daniels, (1975) S.J. No. 98 (Dist. Ct.) (page 168n)

Panorama Developments (Guildford) Ltd. v. Fidelis Furnishing Fabrics Ltd., [1971] 2 Q.B. 711 (C.A.) (page 314n)

Pao On v. Lau Yiu Long, [1979] 3 All E.R. 65 (P.C.) (page 170n)

Paws Pet Food & Accessories Ltd. v. Paws & Shop Inc. (1992), 6 Alta. L.R. (3d) 22 (Q.B.) (pages **356–57**)

Pelley v. Pelley, [2003] 221 Nfld. & P.E.I.R. 1 (C.A.) (pages **394–95**)

Peoples Department Stores v. Wise (2004), 244 DLR (4th) 564 (S.C.C.) (**382, 383–84,** 398n)

P.G. Restaurant Ltd. (c.o.b. Mama Panda Restaurant) v. Northern Interior Regional Health Board (2005), 211 B.C.A.C. 219 (C.A.), reconsideration or rehearing refused by (2005), 41 B.C.L.R. (4th) 55 (C.A.), leave to appeal refused by [2005] S.C.C.A. No. 270 (S.C.C.) (pages **279–80**)

Physique Health Club Ltd. v. Carlsen (1996), 141 D.L.R. (4th) 64 (Alta. C.A.); leave to appeal dismissed [1997] S.C.C. No. 40 (page **449**)

Phytoderm v. Urwin, [1999] O.J. No. 383 (Ont. Gen. Div.) (page 516n)

Poluk v. City of Edmonton (1996), 191 A.R. 301 (Q.B.) (page 262n)

Pontarollo v. Westfair Foods Ltd. (1996), 150 Sask. R. 71 (Q.B.) (page 287n)

Port Arthur Shipbuilding Co. v. Arthurs, [1969] S.C.R. 85 (S.C.C.) (page 520n)

Prebushewski v. Dodge City Auto (1984) Ltd., 2005 SCC 28 (page 593n)

Prinzo v. Baycrest Centre for Geriatric Care (2000) 60 O.R. (3d) 474 (C.A.) (page 535n)

Pro-C Ltd. v. Computer City Inc. (2001), 205 D.L.R. (4th) 568 (Ont. C.A.), rev'g (1999), 7 C.P.R. (4th) 193 (Sup. Ct. Jus.) Leave to appeal to S.C.C. refused, [2002] S.C.C.A. No. 5 (page **18**)

ProCD v. Zeidenberg, 86 F.3d 1447 (7th Cir. 1996) (page 156n)

Punch v. Savoy's Jewellers Ltd. (1986), 33 B.L.R. 147 (Ont. C.A.) (pages **414–15,** 418n, **388**)

Queen v. Cognos Inc. (1993), 99 D.L.R. (4th) 626 (S.C.C.) (pages **498, 499,** 552n)

Quiamco v. Gaspar, [1985] B.C.J. No. 1661 (C.A.) (QL) (page **138**)

R. v. Arthur, Ex parte Port Arthur Shipbuilding Co. (1967), 62 D.L.R. (2d) 342 (Ont. C.A.) (page 520n)

R. v. Bata Industries Ltd. (1992), 9 O.R. (3d) 329 (Prov. Div.); aff'd in (1993), 14 O.R. (3d) 354 (Gen. Div.); varied in (1995), 25 O.R. (3d) 321 (C.A.) (page **386**)

R. v. Big M Drug Mart, (1985) 1 S.C.R. 295 (page **33**)

R. v. Sault Ste Marie (City of) (1978), 2 S.C.R. 1299 (page 256n, 584n)

R. v. D. (W) (1991), 63 C.C.C. (3d) 397 (S.C.C.) (page 226n)

R. v. Edwards Books and Art, [1986] 2 S.C.R. 713 (page **33**)

R. v. Felderhof (2003), 68 O.R. (3d) 481 (C.A.) (page 366n)

R. v. Harper (2000), 232 D.L.R. (4th) 738 (Ont. C.A.) (page 365n)

R. v. Lifchus, [1997] 3 S.C.R. 320 (page 226n)

R. v. Massoudinia, (2002), 65 W.C.B. (2d) 765 (Ont. S.C.J.) (page **304**)

R. v. Nova Scotia Pharmaceutical Society et al., [1992] 2 S.C.R. 606 (page 596n)

R. v. Partridge (1996), 32 W.C.B. (2d) 259 (Sask. C.A.) (page 616n)

R. v. Ron Engineering & Construction Ltd., [1981] 1 S.C.R. 111 (page **178**)

R. v. Weir, [1988] A.J. No. 155 (Alta. Q. B.). (page 511n)

Raso v. Dionigi, [1993] 31 R.P.R. (2d) 3 (Ont. C.A.) (page **203**)

Redfern Farm Services Ltd. v. Wright, 2006 MBQB 4 (CanLII) (page 345n)

Reichmann v. Berlin, [2002] O.J. No. 2732 (Sup. Ct.) (page **281**)

Rhee v. Rhee, [2001] 3 S.C.R. 364 (page 226n)

RJR-MacDonald Inc. v. Canada (A.G.), [1995] 3 S.C.R. 199 (page 25n)

Robert Addie & Sons v. Dumbreck, [1929] A.C. 358 (H.L.) (page 268n)

Robichaud v. The Queen (1987), 40 D.L.R. (4th) 577 (S.C.C.) (page 506n)

Rocket v. Royal College of Dental Surgeons, [1990] 1 S.C.R. 232 (page **33**)

Rockland Industries Inc. v. Amerada Minerals Corporation of Canada (1978), 108 D.L.R (3d) 513 (S.C.C.), rev'g 95 D.L.R (3d) 64 (Alta. C.A.) (pages **298–995**)

Rothmans, Benson & Hedges v. Saskatchewan, [2002], S.J. No. 60673 (C.A.), reversing (2003), SKQB 382. (pages 25n)

Royal Bank of Canada v. Intercon Security Ltd. (2005), 143 A.C.W.S. (3d) 608 (Ont. S.C.J.) (pages **228–29**)

Royal Bank of Canada v. J. Segreto Construction Ltd. (1988), 38 B.L.R. 134 (Ont. C.A.) (page 660n)

Royal Bank of Canada v. Speight, 2006 NSSC 151 (page **657**)

Royal Bank of Canada v. State Farm Fire and Casualty Co., [2005] 1 S.C.R. 779 (page 690n)

Royal Bank of Canada v. Woloszyn (1998), 170 N.S.R. (2d) 122 (S.C.) (page 637n)

Rudder v. Microsoft Corp. [1999], O.J. No. 3778 (Sup. Ct.) (pages **126, 157, 164**)

Russell v. Nova Scotia Power (1996), 150 N.S.R. (2d) 271 (S.C.) (page 541n)

Rylands v. Fletcher (1868), L.R. 3 H.L. 330 (256n)

Salomon v. Salomon Ltd. (1897), A.C. 22 (H.L.) (pages **350, 385, 358**)

Sammut v. Islington Golf Club, Ltd. (2005), 16 C.E.L.R. (3d) 66 (Ont. S.C.J.) (page **272**)

Sawler v. Franklyn Enterprises Ltd. (1992), 117 N.S.R. (2d) 316 (T.D.) (page 266n)

Schimp v. RCR Catering Ltd. (2004), 221 N.S.R. (2d) 379 (C.A.) (page 542n)

Schneider v. Royal Wayne Motel Ltd. (1995) 27 Alta.L.R. (3d) 18 (Prov. Ct.) (page 272n)

Schneider v. The Queen, [1982] 2 S.C.R. 112 (page 25n)

Schwartz v. Maritime Life Assurance Co. (1997), 149 Nfld. & P.E.I.R. 234 (Nfld. C.A.), leave to appeal to S.C.C. refused [1997] S.C.C.A. No. 362 (page 314n)

Seanix Technology Inc. v. Ircha (1998), 78 C.P.R. (3d) 443 (B.C.S.C.) (page 457n)

Selick v. 149244 Canada Inc., (1994), 15 C.C.E.L. (2d) 176 (Q.C.A.) (page **527**)

Semelhago v. Paramedevan (1996), 197 N.R. 379 (S.C.C.) (page **472**)

Shah v. Xerox Canada Ltd., (2000), 49 C.C.E.L. (2d) 166 (Ont. C.A.) (page **529**)

Shelanu Inc. v. Print Three Franchising Corporation (2003), 64 O.R. (3d) 533 (C.A.) (pages **345, 399–400**)

Simpson v. Consumers' Assn. of Canada (2001), 209 D.L.R. (4th) 213 (Ont. C.A.) (page 540n)

Simpson v. Geswein, [1995] 6 W.W.R. 233 (Man. Q.B.) (page 226n)

Slaight Communications v. Davidson, [1989] 1 S.C.R. 1038 (page **33**)

Smith & Osberg Ltd. v. Hollenbeck, [1938] 3 W.W.R. 704 (B.C.S.C.) (page 123n)

Snow v. The Eaton Centre Ltd. (1982), 70 C.P.R. (2d) 105 (Ont. H.C.) (page **444**)

Societa' Gei A Responsabilita' Limitata v. Piscitelli, [1988] O.J. No. 894 (Dist. Ct. (page 123n)

Society of Composers, Authors and Music Publishers of Canada v. Canadian Association of Internet Providers, [2004] 2. S.C.R. 427 (page 445n)

Solar U.S.A. Inc. v. Saskatchewan Minerals, [1992] 3 W.W.R. 15 (Sask. Q.B.) (page 163n)

Specht v. Netscape Communications Corp. 150 F.Supp.2d 585 (S.D. N.Y. 2001), aff'd 306 F.3d 17 (2d Cir. 2002) (page 157n)

Stewart v. Canada Life Assurance Co. (1994), 132 N.S.R. (2d) 324 (C.A.) (page 191n)

Still v. Ministry of National Revenue, [1998] 1 F.C. 549 (C.A.) (page 181n)

Stolle v. Daishinpan (Canada) Inc. (1998), 37 C.C.E.L. (2d) 18 (B.C.S.C.) (page 541n)

Sun Life Assurance Co. of Canada v. Fidler, [2006] SCC 30 (pages **207–08, 705**)

Taylor v. Caldwell (1863), 122 E.R. 309 (C.A.) (page **199**)

T. Eaton Co. v. Smith (1977), 92 D.L.R. (3d) 425 (S.C.C.) (page 710n)

Théberge v. Galerie d'Art du Petit Champlain Inc., [2002] S.C.C. 34 (page **413**)

Thiessen v. Mutual Life Assurance (2002), 219 D.L.R. (4th) 98 (B.C.C.A) (page 492n)

Thornton v. School Dist. No. 57 Bd. of School Trustees, [1978] 2 S.C.R. 267 (page 232n)

Tilden Rent-A-Car Co. v. Clendenning (1978), 83 D.L.R. (3d) 400 (Ont. C.A.) (pages **155,** 180n, 409n, 416n)

Toronto Dominion Bank v. 2047545 Nova Scotia Ltd. and Brace (1996), 148 N.S.R. (2d) 228 (C.A.) (page 191n)

Toronto Marlboro Major Junior 'A' Hockey Club v. Tonelli (1979), 96 D.L.R. (3d) 135 (Ont. C.A.) (page 192n).

Transport North American Express Inc. v. New Solutions Financial Corp., [2004] 1 S.C.R. 249 (page 181n, 662n).

Traquair v. National Arts Centre Corp., [2004] O.T.C. 891 (S.C.J.). (page 286n)

Triple Five Corp. v. Simcoe & Erie Group (1994), 159 A.R. 1 (Q.B.), aff'd [1997] 5 W.W.R. 1 (C.A.), leave to appeal to the S.C.C. denied [1997] S.C.C.A. No. 263 (page **702**)

Trollope & Colls Ltd. v. North West Metropolitan Regional Hospital Board, [1973] 2 All E.R. 260 (H.L.) (page **146**)

Truong v. British Columbia, (1999) 178 D.L.R. (4th) 644 (B.C.C.A.) (page 516n)

Ultramares Corp. v. Touche Niven & Co. (1931), 255 N.Y. 170 (U.S.C.A.) (pages 250n, 550n)

United Artists Pictures Inc. v. Pink Panther Beauty Corp. (1998), 225 N.R. 82 (Fed. C.A.), leave to appeal granted (1998), 235 N.R. 399 (S.C.C.) (page 457n)

Veinot v. Kerr-Addison Mines Ltd., [1975] 2 S.C.R. 311 (page 268n)

Veuve Clicquot Ponsardin v. Boutiques Cliquot Ltee, 2006 SCC 23 (page 439n)

Volkers v. Midland Doherty Ltd. et al. (1985), 17 D.L.R. (4th) 343 (B.C.C.A.) (page 314n)

Vorvis v. Insurance Corporation of British Columbia, [1989] 1 S.C.R. 1085 (page 233n)

Vriend v. Alberta, [1998] 1 S.C.R. 493 (page 494n)

Waldick v. Malcolm, [1991] 2 S.C.R. 456 (pages 269n, 270n)

Wallace v. United Grain Growers, [1997] 3 S.C.R. 701 (page **531**)

Walt Disney Productions v. Triple Five Corp. et al., [1994] 113 D.L.R. (4th) 229 (Alta. C.A.) (pages **277,** 288n)

Waxman v. Waxman (2002), 25 B.L.R. (3d) 1 (Ont. Sup. Ct. Jus.), varied as to damages (2004), 44 B.L.R. (3d) 165 (C.A.), leave to appeal refused, [2004] S.C.C.A. No. 291, reconsideration allowed (2004), 6 B.L.R. (4th) 167 (C.A.) (page 172n)

Weir v. Canada Post Corp. (1995), 142 N.S.R. (2d) 198 (S.C.) (page 162n)

Westman Equipment Corp. v. Royal Bank of Canada (1982), 19 B.L.R. 56 (Man. Cty. Ct.) (page 660n)

Whirlpool Corp. v. Camco Inc., [2000] 2 S.C.R. 1067 (page 433n)

Whirlpool Corp. v. Maytag Corp., [2000] 2 S.C.R. 1116 (page 433n)

Whiten v. Pilot Insurance Co. (2002), 209 D.L.R. (4th) 257 (S.C.C.) (pages 206n, 234n, **704–05, 709**)

Wickman Machine Tool Sales Ltd. v. Schuler, [1974] A.C. 235 (H.L.) (page 203n)

Wiebe v. Bobsien (1985), 14 D.L.R. (4th) 754 (B.C.S.C.), aff'd (1986) 20 D.L.R. (4th) 475 (C.A.), leave to appeal refused (1985), 64 N.R. 394 (S.C.C.) (page **152**)

Williams v. Roffey Bros. & Nicholls (Contractors) Ltd., [1990] 1 All E.R. 512 (C.A.) (page 129n)

Table of Statutes

Act to Amend the Copyright Act and Other Acts in Consequence Thereof, S.C. 1988, c. 65 (page 434n)

Act to Amend the Criminal Code (Criminal Liability of Organizations) S.C. 2003 c. 21 (page **376**)

Act to Amend the Film and Video Classification Act, 2d Sess., 25th Leg., Saskatchewan, 2005–2006

Act to Amend the Patent Act, S.C. 2001, c. 10 (page 433n)

Act to Amend the Professional Code and Other Legislative Provisions as Regards the Carrying on of Professional Activities within a Partnership or Company, S.Q. 2002, c. 35 (page 331n)

Act to Establish a Legal Framework for Information Technology, S.Q. 2001, c. 32 (page 126n)

Act for the Prevention and Suppression of Combinations Formed in Restraint of Trade, S.C. 1889, c. 41 (page 583n)

Act Respecting Labour Standards, R.S.Q. c. N-11 (page 505n)

Act Respecting the Protection of Personal Information in the Private Sector, R.S.Q. cP-39.1 (page 509n)

Act to Repeal the Statute of Frauds, R.S.M. 1987, C. F-158 (page 181n)

Age of Majority and Accountability Act, R.S.O. 1990, c. A.7 (page **168**)

Amusements Act, C.C. S. M., c. A-70 (page **18**)

Arbitration Act (page **78**)

Arthur Wishart Act (Franchise Disclosure), 2000, S.O. 2000, c. 3 (page 337n)

Bank Act, S.C. 1991, c. 46 (pages **620, 648**)

Bankruptcy and Insolvency Act, R.S.C. 1985, c. B-3 (pages 665n, **670, 672, 673, 674, 677, 679**)

Bankruptcy and Insolvency General Rules, C.R.C. 1978, c. 368 (pages **671,** 676n)

Bills of Exchange Act, R.S.C. 1985, c. B-4 (pages **623,** 625n)

Business Corporations Act, R.S.A. 2000, c. B-9 (pages 352n, **357, 358**)

Business Corporations Act, R.S.N. 1990, c. C-36 (page 352n)

Business Corporations Act, R.S.O. 1990, c. B-16 (pages 352n, 517n)

Business Corporations Act, R.S.S. 1978, c. B-10 (page 352n)

Business Corporations Act, S.B.C. 2002, c. 57 (pages 175n, 352n, **359**)

Business Corporations Act, S.N.B. 1981, c. B-9.1 (pages 352n, 554n)

Business Names Act, R.S.O. 1990, c. B-17 (pages 319n, 554n)

Business Practices Act, C. C. S. M: c. B120 (page 175n)

Business Practices Act, R.S.P.E.I. 1988, c. B-7 (pages 175n, 587n)

Business Practices and Consumer Protection Act, S.B.C. 2004, c. 2 (pages 587n, **643**)

Canada Business Corporations Act, R.S.C. 1985, c. C-44 (pages 352n, **359,** 362n, **373,** 375n, **380, 383, 386, 391,** 393n, **397**)

Canada Labour Code, R.S.C. 1985, c. L-2 (page 503n)

Canadian Charter of Rights and Freedoms, Part I of the Constitution Act, 1982, being Schedule B to the *Canada Act 1982* (U.K.), c. 11 (pages **20,·30–31, 33, 36, 37, 42, 43, 45, 46, 47, 494, 498**)

Canadian Human Rights Act, R.S.C. 1985, c. H-6 (pages 493n, 505, 506n, **507**)

Carriage of Goods by Water Act S. C. 2001, c-26 (page **420**)

Charter of the French Language, R.S.Q. c. C-11 (page 580n)

Charter of Human Rights and Freedoms R.S.Q. c. C-12 (page 282n)

Civil Code of Québec (pages **39, 569**)

Class Proceedings Act, 1992, S.OP. 1992, c. 6 (page 83n)

Collection Agencies Act, R.S.O. 1990, c. C-14 (page 644n)

Companies Act, R.S.N.S. 1989, c. 81 (page 352n)

Companies Act, R.S.P.E.I. 1988, c. C-14 (page 352n)

Companies Act, R.S.Q. 1977, c. C-38 (page 352n)

Companies' Creditors Arrangement Act, R.S.C. 1985, c. C-36 (page **666**)

Company Act, R.S.B.C. 1996, c. 62 (page **359**)

Compensation for Victims of Crime Act, R.S.O. 1990, c. C-24 (page 225n)

Competition Act, R.S.C. 1985, c. C-34 (pages 114n, **181, 387, 582, 584, 585, 588, 589, 590, 592, 593, 596, 597, 598–99, 600, 602, 603–07, 610, 611, 614**)

Constitution Act, 1867 (pages **24, 43**)

Constitution Act, 1867 (pages **22, 23, 28, 41, 42**)

Constitution Act, 1982 (pages 23n, 462n)

Constitution Act, 1982 (page 462n)

Consumer Packaging and Labelling Act, R.S.C. 1985, c. C-38 (pages **580,** 582n, **583, 588, 591, 592**)

Consumer Product Warranty and Liability Act, S.N.B. 1978, c. C-18 (pages 202n, 415n, 536n)

Consumer Protection Act, R.S.M. 1987, c.C-200 (pages 126n, 535n)

Consumer Protection Act, R.S.O. 1990, c. C-31 (pages **174,** 536n)

Consumer Protection Act, R.S.Q. c. P-40.1 (pages 587n, 550n)

Consumer Protection Act, S.S. 1996, c. C-30.1 (pages 202n, 536n)

Consumer Protection Act, 2002, S.O. 2002, Sched. A. c. C (page 643n)

Consumer Protection Act, 2002, S.O. 2002, Sched. A, c.30 (pages 186n, 587n, **608**)

Consumer Reporting Act, R.S.O. 1990, c. 33 (page 643n)

Controlling the Assault of Non-Solicited Pornography and Marketing Act of 2003, 15 U.S.C. 7701, *et seq* (pages **3,** 11n)

Copyright Act, R.S.C. 1985, c. C-42 (pages 428n, 434n, 441n, **442–46, 455, 456**)

Criminal Code of Canada, R.S.C. 1985, c. C-46 (pages **3, 5,** 6n, **11, 23, 24, 38, 39, 46, 47, 181, 225, 226, 227, 238,** 274n, **365,** 375n, 376n, **377, 401, 504, 511,** 643n, **644**)

Digital Millennium Copyright Act, 112 Stat. 2860 (1998) (page 446n)

Direct Sellers' Licensing Act, R.S.N.S. 1989, c. 129 (page 605n)

Electronic Commerce Act, S.N. 2000, C. E-52

Electronic Commerce Act, S.N.S. 2000, c. 26 (pages 126n, **284**)

Electronic Commerce Act, S.O. 2000, c. 17 (pages 126n, 185n)

Electronic Commerce Act, S.P.E.I. 2001, c. E-4.1 (page 126n)

Electronic Commerce Act, R.S.Y. 2002, c. 66 (pages 126n, **169**)

Electronic Commerce and Information Act, C.C.S.M. 2000, c. E55 (page 126n)

Electronic Information and Documents Act, S.S. 2000, c. E-7.22 (page 126n)

Electronic Transactions Act, S.A. 2001, c. E-5.5 (page 126n)

Electronic Transactions Act, S.B.C. 2001, c. 10 (page 126n)

Electronic Transactions Act, S.N.B. 2001, c. E-5.5

Employment Equity Act, S.C. 1995, c. 44 (pages 498n, **514**)

Employment Insurance Act, S.C. 1996, c. 23 (page **504**)

Employment Standards Code, R.S.A. 2000, c. E-9 (page 503n)

Employment Standards Act, R.S.B.C. 1996, c. 113 (page 503n)

Employment Standards Act 2000, S.O. 2000, c. 41 (page 535n)

Employment Standards Code, R.S.M. 1987, c. E110 (page 503n)

Execution Act, R.S.O. 1990, c. E-24 (page **677**)

Fair Trading Act, R.S.A. 2000, c. F-2 (pages 175n, 605n)

Film Classification Act, 2005, S.O. 2005, c. 17 (page **18**)

Financial Consumer Agency of Canada Act, S.C. 2001, c. 9 (page 620n)

Food and Drugs Act, R.S.C. 1985, c. F-27 (page **580**)

Franchises Act, R.S.A. 2000, c. F-23 (page 337n)

Franchises Act, R.S.P.E.I 1998, c. F-14.1 (page 337n)

Fraudulent Conveyances Act, R.S.O. 1990, c. F-29 (page 673n)

Guarantees Acknowledgment Act, R.S.A. 2000, c. G-11 (pages 181n, 656n)

Hazardous Products Act, R.S.C. 1985, c. H-3 (pages 385n, 581n, **590**)

Health Disciplines Act (page **33**)

Human Rights Code, S.M. 1987–88, c. 45 (pages **33, 34, 35,** 506n)

Human Rights Code, R.S.O, 1990, c. H-19 (pages 497n, **508**)

Income Tax Act, R.S.C. 1985, c. 1 (pages 46, **354,** 378, 386n, **398,** 674n)

Industrial Design Act, R.S.C. 1985, c. 1-9 (pages **434, 452**)

Infants Act, R.S.B.C. 1996, c. 223 (page **169**)

Innkeepers' Act, R.S.M. 1987, c. H-150 (page 420n)

Innkeepers' Act, R.S.N.S. 1989, c. 229 (page 420n)

Innkeepers' Act, R.S.O. 1990, c. I-7 (page 420n)

Insurance Act, R.S.O. 1990, c. I.8 (pages 175n, 696n)

Integrated Circuit Topography Act, S.C. 1990, c. 37 (page 427n)

Intellectual Property Law Improvement Act, S.C. 1993, c. 15 (pages 428n, **419**)

Internal Revenue Code (page 352n)

Judicature Act, R.S.A. 2000, c. J-2 (page 131n)

Labour Standards Act, R.S.N. 1990, c. L-2 (pages 503n, **530**)

Law and Equity Act, R.S.B.C. 1996, c. 253 (pages 131n, 181n, 184n)

Law Reform (Miscellaneous Amendments) Act, S.M. 1992, c. 32 (page **131**)

Law Reform Amendment Act, S.B.C. 1985, c. 10 (page 181n)

Law Society Act, R.S.O. 1990, c. L.8 (page 554n)

Legal Profession Act, R.S.B.C. 1996, c. 255 (pages 546n, **555**)

Limitation of Actions Act, R.S.N.S. 1989, c. 258 (page 84n)

Limitations Act, R.S.O. 1990, c. L-15 (page 84n)

Mandatory Retirement Statute Law Amendment Act, 2005, S.O. 2005, c. 29 (page **495**)

Manitoba Evidence Act, C.C.S.M. 1987, c. E-150 (page 126n)

Mechanics Lien Act, R.S.N. 1990, c. M-3 (page 419n)

Mercantile Law Amendment Act, C.C.S.M., c. M120 (page 131n)

Mercantile Law Amendment Act, R.S.O. 1990, c. M.10 (page **131**)

Occupational Health and Safety Act, R.S.O. 1990, c. O.1. (page **377**)

Occupiers' Liability Act, R.S.B.C. 1996, c. 337 (page 267n)

Occupiers' Liability Act, R.S.M. 1987, c. O-8 (pages 267n, **269**)

Occupiers' Liability Act, R.S.N.S. 1996, c. 27 (page 267n)

Occupiers' Liability Act, R.S.O. 1990, c. O.2 (pages 267n, **269, 270**)

Occupiers' Liability Act, R.S.P.E.I. 1988, c. O-2 (page 267n)

Occupiers' Liability Act, R.S.A. 2000, c. O-4 (page 267n)

Partnership Act, R.S.B.C. 1996, c. 348 (page 331n)

Partnership Act, R.S.N.B. 1990, c. P-4 (pages 321n, 326n, 331n)

Partnership Act, R.S.N.S. c. 334 (page 331n)

Partnership Act, S.A. 1999, c. 27 amending *Partnerships Act,* R.S.A. c. P-2 (page 331n)

Partnerships Act, R.S.O. 1990, c. p-5 (page 554n)

Partnerships Act, S.O. 1998, c. 2 amending *Partnerships Act,* R.S.O. 1990, c. P. 5 (page 331n)

Partnership Amendment Act 2001, S.S. 2001, c. 27 (page 331n)

Patent Act, R.S.C. 1985, c. P-4 (pages 428n, **433, 452**)

Patents Act (page **431**)

Patriot Act (page **646**)

Pay Equity Act, R.S.O. 1990, c. P-7 (page 506n)

Pay Equity Act, R.S.Q. 1990, c. E-12 (page 506n)

Personal Information Protection Act, S.A. 2003, c.P-6.5 (page 509n)

Personal Information Protection Act, S.B.C. 2003, c.63 (page 509n)

Personal Information and Electronic Documents Act, S.C. 2000, c. 5 (pages 115n, **509**)

Personal Information Protection and Electronic Documents Act (PIPEDA), S.C. 2000, c. 5 (pages **185, 607, 645**)

Personal Property Security Act, R.S.O. 1990, c. P-10 (pages 649n, 651n)

Personal Property Security Act, S.N.S. 1995–96, c. 13 (page 649n)

Petty Trespass Act, R.S.A. 2000, c. P-11 (page 274n)

Petty Trespass Act, R.S.M. 1987, c. P50 (page 274n)

Petty Trespass Act, R.S.N. 1990, c. P-11 (page 274n)

Plant Breeders' Rights Act, S.C. 1990, c. 20 (page 427n)

Precious Metals Marking Act, R.S.C. 1985, c. P-19 (page **583**)

Privacy Act, R.S.B.C. 1996, c. 373 (pages **282,** 427n)

Privacy Act, R.S.C. 1985, c. P-21 (page **509**)

Privacy Act, R.S.M. 1987, c. P-125 (page 282n)

Privacy Act, R.S.N.L. 1990, c. P-22 (page 282n)

Privacy Act, R.S.S. 1978, c. P-24 (page 282n)

Proceeds of Crime (Money Laundering) Act, S.C. 1991, c. 26 (page 621n)

Proceeds of Crime (Money Laundering) Act, S.C. 2000, c. 17 (page 621n)

Public Accountants Act, 1989, R.S.N.S., c. 369 (page 554n)

Public Accounting Act, 2004, S.O. 2004, c.9 as am. By S.O. 2006, c. 19, Sched. B. (page **555**)

Public Health Act, R.S.A. 2000, c. P-37 (page **6**)

Queen's Bench Act, S.S. 1998, c. Q-1.01 (page **131**)

Real Estate and Business Brokers Act, R.S.O. 1990, c. R.4 (page **181**)

Real Estate and Business Brokers Act, 2002, S.O. 2002, c. 30 (pages 293n, 269n)

Red Tape Reduction Act, S.O. 1999, c. 12 (page **149**)

Registry Act, R.S.O. 1990, c. R-20 (page 468n)

Repair and Storage Liens Act, R.S.O. 1990, c. R-25 (pages 418n, 419n)

Repairers' Lien Act, R.S.B.C. 1996, c. 404 (page 419n)

Representation Agreement Act, R.S.B.C. 1996 (Supp.), c. 405 (page 295n)

Sale of Goods Act, R.S.A. 2000, c. S-2 (page **100**)

Sale of Goods Act, R.S.O. 1990, c. S-1 (pages **145–46, 588,** 533n, 538n)

Sarbanes-Oxley Act (pages **379, 557**)

Secure Electronic Signature Regulations S.O.R./2000-30 page **185**)

Securities Act, R.S.O. 1990, c. S-5 (pages **354, 363–64, 365, 368,** 392n)

Sexual Sterilization Act, S.A. 1928, c 37 (page **34**)

Statute of Frauds, R.S.O. 1990, c. S-19 (pages 124n, **183–84, 185–86, 188, 189, 211,** 467n, 654n)

Statute Law Amendment Act, S.O. 1994, c. 27 (page 184n)

Textile Labelling Act, R.S.C. 1985, c. T-10 (pages **546, 580**)

Tobacco Act, S.C. 1997, c. 13 (pages **20, 21, 22, 31, 580, 583**)

Tobacco Act Cigarette Ignition Propensity Regulations, COR/2005-178 (page **46**)

Tobacco Control Act, S.S. 2001, c. T-14.1 (Saskatchewan) (pages **23, 24–26, 36, 41**)

Tobacco Products Information Regulations, S.O.R./2000/272 (page **28**)

Trade Practices Act, R.S.N. 1990, c. T-7 (pages 175n, 587n)

Trade-marks Act, R.S.C. 1985, c.T-13 (pages **277, 436, 438,** 439n, **450, 452**)

Trespass Act, R.S.B.C. 1996, c. 462 (page 274n)

Trespass Act, R.S.N.B. 1973, c.T-11.2 (page 274n)

Trespass to Premises Act, R.S.A. 2000, c. T-7 (page 274n)

Trespass to Property Act, R.S.O. 1990, c. T-21 (page 274n)

Unconscionable Transactions Act, R.S.A. 2000, c. U-2 (page 175n)

Unconscionable Transactions Relief Act, R.S.M. 1987, c. U20 (page 175n)

Unconscionable Transactions Relief Act, R.S.N.B. 1973, c. U-1 (page 175n)

Unconscionable Transactions Relief Act, R.S.N.S. 1989, c. 481 (page 175n)

Unconscionable Transactions Relief Act, R.S.N. 1990, c. U-1 (page 175n)

Unconscionable Transactions Relief Act, R.S.O. 1990, c. U-2 (page 175n)

Unconscionable Transactions Relief Act, R.S.P.E.I. 1988, c. U-2 (page 175n)

Unconscionable Transactions Relief Act, R.S.S. 1978, c. U-1 (page 175n)

Unemployment Insurance Act S.C. 2000, c. 30 (page 504n)

Unfair Contract Terms Act, 1977 (U.K.), c. 50 (page 415n)

Victims' Bill of Rights, 1995, S.O. 1995, c. 6 (page 225n)

Warehouse Lien Act, R.S.B.C. 1996, c. 480 (page 418n)

Warehouser's Lien Act, R.S.N. 1990, c.W-2 (page 418n)

Wildlife Act, R.S.A. 2000, c.W-10 (page 6n)

Integrated Pedagogical System

Basic legal principles and concepts are explained and reinforced through the use of extensive pedagogy designed to help you proceed and learn the material.

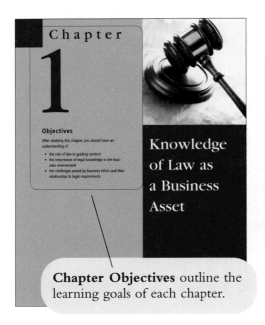

Chapter Objectives outline the learning goals of each chapter.

A **Business Law in Practice** scenario opens each chapter with a business situation containing both legal and managerial implications. A special section before the **Chapter Summary** called **Business Law in Practice Revisited** reviews the questions posed in the scenario with suggested responses.

Business Law in Practice

Janet and Alphonso Owen entered into a contract with Charles Conlin to construct their family home in Vancouver, B.C. Conlin inspired a lot of confidence. He told the Owens that he understood the importance of building the family home with great care and attention. "It's where you're going to live, for goodness sake," he stated. "Your home is an extension of you. Don't worry about anything. My work is second to none." For her part, Janet was particularly excited about a see-through fireplace that would be installed in the centre portion of the proposed house. A see-through fireplace opens onto two rooms, in this case, the living room and dining room.

Pursuant to the contract, Conlin, known as the "Contractor," had a number of obligations including as follows:

> 12. The Contractor covenants to construct in accordance with the relevant sections of the British Columbia *Building Code*.
>
> 13. The Contractor covenants to construct in accordance with plans and

Managing Risk

There are several risks that a business faces when the time comes to perform a contract. It may be that the business cannot perform at all or, that when it does perform, it does so deficiently. A business can attend to these possibilities proactively or reactively. From a proactive perspective, the business can negotiate for clauses to limit or exclude liability as well as for a *force majeure* clause, as appropriate. It may be, however, that the other side is unwilling to agree to such clauses. Another proactive strategy is to ensure that employees are competent and properly trained since any mistakes they make in performance of the contract are attributable to the employer. The better the employees do, the more likely the contract will be performed without incident. Securing proper insurance can also be effective, a matter discussed in Chapter 28 in more detail.

Once the business is in breach of contract, however, matters are now in a reactive mode. The contract breaker is in an unenviable position since it faces liability for all reasonable costs associated with its default. To reduce financial exposure and litigation expenses, the business should consider seeking mediation, arbitration, and other forms of compromise, including settlement offers, as alternatives to going to trial. Depending on the nature of the breach, the loss may be covered by insurance.

Those who contract for the provision of a product or service should undertake to ensure that the supplier is reputable and reliable. This way, legal conflict is perhaps avoided altogether.

When faced with a breach of contract, the innocent party must make a business decision—as much as a legal one—and decide how it should treat that failure. This decision involves evaluating the risks of losing in court; the remedies available including the amount of damages; the likelihood of being able to negotiate a settlement; and whether there is a valuable business relationship to preserve.

Business Law in Practice Revisited

1. **Can the Owens demonstrate all the steps in an action for breach of contract against Conlin?**

The Owens can meet all the steps to succeed in an action for breach of contract. They can show privity of contract between themselves and Conlin. They can show that Conlin breached the contract in multiple ways, including by failing to build the

The real-world application of legal knowledge is reinforced through the **Business Application of the Law,** which provides examples that illustrate how the law affects a business enterprise—such as, for example, the issues to consider when determining whether to pursue a legal conflict.

Business Application of the Law — **Unjustified Performance Claims**

Performance-enhancing products are common, but the manufacturer cannot make claims about their effectiveness without proof of their truth. Three recent cases have involved claims relating to fuel-saving devices, health benefits of tanning, and weight loss.

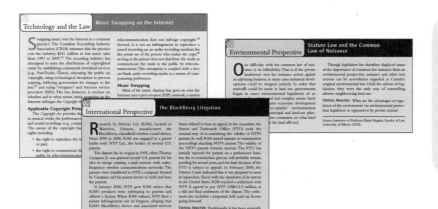

New technologies, globalization, and the environment all have implications for many aspects of business law. Learn how in the **Technology and the Law**, **International Perspective**, and **Environmental Perspective** features.

Peoples Department Stores Inc. (Trustee of) v. Wise (2004), 244 DLR (4th) 564 (S.C.C.).

THE BUSINESS CONTEXT: The *Canada Business Corporations Act* imposes a duty on directors and officers to act honestly and in good faith with a view to the best interests of the corporation (the fiduciary duty) and to exercise the care, diligence, and skill that a reasonably prudent person would exercise in comparable circumstances (a duty of care).[32] There have been questions about whether the duties of directors extend to creditors, particularly when the corporation is financially troubled. In this case, which is now Canada's leading case on directors' duties, the Supreme Court addresses this question.

FACTUAL BACKGROUND: Lionel, Ralph, and Harold Wise were majority shareholders and directors of Wise Stores Inc., a publicly traded company operating about 50 junior department stores in Quebec with annual sales of $100 million. In 1992, Wise Inc. acquired all of the shares of Peoples Department Stores Inc., from Marks & Spencer for $27 million. Peoples owned 81 stores and generated sales of $160 million annually. The Wise brothers became

The **Special Case format** follows a standard analysis for every featured case and landmark case, beginning with an explanation of the BUSINESS CONTEXT that is at issue. Readers are then given the FACTUAL BACKGROUND of the case and presented with the LEGAL QUESTIONS before they actually read the court's RESOLUTION. Each case ends with questions for CRITICAL ANALYSIS. Each of these sections is clearly labelled for easy reference.

Ethical Considerations — The Payday Loans Dilemma

There has been considerable publicity in recent years surrounding what have come to be called payday loans. These are loans usually granted for a short period of time by a storefront operation for the purpose of tiding the borrower over until payday. The concern focuses on the actual cost of these loans, which can amount to 1000 percent when the nominal interest rate is calculated on an annual basis and various fees, commissions, and penalties are added. For example, a plaintiff in a class-action suit borrowed $300 on 19 March, rolled it over five times and repaid it in full on 11 July. He paid the principal of $300 plus $470 in broker fees, $40 in interest, and $22 in transaction fees.

There is concern that borrowers are being exploited by the lenders, both in terms of the cost of credit and their lack of awareness of the actual cost. On the other hand, it is argued that these borrowers are not well served by banks and are attracted to payday lenders by their location, hours of business, and accessibility.

There are many different approaches to this dilemma

- Lenders could be prosecuted under the *Criminal Code* since the actual cost of these loans is well in excess of the permitted 60 percent annual maximum.
- The industry could be made exempt from the criminal provisions and regulated in a noncriminal fashion.

The **Ethical Considerations** feature assists the student in assessing the sometimes uncomfortable compromises that the law forges between competing interests.

The **Landmark Case** and **Business and Legislation** features provide accounts of pivotal case law and historical legislative initiatives.

Carlill v. Carbolic Smoke Ball Co., [1893] 1 Q.B. 256 (Eng. C.A.)

THE HISTORICAL CONTEXT: This case was decided at a time when Victorian England was being inundated with quack cures. Examples of "miracle" cures included Epps Glycerine Jube Jubes and a product called Prosolic, which claimed to prevent marriage ... prevented indigestion. The ad ... that indigestion "Causes Bad ... Peppery Disposition, Domestic ... and—the Divorce Court."[*]

...: This case considers the legal ... resulted from the advertisement ... Smoke Ball Company in a ... the turn of the 19th century. ... the smoke ball as directed for ... ght influenza anyway. When the ... pay her the advertised reward, ... action for breach of contract.

Business and Legislation — Incorporating in British Columbia

The new *British Columbia Business Corporations Act*[20] came into force in March 2004. The act replaces the *Company Act* and represents the first major reform of corporate legislation in B.C. in 30 years.

The act retains the contract model of incorporation (shareholders can specify the nature of their agreement with the corporation) rather than adopting the statutory model that is used in the *Canada Business Corporations Act (CBCA)* and in the companies legislation of most other provinces. The new act does, however, adopt many features of the *CBCA* while including features not found elsewhere.

The major changes embodied in the new act include the following:

- *Directors and officers.* There is now no residency requirement for directors (the CBCA requires 25 percent resident Canadians). Also a company is not required to have a president and secretary (matching the CBCA's requirements).
- *Directors' duties.* The duties of directors and the events that trigger liability are much the same as in the CBCA. However the solvency test for determining liability is simpler. Under the new act it means "the inability to pay debts as they become due in the usual course of business" (under the CBCA there are several definitions). Also now there is no requirement for court ...

FIGURE 6.2

Carbolic Smoke Ball Advertisement

£100 REWARD
WILL BE PAID BY THE
CARBOLIC SMOKE BALL CO.
To any person who contracts the increasing Epidemic, INFLUENZA
Colds, or any diseases caused by taking cold, AFTER HAVING USED THE BALL
3 times daily for two weeks according to the printed directions supplied with each Ball.
£1000
Is deposited with the ALLIANCE BANK, REGENT STREET, showing our sincerity in the matter.
During the last epidemic of Influenza many of our CARBOLIC SMOKE BALLS were sold as Preventives against this Disease, and in no ascertained case was the disease contracted by those using the CARBOLIC SMOKE BALL.

THE LEGAL QUESTION: Was there a contract between the parties, even though Mrs. Carlill did not communicate her acceptance of the Carbolic Smoke Ball Company's offer?

Chapter Study

Key Terms and Concepts

arbitration (p. 8)
breach of contract (p. 6)
business ethics (p. 11)
business law (p. 4)
contract law (p. 7)
law (p. 4)

legal risk management plan ... liability (p. 8)
litigation (p. 7)
mediation (p. 8)
spam (p. 3)

Questions for Review

1. What is the function of law?
2. How does the law protect members of society?
3. How does the law facilitate business activity?
4. In what ways does law facilitate certainty in the marketplace?
5. Does the nature of the business relationship affect the enforcement of legal rights?
6. How does the law resolve disputes?
7. Does dispute resolution always involve going to court?
8. In what way is knowle ... business asset?
9. How might a lack of know ... atively impact a business?
10. Why should a business pu ... management plan?
11. What is the role of busine ...
12. Why are business ethics i ...
13. What is spam?
14. What is the purpose of reg ...

Questions for Critical Thinking

1. Many companies and organizations have codes of conduct; however, there is often a gap between the code and the daily performance of employers. How could the gap be narrowed? What steps could businesses take to ensure a ... more ethical corporate c ... 850 codes of ethics, incl ... http://www.iit.edu/depa ... coe.html.

2. What is the relationship between ethics and law? Are ethical responsibilities the same as legal responsibilities?
3. When in a lawsuit the best response to a legal dispute? What is at risk?
4. Knowledge of the law is a business asset. How can you acquire this asset short of becoming a lawyer? How is ignorance of the law a liability?
5. The legal requirement for UL labels is intended to protect society. What are some other examples of such a law?

Situations for Discussion

1. Joe has recently opened a bar and adjoining restaurant, specializing in seafood. It is named "The Finny Friends" after a restaurant that Joe had visited in Toronto several years ago. In accordance with the law, Joe has a liquor licence from the provincial liquor licensing authority that limits the seating capacity in the bar to 30. As Joe's bar becomes increasing popular, he begins to regularly allow over 60 patrons in at one time. Eventually he is caught, and—having already received two warnings—his operation is closed down for 30 days. Joe is flabbergasted at the severity of the penalty. Soon thereafter, Joe is contacted by a lawyer for The Finny Friends restaurant in Toronto. The lawyer says that Joe has 48 hours to take down his restaurant awning and destroy anything else with the name The Finny Friends on it (including menus, invoices, placemats, napkins, and even match covers) or he will bring an application for a court order to that effect. To make matters worse, a health inspector is on Joe's doorstep saying that there have been several recent reports of food poisoning originating from Joe's restaurant. What has gone wrong in Joe's business and why?

2. Discuss the kinds of legal questions that you think might arise in the following business proposals:
   - Corporation A is planning to launch a new marketing program featuring an advertising campaign that extols the virtues of its product and denigrates the product of Corporation B.

- Corporation C is planning to construct an oil rig at the mouth of a particular river to exploit a recent mineral find.
- Corporation D is planning to expand its manufacturing facilities into a foreign country. In order to finance its operations, it is planning to sell shares to the public.

3. Assume that you have a major dispute with a business on the property next to yours over acceptable use of its land. You find that although zoning allows a small tool shop to operate on the property, the noise is too much for you. Your lawyer tells you that there may be a legal case for you to pursue, but it will be costly and the results are not guaranteed. What alternative approaches might address your problem more effectively?

4. Several provinces across Canada, including Ontario, Manitoba, and Saskatchewan, have proposed or passed legislation that prevents children from buying or renting video games that are expressly violent or sexual, as determined by a ratings board. Businesses found selling these games to minors face penalties that range from fines to having their license revoked.[38] How effective do you think government regulation is in limiting children's access to violent video games? Are there better ways of achieving these types of goals? Is it the role of government to provide legal consequences for the underage renting or purchase of violent video games?

End-of-chapter materials include **Key Terms and Concepts** with page references, **Questions for Review, Questions for Critical Thinking,** and **Situations for Discussion. Questions for Review** will help you to check your understanding of chapter topics; **Questions for Critical Thinking** and **Situations for Discussion** will let you apply the concepts you have learned to other business situations.

16 • PART 1 THE LEGAL ENVIRONMENT OF BUSINESS

NEL CHAPTER 1 KNOWLEDGE OF LAW AS A BUSINESS ASSET • 17

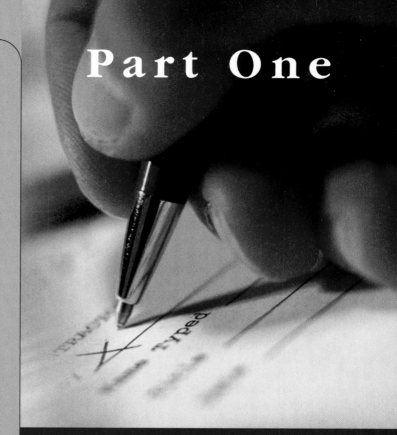

Part One

THIS TEXT DEALS WITH THE IMPORTANCE OF THE LAW to business and, in Parts Two to Nine, presents fundamental legal principles in their relevant business contexts. The text contends that those engaged in business need to manage the legal environment as much as any other aspect of their business. Part One provides the basis for that management by introducing the foundations of business law and the concept of legal risk management. It emphasizes the importance of knowing the law, complying with the law, avoiding unexpected legal problems, and regarding law not as an obstacle, but as a way to facilitate commercial activity.

The Legal Environment of Business

Chapter 1   Knowledge of Law as a Business Asset

Chapter 2   The Canadian Legal System

Chapter 3   Managing Legal Risks

Chapter 4   Dispute Resolution

Chapter

1

Objectives

After studying this chapter, you should have an understanding of

- the role of law in guiding conduct
- the importance of legal knowledge in the business environment
- the challenges posed by business ethics and their relationship to legal requirements

Knowledge of Law as a Business Asset

Business Law in Practice

Louella Lambast has decided to open a gift store. She intends to offer a wide selection of ever-changing, low-priced giftware including T-shirts, novelty toys, costume jewellery, comic books, video games, and household goods. She is tremendously excited about her new venture but cash poor. For this reason, Louella decides to do a lot of the work of setting up her store, including assembling a large glass display case. Louella also takes some immediate steps to make her store known by arranging for mass commercial e-mails to be sent out.

Louella's next decision is to stock all her product from an overseas supplier, including an array of T-shirts bearing the labels of a streetwear manufacturer known as FUBU (For You By Us). Louella tells friends that although she has a pretty good idea that product supplied to her may end up being illegal "knockoffs" of brand name designers, she does not know that with 100 percent certainty. "I'm not legally responsible for what people like my supplier do, anyway," she determines. "Plus, business is a game; I'll handle any fallout as it arises."

Louella also imports some small table lamps. When the lamps arrive, she notices that they do not contain labels identifying them as certified safe by Underwriters' Laboratories of Canada or another approved group. The Underwriters' Laboratories is an international, independent, and not-for-profit organization whose mandate is to evaluate product safety. The UL mark means that the organization has tested samples of the product in question and concluded that requisite safety requirements have been met.[1] Because Louella is completely satisfied that the lamps pose no risk, she decides to attach some counterfeit labels on the lamps to reassure her customers.

A few months later, Louella's world is falling apart. A customer suffers a head injury when the glass display case that Louella had improperly assembled suddenly collapses. A group of demonstrators has begun picketing Louella's business premises protesting the violent kind of comic books she sells. The Underwriters' Laboratories has learned that lamps in Louella's store contain counterfeit labels indicating that they had UL approval, and the police are now involved. Louella's lawyer has explained that she will likely face prosecution for distributing material infringing copyright as well as for violating the *Criminal Code of Canada*.

Just when it seemed that things could not get worse, Louella receives a phone call from an American who has been inundated with her unsolicited commercial e-mail. The individual is livid, advising Louella that she is in breach of recent American legislation that he calls the *CAN-SPAM Act*. The *Controlling the Assault of Non-Solicited Pornography and Marketing Act of 2003*[2] permits e-advertising only under certain circumstances. The **spam** must contain an opt-out mechanism so that the recipient can "unsubscribe"; a valid return e-mail address; a subject line identifying the e-mail as an advertisement or solicitation; and a valid postal (i.e., physical) address of the mailer.[3] The American tells Louella that she could go to jail for five years and faces civil penalties of $250 per e-mail, to a maximum of $2 million.[4] Since Louella's spam did not conform with the legislation, Louella is terrified that she will receive a large fine or possibly end up serving time in an American prison. Needless to say, Louella's business cannot survive this barrage of legal problems. Nor can her reputation.

spam
Unsolicited email advertising a product or service.

---

1. For UL (Canada)'s website, go to this book's website under Chapter 1 and follow the links. Alternatively, go to http://www.ulc.ca
2. To see the entire legislation, go to http://www.spamlaws.com/federal/can-spam.shtml
3. For discussion of these legislative requirements, see http://www.bakernet.com/ecommerce/can-spam-act-memo.pdf. See also the Federal Trade Commission website at http://www.ftc.gov/bcp/conline/pubs/buspubs/canspam.htm
4. For penalties, see sections 4, 5, and 7 of the Act, *supra* note 2.

1. How does the law affect Louella's business?
2. What are the purposes of the laws that affect Louella's business?
3. What has gone wrong in Louella's business, and why?

Law in the Business Environment

The law affects virtually every aspect of society, including the business environment. The law affects most business decisions—from development of the basic business idea through to its implementation, and all the attendant matters in between, including financing, hiring, production, marketing, and sales. As Louella starts her business, for example, she will be involved in a number of transactions and events with significant legal implications.

For instance, to get her business off the ground, Louella has to decide whether to form a corporation, operate as a sole proprietor, or find partners. She also has financing decisions to make: Should she borrow money, use her own funds, or perhaps sell shares in her venture? Louella also needs to find a location for her store, whether by constructing a new building, purchasing an existing structure, or leasing premises from someone else. She requires furnishings, signage, and supplies. While her operation is starting out small, she may ultimately have to hire employees. Louella also has to market her business in order to build and maintain a customer base. All of these decisions have legal aspects, whether Louella recognizes that or not.

By understanding the role of law in the multitude of business decisions that people like Louella must make, an entrepreneur can maximize the protection that the law extends while avoiding its pitfalls. Put another way, knowledge of the law is a business asset that can assist owners and managers in reaching their goals and objectives. This is because **business law**

business law
A set of established rules governing commercial relationships, including the enforcement of rights.

- defines general rules of commerce
- protects business ideas and more tangible forms of property
- provides mechanisms that permit businesspeople to select their desired degree of participation and exposure to risk in business ventures
- seeks to ensure that losses are borne by those who are responsible for them
- facilitates planning by ensuring compliance with commitments

Of course, a businessperson can function with little or no understanding of the law. This lack of knowledge, however, may result in failure to maximize opportunities or in losing out on them altogether. For example, a business that neglects to protect its intellectual property may have its ideas taken by a competitor with impunity; a business that ignores employment and human rights laws may be forced to reverse human resource decisions or pay compensation to wronged employees; a business that fails to explore different modes of carrying out business may suffer unnecessary losses. Perhaps even more seriously, this lack of legal knowledge may result in the business or its owner being subjected to regulatory and judicial sanctions, including being fined, forced to pay penalties, or closed down altogether.

Rules and Principles

law
The set of rules and principles guiding conduct in society.

Broadly defined, the **law** is a set of rules and principles intended to guide conduct in society, primarily by protecting persons and their property; facilitating personal and commercial interactions; and providing mechanisms for dispute resolution.

Protecting Persons and Their Property

Probably the most familiar purpose of the law is to provide protection. Those who violate the *Criminal Code of Canada*—such as by breaking into another person's house, assaulting someone, or committing a commercial fraud—are subject to criminal sanctions, such as fines or imprisonment. From this vantage point, the law protects members of society in two ways: first, it sets rules with penalties in order to encourage compliance and, second, it seeks to make those who break the law accountable for their misconduct.

Business Application of the Law | Fraud on the Public

For reasons of public safety, electrical products must be approved by Underwriters' Laboratories (UL) or another approved group such as the Canadian Standards Association. In defiance of this requirement, San Francisco Gifts Ltd., also called San Diego Gifts, with stores across Canada, has recently admitted in court to attaching fake UL safety labels to table lamps as well as selling counterfeit brand-name products such as Tommy Hilfiger, Playboy, and West Coast Chopper, as reported by the *Edmonton Journal*. The presiding judge was particularly concerned about the phony UL labels: "That is despicable," he stated. "We're talking about electrical appliances causing fires....The exercise of getting cheap stuff somewhere else and dressing it up with false labels and false safety certificates causes me great pause....Quite frankly, this should be described as nothing less than a despicable fraud on the public, bordering on a massive scale." The *Edmonton Journal* also reported that Brian Monks, director of anti-counterfeiting operations for UL, has identified this case as the first instance of such a conviction in Canada.

In a surprising June 2006 development, San Francisco Gifts Ltd. has been accused—yet again—of distributing lamps with counterfeit UL safety labels at the company's 60 stores. According to reporter Trish Audette, the San Francisco chain and its owner are charged with "one count of distributing an infringed copyright under the *Copyright Act* and one count of passing off goods bearing counterfeit trade marks under the *Criminal Code*."

CRITICAL ANALYSIS: What are the alternatives to market regulation by government?

Sources: Gordon Kent, "Angry Judge Slams Chain for Fake Labels on Goods" *Edmonton Journal*, (31 December 2004) at A1 and A14; Trish Audette, "Novelty Store Owner Charged with Infringing Copyright Law" *Edmonton Journal* (28 June 2006) at B2. For a link to the 2004 provincial court judgment in this case, see http://www.cacn.ca/case%20law/san%20francisco%20gifts.HTM (accessed July 6, 2006).

The law also protects businesses by setting penalties and ensuring accountability. For example, if one business misappropriates another business's legally protected commercial idea, the law can step in and sanction that conduct. As well, the law ensures that losses are paid for by the parties responsible for creating them. For example, if a law firm gives negligent advice to a client, that client can sue the firm for associated losses.

Louella's business intersects with the law in both of these ways. First, the law guards her business interests. For example, should a supplier fail to deliver a product to Louella, this is a **breach of contract** and she can sue for damages. If a competitor wrongfully injures Louella's business reputation, she can sue for defamation.[5] However, the law also protects those who deal with Louella's business. Louella must not discriminate in hiring practices. She must not disregard health and safety regulations governing the workplace. She must pay her creditors. Louella must not sell knockoffs of brand name designers—nor it is a defense that she "did not know that with 100 percent certainty" that the product supplied was counterfeit;[6] she is responsible nonetheless. Louella should respect the laws of other countries that may apply to her business operation. In sum, Louella is obliged to abide by the law on a variety of fronts, since failure to comply can have severe consequences, including financial penalties and criminal prosecution.

Business Application of the Law

Coyote Carcasses in Restaurant Freezer

Animal welfare officers notified a Health Inspector after finding four coyote carcasses in the walk-in freezer of an Alberta restaurant. It is contrary to law to sell uninspected meat from an unapproved source, according to Richard Reive, an environmental health officer—and whether "it's a coyote or a wooly mammoth doesn't make much of a difference." The Alberta *Public Health Act* regulations require that all meat served must be inspected.[7]

Dr. Gerry Preddy, medical officer of health for the Capital Health region, told reporter David Howell that the key issue was the lack of inspection. While at least one official suspected that the carcasses were intended for human consumption—particularly as they were found in a restaurant freezer—Preddy was more circumspect, stating: "We're not jumping to any conclusions at this point, until we have more information."

Another legal issue was whether the coyotes were acquired unlawfully. Under the *Wildlife Act*,[8] it is illegal to sell the meat of any wild species, subject to certain exceptions. In the meantime, the restaurant has been closed and, according to press accounts released at the time of the offenses, the owners cannot be found.

CRITICAL ANALYSIS: Should the law prohibit uninspected meat from being served in a restaurant? What are the reasons for regulating this area?

Fish and Wildlife Officer Doug Northstein examining seized carcasses.

Source: David Howell, "Gutted Canine Carcasses Likely Intended for Menu" *Edmonton Journal* (6 November 2003) at A3; "Carcasses in Restaurant Freezer Were Coyotes" (11 November 2003) at B1 and "Suspected Dog Carcasses Found at Edmonton Restaurant" CBC News (5 November 2003) at http://www.cbc.ca/story/news/national/2003/11/05/dogs031105.html (accessed October 17, 2006).

---

5. Defamation is the public utterance of a false statement of fact or opinion that harms another's reputation. For discussion of the tort of defamation, see Chapter 12.
6. Selling products that she "had a pretty good idea" were knockoffs could, among other illegalities, amount to criminal fraud under section 380 of the *Criminal Code*, R.S.C. 1985, c. C-46.
7. Regulations provide that a commercial food establishment must obtain all food that is liable under law to inspection by the Government of Canada or Alberta or by an agency of either from a source that is subject to inspection by that entity. See what is now section 22(1) Alta. Reg. 31, 2006 pursuant to the *Public Health Act*. For further discussion as to what legislation and regulations are, see Chapter 2.
8. Section 62 of the *Wildlife Act*, R.S.A. 2000, c. W-10

Facilitating Interactions

The law facilitates personal interactions by providing rules concerning marriage, adoption, and the disposal of property upon the owner's death, to name a few examples. The law also facilitates commercial activity by providing rules governing the marketplace. The law of contract, for example, provides a way for parties to enter into binding agreements, thereby creating a measure of security and certainty in their business operations. **Contract law** allows business enterprises to plan for the future and to enforce their expectations.

Although the law addresses failed relations—as when one party does not meet its contractual obligations or gives negligent legal advice—it is not primarily about conflict. Rather, the law functions to prevent disputes and to facilitate relationships. It provides certainty for Louella's commercial agreements and enables her to engage in transactions that might otherwise be unstructured and unpredictable.

Nor is the law primarily about rules that constrain commerce. Though the law does forbid certain activities—such as false advertising and operating without a business license—its more significant role is facilitative. Legal rules provide definition and context to doing business. For example, assume that Louella wants to enter into a long-term relationship with a particularly reliable local supplier. Contract law allows her to accomplish this end by providing a mechanism through which Louella and the supplier can describe—and enforce—their commitments to each other. Therefore, Louella can agree in advance with her supplier on what kind of product is to be provided, how much, at what price, over what period of time, and when.

The creation of certainty in business relationships is one of the most important contributions that law can make to the commercial arena. While the necessity of creating certainty means that some anticipated contracts founder when it comes to formalizing their content, the law has not necessarily "failed." It more likely means that the businesspeople involved were not as close to being in agreement as they had initially assumed. Further discussions, perhaps through lawyers, have simply identified problems that, although hidden, were always there.

No contract can recite and provide for all contingencies; there will be some issues left unstated, but often the parties themselves find ways of overcoming these omissions. Generally, they will be guided by the need to achieve the original intent behind the contractual relationship, with the objective of dealing fairly with the unexpected or unaddressed event that has just occurred. In this way, the business relationship "fills in the blanks" in the contractual arrangement. If one or both of the parties involve the legal system, a judge will apply established rules governing contracts that lack the necessary specificity.

The influence of the law on the business environment does not have to be exacting and literal. In fact, parties to a business contract do not always observe their agreement to the letter, preferring to maintain their relationship rather than sue for breach of contract. For example, assume that Louella has a five-year contract with a reputable supplier of plastic bags customized to Louella's specifications. These bags are important to Louella's business since they hold her customers's retail purchases and are also part of her business's look. Owing to poor planning, the supplier will be unable to make its delivery on time and has advised Louella of the delay. Although she may be annoyed at the default, Louella stands to lose more than she would gain from suing, particularly if the supplier is otherwise reliable and the two have a solid working relationship. There is no good reason to risk this relationship and devote resources to **litigation,** that is, the process involved in suing someone else. In this way, the contract between Louella and the supplier provides the legal backdrop to their relationship—by defining rights and obligations—but it is the business relationship that determines whether strict legal rights will be insisted upon. This is an important reality that affects how the law actually operates in the business environment.

Providing Mechanisms for Dispute Resolution

Whether a conflict can or even should be resolved outside the formal legal system depends on the circumstances. If Louella hires an on-site manager who proves to be incompetent, it is in the interests of her enterprise to terminate the person's employment. While Louella may have a case to fire the employee outright, she might also consider offering a small severance package to reduce the possibility of being sued for wrongful dismissal.[9] This is a judgment call, but the time and money saved in avoiding a court battle may more than offset the cost of the severance package. Conversely, it may be that the employee has had his hand in the till and stolen some of the business's daily receipts. Louella is in a different situation now. She not only must ensure that the employee leaves the company immediately, but also will probably want to involve the police and try to recover what the employee has taken. In these kinds of circumstances, a full-blown legal conflict is much more likely and appropriate.

When one party fails to keep a contractual commitment, suing that person may seem to be the best and only response. This is particularly true when someone feels badly treated and believes that an essential principle is at stake in the conflict. However, the desire to stand up for this principle at all costs tends to betray a short-term perspective and should be resisted. Maintaining a good business relationship with the party in breach—or at least minimizing the financial costs of the dispute—is often much more important than proving yourself to be "right" in a court of law. Questions to ask include

- ■ Are legal proceedings absolutely necessary, at least right now?
- ■ Is there a way to resolve the problem from a larger, relationship-preserving perspective, rather than from a strictly legal viewpoint?

mediation
A process through which the parties to a dispute endeavour to reach a resolution with the assistance of a neutral person.

Solutions to a legal dispute exist at various levels of formality. The first logical step is for the parties to try to come to a resolution between themselves and produce, if necessary, a formalized settlement agreement. If this solution does not work, the legal system offers **mediation** and **arbitration** as ways of avoiding litigation. Thus, the law provides a number of mechanisms for settling disputes short of a courtroom battle.

arbitration
A process through which a neutral party makes a decision (usually binding) that resolves a dispute.

Sometimes, however, one business will commence legal action against another and take the matter to court. Perhaps there had been no previous agreement between the parties to refer disputes to arbitration and they have no desire to do so now; perhaps one of the parties refuses to accept mediation; perhaps one of the parties is tremendously unfair and cannot be reasoned with; or perhaps the dispute has reached the point at which a court ruling is the only way to end the matter once and for all. It is essential to a workable business environment that the last-resort solution provided by the litigation process be available to the disputants. In this way, the **liability** of one business to another can be established.

liability
Legal responsibility for the event or loss that has occurred.

---

9. For discussion of wrongful dismissal, see Chapter 21.

Business Application of the Law

Four major Internet services providers (ISPs), including Yahoo, have recently sued some of the leading senders of spam. "We are trying to find the biggest, the baddest and the most notorious," according to Randall Boe, lawyer for America Online. While "casual spammers" are no longer in business, he notes, the object now is to target the "hardcore" group. According to Boe, "You can't not sue. You have to sue. You have to put people in jail who are the most egregious. And you have to filter out spam at the ISP level. It is the combination of methods that will knock these people down and bring us back to a level of sanity we can deal with." CBC Online reports that an estimated 15 billion spam messages are sent every day.

One of the companies sued by Yahoo is the now defunct Gold Disk Canada (based in Kitchener, Ontario), a company run by Eric Head and his family members. Gold Disk Canada was started by Head in 1998, when he was 19 years old. According to *The Globe and Mail*, Yahoo alleges that the Heads' spamming operation sent more than 94 million e-mails in one month alone to Yahoo customers.

This lawsuit has now been settled. The Heads have agreed to pay Yahoo at least US$100 000 though the exact amount is confidential. Eric Head has closed Gold Disk Canada and become a drummer in a rock band. In his prepared statement, Head expressed deep regret and stated, "I urge everyone who is involved in the commercial bulk e-mail business to cease all operations unless and until they are completely compliant with the requirements of the new United States anti-spam laws. There is no substitute for complete compliance." For further analysis of spam, see Chapter 6.

CRITICAL ANALYSIS: Do you think that these lawsuits will stop spam? What were the risks associated with bringing this lawsuit?

Sources: Paul Waldie, "Canada's Spam King Apologizes, Tells Others to Mend Their Ways" *The Globe and Mail* (15 June 2004) at A1; "Web Providers Fire Legal Salvo against Spam," *New York Times* article reprinted in *The Edmonton Journal* (11 March 2004) at A5; and Robin Rowland, "Spam, Spam, Spam: The Cyberspace Wars" CBC News (24 November 2003, updated 12 March 2004) at http://www.cbc.ca/news/background/spam/index.html (accessed October 17, 2006).

How and Why the Law Works

There are any number of ways to resolve a dispute, including trial by ordeal (as in the notorious Salem witch trials of 17th-century America); pistol duel (prevalent in France and England until the 19th century); and even modern-day drive-by shootings. What these methods lack, however, is accordance with modern ideas of what is just, fair, and reasonable.

Canada's legal system stands in opposition to such inequitable, arbitrary, and violent alternatives. While our legal system is far from perfect, it possesses essential improvements over its predecessors because it determines liability in accordance with certain principles and processes that are regarded as just.

For example, assume that Louella is suing a supplier for breach of contract for failure to deliver, and the matter has now come before a judge. The Canadian legal system demands that both the process for determining liability and the rules or laws that are applied in that process are fair and free from bias. Though it is impossible for our legal system to completely reach such a laudable standard, these are its laudable goals.

Louella, as the party who has initiated the complaint of breach of contract, is obligated to prove her case. The judge, in turn, is obligated to be as objective as possible in determining whether Louella has proven her case. Part of the judge's job is to determine what the agreement between the parties actually was, as well as the law governing the matter. The judge must then apply this law as impartially as possible to the situation. In order that the outcome of Louella's dispute with the supplier be seen as just, the law that the judge ultimately relies on must also be fair and reasonable.

For instance, it is a rule of law that a party who suffers a breach of contract is entitled to be put in the position that she would have been in had the contract been fulfilled. If Louella can prove that as a result of the supplier's breach she lost business, for example, a court may well award her damages for loss of profit. The rationale behind the rule is simple: the supplier has broken his contractual promise. The supplier must therefore assume responsibility for any direct and foreseeable financial consequences Louella experiences as a result.

The goals of the Canadian justice system are ambitious and often difficult to achieve. There are also obvious limitations to what the law can actually accomplish, even when it is most successful. Employment equity law will not end discrimination. Reform of bankruptcy law will not prevent business failures. More restrictive copyright laws will not stop unauthorized copying in everyday life. As noted earlier, the law can, however, offer itself as a mechanism for achieving the goals of protection, facilitation, and dispute resolution. For example, bankruptcy law is the vehicle for ensuring that all those affected by a failed business are treated fairly, reasonably, and according to a set of agreed-upon rules. The law is prepared to confront bigotry by providing remedies to those who are the targets. It provides rules for contract formation. And it provides a vast machinery for resolving conflict.

This man claimed to have been locked in a car trunk over an alleged debt owed to his attackers. He was freed from the trunk by firefighters. How is this method of dispute resolution inconsistent with the values informing the Canadian justice system?

Knowledge of the Law as a Business Asset

Entrepreneurs like Louella can use the law to protect and advance their business interests. Conversely, they can cause themselves much anxiety, grief, and financial loss by ignoring the law.

For example, the law holds Louella responsible for the head injuries suffered by her customer because Louella was negligent in how she assembled the display case.[10] Louella also infringed copyright law and the *Criminal Code of Canada* in using the counterfeit UL sticker.[11] Selling products that she "had a pretty good idea" were knockoffs could, among other illegalities, amount to criminal fraud under section 380 of the *Criminal Code of Canada*. As for her problems with the American antispamming legislation, Louella faces penalties that range from fines to imprisonment.[12]

Though the application of a foreign criminal statute is a fact-specific inquiry, in practice it is unlikely that Louella will suffer any antispamming sanctions since she lives in Canada and is therefore outside the personal jurisdiction or reach of an American court.[13] Nor does she appear to have assets in the United States that would be at risk. But even though Louella may have dodged this particular bullet, she has still broken California law and doubtless aggravated a good many people with her spam. Persistence in this line of advertising will further damage her business reputation.

While Louella's negative experience with the law is exaggerated, it illustrates the point that knowing the law is a business asset. Had Louella taken the time to inform herself about the laws governing her operations—as well as about the consequences for failing to abide by them—her business experience presumably would have been much more positive and profitable.

An effective way to avoid Louella's negative business experience and enhance returns is to implement a **legal risk management plan.** This means identifying the legal risks associated with a business and implementing concrete measures for managing those risks. The objective is to identify and plan for risks *before* they occur rather than adopting the reactive mode that Louella favours.[14]

legal risk management plan
A comprehensive action plan for dealing with the legal risks involved in operating a business.

Law and Business Ethics

From the perspective of reputation and profitability, it is not enough for a commercial enterprise simply to comply with the law. **Business ethics** also provide an increasingly important overlay. Business ethics concern moral principles and values that seek to determine right and wrong in the business world. On this basis, while it is ethical for a business to comply with the law, ethics may demand even more. Business ethics require entrepreneurs to conform to principles of commercial morality, fairness, and honesty. Entire books have been written about the ethical problems or dilemmas that a business might face.[15] A few examples follow:

business ethics
Moral principles and values that seek to determine right and wrong in the business world.

- ■ LABOUR PRACTICES. To what lengths should a company go to enhance shareholder return? To reduce costs, should a business employ child labour in those countries where it is legal to do so? What if the child's income is essential to the family's survival?

- ■ EMPLOYEE PRIVACY. Should a business monitor employee e-mails and Internet use on company computers?

---

10. For discussion of the tort of negligence, see Chapter 11.
11. For discussion of copyright, see Chapter 18.
12. See *Controlling the Assault of Non-Solicited Pornography and Marketing Act* (Can-Spam Act), *supra* note 2.
13. For further analysis of the problems of enforcing antispamming legislation, see C.S. Maravilla, "The Feasibility of a Law to Regulate Pornographic, Unsolicited, Commercial E-Mail" (Spring 2002) Tul. J. Tech. & Intell. Prop. 117.
14. See Chapter 3 for a risk management model.
15. For an excellent survey of the kind of ethical questions business must face, see Laura Pincus Hartman, *Perspectives in Business Ethics* (Chicago: Irwin McGraw-Hill, 1998).

- ENVIRONMENTAL PROTECTION. Should a business improve upon the minimum environmental standards required by legislation? Should it move production to countries that have exceedingly low environmental standards?

- ADVERTISING. How far should a company go in extolling the virtues of its product? When does sales talk become deception?

- BLUFFING. Short of lying or fraud, is it ethical to bluff during business negotiations? When does bluffing become a form of corruption?

As for Louella, many of her legal problems actually arise *because* of her unethical perspective and sole focus on "doing the deal" whatever the subsequent cost. On a related front, Louella does not take the law seriously. Both these attitudes can contribute to the demise of a business, as the spectacular collapse of Enron Corp. illustrates.

Louella seems consumed with short-sighted goals, causing her to violate overlapping legal and ethical norms. It is illegal and unethical to misrepresent a product as having passed a safety test when it has not, yet this is exactly what Louella does by using counterfeit UL labels on the imported lamps she retails. Similarly, it is illegal and unethical for Louella to sell knockoffs of FUBU merchandise; she is essentially misappropriating one company's reputation to increase her own sales. Even Louella's spamming has legal and ethical implications since not only is she breaking American law, but also arguably breaching ethical norms by commandeering the time and resources of the recipients without compensation.

Sometimes ethical standards are even stricter than legal ones, as Louella is learning. Though Louella is obviously free to sell any kind of legal product she sees fit—including extremely violent comic books—her choices are not automatically sanitized as a result. Indeed, skirting ethical norms can lead to lost revenue, bad publicity, public demonstrations, and condemnation for contributing to social injustice.

Companies currently accused of breaching legal and ethical standards include Shell (for allegedly contributing to environmental degradation and human rights violations in Nigeria); and Nike (for allegedly paying offshore workers subsistence wages).[16]

Ethical Considerations

The Demise of Enron

Enron—an American company that supplied energy and other commodities to an international customer base—used to be called the "World's Coolest Company" by its then president Jeff Skilling. By 2001, however, it had become one of the largest bankruptcies in U.S. history. Analysts have since identified serious problems in Enron's corporate culture, described by one ethics specialist in the following terms: "This is a company with no core of values, just focused on making a trade. A company without values is a company going to jail."[17] For example, press reports suggest that Enron's senior management placed enormous pressure on employees to take huge risks and enter into business deals, whatever the apparent costs. Whether the deal was ultimately good for Enron or properly recorded on accounting statements was irrelevant. For a time it seemed that nothing could stop Enron's drive to

---

16. Both these companies have sought to rebut their critics via websites. See http://www.shellnigeria.com and http://www.nike.com
17. Miles Moffeit quoting an unnamed ethics specialist in "The Collapse of the Temple of Cool" *Knight Ryder Newspapers*, republished in the *Edmonton Journal* (2 June 2002) at D4.

the top. However, the company was ultimately taken down by growing debt and bad deals that questionable accounting practices could no longer conceal. As Miles Moffeit, a reporter with Knight Ryder Newspapers, observes: "The culture of cool was beginning to sweat."[18]

In the months prior to its bankruptcy, Enron's share prices sank, creditors went unpaid, the U.S. Securities Commission began to ask questions about possible insider trading, and a congressional panel commenced an investigation.[19] One central concern has been the creation of off-the-books partnerships—some named Chewco and JEDI after *Star Wars* characters—through which Enron managed to hide a staggering amount of debt. The fallout has been tremendous for a variety of stakeholders and parties. As the BBC reports on its website, the collapse of Enron meant that thousands of employees lost their life savings because they had invested in Enron stock.[20] Many Enron executives have been convicted of serious crimes. For example, Ken Lay, the founder and former chairman of Enron was recently convicted on six counts of fraud and conspiracy but died soon thereafter of an apparent heart attack.[21] Jeff Skilling, Enron's former chief executive officer, was found guilty on 19 of the 28 charges he faced, including one count of conspiracy and 12 counts of securities fraud.[22] Lea Fastow, wife of Andrew Fastow, was Enron's former assistant treasurer and pleaded guilty to a charge of filing a false income tax return to avoid a trial on conspiracy and tax charges. She was sentenced to 12 months in prison as part of a plea agreement with

prosecutors.[23] Richard Causey, the former chief accountant at Enron, pleaded guilty to a single count of securities fraud as part of a deal with prosecutors to help the U.S. government with its case against Lay and Skilling, and the other 33 charges against him were dropped. Causey was sentenced to seven years in jail but the time could be reduced, provided prosecutors are content with his level of ongoing cooperation.[24] Thus far, a total of at least 19 former Enron executives have either pleaded guilty or been convicted for their part in Enron's demise.[25]

As well, a class action was commenced against several parties for their alleged role in the Enron debacle, including not just Arthur Andersen (Enron's Accountants), but also JP Morgan Chase and Citigroup (Enron's banks), Vinson & Elkins (Enron's lawyers), and members of Enron's board of directors.[26] The lawsuit flatly states: "The apparent success of Enron was a grand illusion—a false picture created by manipulative devices and contrivances."[27]

18. *Ibid.* at D5.
19. Karen Masterson, "Congress Adding Layer to Inquiries into Enron's Past" Houston Chronicle (17 January 2002) at http://www.chron.com/disp/story.mpl/special/enron/nov01/115202 (accessed January 2002).
20. David Schepp, "Enron Probe Won't Restore Pension Funds" at http://news.bbc.co.uk/1/hi/business/1754211.stm
21. See Mary Crane, "Convicted CEO Ken Lay Dies at 64" Forbes online at http://www.forbes.com/home/business/2006/07/05/lay-enron-skilling-cx_mc_0705laydeath.html.
22. "Enron's Lay Found Guilty on All Counts, Skilling on 19" CBC News at http://www.cbc.ca/story/business/national/2006/05/25/enron-decision.html
23. "Lea Fastow Pleads Guilty to Tax Charge, Gets 12 Months Sentence" at http://www.cbc.ca/story/business/national/2004/05/06/fastow_040506.html
24. CBC News at http://www.cbc.ca/story/business/national/2005/12/28//enron-051228.html
25. CBC News at http://www.cbc.ca/news/background/enron
26. See Adrian Michaels, "Class Action Names Players in Enron Scandal" *Financial Times* (8 April 2002) at http://specials.ft.com/enron/FT337OIOSZC.html
27. *Ibid.*

Business Law in Practice Revisited

1. How does the law affect Louella's business?

As Louella starts her business, she will be involved in a number of transactions and events with significant legal implications, including the following:

- BUSINESS FORM. Does Louella want to operate her business alone as a sole proprietor, would she prefer to work with partners, or is she interested in incorporating? Each business vehicle has its own set of rules, which Louella must find out about. For instance, the incorporation process is strictly dictated by federal and provincial law.[28]

- BUSINESS NAME. Louella must be sure to choose a name that is not confusingly similar to the name of another business. Even if she chooses such a name inadvertently, she will be subject to legal consequences, including being sued for damages by the individual or company that has built up goodwill in the name in question.[29]

- FINANCING CONSIDERATIONS. If Louella decides to borrow her operating capital from the bank, she must enter into a specialized form of contract known as a promissory note. In this contract, she promises to repay the loan, with interest, according to a schedule.[30] If Louella decides that she wants to raise money by selling shares, she will definitely have to incorporate a company. As well, should Louella's company end up selling shares to the public, it will have disclosure obligations under securities legislation.[31]

- PROPERTY. Louella must determine whether to buy, build, or lease premises for her business operation. Each option involves a unique set of laws.[32] Furthermore, many aspects of the property used in Louella's business are regulated through health legislation and fire regulations, to name two examples. Furthermore, if customers are injured on her premises, Louella may be held liable and be required to pay damages.

- SERVICES. Louella may ultimately hire staff to run her business. She must become aware of the law concerning unjust dismissal and employment equity, as well as human rights legislation that prohibits discrimination.[33]

- MARKETING. In promoting her store to the public, Louella must be sure to abide by laws prohibiting false and misleading advertising,[34] as well as trademark and copyright law, to name two examples.

- SELLING. Louella must be sure to provide a reasonable level of service to her customers.

Just as Louella must devote resources to monitoring any staff that she might have, attending to proper bookkeeping, and keeping her loans in good standing, she also must spend time managing the legal elements of her business environment. Since the law affects Louella's business from a variety of perspectives, she is much better off accepting this responsibility from the outset, rather than fighting a rearguard action.

---

28. For a discussion of the incorporation process, see Chapter 14.
29. *Ibid.*
30. For a discussion of credit, see Chapter 26.
31. For a discussion of securities law, see Chapter 15.
32. For a discussion of real estate law, see Chapter 19.
33. For a discussion of employment law, see Chapters 20–21.
34. For a discussion of marketing law, see Chapters 23–24.

Once she understands the law, Louella can take simple, proactive steps to ensure that she complies with it; just as importantly, she can plan for the future. A properly devised risk management plan is an invaluable tool to achieving this end.

2. What are the purposes of the laws that affect Louella's business?

One of the most important functions of law in the business environment is to facilitate planning, particularly—though not exclusively—through contract law. Business law also has a protective function in that it seeks to ensure that those who cause a loss are held financially responsible and otherwise accountable for their actions, including through the criminal justice system. Finally, the law provides a series of mechanisms and rules for dispute resolution, thereby making an essential contribution to certainty in the marketplace.

3. What has gone wrong in Louella's business, and why?

The Business Law in Practice scenario provides a lengthy illustration of the kinds of penalties and liabilities Louella faces if she neglects to pay attention to the legal rules that govern her enterprise. Louella's ignorance of her legal obligations—combined with her lack of business ethics—will lead to the demise of her fledgling enterprise.

Chapter Summary

Law is involved in all aspects of business, whether the entrepreneur is aware of it or not. The law protects persons and their property; facilitates commercial interactions, particularly through contract law; and provides mechanisms for dispute resolution.

Though not perfect, the Canadian legal system has much to recommend it. The system strives for just outcomes by demanding that both the process for determining liability and the rules or laws that are applied in that process are fair, objective, and free from bias. No justice system, of course, can consistently accomplish all these goals.

Indeed, there are serious limitations to what the law can realistically achieve when a legal problem arises; thus, it is imperative that a business adopt a proactive approach in managing the legal aspects of its environment through a legal risk management plan. This chapter has emphasized the idea that knowledge of the law is an essential business asset. Informed owners and managers can protect their businesses by ensuring compliance with legal requirements. They can capitalize on the planning function of law to ensure the future of their business by entering into contracts. They also can seek enforcement of legal rules against those who do business or have other interactions with the enterprise. In this way, the property, contractual expectations, and profitability of the business are made more secure. Business ethics—while sometimes but not always coextensive with legal requirements—are also increasingly important to running a successful business.

Chapter Study

Key Terms and Concepts

arbitration (p. 8)

breach of contract (p. 6)

business ethics (p. 11)

business law (p. 4)

contract law (p. 7)

law (p. 4)

legal risk management plan (p. 11)

liability (p. 8)

litigation (p. 7)

mediation (p. 8)

spam (p. 3)

Questions for Review

1. What is the function of law?

2. How does the law protect members of society?

3. How does the law facilitate business activity?

4. In what ways does law facilitate certainty in the marketplace?

5. Does the nature of the business relationship affect the enforcement of legal rights?

6. How does the law resolve disputes?

7. Does dispute resolution always involve going to court?

8. In what way is knowledge of the law a business asset?

9. How might a lack of knowledge of the law negatively impact a business?

10. Why should a business put in place a legal risk management plan?

11. What is the role of business ethics?

12. Why are business ethics important?

13. What is spam?

14. What is the purpose of regulating spam?

Questions for Critical Thinking

1. Many companies and organizations have codes of conduct; however, there is often a gap between the code and the daily performance of employees. How could the gap be narrowed? What steps could businesses take to ensure a more ethical corporate culture? For access to 850 codes of ethics, including Enron's, see http://www.iit.edu/departments/csep/codes/coe.html.

2. What is the relationship between ethics and law? Are ethical responsibilities the same as legal responsibilities?

3. When is a lawsuit the best response to a legal dispute? What is at risk?

4. Knowledge of the law is a business asset. How can you acquire this asset short of becoming a lawyer? How is ignorance of the law a liability?

5. The legal requirement for UL labels is intended to protect society. What are some other examples of such a law?

Situations for Discussion

1. Joe has recently opened a bar and adjoining restaurant, specializing in seafood. It is named "The Finny Friends" after a restaurant that Joe had visited in Toronto several years ago. In accordance with the law, Joe has a liquor licence from the provincial liquor licensing authority that limits the seating capacity in the bar to 30. As Joe's bar becomes increasing popular, he begins to regularly allow over 60 patrons in at one time. Eventually he is caught, and—having already received two warnings—his operation is closed down for 30 days. Joe is flabbergasted at the severity of the penalty. Soon thereafter, Joe is contacted by a lawyer for The Finny Friends restaurant in Toronto. The lawyer says that Joe has 48 hours to take down his restaurant awning and destroy anything else with the name The Finny Friends on it (including menus, invoices, placemats, napkins, and even match covers) or he will bring an application for a court order to that effect. To make matters worse, a health inspector is on Joe's doorstep saying that there have been several recent reports of food poisoning originating from Joe's restaurant. What has gone wrong in Joe's business and why?

2. Discuss the kinds of legal questions that you think might arise in the following business proposals:

   • Corporation A is planning to launch a new marketing program featuring an advertising campaign that extols the virtues of its product and denigrates the product of Corporation B.

   • Corporation C is planning to construct an oil rig at the mouth of a particular river to exploit a recent mineral find.

   • Corporation D is planning to expand its manufacturing facilities into a foreign country. In order to finance its operations, it is planning to sell shares to the public.

3. Assume that you have a major dispute with a business on the property next to yours over acceptable use of its land. You find that although zoning allows a small tool shop to operate on the property, the noise is too much for you. Your lawyer tells you that there may be a legal case for you to pursue, but it will be costly and the results are not guaranteed. What alternative approaches might address your problem more effectively?

4. Several provinces across Canada, including Ontario, Manitoba, and Saskatchewan, have proposed or passed legislation that prevents children from buying or renting video games that are expressly violent or sexual, as determined by a ratings board. Businesses found selling these games to minors face penalties that range from fines to having their license revoked.[35] How effective do you think government regulation is in limiting children's access to violent video games? Are there better ways of achieving these types of goals? Is it the role of governments to provide legal consequences for the underage renting or purchase of violent video games?

5. Pro-C Ltd., a Canadian software company, owns the rights to "WINGEN," a software program, as well as the Canadian and U.S. trademarks associated with that product. The company has recently found out that Computer City, a large computer chain, has been using the WINGEN trademark for its own line of computers, albeit for a line that is not offered for sale in Canada. The owner of Pro-C Ltd., found out about Computer City's use of the WINGEN trademark when he received a mass of e-mails on wingen.com (a domain that the owner has registered) that were actually intended for Computer City. In fact, the owner has received so many of these e-mails that the website has crashed, and he has a hard time locating and responding to his own customers' orders. As a result, the owner's income has dropped by 95 percent. The owner is extremely unhappy with Computer City, and wants to sue the company over its use of the WINGEN trademark.[36] What are the risks of pursuing this course of action?

6. Olivia owns a convenience store and has invested a lot of money in gambling machines for the store. Recently, the government passed a law banning the machines from the store immediately, although pubs are allowed to continue operating these machines. Is this law fair? Does it violate any of the common values associated with the law? Would it make a difference if the law applied only to new businesses? Would it make a difference if the government provided compensation to the convenience stores affected, or phased in the law to allow for a period of adjustment?

For more study tools, visit
http://www.businesslaw3e.nelson.com

35. Based, in part, on "Manitoba Video-Game Legislation Remains in Limbo," Steve Lambert, *The Globe and Mail* (6 January 2005) at A9; and "Manitoba Moves to Rate Violent Video Games" (29 April 2004), CBC News at http://www.cbc.ca/story/canada/national/2004/04/29/vids040429.html. Under the proposed amendments contained in Saskatchewan's Bill 30, it will be an offence to sell, rent, or exhibit video or computer games classified as Mature to a person under the age of 17 and to sell, rent, or exhibit a video or computer game classified as Adults Only to a person under the age of 18. See Bill 30, *An Act to Amend the Film and Video Classification Act*, 2d Sess., 25th Leg., Saskatchewan, 2005–2006. For Manitoba's legislation, see *The Amusements Act*, C.C.S.M., c. A-70. Specifics can be found at http://www.gov.mb.ca/chc/mfcb/game_update.pdf. For Ontario's legislation, see the *Film Classification Act*, 2005, S.O. 2005, c. 17 and its regulations, O. Reg. 452/05.
36. Based, in part, on "Goliath's Revenge: How a Tiny Software Company Got Crushed by Computer City" *Canadian Business* (15 October 2001) 100; and *Pro-C Ltd. v. Computer City Inc.* (2001), 205 D.L.R. (4th) 568 (Ont. C.A.), rev'g (1999), 7 C.P.R. (4th) 193 (Ont. S.C.J.), leave to appeal refused, [2002] S.C.C.A. No. 5.

Chapter

2

The Right Honourable Beverley McLachlin,
Chief Justice of the Supreme Court of Canada

The Canadian Legal System

Objectives

After studying this chapter, you should have an understanding of

- the impact of the Canadian legal system on business
- the role of constitutional law in protecting commercial rights and freedoms
- the government's law-making powers under sections 91 and 92 of the *Constitution Act, 1867*
- the executive's formal and political functions in regulating business
- the judiciary's role in assessing the constitutionality of legislation
- the classifications of law
- how administrative law affects business

Business Law in Practice

Jane Seymour is vice president of marketing for a corporation that produces cigarettes and other tobacco products. She has just received a phone call from a retailer who is very concerned about legislation enacted in Saskatchewan called the *Tobacco Control Act*. Section 6(3) provides:

> (3) No retailer shall permit tobacco or tobacco-related products to be displayed in the retailer's premises so that the tobacco or tobacco-related products are visible to the public if young persons are permitted access to those premises.

[Note: The Act defines a young person as a person under the age of 18 years.]

As a result of this law, retailers in Saskatchewan have been required to either bar young people from their stores or hide their cigarette inventory in cupboards, behind curtains, or under the counter. Fines for violations are significant, especially given the low profit margins of the smaller business. Section 20(1) provides liability:

    (a) for a first offence, to a fine of not more than $3000

    (b) for a second offence, to a fine of not more than $5000

    (c) for a third offence, to a fine of not more than $15 000

    (d) for a fourth or subsequent offence, to a fine of not more than $50 000.

Jane knows that antismoking activists are welcoming the Saskatchewan initiative with open arms. For example, Essential Action (Global Partnerships for Tobacco Control) states:

> This section [s. 6] is precedent-setting and will ban the large displays of tobacco products or "power walls" found in stores. The banning of these displays effectively eliminates one of the remaining methods the tobacco industry has to promote its products to youth…. The tobacco industry in Canada pays retailers … in order to have its power walls of tobacco products. Tobacco companies pay for displays in order to make cigarettes appear to be more popular than they are. The industry installs large "power walls" of cigarette packages, in vast quantities far more than is necessary to supply consumers. These displays are visible to the entire population including children and ex-smokers sending a message that tobacco is as socially acceptable as candy or newspapers. They are inconsistent with the industry's claim that it does not promote to children.[1]

Jane lets the retailer know that her company fully supports the lawsuit initiated in 2002 by Rothmans, Benson & Hedges Inc. against the government of Saskatchewan. One argument Rothmans makes is that Saskatchewan's law is inoperative since the federal government has already passed comprehensive legislation governing the advertising and promotion of cigarettes. The second argument is that the Saskatchewan law violates freedom of expression as protected by the *Canadian Charter of Rights and Freedoms*.

---

1. See http://www.essentialaction.org/tobacco/letter/ca0203.html. André Picard reports in "Top Court Upholds Province's Tobacco Display Law," *Globe and Mail* (20 January 2005) at A11, that tobacco companies pay an average of $875 per retailer to have displays in Canadian stores, amounting to a total of $77 million a year.

The retailer is facing additional costs to build a cabinet to hold his tobacco inventory, not to mention lost revenue from cigarette manufacturers whose products he can no longer display for a fee. He wants to know from Jane if Rothmans's lawsuit will be successful.

1. Is the *Tobacco Control Act* legal?
2. Who assesses whether the legislation is permissible?
3. Are there any moral or ethical questions that arise from this scenario?
4. What can Jane do about the legislation at this point?

Note: To see a copy of Rothmans's **statement of claim** challenging the constitutionality of the *Tobacco Control Act* as well as Saskatchewan's statement of defence, go to the website for this text (http://www.businesslaw2e.nelson.com) and click under Chapter 2.

statement of claim
A document setting out the basis for a legal complaint.

Introduction

The Canadian legal system is the machinery that comprises and regulates government. Government, in turn, is divided into three branches:

- the legislative branch creates law in the form of statutes and regulations
- the executive branch formulates and implements **government policy** and law
- the judicial branch adjudicates on disputes

government policy
The central ideas or principles that guide government in its work, including the kind of laws it passes.

constitutional law
The supreme law of Canada that constrains and controls how the branches of government exercise power.

Constitutional law—which is the supreme law of Canada—is charged with ascertaining and enforcing limits on the exercise of power by the branches of government. It is also charged with upholding "the values of a nation."[2] These values are tied to the political philosophy known as **liberalism.** Briefly put, liberalism elevates individual freedom and autonomy as its key organizing value. A corollary is that any interference with freedom—including the freedom to display a legal product in one's business premises—is inherently suspect and must be justified according to the principles of constitutional law.

liberalism
A political philosophy that elevates individual freedom and autonomy as its key organizing value.

The **Canadian legal system**—along with the constitutional law that governs it—can be an overwhelming and sometimes very technical area. Even so, some basic knowledge is essential for business owners and managers because

Canadian legal system
The machinery that comprises and governs the legislative, executive, and judicial branches of government.

- The legislative branch of government passes laws that impact on business operations. For example, when government enacts a law, failure to comply can result in fines and other penalties, including closure of the business. Ignorance of a law means that business loses out on opportunities to influence government policy and to take advantage of favourable laws. And failure to challenge laws that are unconstitutional means that business is needlessly constrained.
- The executive branch implements and generates policy that may be directed at business. For this reason, companies such as General Motors of Canada Ltd. have a corporate and environmental affairs department that is charged with monitoring government policy as well as tracking and contributing to debates over public policy that could affect GM operations.[3] Smaller business may work

---

2. Peter Hogg, *Constitutional Law of Canada*, vol. 1, looseleaf (Scarborough, ON: Carswell, 1997) at 1-1. Note: Throughout this chapter, Hogg is cited to page number, not paragraph number.
3. Interview with Ms. Miriam Christie, Manager of Government Relations, Corporate and Environmental Affairs Department, General Motors of Canada Ltd. (10 March 2000).

Do "power walls"
normalize smoking?

to influence government on a more modest scale by monitoring issues in-house, hiring lobbyists, and working through industry associations.

■ The judicial branch provides rulings that resolve existing legal conflicts but also impact on future disputes. For example, the Supreme Court of Canada's determination of whether commercial expression is protected speech under the *Canadian Charter of Rights and Freedoms* has an impact on any number of industries, from cigarette producers to toy manufacturers.

Rothmans's challenge to the *Tobacco Control Act* involves all three of these branches. The legislative branch passed the law to which Rothmans objects. The executive branch formulated and advanced the government policy that led to the legislation being enacted. And the judicial branch—by applying constitutional law—will determine whether Rothmans's objections to the law are valid or not.

The Canadian Constitution

The Canadian Constitution is not contained in one document. Rather, it is located in a variety of places, both legislative and political, written and unwritten. While this means that the Constitution may sometimes not be specific, it also means that the Constitution can more easily grow to resolve questions or issues related to government.

The written elements of the Constitution include the *Constitution Act, 1867* (part of which divides legislative power between the federal and provincial governments) and the *Canadian Charter of Rights and Freedoms* (which identifies the rights and freedoms that are guaranteed in Canada). Additionally, relevant decisions by judges concerning constitutional law—discussed later in this chapter—also form part of the Constitution. Though these documents provide some of the framework and values informing Canada's system of government, other important constitutional features (known as constitutional conventions) are not mentioned at all.

constitutional conventions
Important rules that are not enforceable by a court of law but that practically determine or constrain how a given power is exercised.

Constitutional conventions are a "code of ethics that governs our political processes."[4] They are not binding the way that constitutional rules contained in legislation would be. They cannot be enforced in a court of law. Rather, they are in place because politicians historically have agreed to abide by them. One example relates to the office of prime minister. Nowhere in Canada's written Constitution is this important office even mentioned yet no one doubts that the federal government is to be headed by such an officer. In this way, constitutional conventions come to the fore and provide some of the detail of governance.

The Canadian Constitution also attends to a number of other matters, including the admission of new provinces and territories to Canada,[5] provisions for amending the Constitution,[6] and autonomy from the United Kingdom Parliament.[7] Most significantly for our purposes, however, the Canadian Constitution provides for the three branches of government: legislative, executive, and judicial, discussed below.

The Legislative Branch of Government

legislative branch
The branch of government that creates statute law.

statute law
Formal, written laws created or enacted by the legislative branch of government.

The **legislative branch** of government creates a form of law known as **statute law** or legislation. A familiar example of statute law is the *Criminal Code of Canada*, which prohibits a variety of offences, such as assault, theft, and fraud. As noted above, Saskatchewan's *Tobacco Control Act* is also created by the legislative branch, this time at the provincial level.

In fact, three levels of government—the federal, provincial, and municipal levels—make legislation in Canada. Parliament, the federal legislative branch, comprises the House of Commons and the Senate. For legislation to become law, it must first be passed by the House of Commons and then approved by the Senate. Because the Senate assesses the work of the House of Commons, it has been called "the chamber of sober second thought."

Each province also has a law-making body. In British Columbia, for example, it is called the Legislative Assembly, while in Nova Scotia it is called the House of Assembly. At the provincial level, there is no Senate, or upper house.

Municipalities, which are created by provincial legislation, have legislative bodies often called city councils. Their powers are delegated to them by the province in which they are located.

Statute Law and Jurisdiction

jurisdiction
The power that a given level of government has to enact laws.

As already noted, the Constitution—through the *Constitution Act, 1867*—dictates whether each level of government can make a given law or not. Expressed in legal language, each level of government has the **jurisdiction** to pass laws within its proper authority or sphere. Jurisdiction is divided in this way because Canada is a federal state, which means that governmental power is split between the central, national authority (the federal government) and regional authorities (the provincial governments). Additionally, the federal government empowers territorial governments to engage in a form of limited self-government. The provincial governments, in turn, empower municipal governments to legislate in specifically defined areas.

---

4. Bernard Funston & Eugene Meehan, Canada's *Constitutional Law in a Nutshell* (Scarborough, ON: Carswell, 1994) at 7.
5. As Hogg observes, *supra* note 2 at 2-11, s. 146 of the *Constitution Act, 1867,* governs this matter. For a link to constitutional documents, including legislation creating provinces as they are admitted to Canada, see http:/laws.justice .gc.ca/en.index.html
6. See Part V of the *Constitution Act, 1982*, "Procedure for Amending Constitution of Canada" and Hogg, *ibid.* at 4-11 to 4-12 and 4-15 to 4-41.
7. For further discussion of this point, see Hogg, *ibid.* at 3-1 to 3-14.

The federal government has the power, or the jurisdiction, to make laws in those areas set out in section 91 of the *Constitution Act, 1867* (formerly known as the *British North America Act* or the *BNA Act*). Areas in which the federal government may enact laws include the following:

- interprovincial/international trade and commerce
- trade as a whole
- postal service
- navigation and shipping
- currency
- national defence
- criminal law
- all legislative areas not given to the provinces (Note: This is a residual category in the sense that the federal government has all the law-making power not expressly given to the provinces. For example, it is the residual power that justifies federal legislation that creates federally incorporated companies.)

The provincial governments have jurisdiction to make laws in those areas set out in section 92 of the *Constitution Act, 1867*, including the following:

- hospitals
- property and civil rights within the province (e.g., the regulation of contracts)
- administration of justice (e.g., the court system)
- local matters (e.g., highway regulation)
- incorporation of provincial companies

Municipalities have no constitutionally recognized powers. They have only the law-making authority that is delegated to them by provincial government. The municipal governments have jurisdiction to make laws as permitted by the relevant provincial government, for example, in these areas:

- zoning
- subdivision
- taxation for the benefit of the municipality
- licensing

The Constitution specifies that the federal government has jurisdiction over criminal law, which includes the power to define new crimes, provide penalties for breaches of the criminal law, and pass laws with the purpose of protecting the public. Because criminal law falls under federal jurisdiction, there is a *Criminal Code of Canada* but no provincial criminal codes. In fact, if the legislature of Manitoba were to attempt to enact a law known as the *Criminal Code of Manitoba*, for example, this law would be unconstitutional because a provincial government does not have the power to pass such a law. No court would enforce the code because it would be contrary to the Constitution to do so. In short, the federal government has **exclusive jurisdiction** over criminal law.

Sometimes, the federal and provincial governments have shared or **concurrent jurisdiction.** This means that the area being regulated does not fall neatly into federal or provincial jurisdictions but straddles them. Public health is one such area, with both federal and provincial governments legislating in the area. For example, even prior to the Saskatchewan legislation, the federal government had already strictly regulated the tobacco industry through legislation called the *Tobacco Act (Canada)*, S.C. 1997, c. 13. Among other matters, this federal law forbids virtually all forms of tobacco advertising in Canada and requires that health warnings be placed on cigarette packages. Its jurisdiction to do so is solid due to the Supreme Court of

exclusive jurisdiction
Jurisdiction that one level of government holds entirely on its own and not on a shared basis with another level.

concurrent jurisdiction
Jurisdiction that is shared between levels of government.

Canada ruling that such regulation is a valid exercise of the criminal law power, given that the idea or policy behind the law is to protect the public by regulating a dangerous product.[8]

What about Saskatchewan's legislation that prohibits the display of cigarette products? Does the provincial government have jurisdiction to pass such a law? The answer is almost certainly yes. First, over two decades ago, the Supreme Court of Canada confirmed that the province's jurisdiction over matters of a merely local or private nature gives wide powers over public health.[9] Second, the provincial government's jurisdiction over property and civil rights means that it can regulate advertising of a consumer product.[10] Civil rights, in this context, does not refer to matters such as freedom of expression. Rather, it refers to the broad set of rights that someone might have as a result of entering into a contract or owning property.

What the provincial government cannot do, however, is have operative legislation that would create a conflict with federal legislation. That is, in an area of concurrent jurisdiction—such as health or the environment—the doctrine of **paramountcy** applies. This doctrine makes the federal legislation paramount or supreme and the provincial law inoperative, but only to the extent of the conflict. Though a significant doctrine, it is also a limited one. The judiciary has held that paramountcy generally applies only if there is an express contradiction between the two laws. If a person could simply obey the stricter law—and thereby comply with both pieces of legislation—then paramountcy would not apply. Both laws would operate fully.

Note that section 30(1) of the federal legislation (i.e., the *Tobacco Act*) makes virtually any form of tobacco advertising illegal. An exception is the display of the actual product, which is expressly permitted under section 30. That provision states: "... any person may display, at retail, a tobacco product...." The Saskatchewan legislation eliminates a portion of this permission since section 6(3) of the provincial act provides that "no retailer shall permit tobacco ... to be displayed ... if young persons are permitted access to those premises." Is this enough to trigger the paramountcy doctrine to render the provincial law inoperative?

The Supreme Court has recently addressed the matter of paramountcy in this case,[11] determining that two questions were at issue: First, can a person simultaneously comply with s. 6 of the *Tobacco Control Act* (the provincial act) and s. 30 of the *Tobacco Act* (the federal act)? Second, does s. 6 of the *Tobacco Control Act* frustrate or otherwise work against Parliament's purpose in enacting s. 30 of the *Tobacco Act*?

The Supreme Court determined, in response to the first question, that compliance with both pieces of legislation could be effected by following the standard of the stricter one, that is, the provincial law. Put another way, adherence to the provincial law would not lead to a violation of the less strict, federal law. Second, the court found that the provincial legislation did not frustrate or impede the purpose of the federal act. That is, while s. 30(1) of the federal Act provides that, "[s]ubject to the regulations, any person may display, at retail, a tobacco product or an accessory that displays a tobacco product-related brand element," this legislation does not grant retailers a positive *entitlement* or *right* to display such products. On this basis, there was room for the provincial government to legislate in the area and restrict displays. In short, the new provincial legislation was merely prohibiting something that the federal legislation had opted to not to deal with one way or the other. Accordingly, both the general purpose of the federal *Tobacco Act* (to address a national public

paramountcy
A doctrine that provides that federal laws prevail when there are conflicting or inconsistent federal and provincial laws.

---

8. *RJR-MacDonald Inc. v. Canada (A.G.)*, [1995] 3 S.C.R. 199.
9. *Schneider v. The Queen*, [1982] 2 S.C.R. 112.
10. *Irwin Toy v. Que.*, [1989] 1 S.C.R. 927.
11. See *Rothmans, Benson & Hedges v. Saskatchewan*, [2005] 1 S.C.R. 188, 2005 SCC 13.

health problem) and the specific purpose of s. 30 of the federal *Tobacco Act* (to circumscribe the *Tobacco Act*'s general prohibition on promotion of tobacco products set out in s. 19) remain fulfilled. Therefore, the doctrine of paramountcy was not triggered.

Note that Rothmans's other objections to the Saskatchewan legislation will be determined only after a full trial of the matter.

Business is affected by all levels of government, but it is most affected by the provincial and municipal governments. An important exception relates to businesses in banking, international or interprovincial transport, and communication (e.g., telephone and cable). These are areas of federal jurisdiction and, accordingly, such businesses are subject to federal law concerning licensing, labour, and occupational health and safety, to name several examples.

bylaw
A law made by the municipal level of government.

The regulation of business is generally a provincial matter because the provinces have jurisdiction over property and civil rights.[12] Municipalities have jurisdiction to legislate in a broad variety of matters, from levying appropriate taxes and regulating local zoning, parking, and subdivision, to requiring the licensing of businesses and dogs. Municipal legislation takes the form of **bylaws**.

Business Application of the Law | Violating Municipal Bylaws

Even though municipalities have much less legislative power than their federal or provincial counterparts, violation of a municipal bylaw can carry serious consequences, including fines and other penalties. For example, bylaws across the country prohibit smoking in public places, including a Vancouver bylaw that prohibits smoking in any restaurant, casino, bingo hall, or commercial establishment except on a patio or in a smoking room. When several establishments repeatedly disregarded this bylaw, the City of Vancouver launched legal action against them. Depending on the nature of the infraction, fines can reach up $2000 for each offense.

The City of Edmonton also has a smoking bylaw that prohibits smoking in public buildings or structures, including bars. The purpose of the bylaw is "to regulate smoking in certain locations so as to reduce the exposure of others to second-hand smoke."

In response to this bylaw, Tony Burke, owner of T.B.'s Pub, purchased a GMC bus for $1500, installed carpet and insulation, changed the position of the seats so they would line the periphery of the bus, and then parked it outside his establishment. The "butt bus" is where patrons of his bar retreat to in order to have a cigarette. According to Burke: "I can let people smoke on it [the bus] if I want. The city doesn't have control over what people do in their own vehicles. I did my research." However, the bus arguably violated a number of bylaws including the smoking bylaw. Indeed, bylaw enforcement was of the view that the bus had been modified to function as an enclosed structure and therefore the smoking bylaw did apply. Put another way, to permit smoking in the bus, as currently configured, was a bylaw violation.

In the end, however, no action was taken against Burke, because, according to one City official, Burke made some changes. He insured the vehicle and—in addition to permitting his bar patrons to smoke there—began to use it to transport customers. On this basis, the bus was no longer a structure, and the bylaw therefore had no application.

During his dispute with the city, Burke had considerable support from his customers. One patron stated to reporter Katherine Harding: "I'm not one to care about civil liberties and all that, but this is getting out of hand. What's next? Arresting people who are smoking in their own cars?"

---

12. *Supra* note 2 at 21-8.

CRITICAL ANALYSIS: Do "butt buses" violate the spirit of the smoking bylaw? Does it matter whether the bus is used only for patron smoking or, in addition, for the purpose of transporting customers? Should personal habits such as smoking be subject to government regulation? Do you agree with the customer who suggested that the smoking bylaw could lead to further regulation prohibiting people from smoking in their own cars, or would you classify his statement as an exaggeration? What is the difference among smoking in a bar, smoking on a "butt bus," and smoking in your own home or vehicle?

Customers of T.B.'s Pub smoking inside a school bus parked outside the bar.

Source: Neal Hall, "Vancouver seeks tobacco injunction" *The Vancouver Sun* (25 May 2002) at B9; Katherine Harding "'Butt Buses' Ignite Edmonton Furor" *The Globe & Mail* (15 December 2005) at A10; David Aitken, Director of Edmonton bylaw-enforcement; personal communication (8 July 2006).

International Perspective Anti-Smoking Treaty

In response to the millions of deaths caused by tobacco every year, numerous countries, including Canada, have **ratified** a **treaty** known as the "Framework Convention on Tobacco Control." According to the World Health Organization, "the treaty requires countries to impose restrictions on tobacco advertising, sponsorship and promotion; establish new packaging and labelling of tobacco products; establish clean indoor air controls; and strengthen legislation to clamp down on tobacco smuggling." For example, countries would be required to adopt and implement rotating health warnings and messages on tobacco products, occupying at least 30 percent of the display areas. Canada ratified this treaty in 2004.

In 2005, World Health Organization officials reported that the tobacco industry was working hard to limit the number of countries participating in the treaty, including intense lobby efforts in the United States.

CRITICAL ANALYSIS: How might a treaty ratified by multiple countries be more effective in reducing tobacco consumption than if each country simply worked in isolation? What are the advantages of global cooperation? What are the disadvantages?

Sources: Stephanie Nebehay, "UN Anti-Smoking Pact Kicks in as Cigarette Firms Fight Back" *The Globe and Mail* (28 February 2005) at B7 and WHO website at http://www.who.int/features/2003/08/en (accessed 27 October 2006); Health Canada News Release, "Canada Ratifies the Framework Convention on Tobacco Control, the World's First Public Health Treaty" (2 December 2004) online at http://www.hc-sc.gc.ca/ahc-asc/media/nr-cp/2004/2004_63_e.html (accessed 27 October 2006).

FIGURE 2.1

Law-making Jurisdiction

The Constitution Act, 1867

Federal Government
Parliament
—House of Commons
—Senate
• Law-making jurisdiction provided
by s. 91 of the *Constitution Act, 1867*

Provincial Government
Legislature
• Law-making jurisdiction provided
by s. 92 of the *Constitution Act, 1867*

Territorial Governments
• Limited self-government
• Subject to federal control

Municipal Government
• Law-making jurisdiction provided by
the provincial legislature

ratify
To authorize or approve.

treaty
An agreement between
two or more states that
is governed by interna-
tional law.

The Executive Branch of Government

formal executive
The branch of government
responsible for the ceremonial features of government.

political executive
The branch of government
responsible for day-to-day
operations, including formulating and executing
government policy, as well
as administering all departments of government.

The executive branch of government has a formal, ceremonial function, as well as
a political one. From a formal or ceremonial perspective, for example, the executive
branch supplies the head of the Canadian state, the Queen. The **formal executive**
also has a significant role in the legislative process, since the executive branch of
government, represented by the governor general (the Queen's federal representative) or lieutenant governor (the Queen's provincial representative), issues approval
as the final step in creating statute law.

The **political executive** is of great relevance to businesses because it performs
the day-to-day operations of government by formulating and executing government policy and administering all departments of government. It is also the level of
government that businesses typically lobby in order to secure favourable or
improved treatment under legislation or with respect to policy formation.

Business and Legislation — Tobacco Regulation by the Federal Government

egulations are a form of legislation that are
more precisely referred to as subordinate legislation. This is because regulations can be
passed only if that power is accorded by the statute
in question. That said, such power is routinely given.
For example, the *Tobacco Act (Canada)* states that the
governor general in council (i.e., the federal
Cabinet) may make regulations respecting information that must appear on cigarette packages. This
occurred through the *Tobacco Products Information
Regulations* (SOR/2000/272), which require that
graphic health warnings and other information be
placed on cigarette packages.

What determines the images and wording stipulated on
cigarette packages?

The chief executive of the federal government is the prime minister, while the chief executive of the provincial government is the premier. Other members of the political executive—both provincial and federal—include Cabinet ministers, civil servants, and the agencies, commissions, and tribunals that perform governmental functions. It is the political executive at the provincial level whom Jane would contact to voice her concerns about Saskatchewan's legislation.

The **Cabinet**—made up of all the ministers of the various government departments, as well as the prime minister or premier—also has a very significant law-making function. It is often Cabinet that passes **regulations** providing detail to what the statute in question has enacted. When Cabinet enacts regulations, it is known by its formal name: the lieutenant governor in council (provincially) and the governor general in council (federally).

The Judicial Branch of Government

It may seem surprising that the **judiciary** is a branch of government, given that the judiciary is supposed to be independent of government. Expressed more completely, however, the concept is this: the judiciary is to be independent from the legislative and executive branches of government.

The judiciary is composed of **judges** who are appointed by both federal and provincial governments. These judges are required to adjudicate on a variety of matters, including divorce and the custody of children, civil disputes such as those arising from a will, breach of contract, car accidents, wrongful dismissal, and other wrongful acts causing damage or injury. Judges also preside over criminal proceedings. Businesses, however, predominantly rely on the courts to settle commercial disputes.

The System of Courts

Judges operate within a system of courts that vary somewhat from province to province. Despite these variations, each provincial and territorial system of courts has three basic levels: trial, intermediate appeal, and final appeal. Figure 2.2 indicates the hierarchy of courts relevant to commercial disputes.

Trial courts are of two types: inferior and superior. **Inferior courts** are presided over by judges appointed by the provincial government. These courts are organized by type of case, such as criminal, family, and civil. The civil court—sometimes called **small claims court**—handles disputes involving smaller amounts of money. The amount varies from province to province: $25 000 is the limit in British Columbia and Nova Scotia, for example, while $10 000 is the limit in Ontario.[13] These claims can generally be litigated with minimal legal advice and assistance, in part because less is at stake. The process is designed to be simpler, quicker, and less expensive than mainstream litigation. Parties often appear in this court without a lawyer. **Superior courts**—whose judges are appointed by the federal government—have the jurisdiction to handle claims involving any monetary amount. In addition, they are the entry level for the more serious criminal matters. Here, the procedure is much more formal and technical, with parties usually being represented by lawyers.

Cabinet
A body composed of all ministers heading government departments, as well as the prime minister or premier.

regulations
Rules created by the political executive that have the force of law.

judiciary
A collective reference to judges.

judges
Those appointed by federal and provincial governments to adjudicate on a variety of disputes, as well as to preside over criminal proceedings.

inferior court
A court with limited financial jurisdiction whose judges are appointed by the provincial government.

small claims court
A court that deals with claims up to a specified amount.

superior court
A court with unlimited financial jurisdiction whose judges are appointed by the federal government.

---

13. See The Courts of Nova Scotia at http://www.courts.ns.ca/SmallClaims/index_claims.htm; The Ministry of the Attorney General of Ontario at http://www.attorneygeneral.jus.gov.on.ca/english/courts/guides/MakingClaimJun06EN.pdf; and The Ministry of the Attorney General of British Columbia at http://www.ag.gov.bc.ca/courts/civil/smallclaims.

FIGURE 2.2

Courts Dealing with
Commercial Disputes

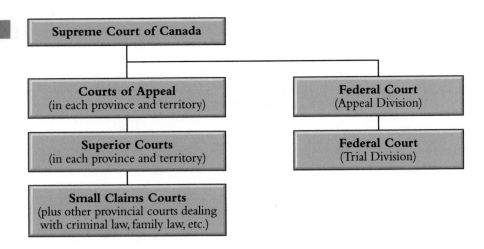

Provincial courts of appeal hear appeals from these lower courts and from there cases go to the **Supreme Court of Canada.** In most commercial cases, litigation tends to end in provincial courts of appeal because appeal to the Supreme Court of Canada is available only after permission or "leave" to appeal is granted by the Supreme Court itself. Ordinarily, the Supreme Court of Canada will hear only appeals that involve questions of national concern or significance.

The **Federal Court of Canada** has special authority to deal with certain cases in which one of the parties is the federal government or one of its agencies.

The *Canadian Charter of Rights and Freedoms*

An important responsibility for judges is determining whether a given law meets the requirements of the Canadian Constitution, including the *Canadian Charter of Rights and Freedoms.* Created in 1982, the *Charter* is intended as a judicially enforceable guarantee that the government will act consistently with the values associated with a liberal democratic state. The right to freedom of expression and of religion, the right to a fair and speedy trial, equality rights, and the right to vote are all examples of *Charter* protections that reflect a set of constitutional values founded on individual freedom. Two protections that are particularly germane to business are contained in sections 2 and 15.

Fundamental Freedoms

2. Everyone has the following fundamental freedoms:

    (a) freedom of conscience and religion;

    (b) freedom of thought, belief, opinion and expression, including freedom of the press and other media of communication;

    (c) freedom of peaceful assembly; and

    (d) freedom of association.

Equality Rights

15. (1) Every individual is equal before and under the law and has the right to the equal protection and equal benefit of the law without discrimination and, in particular, without discrimination based on race, national or ethnic origin, colour, religion, sex, age or mental or physical disability.

Supreme Court of Canada
The final court for appeals in the country.

Federal Court of Canada
The court that deals with some types of litigation involving the federal government.

Canadian Charter of Rights and Freedoms
A guarantee of specific rights and freedoms enshrined in the Constitution and enforceable by the judiciary.

The *Charter* is a powerful constitutional document because it provides protection from improper or oppressive government conduct—conduct that most often takes the form of legislation or policy. In short, section 32 of the *Charter* prohibits government and government alone from violating any of the rights or freedoms recited. By way of contrast, violation of rights in the private sector, such as through employment discrimination, is a matter for provincial and federal human rights codes and thus is addressed according to a separate set of rules.

Rothmans's challenge to Saskatchewan's *Tobacco Control Act* includes a challenge under the *Charter* that the legislation infringes on freedom of expression. This is probably the case since forbidding the display of a product eliminates one of the few methods that Rothmans has left to it to let the public know about its products. Demonstrating a violation of section 2 of the *Charter* does not mean that Rothmans will automatically win its case, however, because the rights and freedoms guaranteed by the *Charter* are not absolute. On the contrary, the *Charter* acknowledges that the government is entitled to restrict freedom of expression—as well as any other right recited in the *Charter*—but only if it has balanced all relevant interests carefully, as required by the very first section of the *Charter*.

1. The *Canadian Charter of Rights and Freedoms* guarantees the rights and freedoms set out in it subject only to such reasonable limits prescribed by law as can be demonstrably justified in a free and democratic society.

Section 1 requires the government to justify why it is infringing a right, as well as to demonstrate that in doing so, it is restricting the right in question in a reasonably measured, controlled, and appropriate way. A court assessing the constitutionality of Saskatchewan's *Tobacco Control Act*, for example, would seek to determine what the government was trying to accomplish through the legislation. It would appear that one objective is to reduce tobacco use and exposure among Saskatchewan's youth. As the government states in one of its communications with retailers: "Keeping tobacco and tobacco-related products out of public view is one way of communicating to Saskatchewan's young people that tobacco use is not a normal behaviour."[14]

Given that this is almost certainly a legislative intent that would justify limiting the tobacco industry's freedom of expression, a court would then go on to assess how that intent was accomplished. If the government could achieve the same legislative goal without interfering as much with the right in question (i.e., freedom of expression), then the law would be vulnerable to legal attack since a more constitutionally acceptable alternative is available. According to Rothmans, denying adult consumers basic information about tobacco products by forbidding their display has no firm connection to discouraging children from smoking. When Rothmans's challenge proceeds through the court system, this is likely the issue that will receive the most attention.

If Rothmans can demonstrate that the *Tobacco Control Act* violates a *Charter* provision and the government cannot prove that its legislation meets the standard set by section 1, a court can order that the legislation be struck down—that is, it can declare the law to be of no force or effect. In essence, the act is thrown out because it is unconstitutional. The court's authority to order such a powerful remedy is set out in sections 24 and 52 of the *Charter*. If Rothmans is unsuccessful, the law stands.[15]

---

14. This is what the government declares the policy to be in "Bulletin #2: *The Tobacco Control Act*: What Retailers Need to Know" at http://www.health.gov.sk.ca/ps_tobacco_control_bulletin_2.pdf.
15. Recent case law from Québec would suggest that Rothmans will have an uphill battle in challenging the Saskatchewan legislation on *Charter* grounds, given its public health objectives. In *J.T.I. Macdonald Corp. c. Canada* (Procureuer Générale), 2005 QCCA 226, the Québec Court of Appeal largely dismissed the tobacco company's action against federal legislation restricting tobacco advertising and was unsympathetic to a vast majority of J.T.I. Macdonald's *Charter* freedom of expression complaints; leave to appeal to the S.C.C. has been allowed, 2006 Carswell Que 2262.

That even a tobacco company could enforce constitutional rights associated with human beings is part of the essence of modern constitutional protections. In a free and democratic society, expression should be as unfettered as is reasonably possible, no matter who the speaker is and no matter what the words are. The Supreme Court of Canada has emphasized the need to protect such expression because

> [o]ver and above its intrinsic value as expression, commercial expression which, as has been pointed out, protects listeners as well as speakers, plays a significant role in enabling individuals to make informed economic choices, an important aspect of individual self-fulfilment and personal autonomy. The Court accordingly rejects the view that commercial expression serves no individual or societal value in a free and democratic society and for this reason is undeserving of any constitutional protection.[16]

Not all Canadians agree with the idea that the judiciary should have the power to strike down legislation as being unconstitutional. Some believe that it is undemocratic for the courts to have the right to eliminate or amend a law duly enacted by elected representatives. However, those who support the *Charter* argue that even a majority (the elected representatives who enacted the legislation) should not have the power to infringe on the rights of others. Put another way, a liberal democratic system of government is not just about majority rule, as suggested in the following statement from Madam Justice Wilson of the Supreme Court of Canada:

> The *Charter* is predicated on a particular conception of the place of the individual in society. An individual is not a totally independent entity disconnected from the society in which he or she lives. Neither, however, is the individual a mere cog in an impersonal machine in which his or her values, goals and aspirations are subordinated to those of the collectivity. The individual is a bit of both. The *Charter* reflects this reality by leaving a wide range of activities and decisions open to legitimate government control while at the same time placing limits on the proper scope of that control. Thus, the rights guaranteed in the *Charter* erect around each individual, metaphorically speaking, an invisible fence over which the state will not be allowed to trespass. The role of the courts is to map out, piece by piece, the parameters of the fence.[17]

Though the court has the power to assess the constitutionality of legislation—and to strike down the law, if need be—it is the legislative branch of government that can have the last word in many cases. This power is enshrined in section 33.

The *Charter* permits the government to override or disregard a judicial decision that a given piece of legislation is unconstitutional or to pre-empt judicial involvement at the start. Section 33 of the *Charter* allows the government to enact legislation "notwithstanding" its unconstitutionality. While the government does not have this option with respect to all rights and freedoms guaranteed by the *Charter*, it does have this option for a great many of them, including the right to freedom of expression.[18]

---

16. *Ford v. Quebec* (A.G.), [1988] 2 S.C.R. 712 at 767.
17. *R. v. Morgentaler* (1988), 44 D.L.R. (4th) 385 at 485 (S.C.C.)
18. Section 33 of the *Charter* permits government to violate a large number of rights and freedoms, including freedom of conscience and religion; freedom of thought, belief, opinion, expression, and peaceful assembly; freedom of association; the right to life, liberty, and security of the person; the right to be free from unreasonable search and seizure; the right to be free from arbitrary detention and imprisonment; the right not to be subject to cruel or unusual punishment; the right against self-incrimination; and the right to equality.

FIGURE 2.3

Sampling of Constitutional Challenges Brought by Business

Case	Nature of alleged *Charter* violation	Result
R. v. Big M Drug Mart, [1985] 1 S.C.R. 295	Federal law that prohibited most commercial activity on Sunday is contrary to the right to freedom of religion.	Action succeeded. The Supreme Court of Canada ruled that the law was unconstitutional since its purpose was "to compel the observance of the Christian Sabbath."
R. v. Edwards Books and Art, [1986] 2 S.C.R. 713	Provincial law prohibiting retail stores from opening on Sunday is contrary to the right to freedom of religion.	Action failed. The Supreme Court of Canada held that the law was valid. Though the law did violate freedom of religion (i.e., its *effect* placed a burden on those who observed a non-Sunday sabbath), the law was saved under s. 1. The court held that the valid secular purpose of the law—to provide a common day off for retail workers—was sufficiently important to justify limiting the right of freedom of religion.
Little Sisters Book v. Canada, [2000] 2 S.C.R. 1120	The federal *Customs Tariff Act* that prohibits importation of "obscene" books and magazines violates the right to freedom of expression.	Mixed result. The Supreme Court of Canada held that the standard of obscenity was valid. However, the court identified discrimination in how the legislation was implemented since homosexual literature was disproportionately and without justification targeted by customs officials.
Ford v. Quebec, [1988] 2 S.C.R. 712	A Quebec law requiring advertisements and signage to be in French violates the right to freedom of expression.	Action succeeded. The Supreme Court of Canada ruled that freedom of expression includes "the freedom to express oneself in the language of one's choice." (*Note: This law was reenacted using s. 33.*)
Irwin Toy v. Quebec, [1989] 1 S.C.R. 927	A Quebec law prohibiting advertising directed at children under 13 years of age violates the right to freedom of expression.	Action failed. Though the law violated freedom of expression, it was saved under s. 1. The Supreme Court ruled that protection of children is important, hence justifying the limitation. As well, since the law permitted the advertisement of toys and breakfast cereals provided cartoons were not used, the ban was only partial in any event.
Rocket v. Royal College of Dental Surgeons, [1990] 1 S.C.R. 232	Ontario's *Health Disciplines Act* violates freedom of expression since it prohibits dentists from advertising their services, including office hours or languages spoken.	Action succeeded. The Supreme Court of Canada held that while maintaining high standards of professional conduct justified some kind of regulation, this act went too far in banning all advertising.
Slaight Communications v. Davidson, [1989] 1 S.C.R. 1038	Labour board order that an employer provide a reference letter to an unjustly dismissed employee violates the right to freedom of expression.	Mixed result. The Supreme Court of Canada held that if the letter were ordered to contain an opinion that the employer did not hold, that would be unconstitutional. Where the letter had only to contain "objective facts that are not in dispute," the order can be justified under s. 1.
Hunter v. Southam, [1984] 2 S.C.R. 145	Powers of search and seizure permitted by the *Combines Investigation Act* violates the right to be free from unreasonable search and seizure.	Action succeeded. The Supreme Court of Canada held that the act did not contain enough safeguards to determine when documents can be seized.
McKinney v. University of Guelph, [1990] 3 S.C.R. 229	Mandatory retirement policy of the university violates prohibition of discrimination on the basis of age.	Action failed. The *Charter* applies only to government or bodies that are not independent from government. Here, the university was classified as a private body. Additionally, the university could rely on the Ontario *Human Rights Code* (which applies to the private sector), which permitted mandatory retirement. Though this provision of the code contravened s. 15, the discrimination was demonstrably justified under s. 1.

There are, of course, political consequences to using section 33, as when the government of Alberta invoked this provision when it introduced Bill 26 on 10 March 1998. This bill would limit the right of recovery to $150 000 for those wrongfully sterilized under that province's *Sexual Sterilization Act*, which was repealed in 1972. As a result of public outcry that the government would deny sterilization victims their right to establish in court that they had suffered damages exceeding $150 000, the government quickly withdrew its proposed legislation.[19]

As noted earlier, the *Charter* governs the relationship between the person and the state, restraining government action that is, for example, discriminatory. By way of contrast, certain kinds of discrimination in the marketplace by one person against another are made illegal primarily by human rights codes as well as by related forms of legislation.[20]

bill
Proposed legislation.

Business and Legislation

Gender-Based Pricing

Ontario Liberal MPP Lorenzo Berardinetti recently introduced to the Ontario Legislative Assembly proposed legislation (called **Bill** 9) to prohibit business from setting prices based on the gender of their customers. He became concerned about this issue when he went clothes shopping with his wife and noted that brand-name men's suits were priced at about one-third less than women's equivalent suits, even though the women's suits used less material. This bill is currently being studied by a legislative committee. What follows is an excerpt from Bill 9:

Preamble

Throughout the course of our recent history, our Province has enacted a Human Rights Code and passed laws to eliminate injustices committed against people on the basis of gender, ethnic and religious persuasions and sexual orientation.

In spite of all of these efforts, a lot of work still needs to be done to eliminate systemic discriminatory practices that continue to this very day.

One such practice is discriminatory pricing on the basis of gender.

---

19. Eoin Kenny, "Klein Government Drops Bill to Compensate Victims" (11 March 1998) online: QL (CP98). Eugenics is a discredited belief that through selective breeding, the "quality" of the human race can be improved.
20. For discussion of human rights codes in relation to employment, see Chapter 20.

In order to create a society where people are judged by the content of their character rather than their physical characteristics, practices such as these must be eliminated.

As a result, it is appropriate to prohibit gender-based discriminatory pricing.

Therefore, Her Majesty, by and with the advice and consent of the Legislative Assembly of the Province of Ontario, enacts as follows:

Definition

1. In this Act," gender-based pricing" means the practice of charging a different price for the same goods or services on the basis of gender.

Prohibition against gender pricing

2. (1) No person shall engage in gender-based pricing.

Limitation

(2) Nothing in subsection (1) prevents price differences that are based upon the cost, difficulty or effort of providing the goods or services.

To see a copy of the entire bill, go to http://www.ontla.on.ca/documents/Bills/38 _Parliament/session2/index.htm#bill9 and look under Bill 9.

Berardinetti commented on the bill as follows: "It's a fairness issue and a human rights issue. It's to amend the *Human Rights Code*. We're not trying to put anyone out of business. We're just telling them to operate fairly."

The online publication *Business Edge* reports that Randy Bridge, then-president of the Toronto-based Ontario Fabricare Association, which represents about 120 dry cleaners in the province, is not a fan of the legislation and provides the following explanation for why women's dry-cleaning is more expensive than men's:

"The automated technology generally used in our industry is specifically designed for larger shirts, those usually worn by men," he says. "Women's sizes are normally smaller and thus require additional hands-on touch-ups."

Business Edge also reports the rebuttal to this argument given by Joanne Thomas Yaccato, author of *The 80% Minority: Reaching the Real World of*

Women Consumers: "Bottom line: If the technology is there for men's apparel, it must be there for cleaning women's garments," she says.

Berardinetti's bill is based on California's gender-based price discrimination law. In 2005, the dating service Lavalife settled a U.S. class action, related to this legislation, which accused Lavalife of improperly discriminating against its male customers by charging them to use certain features of the service while not charging women to use similar or identical features. In a court-approved settlement, Lavalife agreed, among other matters, to provide to the class members 33 minutes of free air time (to an aggregate maximum of $706 464) and to discontinue price differentials based on gender.

The *Toronto Star* reports that the plaintiffs are also seeking recovery of legal fees and costs in the amount of approximately $180 000.

Meanwhile, back in Canada, two Toronto-based online dating services are reportedly opposed to the Berardinetti bill, concerned about similar lawsuits. Lavalife and Quest have even hired a Liberal lobbyist to stop the proposed Ontario legislation.

CRITICAL ANALYSIS: Should government regulate price when it is discriminatory or should that be left to the free market? Do you think that hiring a lobbyist is a good risk management strategy?

Sources: Jack Kohan, "Gender Tax' in Ontario's Crosshairs: Backbencher's Bill Would Eliminate Unequal Pricing" *Business Edge* 1:10 (26 May 2005) at http://www.businessedge.ca/article.cfm/newsID/9591.cfm (accessed 5 November 2006); FindLaw online at http://caselaw.lp.findlaw.com/cacodes/civ/43-53.html (accessed October 27, 2006); CTV.ca News Staff, "Ontario MPP Seeks End to Gender-based Pricing" online at http://www.ctv.ca/servlet/ArticleNews/story/CTVNews/1110908196485_106 317396/?hub=Canada (accessed October 27, 2006); "Ontario Bill Targets 'Gender-based Pricing'" (16 March 2005) online at http://www.cbc.ca/story/canada/national/2005/03/15/haircuts-100-050315.html (accessed 27 October 2006); Robert Benzie, "Liberal Lobbyist Hired to Halt Gender Bill: Lavalife, Quest Say They Will Be Forced to Leave Ontario Ex-McGuinty Aide Will Fight for the Two Dating Companies" *The Toronto Star* (13 March 2006) at A9; Press release: Dating Firms Fight Gender-Price Bill online at http://www.24-7pressrelease.com/view_press_release.php?rID=12114 (accessed 27 October 2006); Christi Dabu, "For Canadian Women, that Haircut May Soon Get Cheaper" *Christian Science Monitor* (10 August 2005) online at http://www.csmonitor.com/2005/0810/p12s02-woam.htm (accessed 27 October 2006).

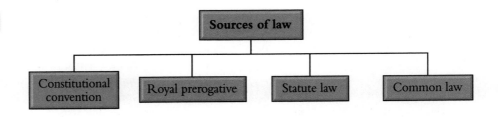

FIGURE 2.4

The Sources of Law

Sources of Law

There are four sources of law in Canada: constitutional convention (discussed earlier), statute law (outlined in the preceding section), the royal prerogative, and the common law.

royal prerogative
Historical rights and privileges of the Crown, including the right to conduct foreign affairs and to declare war.

The **royal prerogative** has diminishing influence in the modern Canadian legal system. Briefly put, the royal prerogative refers to the historical rights and privileges of the Crown, including the right to conduct foreign affairs and to declare war.[21]

common law
Rules that are formulated in judgments.

Common law, unlike statute law, is judge-made law. Common law is the end product of disputes that come before the judiciary. That is, when a judge gives a decision in determining the outcome of a given legal conflict, it is known as a judgment; judgments referred to cumulatively are called the common law.

Ordinarily, a judge does not just give a bald resolution to the dispute in question. Rather, the judge seeks to explain, justify, and account for whatever decision she has reached. In doing so, the court relies on decisions made by other judges in other cases that are relevant to the matter at hand. These cases are known as **precedent.**

precedent
An earlier case used to resolve a current case because of its similarity.

The key principle of precedent can be summarized as "like cases should be treated alike." This means that judges should rule in a given case in a manner consistent with the way judges have adjudicated on or dealt with similar matters in the past. In short, the judge looks to the common law in order to resolve the matter at hand.

There are a number of rules governing the application of precedent, including the following:

- A lower court must follow a relevant precedent created by a higher court within the same jurisdiction.
- Not all precedents are of equal value—the higher the court that created the precedent, the more valued the decision is.
- The Supreme Court of Canada—the highest court in Canada—is entitled to decide a case in any way it sees fit.

When Rothmans's *Charter* challenge goes before the courts, the judges will rely on precedent in determining whether Saskatchewan's *Tobacco Control Act* is constitutional. If, for example, there is a Supreme Court of Canada decision on point, the Saskatchewan courts are required to follow it.

While the process of applying precedent is reasonably easy to describe, it is inevitably riddled with ambiguity, uncertainty, and subjectivity. Although judges endeavour to be impartial, unbiased, and objective, such a standard is probably impossible to consistently achieve. Further, even reasonable people may differ in interpreting whether a given case from the common law applies to the dispute in question. This is not to imply that the study of law is futile or that the judicial application of precedent is without rhyme or reason. It is merely to suggest that the outcome in any case cannot be fully predicted.

---

21. *Supra* note 2 at 1–16.

Judges are free to apply another set of rules, known as rules of **equity.** Like common law, equity originated in England. The role of equity is to provide assistance to the deserving person who otherwise would not receive adequate help under the rules of common law. Equity focuses on what would be fair given the specific circumstances of the case, as opposed to what the strict rules of common law might dictate. In this way, equity seeks to soften the harsh or unfair result that the common law might otherwise cause. This is not to suggest that "anything goes, as long as it's fair." Equity itself is constrained by principles that limit when it can render assistance. For example, assume that a businessperson has transferred some real estate to her spouse in order to hide that asset from creditors. If the spouse later refuses to transfer that property back, the businessperson may be in some difficulty. Should the businessperson seek help from a judge on equitable grounds to get her property back, a court would have the discretion to refuse. This is because—according to an important equitable principle—equity assists only those with "clean hands." There is a good argument that the businessperson fails to meet this description.

Equity also provides its own set of remedies—rectification, *quantum meruit,* rescission, specific performance, and the injunction—which will be described in more detail in later parts of this text.

Judges are bound to apply relevant legislation enacted by the three levels of government even if the legislation has the effect of reversing a common law or judge-made rule. The only exception relates to the constitutionality of the legislation in question. If such legislation violates the division of powers between the levels of government or violates *Charter* provisions, a court may declare that it has no force or effect. Otherwise, statute law trumps or otherwise has priority over the common law. Note too that the courts can make common law about statutes and how to interpret them.

Classifications of Law

The law can be organized according to various categories. It is important for a businessperson to have a basic understanding of these classifications in order to better grasp the nature of the legal problem at issue. Such an understanding will also assist the businessperson to better communicate with legal counsel.

Domestic versus International Law

Domestic law is the internal law of a given country and includes both statute and common law. Domestic law deals primarily with individuals and corporations and, to a lesser extent, the state.

International law governs relations between states and other entities with international legal status, such as the United Nations and the World Trade Organization. An important source of international law is treaty law. International law focuses mainly on states and international organizations.

Substantive versus Procedural Law

Substantive law refers to law that defines rights, duties, and liabilities. Substantive law was at issue in all the cases described in Figure 2.3. They concerned the duty of the government to legislate in accordance with the *Charter* as well as the right of the plaintiff to challenge the government for failing to meet that standard.

Procedural law refers to the law governing the procedure to enforce rights, duties, and liabilities. For example, the fact that a trial judge's decision can be appealed to a higher court is a procedural matter.

Public versus Private Law

Public law describes all those areas of the law that relate to or regulate the relationship between persons and government at all levels. An important aspect of public law is its ability to constrain governmental power according to rules of fairness. Examples of public law are criminal law, tax law, constitutional law, and administrative law.

FIGURE 2.5

Examples of Public Law

Criminal law	Identifies behaviour that is seriously unacceptable. In the interests of maintaining order and security in relations between citizens, the government prosecutes those who transgress basic standards of conduct, and the courts provide sanctions for that conduct, including fines and imprisonment.
Tax law	Sets the rules for the collection of revenue for governmental operation.
Constitutional law	Sets the parameters on the exercise of power by government.
Administrative law	Governs all regulatory activity of the state.

Private law concerns dealings between persons. Many of the major topics in this text fall within private law, including contract law, tort law, property law, and company law.

FIGURE 2.6

Examples of Private Law

Contract law	Provides rules that make agreements between parties binding.
Tort law	Includes rules that address legal wrongs committed by one person against another, apart from a breach of contract. The wrongs may be intentional (as in an assault) or unintentional (as in a case of negligent driving).
Property law	Sets rules that define and protect property in all forms.
Company law	Provides rules concerning the rights, liabilities, and obligations of companies and other business vehicles.

The distinction between public and private law is not absolute. Most of the law of property is private, even if the government is buying, selling, or leasing. However, should the government choose to exercise its executive right to expropriate land, for example, issues of public law would be involved.

Furthermore, a single set of circumstances can have two sets of consequences, one involving private law and the other involving public law. For example, where a personal injury arises from an assault, the Crown may decide to prosecute the perpetrator of the assault under the *Criminal Code*. This is the domain of public law. The victim, however, also has civil rights that can be enforced through tort law, which is the area of private law. Specifically, the victim of the assault can initiate an action in the courts to seek financial compensation for damages from the perpetrator.

Common Law versus Civil Law

While common law refers to judge-made law, it is also used in a totally different sense to describe the system of private law in place in all provinces except Québec. A common law system is one that bases its private law on judicial decisions that—if relevant and binding—must be applied to the case at issue. The private law in nine Canadian provinces, as well as the territories, is governed by common law in this sense of the word.

FIGURE 2.7

Divisions/Classification of the Law

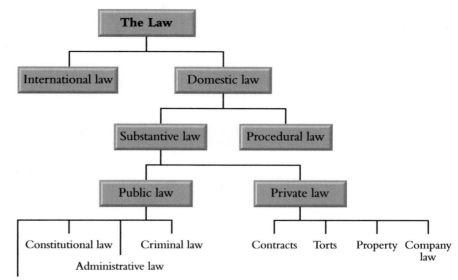

Source: Adapted from Gerald L. Gall, *The Canadian Legal System*, 5th ed. (Scarborough: Carswell, 2005).

Civil Code of Québec
The rules of private law that govern Québec.

The province of Québec is, of course, bound by federal law such as the *Criminal Code*, but it has its own system of private law, which is governed by the *Civil Code of Québec*. Although there are many similarities between common law principles and what would be found in the *Civil Code*, conceptually there are significant differences between the two systems. One key difference is that judges in Québec look to the *Civil Code* for general principles to be applied to the case at hand. They are not bound by how other judges have interpreted the *Code*, though practically speaking, these interpretations would be helpful and relevant.[22] Nor is a judge in a civil code system bound to apply a relevant provision of the code if to do so would produce an unjust outcome.[23]

These various classifications can be applied to the legal problem faced by Jane and the cigarette retailer. The question of the validity of Saskatchewan's *Tobacco Control Act* concerns:

- domestic law (not international law) because the *Tobacco Control Act* was passed by the government of Saskatchewan and does not in any way involve a foreign jurisdiction

- substantive law (not procedural law) because at issue is whether the law violates the right to freedom of expression

- public law (not private law) because at issue is a law that regulates the relationship between tobacco retailers and the government. More specifically, it involves constitutional law because the challenge will concern whether the government has exercised its law-making power appropriately

- common law (not Québec civil law) because the dispute will be resolved by applying Saskatchewan's common law system, not the *Civil Code of Québec*

Administrative Law and Business

administrative law
Rules created and applied by those having governmental powers.

Administrative law is one of the primary legal areas in which government and business interact. This area of law refers to rules created and applied by the various boards, agencies, commissions, tribunals, and individuals who exercise a

22. Gerald L. Gall, *The Canadian Legal System*, 5th ed. (Scarborough, ON: Thomson Carswell, 2004) at 31.
23. Ibid.

governmental function as a result of legislation giving them that power. It also refers to rules of fairness that constrain how administrative bodies exercise their authority.

Administrative bodies have often been established on a needs basis to deal with particular problems or difficulties as they have arisen, rather than pursuant to some overall regulatory plan. This piecemeal nature can make the area somewhat perplexing at times.

The functions of administrative bodies and officials often vary, as well. In some instances, the body or individual carries out purely administrative functions, as when the Employment Insurance Commission processes a claim for benefits; sometimes the body also has judicial functions, such as when the Labour Relations Board settles a dispute between an employer and employee; sometimes the body exercises legislative functions, as when the Canadian Radio and Telecommunications Commisson (CRTC) passes regulations concerning the amount of Canadian content on radio and TV; and sometimes the body has some combination of these functions. As a result, it is often difficult to summarize how businesses are subject to administrative regulation.

Nonetheless, this area of law has a significant impact on business because so much commercial activity is regulated by these bodies—from licensing requests to zoning and subdivision applications and human rights complaints. (See Figure 2.9 for a summary of the administrative bodies and officials that affect business.)

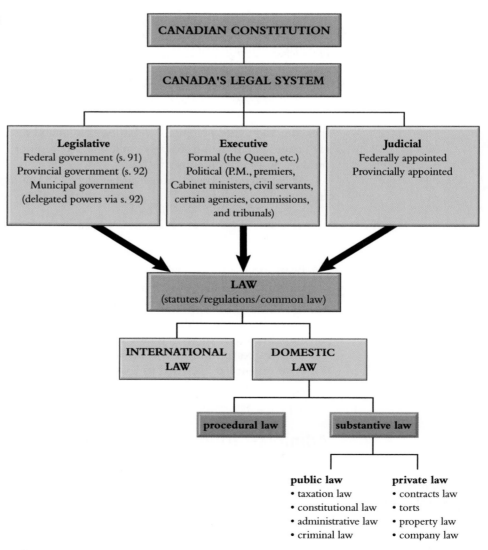

FIGURE 2.8

A Summary of
Constitutional Law

FIGURE 2.9

Administrative Bodies and Officials Affecting Business

Legend: F = federal; P = provincial; M = municipal

If you plan to...	you may interact with...	in regards to...
establish a business	Regional and/or Municipal Licencing Tribunal, Minister, Agency, or Officer (M)	a business permit
construct new facilities or make exceptions to existing zoning regulations	Development Officer/Zoning Board (M) Building Officer (M) Development Appeal Board (M)	a development permit a building permit a denial of permit application
alter the interior or exterior of an existing building	Building Officer (M)	a building permit
hire employees	Workers Compensation Board (P) Labour Relations Board (P) Provincial Human Rights Tribunal (P)	an accident or injury unions, collective agreements discriminatory practices in the workplace
manufacture, sell, or store food or drink	Board of Health (P, M) Food and Drug Agency (F)	a food establishment permit packaging and labelling requirements
sell alcohol	Liquor Control Board or Commission (P)	a liquor licence
manufacture, sell, or advertise products	Consumer Protection Agency (F) trade practices legislation (P)	product/item construction standards fair advertising practices
import products	Federal Import Review Agency (F)	approval
practise in architecture, pharmacy, law, dentistry, medicine, or accountancy	Professional Society (e.g., Law Society of British Columbia and the Public Accountants Council for the Province of Ontario (P)	a licence to practise the profession
sell real estate	Superintendent or Council of Real Estate (P)	a licence to sell
carry on a radio, television, or telecommunications business	Canadian Radio and Telecommunications Commission (F)	structure, scope, and content approval
sell financial products	Securities Commission, Financial Services Commission (P)	licensing and procedural requirements
engage in interprovincial trucking	National Transportation Agency (F)	a business licence
sell a particular agricultural product	Canadian Egg Marketing Agency (F) Canadian Wheat Board (F)	a production and sales licence

Source: Researched and written by Catherine Bradley.

Business Law in Practice Revisited

1. Is the *Tobacco Control Act* legal?

The *Constitution Act, 1867*, sets out jurisdictional constraints that dictate to each level of government the areas in which it can legislate. The provincial government must justify the *Tobacco Control Act* under at least one of the headings of section 92, most likely under the power over property and civil rights as well as under matters of a local nature. The provincial government must also combat, as it successfully did, the allegation that the legislation violated the doctrine of paramountcy. It must also defend the legislation for violating freedom of expression. It must convince a court that this infringement is reasonable given the policy of the legislation to discourage young people from smoking.

2. Who assesses whether the legislation is permissible?

The judiciary makes this assessment. Under the Constitution, judges are mandated to hear challenges to the legal foundation of laws passed by all levels of government. In this example, a judge would consider whether the Saskatchewan government has the jurisdiction under the *Constitution Act, 1867,* to pass the law in question, as well as whether the legislation could be justified under the *Charter.*

3. Are there any moral or ethical questions that arise from this scenario?

Given the persuasiveness of studies demonstrating that cigarettes cause death and serious illness, there are deep moral and ethical issues for anyone in the tobacco industry. However, cigarettes are a legal product and thus tobacco companies are entitled to be in business. It also should be noted that cigarette companies take considerable pains to insist that they do not promote or encourage smoking among children.

If Jane believes that her company's challenge to Saskatchewan's legislation will ultimately encourage smoking among children, her personal ethics may be at odds with her company's strategy. Jane may want to bring her concerns to the company. This is also perhaps in her company's best interests since it would be poor public relations for it to be seen as promoting cigarette use among children in any event. Should this effort fail, however, Jane may decide that she is unable to actively advance the interests of her company. If this is the case, she should resign.

4. What can Jane do about the legislation at this point?

In addition to supporting Rothmans's challenge, Jane can pursue less formal means of dealing with the matter, such as meeting with the provincial Minister of Health and other governmental officials involved. Jane should consider a strategy that accepts the inevitability of some regulation while suggesting less drastic means to address the policy objectives of the legislation. She can also hire a public relations firm to ensure that she handles this sensitive matter in as palatable a way as possible. In this way, a risk management approach can be applied to government-business relations.

Chapter Summary

Canadian society is bound by a set of constitutional values, many of which insist on the importance of the individual and the right to freedom from unreasonable government interference. These values restrain how government operates at all levels—federally, provincially, and municipally. Constitutional law plays an important role in how government does its job by constraining how the three branches of government exercise power.

Each branch of government has its own work to do. The legislative branch creates statutes. The executive branch is responsible for the ceremonial features of government and for day-to-day operations, including formulating and executing government policy, as well as administering all departments of government. The judiciary has a significant role in scrutinizing the legislative and executive branches of government and can be an important resource for those who believe they have been unreasonably limited, such as in how they are permitted to carry out business, or unfairly treated by a governmental officer, board, or tribunal. The judiciary also adjudicates on private disputes.

The Constitution places mandatory limits on the power of the legislature to pass any law it sees fit. The court, as required by the Constitution, insists that the power of government be exercised in a manner that is

- within that body's "jurisdiction," as defined by the *Constitution Act, 1867,* and
- consistent with the values and principles contained within the *Charter*

The judiciary itself is bound by the rules of precedent to help ensure that any given legal dispute is resolved in a manner that is consistent with decisions in previous similar disputes. An important part of precedent involves the court system since only a higher court can bind a lower court. Judges also have discretion, accorded to them by the rules of equity, to ensure that each matter before them is justly resolved.

Canadian law is organized according to classifications reflecting the nature of the legal problem at issue: domestic/international; substantive/procedural; public/private; and common law/civil law. Administrative law provides protection by ensuring that a fair process accompanies any regulatory decisions that affect a business or any other activity.

Chapter Study

Key Terms and Concepts

administrative law (p. 39)

bylaw (p. 26)

bill (p. 34)

Cabinet (p. 29)

Canadian Charter of Rights and Freedoms (p. 30)

Canadian legal system (p. 21)

Civil Code of Québec (p. 39)

common law (p. 36)

concurrent jurisdiction (p. 24)

constitutional conventions (p. 23)

constitutional law (p. 21)

domestic law (p. 37)

equity (p. 37)

exclusive jurisdiction (p. 24)

Federal Court of Canada (p. 30)

formal executive (p. 28)

government policy (p. 21)

inferior court (p. 29)

international law (p. 37)

judges (p. 29)

judiciary (p. 29)

jurisdiction (p. 23)

legislative branch (p. 23)

liberalism (p. 21)

paramountcy (p. 25)

political executive (p. 28)

precedent (p. 36)

private law (p. 38)

procedural law (p. 37)

public law (p. 38)

ratify (p. 28)

regulations (p. 29)

royal prerogative (p. 36)

small claims court (p. 29)

statement of claim (p. 21)

statute law (p. 23)

substantive law (p. 37)

superior court (p. 29)

Supreme Court of Canada (p. 30)

treaty (p. 28)

Questions for Review

1. What is the key idea upon which the Canadian Constitution is based?

2. What does "jurisdiction" mean?

3. What is an example of a constitutional convention?

4. Which document determines whether a government has the jurisdiction to pass a law or not?

5. What is the doctrine of paramountcy?

6. Which level of government does paramountcy seem to favour?

7. How does the authority of a municipal government come into existence?

8. What is the difference between a regulation and a bylaw (or ordinance)?

9. What is the executive branch of government?

10. How is the executive branch different from the legislative branch?

11. What is precedent? Why is a system of courts essential to its creation?

12. What are the two types of trial courts?

13. What is the *Canadian Charter of Rights and Freedoms*?

14. What is the common law? Who creates it?

15. What can a judge do if he determines that a piece of legislation is unconstitutional?

16. If a law is found to violate a person's freedom of expression pursuant to the *Charter*, is it automatically struck down? Is there something in the *Charter* that might allow the government to justify violating that person's freedom of expression?

17. What is the difference between public law and private law?

18. Which Canadian province operates under a civil law system?

19. What is the role of equity?

20. What is one important function of administrative law?

Questions for Critical Thinking

1. Canada has often been described as an overgoverned state. What features of Canada's system of government contribute to this opinion? Do you agree?

2. The Constitution guarantees individual freedoms, such as freedom of religion and freedom of speech, which courts have said can also apply to commercial enterprises. What is the link, if any, between protecting commercial enterprise and protecting the rights and freedoms that individuals are to enjoy?

3. Under a common law system, judges follow precedent when making decisions or resolving disputes. What are the advantages of following precedent? Describe a situation where it might be inappropriate to follow precedent.

4. Why is there so much more statute law now than there was 50 years ago?

5. Review Figure 2.3. In your opinion, how has the *Charter* affected business activity?

6. Do you think that the *Charter* strikes a good balance between protecting the rights of individual citizens and allowing governments to legislate for the benefit of larger groups, or even all members of society? Is section 1 of the *Charter* necessary, or should an individual's fundamental rights and freedoms be absolute?

7. Dozens of administrative tribunals, such as the Atomic Energy Commission of Canada, the Labour Relations Board, the Canadian Radio-television and Telecommunications Commission, the Occupational Health and Safety Commission, and Human Rights tribunals, have been established by both the federal and provincial governments. Why do you think administrative tribunals are such a predominant feature in Canada? Why have they been established?

Situations for Discussion

1. R&D, a Crown corporation, has recently completed a human resource audit and inventory. One of the distressing results of the exercise was the revelation that its workforce is aging and that young recruits are leaving for better opportunities elsewhere. The consulting firm conducting the review has recommended implementing mandatory retirement at age 55. Such a policy would create openings in the higher ranks of the corporation and would help retain younger workers by providing opportunities for promotion. Would such a policy violate the *Canadian Charter of Rights and Freedoms*? What additional information would be useful?

2. In 1999, General Motors and Toyota announced that, working together, they would create the car engine of the future. Ford and DaimlerChrysler formed a partnership to improve fuel-cell engine technology. This initiative was in response to a California law requiring that by 2003, zero-emission vehicles (ZEVs) must make up 10 percent of an auto company's total sales. What is the role of government in regulating industry and protecting the environment, particularly when doing so drives up the cost of the product? Relevant websites include http://www.zevnow.org; http://www.arb.ca.gov/msprog/zevprog/zevprog.htm; and http://www.fuelcellpartnership.org/faq.html.

3. An accounting student is researching the deductibility of business expenses. She has found an amendment to the federal *Income Tax Act* that states that certain expenses are not deductible. However, she has also found case law that states that the expenses are deductible. Which law prevails? What additional information do you require to answer this question?

4. Under regulations in effect as of Oct. 1, 2005, all Canadian cigarette manufacturers must ensure that their product more readily extinguishes itself when left unattended. The purpose of this legislation is to reduce the death, injury, and property loss associated with fires caused by cigarettes. Given that cigarettes are a legal product and the fire loss itself is caused by careless smoking, is it appropriate for government to interfere with the manufacturing process this way? (See *Tobacco Act Cigarette Ignition Propensity Regulations*, SOR/2005-178)

5. Cherry Bomb, a clothing store in St. Catharines, Ontario, was the object of a demonstration in 2004 for selling T-shirts that, critics say, condone violence against women. One T-shirt depicted a bloody hammer with the words "She was asking for it." Other protesters at the demonstration claimed they had the right to wear such T-shirts. The controversy has also raised the question of the T-shirts violating hate crimes legislation, which prohibits someone from wilfully promoting hatred against any identifiable group.[24] In the past, however, this prohibition has been applied only in relation to racist speech. One of the manufacturer's responses to the criticism was that they were "equal opportunity offenders," as they also sold a T-shirt that had a picture of a pair of bloody scissors with the words "He had

---

24. Section 319(2) of the Canadian *Criminal Code*, R.S.C. 1985, c. C-46. The section also provides for the following defences:
    (3) No person shall be convicted of an offence under subsection (2)
    (a) if he establishes that the statements communicated were true;
    (b) if, in good faith, the person expressed or attempted to establish by an argument an opinion on a religious subject or an opinion based on a belief in a religious text;
    (c) if the statements were relevant to any subject of public interest, the discussion of which was for the public benefit, and if on reasonable grounds he believed them to be true; or
    (d) if, in good faith, he intended to point out, for the purpose of removal, matters producing or tending to produce feelings of hatred toward an identifiable group in Canada.

it coming."[25] Is it ethical for a business sell products that may cause deep emotional distress to members of the public? Is it an answer for the manufacturers to claim that they are generally offensive so no particular group should feel singled out? Do you think that the T-shirt offends the hate crimes provision of the *Criminal Code* quoted above? Why or why not?

6. The British Columbia Court of Appeal releases a decision that overturns the province's anti-smoking bylaw for violating the equality provisions of the *Charter*. What effect does this ruling have on other jurisdictions within Canada? Is a trial court in Ontario bound to follow the new ruling? What effect will it have on a decision of the Court of Appeal of Alberta?

7. Assume that Saskatchewan has passed legislation prohibiting children from renting violent videos. How could this legislation be challenged? Explain. Are there any ethical considerations when contemplating such a challenge?

For more study tools, visit
http://www.businesslaw3e.nelson.com

---

25. Chris Dart and Vivian Thomas, "Cherry Bomb Ignites Fury" (21 September 2004), online at http://www.brockpress.com/media/storage/paper384/news/2004/09/21/News/Cherry.Bomb.Ignites.Fury-725578.shtml?norewrite200611051807&sourcedomain=www.brockpress.com; "Domestic Violence T-Shirt Called 'Disgusting'" (23 September 2004), online at http://www.ctv.ca/servlet/ArticleNews/story/CTVNews/1095961654619_91370854/?hub=TopStories (accessed 28 October 2006); Mary Potter, "Offensive T-Shirt: A Joke that is No Laughing Matter" *NCWC Newsletter* (Winter 2005) at 16, at http://www.ncwc.ca/pdf/newsletter_winter_05.pdf#search=%22NCWC%20Winter%202005%20%22 (accessed 28 October 2006); Lynn Crosbie "When Offensive Thoughts Are Worse for the Wear," *The Globe and Mail* (2 October 2004) at R2.

Chapter

3

Objectives

After studying this chapter, you should have an understanding of

- methods of managing the legal environment of business
- the development of a legal risk management plan
- the importance of anticipating and reacting to developments in the legal environment
- methods of managing legal services

Managing Legal Risks

Business Law in Practice

Ideal Business Systems Ltd. (IBS) is a well-established, medium-sized business with its main office in the downtown business district of a typical Canadian town and three branch outlets in the region. It sells and leases a wide range of products and provides related services, such as design, installation, and maintenance. Products include office supplies, furniture and equipment, and computer systems. Its customers are consumers and other businesses. The present owners are the second generation of owners and have expanded the business significantly, especially in sales of computer technology. IBS consults with customers regarding their technology needs, designs computer systems, and recommends suitable hardware and software. IBS is financially healthy and profitable, achieving sales of $6 million last year. IBS owns the three-storey building in which the main office is located. The company uses the main level and leases the other two levels. IBS leases the space for its branch outlets in the towns in which they are located.

Two of the owners recently attended a trade show where one seminar addressed the concept of risk management in the office services industry. When the owners returned, they asked Manon Sevigny, a member of the management team, to explore the possible legal risks in their business.

1. What are the legal risks arising from IBS's business activities?
2. How should IBS handle these risks?

Assessing the Legal Environment

Many factors determine the success of a business organization. It must be able to analyze and evaluate its activities, forecast changes in the business environment, and react effectively to unexpected developments. Of central importance is the ability to strike the right balance between managing the present and planning for the future.

To meet its goal of producing a product or delivering a service at a profit, the business enterprise must have a set of functions and systems in place, including finance, marketing, and human resources. To ensure the smoothest possible operation of these systems, the business also needs to deal intelligently with the legal environment. By doing so, the business is less likely to make mistakes that are

- costly in terms of the expense of legal services and damage claims
- distracting in terms of time and effort
- harmful in terms of relationships and reputation in the industry

This chapter explores how a business can manage its interaction with the law and legal issues. It considers two basic approaches—preventive and reactive. The preventive approach requires a thorough evaluation of the risks associated with the business's activities in order to minimize their impact. The emphasis is on compliance with legal requirements and anticipation of changes in the legal environment. The reactive approach recognizes that legal problems may still materialize, so the firm needs a strategy in place to deal with such developments. These two approaches are combined in a management plan that reduces the impact of **legal risks** on the organization.

legal risk
A business risk with legal implications.

Legal Risk Management Plan

legal risk
management plan
A comprehensive action
plan for dealing with the
legal risks involved in operating a business.

Managing the intersection of law with an organization's activities requires completing a comprehensive assessment of legal risk exposure and developing a **legal risk management plan.** This process is often part of a broader exercise within an organization—enterprise risk assessment, in which all risks, including those with legal implications, are assessed and managed. Large businesses may have a department headed by a senior manager with a title such as risk officer or compliance officer to organize and oversee this process. In smaller organizations, the risk management function may be performed by the chief executive or delegate (such as Manon Sevigny for IBS) or by someone outside the organization, such as an insurance agent or a risk management consultant. Internal or external lawyers are likely to be involved in the process in a variety of roles depending on their familiarity with the legal risks of the business.

Regardless of where primary responsibility lies, it is not a task for one person. Risk management involves the cooperation of managers and others at every level of the organization. The challenge for Manon is to identify those inside and outside IBS who can help her through the steps for developing a useful plan. Those involved may use a variety of methods and approaches such as surveying or interviewing managers and employees or forming workplace committees.

Creating a risk management plan is a four-step process:

- ■ STEP ONE: Identify the legal risks.
- ■ STEP TWO: Evaluate the risks.
- ■ STEP THREE: Devise a legal risk management plan.
- ■ STEP FOUR: Implement the plan.

Applying the Four-Step Process

Identify the Legal Risks

It is a challenge to separate legal risks from the broader business risks. For example, every business runs the financial risk of failure and bankruptcy, but the legal focus of that risk would relate to the impact on the owners of the business. An awareness of the distinction will produce a more legally focused catalogue of risks. There are several methods that a business can use to identify its potential exposure to legal risks. This section explores three possible approaches, which, although reasonably distinct, do sometimes overlap. These approaches would have Manon assessing IBS's functional areas, its business decisions, and its business relationships.

Step One: Identify the legal risks.

 Assess the organization's functional areas.

 Review the organization's business decisions.

 Examine the organization's business relationships and assess those relationships.

Assess Functional Areas

The functional areas of business are those that are traditionally recognized in business organization charts and business school curricula—accounting, finance, marketing, production, human resources, and information systems. Although business and education are moving away from strictly defined functional responsibilities to a more integrated approach, functional areas still provide a useful starting point for risk analysis.

What follows are some possible risks arising in functional areas relevant to our example of Ideal Business Systems.

- Marketing programs are subject to industry codes and government regulation. For example, if IBS decides to mount a large sale on excess inventory, managers should be aware of the consumer protection rules against misleading statements in advertising "regular" and "sale" prices. Without this grounding, managers may cause the organization to break the law.

- Production decisions may entail tradeoffs between efficiency and safety. For example, cost pressures could tempt IBS to cut corners in assembling and installing furniture and equipment, which could lead to claims against IBS for defective products, property damage, or injury.

- Human resources involve a number of serious risks, including harassment, downsizing, and wrongful dismissal. If such matters are not handled according to well-developed policy, the organization runs a greater risk of being sued or having a human rights complaint made against it by a disgruntled employee.

- Information technology poses risks if records are inadequately maintained and protected. For example, timely delivery of products and services is bound to be important to IBS customers. If a proper system of monitoring customer orders is not maintained, IBS may lose future orders and be subject to claims from customers for the consequences of late delivery.

Employees can provide a useful starting point for identifying risks, given their familiarity with operations. As well, Manon needs to involve managers from each functional area in her risk review process.

Review Business Decisions

A review of decisions having possible legal implications can also be used to identify risks.

- IBS must assess the risk in its decisions concerning financial arrangements. How is credit granted to customers? How does IBS obtain credit from suppliers? Who assumes responsibility for defining the terms of credit?

- IBS must assess the risk in its decisions on how its contracts are worded. Sales to customers may involve standard form contracts. These contracts set out terms and conditions that are the same in every sale or transaction. Buying goods and services from suppliers involves dealing with their terms and conditions, also often in standard form. Do the organization's employees understand the content of these documents? Is the organization unwittingly assuming unnecessary risk of loss and liability as a result of these contracts?

- IBS must assess the risk in its decisions regarding the ownership and use of land. IBS is the owner and occupier of part of its building and the landlord of the remainder, as well as the occupier of the space it leases for its branch operations. As occupier, IBS is subject to claims by customers who injure themselves on its premises. As landlord, IBS has leases with its tenants, which may lead to legal problems if the terms are not met (if, for example, tenants fall behind in their rent payments). As a tenant in its branches, IBS depends on its landlords to meet their obligations. Buildings and their contents may be damaged or destroyed by disasters such as fire or flood.

■ IBS must assess the risk in its decisions affecting personnel. IBS faces legal ramifications in hiring, employing, and dismissing employees. These decisions require extensive planning, particularly in setting standards for performance, monitoring performance, and providing feedback to employees.

An inventory of such decisions will provide valuable input into the overall legal risk identification. A team of senior managers is likely in the best position to help Manon with this part of her assessment.

Examine Business Relationships

This approach focuses on the relationships a business has both internally and externally. It has the potential of providing a broad perspective because it identifies

■ those who have relationships with the business, both long and short term
■ the risks involved in those relationships, in both the long and short term

IBS has a number of relationships, all with attendant legal risks, such as the following:

■ Employees may create difficulties with customers or suppliers, be injured at work, or experience discrimination.
■ Suppliers or lenders may claim that they have not been paid. Suppliers may fail to deliver as promised.
■ Regulators may charge that the organization is failing to obey regulations related to business signs or waste disposal.
■ Customers may fail to pay on time or claim that they have not received what was promised.
■ Professionals such as accountants or lawyers may fail to provide the services that are expected.

As noted earlier, there are important interrelationships among these approaches, and all three of them can be used in performing Step One of the risk management plan. After considering the three approaches, Manon and her team at IBS would produce a list of legal risks such as the one illustrated in the following Business Application of the Law box.

This first step in developing a legal risk management program may seem to be unduly negative because it seeks to identify everything that could possibly go wrong in a business operation. The purpose of Step One, however, is to provide a realistic assessment of the potential downside of doing business, with a view toward minimizing loss.

Evaluate the Risks

The techniques used in Step Two vary from a simple, subjective evaluation to a complex statistical approach, involving actuaries and other professionals. These techniques involve assessing both the probability and the severity of loss.

Step Two: Evaluate the risks.

 Assess the probability of loss.

 Assess the severity of loss.

Most organizations have a wealth of information available to assist in performing such assessments, including the organization's loss history, industry statistics on losses, and expert opinion, from both within and outside the organization.

Business Application of the Law — Legal Risks for IBS

1. IBS might have a fire in its building, causing damage to inventory, the building itself, and the property of tenants.
2. Suppliers to IBS may deliver orders late, deliver defective goods, or fail to deliver the goods that were ordered.
3. Customers may fail to pay for orders delivered. They may complain about the quality of the goods or the service provided by IBS.
4. A customer might slip and fall on a slippery floor and be injured.
5. IBS employees may fail to do their jobs properly or make commitments to suppliers or customers that are unacceptable to IBS management.
6. Regulations dealing with such matters as business signs or waste disposal may change, requiring IBS to make significant adjustments and incur expenses.
7. If IBS buys equipment from other countries, trade regulations may change, making continued importation impossible or much more expensive.
8. IBS may get into financial difficulty, which would have serious implications for the owners of IBS and put their personal assets at risk.
9. Accountants (whether employed by IBS or retained as professional advisors) may make a significant error that misleads creditors, owners, or investors.
10. A delivery truck may be involved in a motor vehicle accident, resulting in personal injury and property damage.
11. A customer may complain that a sale price is higher than a competitor's regular price. IBS may be in violation of advertising regulations.
12. A business operated by one of IBS's tenants may fail, leaving IBS with several months of unpaid rent.

What legal risks are involved in delivering customer orders?

A high probability that a particular event will occur can be offset by a relatively low level of loss should the event actually occur. Events that are unlikely to occur also may deserve close attention if the potential loss is high. In the IBS situation, customers may occasionally slip and fall on IBS property, despite the best efforts of staff to prevent such events. However, these falls are unlikely to result in serious injuries that would be catastrophic for IBS. Yet if IBS seriously mishandles a major order from its most important customer, this one event may imperil the future of IBS. Other risks, such as a fire, may have varying consequences depending on their severity.

The point in evaluating risks is to recognize that not all risks are alike, nor should they be treated alike. Some risks crystallize into liability fairly often, but their financial and legal impact is relatively small. Other risks materialize infrequently, but when they do their impact is severe. A business can use this assessment to determine priorities for risk management and as guidance in choosing how to manage a particular risk in Step Three.

Devise a Risk Management Plan

A business can follow a number of methods to limit its exposure to risk, including risk avoidance, risk reduction, risk transference, and risk retention. Choosing one or more approaches involves evaluating the risk matched with the resources, financial or otherwise, of the organization—in other words, doing a cost-benefit analysis.

Step Three: Devise a risk management plan.

- ✓ Avoid or eliminate the risk.
- ✓ Reduce the risk.
- ✓ Transfer the risk.
- ✓ Retain the risk.

risk avoidance
The decision to cease a business activity because the legal risk is too great.

Risk Avoidance   Eliminating risk, or **risk avoidance,** is appropriate when the risk is simply too great or when the undesirable result of the activity, product, or service is greater than the advantages. In the IBS context, the risk that import regulations and conditions may change in ways harmful to IBS may cause the company to avoid committing to an offshore firm as a major supplier. Domestic sources may be less attractive in the short term, but less risky in the long term. Depending on the circumstances, dealing with a major supplier offshore may be judged so risky that the potential downside outweighs the benefits.

Another example of risk avoidance relates to financing the business. If IBS owners need capital for expansion, they may be called upon to pledge personal assets as security for a loan to the business. Despite their confidence about the future of their business, the owners may be unprepared to jeopardize their personal assets. They may, instead, seek other sources of financing—by selling shares in the company, for example—thereby reducing personal risk.

A business involved in heavy industry might decide to discontinue plant tours for the public or a job-shadowing program for school students because of the risk of injury to the visitors.

risk reduction
Implementation of practices in a business to lower the probability of loss and its severity.

Risk Reduction   A business can undertake **risk reduction** in relation to most risks that cannot be avoided. For example, IBS cannot do business without extending credit to customers. The provision of credit inevitably involves the risk that some customers will not pay their accounts. To minimize that risk, IBS should have procedures in place (such as regular credit checks) for evaluating and periodically reassessing the credit-worthiness of customers.

As another example, IBS can reduce the risk of the municipal government's changing regulations in a way that adversely affects the enterprise. IBS management should keep apprised of municipal politics, through contact with municipal representatives, bureaucrats, legal advisors, industry associations, chambers of commerce, and other businesses in the community. By doing so, IBS will see regulatory changes coming and be able to make representations before they become law. At a minimum, IBS will be able to plan for changes and accommodate them in the least disruptive fashion.

To minimize the chance that customers will injure themselves by slipping and falling, IBS can pay extra attention to keeping walkways and other areas frequented by customers clear of possible hazards. Employees delegated to do the maintenance work can be informed about the importance of their work and the nature of the risks to IBS if the work is inadequately performed. IBS also might consider posting warnings for customers in hazardous areas.

IBS also can reduce the risk of accounting errors by carefully hiring and training staff and by choosing professionals based on their reputation and proven performance. IBS can seek professional advice on financial controls and take an active role in the work that its accounting professionals do for the company. For example, before financial results are sent to the bank, IBS management and the accountants should review them for cogency.

Risk Transference   This approach complements risk reduction by transferring the remaining risk to another by contract. Insurance, which is an integral part of most risk management plans, is discussed in detail in Chapter 28. Insurance is likely the best response to many of the risks faced by IBS. Motor vehicles owned by IBS will be covered by vehicle insurance. Slips and falls by customers will be covered by a general liability policy. The risk of fire will be covered by fire insurance. However, it should be noted that insurance can be costly, that some risks (such as potential environmental liability) are difficult to insure against, and that insurance provides coverage only to the extent and in the amount actually purchased. As well, insurance does not prevent loss or the adverse publicity resulting from a high-profile case, even if the insurance company defends or pays the claim.

Although **risk transference** is usually thought of in terms of insurance, it can also involve protection such as limited or excluded responsibility that can be provided by contract (see Part Two).

The most common transaction in the business of IBS is the delivery of goods to customers. Many things can go wrong that may cause loss to the customer, resulting in a claim against the business. The product may be delivered late, it may fail to meet the customer's expectations, or it may be defective. One common approach to such risks is to create a contract for all customers that limits the liability of the business for such claims. For example, IBS might include a clause in its customer contracts providing that in event of the failure of an IBS product to meet the customer's needs, IBS is liable only to pay the customer a specified portion of the purchase price in damages.

The challenge in such a contract is to create terms and conditions that achieve the business objective of risk transference, that are reasonable and acceptable to customers, that are clearly written and explained to customers, and that are legally enforceable if a dispute arises. Lawyers can create these standard form contracts only if they fully understand the risks involved and are able to work closely with the business to ensure that the terms achieve their purpose in a reasonable manner.

Risk Retention   Keeping or absorbing all or part of the risk within the organization is known as **risk retention.** This approach is appropriate when the cost of avoiding or transferring a risk is greater than the impact on the business if the risk materializes. In effect, the organization pays losses out of its own resources. The organization can do this in several ways:

- SELF-INSURANCE. The organization can establish a funded reserve.

- INSURANCE POLICY DEDUCTIBLES. The organization can retain risks to a certain dollar amount.

- NONINSURANCE. The organization can charge losses as an expense item.

risk transference
The decision to shift the risk to someone else through a contract.

risk retention
The decision to absorb the loss if a legal risk materializes.

There has been a marked increase recently in the use of risk retention, owing in part to significant increases in insurance premiums in many industry sectors or even the refusal of insurance companies to cover certain risks such as terrorism or sexual abuse in volunteer organizations. There are also some risks that cannot be avoided or reduced to zero. These risks must be absorbed by the business. For example, IBS cannot avoid local regulations. If waste disposal rules change, IBS may face significant expense, despite its best efforts to anticipate and adapt to the changes.

Another example concerns dissatisfied customers. Even if employees are thoroughly trained to deal with customers (with a view to meeting the best interests of both IBS and customers), some customers will make complaints that have significant financial consequences. Perhaps a customer has bought a computer system on the advice of IBS, and the system has turned out to be completely inappropriate for the customer's real needs. This is a situation that IBS must resolve, and it represents a risk that cannot be completely avoided.

Ethical Considerations · Exploding Gas Tanks

In the 1970s, General Motors discovered that because the gas tank of its Chevrolet Malibu was placed behind the rear axle instead of in front, there was a risk that the gas would explode if the vehicle was hit from behind. To assess the risk, GM did a cost-benefit analysis that showed that based on the projected number of related accidents, it would cost $2.20 per auto to settle claims involving fatalities caused by exploding tanks versus $8.59 per car to fix the problem beforehand.

Which factors—legal, financial, or ethical—are most important in developing a plan to deal with this risk? How would each of the approaches (avoidance, reduction, transference, retention) apply to this risk?

GM decided not to fix the problem, and to retain the risk and cost of injuries caused by the defect. On Christmas Eve 1993, a mother, her four children, and a friend were driving in a 1979 Malibu when a drunk driver hit the rear of the Malibu at 80 to 110 km per hour. All six occupants in the car were injured. The children were trapped in the back seat and badly burned. Those injured sued GM, and in the course of the trial, the GM cost-benefit analysis was revealed. In its defence, GM argued that the speeding drunk driver was responsible for the crash and that most cars made in the 1970s had the gas tank in the same position as the Malibu.

The jury found GM responsible for the injuries and awarded the claimants a total of $4.9 billion—

$107 million in compensation and $4.8 billion in punitive damages to punish GM. The punitive damages were later reduced to $1.09 billion. Brian Panish, lead attorney for the victims, said: "Without the risk of juries holding companies accountable for their reprehensible conduct, GM and other automobile manufacturers would have little reason to put passengers' safety first."

CRITICAL ANALYSIS: Do you agree with Mr. Panish? How might this case affect GM's management of similar risks in future?

Source: Michael White, "Jury Orders GM to Pay Crash Victims $4.9-Billion (U.S.)" *The Globe and Mail* (10 July 1999) at B3.

"How can this risk be managed?"

Any plan devised in Step Three must be reasonable in terms of its cost and complexity. No plan can eliminate all risk. The goal is to be aware of risks and to make conscious decisions about dealing with them. To assist in this process, managers may turn to legal professionals for balanced advice, either on a lawyer-client basis or through in-house counsel. However, the lawyer must know the business and the industry in which it functions in order to provide useful input.

Implement the Plan

Once a business has devised a risk management plan, it must put the plan into action and assess its effectiveness on an ongoing basis.

Step Four: Implement the plan.

 Carry out the plan.

 Monitor and revise the plan.

Responsibility for implementing the risk management plan must be clearly assigned. Much of this allocation may be obvious. For example, if the analysis has suggested a quality-control problem, the plan must identify those responsible for both monitoring quality and delivering the service or producing the product. It will not be enough, however, to simply advise the appropriate personnel of the problem. The employees must be educated as to why the problem requires correction and what techniques should be adopted to ensure that the problem is corrected. In addition, guidelines for carrying out the procedures should be collected in a manual for immediate reference. The document should include, as appropriate, a schedule of inspections of facilities, a formal system of ensuring that those inspections take place as scheduled, an accident-reporting system, and information on any insurance coverage in place. Such a manual can be a two-edged sword, however. If IBS is sued for injury or loss and it is shown that IBS neglected to follow its own policy on the matter, the claimant may have grounds for establishing liability.

The plan must be continually monitored and revised as necessary. Management should have a regular review process in place to determine whether the plan is working, and, if not, why. The frequency and severity of events anticipated in the plan will provide feedback on the plan's effectiveness. For example, as a result of the exploding gas tanks, GM will reconsider its retention of the risk in relation to the Malibus and the design of all of its vehicles.

The nature of the business conducted by a firm may change, requiring major reconsideration of the plan. For example, one of the many causes of the Enron failure in 2001 was the rapid evolution of its business from a traditional energy distribution company to a provider of wholesale services utilizing risky strategies of trading in commodities and derivatives and generating vastly increased revenues. There is some question whether Enron's previously sound risk management approach was appropriate for its changed business and whether the approach was adequately adapted and altered.[1] Risks may frequently change and practices will need to be adapted, but a routine review process can help to ensure that the requisite adjustments are made.

---

1. George Stevens, "Is the Firm Enron-Proof?" *The Lawyers Weekly* (26 April 2002) at 6.

Summary of the Legal Risk Management Model

Step One:	Identify the legal risks.
✓	Assess the organization's functional areas.
✓	Review the organization's business decisions.
✓	Examine the organization's business relationships.

Step Two:	Evaluate the risks.
✓	Assess the probability of loss.
✓	Assess the severity of loss.

Step Three:	Devise a risk management plan.
✓	Avoid or eliminate the risk.
✓	Reduce the risk.
✓	Transfer the risk.
✓	Retain the risk.

Step Four:	Implement the plan.
✓	Carry out the plan.
✓	Monitor and revise the plan.

A risk management plan need not be a lengthy or complicated document. The key is for managers like Manon to identify and evaluate legal risks and then rely on a cost-benefit analysis to devise an action plan in response. For example, the cost of checking in detail the background of prospective tenants may outweigh the possible cost of a tenant's defaulting on the rent. The cost of prevention is a certainty, while risks and the resulting losses may never materialize. Figure 3.2 outlines a possible plan for IBS that Manon might develop with the management team by applying the risk management model. It addresses the 12 risks identified in the Business Application of the Law box on page 53.

FIGURE 3.2

Legal Risk Management Plan for Ideal Business Systems

Risk 1:	IBS might have a fire in its building, causing damage to inventory, the building itself, and the property of tenants.
Action:	IBS could identify potential fire hazards (such as paper stored near a heat source); implement a fire prevention plan by assigning the duty of conducting and documenting regular inspections and reporting any hazards; have insurance coverage that includes the fire risks and covers losses to property, personal injury, and loss of business; and review its coverage with the insurance broker at least once a year.
Risk 2:	Suppliers to IBS may deliver orders late, deliver defective goods, or fail to deliver the goods that were ordered.
Action:	IBS could choose suppliers carefully, based on reputation with industry associations and other firms in the industry; attempt to negotiate agreements with suppliers that set clear standards of performance (specific delivery dates) and specify compensation for performance failures (for example, the right to obtain the goods elsewhere and claim extra costs); and carefully monitor suppliers' quality of performance.

Risk 3: Customers may fail to pay for orders delivered. They may complain about the quality of the goods or the service provided by IBS.

Action: IBS could screen customers carefully before extending credit (by doing checks through credit-reporting agencies); monitor payment history; and use standard form contracts to clearly indicate who is responsible for what in their transactions. In terms of the quality of its goods and services, IBS could have detailed customer service practices in place (such as on-time delivery and time limits for response to customer complaints) and regularly gather feedback from customers (through telephone follow-up).

Risk 4: A customer might slip and fall on a slippery floor and be injured.

Action: IBS could identify hazards (such as a slippery floor or inventory obstructing an aisle in the showroom); ensure that procedures are in place for regular patrol and maintenance of those areas; post warning signs for visitors; and have insurance coverage in place for any injuries that do occur.

What risks are shown here?

Risk 5: IBS employees may fail to do their jobs properly or make commitments to suppliers or customers that are unacceptable to IBS management.

Action: IBS needs to set clear performance standards for employees (such as sales quotas or number of customer complaints) and carefully recruit, train, and regularly evaluate employees.

Risk 6: Regulations dealing with such matters as business signs or waste disposal might change, requiring IBS to make significant adjustments and incur expenses.

Action: IBS should keep attuned to local politics so that changes do not come as a surprise, be prepared to contribute to public debate over proposed changes, and be able to formulate coordinated efforts to deal with adaptation to regulatory changes. For example, if sign regulations change, the marketing manager could be assigned the task of consulting all those affected by the signs and deciding exactly what needs to be done to comply with the changes.

Risk 7:	If IBS buys equipment from other countries, trade regulations may change, making continued importation impossible or much more expensive.
Action:	IBS should obtain expert advice (legal or otherwise) on the situation in the relevant countries and be in a position to anticipate changes there, just as it would with local regulations. If the situation is deemed too unstable, IBS could seek other sources of supply.
Risk 8:	IBS may get into financial difficulty, which would have serious implications for the owners of IBS and put their personal assets at risk.
Action:	IBS owners need to structure their business and personal affairs to achieve a level of comfort with their degree of personal risk, relating to the legal structure of the business (for example, partnership versus corporation) and the extent to which the owners accept responsibility for business losses through such vehicles as guarantees. They also need to keep on top of the financial position of the firm and anticipate financial problems, rather than be caught by a crisis.
Risk 9:	Accountants (whether employed by IBS or retained as professional advisors) may make a significant error that misleads creditors, owners, or investors.
Action:	IBS should choose all professional advisors carefully (based on record and reputation) by consulting professional associations and others involved in the industry and community; work closely with those advisors and not rely completely on their advice; carefully choose accounting employees based on ability and trustworthiness; and obtain professional advice about a system of financial controls to prevent mistakes.
Risk 10:	A delivery truck may be involved in a motor vehicle accident, resulting in personal injury and property damage.
Action:	IBS should carefully recruit drivers of company vehicles; provide appropriate specialized training programs; ensure that complete vehicle insurance coverage is in place; and review coverage at least annually with an insurance broker.
Risk 11:	A customer may complain that a sale price is higher than a competitor's regular price. IBS may be in violation of advertising regulations.
Action:	IBS marketing personnel should be familiar with relevant advertising regulations and seek prior approval from regulators if there is any doubt about compliance.
Risk 12:	A business operated by one IBS's tenants may fail, leaving IBS with several months of unpaid rent.
Action:	IBS should choose tenants carefully (by checking references and general reputation); avoid long-term leases with unproven tenants; be aware of how tenants are using their property; and be on the lookout for any signs of financial difficulty (such as decreased business traffic or employee layoffs).

To create this kind of plan, management needs to analyze business activities, develop practices to minimize risks, and know when to seek assistance outside the business, whether by securing insurance or retaining professionals for advice. Risk 7, involving offshore suppliers, is the only one of the 12 risks for which the recommended action may be risk avoidance. All other risks are dealt with through a combination of risk reduction, transference, and retention.

The management of legal risks can be an even greater challenge in the international arena. The following International Perspective describes some of the risks of doing business in the global marketplace.

The emerging economies of the countries in the former Soviet Union, Eastern Europe, Central and South America, Asia, and Africa provide tremendous opportunities for investment. Although the rewards from doing business in these countries can be great, so can the risks. Consider the following examples of serious legal difficulties faced by Canadian companies operating in foreign countries:

- PetroKazakhstan (PetroKaz) entered a lucrative partnership with a Russian oil company in 1996 to acquire oil reserves in Kazakhstan. After several years of profitability, PetroKaz is now in dispute with its partner over the split of the oil supply and with the government regulator over price controls.

- The Bolivian government has recently decreed that ownership of all oil fields be transferred to the government and future sales be processed through a state-owned company. Foreign producers have been given six months to renegotiate contracts or face the seizure of their assets.

- Niko Resources of Calgary successfully revived gas fields in India for 14 years. When the company attempted to duplicate its business in neighbouring Bangladesh, it encountered a radically different political and legal climate. Following two gas blowouts, Niko now faces compensation claims from citizens, businesses, and government. It is in dispute with government over gas prices, has had assets frozen, and found itself in the middle of the election campaign.

- IMP Group of Halifax entered a partnership with the Russian airline, Aeroflot, to lease the Aerostar Hotel in Moscow from the Russian government. Over 10 years, the partners invested $45 million to develop the luxury hotel. In 2004, the hotel was seized and IMP evicted by a small Russian company claiming a deficiency in the lease.

Aerostar Hotel in Moscow

IMP has been unable to pursue its claim for return of the hotel through the Russian courts.

If businesses in foreign countries are to proceed and succeed, potential risks such as those described above need to be evaluated and managed. However, forecasting political risk is extremely difficult. Furthermore, the scope of the loss if the political risk materializes could be catastrophic. There are, however, steps that businesses can take to manage international risks:

- Plan early, keeping in mind that the foreign legal environment may be different in terms of its laws and their enforcement.

- Access all available sources of information, including the Department of Foreign Affairs, business associations, consultants, and people who have experience with the foreign country.

- Consider local customs concerning contract negotiations and ethical behaviour.

- Become aware of the regulatory climate.

- Determine how competitors are handling risks in the industry.

- Consider relying on local partners in managing indigenous issues before they become a problem.

- Seek the assistance of the political risk insurance market to put the risks into context and quantify the costs of transferring them. Determine the available coverage and the costs.

CRITICAL ANALYSIS: How should the legal risk management model be adapted for conducting international business? Which of the four steps of the model are most important?

Sources: Eric Reguly, "PetroKaz's Woes in Kazakhstan a Cautionary Tale" *The Globe and Mail* (7 May 2005) at B2; Juan Forero, "Step 1 in Bolivian Takeover: Audit of Foreign Companies" *The New York Times* (4 May 2006) online at http://www.nytimes.com (accessed 18 October 2006); Geoffrey York, "Blowout in Bangladesh" *The Globe and Mail* (1 April 2006) at B4; and Michael Tutton, "IMP Loses Court Bid" *The Chronicle Herald* (15 June 2005) at E2.

Interacting with the Legal Environment

Reacting When Prevention Fails

Prevention of loss is the primary goal of a risk management plan, but some risks cannot be avoided. Disputes inevitably arise; products and services sometimes fail; the business climate, the attitude of government toward business, or the marketplace can change. The value of a risk management plan is that when a risk does materialize, the business already has in place an effective way of addressing it and can more readily assess when legal advice may be necessary.

In the IBS example, a potential risk involves the serious problem of computer hackers, who spend their time probing computer systems in order to gain unauthorized access. IBS is a distributor of computer hardware and software and therefore relies on the manufacturers to build security into those products. An IBS customer whose computer system and data are compromised by a hacker could allege that IBS recommended and sold a system that was especially vulnerable to hackers because it lacked the most current security protection. When IBS investigates the complaint, it may discover that several other customers have bought a similar system and are also vulnerable. IBS could view this problem as one that the manufacturer is responsible for, but since the customer also relied on IBS for advice, IBS may have considerable legal risk. In the meantime, the customer may contact other businesses and disparage IBS products and services. Not surprisingly, IBS would worry about damage to its reputation in the business community.

Although IBS's risk management plan (see Figure 3.2, page 58) does not specifically include hacking as a potential risk, it has identified customer dissatisfaction as a significant legal risk (Risk 3). Details of the action plan should include guidelines as to how employees are to address customer complaints; what kind of investigation, if any, is to take place; how solutions are to be developed; what kind of record is to be made of the complaint; what follow-up is to be done to ensure that the customer is satisfied; and what steps are to be taken to prevent such a problem from recurring. As well, the plan would indicate when senior management should be alerted about a customer concern. In the scenario above, the employee should immediately involve senior managers because the customer's complaint about computer security is serious, ongoing, and potentially far-reaching. IBS's risk management plan will also direct senior managers as to when formal legal advice is required. Ideally, that legal advisor will be someone with intimate knowledge of the organization and the personalities within it.

The current problem that IBS faces requires the help of a lawyer, since it involves issues of breach of contract and defamation. The contract issue relates to the possibility that IBS supplied defective equipment. If IBS did so, it may be in breach of contract. The second legal issue relates to the possibility that the customer is defaming IBS and ruining its business reputation. Management may need specialized legal advice on this issue. Whether IBS should take formal steps to stop the customer from denigrating IBS's products and services depends on that legal advice, on IBS's assessment of the need to restore its reputation, and on the resources necessary to pursue such a claim.

IBS's risk management plan should address dispute resolution procedures, which are discussed in Chapter 4. The challenge of managing legal services is discussed below.

Managing Legal Services

Legal advice and input are key components in successful legal risk management. Lawyers may be part of the risk management team or consulted by the team at various stages of the process. They can help in identifying and assessing legal risks, and suggesting options for the risk management plan. The challenge for a business is to make optimal use of legal advisors.

When to Seek Legal Advice

Knowing when to seek legal advice is central to successful management of legal services. Consulting lawyers too soon and too often is expensive and cumbersome. Consulting them infrequently to save money may be more expensive in the long run. Government regulation is becoming more prevalent and complicated, and penalties for violation are generally increasing. Seeking advice at the appropriate time is preferable to waiting for problems to develop. A healthy, ongoing relationship with legal professionals will guide the business in this regard.

IBS has a comprehensive risk management plan and will already have identified the most serious areas of potential liability. Legal advice may be necessary to understand the legal process, especially in regulatory matters. It may be more efficient for a lawyer to clarify sign regulations, waste disposal guidelines, and import requirements than for an ill-informed business to explore such issues on its own. Even if a dispute is unlikely to go to court, the legal issues and options are important in negotiations. If a formal legal process has begun or is imminent, the business should seek legal advice. Otherwise, it may lose the dispute by failing to respond.

It is important to clarify within the organization who should decide when a matter requires legal advice. Assigning responsibility depends on whether or not the business has its own internal law department.

If there is an internal law department, likely those in that department will make the decisions about whether to go to outside lawyers and which lawyers to consult. To allow other employees to unilaterally approach external lawyers seriously undermines both the credibility and the effectiveness of the law department. Organizations may allow employees to go directly to external lawyers only if they have prior authorization from the internal law department. Employees should understand that all legal services involve a cost and should be discouraged from referring nonlegal or trivial problems to the legal department and distracting it from more serious legal concerns.

If there is no internal law department, there must be clear guidelines as to who has the authority to seek outside counsel and when. If external legal advice is sought, the organization must clearly indicate which services are desired, what authority the lawyer has, and the extent to which the business will continue to be involved in the proceedings. Lawyers may define the boundaries of the relationship if the organization fails to do so, and such an approach could prove both costly and inefficient.

Lawyers can seldom resolve disputes instantly. Their role is to provide assistance. For this reason, the business must remain actively involved. Lawyers are integral to the prevention of legal disputes and reaction to developments in the legal environment, but can also contribute to the success of the business.

How to Choose a Lawyer

lawyer
A person who is legally qualified to practise law.

A **lawyer** provides expert advice on legal matters of concern to a business. The business should manage legal services in the same way as any other service. The first step is to find the lawyer or firm appropriate to the business's needs in terms of expertise and approach to dealing with clients. The selection will be much easier if the client has a clear idea of the nature and the volume of the advice required, as well as the allocated budget for legal services. Those responsible for engaging legal services need to discuss a legal services agreement with a number of potential legal service providers in order to achieve the right fit.

The legal profession is one of a number of self-governing professions (see Chapter 22). The governing body determines who is qualified to practise and requires members to be insured against professional negligence, but does not certify specialization or experience. Lawyers may practise on their own as sole practitioners or be members of a **law firm.** Firms can range in nature and size from small and local to large and multinational. Not all lawyers are appropriate for all situations; an organization needs a lawyer with the expertise for the particular issue, although that lawyer may not be part of the law firm the organization typically uses. Lawyers will normally recognize the limitations to their firm's expertise and refer clients to other firms when necessary.

law firm
A partnership formed by lawyers.

There are many sources available for identifying lawyers, although there is no easy way to decide who are the most competent or appropriate for a particular business. Friends, relatives, and business associates of management may be able to recommend lawyers who have served them well. Local and provincial bar associations maintain lists of members by geographical area and preferred type of practice. *The Canadian Law List*[2] is a publication available in libraries and online that includes basic biographical information about most lawyers in private practice.

Some advice follows for choosing from among a group of lawyers or firms:

- Consult with business associates with similar legal problems and needs about the service they have received from any of the prospects.

- Consider meeting with each lawyer or with a representative of each firm to discuss the need of the business for legal advice in general or in relation to a particular legal problem. Lawyers have a strict professional duty to maintain the confidentiality of client affairs.

- Discuss alternative fee structures with the prospects. Lawyers are increasingly willing to provide a fee structure that suits the client, such as billing at an hourly rate, setting a standard fee for routine work, working on an annual retainer, or accepting a percentage fee. The client should expect an itemized billing on a schedule that suits the business's financial cycle. An increasingly popular option is to put the provision of legal services out to tender. This requires detailed knowledge of the services required over a period of time.

- Evaluate the prospects according to a predetermined list of criteria that suit the needs of the business in terms of expertise, availability, willingness to understand the business, and willingness to communicate.

---

2. See http://www.canadianlawlist.com

The object of the exercise is to develop a productive, long-term relationship between the business and the legal advisor. For this reason, there is also a need to continually monitor and evaluate the relationship, primarily to ensure that the business is receiving the advice and assistance it needs at a cost it can afford.

Businesses must be prepared to change law firms if circumstances warrant. Whatever loyalty may develop between lawyer and manager, a critical evaluation of the value of the law firm's services may identify the need for a move to another firm.

In the following Business Application of the Law, two lawyers discuss their contributions to their business clients.

Business Application of the Law — The Role of Lawyers

Lawyers perform different roles and bring different perspectives depending on whether they are employed in-house or consulted as independent professionals.

Lawyers in private practice provide advice as requested by their clients. Kathryn Dykstra has been advising corporate-commercial clients for over 15 years. She states:

> When business clients come to see me, I know there are many issues that they haven't thought about in the push to "get the deal done." The job of a lawyer is not to send them away with ten more problems than they started with, although it is clearly our job to raise those legal issues that have to be addressed in order to complete the transaction properly. Lawyers should not be seen as "deal-breakers," that is, people who point out so many potential problems that the transaction never goes through. Rather, the lawyer is retained to act in her client's best interest, and this includes providing a range of solutions to meet that end.

Corporate (in-house) counsel can identify business opportunities as well as give legal advice.

Richard Bailey is senior vice president and deputy general counsel for Kraft Foods North America. He spends a lot of time advising other corporate lawyers of the need to integrate their department's work with the company's business. Otherwise, corporations tend to see a legal department as a necessary expense that deals with legal problems but contributes nothing to the bottom line. In-house counsel must do more than handle lawsuits. They must help the corporation avoid lawsuits, and they can do so only if actively involved in management. They cannot simply wait to be asked for their advice.

Bailey formerly worked for Kraft Canada, which ships a huge volume of products to the U.S. market and is therefore subject to all the regulations under NAFTA. Many managers at Kraft perceived these regulations as a significant barrier to exporting. Bailey's department did an audit to determine which perceived barriers were real. The lawyers discovered that many barriers had disappeared or were subject to challenge before trade tribunals. The result was that Kraft Canada identified $8 billion in additional export opportunities.

Bailey says, "When I'm asked to show what value our department has added to the bottom line, I'm not going to tell management we successfully challenged regulation such-and-such. I'm going to tell them about the business opportunity we found."

Sources: Michael Fitz-James, "Legal Departments Add Value, Counsel Argues" *Financial Times* (11 September 1997) at 22; Kathryn Dykstra, Lawyer, Parlee McLaws.

Business Law in Practice Revisited

1. What are the legal risks arising from IBS's business activities?

Manon Sevigny and the team she assembles to assist her can study IBS in order to identify the legal risks that exist. Manon and her team can use the three suggested approaches: assess IBS's functional areas, review its business decisions, and examine its business relationships. This process will enable the team to compile a list of risks such as the 12 presented in the Business Application of the Law on page 53.

2. How should IBS handle these risks?

Manon and her team need to evaluate the identified risks by assessing the probability and the severity of each potential loss. They must then develop a risk management plan by deciding how to address each risk—by avoiding, reducing, transferring, retaining, or through some combination of those options. The plan must contain specific actions for dealing with each risk and assign responsibility for each action. Figure 3.2 presents the outline of a plan that Manon might produce. Top management must support the plan, and all affected employees must be familiar with it. Risk management is a continuous process, so Manon or others must monitor the plan to measure its effectiveness in dealing with risks and be prepared to recommend any necessary adjustments.

A key part of the risk management process is managing legal services. Manon should have legal advice as she develops her plan. To be effective, the IBS lawyers must be familiar with the business and be involved in all stages of developing and maintaining the plan. IBS needs a stable relationship with lawyers outside the business, even if IBS decides that the volume and nature of the legal work that IBS requires warrants in-house counsel. IBS also needs a plan to acquire specialized legal advice as the need arises from unexpected events.

Chapter Summary

A business can manage its legal environment by assessing that environment, developing a risk management plan, reacting to changes in the legal environment, and managing its legal services.

It is crucial for a business to actively manage the legal risks arising from its activities in order to avoid and minimize legal claims and expenses. Legal risk management involves a four-step process: identifying legal risks, assessing those risks, devising a risk management plan, and implementing the plan. Risks can be identified through assessment of the functional areas of the business, the decisions made within the organization, and the internal and external relationships maintained by the business. The risks are then assessed in terms of how likely they are to occur and how severe the losses might be. There must be an action plan for dealing with each risk. Should the risk be avoided? If not, how can it be reduced or transferred to someone else? To what extent must the risk be retained?

Management must assemble a knowledgeable team of employees and experts in order to make the plan work. A business also must monitor and revise its plan to ensure that it is current and effective. No risk management plan can anticipate and deal with all possible developments. A business must be prepared to react in a coordinated and timely fashion to unexpected events.

A business also needs to actively manage its legal services, whether it is employing outside lawyers or in-house counsel. This management involves identifying the legal services that are needed and carefully searching out an appropriate lawyer or firm. Every business needs a stable relationship with its legal advisors, whether they are external or internal, and must be prepared to seek specialized advice as needed.

Chapter Study

Key Terms and Concepts

law firm (p. 64)

lawyer (p. 64)

legal risk (p. 49)

legal risk management plan (p. 50)

risk avoidance (p. 54)

risk reduction (p. 54)

risk retention (p. 55)

risk transference (p. 55)

Questions for Review

1. What is meant by the preventive and reactive approaches to legal issues in a business?

2. What is the primary goal of a legal risk management plan?

3. How does a legal risk management plan relate to enterprise risk management?

4. What is the value of a legal risk management plan?

5. What steps are involved in the legal risk management model?

6. How does a business identify legal risks by assessing the functional areas of the business?

7. What business decisions can be assessed to identify legal risks?

8. Which business relationships are crucial in identifying risks?

9. What additional legal risks are involved in doing business internationally?

10. Which of the four approaches to risk management should be considered before deciding to do business internationally?

11. Which of the four approaches did General Motors use with regard to the risk of exploding gas tanks?

12. What methods can a business use to limit its exposure to risk?

13. Outline the procedures to implement a risk management plan.

14. How can a business keep its risk management plan current and relevant?

15. What titles could be given to the employee primarily responsible for risk management in a business?

16. When should a business seek legal advice?

17. What are the different fee structures that can be used for legal services?

18. What are some benefits of employing in-house counsel?

Questions for Critical Thinking

1. The active involvement and commitment of employees at all levels of an organization is crucial for successful risk management. Who is ultimately responsible for managing legal risks and legal services? What factors are relevant for assigning responsibility within an organization?

2. Risk avoidance is an appropriate strategy when the potential losses seriously outweigh the likely benefits. What factors should be considered on the cost and benefit sides of the analysis? At what point should a business decide to discontinue an activity rather than try to manage the risk involved? What are some examples of risk avoidance?

3. Risk retention is an appropriate strategy when the costs resulting from avoidance or transfer of the risk are greater than the probable loss if the risk should occur. The analysis required to employ such a strategy is complicated. What factors are relevant? Since the destruction of the World Trade Center in New York, insurance companies have raised premiums significantly or refused coverage entirely on potential terrorist targets. How far is this trend likely to extend? What are the implications for risk management?

4. Risk management is a continuous process that requires commitment, time, and expense. On the other hand, the benefits are often difficult to identify because they arise largely from prevention. How can a business decide whether the benefits of a risk management plan compensate for the time and expense involved in its design and implementation?

5. A common method of controlling the cost of legal services is to refrain from consulting a lawyer until a serious legal problem absolutely requires it. Another approach is to hire or retain lawyers on an ongoing basis to provide advice as business decisions are made. Which approach is the most expensive? What should a business consider in making that choice?

6. In order to provide timely advice, a company's lawyer should be familiar with the company's business activities. Over time, the company may come to depend on a particular lawyer more and more. How can a company develop and benefit from a long-term relationship without becoming overly dependent on a lawyer or law firm?

Situations for Discussion

1. Johann is the comptroller of Super Tech Inc., a highly aggressive firm in the high-tech industry that specializes in software development. Sally, the CEO, prides herself on her ability to make fast decisions and doesn't worry about documenting her actions. Her favourite sayings are, "If I had wanted red tape, I would have joined the government," and "Why worry? That's why we have insurance." This approach appears to have served her well, at least in the initial years of the business. Johann is concerned, however, because he is often faced with legal bills without having any knowledge of the issues involved.

   The firm's legal costs are steadily increasing. How should Johann present a recommendation to Sally that Super Tech should develop a legal risk management plan?

2. If Sally accepts Johann's recommendation in Situation 1, whom should he recruit for the risk management team? Should he be the leader of the team? How should he go about identifying the legal risks in the firm's business? Whom should he consult?

3. Johann's review has identified a particular problem with Super Tech's software designers. When used by customers, their designs are failing at a higher

rate than the industry norm. The designers are unwilling to go back and correct problems because they prefer to develop new products and are under pressure to do so. Super Tech is faced with legal claims and lost customers. How should Johann evaluate and address this problem in the context of his risk management plan, taking into consideration the software designers and the company's profitability? Which of the four approaches to dealing with a risk are appropriate?

4. Pascal is the manager of software development for Super Tech. He discovers that Bill, the lead software designer, has announced that he is leaving the company next week. Pascal finds that Bill has accepted a job with Super Tech's main competitor. Pascal fears that in his new job Bill will use technology developed while at the company and disclose the identities of key customers. How could Pascal and Super Tech have identified and addressed this risk? What should Pascal do now?

5. A routine review of Super Tech's accounts receivable discloses a recurring problem with collections from one important customer. What factors should Super Tech consider in its review of this account? How could a risk management plan help Super Tech in determining its course of action regarding this customer? Which steps of the process would be most important?

6. Birnbaum is the vice president of administration of Super Tech. She notices that a trend has developed where managers have started "passing things by the lawyer" when they are not sure whether a legal issue is involved. Birnbaum suspects that this trend flows from the close acquaintance of Sally (the CEO) with the senior partner of the law firm used by Super Tech; they both sit on the board of a local charity and socialize frequently. Birnbaum is concerned that legal costs are getting out of hand. There is no internal law department. How should Birnbaum approach Sally about Super Tech's management of legal services? What factors should Birnbaum consider? What recommendations should she make to Sally?

7. Anna, a customer in a Wendy's Restaurant claimed that she bit into a piece of a human finger in bowl of chili. Anna filed a claim for damages. The event attracted wide media attention. Anna gave several interviews in which she graphically described the trauma that she experienced. The volume of business at all Wendy's outlets in the region plummeted. After several weeks, Wendy's accused the customer of deliberately placing the finger fragment in the chili. When the finger was examined, it proved to be uncooked. Anna and her husband were eventually charged and convicted of several criminal offences. The finger came from a co-worker of Anna's husband, who lost it in a workplace accident. Apparently Anna and her husband have a history of filing false injury claims.[3] Apply the legal risk management model to this situation. What plan should organizations such as Wendy's have in place to deal with this risk?

8. Research in Motion (RIM) is a Canadian company whose major product and service is the BlackBerry wireless e-mail device. RIM has over 3 million customers in the United States. The success of the BlackBerry is largely dependent on five patents held by RIM. If these patents cannot be successfully defended by RIM, then competitors will be free to duplicate the BlackBerry and erode RIM's significant share of the market. Patents in information technology are complicated and often overlapping so that there can be disagreement over which patents relate to a particular product and who legally controls those patents. Another threat in this industry comes from companies that are formed solely for the purpose of holding patents and preventing other companies from violating them.[4] Apply the legal risk model to the environment and circumstances faced by RIM. How well does the model work when the survival of the business depends on a vulnerable form of intellectual property such as these patents?

For more study tools, visit
http://www.businesslaw3e.nelson.com

---

3. Based in part on The Associated Press, "Finger-in-chili Caper Nets Wife 9 Years, Hubby 12" *The Edmonton Journal* (19 January 2006) at A3.
4. Based in part on Barrie McKenna, Paul Waldie, and Simon Avery, "Patently Absurd: The Inside Story of RIM's Wireless War," *The Globe and Mail* (28 January 2006) at B4. See also Chapter 18.

Chapter

4

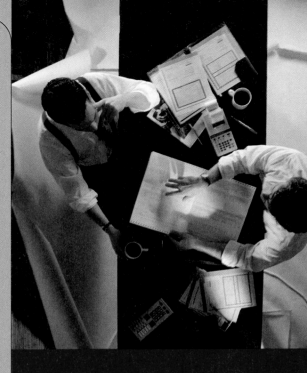

Objectives

After studying this chapter, you should have an understanding of

- how business activities may lead to legal disputes
- the options for resolving a legal dispute
- alternative dispute resolution
- the litigation process

Dispute Resolution

Business Law in Practice

Ideal Business Systems Ltd. (IBS) developed a risk management plan using the approach outlined in Chapter 3. The basic elements of the plan are presented in Figure 3.2. Over the course of a year, a number of events occurred that related to the risks anticipated by IBS management, including the following:

- THE "SLIP AND FALL."[1] A customer slipped on a patch of wet floor and suffered a bruised elbow and a strained back.

- THE BYLAW CHANGE. The municipal authorities changed the bylaw for waste disposal in order to increase recycling and limit the size of landfills. An environmental handling fee has been imposed on electronic devices at the time of purchase, and electronic waste is now banned from landfills. This change affects IBS's prices and its policy of accepting customers' unwanted computers for disposal when customers buy new equipment.

- THE DELINQUENT CUSTOMER. A customer failed to pay its account within the usual 30 days. When IBS investigated, it discovered that the customer was in serious financial difficulty.

- THE DISSATISFIED CUSTOMER. A customer failed to pay its large account to IBS, and when contacted about this matter, informed the company that the computer system that IBS recommended, supplied, and installed was not functioning properly and was inadequate to perform the needed tasks.

- THE DAMAGED GOODS. IBS received from a supplier a shipment of office furniture that was seriously dented and scratched. When IBS contacted the supplier about this problem, the response was that the damage must have occurred in transit and was therefore the responsibility of IBS.

- THE PROBLEM EMPLOYEE. Without authorization, a salesperson gave a customer a large discount in order to make a sale. The price was so low that IBS will incur a loss on the contract.

- THE MOTOR VEHICLE ACCIDENT. An IBS delivery truck was involved in a collision with a car. Both vehicles were considerably damaged, but there were no injuries.

1. How well does IBS's current risk management plan deal with these events?
2. What approaches should IBS use in dealing with these events?
3. What are the possible outcomes?

Introduction

As emphasized in Chapter 3, business organizations require a risk management plan to minimize the potentially adverse impact of the legal environment through prevention of loss to the extent possible, and planned reaction to adverse events. Legal problems cannot always be avoided, however, and sometimes arise even when sound management practices are in place. This chapter focuses on the reactive aspect of risk management.

It is not in the best interest of a business to avoid all legal conflict at all costs. For example, if IBS is not being paid on a large account, it must risk a legal dispute or face the unpalatable alternative of a substantial write-off. It could spell the end

---

1. A "slip and fall" is an expression lawyers use to refer to an incident in which someone slips on a wet floor, ice, or some other slippery surface and suffers an injury.

of IBS if management were simply to concede defeat any time a legal problem seemed to be developing. Businesses like IBS should seek, instead, to manage such disputes with the express goals of

- avoiding time-consuming and expensive litigation
- preserving desirable long-term commercial relationships

Business Activities and Legal Disputes

Business operations—both internal and external—involve numerous interactions that have potential legal consequences. Consider the following analysis of how well the plan anticipated and dealt with the events in the Business Law in Practice scenario.

The "Slip and Fall"

IBS must report the incident and possible injuries to its insurer as soon as possible. If IBS has arranged for the proper coverage and has kept its policy in good standing, the insurer will deal with any legal claim made by the injured party. IBS must provide the insurer with immediate, complete, and accurate information concerning the accident. If the insurance company decides that the injured party is seeking greater compensation than is justified, it may resist paying the injured party, and the matter may ultimately be decided before a judge. In such a case, IBS is obliged to cooperate with the legal counsel appointed by the insurer, such as by providing sworn testimony in court.

IBS will probably experience an increase in its insurance premiums, particularly if the accident occurred because the company neglected to keep the floors free of water or other hazards. IBS management should investigate the accident to determine whether it was caused by a failure to follow maintenance practices or was an isolated and unavoidable incident.

Provided that the insurance company pays the claim, there is an excellent chance that this "slip and fall" will be resolved with minimal involvement of the legal system. A legal dispute is unlikely to emerge. IBS's risk management plan has been successful because it calls for comprehensive insurance coverage. However, prevention procedures should be reviewed in order to reduce the risk in the future.

The Bylaw Change

IBS may not have properly implemented its risk management plan in this instance if IBS was unaware of the proposed amendments to the bylaw before those changes went before the municipal council; if prior to the passage of the bylaw, IBS failed to contact the municipality to point out problems with the proposal; or if IBS failed to propose a compromise, such as a period of transition during which existing practices could be changed.

Now that the bylaw has been changed, however, IBS must observe it and make whatever alterations are required to ensure that its waste disposal practices comply. Assuming that the municipality was given the power by the province to regulate waste management, and has done so in the proper exercise of that jurisdiction, there is little chance of successfully challenging the bylaw in court. IBS could consider approaching the municipal council and asking for an amendment, but it may simply be too late at this point to effect any change.

On this basis, there is little possibility that a legal dispute will arise from this matter, since IBS has no other viable option but to comply. As a result, IBS can decide to continue its policy of disposing of customers' used property and bear the additional cost, or change its policy and risk customer dissatisfaction. IBS must also decide whether to pass on the environmental handling fee to customers through increased prices.

The Delinquent Customer

The customer's refusal to pay its account may indicate that IBS has failed in its procedures for extending credit. Management should explore this possibility to prevent recurrences. In the meantime, IBS must decide if it should give the customer an opportunity to recover before demanding payment; offer to accept less than the full amount; write off the debt altogether; or take steps to be paid on its account, such as selling the debt to a collection agency at a discount, suing for the debt, or filing a claim if the customer is involved in bankruptcy proceedings.

Setting guidelines for granting credit to customers does not guarantee that every debt will be collectible. If this debt is not large and this customer is in serious financial difficulty, coming up with a negotiated repayment plan or writing it off may be more practical than spending money to try to collect it. The debtor is certain to welcome such a proposal, and therefore no legal dispute will arise from this event.

The Dissatisfied Customer

IBS's problem with this customer goes beyond the immediate challenge of collecting what it is owed. If the customer's business has been disrupted by a malfunctioning or inadequate system, the customer may sue IBS for compensation. The long-term relationship with this customer is also in jeopardy. IBS should consult the contract between them to determine the extent of its liability, if any, and avoid any hasty actions that might harm its ability to resolve this matter amicably. For example, it would be imprudent for IBS to acknowledge or deny responsibility without knowing more about the substance of the allegations.

IBS may also have a form of commercial liability insurance. This insurance provides coverage should IBS be sued by customers who allege that they have been provided with substandard goods or services. If such a policy is in place, IBS must immediately notify its insurer of the potential claim.

This matter is now a legal dispute, since the customer is refusing to pay an account that is too large to write off and, furthermore, is maligning the goods and services IBS provided.

The Damaged Goods

IBS has received a shipment of furniture that cannot be sold to its customers, except at a discount. IBS should review its contract with the supplier—which, it is hoped, is in writing and clearly worded—because this is what should determine who is responsible for damage to goods in transit. If the contract identifies the supplier as being responsible for the damage, a legal conflict may still arise if the supplier is unable or unwilling to pay compensation or does not agree that the damage was as extensive as alleged by IBS. If the contract does not specify which party is responsible, the supplier may take the position that IBS was responsible and should bear any loss.

This matter may develop into a legal dispute. In the meantime, IBS managers should review their practices for negotiating and recording contracts. Specifically, they must be sure that IBS contracts state who bears the risk of loss or damage to goods in transit—the buyer or the seller—in a manner that is acceptable to IBS.

The Problem Employee

Generally, IBS must honour the terms of the sale to the customer, even though the contract is not to its liking and not one that it authorized.[2] The problem with the employee is an internal matter for which the customer is not responsible.

A risk management plan would ensure that IBS's policy manuals, company rules, and the relevant job description already specify the employee's authority, as well as the consequences for exceeding that authority or otherwise being insubordinate. Performance appraisals and discipline records should document any previous infractions by this employee.

This matter will likely develop into a legal dispute if IBS decides to fire the employee with no termination pay or with an amount that the employee considers inadequate.[3]

The Motor Vehicle Accident

IBS must immediately report this accident to its insurer and cooperate fully in the investigation. Assuming that appropriate insurance coverage is in place, the insurance company will deal with the matter in a similar way to how it dealt with the slip and fall, and a legal dispute is unlikely to arise.

As the foregoing analysis suggests, IBS's risk management plan predicted and planned for several events that did in fact occur. As a result, a legal dispute is unlikely to arise from them. For example, the insurance company will likely sort out the slip and fall incident, as well as the motor vehicle accident. Other events will not develop into legal disputes because the company has no other viable option but to live with what has happened. That is, IBS will likely write off the delinquent customer's bad debt as an anticipated cost of doing business; IBS will not throw away its resources on a lost cause. Similarly, there is little point in launching a legal challenge to the waste disposal bylaw because the chances of success are remote. Yet other events may result in legal conflict, including the problems with the dissatisfied customer, the supplier of damaged furniture, and the discount-granting employee.

IBS's challenge with these latter issues is to actively and effectively manage them—just as it would any other aspect of the business's environment. Managing disputes does not mean simply proceeding to court. There are many ways to resolve a dispute that do not involve litigation. See Figure 4.1 on page 91 for a summary of the various methods of dispute resolution that are discussed in the following sections. These methods, from negotiation through litigation, are progressively more complicated and expensive. The most desirable and common method is negotiation.

Resolving Disputes through Negotiation

Clarification of the Situation

The first step for a manager faced with an apparent conflict is to investigate the situation to determine the nature and extent of the dispute. The manager should contact the individuals involved in his own organization and the appropriate people on the other side of the dispute to clarify the situation before formulating an approach to its resolution.

---

2.   For more discussion of this point, see Chapter 13.
3.   The law concerning wrongful dismissal is discussed in Chapter 21.

Managers must contend with numerous disputes in the operation of their business organization, and not all are of equal importance. Managers must set priorities, decide which disputes justify the use of the firm's resources, and determine when professional legal advice is required.

Even if a dispute escalates, the objective is still to resolve the matter as quickly as is reasonably possible. Prolonging legal conflict is expensive, in terms of both dollars spent and managerial hours unproductively consumed. A quick resolution will produce real cost savings for all concerned and a greater chance that relationships between the parties will not be irreparably harmed.

Negotiation is a tool that owners and managers can use effectively to assess, evaluate, and develop resolutions to legal disputes on a relatively informal and inexpensive basis. The goal is to reach a fair and acceptable outcome without having to activate more formal processes, particularly the burdensome, costly, and unpredictable machinery associated with formal litigation. The process of negotiation is not governed by technical rules; it can operate in whatever way the parties wish to solve their problem. With a negotiated resolution or settlement, all parties agree to a compromise that is preferable to allowing someone else, such as a judge, to impose a resolution on them.

In fact, although some disputes go to court through the litigation process, the overwhelming majority are resolved through negotiation between the parties involved or through other informal methods of dispute resolution that do not involve judges or even lawyers.

There are some situations where negotiation is not the proper way to proceed, even as a first step, such as when insurance covers the risk that is the subject of the dispute. In such circumstances, the business is required to allow the insurer to conduct settlement negotiations. Any attempt by the business to negotiate privately may jeopardize the coverage.

> **negotiation**
> A process of deliberation and discussion used to reach a mutually acceptable resolution to a dispute.

The Negotiation Process

Assuming that there are no insurance issues, negotiating an end to the dispute should become management's focus once a good understanding of the dispute has been achieved. Whether negotiations will succeed depends on a number of factors, including the following:

- the willingness of the parties to compromise and negotiate in good faith
- the nature and significance of the dispute
- the priority the parties give to its resolution
- the effectiveness of those involved in the negotiations

The parties choose their own negotiators. They could be employees, lawyers, or professionals who specialize in bringing parties together.

IBS has three legal disputes that it may well be able to resolve through negotiation.

The Dissatisfied Customer

In order to get negotiations off on the right foot, IBS must assure its dissatisfied customer that it is looking into its concerns; it must also quickly choose the appropriate IBS manager to investigate the matter internally. The investigation will involve a review of documentation, as well as consultation with the IBS employees who provided the advice and computer products. The customer should then be contacted for its full version of events.

IBS's problems with the dissatisfied customer may appear to be exclusively about money, owing to the unpaid account and the financial losses—present and future—that the customer may claim as a result of the allegedly substandard service and products IBS supplied. Also at risk, however, is the opportunity for future dealings with this customer, as well as the reputation of IBS in the marketplace.

Negotiation should occur at the senior management level in both organizations, and legal advice will be needed. Perhaps the customer's complaints are a means to get IBS to reduce its account, or perhaps there is some merit to the allegations. To try to end the dispute and also to test the customer's reaction, IBS could offer to compromise by making a reduction in its account or provide assistance to make the system work better. However, IBS must be prepared for its compromise to be rejected; if it is, IBS must then reconsider its options.

The Damaged Goods

IBS could use a similar approach to manage the situation involving the supply of damaged goods by first designating an IBS manager to determine the background to the problem. This would include checking documentation and consulting with the IBS employees who were involved in the transaction. IBS can then contact the supplier for clarification of its position.

While any conflict with the supplier of damaged office furniture is primarily financial, the trading relationship between the parties is an important factor in the dispute and its possible resolution. For example, if IBS is a major customer of the supplier, IBS can use this fact as leverage to achieve a favourable compromise with respect to this transaction or, perhaps, to secure concessions with respect to future orders.

IBS has a good chance of informally negotiating a settlement with the supplier. The stakes (financial and otherwise) appear to be relatively low and are unlikely to justify taking the matter further, particularly if the supplier shows some flexibility.

The Problem Employee

Resolving issues related to the problem employee should involve less investigation, particularly if IBS's general policies are documented and this salesperson's performance record and job responsibilities have been clearly established and documented.

Management may decide to simply discuss with the employee the problems she has caused by the money-losing contract and ask her to respect the limits on her authority in the future. The employee may have a reasonable explanation for her conduct and should be given an opportunity to provide her side of the story. In the end, IBS may decide not to discipline the employee but to simply remind her to clear discounts with her supervisor before agreeing to provide them to customers under any circumstances. She should be warned that further incidents of this kind might lead to her dismissal from the company.

When Negotiations Fail

In the majority of disputes, such as the ones explored here, parties reach settlement informally, often without the involvement of lawyers. Other times, an impasse is reached where neither party is prepared to compromise further. If the damaged goods problem can be settled through negotiation, the legal issues remaining from the Business Law in Practice scenario are reduced to two: the dissatisfied customer and the problem employee. More information (such as the following) is required to continue these illustrations.

IBS's negotiations with DC (the dissatisfied customer) have been disappointing. DC is unwilling to pay anything on IBS's account of $100 000 and is insisting that IBS compensate it for a loss of $250 000. IBS is not prepared to accept responsibility for any loss and considers this an unreasonable claim. IBS's employee has failed on three more occasions to follow company policies and other limitations on her authority to provide discounts. At the same time, she wants to remain employed by IBS. Management is disturbed by PE's (the problem employee) attitude but is reluctant to fire her because of the sales she has generated for IBS.

When impasses such as these are reached, the business is faced with a difficult choice: concede and cut its losses or risk the expenditure of more time and money. IBS can abandon its claim against DC or become more aggressive in its efforts to collect, knowing that the customer must decide what to do about its claim for business disruption losses. In dealing with PE, IBS can tolerate her behaviour and realize that it is likely to persist, or consider beginning the termination process.

Whether IBS should continue or abandon these legal conflicts depends on its analysis of what is in the best interests of the organization in the long term. The key questions are posed in the Business Application of the Law below.

If IBS decides to continue its dispute with DC, it faces the possibility of having to sue that customer or being sued by it. If IBS decides to pursue the matter with its employee—perhaps culminating in her termination—IBS could end up being sued for wrongful dismissal. In both situations, however, both parties have a strong incentive to avoid litigation because it is a cumbersome, expensive, and uncertain process. They should consider the alternatives to litigation, known collectively as **alternative dispute resolution (ADR).**

alternative dispute resolution (ADR)
A range of options for resolving disputes as an alternative to litigation.

Business Application of the Law

To Proceed or Not to Proceed with a Legal Dispute

Consider these questions when deciding whether to proceed with a legal conflict that could not be resolved through negotiation:

- What further steps are available and how long will they take?

- Can the business devote the resources necessary to proceed with the dispute, in terms of both the commitment and the time of business personnel?

- Will a lengthy dispute affect the public profile and reputation of the business?

- Is the relationship with the other side valuable?

- Will that relationship be harmed, whatever the outcome?

- What is the likely cost in terms of legal fees and company time?

- Are there worthwhile principles at stake that go beyond the particular dispute?

- If the dispute goes to court, what are the chances of winning?

- If the court decides in favour of the business, does the other side have the assets to pay the claim?

CRITICAL ANALYSIS: Which of these factors is most important?

Alternative Dispute Resolution

How ADR Works

ADR refers to a broad range of options for resolving disputes that are often considered alternatives to litigation, but it also includes ways to avoid disputes entirely as part of a risk management approach to resolving disputes as quickly and as efficiently as possible.

The most common forms of ADR are mediation and arbitration. Both involve a person who is independent of the parties and who has expertise in resolving disputes. The function of a **mediator** is to help the parties reach their own compromise. The mediator brings the parties together to clarify the situation and to assist them in appreciating the validity of the other's position. A mediator normally refrains from evaluating positions or in any way judging the parties or deciding the outcome.

An **arbitrator** fulfills a more formal role by hearing from the various sides their positions and desired outcomes. The role is also more formal than in mediation in that the arbitrator makes a definite ruling after considering the submissions of the parties. This ruling is in the form of a decision that is usually binding on the parties (depending on the arbitrator's terms of reference). **Binding** means that the decision is final—it generally cannot be appealed, and it is enforceable in the courts. Arbitration is usually chosen by the parties before a dispute arises, through a term in the contract providing that disagreements arising from the contract are to proceed to arbitration in accordance with the terms of the *Arbitration Act* in the relevant jurisdiction. However, the arbitration process can be adopted at any point in a dispute if the parties agree.

mediator
A person who helps the parties to a dispute reach a compromise.

arbitrator
A person who listens to both sides of a dispute and makes a ruling that is usually binding on the parties.

binding
Final and enforceable in the courts.

Business Application of the Law — ADR in Big Business

Major corporate battles involving Molson Breweries, Maple Leaf Gardens Ltd., Groupe Videotron Ltée, and McCain Foods Ltd. have been resolved outside the regular court system through private mediation or arbitration. Mediation is often completed in a single day, and arbitration in a matter of weeks, while complicated litigation can drag on for years.

ADR is most popular in disputes between companies that wish to continue a business relationship, such as a franchise agreement. It is less effective when one party decides to delay rather than settle quickly—for example, when there is a claim for one side to pay out a large sum, says Samuel Rickett, a lawyer at Fasken Campbell Godfrey in Toronto.

Noel Rea, in-house counsel at Imperial Oil and chair of the Canadian Bar Association's ADR section, says that the use of ADR in international oil and gas disputes is increasing rapidly. According to Earl Cherniak, a lawyer with Lerners and a prominent

ADR can be used in large corporate battles as well as small disputes.

arbitrator, "It would be a very rare significant commercial contract in my experience now, whether domestic or international, that would not have an arbitration clause in it." The ADR mechanisms are private and fast, and the parties involved pick their own facilitator.

As Mr. Rickett says, "You get to select an arbitrator or a panel who is acceptable to you, instead of taking your chances with a judge who may or may not be familiar with the business area under dispute."

A survey of Fortune 1000 corporations showed that 88 percent had used ADR internationally in the past three years. Users said that ADR saved costs (91 percent), provided better outcomes than litigation (61 percent), and preserved good business relationships (59 percent).

CRITICAL ANALYSIS: Is ADR always the best way to resolve disputes in big business?

Sources: Janet McFarland, "Companies Move Away from Courtroom Battles" *The Globe and Mail* (22 November 1996) at B13; Michael Lewis, "Borderline Settlements" *The National* (March–April 2002) at 39; and Beppi Crosariol, "Corporate Arbitration Sweeps the Nation" *The Globe and Mail* (21 September 2005) at B10.

There are no mandatory qualifications for ADR practitioners as there are for professionals such as lawyers, but there are many training programs available through universities[4] and the private sector. Mediators and arbitrators are often lawyers[5] or retired judges, but anyone is eligible to become a full- or part-time practitioner. Success depends on securing referrals from satisfied clients, which in turn depends on building a reputation for achieving results. The practitioner builds a reputation by demonstrating the qualities needed in an impartial, respected facilitator. Although mediators are primarily facilitators, and arbitrators are decision makers, both need to be good at listening, adapting, grasping situations quickly, and gaining the trust of the participants. There are provincial and national associations[6] that maintain directories of those available for service and make referrals for interested clients.

Although ADR usually happens with the parties meeting face to face, it can also be conducted through video conference or even online[7] if more convenient for the parties and appropriate for the type and size of dispute.

ADR has many positive features. The parties control the process, the timing, and the selection of the facilitator, who can be chosen based on expertise in the subject of the dispute. The process is usually faster and cheaper than litigation and can be kept confidential.

There are also some negative aspects. The process does not always produce a resolution, so time and money may be invested, only to have the matter proceed to litigation. There is a long-term concern that widespread use of ADR will result in diminished openness and accountability of the legal system. Because ADR is usually a private process, the outcomes do not provide the guidance to the business community that court decisions do.

When ADR Works

Every dispute is theoretically capable of being resolved through one or more forms of ADR, but the nature of the relationship between those involved and the particular circumstances of the disagreement will affect the suitability of ADR and its chance of success. ADR is likely to be successful when

■ The parties are interested in considering each other's position with the goal of achieving a compromise and settling the dispute.

---

4. For example, the Centre for Conflict Resolution Studies at the University of Prince Edward Island and the John V. Decore Centre for Alternative Dispute Resolution at the University of Alberta.
5. For example, the Nova Scotia Barristers' Society enables its members to be listed on its *Civil Mediation Roster* (see http://www.nsbs.ns.ca).
6. Such as the Arbitration and Mediation Institute of Canada.
7. See, for example, Cybersettle.com and the Quebec National and International Commercial Arbitration Centre at http://www.cacniq.org.

- The parties wish to maintain their commercial relationship.
- The parties need a quick resolution of minor problems as they arise in an ongoing transaction.
- The dispute is complicated, meaning that litigation is likely to be costly.
- The dispute involves sensitive or emotionally charged issues that the parties wish to keep private or confidential.

The suitability of disputes for ADR is not dependent on the type of law involved. ADR can work well whatever the nature of the legal rules that apply. ADR has worked effectively in these types of legal disputes:

- commercial or contract matters (disputes about payment for goods or the quality of goods)
- personal injuries (claims by a customer who slips and falls or who is injured by a defective product)
- employment matters (claims of improper dismissal or discrimination)
- environmental protection (application of waste storage regulations)
- trade matters (difficulty with import documentation)
- intellectual property (claims of patent infringement)
- professional/client matters (an accountant's difficulty collecting fees or a client's complaint about the quality of service)
- partnerships (disagreement by partners on contributions of work or compensation)
- real estate (dispute among adjoining landowners about a common boundary)
- franchising (a dispute arising from a franchise agreement)

IBS's two outstanding matters—involving DC and PE—are types of disputes in which ADR has been successfully employed. A key factor in the customer dispute is the need to preserve the relationship and come to a fair resolution. The employee problem may benefit from the involvement of an objective outsider who can help each party appreciate the other's view of the matter.

Both disputes are candidates for mediation. The employee problem, as an internal situation, is especially appropriate. A mediator might, for example, help IBS and the employee better understand the situation or agree that the relationship cannot survive. The mediator could also assist the parties in devising a termination package that would provide the employee with time-limited financial assistance while she seeks a new job; finally, it would enable IBS to avoid a lengthy wrongful dismissal action.

The situation with the customer involves a contract between the two parties that may specify a process for resolving disputes arising from the transaction. For example, if the contract calls for arbitration, it will pre-empt litigation and likely result in a binding decision. If the contract is silent, the parties could try mediation or agree at any time to resort to arbitration.

ADR Sources

There are several ways in which a form of ADR may become the means of resolving a dispute. Businesses should anticipate the possibility of a dispute arising in the course of a particular transaction or a longer-term relationship. They may include a dispute resolution process as part of their agreement for the purpose of diverting potential disputes away from litigation and into a process that they define and control. The agreement between IBS and its customer may contain such a clause.

If parties do not agree in advance on ADR, they can do so at any later time. They are always free to agree on a process of dispute resolution that serves their mutual needs. IBS should suggest ADR to the customer and the employee, and attempt to agree on an appropriate process. As litigation looms or progresses, the incentive to agree on an alternative process becomes greater. As the following International Perspective explains, ADR by agreement is especially prevalent in international transactions, where litigation is complicated by competing sets of rules and procedures.

International Perspective

ADR Is the Norm in International Transactions

Litigation of a business dispute in a domestic transaction can be a time-consuming, damaging, and expensive process. If the dispute arises in an international transaction, problems are compounded by questions of which country's law applies, which country's courts will hear the case, and whether the courts of one country will recognize and enforce a judgment obtained in another country. There is no international court for the resolution of commercial disputes, nor is there a comprehensive international system for the enforcement of awards obtained in domestic courts of other countries. Individual countries may have agreements with other countries that provide for the reciprocal enforcement of judgments. For example, there is a convention between Canada and the United Kingdom that each country will recognize and enforce judgments from the other in civil and commercial matters. Such a convention is the exception rather than the norm, however.

For these reasons, ADR mechanisms are extremely popular for settling international commercial disagreements. In international commercial contracts, arbitration has emerged as the favoured form of settlement, and arbitration clauses are the norm. The arbitration process has been greatly enhanced by the adoption in many countries of standardized rules and procedures and provisions for the reciprocal recognition and enforcement of the arbitral award. In Canada, the federal government and each province have implemented the 1958 New York Convention on the Recognition and Enforcement of Foreign Arbitral Awards. This convention established rules for the recognition of arbitration clauses in contracts and has been adopted by more than 70 countries. As well, all jurisdictions in Canada have enacted legislation based on the *UNCITRAL Model Law on International Commercial Arbitration*, an international convention that deals with international arbitration procedures and enforcement.

A further development was the adoption in 2002 of the *UNCITRAL Model Law on International Commercial Mediation*. A federal commercial mediation act has been adopted by the Uniform Law Commission of Canada and is under consideration by the federal and provincial governments. These developments should make mediation more prevalent and consistent in commercial disputes, although the uniform laws lack a mechanism for enforcing settlements reached through the mediation process.

CRITICAL ANALYSIS: Is arbitration of international disputes a positive development? Why is commercial arbitration being adopted more slowly in domestic business arrangements?

Sources: Mary Jo Nicholson, *Legal Aspects of International Business* (Scarborough: Prentice-Hall, 1997) at 226–233; and Daryl-Lynn Carlson, "Worldwide Mediation" *The National* (November 2004) at 30.

Some industries have recognized the need to provide customers with a means of submitting and resolving complaints about the quality of goods or services provided. For example, the Canadian Bankers Association has a code of conduct[8] governing relations between its members and small business customers. This code requires commercial banks to have their own systems for resolving disputes. The Canadian Motor Vehicle Arbitration Plan[9] is available to consumers and vehicle manufacturers to settle differences over alleged defects or warranties for purchased or leased vehicles.

The Investment Dealers Association of Canada has an arbitration system to deal with complaints by clients against their brokers, which can be accessed by phone and online.[10] Cases are decided by independent arbitrators, through a designated dispute resolution body in each province. Clients pay an administration fee for the service. This type of industry-related ADR is a competitive tool for increasing customer satisfaction.

Many regulatory bodies now have an ADR element for the purpose of attempting to resolve disputes without the cumbersome process of a tribunal proceeding. For example, human rights complaints go through a mediation stage, and the Competition Bureau has a process for attempting to resolve allegations of misleading advertising.

If none of the ADR possibilities results in resolution of the dispute, then litigation is the last resort.

The Litigation Process

If IBS succeeds in resolving its employee dispute through mediation, only the dispute with the dissatisfied customer remains. If IBS's contract does not require arbitration, and if the company and its dissatisfied customer have not been able to agree on a form of ADR, then litigation is the only option.

Litigation should not be undertaken without an understanding of its potentially adverse consequences. Court backlogs have made the system slower to access and can seriously harm commercial relationships by prolonging disputes for years. There is no guarantee of success, either in obtaining a favourable decision from the court or in collecting a judgment from the defendant. When and if success is achieved, it comes only after a significant investment of money, time, and commitment. In particular, complicated litigation can be a significant drain on corporate resources, an unproductive diversion from profitable business activities, and a source of stress for those involved in the process. Litigation is a slow, expensive, and risk-ridden process. It should be deployed only when all other feasible methods have failed and the claim cannot realistically be abandoned.

Commercial litigation arises when one business makes a deliberate decision to take legal action against another. The legal foundation and outcome of the claim are governed by the legal rules contained in relevant common law and statute law. IBS could sue (initiate legal action, known as a lawsuit or litigation) to recover money owed by DC. If the dispute with PE had not been resolved through mediation, the employee could have sued IBS to secure compensation for being wrongfully dismissed. The common law and statute law are the substantive rules applicable to the matter. How the claim is carried through the civil justice system is dictated by the procedural rules— that is, the rules that mandate such matters as what documents are to be filed with the court, what the process leading up to the trial will be, and how the trial will proceed.

---

8. See http://www.cba.ca
9. See http://www.camvap.ca
10. See http://www.ida.ca

A business faces the possibility of litigation involving its business customers, suppliers, investors, and employees. If the products of the business are used by individual consumers, the business is also exposed to potential lawsuits initiated by those consumers. This exposure becomes much more significant in the form of a class action as opposed to a number of separate claims from individual claimants.

A **class action** is a lawsuit launched by one person representing a larger group whose members have similar claims against the same defendant. Claimants are able to combine their resources economically in a single action rather than a large number of less economic individual actions, and the court system is relieved of the burden of a large number of potential small claims. Legislation has been passed in most provinces[11] to broaden the availability of class actions. Generally, the legislation enables a class action to be certified or approved by the court if the class can be clearly defined, there are common issues of fact or law, success for one class member means success for all, and the proposed representative adequately reflects the common interests of class members. In provinces without legislation, class actions may be allowed to proceed based on similar common law criteria.

Although class actions improve claimants' accessibility to the court system for relatively small claims, there are several difficulties—for example, how to decide who is in the class (particularly when members are in different provinces, each with his own legislation), how to communicate with members of a class containing thousands of members; how to accommodate claimants who do not wish to be part of the class; and how to deal with a large number of claims that have common issues but individual circumstances. There is also the need to balance the goals of increased access to the legal system and corporate accountability with the rights of defendants to defend themselves against potentially crippling claims.

Here are some examples of class action situations:

- Diet drugs cause life-threatening illness in a large group of consumers.

- A credit card company charges interest rates that are not permitted by the cardholder agreement.

- Purchasers of an online service dispute the enforceability of the seller's standard terms.

- Employees dispute the employer's use of surpluses in the company's pension fund.

- A hard drive containing personal data for thousands of consumers is lost through lax security.

- Investors claim they were misled by information provided when a company's shares were put on the market. See Chapter 14.

- Residents claim that health problems and property damage resulted from long-term pollution by a mining company.

CRITICAL ANALYSIS: Does the improved access to the legal system for claimants justify the large risk for sellers created by class actions? How can a business address class actions in its risk management?

What "class" might be harmed by these activities?

---

11. See, for example, *Class Proceedings Act, 1992*, S.O. 1992, c. 6.

class action
A lawsuit launched by one person who represents a larger group whose members have similar claims against the same defendant.

limitation period
The time period specified by legislation for commencing legal action.

A crucial set of rules affects litigation in each province by establishing specific time periods for commencing legal action. **Limitation periods** vary widely, depending on the nature of the lawsuit and the province in which the litigation will occur. For example, in many provinces[12] an action based on breach of contract (such as failure to pay money owing) must begin within six years of the time when the right to collect arises. Other limits are much shorter. Ontario has recently set a basic limitation period of two years for civil litigation. In some provinces,[13] the courts can permit actions to proceed after the limitation has expired if there is a reasonable explanation for the delay, but the general rule is that the right to sue is lost after the specific period of time ends. The rationale for these limits is that there is a need to bring closure to legal disputes by preventing claimants from indefinitely delaying the initiation of lawsuits. These rules are an important reason legal advice should be sought at an early stage in disputes with significant financial consequences. Lawyers in such cases must be aware of the relevant limitation period and ensure that litigation is commenced if settlement does not occur within that period.

Commercial litigation is known as private (or civil) litigation. The costs of bringing a matter through the judicial system are borne by the litigants, and any recovery of compensation comes from the losing party. The only involvement of government in the process is through the provision of the administrative structure, the court facilities, the judges, and other court officials. There is no government funding for the private litigants themselves, with the limited exception of legal aid programs, which assist in certain civil matters, such as divorce and custody lawsuits, but not in commercial disputes.

Every province and territory has its own system of courts and rules for civil litigation. This section describes those features generically, largely from the viewpoint of the key elements that are relevant to business.

plaintiff
The party that initiates a lawsuit against another party.

defendant
The party being sued.

A business may become involved in litigation by starting a lawsuit as a **plaintiff** or being sued as a **defendant.** In the IBS–DC dispute, the likely scenario is that IBS will be the plaintiff and begin the suit for the unpaid account.

In a lawsuit such as this one, in which one business is suing another for nonpayment, the amount of the claim determines the court in which the action would commence. Relatively small claims can be processed in the local equivalent of a small claims court. The name and monetary limit vary from province to province, ranging from $10 000 to $25 000. These claims can be litigated with minimal legal advice and assistance, in part because less is at stake. The process is designed to be simpler, quicker, and less expensive than mainstream litigation. Parties often appear in this court without a lawyer. Some provinces provide a "simplified procedure" for claims in an intermediate range (for example, $10 000 to $25 000 in Ontario). Claims in excess of these designated small and intermediate amounts must be pursued in the local equivalent of the superior court, which has unlimited monetary jurisdiction. Since IBS is claiming that there is an outstanding account of $100 000 with DC, the claim must be brought to superior court.

Stages of a Lawsuit

There are four formal stages in a lawsuit that goes through the full court process, although the majority of lawsuits are settled informally by the parties at some stage in the process. Settlement out of court after litigation begins is generally preferable to going to trial, for many reasons:

- It saves time, legal expenses, and effort by company personnel.
- It provides a better chance of preserving a commercial relationship.

---

12. See *Limitations Act 2002*, S.O. 2002, c. 24, Sched. B; *Limitation of Actions Act*, R.S.N.S. 1989, c. 258.
13. For example, Nova Scotia, *ibid.*, s. 3.

- It offers a certain result, rather than the unpredictable decision of a trial judge.
- It keeps the outcome private by avoiding the publicity of a public trial.

There is a public interest in promoting out–of-court settlements to the extent that lawyers are now ethically required to advise and encourage their clients to settle legal disputes where there is a reasonable possibility of doing so.

Litigation, other than small claims, is ordinarily conducted by a lawyer in consultation with the client. It is technically permissible but inadvisable for a business to attempt to meet the many formal requirements of the litigation system without the benefit of legal advice. This practicality raises the issue of accessibility to the system by those who cannot afford the services of a lawyer. The litigation process is governed by complicated and technical rules of court in each province.

Pleadings

pleadings
The formal documents concerning the basis for a lawsuit.

claim
The formal document that initiates litigation by setting out the plaintiff's allegations against the defendant.

The first stage is known as **pleadings** and involves the exchange of the formal documents outlining the basis of the suit. The plaintiff initiates the action by preparing a document that contains the allegations supporting the **claim.** For example, in IBS's claim for payment of goods and services, the initial document would describe the contract; state that IBS had provided the goods and services pursuant to the contract; and observe that in breach of contract, the customer had not yet paid the account. This document is a notice of the claim and is registered, or "filed," with the appropriate court office. It is then delivered to the party being sued (the defendant), through a process known as service. If the defendant has retained a lawyer, that lawyer may accept service of the documents on the defendant's behalf.

This first stage does not include evidence, but instead outlines the key points that the plaintiff needs to prove at trial in order to succeed. The defendant has a short period of time (for example, 20 days in Ontario) in which to respond to the allegations. Failure to respond within the allowed time is equivalent to admitting the claim. If the amount claimed is not in dispute and the reason for nonpayment is financial, the defendant will likely choose not to incur legal expenses to contest the claim. Instead, the defendant will concede responsibility and allow the plaintiff to "win" the case. The plaintiff, in turn, simply explains to the judge that the defendant has conceded the case. The court gives judgment to the plaintiff, who is then free to move to the collection stage.

defence
The defendant's formal response to the plaintiff's allegations.

counterclaim
A claim by the defendant against the plaintiff.

If there are matters in dispute, the defendant will likely seek legal advice and prepare a formal response to the claim, known as a **defence.** The lawyers may agree to allow the defendant longer than the minimum period in which to prepare the defence. This document might allege, for example, that the goods and services provided by IBS were inadequate or of no value at all. The defence is then filed with the court and delivered to the plaintiff. The defendant may also consider suing the plaintiff by preparing a document known as a **counterclaim.** In this counterclaim, DC can seek to recover compensation for its business disruption losses caused by IBS's deficient goods and services (in this case $250 000). It is also at this stage that the parties may consider expanding the suit to include other parties. For example, if DC alleges that the computers delivered under the contract were defective, IBS may decide to sue the manufacturer and supplier of the computers, on the theory that these are the people who caused all the problems in the first place.

Discovery

discovery
The process of disclosing evidence to support the claims in a lawsuit.

Once the basic claims and allegations have been made and clarified, the suit proceeds to the second stage, commonly known as **discovery.** Both parties must now reveal and demonstrate the facts that support their allegations. These facts are found in documents, in the oral testimony of those directly involved in the situation, and in expert reports. In this context, documents include electronic data and give rise to complicated issues of preservation and access. Electronic data is easier to access, organize, and distribute, but can be challenging to find and control. The time frame for this stage is undefined and depends largely on the degree of complexity of the case. The purpose of this stage is to test the strength of the opposing positions, so that the parties will be encouraged to reach a compromise, based on their greater appreciation of the strengths and weaknesses in both sides of the case. In the IBS case, the key information for discovery will be the contract and other documentation supporting the IBS claim for $100 000, the testimony of personnel on both sides who were involved in the original deal and in the subsequent events, and the details of the basis of the customer's claim for $250 000. Computer technology can help track the numerous documents in complicated cases.

At this stage, several initiatives in the various provinces come into play for the purpose of clearing the backlogs in the courts and streamlining the litigation process. Generally, these initiatives require the parties involved in litigation to engage in a formal attempt to resolve their dispute before it actually goes to court. These attempts may require the parties to engage in a process of mediation, whereby a facilitator, who may be a judge, helps them reach a compromise and avoid a trial. There are strict time frames for such dispute resolution initiatives, and only when this process is completed without successful resolution can the parties proceed to trial. Besides these mandatory dispute resolution methods, the parties are required to participate in a pretrial conference, the purpose of which is to narrow the issues in dispute and make the actual trial as short as possible in the event that it does occur.

How does shredding documents relate to the discovery process?

Trial

trial
A formal hearing before a judge that results in a binding decision.

burden of proof
The obligation of the plaintiff to prove its case.

evidence
Proof presented in court to support a claim.

If no settlement is reached at the discovery stage, the plaintiff can proceed to **trial**. The timing will depend on the availability of the courts and on how long it takes the parties to prepare for the formalities of the trial. Most trials proceed with a single judge and no jury. Jury trials are available for commercial matters, but a jury trial can be opposed if, for example, the case is deemed too complex for a jury to understand. At trial, the **burden of proof** falls on the plaintiff. The plaintiff must formally introduce **evidence** according to established rules to prove that its version of events is more likely true than not, known as "proving the case on the balance of probabilities." Expressed numerically, the plaintiff must prove that there is a better than 50 percent chance that the circumstances of the contract are as it contends they are and that, furthermore, these circumstances entitle it to receive what it claimed. The defendant has the opportunity to challenge the plaintiff's witnesses and documents, and to introduce its own account of events to oppose the claim. The judge must decide what happened between the parties and what the nature of their contract, if any, was. This is not generally a straightforward task, as the parties typically have widely differing versions of events. Once the facts have been established, the judge is then in a position to consider and apply the relevant case law.

The parties make submissions about the legal rules and precedents that support their desired conclusion. The judge then identifies and applies relevant legal rules to those factual findings to produce a decision. The decision may be given by the judge immediately at the end of the trial or reserved until a later time, to allow her some time for deliberation.

The *IBS v. DC* trial is likely to proceed before a judge without a jury, unless one side feels that a jury might be more sympathetic to its position than a judge. In a commercial matter such as this, that is unlikely to be the case. IBS will present its evidence to support its claim and oppose DC's counterclaim. DC will produce evidence in opposition to the IBS claim and in support of its counterclaim. In this case, the crucial issues are likely to be the quality of the goods and services provided, the interpretation of the terms of the contract, the effect of any statements IBS personnel may have made to DC concerning the application of those terms, and DC's actions following its identification of the problems with the system, including steps to limit its losses for any disruption of business that might have occurred.

Decision

decision
The judgment of the court that specifies which party is successful and why.

costs
Legal expenses that a judge orders the loser to pay the winner.

The judge's **decision** contains her resolution of the case—who must pay how much to whom—supported by the appropriate justification based on the evidence and legal rules. While IBS is seeking a monetary award, other remedies are available in exceptional circumstances, such as when the successful party requests an order from the court for the losing party to perform a specific act (e.g., transfer a piece of land) or cease some activity (e.g., trespassing on property).

Any monetary award includes the basic amount of the claim (e.g., the unpaid price of the goods) plus interest, and, in the usual case, the legal **costs** of the successful party. These costs usually fall far short of fully compensating the winning party for all its legal expenses. They are awarded by the judge based on a predetermined scale, combined with her view of the complexity of the case. In any event, these costs provide only a partial recovery with the result that even successful litigation involves expense. The downside for the losing party is significant: it is likely to be required to pay "costs" to the winner, as well as pay its own legal expenses.

In exceptional cases where the conduct of the losing party has been seriously objectionable, the court will award against it what are known as solicitor and client costs. This award reflects the actual legal expenses to a greater extent than the predetermined scale.

The many possible outcomes to the IBS case depend on the evidence presented, the persuasiveness of the lawyers, and the judge's view of the case. For purposes of illustration, here is one possible outcome:

IBS v. DC. The judge concluded that DC did order and receive the computer system and services in question and that DC was not misled by IBS personnel about the capacity and suitability of the system for its needs. However, there were some significant, but only partial, defects in the system's performance. The judge therefore awarded IBS $75 000 ($25 000 less than IBS claimed). This reduction was intended to take into account the fact that the system and services provided by IBS caused some disruption to DC's operations and made the system itself less valuable. DC's counterclaim for $250 000 was disallowed.

In addition, IBS was awarded interest on its claim (from the time when payment was due to the date of the decision) of $5000 and legal costs of $20 000, for a total of $100 000. DC must pay this amount, along with its own legal costs, and absorb the remainder of the cost of the adverse impact on its business. Recovery by IBS will be less than complete because the legal expenses of IBS are likely to be well above the recovered costs of $20 000.

Enforcement

judgment debtor
The party ordered by the court to pay a specified amount to the winner of a lawsuit.

The winner of the suit must enforce the judgment with the assistance of the court. The judge issues a judgment for a certain amount of money ($100 000 in the IBS case), which, in turn, can be enforced against the loser, now known as the **judgment debtor.** Court officials or other designated persons will assist in proceeding against the assets of the judgment debtor, which may include land, vehicles, houses, monthly income, and other assets. Laws in every jurisdiction limit the extent to which the winning party can take assets from the losing party, the point being to ensure that the person is not left destitute.

The winner recovers the judgment only to the extent that the loser's assets provide. There is no public fund from which these judgments are paid. Therefore, it is advisable for a prospective plaintiff to investigate the defendant's ability to pay before commencing the suit. IBS should not sue DC without reasonable certainty that DC is financially healthy. A judgment in any amount is of little value if DC has insufficient assets to pay, has a large number of other unpaid creditors, or is in bankruptcy proceedings.

Chances are that in a commercial dispute of this sort, DC will acknowledge the result and pay the debt, if at all possible. A judgment is valid for a long period (up to 20 years depending on the jurisdiction) and can be extended.

Appeals

appeal
The process of arguing to a higher court that a court decision is wrong.

A party who does not wish to accept the trial decision may consider an **appeal** to the next court in the hierarchy. An appeal must be initiated within a specific period of time (such as 30 days). There are several reasons an appeal should be undertaken only after careful consideration. In addition to the time and commitment required to pursue an appeal, the chances of success are limited. An appeal is not a rehearing of the case, but merely an opportunity to argue that the trial decision contains significant errors in how the law was applied. It is normally not possible to dispute the conclusions regarding what events actually transpired between the parties (i.e., what the trial judge found the "facts" to be), but only to dispute the judge's understanding and application of the law. Appeal courts tend to confirm trial decisions unless serious errors have been demonstrated.

Appeals at higher levels are normally conducted by a panel of at least three judges. No new evidence is presented. The lawyers representing the **appellant** (who makes the appeal) and the **respondent** (who defends the appeal) make written and oral submissions to the appeal judges, who then decide whether to confirm the original decision, vary it in some way, reverse the decision, or, in exceptional cases, order that another trial be conducted. In the IBS case, it is unlikely that either party will appeal, considering the amount in dispute and the legal costs already incurred. However, if DC still feels strongly about its counterclaim and legal advice indicates possible serious error by the trial judge, an appeal may be viable. Since the IBS action was brought in superior court, the potential appeals would be to the provincial court of appeal and ultimately to the Supreme Court of Canada.

IBS appears to be the winner in its case by recovering 75 percent of its claim, but it has incurred significant legal costs and experienced disruption of normal business activities. The relationship with the customer is destroyed, and the reputation of IBS has possibly been harmed. It is often difficult to decide whether litigation has been worthwhile, even when it has been successful.

Developments in litigation (in particular, contingency fees, punitive damages, and class actions) are addressed in the following comparison of the systems in Canada and the United States.

appellant
The party who begins or files an appeal.

respondent
The party against whom an appeal is filed.

contingency fee
A fee based on a percentage of the judgment awarded, and paid by the client to the lawyer only if the action is successful.

The judges in the Supreme Court of Canada.

The Supreme Court of
Canada building in Ottawa.

International Perspective

Litigation in the United States

Largely owing to the dominance of the U.S. media in Canada, the public's perception of litigation in Canada is often skewed toward the U.S. system. In fact, there are many differences in attitude, perception, and practice between the two systems:

- Americans tend to be more litigious than Canadians, perhaps because they are more conscious of their civil rights and property rights and are more willing and eager than Canadians to take legal action to protect those rights.

- There are more lawyers per capita in the U.S. system, and Americans tend to make more use of legal services.

- More civil cases are decided by juries in the United States, so that damage awards are less predictable and potentially higher.

- The U.S. system does not provide for partial recovery of costs by the successful party, so there is no risk of being required to pay any legal expenses of the other side.

- The use of **contingency fees**[14] is more widespread in the United States. Contingency fees are a means for a lawyer to bear the risk that litigation may fail. If it does, the client pays only the actual expenses, not fees. If the suit succeeds, the lawyer receives (by prior agreement) a significant portion of the judgment as compensation for services.

- American juries have more latitude to award punitive damages (to punish the loser) in addition to damages to compensate the victim.[15] Punitive damages are

---

14. Contingency fees can result in more litigation by improving accessibility to the legal system by claimants who might otherwise lack the resources to sue. This has serious implications for risk management of the businesses that may be the target of such litigation.
15. See Chapter 10.

rarely awarded in Canadian cases and usually only by judges, rather than juries.

- Class actions are more widely available in the United States. These suits enable individuals with similar claims to unite and pursue their claim as a group, with representation by the same lawyer. For example, consumers who have been harmed by the same defective product can unite to sue the manufacturer. However, in recent years (as described earlier in this chapter), class actions are becoming more accessible and more widely used in Canada as well.

- American consumers can more easily hold manufacturers liable for defective products based on the principle of strict liability.[16]

CRITICAL ANALYSIS: Class action suits and contingency fees are becoming increasingly common in Canada. Are these positive developments? What do the number of lawyers and the volume of litigation in a country tell us about the business climate in that country?

FIGURE 4.1

Forms of Dispute Resolution

	Negotiation	Mediation	Arbitration	Litigation
Who is involved	Parties only	Parties and facilitator	Parties and arbitrator (maybe lawyers)	Parties, lawyers, and a judge
When it is used	Anytime	By negotiation	By negotiation or contract	When one party sues the other
How it works	Parties decide	Mediator helps the parties	A formal hearing is held	The dispute goes through a four-stage process, ending in trial
Outcome	Settlement	Settlement	Binding decision (usually)	Court order
Advantages	Quick, cheap, controllable, private, preserves relationships	Quick, cheap, controllable, private, preserves relationships	Avoids litigation, final, preserves relationships	Final
Disadvantages	May fail	May fail	Imposed decision, unpredictable	Imposed decision, unpredictable, public, destroys relationships

---

Business Law in Practice Revisited

1. How well does IBS's current risk management plan deal with these events?

The IBS plan had mixed success. While it anticipated several possible events that could give rise to legal consequences, IBS failed to always implement the plan effectively. The surprise concerning the change to the waste disposal bylaw is evidence of that failure. In other respects, the plan worked well. IBS bought insurance coverage against some risks. As a result, the motor vehicle accident and slip and fall were expeditiously resolved through the insurer. Other issues, such as the matters involving the problem employee and the dissatisfied customer, were anticipated but proved difficult to manage. These disputes do not mean that IBS's risk management plan failed with respect to these more tenacious matters; some legal conflicts are inherently difficult to resolve.

---

16. See Chapter 11.

2. What approaches should IBS use in dealing with these events?

This chapter proposed that how IBS should deal with each event depends on the particular circumstances. The chapter also made several suggestions on how management might proceed. It is important to emphasize, however, that there is no clear path or set of procedures that the decision makers should follow in every event. The best courses of action depend on

- the objectives each party has in relation to the particular dispute
- the attitudes of the parties: Are they more interested in resolution or in making a point to the other side?
- the amount of money at stake
- the resources the parties are prepared to devote to the dispute
- risk analysis and cost-benefit analysis of prolonging the dispute
- the nature of the relationship between the parties

The key is to adopt and follow a rational approach to dispute resolution and to avoid litigation, with all of its pitfalls, if at all possible.

3. What are the possible outcomes?

This chapter presented a hypothetical outcome for each of the events outlined at the beginning. Actual outcomes depend on the circumstances, the other party, the way IBS chooses to proceed, and the influence of outside decision makers, such as the courts:

- Insurance covered the slip and fall and the motor vehicle accident.
- IBS complied with the bylaw changes and considered attempting to have them reconsidered.
- IBS wrote off the delinquent customer's account as a bad debt.
- IBS resolved the damaged-goods problem through negotiation with the supplier.
- Mediation resolved the dispute with the problem employee.
- IBS sued the disgruntled customer and was partly successful.

To improve its management of legal risk, IBS must review each resolution and decide whether its plan needs adjustment in order to prevent or deal more effectively with similar events in the future.

Chapter Summary

This chapter has explored a range of disputes in which a business such as IBS might become involved. A risk management plan that is well developed and carefully implemented can minimize the number of disputes that arise and provide guidance for dealing with those that do. Legal disputes should be approached with a view to achieving an acceptable resolution, rather than winning at all costs.

There are a wide variety of techniques for resolving disputes that avoid litigation altogether or enable the parties to minimize damage to the businesses and their commercial relationships. The parties can negotiate their own resolution, or if that is not possible, they can involve another person as a mediator to assist them or as an arbitrator to make a decision for them. If the parties resort to litigation, they are involving themselves in a lengthy, costly, public, and risky process with strict procedural rules. The process has four stages—pleadings, discovery, trial, and decision. The winner must collect the amount awarded by the court. That amount usually does not include full recovery of the legal expenses incurred to win the lawsuit.

Chapter Study

Key Terms and Concepts

alternative dispute resolution (ADR) (p. 77)

appeal (p. 88)

appellant (p. 89)

arbitrator (p. 78)

binding (p. 78)

burden of proof (p. 87)

claim (p. 85)

class action (p. 83)

contingency fee (p. 90)

costs (p. 87)

counterclaim (p. 85)

decision (p. 87)

defence (p. 85)

defendant (p. 84)

discovery (p. 85)

evidence (p. 87)

judgment debtor (p. 88)

limitation period (p. 84)

mediator (p. 78)

negotiation (p. 75)

plaintiff (p. 84)

pleadings (p. 85)

respondent (p. 89)

trial (p. 87)

Questions for Review

1. What are some potential business law disputes arising from the operation of a fast-food restaurant?

2. What is the goal of negotiation in resolving legal problems?

3. What happens when negotiations fail?

4. What is the process for attempting to resolve disputes informally?

5. What issues should a business consider before deciding to proceed with a legal dispute rather than abandon it?

6. What are three reasons for using ADR?

7. What are the differences between mediation and arbitration?

8. Why is ADR particularly attractive in international disputes?

9. Why should litigation be avoided, if possible?

10. What are the major steps in the litigation process?

11. What happens during the "discovery" stage of litigation?

12. Why is settlement out of court preferable to going to trial?

13. How does a class action differ from a normal lawsuit?

14. Who provides the funds to finance a lawsuit?

15. To what extent does the winner of a lawsuit recover the expenses of the litigation?

16. How does the winner of a lawsuit enforce the judgment?

17. What factors should be considered before appealing a court decision?

18. What is a contingency fee?

Questions for Critical Thinking

1. How could management use the various options for dispute resolution to deal with the disputes you identified in Question for Review 1, above? Which might be suitable for negotiation? ADR? litigation?

2. The Canadian system of litigation partially compensates the winning party for its legal expenses through an award of "costs," to be paid by the loser in addition to any damages awarded by the court. It has been argued that the ultimate losers in litigation are not the businesses involved, but rather their customers and shareholders. Are the costs of litigation ultimately borne by the consumers of goods and services through higher prices or shareholders through lower profits?

3. Class actions are growing in popularity as a way for a large number of small consumer claims to be brought against a corporation that might otherwise have been ignored. However, is a class action merely a process for compensating some consumers at the expense of others? Will corporations simply pass on class action damages through higher prices?

4. Most jurisdictions in Canada now have an element of mandatory ADR in their systems of litigation. Parties are required to consider or use a form of ADR before proceeding to trial. These requirements are meant to encourage settlement and ease the backlog of cases in the courts. Is it logical to make ADR mandatory rather than consensual? Are weaker litigants at the mercy of stronger parties?

5. Government involvement in litigation is mainly to provide a set of procedural rules, court facilities, and judges. Should government be expected to provide whatever resources are needed to deal efficiently with the volume of litigation, or should government instead be attempting to limit the extent of litigation?

6. The volume of electronic business (e-business) is rapidly increasing. In transactions between consumers and business, consumers are buying such items as books, food, and clothing on the Internet. Consumers are not always satisfied with every aspect of their purchases. Their complaints concern delivery of the wrong items, failure of items to meet statements and descriptions made on business websites, late delivery, refusal of returns, and problems with warranties. Consumers sometimes have difficulty contacting sellers and getting them to deal effectively with complaints. Consumers, government, and business are all concerned about the volume of complaints and are interested in devising a system to deal with them. Who should take responsibility for developing a dispute resolution mechanism for these complaints? What should be the goals of the mechanism? What procedures are needed?

Situations for Discussion

1. Manon Blanchard is in charge of purchasing for Best Produce Ltd. (BP), a wholesale dealer in fruit and vegetables. She is informed by the Receiving Department that BP has just received a large shipment of tropical fruit from a supplier, Tropical Delights Ltd. (TD), that has been reliable in the past. Not only is the shipment significantly short, but the quality is poor and about 20 percent cannot be used. Identify the informal steps Manon could take to address this problem.

2. Tropical Delights has a new sales manager, Brad Carpenter, who is unwilling to concede anything. TD insists on full payment of $50 000 for the shipment in situation 1 above. Manon thinks a reduction in price of $15 000 would be fair for BP. What critical factors should Manon consider in deciding whether to pursue this dispute further?

3. Manon consults the legal department of BP and is advised to consider mediation as a means of resolving this dispute. Manon is not optimistic about the prospect of successful mediation in view of her recent dealings with Brad, but she knows that BP needs TD as a supplier of exotic fruit and suspects that TD values her company as a customer. Suggest how Manon might use mediation in this situation.

4. Mediation failed and TD was unwilling to consider arbitration. Manon was unable to find another reliable supplier of exotic fruit. Meanwhile, TD sued BP for $50 000. Manon's CEO is puzzled and upset about TD's attitude. He is about to refuse to buy anything ever again from TD and to advise outside counsel to "take them to the Supreme Court, if necessary." What arguments could Manon use to persuade him that this may not be the best approach? Can Manon use her experience with TD to improve her relationship with suppliers in future?

5. Sarah Rickard, the CEO of Tropical Delights, was not consulted about the decision to sue Best Produce. When she became aware of the litigation, Sarah was upset about the prospect of losing BP as a customer. When she investigated further, she discovered that several TD customers were unhappy with the service provided by TD in recent months and were seeking other suppliers. What should Sarah do about the BP lawsuit and her other dissatisfied customers?

6. The Loewen Group, based in Burnaby, B.C., and founded by Ray Loewen in the 1960s, was one of the largest owners of funeral homes in North America. Throughout the 1980s and 1990s, the company pursued a strategy of growth through the aggressive acquisition of U.S. funeral homes. In 1990, Loewen purchased Wright & Ferguson, the largest funeral operation in Jackson, Mississippi. Shortly after the purchase, a dispute arose concerning an earlier contract between Wright & Ferguson and Gulf Insurance regarding the sale of insurance policies for funeral services. Gulf alleged that Loewen had breached this earlier contract and sued Loewen. An initial settlement was reached for $10 million, but never completed. Gulf then amended its original claim to include charges of fraud, breach of good faith, and malicious monopoly. Gulf asked for damages of $107 million. In 1995, a Jackson jury awarded the plaintiff $100 million in compensation and $400 million in punitive damages. The award equalled almost half the value of Loewen's assets and almost 13 times its 1994 profit of $38.5 million. Jury foreman Glenn Miller told *The New York Times*: "[Ray Loewen] was a rich, dumb Canadian politician who thought he could come down and pull the wool over the eyes of a good ole Mississippi boy. It didn't work." The jury award was subsequently upheld by a Mississippi judge.

Loewen vowed to appeal. However, under Mississippi law, Loewen was required to post a bond of 125 percent of the award—$625 million—while appeals were pending. Rather than face several years of uncertainty, the company agreed to a settlement worth about $175 million.[17] Despite the settlement, the litigation seriously undermined Loewen's equity value and credit rating. The company eventually went bankrupt. Shareholders who lost their equity filed claims under NAFTA, but were unsuccessful. What does this case illustrate about the risks of doing business internationally and the uncertainties of litigation? How could Loewen have tried to avoid these uncertainties?

7. The Eirik Raude is one of the largest semi-submersible oil rigs in the world. It is owned by Ocean Rig ASA (OR), a company based in Norway. OR engaged Irving Shipbuilding Inc. (ISI) to do extensive mechanical work on the rig in Halifax. The work was initially expected to cost $60 million, but eventually cost $190 million. ISI used legal remedies to collect the final $30 million from OR. Their contract contained a clause requiring arbitration to settle any disputes. Without warning to ISI, OR gave notice that it would use arbitration to recover some of the large cost overrun on the job. These overruns related to ISI's alleged mismanagement of the project.[18] What are ISI's options? Must ISI participate in the arbitration process?

8. Research in Motion (RIM) is a Canadian company that has achieved huge success based on its main product, the BlackBerry wireless e-mail device. This success is largely based on five patents that RIM has registered in Canada and the U.S. NTP Ltd. is an American company whose only assets are U.S. patents. NTP claimed that RIM violated its patent rights through sale of the BlackBerry. NTP claimed significant damages and a court order prohibiting RIM from selling BlackBerrys. The dispute went to trial and a jury found that RIM had violated NTP's patents. RIM later challenged NTP's patent registrations. The two companies reached a tentative settlement of $450 million, but it failed due to certain conditions that were attached. It was left to the court to make a final decision on the remedies against RIM based on the jury's verdict. RIM's profit forecast and share price suffered and its planned expansion into China was jeopardized. Shortly before the judge was to make his decision, the companies reached a final settlement of $612 million.[19] Evaluate the strategy employed by RIM in this high-stakes litigation.

For more study tools, visit
http://www.businesslaw3e.nelson.com

---

17. Based on *O'Keefe v. Loewen Group* (1995), *The National Law Journal* http://www.law.com/jsp/nlj/index.jsp (11 December 1995) (accessed 29 October 2006).
18. Based in part on Tom Peters, "Ocean Rig Files Legal Action Against Irving Shipbuilding" *The Chronicle Herald* (8 July 2006) at D3.
19. Based in part on Simon Avery and Barrie McKenna, "Marathon Talks This Week Led to Agreement" *The Globe and Mail* (4 March 2006) at B3. See also Chapter 18.

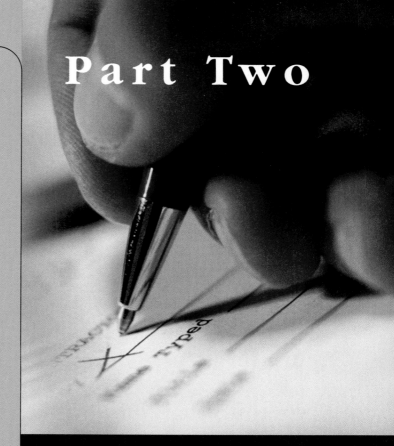

Part Two

BUSINESS RELIES ON CONTRACT LAW—MORE THAN any other area of law—to facilitate commerce. Contract law provides a structure through which individuals and organizations are able to create legally binding, commercial commitments. Essentially, parties must keep their contractual promises or pay damages to the other side for breach.

A working knowledge of contract law is essential to anyone involved in business. This knowledge is crucial because the law advances commercial activities and can be used to build productive and cooperative business relationships. In fact, contract law forms the basis of many commercial relationships, including employment, credit, property, and insurance dealings, as well as the sale of goods and services.

Contracts

Chapter 5   An Introduction to Contracts

Chapter 6   Forming Contractual
Relationships

Chapter 7   The Terms of a Contract

Chapter 8   Nonenforcement of Contracts

Chapter 9   Termination and Enforcement
of Contracts

Chapter

5

Objectives

After studying this chapter, you should have an understanding of

- the general concept of a contract
- the legal factors in the contractual relationship
- the business factors influencing the formation and performance of contracts

An Introduction to Contracts

Business Law in Practice

Amritha Singh is a middle manager with Coasters Plus Ltd. (Coasters), a company that designs and manufactures roller coasters for amusement parks across North

America. She has been appointed one of the project managers for the design and delivery of a special roller coaster for the Ultimate Park Ltd., an American customer. A major component of the project is the steel tracking, and one possible source is Trackers Canada Ltd. (Trackers). Amritha's supervisor has asked her to negotiate the necessary contract. This task causes Amritha some concern, since she has never been solely responsible for contractual negotiations before. She does know, however, that Coasters needs a reliable supplier that can deliver high-quality tracking for under $2 million, and in good time for installation at the Ultimate Park site.

1. How should Amritha approach her task of securing the necessary tracking?
2. How can the law facilitate Amritha's acquisition task?
3. What rules apply to a commercial relationship between a manufacturer (such as Coasters) and a supplier (such as Trackers), and how are disputes resolved?
4. What are the legal consequences to Coasters of assigning the negotiation task to Amritha?
5. What are the nonlegal factors contributing to the proposed legal agreement?

Introduction to Contract Law

Amritha needs to extract a firm commitment from Trackers to ensure that Coasters receives the necessary tracking in a timely fashion at the agreed-upon price (see Figure 5.1). The flip side of her task is to ensure that—should Trackers renege—Coasters can sue Trackers to recover for any related financial loss. Simply put, Amritha needs to negotiate and secure a contract with Trackers on behalf of her company.

contract

An agreement between two parties that is enforceable in a court of law.

A **contract** is a deliberate and complete agreement between two or more competent persons, not necessarily in writing, supported by mutual consideration, to do some act voluntarily. By definition, a contract is enforceable in a court of law.

What follows is a brief synopsis of these elements, which are analyzed more comprehensively in subsequent chapters.

■ AN AGREEMENT. An agreement is composed of an offer to enter into a contract and an acceptance of that offer. This is a matter explored in Chapter 6. The promises contained in the agreement are known as terms. These are discussed in Chapter 7. The informing idea behind a contract is that there has been a "meeting of the minds"—that the parties have agreed on what their essential obligations are to each other.

- COMPLETE. The agreement must be complete, that is, certain. Certainty is explored in Chapter 6.
- DELIBERATE. The agreement must be deliberate, that is, both parties must want to enter into a contractual relationship. This matter—formally known as an intention to create legal relations—is discussed in Chapter 6.
- VOLUNTARY. The agreement must be freely chosen and not involve coercion or other forms of serious unfairness. This is explored in Chapter 8.
- BETWEEN TWO OR MORE COMPETENT PERSONS. Those who enter into a contract are known as parties to the contract. There must be at least two parties to any contract, who must have legal capacity—a matter discussed in Chapter 8. As a general rule, only parties to a contract can sue and be sued on it. This matter is discussed in Chapter 9.
- SUPPORTED BY MUTUAL CONSIDERATION. A contract involves a bargain or exchange between the parties. This means that each party must give something of value in exchange for receiving something of value from the other party. Expressed in legal terminology, a contract must be supported by mutual consideration. This is discussed in Chapter 6.
- NOT NECESSARILY IN WRITING. As a general rule, even oral contracts are enforceable, though it is preferable for negotiators to get the contract in writing. That said, in most Canadian jurisdictions there are certain kinds of contracts—such as those involving an interest in land—that must be in writing in order to be enforceable. These exceptions are discussed in Chapter 8.

The genius of contract law is that once a contract is created, it permits both parties to rely on the terms they have negotiated and plan their business affairs accordingly. If a dispute arises between the two parties, there are various options for dispute resolution, outlined in Chapter 4. This includes taking the matter to court and suing for losses sustained. In short, contract law ensures that each party gets what it bargained for—namely, performance of the promises made to it or monetary compensation in its place. Chapter 9 discusses the termination and enforcement of contracts.

For the most part, the rules governing contracts are based on common law. The common law, as discussed in Chapter 2, refers to judge-made laws, as opposed to laws made by elected governments. This means that a judge resolving a contractual conflict is usually relying not on statute law to guide deliberations, but rather on what other judges have said in past cases that resemble the current case. As noted in Part One, these past cases are known as precedents because they contain a legal principle found in a past situation similar to the one being litigated. The judge will hear evidence from the two parties in support of their respective positions and then determine which common law rules of contract are applicable to the situation and what the outcome should be. Depending on the nature of the contract, legislation such as the *Sale of Goods Act* may also be relevant.

FIGURE 5.1	
A Contract Contains Binding Promises	Through a contract: **Trackers** *makes binding promises concerning price, quantity, and delivery of tracking to* → **Coasters** **Coasters** *makes a binding promise to pay the purchase price to* → **Trackers**

Contracts are the legal cornerstone of any commercial operation. Through a contract, the business enterprise can sell a product or service, hire employees, rent office space, borrow money, purchase supplies, and enter into any other kind of binding agreement it chooses. In this way, contract law is facilitative: it allows participants to create their own rights and duties within a framework of rules that a judge will later enforce, if called upon to do so.

CASE ▼

Ky Zur Investments Ltd. v. David Friesen Holdings Ltd. (1994), 160 A.R. 378 (Q.B., Master in Chambers)

THE BUSINESS CONTEXT: When buying and selling, businesses enter into contracts to establish obligations on both sides. Even in detailed contracts, however, the parties may not always agree on what a contractual term includes in light of subsequent events.

FACTUAL BACKGROUND: Ky Zur Investments, the plaintiff, purchased an entire condominium project from the defendant, David Friesen Holdings Ltd. The contract included a promise by David Friesen Holdings Ltd. that the lands were free of defects. In fact, in at least one of the buildings, the "out lines" for the sanitary sewer system and storm sewer system were improperly connected. As a result, the city issued an order requiring the plaintiff to correct the problem.

Ky Zur Investments sued the vendor for damages for breach of contract, stating that the improper connections amounted to a breach of the promise that the lands were free of defects.

THE LEGAL QUESTION: Was there a breach of contract?

RESOLUTION: Defendant's counsel advanced several interpretations of the contract that would suggest his client had no responsibility for the improperly connected out lines. For example, counsel argued that only problems *on* the land itself would be covered by the contractual promise that the lands were "free of defects." Since the sewer and storm connections had to take place *off* the land, the soundness or defects in those connections were not part of the contract. Master Funduk agreed that the two "out lines" from the building (one for storm and one for sewer) must run out into the street to connect to the city's lines. However, he ruled, the out lines from a residential building are still part of the building. Master Funduk therefore granted judgment, on a summary basis,[1] to the plaintiffs, determining the defendants were in clear breach of contract.

CRITICAL ANALYSIS: Why would David Friesen Holdings Ltd. resist the lawsuit instead of admitting liability?

Contracts come in a wide variety. A contract for the purchase and sale of a box of pens from the corner store, for example, is casually conducted and instantly completed. The only document that will be produced is the sales receipt. Other contracts, such as for the purchase and sale of high-quality steel tracking, will require lengthy negotiations, considerable documentation, and time to perform. Some contracts are one-shot deals, in that the parties are unlikely to do business with each other again. Other contracts are part of a long-standing and valued commercial relationship, as one might find between supplier and retailer. Regardless of the context, however, every contract is subject to the same set of mandatory legal rules. This means that contract law principles will be applied by a judge to resolve a contractual dispute between the parties, whether the parties were aware of those principles or not.

---

1. As in this case, if one party believes that it is clearly in the right in the sense that there is no genuine issue for trial, it may consider seeking summary judgment. This entitles that party to win its case without having to go through a full-blown trial. Needless to say, this approach can save tremendous expense, though courts generally err on the side of sending matters to trial rather than granting summary judgment.

Amritha's attention is currently focused on one transaction: her company's acquisition of tracking from a suitable supplier. Her goal should be to enter into a contract with a supplier like Trackers, because Coasters requires legally enforceable assurances that its supplier will fulfill its commitments. The alternative to a contract—in the form of a casual understanding—makes little business sense, even if Trackers is highly reputable and trustworthy, because cooperation and goodwill between parties can suddenly evaporate when an unforeseen conflict or problem arises. Personnel can change; memories may become selective and self-serving; and genuine differences of opinion may arise. At this point, Amritha's company needs the protection of a well-constructed contract—including the right to commence a lawsuit based upon it—not the vague assurances she may have received from Trackers personnel sometime in the past.

This is not to say that informal business arrangements never succeed, but only that there is no remedy in contract law should one of the parties fail to keep its word. This is a risk that a business should ordinarily not be prepared to run.

This chapter has thus far introduced the *legal* elements to a contract, but *business* factors also figure prominently in contractual relationships. The next section locates important legal factors in their business context. Without this context, the legal ingredients of a contract cannot be properly understood.

Legal Factors in Their Business Context: Creating the Contract

Communication

Most contractual relationships begin with communication, which may originate in a number of ways—through informal contact between individuals in different businesses who recognize mutual needs, or perhaps through a general inquiry made to a supplier concerning price and availability of materials. Amritha may initiate contact with potential suppliers based on recommendations from others in her company who have purchasing experience, from colleagues in the industry, or from industry organizations. And, of course, Coasters may be approached periodically by tracking suppliers. Regardless of who makes the first move, Amritha will likely communicate with a number of businesses in order to determine who can give her company the most favourable terms.

Communication is not just about discussing possibilities with the other side, however. Communication—in the form of contractual negotiations—is automatically laden with legal meaning. It is therefore important for the businessperson to know when simple business communications crystallize into legal obligations.

Ethical Considerations

Is It Ethical to Bluff during Business Negotiations?

Albert Carr, in a well-known article published in the *Harvard Business Review*, argues that business is a game and therefore is not subject to the same ethical standards that govern one's private life. On this footing, it is perfectly acceptable for a businessperson to bluff during negotiations since it is merely strategic—just as it is in poker—and does not reflect on the morality of the bluffer. Carr goes on to argue as follows:

> Most executives from time to time are almost compelled, in the interests of their companies or themselves, to practice some form of deception when negotiating with customers, dealers, labor unions, government officials, or even other departments of their companies. By conscious misstatements, concealment of pertinent facts, or exaggeration—in short, by bluffing—they seek to persuade others to agree with them. I think it is fair to say that if the individual executive refuses to bluff from time to time—if he feels obligated to tell the truth, the whole truth, and nothing but the truth—he is ignoring opportunities permitted under the rules and is at heavy disadvantages in his business dealings.

Carr goes on to argue that, like every poker player, a businessperson can be faced with a choice between certain loss or "bluffing within the legal rules of the game." The individual who wants to win and have a successful career "will bluff—and bluff hard."

Carr is not suggesting that businesspeople break the law to seek an advantage in business negotiations. He is, however, claiming that morality of the businessperson who conceals, exaggerates, or misstates is simply not in question. Short of fraud or actionable misrepresentation, bending the truth a little is simply playing the game of business.

What are the dangers of Carr's approach to business ethics? What are the possible benefits?

Source: Albert Z. Carr, "Is Business Bluffing Ethical?" in Robert A. Larmer, *Ethics in the Workplace: Selected Readings in Business Ethics* (Minneapolis/St. Paul: West Publishing Company, 1996) at 4.

First and foremost, contract law concerns itself with what the negotiators say and do, not with what they think or imagine. For example, if Amritha makes what looks like an offer to purchase tracking, the other side is entitled to accept that offer whether it was intended as one or not. This is because contract law is governed by the **objective standard test.** This test asks whether the reasonable person, observing the communication that has occurred between the negotiators, would conclude that an offer and acceptance had occurred. Assuming that all the other ingredients of a contract are in place, the parties are completely bound.

objective standard test
The test based on how a "reasonable person" would view the matter.

Bargaining Power

The kind of contract a businessperson ends up creating is very much influenced by her bargaining power. The business reality is that negotiating parties rarely have equal bargaining power. It is almost invariably the case that one side will have more experience, knowledge, market leverage or other advantages. The greater one's bargaining power, of course, the more favourable terms one will be able to secure.

The law, however, does not recognize or attach legal significance to this business reality. On the contrary, contract law is constructed on the basic assumption that those who negotiate and enter into contracts have **equal bargaining power,** meaning that they are capable of looking out for themselves and will work to maximize their own self-interest. As a result, courts are normally not entitled to assess the fairness or reasonableness of the contractual terms the business parties have chosen. Courts will generally assume that the parties had their eyes open, considered all the relevant factors, evaluated the risks, and were prepared to accept both the costs and benefits of the contract.

equal bargaining power

The legal assumption that parties to a contract are able to look out for their own interests.

Business Application of the Law

Inequality of Bargaining and the Standard Form Contract

An important, practical, and modern form of inequality of bargaining is found in the proliferation of the standard form contract. Sales and rental businesses frequently require their customers (consumer and commercial) to consent to a standard set of terms that have been developed by the business over years of operation. Such terms often heavily favour the business that created them and normally are not open to negotiation. For this reason, such contracts are known colloquially as "take it or leave it" contracts. Examples include renting a car and borrowing money from the bank.

Even in circumstances such as these, where bargaining is not contemplated, the law expects people to take care of themselves. While there is provincial consumer protection legislation that may be of assistance in certain consumer transactions, the better course—particularly in a contract of some importance—is to read and understand the standard form contract before signing it.

Why do you think the standard form contract is so common in the car rental business?

The law applies the principle of equality of bargaining power even though, in almost every situation, one party will have some distinct advantage over the other. The rationale is that parties should be able to rely on contractual commitments. Though one party may have agreed to a price she now considers too high or, in fact, may have made a bad deal, none of this is justification for securing the court's assistance and intervention. People are simply expected to take care of themselves.

Occasionally, however, circumstances favour one party over the other to such an extent that the court will come to the assistance of the weaker party and set the contract aside. Such judicial assistance is very much the exception, not the rule.

The fact that Amritha may have less bargaining power than the tracking supplier she contracts with does not generally affect the enforceability of their concluded contract. On the contrary, Amritha must be careful to protect her company's position and not enter into a bad bargain. Coasters is unlikely to succeed in having any contract set aside because Amritha was an inexperienced negotiator or because the supplier was a relatively bigger, more powerful company.

Legal Factors in Their Business Context: Performing or Enforcing the Contract

Business Relationships

Businesspeople regularly breach contracts. For example, a purchaser may fail to pay invoices on a timely basis. A supplier may deliver the wrong product, or the wrong amount of product, or a defective product. All these amount to breaches of contract. Whether the other side sues for breach of contract, however, is as much a business decision as it is a legal one.

Contract law is narrow in scope: its emphasis is often on a specific transaction, such as a single sale, and is not traditionally concerned with longer-term business relationships. Because contract law does not focus on the longer-term relationship, one may be misled into thinking that when faced with a legal wrong, the best response is a lawsuit. When the business context is considered, however, this approach reveals itself to be counterproductive in many circumstances. For example, if Coasters's supplier is late in delivering its tracking, the supplier is in breach of contract, and Coasters will be entitled to compensation for any resulting loss, such as that caused by late completion of the project for the Ultimate Park. However, if Coasters insists on that compensation, the relationship with that supplier may be irreparably harmed. Absorbing the loss in this instance—or splitting the difference—may be a small price to pay in the long term, particularly if the supplier is otherwise reliable and Coasters is not interested in investing time and money in finding a replacement. Put another way, insisting on one's strict legal rights may not be the best business option.

The expense and uncertainty of litigation are also reasons to avoid a full-blown legal conflict.

Business Application of the Law

Seeing the Big Picture

Even with a comprehensive contract in place defining the obligations and relationship between a customer and service provider, issues can arise because contracts can never be entirely black and white. There is an inevitable grey area. In dealing with a customer who seeks to expand or restrict a contract on a large project, for example, owners and managers can approach the question with a number of objectives in mind, including

- maintaining the project's profitability.

- treating the customer with respect while seeking a standard of reasonableness in return.

- ensuring that the work is completed on a safe and timely basis without incident.

- not approaching matters legalistically. Down the legal road, one faces intractable positions and an ultimate settlement based not on the "correct answer" but on how each side perceives its risk of losing the lawsuit. It is much more preferable to find practical ways of interpreting contracts to arrive at resolutions to issues.

- understanding that business relationships are long term and so is reputation.

CRITICAL ANALYSIS: Why is a contract an imperfect tool for defining the rights and obligations of a service provider and customer?

Source: Terry Freeman, C.A. Chief Financial Officer of Flint Energy Services Ltd. For information on Flint Energy Services, go to http://www.flintenergy.co.

Economic Reality

Though contract law exists to create legally binding commitments, it is not always the best economic decision for a party to keep that commitment. The law has some built-in flexibility, since it requires contractual obligations to be performed or compensation to be paid for nonperformance. Accordingly, there may be situations where the cost of compensation is a perfectly acceptable price to pay for release from obligations. For example, a business whose production is committed to a one-year contract may be quite willing to pay what is necessary to be relieved of the one-year obligation if a more profitable, long-term deal becomes available for the same production. This idea is explained further in the Business Application of the Law box below.

Reputation Management

A business that makes a practice of breaching contracts due to bad planning or to pursue an apparently more lucrative business opportunity will certainly be within its legal rights to breach and pay damages in lieu of performance. Such a business is also likely to acquire a reputation in the industry as an unreliable and undependable company. The long-term viability of a business organization is undoubtedly compromised if customers, suppliers, and employees grow reluctant to deal with it.

Similarly, a business that insists on strict observance of its legal rights may damage its reputation in the marketplace. Although a manufacturer may have a valid defence for having produced a defective product that injures a customer, for example, it may be better, in the end, to compensate the customer voluntarily rather than fight out a lawsuit. A lawsuit in the circumstances of this example may result in a serious blow to reputation and a public relations disaster.

Business Application of the Law

Economic Breach

Suppose Trackers signs a contract to deliver 900 metres of tracking to Coasters for $2 million, in 2 equal installments. After Trackers has delivered half the order, Thriller Rides Ltd. (a competitor of Coasters) contacts Trackers and explains that, owing to an emergency, it desperately needs 450 metres of track to complete a major project. Thriller offers Trackers $2 million to supply the necessary tracking—double the price Trackers would receive from Coasters for the same amount of tracking. Trackers has several options in response to Thriller's request:

- *Option 1*: Complete delivery to Coasters as agreed and decline Thriller's request.

- *Option 2*: Try to persuade Coasters to accept late delivery of the remainder of its order and offer a price break as an incentive.
- *Option 3*: Abandon the balance of Coasters's contract and fill Thriller's order.

Each option has its own economic and legal consequences:

- *Option 1* respects the Coasters contract and maintains good relations with Coasters but concedes the extra profit and the potential relationship to be gained from filling Thriller's order
- *Option 2* has the potential to satisfy both customers and to gain from Thriller (less some portion for Coasters as compensation).
- *Option 3* generates extra profit and a potential long-term relationship with Thriller, but it destroys any relationship with Coasters and likely will lead to a claim for compensation from Coasters for its extra tracking cost and potential losses from late delivery to the Ultimate Park.

Before accepting the Thriller order, Trackers needs to assure itself that the extra profit generated from Thriller will offset the damages it will have to pay to Coasters for breach of contract. Those damages could be quite high, depending on the circumstances, and difficult for Trackers to assess.

There is no question that Trackers has a legal obligation to Coasters, but that does not preclude Trackers from considering other opportunities. If Trackers chooses to breach the contract, there are also nonfinancial factors to be considered, such as future relations with Coasters; but in legal terms, a business that is prepared to pay damages for breach of contract can always refuse to perform its contractual obligations. Contract law provides compensation for breach, rather than punishment. There are no criminal consequences to breach of contract, and the law has traditionally refrained from making moral judgments about business activities.

Note: For further discussion of economic breach, see Richard Posner, *Economic Analysis of Law*, 5th ed. (New York: Aspen Law & Business, 1998).

Business Law in Practice Revisited

1. How should Amritha approach her task of securing the necessary tracking?

Given the size and expense of the proposed acquisition of tracking, Amritha should make it a priority to enter into a contract with a supplier such as Trackers. Nothing less than a contract will do, since Coasters must be able to exercise its legal right to sue, should Trackers fail to perform as promised.

2. How can the law facilitate Amritha's acquisition task?

Legal knowledge will help Amritha ensure that her negotiations produce an enforceable contract that meets her employer's needs and protects its interests. If Amritha does not know what a contract is, how it is formed, and what its legal significance might be, she is not competent to accomplish the task her employer has set for her.

3. What rules apply to a commercial relationship between a manufacturer (such as Coasters) and a supplier (such as Trackers), and how are disputes resolved?

The rules governing contracts are found in the common law (which develops through the decisions of the courts on a case-by-case basis), and to a lesser extent in statute law. If a dispute arises between Coasters and Trackers, there are several options available for attempting to resolve the dispute, including mediation and arbitration. Litigation is a last resort and will bring the matter to court. A judge will evaluate the terms of the contract and the conduct of the parties, apply the relevant law, and then come to a determination.

4. What are the legal consequences to Coasters of assigning the negotiation task to Amritha?

Amritha is representing her employer in negotiations. She will therefore need to appreciate at what point legal commitments are being made by both sides. Coasters should consider its relative bargaining position with available suppliers and ensure that Amritha has adequate support in her negotiations. Her inexperience and Coasters's size and expertise in contract negotiations will not relieve Coasters of its obligations. The contract itself will be between Coasters and the supplier (as the parties to the contract). They are the only parties able to enforce rights and the only parties that are subject to the obligations in the contract.

5. What are the nonlegal factors contributing to the proposed legal agreement?

If Coasters has a good working relationship with companies that can supply the required tracking, those suppliers are the logical candidates for Amritha's project. Their business practices and reliability will be known to Coasters, and negotiating a contract with them is likely to be more efficient than with a new supplier. Even a significant price advantage from a new supplier may not justify endangering long-term relationships with others.

Although both parties are obligated by the terms of any contract they make, there may be developments in the market or in the situation relating to the operations of Coasters or Trackers. The request to Trackers from a competitor of Coasters for the supply of tracking is only one example of an event that may cause these companies to reconsider their business and legal relationship. They must weigh all factors, including long-term business dealings and their reputation in the industry, when faced with a decision about whether to honour the contract, seek adjustment, or consider breaching the contract.

Chapter Summary

Through an awareness of contract law, business organizations are better able to protect themselves when forming and enforcing contracts. Contracts generally are not required to be in a particular form, but clear agreement on all essential terms is necessary. Those involved in negotiating contracts should be aware of the legal impact of their communication with each other, and they should realize that they are largely responsible for protecting their own interests before agreeing to terms. Contract rules are understood best when assessed in the broader business context, which includes the impact that any given legal decision by a business may have on its reputation with other businesses, with its customers, and in the community at large. A business must also assess its legal options in light of the business relationship at issue, the need to generate a profit, the uncertainty of the marketplace, and the importance of conducting operations with a sense of commercial morality, honesty, and good faith.

Chapter Study

Key Terms and Concepts

contract (p. 99)

objective standard test (p. 103)

equal bargaining power (p. 104)

Questions for Review

1. What is a contract?
2. What are the elements of a contract, according to the common law?
3. Must all contracts be in writing in order for them to be legally binding?
4. What is a standard form contract?
5. Name two industries that rely on standard form contracts.
6. What are the purposes of contract law?
7. Is the matter of whether a contract exists judged according to a subjective standard or an objective one? Explain.
8. Contract law assumes that parties have equal bargaining power. What is the effect of this assumption?
9. What is the role of public relations in contracts?
10. Why might a business elect to not perform on a contract, and what are some of the consequences that may arise from this decision?

Questions for Critical Thinking

1. Is there a better way to resolve disputes about contracts than by applying common law rules in litigation?
2. Should the law insist that there be actual equal bargaining power between the parties before a contract can be formed? What would the dangers of such a rule be?
3. Why are the nonlegal factors in a contractual relationship so important? Why is it important to place contract law in a business context?
4. Should negotiators follow a course of strict and absolute honesty in contractual negotiations? Why or why not?
5. How important is it to be aware of the law when negotiating a contract? Does it depend on who you negotiate with? Does it depend on the size and complexity of the contract in question?

Situations for Discussion

1. Trackers is a manufacturer of steel tracking, which is used by customers in a variety of applications, including rides for amusement parks.

   Trackers's business is booming, and its scheduling is tight for meeting delivery commitments. Trackers is contacted by a representative of Coasters, who inquires whether Trackers is capable of providing track for a special roller coaster in Florida and, if so, what price Trackers could offer and when it could deliver. Trackers knows that Coasters is a leader in the industry and would be a valuable customer. What factors should Trackers consider before responding to the Coasters inquiry? What are the risks and benefits of agreeing to fill Coasters's order?

2. Representatives of Trackers and Coasters discuss the key terms of their agreement over several weeks. Finally, in a meeting they agree on price, quality, delivery, and terms of payment. Trackers representatives volunteer to draw up the formal contract, based on the results of the meeting. When Coasters receives the contract the following week, it contains the key terms as agreed, but it also includes several complex terms that appear to protect Trackers if it fails to deliver, and it places responsibility on Coasters for shifts in the market or transportation difficulties. When Coasters inquires about the "extra" terms, Trackers replies that these terms are standard for all of its customers. How should Coasters deal with the standard terms? What role does bargaining power play in these negotiations?

3. Systems Unlimited (SU) is a well-established and successful retailer of computer systems. Mega Computers (MC) has been a major supplier to SU for many years. MC is having difficulty meeting the demand from all of its customers and decides that it needs to focus on a number of key customers, which do not include SU. The loss of MC as a supplier will be a major blow to SU's business. Does MC have any legal obligation to continue supplying SU? How should MC approach SU with its policy change? Could SU have prevented this situation from arising?

4. Melissa, an accounting student, interviews for a job with two firms. She really wants to work for Firm X but gets an offer of employment from Firm Y first and accepts it. A week later she receives an offer from Firm X, which she also accepts. She does so because she believes she is economically better off with firm X and will be able to "cancel" her acceptance with Firm Y.
   a. What is Melissa's legal situation now?
   b. Even assuming that she is better off economically by joining Firm X, what other costs does she face?
   c. Do you think that Firm Y will sue Melissa for breach of contract because she has accepted an employment offer elsewhere?
   d. What could Melissa have done to prevent this situation from occurring in the first place?
   e. What should Melissa do now?

5. Samantha Jones entered into a contract with Peter Black to act as a contractor for a new house she is having built in Calgary. She was anxious to have the house built as soon as possible, and upon receiving Peter's estimate that the work, including labour and materials, will cost $250 000, she immediately paid a $50 000 deposit. However, since receiving Samantha's deposit, Peter has been contacted by a developer who is willing to pay him a significant amount more to work on a new housing development, provided that he begin immediately. Peter does some calculations based on the current market. He decides that the amount the developer is offering is enough that he can afford to return the deposit, compensate Samantha for breaching the original contract, and still come out ahead on the development contract. He lets Samantha know that she will have to find a new contractor, and begins work on the housing development. When he calls Samantha a few months later to offer her compensation, she informs him that she has finally been able to hire a new contractor, but that the estimate for the work has now doubled. In the intervening months, the costs of labour and materials have skyrocketed. The house that originally would have cost $250 000 will now cost her $500 000. Do you think that Peter should be responsible for the additional costs of building Samantha's house, even though they very much exceed his original estimates?

For more study tools, visit http://www.businesslaw3e.nelson.com

Chapter

6

Objectives

After studying this chapter, you should have an understanding of

- how negotiations lead to a contractual relationship
- how negotiations can be terminated
- the legal ingredients of a contract
- how contracts can be amended or changed

Forming Contractual Relationships

Business Law in Practice

Amritha, introduced in Chapter 5, began negotiations with Jason Hughes. Jason is a representative of Trackers, the steel tracking manufacturer willing to supply tracking to Coasters, Amritha's employer. Amritha provided Jason with the plans and specifications for the roller coaster, and they negotiated a number of points, including price, delivery dates, and tracking quality. A short time later, Jason offered to sell Coasters a total of 900 metres of track in accordance with the plans and specifications provided. Jason's offer contained, among other matters, the purchase price ($1.5 million), delivery date, terms of payment, insurance obligations concerning the track, and a series of warranties related to the quality and performance of the tracking to be supplied. There was also a clause in the offer that stated: "Trackers will use its best efforts to secure insurance from the insurer named by Coasters." Another clause, inserted at Amritha's express request, required Trackers to pay $5000 to Coasters for every day it was late in delivering the tracking.

After reviewing the offer for several days, Amritha contacted Jason and said, "You drive a hard bargain, and there are aspects of your offer that I'm not entirely happy with. However, I accept your offer on behalf of my company. I'm looking forward to doing business with you."

Within a month, Trackers faced a 20 percent increase in manufacturing costs owing to an unexpected shortage in steel. Jason contacted Amritha to explain this development and worried aloud that without an agreement from Coasters to pay 20 percent more for the tracking, Trackers would be unable to make its delivery date. Amritha received instructions from her supervisor to agree to the increased purchase price in order to ensure timely delivery. Amritha communicated this news to Jason, who thanked her profusely for being so cooperative and understanding.

Jason kept his word and the tracking was delivered on time. However, Coasters has now determined that its profit margin on the American deal is lower than expected, and it is looking for ways to cut costs. Amritha is told by her boss to let Jason know that Coasters would not be paying the 20 percent price increase and would remit payment only in the amount set out in the contract. Jason and Trackers are stunned by this development.

1. At what point did the negotiations between Jason and Amritha begin to have legal consequences?
2. In what ways could negotiations have been terminated prior to the formation of the contract?
3. Can Coasters commit itself to the price increase and then change its mind with no adverse consequences?
4. How could Trackers have avoided from the outset this situation related to cost increases?

The Contract

Chapter 5 emphasized that Amritha must enter into a contract with Trackers in order to secure the product that Coasters needs. This chapter accounts for several of the basic elements of a contract, namely that it is

- an agreement (i.e., composed of offer and acceptance)
- complete (i.e., certain)
- deliberate (i.e., intention to create legal relations is present)
- supported by mutual consideration

In short, this chapter sets out the legal ingredients that transform a simple agreement—which can be broken without legal consequences—into an enforceable contract.

An Agreement

Before a contract can be in place, the parties must be in agreement, that is, have reached a consensus as to their rights and obligations. This agreement takes the form of offer and acceptance.

Offer

Definition of Offer

offer
A promise to perform specified acts on certain terms.

An **offer** is a promise to enter into a contract, on specified terms, as soon as the offer is accepted. This happened in negotiations between Amritha and Jason when Jason committed to provide tracking to Coasters in the concrete terms noted: he named his price, terms of payments, delivery date, and other essential matters. At this point, negotiations have taken an important turn because Amritha is entitled to accept that offer, and, upon her doing so, Trackers is obligated to supply its product exactly as Jason proposed, assuming that the other ingredients of a contract are established.

Certainty of Offer

Only a complete offer can form the basis of a contract. This means that all essential terms must be set out or the contract will fail for uncertainty. An offer does not, however, have to meet the standard of perfect clarity and precision in how it is expressed. If the parties intend to have a contract, the courts will endeavour to interpret the alleged offer in as reasonable a fashion as possible and thereby resolve ambiguities. For example, Jason's offer promised that "Trackers will use its best efforts to secure insurance from the insurer named by Coasters." Is the idea of using "best efforts" so vague that the offer lacks sufficient certainty? A court would likely say no and conclude that such a promise was enforceable—"best efforts" in this context would require Trackers to take conscientious and reasonable steps to secure insurance from the company Coasters named.[1]

An offer can achieve the requisite standard of certainty even if it leaves certain matters to be decided in the future. For example, Jason's offer could have made the final price for the tracking contingent on the market price of steel, as determined by a given formula. Though the price is not set out in the offer, a workable way of determining price would have been established, and a contract can be entered into on that basis. A court will not speculate, however, on what the parties would have agreed had they completed their negotiations.

Invitation to Treat

invitation to treat
An expression of willingness to do business.

An offer is different from a communication that merely expresses a wish to do business. In law, the latter form of communication is called an **invitation to treat** and has no legal consequences. Whether a communication is an offer or an invitation to treat depends on the speaker's intention, objectively assessed. Subjective intent is of no legal relevance.

---

1. For a discussion of what "best efforts" means, see *CAE Industries Ltd. v. R.* (1985), 20 D.L.R. (4th) 347 (Fed. C.A.), leave to appeal to S.C.C. refused (1985), 20 D.L.R. (4th) 347n.

When Amritha provided Jason with plans for the roller coaster, she was not offering to buy tracking from Jason at that point but merely indicating her interest in receiving an offer from him. This was an invitation to treat. Similarly, if Jason had offered to sell tracking to Coasters during negotiations but provided no other detail, he would simply be demonstrating his wish to do business with Coasters. Such expressions of interest have no legal repercussions because they essentially have no content. Vague commitments to buy or sell tracking are invitations to treat and not offers because they fail to specify the terms or scope of the proposed arrangement.

To assist in the sometimes difficult task of classifying whether a communication is an offer or an invitation to treat, the common law has devised a number of rules. A rule of particular significance to business relates to the advertising and display of goods for sale in a store.

Enterprises such as retail outlets prosper by attracting customers to their premises. They do this through advertising their existence, as well as describing the products they sell and prices they charge, especially when those prices have been reduced. For practical reasons, these advertisements are generally not classified as offers.[2] If advertisements were offers, the store owner would be potentially liable for breach of contract if the store ran out of an advertised item that a customer wished to purchase. By classifying the advertisement as an invitation to treat, the law ensures that it is the customer who makes the offer to purchase the advertised goods. The owner is then in a position to simply refuse the offer if the product is no longer in supply. As a result of this refusal, no contract could arise.[3] In this way, the law seeks to facilitate commercial activity by permitting a businessperson to advertise goods or services without ordinarily running the risk of incurring unwanted contractual obligations.

Similarly, the display of a product in the store is not an offer by the store to sell. The display is simply an indication that a product is available and can be purchased. In short, it is an invitation to treat and, by definition, is not capable of being accepted. In this way, the store maintains the option of refusing to complete the transaction at the cash register.[4] (see Figure 6.1).

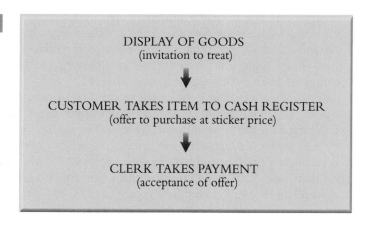

FIGURE 6.1

Legal Analysis of the Retail Purchase

DISPLAY OF GOODS
(invitation to treat)

⬇

CUSTOMER TAKES ITEM TO CASH REGISTER
(offer to purchase at sticker price)

⬇

CLERK TAKES PAYMENT
(acceptance of offer)

2. An exception to this general rule occurs when the advertisement is so clear and definite that there is nothing left to negotiate. See *Lefkowitz v. Great Minneapolis Surplus Store, Inc.*, 251 Minn. 188, 86 N.W. 2d. 689 (1957).
3. A store owner may have other legal problems if she runs out of an advertised sale product. For example, the "bait and switch selling" provision of the *Competition Act*, R.S.C. 1985, c. C-34, s. 74.04(2) provides

    A person engages in reviewable conduct who advertises at a bargain price a product that the person does not supply in reasonable quantities having regard to the nature of the market in which the person carries on the business, the nature and the size of the person's business and the nature of the advertisement.

    Subsection (3) provides defences for contravening (2). Note that 74.1 (1) provides for fines in an amount not exceeding: (i) in the case of an individual, $50,000 and, for each subsequent order, $100,000, or (ii) in the case of a corporation, $100,000 and, for each subsequent order, $200,000.
4. Note, however, that human rights legislation across the country prohibits a business owner from refusing to serve a customer on the basis of race, gender, and other discriminatory grounds.

Some contracts, like the purchase of photocopying paper from an office supply store, are formed without any negotiations whatsoever. The customer simply takes the purchase to the cashier—thereby offering to purchase the item at its sticker price—and the cashier accepts the offer by receiving payment. Other contracts arise only after protracted discussions.

When negotiations are complicated, it is important for the parties to know when an offer has been made, since at that moment significant legal consequences arise, whether the parties intend them to or not. A fundamental rule is that a contract is formed only when a complete offer is unconditionally accepted by the other side. The key factor in deciding whether an offer has been made is this: if the purported offer is sufficiently comprehensive that it can be accepted without further elaboration or clarification, it is an offer in law. Jason's proposal to Amritha, outlined in the opening scenario, contains the requisite certainty and completeness. On this basis, the first building block to a contract between Trackers and Coasters is in place.

Business Application of the Law   Spamming on the Internet

Unsolicited bulk commercial e-mail (sometimes called spam) is an increasingly common way of advertising goods and services on the Internet. Like traditional advertising, spam is likely to be classified as an invitation to treat, though if it contained enough specificity, it could constitute an offer.

As noted by Industry Canada, spamming itself is currently legal in Canada,[5] though—due to increasing misuse of the Internet—this matter is under review by the federal government. In 2005, the task force on Spam, constituted by the federal government, reported that spam made up 80 percent of all global e-mail, representing a sharp increase from the 10 percent levels of 2000. According to the task force, such volume causes a rash of problems, including wasting employee time, tying up Internet services providers, and causing injury to legitimate Internet marketers. And frauds associated with spam make the public less likely to trust the Internet as a vehicle for conducting business.[6] As the report states

> The new mutations of spam undermine consumer confidence in the Internet as a platform for commerce and communications. Because of this, the potential of information and communications technology to buttress productivity, and the ability of e-commerce to attract investment, create jobs and enrich our lives, is constrained not only by torrents of spam, but by the deceptive, fraudulent and malicious activities that sometimes accompany it.

5. Industry Canada, "E-mail marketing: Consumer choices and business opportunities" (January 2003) at http://e-com.ic.gc.ca/epic/internet/inecic-ceac.nsf/en/gv00189e.html (accessed 1 November 2006).
This government website also notes that e-mail addresses are classified as personal information under the *Personal Information Protection and Electronic Documents Act*, S.C. 2000, c. 5. As a result, businesses can run afoul of this law by using their customers' e-mail addresses for secondary purposes—such as commercial solicitation—without securing the necessary consents. The website also notes that in October 2002, the privacy commissioner determined that several major organizations that provide communications services were at fault for failing to secure such consents prior to using the addresses for commercial solicitation. For more recent privacy violations related to unsolicited e-mail, see the website for the Office of the Privacy Commissioner of Canada at http://www.privcom.gc.ca/cf-dc/2005/297_050331_01_e.asp
6. Industry Canada, "Stopping Spam: Creating a Stronger, Safer Internet" (May 2005) at http://e-com.ic.gc.ca/epic/internet/inecic-ceac.nsf/en/h_gv00317e.html (accessed 1 November 2006). Spam is often used to promote illegal schemes as well as schemes that should be illegal, as the task force notes. What follows is a quotation from the report that sets out the dangers of spam, including:

    malicious actions that cause harm to computers, networks or data, or use personal property for unauthorized purposes (e.g., viruses, worms, Trojan Horses, denial of service attacks, zombie networks);

    deceptive and fraudulent business practices, including online versions of traditional mail-based frauds (e.g., the "Nigerian bank account" or "419" scam, and "spoofed" websites masquerading as legitimate businesses);

    phishing emails designed for identity theft or to steal money; and

    invasions of privacy (e.g., email-address harvesting, spyware).

    For definitions of many of these words, go to the Webopedia at http://www.webopedia.com (accessed 1 November 2006). For a description of the Nigerian bank account or 419 scams, go to http://www.snopes.com/crime/fraud/nigeria.asp (accessed 1 November 2006).

As one aspect of a multipronged strategy to combat spam, the task force recommends that certain e-mail activities be made offences in spam-specific legislation, noting that these proposed offenses may also be reflected, in whole or in part, in existing legislation:

- the failure to abide by an opt-in regime for sending unsolicited commercial e-mail
- the use of false or misleading headers or subject lines (i.e., false transmission information) designed to disguise the origins, purpose, or contents of an e-mail, whether the objective is to mislead recipients or to evade technological filters
- the construction of false or misleading URLs and websites for the purpose of collecting personal information under false pretences or engaging in criminal conduct (or to commit other offences listed)
- the harvesting of e-mail addresses without consent, as well as the supply, use, or acquisition of such lists
- dictionary attacks

According to the Webopedia (http://www.webopedia.com), a "dictionary" attack is method of breaking security systems whereby the attacker runs through all the words in a dictionary in order to establish someone's password.

Other aspects of the task force's recommended strategy to combat spam include

- securing action and assistance from Internet services providers and other network operators
- cooperation from e-mail marketers
- user education and awareness
- global cooperation
- the establishment of a coordinating body

For further discussion of this strategy, see "Stopping Spam: Creating a Stronger, Safer Internet," a report of the Task Force on Spam (May 2005), at http://strategis. ic.gc.ca/epic/internet/inecic-ceac.nsf/en/h_gv00317e.html.

CRITICAL ANALYSIS: Do you agree that legislation should be part of Canada's strategy to combat spam? Why not leave the problem of spam to the marketplace to resolve?

Why is spam objectionable?

---

offeror
The person who makes an offer.

offeree
The person to whom an offer is made.

The person who makes an offer is known as the **offeror.** The person to whom an offer is made is known as the **offeree.** In the Business Law in Practice scenario, Jason is the offeror and Amritha is the offeree.

Termination of Offer

An offer can be accepted only if it is "alive," meaning that it is available to be accepted. If the offer has been legally terminated, no contract can come into existence, since one of its essential ingredients—the offer itself—is missing.

An offer can be terminated or taken "off the table" by any of the following events:

- revocation
- lapse
- rejection
- counteroffer
- death or insanity

What factors will determine whether a contract will be the result of lengthy negotiations or will be easily and quickly concluded?

CASE ▼

Bigg v. Boyd Gibbins Ltd., [1971] 2 All E.R. 183 (C.A.)

THE BUSINESS CONTEXT: For the purpose of entering into a contract, parties may negotiate considerably. Difficulties arise when one party believes that a contract has been concluded while the other party disputes that conclusion.

FACTUAL BACKGROUND: Plaintiff and defendant negotiated extensively for the purchase and sale of real estate by the plaintiff to the defendant. The negotiation over this property—known as Shortgrove Hall—took the form of correspondence that the plaintiff/vendor claims culminated in a contract. The first legally important letter from the plaintiff stated

> Thank you for your letter received last week.... As you are aware that I paid £25,000 for this property, your offer of £20,000 would appear to be at least a little optimistic. For a quick sale I would accept £26,000, so that my expense may be covered.

In response, the defendant wrote

> I have just recently returned from my winter holiday and, turning this matter over in my mind now, would advise you that I accept your offer.

The plaintiff replied

> I thank you for your letter . . . accepting my price of £26,000 for the sale of Shortgrove

Hall. I am putting the matter in the hands of my solicitors. . . . My wife and I are both pleased that you are purchasing the property.

The defendant denies a contract was formed, asserting that the parties had merely agreed on price.

THE LEGAL QUESTION: Is there a contract between the parties?

RESOLUTION: The court found for the plaintiff. There was a contract for the purchase and sale of Shortgrove Hall. To reach this conclusion, the court carefully analyzed the correspondence provided and acknowledged the defendant's argument that agreement on price does not necessarily mean that the parties have reached a full agreement. On these facts, however, a contract did exist. As the court concluded, "the impression conveyed to my mind by these letters, and indeed the plain impression, is that the language used was intended to and did achieve the formation of . . . [a] contract. As I have indicated, in the last letter stress was laid on the phrase 'accepting my *price* [emphasis added] of £26,000 for the sale of Shortgrove Hall.' I think, in the context of the letters that preceded that, it is to be read, as I have said, as 'accepted my *offer* [emphasis added] to sell Shortgrove Hall at that price.'"

CRITICAL ANALYSIS: Who is the offeror and who is the offeree in this case? Do you agree with the court that a contract was in place? Should courts hold parties to the meaning of the exact words they use, or should words be interpreted in their larger context?

Revocation

revocation
The withdrawal of an offer.

The offeror can **revoke** his offer at any time before acceptance simply by notifying the offeree of its withdrawal. An offer that has been revoked does not exist anymore and therefore cannot be accepted.

In the opening scenario, there were several days between the communication of Trackers's offer and Amritha's acceptance of that offer. During this time, Jason would have been legally entitled to revoke his offer by simply advising Amritha of that fact. Amritha's alternatives would then be reduced, since she cannot accept an offer that has been revoked, nor can she make Trackers do business with her if it is no longer interested.

As the following case illustrates, the law even permits offerors to revoke their offers despite a promise to leave the offer open for a set period of time. In short, such a promise is enforceable only if the other party has purchased it or otherwise has given the offeror something in return for the commitment. Accordingly, if Jason had promised to leave his offer to sell tracking open for 30 days, but Amritha did not provide something in return for this promise—like the payment of a sum of money—she would have no legal recourse if Jason were to break his word and revoke his offer the next day.

Landmark Case ▼

Dickinson v. Dodds, [1876] 2 Ch.D. 463 (C.A.)

THE HISTORICAL CONTEXT: This case is the leading decision—valid even today—on whether an offeror can renege on a commitment to hold an offer open for a specified period of time.

FACTUAL BACKGROUND: On Wednesday, June 10, Dodds delivered to Dickinson a written offer to sell his property to Dickinson for £800. The offer stated that it would be open for acceptance until 9 a.m. on Friday, June 12. On Thursday, Dickinson heard that Dodds had been offering or was agreeing to sell the property to Mr. Allan. That evening, Dickinson delivered an acceptance to the place where Dodds was staying, and at 7 a.m. on Friday morning—a full two hours before the deadline—he personally delivered an acceptance to Dodds. Dodds declined the acceptance, stating: "You are too late. I have sold the property." Dickinson sued Dodds, alleging there was a contract between them.

THE LEGAL QUESTION: To determine whether Dickinson's action should succeed, the court had to decide whether Dodds was entitled to revoke his offer prior to the deadline he had set. This decision was necessary because if the offer had been properly revoked, it was not capable of being accepted, and, accordingly, there could be no contract between the two men.

RESOLUTION: The court decided that what Dodds did was permissible: "[I]t is a perfectly clear rule of law . . . that, although it is said that the offer is to be left open until Friday morning at 9 o'clock, that did not bind Dodds. He was not in point of law bound to hold the offer over until 9 o'clock on Friday morning."

On this footing, a firm offer can be revoked at any time before acceptance. More controversially, the court also held that Dodds's offer had been effectively revoked prior to acceptance because Dickinson learned in advance—from a presumably reliable source—that Dodds was selling the property to someone else.

CRITICAL ANALYSIS: Being guided primarily by legal principles is certainly an acceptable way of doing business. However, what might be the impact on your business reputation of going back on your word and revoking an offer sooner than you had promised you would? Do you think that the method used by Dodds for revocation (i.e., relying on the fact that Dickinson had learned that Dodds was selling to someone else) is the usual way of revoking an offer? What would be a more certain way and reliable way of effecting revocation?

option agreement
An agreement where, in exchange for payment, an offeror is obligated to keep an offer open for a specified time.

One way to avoid application of the rule in *Dickinson v. Dodds* that firm offers can be revoked prior to their deadlines is for the parties to form an **option agreement,** whereby the offeree pays the offeror to keep the offer open for the specified time. An option agreement is a separate contract that may or may not lead to the acceptance of the offer and a resulting agreement of purchase and sale. Its purpose is simply to give the offeree a guaranteed period of time within which to deliberate whether to accept the offer or not. If the offeror withdraws the offer before the option agreement permits, she has committed a breach of contract, and the offeree can sue for damages.

Option agreements are commonly found in real estate developments—the developer will buy a number of options to purchase land from owners in the development area. The developer can choose whether to exercise the options and knows that during the option period, the owners are contractually bound to not withdraw their offers to sell at the specified price.

Dickinson v. Dodds also demonstrates that an offer does not have to be directly revoked by the offeror—that revocation can take place through a reliable third-party source. This method of revocation, however, is both unusual and unreliable. Prudent business practice would have the offeror expressly revoking offers as necessary.

Lapse

lapse
The expiration of an offer after a specified or reasonable period.

An offer **lapses** in one of two ways. It may contain a date upon which it expires. After this date, it is no longer "alive" and therefore cannot be accepted. If the offer contains no expiry date, it will remain open for a reasonable period of time, which, in turn, will depend on all the circumstances of the case, including the nature of the transaction at issue. For example, an offer to sell a piece of woodland that is sitting idle would probably remain open longer than an offer to sell a piece of property that is about to be commercially developed. A judge will bring as much precision as possible to the question of when an offer lapses, but the whole exercise is inherently speculative.

With this in mind, an offeror should consider specifying an expiry date for the offer and thereby avoid the debate altogether. For his part, the offeree should act promptly, because of the principle in *Dickinson v. Dodds* permitting revocation prior to the expiry date, or at least keep in contact with the offeror to ensure that the status of the offer is known.

Rejection

rejection
The refusal to accept an offer.

It is important for those involved in contractual negotiations to know that an offer is automatically terminated when it is rejected by the offeree. The offer can be accepted only if the offeror revives it by offering it anew or if the offeree presents it as his own offer, which can then be accepted or **rejected** by the original offeror. The risk in rejecting an offer is that it may never be renewed by the other side.

Counteroffer

counteroffer
The rejection of one offer and proposal of a new one.

A **counteroffer** is a form of rejection. Through a counteroffer, the offeree is turning down the offer and proposing a new offer in its place. The distinction between an acceptance and a counteroffer is not always readily apparent. For example, suppose that a seller offers 100 widgets to the buyer at $10 per widget, and the buyer responds, "Great, I'll take 800." Or suppose a seller offers a car for $10 000, and the buyer says, "I'll take it. I'll give you $5000 today and the balance next week." In both situations, it looks like the buyer has accepted, but in law he or she has made a counteroffer. Any change to a term of an offer—including to price, quantity, time of delivery, or method of payment—is a counteroffer. Because a counteroffer is a rejection, the original offer is automatically terminated and can be accepted only if it is renewed by one of the parties. Whenever a party makes a counteroffer, she jeopardizes the chance of being able to accept the original offer.

Death or Insanity

While the matter is not free from controversy, it would seem that an offer generally dies if the offeror or offeree dies. However, if the offer concerns a contract that would not require the affected party to personally perform it, a court may decide that the offer could be accepted notwithstanding that party's death.

Someone who makes an offer and then subsequently becomes insane would not be bound, as a general rule.

Acceptance

Definition of Acceptance

acceptance

An unqualified willingness to enter into a contract on the terms in the offer.

When an offer made by one party is unconditionally and unequivocally accepted by the other party, a contract is formed. To be effective, the **acceptance** must demonstrate an unqualified and complete willingness to enter into the contract on the precise terms proposed. If the purported acceptance does not mirror the offer by agreeing to all its content, it is a counteroffer and no contract has been formed.

In the opening scenario, Amritha clearly accepted Jason's offer—she did not propose modifications or alterations to his proposal. While she expressed some reservations, saying that she was not entirely happy with the offer, this was not a rejection. Rather, she went on to fully and completely accept his offer. At this point, two of the building blocks of a contract between Coasters and Trackers are in place—namely, offer and acceptance.

Communication of Acceptance

In order to effect legal acceptance, the offeree must communicate—by words or by conduct—an unconditional assent to the offer in its entirety. This message of acceptance can be conveyed in any number of ways: in person, in writing, by mail, by fax, by e-mail, by telephone, and by other actions. In fact, any manner of communication that is reasonable in the circumstances ordinarily will do. However, the offer must be scrutinized to determine if it requires a specific method of communicating an acceptance. If it does, and by the terms of the offer that method of communication is mandatory, then the offeree must follow that method of communication in order to ensure legal acceptance. For example, if a company offers, by telephone, to sell a given item but specifies that acceptance must be in writing, then the offeree's calling back with a purported acceptance will be ineffective. In this case the offeror is entitled to insist on written acceptance before it is bound.

Why might a business decide to accept an offer by conduct instead of formally communicating acceptance to the other side? What are the risks of doing so?

Since entering a contract is about assent, the law determines that the offer is effective only when it has been communicated to the offeree. In this way, the offeree becomes aware of its terms and can respond. Similarly, the acceptance, if any, must be communicated to the offeror so that the offeror is aware of the unqualified acceptance. Acceptance is achieved expressly, as when the offeree accepts in person or sends a message through some medium to the offeror. Occasionally, however, acceptance can be indicated by conduct, as the following case illustrates.

CASE ▼

Lowe (D. J.) (1980) Ltd. v. Upper Clements Family Theme Park Ltd. (1990), 95 N.S.R. (2d) 397 (S.C.T.D.)

THE BUSINESS CONTEXT: Businesses often have to act quickly to address a problem that has developed. In such circumstances, proper attention may not be given to the legal requirements of contract formation. This lack of focus can lead to disappointed expectations.

FACTUAL BACKGROUND: Mr. Bougie, construction manager of Upper Clements Family Theme Park, was under a tight construction schedule and needed a crane quickly to complete construction of a theme park. He discussed leasing a crane from Mr. Lowe's company, but the two men could not come to an agreement. Lowe insisted that the crane be leased for a minimum period of two months, whereas Bougie did not want to commit to that length of a term, preferring to prorate[7] charges based on a monthly rental. The next day, however, Bougie delivered the following letter to Lowe from Mr. Buxton, the general manager of Family Theme Park:

November 24, 1988

D.J. Lowe (1980) Limited
Deep Brook
Anna Co., Nova Scotia
B0S 1J0

Dear Sirs:

Further to your verbal agreement with our Construction Manager, I can confirm the following arrangements with respect to the hiring of a crane for the erection of steel to the flume ride:

1. The Upper Clements Family Theme Park Limited agrees to pay the sum of $10 000 (ten thousand dollars) per month, pro rated for partial months for crane hire.
2. The Upper Clements Family Theme Park Limited agrees to supply the crane operator.
3. D.J. Lowe (1980) Limited agrees to supply fuel and maintenance for the above crane.

If you are in agreement with these conditions, kindly sign one copy of this letter and return to me.

Yours truly,

(Signed)
PAUL G. BUXTON, P.Eng.

GENERAL MANAGER
SIGNATURE OF AGREEMENT
D.J. LOWE (1980) LIMITED

This letter did not, in fact, reflect the parties' agreement and was never signed by the Lowe company, but Lowe did send a crane to the construction site. Lowe apparently believed that he and the Theme Park personnel could come to an agreement on price, and within two days of delivering the crane, approached Bougie with a draft agreement setting out a monthly rate for a two-month term. Bougie said that he had no authority to deal with the document, and it would have to wait for Buxton's return from an out-of-town trip. In the end, the Theme Park had the crane onsite for four days and then immediately returned it, along with payment of $1250. Lowe's company sued for the balance, claiming that it was owed a total of $20 000.

THE LEGAL QUESTION: Is there a contract between the parties? If so, did Buxton's terms on price prevail or did Lowe's?

RESOLUTION: The trial judge determined that there was a contract between the parties for the rental of the crane. Whether Buxton's letter was classified as an acceptance or a counteroffer,

> it was the serious expression of an intention by the Theme Park to enter into a contract with the Lowe company. . . . Having received that letter, Mr. Lowe had his company go ahead with delivery of the crane, knowing it was essential that the Theme Park have it at the earliest possible moment. Rather than risk losing the contract, Lowe accepted the offer by delivering the crane and acquiescing in the Theme Park's use of it.
>
> In doing so Mr. Lowe was not intentionally capitulating to an unfavourable counter-offer. Based upon his experience in the industry and his previous dealings with the Theme Park, Mr. Lowe was taking a calculated risk that even though his company was entering into a contract, he could later negotiate more satisfactory terms. . . . His expectations were not unreasonable. However they were frustrated first by Mr. Buxton's absence and then by his own. . . . The two-month term [set forth in the draft lease that Lowe subsequently presented to Bougie] was not part of the contract that was entered into. The governing provision is in

---

7.   When a sum is prorated, it means that what is charged is determined in relation to a certain rate. In this example, the monthly rate is $10 000. Based on a 30-day month, the prorated daily charge would be $10 000 divided by 30, or $333.

Mr. Buxton's letter of November 24th. . . . That is the provision of the counter-offer Mr. Lowe wished to avoid, but it is the one that governs. The Theme Park is entitled to return the crane for the monthly rental prorated for the partial month when it had possession of the crane. . . . The amount to be paid was calculated at $1250.00 by the Theme Park and previously tendered to the Plaintiff. I accept that calculation and award the Plaintiff damages.

CRITICAL ANALYSIS: How can a business avoid unwanted obligations when there is insufficient time to properly negotiate a contract? Is it reasonable for the judge to decide the case based on the terms of one letter?

It is also possible—though less than usual—for the offer to be expressed in such a way that no communication of acceptance is needed.

Landmark Case ▼

Carlill v. Carbolic Smoke Ball Co., [1893] 1 Q.B. 256 (Eng. C.A.)

THE HISTORICAL CONTEXT: This case was decided at a time when Victorian England was being inundated with quack cures. Examples of "miracle" cures included Epps Glycerine Jube Jubes and a product called Pepsolic, which claimed to prevent marriage breakups because it prevented indigestion. The ad for this product noted that indigestion "Causes Bad Temper, Irritability, Peppery Disposition, Domestic Quarrels, Separation and—the Divorce Court."[8]

FACTUAL BACKGROUND: This case considers the legal obligations that resulted from the advertisement placed by the Carbolic Smoke Ball Company in a London newspaper at the turn of the 19th century.

Mrs. Carlill used the smoke ball as directed for two weeks but caught influenza anyway. When the company refused to pay her the advertised reward, she commenced an action for breach of contract.

FIGURE 6.2

Carbolic Smoke Ball Advertisement

> **£100 REWARD**
> WILL BE PAID BY THE
> **CARBOLIC SMOKE BALL CO.**
> To any person who contracts the increasing Epidemic,
> **INFLUENZA**
> Colds, or any diseases caused by taking cold, AFTER HAVING USED the BALL
> 3 times daily for two weeks according to the printed directions supplied with each Ball.
> **£1000**
> Is deposited with the ALLIANCE BANK, REGENT STREET, showing our sincerity in the matter.
> During the last epidemic of Influenza many of our CARBOLIC SMOKE BALLS were sold as Preventives against this Disease, and in no ascertained case was the disease contracted by those using the CARBOLIC SMOKE BALL.

THE LEGAL QUESTION: Was there a contract between the parties, even though Mrs. Carlill did not communicate her acceptance of the Carbolic Smoke Ball Company's offer?

8. A.W.B. Simpson, "Quackery and Contract Law: The Case of the Carbolic Smoke Ball" (1985) 14 J. *Legal Stud.* 345 at 356. The historical information contained in this box draws heavily on Simpson's analysis.

RESOLUTION: While communication of acceptance is generally required, this is not always the case. Because the Carbolic Smoke Ball Company—the offeror—had chosen to dispense with the necessity of notice, it could not complain about Mrs. Carlill's failure to communicate acceptance now. In the end, the court found that Mrs. Carlill had accepted the company's offer of a reward by using the smoke ball as requested and that, upon becoming sick, she was contractually entitled to the £100.

CRITICAL ANALYSIS: This case is an example of an offer of a unilateral contract, though the court did not identify it as such. Through such an offer, the offeror promises to pay the offeree a sum of money if the offeree performs the requested act. For example, a company might offer a $200 reward to anyone who finds a missing laptop computer. Unlike the ordinary business contract, where both parties have obligations, in the unilateral contract only the offeror is bound because the offeree can perform the requested act—find the laptop—or not. He has no obligation even to try. If he does find the computer and returns it, the contract is complete, and the offeror is contractually required to pay. For obvious reasons, this kind of offer typically does not require people who decide to look for the computer to advise the company of their intention to do so. From the company's perspective, it is enough to hear from the person who actually finds the computer.

Ordinarily, however, communication of acceptance is expected and required. In practical terms, the offeror needs to be aware of the acceptance in order to appreciate that the contract exists and that performance of the obligations in it should proceed.

A problem arises if the offeree sends an acceptance that for some reason never reaches the offeror. Perhaps a letter gets lost in the mail, an e-mail message goes astray, or a fax gets sent to the wrong number. Has there been acceptance or not? Normally, the answer would be that no acceptance has occurred until actually received. Put another way, acceptance is effective only when communicated—it is at this moment that a contract comes into existence.

A specific exception to this general rule is the "postbox rule," also called the "postal rule." If it is clear that the offeror intends the postbox rule to apply to her offer, then acceptance is effective at the time of mailing the acceptance, rather than the time of delivery. Even if the letter containing the acceptance is never delivered to the offeror, a contract has been formed. Since application of the postbox rule means that an offeror could end up being in a contract without even knowing it, that person is best advised to avoid application of the postbox rule by making it clear in the offer that actual communication or notice of acceptance is absolutely required.

When a court will apply the ordinary rule and when it will apply the postbox rule depends on the facts of the case. As Lord Wilberforce states: "No universal rule can cover all such cases; they must be resolved by reference to the intentions of the parties, by sound business practice and in some cases by a judgment where the risks should lie. . . ."[9] Courts have suggested that the postbox rule applies to telegrams but only where the offeror had impliedly constituted the telegraph company as his agent for the purpose of receiving the acceptance.[10] Otherwise, the ordinary rule applies and the acceptance by telegram is effective only upon receipt.[11] The postbox rule has also been applied where the acceptance was delivered by courier.[12]

9. *Brinkibon Ltd. v. Stahag Stahl Und Stahlwarenhandelsgesellschaft mbH*, [1983] 2 A.C. 34; the rule in *Brinkibon* was adopted in Canada by *Eastern Power Ltd. v. Azienda Comunale Energia & Ambiente* (1999), 178 D.L.R. (4th) 409 (Ont. C.A.).
10. *Smith & Osberg Ltd. v. Hollenbeck*, [1938] 3 W.W.R. 704 (B.C. S.C.).
11. *Societa' Gei A Responsabilita' Limitata v. Piscitelli*, [1988] O.J. No. 894 (Dist. Ct.).
12. *Nova Scotia v. Weymouth Sea Products Ltd.* (1983), 4 D.L.R. (4th) 314 (N.S. C.A.) and *Fp Bourgault Ind. Cultivator Division Ltd. v. Nichols Tillage Tools Inc.* (1988), 63 Sask. R. 204 (Q.B.).

That said, it is much more common for the courts to apply the ordinary rule—that acceptance is effective only when communicated. They have done so with respect to all forms of instantaneous communication, including the telephone, the telex, and the fax.[13]

The practical application of the rules governing offer and acceptance is affected by the requirement of proof that the necessary events occurred. Someone who seeks to enforce a contract that the other party denies exists must be able to prove that offer and acceptance occurred. While ideally this proof is created through documentary evidence, documents are not always available. In such circumstances, the individual seeking to rely on the contract must convince the court of its existence without the benefit of extraneous proof. Oral agreements are very difficult to prove without some independent verification or corroboration—by a witness to the negotiations, for example—of what was said.

Business Application of the Law

Get It in Writing

Even though most oral contracts are enforceable,[14] it is an excellent business practice to get them in writing. This risk management strategy can prevent disputes from subsequently arising as well as help to prove one's case, should the matter go to trial.

When nine coworkers at a Mission B.C. A&W went to claim a $14.5 million jackpot from the B.C. Lottery Corp., four other coworkers came forward, including Megan Lee Weisgarber, saying that they, too, should share in the prize.

While the facts of the case remain unclear, Ken MacQueen for *Maclean's* was able to report two versions of the story, on 28 September 2005. One version is that, on 20 August, employee Marge Toyryla went into work early in order to encourage her coworkers to participate in that evening's 6-49 lottery draw. She passed around an envelope and those who wanted to be part of the ticket purchase placed $2.00 inside and wrote their name on the outside of the envelope. Some rules applied to the process—including that people paid up front for their tickets. According to Manager Shirley Marshall, this was because it would be "too hard to collect money after a losing draw."

Weisgarber and another coworker contended that they should share in the winnings as each contributed money on 17 August 2005, to the pool and that a portion of that money should have been used

Megan Lee Weisgarber is one of four A&W workers who claimed in August 2005 to have been unfairly excluded from the lottery jackpot.

to purchase what turned out to be the winning ticket. They also dispute the version of the story recounted, claiming that Toyryla never used envelopes and that she did not regularly write down the names of people who had contributed. Two other coworkers claimed that they were asked to

---

13. *Eastern Power Ltd. v. Azienda Communale Energia* (1999), 178 D.L.R. (4th) 409 (Ont. C.A.), application for leave dismissed, [1999] S.C.C.A. No. 542.
14. But see Chapter 8 for discussion of the *Statute of Frauds*.

participate in the workplace lottery and had been told that they could pay later. The four filed suit with the British Columbia courts, laying a claim to the lottery win. Since then, three of the four—including Weisgarber—have ended their claims, according to a story in *The Province*.

The only remaining claim—by A&W worker Rani Johnson—will be going to trial, but it is not known when this will happen.

Western Canada Lottery Corporation spokesman John Matheson recommends that any group wishing to buy lottery tickets should have a written agreement in place. He advises that the deal should include

- a list of participants
- their contact information
- the group's trustee
- what happens when someone who ordinarily participates is away

For a group-buying agreement created by the Western Canada Lottery Corporation, see http://www.wclc.com/download/wclc/group_buying_agreement.pdf

CRITICAL ANALYSIS: When coworkers pool funds to buy lottery tickets, how is the contract formed? In the case of the contract among A&W workers, what do the terms seem to be? How would a written agreement, such as suggested that by the Western Canada Lottery Corporation, have assisted in the A&W dispute?

Sources: Keith Fraser, "Brenner Orders Another $3 Million Be Released to Group of Nine Original Winners" *The Province* (22 March 2006) at A4; Ken MacQueen, "Tough Luck: An A&W Workers' Dispute in Mission, B.C. over a $14.5-Million Lottery Ticket Has Turned Nasty, with Allegations of Lies, Deceit—Even Threats of Physical Harm" *Maclean's* (28 September 2005) at http://www.macleans.ca/topstories/canada/ article.jsp?content= 20051003_113095_113095; Gary Mason, "Jackpot Proving to Be a Bear for A&W Workers" *The Globe and Mail* (27 August 2005) at A12; Sarah O'Donnell, "Lottery Ticket Office Pools a Canadian Tradition" *Edmonton Journal* (29 October 2005) at A2.

Developments in technology have created new methods of doing business that test the relevance and applicability of the older common law rules regarding offer and acceptance to which this chapter has already alluded.

Technology and the Law · Electronic Contracting

Electronic business—such as the sale of goods and services, the exchange of commercial information, and the payment of debts conducted over public and private computer networks—has grown tremendously over the last decade.

In an effort to facilitate the growth of electronic business, the Uniform Law Conference of Canada has adopted the *Uniform Electronic Commerce Act (UECA)*[15] based on the United Nations Commission on International Trade Law's (UNCITRAL) Model Law on Electronic Commerce.[16] The UECA, which is designed to remove barriers to electronic commerce, is intended to serve as the basis for provincial and federal electronic commerce legislation. The model law has three parts. The first sets out basic functional equivalency rules. To remove any doubts pertaining to the legal recognition of electronic contracts, the model legislation provides that a contract shall not be denied effect on the sole ground that it was entered into electronically.[17] Part 2 deals with special rules for the formation and operation of contracts, the effect of using automated transactions, corrections of errors when dealing with a computer, and the sending and receipt of computer messages. Part 3 makes special provision for the carriage of goods. Virtually all of the provinces and the territories have enacted electronic commerce

---

15. Available at http://www.ulcc.ca/en/us/index.cfm?sec=1&sub=1u1 (accessed 1 November 2006).
16. Available at http://www.uncitral.org/uncitral/en/uncitral_texts/electronic_commerce/1996Model.html (accessed 1 November 2006).
17. The UECA provides a requirement that information in writing can be satisfied by information in electronic form. Contractual writing requirements are discussed in Chapter 8.

legislation.[18] In most cases the legislation is the same or similar to the UECA; however, important variations do exist.

The UECA and the legislation that it has spawned do not modify or change the general rules applicable to contracts. The formation of electronic contracts is governed by the same general rules as other contracts. There must be an offer, acceptance, and communication of the acceptance.

OFFER: The UECA provides that an offer may be expressed electronically. The legislation does not, however, specify whether communication displayed on a website is an offer or an invitation to do business. Generally, advertisements in catalogues and goods displayed in a store are not viewed as offers on the basis that merchants have only a limited supply and therefore could not reasonably be making offers to everyone. Presumably, electronic catalogues, advertisements, and price lists would be subject to the same rule. However, if the website displaying goods or services for sale not only indicates the price but also indicates that the item is in stock then the online advertisement could conceivably be considered an offer.[19]

ACCEPTANCE: The UECA provides that acceptance of an offer can be made electronically. Thus an offer made electronically may be accepted electronically unless the party making the offer insists on some other means of communication. Case law has recognized that an offer made electronically can be accepted by clicking on an online icon or an "I agree" button. In *Rudder v. Microsoft*,[20] an Ontario court held that an online membership agreement became enforceable against the subscriber once the subscriber clicked on the "I Agree" button.[21] The UECA also recognizes that an acceptance (as well as an offer) can be affected by an electronic agent.[22]

COMMUNICATION OF ACCEPTANCE: An acceptance of the offer must be communicated to the offeror to take effect. Where the acceptance is effective usually determines where the contract is formed and consequently what law applies to the transaction. In the absence of an agreement, an acceptance using an instantaneous means of communication (telephone, telex, facsimile) takes effect where the offeror receives the communication whereas, generally speaking, acceptance using a noninstantaneous means of communication (such as the mail) can be effective on sending, that is, where the offeree is located. What then of communication by electronic means? Is this an instantaneous means of communication? Electronic mail is not quite like ordinary mail because, generally, it is significantly faster and it is often dependent on the actions of the recipient for arrival; it is not quite like a telephone because there is no direct line of communication between the parties and it is not always possible to verify whether the intended recipient has heard the message. Communications on the World Wide Web, however, can be interactive and in real time, therefore exhibiting characteristics of instantaneous means of communication.[23] The UECA has provisions specifying when a message is sent and when it is received, but it does not specify where an acceptance becomes effective. Therefore, unless electronic traders specify where acceptance becomes effective, the question of where an electronic contract is formed will be presumably decided on a case-by-case basis.

CRITICAL ANALYSIS: Legislation has removed some of the uncertainty about online contracting. However, questions still remain concerning whether communications on a website are an offer or invitation to do business and whether an electronic acceptance is effective on sending or receipt. What risks do these uncertainties pose for business? What steps can a business take to minimize these risks and avoid contractual disputes?

---

18. In Alberta, the *Electronic Transactions Act*, S.A. 2001, c. E-5.5; in British Columbia, the *Electronic Transactions Act*, S.B.C. 2001, c. 10; in Manitoba, the *Electronic Commerce and Information Act*, C.C.S.M. 2000, c. 32 plus amendments to the *Consumer Protection Act*, R.S.M. 1987, c.C-200 and the *Manitoba Evidence Act*, C.C.S.M. 1987, cE-150; in New Brunswick, the *Electronic Transactions Act*, S.N.B. 2001, c. E-5.5; in Newfoundland, the *Electronic Commerce Act*, S.N. 2000, c. E-5.2; in Nova Scotia, the *Electronic Commerce Act*, S.N.S. 2000, c. 26; in Ontario, the *Electronic Commerce Act*, S.O. 2000, c.17; in Prince Edward Island, the *Electronic Commerce Act*, S.P.E.I. 2001, c. 31; in Quebec, *An Act to Establish a Legal Framework for Information Technology*, S.Q. 2001, c. 32; in Saskatchewan, the *Electronic Information and Documents Act*, S.S. 2000, c. E-7.22; and in the Yukon, the *Electronic Commerce Act*, R.S.Y. 2002, c.66.
19. Barry Sookman, *Computer, Internet and Electronic Commerce Law*, vol. 3, looseleaf (Toronto: Carswell, 2002) at 10-15.
20. [1999] O.J. No. 3778 (Sup. Ct.).
21. The enforceability of these type of contracts—known as click-wrap agreements—is discussed in Chapter 7.
22. According to the UECA, s.19, an electronic agent is a computer program or electronic means used to initiate an action or to respond to electronic documents in whole or in part without review by an actual person at the time of the response or action. Electronic agents are discussed in Chapter 13.
23. *Supra* note 19 at 10-7.

Formalization

Even though the parties may have reached an agreement through offer and acceptance, this will not always produce an enforceable agreement. This is because a court will not enforce an agreement that the parties have decided will not be effective until the exact wording of the contract has been agreed upon and the contract has been written and signed. This kind of intention is signalled by phrases such as "this agreement is subject to formal contract." Unless and until the formal contract comes into existence, there are generally no enforceable obligations between the parties.

Consideration

The Nature of Consideration

consideration
The price paid for a promise.

A contract is a set of commitments or promises. It therefore entails a bargain or an exchange between the parties. Each party must give up something of value in exchange for receiving something of value from the other contracting party. In the example of the agreement between Jason and Amritha, it is clear that there is **consideration** on both sides of the transaction: the buyer promises to pay the purchase price in exchange for the seller's promise to provide tracking of the specified quality and quantity. Seen from the other perspective, the seller promises to provide tracking of the specified quality and quantity in exchange for the buyer's promise to pay the purchase price (see Figure 6.3). This bargain, or exchange of promises, is a classic example of the legal requirement of consideration.

Consideration is a key ingredient that distinguishes a legally enforceable promise from one that is not legally enforceable. If Trackers promises to provide tracking to Coasters at no charge and later changes its mind, Coasters cannot sue for breach of contract. Coasters has not given something back to Trackers in order to purchase Trackers's promise; accordingly, there is no contract in place, and any lawsuit by Coasters will fail. In law, Trackers has made a **gratuitous promise**—that is, a promise unsupported by consideration. Such promises can be broken with legal impunity. Conversely, if the parties have exchanged promises or something else of value, their obligations are contractual and therefore enforceable.

gratuitous promise
A promise for which no consideration is given.

As the above examples illustrate, a "price" must be paid for a promise before a party can sue when it is broken. Most commonly, the price for a promise to supply goods or services takes the form of another promise—including a promise to pay an agreed-upon sum in the future—or immediate payment of money. However, the consideration need not be monetary. The only requirement is that something of value be given up by the party seeking to purchase the promise of another. Furthermore, that item of value may be conferred on a third party and still amount to consideration, provided it was conferred at the request of the other side. For example, if Jason requested that the purchase price of the tracking be paid to a creditor of Trackers, Coasters's agreement to do so would support Trackers's promise to supply the tracking.

FIGURE 6.3

Consideration as an Exchange of Promises

Coasters

 promises to pay in consideration for Trackers's promise to supply

Trackers

 promises to supply in consideration for Coasters's promise to pay

---

The requirement for consideration is strongly linked to the idea of freedom of bargaining. Although the law requires that consideration be present on both sides of the transaction, it is up to the parties to negotiate a deal that is mutually acceptable. They, not a judge, decide what is a fair and reasonable price. Therefore, the adequacy of consideration is normally not open to challenge. If Amritha has agreed to pay a price for the tracking that turns out to be well above its market value, that is her choice. She cannot later go to a judge and ask that the price be lowered on that basis alone. The law will generally enforce a contract even where one party has agreed to pay too much because the parties are responsible for being fully informed of all aspects of the transaction and for evaluating the risks involved. If Amritha is concerned that she may end up paying too much for tracking, she should consult experts in the field and seek competing bids to help her establish a fair market price before accepting Jason's offer. Similarly, if one or both of the parties is concerned that the value of the goods or services contracted for may change between the time of agreement and the time of performance, a clause allowing the contract price to be adjusted for market fluctuations should be included in the contract. In short, parties are expected to take care of themselves and plan for contingencies.

Pre-existing Legal Duty

Just as a contract can be viewed as a set of promises, it can also be viewed as a set of duties. The consideration for each party's duties is the other party's duties. Once those duties or promises have been finalized, the contract is concluded. If the parties agree to alter the contract in a way that benefits only one of them, that alteration is unenforceable. In other words, a new promise needs new or fresh consideration. For example, if a contract provides that a project is to be completed on a particular date, a promise by the owner to pay an additional sum of money, say $2000, to ensure completion on that date is unenforceable. The promise to pay an additional $2000 is not supported by fresh consideration because completion on a particular date is already required under a contract. In short, it is a **pre-existing legal duty.**

pre-existing legal duty
A legal obligation that a person already owes.

CASE ▼

Gilbert Steel Ltd. v. University Construction Ltd., [1976], 12 O.R. (2d) 19 (C.A.)

THE BUSINESS CONTEXT: A business may enter into a contract that suddenly becomes unfavourable because of changes in the market. If it secures a concession from the other side in response to these changes, without regard to legal requirements, the concession may prove to be unenforceable.

FACTUAL BACKGROUND: Gilbert Steel (Gilbert) and University Construction (University) were in a contract that required Gilbert to supply a set amount of fabricated steel at an agreed-upon price. When steel prices rose dramatically, Gilbert asked University if it would pay more for the steel. University agreed but later refused to pay the increase and sent only payment for the originally agreed-upon price. Gilbert sued for breach of contract.

THE LEGAL QUESTION: Is there consideration supporting University's promise (i.e., what is Gilbert doing in return for University's promise to pay more for the steel)?

RESOLUTION: There is no consideration from Gilbert for University's promise, and it is therefore unenforceable. Gilbert is doing only what it is already contractually obliged to do—namely, supply steel to University. Put another way, Gilbert has a pre-existing legal duty to provide the steel and, accordingly, is giving nothing "extra" to University to support University's promise to pay more. The promise is therefore unenforceable, even though University made the second promise in good faith, possibly with a full intention to pay the higher price. Gilbert's action for breach of contract therefore fails.

Gilbert should have contemplated a rise in the cost of steel when setting the original price and built into the contract a formula permitting an increase in the contract price. Alternatively, it could have provided something in return for the higher price, such as earlier delivery or any other benefit that University requested. A final option would have been to get University's promise under seal (see below).

CRITICAL ANALYSIS: Does this rule concerning performance of a pre-existing legal duty reflect the reasonable expectations of both the parties involved and the broader business community?[24]

Variation of Contracts

The rule that performance of a pre-existing legal duty is not good consideration for a new promise also finds expression in the rule that all variations of a contract must be supported by "fresh" consideration. As *Gilbert Steel Ltd. v. University Construction Ltd.* illustrates, just as a contract needs to reflect a two-sided bargain, so must variations or changes to that contract. This is why University's promise to pay more for the steel is worthless without some corresponding concession from Gilbert.

If parties decide to terminate their contract and replace it with a new agreement altogether, consideration is automatically present because both sides have given something up—namely, the old contract. However, a judge will consider the substance of the transaction. If in reality only one side has given something up, then a variation has occurred, and a court will insist on evidence of fresh consideration to support it.

When Trackers, through Jason, asked Amritha's company to pay more for the steel, it was seeking a variation of the contract. Because Trackers did not provide anything new to Coasters in return, Coasters's commitment to pay an increased price was a gratuitous promise. The fact that Trackers supplied the steel on time does not count as consideration because Trackers had a pre-existing duty to do just that. On this basis, Coasters is not bound by its promise to pay more. Its only obligation is to pay the price recited in the contract that Amritha first negotiated. From a business perspective, however, its refusal to abide by its own promise will almost certainly destroy any possibility of Coasters and Trackers ever doing business together again.

Promises Enforceable without Consideration

Consideration is not always necessary for a contract or contractual variation to be enforceable. Important exceptions to the consideration requirement are promises under seal, promissory estoppel, and, in some jurisdictions, partial payment of a debt.

Promise under Seal

Before commercial negotiations became as commonplace and sophisticated as they are today, and before the rules of contract were fully developed, a practice originated to authenticate written agreements by putting hot wax beside the signature on a document and placing an imprint in the wax, unique to the person who signed. The use

---

24. In England, the law appears to be changing on this point. In *Williams v. Roffey Bros. & Nicholls (Contractors) Ltd.,* [1990] 1 All E.R. 512 (C.A.), the court held that variations of a contract do not always require legal consideration to be enforceable; a practical benefit is sufficient.

What is the purpose of placing a seal on a document?

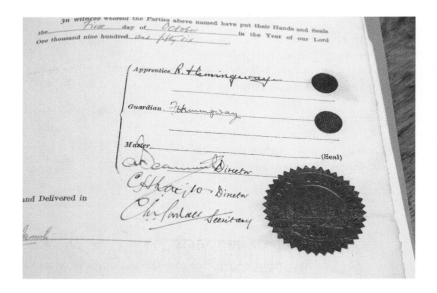

of a seal has evolved so that today the seal takes the form of a red gummed circle or wafer attached to the document beside the signature of the party making the promise. The legal effect is the same, however. If the document containing the promise is signed and the seal affixed, the fact that there may not be consideration for the promise is irrelevant. The seal is taken as evidence of serious intent by the promisor and amounts to an acknowledgment that the promise is enforceable, even if it is gratuitous. Contracts of guarantee, for example, typically have seals attached.[25]

Promissory Estoppel

Without a seal, a gratuitous promise is simply not enforceable at common law, even if made with great deliberation, and regardless of the adverse consequences to the person who relied on the promise. In response to the harshness that this common law rule could sometimes generate, courts began to assist parties through the equitable doctrine of **promissory estoppel.**

promissory estoppel
A doctrine whereby someone who relies on a gratuitous promise may be able to enforce it.

Promissory estoppel focuses on the idea of fairness, but since fairness is relatively subjective and courts are reluctant to stray too far from the doctrine of consideration, the party seeking to rely on the doctrine (Party A) must show that a number of distinct factors also exist in relation to the promise made by Party B, as listed below:

- Party B has, by words or conduct, made a promise or an assurance to Party A that was intended to affect their legal relationship and to be acted on.
- In reliance on the representation, Party A acted on it or in some way changed its position.[26]
- Party A's own conduct has been above reproach and, in this way, Party A is deserving of the court's assistance.

A final requirement is that promissory estoppel can be used only as a defence to legal claims made by the promise-breaker.[27]

---

25. Guarantees are discussed in detail in Chapter 26.
26. *Maracle v. Travellers Indemnity Co. of Canada*, [1991] 2 S.C.R. 50.
27. Most Canadian courts insist that promissory estoppel can be used only as a defence, though there is some case law to the contrary. See, for example, *Robichaud c. Caisse Populaire de Pokemouche ltée* (1990), 69 D.L.R. (4th) 589 (N.B.C.A.). Note that the doctrine of promissory estoppel cannot be used by Trackers to enforce Coasters's promise to pay more for the tracking. Trackers cannot sue on the promise—it can use it only as a defence.

Assume, for example, that Jason contacts Amritha one month before the delivery date specified in their contract. Jason tells her that Trackers is having minor production difficulties and so there is a chance that the tracking will be delivered three days late. He asks Amritha if this will be a problem for Coasters. He also wants to know if Coasters will insist on enforcing the late delivery clause in their contract obligating Trackers to pay $5000 per day for every day it is late. After securing instructions from her supervisor, Amritha gets back to Jason and tells him not to worry: "Jason, it poses no problem for us if you are up to one week late, and no, we won't come after you for late charges. We just want our tracking in good time." In the end, the tracking is delivered three days late, and Coasters suddenly takes the position that it is owed $15 000.

Coasters's promise not to rely on the late charges clause is unenforceable at common law because there is no consideration supporting it. Trackers is giving nothing back to Coasters in exchange for Coasters's promise to accept late delivery without complaint. For this reason, the common law would allow Coasters to go back on its word and collect the $15 000. However, there is an excellent chance that the doctrine of promissory estoppel would be applied by a judge to prevent this outcome because:

- Coasters promised not to rely on its contractual right to collect late charges.
- Trackers relied on this promise and changed its position by scheduling production accordingly and taking no additional steps to speed up its schedule.
- Trackers's conduct throughout has been beyond reproach—it did not threaten Coasters or otherwise place undue pressure on it to accept late delivery.
- Trackers is using the doctrine to defend itself from a claim by Coasters for the late charges.

For these kinds of reasons, Coasters would be estopped from relying on the late charges clause, and its action for $15 000 would fail.

Promissory estoppel is a relatively complicated doctrine and cannot be fully detailed here. The foregoing analysis is offered only as an introductory account of how the doctrine might arise in a business context.

Partial Payment of a Debt

A common difficulty encountered by a business arises when the customer cannot pay its account but offers a smaller amount to settle the debt in full. Can the business agree to the customer's proposal, accept the smaller amount, and then sue for the balance? Put another way, does the compromise on a bill amount to a binding contract, or is it simply a gratuitous promise by the creditor to accept a lesser amount? The discussion under promissory estoppel illustrates that equity may provide assistance to the debtor and enforce the creditor's promise. As well, the debtor may have recourse because she has provided consideration or because the new agreement is under seal. Finally, there may be a statute that makes the creditor's promise binding.

The rule that a creditor can go back on a promise to accept a lesser sum in full satisfaction of the debt has been reversed by legislation in several jurisdictions, including Ontario. Section 16 of Ontario's *Mercantile Law Amendment Act*, for example, essentially provides that once the lesser amount has been freely agreed upon and paid, the creditor cannot latter claim the full amount.[28] A policy rationale for the legislation is to promote settlement of debts on a final basis.

---

28. The *Merchantile Law Amendment Act*, R.S.O 1990, c. M.10, s. 16 states: "Part performance of an obligation either before or after breach thereof when expressly accepted by the creditor or rendered in pursuance of an agreement for that purpose, though without any new consideration, shall be held to extinguish the obligation." Similar provisions are in effect in British Columbia (*Law and Equity Act*, R.S.B.C. 1996, c. 253, s. 43); Manitoba (*Mercantile Law Amendment Act*, C.C.S.M., c. M120, s. 6 as amended by the *Law Reform (Miscellaneous Amendments) Act*, S.M. 1992, c. 32, s. 10); Saskatchewan (*Queen's Bench Act*, S.S. 1998, c. Q-1.01, s. 64); and Alberta (*Judicature Act*, R.S.A. 2000, c. J-2, s. 13).

For example, assume that Coasters has fallen on hard times and has been able to pay only $1 million on its account with Trackers. Therefore, $500 000 is outstanding. Trackers agrees to accept $300 000 from Coasters and write off the balance. At common law, Trackers can go back on its word and sue for the remaining $200 000 because its promise to accept a smaller sum is gratuitous. There is no consideration from Coasters supporting Trackers's promise to accept less than what is owed. Since Coasters has a pre-existing legal duty to pay $500 000, paying $300 000 is not consideration for Trackers's promise to forgive the balance. Put another way, Coasters is not giving Trackers anything in return for Trackers's promise, except a $300 000 payment that it was obligated to make in any event.

In jurisdictions that have legislation making such agreements binding, the creditor cannot sue for the balance once she has received from the debtor the smaller amount promised. In jurisdictions without such legislation, the creditor's promise is not enforceable. The consideration rule remains in force so that in order for the promise to be enforced, the creditor must give the promise under seal or receive something in return for her promise to accept less (such as payment earlier than required). Another alternative for the debtor seeking to enforce the creditor's promise is to rely on promissory estoppel, if circumstances permit.

Another question arises in jurisdictions governed by legislation on point when the debtor has agreed to pay a lesser sum by installments, over a period of time instead of all at once. What if creditor changes her mind halfway through and seeks repayment of the entire amount owed? While case law is somewhat unclear on this point, it would seem that the legislation, as drafted, does not cover such a scenario and therefore the common law applies. In such a situation, the creditor may well be able to sue for the entire amount owing.[29]

The varying status of how partially paid debts are handled across Canada illustrates two important aspects of contract law. First, provincial legislatures may intervene at any time to alter or override a common law rule governing contracts. Second, though largely uniform across the country, contract law is under provincial control and is therefore subject to important provincial variations.

Intention to Contract

The last important ingredient in a contract is the intention to contract. In order for one party to enforce the promise of another, the promise at issue must have been intended to be a contractual one, that is, one that would be enforceable by a court of law. Absent such an intention, there is no contract between the parties.

Business Agreements

Most agreements in the commercial world, such as the one between Trackers and Coasters, are quite obviously intended to be contractual. The common law recognizes this reality through the rule stating that in the marketplace, the intention to contract is *presumed*. Therefore, if Trackers ends up suing Coasters for breach of contract, it will not have to prove that the agreement between them was intended to be a contractual one. The law gives Trackers a presumption to this effect. The presumption is **rebuttable,** however. This means that while the court will assume that intention was present, Coasters can try to displace that presumption by proving a lack of intent to contract, judged objectively. Given the circumstances of its relationship with Trackers, Coasters faces an uphill battle on this point.

rebuttable presumption
A legal presumption in favour of one party that the other side can seek to rebut or dislodge by leading evidence to the contrary.

29. Christine Boyle and David Percy, eds. *Contracts: Cases and Commentaries,* 7th ed. (Scarborough: Carswell, 2004) at 216.

Family Agreements

Agreements between family members are regarded differently in law because of the personal nature of the underlying relationship. In fact, the common law presumes that promises between family members are noncontractual. Therefore, people who want to enforce an alleged contract against their parents or siblings, for example, must demonstrate to a court that there was an intention to contract. If they cannot positively prove that intent, their action will fail.

Managing the Risks in Contract Formation

Negotiators such as Jason and Amritha face two main risks. The first is the risk of misunderstanding when statements and conduct have legal consequences. For example, if Amritha makes what objectively looks like an offer to Jason, he is entitled to accept it and a contract is thus formed. Amritha cannot then go back and unilaterally amend the terms of her offer. The second risk is failing to anticipate and plan for contingencies that might occur after the contract has been formed. For example, if Jason agrees to supply tracking at a set price and later faces a substantial increase in production costs, Trackers still must provide the tracking as agreed, even though this will cause enormous financial hardship to Trackers. Customizing contractual terms in order to accommodate future contingencies such as these is discussed further in Chapter 7.

Business Law in Practice Revisited

1. At what point did the negotiations between Jason and Amritha begin to have legal consequences?

When Jason made an offer to sell tracking on specific terms, his negotiations with Amritha took a legal turn. At this point, Amritha was in a position to accept Jason's offer and, if she did, Trackers would be obligated to supply tracking on precisely those terms.

2. In what ways could negotiations have been terminated prior to the formation of the contract?

Amritha could have ended her negotiations by rejecting Jason's offer and telling him that Coasters would be looking elsewhere for its tracking. Though Amritha is not legally obligated to reject an offer, it is helpful to do so to ensure clarity and to avoid misunderstandings and disappointed expectations later on. Amritha should also withdraw any offer she may have made on behalf of Coasters to prevent Jason from accepting it sometime down the road. While the doctrine of lapse will prevent Jason from accepting after a certain point in time, it is difficult to predict how long a court would consider the offer to be open. It is preferable to simply withdraw the offer and avoid the debate altogether.

3. Can Coasters commit itself to the price increase and then change its mind with no adverse consequences?

Trackers has a pre-existing legal duty to supply the tracking at the price stated in the contract. Since it has given Coasters nothing in return for its promise to pay more, Coasters has no legal obligation to pay the increase. Put another way, the promise is gratuitous. Any change to a contract—known in law as a "variation"—must be supported by consideration or be under seal in order to be enforceable.

There is, however, a significant consequence to Coasters's decision from a business perspective: its relationship with Trackers will be seriously harmed and possibly destroyed. If Coasters ever needs tracking again, it is unlikely that Trackers will agree to be its supplier.

4. **How could Trackers have avoided from the outset this situation related to cost increases?**

Trackers should have negotiated a clause in the contract that included a formula for varying the price according to prevailing market conditions, as established by a third party, trade journal, or other source. Other possibilities include negotiating a "cost plus contract," meaning the contract price would comprise the tracking manufacturer's actual costs, plus a set percentage of profit. Another alternative would have been to charge a higher price to begin with to cover unexpected cost escalations.

If Trackers were unsuccessful in getting such price adjustment mechanisms into the contract, it would assume the full risk of unanticipated cost increases. If Coasters did subsequently agree to pay more for the steel, Trackers should provide consideration for that promise or get it under seal.

Chapter Summary

A contract comprises four essential elements: an offer, an acceptance, consideration, and an intention to contract. Before a contract can be formed, one party must make an offer on a complete set of certain terms. An offer can be terminated in a number of ways, including by revocation, lapse, rejection, counteroffer, death, or insanity. Assuming that an offer is on the table, the other party must unconditionally accept all the terms of the offer. Each party must give something (called consideration) in exchange for the promise or performance of the other. The parties must intend their bargain to be a contractual one. If any one of these elements is missing, the relationship is noncontractual by definition.

There are rare occasions, however, when the law will enforce a promise that is not supported by consideration. In short, if the promise is under seal, meets the requirements of promissory estoppel, or is subject to a specialized statutory scheme, such as the partial payment of debt, it will be enforceable. Aside from these exceptions, a gratuitous promise is not binding, no matter how seriously it was intended and no matter how much the other party may have relied on it. This legal reality is particularly important when varying a term in an existing contract.

While the conditions for creating a legal agreement may seem stringent, they serve an important purpose. Contract law is about creating voluntary agreements and is therefore facilitative. In sum, it helps those in the marketplace to determine—in advance of litigation—the legal enforceability of commitments they have received, and thereby lets them do business more effectively.

Chapter Study

Key Terms and Concepts

acceptance (p. 120)

consideration (p. 127)

counteroffer (p. 119)

gratuitous promise (p. 127)

invitation to treat (p. 113)

lapse (p. 119)

offer (p. 113)

offeree (p. 116)

offeror (p. 116)

option agreement (p. 119)

pre-existing legal duty (p. 128)

promissory estoppel (p. 130)

rebuttable presumption (p. 132)

rejection (p. 119)

revocation (p. 118)

Questions for Review

1. What must an offer contain?

2. Is an advertisement an offer or an invitation to treat? Why?

3. Are oral contracts enforceable?

4. Explain why it might be a good idea to get a contract in writing.

5. Does the acceptance of an offer have to mirror it exactly, or are slight variations permissible?

6. What is the "postal rule"?

7. How is the postal rule different from the "ordinary rule" for acceptance?

8. When must an offeree communicate acceptance to the offeror in a specific form?

9. What is the effect of a counteroffer?

10. When can an offeror revoke or withdraw an offer?

11. What is consideration?

12. What is an option agreement? How is the concept of consideration related to the enforceability of such an agreement?

13. What is the key question relating to consideration in the enforceability of a promise?

14. What is a pre-existing legal duty?

15. Why is a promise to pay more for performance of a pre-existing legal duty generally not enforceable?

16. What is a gratuitous promise? Give an example.

17. Are the rules governing the formation of electronic contracts any different than those for written or oral contracts?

18. How does the relationship between the parties affect presumptions concerning their contractual intent?

Questions for Critical Thinking

1. Even when a promise is relied on, this is ordinarily not enough to make it enforceable. Only if the promise is supported by consideration does it become contractual. Is the consideration requirement reasonable, or should all promises be legally enforceable if they were seriously intended?

2. Family members are presumed not to intend legal relations, while businesspeople are subject to the opposite presumption, namely that an intention to create legal relations is intended. Why should the relationship between the parties affect the enforceability of their promises?

3. When the common law rules of contract were being formed by the judiciary, paper correspondence was the only form of distance communication. Are the traditional rules of contract formation appropriate for modern methods of communication?

4. What risks do negotiators face if they lack knowledge of the rules of contract?

5. Do you agree with the following quotation posted by the Coalition Against Commercial Email, attributed to Mr. Vint Cerf (frequently called the father of the Internet):

   > Spamming is the scourge of electronic-mail and newsgroups on the Internet. It can seriously interfere with the operation of public services, to say nothing of the effect it may have on any individual's e-mail system. . . . Spammers are, in effect, taking resources away from users and service suppliers without compensation and without authorization. (Note: See http://www.cauce.org/about/problem.shtml.)

6. Given our current reliance on electronic technology, electronic contracting will undoubtedly become increasingly common in the commercial arena. What are some of the advantages of this development? What might be some of the disadvantages?

Situations for Discussion

1. Mr. Gaff made the following written offer to Ms. Paulo:

   MEMO FROM: J. Gaff
   TO: R. Paulo
   DATE: June 7, 2000
   I hereby agree to sell to R. Paulo my entire fleet of Rolls-Royce automobiles for the sum of $1 million.
   This offer is open until Friday, June 9, 2000, at 9:00 a.m.

   On Thursday, June 8, Gaff decided to sell the cars to his well-to-do neighbour instead. Paulo heard about the alleged sale later that same day and rushed over to Gaff's house, stating that she wished to accept Gaff's offer. Gaff smiled and said, "Sorry, you're too late. I've sold to someone else." Is Gaff obligated to keep the offer open until the specified time? What could Paulo have done to better protect her position?

2. An advertisement similar to the following appeared in a popular Canadian business magazine. What legal obligations does it create for Star?

At ★Star★ We try harder!!

Any car rental company will reserve you a car.
Only ★Star★ tries harder to get you where you're going.

3. Greedy Cablevision provided various packages of cable television channels to its customers. When the regulatory authority approved five new channels, Greedy provided the new channels free for one month. Greedy informed its customers in a letter included with their regular monthly bills that unless customers notified Greedy by a specific date that they did not want the extra channels, a $5 monthly charge would be added to each bill. Does Greedy's policy on the new channels fit the rules of offer and acceptance? Are customers obligated to pay if they fail to notify Greedy? What other methods could Greedy use to persuade customers to order the new channels?

4. On 30 October, Casgrain offered to purchase some farmland from Butler for $14 500 with possession in January. On 15 November, Butler counteroffered, by telegram, at $15 000. The telegram was delivered to Casgrain's home on 20 November but Casgrain was absent on a hunting trip. Casgrain's wife opened the letter and wrote back to Butler saying that her husband was away for ten days and asked that he hold the deal open until Casgrain could consider the matter. Butler did not respond. On 10 December, Casgrain returned home and immediately wired Butler, purporting to accept Butler's offer of $15 000. The wire was received on 12 December. By this time, Butler had already sold the land to someone else. Has Casgrain accepted the offer in time or has it lapsed?[30]

5. Cogan was a long-standing season ticket holder to Toronto Blue Jays baseball games and had made a practice of allowing his friends and business associates—Sherman and Fingold—to purchase some of those tickets. It was agreed that Cogan would provide them with a total of six tickets per season. After ten years, Cogan decided to discontinue this practice, since he no longer had any social or business dealings with these individuals and his children had expressed the wish to have additional baseball tickets. Do Cogan and his friends have a contractual relationship? Which of the four requirements for a contract is in doubt?[31]

6. Jawa supplied a product to Luke but Luke has yet to pay Jawa's account of $1000. Luke has told Jawa that he cannot and will not pay the full amount and that Jawa had just better be satisfied with a cheque for $500. "Take it or leave it," said Luke. Jawa took the cheque and cashed it, feeling that he had no choice in the matter. He would now like to go after Luke for the balance. Can he do so?

7. April manufactures leather chairs and sofas, and is happy because she has just negotiated a contract with Bob's Fine Furnishings, Ltd., to supply them with her handmade furniture. The terms of the contract are that on the first Monday of every month, April is to send over ten chairs and two sofas, and Bob's Fine Furnishings will pay her $7000. She is excited to learn that her furniture is so popular that Bob's Fine Furnishings has a waiting list of customers who have pre-paid for their chairs, as her last shipment sold out in only a week. April is a little worried, however, as she has just received a phone call saying that her leather supplier will not be able to send her any

30. Based, in part, on *Barrick v. Clark*, [1951] S.C.R. 177.
31. Based, in part, on *Fobasco Ltd. v. Cogan*, [1990] 72 O.R. (2d) 254 (H.C.J.).

leather for the next three months, as there is a local shortage. Without the leather, she knows she cannot fill her order for Bob's Fine Furnishings by the first Monday of the month, much less for the two months after that. What could April have done when negotiating the contract with Bob's Fine Furnishings to help manage the risk of a situation like this? What should she do now that the contract is already in place?

8. Quentin, a friend, was helping to renovate George's home. George realized he needed some pipe to complete a plumbing installation, but didn't have any cash on him, so Quentin gave him $5.00. In consideration of that, George said that he would share his $10.00 Super Lotto ticket with Quentin. George then took the $5.00, bought the pipe, and Quentin installed it. Later that month, George was declared the winner of the lottery draw, in the amount of $1 000 000. He tried to hide that fact that he had won, denying to Quentin that he was the winner. He later told him that he had won only $50 000 and, in any case, that the winner was one of five tickets he had purchased after the one he said he'd split with Quentin.[32] Does Quentin have an enforceable contract with George, such that he's entitled to half of the $1 000 000? What do you think his chances are if he tries to sue George to enforce the contract? Would they be better or worse if George hadn't denied winning in the first place?

For more study tools, visit
http://www.businesslaw3e.nelson.com

---

32. Based, in part, on *Quiamco v. Gaspar*, [1985] B.C.J. No. 1661 (C.A.) (QL).

Chapter

7

Objectives

After studying this chapter, you should have an understanding of

- the difference between implied and express terms
- how judges determine and interpret the content of a contract
- how a party can use terms as a business tool to protect itself from liability

ITATION OF REMEDIES.

SELLER

By_____

Title:____

dges he/she ___ ad, understands
RRANTY, ___ ATIONS OF
GES and is aut ___ to execute th

TERMS A ___ COND

bject to the follow ___ and c

The Terms
of a
Contract

Business Law in Practice

The dispute discussed in Chapter 6 between Coasters and Trackers over the purchase price was resolved reasonably amicably—the parties agreed to split the increased cost of the steel required to manufacture the tracking and thereby avoid the expense and disruption of litigation. All the tracking has been delivered, and the new purchase price has been paid. Jason is tremendously relieved but also wants to improve his performance as a negotiator, since matters did not proceed entirely smoothly. He is reviewing the Coasters–Trackers contract to determine whether it did, in fact, contain the terms Trackers needed to protect itself.

The contract between Coasters and Trackers covered a number of terms already discussed in the previous chapter, including price ($1.5 million); quantity (900 metres); delivery dates; and late-delivery charges ($5000 a day). Other significant clauses are excerpted below.

Excerpt from the contract between Trackers (the "Seller") and Coasters (the "Buyer") for the purchase and sale of tracking (the "Goods")

...

12. Warranties—Guarantees.

    Seller warrants that the goods shall be free from defect in material, workmanship, and title and shall conform in all respects to the design specifications provided by Buyer and attached as Appendix A to this contract. Where no quality is specified, the quality shall be of the best quality.

    If it appears within one year from the date of placing the goods into service for the purpose for which they were purchased that the Goods, or any part thereof, does not conform to these warranties, Buyer, at its election and within a reasonable time after its discovery, may notify Seller. If notified, Seller shall thereupon promptly correct such nonconformity at its sole expense.

...

13. Limitation of Seller's Liability.

    Except as otherwise provided in this contract, Seller's liability shall extend to all damages proximately caused by the breach of any of the foregoing warranties or guarantees, but such liability shall in no event exceed unit price of defective Goods and in no event include loss of profit or loss of use.

...

14. Exemption of Seller's Liability.

    Seller is exempted from all liability in respect to losses, damages, costs, or claims relating to design of Goods.

...

20. Entire Contract.

    This is the entire agreement between the parties, covering everything agreed upon or understood in connection with the subject matter of this transaction. There are no oral promises, conditions, representations, understandings, interpretations, or terms of any nature or kind, statutory or otherwise, as conditions or inducements to the execution hereof or in effect between the parties or upon which the parties are relying relating to this agreement or otherwise.

---

1. How is the scope of Trackers's and Coasters's obligations determined?
2. Are there any ambiguous or unclear terms in the contract?
3. Are there any additional terms that Jason should have tried to have included?
4. Does the contract relieve the parties from responsibility for inadequate performance?

The Content of a Contract

This chapter is about the content—or terms—of a contract and how the courts interpret those terms. The terms of a contract simply refer to promises made by one party to another by virtue of offer and acceptance. From a risk management perspective, a contract is a business tool that can be used to manage a business's exposure to liability—also the subject matter of this chapter.

Terms

Contractual terms can be express or implied.

Express Terms

express term
A provision of a contract that states a promise explicitly.

An **express term** is a provision of the contract that states or makes explicit one party's promise to another. In the Coasters–Trackers contract, for example, a number of terms are express, including the price, quantity, and warranties associated with the tracking. It is important that the essential terms of a contract be express so that each party knows its obligations and the obligations of the other side. Parties negotiating a contract should be very careful not to make assumptions about any aspect of the transaction, as only terms, not assumptions, have legal weight.

Judicial Interpretation of Express Terms

Vague or Ambiguous Language Even when a term is express, there may be problems interpreting what it means because the language is vague or ambiguous. Assuming that the existence of the contract is not in doubt, the court assigns as reasonable a meaning as possible to vague or ambiguous terms.[1] As well, if the contract has been drafted by one of the parties, any ambiguity in language will be construed against that party in favour of the other.[2] The policy rationale for this rule is that the drafter should bear the risk of unclear language.

The reference to "best quality" in clause 12 of the Coasters–Trackers contract is somewhat nebulous, as it introduces an express element of subjectivity: What, exactly, is "best quality?" If faced with such a question, a court would conclude that "best quality" refers to the highest quality available, which, in turn, is a matter that expert evidence would establish. A court would not set the contract aside for uncertainty because some meaning can be assigned to the phrase "best quality."

There is a point, however, at which language is so ambiguous that the contract cannot be understood. In such cases, the contract will fail for uncertainty, and none of the promises it contains will be enforceable.

rules of construction
Guiding principles for interpreting or "constructing" the terms of a contract.

It can be very difficult to predict how a court will interpret any given contract because **rules of construction**—that is, guiding principles for interpreting or "constructing" the terms of a contract—are often conflicting. For example, on the

---

1. Christine Boyle & David R. Percy, eds., *Contracts: Cases and Commentaries*, 7th ed. (Scarborough: Carswell, 2004) at 127.
2. *Ibid.* at 540.

one hand, courts are required to enforce the contract as it is written and to rely primarily on the plain, ordinary meaning of the words that the parties have chosen. The court simply asks how a reasonable person would regard the term in question and can refer to dictionaries, legal reference materials, and cases that have considered such terms in the past. On the other hand, courts are to give effect to the parties' intentions. Both of these rules make sense standing alone, but they do not provide a solution to the situation in which the parties' intentions may be inadequately reflected in the written contract itself. Should the court apply the plain-meaning rule or give effect to the parties' intentions? Which rule should prevail?

In the Coasters–Trackers contract, Trackers promised to pay $5000 to Coasters for every day it was late in delivering the tracking. The intent of the parties, objectively assessed, may have been to motivate Trackers to do everything in its power to provide the tracking by the contractual delivery date. On this basis, if Trackers were late delivering because of a mechanical problem in its plant, the clause would apply. It would be more contentious to apply the clause if late delivery were caused by an event completely outside Trackers's control—such as a severe lightning strike disrupting electricity to its plant for several days. Trackers might advance the position that to apply the clause in such circumstances would be contrary to the parties' intention.

In response, Coasters would ask that the court apply the plain-meaning rule and disregard evidence of the parties' intention. On the basis of the plain-meaning rule, a court could easily conclude that the late-delivery clause speaks for itself and is unconditional: if Trackers delivers late, it has to pay $5000 per day. Whether a court would use the plain-meaning rule standing alone or allow the clause's plain meaning to be tempered with evidence of what the parties intended the term to mean is impossible to predict—another inherent risk of litigation.

Trackers could face further problems in convincing a court of its interpretation of the late-delivery clause based on the parties' intention. Two possible sources of problems are the parol evidence rule and the fact that the Coasters–Trackers contract contains what is known as an entire contract clause. Both matters are discussed later in this chapter.

When parties fail to address an important aspect of their contractual relationship, the law may help to "fill in the blanks" through implied terms, discussed below. The assistance that implied terms can provide, however, is sporadic and cannot be relied on with any certainty.

Implied Terms

When an event arises that is not addressed in the contract through express terms, courts may be asked to imply a term in order to give effect to the parties' intention. A judge will do so if satisfied that not all of the terms that the parties intended to include in the contract were in fact included. In the classic scenario, the plaintiff argues to include an **implied term** but the defendant asserts that no such term was intended. Since the plaintiff carries the burden of proof, she will lose unless she can demonstrate that the term exists based on the balance of probabilities (i.e., she needs to prove that it is more likely than not that the parties intended such a term to be included).

Courts will imply terms based on a number of grounds, such as those listed below.

implied term

A provision that is not expressly included in a contract but that is necessary to give effect to the parties' intention.

Business Efficacy Through the doctrine of business efficacy[3] a judge is entitled to imply terms necessary to make the contract workable. For example, if Trackers promised to use a certain grade of steel, "providing it is available," a court will almost certainly imply a promise by Trackers to put reasonable effort into trying to find that grade of steel. Though Trackers has not expressly committed itself to make systematic efforts in this regard, business efficacy makes the obligation implicit. Were it otherwise, the express term in relation to the quality of steel would mean next to nothing.[4]

A term that courts are increasingly willing to imply as part of commercial contracts is that of good faith, owing, in large part, to the influence of the following case.

Landmark Case ▼

Gateway v. Arton Holdings Ltd. (1991), 106 N.S.R. (2d) 180 (S.C.), aff'd (1992), 112 N.S.R. (2d) 180 (C.A.)

THE BUSINESS CONTEXT: Businesspeople may assume that the only obligations they owe the other party are those recited in the contract between them. This assumption may prove to be unfounded, particularly in the situation where one party is in a position to adversely affect the interests of the other.

FACTUAL BACKGROUND: Gateway owned a shopping mall in which Zellers was the anchor tenant. The lease permitted Zellers to occupy the premises, leave them vacant, or assign them to a third party without any obligation to secure the consent of the landlord. After being approached by Arton, a competitor of Gateway, Zellers agreed to locate in Arton's mall. As part of this arrangement, Arton agreed to take an assignment of Zellers's lease with Gateway. As a result, a large part of Gateway's mall had been assigned to its competitor. Pursuant to a subsequent contract between Gateway and Arton, the companies agreed to use their best efforts to get a tenant for the space formerly occupied by Zellers. Arton, however, rejected all prospective tenants. Gateway then sued, alleging that Arton was in breach of contract for declining prospective tenants. From Gateway's perspective, Arton was simply trying to undermine the economic viability of the mall by letting a large portion of it remain unoccupied.

THE LEGAL QUESTION: Is there an implied obligation of good faith on Arton's part to take reasonable steps to sublet the premises?

RESOLUTION: The court found that Arton breached the express obligation to use its "best efforts" to find a tenant, as well as an implied term to act in good faith.

According to the court

> The law requires that parties to a contract exercise their rights under that agreement honestly, fairly and in good faith. This standard is breached when a party acts in a bad faith manner in the performance of its rights and obligations under the contract. "Good faith" conduct is the guide to the manner in which the parties should pursue their mutual contractual objectives. Such conduct is breached when a party acts in "bad faith"—a conduct that is contrary to community standards of honesty, reasonableness or fairness.

The court went on to say

> In most cases, bad faith can be said to occur when one party, without reasonable justification, acts in relation to the contract in a manner where the result would be to substantially nullify the bargained objective or benefit contracted for by the other, or to cause significant harm to the other, contrary to the original purpose and expectation of the parties.

---

3. G.H.L. Fridman, *The Law of Contract in Canada*, 4th ed. (Scarborough: Carswell, 1999) at 502.
4. For a case that follows this analysis, see *Dawson v. Helicopter Exploration Co.*, [1955] S.C.R. 868.

Customs in the Trade of the Transaction   Relying on trade customs to imply a term is rarely successful, since it must be proved that the custom is so notorious that the contract in question must be presumed to contain such an implied term.[5] Though a party is occasionally successful in relying on custom in a trade, the more prudent course is to ensure that all important terms in a contract are expressly recited.

CASE ▼

Glenko Enterprises Ltd. v. Ernie Keller Contractors Ltd., [1994] 10 W.W.R. 641 (Man. Q.B.), aff'd [1996] 5 W.W.R. 135 (Man. C.A.)

THE BUSINESS CONTEXT: Unpaid accounts are an unfortunate reality of the business world. Even when the customer admits that the account is owed, disputes can arise on the rate of interest payable if the contract does not expressly address this matter.

FACTUAL BACKGROUND: Though a number of factual and legal matters were at play in this case, it is most germane to note that the subcontractor, Glenko Enterprises Ltd., worked on a project but was not paid by the project contractor (Ernie Keller Contractors Ltd.). The contractor admitted that it owed $123 862.75 but insisted that since no interest had been stipulated in the contract, no interest on the overdue account should be payable. The plaintiff stated that interest was owed at the rate of 1.5 percent per month or 18 percent per annum on accounts over 30 days for three reasons:

- there was an implied agreement that such interest was payable based on the term being contained in the invoices sent to the contractor

- the contractor did not object to the term regarding interest and, on the contrary, continued to deal with the subcontractor

- it is a common trade practice to be charged and to pay interest on overdue accounts. The contractor itself included such an interest provision in its own invoices.

THE LEGAL QUESTION: Since the contract between the contractor and subcontractor was silent on the point of interest, what interest, if any, would be payable? Could a term be implied based on trade custom?

RESOLUTION: Even though this matter was not extensively discussed at trial, the judge ruled that the contractor was aware of and followed an industry practice of charging interest on overdue accounts. This was largely because the contractor had itself included a provision for interest in its own invoices. The plaintiffs were therefore entitled to the interest as claimed.

CRITICAL ANALYSIS: Why should industry or trade practice be relevant to understanding the parties' contractual obligations? Would it not be simpler for a court to apply the contractual terms as stated and refuse to look outside that document? What are the risks of relying on industry practices as a way of implying terms into a contract?

---

5.   *Supra* note 3 at 512.

Previous Dealings between the Parties If parties have contracted in the past, it may be possible to imply that their current contract contains the same terms.[6] A risk management perspective would suggest, however, that the parties clarify the basis of their contractual relationship each time they do business with each other.

Statutory Requirements An important source of terms implied by statute[7] is found in provincial sale-of-goods legislation, which is largely uniform across the country. This legislation provides that certain terms are a mandatory part of every contract for the sale of goods unless specifically excluded by the parties.[8] Specialized rules governing the sale of goods and the extent to which consumer transactions can exclude their application are discussed in more detail in Chapter 23.

If Trackers delivers too much tracking to Coasters under its contract, the Ontario *Sale of Goods Act*,[9] for example, would resolve the situation according to the following rule:

> 29. (2) Where the seller delivers to the buyer a quantity of goods larger than the seller contracted to sell, the buyer may accept the goods included in the contract and reject the rest, or may reject the whole, and if the buyer accepts the whole of the goods so delivered, the buyer shall pay for them at the contract rate.[10]

contractual *quantum meruit*
Awarding one party a reasonable sum for the goods or services provided under a contract.

Business Application of the Law

A Request for Goods or Services: Implying a Promise to Pay

When someone requests the supply of goods or services, the law—be it through common law or by applicable legislation such as the *Sale of Goods Act*—will imply a promise to pay a reasonable price for those goods or services. The law draws this conclusion because, in a business situation, it is the intention of the parties that goods or services are not to be provided for free, but rather are to be purchased. Implying such a term reflects what can only be the reasonable expectation of the parties—especially that of the seller—and is needed to give purpose and effect to the rest of the contract. If the goods or services have already been provided but there has been no agreement on price, a term must be implied to require payment. The obligation on the customer is not to pay whatever the supplier chooses to charge or whatever the customer is willing to pay, but to pay a reasonable amount, as determined by the judge. This is known as a **contractual *quantum meruit*,** which is Latin for "as much as is merited or deserved." Given the expense and uncertainty of judicial proceedings, it is in the interests of both parties to agree on the price, in advance, as an express term. The objective is to avoid the surprises and misunderstandings that may lead to a legal dispute.

---

6. *Supra* note 3 at 510.
7. For discussion, see *supra* note 3 at 514.
8. For a discussion of sale of goods legislation, see G.H.L. Fridman, *Sale of Goods in Canada*, 5th ed. (Scarborough: Carswell, 2004).
9. R.S.O. 1990, c. S-1.
10. Sale of goods legislation imports a number of other rules governing a contract for the sale of goods, discussed further in Chapter 23.

In general, terms are not easily implied except in routine transactions or unless the *Sale of Goods Act* applies. It must be clear that both parties would have included the term in question, had they addressed the matter.

CASE ▼

Abramowich v. Azima Developments Ltd.
(1993), 86 B.C.L.R. (2d) 129 (B.C. C.A.)

THE BUSINESS CONTEXT: When a housing development company markets its projects to potential consumers, there can be a variety of promotional literature designed to increase sales. If a purchaser later complains that the house or condominium purchased is contractually deficient because it does not accord with descriptions in the promotional material, the developer may be sued for breach of contract. Whether the action is successful depends on what the court decides are the terms of the contract in question.

FACTUAL BACKGROUND: The plaintiff (purchaser) entered into a contract with the defendant (vendor) for the purchase of a condominium that was to be built. The plaintiff was dissatisfied with the condominium ultimately delivered to him for a number of reasons, including that it did not accord with the description contained in a sales brochure prepared by the defendant. The plaintiff sued, claiming, among other matters, that it was an implied term of the contract that the condominium would match the standards described in a brochure. The brochure stated that the condominium would be a "luxurious city home"; of "exceptional quality"; have an "architect designed interior"; and have "first class finishings."

THE LEGAL QUESTION: Was there an implied term in the contract that the condominium would correspond to the description in the brochure?

RESOLUTION: The British Columbia Court of Appeal agreed with the trial judge that no such term should be implied. Not only was it difficult to determine what standard the brochure description mandated, it was also the case that courts imply terms only in limited circumstances. Both the trial judge and the Court of Appeal relied on the following quotation from an English decision known as *Trollope & Colls Ltd. v. North West Metropolitan Regional Hospital Board*:[11]

> An unexpressed term can be implied if and only if the court finds that the parties must have intended that term to form part of their contract: it is not enough for the court to find that such a term would have been adopted by the parties as reasonable men[12] if it had been suggested to them: it must have been a term that went without saying, a term necessary to give business efficacy to the contract, a term which, although tacit, formed part of the contract which the parties made for themselves.

The Court of Appeal agreed that business efficacy did not require implying the term advanced by the plaintiff. It was enough to imply that the vendor was required to complete the condominium in accordance with the unit's plans and specifications.

CRITICAL ANALYSIS: Why did the court decide that the brochure description was not an implied term of the contract? Do you agree with the court's analysis? How should the purchaser have ensured that the description in the brochure was a part of the contract? Would this have changed the outcome in the case?

entire contract clause
A term in a contract in which the parties agree that their contract is complete as written.

Similarly, courts ordinarily will not imply terms when the parties have agreed that their contract is complete as written. The clearest way parties can signal this intention is through an **entire contract clause** like the one in the Coasters–Trackers contract excerpted earlier in this chapter. The function of this clause is to require a court to determine the parties' obligations based only on what is recited in the contract itself. Such a clause is not essential to exclude implied terms, however, as the *Abramowich* case above illustrates.

---

11. [1973] 2 All E.R. 260 (H.L.) at 268.
12. Regrettably, it is only recently that the judiciary has begun to use inclusive language.

The Parol Evidence Rule

Contracts can take three possible forms:

- entirely oral (i.e., the terms of the contract are based on a conversation)
- entirely written (i.e., the terms of the contract are contained in a written contract)
- both oral and written (i.e., some of the agreement is written down and other assurances are not). For example, if Jason gave Amritha an oral assurance that Trackers would provide expert advice on how to install the tracking as a service included in the contract price, their contract would be both oral and written.

Except in a few specialized instances discussed in Chapter 8, the form a contract takes does not affect its enforceability. So long as the party claiming that there is a contract can prove it—through witnesses, for example—the fact that the parties only "shook hands" on the deal is not an impediment. Nevertheless, from the perspective of proving the contract, a written contract is always best.

There is an important consequence to having a written contract. Such contracts may trigger the **parol evidence rule** when a court is asked to determine— according to the parties' intentions—what a contract means and includes. "Parol" means "oral" or "spoken" but in this context refers to any kind of evidence that is extrinsic to the written agreement. The rule forbids outside evidence as to the terms of a contract when the language of the written contract is clear and the document is intended to be the sole source of contractual content. In the example just above, the parol evidence rule may prohibit Amritha from bringing forward evidence of Jason's oral promise to provide expert installation advice. For this reason, a businessperson must be careful not to rely on oral assurances made by the other party, because if the assurance is not in the contract, a court may decline to enforce it as a contractual term.

parol evidence rule
A rule that limits the evidence a party can introduce concerning the contents of the contract.

Entire contract clauses are used to ensure application of the parol evidence rule to the contract in question. As noted earlier, such clauses generally operate to prevent a party from arguing that the terms of the agreement were found not just in the written document, but also in oral form. Clause 20 of the Coasters–Trackers contract is an entire contract clause. Such a clause is intended to ensure that any oral commitment made by one side to the other that is not ultimately written into the contract simply dies.

The parol evidence rule emphasizes the sanctity of the written agreement and means that the parties should, before agreeing to a written contract, ensure provision of all terms important to them. Failure to do so may mean that the rule is invoked against the party that cannot support its interpretation of the contract without leading evidence "outside" the contract.

The parol evidence rule has itself become the subject of judicial consideration, which in turn has justifiably limited its operation. Indeed, there are several situations where evidence outside the contract is important and is considered:

- If there is an alleged problem going to the formation of the contract—because one party alleges fraud at the hands of the other or asserts that there has been a mistake, for example—a party may bring to the court evidence to establish that allegation. Chapter 8 considers problems going to the formation of a contract in more detail.
- If the contract is *intended* to be partly oral and partly in writing, the rule has no application. The rule applies only when the parties intended the document to be the whole contract.
- If the promise to be enforced is contained in a separate (collateral) agreement that happens to be oral, the rule does not apply. For example, an agreement to sell for a set price a building with all the equipment in it may not include the equipment if the written agreement fails to mention it. If there is a separate agreement and a separate price for the equipment, however, the fact that the agreement for the building says nothing about the equipment is likely not a concern. The difference in the two situations is in the matter of there being separate consideration for the building and the equipment. If there is only one agreement and one price, the rule likely applies to the detriment of the party seeking to enforce the purchase and sale of the equipment.
- If the language in the contract is ambiguous, evidence outside the written contract can be used to resolve the ambiguity.

The following case demonstrates how even an entire contract clause may not prevent a court from considering parol evidence.

CASE ▼

Corey Developments Inc. v. Eastbridge Developments (Waterloo) Ltd. (1997), 34 O.R. (3d) 73, aff'd (1999), 44 O.R. (3d) 95 (C.A.)

THE BUSINESS CONTEXT: The parol evidence rule in its absolute form may cause manifest injustice and defeat the true intentions of the parties. Thus, almost from its inception, it has been subject to many exceptions. In recent times, the rule has also received disapproval from various law reform commissions. As well, several provinces have abolished the rule altogether in consumer situations. Consumer protection legislation in these provinces effectively makes oral precontractual statements supersede written terms.

In commercial transactions, the parol evidence rule has generally prevented the introduction of extrinsic evidence in challenging the written document (usually a standard form contract) and establishing the existence of oral promises. This treatment of the parol evidence rule as an absolute bar in commercial transactions has recently come under attack, however.

FACTUAL BACKGROUND: Corey Developments Inc. signed an agreement of purchase and sale with Eastbridge Developments Ltd., which was controlled by Mr. Ghermezian, a well-known Alberta developer. Corey gave a deposit of $201 500 to Eastbridge. According to Corey, as the money was to be used by Eastbridge to fund the costs of obtaining subdivision approval, Ghermezian said he would give his personal guarantee for the return of the deposit if the agreement did not close. The agreement of purchase and sale, however, made no mention of the personal guarantee, and Ghermezian denied ever having made such a promise. Evidence, including various letters between the parties, established the existence of the promise. The agreement of purchase and sale, however, contained an entire contract clause indicating that the agreement was intended to be the whole agreement. Therefore, by strict application of the parol evidence rule, the judge could not admit the oral evidence of Corey or the other documentary evidence.

THE LEGAL QUESTION: Was Ghermezian's personal guarantee to return the deposit a part of the contract?

RESOLUTION: Justice MacDonald referred to *Gallen v. Allstate Grain Ltd.*,[13] in which Mr. Justice Lambert found that the parol evidence rule provided only a presumption that the written terms should govern and allowed the extrinsic evidence. Justice MacDonald went on to state, "The court must not allow the rule to be used to cause obvious injustice by providing a tool for one party to dupe another."

Applying the principle from *Gallen*, Justice MacDonald ruled that Ghermezian's personal guarantee was part of the contract between the parties, notwithstanding the entire contract clause and the parol evidence rule.

CRITICAL ANALYSIS: Is the *Corey* decision a welcome development? What are the justifications, if any, for abolishing the parol evidence rule in a commercial context?

Source: Jan Weir, "The Death of the Absolute Parol Rule" *The Lawyers Weekly* (6 February 1998) at 3.

B Business and Legislation · Evidence of Electronic Contracts

Those who seek to enforce a contract must be able to prove that the contract was formed and that its terms support the claim that is made. Traditionally, that proof takes the form of witness testimony and documents that are submitted to the court as evidence. Of course, in proving the contract, the parties will have to respect the parol evidence rule and other rules of evidence.

With the growth of electronic business, contracts are increasingly negotiated online and the terms are recorded electronically, without a paper version. This method of doing business creates difficulty if it becomes necessary to produce the "original" contract in court. In response, governments across Canada have begun to enact legislation addressing this point.

In 1997, the Uniform Law Conference of Canada proposed draft legislation—called the *Uniform Electronic Evidence Act*, or "UEEA" for short—to make the proof of electronic contracts subject to a uniform set of rules. This draft legislation has since been implemented in a number of jurisdictions. For example, Ontario implemented the UEEA by amending its *Evidence Act* through the *Red Tape Reduction Act*, S.O. 1999 c. 12. Section 34 of that act provides

Authentication

(4) The person seeking to introduce an electronic record has the burden of proving its

---

13. (1984), 9 D.L.R. (4th) 496 (B.C. C.A.).

authenticity by evidence capable of supporting a finding that the electronic record is what the person claims it to be.

Application of best evidence rule

(5) Subject to subsection (6), where the best evidence rule is applicable in respect of an electronic record, it is satisfied on proof of the integrity of the electronic records system by or in which the data was recorded or stored.

For access to the entire legislation from Ontario as well as other jurisdictions, see http://www.canada.justice.gc.ca/en/ps/ec/sriec.html.

Using Contractual Terms to Manage Risk

The planning function of law permits a businessperson to use contractual terms as a buffer against future, uncertain events as well as a way of limiting liability.

Changed Circumstances

Numerous circumstances may arise that prevent a party from performing its contractual obligations or that make performance much more expensive than anticipated. The rule, however, is that the terms of a contract are settled at the time of acceptance. Therefore, if disaster strikes—such as when a plant burns, railways go on strike or are closed, trade regulations change, or an entire manufacturing process becomes obsolete—the obligations in a contract are enforceable, unless a clause to the contrary is included. Though the legal doctrine of "frustration" occasionally relieves parties from their obligations (see Chapter 9), it operates in very limited circumstances and cannot be counted on to provide an avenue of escape.

It is therefore particularly important in longer-term contracts that negotiators evaluate risks, speculate on possible changes in the business environment, and be wary of making inflexible commitments. Taking these precautions is essential because changed circumstances may render a contract extremely disadvantageous to one party. For example, the price for the steel that Trackers needed to fill Coasters's order for tracking dramatically increased, making it very expensive for Trackers to

Why do well-drafted contracts anticipate events that can affect performance?

complete its end of the bargain. Rather than run such a risk, Trackers could have negotiated for a term that would permit the contract price for the tracking to rise should the price of steel increase. A contractual term could

- provide a formula setting the price of the goods supplied, in a manner that is tied to market value
- set the price according to the cost of materials, plus a specific percentage for profit
- allow the parties to reopen negotiations or terminate the contract altogether if specified events occur, such as a commodity price reaching a certain level

Instead of having to go to Coasters for some kind of accommodation, Trackers could have included a clause protecting its interests. Though the approach of voluntarily altering the agreement as the need arises can be successful, legally there is no obligation on either party to reach agreement. Furthermore, as discussed in Chapter 6, the voluntary agreement is unenforceable unless fresh consideration is given, promissory estoppel applies, or the document is put under seal.

Parties must try to build some flexibility into their agreements, while avoiding creating a document that is so vague that they run the risk of having no contract at all. If in negotiations a customer such as Coasters refuses to accept a price-variation clause of any description, the supplier must then choose to risk an adverse change in market conditions, try to negotiate a higher price to compensate for possible market changes, or lose the order altogether.

Conditional Agreements

Conditional agreements are essential when one party wants to incur contractual obligations but only under certain circumstances. For example, a business enterprise may be interested in buying a warehouse but only if it is able to secure financing from the bank. If the business simply agrees to purchase the warehouse without making its agreement conditional on securing financing, it will be obligated to complete the transaction even if the bank refuses the request for a loan. This outcome could have devastating financial consequences for the business in question. Conversely, if the business makes an offer to purchase the property subject to financing,[14] and that offer is accepted by the vendor, the business is obligated to complete only if and when the financing is approved.

From a risk management perspective, it is important that the law provide a mechanism not only for making the contractual obligation conditional on a certain event happening, but also for binding the parties in some way during the time set aside for that condition to occur. If the vendor of the warehouse were entitled to sell to someone else while the business enterprise was trying to secure necessary financing, the whole arrangement would be somewhat futile.

To bind the other side during the time set aside for the condition's fulfillment, the law provides two mechanisms: the condition subsequent and the condition precedent. **Conditions subsequent** will always bind the parties to a contract pending the fulfillment of the condition. The occurrence of a condition subsequent operates to terminate the contract between the parties—that is, it must, by definition, relate to an existing contract. For example, parties to an employment contract may agree that an employee is to work for an organization unless her sales drop

condition subsequent
An event or circumstance that, when it occurs, brings an existing contract to an end.

---

14. Such a clause must contain sufficient detail; otherwise, it will be unenforceable owing to uncertainty. For discussion of such clauses, see Gwilym Davies, "Some Thoughts on the Drafting of Conditions in Contracts for the Sale of Land" (1977) 15 *Alta. L. Rev.* 422.

below a certain amount. This is a contract subject to a condition subsequent. If the condition occurs—that is, if the employee's sales fall below the threshold—the contract automatically comes to an end.

For the most part, **conditions precedent** work in the same way—that is, there is a contract between the parties.[15] However, unlike the condition subsequent situation, where parties perform their contractual obligations until the condition occurs, the condition precedent situation means that the parties' obligations to perform are not triggered pending fulfillment of the condition. That is, a contract exists between the parties, but the obligation to perform the contract is held in abeyance pending the occurrence of the event. Because there is a contract between the parties, the law is able to imply certain terms binding on the parties in the meantime. In the real estate situation, for example, a court would imply a term that the vendor must wait until the time for fulfilling the condition has passed before it can sell to someone else. Similarly, a court would imply a term on the purchaser to make good-faith efforts to secure the necessary financing. Without a contract between the parties, these kinds of terms could not be implied, because without a contract, there are no terms whatsoever.[16]

Purchasers of real estate, for example, frequently rely on the conditional agreement by making the contractual obligation to buy and sell subject to

- rezoning
- subdivision approval
- annexation of the property by a municipality
- mortgage financing
- provision of adequate water and sanitary sewer services to the property

CASE ▼

Wiebe v. Bobsien (1984), 14 D.L.R. (4th) 754 (B.C.S.C.), aff'd (1986), 20 D.L.R. (4th) 475 (C.A.), leave to appeal refused (1985), 64 N.R. 394 (S.C.C.)

THE BUSINESS CONTEXT: Because the purchase of real estate can involve a large expense, businesses and individuals alike often require time to either borrow the money necessary to make the purchase or divest themselves of an existing property, the proceeds of which can be applied to the contemplated purchase. Such a process can take weeks or months, during which time the freedom of the vendor to deal with other buyers or back out of the arrangement altogether can become an issue.

FACTUAL BACKGROUND: Dr. Wiebe made an offer to purchase a house owned by Mr. Bobsien. This offer was made conditional on Wiebe being able to sell his current residence on or before August 18, 1984. Wiebe's offer was accepted by Bobsien. However, on July 22, 1984, Bobsien changed his mind and informed Wiebe that their agreement was "cancelled." Wiebe did not accept this cancellation and on 18 August he informed Bobsien that he had obtained a buyer for his current house and that, since the condition had been fulfilled, the main transaction had to go through. Bobsien refused to complete the sale, saying that he had no contractual obligation to do so.

---

15. Not all conditions precedent operate within the context of a contract, however, and this is where the law can become somewhat confusing. As a rule, conditions precedent will bind the parties to a contract if the condition itself is reasonably certain and objective. Conditions that are tied to whim, fancy, or extreme subjectivity—as in, "I'll buy your house if I decide that I like it"—do not bind the parties because they essentially have no objective content. These are known as illusory conditions precedent and leave the parties free to do as they please, since there is no contract between them. For obvious reasons, illusory conditions precedent are rare. For discussion and case law on this point, see Christine Boyle & David R. Percy, *supra* note 1 at 339–376.

16. It is beyond the scope of this text to discuss the issue of waiver of conditions precedent. For an assessment of this particularly thorny problem, see Gwilym Davies, "Conditional Contracts for the Sale of Land in Canada" (1977) 55 *Can. Bar Rev.* 289.

THE LEGAL QUESTION: Was there a contract between Wiebe and Bobsien such that Bobsien was obligated to wait until August 18 to see whether Wiebe could fulfill the condition?

RESOLUTION: According to the court, the condition precedent that Wiebe be able to sell his current residence merely suspended the obligation to perform the contract pending occurrence of that event. On this basis, Wiebe had a contractual obligation to take all reasonable steps to sell his house, and if he failed to take those reasonable steps, he would be in breach

of contract and liable in damages to Bobsien. As for Bobsien, he was contractually bound to wait and see if Wiebe would be successful in selling his current residence and did not have the legal right to "cancel" the contract on July 22. Since Wiebe fulfilled the condition within the time provided in the contract, Bobsien was contractually bound to sell to him. Bobsien's failure to do so was a breach of contract.

CRITICAL ANALYSIS: Do conditions precedent introduce too much uncertainty into contracts?

Conditional agreements might also arise in other contexts. For example, a business may be willing to commit to perform a contract provided it can

- access a certain source of supply
- engage people with the necessary expertise
- obtain a licence to use certain intellectual property

Conditional agreements would permit such an enterprise to contract with the other side but would provide an established reason to escape the obligation to perform.

Limitation of Liability Clause

When a party fails to meet its contractual obligations, it is liable for breach of contract and is responsible to the other side for any reasonably foreseeable damages the breach may have caused.[17] For example, in the Coasters–Trackers contract, a failure by Trackers to deliver adequate tracking may result in Coasters losing its contract with the American amusement park, the ultimate purchaser of the ride.

FIGURE 7.1

Trackers's Liability to Coasters

1. **Trackers ➔ ➔ ➔ ➔ to Coasters**
   breaches contract by supplying substandard tracking

2. **Coasters ➔ ➔ ➔ ➔ to American customer**
   breaches contract by failing to deliver tracking

3. **American customer finds an alternative supplier and terminates contract with Coasters.**

4. **Coasters loses $1 million in profit on contract with American customer.**

---

17. The classic test for foreseeability in contract, discussed further in Chapter 9, is stated in *Hadley v. Baxendale* (1854), 9 Exch. 341:

    Where two parties have made a contract which one of them has broken, the damages which the other party ought to receive in respect of such breach of contract should be such as may fairly and reasonably be considered either arising naturally, i.e., . . . such as may reasonably be supposed to have been in the contemplation of both parties, at the time they made the contract, as the probable result of the breach of it. Now, if the special circumstances under which the contract was made were communicated by the plaintiffs to the defendants, and thus known to both parties, the damages resulting from the breach of such a contract, which they would reasonably contemplate, would be the amount of injury which would ordinarily follow from a breach of contract under these special circumstances so known and communicated.

On the basis of this scenario, Coasters could recover from Trackers its loss of profit, particularly since Trackers knew very well that Coasters needed the tracking to fulfill contractual obligations to an American amusement park. However, since contracts are about consensus and choice, parties can agree to limit liability for breach to something less than would otherwise be recoverable. This is precisely what the parties to the Coasters–Trackers contract accomplished. Clause 13 of the contract (set out in the opening scenario) is a **limitation of liability clause.** It provides that Trackers's liability shall in no event exceed the unit price of the tracking, and in no event shall it include loss of profit. Therefore, by the clear words of the contract, any loss of profit that Coasters may suffer from Trackers's breach is not recoverable. Since the parties agreed to place such a limit on damages when they entered into the contract, Coasters is bound.

limitation of liability clause
A term of a contract that limits liability for breach to something less than would otherwise be recoverable.

Exemption Clause (or Exclusion Clause)

exemption clause
A term of a contract that identifies events causing loss for which there is no liability.

Through an **exemption clause,** a party to a contract can identify events or circumstances causing loss for which it has no liability whatsoever. Clause 14 in the Coasters–Trackers contract achieves such an end, since it exempts Trackers from all liability in respect to losses, damages, costs, or claims relating to design of tracking. This means that if there is a problem with the design, Coasters cannot sue Trackers for any loss it might sustain to replace or alter the tracking, for example.

Business Application of the Law

Standard Form Contracts

Standard form contracts are a common feature of the modern commercial world and pose a set of unique problems. A standard form contract is one in which the main terms cannot be changed through negotiation. The terms are offered to the other side on a "take it or leave it" basis. Such contracts save transaction costs because resources are not put into negotiating fresh terms with each new customer. Furthermore, in many situations, such as renting a video, neither party has the time or the inclination to negotiate.

Standard form contracts are also common for more significant agreements, such as obtaining a credit card, renting a car, buying insurance, or signing a guarantee of another's debt. Key terms—such as price, terms of payment, and basic obligations—are likely to be discussed. The remaining terms in these agreements are common to every transaction and are not subject to negotiation.

Most transactions proceed smoothly (the supplier provides the goods or services, and the customer pays), so that the standard terms do not come into play. However, if a transaction does not go as planned and the parties resort to the agreement to sort out the situation, the standard terms may be a problem. The customer may have agreed to the terms without reading them, understanding them, or even being aware that they formed part of the contract. The terms are often expressed very legalistically because suppliers develop and refine the language over time to achieve their goals. These goals often involve maximum protection for the supplier at the expense of the customer. The supplier's liability may be severely limited, to the consternation of the customer.

Parties to a standard form contract are expected to protect their own interests and ensure they understand the terms before accepting them. If someone agrees to terms without fully investigating, that person ought to be the one who suffers the consequences. The rule is even more stringently applied if the customer signs a contract, since signing is evidence that the customer has agreed to its terms. However—particularly in the consumer contract situation—the law places some responsibility on the supplier who creates the standard form agreement. There is, for example, an obligation on suppliers to make customers aware of the restrictive, unexpected terms in the agreement, including limitation clauses and exemption clauses. The more restrictive the terms, the greater the duty of the suppliers to bring the terms to the customer's attention. Perhaps even more so than in the customized contract, courts are apt to construe ambiguous language in a standard form contract against its maker.

Landmark Case ▼

Tilden Rent-A-Car Co. v. Clendenning (1978), 83 D.L.R. (3d) 400 (Ont. C.A.)

THE BUSINESS CONTEXT: A business may decide to use a standard form contract with its customers in order to save money. However, this may prove to be a false economy should the business fail to properly explain to the consumer the consequences of the standard form contract in question. Such a business runs the risk of a court taking the customer's side and disallowing a term that would otherwise protect the business.

FACTUAL BACKGROUND: Mr. Clendenning rented a car from Tilden at the Vancouver airport. At the time of entering into the agreement, he was asked if he wanted additional insurance, which involved a higher fee but did provide full, nondeductible coverage. Thinking that this would protect him if the car were damaged in his possession, he agreed. As he was in a hurry, he signed the long and complicated rental agreement without reading it. An exemption clause, on the back of the agreement and in very small type, provided that the insurance would be inoperative if the driver had consumed any alcohol whatsoever at the time the damage occurred. Clendenning was unaware of the clause. When the car was damaged—Clendenning drove into a pole after consuming some alcohol—Tilden sued to recover the full cost of repairing the vehicle.

THE LEGAL QUESTION: Can Clendenning rely on the clause providing him with full, nondeductible coverage, or is that clause inoperative because Clendenning had consumed some alcohol?

RESOLUTION: The Ontario Court of Appeal held that Clendenning's signature on the contract was not a true assent to the terms of the contract and, therefore, Tilden could not rely on the exemption clause denying insurance coverage to Clendenning. The clerk who had Clendenning sign knew that he had not read the contract and knew therefore that the contract did not represent his true intention. Given that the contract contained "stringent and onerous provisions," it was incumbent on Tilden to show that it took reasonable measures to draw these terms to Clendenning's attention. This did not occur and therefore Tilden could not rely on the exemption clause. The court went on to observe that since the trial judge had accepted that Clendenning was capable of proper control of a motor vehicle at the time of the accident, and since Clendenning had paid the premium, he was not liable for any damage to the vehicle.

CRITICAL ANALYSIS: Courts may be less helpful to the customer in a nonconsumer context, since parties are expected to look after their own interests. In a 1997 decision from the Ontario Court of Appeal, for example, the court emphasized that inadequate notice of the kind complained of in the *Tilden* case will not ordinarily be grounds for attacking an exemption clause in a commercial situation. The court affirmed the rule that a person will be assumed to have read and understood any contract that she signs.[18] Should consumer and commercial contracts be treated differently?

---

18. See *Fraser Jewellers (1982) Ltd. v. Dominion Electric Protection Co. et al.* (1997), 34 O.R. (3d) 1 (C.A.). Note that the *Abrams v. Sprott Securities Ltd.* (2003), 67 O.R. (3d) 368 (C.A.) distinguished *Fraser Jewellers*, by narrowing the proposition in three ways: first, the *Fraser* proposition depends on the absence of misrepresentation by the party seeking to rely on the written agreement (the party seeking to rely on the clause had no legal obligation to draw it to the other party's attention); second, it depends on there being no special relationship between the parties; and finally, a person cannot rely by way of estoppel on a statement induced by his or her own misrepresentation.

What risks do lengthy contracts—as found in the car rental industry—pose to the consumer and to the business supplying the vehicle?

Technology and the Law

Shrink-Wrap, Click-Wrap, and Browse-Wrap Agreements

Even when terms are written down, one party may claim not to have known that certain terms were actually part of the contract. As noted above, this can arise in the standard form contract, for example, when a customer of a car rental company signs a lengthy agreement without having read it. Questions of enforceability of terms also arise in the more modern context of shrink-wrap, click-wrap, and browse-wrap contracting practices.

Shrink-Wrap Agreements: A shrink-wrap agreement (also referred to as a shrink-wrap licence) is an agreement whose terms are enclosed with a product such as prepackaged software. Usually there is also a notice to the effect that opening the package constitutes agreement to the terms. The terms normally cover warranties, remedies, or other issues relating to the use of the product.

At one time, the practice was to put the terms on the box containing the software disk and wrap the box tightly in cellophane so that the purchaser could see the terms before buying. Today, the common practice is to put the terms inside the box (i.e., sometimes in a printed manual or on the envelope containing the disk) to which reference is made on the outside of the box.

In Canada,[19] there is uncertainty as to whether shrink-wrap agreements are enforceable, particularly where the packaging fails to alert the purchaser that he will not have full rights to the product inside the box. In *North American Systemshops Ltd. v. King*,[20] a software program was distributed on a floppy disk that was contained inside a shrink-wrap manual. A licence agreement—which restricted use of the program—was contained inside the packaging but was not visible at the time of purchase. The Alberta Court of Queen's bench found that the licence enclosed in the program manual was not binding on the purchaser as the terms of the licence were not made known at the time of sale. As noted by the court

> In the case at bar, the plaintiff manifestly did not bring home to the defendants, or any of them, that there were restrictions on the purchase. Not one of the simple, cheap, obvious methods to do this were used by the plaintiff.[21]

---

19. In the United States, shrink-wrap agreements are enforceable unless the terms are objectionable on grounds applicable to all agreements; see *ProCD v. Zeidenberg*, 86 F.3d 1447 (7th Cir. 1996).
20. (1989) 68 Alta. L.R. (2d) 145 (Q.B.).
21. *Ibid.* at 155.

Click-Wrap or Web-Wrap Agreements: A click-wrap or web-wrap agreement (also referred to as a licence) is an agreement that appears on a user's computer screen when a user attempts to download software or purchase goods or services online. The user is instructed to review the terms prior to assenting by clicking an "I Accept" button, a hyperlink, or an icon. Usually the user cannot proceed any further without agreeing to the terms.

In Canada, the validity of this method of contracting has been upheld. In *Rudder v. Microsoft Corp.*,[22] the plaintiffs brought a class action suit against Microsoft (MSN) alleging that MSN had breached the member service agreement. MSN applied for a permanent stay of proceedings based on a clause in the click-wrap agreement that indicated that all MSN service agreements are governed by the laws of the state of Washington and that all disputes arising out of the agreement would occur in that state's courts. The Ontario Superior Court granted the application. In response to the plaintiffs' argument that they did not receive adequate notice of the term, Mr. Justice Winkler said

> All of the terms of the Agreement are the same format. Although there are certain terms of the Agreement that are displayed entirely in upper-case letters, there are no physical differences which make a particular term of the agreement more difficult to read than any other term. In other words, there is no fine print as the term would be defined in a written document. The terms are set out in plain language, absent words that are commonly referred to as 'legalese'. Admittedly, the entire Agreement cannot be displayed at once on the computer screen, but that is not materially different from a multi-page written document which requires a party to turn the pages.[23]

Browse-Wrap Agreements: Also of recent interest has been the validity of browse-wrap agreements. Browse-wrap agreements are said to be formed on this basis: the user agrees that—by virtue of accessing the website—he or she is bound by the terms of use associated with the website and agrees that those terms are part of a binding contract between the parties. In short, a browse wrap agreement is formed not because the user has clicked on an "I Accept" button. Rather, the webpage presents a link or button that takes the user to the terms and conditions that apply to the transaction. Because the browse wrap agreement does not require the user to do anything unequivocal to signify assent—such as electronically checking a box—its status as a contract has sometimes been controversial in the United States.[24] Nonetheless, in a 2005 decision, a browse-wrap contract was completely upheld by the Illinois Appeals Court.[25] In this case, the court held that those who had purchased Dell computers over the Internet were bound by the Terms and Conditions of Sale even though they were not required to do *anything* to manifest assent. It was sufficient that Dell included a blue hyperlink to the "Terms and Conditions of Sale" on each of the five pages that the purchaser had to complete in order to purchase the computer. According to the court, this approach meant that purchaser had to know that more information would be available by clicking on the link. Furthermore, as the court observes: "The blue hyperlink simply takes a person to another page of the contract, similar to turning the page of a written paper contract." On this basis, the purchasers were bound by all those terms.

While there is no definitive Canadian ruling on point, the Québec Superior Court recently considered the matter. In *The Canadian Real Estate Association v. Sutton Real Estate Services Inc.*[26] at issue was the unauthorized downloading or "data scraping" by Sutton from the MLS real estate website. Note that the website's Terms of Use prohibited commercial use of the site as well as any republishing of the data found on the site and further stated: "By downloading the property listings and data, the user confirms agreement with and acceptance of the foregoing conditions of use." Notwithstanding, Sutton refused to stop its data- or screen-scraping activity and even managed

---

22. (1999), 47 C.C.L.T. (2d) 168 (Ont. S.C.J.).
23. *Ibid.* at 173.
24. Some U.S. courts have rejected the browse-wrap as creating a contract, particularly where the website is ambiguous. In *Specht v. Netscape Communications Corp.* 150 F.Supp.2d 585 (S.D. N.Y. 2001), aff'd 306 F.3d 17 (2d Cir. 2002), the court rejected the argument that a browse-wrap agreement mandating arbitration had been created. This is because Netscape did not make it clear to users that a contract was being formed—all that was in evidence was a small box that "requested" the user to review the terms of the licence agreement before downloading.
25. *Hubbert v. Dell Corp.* 359 Ill. App. 3d 976 (2005).
26. [2003] J.Q. No. 3606 (Que. C.S.) (QL).

to break through technology that The Canadian Real Estate Association (CREA) erected to try to stop Sutton's unwelcome activity. CREA then sued Sutton for breach of the terms of use and sought a court order—in this case an injunction—prohibiting Sutton breaching the terms of use governing the site. The court agreed to issue a pretrial injunction for a number of reasons, including the irreparable harm that would otherwise result to CREA and its members. This is because certain CREA members were threatening to stop participating in the MLS website if Sutton continued to "scrap, modify and republish the images and date they provided regarding their properties."[27]

This case does not decide the question as to whether a contract existed between CREA and Sutton simply by virtue of Sutton's use of the MLS website. This matter can be determined only after a full trial of the issue. The injunction issued by the court will be in place until then, thereby protecting CREA interests pending trial.

CRITICAL ANALYSIS: The enforceability of terms in click-wrap agreements depends on notification prior to assent. What steps can a business take in preparing and presenting an agreement to ensure that the terms will be found to be enforceable? What steps could a business take to increase the chances that a shrink-wrap agreement is found enforceable? Do you think that browse-wrap agreements should be enforceable? Why or why not? As a businessperson, how confident would you be at this point concerning the enforceability of a browse-wrap contract in Canada?

Liquidated Damages Clause

data or screen scraping
Gathering and assembling information from other Internet websites.

liquidated damages clause
A term of a contract that specifies how much one party must pay the other in the event of breach.

A **liquidated damages clause** sets out—in advance—what one party must pay to the other in the event of breach. Through such clauses, the parties themselves decide before a breach has even happened what that breach would be worth by way of compensation. Provided that the clause is a genuine pre-estimate of the damages that the innocent party will suffer, it is enforceable.[28] The clause will not be enforceable, however, if it sets an exorbitant amount as a remedy for the innocent party. If so, the clause is a penalty clause—it intends to punish, not compensate—and a court will simply disregard it in assessing damages for the breach in question. As noted in Chapter 6, Amritha had insisted on a contractual clause that Trackers pay $5000 to Coasters for every day it was late in delivering the tracking. Such a clause is enforceable only if it fits the definition of a liquidated damages clause. If it is simply a clause meant to scare or terrorize Coasters into timely performance because of the financial punishment it would face in the event of delay, the court will simply not enforce it.

These three kinds of clauses—the limitation of liability clause, the exemption clause, and the liquidated damages clause—illustrate the planning function of the law. Through such clauses, a businessperson can manage the kind and extent of liability he faces.

Business Law in Practice Revisited

1. How is the scope of Trackers's and Coasters's obligations determined?

If the parties cannot resolve a dispute concerning obligations by themselves, a judge will determine whether there is a contract between the parties and, if so, what its content is. Every contract must cover certain essentials in order to be enforceable.

27. Per Bradley J. Freedman's analysis of this case in "Website Terms and Conditions—Canadian Real Estate Association v. Sutton," at http://www.cle.bc.ca/CLE/Analysis/Collection/03-cdnrealestate?practiceAreaMessage=true&practiceArea =Technology%20Law (accessed 3 November 2006). As the *Sutton* decision is not available in English, Freedman's analysis is particularly useful and welcome.
28. See Harvey McGregor, *McGregor on Damages*, 16th ed. (London: Sweet & Maxwell, 1997) at para. 491.

If key terms are missing, the court may conclude that the parties were still at the point of negotiating and had not actually entered into a contract yet. The other possibility is that the court will imply a term that one or the other party finds unsatisfactory or contrary to expectations.

The Coasters–Trackers contract was complete because it contained all the terms that the circumstances of the case would identify to be essential, as well as some clauses that defined the relationship in more detail. For example, the contract identified the following terms:

Parties: Coasters and Trackers
Price: $1.5 million
Delivery dates: as specified
Product: tracking
Quantity: 900 metres
Quality: as per specifications and where no specifications, of the best quality
Guarantees: tracking to be free from defect for one year
Limitations on/exemptions of liability: liability not to exceed unit price; no liability for design defects; no liability for defects after one year
Insurance: vendor to insure tracking

2. Are there any ambiguous or unclear terms in the contract?

While certain aspects of the contract were somewhat ambiguous, such as the term specifying that the quality was to be of the best quality, a court would have been able to assign meaning to the term because there was a contract between the parties and expert evidence would have been available to establish what the phrase meant.

3. Are there any additional terms that Jason should have tried to have included?

Jason managed to negotiate a reasonably complete contract, as noted above. He included a number of clauses to limit the liability of Trackers, which was prudent, but he should have gone further and included a clause expressly eliminating application of the *Sale of Goods Act*. This term would have ensured that the act would have no application in a contractual dispute with Coasters sometime down the road. It was wise from Trackers's perspective to include, as it did, an entire contract clause, as this would have helped forestall any arguments from Coasters that there were additional warranties or guarantees not expressly recited in the contract.

Jason probably should have included a price-variation clause to deal with the problems that arose when the price of steel rose dramatically. In addition, an arbitration or mediation clause might have proven useful to deal with conflicts, although, as it turns out, the parties negotiated their own resolution to the pricing dispute that arose.

4. Does the contract relieve the parties from responsibility for inadequate performance?

The contract limited Trackers's liability for defective tracking for one year and to an amount not exceeding the unit price. Trackers had no liability for problems in the design of the tracking.

Coasters's obligation to pay the purchase price was not qualified by the express terms of the contract. Of course, if Trackers had failed to deliver, Coasters would not have had to pay. If Trackers had delivered seriously defective goods, Coasters would have had the option to refuse delivery. If the defect had been less significant, Coasters probably would have remitted payment in a reduced amount, to reflect the track's lesser value or the cost of repairing the defects in the tracking. Clauses to this effect are not necessary and probably do not help in establishing certainty, in any event. Whether the tracking was seriously defective or only somewhat so would have been a question of fact and therefore a matter of debate, which no clause in a contract can resolve. If the parties cannot resolve that question informally, it will be determined by a judge in an action by Trackers against Coasters for the purchase price set out in the contract.

Chapter Summary

The nature, scope, and extent of the obligations of the parties to a contract are known as the terms of the contract. The terms may be express, as when they have been specifically mentioned and agreed upon by the parties, or they may be implied. Since the court has considerable discretion to imply a term or not, parties are best advised to make their agreement as clear and explicit as possible.

How courts will resolve a contractual dispute over terms is an open question, as is any matter that proceeds to litigation. An important evidential rule that guides a judge is known as the parol evidence rule. It prevents the introduction of evidence that varies or adds to the terms of a written contract when the contract is clear and intended to be the sole source of the parties' obligations. Entire contract clauses are used to propel a court to apply the parol evidence rule in any given case.

An important planning function of contract law lies in the fact that it permits parties to manage the risk of future uncertainties. Additionally, it permits them to establish, in advance, the extent of responsibility for breach through limitation clauses and exemption clauses. Furthermore, parties can bargain for what will be payable in the event of breach. Such a term will be enforceable, provided the amount is a genuine pre-estimate of damages and not a penalty.

Both standard form contracts and electronic contracts are a fixture of modern business practice. Courts may refuse to apply a clause that disadvantages a consumer if the business in question failed to take reasonable steps to ensure that the consumer was alerted to the clause in question. Courts are less likely to assist the commercial or industrial customer, however, on the basis that sophisticated business interests should be left to take care of themselves.

Chapter Study

Key Terms and Concepts

condition precedent (p. 152)

condition subsequent (p. 151)

contractual *quantum meruit* (p. 145)

data or screen scraping (p. 158)

entire contract clause (p. 146)

exemption clause (p. 154)

express term (p. 141)

implied term (p. 142)

limitation of liability clause (p. 154)

liquidated damages clause (p. 158)

parol evidence rule (p. 147)

rules of construction (p. 141)

Questions for Review

1. What is the difference between an express and an implied term?

2. What are two major rules of construction used by the courts in interpreting a contract?

3. Who decides the content of a contract and on what basis?

4. What are four sources that the court can rely on to imply terms?

5. Why are express terms preferable to implied terms?

6. How does the doctrine of business efficacy affect the interpretation of implied terms?

7. How do the courts deal with ambiguities in the contract?

8. What is the expression used to describe an implied legal promise to pay a reasonable price for goods or services?

9. What are three ways that a party can control its exposure to liability for breach of contract?

10. What is a limitation of liability clause?

11. How is a limitation of liability clause different from an exemption clause?

12. Why are conditional agreements important?

13. What is the parol evidence rule?

14. What is a separate or collateral agreement?

15. Why does business make extensive use of standard form agreements?

16. What assumptions do the courts make about how contract terms relate to changing circumstances?

17. What is the difference between a click-wrap agreement and a browse-wrap agreement?

18. What is a liquidated damages clause?

Questions for Critical Thinking

1. Joe and Susan are negotiating a contract for the sale and purchase of furniture for Joe's new boardroom. What are some factors that business-people should consider before negotiating a contract?

2. Entering a contract can create a great deal of risk for the parties. What are examples of these risks, and how can they be managed?

3. The use of standard form agreements is common in a number of industries, such as banking and dry-cleaning. Should the use of standard form agreements be regulated by legislation?

4. Standard form contracts are also common in rental agreements. Why do you think that standard form contracts in this area are so prevalent? What are their advantages and disadvantages?

5. Do you agree that contracts should be interpreted based on an objective assessment of the parties' intentions? What would be the advantages and disadvantages of interpreting contacts based on evidence of what the parties subjectively intended?

Situations for Discussion

1. Laba Karl owned two adjacent businesses: a grocery store and a bakery. Both were served by the same parking lot. Laba agreed to sell the grocery store to Azar. The agreement of purchase and sale contained this clause:

   > The premises shall include use of the parking located at the rear of the store for customers, on the understanding that such parking shall be shared with the vendor with regards to his operation of the bakery.

   A disagreement developed about the use of the parking. Azar's position was that she was to have full use of the lot for herself and her customers, subject only to Laba's right to park two delivery vehicles. Laba argued that it was intended that he be able to use the lot for his bakery business, his employees, and his tenants.[29] What is the most reasonable meaning of the clause? How could the language be better expressed?

2. Louise purchased a shrink-wrapped piece of software from a local software developer. She used the software properly but much to her dismay, the product contained a virus that destroyed the hard drive of her computer. When Louise looked in the software packaging, she found a card that contained a number of terms of conditions, including a limitation of liability clause. Is this term a part of the contract, or can Louise argue that she is not bound by it? Explain.

3. Weir was engaged by Canada Post to deliver ad flyers for a five-year term. She was entitled to payment on a per piece basis. The contract provided that Canada Post could terminate the agreement on 60 days' notice if it changed its ad flyer distribution system and "alternatively, Canada Post may in its sole discretion terminate this agreement immediately on giving written notice to the Contractor." Payment per piece became costly for Canada Post, and two years later it instituted a new payment system based on packages (containing several pieces).[30] Is Canada Post entitled to terminate the contract with Weir? What evidence is relevant? Is it a contract at all when one party has so much discretion?

---

29. Based, in part, on *Azar v. Fancy Pastry Shop Ltd.* (1984), 63 N.S.R. (2d) 124 (S.C.T.D.).
30. Based, in part, on *Weir v. Canada Post Corp.* (1995), 142 N.S.R. (2d) 198 (S.C.).

4. Jolly Games Ltd. and Yahoo College signed a two-year agreement stating that Jolly would supply and maintain electronic videogames for the college. The contract included insurance, a machine rotation plan, and a payment schedule for commission on receipts to be paid to the college (including a guaranteed minimum payment). Shortly after the machines were installed, Jolly began to experience problems with vandalism. Machines were upset, glass broken, cords and plugs removed, cash boxes broken into, and drinks poured into the machines. Jolly employees serviced most of their machine sites once a week, but they had to service the college sites every day. Jolly requested that the college provide security for the machines, but the vandalism continued. Jolly earned no commissions and refused to make any payments to the college, claiming that security was the college's responsibility as an implied term.[31] Is this the sort of situation where a term should be implied? How could the issue have been resolved through an express term?

5. In July, Zola saw an advertisement for a Celtic Twilight Holiday from Gougemaster Tours Ltd. Zola went to her local travel agent and picked up a brochure that contained six glossy, colourful pages of print with several photos of hotels, villages, and beaches with sunbathers.

   Zola booked her 14-day holiday over the Christmas period for $1899. She paid the full amount and received tickets that detailed her flight schedules, seven-day coach tour, and seven nights in the Water Spirit Hotel in Dublin. The travel agent did not discuss with Zola the terms of the contract, other than noting that half the price was nonrefundable if Zola changed her mind.

   Zola was dissatisfied with her holiday from the beginning. The seven-day coach tour was unguided and appeared to Zola to consist of endless wandering through boring villages and countryside. The bus was hot, dirty, and slow. Because there was no guide, Zola could find no one to whom she could complain. In Dublin, Zola was escorted to the El Sleezo Hotel because the Water Spirit Hotel was full. The El Sleezo had a small, unremarkable restaurant and lounge. There was no swimming pool, and Zola's room contained only a bed, bureau, and chair. She shared a bathroom with three other guests. She was 3 kilometres from the city centre. Zola would have flown home in the second week, but she could not afford to buy a new ticket.

   Zola was depressed for months afterward and could think only of getting compensation from Gougemaster Tours. She finally sued. In response, Gougemaster Tours pointed out to Zola several paragraphs in the holiday brochure, including the following:

   Hotel Changes: Gougemaster Tours has contracted with the hotels shown in this brochure to supply accommodation. From time to time the accommodation reserved is unavailable and a substitute hotel is provided. There are several reasons this may occur, including unexpected maintenance problems, guest stayovers, and hotel overbookings. The chances of a hotel change are remote, but we would like you to be aware that the possibility exists.

   Gougemaster's Responsibility: Gougemaster Tours Ltd. does not assume responsibility for any claims, losses, damages, costs, or expenses arising out of loss of enjoyment, upset, disappointment, distress, or frustration, whether physical or mental, resulting from the following:

   (a) the need for us to change itineraries or substitute accommodation, hotels, or services, provided that every effort is made to supply the most comparable service and accommodation available

   (b) cancellation of a tour by Gougemaster, provided that full refund of all monies paid is made to the passenger

---

31. Monique Conrad, "Security for Games Is Implied Term of Contract" *The Lawyers Weekly* (3 May 1991) at 2.
32. Based, in part, on *Solar U.S.A. Inc. v. Saskatchewan Minerals*, [1992] 3 W.W.R. 15 (Sask. Q.B.).

It appeared that the hotel change in the second week was caused by Gougemaster's policy of overbooking. To what extent has Gougemaster limited its liability? Is the brochure part of the contract? Is Zola subject to the terms if she hasn't read them?

6. Lunar Inc. had developed a mechanism that harnessed heat from the sun. What the company lacked, however, was a method for storing the heat until it was needed. Trays-R-Us had developed a unique tray that appeared to solve this problem, so the parties entered into negotiations. It was agreed that Trays would sell the trays to Lunar at a set unit price per tray, for a term of one year. No particular sales volume for the year was agreed upon or guaranteed. After the trays were produced, however, Trays discovered that they leaked and were unable to hold any solar heat, owing to a design flaw that could not be fixed. As a result, Trays refused to fill any orders for the trays placed by Lunar. Lunar sued for breach of contract, alleging that there was an implied term in the contract that Trays would make trays available to Lunar as required.[32] Does the business efficacy rule require that such a term be implied in the contact between Trays and Lunar? Do you think that such a term might have been left out on purpose? How can a business avoid having terms implied into a contract?

7. Kristin signed a user agreement with Hagel's Cable, Inc. upon installation of high-speed Internet service in her home. Included in the agreement was a provision that the agreement could be amended at any time, and that customers would be notified of changes on Hagel's website, by e-mail, or through regular mail. Hagel's later added a clause to the agreement that any right to commence or participate in a class action suit was waived. The agreement, including the new clause, was posted on its customer support website, and a notice was posted on the main website that the agreement had been amended. Kristin has continued using the service since this time. However, she now wants to join a class action suit that is alleging a number of breaches of the agreement.[33] Will the clause in the amended user's agreement prevent her from bringing such an action? Did she receive adequate notice of the amended term? Does the fact that the user agreement relates to Internet services make a difference in whether the notice was adequate? How is this situation similar to the *Rudder v. Microsoft Corp.* case, discussed on p. 157?

8. Trackers is three days late in delivering the tracking to Coasters. Amritha now wants to rely on the clause in the contract that Trackers will pay $5000 for each day that the tracking is late, and is claiming that Trackers owes Coasters $15 000. However, Trackers points out that Amritha has not been inconvenienced by the late delivery, because construction on the roller coaster had already been delayed by two weeks. It has been a week and a half since Trackers was able to deliver the tracking, and Coasters has still been unable to use it. Is Amritha entitled to rely on the clause and collect the $15 000? Do you need any additional information to make your decision?

For more study tools, visit
http://www.businesslaw3e.nelson.com

---

33. Based, in part, on *Kanitz v. Rogers Cable Inc.*, [2002] O.J. No. 665 (S.C.).

Chapter

8

Objectives

After studying this chapter, you should have an understanding of

- why enforcement of contracts is the norm
- the exceptional circumstances in which contracts are not enforced
- which contracts must be in writing, and why

Non-enforcement of Contracts

Business Law in Practice

Martha Smith bought a fitness club in downtown Toronto and renamed it "Martha's Gym." She invested $50 000 of her own money and financed the remainder through a business loan from the local bank. Martha tried to attract a large clientele to the facility, but the volume of business failed to meet her expectations. She began to run short of cash and fell behind in her monthly loan payments to the bank. Eventually, the bank called the loan, which had an outstanding balance of $20 000. The bank told Martha that unless she paid off the entire balance in two weeks, it would start seizing assets from the fitness club.

Martha convinced her elderly parents, Mr. and Mrs. Smith, to help her by borrowing $40 000 from the same bank. She explained that through such a cash infusion, she would be able to retire her own loan with the bank and use the balance as operating capital for her business. Martha assured her parents that the problems at the fitness club were temporary and that by hiring a new trainer, she would be able to quickly turn the business around.

Martha and her parents went to meet Kevin Jones, the branch manager, who had handled Mr. and Mrs. Smith's banking for over 35 years. Kevin said that he would give the Smiths an attractive interest rate on the loan—namely, 8 percent—but insisted that the loan be secured by a mortgage on their home. Since the Smiths had no other means of paying back the loan and the house was their only asset, they were nervous about the proposal, which they did not fully understand. However, they did not want Martha to go through the humiliation of having her fitness equipment seized and sold at auction.

For his part, Kevin was tremendously relieved that the Smiths had come in to see him. Kevin was the one who had approved Martha's ill-fated business loan in the first place, and he had failed to ensure that it was properly secured. He saw this as an opportunity to correct his own error and get Martha's loan off his books altogether.

Kevin had the mortgage documents prepared and strongly encouraged the Smiths to sign, saying that this would protect Martha's assets from seizure. He also told them that to a large extent, signing the mortgage was just a formality and that he was confident that nothing would come of it.

In the end, the Smiths decided to put their trust in Kevin that he would not let them enter into a contract that could bring about their financial ruin. They simply signed the mortgage. Immediately, $20 000 went to the bank to pay the outstanding balance on Martha's loan. The remaining $20 000 was paid directly to Martha.

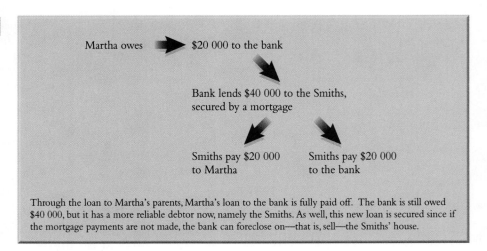

FIGURE 8.1

Martha's and Her Parents' Financial Arrangements with the Bank

Martha owes ➡ $20 000 to the bank

Bank lends $40 000 to the Smiths, secured by a mortgage

Smiths pay $20 000 to Martha

Smiths pay $20 000 to the bank

Through the loan to Martha's parents, Martha's loan to the bank is fully paid off. The bank is still owed $40 000, but it has a more reliable debtor now, namely the Smiths. As well, this new loan is secured since if the mortgage payments are not made, the bank can foreclose on—that is, sell—the Smiths' house.

Martha's business continued to operate until the additional capital was completely expended. Its prospects failed to improve, as Martha was still unable to attract customers and the new trainer quit. Eventually, neither Martha nor her parents could make the payments on the mortgage, and the bank began to foreclose on the Smiths' home. Mr. and Mrs. Smith are in shock—they never believed that it would come to this.[1]

1. Did Kevin manipulate or pressure the Smiths into signing the mortgage? If so, what legal remedies do the Smiths have?
2. Did Mr. and Mrs. Smith enter into the contract on the basis of mistake's or misrepresentation? If so, what legal remedies do they have?
3. How could Kevin have managed this transaction better?

The Importance of Enforcing Contracts

Once negotiators reach an agreement that appears to contain their consensus on the essential elements of a bargain, a contract is formed. The law then focuses on enforcing that agreement in order to preserve the integrity, reliability, and predictability of contractual relationships. Were it otherwise, the business world would be unable to predict with any certainty which agreements would be binding.

At the same time, the Canadian legal system recognizes the injustice of enforcing contracts without any provision for exceptional circumstances. Accordingly, the law endeavours to achieve a balance between two competing goals. On the one hand, it must prevent people from pulling out of deals because they have found better opportunities elsewhere or have failed to conduct diligent negotiations. On the other hand, it must remedy situations where an apparently valid contract fails to reflect the real agreement of both parties, or is fundamentally unjust.

This chapter presents a number of legal doctrines—developed through common law and statute—that are exceptions to the general rule that a contract, once formed, is enforceable. It categorizes these doctrines on the basis of there being

- an unequal relationship between the two parties
- misrepresentation or important mistakes concerning the contract
- a defect within the contract itself

If the aggrieved party can bring itself within one of the doctrines discussed in this chapter, there are two possible outcomes. In certain circumstances, he may elect whether to keep the contract in force or have it brought to an end. Where this option is available, the contract is said to be **voidable.** For example, when someone signs a contract under duress, it is that person's choice whether to abide by the contract or seek to have it set aside by a judge. In other, more limited instances, the legal problem is so serious that the aggrieved party has no choice in the matter: a court must declare the contract to be null and void. In other words, because of some tremendously substantial defect—such as the illegality that underlies the "hitman" contract—the contract is considered never to have existed at all and, for that reason, to be of no force or effect. This is known as a **void contract.**

voidable contract

A contract that, in certain circumstances, an aggrieved party can choose to keep in force or bring to an end.

void contract

A contract involving a defect so substantial that it is of no force or effect.

---

1. This Business Law in Practice scenario is based on *Morrison v. Coast Finance Ltd.* (1965), 55 W.W.R. 257 (B.C.C.A.) and *Lloyds Bank v. Bundy,* [1975] Q.B. 326 (C.A.).

Contracts Based on Unequal Relationships

Legal Capacity

In general, the law assumes that individuals and properly constituted organizations have the **legal capacity** to form contracts. Contract law also emphasizes the importance of consent and voluntariness. Because they may be unable to give true consent to their agreements, certain kinds of people—namely, children and those with mental incapacities—are given the benefit of special legal protection.

Minors

The **age of majority** is the age at which a person is recognized as an adult for legal purposes. Those under the age of majority (minors or infants) are in a very different position concerning their ability to enter contracts than are those who have attained the age of majority. To protect minors from the enforcement of contracts that may not be in their best interests, the general rule is that minors are not obligated by the contracts they make.

However, since the goal of the law in this area is to protect the underaged, minors have the option to fulfill their contractual commitments and can enforce a contract against the other party should that party be in breach. In this way, contracts with a minor are usually voidable, at the option of the minor alone.[2]

The age of majority—which defines who is not a minor—is within provincial control and is set at 18 or 19 years of age, depending on the province.[3] For example, the Ontario *Age of Majority and Accountability Act*[4] sets the age of majority at 18.

Because minors may have to provide for their own welfare in certain circumstances, there are exceptions to the general common law rule of immunity from liability. Minors are obligated by contracts for essentials, known in law as "necessaries," and are required to pay a reasonable price for them. What amounts to a necessity in a given case is legally determined in relation to two questions:

1. Is the item being acquired necessary to this minor?[5]
2. Does this minor already have an adequate supply of the item?[6]

While food, shelter, and clothing are the most common categories of necessaries, the two-step test must still be satisfied in order for the supplier to be able to enforce the specific contract. Suppliers should also be aware that even when the contract is one for necessaries, problems of enforcement can arise. Suppliers may be faced with the presumption that a minor who lives with a parent or guardian is already adequately provided for and has no outstanding needs.[7]

Contracts known as beneficial contracts of service are also binding if they are considered largely for the benefit of the minor. For example, an employment contract with a minor is enforceable if the employer can show that the contract involves a significant

---

2. It is beyond the scope of this chapter to discuss whether there is a category of void minors' contracts. For discussion see G.H.L. Fridman, *The Law of Contract in Canada*, 4th ed. (Scarborough: Carswell, 1999) at 162 and following.
3. *Ibid.* at 152.
4. R.S.O. 1990, c. A.7.
5. Courts are entitled to consider the infant's socioeconomic status in determining the answer to this question. See, for example, *Merchant Retail Services Ltd. v. Mustoe* (1990), 115 A.R. 210 (Prov. Ct.) and *Ottenbreit v. Daniels*, [1975] S.J. No. 98 (Dist. Ct.).
6. *Supra* note 2 at 155. This common law rule has been codified in sale of goods legislation in Canada. For example, s. 4 of the Alberta legislation, R.S.A. 2000, c. S-2 states:
   4(2) When necessaries are sold and delivered to a minor or to a person who by reason of mental incapacity or drunkenness is incompetent to contract, the minor or person must pay a reasonable price for them.
   (3) In this section, "necessaries" means goods suitable to the condition in life of the minor or other person and to the minor's or person's actual requirements at the time of the sale and delivery.
7. See David Percy (Institute of Law Research and Reform), *Minor's Contracts—Report 14* (Edmonton: Institute of Law Research and Reform, 1975) at 5.

element of training and career development, such as one would expect in a program required to enter or progress through a trade or profession. Enforceability in this context means that the employer can be awarded damages for breach of contract.

Business Application of the Law — Dealing with Minors

Although there may be sound business reasons for entering into a contract with a minor, there is considerably more risk of nonperformance and unenforceability than when contracting with an adult. If the contract is for any significant value, a contractor should consider either contracting with the parent or guardian instead of the minor, or requiring an adult to cosign or guarantee the performance of the minor.

In the employment context, in order for the employment contract to be enforceable against the minor, the employer must be able to prove that the minor is receiving a significant benefit. Otherwise, the minor can simply abandon the contract, at her sole option.

The common law generally provides that when a minor reaches the age of majority, there is no impact on contracts formed when underage. They remain unenforceable against the minor unless they involve necessaries or beneficial service contracts. Only if the person—now of legal age—expressly adopts or ratifies the agreement does it become enforceable. The one exception to this rule is where the agreement is of a permanent or continuous nature, such as a partnership agreement. In such a case, the minor, upon attaining the age of majority, must reject (repudiate) this obligation, even if it is for non-necessaries. If he fails to do so, liability will be imposed from the time the minor becomes of age.[8]

In all Canadian jurisdictions except British Columbia, the common law governs the contractual capacity of minors.[9] In British Columbia, a different set of rules applies, as set out in the *Infants Act*.[10] This legislation provides even more protection for the infant than is present at common law, since generally, even contracts for necessities and beneficial contracts of service are unenforceable at the election of the minor.[11] However, a court has a number of powers under the legislation and can order, for example, that compensation be paid by or to any of the parties to the contract.

Mental Incapacity

In order for a contract to be formed freely and voluntarily by both parties, both must be able to understand the nature and consequences of their agreement. If people are mentally impaired through illness or intoxication by alcohol or drugs, such that they are unable to understand the consequences of their actions, and the other party was

---

8. *Supra* note 2 at 158 and following.
9. *Supra* note 2 at 153 and following.
10. See Part 3 of the *Infants Act*, R.S.B.C. 1996, c. 223.
11. *Supra* note 2 at 169 describes the operation of B.C.'s *Infants Act* in the following terms:
    A contract by a minor, i.e., someone who was an infant at the time the contract was made, is unenforceable against him unless: (a) the contract is enforceable against him by some statute; (b) the minor affirms the contract on attaining majority; (c) it is wholly or partially performed by the minor after majority; or (d) was not repudiated by the minor within a year after majority. However, the minor can enforce the contract against the adult party as if the minor had been an adult at the time of contracting. In the case of an unenforceable contract, the minor or another party (if the minor has repudiated the contract or is in breach) can apply to a court for relief.... [footnotes deleted]

aware of their state, they may be able to avoid the contract[12] at their option.[13] And to the extent that the other party has unfairly exploited the party who is lacking capacity, there are additional grounds for attacking the contract's validity—namely, duress, undue influence, and unconscionability. All three are considered below.

The fact that Martha's parents are elderly does not, of itself, mean that they lack mental capacity to enter into financial transactions. Rather, before Martha's parents can avoid paying the mortgage on this ground, a court will have to be satisfied that their advanced age has affected their sanity or mental competence—an unlikely outcome on the facts of this scenario. They may be old and overly trusting, but not legally incompetent.

Duress

Contracts that are made as a result of one of the parties being threatened with physical harm are obviously not enforceable. The presence of this extreme form of duress indicates that the threatened party did not freely consent to the terms of the contract and, in fact, was the victim of a crime.

duress
The threat of physical or economic harm that results in a contract.

In the more difficult cases—those more likely to arise in commercial dealings—**duress** takes the form of one party financially pressuring the other. For example, a company might threaten to break a contract that it knows is crucial to the other side unless the other side gives certain financial concessions or payments in return.[14] These concessions will be unenforceable if it is shown that the coercion went beyond ordinary commercial pressure to a force or compulsion that prevented the other side from giving true consent to the proposal.[15] In such circumstances, the contract is voidable at the option of the party who was subject to the duress.

There is no possibility that Martha's parents can rely on the doctrine of duress to avoid their obligations under the mortgage. Though the bank was going to seize Martha's fitness club equipment and offer it for public sale, this "threat" did not amount to duress. Certainly, her parents may have been very upset and worried by the situation, but this would not force them to borrow $40 000 from the bank. Furthermore, the bank is fully within its legal rights to seize property when a loan has fallen into arrears.

Undue Influence

Since the basic premise of contract formation is that both parties have chosen to enter into the contract, surrounding circumstances that put in question the ability of one of the parties to exercise free will are of great concern. If these factors are sufficiently strong, then the contract is voidable at the option of the party whose free will was lost because of the **undue influence** of the other contracting party.

undue influence
Unfair manipulation that compromises someone's free will.

Undue influence traditionally operates in two circumstances:

- *Actual pressure.* Sometimes a transaction—commercial or otherwise—arises because one party has exerted unfair influence on the other. In such a case, the party who seeks relief from the contract must show that the influence existed, was exercised, and resulted in the agreement in question.[16] If an elderly person is pressured into signing over her estate to caregivers in return for care, such a transaction could be set aside for undue influence.

---

12. *Supra* note 2 at 174–175 and G.H. Treitel, *The Law of Contract,* 11th ed. (London: Sweet & Maxwell, 2003) at 557 and following.
13. *Supra* note 2 at 170–174.
14. This was held to amount to duress in *North Ocean Shipping Co. Ltd. v. Hyundai Construction Co. Ltd.,* [1978] 3 All E.R. 1170 (Q.B.).
15. The leading case in the area is *Pao On v. Lau Yiu Long,* [1979] 3 All E.R. 65 (P.C.).
16. G.H. Treitel, *The Law of Contract,* 11th ed. (London: Sweet & Maxwell, 2003) at 409.

- *Presumed pressure.* Sometimes the relationship that already exists between the parties gives rise to a presumption that the ensuing agreement was brought about by one party's unfair manipulation of the other. For example, when the contract is formed between family members or between lawyer/client or doctor/patient, for example, the court is entitled to assume that undue influence has been exerted. Other kinds of relationships—as between banker and customers, for example—do not import this presumption. When the presumption is in place, however, it then falls to the more powerful party to prove that no undue influence was present.[17]

CASE ▼

Bank of Montreal v. Duguid (2000), 47 O.R. (3d) 737 (C.A.)

THE BUSINESS CONTEXT: When a bank lends money to a customer, it wants to ensure that, in the event of default, the customer has provided sufficient collateral to cover any shortfall. If the customer does not have satisfactory collateral, the bank may refuse to make the loan unless a third party either cosigns or guarantees the loan. This situation can pose serious risks for the third party, given its responsibility that loan payments must be made.

FACTUAL BACKGROUND: In 1989 Mr. Duguid and a business partner applied to the Bank of Montreal for a loan to finance their investment in a condominium project. The bank said that it would make the loan only if Mrs. Duguid would cosign it.

Mr. Duguid approached his wife, a real estate agent, who did sign the loan. Contrary to the bank's usual policy in such matters, its representative failed to recommend to Mrs. Duguid that she secure independent legal advice prior to signing. In short order, the loan went into default, Mr. Duguid declared bankruptcy, and the bank sued Mrs. Duguid for the amount outstanding on the loan, namely $87 000 plus interest.

THE LEGAL QUESTION: Did Mrs. Duguid cosign the loan as a result of her husband's undue influence?

RESOLUTION: Though the bank itself did not exert undue influence, any undue influence exerted by the husband would release the wife from her obligation under the loan if the bank knew or should have known about the undue influence and did nothing about it. Because Mr. Duguid was in a close, personal relationship with the other debtor—namely, his wife—the bank had a duty to make inquiries since the loan was clearly to the wife's disadvantage. If there were any undue influence, this failure by the bank would lead to the wife's loan being set aside.

A majority of the Ontario Court of Appeal said, however, that there was no undue influence. Only if the wife could demonstrate that she reposed "trust and confidence" in her husband concerning financial matters would there be a presumption of undue influence. As a real estate agent, she knew the risks of her husband's investment, and there was no potential for domination. On this basis, undue influence could not be presumed. Even if it could be presumed, the bank had rebutted that presumption, given Mrs. Duguid's knowledgeable background. On this basis, the loan was enforceable against her.

The dissenting judge would have set the loan aside based on undue influence. The dissent said that while Mrs. Duguid did not repose trust and confidence in her husband in the classic sense, she did fear "destroying the relationship between herself and her husband" should she refuse to cosign. Her background as a real estate agent was simply irrelevant to this more emotional question. Given that Mrs. Duguid agreed to the loan during a low ebb in her marriage and that she signed in order to maintain "some level of tranquility" in the household, a presumption of undue influence had been established. This presumption was not rebutted by the bank since it knew that the transaction was to the wife's disadvantage and that there was a substantial risk

---

17. It is beyond the scope of this text to discuss whether it must also be proven that the contract was a "manifest disadvantage" to the party seeking to have it set aside. For discussion of this point, see Fridman, *supra* note 2 at 341–342 and following.

that her husband would pressure her to sign. Since the bank failed to advise her to get independent legal advice, Mrs. Duguid's loan should be set aside due to undue influence.

There is a chance that the elderly Mr. and Mrs. Smith would succeed in having the $40 000 mortgage set aside as having been procured by undue influence, either actual or presumed. The Smiths could argue that they entered into the mortgage with the bank only because the bank manager insistently preyed on their overwhelming need to help their daughter. If so, they could then win on the grounds of actual pressure. An argument could also be advanced on the grounds of presumed pressure. Though courts will not ordinarily presume that a bank has undue influence over its customers, the Smiths may succeed by proving that they placed themselves entirely in the hands of their long-standing bank manager and had received no qualified outside guidance.[18] It would then fall to the bank to show that the mortgage was freely and independently entered into by the Smiths.[19]

One way of proving that the contract was freely chosen is to arrange for the weaker party—such as the Smiths—to get independent legal advice concerning the transaction before it is entered into. The lawyer providing that advice will also produce what is called a "certificate of independent legal advice," which is then appended to the mortgage or other document in question. In the certificate, the lawyer attests that

- he or she has explained the proposed transaction to the weaker party
- the weaker party appears to understand the proposed transaction
- the weaker party is proceeding with the transaction on a free and informed basis

Unconscionability

unconscionable contract
An unfair contract formed when one party takes advantage of the weakness of another.

Where one party stands in a position of being able to take advantage of someone and causes that person to enter into an unfair or improvident agreement, an **unconscionable contract** is the result. According to the Supreme Court of Canada, proof of unconscionability involves a two-step process:

- proof of inequality between the parties
- proof of an improvident bargain or proof of exploitation.[20] If the transaction is sufficiently divergent from community standards of commercial morality, this is a "strong indication of exploitation."[21] At this point, the court will presume unconscionability. It then falls to the stronger party to show that the contract was, in fact, fair.

---

18. This argument is based on *Lloyds Bank Ltd. v. Bundy, supra* note 1.
19. *Supra* note 16 at 419 and following.
20. *Norberg v. Wynrib* (1992), 12 C.C.L.T. (2d) 1 (S.C.C) (pages 172n, 224n) at 23, for the majority. Though this case involved noncommercial facts, courts have recently considered *Norberg* in a commercial context. See, for example, *Waxman v. Waxman* (2002), 25 B.L.R. (3d) 1 (Ont. Sup. Ct. Jus.), varied as to damages (2004), 44 B.L.R. (3d) 165 (C.A.), leave to appeal refused, [2004] S.C.C.A. No. 291, reconsideration allowed (2004), 6 B.L.R. (4th) 167 (C.A.); and *Ellis v. Friedland,* [2001] 2 W.W.R. 130 (Alta. Q.B.), aff'd (2003), 277 A.R. 126 (C.A.). Note that in *Norberg,* Justice Sopinka in dissent took the position that the doctrine of unconscionability had not yet been settled, at 634.
21. *Norberg, ibid.*

Inequality between the Parties

The required inequality may result because one party is unsophisticated, is poorly educated, lacks language facility, or has lower economic standing than the stronger party. Parties to a contract are never on strictly equal bargaining terms; therefore, disparity between them is, on its own, insufficient to upset a contract.

Since the Smiths are inexperienced and unsophisticated senior citizens who received no independent legal advice prior to signing the mortgage, this element could arguably be established, particularly if a court were sympathetic to their plight.

An Improvident Bargain

The party seeking to have the contract set aside must also be able to demonstrate that its terms greatly advantaged one party over the other. In short, there must be proof of substantial unfairness.

In the case of the Smiths' mortgage to the bank, the rate of interest was set at 8 percent and, from that perspective, was more than reasonable. However, there is a strong argument that the transaction was nonetheless a very unfair bargain for them. Through the mortgage, the Smiths put at risk their only substantial asset, for a loan they could never repay from their own resources. In fact, while the bank and Martha stood to gain enormously from the transaction, the Smiths stood to lose everything for absolutely no return.

Why should contracts that appear normal on the surface be subject to challenge on the basis of the relations between the parties or the surrounding circumstances?

CASE ▼

Atlas Supply v. Yarmouth Equipment
(1991), 103 N.S.R. (2d) 1 (N.S. C.A.)

THE BUSINESS CONTEXT: Businesses are expected to obtain necessary information and not agree to terms until they have an agreement they can live with. Sometimes, however, one party takes such extreme advantage of the other that the court agrees to intervene.

FACTUAL BACKGROUND: Atlas was a subsidiary of Esso that supplied parts and accessories to Esso auto service stations. Atlas decided to franchise its operations because its profits were declining. Mr. Murphy's company, Yarmouth Equipment, was interested in purchasing the franchise for a particular area. Atlas prepared two sets of financial projections for the business in that area. The projections given to Murphy portrayed a viable operation. The other set showed that the franchise was not viable at all. Yarmouth bought the franchise in reliance on the optimistic written projections supplied to him as well as on other oral assurances. The contract Murphy signed with Atlas, however, contained an "entire agreement" clause stating: "Except as provided herein, there are no conditions, representations, warranties, undertakings, inducements, promises or agreements...." This would mean that the written projections and other oral assurances were not to form part of the contract. Another clause recited: "The Franchisee [Murphy] further acknowledges that it has had an adequate opportunity to be advised by advisors of its own choosing regarding all pertinent aspects of the franchise business, Atlas and this agreement."

Murphy's operation failed and closed in less than a year. Murphy was called upon to pay a substantial sum under his personal guarantee of Yarmouth's debt to Atlas. In defence, Murphy argued that Atlas's positive income projection was a term of the contract and that Atlas was in breach of that term. On a related front, he argued that the exclusion clauses—which would suggest that Atlas's income projection formed no part of the contract—should not apply, given Atlas's unconscionable conduct. The trial judge found in Murphy's favour. Atlas appealed.

THE LEGAL QUESTION: Do Atlas's income projections constitute a contractual warranty or do the exclusion clauses prevent this conclusion? Is Murphy liable on his guarantee to Atlas?

RESOLUTION: The appeal court ruled 2 to 1 in favour of Murphy. Justice Matthews found that the agreement "was entered into on the one hand by a national company with international connections through its parent, Imperial Oil, and on the other by a small businessman who, though no neophyte, had little or no retail experience." He concluded that it was unconscionable for Atlas to give Murphy misleading information while withholding contrary information. On this footing, he refused to allow Atlas to rely on the exclusion clauses. This meant that Atlas was in breach of its contractual warranty. The court also partially released Murphy from his guarantee to Atlas, given all the circumstances, including Atlas's unconscionable conduct.

The dissenting judge found that Murphy was a very experienced businessperson who was aware of the basis for the financial projections and was not compelled to agree to the terms, which were clearly expressed. He cautioned that the courts should be very reluctant to set aside business deals such as this one.

CRITICAL ANALYSIS: Should a large business with the advantage in information (such as Atlas) be allowed to take advantage of a small, relatively uninformed one (such as Yarmouth)? Which of the judges do you find to be the most persuasive?

Business and Legislation — Unconscionability

Many provinces have enacted legislation that relies on unconscionability as a standard against which to assess the fairness of a consumer transaction. For example, the Ontario *Consumer Protection Act*, gives remedies—including damages and the right to have the contract set aside—to the consumer who has entered into a contract on the basis of an unfair practice, which includes unconscionable representations. In determining whether to assist the consumer, the court is directed by the legislation to consider whether the person making the representation knows or ought to have known that, for example

- the consumer was not reasonably able to protect his interests because of his physical infirmity, ignorance, illiteracy, inability to understand the language, or similar factors

- the price grossly exceeded the price at which similar goods or services are readily available to like consumers
- there was no reasonable probability of payment of the obligation in full by the consumer.[22]

Many jurisdictions also have legislation that applies when the cost of the loan is excessive. In such circumstances, the courts have a range of options open to them, including redrafting the loan agreement so that it is fair.[23]

CRITICAL ANALYSIS: Does such legislation fill a real need in commercial transactions? Does it unfairly restrict business?

People seeking to avoid a contract owing to mental capacity, duress, undue influence, or unconscionability must do so as promptly as possible or risk losing their case.

Misrepresentations and Important Mistakes

Misrepresentation of Relevant Facts

Parties involved in negotiating a contract are usually not obligated to volunteer information. The basic principle or rule is that both parties are to look out for their own interests and if they want information, they should ask for it.

Sometimes parties do owe a duty to disclose information without being prompted, however.[24] Consider the follow scenarios:

- *One party provides only partial information to the other side.* This may amount to a misrepresentation since once information is offered, it must not be misleading or incomplete.

- *One party actively conceals the truth.* If the vendor of a building, for example, takes steps to conceal a crack in the foundation, this must be disclosed or will amount to a misrepresentation.

- *One party neglects to correct an earlier assertion that, when stated, was correct but now no longer is so.* If a physician selling his practice gives initial information regarding its value that later becomes inaccurate, the physician must go back and disclose this new fact to the prospective purchaser.

- *The parties are in a relationship requiring utmost good faith.* Insurance law provides an example of this. The person applying for insurance coverage has a duty to disclose all information that would be relevant to the insurer who is assessing the risk of accepting the application.[25]

---

22. See too the *Fair Trading Act*, R.S.A. 2000, c. F-2 (Alberta); the *Business Practices and Consumer Protection Act*, S.B.C. 2004, c. 2, (British Columbia); the *Business Practices Act*, S.M. 1990-91 c. 6 (Manitoba); the *Trade Practices Act*, R.S.N. 1990, c. T-7 (Newfoundland); and the *Business Practices Act*, R.S.P.E.I. 1988, c. B-7 (Prince Edward Island).
23. For legislation concerning unconscionability, see, for example, the *Unconscionable Transactions Act*, R.S.A. 2000, c. U-2 (Alberta); the *Unconscionable Transactions Relief Act*, R.S.M. 1987, c. U-10 (Manitoba); the *Unconscionable Transactions Relief Act*, R.S.N.B. 1973, c. U-1 (New Brunswick); the *Unconscionable Transactions Relief Act*, R.S.N.S. 1989, c. 481 (Nova Scotia); the *Unconscionable Transactions Relief Act*, R.S.N. 1990, c. U-1 (Newfoundland); the *Unconscionable Transactions Relief Act*, R.S.P.E.I. 1988, c. U-2 (Prince Edward Island); the *Unconscionable Transactions Relief Act*, R.S.S.1978, c. U-1 (Saskatchewan); the *Business Practices and Consumer Protection Act*, S.B.C. 2004, c. 69 (British Columbia); and the *Unconscionable Transactions Relief Act*, R.S.O. 1990, c. U-2 (Ontario).
24. There are a number of areas in which a duty to disclose can arise. For discussion, see Shannon O'Byrne, "Culpable Silence: Liability for Non-Disclosure in the Contractual Arena" (1998) *30 Can. Bus. L. J.* 239.
25. The first four examples in this part of the text are based in case law and are taken from John McCamus, *The Law of Contracts* (Toronto: Irwin Law Inc., 2005) at 332–333. For discussion of the insurance contract scenario, see *supra* note 2 at 326–327. Note that the common law duty to disclose information is also repeated in legislation governing insurance contracts. See for example, *Insurance Act*, R.S.O. 1990 c. I-8, section 148.

■ *A statute imposes a positive obligation to disclose information.* For example, and as discussed in Chapter 16, legislation requires directors of a corporation to disclose their interest in certain kinds of contracts involving the corporation they serve.[26]

The difference between a statement made in the contract and one that is made prior to entering into the contract is crucial in this area of law.[27] If the statement is made in the contract, it is a promise or a term of the contract. If it proves to be untrue, a breach of contract has occurred. However, if the statement is made *prior to entering into* the contract but is not a term, it still can have legal consequences. A statement that meets the conditions set out below is known in law as an actionable **misrepresentation.**

Contract law allows the party who has relied on a misrepresentation to have the contract cancelled. This cancellation is called **rescission** and involves putting the parties back into their precontractual positions. Because rescission is an equitable remedy, the court requires the person seeking such assistance to act promptly in bringing the complaint forward.

Where rescission is not possible, such as when one party has substantially altered the subject matter of the contract, the courts will endeavour to do what is practically just so that the innocent party receives some redress, including monetary compensation.[28]

Ingredients of an Actionable Misrepresentation

The law provides that a negotiating party must answer inquiries accurately and that any information volunteered must be correct. Whether or not a statement is a misrepresentation that allows the other party a remedy depends on its nature and effect. To count as a misrepresentation, it must be proven that the statement is

■ false

■ clear and unambiguous

■ material to the contract; that is, it must be significant to the decision of whether or not to enter into the contract

■ one that actually induces the aggrieved party to enter into the contract

■ concerned with a fact and not an opinion, unless the speaker claims to have special knowledge or expertise in relation to an opinion

Categories of Actionable Misrepresentations

The law further divides misrepresentations into three categories:

■ *Fraudulent misrepresentation.* The speaker has a deliberate intent to mislead or makes the statement recklessly without knowing or believing that it is true.

■ *Negligent misrepresentation.* The speaker makes the statement carelessly or negligently.

■ *Innocent misrepresentation.* The speaker has not been fraudulent or negligent, but has misrepresented a fact. By process of elimination, the misrepresentation, is merely innocent.

---

26. See, for example, discussion of the self-dealing contract in Chapter 16. Directors must disclose their interest in certain kinds of corporate contracts.
27 Consumer protection legislation in some jurisdictions, however, specifies that precontractual representations are part of the contract. The distinction between precontractual representations and terms of the contract, while important in the commercial context, is less important when a business deals with a consumer.
28. See, for example, *Kupchak v. Dayson Holdings Ltd.,* [1965] 53 W.W.R. 65 (B.C. C.A.).

misrepresentation
A false statement of fact that causes someone to enter a contract.

rescission
The remedy that results in the parties being returned to their precontractual positions.

When Kevin told the Smiths that signing the mortgage was a formality, this statement amounted to a misrepresentation, since a mortgage is in fact a legal instrument with far-reaching consequences, the most serious being that the bank could foreclose on the Smiths' house. If the Smiths can prove that they relied on that representation in deciding to sign the mortgage, they will probably succeed in establishing an actionable misrepresentation. Minimally, this statement was negligent but, given the likely state of Kevin's banking knowledge, the statement might even be fraudulent.

When Kevin told the Smiths he was confident that nothing would come of their signing the mortgage, this was arguably an expression of opinion—not a statement of fact—and therefore not actionable. A court might find, however, that since Kevin is an expert in the area of mortgages and other banking matters, his statement was one of fact, and order a remedy on that basis. While a court would be unlikely to find this statement to be a fraudulent misrepresentation, given the sparse facts, it may well find it to be negligent.

Remedies for Misrepresentation

Besides entitling courts to rescind or set aside a contract, certain kinds of misrepresentations are torts, which provide for a remedy in damages. If the misrepresentation is fraudulent or negligently made, damages in tort can be awarded in addition to the remedy of rescission provided by contract law. Where the misrepresentation is neither fraudulent nor negligent, an action is still available to set the contract aside based on innocent misrepresentation. Negligence and fraud (or deceit) are discussed further in Chapters 11 and 12.

FIGURE 8.2			

Remedies for Misrepresentation

	Type of Misrepresentation		
	Fraudulent	Negligent	Innocent
Remedy	Rescission in contract Damages in tort	Rescission in contract Damages in tort	Rescission in contract

Upon the Smiths demonstrating an innocent misrepresentation, the court can order that their contract with the bank be set aside. If the Smiths can go on to prove that the bank—through Kevin—is responsible for the tort of negligence or fraud, they are entitled to damages as well, though these are probably not large.

Given the cost of litigation—and the fact that the innocent party may fail to prove her case on the balance of probabilities that an actionable misrepresentation had been made—prevention is the best medicine. It is prudent to insist that important terms be an express part of a written contract, so as to achieve the goal of clarity between the parties. It is generally easier to prove breach of a written term than to establish that an oral statement made during contractual negotiations amounts to a misrepresentation in law. If the other party balks at reciting an important representation as an express, written term, the customer would be best advised to do business elsewhere.

Mistake

The doctrine of legal **mistake** is one of the most difficult aspects of contract law. In the course of its development by the courts, the law of mistake has become so complex and confusing that it presents a major challenge even to seasoned lawyers and judges. In practice, legal mistake is rarely proven but when it is, the court is entitled to set the contract aside as a remedy.

CASE ▼

R. v. Ron Engineering & Construction Ltd., [1981] 1 S.C.R. 111

THE BUSINESS CONTEXT: Owners commonly secure competitive bids to build large projects through a call for tenders. In response, contractors submit tenders that set out a price for the work to be done. Though this is a fact-specific matter, the tendering rules can require the contractors to submit a tender deposit that is forfeited by the contractor who is chosen if he refuses to undertake the job. It is therefore important that the tender price is accurately tabulated *before* the tender is submitted to the owner since it can be difficult to withdraw after the fact, at least not without risking the deposit.

FACTUAL BACKGROUND: Ron Engineering submitted a tender on a project for a price of $2 748 000 along with a certified cheque for $150 000 as the tendering rules required. The tendering rules—contained in the Information for Tenderers—stipulated that tenders could be withdrawn up to the official closing time, after which they would be irrevocable. The rules also provided that the deposit was forfeited by the successful contractor if the successful contractor refused to proceed with the project.

Tenders closed at 3:00 p.m. and soon thereafter, Ron Engineering realized that, due to a simple miscalculation, it had submitted a bid that was $750 000 less than it had intended to submit. Though this error was detected by Ron Engineering and explained to the owner within 72 minutes of closing, the owner insisted that Ron Engineering proceed with the project or forfeit its deposit.

THE LEGAL QUESTION: Does the law of mistake provide Ron Engineering with a route of escape or is it obligated to either perform or forfeit its tender? Is it too late for Ron Engineering to withdraw its tender?

RESOLUTION: The Supreme Court of Canada ruled that tenderers in the position of Ron Engineering could not withdraw tenders after the official closing time. Upon submission of its tender, Ron was in a preliminary contract with the owner. This preliminary contract (known as Contract A) required the owner to respect the rules on *how* to evaluate tenders. On these facts, it also required tenderers not to withdraw their tenders after the official closing time. The larger contract to perform the work tendered for is known as Contract B. Only the successful tenderer would enter into a Contract B with the owner.

Ron Engineering unsuccessfully argued that the law of mistake prevented Contract A from ever coming into existence. According to the court, since Ron Engineering intended to submit the very tender submitted, including the named price, there was no mistake in any legal sense. Furthermore, even though the tender was $750 000 less than intended, this error was not so large as to suggest to the other side that there had been a miscalculation. Unless there was something seriously amiss with the tender—such as an entire page being missing—Contract A would come into existence. Since no such circumstances existed here, Ron Engineering lost its deposit. The court insisted that such strictness was essential to protecting the integrity of the tendering process.

CRITICAL ANALYSIS: Is the law of mistake too harsh? What would the consequences be if a party could escape its contractual obligations simply because it had made a mathematical error?

The central point is that legal mistake is much narrower than the everyday idea of a mistake. A simple oversight or error by one negotiating party does not constitute a legal mistake and provides no basis for voiding a contract. As previously noted, negotiators are expected to look after themselves and to exercise appropriate caution before making legal commitments.

Compare the following two examples:

EXAMPLE 1 Kerry intends to make an offer to sell her car for $11 000 and in error sends a written offer to Sean for $10 000. Sean accepts her offer.

EXAMPLE 2 Kerry makes a written offer to sell her car for $1100 rather than $11 000, and Sean promptly accepts. There is no reason to believe that the car, worth approximately $11 000, should be sold at a substantially lower price. Moreover, there is nothing in the relationship that would suggest that Kerry would give Sean a break in price.

In both cases, Kerry has made a mistake according to the common understanding of that word. However, in all likelihood, only in Example 2 would this be interpreted at law as a mistake worthy of a remedy. The error Kerry has made in Example 1 is not one that would surprise Sean. This could be exactly the price for which Kerry intends to sell her car. In contrast, in Example 2, Sean could not reasonably expect that the price would be so low, especially if Kerry and Sean have had earlier discussions about the possible price range. Kerry has made an error, and any reasonable person in Sean's position would realize that. In the latter example, there can be no true agreement for $1100. The law will not permit Sean to "snap up" Kerry's offer in this way.

CASE ▼

Craig Estate v. Higgins (1993), 86 B.C.L.R. (2d) 64 (S.C.)

THE BUSINESS CONTEXT: Businesspeople regularly engage in protracted contractual negotiations that can involve a series of offers and counteroffers over time. One party may find itself in a very disadvantageous contract due to an error.

FACTUAL BACKGROUND: The plaintiff was responsible for "executing" her deceased brother's will, meaning it was her job to gather up his assets, pay off his debts, and distribute the net assets to those named in the will. A conflict arose with the defendant as to whether she should have to return $100 000 in her possession because it belonged to her brother or whether the brother had given her that money as a

gift prior to his death. Negotiations to settle this dispute began. The plaintiff offered to accept $93 000 from the defendant as a compromise. Prior to that, the defendant offered to give $50 000 to the plaintiff as a compromise. Two days before this matter was to go to trial, the defendant's lawyer received from the plaintiff's lawyer an offer to accept $1.00 to end the matter. Defendant's counsel quickly accepted. Soon thereafter, the plaintiff and her lawyer claimed that this offer had been made in error. The intended offer had been to accept in settlement the amount of the claim *less* $1.00.

THE LEGAL QUESTION: Is there a settlement contract between the parties such that the defendant only has to pay $1.00 to settle the dispute?

RESOLUTION: Courts are very reluctant to interfere with contracts simply because they are unfair or unreasonable. Before a court will assist a party who claims that the contract was entered into under a legal mistake, the plaintiff must establish:

1. That the defendant knew or ought to have known that the offer contained an error; and
2. It would be "unjust, inequitable or unconscionable" for the court to permit the contract to go ahead.

The court found that the defendant ought to have known that the plaintiff's offer contained an error, given how drastically low it was in relation to previous negotiations. The court also found that it would be inequitable to enforce the contract, given the prejudice this would cause to the plaintiff and because, from the defendant's perspective, there was no reasonable explanation for the offer being other than in error. On this basis, the court ordered the plaintiff's offer to settle to be set aside and the matter was to be set down for trial, instead.

CRITICAL ANALYSIS: Is it important to the outcome of this case that there was no apparent explanation of why the plaintiff would suddenly make such a low offer to settle? How is this case different from the *Ron Engineering* case?

A legal mistake may also occur if both parties have made the same error. If Kerry's car appears to be old and relatively worthless, and she and Sean negotiate on that basis for a relatively low price, their agreement is based on a common mistake if the car turns out to be a valuable antique. Only if the error is such that the car purchased is a totally different thing from what the parties thought it was will the contract be set aside on the basis of mistake. For example, if the difference is between low-grade transportation (what the parties thought the car was) and a classic car to be displayed and never driven (what the car actually is), a mistake in law could possibly be established. To the extent that the error is simply a mistaken assumption about the quality of the car (i.e., in terms of value), however, no legal mistake has occurred, and the purchaser is entitled to retain what may appear to be a windfall. Needless to say, such distinctions can be subtle.

Under the Business Law in Practice scenario, Martha's parents may have signed the mortgage under the mistaken belief that Martha's business problems were temporary and reversible. This is not a legal mistake, however, and there is no possibility that the mortgage would be set aside on the basis of this misapprehension.

An argument that is often made, though seldom successfully, concerns signed documents. The signer may misunderstand the type or nature of the document. Perhaps the signer thinks he is signing a guarantee of a debt, but the document is actually a mortgage on his residence. Or the document is a transfer of land, and the signer thought she was signing an option to sell the property. The argument is, "I never intended to sign this type of contract." In practice, this argument tends to succeed only when there is a good reason for the signer's failure to more closely examine the document before signing—as when the signer is poorly educated, illiterate, or otherwise dependent on the creator of the document (the other party) for an explanation of what it is. Simple carelessness in signing a document without attention to what it is or to what its consequences might be is not enough to avoid enforceability.[29]

---

29. For an exception to this statement see discussion in Chapter 7 concerning *Tilden Rent-A-Car Co. v. Clendenning* (1978). 83 D.L.R. (3d) 400 (Ont. C. A.).

Contracts Based on Defects

Illegality

Under the classical model of illegality, even a freely chosen contract will be unenforceable if it

- is contrary to a specific statute and/or
- violates public policy

These contracts are void and of no effect unless the court decides that the offending portions of the contract can be deleted, or severed, and the remaining portions saved. In such a case, only some of the contract will remain in effect and be enforceable. What a court will not do, however, is redraft the offending portions to make them comply with the law.

Contracts that are illegal may or may not be criminal. In this context, an **illegal contract** is simply one that violates statute law or public policy.[30]

Illegal by Statute

Numerous kinds of contracts are made illegal by legislation. For example

- The *Criminal Code*[31] forbids loans at a rate of interest considered "criminal"— defined as a rate exceeding 60 percent per year. The courts may or may not invalidate the entire transaction, depending on whether it is possible to sever the clauses dealing with the criminal rate of interest from the rest of the contract.
- The federal *Competition Act*[32] invalidates a range of commercial transactions that unduly restrict competition. For example, resale price maintenance contracts are prohibited because, through them, manufacturers attempt to influence retail prices in the stores by keeping them high. Entering into such contracts can lead to criminal sanctions.
- The Ontario *Real Estate and Business Brokers Act*[33] provides that an unlicensed realtor cannot maintain an action for services rendered.

Business enterprises should take care to meet their statutory and regulatory obligations lest they be faced with a challenge to the legality of a contract they have entered into. Increasingly, however, the consequences of statutory illegality depend on all the circumstances of the case.[34] As one leading text in this area of law states, "If every statutory illegality, however trivial in the course of performance of a contract, invalidated the agreement, the result would be an unjust and haphazard allocation of loss without regard to any rational principles."[35] This statement signals a more flexible perspective, which may fully eclipse the strict, traditional approach that says that illegal contracts are automatically unenforceable.

---

30. See Christine Boyle & David R. Percy, eds., *Contracts: Cases and Commentaries*, 7th ed. (Scarborough: Carswell, 2004) at 771.
31. *Criminal Code*, R.S.C. 1985, c. C-46, s. 347.
32. *Competition Act*, R.S.C. 1985, c. C-34.
33. *Real Estate and Business Brokers Act*, S.O. 2002, C. 30 Schedule C, s. 9.
34. See *Still v. Minister of National Revenue*, [1998] 1 F.C. 549 (C.A.), whose analysis was approved by the Supreme Court of Canada in *Transport North American Express Inc. v. New Solutions Financial Corp.*, [2004] 1 S.C.R. 249.
35. S.M. Waddams, *The Law of Contracts*, 5th ed. (Toronto: Canada Law Book, 2005) at 406.

B | Securing Contracts Illegally—Paying Bribes to Foreign Officials

Canadian business may feel compelled to pay bribes in order to close deals overseas but they also face serious liability for doing so. A Toronto-based engineering firm, Acres International Ltd., was initially convicted of two counts of bribery for attempting to secure contracts for a US$2.4 billion water project funded by the World Bank. Acres was accused of bribing the former head of the water project in the African kingdom of Lesotho, in return for contracts worth about CDN$21 million. The bribes totalled $674 000 over seven years.

In 2005, Acres's appeal was partially successful, with one of the bribery convictions being overturned by the Lesotho Court of Appeal. Acres's fine was also reduced to $2.8 million from $4.2 million. Since then, the World Bank has imposed its own penalty, banning Acres from bidding on Bank-financed projects for three years. Probe International, a Toronto-based lobby group, endorsed the World Bank's decision. "This is a sad day for Acres employees," stated Patricia Adams, executive director of Probe International, "but an important precedent and a strong signal that corruption doesn't pay."

Source: Karen MacGregor and Karen Howlet, "World Bank Penalizes Canadian Company" *The Globe and Mail* (24 July 2004) at B2; and Karen MacGregor, "Acres Int'l Convicted in African Bribery Case; Engineering Firm Shocked; Plans Appeal" (18 September 2002) at http://www.theglobeandmail.com (accessed 3 November 2006).

Sytze Alkema, a barrister who represented the Canadian engineering firm Acres International, leaves the Lesotho High Court whose decision in the case was partially reversed on appeal.

Contrary to Public Policy

public policy
The community's common sense and common conscience.

At common law, contracts are contrary to **public policy** when they injure the public interest. For example, some employment contracts contain a noncompetition covenant (or clause) preventing the employee from competing with the employer for a certain period of time after the contract ends. Similarly, noncompetition clauses are often found in an agreement for the purchase and sale of a business. If these clauses are drafted too broadly, the courts will not enforce them because they are contrary to public policy. In short, they unduly interfere with an individual's ability to earn a livelihood, and they reduce competition within a sector.

The enforceability of noncompetition clauses is discussed in the Elsley case.[36]

---

36. Written and researched by Dion Legge.

Elsley v. J.G. Collins Insurance Agencies Limited, [1978] 2 S.C.R. 916

THE BUSINESS CONTEXT: The purchaser of a business often wants to prevent the vendor from competing against him for a specified period of time in order to prevent the vendor from setting up a similar business across the street. If the purchaser hires the vendor to work at the business, the employment contract may also contain a noncompetition covenant for a related reason.

FACTUAL BACKGROUND: Elsley and Collins entered into a purchase and sale agreement, whereby Collins purchased Elsley's general insurance business. This agreement contained a noncompetition covenant, which stipulated that Elsley was restricted from carrying on or engaging in the business of a general insurance company within a certain geographic area for a period of ten years. By a separate employment agreement, Elsley worked as a manager for Collins. This agreement also contained a noncompetition covenant covering the same geographic area, whereby Elsley could not compete with Collins for a period of five years after he ceased to work for Collins. After 17 years, Elsley resigned and opened his own general insurance business, which took some of Collins's customers.

THE LEGAL QUESTION: Is the noncompetition covenant in Elsley's employment contract valid?

RESOLUTION: In finding the noncompetition covenant to be valid, the court stated:

> A covenant in restraint of trade is enforceable only if it is reasonable between the parties and with reference to the public interest. As with many of the cases which come before the Courts, competing demands must be weighed.

There is an important public interest in discouraging restraints of trade, and maintaining free and open competition unencumbered by the fetters of restrictive covenants. On the other hand, the courts have been disinclined to restrict the rights to contract, particularly when the right has been exercised by knowledgeable persons of equal bargaining power. In assessing the opposing interests the word one finds repeated throughout the cases is the word 'reasonable'. The test of reasonableness can be applied, however, only in the peculiar circumstances of the particular case....

After stating that noncompetition clauses in employment contracts are to be more strictly interpreted than those contained in an agreement for the sale of a business, the court provided guidelines for determining whether such clauses are enforceable as being reasonable between the parties. According to the court, the assessment of noncompetition clauses involves considering whether

- the employer has a proprietary interest that he is entitled to protect
- the temporal and geographic restrictions are reasonable
- the restrictions are reasonably necessary to protect the employer, given the nature of the business and the nature and character of the employment

Once the reasonableness of a restrictive covenant has been established, it is enforceable unless it runs contrary to the public interest.

In this case, the clause was reasonable and therefore fully enforceable. The plaintiff was entitled to an injunction and damages for breach of the clause.

CRITICAL ANALYSIS: Why are noncompetition clauses in employment contracts less likely to be enforced than similar clauses in sale of business agreements? What are an employer's "proprietary interests"?

Writing as a Requirement

As a general rule, contracts do not have to be written down in order to be enforceable. A party to an oral contract must find other means to prove its existence, such as calling of witnesses. Sometimes, however, a contract *must* be evidenced in writing due to the *Statute of Frauds*.

The *Statute of Frauds* was imported to Canada from England. Except in Manitoba, where it has been completely repealed,[37] it applies to differing extents in all common law provinces.

The purpose of the *Statute of Frauds* is to prevent fraud and perjury by requiring written proof of certain kinds of contracts. The categories discussed below are the most relevant to business. A contract falling into these categories must have its essential terms contained in a document or documents signed by the party against whom the contract is to be enforced. Several documents can be combined to meet the requirement if each of the documents can be connected with the others. If the writing requirement cannot be met, however, the contract is generally unenforceable.

Contracts of Guarantee

A **guarantee** is a promise to pay the debt of someone else, should that person default on the obligation. A guarantee must generally be evidenced in writing.[38]

The province of Alberta has gone even further than the *Statute of Frauds* by requiring additional formalities from noncorporate guarantors, including the requirement that the written guarantee be accompanied by a notary's certificate. In this certificate, the notary attests that the guarantor understands the consequences of entering into the guarantee and that the guarantee is freely given.[39]

Contracts Not to Be Performed within a Year

The rationale for requiring a written record of these kinds of contracts is the difficulty of proving promises that were possibly made in the distant past. Since the arbitrary cutoff of one year is bound to be unfair in some cases, the courts have been known to interpret the *Statute of Frauds* in such a way as to avoid an injustice.

The requirement of writing for this kind of contract has been repealed in several jurisdictions such as Ontario,[40] British Columbia, and Manitoba.

Technology and the Law

E-Signatures

Commercial contracts are generally enforceable, no matter what form they take, but there are important exceptions. For example, signature requirements exist in statutes such as the *Statute of Frauds*.

A common definition of a signature is a "physical, handwritten mark that authenticates a document." The courts, however, have been quite liberal in applying the signature requirement and have accepted typewritten names, initials, and the like as signatures. Whether an electronic signature, such as a personal identification number, fits the definition of signature is unclear and has not, to date, been the subject of established case law.

The term "electronic signature" itself refers to any number of ways in which a person may indicate association with an electronic document. It can include a name typed at the bottom of an e-mail message; a digitized form of a handwritten signature; a unique password, code, or personal identification

---

37. *An Act to Repeal the Statute of Frauds*, R.S.M. 1987, c. F-158. British Columbia has also repealed the *Statute of Frauds* with the *Law Reform Amendment Act*, S.B.C. 1985, c. 10, s. 8. However, s. 59 of the *Law and Equity Act*, R.S.B.C. 1996, c. 253 requires contracts for land or a disposition of land, as well as contracts of guarantee and indemnity, to be in writing in order to be enforced unless the transaction fits within an exception contained in s. 59.
38. Manitoba is an exception to this rule.
39. See the *Guarantees Acknowledgment Act*, R.S.A. 2000, c. G-11. British Columbia has extended the writing requirement to indemnities owing to the *Law and Equity Act*, R.S.B.C. 1996, c. 253, s. 59(6).
40. *Statute of Frauds*, R.S.O. 1990, c. S-19, s. 4, amended by *Statute Law Amendment Act*, S.O. 1994, c. 27, s. 55.

number; or a signature created through the use of encryption technology. Of course, some forms of electronic signatures are by nature more secure than others. For example, a "digital signature" is a specific type of electronic signature, and is generally unique to a particular signer, capable of verification, and capable of indicating whether the record to which it is attached was changed after it was signed.

Legislators have begun to recognize the need for guidance in this area. Section 11(1) of Ontario's *Electronic Commerce Act*, 2000, for example, provides that, with some exceptions, "a legal requirement that a document be signed is satisfied by an electronic signature." Section 1(1) defines an "electronic signature" to mean "electronic information that a person creates or adopts in order to sign a document and that is in, attached to, or associated with the document."

Federally, the validity of e-signatures is addressed in the *Personal Information Protection and Electronic Documents Act* (*PIPEDA*), S.C. 2000, c. 5, ss. 31 and 43. The *Secure Electronic Signature Regulations*, issued in 2005 pursuant to the *PIPEDA*, provide for a "secure electronic signature," much like the "digital signature" mentioned above, that is to be used for electronic documents that are originals, declarations, sealed, sworn, or witnessed. The secure electronic signature technologies must ensure that the signature is unique to the signer, that the application of the signature was under the signer's sole control, that the signer is identifiable, and the technologies can be used to determine if the document was changed after it was signed.

CRITICAL ANALYSIS: Are electronic signatures more or less reliable than the hand-written variety?

For legislation in other jurisdictions, see http:www.canada.justice.gc.ca/en/ps/ec/sriec.html. Most provinces have provided for electronic signatures according to rules of varying stricture. In most jurisdictions, the validity of an e-signature is subject to tests of identification and reliability.

Sources: Michael Erdle, "Legal Issues in Electronic Commerce" (1996) 12 C.I.P.R. 251; Alan Gahtan, et al., *Internet Law: A Practical Guide for Legal and Business Professionals* (Scarborough: Carswell, 1998) at 313; Bradley J. Freedman, "Digital Signatures and Authentication Processes" (12 July 2004) at http://www.cle.bc.ca/CLE/Analysis/Collection/04-54321-signatures; and Michael Deturbide, "Canadian Laws on e-Contracting Still Leave Many Questions Unanswered" *The Lawyers Weekly* (27 January 2006) at 14 and 16.

Contracts Dealing with Land

Contracts concerning land—including leases and sales—generally must be evidenced in writing in order to be enforceable.[41] Nevertheless, in the interest of fairness, the courts have also created an exception to the absolute requirement for writing in the case of "part performance." If the person attempting to enforce an oral agreement for purchase and sale of land has performed acts in relation to the land that could be explained by the existence of an agreement, that performance may be accepted in place of a written agreement.[42]

The mortgage given by the Smiths to the bank must comply with the *Statute of Frauds*, since it concerns an interest in land. That is, through the mortgage, the bank acquires the right to sell the land and apply the proceeds against the Smiths' loan, should they default on payments. The mortgage prepared by the bank appears to meet the requirements of the *Statute of Frauds* because the agreement is a written contract and has been signed by the Smiths.

41. Even in Manitoba—where the *Statute of Frauds* has been repealed—courts have been known to insist that contracts dealing with land be in writing, particularly when the offer is made in writing, as in *Jen-Den Investments Ltd. v. Northwest Farms Ltd.*, [1978] 1 W.W.R. 290 (Man. C.A.). See too *Megill-Stephenson Co. Ltd. v. Woo* (1989), 59 D.L.R. (4th) 146 (Man. C.A.).
42. It is beyond the scope of this text to discuss the varying tests for part performance that exist at common law.

Contracts for the Sale of Goods

All provinces have a version of the *Sale of Goods Act*, and most[43] contain a provision that contracts for the sale of goods above a specified amount must be in writing to be enforceable by the courts. The amount is generally set at between $30 and $50, not adjusted to reflect inflation. Thus, it would appear that most sales of goods are caught by the act. Since written contracts are generally not produced for routine transactions, it is fortunate that sale of goods legislation also contains very broad exceptions that limit the application of the rule. For example, if partial payment is made by the buyer, or if the buyer accepts all or part of the goods, no written evidence is required for the contract to be enforceable.

Even without *Statute of Frauds* requirements, creating a record of an agreement is generally a prudent business decision. Personnel may change and memories may fade, and genuine disagreement as to the terms of a contract can result. Through a well-recorded written document, such disagreements—and perhaps the expense of litigation—can be avoided.

That said, businesses and individuals must strike a reasonable balance between the comfort of complete records and the time and effort required to produce them, particularly in small transactions.

B Business and Legislation | Internet Contracts

Even where a contract is not caught by *Statute of Frauds* requirements such that it must be in writing, other legislation may nonetheless require the business in question to produce a written copy of the contract. That is, governments may decide it is in the best interests of consumers to give them additional protection and safeguards when entering into certain kinds of transactions.

Several provinces, including Manitoba, Alberta, Nova Scotia, Ontario, and British Columbia, have passed legislation reflecting the consumer protection measures of the *Internet Sales Contract Harmonization Template*. The template was released by the Consumer Measures Committee, and endorsed by all federal, provincial, and territorial ministers responsible for consumer affairs. The template and its various counterparts apply to consumer purchases of goods and services over the Internet, and require sellers to clearly disclose certain information to the buyer before an online contract is formed. The information to be disclosed includes the seller's business name and address (including e-mail address), a fair and accurate description of the goods and services, all costs (including taxes and shipping), delivery arrangements, and return policies. All of this information must be accessible such that it can be printed and retained by the consumer, and must be clearly and prominently displayed. Consumers must also be given an opportunity to accept or decline the terms of the agreement, and to correct errors before the contract is formed.

Some provinces' legislation goes beyond the minimum requirements set out in the template. For example, Ontario's *Consumer Protection Act* requires a supplier to deliver to a consumer who has entered into an Internet agreement a copy of that agreement. If the supplier fails to do so within a specified time, the consumer may cancel the agreement and it becomes unenforceable.

By requiring that the supplier provide a written contract to the consumer, the consumer is better able to confirm what rights and liabilities exist under the contract. The consumer is also able to confirm whether the written agreement reflects her understanding of the contract.

Researched and written by Meredith Hagel.

Sources: Michael Deturbide, "Canadian Laws on e-Contracting Still Leave Many Questions Unanswered" *The Lawyers Weekly* (27 January 2006) at 14 and 16; See also s. 39(1) and s. 40(2) of the *Consumer Protection Act, 2002*, S.O. 2002, Sched. A, c. 30.

---

43. The exceptions include New Brunswick, Manitoba, Ontario, and British Columbia. See too G.H.L. Fridman, *Sale of Goods in Canada*, 5th ed. (Toronto: Carswell, 2005) at 43.

Managing the Risks of Unenforceability

When contracts are entered into, a business runs the risk that they may ultimately be unenforceable. Since a contract is only as good as the process leading up to its formation, businesses should train their employees carefully in how to negotiate contracts. Matters to be concerned about include

- Are the parties to the contract under any legal incapacities?
- Has one party taken unfair advantage of the other?
- Has one party misled the other?
- Has a substantial mistake been made?
- Is the contract contrary to legislation or in violation of public policy?
- Is the contract required to be in writing?

An affirmative response to any of the foregoing may signal a possible problem if suing becomes necessary. Securing a deal at any cost may end up producing no deal at all.

Business Law in Practice Revisited

1. Did Kevin manipulate or pressure the Smiths into signing the mortgage? If so, what legal remedies do the Smiths have?

While the Smiths have the capacity to contract and were not subject to duress by Kevin, the mortgage transaction is probably unconscionable. There was inequality between the parties—namely the bank and the Smiths—because the Smiths were inexperienced senior citizens who had received no prior independent legal advice. As well, the transaction was very unfair, since the Smiths were risking their only substantial asset for a loan they could never repay on their own. In short, only the bank and Martha would benefit from the transaction, while the Smiths stood to lose everything. On this basis, both of the steps necessary to establish unconscionability have been met, and a court will set the mortgage aside unless the bank can somehow show that the transaction was fair.

The mortgage transaction is also liable to be set aside at common law on the grounds that it was signed on the basis of undue influence. There is a good argument that the Smiths did not freely enter into the mortgage but did so only because Kevin preyed on their deep need to help Martha, their daughter. As well, it appears that the Smiths put their entire trust in Kevin, which is another basis for a court to find undue influence.

2. Did Mr. and Mrs. Smith enter into the contract on the basis of mistake or misrepresentation? If so, what legal remedies do they have?

The Smiths could argue that they did not understand what they were signing and that the whole thing was a "mistake." This may be true from their point of view, but they did sign the mortgage document. The law ordinarily expects people not to sign documents unless they understand them. Accordingly, the mortgage is unlikely to be set aside on the grounds of mistake.

There is a very strong argument, however, that Kevin misrepresented the nature of the transaction by telling the Smiths that signing the mortgage was just a formality and that likely nothing would come of it. While it could be argued that this statement was merely an opinion, this defence is unlikely to succeed since the words were spoken by a banker who should know better. While it also could be argued that the Smiths did not rely on Kevin's statement—in other words, that they knew very well that their house could be foreclosed upon if Martha failed to make the payments—a judge is much more likely to take the Smiths' side. There is an excellent chance that the mortgage would be set aside on the basis of Kevin's misrepresentation.

3. How could Kevin have managed this transaction better?

Since the essence of a contract is the free and voluntary adoption of obligations, Kevin should never have asked the Smiths to sign the mortgage until they had secured independent legal advice.

Furthermore, it would probably have been better for Kevin not to have been involved in the transaction at all, and instead to have sent the Smiths elsewhere. Most of the legal problems in this scenario arose because Kevin was trying to get a bad loan he had given to Martha off his books. This motivation may have interfered with his judgment in how to handle the Smiths from the outset.

Chapter Summary

There is a broad range of doctrines available to cancel all or part of a contract, but they apply only in relatively unusual or extreme circumstances. Moreover, courts are justifiably demanding in what parties must prove in order to be released from their obligations. Courts expect parties to negotiate carefully and deliberately to ensure that any commitment they make accurately reflects their intentions. If the deal merely turns out to be less desirable than expected, the doctrines in this chapter are unlikely to apply.

With limited exceptions, contracts made by minors are not enforceable against them. At common law, unless the contract is for a necessary or amounts to a beneficial contract of service, it is unenforceable at the election of the minor. In British Columbia, minors have even more protection through legislation. Persons suffering from a mental impairment also do not generally have the capacity to contract when they are incapable of understanding the transaction.

The doctrine of duress permits a court to set aside a contract when one of the parties was subjected to such coercion that true consent to the contract was never given. The doctrine of undue influence permits the same outcome if one party, short of issuing threats, has unfairly influenced or manipulated someone else into entering into a contract. Unconscionability also considers the unequal relationship between the two contracting parties. If both inequality between the parties and an improvident bargain can be established, the contract can be rescinded by the court. If the transaction is sufficiently divergent from community standards of conduct, this may signal the presence of exploitation and lead to a finding of unconscionability.

Misrepresentation concerns the parties' knowledge of the circumstances underlying a contract. If one party misrepresents a relevant fact and thereby induces the other side to enter into the contract, the innocent party can seek to have the contract set aside or rescinded. If the misrepresentation also counts as a tort, the innocent party is entitled to damages as well.

A party who has entered into a contract based on wrong information can try to have the contract set aside on the basis of mistake, but this strategy will rarely be successful because mistake is an exceedingly narrow legal doctrine.

Contracts that are illegal because they violate a statute or are at odds with public policy can also be rescinded. Courts are increasingly looking at all the circumstances surrounding the contract and will not automatically set them aside.

The *Statute of Frauds*, in its various forms, seeks to prevent fraud and perjury by requiring written proof of certain kinds of contracts. With the use of electronic and Internet contracts becoming more and more common, modern legislation also seeks to address the same types of problems in the new environment of technological commerce.

Chapter Study

Key Terms and Concepts

age of majority (p. 168)

duress (p. 170)

guarantee (p. 184)

illegal contract (p. 181)

legal capacity (p. 168)

misrepresentation (p. 176)

mistake (p. 178)

public policy (p. 182)

rescission (p. 176)

unconscionable contract (p. 172)

undue influence (p. 170)

void contract (p. 167)

voidable contract (p. 167)

Questions for Review

1. Explain the difference between a void and a voidable contract.

2. Who has the legal capacity to form contracts?

3. What must be proven by someone seeking to avoid a contract based on mental impairment?

4. Describe the doctrine of undue influence.

5. What is duress? How does it relate to the idea of consent?

6. What is an unconscionable transaction?

7. Give an example of economic duress.

8. What is a misrepresentation?

9. How does the concept of a legal mistake differ from its ordinary meaning?

10. Name one statute that makes certain kinds of contracts illegal.

11. What is the role of public policy in contract enforcement?

12. How are noncompetition covenants used in employment contracts?

13. How does the *Statute of Frauds* affect contracts?

14. What four types of contracts relevant to business law are required to be in writing?

15. How might the fact that a contract is electronic affect its enforceability?

16. Is an electronic contract subject to the same basic principles as a traditional contract?

17. Who is a minor?

18. Are contracts with minors binding?

Questions for Critical Thinking

1. Though contracts are generally enforceable, there are important doctrines that provide exceptions to this general rule. Do these exceptions undermine the notion of sanctity of contracts—the principle that once a contract is made, it should be enforced? Do these doctrines give the courts too much discretion to set aside a contract?

2. As a general proposition, negotiators have no duties of disclosure to the other side. Do you agree with this proposition, or do you think negotiators should be required to disclose all information relevant to a transaction?

3. What factors should a business consider in developing a policy on documentation of commercial relationships? Should it insist that all contracts be in writing, or is more flexibility in order?

4. Which doctrines discussed in this chapter would be unlikely to arise in an online transaction? Why?

5. How can a business use a risk management plan in order to reduce the chances that it will enter into an unenforceable contract?

Situations for Discussion

1. Carlsen was sued by Financial Collection Services for outstanding principal and interest on a student loan. He claimed he had no recollection of receiving money from a student loan or of signing loan agreements and that he has been mentally unstable for most of his life. A letter from a psychiatrist indicated that Carlsen had severe mental problems for a long time.[44] Is the loan agreement enforceable? What are the implications for the lending policies of those who grant student loans?

2. Tim Donut Ltd. was founded by Tim Horton, a professional hockey player, in 1964. Ron Joyce, the company's first franchisee, became an equal partner with Horton in 1966. Tim Horton died in 1974, and his wife inherited his share of the business. In 1975 she sold that share to Joyce for $1 million. Mrs. Horton subsequently claims that, after the death of her husband, she became addicted to drugs and did not know what she was doing when she sold her share. She says she was unaware for days that she had sold her

interest and remembers little from the day of the sale, other than sitting in an office and signing some papers. She now seeks to have the contract cancelled.

What doctrines in this chapter are relevant to the situation? What further information is needed to apply those doctrines? What are the major challenges that Mrs. Horton faces to succeeding on her claim?

3. Stewart bought a business operating in rented space in a shopping mall. Shortly after she took over the business, the landlord pressured her to sign a lease that made her responsible for the arrears in rent of the previous tenant. The landlord secured Stewart's agreement by exerting tremendous pressure on her. For example, he called in the sheriff to execute a distress for rent when, at that time, Stewart was in arrears only for the month of January. The landlord told Stewart that if she did not pay the former tenant's arrears, "she would be the one to suffer." The landlord

---

44. Based, in part, on *Financial Collection Services Ltd. v. Carlsen* (1995), 166 A.R. 78 (Q.B.).

knew that Stewart was unsophisticated in business dealings and signed the lease without seeking advice.[45] Is she obligated by the lease?

4. Brace was considering the purchase of a mortgaged apartment building. He incorporated a numbered company to be the purchaser. He visited the bank holding the mortgage in order to have the mortgage transferred to him. Brace alleges that the bank employee with whom he spoke assured him that the building was worth more than the purchase price and was an excellent investment in an expanding market but, since a company was buying the building, Brace would be required to give a personal guarantee of the mortgage debt. Brace bought the building, took over the mortgage, and signed the guarantee. In the months following the purchase, the value of the building fell sharply, owing to an economic downturn, deterioration of the building, a high vacancy rate, a glut of similar accommodation, and a lack of investment in property in the area. Brace defaulted on the mortgage, and the bank foreclosed and claimed on the guarantee. Brace now claims that the bank employee misled him and that he did not understand the nature of the guarantee he signed.[46] Can he avoid his obligations?

5. The Craig Agency operates an employment agency business by obtaining orders for job openings from employers, obtaining job applicants, and then trying to match the applicant with the job opening. Bennett and Leek were employed as counsellors with the agency, and their employment contracts included this covenant:

> 8. Non-Competition.... It is understood and agreed that in the event of the cancellation of this Agreement, Counsellor shall not, for a period of three months from the date of said termination, engage in the employment agency business, directly or indirectly, or as an owner, operator, partner, officer, director, shareholder, employee or contractor of another employment

agency situated or operated within a radius of 25 miles of Agency. Counsellor warrants and represents to Agency that in the event that the restrictions set forth herein become operative, he will be able to engage in other business or businesses for the purpose of earning a livelihood.[47]

Are Bennett and Leek bound by the non-competition clause? What are the relevant factors? What should they do if they decide to leave Craig and open their own agency?

6. Wendy and Sam were shareholders of a corporation that built and sold homes. Symphony and Rose were the developers and builders of high-rise condominium projects. They told Wendy and Sam that a penthouse apartment was still available in their project. Wendy and Sam provided Symphony and Rose's real estate agent with information relevant to the purchase and delivered cheques for the various deposits. The agent told them that in a few days they would be required to sign an offer on Symphony and Rose's standard form. They thought they had a deal. A few days later, a senior representative of Symphony and Rose contacted Wendy and Sam to tell them that the penthouse had already been sold and 40 units were currently available.[48] Do Wendy and Sam have an enforceable agreement? Should they have done anything differently?

7. John Tonelli was an exceptionally talented young hockey player who, in 1973 at the age of 16, entered into a two-year contract with the Toronto Marlboro Major Junior "A" hockey club, a team in the Ontario Major Junior "A" Hockey League. The Junior league had an agreement with the NHL (National Hockey League) that prevented the drafting of underage players, and that called for the payment of certain fees once a player was drafted at the end of his junior career. However, a similar agreement could not be reached with the WHA (World Hockey Association). John—like all other Junior hockey

---

45. Based, in part, on *Stewart v. Canada Life Assurance Co.* (1994), 132 N.S.R. (2d) 324 (C.A.).
46. Based, in part, on *Toronto Dominion Bank v. 2047545 Nova Scotia Ltd. and Brace* (1996), 148 N.S.R. (2d) 228 (C.A.).
47. Based, in part, on *Craig Agency of Ontario v. Bennett* (1977), 14 O.R. (2d) 740 (H.C.J.).
48. Based, in part, on *Bay Tower Homes v. St. Andrew's Land Corp.* (1990), 10 R.P.R. (2d) 193, Ont. H.C.J.).

players of his time—was forced to sign a new contract as a condition of continuing to play in the Junior league. This new contract essentially bound him to play three years longer than his earlier contract with the Toronto Marlboros; in addition, it imposed monetary penalties if he signed with a professional team within that time frame, or within a period of three years after he ceased to be eligible to play in the Junior league. As soon as he turned 18 (the age of majority), John abandoned the contract with the Toronto Marlboros and signed with the Houston Aeros, a professional team. The Marlboros sued him for breach of contract.[49] Is John's contract enforceable against him? If yes, does this seem fair, and from whose point of view? If no, is it fair that John can sign a contract and then ignore his obligations under it?

8. Sam Moore, an alert and intelligent 52-year-old businessman, tried without success to purchase a piece of farmland from Louis Wells. When he heard that Louis's brother, James, was willing to sell his nearby farm, he went to see him at his nursing home to make an offer to purchase it. James was 62 years old, and unbeknownst to Sam, was suffering from brain damage. Sam offered to purchase the land for $7000. James signed an acceptance to the offer, and received a deposit of $100, without receiving any independent advice on the transaction. The land in question was worth quite a bit more than $7000—in fact, the farmer who was leasing James' land at the time had offered to pay $14 000 to $15 000 for it just the year before. Since then, a trust company was appointed under the *Mentally Incapacitated Persons Act*, and took over the management of James' affairs. The trust company refused to transfer the farm to Sam, who decided to sue in order to enforce the contract he entered into with James.[50] Is the contract for the sale of the farm enforceable? If yes, does that seem like a just result? If not, what legal doctrine would likely be used to rescind it? If the contract is not enforceable, do you think that it is fair to Sam, who did not know about James's mental state? Or is it reasonable to expect that he make sure that the person he is contracting with is mentally capable of entering into a contract? What factors ought Sam have taken into account?

For more study tools, visit
http://www.businesslaw3e.nelson.com

---

49. Based, in part, on *Toronto Marlboro Major Junior 'A' Hockey Club v. Tonelli* (1979), 96 D.L.R. (3d) 135 (Ont. C.A.).
50. Based, in part, on *Marshall v. Canada Permanent Trust Co.* (1968), 69 D.L.R. (2d) 260 (Alta. S.C.).

Chapter

9

Objectives

After studying this chapter, you should have an understanding of

- the termination of a contract by performance
- the termination of a contract by agreement
- the termination of a contract by frustration
- the methods of enforcing contracts
- the concept of privity
- remedies for breach of contract

Termination and Enforcement of Contracts

Business Law in Practice

Janet and Alphonso Owen entered into a contract with Charles Conlin to construct their family home in Vancouver, B.C. Conlin inspired a lot of confidence. He told the Owens that he understood the importance of building the family home with great care and attention. "It's where you're going to live, for goodness sake," he stated. "Your home is an extension of you. Don't worry about anything. My work is second to none." For her part, Janet was particularly excited about a see-through fireplace that would be installed in the centre portion of the proposed house. A see-through fireplace opens onto two rooms, in this case, the living room and dining room.

Pursuant to the contract, Conlin, known as the "Contractor," had a number of obligations including as follows:

> ...
>
> 12. The Contractor covenants to construct in accordance with the relevant sections of the British Columbia *Building Code.*
>
> 13. The Contractor covenants to construct in accordance with plans and specifications attached to this Contract.
>
> ...
>
> 20. The Contractor covenants to complete construction on or before 30 June 2006.

The plans and specifications were duly attached to the contract and included a provision for the see-through fireplace that Janet loved so much.

The Owens' covenanted to pay a total of $500 000 and provide advances on a regular basis. Over time, the Owens advanced $300 000 to Conlin and looked forward to the day when they would be able to move in. Their excitement about their new home construction eventually turned to disappointment when Conlin failed to complete construction according to schedule. The Owens gave several extensions but when Conlin missed the last deadline, the Owens went to talk to him at the job site. Upon arrival at the site, Alphonso noted that the house was only half-built and did not even look structurally sound (the centre of living room ceiling drooped in dramatic fashion). He asked Conlin for an explanation and a progress report. Conlin became absolutely enraged, stating: "You're complaining about things here just to grind me down on my price. Well, at least my wife isn't ugly like yours is." This was the last straw. The Owens ordered Conlin and his crew to leave the property. They took possession of the house and promptly changed the locks.

About two weeks later, the Owens' luck changed for the better. A well-known house building expert, Mr. Holmstead, agreed to assist the Owens. The Owens hired Holmstead to fix the problems and finish the house.

In addition to creating structural problems, Conlin's employees had defectively constructed the see-through fireplace. When in use, it filled the entire living area with smoke due to the failure of the chimney to draw. Holmstead took the view that, in order for it to properly function as a fireplace, parts of it would have to be dismantled and rebuilt. When consulted on this, Conlin took the position that the problem could easily be solved by simply bricking in one side of the fireplace since this would create the draw needed to carry the smoke up and out the chimney. "My solution will cost about $200," said Conlin. "Your so-called solution will cost at least $5000. It's insane." Notwithstanding, the Owens decided to have Holmstead rebuild the fireplace and deal with Conlin later.

All in all, the Owens paid $300 000 to Holmstead who fixed and completed the house to high standards.

In the meantime, Janet has been suffering considerable distress. Her disappointment in Conlin's work became overwhelming and every day seemed to get harder. Though not clinically depressed, Janet found herself bursting into tears and waking up in the middle of the night, worrying about the house.

1. Can the Owens demonstrate all the steps in an action for breach of contract against Conlin?
2. Are the Owens themselves in breach of contract for refusing to permit Conlin to complete the contract?
3. Did the Owens properly mitigate their damages?
4. What damages can the Owens receive?

Termination of Contracts: An Overview

What kind of issues can a construction contract raise in relation to the termination and enforcement of contracts?

When parties enter into a contract, there are several ways in which it can be brought to an end—known, in law, as "termination":

- *Through performance.* When both parties fulfill their contractual obligations to each other, they have performed the contract. This is generally the ideal way of concluding a contractual relationship.

- *Through agreement.* Parties are always free to voluntarily bring their contract to an end. Both parties could agree to simply walk away from their agreement, or one party could pay a sum to the other side by way of settlement in exchange for agreeing to end the contract.

- *Through frustration.* The doctrine of frustration applies when, after the formation of a contract, an important, unforeseen event occurs—such as the destruction of the subject matter of the contract or the death/incapacity of one of the contracting parties. The event must be one that makes performance functionally impossible or illegal.[1] When a contract is frustrated, it is brought to an end.

- *Through breach.* A breach of contract, when it is particularly serious, can release the innocent party from having to continue with the contract if that is his wish. Less significant breaches generally entitle such a party to damages only.

What follows is a discussion of these four methods of termination and an outline of the remedies available for breach of contract.

Termination through Performance

What amounts to termination by performance depends on the nature of the contract, as in the following examples:

- A contract to provide an audit of a corporation is performed when the audit is competently completed and the auditor's account for service rendered is paid in full.

---

1. G.H. Treitel, *The Law of Contract*, 11th ed. (London: Sweet & Maxwell, 2003) at 866.

- A contract to buy and sell a house is performed when the purchase price is paid and title to the property is transferred to the buyer.
- A contract to provide a custom-designed generator is complete when a generator conforming with contract specifications is delivered and the purchase price is paid.

In short, a contract is performed when all of its implied and express promises have been fulfilled. When a contract is terminated through performance, this does not necessarily mean the end of the commercial relationship between the parties, however. They may continue to do business with each other by means of new, continuing, and overlapping contracts.

Performance by Others

The law easily distinguishes between those who have the contractual obligation to perform and those who may actually do the necessary work. When a corporation enters into a contract to provide goods or services, for example, it must by necessity work through employees/agents. Even when the contracting party is an individual, employees may still have an important role. In both cases, the employee/agent is ordinarily not a party to the contract. Expressed in legal terms, such an employee/agent lacks privity of contract and therefore cannot sue or be sued on the contract, though there may be liability in tort. Privity is discussed in more detail later in this chapter. Agency is discussed in Chapter 13.

vicarious performance
Performance of contractual obligations through others.

It is permissible to use employees to **vicariously perform** a contract in question, as long as personal performance by the particular contracting individual is not an express or implied term of a contract. For example, if a client engages an accountant and makes it clear that only that particular accountant is to do the work, performance through other accountants is not permitted. If there is no such term, the accountant is free to delegate the work to others in the firm while remaining contractually responsible for the timing and quality of the work.

In the case of Conlin and the Owens, there was nothing in the contract requiring Conlin to perform the contract unassisted. In fact, it would appear that the Owens fully understood that Conlin would use staff members to help him. For this reason, Conlin is not in breach of contract simply because he did not perform every aspect of the contract himself. He is, however, in breach of contract because his employees failed to properly perform aspects of the contract: the structural defects mean that the house was not built to Code and the fireplace was not constructed in accordance with plans and specifications since it could not draw air properly. The law holds Conlin responsible for his employees' incompetence.

Termination by Agreement

By Agreement between Parties

Parties may enter into an agreement that becomes unfavourable for one or both of them. In response, they may decide to

novation
The substitution of parties in a contract or the replacement of one contract with another.

- *Enter into a whole new contract.* This is known as **novation.** Provided both parties benefit from this arrangement, the agreement will be enforceable by the court as a new contract. For example, if the Owens subsequently decide that they want to buy an entirely more luxurious home than they have contracted for from Conlin, they and Conlin are free to negotiate a new contract and cancel the old one.
- *Vary certain terms of the contract.* If the Owens decide that they would like upgraded bathroom fixtures installed instead of the ones provided for in the

plans and specifications, they can seek a variation of contract. As discussed in Chapter 6, the party benefiting from the variation (the Owens) must provide consideration to the other side (Conlin). Without consideration, a variation is usually not enforceable. In a case like this, the typical consideration would be an increase in the contract price, reflecting the additional cost of the acquiring and installing upgraded bathroom fixtures.

- *End the contract.* The parties may decide to simply terminate the contract, with both parties agreeing not to enforce their rights or with one party paying the other to bring his obligations to an end.

- *Substitute a party.* The law permits a more limited form of novation whereby one party's rights and obligations are transferred to someone else. In short, a new party is substituted, and the old party simply drops out of the contract altogether. For example, if Conlin discovered that he had double-booked himself and could not in fact build the Owens' house, he might be able to recommend someone else who would step into his "contractual shoes." This new contractor would assume all of Conlin's obligations but also be entitled to payment by the Owens. However, everyone—the Owens, Conlin, and the new proposed contractor—must agree to this substitution in order for it to be effective. Of course, if the Owens are unhappy with Conlin's proposal, they are free to insist on performance by him and sue for breach of contract if he fails to perform.[2]

An agreement between the parties is almost always the best way of dealing with events that make the contract disadvantageous in some respect. By taking such a route, the parties are able to avoid the expense and uncertainty of litigation.

Transfer of Contractual Rights

A party who wants to end his involvement in a particular contract has the option—in certain circumstances—to transfer it to someone else. This transfer does not terminate the contract but does have the effect of eliminating the transferor's role in it. In short, while contractual duties or obligations cannot be transferred to someone else without agreement by the other side, contractual rights can be transferred without any such permission being required.

This means that Conlin cannot unilaterally transfer to another contractor his obligation to build the Owens' home. The Owens have contracted for performance by Conlin and his employees. They cannot be forced to deal with a new contractor altogether. However, Conlin can transfer his right to be paid for the building job to someone else.

assignment

The transfer of a contractual right by an assignor to an assignee.

In law, when one party transfers a contractual right to someone else, this is known as an **assignment** (see Figure 9.1). The person who is now or will be entitled to payment from a contract is known as a creditor. The party who is obligated to make the payment is known as a debtor.

The law of assignment of rights permits the creditor (the assignor) to assign the right to collect to another person (the assignee) without the agreement of the debtor. However, to be effective, the debtor must have notice of the assignment so that she knows to pay the assignee rather than the creditor. The assignee is entitled to collect the debt despite not being involved in the creation of the contract that produced the debt. Conversely, after receiving notice of the assignment, the debtor can perform his obligation only by paying the assignee. If the same debt is assigned to more than one assignee, normally the assignee who first notifies the debtor is entitled to payment.[3]

---

2. If they choose this route, the Owens still have a duty to mitigate, as discussed later in this chapter.
3. *Supra* note 1 at 682.

FIGURE 9.1

The Steps in Assignment

Step One: Creditor–Debtor Relationship
C (creditor) ⟷ D (debtor)
Contract is entered between C and D, whereby D owes money to C for services rendered.

Step Two: Assignor–Assignee Relationship
C (assignor) ⟷ A (assignee)
Contract is entered between C and A, whereby C assigns the debt he is owed by D.

Step Three: Assignee–Debtor Relationship
A (assignee) ⟷ D (debtor)
A gives notice to D.
D is now obligated to pay debt directly to A.

Expressed in legal language, the rule is that the assignees who take in good faith rank in the order that they have given notice to the debtor. This means that a later assignee may end up collecting from the debtor ahead of an earlier assignee simply by being the first to give notice to the debtor. In the meantime, the disappointed assignees can sue the assignor for breach of the contract of assignment; however, doing so is usually pointless if the assignor has disappeared or has no resources to pay damages.

The advantage of an assignment for a creditor such as Conlin is that he can "sell" rights for cash now and let the assignee worry about collecting from the Owens. Of course, Conlin will pay a price for this advantage by accepting less than the face value of the debt from the assignee. This discount will reflect the cost of early receipt, as well as the risk that the debtor cannot or will not pay.

Additionally, the assignee's right to payment is no greater than the right possessed by the assignor. This means, for example, that if Conlin breaches his contract with the Owens and becomes entitled to less than the full contract price, Conlin's assignee is likewise entitled to less. The objective is to ensure that the debtor—in this case, the Owens—is not disadvantaged by the assignment.[4]

Termination by Frustration

When a significant, unexpected event or change occurs that makes performance of a contract functionally impossible or illegal, the contract between the parties may be **frustrated.** In such circumstances, both parties are excused from the contract and it comes to an end. Neither side is liable to the other for breach.

frustration

Termination of a contract by an unexpected event or change that makes performance functionally impossible or illegal.

Unlike the doctrine of mistake—which relates to severely erroneous assumptions concerning existing or past circumstances surrounding a contract at its formation—frustration deals with events that occur after the contract has been formed. Like mistake, however, the defence of frustration is difficult to establish, given that the purpose of contract law is to enforce voluntarily chosen agreements.

The person claiming frustration must establish that the event or change in circumstances

■ was dramatic and unforeseen

■ was a matter that neither party had assumed the risk of occurring

---

4. *Supra* note 1 at 691. Note that in certain jurisdictions, there is also legislation related to assignments. These are discussed in G.H.L. Fridman, *The Law of Contract in Canada*, 4th ed. (Scarborough: Carswell, 1999) at 720 and following.

- arose without being either party's fault
- makes performance of the contract functionally impossible or illegal[5]

All of these elements must be demonstrated.

Sometimes events that would amount to frustration are expressly dealt with in the contract through a *force majeure* or other clause. That is, rather than leaving it to a judge to decide whether the occurrence of a given event amounts to frustration, the parties contractually define for themselves—in advance—what events would frustrate the contract.

Many circumstances that may appear to frustrate a contract do not amount to frustration in law. For example, if Conlin finds that construction material has unexpectedly tripled in price, and thus he will suffer a substantial loss on the contract, this circumstance would not amount to frustration. It has become financially disadvantageous to perform the contract, but it is still possible to do so. Similarly, if Conlin contracts to provide a certain kind of building material and no other, and that material proves to be unavailable at any price, that part of the contract has not been frustrated either. Conlin has simply made a promise that he cannot keep and is in breach. As a final example, if Conlin is unable to perform the contract because he has fired all his employees at the last minute, the contract may have become impossible to perform, but owing only to Conlin's own conduct. Self-induced impossibility does not count as frustration in law.

Landmark Case ▼

Taylor v. Caldwell (1863), 122 E.R. 309 (C.A.)

THE BUSINESS CONTEXT: A common situation giving rise to frustration occurs when the subject matter of the contract is destroyed, as discussed below.

FACTUAL BACKGROUND: Taylor rented from Caldwell the Surrey Gardens and Music Hall for four days to be used for a series of concerts. Prior to the scheduled concerts, the music hall was destroyed by a fire for which neither party could be faulted, and all of the concerts had to be cancelled. Taylor sued for his expenses related to advertising and other preparations, which were now wasted.

THE LEGAL QUESTION: Was Caldwell in breach of contract for failing to supply the music hall as promised?

RESOLUTION: Since the parties had not expressly or implicitly dealt with who would bear the risk of the music hall being destroyed by fire, the court had to decide whether the contract had been frustrated or not. It reasoned that the existence of the music hall was essential to performance of the contract, or, put another way, its destruction defeated the main purpose of the contract. On this basis, the contract had been frustrated, and Taylor's action failed.

CRITICAL ANALYSIS: Why did the court not simply decide that the owner of the music hall was liable when he failed to supply the promised venue, no matter how extenuating the circumstances?

In those rare cases in which a contract is terminated by frustration—as when the contract expressly states that the goods to be supplied must come from a particular source, which fails[6]—the consequences for the parties are often unsatisfactory. At the moment frustration occurs, any further obligations under the contract cease. If neither party has performed, they are left where they were before the contract was formed. If one party has begun to perform and incurred costs, there is no easy way to compensate that party, the reason being that, by definition, the contract

---

5. *Supra* note 1 at 866 and following, as well as Fridman, *supra* note 4 at 675 and following.
6. *Howell v. Coupland* (1876), 1 Q.B.D. 258 (C.A.).

has ended through the fault of neither party. Shifting the loss to the other would be no more just than leaving it where it lies. There are complicated and uneven developments in the common law and in the statutes of some provinces that attempt to address these problems, but these are beyond the scope of this book.[7]

International Perspective

Force Majeure Clauses

The commercial objective of parties to a contract sometimes can be defeated by circumstances beyond their control. Unforeseen events, both natural and human-made, may occur that make performance onerous or even impossible. The risk of unforeseen events is particularly great in international transactions. Storms, earthquakes, and fires may destroy the subject matter of the contract. Wars, blockades, and embargoes may prevent the performance of the contract. Hyperinflation, currency devaluation, and changes in government regulation may create hardship for the parties to the contract.

Legal systems, for the most part, recognize that the occurrence of some unforeseen events may be a valid excuse for nonperformance. This notion finds expression in various doctrines, such as commercial impracticality, impossibility, and frustration. The difficulty for traders is that, although legal systems recognize this kind of defence, there are varying rules governing when nonperformance is excused without liability on the part of the nonperforming party. It is difficult to predict precisely which events will release a party from contractual obligations. Additionally, exemption from performance is normally restricted to situations where it is impossible to perform—hardship or additional expense involved in performance is usually not an excuse. For these reasons, it is common business practice both in domestic and international contracts to include *force majeure* clauses.

A *force majeure* clause deals with the risk of unforeseen events. It allows a party to delay or terminate a contract in the event of unexpected, disruptive events such as the following:

- fire, flood, tornado, or other natural disaster
- war, invasion, blockade, or other military action
- strike, labour slowdown, walkout, or other labour problems
- inconvertibility of currency, hyperinflation, currency devaluation, or other monetary changes
- rationing of raw materials, denial of import or export licences, or other governmental action

CRITICAL ANALYSIS: What is the problem with drafting a clause that is very simple, such as, "In the event of a *force majeure*, the affected party may terminate its obligations under a contract"? Similarly, what is the problem with drafting a very specific clause that lists the events that allow a party to terminate the contract?

Source: Mary Jo Nicholson, Legal Aspects of International Business (Scarborough: Prentice Hall, 1997) at 175–179.

Enforcement of Contracts

balance of probabilities
Proof that there is a better than 50 percent chance that the circumstances of the contract are as the plaintiff contends.

When one party fails to perform its contractual obligations, it is in breach of contract and subject to a lawsuit. To succeed in its action for breach of contract, the plaintiff (the person who initiates the lawsuit) is obligated to demonstrate the following elements to the court's satisfaction, that is, on the **balance of probabilities:**

- *Privity of contract.* The plaintiff has to establish that there is a contract between the parties.

---

7. For a discussion of statute law applying to frustration, see Fridman, *supra* note 4 at 704 and following.

- *Breach of contract.* The plaintiff must prove that the other party (the defendant) has failed to keep one or more promises or terms of the contract.
- *Entitlement to a remedy.* The plaintiff must demonstrate that it is entitled to the remedy claimed or is otherwise deserving of the court's assistance.

As noted in Chapter 4, the balance of probabilities means that the plaintiff must prove there is a better than 50 percent chance that the circumstances of the contract are as it contends they are and, furthermore, that these circumstances entitle it to receive what is claimed.

Privity of Contract

Privity is a critical ingredient to enforcing a contract. It means that, generally speaking, only those who are parties to a contract can enforce the rights and obligations it contains.[8]

Because a strict application of the doctrine of privity can lead to serious injustices, courts have recently shown a willingness to allow third parties to rely on contractual clauses placed in the contract for their benefit. For example, a contract between a business and a customer may have an exclusion clause protecting employees from liability in the event that the customer suffers a loss. Under a classical approach to privity, employees would not be permitted to rely on such clauses as a defence to any action brought by a disgruntled customer because they are not parties to the contract—only their employer and the customer are. In the following case, however, the Supreme Court of Canada refused to apply privity in this way, choosing instead to create a limited exception to its application.

CASE ▼

London Drugs Limited v. Kuehne & Nagel International Ltd. (1992), 97 D.L.R. (4th) 261 (S.C.C.)

THE BUSINESS CONTEXT: Businesses may try to protect their employees from being successfully sued by including clauses in their contracts with customers that shelter employees from liability.

FACTUAL BACKGROUND: Kuehne & Nagel International Ltd. (K&N) stored a variety of merchandise for London Drugs, including a large transformer. A term in the storage agreement limited K&N's liability on any one item to $40. Owing to the negligence of two K&N employees, the transformer was dropped while it was being moved and sustained over $33 000 in damage. London Drugs brought an action for the full amount of damages against both the employees and K&N. It was acknowledged that K&N's liability was limited to $40.

THE LEGAL QUESTION: Can the employees rely on the clause limiting liability to $40?

RESOLUTION: The trial judge agreed that the negligent employees could be sued by the customer. Expressed in more technical legal language, the court applied the rule that employees are liable for torts they commit in the course of carrying out the services their employer has contracted to provide. Because the K&N employees were negligent in their attempt to lift the transformer, they were liable for the full extent of London Drugs' damages. The employees could not rely on the clause limiting recovery to $40 because this clause was found in a contract to which they were not a party. Put another way, the employees lacked privity to the contract between London Drugs and K&N.

---

8. There are a number of ways in which someone who is not a party to a contract (called a third party) may acquire an enforceable benefit, but this chapter discusses only one of them, in the employment context.

In response to the harshness that the strict doctrine of privity creates in this kind of situation, the Supreme Court of Canada created an exception to its application. As Justice Iacobucci explains,

> This court has recognized . . . that in appropriate circumstances, courts have not only the power but the duty to make incremental changes to the common law to see that it reflects the emerging needs and values of our society. . . . It is my view that the present appeal is an appropriate situation for making such an incremental change to the doctrine of privity of contract in order to allow the . . . [employees] to benefit from the limitation of liability clause. . . . I am of the view that employees may obtain such a benefit if the following requirements are satisfied: (1) the limitation of liability clause must, either expressly or impliedly, extend its benefit to the employees (or employee) seeking to rely on it; and (2) the employees (or employee) seeking the benefit of the limitation of liability clause must have been acting in the course of their employment and must have been performing the very services provided for in the contract between their employer and the plaintiff (customer) when the loss occurred.

The court went on to hold that the employees could rely on the limitation of liability clause. This is because the clause in question did extend its protection to the employees and, when the transformer was damaged, it was due to the negligence of the employees while doing the very thing contracted for, as employees. Though the negligence of the employees caused London Drugs' damages in the amount of $33 955.41, it was entitled to recover only $40 from the employees.[9]

CRITICAL ANALYSIS: Do you agree with Justice Iacobucci's decision? Should employees be able to rely on a clause in a contract to which they are not parties? How could employees protect themselves if they were not permitted to rely on such a clause?

The Owens could easily establish a critical step in a successful breach of contract action against Conlin—namely, privity of contract. Conlin and the Owens entered into a contract whereby Conlin would supply certain goods and services to the Owens in exchange for payment.

The Owens may well have an action against Conlin's employees, but only for the tort of negligence (discussed in detail in Chapter 11). There is no action in contract against the employees, however, because there is no contract between them and the Owens. The contract is between only the Owens and Conlin.

Statutory Modifications of the Doctrine

The common law of privity has also been modified by statute in two important areas: consumer purchases and insurance. In certain jurisdictions such as Saskatchewan, consumer protection legislation provides that a lack of privity is no defence to an action brought under the act for breach of warranty brought against a manufacturer, for example.[10] Similarly, insurance legislation across the country permits the beneficiary under a life insurance contract to sue the insurer even though the beneficiary is not a party to the contract (i.e., even though the beneficiary lacks privity).

---

9. Those who are not party to a contract containing exclusion clauses should not automatically assume that they can rely on those clauses notwithstanding the outcome in *London Drugs*. In *Haldane Products Inc. v. United Parcel Service* (1999), 103 O.T.C. 306 (Sup. Ct. Just.), for example, the plaintiff contracted with UPS to deliver industrial sewing needles to British Columbia. The contract contained a limitation of liability clause but there was no stipulation that anyone other than UPS employees would discharge UPS contractual obligations. UPS's subcontractor—who was transporting a UPS trailer containing the package—failed to deliver due to a fire in the trailer. The subcontractor was found liable for over $40 000 because the court refused to allow it to shelter under the exclusion clause in the UPS–Haldane contract.

10. *The Consumer Protection Act*, S.S. 1996, c. C-30.1, s. 55. See too *Consumer Product Warranty and Liability Act*, S.N.B. 1978, c. C18.1, s. 23.

Breach of Contract

Classification of the Breach

Virtually every breach of contract gives the innocent party the right to a remedy. When determining what that remedy should be, the courts will first consider whether the term breached can be classified as a condition or a warranty.

A contractual term will be classified as a condition or warranty only if that is the parties' contractual intention. Courts will consider all the circumstances surrounding the contract, including the language chosen by the parties in the contract itself, in making this determination.

condition
An important term that, if breached, gives the innocent party the right to terminate the contract and claim damages.

A **condition** is an important term that, if breached, gives the innocent party the right to not only sue for damages, but also, to treat the contract as ended. This latter right means that, if she so chooses, the nondefaulting party can consider herself to be freed from the balance of the contract and to have no further obligations under it. For example, it is an implied term of the contract between the Owens and Conlin that Conlin will be reliable. His multiple breaches of contract and insulting behaviour strongly suggest that he will not properly perform the contract in the future. On this basis, it could be argued that Conlin has breached a condition of the agreement, and the Owens are not obligated to continue in the contract with him.[11]

warranty
A minor term that, if breached, gives the innocent party the right to claim damages only.

A term classified as a **warranty** is a promise of less significance or importance. When a warranty is breached, the innocent party is entitled to damages only. Viewed in isolation, Conlin's failure to build the fireplace properly is likely to be regarded as a breach of warranty, entitling the Owens to damages only.

innominate term
A term that cannot easily be classified as either a condition or a warranty.

Even after the parties' intentions have been assessed, some terms cannot easily be classified as warranties or conditions and are known in law as **innominate terms.** In such circumstances, the court must look at exactly what has happened in light of the breach before deciding whether the innocent party is entitled to repudiate the contract. For example, it is a term of the contract that the house be built to *Code*. It would be difficult to classify such a term as either a condition or a warranty of the contract. The contract is unclear on this point and the term is one that could be breached in large and small ways. If Conlin failed to install shingles on the roof that were *Code* approved, this is likely a breach of a warranty-like term, giving rise to a claim for damages only. On the other extreme, Conlin's failure to provide a structurally sound home would be a breach of a condition-like term, allowing the Owens to end the contract on the spot, as they have done. Provided that the plaintiffs can establish just one breach of condition or condition-like innominate term, they are entitled to end the contract.

Note, however, that if the Owens end the contract on the erroneous assumption that such a serious form of breach has occurred, they themselves will be in breach of contract and subject to a lawsuit by Conlin.

Parties are free to classify a term in advance within the contract itself by setting out the consequences of breach. The court will generally respect this classification if it has been done clearly.[12]

Exemption and Limitation of Liability Clause

As already noted, parties are free to include a clause in their contract that limits or excludes liability for breach. This is what the storage company did in the *London Drugs* case discussed earlier. Historically, courts have been reluctant to allow the party in breach to rely on such a clause when the breach in question was severe and undermined the whole foundation of the contract. This is known as a **fundamental breach.** The argument is that such a breach automatically renders the entire contract

fundamental breach
A breach of contract that affects the foundation of the contract.

---

11. This analysis is based on John McCamus, *The Law of Contracts* (Toronto: Irwin Law Inc., 2005) at 635 and cases cited therein.
12. *Wickman Machine Tool Sales Ltd. v. Schuler*, [1974] A.C. 235 (H.L.).

(including the exclusion clauses) inoperative, and therefore the innocent party should be compensated. While such judicial concern might be helpful in a consumer contract, it is less welcome in a commercial context. The Supreme Court of Canada has therefore weighed in on the issue in *Hunter Engineering Co. v. Syncrude Canada Ltd.* but this case provides limited assistance because the judges split between two competing approaches,[13] making the law in the area unclear.

CASE ▼

Hunter Engineering Co. v. Syncrude Canada Ltd. (1989), 57 D.L.R. (4th) 321 (S.C.C.)

THE BUSINESS CONTEXT: Those who provide goods and services frequently include contractual clauses to limit or exclude their liability in the event of breach. Sometimes these clauses are intended to cover the situation of fundamental breach.

FACTUAL BACKGROUND: Syncrude purchased gearboxes to drive conveyor belts at its oil sands operation in Alberta. These gearboxes were purchased from Hunter Engineering and from Allis-Chalmers. Both the Hunter and Allis-Chalmers gearboxes were designed by Hunter and manufactured by a subcontractor. Both purchase contracts contained express warranties with time limits. Additionally, the contract between Syncrude and Allis-Chalmers contained a clause expressly excluding any other warranty or condition, "statutory or otherwise."

After the expiry of the express warranties and conditions, the gearboxes failed owing to a design defect in the manner in which the gears were welded. Syncrude repaired the gearboxes at its own considerable expense and brought an action against both Hunter Engineering and Allis-Chalmers for breach of contract.

THE LEGAL QUESTION: What is Hunter's liability under its contract with Syncrude? What is Allis-Chalmers' liability under the doctrine of fundamental breach? Can it rely on the exclusion clause in its contract with Syncrude, given the nature of its breach?

RESOLUTION: The Supreme Court held that the welding design details were the seller's responsibility, and that the failure of the gearboxes constituted a breach of a condition that the gearboxes be fit for the purpose sold. The presence of an express warranty or condition did not exclude the statutorily implied terms. Thus, Hunter was liable to Syncrude on this basis. Allis-Chalmers, however, was not liable because of the express exclusion of statutory warranties and conditions.

The court also discussed the issue of whether an exclusion of liability was effective when there is a fundamental breach of contract. Two judges, including Chief Justice Dickson, held that the breach in this case was not a fundamental breach, and in any event, an exclusion of liability for fundamental breach was enforceable unless it was unconscionable.

As Chief Justice Dickson explained,

> The doctrine of fundamental breach in the context of clauses excluding a party from contractual liability has been confusing at the best of times. Simply put, the doctrine has served to relieve parties from the effects of contractual terms, excluding liability for deficient performance where the effects of these terms have seemed particularly harsh.
>
> In light of the unnecessary complexities the doctrine of fundamental breach has created, the resulting uncertainty in the law, and the unrefined nature of the doctrine as a tool for averting unfairness, I am inclined to lay the doctrine of fundamental breach to rest, and where necessary and appropriate, to deal explicitly with unconscionability. . . . It is preferable to interpret the terms of the contract, in an attempt to determine exactly what the parties agreed. If on its true construction the contract excludes liability for the kind of breach that occurred, the party in breach will generally be saved from liability. Only where the contract is unconscionable, as might arise from situations

---

13. As Fridman notes, *supra* note 4 at 634, "Far from resolving . . . issues relating to fundamental breach and its effect on exclusion clauses, the decision of the Supreme Court of Canada . . . can be said to have left a legacy of more uncertainty. In it two different views were expounded as to the proper method of dealing with such clauses where a fundamental breach occurred, although, in the case in question, no such breach was held to have been involved."

of unequal bargaining power between the parties, should the courts interfere with agreements the parties have freely concluded.

Two other judges, including Madam Justice Wilson, took a different approach and would preserve a role for fundamental breach in certain circumstances, though they agreed that no fundamental breach had occurred in this particular case. For these judges, a fundamental breach would render an exclusion clause inoperative or ineffective if, in light of what happened, it would be unfair and unreasonable to allow the defendant to rely on the clause.

CRITICAL ANALYSIS: A clause that excludes or limits liability even for a profoundly serious breach of contract is enforceable, provided it is not unconscionable or would not be unfair or unreasonable. Would it not be better to simply apply the contract and expect parties to take care of themselves, at the bargaining stage, particularly in a contract involving sophisticated businesspeople?

Ethical Considerations — Is It Unethical to Breach a Contract?

Contract law generally does not punish a contract breaker but rather compensates the innocent party for any loss associated with the breach. According to famous jurist Oliver Wendell Holmes

> The duty to keep a contract at common law means a prediction that you must pay damages if you do not keep it—and nothing else.... If you commit [to] a contract, you are liable to pay a compensatory sum unless the promised event comes to pass, and that is all the difference. But such a mode of looking at the matter stinks in the nostrils of those who think it advantageous to get as much ethics into the law as they can.

This is known as the "bad man" theory of breach and coincides with the concept of economic breach already discussed in Chapter 5. Economic breach means that the potential contract breaker measures the cost of breach against the anticipated gains. If the projected benefits exceed the probable costs, the breach is efficient. The difficulty with this strictly economic perspective on the question of breach is that it purposely ignores or marginalizes the ethical implications of breaking a promise.

What, then, is the role of ethics in the realm of contract law? It must have at least a limited role, according to Robert Larmer, since morality is essential for a functioning business environment:

> [U]nless those in business recognize the obligation to keep promises and honour contracts, business could not exist. This is not to suggest that business people never break contracts, but if such behaviour ever became general, business would be impossible. Just as telling a lie is advantageous only if most people generally tell the truth, shady business practices are advantageous only if most business people recognize the existence of moral obligations. Immorality in business is essentially parasitic because it tends to destroy the moral environment which makes its very existence possible.

CRITICAL ANALYSIS: Should contract law start punishing more regularly those who breach contracts because such conduct amounts to a betrayal of trust and may lead to the market being undermined? Is it practical to ask the law to enforce a moral code or is Holmes's approach preferable? What nonlegal penalties might a contract breaker face?

Sources: Robert Larmer, ed. *Ethics in the Workplace: Selected Readings in Business Ethics* (Minneapolis/St. Paul: West Publishing Company, 1996) at 3; and Oliver Wendell Holmes, "The Path of the Law" (1897), 13 *Harv. L. Rev.* at 457.

Timing of the Breach

anticipatory breach
A breach that occurs before the date for performance.

A breach of contract can occur at the time specified for performance—as, for example, when one party fails to deliver machinery on the date recited in the contract. A breach can also occur in advance of the date named for performance—as, for example, when one party advises the other, in advance of the delivery date, that no delivery with be forthcoming. This is known as an **anticipatory breach.** Anticipatory breaches are actionable because each party to a contract is entitled to a continuous expectation that the other will perform during the entire period between the date the contract is formed and the time for performance. This means that the innocent party can sue immediately for breach of contract and is not required to wait and see if the other party has a change of heart.

When the anticipatory breach is sufficiently serious, the innocent party is not just entitled to damages. She can also treat the contract as at an end. This option puts the innocent party in somewhat of a dilemma, since she will not know for sure whether the contract can legally be treated as at an end unless and until the matter is litigated—an event that will occur months or, more likely, years later.

Entitlement to a Remedy

The final step in an action for breach of contract is for the plaintiff to satisfy a court that he is entitled to a remedy. In the usual case, damages—or monetary compensation—are awarded, but in specialized circumstances, a plaintiff is entitled to an equitable remedy.

The Measure of Damages

damages
Monetary compensation for breach of contract or other actionable wrong.

The purpose of **damages** in contract law is to compensate a plaintiff for loss, not to punish[14] the defendant for breach. Expressed in legal language, the plaintiffs, in this case the Owens, are entitled to compensation that puts them, as much as possible, in the financial position they would have been in had the defendant, Conlin, performed his obligations under the contract.

This section will provide the necessary background to assess the kinds of damages that the Owens may have sustained owing to Conlin's breaches of contract.

Pecuniary and Nonpecuniary Damages

As will be discussed in detail in Chapter 10, damages in tort can be pecuniary (for financial loss) and nonpecuniary (for loss of enjoyment, mental distress, and other emotional consequences). The same holds true in contract law, except that recovery for nonpecuniary damages is historically unusual. In law, a defendant is responsible only for the reasonably foreseeable damages sustained by the plaintiff and not for absolutely every adverse consequence experienced by the innocent party after the contract has been breached.[15] While pain and suffering or other emotional distress is reasonably foreseeable when one person negligently injures another in a car accident, it is not generally anticipated as being the consequence of a breach of contract.

Test for Remoteness The kinds of damages recoverable in contract law are determined by the test for remoteness, which was established in the still-leading decision of *Hadley v. Baxendale.*[16] That test states that the damages claimed are recoverable provided

- the damages could have been anticipated, having "arisen naturally" from the breach, or

---

14. Though exceptional, punitive damages in contract are available. See discussion of *Whiten v. Pilot Insurance Co.* (2002), 209 D.L.R. (4th) 257 (S.C.C.) in Chapter 28.
15. It is beyond the scope of this book to discuss whether the test for remoteness is stricter in contract than it is in tort.
16. (1854), 9 Exch. 341.

■ the damages—although perhaps difficult to anticipate in the ordinary case—are reasonably foreseeable because the unusual circumstances were communicated to the defendant at the time the contract was being formed.

Any claim for damages in contract must pass one of the remoteness tests set out above; otherwise, it is simply not recoverable. The policy rationale of such a rule is the need to ensure that defendants do not face unlimited liability for the consequences of a breach and to allow them, by being informed of special circumstances, the option of turning down the job, charging a higher price to compensate for the increased risk, or, perhaps, purchasing the necessary insurance.

Recovery of Nonpecuniary Damages   As already noted, recovery for nonpecuniary damages—such as for mental distress—is traditionally viewed with suspicion in contract law. This traditional approach has been challenged, however, due to a recent decision of the Supreme Court of Canada. Based on this new case, Janet Owen has a very reasonable chance of recovering damages for mental distress caused by Conlin's breaches of contract.

CASE ▼

Sun Life Assurance Company of Canada v. Fidler, [2006] 2 S.C.R.

THE BUSINESS CONTEXT: When a supplier of goods or services fails to meet contractual obligations, the customer may experience frustration and distress. Depending on the kind of contract involved, the customer may be entitled to damages for enduring such upset, thereby driving up the size of the damage award.

FACTUAL BACKGROUND: Ms Fidler worked as a receptionist at a bank in British Columbia. She was covered by a long-term disability policy that would provide her with an assured income should she become ill and unable to work. Ms Fidler began to receive benefits when she was diagnosed with chronic fatigue syndrome and fibromyalgia. The insurer later cut her off from payments, citing video surveillance that detailed activity proving that she could work. In face of medical evidence that Fidler could not, in fact, work, the insurer refused to reinstate her benefits. Fidler sued the insurer for breach of contract. Just before trial, the insurer agreed to reinstate benefits, leaving only a few issues to be determined at trial, including the one described below.

THE LEGAL QUESTION: Was the plaintiff entitled to recover damages for mental distress caused by the defendant's wrongful denial of benefits?

RESOLUTION: The Supreme Court of Canada rejected the traditional notion that damages for mental distress should be tightly controlled and exceptional. On the contrary, the court should simply ask the question "what did the contract promise?" and provide damages on that basis. More specifically, the plaintiff seeking recovery for mental distress must show:

1. that the object of the contract was to secure a psychological benefit that brings mental distress upon breach within the reasonable contemplation of the parties [i.e., the test in *Hadley v. Baxendale* cited above]; and

2. that the degree of mental suffering caused by the breach was of a degree sufficient to warrant compensation

The court ruled that—as disability insurance contracts are to protect the holder from financial and emotional stress and insecurity—mental distress damages should be recoverable. On this basis, Fidler was able to bring herself with the first step of the test above. And because Fidler's distress was of a sufficient degree, she met the second part of the

It would seem that Janet Owen has a particularly strong claim for mental distress damages. A c kontract to construct a home—given its personal nature—has as one of its objects the provision of a psychological benefit that brings mental distress upon breach within the reasonable contemplation of the parties. Second, since Janet has been very upset due to Conlin's breach, and is even having trouble sleeping, it would seem that the degree of mental suffering caused by the breach is of a degree sufficient to warrant compensation.

Recovery of Pecuniary Damages

Those who have suffered a breach of contract can recover all their resulting pecuniary (or monetary) losses unless a clause is included that limits, excludes, or fixes liability at a set amount.[17] Recovery of pecuniary damages is possible in situations such as the following:

- A purchaser of a warehouse with a leaky roof can recover the cost of repairing the roof provided the roof was warranted to be sound.
- A client who suffers a financial loss owing to negligent legal advice can recover those losses from the lawyer in question.
- A person whose goods are stolen while they are in storage can recover the cost of those items from the warehouse owner.

Similarly, because Conlin did not construct and complete the house properly, the Owens are entitled to recover additional damages that flow from that breach. This is discussed in the next section of the text.

Business Application of the Law

Damages for Cramped Seat

Though suing for breach of contract is ordinarily a last resort, successful litigation can still be tremendously satisfying.

Mr. Brian Horan knows the feeling. On his return by air to England from a ski vacation in Banff, Alberta, Horan was forced to endure extremely cramped conditions. "It was like being in a veal crate," he said. "I sat for eight hours at an angle. I was unable to read because the seat in front was too close. Eating was a nightmare and it wasn't possible to sleep." Soon after his arrival in England, Horan experienced terrible leg cramps and was concerned that he had developed deep vein thrombosis. Though this was not in fact the case, Horan felt badly treated and wrote to the company that had sold him the vacation package. When he received no reply, Horan decided to take the matter to small claims court in England, alleging breach of contract.

Judge Andrew Wallace awarded Horan the equivalent of CDN$1140 in damages, accepting that Horan had suffered considerable discomfort on the trip home. According to Judge Edwards, what Horan had to contend with "was not merely uncomfortable, it was intolerable," especially because the flight was eight hours long. The judge went on to recommend

---

17. Liquidation of damages clauses are discussed in Chapter 7.

that airlines should provide seats with a minimum pitch or distance between rows of seats of 35 inches. Seat pitch on Horan's flight was 29 inches.

After the hearing, Horan stated to the press that his case was a victory for everyone who takes vacations and travels by air: "I have not done this just for me. Today I was standing up for the greater body of the travelling public."[18]

CRITICAL ANALYSIS: How should the service provider have handled Horan's complaint from the outset? Do you agree with the court's decision?

Should cramped airplane cabins be actionable?

Sources: Keith McArthur, "Cramped Airline Passenger Wins Case" *The Globe and Mail* (18 April 2002) at A1; Rosemary Behan, "Travel News—Cramped Seats—Now You Can Sue: Judge Upholds Payout to Passenger" *The Daily Telegraph* (20 April 2002) ; and Nigel Bunyan, "Airline Passenger Awarded Damages over Cramped Seat" *The Daily Telegraph* (24 January 2002) at http:www.telegraph.co.uk/news/main.jhtml?xml=/news/2002/01/24/nfly24.xml (accessed 5 November 2006).

---

duty to mitigate
The obligation to take reasonable steps to minimize the losses resulting from a breach of contract or other wrong.

Duty to Mitigate   Everyone who suffers a breach of contract has a **duty to mitigate.** This means that they must take reasonable steps to minimize losses that might arise from the breach, as in the following examples:

- A person who is fired from his job, in breach of contract, has a duty to mitigate by trying to find replacement employment.
- A landlord whose tenant breaches a lease by moving out before the expiry of its term has a duty to mitigate by trying to find a replacement tenant.
- The disappointed vendor whose purchaser fails to complete a real estate transaction has a duty to mitigate by trying to find a replacement purchaser.

If the plaintiff fails to mitigate, its damage award will be reduced accordingly. For example, if the employee making $100 000 a year had one year left on his contract before he was wrongfully terminated, his damages would be $100 000. However, his duty to mitigate requires him to look for comparable employment. If he immediately does so and secures a job at $80 000, his damages drop to $20 000. If he fails to mitigate—by, for example, refusing such a job—a court will reduce his damages by $80 000, since that loss is more attributable to him than to his former employer.

By the same token, any reasonable costs associated with the mitigation are recoverable from the party in breach. An employee could, in addition to damages related to salary loss, also recover reasonable expenses related to the job search.

In the Owens' case, mitigation took the form of hiring Holmstead to finish and repair the house for $300 000. Assuming that this is reasonable, the Owens will be able to recover $100 000 from Conlin. This is because the Owens have had to pay an extra $100 000 for their house over and above what they had committed to pay Conlin. The calculation is based on the following analysis: The Owens were going

---

18. According to Professor David Grant, this ruling would apply only to flights that come with a package holiday. The legal relationship between the airline and passenger is governed by the Warsaw Convention where "discomfort probably doesn't apply." See Rosemary Behan, "Travel News—Cramped Seats—Now You Can Sue: Judge Upholds Payout to Passenger" *The Daily Telegraph* (20 April 2002) (accessed September 2002 from www.factiva.com/upgrade/Loginredirect)

to spend $500 000 on the house but have paid Conlon $300 000 and Holmstead $300 000 for a total of $600 000. Since this extra cost of $100 000 to obtain their bargain flows from Conlin's breach of contract, it is recoverable. Note that even the $5000 to rebuild the see-through fireplace (which is included in Holmstead's $300 000 bill) is recoverable. A court will almost certainly agree that the Owens are entitled to the price of rebuilding the fireplace even though this amount is much higher than Conlin's solution of simply bricking in one of the fireplace walls. In short, the Owens had contracted for a see-through fireplace and are entitled to it.

Equitable Remedies

In those relatively rare situations in which damages would be an inadequate remedy for breach of contract, the court may exercise its discretion to grant one of the equitable remedies discussed below.

Specific Performance   An order by the court for the equitable remedy of specific performance means that instead of awarding compensation for failing to perform, the court orders the party who breached to do exactly what the contract obligated him to do. This remedy is available only when the item in question is unique and cannot be replaced by money. The classic situation for specific performance is a contract for the sale of land, where the particular piece of land covered by the contract is essential to the buyer's plans, perhaps as part of a major development project. Without the remaining piece, the project cannot proceed, so damages would fail to provide a complete remedy.

Because specific performance is an equitable remedy, a court can refuse to order it, at its discretion, as in the following circumstances:

- *Improper behaviour by the plaintiff.* Any improper motive or conduct on the part of the plaintiff may disqualify him from being granted such special assistance. Rules governing equity, like "he who seeks equity must do equity" or "she who comes to equity must come with clean hands," mean that only the deserving plaintiff will succeed.
- *Delay.* Failure by the plaintiff to bring her claim promptly can be grounds for denying her an equitable remedy.[19]
- *Impossibility.* A court will not order a defendant to do something that is impossible, such as convey land she does not own.[20]
- *Severe hardship.* If specific performance would cause a severe hardship to the parties, or to a third party, a court may refuse to order it.
- *Employment contracts.* A court will not, ordinarily, order specific performance of an employment contract because being forced to work for someone else against his wishes would interfere too much with the employee's personal freedom.

Injunction   If a contract contains promises not to engage in specified activities, disregarding those promises by engaging in the prohibited acts is a breach of contract. While an award of damages is of some help, additionally, the plaintiff would want a court order requiring the offender to refrain from continued violation of the contract. For example, if the vendor of a business agrees not to compete with the new owner and the relevant clauses are reasonable restrictions (see Chapter 8), damages alone are an inadequate remedy for breach because they fail to prevent the

---

19. For a discussion and excerpts of relevant case law concerning equitable remedies and defences thereto, see Christine Boyle & David R. Percy, eds., *Contracts: Cases and Commentaries*, 7th ed. (Toronto: Carswell, 2004) at 950 and following.
20. See *Castle v. Wilkinson* (1870), 5 L.R. Ch. App. 534.

vendor from competing. Only an order to cease doing business will provide the buyer with a complete remedy.

Like an order of specific performance, an injunction is an equitable remedy and is subject to the court's discretion. However, it is commonly ordered to restrain a party from breaching a promise not to do something, as noted above. There are occasions where a court will not order an injunction, however, as when the plaintiff does not have "clean hands" (e.g., is undeserving) or delays in bringing the matter before the court.

Courts also have the jurisdiction to order an injunction for a limited period of time. This type of injunction, known as an **interlocutory injunction,** requires someone to stop doing something until the whole dispute can be resolved through a trial.

Rescission   It may be appropriate, in some cases, to restore the parties to the situation they were in before the contract was formed, rather than use compensation to put the innocent party in the position it would have been in had the contract been completed. For example, many of the doctrines in Chapter 8 for avoiding contracts provide rescission as the contractual remedy.

As with other equitable remedies, there are bars to receiving rescission of a contract. For example, where parties cannot restore each other to their precontractual positions—because, perhaps, the subject matter of the contract has been altered—the court has the power to do what is practically just, including the power to order that the innocent party be compensated. Another bar to rescission is delay by the plaintiff in seeking the court's assistance.

Restitutionary Remedies

Sometimes a contractual claim fails not because the plaintiff is undeserving but because he cannot prove that an enforceable contract is in place. The law of restitution gives recourse to a plaintiff who has conferred benefits on the defendant in reliance on a contract that cannot be enforced due, for example, to noncompliance with the Statute of Frauds.[21] For example, if the plaintiff has done work for the defendant pursuant to an unenforceable contract for the purchase of land, the plaintiff may end up being recompensed by the defendant, not under contract but pursuant to the law of restitution.

Restitution is a complex area of law but its main objective is clear—to remedy unjust enrichment. **Unjust enrichment** occurs when the defendant has undeservedly or unjustly secured a benefit at the plaintiff's expense. In such circumstances, the court will ordinarily order that the benefit be restored to the plaintiff or otherwise be accounted for by the defendant.

In response to an unjust enrichment, the court has several options, including ordering the defendant to

- pay a **restitutionary** *quantum meruit;* that is, an amount that is reasonable given the benefit that the plaintiff has conferred.[22]
- pay compensation; that is, an allowance of money to put the plaintiff in as good a position as she was in prior to conferring the benefit.[23]

interlocutory injunction
An order to refrain from doing something for a limited period of time.

unjust enrichment
Occurs when one party has undeservedly or unjustly secured a benefit at the other party's expense.

restitutionary *quantum meruit*
An amount that is reasonable given the benefit the plaintiff has conferred.

---

21. See Chapter 8.
22. Contractual *quantum meruit* has already been discussed in Chapter 7.
23. G.H.L. Fridman, "*Quantum Meruit*" (1997), 37 *Alta. L. Rev.* 38; M.M. Litman, "The Emergence of Unjust Enrichment as a Cause of Action and the Remedy of Constructive Trust" (1987/88) 26 *Alta. L. Rev.* 407–470.

Managing Risk

There are several risks that a business faces when the time comes to perform a contract. It may be that the business cannot perform at all or, that when it does perform, it does so deficiently. A business can attend to these possibilities proactively or reactively. From a proactive perspective, the business can negotiate for clauses to limit or exclude liability as well as for a *force majeure* clause, as appropriate. It may be, however, that the other side is unwilling to agree to such clauses. Another proactive strategy is to ensure that employees are competent and properly trained since any mistakes they make in performance of the contract are attributable to the employer. The better the employees do, the more likely the contract will be performed without incident. Securing proper insurance can also be effective, a matter discussed in Chapter 28 in more detail.

Once the business is in breach of contract, however, matters are now in a reactive mode. The contract breaker is in an unenviable position since it faces liability for all reasonable costs associated with its default. To reduce financial exposure and litigation expenses, the business should consider seeking mediation, arbitration, and other forms of compromise, including settlement offers, as alternatives to going to trial. Depending on the nature of the breach, the loss may be covered by insurance.

Those who contract for the provision of a product or service should undertake to ensure that the supplier is reputable and reliable. This way, legal conflict is perhaps avoided altogether.

When faced with a breach of contract, the innocent party must make a business decision—as much as a legal one—and decide how it should treat that failure. This decision involves evaluating the risks of losing in court; the remedies available including the amount of damages; the likelihood of being able to negotiate a settlement; and whether there is a valuable business relationship to preserve.

Business Law in Practice Revisited

1. Can the Owens demonstrate all the steps in an action for breach of contract against Conlin?

The Owens can meet all the steps to succeed in an action for breach of contract. They can show privity of contract between themselves and Conlin. They can show that Conlin breached the contract in multiple ways, including by failing to build the house according to Code and providing the fireplace contracted for. Finally, the Owens can show that they are entitled to a remedy. Both have suffered both pecuniary loss and, in addition, Janet has suffered nonpecuniary damages in the form of mental distress.

2. Are the Owens themselves in breach of contract for refusing to permit Conlin to complete the contract?

Conlin's multiple breaches of contract and insulting behaviour strongly suggest that he will not properly perform the contract in the future. A court may well conclude that this amounts to a breach of a condition of the contract—namely that he will be reliable. If the Owens can prove a breach of condition, they have the right to end the contract. They are therefore not in breach of contract for refusing to permit him to complete.

The term that the house be built to Code may be hard to classify as a condition or warranty upfront since the parties' intentions are not clear and the term itself can be breached in large ways and small. On this basis, the court will look to how serious the structural defects are. If they are serious, the breach will be of a condition-like innominate term, also bringing with it the right to treat the contract as at an end.

3. Did the Owens properly mitigate their damages?

Assuming that there has been a breach of condition or condition-like innominate term, the Owens properly mitigated their loss in hiring Holmstead to repair and complete the home. This is also based on the assumption that the extra cost was reasonable.

4. What damages can the Owens receive?

The Owens stand a good chance of receiving considerable pecuniary and nonpecuniary damages.

Pecuniary Damages Because the Owens had to hire Holmstead to finish and repair the house for $300 000, they paid an extra $100 000 for their home. That is, the contract price with Conlin was $500 000. They have already paid Conlin $300 000 and will be paying Holmstead another $300 000. Assuming that Holmstead's fees were reasonable, the Owens will be able to recover $100 000 from Conlin.

Note that even the $5000 to rebuild the see-through fireplace (which is included in Holmstead's $300 000 bill) is probably recoverable even though a cheaper "solution" was offered by Conlin. The Owens contracted for a see-through fireplace and therefore Conlin's idea of simply bricking in one of the fireplace walls is not acceptable. Note that the recovery of $5000 is already included in the $100 000 discussed above. It cannot be claimed and recovered twice.

The Owens' pecuniary damages are $100 000.

Nonpecuniary Damages Janet Owens may also be able to recover damages for mental distress and suffering because Conlin's breach of contract caused her mental distress. A contract for home construction arguably has, as one of its objects, the provision of a psychological benefit so the first step in *Fidler* is met. The second step is also met since Janet has suffered mental distress to a degree sufficient to warrant compensation. She has experienced great upset and even has had trouble sleeping.

It is difficult to predict how much a court will award for nonpecuniary damages but based on existing case law, it is unlikely to exceed $5000.[24]

Chapter Summary

In the vast majority of situations, a contract terminates or ends when the parties fully perform their obligations. Less common are situations where the contract ends because the parties find it impossible or tremendously difficult to perform their obligations. In such cases, prudent business parties will have addressed such a possibility through a *force majeure* clause or equivalent.

A more usual and complicated situation, from a business perspective, occurs when one party breaches the contract by failing to perform or by performing inadequately.

There are several ways that a contract is terminated: by performance, by agreement, through frustration, and through breach.

When a contract is terminated by performance, the parties have fulfilled all their implied and express promises. The work necessary to achieve performance may be done by the parties personally or through their agents/employees, unless a term to the contrary is included.

---

24. For discussion of quantum, see Shannon Kathleen O'Byrne, "Damages for Mental Distress and Other Intangible Loss in a Breach of Contract Action" (2005) 28 *Dalhousie Law Journal* 311–352.

Sometimes, parties terminate a contract by agreement. For example, the parties may agree to end the contract entirely or to replace it with a new one. Alternatively, the parties may vary certain terms of the contract or substitute a new party who, in turn, assumes rights and duties under the contract.

Contract law allows one party to assign her right under a contract but not the liabilities. The law of assignment permits the creditor to assign his right to collect under a contract to another (the assignee) without the agreement of the debtor. Once the creditor (assignor) has given notice to the debtor, the latter can perform the obligation only by paying the assignee.

The doctrine of frustration terminates a contract, but only in very limited circumstances. It must be shown that an unanticipated event or change in circumstances is so substantial that performance has become functionally impossible or illegal. Provided the risk of such an event has not been allocated to one party or the other, and provided the event did not arise through either party's fault, the contract has been frustrated.

When one party fails to perform its contractual obligations, it is in breach of contract and subject to a lawsuit. To succeed in its action for breach of contract, the innocent party must establish the existence of a contract, breach of contract, and entitlement to a remedy.

Privity means that, with limited exceptions, only those who are parties to a contract can enforce the rights and obligations it contains.

When a party to a contract fails to keep his promise, he has committed a breach of contract and is liable for such damages as would restore the innocent party to the position she would have been in had the contract been performed. If there is an exclusion or limitation of liability clause in the contract, the defendant's liability will be reduced or eliminated, depending on the circumstances.

Damages in contract are ordinarily pecuniary, but in some circumstances, the innocent party is entitled to nonpecuniary damages for mental suffering and distress.

When one party suffers a breach of contract, she must take reasonable steps to mitigate. If the party fails to do so, the damage award will be reduced accordingly. By the same token, any reasonable costs associated with mitigation are also recoverable from the party in breach.

Contract law also offers equitable remedies, such as specific performance and injunction, when damages are an inadequate remedy. On occasion, the best solution is to rescind the contract—that is, return the parties to their precontractual positions.

The law of restitution also provides remedies in a contractual context because its main objective is to remedy unjust enrichment. Unjust enrichment occurs when the defendant has undeservedly or unjustly secured a benefit at the plaintiff's expense.

Whether the innocent party takes the contract breaker to court is as much a business decision as it is a legal one.

Chapter Study

Key Terms and Concepts

anticipatory breach (p. 206)

assignment (p. 197)

balance of probabilities (p. 200)

condition (p. 203)

damages (p. 206)

duty to mitigate (p. 209)

frustration (p. 198)

fundamental breach (p. 203)

innominate term (p. 203)

interlocutory injunction (p. 211)

novation (p. 196)

restitutionary *quantum meruit* (p. 211)

unjust enrichment (p. 211)

vicarious performance (p. 196)

warranty (p. 203)

Questions for Review

1. What are the four major ways that a contract can be terminated?

2. What is an assignment? What risks does the assignee of a contractual right assume?

3. What is privity of contract?

4. How is vicarious performance used by business?

5. How is a new contract created through novation?

6. When is a contract frustrated?

7. What is a *force majeure* clause?

8. What elements need to be established in a successful action for breach of contract?

9. How is the severity of a breach of contract evaluated?

10. What is the difference between a warranty and a condition?

11. What is the purpose of awarding damages for breach of contract?

12. When is a plaintiff entitled to damages for mental distress?

13. What is unjust enrichment?

14. What is restitutionary *quantum meruit*?

15. What is specific performance?

16. When will a court grant an injunction?

17. What is the remedy of rescission?

18. When can the innocent party treat the contract as at an end?

Questions for Critical Thinking

1. A contract is considered frustrated only in very unusual situations. Should the doctrine of frustration be applied more often? Would a broader application produce fairer results? What is the downside of such a change in commercial contracts?

2. Damages for breach of contract are meant to compensate the victim for financial loss resulting directly from the breach. Would compensation be more complete if the courts took a broader approach to damages and considered factors such as inconvenience, harm to reputation, or upset of a business caused by the breach? Should the motive or reason for the breach of contract also affect the amount of damages?

3. The privity rule is one of the basic elements of contract law. Is it too restrictive? On the other hand, is there a danger in creating too many exceptions to the rule?

4. Contract law is intended to facilitate commercial activities and to enable businesses to conduct their affairs so that their legal obligations are certain. Do you think, after considering the material in the last five chapters, that contract law achieves its goals? Can you think of ways to improve the effectiveness of contract law?

5. The Supreme Court of Canada stated that mental distress damages for breach of contract can be awarded when an object of the contract was to secure a psychological benefit. What kinds of contracts can you think of that promise a psychological benefit?

6. Everyone who suffers a breach of contract still has a duty to mitigate his or her damages. Do you think it is fair to impose a positive duty on someone when a contract is breached through no fault of his own? How strict do you think courts should be in analyzing whether someone has fulfilled his duty to mitigate?

Situations for Discussion

1. Total Waste Disposal Ltd. (TWD) made a contract with the City of Kingsville for collection of garbage in a growing area of the city. When the contract was made, there were 3000 households in the collection area. The contract was for three years, and TWD estimated that in three years' time there would be 1000 more households in the area. TWD agreed to remove all garbage in the defined area for three years for $400 000 a year. TWD projected a profit of $75 000 on the contract. The area developed more quickly than expected. By the end of the first year, there were 4000 households and more growth appeared likely. TWD broke even in year one, but it now predicts significant losses in years two and three. TWD is considering whether to approach the city for renegotiation of the contract for years two and three.

How does this contract allocate the risk? How else could the risk have been allocated? Should TWD request renegotiation? On what terms? What factors should the city consider in responding to the request? Has the contract been frustrated? Should TWD try to buy its way out of the contract? What is the best strategy for TWD?

2. Action Distributors (AD) and Bonny Toys (BT) had an agreement whereby AD was the sole distributor of BT's toys in Canada. The agreement made no provision for termination. Two years into the contract, BT was bought by AD's major competitor, Entertainment Plus (EP). Shortly after the takeover, BT terminated its contract with AD without notice. By this time, BT's toys made up 75 percent of AD's business. AD was unable to find another supplier and eventually went out of business. AD estimates that as a result of BT's termination, it lost $450 000 in profit and $625 000 in the value of the business as a going concern.[25]

   Was BT entitled to terminate the contract? Should AD have received notice of BT's intention? Can AD hold EP responsible for BT's termination? Are AD's losses the result of the termination? How could this contract have been better designed?

3. Cartright owned a large house, which he converted into five small apartments. He leased the apartments to tenants for monthly rents ranging from $900 to $1500. Cartright decided to sell the property, and Luxury Developments (LD) agreed to buy it for $500 000. In the agreement, Cartright promised that "the property may continue to be lawfully used as it is presently being used" and that all zoning bylaws had been observed. When LD's lawyer investigated the property, she discovered that the applicable zoning regulation permitted a maximum of three rental units for each property.[26]

   How significant to the contract is the three-unit restriction? Can LD demand that Cartright attempt to have the regulation changed? Can LD demand a reduction in the price? If so, how much? Can LD choose to terminate the contract? How would you advise each party to deal with the situation?

4. Atlantic Fertilizer (AF) operates a fertilizer plant in New Brunswick. AF made a major sale to the government of Togo in Africa and engaged Pearl Shipping (PS) to transport the fertilizer to Togo for a fee of $60 000. The contract between AF and PS specified that AF would deliver the cargo to PS for loading on its ship between 25 and 31 March and that AF would pay $1000 (in addition to the shipping charges) for each day after 31 March that the cargo was delayed. AF had difficulty in filling the large order in its plant and notified PS that delivery would be sometime after 31 March.[27]

   PS is contemplating AF's message and deciding how it should react. Options under consideration are to wait for AF to deliver and add the $1000 daily charge to the bill; give AF a firm date by which it must deliver; or terminate the contract with AF and seek another cargo for its ship. Which options are legally available to PS? Which should PS choose?

5. ABC Ltd. was in a contract to supply 1000 widgets at $1.00 each to XYZ Ltd. by a specified date. Due to a mechanical failure at its factory, ABC Ltd. cannot fill the order on time and has advised XYZ Ltd. to expect delivery to be two months late. XYZ Ltd. planned to use the widgets as components in a machine that it had already contracted to sell for an anticipated profit of $30 000. It cannot wait the two months without jeopardizing that sale. What is XYZ Ltd. obligated to do now? What if the only other source for replacement widgets is from a manufacturer that is proposing to sell at an exorbitant sum? What other costs can XYZ Ltd. seek to recover?

6. Wigmore Farms ("Wigmore") grows lentils on its farms. Wigmore entered into a contract with A & BB Rice, Inc. ("ABB"), a lentil, chickpea, and rice wholesaler, to supply ABB with lentils from its farms. This relationship continued for two years, until, due to unforeseen weather conditions, Wigmore's lentil crop failed, and it was unable to deliver the product to ABB.[28] If ABB sues Wigmore for breach of contract, will

---

25. Based, in part, on *Cosco Inc. v. Cambridge Recreation Products Inc.*, [1995] O.J. No. 717 (Gen. Div.) (QL, O.J.).
26. Based, in part, on *Jorian Properties Ltd. v. Zellenrath* (1984), 26 B.L.R. 276 (Ont. C.A.).
27. Based, in part, on *Armada Lines Ltd. v. Chaleur Fertilizers Ltd.* (1994), 170 N.R. 372 (F.C.A.), rev'd [1997] 2 S.C.R. 617.
28. Based, in part, on *A & BB Rice Inc. v. Wigmore Farms Ltd.* (2005), 141 A.C.W.S. (3d) 559 (Ont. S.C.J.).

Wigmore be able to successfully advance the defence of frustration? Is there any other information you need before deciding?

7. Imperial Brass Ltd. wanted to computerize all of its systems. Jacob Electric Systems Ltd. presented Imperial with a proposal that met Imperial's needs. In August, Imperial accepted the proposal, along with Jacob's "tentative" schedule for implementation, which led Imperial to expect a total computerized operation by mid-January, with the possibility of a 30-day extension. In October, it became clear that there were problems with the software being developed, and Imperial asked for corrections to be made. At the end of October, the hardware and two software programs were delivered to Imperial, and Imperial's employees attempted to begin to use the programs. Very little training was provided, however, and there were major problems with the computer screens freezing, and data being lost. More programs were delivered in January, along with some operating instructions, but Imperial's employees were still unable to make any use of the programs they had. The programmer Jacob assigned to Imperial's contract, Mr. Sharma, continued to work on the remaining programs. In May, however, Jacob informed Imperial that Sharma would be leaving the company, and Imperial informed Jacob that if that were to happen, given the problems and delays the company had already experienced, Imperial would be forced to end the contract with Jacob.[29] Is the breach by Jacob serious enough to permit the innocent party, Imperial, to treat the contract as at an end?

8. Canadian Pacific Airlines (CP) agreed to safely transport the Newells' two pet dogs on a flight from Toronto to Mexico City. The Newells were concerned about the safety and welfare of their dogs, but CP's employees reassured them that the dogs would be safe in the cargo compartment of the aircraft, and reported to them before they boarded that their dogs had been safely placed in the cargo area. When the flight arrived in Mexico City, one dog was dead and the other was comatose. The Newells sued CP for general damages to compensate them for "anguish, loss of enjoyment of life and sadness" that they allege resulted from the breach of contract.[30] Are the Newells entitled to anything other than compensation for their direct financial loss (i.e., the value of the dogs)? If so, what would be an adequate amount to compensate for the mental distress suffered by the Newells?

For more study tools, visit
http://www.businesslaw3e.nelson.com

---

29. Based, in part, on *Imperial Brass Ltd. v. Jacob Electric Systems Ltd.* (1989), 72 O.R. (2d) 17 (H.C.J.).
30. Based, in part, on *Newell v. Canadian Pacific Airlines Ltd.* (1976), 14 O.R. (2d) 752 (Co. Ct.).

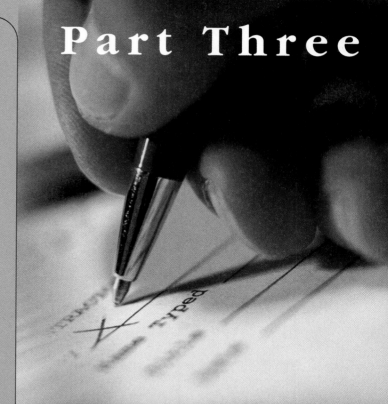

Part Three

TORT LAW PROVIDES REMEDIES TO PERSONS WHO have suffered physical harm and/or economic loss due to the intentional or careless actions of another. Business is exposed to tort risks on a variety of fronts. A paper mill may release toxins into a nearby river and ruin the water downstream. A customer may slip on the floor of a store and suffer serious injury. One business may intentionally seek to drive a competitor out of business by spreading lies. An accountant or lawyer may provide negligent advice that causes the client to lose money. Tort law provides a set of rules through which the innocent party can recover financial compensation for the loss sustained. The next three chapters consider the risk exposure of business in the context of tort law.

Business Torts

Chapter 10 Introduction to Tort Law

Chapter 11 The Tort of Negligence

Chapter 12 Other Torts

Chapter

10

Objectives

After studying this chapter, you should have an understanding of

- the broad scope of tort law
- the differences between a civil action and a criminal action
- the purpose of tort remedies
- how business can manage its potential liability in tort

Introduction
to Tort Law

Business Law in Practice

Bar-Fly is a large bar operating in Eastern Canada. Though most of its staff members are trained to diffuse hostility and aggression among patrons, fights occasionally occur. At least one bouncer is on duty to handle such situations.

Sam, a university student, visits Bar-Fly one night with several of his friends. Though Sam and his friends stick to themselves, an altercation breaks out at the table beside them. It is soon quelled by Bar-Fly staff. Mike, one of the bouncers, then accuses Sam of starting the fight and demands that he leave. When Sam protests his innocence, Mike begins to gesture wildly very close to Sam's face. He then grabs Sam by his shirt collar and throws him from the premises with such force that Sam suffers serious spinal injuries. While all this is going on, one of Sam's friends slips in the men's room on spilt beer that had been accumulating for hours. He lands hard and breaks his arm.

1. What kind of tort action does Sam's friend have as a result of breaking his arm?
2. What potential legal actions result from the altercation between Sam and Mike?
3. Is Bar-Fly responsible for Mike's actions?
4. What risk management actions could Bar-Fly have taken to prevent this altercation and the fall in the men's room?

Defining Tort Law

tort

A harm caused by one person to another, other than through breach of contract, and for which the law provides a remedy.

The word **tort**[1] describes any harm or injury caused by one person to another—other than through breach of contract—and for which the law provides a remedy.[2] According to the Supreme Court of Canada, tort law provides a means whereby compensation, usually in the form of damages, may be paid for

> injuries suffered by a party as a result of the wrongful conduct of others. It may encompass damages for personal injury suffered, for example, in a motor vehicle accident or as a result of falling in dangerous premises. It can cover damages occasioned to property. It may include compensation for injury caused to the reputation of a business or a product. It may provide damages for injury to honour in cases of defamation and libel. A primary object of the law of tort is to provide compensation to persons who are injured as a result of the actions of others.[3]

Given this diversity, the law historically evolved so as to break torts down into distinct categories, each with its own discrete definition. What follows is a brief sampling:

trespass to land

Interference with someone's possession of land.

deceit or fraud

A false representation intentionally or recklessly made by one person to another that causes damage.

- *Trespass to land.* **Trespass to land** involves interference with someone's possession of land.[4] Parking garage operators might rely on the tort of trespass when drivers leave their cars in the lot but fail to purchase the required ticket from the automated ticket dispenser. The driver is responsible for the tort of trespass because he has left the vehicle on the property without permission.

- *Deceit or fraud.* This tort is based on a false representation intentionally or recklessly made by one person to another that causes damage.[5] The tort of **deceit or fraud** occurs when, for example, a customer purchases a vehicle based on

---

1. The word "tort" is derived from the Latin word meaning "crooked" and the French word meaning "wrong." See Lewis Klar, *Tort Law*, 3rd ed. (Toronto: Carswell, 2003) at 1.
2. See J. Fleming, *The Law of Torts*, 9th ed. (Sydney: Law Book Co., 1998) at 1 for further discussion.
3. *Hall v. Hebert*, [1993] 2 S.C.R. 159 at para. 58, per Cory J.
4. *Supra* note 1 at 97–98.
5. *Supra* note 1 at 599 and following.

the vendor's intentional representation that the vehicle has a new engine when, in fact, it does not. The vendor has committed the tort of deceit because he made an untrue statement, which the purchaser relied on in deciding to make the purchase.

negligence
Unreasonable conduct, including a careless act or omission, that causes harm to another.

■ *Negligence.* The tort of **negligence** compensates someone who has suffered loss or injury due to the unreasonable conduct of another.[6] It is one of the most common torts to arise in a business context. For example:

— when a taxi driver is injured due to an unsafe lane change by another, he is the victim of the tort of negligence. The driver causing the injury is responsible for the tort of negligence because she has made the unsafe lane change and failed to show the care and attention that the circumstances required.

— when lawyers, accountants, or other professionals give their client incompetent advice that causes loss, they have committed not only a breach of contract but also the tort of negligence, more specifically known as professional negligence.

— when consumers purchase a defective product, they may have an action against the manufacturer for negligence if the product was improperly designed and/or produced. This area of law is known more specifically as product liability, but its foundations are in negligence.

— when a bar overserves a customer, it may be found negligent if that intoxicated customer is injured or causes injury to others.

The law of torts will not automatically provide a remedy when someone has been physically or economically injured. One of the key objectives of tort law is to distinguish between a situation in which the loss suffered by an injured individual should remain uncompensated and one in which responsibility for the loss should be "shifted" to another party considered responsible for causing the loss, known as the **tort-feasor.** Tort law provides an evolving set of rules for making that determination.

tort-feasor
Person who commits a tort.

To a large extent, tort law seeks to impose liability based on fault, as the following two examples illustrate:

EXAMPLE 1 A truck driver falls asleep at the wheel. As a result, his rig crashes into a parked car, causing substantial property damage.

■ The driver has committed the tort of negligence. His careless acts or omissions have caused harm or loss to another, namely the owner of the parked car. The owner can successfully sue in tort.

EXAMPLE 2 A truck driver—with no previous history of health problems—suffers a heart attack while at the wheel. As a result, his rig crashes into a parked car, causing substantial property damage.

■ Assuming that the driver's heart attack was not reasonably foreseeable or reasonably preventable, no tort has been committed by the driver. Though his rig caused property damage, it was not due to a careless act or omission.

---

6. *Supra* note 1 at 151.

It is important to note that liability in these examples will vary from province to province depending on the no-fault elements of the provincial *Insurance Act* as relating to auto insurance that may be in place. A pure no-fault system eliminates the ability to claim in tort. No-fault insurance is discussed further in Chapter 28.

A central function of tort law is to compensate an injured party when the injury is the result of someone else's blameworthy conduct. While one may feel sympathy for anyone who suffers damages, tort law does not provide a remedy in all circumstances.

As noted in Chapter 2, courts are governed by precedent when determining the law in any particular case. The nature of precedent is inherently historical, meaning that judges can reach back and rely on old cases as well as more recently decided ones. The case below, for example, was decided in 1948 but maintains the status of a reliable and useful precedent even today.

CASE ▼

Jones v. Shafer Estate, [1948] S.C.R. 166

THE BUSINESS CONTEXT: Those who transport goods along the nation's highways may encounter serious mechanical problems while en route. When leaving the truck or other vehicle at the side of the road, they must be concerned about not putting other drivers in danger but, at the same time, are not responsible for every untoward event that subsequently occurs.[7]

FACTUAL BACKGROUND: Jones was driving a Diamond T. oil truck, loaded with gasoline, along a highway in Western Canada. He realized that one of his wheels was coming off and so pulled to the side of the road, leaving ample room for other vehicles to get by his truck. Jones inspected the vehicle and saw that the outer bearing of his left wheel was gone and the brakes could not be used. Since it was impossible for him to move the truck until the next morning, he placed two oil-powered flares out on the road to alert other drivers. Jones then left. Several hours later, between 10:00 and 11:00 p.m., the flares were stolen by an unknown person. A police officer was called to the scene when notified by a passerby that a truck was parked on the side of the highway without warning flares or lights in place. The police

officer broke into the truck, turned on the vehicle's marker lights, and also left.

The next morning, conditions were foggy and visibility was poor. Mr. Shafer, the deceased, was driving alone. He collided with Jones' broken-down truck and was killed. It appeared that there had been a head-on collision of Shafer's car and Jones' truck, which was still parked on the highway shoulder. Had the flares not been removed, they would have been burning at the time of the accident.

THE LEGAL QUESTION: Did Jones commit the tort of negligence?

RESOLUTION: The Supreme Court of Canada reversed both the trial and appellate judges, instead ruling that there had been no negligence. Jones' duty was not to guarantee that there could never be an accident associated with his parked truck but merely to exercise the care of a reasonable person in all the circumstances. As Justice Estey observed, Jones was not required, in this particular case, to anticipate that someone else would commit the "contemptible act" of stealing the flares he placed on the highway as a warning to others.

Another Justice of the Supreme Court of Canada, Justice Locke, criticized the trial judge's reasoning that Jones was liable in negligence since he could have done more to prevent the accident. As Justice Estey points out: "[T]his is hardly the true test in deciding the question of his liability: it was

---

7. The law of nuisance can also be triggered in such situations. Nuisance is discussed in Chapter 12.

What are the risks here and how can they be managed?

How Torts Are Categorized

Torts can generally be categorized as falling into two main groups: torts committed intentionally and torts committed through negligence. The first, called **intentional torts,** are harmful acts that are committed on purpose. For example, when Bar-Fly's bouncer gestured wildly in Sam's face, he committed the tort of **assault.** Assault involves a threat of imminent physical harm without there being any actual physical contact. When the bouncer ejected Sam from the premises, he committed the intentional tort of **battery.** Battery involves the intentional infliction of harmful or offensive physical contact.[8] Chapter 12 examines several kinds of business-related torts, most of which are intentional.

Torts committed through negligence comprise another large group. When someone is negligent, she is liable for damages even though she did not intentionally cause the event in question. For example, Bar-Fly has a responsibility to keep the floor of the men's room in a good and safe condition.[9] It did not intentionally cause Sam's friend to fall and break his arm, but its failure to maintain the floor properly brought about the injury. Under these circumstances, Sam's friend can sue Bar-Fly in negligence. The tort of negligence is assessed in more detail in Chapter 11.

This chapter discusses tort law from a more general perspective in order to lay the foundation for subsequent discussion.

intentional tort
A harmful act that is committed on purpose.

assault
The threat of imminent physical harm.

battery
Intentional infliction of harmful or offensive physical contact.

---

8. *Norberg v. Wynrib* (1992), 12 C.C.L.T. (2d) 1 at 16 defines battery as the "intentional infliction of unlawful force on another person."
9. This situation can also be treated under occupier's liability. See Chapter 12.

Tort Law and Criminal Law

The same event can give rise to two distinct legal consequences: one in tort and one in criminal law. For example, since Sam has been seriously attacked by Mike the bouncer, section 268(1) of the *Criminal Code* of Canada[10] likely applies. That section states

> Everyone commits an offence of aggravated assault who wounds, maims, disfigures or endangers the life of the complainant.

According to section 268(2), a person who commits aggravated assault

> ... is guilty of an indictable offence and liable to imprisonment for a term not exceeding fourteen years.

Mike could be charged with aggravated assault by the police, and he could be sued by Sam in tort.

Put another way, Mike's behaviour and its consequences give rise to two separate legal actions. This is because, in addition to tort law, the *Criminal Code* prohibits one person from assaulting another, except in self-defence. There are important differences between tort claims and criminal prosecutions.

Purposes of the Actions

The purpose of a criminal prosecution is to sanction behaviour—such as the assault that Sam experienced at the hands of Mike—and secure the punishment of a fine, imprisonment, or both. The action is brought because the Parliament of Canada has determined that anyone who violates the *Criminal Code* should be punished and deterred from such conduct in the future. Prosecution is considered to be critical to maintaining a rights-respecting society.

In tort law, on the other hand, the objective is to compensate the victim for the harm suffered due to the culpability of another. It enforces the victim's private right to extract compensation from the party who has caused the loss.[11]

Commencing the Actions

In criminal law, the legal action is called a prosecution and is brought most often by Crown prosecutors employed by the federal or provincial governments. Rarely do the injured parties bring the prosecution, though it is technically possible for them to do so.[12] In a criminal action, Mike, the bouncer, would be known as the "accused" or "defendant" and Sam, the injured party, as the "complainant."

In tort law, the injured party brings the legal action. This means that Sam would sue in order to enforce his personal or private right to secure compensation for Mike's attack. His action is called a civil action because it is enforcing a right belonging to an individual. In a civil action, Sam is known as the "plaintiff" and Mike as the "defendant."

---

10. R.S.C. 1985, c. C-46.
11. Note, in Ontario, for example, victims of crime also have access to a fund that allows some compensation for their loss or suffering: *Compensation for Victims of Crime Act*, R.S.O. 1990, c. C-24. In Ontario there is also the *Victims' Bill of Rights, 1995*, S.O. 1995, c. 6 and *An Act to Protect Victims by Prohibiting Profiting from Recounting of Crime, 2002*, S.O. 2002, c. 2.
12. Private prosecutions, that is, those brought by the victim or anyone else who is not an agent of the Crown, are uncommon but permissible. Law Reform Commission of Canada, *Private Prosecutions*, Working Paper No. 52 (Ottawa: Law Reform Commission of Canada, 1986) at 51–59.

Proving the Actions

To secure a conviction under section 268(1) of the *Criminal Code*, the Crown must prove that force was applied, that it was intentional, and that the actions were so serious as to "wound, maim, disfigure or endanger" Sam's life. The Crown would have to establish that Sam was not the aggressor; that even if Sam were the aggressor, the response from Mike was not reasonable in light of Sam's actions; that Mike did indeed use excessive force; and that it was this force that caused Sam's injuries.

The Crown has the burden of proof in a criminal action. This means that the prosecutor must prove all the elements of the offence beyond a reasonable doubt based on "reason and common sense," not on "sympathy or prejudice." Guilt must be a logical deduction from the evidence, and it is not sufficient that the jury or judge believed the accused "probably" committed the act.[13]

In tort, by way of contrast, the injured party, Sam, must prove that Mike is responsible for the assault and battery, on the balance of probabilities. Put another way, Sam must establish that it is more likely than not that assault and battery took place. Represented in numerical terms, Sam must convince the judge that there is a better than 50 percent chance that he was harmed by the defendant.

Given the different burdens, it is obviously easier to prove a civil case than a criminal case, and for good reason (see Figure 10.1). Criminal convictions can result in depriving persons of their liberty. This has always been considered to be far more serious than requiring them to pay damages in a civil action. While the odds are high that the plaintiff will succeed in tort if the defendant has already been convicted under criminal law, this is not a certainty since the definitions of the individual torts and crimes are not always exactly the same. Furthermore, only recently have some courts decided that evidence of a conviction for conduct constituting a crime is relevant to establishing the existence of a related tort.[14]

In a case with similarities to the scenario involving Mike and Sam,[15] a bouncer was convicted of aggravated assault and sentenced to 18 months, to be served in the community, and prohibited from owning a gun for 10 years. In addition, he was ordered by the judge to

- perform 240 hours of community service
- speak to bouncers about their responsibilities
- take anger-management courses
- pay a $1000 victim surcharge

The victim started a civil action against all parties involved, including the bar. The case was settled out of court for an undisclosed amount. The victim was provided with what is known as a "structured settlement." He receives an annuity that provides him with annual, tax-free benefits.

---

13. *R. v. D. (W)* (1991), 63 C.C.C. (3d) 397 (S.C.C.); *R. v. Lifchus*, [1997] 3 S.C.R. 320. See too Arbour J.'s decision in *Rhee v. Rhee*, [2001] 3 S.C.R. 364 at para. 20.
14. *Simpson v. Geswein*, [1995] 6 W.W.R. 233 (Man. Q.B.). For a further discussion of this point, including relevant statute law, see Klar, *supra* note 1 at 36–38.
15. "Judge Wants Bar Bouncer Training" *Canadian Press* (19 January 1997) (QL).

FIGURE 10.1

Differences between
Civil and Criminal
Actions

Type of action	Commencing the action	Proving the action	Outcome
Assault and battery as torts	Sam files a claim against Mike based on the torts of assault and battery.	Sam must prove his case on the balance of probabilities.	A court orders Mike to pay Sam compensation for his injuries.
Aggravated assault as a crime	The Crown prosecutes Mike based on section 268(1) of the *Criminal Code.*	The Crown must prove its case beyond a reasonable doubt.	A court orders Mike to be fined, imprisoned, or both.

Liability in Tort

Primary and Vicarious Liability

There are two kinds of liability in tort law: primary and vicarious. Primary liability arises due to one's own personal wrongdoing. Mike the bouncer, for example, has primary liability for the torts of assault and battery because he is the individual who actually attacked Sam. **Vicarious liability,** by way of contrast, arises due to the relationship that someone has to the person who actually commits the tort. For example, the doctrine of vicarious liability makes an employer liable for the torts committed by its employees acting in the ordinary course or scope of employment.

Traditionally regarded, an employee's wrongful conduct is within the ordinary course or scope of employment if it is

- authorized by the employer; or
- is an unauthorized mode of doing something that is, in fact, authorized by the employer.

It can be particularly difficult to distinguish between an unauthorized "mode" of performing an authorized act that attracts liability and an entirely independent "act" that does not. This problem is illustrated in the application of vicarious liability to sexual assaults and other intentional, as opposed to negligent, acts committed by employees.[16] To provide further context, the Supreme Court of Canada states in *Blackwater v. Plint*:

> Vicarious liability may be imposed where there is a significant connection between the conduct authorized by the employer ... and the wrong. Having created or enhanced the risk of the wrongful conduct, it is appropriate that the employer or operator of the enterprise be held responsible, even though the wrongful act may be contrary to its desires .... The fact that wrongful acts may occur is a cost of business.[17]

To what extent this test overtakes or co-exists with the traditional test is unclear at this time. There is a good argument, however, that the "significant connection" test is not limited to intentional torts.

The Supreme Court of Canada's analysis in *Plint* is applied in the following case.

vicarious liability
The liability that an employer has for the tortious acts of an employee committed in the ordinary course or scope of employment.

---

16. See, for example, the Supreme Court of Canada's analysis in *Bazley v. Curry*, [1999] 2 S.C.R. 534.
17. *Blackwater v. Plint*, [2005] 3 S.C.R. 3 at para. 20, per McLachlin C.J.

CASE ▼

Royal Bank of Canada v. Intercon Security Ltd. (2005), 143 A.C.W.S. (3d) 608 (Ont. S.C.J.)

THE BUSINESS CONTEXT: Employers are generally not in a position to supervise everything that an employee does on the job, let alone when not on duty. Even when an employee commits a tort while off duty, the employer may find itself being sued on the basis of vicarious liability.

FACTUAL BACKGROUND: An Ontario security company, Intercon, provided alarm response security to a number of banks, including the plaintiff bank, RBC. During this time, David Hornett broke into numerous branches of RBC and stole over $1 million from the automated teller machines (ATMs) on site. Hornett was employed as a security officer by Intercon when he committed five of the thefts. The last six thefts occurred after he had voluntarily resigned his position and was still the unknown culprit.

Hornett gained access to the banks after hours and when he was not on shift. He used a key that he stole from his employer. On the first occasion, Hornett and his accomplice used the stolen key and entered the ATM room of the bank. Slots in the mini-safes inside the ATMs contained pieces of paper with the combinations written on them but Hornett could still not open the safes. This is because the safes were complicated and did not operate like high school locker combinations. He and his accomplice were close to giving up when they noticed an ATM manual on a nearby shelf. They consulted the manual and learned the procedure for using the combinations. With this knowledge, they were able to open the safes and get away with cash. Hornett and various accomplices went on to commit a series of thefts, both before and after he left the employment of Intercon. Hornett was later arrested. He ultimately pleaded guilty to multiple counts of theft and was sentenced to four years imprisonment.

THE LEGAL QUESTION: Was Intercon vicariously liable for the deliberate acts of Hornett?

RESOLUTION: The court decided that there was no significant connection between the creation or enhancement of the risk of theft and the thefts that Hornett actually committed. As Justice Dambrot states, in para. 56 of the judgment:

> Undoubtedly the wrongs committed by Mr. Hornett were unrelated to the defendant's desires. But were they sufficiently related to conduct authorized by the employer to justify the imposition of vicarious liability? In my view they were not. Not only did the defendant not authorize Mr. Hornett to commit the thefts, it also did not authorize him to be on the Bank's premises when he was not responding to an alarm, it did not authorize him to be on the Bank's premises when he was off duty, it did not authorize him to be in possession of any key to the Bank's premises when he was off duty and it did not authorize him to be in possession of its radio equipment when he was off duty. In short, for these reasons alone I am of the view that the wrongs committed by Mr. Hornett were not sufficiently related to conduct authorized by the employer to justify imposition of vicariously liability.

The court went on to add that, even if the defendant had been negligent in how it controlled keys to RBC branches, this event did not create a sufficient connection between the risk of employee theft and what Hornett did. In short, the bank did not have strong security in place to begin with and, therefore, Hornett's ability to gain access to the interior of the bank was "no more than a small factor contributing to Mr. Hornett's ability to commit the thefts" according to the court. As the court summarizes the matter, at para 58:

> While undoubtedly Mr. Hornett's employment by Intercon led him to the idea of stealing from the Bank's ATM's, and provided him with an opportunity to acquire keys to enter the branches, it did not provide him with the means to enter the machines to steal money. Those means were readily provided by the Bank to any clever intruder. The combinations to the machines were conveniently available in boxes near the ATMs with slots in

the boxes enabling the combinations to be removed. And the intricate method for using the combinations was described in manuals that were readily available to intruders on shelves above the ATMs.

On this basis, there was no vicarious liability on the part of Hornett's employer.

CRITICAL ANALYSIS: Do you agree with the court's analysis? What factor do you think was the most important factor leading to the court's decision of no vicarious liability on Hornett's employer?

Applying the law to the Business Law in Practice scenario, the court must decide whether there is a "significant connection" between the conduct authorized by the employer and the wrong committed by the employee to justify making the employer vicariously liable. Since there is, in fact, a strong relationship between Mike's job as a bouncer and his assault and battery of Sam, Bar-Fly will almost certainly be vicariously liable for Mike's tortious conduct. By way of contrast, if Mike assaulted a friend whom he had invited to the Bar-Fly—after hours and without his employer's permission—the doctrine of vicarious liability is unlikely to have any application. Though it may seem unfair to make an employer responsible for a tort committed by its employees, the doctrine of vicarious liability has been justified on the following basis:

- employers have the ability to control employees and therefore should be liable for the employee's conduct;
- the person who benefits from a business enterprise (the employer) should bear the associated costs[18]
- innocent plaintiffs have a better chance of being compensated [19]
- the employer should be given an incentive to try to prevent torts from occurring in the first place[20]

Vicarious liability is discussed further in Chapter 20.

Liability and Joint Tort-Feasors

joint tort-feasors

Two or more persons whom a court has held to be jointly responsible for the plaintiff's loss or injuries.

When a person is injured due to the tortious conduct of more than one person, those culpable are known as "**joint tort-feasors.**" For example, if Sam were attacked by Mike and another employee, Mike and his coworker would have joint liability for Sam's injuries. Legislation passed across Canada states that if the negligence of more than one person is responsible for the loss, the victim or plaintiff can sue any or all of them, with recovery apportioned between the joint tort-feasors according to their level of responsibility. Notwithstanding the apportionment of liability *between* the joint tort-feasors, the plaintiff can recover 100 percent of her judgment from any of those defendants whom a court has held to be jointly responsible for the loss or injuries.[21]

---

18. Klar, *supra* note 1 at 581.
19. *Ibid.*
20. *Ibid.*
21. For example, *Negligence Act*, R.S.O. 1990, c. N-1; *Contributory Negligence Act*, R.S.N.B. 1973, c. C-19; *Contributory Negligence Act*, R.S.N.S. 1989, c. 95; *Negligence Act*, R.S.B.C. 1996, c. 333.

Business and Legislation

Workers' Compensation

Although tort law remains primarily a common law matter, it has also been modified by statute law. **Workers' compensation legislation,** for example, provides monetary compensation to employees for work-related injuries and illnesses. At the same time, it prohibits the employee from suing the employer for any negligence that might have caused the problem. In this way, the statute takes away the employee's common law right to sue but provides compensation no matter who is at fault.

workers' compensation legislation
Legislation that provides no-fault compensation for injured employees in lieu of their right to sue in tort.

contributory negligence
A defence claiming that the plaintiff is at least partially responsible for the harm that has occurred.

Liability and Contributory Negligence

Tort victims may be at least partially responsible for their own injuries. If the defendant successfully argues that the plaintiff was responsible for at least a part of the loss—that is, the defendant uses the defence of **contributory negligence**—the amount of damages that the plaintiff is awarded is reduced by the proportion for which the plaintiff is responsible. Contributory negligence is a common defence used in lawsuits involving car accidents. If the plaintiff was not wearing a seat belt at the time of the accident, the defendant may well be able to establish that the injuries sustained were worse than they otherwise would have been. The court will then go on to decrease the plaintiff's damages award in proportion to the plaintiff's degree of contributory negligence. For example, if the plaintiff's damages are set at $100 000 and the court finds the plaintiff to have been 20 percent contributorily negligent—that is, responsible for 20 percent of the loss—the plaintiff's damages award will be reduced to $80 000.

CASE ▼

Alberta Wheat Pool v. Northwest Pile Driving Ltd. (1998), 80 A.C.W.S. (3d) 692 (B.C. S.C.), reversed in part (2000), 80 B.C.L.R. (3d) 153 (C.A.)

BUSINESS CONTEXT: Owners of large commercial facilities often rely on outside companies to perform necessary repairs and improvements. When the outside company does the work improperly, the owner can sustain considerable damage and also be implicated as one of the causes of the loss, via the doctrine of contributory negligence.

FACTUAL BACKGROUND: The plaintiff hired the defendant to renovate the wooden wharf that the plaintiff owned in British Columbia. The wharf was part of the plaintiff's grain loading facility in Vancouver Harbour. During this renovation process, the wharf was seriously damaged by fire. The fire was started by molten slag from an oxyacetylene torch operated by the defendant's employee.

The trial judge found that the defendant indisputably owed a duty of care to the plaintiff and had been negligent in failing to minimize the fire hazard created by the torch. Among other deficiencies, the defendant's employees failed to wet the combustible surfaces before using the torch and failed to keep a proper fire watch during cutting operations so that any slag that landed would be doused with water. She valued the plaintiff's damages at $1 525 520.

The trial judge went on to reduce this amount on the basis of the plaintiff's contributory negligence. She agreed with the defendant's argument that the plaintiff failed to install and maintain an adequate fire protection system. The trial judge decided that—as the defendant caused the fire — it carried the primary fault and should therefore carry a majority of the liability. On this basis, the plaintiff's contributory negligence was set at 25 percent.

On appeal, most of the trial judge's decision was upheld. However, the Court of Appeal said that, in these circumstances, the plaintiff should be found 50 percent contributorily negligent. According to legislation governing the matter, the court must assess each party's "fault" in apportioning liability. Measuring what each party did wrong, it would seem that both were at fault equally. As the Court of Appeal notes:

> On this analysis, I do not see how the fault of one party can be said to be greater than the fault of the other party. Both were aware, or must be taken to have been aware, of the circumstances giving rise to the risk of fire, and to its rapid propagation. The defendant failed, for no good reason, to guard against fire by dousing the area with water and keeping a constant fire watch before, during and after the oxyacetylene torch cutting operation took place. The plaintiff failed, for no good reason, to install an adequate fire protection system which it could have done at a reasonable cost either in 1977, or at the time of renovations in 1994. While the fault of the two is different in kind, I do not see how one can justify a conclusion that their faults differ in degree .... [L]iability in these circumstances must be apportioned equally.

CRITICAL ANALYSIS: Does it make sense to deduct from the plaintiff's award for contributory negligence when, after all, it has been the victim of a tort? Do you think it would be preferable to simply place all the liability on the defendant? Why or why not?

Damages in Tort

The Purpose of Damages

The primary goal of a tort remedy is to compensate the victim for loss caused by the defendant. Generally, this is a monetary judgment. Less common alternatives are equitable remedies, such as an injunction—a court order requiring or prohibiting certain conduct. An injunction would be ordered if money would not suffice—for example, in the case of a recurring trespass where there is little economic harm, but the plaintiff simply wants the trespasser to stop coming onto the land in question. Financial compensation means the defendant is ordered by the court to pay a sum of money to the successful plaintiff. Such a remedy has obvious limitations. For example, where the plaintiff has suffered serious physical injuries, how can money truly compensate someone for the permanent loss of health? However, in personal injury cases there are no ready alternatives to financial compensation such as in the trespass example above.

Tort law compensates not only for physical injury or loss but also for mental pain and suffering and other forms of emotional distress. These latter areas are approached with more caution by the judiciary but are compensable if proven through psychiatric and other expert evidence.

Because any award or out-of-court settlement is final, a plaintiff's lawyer will not usually settle or bring the case to court until the full extent of damages is known.

Pecuniary and Nonpecuniary Damages

Under Canadian law, the losses for which damages are awarded are categorized as being either pecuniary (that is, monetary) or nonpecuniary.

nonpecuniary damages
Compensation for pain and
suffering, loss of enjoyment
of life, and loss of life
expectancy.

Nonpecuniary losses—sometimes called general damages—are damages that are awarded to compensate the plaintiff for

- pain and suffering
- loss of enjoyment of life
- loss of life expectancy

Because Mike's attack on Sam caused him severe spinal injuries, Sam undoubtedly has suffered a considerable amount of general damages. These damages are nonpecuniary in the sense that they are not out-of-pocket, monetary losses, but they are nonetheless both real and devastating. The quality of Sam's life has been seriously diminished due to a loss of mobility and independence. His life expectancy has likely been reduced. A judge will award damages based on these facts, as well as on expert testimony as to how badly Sam has been injured. The more serious and permanent the injury is, the higher the general damages will be. Courts have developed precedents to assist in this process, and the Supreme Court of Canada has set a clear upper limit on what can be awarded for general damages.[22]

pecuniary damages
Compensation for out-of-
pocket expenses, loss of
future income, and cost of
future care.

Pecuniary losses fall into three main categories:

- cost of future care
- loss of future income
- special damages

Cost of Future Care

A plaintiff like Sam is entitled to an award sufficient to provide him with all the care and assistance his injury will necessitate. This can include the cost of a personal care attendant for the rest of his life, modifications to his living accommodations to increase accessibility, and the costs related to equipment and treatment of his condition. As in other areas of damages, what the plaintiff is ultimately awarded will be based on the testimony of experts, including occupation, rehabilitation, and medical experts.

Loss of Future Income

A judge will value the plaintiff's diminished earning capacity resulting from the injury. This calculation can be complex, involving the input of vocational experts, labour economists, accountants, and actuaries. Since Sam has suffered a serious injury as a result of Mike's attack and he is a young person, his loss of future income will likely be considerable.

Special Damages

These relate to out-of-pocket expenses resulting from the injury-causing event. These expenses may include any number of items, including ambulance costs, medication costs, housekeeping, and yard work. Sam should keep records and receipts of such costs and expenses in order to prove them in court. In some provinces medical costs must be claimed as special damages, although these will be repaid to the provincial health insurer under the insurance principle of subrogation.[23]

---

22. *Andrews v. Grand & Toy Alberta Ltd.,* [1978] 2 S.C.R. 299; *Arnold v. Teno,* [1978] 2 S.C.R. 287; and *Thornton v. School Dist. No. 57 Bd. of School Trustees,* [1978] 2 S.C.R. 267. In *Andrews,* the Supreme Court of Canada placed a ceiling on recovery for general pain and suffering at $100 000. In 2006 dollars, this amounts to approximately $300 000.
23. It is beyond the scope of this text to discuss the law governing health care expense subrogation.

Punitive or Exemplary Damages

punitive damages
An award to the plaintiff to punish the defendant for malicious, oppressive, and high-handed conduct.

Punitive damages—also known as exemplary damages—are an exception to the general rule that damages are intended only to compensate the plaintiff. Punitive damages are awarded to punish the defendant for malicious, oppressive, and high-handed conduct or where the defendant might otherwise profit from the behaviour.[24] If, for example, the bouncer or the bar refused to call an ambulance for the seriously injured Sam, punitive damages would almost certainly be awarded. The court would seek to punish such offensive conduct.

Aggravated Damages

aggravated damages
Compensation for intangible injuries such as distress and humiliation caused by the defendant's reprehensible conduct.

Aggravated damages compensate the plaintiff for intangible injuries such as distress and humiliation caused by the defendant's reprehensible conduct.[25] For example, when store detectives unlawfully restrain a customer, they have committed the tort of false imprisonment. If, in restraining the customer, they treat the person in a humiliating or degrading fashion, a court may well award aggravated damages to compensate the plaintiff for the mental distress the whole experience caused.

Business Application of the Law
Punitive Damages in the United States and Canada

The Canadian Press regularly reports instances of high punitive awards given by American juries to sympathetic plaintiffs in the United States. Most famously, Stella Liebeck of Albuquerque, New Mexico, was awarded nearly $3 million in punitive damages from McDonald's when she suffered serious burns upon opening a cup of coffee that she had placed between her legs. Due to severe scalding, she remained hospitalized for eight days. According to *The New York Times*, the jury was influenced by McDonald's knowledge that at least 700 of its customers had also been burned. The *Times* also reports what is less commonly known, namely that the plaintiff was found 20 percent contributorily negligent and that an out-of-court settlement reduced her damages award significantly.[26]

Jury trials are much less common in Canada than they are in the United States. This is at least one factor that keeps punitive damages lower since judges may

Should the defendant's ability to pay be a consideration in the awarding of punitive damages?

be less easily influenced to make large awards than members of the public who compose juries. Second,

---

24. *Supra* note 1 at 108–109.
25. *Vorvis v. Insurance Corporation of British Columbia*, [1989] 1 S.C.R. 1085.
26. In *Bogle v. McDonald's Restaurants Ltd.*, [2002] EWHC 490 (Q.B.), an English court was much less sympathetic to a similar claim by plaintiffs who had been burnt by hot beverages at McDonald's outlets in the United Kingdom. According to that judge, "Persons generally expect tea or coffee purchased to be consumed on the premises to be hot. . . . Persons generally know that if a hot drink is spilled onto someone, a serious scalding injury can result. . . . [T]he allegations . . . that McDonald's are legally liable for these unfortunate injuries have not been made out."

the specter of "uncontrolled and uncontrollable awards of punitive damages in civil actions"[27] is a matter that the Supreme Court of Canada guards against by insisting on "proportionality" as the measure for punitive damages. Any punitive award must be rationally related to and be no more than necessary to punish the defendant, deter wrongdoers, or convey denunciation of the defendant's conduct. Moreover, the court has insisted that punitive damages should be exceptional, leaving criminal law as the main venue of punishment.

CRITICAL ANALYSIS: Should punitive damages be closely controlled, as they are in Canada, or is the American approach, which tolerates much higher awards, to be preferred? How can businesses avoid being ordered to pay punitive damages?

Sources: *Bogle v. McDonald's Restaurants Ltd.*, [2002] EWHC 490 (Q.B.); *Whiten v. Pilot Insurance Co.* (2002), 209 D.L.R. (4th) 257 (S.C.C.); and Anthony Ramirez, "For McDonald's, British Justice Is a Different Cup of Tea" *The New York Times* (7 April 2002) at 7.

Tort Law and Contract

Sometimes the same set of facts can give rise to liability in tort and in contract. For example, when Mike attacked Sam, he committed a tort. Mike's tortious conduct is attributed to his employer by way of vicarious liability and, by that same fact, *also* places Bar-Fly in breach of its contract with Sam. That is, it would be an implied term in the contract for the purchase of beverages that Bar-Fly would provide a reasonably safe environment for their consumption. When Sam was attacked by Mike the bouncer, this term was breached.

Overlapping liability in contract and tort is also common when a professional—such as an accountant, lawyer, or banker—gives advice to her client. If that advice is incompetent, the professional is in breach of contract *and* has committed the tort of negligence. This matter is explored further in chapters 11 and 22.

Managing Tort Risk

Chapters 3 and 4 discussed extensively the issues of risk management and dispute resolution. Businesses are exposed to a wide variety of risks related to tort actions, particularly in the area of negligence. In addition, they are vulnerable due to the doctrine of vicarious liability.

No business can eliminate all risk. It must, however, assume active measures to minimize it. This is because ignoring tort risk can result in

- incurring the costs of a tort that could have been avoided, including lawyers' fees, management time devoted to defending the claim, and the amount of the actual judgment awarded to the successful plaintiff
- losing insurance coverage because of a poor claims history
- losing a hard-earned business reputation

Risk management strategies that business operations such as Bar-Fly might deploy are set out in the next section of this chapter (Business Law in Practice Revisited).

---

27. *Whiten v. Pilot Insurance Co.* (2002), 209 D.L.R. (4th) 257 (S.C.C.). This case is summarized in Chapter 28.

Business Law in Practice Revisited

1. What kind of tort action does Sam's friend have as a result of breaking his arm?

Sam's friend has an action in negligence against Bar-Fly for failing to take reasonable steps to ensure that the washroom floor was free of hazards. He likely also has an action for breach of contract due to this same failure.

2. What potential legal actions result from the altercation between Sam and Mike?

Mike could be prosecuted for a criminal offence, perhaps that of aggravated assault. If successful this could lead to imprisonment. Mike can also be sued by Sam, who will be seeking compensation by way of civil action—here a complaint based on the torts of assault and battery—for the damages he has suffered.

3. Is Bar-Fly responsible for Mike's actions?

Sam will claim that Bar-Fly is responsible for Mike's actions based on the principle of vicarious liability. Since Mike is an employee of Bar-Fly and it appears that there is a significant connection between Mike's job and the tort he committed, Bar-Fly will probably be responsible for Mike's tortious actions.

4. What risk management actions could Bar-Fly have taken to prevent this altercation and the fall in the men's room?

Bar-Fly's risk of liability in tort can be reduced through a risk management plan. Possibilities include

- reducing risk by hiring employees with care and instituting training programs to help them perform their jobs well. Employees should be hired for their good judgment and interpersonal skills and not simply their brawn. They should be instructed as to both the parameters of acceptable behaviour and how to address patrons. Employees should learn what they are entitled to do and when they have to call in the police, as much for their own safety as for that of patrons. It may be appropriate to have employees working in pairs to ensure they have backup and are able to monitor each other's behaviour and well-being.

- reducing risk by setting up a system of checks so that floor surfaces in the bar remain hazard free.

- transferring risk by purchasing insurance to cover the business's liability to patrons who are injured on its premises.

Chapter Summary

Tort law has a significant impact on business enterprises, particularly in the area of negligence. Tort law permits someone who has been injured or suffered a loss to sue the responsible person for damages. The objective of a damages award is to compensate the plaintiff, though punitive damages are sometimes available if the defendant's conduct has been particularly egregious. Aggravated damages are also available to compensate the person who suffers intangible injuries such as distress or humiliation caused by the defendant's reprehensible conduct. Less commonly, the injured party will seek an injunction or other form of equitable remedy.

Criminal law also affects a business, though to a lesser degree. As the purpose of a criminal law is to punish the offender—through fines and imprisonment—distinct procedures are in place to help ensure that only guilty people are convicted.

For example, in a criminal prosecution the Crown must prove its case beyond a reasonable doubt. By way of contrast, the plaintiff in a tort action need only demonstrate his case on the balance of probabilities.

Liability in tort can be primary and vicarious. Primary liability arises due to one's own personal wrongdoing. Vicarious liability arises due to the relationship one has with the actual tort-feasor, as in an employer–employee context. Since a business may have several employees, its exposure in this area can be considerable.

When a person is injured due to the tortious conduct of more than one person, those culpable are known as joint tort-feasors. A court can apportion liability between them but the victim or plaintiff can recover 100 percent of her judgment from any one of them.

When a tort victim is at least partially responsible for his own injuries, he has been contributorily negligent. The amount that the plaintiff is awarded will be reduced by the proportion for which he is responsible.

Sometimes, the same set of facts can give rise to liability in tort and in contract, particularly in the context of a professional advice giver such as a lawyer or accountant.

The best response a business can have to its potential liability in tort is to establish a risk management plan that reduces, eliminates, or transfers risk.

Chapter Study

Key Terms and Concepts

aggravated damages (p. 233)

assault (p. 224)

battery (p. 224)

contributory negligence (p. 230)

deceit or fraud (p. 221)

intentional tort (p. 224)

joint tort-feasors (p. 229)

negligence (p. 222)

nonpecuniary damages (p. 232)

pecuniary damages (p. 232)

punitive damages (p. 233)

tort (p. 221)

tort-feasor (p. 222)

trespass to land (p. 221)

vicarious liability (p. 227)

workers' compensation legislation (p. 230)

Questions for Review

1. What does the term "tort" mean?

2. Give an example of a tort.

3. What are the two main categories into which torts are organized?

4. What is the difference between the tort of assault and the tort of battery?

5. The goals of tort and criminal law are quite distinct, even when they stem from the same event. Explain the differences.

6. What is a joint tort-feasor?

7. What does burden of proof mean?

8. How does the burden of proof differ between a criminal case and a tort action?

9. What is the difference in the way tort and criminal actions are initiated?

10. What is the purpose of damages in tort?

11. Under what circumstances might an injunction be awarded in tort?

12. Vicarious liability is an essential feature of modern tort law. What is it?

13. What might be a defence to a claim for vicarious liability?

14. How does contributory negligence affect the amount of damages a plaintiff may receive?

15. Explain the difference between pecuniary and nonpecuniary damages.

16. How are pecuniary damages typically calculated?

17. What are punitive damages?

18. When is overlapping liability in tort and contract common?

Questions for Critical Thinking

1. What are the justifications for the basic legal principle that the standard of proof is higher in a criminal matter than in a civil one?

2. Punitive damages are somewhat controversial even in jurisdictions where they are relatively common. At the same time, there are circumstances in which a person's tortious actions have been particularly callous and calculating, yet the actual loss suffered by the plaintiff is not extensive in monetary terms. In these latter cases, what are the compelling reasons for allowing the plaintiff additional recovery over and above her actual loss? Should the compensation principle of tort law be compromised in this way?

3. The concept of vicarious liability developed in the business world, where the company is out to make a profit and its activities are for the most part directed to generating profit. Is it appropriate to apply a test developed in this context to a charitable organization? What are the pros and cons for holding organizations liable for the conduct of their employees?

4. Does the idea of contributory negligence reflect the major aims and purposes of tort law? Does it make sense to reduce the amount of damages available to a plaintiff, when he may not have suffered the loss to the same extent, or at all, but for the negligence of someone else?

5. Without permission, Angela borrows Jacob's car. Has Angela committed a crime? Do you think that her conduct might be tortious as well?

Situations for Discussion

1. It was Susan's turn to drive her three classmates to university, this time for the final exam in the business law course. Unfortunately she had left home late, and by the time she had picked up everyone else, they were in serious risk of arriving at least ten minutes after the exam began. The weather was not good and the roads were obviously slippery—there were cars off to the side of the road in a number of locations. Susan's friends urged her to speed up, which she did, although as a relatively inexperienced driver she was uncomfortable handling the car under these conditions. As she approached a major intersection the light turned amber and Susan braked. The car began sliding and Susan instinctively braked harder, causing the car to go out of control and enter the intersection into the path of a car proceeding on a green light from the cross street. In the subsequent collision, one of the passengers in Susan's car, Jean-Guy, was seriously injured.

The police arrived and, after investigating the case, charged Susan with dangerous driving under the *Criminal Code*. In time it became clear that Jean-Guy's injuries had resulted not only in short-term harm—for example, he could not sit his exam and had fallen behind one term in his program—but also permanent damage. In particular, his right arm and wrist were shattered and, being right-handed, he has and will continue to have limited manual dexterity. He was planning a career in IT and finds that these injuries severely affect his ability to perform basic tasks. For which categories of damages will Jean-Guy seek compensation?

2. Discuss the relationship between criminal and civil law in relation to Situation 1. How will each case be proven and by whom?

3. Security Services-R-Us was hired by the Ferry Corporation to provide security for its premises. Mr. Brown, the security guard sent to the site, fell

asleep during his watch. A break-in occurred and valuable computer equipment owned by Ferry Corporation was stolen. Later that same night, Brown intentionally destroyed an outbuilding by pouring an accelerant around the periphery of the building and igniting it. The Ferry Corporation is now suing both Brown and his employer, Security Services-R-Us, for damages arising from the theft and Brown's arson.

Why would Ferry Corporation sue both Brown and his employer? To what extent is the security company responsible for its employee's behaviour?[28]

4. Mr. Hunter was driving his van at night in the winter on an isolated two-lane portion of the Trans Canada highway when he hit a moose. At the time, he was not driving above the posted speed limit of 100 km/h. Almost immediately, Mr. Hartson, who was driving his truck in the opposite direction, struck the same moose. The moose had been dealt a "glancing blow" by Mr. Hunter's van, and was pushed into the opposite lane. The moose crushed the windshield and cab of the truck and Mr. Hartson was injured. Mr. Hartson is suing Mr. Hunter, claiming that he was driving too fast for the conditions, and should have reduced his speed to 75 or 80 km/h.[29] Did Mr. Hunter breach the standard of care expected of him by driving 100 km/h at night in the winter on an isolated stretch of highway? Does it make any difference that even if Mr. Hunter had driven at the "more reasonable" suggested rate, Mr. Hartson would still have hit the moose and suffered the same injuries?

5. Identify the tort liability that the business in question faces:

a. ABC Ltd. is in the business of renting chainsaws and other construction material to "do-it-yourselfers."

b. Susan sells hotdogs downtown, out of her portable hotdog stand.

c. Roger would like to start a new student newspaper. He is concerned about his liability in tort law and in relation to hate crimes legislation that prohibits the willful promotion of hatred against any identifiable group.[30] What steps can he take to manage the risks of his proposed business?

d. XYZ Ltd. offers driver training courses to prospective new drivers.

For more study tools, visit
http://www.businesslaw3e.nelson.com

---

28. Based, in part, on *British Columbia Ferry Corp. v. Invicta Security Corp.* (1998), 167 D.L.R. (4th) 193 (B.C.C.A.).
29. Based, in part, on *Hartson v. Hunter*, 2006 NLTD 59 (S.C. T.D.).
30. For an excerpt of this legislation, see footnote 24 in Chapter 2.

Chapter

11

Objectives

After studying this chapter, you should have an understanding of

- the conduct that the law of negligence addresses
- the principles of the law of negligence
- the defences in a negligence action
- the common kinds of negligence actions businesses face
- the difference between negligence and strict liability

The Tort of Negligence

Business Law in Practice

Pierre Bouffard is vice president of operations at Excel-Fibreglass Canada Ltd. (Excel). Excel produces fibreglass repair kits that are used primarily in auto-body work. Each kit comes with a piece of fibreglass cloth, a can of liquid resin, and several tubes of liquid hardener. Since the liquid hardener contains corrosive chemicals, the tube carries the following warning, in small print:

> **Warning:** Flammable material. Store in a cool place away from sunlight and other sources of heat. Keep out of reach of children. Can cause skin irritation and blindness—not to be taken internally. If swallowed, dilute stomach contents and induce vomiting. In case of contact with skin or eyes, flush with liberal quantities of water. For eye contact, get immediate medical attention. Composition: 60% Methyl Ethyl Ketone Peroxide in Pi-Methyl Phthalate.

Pierre has recently received a disturbing phone call from a lawyer representing Hugh Thomkins. According to the lawyer, Hugh was seriously injured by Excel's product. It seems that Hugh had purchased Excel's repair kit from a local retailer and brought it home to do repairs on his car. Hugh perforated the nib of the tube of the hardener and pointed the tube downward in order to add a few drops into the bowl of resin. When Hugh squeezed the tube, the seal on the bottom failed, squirting the corrosive product in Hugh's eyes. Hugh experienced tremendous pain, was hospitalized for seven days, and has only recently regained his sight. He was unable to work for four months following the accident and still suffers serious eye irritation.

Pierre is now gathering documents to bring to Excel's lawyer. Included is a memo that outlines Excel's quality control program to check for defects in the sealed tubes of hardener. According to the memo, workers squeeze the tubes by hand at two stages of production. The first occasion is when the tubes are filled with the hardener—one of every six tubes is tested this way. The second occasion for testing the seals is when the tubes are packed into the kit boxes. Nine out of ten tubes are squeezed at this point, but there is no standard as to how much pressure employees should put on each tube nor any way of measuring the pressure exerted, in any event.[1]

1. What will Hugh need to establish in order to succeed in a negligence action?
2. How could Excel better manage its risk of tort liability?

The Law of Negligence

What Is Negligence?

reasonable care
The care a reasonable person would exhibit in a similar situation.

Chapter 10 defined the tort of negligence as a careless act that causes harm to another. The law understands carelessness as a failure to show **reasonable care,** that is, the care that a reasonable person would have shown in a similar situation.

Negligence is a very common tort action in the commercial world because it covers a broad range of harmful conduct. For example, a negligence action can be brought by someone

- who has been injured by the dangerous driving of a delivery truck driver
- who has suffered loss by relying on poor advice provided by an accountant, lawyer, architect, or engineer
- whose furniture has been damaged in transit by a moving company

---

1. Based, in part, on *LeBlanc v. Marson Canada Inc.* (1995), 139 N.S.R. (2d) 309 at paras. 17–18, aff'd (1995) 146 N.S.R. (2d) 392 (C.A.).

The plaintiff need not show that the defendant intended to cause the damage or that there were deliberate acts that gave rise to the damage. Instead, the tort of negligence makes the defendant liable for failing to act reasonably—for driving too fast, for giving unprofessional advice, or for not taking proper care of furniture entrusted to its care.

In the Business Law in Practice scenario above, Hugh has an action in negligence against Excel on two grounds. First, it appears that Excel has failed to use reasonable care in the production and testing of the tubes containing the hardener, since the company's quality control program is probably deficient. As well, the warning on each tube appears inadequate, given that the hardener is corrosive. The warning states that the contents can cause skin irritation and blindness but does not recommend that protective gear, such as safety goggles, be worn while the product is in use. For both these reasons, it may well be that Excel has been negligent and is therefore liable to Hugh for his damages.

Negligence law—like tort law in general—seeks to compensate victims for their loss or injury. It provides this compensation after applying rules that determine who is liable to compensate another, on what basis, and for how much. Without such limiting rules, business and professional people might be reluctant to produce goods and services because the risk of liability in negligence would be unknowable. Those goods and services that did reach the market would be relatively more expensive since the price would need to reflect the increased risk flowing from widespread liability.

With these kinds of factors in mind, the courts have the task of balancing competing interests. They must compensate victims of negligence, but without discouraging legitimate activity and without making the legal standards a business must meet unreasonably exacting.

Steps to Negligence Action

The rules that limit when a plaintiff like Hugh will succeed in a negligence action are set out in a series of classic steps, as summarized in Figure 11.1.

FIGURE 11.1

Steps to Negligence Action

Step 1: Does the defendant owe the plaintiff a duty of care? If yes, proceed to the next step.

Step 2: Did the defendant breach the standard of care? If yes, proceed to the next step.

Step 3: Did the defendant's careless act (or omission) cause the plaintiff's damage? If yes, proceed to the next step.

Step 4: Was the damage suffered by the plaintiff too remote? If not, the plaintiff has proven negligence.

The steps in a tort action, by design, lack a certain specificity. Their purpose is to describe general standards or markers that help a court assess whether the defendant in any given case has been negligent.

duty of care
The responsibility owed to avoid carelessness that causes harm to others.

Step 1: Does the defendant owe the plaintiff a duty of care?
The defendant Excel will be liable to Hugh only if it owes Hugh what is known in law as a duty of care. A defendant owes a **duty of care** to anyone who might reasonably be affected by the defendant's conduct. This is known as the **neighbour** principle, as formulated by the House of Lords in *Donoghue v. Stevenson*.[2]

neighbour
Anyone who might reasonably be affected by another's conduct.

2. *Donoghue v. Stevenson*, [1932] A.C. 562 (H.L.).

Landmark Case ▼

Donoghue v. Stevenson, [1932] A.C. 562 (H.L.)

THE BUSINESS CONTEXT: Before large-scale production, most goods were sold directly from producer/artisan to consumer. By the 20th century, a multistage distribution chain was the norm, which comprised several distinct transactions or contracts—from manufacturer, to supplier, to retailer, to the ultimate consumer.

FACTUAL BACKGROUND: A customer bought some ice cream and an opaque bottle of ginger beer for her friend, Donoghue. Some of the ginger beer was poured over the ice cream and some was drunk by Donoghue. When the remainder of the beer was being poured into a tumbler, a decomposed snail was discovered in the contents. Donoghue became ill and subsequently sued the manufacturer for damages, based on negligence.

THE LEGAL QUESTION: At this time, the extent of the manufacturer's duty of care was severely constricted: the manufacturer was responsible only to those with whom it had a contractual arrangement. Most consumer "victims" were prevented by this limited responsibility from recovering from the manufacturer. There was almost certainly a retailer in the transaction and no direct contractual relationship between the manufacturer and consumer.

RESOLUTION: Lord Atkin, for the majority, wrote the following classic statement when discussing how to determine to whom a duty of care is owed in negligence:

> The rule that you are to love your neighbour becomes in law, you must not injure your neighbour, and the lawyer's question, Who is my neighbour? receives a restricted reply. You must take reasonable care to avoid acts or omissions which you can reasonably foresee would be likely to injure your neighbour. Who, then, in law, is my neighbour? The answer seems to be—persons who are so closely and directly affected by my act that I ought reasonably to have them in contemplation as being so affected when I am directing my mind to the acts or omissions which are called in question.

CRITICAL ANALYSIS: Is it reasonable to make manufacturers liable for their products to end users? Would it be enough simply to make the retailer liable for breach of contract and leave the manufacturer out of the equation?

Since *Donoghue*, the Supreme Court of Canada has continued to refine the test for whether a duty of care is owed. On numerous occasions, it has confirmed that the statement of law from an English case—*Anns v. Merton London Borough Council*[3]—is good law in Canada.[4] As formulated by the Supreme Court of Canada, the *Anns* test is as follows:

prima facie
At first sight or on first appearances.

- Is "a ***prima facie*** duty of care owed?" (That is, is there a relationship of proximity between the parties? In the words of Lord Atkin, quoted above, are the parties neighbours? Put another way still, is it reasonably foreseeable that carelessness by one party would adversely affect the other?) If the answer is yes, then a duty of care is owed, subject to one more question, which follows.

- Is this duty "negated or limited by policy considerations?" (That is, are there any considerations that should scale back the duty owed or eliminate it entirely?)

---

3. (1977), 2 All E.R. 492 (H.L.).
4. See, for example, *Hercules Managements Ltd. v. Ernst & Young*, [1997] 2 S.C.R. 165; *Cooper v. Hobart* (2001), 206 D.L.R. (4th) 193 (S.C.C.); and *Kamloops (City) v. Nielsen*, [1984] 2 S.C.R. 2.

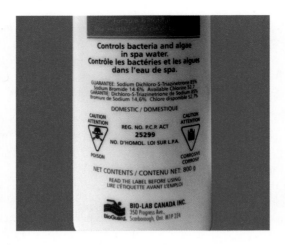

For a business like Excel, virtually everyone who comes into contact with the fibreglass repair kit product would be Excel's neighbour. This is because Excel manufactures a product for mass consumption. It is reasonably foreseeable that carelessness in the production process could injure the ultimate user, whomever that person might be, and wherever he or she might live in the world. For this reason, the manufacturer's duty extends to all purchasers and consumers of the product, not just those with whom the manufacturer has a contract.

To conceptualize how the first step in the test for duty of care is applied, assume that the events leading up to Hugh's injury were captured on film. The defective tube slips through the quality control program undetected. It is packaged into the kit and shipped to the retailer. Hugh purchases the kit, returns home, and begins to use the product. He perforates the nib of the hardener tube, points it downward into a bowl of resin, and squeezes the tube. At this point, imagine stopping the film and asking the audience the following question: Who is reasonably likely to be affected by Excel's defectively produced hardener tube? The answer is clear: Hugh and anyone else who could have come into contact with the product. On this basis, Hugh is Excel's neighbour.

The only difference between the exercise described above and one that might occur in a court of law is that now the audience is a judge and the judge knows the outcome—the tube failed and the hardener injured Hugh. What judges must do is place themselves in the hypothetical position of observing the events as they are about to occur. While this might appear to be a somewhat strained exercise, it is a process with which judges are very familiar.

Once a trial judge has determined that the defendant owes a duty of care to the plaintiff, the judge must go on to assess whether there are any considerations that ought to eliminate or reduce that duty. The objective of this is to ensure that businesses and other defendants are not made liable to an unreasonably broad, unknowable, and indeterminate extent. In practice, considerations that eliminate or reduce a defendant's duty of care are more likely to arise in the area of pure economic loss—such as loss of profit—than in cases of physical harm. Such concerns are prevalent in the context of negligent misstatement, a tort that is discussed later in this chapter.

In Excel's case, a judge is very unlikely to find that such a consideration exists because of the nature of Excel's business—Excel wants people like Hugh to use its product. If consumers are injured in the process, what possible reason could there be to suggest that Excel should not owe a duty of care to them?

Step 2: Did the defendant breach the standard of care?

Once it is established that Excel owes a duty of care to Hugh, the next formal question is whether there has been a breach of the standard of care associated with that duty. In short, did Excel show a lack of reasonable care in the preparation of the fibreglass hardener tube and instructions for use?

In general, the defendant's conduct is judged according to the standards of behaviour that would be observed by the reasonable person in society. In law, a **reasonable person** is regarded as being an ordinary person of normal intelligence who uses ordinary prudence to guide his conduct. The law does not demand that the reasonable person be perfect.

Where the defendant exercises specialized skills, the standard of the reasonable person described above is not applied. Professionals such as doctors, accountants, engineers, and lawyers must meet a higher or specialized standard of care because the level of expertise of the average member of society is simply inadequate as a measure of competence. In cases involving specialized tasks, courts introduce the standard of the "reasonable" person with that specialized training—the reasonable electronics engineer, or the reasonable heart surgeon, for example. To determine just what the standard is on the facts before it, the court will hear from expert witnesses who, in turn, will present evidence of what that standard is.

Where the activity or product poses a high risk, the law imposes a higher standard of care. The policy reason for this higher standard is to encourage competence and caution in light of the very serious harm that could result if the task were poorly performed.

In assessing whether Excel breached its duty of care, a court will likely apply a higher standard because of the inherent dangers in the Excel product. A central issue will be Excel's quality control procedures. As noted earlier, these procedures involve employees squeezing the tubes by hand at two separate steps in the production process. This is a factor suggesting that Excel fulfilled its duty of care—the tubes were checked and passed the squeeze test. On the other hand, the quality control measure may itself be inadequate. In fact, the procedure for assessing whether the tube was properly sealed could be described as totally haphazard, unscientific, and uncontrolled[5] since, among other problems, there was no way of measuring the pressure exerted by an employee at any given time. If this second argument prevails, a court will find that Excel did breach the standard of care it owed to Hugh in how it packaged the fibreglass hardener.

There is another basis upon which Excel may have breached the standard of care. The warning label on the tube noted that the product was flammable and could cause skin irritation and blindness. The label did not recommend that any special precautions be taken, such as the wearing of protective gloves and goggles. Furthermore, there was no warning to the user to exercise caution in applying pressure to the tube. Given the very hazardous quality of the fibreglass hardener, such deficiencies in Excel's warning are likely fatal to its case.

In sum, there is a very strong argument that Excel failed to meet a reasonable standard in packaging its products: Excel's quality control procedures were inadequate, as were the warning and other information on its product.

---

reasonable person
The standard used to judge whether a person's conduct in a particular situation is negligent.

---

5. This is how the trial judge described the process in the case upon which aspects of the Excel–Hugh scenario is based. See *LeBlanc v. Marson Canada Inc.*, *supra* note 1 at paras. 17–18.

causation

The relationship that exists between the defendant's conduct and the plaintiff's loss or injury.

Step 3: Did the defendant's careless act (or omission) cause the plaintiff's damage? While the legal test for **causation** is sometimes debated, courts generally have little difficulty reaching a decision on causation by asking this simple question: Would the harm not have occurred *but for* the defendant's actions?[6]

It seems relatively clear that Excel's failure to use reasonable care in the production process and to provide proper warnings on the product caused Hugh's injury. But for these failures, Hugh would not have been injured.

CASE ▼

Kauffman v. Toronto Transit Commission, [1960] S.C.R. 251

THE BUSINESS CONTEXT: Even when a customer is injured on business premises, it may be that the injury was not caused by a negligent act or omission by the business itself but for other reasons. If so, the business would have a complete defence to any claim brought against it by the injured party.

FACTUAL BACKGROUND: Mrs. Kauffman was riding up the escalator owned by the Toronto Transit Commission (TTC). The escalator was equipped with a metal-clad handrail instead of the rubber type, which presumably would have been less slippery. Several youths, riding the same escalator just above Kauffman, began pushing each other around. They ultimately fell on Kauffman, knocking her over and severely injuring her. Kauffman sued the TTC for damages, claiming that it had been negligent in installing an untested handrail made of metal. Furthermore, she argued that the defendant had failed to supply proper supervision of those using the escalators and was therefore liable.

RESOLUTION: The Supreme Court of Canada ruled that the TTC did not cause the loss suffered by Kauffman. The cause of the fall was the wrongful and grossly negligent conduct of the youths who fell on her. The nature of the grip on the handrail—though not as effective as a rubber grip—did not contribute to the accident. As one of the judges observed

It is impossible to seriously suggest that when the weight of three men amounting to approximately 450 lbs. was projected suddenly from above against this elderly lady she would not have fallen backwards, whatever the nature of the grip on the handrail.

Furthermore, the court determined that the defendant did not owe a duty to supply supervision of those using the escalator. While it was required to use all due, proper, and reasonable care, it was not an insurer of the safety of those using the escalators.

CRITICAL ANALYSIS: Do you agree with the court's analysis? Should not a business be liable whenever one of its customers is hurt?

What steps could the owner of the escalator take to reduce accidents?

---

6. Lewis Klar, *Tort Law*, 3rd ed. (Toronto: Carswell, 2003) at 389.

Step 4: Was the damage suffered by the plaintiff too remote?

At this point in the test for negligence, a court asks, "Even if there is an obligation to take reasonable care and it was breached, how far will the legal liability of the defendant stretch?"[7] The idea is that there must be some limit on the defendant's responsibility for the consequences of his negligence.

Because Hugh suffered a corrosive product in his eye due to Excel's negligence, he was unable to work at any job for four months after the injury. His loss of income due to this enforced period of unemployment is foreseeable, and Excel will be ordered to pay damages accordingly. While Excel is not responsible for every negative event in Hugh's life after the accident, it is certainly responsible for his inability to work in the months following his hospitalization.

By way of contrast, assume that Hugh's fiancée—who is involved in a start-up company with a bright future—cannot cope with the stress caused by Hugh's injury. She calls off the wedding. Hugh cannot argue that the injury prevented him from becoming a millionaire because he otherwise would have married his fiancée and reaped the future financial success of her company. Such a claim would fall into the category of **remoteness of damage.**

In assessing Excel's responsibility for Hugh's damages, a court need only be satisfied that the type of damage he suffered was foreseeable. It is not necessary, in addition, to foresee the full extent of the damage of any given type. If Hugh is a world-famous neurosurgeon whose loss of income claim amounts to millions of dollars, Excel is still liable for the full amount. Provided that it is reasonably foreseeable that someone injured by the fibreglass hardener would have employment income, it is not necessary to foresee that the person injured may work in a particularly lucrative field.

The principle that only the type of the loss must be foreseeable also finds expression in the **thin skull rule.** This rule protects the plaintiff who has an inherent weakness or "thin skull" that makes a given injury more serious than one might otherwise reasonably anticipate. The rule states that such a plaintiff is still entitled to the full extent of the loss. For example, if Hugh's recovery from his eye injury takes a longer period of time than would normally be anticipated because he has an impaired immune system, his damages will not be reduced for that reason. Though the condition impairing the immune system is reasonably rare, Excel cannot use this fact to escape liability for Hugh's entire loss of income claim.

While the thin skull rule traditionally applies to physical infirmities, it has been extended to psychological infirmity as well.[8]

Hugh is clearly entitled to recover for damages related to the personal injuries caused by a defective product such as the fibreglass hardener. What tort law traditionally is reluctant to permit is recovery for **pure economic loss,** that is, loss that is only financial and involves no personal injury or property damage to the plaintiff. When a person not in a contractual relationship causes someone else to suffer a financial detriment only, such a loss is generally not recoverable. One explanation is that the rule prevents defendants from being overwhelmed with liability.[9] A related explanation is that to permit recovery of damages in such cases would cause too much litigation in the courts. It is only in a relatively few areas, such as negligent misstatement (discussed later in this chapter), that a plaintiff can recover for pure economic loss.

remoteness of damage
The absence of a sufficiently close relationship between the defendant's action and the plaintiff's loss.

thin skull rule
The principle that a defendant is liable for the full extent of a plaintiff's loss even where a prior vulnerability makes the harm more serious than it otherwise might be.

pure economic loss
Financial loss that results from a negligent act where there has been no accompanying property or personal injury damage to the person claiming the loss.

---

7. *Ibid.* at 417.
8. See, for example, *Dunne v. Gauthier*, [2000] B.C.J. No. 2404 (S.C.) (QL); and *Costello v. Blakeson*, [1993] 2 W.W.R. 562 (B.C. S.C.).
9. For a general discussion of these points, see Klar, *supra* note 6 at 202.

The law requires the plaintiff to prove *each and every step* in a negligence action. It is not enough to establish some of the steps or even most of them. In short, the plaintiff must show that the defendant owed a duty of care and breached the standard of care associated with that duty. Provided that the breach in question caused the plaintiff's loss and that the loss was not too remote, the plaintiff has won the negligence action.

Defences to a Negligence Action

Though a court may find the defendant to have been negligent, the plaintiff is not automatically entitled to recover all of her damages. The defendant may raise defences against the plaintiff in order to place at least some of the responsibility for the loss on that party. This section explores two such defences: the defence of contributory negligence and the defence of *volenti non fit injuria*—that the plaintiff has voluntarily agreed to assume the risk in question.

Contributory Negligence

The defence of contributory negligence was introduced in Chapter 10. It refers to unreasonable conduct by the plaintiff that contributed—or partially caused—the injuries that were suffered.[10] This defence recognizes that in many instances, both the defendant and the plaintiff may have been negligent. For example, Hugh may have partially caused his own injury by squeezing the hardener tube with extreme pressure. Since the tube was marked as containing a corrosive and potentially harmful substance, he arguably should have been more cautious in how he handled it.

If Hugh is found to have been part author of his own misfortune, Excel has made out its defence of contributory negligence. As noted in Chapter 10, provincial legislation[11] will then come into play. It provides that responsibility for the tortious event must be apportioned between or among the respective parties, in this case, Hugh and Excel. Through this mechanism, Hugh's damages award is then reduced in proportion to his own negligence.

Voluntary Assumption of Risk

voluntary assumption of risk

The defence that no liability exists as the plaintiff agreed to accept the risk inherent in the activity.

When the court makes a finding of *volenti non fit injuria* or **voluntary assumption of risk,** it is concluding that the plaintiff consented to accept the risk inherent in the event that gave rise to the loss. *Volenti non fit injuria* is therefore a complete defence to the lawsuit, and the plaintiff will be awarded nothing by a judge even though the defendant had been negligent.

To succeed on the defence, the defendant must show that the plaintiff—knowing of the virtually certain risk of harm—released his right to sue for injuries incurred as a result of any negligence on the defendant's part.[12] In short, both parties must understand that the defendant has assumed no legal responsibility to take care of the plaintiff and that the plaintiff does not expect him to.[13] Since this test is not easy to meet, *volenti non fit injuria* is a very rare defence.

---

10. *Supra* note 6 at 455–56.
11. *Supra* note 6 at 458. Each common law province has contributory negligence legislation, which has replaced the common law.
12. *Dubé v. Labar*, [1986] 1 S.C.R. 649.
13. *Ibid.*

THE BUSINESS CONTEXT: When a business sponsors promotional events, it runs the risk of being held legally responsible for any injuries that might occur.

FACTUAL BACKGROUND: Crocker entered an inner tube race at an event put on by Sundance, the operators of a ski slope. He decided to do so having seen a video of the event held in the previous year. Like other participants, Crocker was required to sign a waiver—that is, a commitment not to sue the promoters for any loss or injury associated with participating in the event. Crocker signed the waiver without reading it or knowing what it involved.

It was obvious to the manager of the facility that Crocker had been drinking. In fact, on Crocker's second trip down the hill, the manager advised him not to proceed with the race. Crocker did not listen. On his way down the hill, Crocker fell off the tube, broke his neck, and was rendered quadriplegic. Crocker sued.

THE LEGAL QUESTION: Was Sundance negligent? Did Crocker voluntarily assume the risk (i.e., could Sundance rely on the defence of *volenti non fit injuria*)? Was Crocker contributorily negligent?

RESOLUTION: The Supreme Court of Canada ruled that Sundance owed a duty of care to the participants because it had set up an "inherently dangerous competition in order to promote its resort and improve its financial future." It was therefore obligated to take all reasonable care to prevent Crocker—

who was clearly drunk—from competing in the event at all. Management's suggestion to Crocker that he not continue with the race was insufficient to meet the standard of care associated with the duty. On the contrary, Sundance allowed and even assisted a visibly intoxicated person to participate in a dangerous event it had organized. Sundance was therefore liable for the resulting damages.

The court rejected Sundance's defence of *volenti non fit injuria.* The court stated that while Crocker's participation in the event could be regarded as an assumption of the *physical* risks involved, even this was a questionable conclusion given that Crocker was inebriated. But leaving this aside, Crocker had certainly not consented to the *legal* risk. As the court observed: "Sliding down a hill in an oversized inner tube cannot be viewed as constituting per se a waiver of Crocker's legal rights against Sundance." Even though Crocker had signed a waiver, this had no legal effect since he had not read the waiver nor did Sundance have any reasonable grounds for concluding that the signed waiver expressed Crocker's true intention. The defence of *volenti non fit injuria* therefore failed.

The trial judge's finding that Crocker was 25 percent contributorily negligent for his own injuries had not been appealed to the Supreme Court and therefore was not disturbed. Crocker was awarded 75 percent of his damages because his voluntary intoxication had contributed to the accident.

CRITICAL ANALYSIS: Was Crocker treated too harshly by the court in deducting 25 percent from his award for contributory negligence? Was Crocker treated too leniently given that Sundance's defence of *volenti non fit injuria* failed?

Negligent Misstatement (or Negligent Misrepresentation)

**negligent misstatement
or negligent
misrepresentation**
An incorrect statement
made carelessly.

When negligence takes the form of words, the tort is known as a **negligent misstatement** or **negligent misrepresentation.** The plaintiff's loss does not arise due to the defendant's physical actions but due to the defendant's careless oral or written statements.

Historically, the tort of negligent misstatement was governed by a specialized test that the courts used to determine whether the tort had been committed or not. This is no longer the case. The Supreme Court of Canada, in *Hercules Managements v. Ernst & Young,*[14] reconfirmed that the two-step *Anns* test—referred to earlier in this chapter—applies to *all* negligence actions. Put another way, there is no specialized test for negligent misstatement.

professional
Someone engaged in an occupation requiring the exercise of special knowledge, education, and skill.

From a business perspective, it is **professionals**—such as accountants, lawyers, engineers—who are most likely to commit the tort of negligent misstatement by giving bad advice or providing the client with an incompetent report. The professional who gives poor advice to his client not only faces liability for the tort of negligent misstatement but also is in breach of his contract with the client. That is, providing incompetent advice is both a tort and a breach of contract. This is a matter discussed more fully in Chapter 22.[15]

When professionals are sued by their clients, they are clearly not faced with an unduly broad scope of liability. If a professional takes someone on as a client and performs her service negligently, a lawsuit is perfectly justifiable. The justification is considerably less strong when the professional gives incompetent advice or provides a negligent report that is relied upon by a **third party** (that is, someone other than the client). Should that third party have an action in negligence? Keep in mind that in many cases, the professional has had no dealings with that third party and may not even know that third party exists until she is sued. Courts are legitimately concerned that the professional could face an unreasonable level of liability. In fact, they have stated that such defendants should not be exposed to liability "in an indeterminate amount for an indeterminate time to an indeterminate class."[16]

third party
One who is not a party to an agreement.

Also tied up in the analysis of professional liability is the idea that, generally speaking, professionals cause pure economic loss as opposed to physical loss or injury. When the loss is merely economic—that is, purely monetary—the law is simply less solicitous of the victim. From tort law's perspective, monetary loss is simply not as worthy of compensation as is property damage or personal injury.

CASE ▼

Hercules Managements Ltd. v. Ernst & Young, [1997] 2 S.C.R. 165

THE BUSINESS CONTEXT: Accountants are regularly hired by corporations to prepare the audited financial statements that many corporations are required to present to shareholders at their annual general meeting. The audit reports—though prepared for the corporate client—are in fact reviewed by a variety of people from directors and officers, to shareholders, to prospective investors across the world.

FACTUAL BACKGROUND: Ernst & Young prepared audited financial statements for two companies. These financial statements were the result of incompetent work by the auditors. Shareholders in the

two companies claimed that they relied on the financial statements in deciding to invest further in the companies. These shareholders lost hundreds of thousands of dollars when the companies failed to perform.

THE LEGAL QUESTION: Do the auditors owe a duty of care to the shareholders such that they are responsible to the shareholders for negligent misstatement?

RESOLUTION: According to the court, the two-step *Anns* test—discussed earlier in this chapter—is a fixture of Canadian law and should be used in all negligence cases.

The court agreed that the first part of *Anns* had been met. The accountants owed the shareholders a *prima facie* duty of care because there existed between them a neighbour relationship (or relationship of proximity). The auditors would have realized

---

14. *Hercules, supra* note 4.
15. As Chapter 22 discusses, such conduct can also be a breach of fiduciary duty.
16. *Ultramares Corp. v. Touche Niven & Co.* (1931), 255 N.Y. 170 (U.S. C.A.).

By way of contrast to the court's approach in *Hercules*, when the negligent misstatement causes physical harm (i.e., personal injury or property damage), courts are much more willing to assist the plaintiff. Almost certainly, a judge would not cut back a *prima facie* duty of care when such circumstances exist. For example, if Excel gave erroneous first aid instructions on the product labelling and these instructions resulted in permanent vision loss to Hugh, Hugh has suffered physical harm. He will easily pass the two-part *Anns* test because he is Excel's neighbour and there are no considerations that should limit the duty of care that Excel owes to him. Excel's negligent words injured Hugh, and the company should be fully responsible for Hugh's injuries.

Negligence and Product Liability

product liability

Liability relating to the design, manufacture, or sale of the product.

The law imposes a standard of care on manufacturers in relation to the design, manufacture, or sale of their products. This area of law is known generically as **product liability.** The scenario under discussion in this chapter is a product liability case because Excel breached the standard of care it owed Hugh by manufacturing an unsafe tube. It also failed to exercise proper care in marketing—it did not adequately advise users of the precautions they should take to minimize the risk of harm.

Product liability cases often involve contract law as well. Besides being able to sue Excel in negligence, Hugh has an action for breach of contract against the retailer who provided him with the defective fibreglass repair kit. The retailer is in breach of contract because it supplied Hugh with a product that was not fit to be sold. Hugh does not, of course, have a contract action against the manufacturer, since there is no contract between them.

Hugh's contract action against the retailer will probably be more straightforward than his negligence action against Excel. This is because liability for breaching a contractual term is strict. Since the retailer's promise to supply a nondefective product is not qualified in any way, there is no defence for breaching that promise. It is no defence to the contract action for the retailer to prove that it purchased from a reputable supplier, for example, or that there was no way of telling that the product was defective apart from opening the package and performing a squeeze test on-site. To succeed in negligence against the manufacturer, however, Hugh has to demonstrate all the steps in the action, as outlined earlier in this chapter. It is not enough for Hugh simply to show that the tube seal broke, leading to a serious eye injury. Hugh has to show that the break in the tube was due to Excel's negligence.

Because of the nature of product liability, Hugh has two defendants he can sue and is well advised to proceed against both of them. Having two defendants increases the chances that Hugh will be able to collect at least something on any judgment in his favour. For example, if the retailer is out of business by the time the matter goes to trial, Hugh will still have the manufacturer left as a source of payment of damages and vice versa.

The nature of product liability in foreign jurisdictions is discussed at the end of this chapter. Chapters 23 and 24 offer further discussion of liability relating to the manufacture, distribution, and sale of products.

Negligence and the Service of Alcohol

Commercial establishments serving alcohol owe a duty of care to impaired patrons to assist them or prevent them from being injured.[17] Similarly, these establishments can be liable to members of the public who are injured by the conduct of one of their drunken customers,[18] most notably through drunk driving. An important rationale for this duty is that clubs, bars, and taverns benefit economically from serving drinks to their patrons. It stands to reason that such commercial establishments should also have some positive obligation to the inebriated patron and to others put at risk by that patron.[19] This economic relationship between the commercial host and patron provides an important rationale for extending the law of negligence in this way.

Another example of a relationship leading to liability in relation to the service of alcohol relates to the office party. Liability imposed on employers in this context is based on the employer's larger duty to provide a safe working environment.[20]

CASE ▼

Hunt v. Sutton Group Incentive Realty Inc. (2001), 52 O.R. (3d) 425 (Sup. Ct. Jus.), rev'd on other grounds (2002), 215 D.L.R. (4th) 193 (C.A.)

THE BUSINESS CONTEXT: Employers regularly host social events for their employees at which alcohol is served. Employers face liability should a drunken employee get behind the wheel and become injured in a car accident.

FACTUAL BACKGROUND: The plaintiff employee, Linda Hunt, became drunk at the office Christmas party. When she was leaving the event, her employer grew concerned and offered to call her spouse to pick her up. The plaintiff declined and went with several other employees to a bar. The plaintiff consumed at least two drinks at this new location. Notwithstanding a snowstorm and her own impairment, the plaintiff subsequently drove home and was in a serious accident resulting in her suffering brain injuries and multiple fractures.

THE LEGAL QUESTION: Does the employer owe a duty of care to the employee to keep her out of harm's way? Does the commercial host (the bar that the employee visited after the office party) owe her a similar duty of care? Was the employee contributorily negligent?

RESOLUTION: The trial judge found both the employer and the commercial host partially responsible for the

---

17. See Klar, *supra* note 6 at 178.
18. See, for example, discussion in *Stewart v. Pettie* (1995), 121 D.L.R. (4th) 222 (S.C.C.).
19. See Klar, *supra* note 6 at 178.
20. *Ibid.* at 190.

plaintiff's injuries. The court also found that the plaintiff was contributorily negligent. According to the court,

> [the employer] not only owed its employee an obligation to take reasonable care to avoid acts or omissions which it could reasonably have foreseen would likely cause her some harm, it also owed its employee an overriding managerial responsibility to safeguard her from an unreasonable risk of personal injury while on duty.

To discharge this duty, the defendant should have personally intervened to prevent her from driving. As the court observed:

> It was open to the defendant to send the plaintiff home by taxi, if necessary to take her car keys away and to take custody of her car. Alternatively, it should have taken steps to call her common law husband to come and pick her up. Alternatively, he could have taken her to a local hotel or found somebody else who had not been drinking to do so or to drive her home.

The court also found that this breach caused the accident. Although weather was a factor, the plaintiff's degree of intoxication played a "major role." Furthermore, the accident was foreseeable.

The commercial host also shared some liability for the accident since it served alcohol to the already visibly impaired plaintiff. According to the court,

> the defendant Pub owed an obligation to take positive steps to care for its patron from foreseeable and unreasonable risk of harm through its act of commission or omission. . . .
>
> I . . . find that the Pub owed a duty to the plaintiff to find her alternative methods of getting home other than driving her own motor vehicle. This duty is a "positive duty" which includes taking positive steps not only to oversee her consumption of alcohol while on [the] premises but also, if necessary, to get her a taxi home, to require her to hand over the keys to her motor vehicle or alternatively, and if necessary, even to call the police.

The court ruled that the accident and resulting damages were also foreseeable because the pub allowed the plaintiff "to drive home in the dark, in the middle of a snowstorm when her ability to drive was obviously impaired by alcohol."

Finally, the court also determined that the plaintiff was 75 percent contributorily negligent. According to the court:

> I find that turning her back to the dangers that she ought to have foreseen by allowing herself to drink and then drive home in such weather conditions as existed at the time in question was negligent on her part. She ought to have foreseen that by becoming intoxicated, her judgment would then become impaired.

On appeal, one of the grounds raised was that the judge had been in error to grant the plaintiff's counsel's motion to discharge the jury. The court of appeal agreed and ordered a new trial on this basis alone. It is an open question whether the trial judge's analysis will be followed by future courts,[21] particularly as this matter has since been settled.

CRITICAL ANALYSIS: Do you think that the court put too much responsibility on the employer and commercial host?

Linda Hunt's case recently settled out of court.

---

21. Sharon Duffy, "Ont. C.A. Fails to Clarify Workplace Alcohol Liability" *The Lawyers Weekly* (11 October 2002) at 12.

Business Application of the Law

How Employers Can Manage the Risk of Alcohol-Related Liability

In an article in *The Lawyers Weekly*, Norman MacInnes relies on employment lawyer Soma Ray to provide a list of the top ten steps that companies can follow to reduce liability for alcohol-related lawsuits associated with company parties.

1. Control the amount of alcohol served.
2. Stop serving a couple of hours prior to the end of the party.
3. Ensure that the bar is attended, with instructions to the bartender that no one who appears to be intoxicated should be served alcohol.
4. Draft language in the contract with the hotel to the effect that identified company management needs to be informed of any employees to whom the bartender has refused to serve alcohol.
5. Inform employees that intoxicated employees will be put into taxicabs (but stress that it would be preferable if individuals did not drink to that point).
6. Encourage car pools and pay mileage to the designated driver.
7. Provide reduced rates at hotels.
8. Provide taxi chits.
9. Remind employees prior to the party (via e-mail, for example) and at the party not to drink and drive.

The tenth possible suggestion offered—making employees sign a waiver—actually isn't a good idea, according to Ray. "It's not likely to reduce liability. ..."

CRITICAL ANALYSIS: Why do you think having employees sign waivers may prove ineffective?

Source: Norman MacInnes, "Alcohol at Work: How Employers Can Avoid Liability," *The Lawyers Weekly* (23 February 2001) (Lexis).

CASE ▼

Childs v. Desormeaux (2006), 266 D.L.R. (4th) 257 (S.C.C.)

BUSINESS CONTEXT: There is no business context to the *Childs* case, since it involved a social gathering between friends where alcohol was consumed. It may, however, shed light on the potential liability of the employee who invites office colleagues over for drinks after work. Is this latter scenario more like the social host situation or more like the situation involving an office party hosted by the employer?

FACTUAL BACKGROUND: Desormeaux was attending a B.Y.O.B. social event hosted by two friends who knew that he was a heavy drinker. Desormeaux drank 12 beers in two and a half hours (though this was unknown to his hosts) and drove away in his car (which they did know about). Desormeaux was uninsured and already had two convictions for impaired driving. He drove his vehicle into ongoing traffic and caused a head-on collision with the car in which 17-year-old Zoe Childs was a passenger. Childs was paralyzed from the waist down due to this accident. She sued the hosts of the party Desormeaux was attending. If she were successful, this would give her access to the defendants' insurance and mean that she would have a better chance of recovering her damages, calculated to be in the millions of dollars. The uninsured Desormeaux would almost certainly never be able to pay.

THE LEGAL QUESTION: Do Desormeaux's social hosts owe a duty of care to the plaintiff as she was injured by one of their intoxicated guests?

RESOLUTION: The Supreme Court of Canada ruled that, on these facts, the social hosts did not even owe Childs a *prima facie* duty of care as articulated in *Anns* and discussed earlier in this chapter. Since Desormeaux was not showing signs of intoxication, it was not reasonably foreseeable to his hosts that he would be a danger on the highways. As well, there was no real link or nexus between the social hosts and the plaintiff such that the law would require the social hosts to take *positive* steps to stop the event from happening. As the court states in para. 31:

> Although there is no doubt that an omission may be negligent, as a general principle, the common law is a jealous guardian of individual autonomy. Duties to take positive action in the face of risk or danger are not free-standing. Generally, the mere fact that a person faces danger, or has become a danger to others, does not itself impose any kind of duty on those in a position to become involved.

A positive duty to act is imposed only in rare circumstances, as where, for example, the defendant invites others to participate in dangerous activity that he has created or controlled. An example is *Crocker v. Sundance Northwest Resorts Ltd.*, (see analysis of this case earlier in this chapter). Another example is when one is engaged in commercial activity that brings with it responsibilities to the public, as in the situation of commercial hosts. Holding a house party would not be classified in law as a dangerous or risky activity, unless, perhaps, the hosts did something to make the situation risky by continuing to serve alcohol to a visibly intoxicated guest who the host knew would be driving home. According to the court:

> Short of active implication in the creation or enhancement of the risk, a host is entitled to respect the autonomy of a guest. The consumption of alcohol, and the assumption of the risks of impaired judgment, is in almost all cases a personal choice and an inherently personal activity. Absent the special considerations

that may apply in the commercial context, when such a choice is made by an adult, there is no reason why others should be made to bear its costs. The conduct of a hostess who confiscated all guests' car keys and froze them in ice as people arrived at her party, releasing them only as she deemed appropriate, was cited to us as exemplary. This hostess was evidently prepared to make considerable incursions on the autonomy of her guests. The law of tort, however, has not yet gone so far.

The court did not proceed to consider whether the second step in *Anns* had been met, since the plaintiff had already failed on the first step. Zoe Childs lost her case.

CRITICAL ANALYSIS: Do you think that the hosts should have been found liable? How is the case different from a party hosted by an employer, as in the *Hunt* case? Should the court have taken into consideration the fact that Desormeaux had no insurance?

Source: Christin Schmitz, "SCC finds no duty on this particular set of social hosts" *The Lawyers Weekly* (16 May 2006) at 1.

Zoe Childs's case was recently heard by the Supreme Court of Canada

The Negligence Standard versus Strict Liability

strict liability
The principle that liability will be imposed irrespective of proof of negligence.

Strict liability makes the defendant liable for the plaintiff's loss even though the defendant was not negligent and, by definition, had exercised reasonable care.[22] Given that Canadian tort law is founded on a fault-based system, the scope of strict liability is necessarily limited.[23] These exceptions are largely confined to liability for fires, for dangerous animals, and for the escape of dangerous substances.[24]

Another reason strict liability is so unusual is because the law of negligence has expanded to provide a remedy to most victims of accidents who merit compensation.[25]

Though strict liability[26] makes only rare appearances in the law of torts, it would be wrong to conclude that businesses rarely face strict liability. As already noted, there are significant areas where liability is strict, including

- *Liability in contract.* When a business makes a contractual promise that it breaches or fails to perform, that business is liable for breach of contract. The absence of negligence is no defence.

- *Vicarious liability.* As already discussed in Chapter 10, vicarious liability is a form of strict liability. An employer is *automatically responsible* for the torts of his employee when, for example, there is a significant relationship between what the employer was asking the employee to do and the employee's tort.

A third relevant instance of strict liability is described in the following box.

International Perspective — Strict Liability

Some of Canada's major trading partners, such as members of the European Union (EU) and areas in the United States, use a strict liability rather than a fault-based standard in defective-product liability cases.

For example, all EU member states are subject to a directive requiring that manufacturers be strictly liable for their defective products. The directive provides that a product is defective when it does not provide the safety that a person is entitled to expect, taking into consideration all the circumstances.

Relevant considerations include the presentation of the product, expectation of use, and the time the product was put into circulation. The directive also provides for a "state of the art" defence by stating that a product will not be considered defective for the sole reason that a better product is subsequently put on the market.

The effect of a strict liability standard is that manufacturers can be held liable for unsafe products even if they were not negligent in any way and exercised due care. This is markedly different from the result

---

22. *Supra* note 6 at 553.
23. *Supra* note 6 at 553.
24. *Supra* note 6 at 554. This is the *Rylands v. Fletcher* tort. The tort is "no fault," and the mere fact that the dangerous substance escapes from one's non-natural use of land is enough to make the defendant tortiously liable, even if the escape was not due to negligence/lack of due care. What constitutes non-natural use is a matter of debate beyond the scope of this text. For discussion, see Klar at 556 and following.
25. *Supra* note 6 at 553–54.
26. Note that strict liability in the context of tort law is different from strict liability in the context of regulatory offences. Governments enact regulatory statutes—creating regulatory offences—in order to protect the public interest. According to the leading case of *R. v. City of Sault Ste. Marie* (1978), 85 D.L.R. (3d) 161 (S.C.C.), regulatory statutes such as environmental protection legislation contemplate three classes of offences, one of which is known as a *strict liability offence.* In this context, strict liability does not mean that an offence is created to which there is no defence. For strict liability offences in the regulatory context, a person charged can raise the defence of due diligence. That is, if such a person can show that she took all reasonable care, there will be no liability.

under a fault-based standard. In the latter case, if the manufacturer takes due care at all stages of product production—in designing the product, in selecting a production process, in assembling and testing, and in packaging and labelling—there is no liability regardless of defects. Strict liability, on the other hand, is imposed irrespective of fault.[27]

CRITICAL ANALYSIS: Which approach to liability do you prefer and why?

Business Law in Practice Revisited

1. What will Hugh need to establish in order to succeed in a negligence action?

Hugh must establish that he is owed a duty of care by Excel. This will be straight-forward, as manufacturers such as Excel owe a duty of care to consumers. That is, Hugh is clearly Excel's neighbour and he is therefore owed a *prima facie* duty of care. There are no policy considerations that should reduce or eliminate this duty. Next, Hugh will also have to establish that Excel breached the standard of care by failing to have an adequate quality control program in place and/or by failing to put an adequate warning on its product. Excel's failure to recommend the use of goggles alone will probably be sufficient to meet this step of the negligence test, but there were other failures including poor quality control and poor labelling. In terms of causation, Hugh will almost certainly be able to show that "but for" this failure to recommend goggles, Hugh would not have been injured. Another angle would be for Hugh to show that "but for" the poor quality control and the incomplete warning on the package, he would not have suffered an eye injury. Finally, Hugh will need to establish that his damages—including his claim for loss of future income—were not too remote. This will also be straightforward, as it is entirely foreseeable that someone injured by an Excel product would have a job and that such a person would be unable to work during convalescence.

2. How could Excel better manage its risk of tort liability?

Excel is producing a consumer good with considerable dangers. A risk management plan as discussed in Chapter 3 would certainly assist this company. There are at least three areas related to Excel's operations that need immediate attention:

Quality Control Since the chemicals in Excel's product are corrosive, great care should be taken to ensure that tubes can withstand the normal wear and tear caused by average use. Excel cannot destructively test every tube it produces but no doubt it can make improvements to its existing system. For example, since testing is manual and there is therefore no way of measuring the pressure exerted, perhaps Excel could move to a more controlled and reliable method of ensuring product safety. It may well be that the quality control staff require better training. Additionally, Excel should consider hiring a consultant to evaluate its business and produce recommendations on how Excel's operation can be improved.

---

27. EC, Council Directive 85/374/EEC of 25 July 1985 on the approximation of the laws, regulations, and administrative provisions of the Member States concerning liability for defective products, [1985] O.J. L 210/29; G. Howells, *Comparative Product Liability* (Aldershot, England: Dartmouth, 1993); and S.N. Hurd & F.E. Zollers, "Product Liability in the European Community: Implications for United States Business" (1993) 31 Am. Bus. LJ. 245.

Better Instructions to Users While the current warning on Excel's product alerts the user to some of its dangers, the warnings must be more express. Excel's product can cause serious eye injury, including blindness. This danger should be identified on the outside of the package and on the instructions—not just on the tube itself. As well, this warning should be as prominently displayed as possible, perhaps through using a larger font and a different-coloured ink for the warning itself.

It may well be that the contents of the tube sometimes deteriorate and harden or otherwise block the nib. Excel should ensure that its tubes can withstand the additional pressure that a consumer might exert in such circumstances. It should also provide appropriate warnings to the consumer as to how to safely unblock the tube and advise users not to place the tube under undue pressure.

Most importantly from a preventive perspective, Excel should instruct users to wear goggles or other eye protection.

Insurance Excel likely maintains third-party liability insurance so that, in the event of injury, Excel can use insurance proceeds to pay out on any damages award made against the company. Insurance, which is discussed further in Chapter 28, is a central element in any risk management plan.

Additionally, Excel should institute a formal review process for when accidents do occur. This is likely a step that Excel's insurer will insist upon in any event.

Chapter Summary

Donoghue v. Stevenson is the foundation of the modern negligence law. Negligence law is an inherently flexible, growing legal area. It seeks to provide a remedy to the plaintiff who has suffered a loss or injury due to the culpable though unintentional conduct of the defendant.

The four steps to a negligence action describe general standards or markers that help a court assess whether the defendant in any given case has been negligent.

One of the most common defences to a negligence claim is that of contributory negligence. The plaintiff's damages award will be reduced in proportion to her own culpability in causing the loss, for example, by failing to wear a seat belt or drinking to the point of impairment.

A less common defence is to allege that the plaintiff voluntarily assumed the risk. This defence is rarely established since the defendant must prove that the plaintiff consented not only to the *physical* risk of harm but also agreed to accept the *legal* risk of not being able to sue the defendant for resulting loss or injury.

Negligent misstatement or negligent misrepresentation holds the defendant responsible for negligence taking written or oral form. Professionals such as accountants and lawyers are most likely to commit this kind of tort. Courts guard against the professional facing liability in "an indeterminate amount for an indeterminate time to an indeterminate class." This sheltering of the professional is also partially justifiable in light of the fact that a professional's negligent misstatement is likely to cause only pure economic loss as opposed to personal injury or property loss. Tort law has been historically less concerned when the plaintiff's loss is purely monetary.

Business is also affected by product liability. Product liability involves both negligence law and the law of contract. The manufacturer of a poorly produced or designed product will face an action in negligence by the disappointed purchaser. The retailer will face a breach of contract action by that same person and—if the retailer was also negligent—an action in negligence as well.

Another area of liability for business relates to the service of alcohol. Commercial servers of alcohol, such as bars, taverns, and restaurants, owe a duty of care to protect against the foreseeable risks of intoxication. This duty extends broadly, including the employer who hosts a social event where alcohol is served. The Supreme Court of Canada has confirmed, on the facts of the case before it, that there is no social host liability in Canada, at least as yet.

Strict liability is a liability imposed even where the defendant has not been negligent. This is a rare phenomenon in tort law, but there are other areas of law in which strict liability is common. The two most important areas relate to liability for breach of contract and vicarious liability for the torts of one's employees. As well, some of Canada's major trading partners, including the EU and parts of the United States, use strict liability rather than a fault-based standard in defective-product liability cases.

Chapter Study

Key Terms and Concepts

causation (p. 246)

duty of care (p. 242)

negligent misstatement or
  negligent misrepresentation (p. 249)

neighbour (p. 242)

prima facie (p. 243)

product liability (p. 251)

professional (p. 250)

pure economic loss (p. 247)

reasonable care (p. 241)

reasonable person (p. 245)

remoteness of damage (p. 247)

strict liability (p. 256)

thin skull rule (p. 247)

third party (p. 250)

voluntary assumption of risk (or *volenti non fit
  injuria*) (p. 248)

Questions for Review

1. What competing interests must a court balance in deciding a negligence action?

2. What are the four steps in a negligence action?

3. Before *Donoghue v. Stevenson*, what defence could most manufacturers of goods raise when faced with a claim for negligence brought by an injured user of those goods?

4. How does the foreseeability test help in defining the neighbour principle in negligence?

5. What is the standard of care in negligence?

6. How is causation usually determined in negligence?

7. Does the normal standard of care vary in any specific circumstances? Explain.

8. Does tort law generally allow recovery for pure economic loss?

9. What does contributory negligence mean and what are the consequences of it being found to exist?

10. What is the consequence of a *volenti non fit injuria* finding? What might be an example of it being applied?

11. What kinds of plaintiffs will be likely to succeed in an action for negligent misstatement against a professional?

12. What second part of the test for duty of care did the Supreme Court of Canada apply in the case of *Hercules Managements v. Ernst & Young*?

13. What other area of law (other than tort law) do product liability actions often involve? Why are actions in that area often more straightforward than in tort law?

14. Does the employer always owe his impaired employee a duty of care? What must the employer do to discharge that duty of care?

15. Is the commercial host liable if one of its patrons is injured due to his own impaired driving? Explain.

16. Why do social hosts not have liability for their drunken guests?

17. Why is strict liability rare in Canada's tort regime?

18. Name two areas where strict liability is common.

Questions for Critical Thinking

1. The principles of *volenti non fit injuria* have been restricted to allow the defence to apply only in limited circumstances. Are these circumstances too limited? For example, should the person getting into the car with an impaired driver still be allowed to recover in negligence? Is there not sufficient public knowledge of the dangers of impaired driving for people to understand the risk they assume? What about those who deliberately choose not to wear a seat belt? Why should they potentially recover?

2. From time to time, it has been proposed that the principles of strict liability be applied to product liability in Canada as they are in certain other jurisdictions. What are the pros and cons of applying this concept in Canada? What changes would result for producers of goods and services, as well as for consumers? Are there inherent risks that might arise for society as a whole if strict liability was imposed in certain industries?

3. One of the areas in which liability for negligence is expanding is in the case of those serving alcohol both as a business and at office parties. Think of the contexts in which businesses might be exposed to these risks either because they make their money from selling alcohol or because they are conducting a social event. To what extent should the business be held liable for negative outcomes of the overconsumption of liquor? How should the business protect itself?

4. It is relatively new for courts to allow recovery for pure economic loss in negligence, that is, loss unrelated to any physical loss. Some would argue that extending negligence in this regard potentially places an unfair burden on some occupations and service providers. In our society, people should accept that there are some losses for which recovery cannot be obtained. What are the pros and cons of allowing recovery for purely economic loss?

5. The application of the "thin skull" rule often places a considerable burden on a defendant who is found liable in negligence, above and beyond what would normally be "reasonably foreseeable." Is it fair that the negligent party assume the burden of these extra costs? Does the "thin skull" rule make sense when considered alongside the rule about remoteness of damage?

6. A delivery truck driver swerves to avoid hitting a large dog that has run onto the highway. The driver loses control of the van and it turns over, seriously injuring his co-worker. Is the driver negligent? What further facts would you be interested in knowing?

Situations for Discussion

1. Paul was shot and killed by an unknown assailant as he was coming out of the front door of a night club late one night. Paul's wife sued the nightclub in negligence. She claimed that the nightclub was negligent in failing to provide uniformed guards outside the front door. Assuming that this failure was negligent, does this prove causation between the negligent act and Paul's murder?[28] Do you think that Paul's wife will win her case? Explain.

2. Max invited some of his co-workers to his home for after-work drinks. Sasha, a new employee, drank a great deal in part because she was an avid participant in various drinking games that Max had planned. When the last game concluded, Sasha drove herself home. She was in a serious car accident and now wants to sue Max in negligence. What are the strengths and weaknesses of her case?

3. Klutz won a contest sponsored by a radio station, entitling him to play in a twilight golf tournament. He went to the radio station and signed a form releasing the station from any liability connected with the tournament. The event was held at the Dark Side Country Club, beginning at 11 p.m. Klutz attended a pre-tournament instructional meeting and was told that his team was to tee off on the second hole. While the team headed for that spot, Klutz hurried to his car to get his clubs and golf shoes. As he sprinted down the path to the parking lot, he ran into one of a series of black iron posts embedded in the asphalt path at the point where the walkway and parking lot met. Klutz somersaulted several times, ending up on the driveway with banged knees and a badly bruised elbow. He played seven holes of golf, but could not carry on. Prior to the accident he was a self-employed upholsterer. Following the accident, he was unable to work for three months. After that his production was down 20 percent. His ability to participate in household and leisure activities was also reduced.[29]

   Apply the principles of tort law to this situation. Suggest a result. What further information would be useful?

4. Burger Heaven (BH) is a large chain of restaurants specializing in burgers and fries. In response to customer demand, BH added coffee to its menu. The temperature of the coffee and the style of container and lids were part of BH operating standards to be followed by all restaurant operators and staff. BH restaurants provide counter and drive-through service. Sandra bought coffee at the drive-through for herself and her husband, Morley. Sandra passed both cups of coffee to Morley. The car hit a big bump and the coffee spilled in Morley's lap, burning him severely.

   What should BH do about this particular incident? Is Morley likely to be successful in any claim for negligence? What defences might BH raise? How can BH manage the risk of a similar incident occurring in the future? Can any preventive steps be taken?

5. Compare and contrast the following two scenarios:

   Example 1: Shannon is walking down a staircase in a mall. Unfortunately, the handrail is not properly attached to the wall and pulls away as Shannon tries to grab it. Shannon loses her balance, falls down the stairs, and suffers serious injuries. Would the accident have occurred "but for" the improperly installed handrail?

---

28. Based, in part, on *Ortega v. 1005640 Ontario Inc. (C.O.B. Calypso Hut 3)*, [2004] O.J. No. 2478 (C.A.), leave to appeal refused, [2004] S.C.C.A. No. 377.
29. Based, in part, on *Poluk v. City of Edmonton* (1996), 191 A.R. 301 (Q.B.).

Example 2: Shannon is walking down the staircase in a mall. Someone on the stair above her accidentally drops some packages and these come cascading down the stairs. Shannon trips on the packages and loses her footing. When Shannon grabs for the handrail, it pulls out of the wall. Shannon continues her fall down the stairs and suffers serious injuries. Would the accident have occurred "but for" the improperly installed handrail?

6. FunTime manufactures children's toys in Winnipeg. It has a new product that is a variation on a bow and arrow: there are suction cups instead of points on the end of arrows. The products are solidly manufactured of plastic in a variety of fluorescent colours. The product, if correctly used, is completely safe. It is possible, however, for a determined child to remove the suction cup, rendering the arrow dangerous. FunTime, mindful of this potential, takes great pains to ensure that all parts of the packaging are labelled with a warning to consumers that this toy should not be given to children under age 5.

   FunTime embarks on an aggressive pre-Christmas advertising campaign in which the new bow and arrow set is its showcase product. The primary focus of the campaign is children's television cartoons. The most popular advertisement shows a group of small children playing a game of hide-and-seek in an imaginary location; the advertisement highlights the attractive colours of the product; and the entire ad is bright, loud, and appealing. The marketing strategy has resulted in most of the advertisements being placed in the 9 a.m. to 11 a.m. time slot on weekdays and weekends. The jingles soon become a favourite theme with young children, the campaign is a great success, and sales increase dramatically.

   Ms Wong, a grandmother, is persuaded by her persistent young grandchildren, age 4 to 7, to buy the product. Unfortunately, the youngest child gets in the habit of chewing on the arrows while watching TV. The suction cups disintegrate, but the children keep playing with the toy. Inevitably one suffers a serious eye injury as a result of the misuse of a damaged arrow.

   Assuming that the injured child, through his parents, now sues FunTime for negligence, review the arguments that might be used by both parties in the case. What defences might FunTime raise? Should it consider "joining" any other parties (arguing that they are responsible)?

   In light of the litigation, FunTime is engaging in an internal review of its policies to ensure that the risk of this type of suit is minimized. Discuss the failings of corporate practices in the above case, and present a proposal for a risk reduction program.

7. Big Pizza, a province-wide pizza chain, has a new promotional campaign. The chain guarantees that all pizzas will be delivered within 30 minutes or they will be free. While this promise is readily kept in small cities and towns, it places considerable stress on franchises in large urban areas. Franchisees are required by their franchise agreement to pass on this stress to drivers by fining them half of the cost of any pizza not delivered within the requisite time. To overcome this threat, drivers often are forced to drive well above the speed limit. A driver, attempting to meet the deadline, fails to notice another vehicle in its path and collides with it, seriously injuring the passengers in that vehicle.

   Assuming that the issue of negligence by the driver is clear-cut and that the driver is an employee, can the injured persons claim damages from the franchisee for the actions of the employee? Why or why not? Is there any argument that Big Pizza has itself been negligent? Present arguments for both sides of the case, and determine whether liability will be upheld.

8. The Bridge Engineering Company contracted to build a bridge between a suburb and the downtown of a medium-sized town. For years the two communities were joined by a one-lane bridge, and this new four-lane bridge was a major improvement. Indeed, as a result of the new bridge, a local contractor began building a new housing project of 30 homes. Just before the first home sales were made, a major defect

was discovered in the bridge design that meant that the bridge would be unusable for at least two years. Residents would be forced to use a lengthy detour that added approximately 30 minutes to the average drive between the suburb and downtown, where the majority of the residents worked. The market for the new housing project immediately collapsed, and the contractor was unable to sell any houses. The contractor is considering litigation but realizes that he has no claim in contract against the engineering company. Are there any alternatives? Explain.

For more study tools, visit
http://www.businesslaw3e.nelson.com

Chapter

12

PRIVATE PROPERTY

NO TRESPASSING

TRESPASSERS WILL BE PROSECUTED

Other Torts

Objectives

After studying this chapter, you should have an understanding of

- the range of torts that are relevant to business organizations
- how torts arise from the use of property
- how torts arise from business operations
- how a business can manage the risk of liability in tort

Business Law in Practice

Ron Smithson owns and operates a small manufacturing business in St. John's, Newfoundland. The business supplies specially crafted items for gift stores, specialty boutiques, and craft shops. Ron sells mostly through trade shows, although online sales are beginning to account for a sizable part of his business. He also has a small factory outlet. Ron conducts business in a two-storey building that he owns in a historic part of the city. The basement houses a manufacturing facility consisting of pottery wheels, kilns, and a decorating and glazing studio. The main floor is used for warehousing and storage, packing, and shipping. The second floor, with the exception of a small unit devoted to the factory outlet, is leased to a number of other small businesses.

Ron has had a successful year, although there are two situations that have the potential to jeopardize the bottom line:

- Julie Osbourne, a local resident, suffered serious injuries on Ron's premises. Julie had planned to visit the factory outlet to purchase some gifts for visitors. To access the store, she had to use the elevator. As she travelled between floors, the steel plate covering the indicator lights above the elevator door became unhinged and fell, hitting her on the head, neck, and shoulders. Apparently, the plate fell off because the elevator maintenance company, Elevator XL Services, which had been hired by Ron to maintain all features of the elevator, had run out of plate clips to keep the plate itself in place. It instructed its employee to use a broken clip for the time being rather than leave the steel plate off altogether. Ron knew that a broken clip had been used on the steel plate but had also been assured by the elevator maintenance company that a proper clip would be installed on the very next business day.

- While visiting a trade show on the mainland, Ron saw a replica of his best-selling figurine "Old Man of the Sea." The replica was dressed in the same fisher garb as Ron's figurine, was decorated with the same colours, and had the same style of packaging and labelling. The only differences were that the replica was made with cheap plastic and that it was named "Man of the Sea." Ron is concerned about the impact that sales of this competing figurine will have on his business.[1]

1. What potential legal actions does Julie have against Ron's business?
2. What is the responsibility of Elevator XL Services?
3. Does Ron have any recourse against the manufacturer of the replica figurine?
4. How can Ron manage the risk his business faces of potential tort liabilities?

Introduction

Business activity—whether it involves generating electricity, cutting hair, filing tax returns, or selling automobiles—involves interactions that may ultimately have a negative impact on others and their property. Consider these examples:

- A customer in a grocery store slips on a lettuce leaf and falls, breaking his ankle.
- A store detective detains a shopper, assuming, incorrectly, that the shopper has stolen merchandise.

---

1. Based, in part, on *Sawler v. Franklyn Enterprises Ltd.* (1992), 117 N.S.R. (2d) 316 (T.D.).

- A salesperson intentionally overstates an important quality of a product because she wants to close a sale.
- A golf course impacts on an adjacent landowner because players continually drive balls into her yard.

In each of these examples, the business may have interfered with a legitimate interest of another and could, as a result, be subject to a tort action.

The laws that make a business liable for its tortious conduct also operate to protect that same business when it is the victim of a tort. Consider these examples:

- A newspaper columnist maligns the environmental record of a business.
- Vandals continually spray paint graffiti on factory walls.
- A competitor entices a skilled employee to break his employment contract and join the competitor's business.
- A new business creates a logo that is remarkably similar to that of an existing business in the same market.

Tort actions relevant to businesses can be conveniently divided between those that arise because a business occupies a property and those that arise because of actual business operations.

Torts and Property Use

occupier

Any person with a legal right to occupy premises.

Tort actions may arise in relation to property in a number of ways, most commonly when the occupier of the property harms others. An **occupier** is generally defined as someone who has some degree of control over land or buildings on that land. An enterprise conducting business on property is an occupier, whether it is the owner, a tenant, or a temporary provider of a service. Following from this definition, it is entirely possible to have more than one occupier of land or a building.

Ron, as owner and user of the building, is an occupier. His tenants on the second floor are occupiers of that space. Elevator XL Services Ltd. was hired to service and maintain the elevator. As such, Elevator XL Services had control of the elevator at a critical time and can also be classified as an occupier, although for a much more fleeting moment. The main tort actions in relation to occupation of property relate to occupiers' liability, nuisance, and trespass.

Occupiers' Liability

Occupiers' liability describes the liability that occupiers have to anyone who enters onto their land or property. This area of the law varies by jurisdiction. New Brunswick, Newfoundland, Quebec, and Saskatchewan retain the common law. Other provinces have occupiers' liability legislation.[2]

Liability at Common Law

The liability of the occupier for mishaps on property is not determined by the ordinary principles of negligence. Rather, liability is determined by classifying the visitor as a trespasser, licensee, invitee, or contractual entrant. Each class is owed a different standard of care, with the trespasser being owed the lowest standard and

---

2. *Occupiers' Liability Act*, R.S.A. 2000, c. O-4 (Alberta); *Occupiers' Liability Act*, R.S.B.C. 1996, c. 337 (British Columbia); *Occupiers' Liability Act*, R.S.M. 1987, c. O-8 (Manitoba); *Occupiers' Liability Act*, R.S.O. 1990, c. O.2 (Ontario); *Occupiers' Liability Act*, R.S.N.S. 1996, c. 27 (Nova Scotia); and *Occupiers' Liability Act*, R.S.P.E.I. 1988, c. O-2 (Prince Edward Island).

the contractual entrant being owed the highest. This area of law is often criticized for the difficult distinctions between the different classes of visitors, the blurring of duties owed between the various classes, and the severity of the result when the visitor is classified as a trespasser.

A **contractual entrant** is someone who has contracted and paid for the right to enter the premises.[3] Visitors to the premises who have bought tickets to see a pottery exhibit would be contractual entrants. The duty owed to this class (in the absence of a contract specifying the duty) is akin to the negligence standard—that is, the standard of reasonableness.

An **invitee** is someone whose presence on the property is of benefit to the occupier, such as store customers and delivery or service personnel. The occupier owes a slightly lower duty to the invitee than to the contractual entrant. He must warn the invitee of any "unusual danger, [of] which he knows or ought to know."[4] There is no requirement to warn of usual or common danger that "ordinary reasonable persons can be expected to know and appreciate."[5]

Julie is clearly an invitee, and the improperly fastened steel plate would be classified as an "unusual danger." She is therefore entitled to hold the owner and elevator maintenance company liable for injuries suffered as a result of that unusual danger.

A **licensee** is someone who has been permitted by the occupier to enter for the benefit of the licensee.[6] If Ron allows people accessing an adjacent business to take a shortcut through his building, those users would be licensees. A licensee might also include guests invited to someone's property for a social occasion.

The general rule is that occupiers are responsible to licensees for any unusual danger of which they are aware or that they have reason to know about. The latter part of the rule is a recent addition and tends to blur the distinction between the duty owed an invitee and the duty owed a licensee.[7] Since there is no strong rationale for distinguishing between a licensee and invitee to begin with, this blurring is entirely justifiable.

A **trespasser** is someone who "goes on the land without invitation of any sort and whose presence is either unknown to the occupier, or if known, is practically objected to."[8] A burglar clearly fits the definition of a trespasser.

An occupier still owes some responsibility to a trespasser. In particular, the occupier will be liable for any act done with the deliberate intention of doing harm to the trespasser, or an act done with reckless disregard for the presence of the trespasser.[9] Though the trespasser is not owed a common law duty of care described in *Donoghue v. Stevenson*,[10] the occupier does owe him "at least the duty of acting with common humanity towards him."[11]

Though a trespasser is owed a very low duty, courts have often mitigated the harshness of this result, particularly when the trespasser is a child. For example, courts have at times reclassified the trespasser as a licensee, interpreted the duty owed the trespasser very generously, and even brought the children's claims under the ordinary law of negligence.

---

contractual entrant
Any person who has paid (contracted) for the right to enter the premises.

invitee
Any person who comes onto the property to provide the occupier with a benefit.

licensee
Any person whose presence is not a benefit to the occupier but to which the occupier has no objection.

trespasser
Any person who is not invited onto the property and whose presence is either unknown to the occupier or is objected to by the occupier.

---

3. Allen M. Linden & Lewis. N. Klar and Bruce Feldthusen, *Canadian Tort Law: Cases, Notes & Materials*, 12th ed. (Toronto: Butterworths, 2004) at 613.
4. *Indermaur v. Dames* (1866), L.R. 1 C.P. 274 at 288.
5. *McErlean v. Sarel* (1987), 61 O.R. (2d) 396 (C.A.) at 418, leave to appeal to S.C.C. refused (1988), 63 O.R. (2d) x (note).
6. Lewis Klar, *Tort Law*, 3rd ed. (Toronto: Carswell, 2003) at 529.
7. *Mitchell v. Canadian National Railway Co.* (1974), 46 D.L.R. (3d) 363 (S.C.C.).
8. *Robert Addie & Sons v. Dumbreck*, [1929] A.C. 358 at 371 (H.L.).
9. *Ibid.* at 365
10. [1932] A.C. 562 (H.L.).
11. *British Railways Board v. Herrington*, [1972] A.C. 877 (H.L.), quoted with approval by the Supreme Court of Canada in *Veinot v. Kerr-Addison Mines Ltd.*, [1975] 2 S.C.R. 311.

Liability under Occupiers' Liability Legislation

Alberta, British Columbia, Manitoba, Nova Scotia, Ontario, and Prince Edward Island have enacted occupiers' liability legislation.[12] Although there are differences in the legislation from one jurisdiction to the next, there is also considerable common ground. One objective of the legislation is to simplify the common law. As the Supreme Court of Canada confirmed in the context of Ontario's *Occupiers' Liability Act*, the legislative purpose was "to replace the somewhat obtuse common law of occupiers' liability by a generalized duty of care based on the 'neighbour' principle set down in *Donoghue v. Stevenson*."[13]

Indeed, legislation across the country provides for a high duty of care—equivalent to the negligence standard—to be owed to entrants who are on the property with express or implied permission (at common law, contractual entrants, invitees, licensees). Responsibility to trespassers differs among the various statutes. In general, however, an occupier must not create deliberate harm or danger, and the responsibilities increase where the trespassers are children.[14]

If Ron's business were located in Ontario where occupiers' liability legislation is in place, the court would likely still find both the elevator company and Ron liable to Julie. This is because under section 3 of the act, an occupier owes a statutory duty of care as "in all the circumstances of the case is reasonable to see that persons entering on the premises, and the property brought on the premises by those persons are reasonably safe while on the premises." Specifically, a court would find that the elevator company ought to have foreseen that harm could occur as a result of a defective clip. Likewise, since Ron was aware of the use of the defective clip and was prepared to allow the elevator to remain in service, he too is liable.

In the context of Ron's business, the outcomes using either statutory or common law applications are, for all intents and purposes, the same. Nonetheless, it remains important to apply the correct principles to the specific provincial context, as responsibilities can and will vary at times.

CASE ▼

Frame v. The Fort Garry Hotel (2002), 162 Man. R. (2d) 267 (Q.B.)

THE BUSINESS CONTEXT: A "slip and fall" incident is one of the most common tortious events that a business will encounter. Ice and snow on sidewalks leading up to the business as well as hazards within the business premises can all lead to liability.

FACTUAL BACKGROUND: Ms. Frame was a guest at the defendant hotel. She slipped and fell on the bathroom tiles, having just used the shower. Though the plaintiff alleged several reasons for the accident, the main ones were that the tiles in the bathroom were not slip-resistant and the cleaner used for those tiles made them additionally hazardous when wet.

THE LEGAL QUESTION: Did the defendant—an occupier—breach its duty to take reasonable care to ensure that the plaintiff was reasonably safe while in the bathroom?

RESOLUTION: According to the court, while the occupier is required under Manitoba's *Occupiers' Liability Act* to take reasonable care, the occupier is not obligated to guarantee the safety of entrants but it does, however, have a duty to exercise reasonable care to ensure that the premises are reasonably safe. The plaintiff's use of the bathroom was in no way unusual.

---

12. *Supra* note 2.
13. *Waldick v. Malcolm*, [1991] 2 S.C.R. 456 at 466 quoting with approval the appellate judge from (1989), 70 O.R. (2d) 717 (C.A.). Note however that in Alberta, for example, separate categories for trespassers and child trespassers are retained. As well, in some jurisdictions, snowmobilers are treated according to specialized rules. See Klar, *supra* note 6 at 549–50.
14, Klar, *ibid.* at 542–52.

While the water on the floor came from the plaintiff's shower, expert evidence established that improper tiles had been used in the bathroom. As well, the particular cleaner used on those tiles was a poor choice because its alkaline level would also result in a slippery surface. That someone might lose her footing under these circumstances was entirely foreseeable. The court therefore found for the plaintiff.

CRITICAL ANALYSIS: Do you think that the plaintiff was contributorily negligent for walking on wet tiles? What can businesses do to prevent "slip and fall" incidents?

Ethical Considerations
Legal Arguments, NHL Arena Safety Nets, and Doing the Right Thing

When spectators are injured by pucks at a sporting event, they might sue for breach of contract, in negligence, or pursuant to occupiers' liability—whether at common law or by legislation. Under occupiers' liability legislation in Ontario, for example, the argument would be that the club and facility owner failed in their duty to take reasonable care under section 3 of the Act noted above. The argument in contract would be that the hockey club failed to provide the spectator with a reasonably safe environment, in breach of an implied term or promise to do so. The argument in tort would be that this same deficiency amounted to negligence. In short, whether by contract, tort, or statute, the hockey club and/or facility owner must ensure that the premises are reasonably safe.

One defence to an action based on occupiers' liability would be to show that the spectator assumed the risk that the premises were not safe. Under section 4 of the Ontario *Occupiers' Liability Act*, the club and facility owner's duty to take reasonable care does not apply to risks willingly assumed by the person who enters.[15] According to several courts across the country, this kind of provision codifies the common law of *volenti non fit injuria* already discussed in Chapter 11.[16] *Volenti non fit injuria* requires the defendant to show that the plaintiff assumed both the physical and legal risks involved.

From a contractual perspective, the argument of breach of contract would likely be met by the club because the ticket doubtless contains an exemption clause. Such a clause—discussed in Chapter 7— would seek to exclude liability for any injury caused by hockey pucks or other objects. Even if such a clause were absent, the club could point out that there was no promise of absolute safety. It would be sufficient under the contract that the seat provided was reasonably safe.

And yet another defence would be to argue that the plaintiff failed to properly watch for pucks and was therefore contributorily negligent.

Setting aside the possibility that the club's legal defences might well fail,[17] what kind of ethical resonance does it have in the context of a serious injury or fatality? Whatever the standard of safety in an NHL rink must be from a *legal* perspective, is it good enough from an *ethical* one?

In March 2002, a young spectator died after being hit by a puck at a National Hockey League game. In light of this tragedy, the NHL's board of governors ordered that safety netting be installed at all league rinks. The board also ordered that plexiglass inside the blue-lines be raised to a minimum of

---

15. Note that even under the circumstances where risk is willingly assumed, the occupier still owes a duty not to create a danger with reckless disregard (s. 4).
16. See *Waldick v. Malcolm, supra* note 13.
17. It may be that a judge would now find that flying pucks are dangers that the club should have reasonably anticipated. See Michael Hirshfeld, "Do Spectator Safety Standards Miss the Net?" *The Lawyers Weekly* (7 June 2002).

5 feet (1.52 metres). "It's the right thing to do," said Oilers president Patrick LaForge.

CRITICAL ANALYSIS: If the NHL can make the ice arenas safer, is the NHL legally or morally obligated to do so—even though fatalities are extraordinarily rare and some fans will complain that such measures obscure their view of the ice? Does it affect the analysis whether the safety measures are more or less

expensive? Should ethics be part of a business's risk management plan? If so, to what extent?

Sources: Jim Matheson, "'Right Thing to Do' NHL Arenas Now Get Safety Nets" *The Edmonton Journal* (21 June 2002); John Heinzl, "Protective Mesh at Hockey Rinks Would Save Lives" *The Globe and Mail* (21 March 2002); and *Hagerman v. City of Niagara Falls* (1980), 29 O.R. (2d) 609 (H.Ct.Jus.).

The Tort of Nuisance

nuisance

Any activity on an occupier's property that unreasonably and substantially interferes with the neighbour's rights to enjoyment of her property.

The tort of **nuisance**[18] addresses conflicts between neighbours stemming from land use. It concerns intentional or unintentional actions taken on one neighbour's land that cause harm of some sort on another's, as in these examples:

- Noise from a steel fabricator's 800-ton press seriously interrupts the neighbours' sleep.
- Ashes and unpleasant odours escaping from a rendering company because of dated technology are carried onto neighbouring properties.
- Sophisticated electronic equipment installed on the roof of a taxi company interferes with the television reception of neighbours who do not have cable.

The focus of nuisance is on one's right to enjoy the benefits of land/property uninterrupted by the actions of neighbours. The general test is whether the impugned activity has resulted in "an unreasonable and substantial interference with the use and enjoyment of land."[19] For example, Ron may vent the kiln and the decorating and glazing operation in the direction of the window his neighbour must routinely leave open in the summer for cool air. Conversely, the restaurant/bar in the building next door may begin hiring bands that play so loudly that Ron's tenants are threatening to leave.

How can locating houses and factories adjacent to each other lead to claims in nuisance?

---

18. As Klar, *supra* note 6 at 641, indicates, there are two distinct causes of actions in nuisance: public nuisance and private nuisance. Since public nuisance plays only a "peripheral role in contemporary law," this text will focus only on private nuisance.
19. *Supra* note 6 at 651.

CASE ▼

Sammut v. Islington Golf Club, Ltd. (2005),
16 C.E.L.R. (3d) 66 (Ont. S.C.J.)

THE BUSINESS CONTEXT: As cities grow, owners of recreational venues, such as golf courses, may encounter problems arising from new houses springing up in what had formally been undeveloped land. Whether the business is responsible for solving those problems depends on whether or not the plaintiff landowner can establish nuisance.

FACTUAL BACKGROUND: Mr. and Mrs. Sammut built a home in a new development, directly to the east of the Islington Golf Club ("IGC"), which had been incorporated in 1923. IGC had initially opposed the building of any homes immediately adjacent to the golf course, on the east, and was successful on first instance. Pending appeal to the Ontario Municipal Board by the developers, the developers and ICG entered into an agreement that permitted redevelopment on certain conditions. Included in this agreement was a clause inserted at ICG's insistence that a narrow, "no touch" zone be established between the Sammuts' proposed home and the third fairway.

The Sammuts build their house very close to the border of the "no touch" zone, which concerned IGC. It viewed this as a violation of the spirit of the agreement.

The tee-box for the third hole abuts the Sammuts' property. The Sammuts found their house and property being peppered by golf balls, causing property damages to their garage door and stucco on the exterior walls. Golf balls also cracked shatterproof windows in the house and gazebo, and destroyed at least one ornamental statue. In addition, the Sammuts were not able to make use of their yard because they were afraid of being hit by high-speed golf balls, known as "screamers." The Sammuts sought damages as well as an injunction.

THE LEGAL QUESTION: Has ICG committed the tort of negligence and nuisance?

RESOLUTION: The Ontario Superior Court agreed that ICG was negligent for failing to develop a method to prevent the balls from falling on the Sammuts' property. ICG also committed the tort of nuisance.

According to the court, the law of nuisance requires the judge to undertake a balancing act and compare competing interests. It is not enough to simply ask whether the ICG has made "reasonable" use of its own property. The court must also enquire whether this conduct is reasonable given that it has a neighbour, namely the Sammuts. The court concluded that IGC was committing the tort of nuisance given the "barrage" of golf balls to which the Sammuts were being subjected.

The court valued damages at $9000 for cost of repairs and $5000 for inconvenience and annoyance. In addition, the court issued an injunction such that IGC could not permit members or guests to play the third hole in any way that would result in balls being hit onto the Sammuts' property. The court ordered that this injunction would go into force into two weeks to permit the club to review its available options and modify the course as required. The court expressed its hope that a solution would be found that would not involve redesign of the third hole but would rely on screening, landscaping, and a possible repositioning of the third-hole tee-boxes.

CRITICAL ANALYSIS: Given that the golf course was built first and the Sammuts built their house right up beside it, are you surprised by the court's decision? Do you agree with Canadian common law principle that, regardless of who was there first, the court must balance the competing interests of the two landowners?[20] Do you think an important factor in the Sammuts case is that the golf course agreed to the development, subject to a "no touch" zone that turned out to be inadequate?

★Note: Subsequent to this decision, ICG erected a 22 foot chain-link screening fence directly in front of and across the Sammuts' property. On subsequent application by the Sammuts, the court agreed that the fence was a great inconvenience and serious eyesore. The court gave the golf course more time to come up with a reasonable solution, noting that the Sammuts too had to be reasonable in their expectations. See *Sammut v. Islington Golf Course* [2005] O.J. 2780, (S.C.J.)

---

20. See for example, *Schneider v. Royal Wayne Motel Ltd.* (1995) 27 Alta.L.R. (3d) 18 (Prov. Ct.), which concerned a nuisance claim by home-owners who built on land adjacent to an existing golf course. According to the court, the fact that the golf course was there first did not give it the right to commit nuisance.

In striking a balance between the respective parties, courts have developed the following guidelines:

- Intrusions must be significant and unreasonable.

- Nuisance typically does not arise where the intrusion is only temporary. For example, construction and demolition may be unpleasant, but are likely to be considered temporary and will not lead to a remedy in nuisance.

- Not all interests are protected by the tort of nuisance. For example, the right to sunlight is an unprotected interest as far as the law of nuisance is concerned.

- In nuisance actions courts will consider tradeoffs in interest. When the noise in question is reasonable and for the public good, the action in nuisance will fail.[21]

Environmental Perspective | Statute Law and the Common Law of Nuisance

One difficulty with the common law of nuisance is its inflexibility. That is, if the private landowner won her nuisance action against an adjoining business, in many cases industrial development could be stopped entirely. In order that tradeoffs could be made in land use, governments began to enact environmental legislation of an increasingly sophisticated and complex nature. Such legislation seeks to balance economic development with a degree of "acceptable" environmental damage. In addition, municipal and land-use planning laws have put further constraints on what kind of activity can occur on the land affected.

Though legislation has therefore displaced some of the importance of common law nuisance from an environmental perspective, nuisance and other tort actions can be nonetheless regarded as Canada's original environmental law. Until the advent of legislation, they were the only way of controlling adverse neighbouring land use.

CRITICAL ANALYSIS: What are the advantages of regulation of the environment via environmental protection legislation as opposed to by private action?

Source: Interview of Professor Elaine Hughes, Faculty of Law, University of Alberta (2002).

Trespass to Property

The tort of trespass protects a person's possession of land from "wrongful interference."[22]

Trespass arises in several ways:

trespass
The act of coming onto another's property without the occupier's express or implied consent.

- A person comes onto the property without the occupier's express or implied permission.

- A person comes onto the property with the occupier's express or implied consent but is subsequently asked to leave.[23] Any person who refuses to leave becomes a trespasser.

- A person leaves an object on the property without the occupier's express or implied permission.

---

21. *Mandrake Management Consultants Ltd v. Toronto Transit Commission* (1993), 102 D.L.R. (4th) 12 (Ont. C.A.).
22. *Supra* note 6 at 97.
23. It should be noted that there are statutory restrictions on a businessperson's common law right to do business with whom she or he sees fit. Alberta human rights legislation, for example, prohibits discrimination by those who offer goods or services that are customarily available to the public. This means that if a businessperson refused to serve a customer because of that customer's ethnicity or gender, for example, and that customer refused to leave, a trespass has occurred. However, the businessperson would also be subject to a penalty for violating human rights legislation.

The tort of trespass is important for resolving boundary/title disputes and, more generally, for protecting property rights. It also protects privacy rights and the right to "peaceful use of land."[24] For these kinds of reasons, trespass is actionable without proof of harm or damage. In the exceptional case where the occupier suffers monetary damages due to another's trespass, however, those damages are recoverable. More commonly, the plaintiff will seek an injunction requiring the trespasser to stop trespassing. Provincial legislation in several jurisdictions also provides for fines against the trespasser.[25]

Torts from Business Operations

Business operations involve a broad range of activities from which tort action can arise. A useful way of categorizing these torts is to consider separately torts involving customers or clients and those more likely to involve competitors.

Torts Involving Customers

Chapter 11 considered the most important tort arising in this context: negligence. Product liability, motor vehicle accidents, alcohol-related liability, and negligent misrepresentations are all examples of negligence affecting the business/consumer relationship.

In this section additional torts will be considered.

False Imprisonment

false imprisonment
Unlawful detention or physical restraint or coercion by psychological means.

False imprisonment occurs most often in retail selling. It arises where any person detains another without lawful justification.

In order for a false imprisonment to have occurred, the victim must have been prevented from going where he has a lawful right to be. The tort includes both either physically restraining that person or coercing them to stay by psychological means.

The tort of false imprisonment presents retailers in particular with a real dilemma. To defend against the tort of false imprisonment, the retailer and/or its employees must comply with the requirements of section 494 of Canada's *Criminal Code*.[26] While there is some legal controversy on this matter, the bulk of the case law requires the following to be established as a defence:

- reasonable grounds to detain the person; and
- proof that a crime such as theft or fraud (or other indictable offence) was committed.

Note that a minority of cases are less exacting—it is enough for the defendant to show that it reasonably appeared to him that the person was committing a crime such as theft or fraud.[27]

24. *Supra* note 6 at 98.
25. Several jurisdictions have enacted legislation that permits trespassers to be fined. See, for example, *Trespass to Premises Act*, R.S.A. 2000, c. T-7 and *Petty Trespass Act*, R.S.A. 2000, c. P-11 (Alberta); *Trespass Act*, R.S.B.C. 1996, c. 462 (British Columbia); *Petty Trespass Act*, R.S.N. 1990, c. P-11 (Newfoundland); *Trespass Act*, S.N.B. 1983, c. T-11.2 (New Brunswick); *Petty Trespass Act*, R.S.M. 1987, c. P-50 (Manitoba); *Trespass to Property Act*, R.S.O. 1990, c. T-21 (Ontario). Note too that the Ontario legislation, for example, also provides for damages to be awarded against the trespasser.
26. Under section 494(1) of the *Criminal Code*
   Any one may arrest without warrant
   (a) a person whom he finds committing an indictable offence; or
   (b) a person who, on reasonable grounds he believes
      (i) has committed a criminal offence, and
      (ii) is escaping from and freshly pursued by persons who have lawful authority to arrest that person.
27. *Supra* note 6 at 134

Whatever the predicament of storekeepers facing serious shoplifting problems, neither they nor their store detectives have any greater rights to detain than does any other citizen. A suspicion that someone committed a crime is not a justification under statute law for the restraint. Furthermore, when they detain a customer in reliance on section 494, the *Criminal Code* requires them to "forthwith deliver the person to a police officer." This means that they must immediately call the police.

Business Application of the Law

Managing the Risk of Retail Theft and Fraud

According to a 2003 report by the Retail Council of Canada, retailers report (via a survey) that they lose $8 million dollars a day in "inventory shrinkage," or nearly $3 billion in total. This inventory shrinkage is attributed to a number of causes:

- Customer theft—35 percent
- Employee theft—40 percent
- Administrative errors—18 percent
- Vendor dishonesty—7 percent

According to the Retail Council of Canada, losses that are not covered under the "shrinkage umbrella" include losses caused by credit card fraud, counterfeit bills, robberies, and other criminal activities such as fraudulent returns.

While retailers can fight a rear-guard action of apprehending the perpetrators and pressing charges, it is much cheaper to prevent loss from occurring in the first place. For this reason, the Alberta branch of the Retail Merchants Association of Canada and the Heads Up Fraud Prevention Association have begun a joint program to educate business owners on security issues, including how to train staff to recognize fraud. The police will also use e-mail and faxes to advise businesses if there are new "scams" or counterfeit bills being circulated in the community. A similar program is underway in British Columbia. As Fugi Saito, then-chair of Heads Up Fraud Prevention Association, states: "It's cheaper to pay for prevention than it is to pay for the damage."

Sources: "City Merchants Target Shoplifters" *The Edmonton Journal* (26 March 2002) at F-1; Retail Council of Canada 2003 Canadian Retail Security Report, Executive Summary at http://www.tagcompany.com/filesttc/Canadian%20Retail%20Security%20Report%202003.pdf#search=%22%22retail%20council%20of%20canada%22%20customer%20theft%22 (accessed 8 November 2006); and the Retail Council of Canada "Resources Protection—Theft and Fraud in Retail" (9 March 2005) at http://www.retailcouncil.org/submissions/submission_bcprivacy_rp.asp

This 2002 photo shows John Wojcicki, of the Retail Merchants Association of Canada, and Fugi Saito, representing the Heads Up Fraud Prevention Association. What are the risks for shopkeepers in apprehending suspected shoplifters?

Assault and Battery

The torts of assault and battery (introduced in Chapter 10) are not common in a business or professional context although they may occur. For example, security personnel may commit the torts of assault and battery when seeking to apprehend a suspected shoplifter or eject a patron. An assault is the threat of imminent physical harm by disturbing someone's sense of security. Battery is the actual physical contact or violation of that bodily security. The contact need not cause actual harm,[28] though it must be harmful or offensive.

Where the torts of assault or battery are proven, the most common remedy is damages.

Deceit

deceit
Misrepresentations that are made fraudulently or recklessly, causing loss.

The tort of **deceit** arises out of misrepresentations, causing loss, that are made either fraudulently or with reckless disregard for their truth. When deceit arises in a contractual context, one of the remedies available is release from the contract (see Chapter 8) in addition to any other damages in tort that the plaintiff can establish. Though the tort of deceit is not confined to the contractual area, this is where it is most commonly found from a business perspective.

Business to Business Torts

Passing Off

passing off
Presenting another's goods or services as one's own.

The tort of **passing off** occurs when one person represents her goods or services as being those of another. While it may be common to think of the tort in terms of the "dirty tricks" some businesses might adopt to compete unfairly with others, the tort can also be committed inadvertently or innocently.

The tort of passing off arises, for example, when a business name is used that is so similar to an existing business name that the public is misled into thinking that the businesses are somehow related. It also may occur where a competing company markets a product that is similar in presentation or overall look to a product already established on the market.

CASE ▼

Ciba-Geigy Canada Ltd. v. Apotex Inc.
[1992] 3 S.C.R. 120.

BUSINESS CONTEXT: Manufacturers of a product generally become concerned if a competitor starts to copy the look or "get-up" of its product. This is because consumers will assume that the goods of the competitor are actually the original manufacturer.

FACTS: The plaintiff, Ciba-Geigy Canada Ltd., manufactured and sold the drug metoprolol tartrate in Canada. The defendants later began to manufacture and sell the same drug in Canada. The parties' products were officially designated as "interchangeable," meaning that the pharmacist could, in filling a prescription, give the defendant's product in place of the plaintiff's product provided the prescription did not contain a "no substitution" notation.

The plaintiff brought an action in passing off against the defendants (Apotex and Novopharm) on the basis that the defendants were copying the plaintiff's "get up" in relation to the size, shape and colour of the pills. The plaintiff claimed that this was creating confusion that the Apotex/Novopharm product was actually a Ciba-Geigy product and sued for passing off.

THE LEGAL QUESTION: What must the plaintiff prove in order to succeed in its action for passing off? More specifically, the issue in this aspect of the litigation was as follows: in seeking to prove that there is confusion caused by the defendants, is the plaintiff limited to showing confusion in the mind of professionals (such as doctors and pharmacists) or can it also rely on confusion in the mind of the ultimate consumer (i.e: the patient)?

RESOLUTION: The Supreme Court of Canada confirmed "that competing laboratories must avoid manufacturing and marketing drugs with such a

---

28. *Supra note 6 at 43.*

similar get-up that it sows confusion in the customer's mind." The court also confirmed that there are three steps to proving the tort of passing off:

1. the existence of goodwill[29] (i.e., in this case, the plaintiff must show that there is goodwill in respect of the "look" or distinctiveness of the product);[30]

2. deception of the public due to a misrepresentation by the defendant (the misrepresentation may be intentional but it also includes negligent or careless misrepresentation); and

3. actual or potential damage to the plaintiff.

Under step two, the plaintiff must show that the competing product is likely to create a risk of confusion in the public mind. On this latter point, the Supreme Court was clear that the plaintiff is not limited to showing confusion in the mind of professionals. Confusion in the mind of the patient who uses the product may also be included.

CRITICAL ANALYSIS: Do you think it is right that a manufacturer should receive legal protection for the features of its product, including colour?

Based on the Supreme Court of Canada's analysis above, Ron will need to establish the following in order to prove passing off.

1. Goodwill or a reputation is attached to his product.

Ron's "Old Man of the Sea" product already has a well-established and valuable reputation among the relevant buying public. In other words, he holds goodwill in the product, and that goodwill, or ability to attract buyers, flows either from the look of the product or from its name, or from both.

2. A misrepresentation—express or implied—by the maker of the cheap replica has led or is likely to lead members of the public into believing that it is Ron's product or a product authorized by Ron.

Whether the competitor actually intended to confuse the public does not matter. Given the similarity of the two figurines, the competitor will make many of its sales by falsely associating itself with the established reputation of Ron's "Old Man of the Sea" product. Ron could prove his point by commissioning a survey of the relevant sector of the buying public.

3. He has or will likely suffer damages.

Ron must show that he has lost sales, or is likely to lose sales, because of the replica product.

While the award of damages is one remedy for a passing-off action, businesses claiming they are being harmed in this way will often seek an injunction forbidding the defendant from continuing the deceptive copying. In the case of *Walt Disney Productions v. Triple Five*,[31] for example, Walt Disney Productions secured a permanent injunction prohibiting the use of the name Fantasyland at West Edmonton Mall's amusement park.[32]

The *Trade-marks Act*[33] contains a statutory form of action that bears a strong resemblance to the tort of passing off. Such legislation will be considered more thoroughly in Chapter 18. Where the legislation is not relevant, as in the *Walt Disney Productions v. Triple Five* case, the plaintiff is entitled to pursue her action for passing off at common law.

---

29. Goodwill refers to the reputation of the business and its expectation of patronage in the future.
30. This means that the product has a "secondary meaning" in the mind of the public.
31. *Walt Disney Productions v. Triple Five Corp.* (1994), 113 D.L.R. (44ʰ) 229 (Alta. C.A.).
32. *Ibid.*
33. R.S.C. 1985, c. T-13, s. 7.

Interference with Contractual Relations

interference with
contractual relations
Incitement to break the
contractual obligations of
another.

The tort of **interference with contractual relations** is known by a variety of names, including interference with contract, inducement of breach of contract, and procuring a breach of contract.[34] It has its origins in the relationship of master and servant. The common law made it actionable if one master attempted to "poach" the servant of another. In legal terms, the "poacher" was seen as enticing the servant to break his existing contract of employment, which, in turn, caused economic harm to the master. Over time, this tort extended beyond master/servant relations to any form of contractual relationship.

The tort prohibits a variety of conduct, including conduct whereby the defendant directly induces another to breach her contract with the plaintiff.

In Ron's business, the tort of interference with contractual relations could be important in at least two different contexts:

- Ron employs a skilled potter who makes the "Old Man of the Sea" product. The potter has a three-year employment contract. A competitor approaches the potter in the second year of the contract and encourages the potter to work for him with promises of higher wages and better conditions. The competitor's conduct is tortious because he knew about the contract and acted with the objective of convincing the potter to join him. Since this could happen only if the potter were to breach his contract with Ron, the tort has been made out.

- Ron's largest and most lucrative supply contract is with one of the leading tourism organizations in Nova Scotia. The owner of the competing business making "Man of the Sea" products approaches the tourism organization and suggests that if it breaks the contract with Ron and buys from her, she can offer larger profit margins and the final product can sell for less, thus increasing the volume of sales.

In both cases, then, Ron could likely make out the tort of interference with contractual relations. While he will sue for damages, he may also seek an injunction to prevent a breach of contract occurring if he finds out in time. A court would never order the potter to work for Ron—courts will not award specific performance with contracts of personal service—but it can order damages against the potter for breach of contract and damages and/or an injunction against the competitor for the tort of interference with contractual relations.

An example of a successful tort action is *Ernst & Young v. Stuart*.[35] A partner left the accounting firm of Ernst & Young to join the firm of Arthur Andersen. In so doing, the partner violated a term of the partnership agreement requiring one year's notice of intention to retire from the partnership. Ernst & Young sued both the partner and the new firm, the latter for interfering with contractual relations. Both actions were successful.

Defamation

defamation
The public utterance of a
false statement of fact or
opinion that harms
another's reputation.

The tort of **defamation** seeks to "protect the reputation of individuals against unfounded and unjustified attacks."[36] Though all jurisdictions in Canada have legislation modifying the common law of defamation to some extent, the fundamentals of the common law action remain.[37]

---

34. P. Burns, "Tort Injury to Economic Interests: Some Facets of Legal Response" (1980) 58 *Can. Bar Rev.* 103 cited by Klar, *supra* note 6 at 610, his footnote 81.
35. (1997), 144 D.L.R. (4th) 328 (B.C. C.A.).
36. *Supra* note 6 at 669.
37. *Ibid.* at 670–71.

Common terms for defamation are slander (typically for the oral form) and libel (usually the print form). These terms are not always consistently applied, and the correct legal usage for either is defamation.[38]

The key ingredients to the tort are as follows:

- The defendant has made a statement about the plaintiff.
- The statement presents the defendant in an uncomplimentary light.
- The statement would have had the effect of lowering the plaintiff's reputation in the mind of a reasonable person hearing it.
- The statement has been communicated to at least one person who is not the person being defamed.[39]

The plaintiff will then succeed if the defendant is unable to establish a defence to the action. If, for example, the defendant can show that the statement is true, he has a complete defence.[40]

From a business perspective, a potential defamation scenario occurs, for example, when an employer provides a reference for an ex-employee. If the letter contains a defamatory statement that is true, the employer may have a defence. Other defences that might be available, however, include that of **qualified privilege.** That is, if the employer's statement is relevant, made without malice, and communicated only to a party who has a legitimate interest in receiving it, the defence is established.

qualified privilege
A defence to defamation based on the defamatory statement being relevant, without malice, and communicated only to a party who has a legitimate interest in receiving it.

CASE ▼

P.G. Restaurant Ltd. (c.o.b. Mama Panda Restaurant) v. Northern Interior Regional Health Board (2005), 211 B.C.A.C. 219 (C.A.), reconsideration or rehearing refused by (2005), 41 B.C.L.R. (4th) 55 (C.A.), leave to appeal refused by [2005] S.C.C.A. No. 270 (S.C.C.)

THE BUSINESS CONTEXT: Businesses that provide goods and services to the public can be particularly vulnerable to media scrutiny. When damaging news articles are published about a business, this may severely impact its ability to remain profitable.

FACTUAL BACKGROUND: In a northern B.C. restaurant, a patron became ill and vomited on one of the buffet tables. A supervisor and an employee promptly tended to the situation by removing most of the food from the buffet itself, wiping up with a cloth soaked in a weak bleach solution, and by mopping the floor. They then replaced the food in the buffet and carried on business.

Thirteen people at the restaurant that day later became ill with the Norwalk virus, a highly contagious pathogen that is easily spread and is not deactivated with standard disinfecting solutions. A small local newspaper ran a story about the incident on its front page, with the headline "Vomit serves up virus at buffet." The article stated that 13 people had become sick, and suggested that the illnesses were caused by "eating from a buffet that a customer had vomited on." The article went on to quote the manager, who said that the illnesses were not caused by the restaurant's food, and the chief environmental health officer, who noted that it was an atypical event. The officer suggested that the virus was likely spread by contact with contaminated surfaces and may not have involved the buffet food at all.

Immediately after the article appeared, the restaurant's business dropped by 50 percent, and it was eventually forced to close. The restaurant sued the newspaper and the reporter for defamation, alleging that the article gave the impression both that the restaurant had served tainted food, and that, as a result of eating tainted food, customers had contracted food poisoning.

---

38. The distinction between libel and slander has been abolished by statute in a number of provinces.
39. *Supra* note 6 at 672–84.
40. *Ibid.* at 685.

At trial, the judge held that the article was defamatory. The restaurant's reputation suffered from the public impression conveyed by the article that people had become ill from eating food with vomit on it, and that the vomit had not been adequately cleaned off the buffet table. The court also held that the newspaper did not present an adequate defence, and so awarded the restaurant damages in the amount of $633 423, one of the largest awards of its kind in Canadian history.

THE LEGAL QUESTION: Was the article defamatory and, if so, was the newspaper able to establish a defence?

RESOLUTION: On appeal, Justice Saunders found that the statements in the article, though injurious to the restaurant's reputation, were justified. The trial judge had mistakenly concentrated on only the headline

and the first couple lines of the story. In fact, the article, read as a whole, did not leave the reader with the impression that patrons consumed food with vomit on it, but merely described an event wherein a patron vomited on food, and the cleanup was not adequate to eradicate the virus. As these allegations were true, the newspaper successfully advanced the defence of justification.

CRITICAL ANALYSIS: Which court's analysis do you prefer? What should the management of the B.C. restaurant have done differently? What measures could have been taken immediately following the vomiting incident? Is the risk of a customer contracting the Norwalk virus simply the cost of doing business?

Source: Researched and written by Meredith Hagel.

If the plaintiff can prove actual monetary loss as a result of the defendant's defamation, this loss is recoverable. The law recognizes, however, that much of the damage suffered is intangible. Therefore, the court is permitted to assess damages from an alternate perspective. This includes considering the seriousness of the defamation, how widely the defamation was published, the malice of the defendant, and the amount of demonstrable damages that have been caused.[41] Where the defendant's conduct has been particularly reprehensible and oppressive, a court is entitled to award punitive damages, as the following box illustrates.

Technology and the Law

E-Torts: Defamation on the Internet

A growing objective for business is to guard against defamation via electronic media. The danger of e-mails, in particular, is that once they are sent they cannot be retrieved, yet they can be instantaneously transmitted to an enormous audience. There is likely no one who has not hit the Send key and then realized he was transmitting to unintended recipients. Since the legal process allows for the discovery or tracing of electronic words to their author, electronic defamation can most certainly be established even long after a defamatory message has apparently been deleted.

Defamation can also occur on websites found via the Internet. In a recent decision from the Ontario

Superior Court, damages were awarded to the plaintiff— Mr. Reichmann—for just this form of defamation. Reichmann sued because the defendants had defamed him as part of an extortion campaign. They told Reichmann that if he failed to pay them a large sum of money, they would publish statements on the Internet that he had lied and cheated an innocent man of his inheritance. When Reichmann refused to pay, the defendants distributed cards to Reichmann's neighbours alerting them to a website containing these false allegations. Given the egregious circumstances—including that fact that Internet publication instantly communicates information to the entire world—the court awarded

41. *Ibid.* at 711.

a total of $400 000 in damages, including $100 000 in punitive damages.

CRITICAL ANALYSIS: How can a business protect its reputation from attack on the Internet?

Sources: *Reichmann v. Berlin*, [2002] O.J. No. 2732 (Sup. Ct.); and Bradley J. Freedman, "Ontario Court Orders $400,000 in Damages for Internet Defamation" (25 July 2002) at http://www.cle.bc.ca/CLE/Stay+Current/Collection/2002/7/02-onthcj-reichmann (accessed 2004). See also http://cle.bc.ca

Injurious Falsehood or Product Defamation

injurious or malicious falsehood

The utterance of a false statement about another's goods or services that is harmful to the reputation of those goods or services.

Injurious or malicious falsehood concerns false statements made not about a person but about the goods or services produced by that person. Sometimes the distinction between injurious falsehood and defamation is subtle; for example, if the statement is made that a particular company routinely provides shoddy maintenance, is this a negative reflection on the quality of the people doing the work or on the company's services? In such a situation, the complainant would sue in both defamation and injurious falsehood.

Injurious falsehood requires the plaintiff to establish that the statement about the goods or services was false and was published (uttered) with malice or improper motive. It is not necessary to prove that the defendant intended to injure the plaintiff. A reckless disregard for the truth or falsity of the statement is sufficient.

Injurious falsehood can be particularly problematic in the context of comparative and negative advertising, as the following case shows.

CASE ▼

Mead Johnson Canada v. Ross Pediatrics
(1996), 31 O.R. (3d) 237 (Gen. Div.)

THE BUSINESS CONTEXT: It is relatively common for sellers to engage in comparative advertising. In this case, Mead Johnson Canada (Mead) was claiming that Ross Pediatrics (Ross) uttered a false statement (injurious falsehood) in its promotional materials. It sought an interim injunction to prevent the continued distribution of the material.

FACTUAL BACKGROUND: Ross began selling a new infant formula, Similac Advance, using promotional materials that included many representations to which Mead, the maker of a competing infant formula, Enfalac, objected.

Mead representatives obtained samples of the professional brochure and some of the consumer materials. Research Management Group conducted market studies for Mead, which suggested that 81 to 91 percent of new parents, having seen the promotional materials, would choose the new product.

Mead argued that the Similac Advance materials were false and misleading in claiming that Similac was superior to other formulas; similar to breast milk; and clinically proven to strengthen infants' immune systems.

THE LEGAL QUESTION: Had injurious falsehood occurred? Ross argued that Mead and Enfalac were not identified by the Ross promotional materials. No injurious falsehood could be established where there was no identification of the injured party.

RESOLUTION: While it was true that Enfalac was not identified in the brochure materials, Enfalac was identified as a target in the materials distributed to the Ross sales force. It was also true that Enfalac, being the other major competitor in this marketplace, would be identified by implication. On this basis, the court held that all of Ross's competitors, including Mead, might have a cause of action if the representations were false and misleading.

CRITICAL ANALYSIS: Many companies engage in comparative advertising. What could Ross have done that would have avoided any suggestion of injurious falsehood? If the injunction continued, what would be the business implications for Ross? What recommendations might you have for senior management in order to avoid a similar episode in the future?

The common law protects privacy interests in a variety of ways. The tort of defamation protects reputation. The torts of trespass and nuisance protect the right to enjoy one's property. The torts of assault, battery, and false imprisonment protect the person's right to dignity. In this way, the common law produces a patchwork of protection though there is no general recognition of a tort for the invasion of privacy.

However, some Canadian jurisdictions have sought to protect the privacy interest through legislation that deals with the collection, use, and disclosure of personal information by organizations in the course of commercial activities.[42] In addition, certain provincial governments have passed legislation that creates the tort of breach of privacy.[43] British Columbia's *Privacy Act*,[44] for example, states:

1(1) It is a tort, actionable without proof of damage, for a person, willfully and without a claim of right, to violate the privacy of another.

(2) The nature and degree of privacy to which a person is entitled in a situation or in relation to a matter is that which is reasonable in the circumstances, giving due regard to the lawful interests of others.

(3) In determining whether the act or conduct of a person is a violation of another's privacy, regard must be given to the nature, incidence and occasion of the act or conduct and to any domestic or other relationship between the parties.

(4) Without limiting subsections (1) to (3), privacy may be violated by eavesdropping or surveillance, whether or not accomplished by trespass.

In *Hollinsworth v. BCTV*, [1996] 6 W.W.R. 54 (B.C. C.A.), the plaintiff successfully relied on this statute to bring his action against Look International Enterprises for releasing to BCTV a videotape showing the plaintiff undergoing an operation to have a hairpiece surgically attached to his head. Since Look International Enterprises had done so without the plaintiff's knowledge and consent, this amounted to a willful invasion of privacy, a clear violation of the statute. In response, the court awarded the plaintiff $15 000 in damages.

Source: Lewis Klar, *Tort Law*, 3rd ed. (Toronto: Carswell, 2003), at 77–80.

Managing the Risk of Diverse Commercial Torts

Each of the torts discussed in this chapter exposes a business to liability. A risk management analysis should address the fundamental problems that may arise, always taking into account that business activities are usually engaged in by employees in the course of employment. As discussed in Chapter 10, an employer is responsible under the doctrine of vicarious liability for the torts of its employees.

An occupier's liability risk management plan would ask the following questions:

- Are there dangers on the property? Are adequate warnings and protections given to visitors?

- Are there known trespassers, in particular children, who come onto the property?

- What could be done to eliminate or reduce the risk flowing from the dangers?

---

42. For discussion of this legislation, see Chapters 20, 24, and 26.
43. See *Privacy Act*, R.S.B.C. 1996, c. 373 (British Columbia); *Privacy Act*, R.S.S. 1978, c. P-24 (Saskatchewan); *Privacy Act* R.S.M 1987, c. P125 (Manitoba); and *Privacy Act* R.S.N.L. 1990, c. P-22 (Newfoundland). See too Quebec's *Charter of Human Rights and Freedoms* R.S.Q. c. C-12, s. 5, which provides that "[e]very person has a right to respect for his private life."
44. *Ibid.*

- Has the occupier complied with all legislative obligations? Examples include provincial legislation concerning workers' health and safety, as well as municipal bylaws providing for snow and ice removal.
- Is adequate insurance in place?

Although the classification of entrants under the common law of occupiers' liability may be a useful exercise after an incident occurs (it helps determine liability), from a risk management perspective the process is not particularly helpful since the business that occupies property cannot easily predict what class of entrant will be injured on its property. Maintaining safe premises as a preventive measure is much better than having to debate, after the fact, what class of entrant the injured plaintiff is and what standard is owed.

For each additional tort discussed in this chapter, a similar list of questions could be generated. For example, if the business designs and creates consumer goods:

- Do staff understand that they cannot innovate by copying others?
- Is a program in place to review new product ideas, including all aspects of design, to ensure there is no passing off?
- Is a climate in place that allows a manager to step in and say, "This cannot be done because I believe we have crossed the line"?

Tort law evolves to reflect changing social values. What at one time might have been acceptable behaviour may no longer be considered appropriate. This can be seen, for example, in the changing approach to the environmental effects of commercial activities. When a business is assessing its tort exposure, it cannot assume that existing legal rules will apply in perpetuity. Also, it must consider how it can influence public opinion and social values, as those will determine the bounds of future tort liability.

Business Law in Practice Revisited

1. What potential legal actions does Julie have against Ron's business?

Ron is the occupier of the building. As such, he is responsible to different classes of people who come onto his property both lawfully and unlawfully. The extent of the responsibility varies depending on why the person is on the premises and whether he is in a common law or statutory jurisdiction.

In Newfoundland, common law principles apply. Julie is clearly an invitee and, as such, Ron owes a duty to warn of "any unusual danger [of] which he knows or ought to know." In this case, it appears he was aware of the inadequate, temporary repair job on the elevator, and therefore had the requisite knowledge.

If these events occurred in a jurisdiction where statute law has replaced the common law of occupier's liability, the responsibility to Julie, a person on the property legitimately, would be very similar to that of the tort of negligence. In all likelihood Ron would be equally responsible.

2. What is the responsibility of Elevator XL Services?

Elevator XL Services is an occupier, since it had control over the elevator in order to conduct the repairs. This was also the time when the harm occurred. Following the same analysis as used in question 1 above, Elevator XL Services will be liable to Julie under both common and statute law. Julie was on the property lawfully and, at common law, was an invitee.

3. Does Ron have any recourse against the manufacturer of the replica figurine?

Ron can take action based on the tort of passing off. He can claim that the actions of the competitor met the conditions of the tort of passing off, and as such he will either seek an injunction to stop any further action by the competitor, or damages, or both. He will need to prove that his "Old Man of the Sea" figurine existed prior to the "Man of the Sea" product, that it had an established reputation that was of value, that the products' names and appearances were similar enough to result in confusion in the minds of the potential purchasers, and that the confusion has resulted or will result in loss of sales or harm to Ron's business. It is sufficient that the defendant's conduct compromises Ron's control over his own business reputation.

4. How can Ron manage the risk his business faces of potential tort liabilities?

Ron, as owner/occupier of the premises, should do a safety audit of all parts of the building to ensure that neither his tenants nor his visitors (lawful or otherwise) could be harmed by any hazards. Ron should consider all aspects of his business operations, including the building itself, obvious hazards such as the kiln, maintenance of elevators, clearing of sidewalks, hiring and training of all employees, and insurance coverage.

In terms of Ron's products, Ron should

- monitor the activity of competitors and potential competitors to ensure that there is no inappropriate copying of his designs
- ensure that the glazes and materials he uses are lead-free and otherwise harmless
- hire staff who know how to treat customers well and are trained as to their obligations should they have to handle shoplifters

Chapter Summary

While negligence is the most common tort a business will encounter, various other commercially relevant torts merit analysis. These torts can be categorized and assessed according to whether they would arise because the business is an occupier of property or because it provides a product or service. Furthermore, torts that could be committed against a competitor can be grouped separately from those more likely to involve a consumer. Though these distinctions are not definitive, they provide a useful way of organizing the variety of torts that affect the commercial world.

As an occupier, a business must be sure to keep its property safe so that people coming on-site are not injured, otherwise it faces occupiers' liability according to a regime that classifies the entrant in question under common law or by statute. To avoid committing the tort of nuisance, a business must not unreasonably and substantially interfere with the right of its neighbours to enjoy their property. The law governing trespass gives occupiers a right to exert control over who comes onto their premises, subject to human rights codes.

Torts arising from business operations in relation to customers are false imprisonment, assault and battery, and deceit. Through these torts, the law seeks to ensure people's right to move about as they please, to have their bodily integrity respected, and not to be misled about the quality of a product or service.

Torts more likely to be committed against a competitor include passing off, interference with contractual relations, defamation, and injurious falsehood or product defamation. These torts endeavour to protect a business's property and its own reputation. This means that one business cannot falsely represent its goods or services as being someone else's, nor can it malign the reputation of another business or the product or service it sells.

Given the diverse and wide-ranging nature of a business's potential liability in tort, preventing torts from ever occurring should be one of management's top priorities.

Chapter Study

Key Terms and Concepts

contractual entrant (p. 268)

deceit (p. 276)

defamation (p. 278)

false imprisonment (p. 274)

injurious or malicious falsehood (p. 281)

interference with contractual relations
 (p. 278)

invitee (p. 268)

licensee (p. 268)

nuisance (p. 271)

occupier (p. 267)

passing off (p. 276)

qualified privilege (p. 279)

trespass (p. 273)

trespasser (p. 268)

Questions for Review

1. How does the law define the occupier of property?

2. Who is an occupier?

3. What are the four different classes of visitors in the law of occupiers' liability?

4. What is the standard of care owed to each of the four classes of visitors?

5. What is the major change made by legislation in many provinces of Canada to the common law of occupiers' liability?

6. What is a nuisance in tort law?

7. The courts have developed pragmatic rules for resolving inherent conflicts that arise in applying the tort of nuisance. Give two examples of these rules.

8. Under what conditions can trespass arise?

9. What are the limitations to the ability of a store detective to detain a customer who is suspected of shoplifting?

10. Describe how a false imprisonment claim might arise, other than by a person being physically restrained.

11. How can a business manage the risk of retail theft and fraud?

12. Identify what must be established to prove deceit.

13. What is "passing off," and what practices was this tort created to prevent?

14. Describe a situation that might amount to the tort of interference with contractual relations.

15. What are the two forms of defamation, how do they arise, and what is a complete defence to this tort?

16. When is a court entitled to award punitive damages for the tort of defamation?

17. What is injurious falsehood?

18. Give a practical example of an injurious falsehood.

Questions for Critical Thinking

1. One of the controversial aspects of occupiers' liability and its more recent statutory form arises out of the rights afforded trespassers. One possible change to the law would be to eliminate all rights. What would be the consequences of this approach? Are there some trespassers that you would feel uncomfortable leaving without protection?

2. An example of a modern nuisance claim involves a couple who realize their rural dream by buying land 30 kilometres outside town. Unfortunately, this is an active agricultural area and the local farmers engage in the practice of spreading liquid manure over their fields each spring. Not surprisingly, this is not a welcome addition to the lifestyle of the newcomers to the area. In this example of competing interests, what issues do you think it is relevant for courts to consider? Would it make any difference if it was the offending farmer who broke up the land to sell as building lots? Are these issues relevant to the common law?

3. Retailers suffer extensive losses due to "inventory shrinkage" or shoplifting. This cost is passed on to all virtuous shoppers who have no intention of engaging in theft. The tort of false imprisonment places serious limitations on any action the retailer can take to detain suspected shoplifters. What are the pros and cons of these limitations? Are they fair? What are the countervailing interests at stake?

4. The tort of interference with contractual relations has its origins in the ancient master/servant relationship. Today, however, there is greater recognition of mobility rights, and those in business are generally used to competing in an aggressive marketplace. Given that the aggrieved party has the right to sue for breach of contract, should this tort be retained? What rights might not be protected if the tort of interference with contractual relations were to be abolished? Are these important?

5. A major aim of the tort of defamation is to seek to "protect the reputation of individuals against unfounded and unjustified attacks." However, it is relatively easy for a plaintiff to make out the tort, as it basically encompasses any statement that presents another in an uncomplimentary light. The major burden of the action then shifts to the person who made or published the statement to provide a defence. Do you think that the tort of defamation is too easily proven? Is it unfair to place such a heavy burden on someone to defend the statements they make, especially given that freedom of speech is such an important principle in Canada?

6. During rehearsal, a trombonist fell from a riser at the National Arts Centre (NAC) and suffered serious injury. When he adjusted his chair, it caught in a gap where two sections of the risers joined together and he toppled. How does this situation show that the NAC failed to take "reasonable care" for the safety of those on its premises? What should it have done differently?[45]

---

45. Based, in part, on *Traquair v. National Arts Centre Corp.*, [2004] O.T.C. 891 (S.C.J.).

Situations for Discussion

1. A convenience store owner has suffered several burglaries in the past few months. He is very concerned, as he believes this trend means he will likely lose his livelihood. He elects to arm himself with a shotgun for self-protection: the most recent break-in was by armed thieves. One evening, three thieves enter the premises. He shouts at them to leave as they approach the till and he brings out his shotgun. The thieves immediately start running from the store. The store owner shoots one of them as he is leaving. Has the injured thief any right to compensation? How could the owner have better managed the risk of theft and burglary?

2. A customer fell in a puddle of dishwashing soap that had dripped onto the floor of a supermarket. She was wearing high-heeled shoes and, although she saw the puddle, she was reasonably confident that she could walk through it safely. Instead, she fell and sustained serious injury. She is now suing for compensation for her injuries. What are the chances of her suit succeeding?[46] How should supermarkets manage the risk of customers slipping and falling on the premises?

3. Gum Company manufactures the dominant brand of sugarless peppermint gum in Canada. Chewing Company wants to compete by introducing a new product. Chewing sells gum in a package that looks very similar to Gum's product: both products are white with red lettering, each has red on the end of the packages, and the packages are soft foil and paper combinations. A closer analysis of other sugarless and sugar-containing peppermint gum products shows that all packages are some combination of white and red and that the majority are made of similar types of materials. What action can Gum pursue, and what are the chances of success?

4. The Kumar family are long-time residents of an older neighbourhood of a major city. They inherited their home from Ms. Kumar's parents. Their own family is now grown up and gone, and Mr. and Ms. Kumar enjoy the pleasures of the quiet and beautifully maintained back garden—that is, until the past few months. The neighbours on one side of the Kumars sold their property about a year ago, and the new owners have shown the Kumars their plans for the property. The plans involve demolishing the home and building a much larger house, very close to the boundaries of the property. Because the building will be three storeys high and because of its size and location, all afternoon sun will effectively be blocked from the Kumars' garden. Moreover, they will lose their privacy. The Kumars are distraught. They are also very concerned about the noise and disruption from the demolition and construction. Finally, they have noticed that large and noisy air-conditioning and heating units will be placed adjacent to their property, right beside their bedroom wall. Assuming that all these changes are within the local planning rules, what are the Kumars' rights? What factors should the Kumars consider before launching a legal action?

5. The Happy Bar operates in Fergus, Ontario. The bar routinely attracts large numbers of students from the local universities. Because of its location, students have to drive at least 20 kilometres. The owners of the bar are acutely aware of their responsibilities both to ensure that no underage students drink and that all patrons leave the bar in a vehicle driven by a designated driver. On peak nights the bar brings in additional staff to ensure compliance with its policies. On one Saturday night, a regular staff member calls in sick, but recommends his friend, who is a law and security student at the local community college. He assures the manager that this friend is familiar with the appropriate practices and guidelines and is fully responsible. The friend is hired for the night and

---

46. Based on *Pontarollo v. Westfair Foods Ltd.* (1996), 150 Sask. R. 71 (Q.B.).

appears to the manager to be capable. Around 11:30 p.m., a group of young people become particularly rowdy, and one moves toward the door, car keys in hand and shouting to her friends to get into the car quickly so they can find a "really good party." The new staff member is the only employee nearby and able to intervene. He rushes to the young woman, pins her arms behind her with one hand, and puts a choke hold around her neck. He demands she throw down her keys. Unfortunately, the woman suffers from epilepsy. This action precipitates a seizure, and in the course of the seizure, perhaps in part because of the amount of alcohol consumed, the woman chokes. She is unconscious for ten minutes and suffers serious brain damage. Discuss the tort principles that arise in this case. Who will be sued and for what? What are the merits of the case?

6. Mandrake Ltd. were owners and occupiers of an office building. Mandrake complained about the noise and vibration coming from a nearby subway system of the Toronto Transit Commission.[47] Will Mandrake be successful in an action for nuisance? In particular, would the ordinary and reasonable resident of that locality view the disturbance as a substantial interference with the enjoyment of land? What factors will a court consider in determining whether there is nuisance or not? At what point should legitimate activities be curtailed because of the unavoidable consequences to other nearby businesses?

7. Beginning in 1955, Disney started opening outdoor amusement parks around the world, and now owns a number of parks, including those in California, Florida, Europe and Japan. Each amusement park contains various theme parks, one of which is called Fantasyland. In 1981, Triple Five opened an indoor amusement park in the West Edmonton Mall, also called Fantasyland.[48] Has Triple Five committed the tort of passing off? What would a court take into account in determining whether the tort has occurred? If the tort is made out, do you think it is legitimate to give Disney a monopoly over the word "Fantasyland" in association with all amusement parks?

For more study tools, visit
http://www.businesslaw3e.nelson.com

---

47. Based, in part, on *Mandrake Management Consultants Ltd. et al v. Toronto Transit Commission* (1993), 102 D.L.R. (4th) 12 (Ont. C.A.).
48. Based, in part, on *Walt Disney Productions v. Triple Five Corp.* (1994), 113 D.L.R. (4th) 229 (Alta. C.A.).

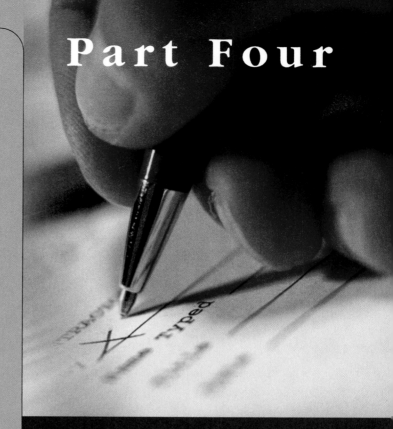

Part Four

ENTREPRENEURS WITH SERVICES OR PRODUCTS READY for market need to select a business vehicle—or ownership structure—through which to offer them. This choice, essentially limited to three basic forms, has broad legal consequences because each kind of business vehicle comes with a specific set of rights and liabilities.

- A *sole proprietorship* refers to an individual carrying on business alone. The actual business activity may be conducted by others, such as agents or employees, but ownership remains the responsibility of one person.

- A *partnership* involves two or more persons sharing ownership responsibilities either equally or in some proportion among the partners.

- A *corporation* is a separate legal entity that is owned by one or more shareholders.

Regardless of its form, the business will almost certainly rely on agency and employment relationships for its day-to-day operations. An agency relationship involves the business relying on someone else to act on its behalf. In law, the actions of the agent are often treated as the actions of the business itself.

Structuring Business Activity

Chapter 13 The Agency Relationship

Chapter 14 Business Forms and Arrangements

Chapter 15 The Corporate Form: Organizational Matters

Chapter 16 The Corporate Form: Operational Matters

Chapter

13

Objectives

After studying this chapter, you should have an understanding of

- the agency relationship and its relevance to business
- how an agency relationship comes into being
- agency duties and liabilities
- how the agency relationship ends

The Agency Relationship

Business Law in Practice

Lisa Jamieson owned and operated a high-end women's clothing store in Vancouver. Every year she made numerous trips to Europe and eastern Canada to purchase clothing to sell in her store. As Lisa's business became increasingly successful, she found it hard to find the time to make these journeys herself. Lisa therefore began sending Leonard Van Wart, her marketing manager, to do the job.

Leonard became well known in the fashion industry as Lisa's amazing buyer who had developed an unfailing eye for what would sell in Lisa's store. Eventually, Lisa left all purchasing decisions up to Leonard, since his judgment was sound and he had built up considerable expertise in the area.

While in Toronto recently on a buying trip for Lisa, Leonard uncharacteristically became involved in two unfortunate contracts:

- THE UGLY CLOTHES CONTRACT. Leonard purchased $90 000 of clothing from a line that, to Lisa, amounted to the ugliest, most bizarre and impractical clothes she had ever seen. Lisa wants to return the clothes to the Toronto manufacturer for a full refund because she is reasonably sure that she will be able to sell them in her store only at a loss.

- THE ATROCIOUSLY EXPENSIVE CONTRACT. Leonard agreed to pay $200 000 to a Montreal fashion house to supply Lisa's business with a variety of women's business suits. Lisa likes the suits but is sure that Leonard has agreed to pay too much. She wants to renegotiate the contract herself. She is also particularly annoyed with Leonard since she expressly told him he could not enter into any contracts on her behalf in excess of $100 000 without getting her permission first.

1. What is the nature of the legal relationship between Lisa and Leonard?
2. Is Lisa bound by the two contracts Leonard entered into during his Toronto buying trip?
3. How should Lisa have handled this agency relationship from the outset?

The Nature of Agency

agency
A relationship that exists when one party represents another party in the formation of legal relations.

agent
A person who is authorized to act on behalf of another.

principal
A person who has permitted another to act on her behalf.

Agency is the relationship between two persons that permits one person, the **agent,** to affect the legal relationships of another, known in law as the **principal**.[1] These legal relationships are as binding on the principal as if that person had directly entered them herself.

Agency is about one person representing another in such a way as to affect the latter's relationships with the outside world. In business, agency is a common relationship, as is shown in the following examples:

- A sports agent negotiates a multimillion-dollar deal on behalf of a hockey player.
- An insurance agent sells fire and theft insurance on behalf of several insurance companies.
- A travel agent sells tickets, cruises, and vacation packages on behalf of carriers and hotels.
- A booking agent negotiates fees and dates on behalf of entertainers.
- A stockbroker buys and sells shares on behalf of individuals and companies.

---

1. G.H.L. Fridman, *Fridman's Law of Agency*, 7th ed. (Toronto: Butterworths, 1996) at 11.

In each case, the agent is acting for someone else (the principal) and is doing business on that person's behalf. This kind of relationship is essential to the success of the principal, who may not necessarily have the expertise to handle the given matter—as may be the case with an athlete or an investor—or who cannot manage and promote his business single-handedly. For this latter reason, insurance companies, hotels, carriers, and entertainers rely on agents regularly.

In the Business Law in Practice scenario, Leonard was needed for just these kinds of reasons. He had acquired expertise in the area of buying that outmatched Lisa's, and she also required his assistance because she could not run her business alone. Consequently, Leonard became Lisa's purchasing agent.

Many of the examples of agency given so far are familiar because they involve businesses engaging external specialists or experts to act on their behalf in various transactions. The scope of agency, however, is considerably broader than these examples would suggest.

In fact, in almost every business transaction, at least one of the parties is acting as an agent. A corporation enters into a contract through the agency of one of its directors or employees. A partnership is likewise bound to a contract through the agency of one of its partners or a firm employee. Even in a sole proprietorship, the owner may hire others, such as office managers and sales clerks, to carry out critical tasks on her behalf. In short, the agency relationship—which formally recognizes the delegation of authority from one party to another—is a cornerstone of business activity. It is a relationship that makes it possible for businesses to conduct a wide array of transactions.

Agency Defined

Agency relationships, like contractual relationships in general, operate for the most part with few difficulties—agents simply represent principals in transactions with others. This is not to say, however, that problems cannot occur. The fact that parties use agents instead of dealing with each other face to face can result in complications and questions. There are two key relationships at play in an agency situation. The first is the relationship between the agent and the principal (see Figure 13.1).

FIGURE 13.1

The Agent–Principal Relationship

This aspect of agency raises numerous questions, such as the following:

- How does A become an agent? When is one person considered to be an agent for another?
- What is the authority of A? What types of transactions can A enter on behalf of P?
- What are A's duties?
- What are P's obligations?

outsider

The party with whom the agent does business on behalf of the principal.

The second relationship in agency is between the principal and the party with whom the agent does business (see Figure 13.2). Such parties are known as **outsiders** because they are "outside" the agency relationship between principal and agent. The outsider is also sometimes called the third party.[2]

---

2. The principal and agent are the first and second parties.

FIGURE 13.2

The Outsider–Principal
Relationship

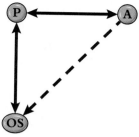

(Outsider or Third Party)

This relationship raises questions, including

- When is the principal liable to the outsider?
- When is the agent himself liable to the outsider?

law of agency
The law governing the relationship where one party, the agent, acts on behalf of another, the principal.

The complications resulting from these relationships have necessitated rules of law to regulate and resolve them. These rules are known as the **law of agency,** which, in turn, is derived largely from tort and contract law. There is very little legislation pertaining to agency as such, other than special statutes that govern the duties and responsibilities of specific kinds of agents.[3]

The remainder of this chapter will explore how the common law of agency has dealt with the kinds of questions and problems posed above.

Creation of Agency

Agency relationships are created in a variety of ways. Most often, particularly in a business context, the relationship arises by contract between the parties. At other times, the relationship arises by conduct. The parties do not specifically agree to an agency relationship, but by words or actions outsiders are led to believe the relationship is one of agency.

Agency by Agreement

An agency relationship created by contract normally involves the principal authorizing an agent to act on her behalf and the agent agreeing to do so in return for some fee or other remuneration. This often occurs through a contract created expressly and only for that single purpose, as illustrated in this example:

- A retired public figure who wishes to earn income by speaking about his experiences in office may engage an agent to contact organizations, negotiate fees, and book engagements on his behalf. In return the public figure will pay the agent a certain sum, perhaps a percentage of his fee.

In other situations, the agency relationship may arise as part of another, broader contract:

- An employment contract may provide for a person to be paid a salary in return for carrying out certain duties including entering into contracts on behalf of the employer. For example, a sales clerk, besides greeting and assisting customers and stocking shelves, would have the authority to enter into sales transactions—

---

3. For example, insurance brokers, mortgage brokers, and mercantile and real estate agents are regulated by legislation that provides for their registration, their training, the regulation of their conduct, and so forth. See, for example, *Real Estate and Business Brokers Act, 2002*, S.O. 2002, c. 30, Sched. C.

at least at the sticker price—on behalf of his employer. Similarly, it was through his employment contract as Lisa's marketing manager that Leonard also came to be her buying agent.

Of course, not all employees are agents for the businesses that employ them. A clerk/typist is not normally an agent, but, if asked to take money from petty cash and purchase a gift for a departing employee, then in this situation and for this purpose, the clerk/typist is an agent for the employer.

The Concept of Authority

The authority of the agent is a key aspect of the agency relationship. It determines whether there is a contract between the principal and the outsider. When an agent acts within the scope of her authority and negotiates a contract for the principal, the principal is bound by the contract, whether the principal likes it or not. However, even when the agent has acted outside the scope of her authority in entering into the contract—that is, by exceeding the powers she has been given—the contract may still bind the principal.

The principal will be obligated by the contract when the agent has actual authority or when the agent has apparent authority.

Actual Authority

actual authority
The power of an agent that derives from either express or implied agreement.

An agent's **actual authority** can be both express and implied. Express authority is the written or oral authority granted by the principal to the agent and is an authority that the agent actually has. Implied authority is also an authority that the agent actually has, but it is present by implication only. An agent will have implied authority when that authority

- is inferred from the position the agent occupies
- is reasonably necessary to carry out or otherwise implement the agent's express authority
- arises by virtue of a well-recognized custom in a particular trade, industry, or profession

Like other contracts, then, the agency contract can contain implied terms concerning the nature and extent of the agent's authority. It is important to remember that these terms are not any less "real" than express terms. They just exist in another, less tangible form.

In the Business Law in Practice scenario, it is clear that Lisa's agent, Leonard, has the actual authority to buy clothes on Lisa's behalf, but she has limited this authority to $100 000 per contract. Above that amount, he is required to secure Lisa's approval before proceeding. What kind of implied authority might Leonard have? This is always a fact-specific inquiry, but since Leonard is empowered to purchase clothes, he almost certainly has the power to arrange for their transportation to Vancouver. This, in turn, would also include the power to acquire insurance to cover any loss or damage to the goods while in transit. For this reason, transportation and insurance contracts will be binding on Lisa.

In a similar vein, the manager of a business may have aspects of his authority expressly recited in his employment contract or job description. To the extent that these documents are not exhaustive on the subject, other components of his authority exist due to the nature of his position and as a result of what is reasonably necessary to manage the business. For example, if he were the general manager of an automotive dealership, he presumably would have the implied power to purchase merchandise, order office supplies, arrange for appropriate advertising of the business, and hire and fire employees. A manager of another kind of business—a fast food outlet or a convenience store—would have less implied power.

The nature of the authority given to the agent is inherently flexible and easily customized. For example, it can be

- very broad or very narrow
- for only one transaction or for several
- for a short, long, or indefinite period of time
- very formal, as in the case of a power of attorney, or very informal, in that it is included in the job description of an employee or merely consists of oral instructions

Business Application of the Law

A Power of Attorney

A power of attorney is a written document in which one person gives authority to another person to act on her behalf. The person receiving the power is most often referred to as "attorney," "agent," or "donee." The person giving the power is usually called the "donor" or "principal."

The rules regulating power of attorney vary considerably among provinces. Variations exist in such matters as who may witness a power of attorney, who is excluded from acting as an attorney, whether the power of attorney must be registered, the forms that must be used to execute a power of attorney, and, most importantly, the kinds of power of attorney that are available.

Typically, however, the kinds available are as follows:

- *a general power of attorney*: the agent has full authority to exercise all the principal's rights in relation to her property and financial affairs, e.g, cash or deposit cheques; pay bills; withdraw money from bank accounts; make payments on loans; purchase, sell, or deal with stocks or bonds; collect rents, profits, or commissions; manage, buy, and sell real estate; and conduct business operations.
- *a specific power of attorney*: the agent has the authority to act for the principal only in relation to certain matters or in certain

specified circumstances, e.g., sell a car, cash a pension cheque, or accept an offer for the purchase of property.

- *a personal care power of attorney*: the agent has authority to act for the principal in relation to personal matters such as housing and health.

A power of attorney may be noncontinuing, meaning that it is automatically revoked if the principal becomes incapacitated (e.g., by death, mental incapacity, or bankruptcy), or it may be continuing or enduring, that is, the power of attorney continues to operate when the donor becomes incapacitated and unable to manage her business.[4] A variation of the enduring power of attorney, available in some provinces, is the "springing power of attorney," which "springs" to life when an event specified in the power of attorney has taken place.[5]

A power of attorney can be a useful tool for conducting business in the event of health problems or other circumstances that would prevent people from managing their own business affairs. However, it also presents an obvious potential for abuse. An attorney with unlimited power over a donor's affairs can easily take advantage of the situation.

CRITICAL ANALYSIS: How may a businessperson manage the risk that her power of attorney may be misused?

---

4. At common law, a power of attorney ended on the principal becoming incapacitated; however, all provinces have passed legislative provisions allowing for a continuing or enduring power of attorney.
5. In British Columbia, representation agreements that allow a person to appoint a representative to cover all areas of his life including financial, legal, health, and personal care are intended to replace the enduring power of attorney, which applies only to financial, property, and legal matters. See *Representation Agreement Act*, R.S.B.C. 1996 (Supp.), c. 405.

Leonard has entered into two contracts on behalf of Lisa. Were they within his actual authority, thereby binding Lisa?

- *The ugly clothes contract.* This contract is almost certainly binding on Lisa because it was concluded within Leonard's actual authority. It is a contract for clothes that was within his allowable monetary range. That he may have exercised poor taste on this occasion is no reason Lisa should be able to renege and send the clothes back to the manufacturer for a refund. Lisa is bound by this contract, whether she wants to be or not.

- *The atrociously expensive contract.* The facts surrounding this contract establish that Leonard acted outside his actual authority because the contract is worth more than $100 000. As his principal, is Lisa bound by the contract anyway? Or can she use this as an opportunity to negotiate a better price with the fashion house?

The answer to these questions depends on whether Leonard has the apparent authority to enter into contracts over that monetary limit.

Apparent Authority

apparent authority

The power that an agent appears to have to an outsider because of conduct or statements of the principal.

Sometimes called ostensible authority, **apparent authority** is the authority that a third party or outsider would reasonably believe the agent has, given the conduct of the principal. For example, as Leonard is acting as Lisa's purchasing agent, it would be reasonable for the outsider to infer that he had the usual authority of someone in such a position. It would not be reasonable to expect clothing manufacturers and suppliers to guess that Leonard's authority to contract on Lisa's behalf had been limited to contracts for less than $100 000. Lisa is sending Leonard into the fashion world as her buying agent without telling outsiders that his authority is in any way limited. She must bear the risk of Leonard exceeding the monetary limit she has privately set for him.

In sum, so long as an agent is acting within his apparent authority the principal will be bound by the transaction unless the third party knew or ought reasonably to have known of the limitation on the agent's authority.

CASE ▼

Doiron v. Devon Capital Corp. (2003), 339 A.R. 371 (Alta. C.A.).

THE BUSINESS CONTEXT: Actual authority exists when a principal expressly confers authority on the agent. Apparent or "ostensible" authority arises when the principal represents that an "agent" is authorized to act on his behalf or allows a third party to believe that the "agent" has been authorized to act on his behalf. The doctrine of apparent authority is particularly relevant when an investment adviser, financial planner, insurance broker, or the like, misappropriates client funds, leaving the client looking for a solvent defendant.

FACTUAL BACKGROUND: In 1998 Glennis and Elliot Doiron sold their home in Calgary and decided to invest the net proceeds of $60 000 for a short term until they required the money for a down payment on their new home. They contacted William Demmers for investment advice as he had previously placed their life insurance and RRSPs with Manulife Financial and was known to them as a Manulife investment advisor. The Doirons were unaware that Demmers had a nonexclusive agency agreement (called a producer's agreement) with Manulife, which provided that he could not bind Manulife without written authorization.

The Doirons gave Demmers a cheque for $60 000 and Demmers filled in the payee as Devon Capital Corporation. The Doirons believed that they were investing in a Manulife product or one guaranteed by

Manulife because they believed that Demmers was a Manulife employee and sold only Manulife products. When the investment became due, the Doirons received a cheque from Devon, which was dishonoured. It turned out that Devon was a sham and the Doirons lost their entire investment.

THE LEGAL QUESTION: Is Manulife liable for the investment losses of the Doirons?

RESOLUTION: A principal is liable for the acts of an agent as long as the agent is acting within the scope of his or her actual or ostensible (apparent) authority. Demmers was not an agent of Manulife in the transaction with the Doirons and had no actual authority to bind Manulife as the guarantor of investments in Devon. However, the doctrine of ostensible authority gives an agent authority to bind a principal to agreements made with third parties when the principal represents to the third party that the agent has authority to enter into a contract and the third party relies on the representation. The representation may be express or implied. Manulife had cloaked Demmers with ostensible authority by providing him with business cards, stationery and other Manulife paraphernalia, and encouraging him to use it, and by

allowing him to be contacted through the Manulife main switchboard. Also Manulife had a co-op advertising programme in which it ran advertisements in newspapers with the "producer's" (i.e., salesperson like Demmers) picture and the Manulife logo.

Although Demmers did not represent that the Devon investment was a Manulife product, the Doirons were entitled to assume that that they were investing in Manulife because they had instructed Demmers to invest in a low-risk Manulife product, Demmers provided no written information regarding the investment before accepting their money and Demmers did not tell them that Devon was not a Manulife product or was unconnected with Manulife. Therefore, given that Demmers purported to contract on behalf of Manulife and the ostensible authority conveyed by Manulife to Demmers, Manulife was bound by the contract.

CRITICAL ANALYSIS: How can companies like Manulife minimize the risk of liability for the actions of its "producers" (i.e., salespeople)? How can companies gain the benefits that accrue from representation without incurring the risk of liability?

Agency by Estoppel

In the preceding section, one of the risks of agency was illustrated: an agent may exceed his actual authority but act within his apparent authority and thereby bind a principal to a contract against her wishes. Lisa is bound to pay for the expensive clothes even though the contract is for an amount above Leonard's authority. This is because the contract was within Leonard's apparent authority and the clothing manufacturer was unaware of the limitation on Leonard's authority. This is an application of what is known in law as **agency by estoppel.** The relationship between Lisa and Leonard has been broadened or extended, not through their mutual consent but by conduct. Lisa is not entitled to deny Leonard's apparent authority unless she actually informs the outsider in advance that Leonard's authority is limited.

agency by estoppel
An agency relationship created when the principal acts such that third parties reasonably conclude that an agency relationship exists.

A less common situation in which an agency relationship can be created by estoppel involves one in which the principal indicates that another is his agent when, in fact, no agency relationship exists. For example, suppose that the owner of a business—in a burst of effusiveness—introduces a prospective employee to a customer, saying, "I want you to meet Terrence, my new vice president of marketing." It would be usual and reasonable for the customer to infer that Terrence has the authority to act on behalf of the owner with respect to selling, promotions, and advertising. Suppose, however, that ultimately Terrence is not hired and, unfortunately, the owner forgets all about having introduced him as the new vice president of marketing. Terrence—now sorely disappointed and wishing to extract some revenge—contacts the customer and enters into a transaction with him, pretending to act on behalf of the owner. Is the owner liable? Assuming the contract is marketing- or sales-related and assuming the customer was unaware of the truth, then the owner probably will be liable. In such a situation, the principal's actions (introducing his "new vice president of marketing") creates the appearance of an agency relationship. The principal will therefore be estopped from denying the relationship and be bound by the contract with the customer. Put another way, the principal is not permitted to avoid the contract by claiming—albeit truthfully—that no agency relationship existed, because she gave every appearance that one did.

Is it fair to place all responsibility on the owner like this? The difficulty is that someone—either the owner of the business or the customer—will end up being adversely affected by Terrence's conduct. That is, either the owner will be stuck with a contract that she never wanted or the customer will be denied the benefit of a contract that he negotiated in good faith. Between these two competing claims, the law sides with the customer through estoppel. In theory, at least, the owner can sue Terrence for misrepresenting himself as an agent, but this can be of little value if Terrence has few assets.

A third situation in which agency by estoppel may operate to bind a principal is that in which an agency relationship has been terminated or an agent's authority has been curtailed. In both situations the agent had at one time the actual authority to bind the principal, but now the authority has been taken away or reduced.

CASE ▼

Rockland Industries Inc. v. Amerada Minerals Corporation of Canada (1978), 108 D.L.R. (3d) 513 (S.C.C.), rev'g 95 D.L.R (3d) 64 (Alta. C.A.)

THE BUSINESS CONTEXT: This case concerns an agent whose authority has been reduced. The same general principles will apply where the agency relationship has been completely severed.

FACTUAL BACKGROUND: Rockland was a textile manufacturer that also engaged in the purchase and resale of sulphur. Amerada was a producer of natural gas. One of the byproducts of the gas processing procedure is sulphur. Mr. Kurtz was the manager of Amerada's petrochemical products with responsibility for domestic and foreign sales and the marketing of petrochemicals, including sulphur. He reported to Mr. Deverin, a senior vice president and a member of the executive operating committee.

After protracted negotiations between Amerada represented by Kurtz, and representatives of Rockland, an agreement was reached for the sale by Amerada to Rockland of 50 000 tons of sulphur at $8 per ton. This agreement was concluded by telephone on 5 September 1974. In the meantime, on 3 September 1974, Deverin had informed Kurtz that he would need to get the approval of the executive operating committee for the sale to Rockland. In other words, Kurtz no longer had the authority to conclude the sale on behalf of Amerada.

The agreement, concluded on 5 September, was not performed by Amerada, and Rockland sued for breach of contract. Amerada argued that there was no contract between the parties as Kurtz did not have the authority to act on Amerada's behalf.

THE LEGAL QUESTION: Was Amerada bound by the contract negotiated by Kurtz?

RESOLUTION: The court determined that Kurtz had actual authority to act on behalf of Amerada in negotiating and entering the contract with Rockland up until 3 September. At that time his actual authority was curtailed. This limitation on Kurtz's authority, however, was not communicated to Rockland. The court held that the onus was on Amerada to notify Rockland of the limitation—it was not up to Rockland to inquire as to Kurtz's authority. Amerada, by permitting Kurtz to act in its business by conducting negotiations, had represented to Rockland that he had permission to act. In short, there was a representation of authority by Amerada on which Rockland relied.

CRITICAL ANALYSIS: How could Amerada have prevented this situation?

The situations described in this section illustrate several of the risks associated with agency. The onus is on the principals to inform outsiders when a person ceases to be their agent; otherwise the principals continue to be liable for the agent's actions. Similarly, the principals have a responsibility to inform outsiders of any limitation on their agent's usual authority; otherwise the principals run the risk of being bound if the agent exceeds his actual authority but acts within his apparent authority. A principal can inform outsiders by contacting them by letter, telephone, or other means; by taking out advertisements in trade publications and newspapers; by clearly indicating on company forms what constitutes necessary approvals; and by otherwise indicating that only properly documented transactions will be binding.

Business Application of the Law

Real Estate Agents

The real estate agent is one of the most familiar and common types of agents. Most sales of property, especially those involving residential property, involve the services of a real estate agent. The real estate agent, however, is somewhat of an anomaly in agency law. Unlike most other agents, usually a real estate agent has no authority to make a binding contract of sale on behalf of his principal, the homeowner. Normally the agreement between the owner of property and the real estate agent—often taking the form of a standard listing agreement—does not confer any authority on the agent to enter a contract on behalf of the property owner. The real estate agent's role is usually limited to listing and advertising the property, showing the property to prospective purchasers, and introducing and bringing together the parties. In short, a real estate agent usually does not have the actual authority to contract on behalf of the principal. As well, a real estate agent does not have the apparent authority to enter a contract on behalf of a homeowner. A principal could, of course, grant actual authority to a real estate agent to enter a contract on her behalf. However, such a grant of authority, to be

Does a real estate agent act for the vendor or the purchaser of property?

effective, would need to be conferred by very clear, express, and unequivocal language.[6]

The case of real estate agents illustrates an important point. The term "agent" is often used very loosely

---

6.   William F. Foster, *Real Estate Agency Law in Canada*, 2nd ed. (Toronto: Carswell, 1994) at 99.

to refer to anyone who represents another, and is not always restricted to relationships where the agent enters into contracts on behalf of the principal. It is always necessary to look at the essence of a relationship rather than merely relying on what the parties call themselves. Just as agents are not always agents in the strict legal sense, so too there may be an agency relationship even though the parties have not labelled it as such.

CRITICAL ANALYSIS: How is the authority of a real estate agent determined?

Agency by Ratification

agency by ratification
An agency relationship created when one party adopts a contract entered into on his behalf by another who at the time acted without authority.

Agency by ratification occurs when a person represents himself as another's agent even though he is not, and when the purported principal adopts the acts of the agent. For example, suppose Ahmed is keenly interested in obtaining a franchise for a certain fast food restaurant, and his friend Frank is aware of this interest. An opportunity comes on the market, but Frank cannot reach Ahmed to tell him about it. Feeling pretty sure of himself, Frank goes ahead and purchases the franchise on Ahmed's behalf although he does not have any authority to do so. Though Frank acted with good intentions, Ahmed has no responsibilities unless he chooses to adopt the contract. When and if he does adopt the transaction, an agency relationship will be created between Frank and him. The result is that Ahmed's rights and duties under the franchise contract are identical to what they would have been had Frank been properly authorized to act as Ahmed's agent all along.

In both agency by estoppel and agency by ratification, the agent has no authority to do what he does. What distinguishes the two doctrines is whether the principal has conducted himself in a misleading way. Agency by estoppel forces the principal to be bound by the unauthorized contract because the principal has represented someone as his agent and must live with the consequences when that agent purports to act on his behalf. Under agency by ratification, the agent is perhaps equally out of line but not due to any fault of or misrepresentation by the principal. For this reason, the law does not force the principal to adopt the contract, but rather permits him to make that decision for himself, according to his own best interests.

FIGURE 13.3		How Created	Agent's Authority
Summary of Creation of Agency and Agent's Authority	Agency by Agreement	P, expressly or impliedly, appoints X as an A	Actual: Express and/or Implied Apparent
	Agency by Estoppel	*Representation of Authority* P represents to OS that X has authority to act as an A even though no actual authority given	Apparent
		Extension of Existing Authority P represents to OS that A has authority in excess of actual authority given	
		Termination or Reduction of Authority P terminates or reduces A's authority but does not give notice to OS	
	Agency by Ratification	P adopts actions of X, and X retroactively becomes an A	No authority until P adopts X's actions

Duties in the Agency Relationship

Duties of the Agent

An agency relationship created by contract imposes on an agent certain duties to perform. If the agent fails to perform these duties, he is in breach of the contract. An agent is required to perform in accordance with the principal's instructions. In the event that the principal has not given any instructions as to how the performance is to be carried out, performance must meet the standard of the particular trade or industry. For example, a real estate agent's duties would normally include appraising property, estimating the revenue and expenses of property the principal wishes to acquire, checking the dimensions of property, advising the principal of the financial implications of transactions, and ensuring properties the principal wishes to acquire do not contravene bylaws or other municipal regulations, among other matters.[7]

Normally, it is expected that the agent will personally perform the obligations. However, there may be an express or implied provision for delegation—that is, the agent may be permitted to "download" responsibility for performance onto someone else. For example, it may be that Leonard and Lisa have an understanding that Leonard can send his own assistant on less important buying trips to act in his place.

Business Application of the Law

Duties of the Insurance Agent

An insurance agent owes a principal a duty of care in the performance of his responsibilities. The content of that duty varies according to the agreement between the principal and the agent and the surrounding circumstances. For example, if a business engages an insurance agent or broker[8] to obtain insurance coverage, the insurance agent or broker has strict duties to provide information and advice to ensure that the business has the coverage it requires.

In *Fine's Flowers Ltd v. General Accident Assurance Co. of Canada,*[9] Fine's Flowers instructed an insurance agent to obtain "full coverage" for its greenhouse operation. The agent obtained insurance to cover a number of risks but failed to obtain "wear and tear" coverage. Fine's Flowers lost all of its plants in a frost when the heating pumps failed to operate—the cause of the malfunction was "wear and tear." The court held that the insurance agent was responsible for Fine's Flowers losses because the agent's undertaking to obtain "full coverage" created

an obligation to ensure that Fine's Flowers was covered for all foreseeable and normal risks. The agent had a duty to advise Fine's Flowers what risks were not covered so that it could take steps to protect its business against these uninsured risks.

As a result of *Fine's Flowers* an agent who has been instructed to obtain "full coverage" has onerous standards to meet to fulfill her duty of care. At a minimum, the agent must

- identify all of the client's foreseeable risks

- take all reasonable steps to determine if the market provides coverage for the risks identified

- provide information to the client about the coverage available

- procure the coverage if it is available

- advise the client if the coverage is unavailable so that the client can take other measures to reduce the risk

---

7. *Ibid.* at 218–219.
8. The distinction between an agent and a broker is discussed in Chapter 28.
9. (1977) 81 DLR (3d) 139 (Ont. C.A.).

CRITICAL ANALYSIS: An agent/broker may face a broad array of duties and be subject to onerous liability for breach of these duties. How can an agent manage her exposure to the risk of liability?

Source: Najma Rashid, "You and Your Insurance Broker" *Howard Yegendorf & Associates News* (31 January 2005) at http://www.yegendorf.com/news.asp?nID=110 (accessed 23 November 2006).

fiduciary duty

A duty imposed on a person who has a special relationship of trust with another.

fiduciary

A person who has a duty of good faith toward another because of their relationship.

An agent also owes a **fiduciary duty** to the principal. This duty requires the agent to show what the law describes as "utmost good faith to the principal." This duty is often expressed as a "profit rule"—a **fiduciary** must not personally profit by virtue of her position—and a "conflict rule"—a fiduciary must not place herself in a position where her own interests conflict with the interests of the principal. For example, it would be a breach of his fiduciary duty for Leonard to go on a buying trip for Lisa and acquire clothes for a store that he is secretly running on the side.

The content of the fiduciary duty will vary with the circumstances. However, as a general rule, an agent has the duty to

- make full disclosure of all material information that may affect the principal's position (i.e., Leonard must disclose to Lisa any good deals or bargains on clothes that he discovers)

- avoid any conflict of interest that affects the interests of the principal (i.e., Leonard must avoid acting as a buyer for both Lisa and any of her competitors)

- avoid acting for two principals in the same transaction (i.e., Leonard must not represent both Lisa and a clothing manufacturer in a sales transaction)

- avoid using the principal's property, money, or information to secure personal gain (i.e., Leonard must avoid using contacts that he has gained through acting as Lisa's agent to set up his own business, and he must not sell or use Lisa's customer lists and records for personal gain)

- avoid accepting or making a secret commission or profit (i.e., Leonard must avoid taking payments from clothing manufacturers for doing business with them)

What are the duties of an insurance agent?

There is not, however, an absolute prohibition against conflicts such as acting for two principals or using the principal's property. The agent simply must not do any of these activities secretly, and he must obtain the fully informed consent of the principal prior to the event.

CASE ▼

Raso v. Dionigi, [1993] 31 R.P.R. (2d) 1 (Ont. C.A.)

THE BUSINESS CONTEXT: As a general rule, an agent is precluded from acting for both the vendor and the purchaser in the same transaction. There is, however, an exception to the rule. An agent may act for both and not be in breach of fiduciary duties if full and fair disclosure of all material facts has been made to the principals prior to any transaction.

FACTUAL BACKGROUND: Raffaela Sirianni and her husband wanted to invest in income-producing property. They informed her brother-in-law, Guerino Sirianni, who was a real estate agent, that they were prepared to invest $250 000 to $300 000. He located a sixplex owned by Mr. and Mrs. Dionigi. The sixplex was not for sale; however, Sirianni actively prevailed upon the Dionigis to sign a listing agreement. Eventually they did sign an agreement with Sirianni's employer, a real estate agency. The listing price was $299 900. Sirianni presented an offer of $270 000 on behalf of "R. Raso in trust." Raso is the maiden name of Raffaela Sirianni. Sirianni never told the Dionigis that the purchasers were his brother and sister-in-law. The Dionigis counteroffered at $290 000, but this was not accepted. Sirianni persisted and the Dionigis ultimately accepted an offer of $285 000. A few days later, the Dionigis became aware of the purchasers' relationship with the agent, and they refused to complete the action. Raffaela Sirianni sued for specific performance of the contract, and Sirianni and the real estate agency sued for their commission.

THE LEGAL QUESTION: Did Sirianni owe a fiduciary duty to the Dionigis? If so, did he breach the duty? Would a breach preclude him from claiming a commission?

RESOLUTION: Sirianni was not a mere middleman in the sense of introducing the parties but rather, he took an active role in the transaction. A real estate agent who acts for both sides of a transaction has a fiduciary duty to both his principals to disclose all material facts with respect to the transaction. Sirianni breached his fiduciary duty to the Dionigis by failing to disclose that the purchasers were his brother and sister-in-law, and by failing to advise of the amount of money that the purchasers had available to purchase the property. A fiduciary who breaches his duty of disclosure of material facts is not entitled to prove that the transaction would have concluded had disclosure been made. In other words, it is immaterial whether the transaction is fair and it is irrelevant whether the principal would still have entered the transaction if disclosure had been made.

Where an agent has breached a fiduciary duty in this manner, the agent is precluded from claiming any commission. It also follows that the purchasers are not entitled to specific performance as they not only had knowledge of the agent's breach but also actively participated in the scheme.

CRITICAL ANALYSIS: What are the distinguishing features of a fiduciary relationship? What consequences flow from the designation of a relationship as a fiduciary one? If Guerino Sirianni had disclosed to the Dionigis just how much money Mr. and Mrs. Sirianni had available to purchase the property, would this disclosure have been a breach of his fiduciary duty to the Siriannis? What does this tell you about the perils of acting for both parties to a transaction?

A fiduciary duty is not unique to the relationship between a principal and an agent. This duty is present, as a matter of course, in many other relationships found in business such as the relationships between

■ lawyers and their clients
■ accountants and their clients

- partners
- directors and senior officers of a corporation and the corporation
- senior employees and employers

The categories of fiduciary relationships are not closed. A fiduciary relationship has been found to exist, in some circumstances, in other relationships such as the relationship between financial advisors (e.g., bankers, stockbrokers, and investment counsellors) and their clients. A fiduciary duty can arise in any relationship where the facts indicate sufficient elements of power and influence on the part of one party and reliance, vulnerability, and trust on the part of the other.[10] For example, the relationship between an investor and a broker will not normally give rise to a fiduciary duty where the broker is simply a conduit of information and merely takes orders. However, where the client reposes trust and confidence in the broker and relies on the broker's advice in making business decisions, the relationship may be elevated to a fiduciary relationship.

Because professional relationships can be easily categorized as fiduciary, it is incumbent on those who offer their services to others to understand the indicia of the fiduciary relationship. In addition, it is noteworthy that where fiduciary duties are found to exist, the innocent party can look to a wider range of remedies than found in contract or tort. The whole range of equitable remedies is available, and with the spectre of these remedies, it is important for businesspeople to comprehend not only when a fiduciary relationship exists but also the ambit of the duties.

Business Application of the Law — Rogue Agents

Scams, swindles and schemes are, unfortunately, a part of the business world. Agency relationships seem to be particularly vulnerable to fraud—the sports agent who steals from his client, the stockbroker who misappropriates her client's funds, the real estate agent who defrauds his principal, and the marriage broker who pockets her customer's money. The prevalence of wrongdoing in agency relationships is due, in part, to the nature of the agency relationship. The principal usually puts a great deal of trust in the agent to represent her interest and act on her behalf. The principal does not usually deal face-to-face with a third party but relies on the services and good faith of the agent. The reliance inherent in agency increases the opportunity for fraud. Consider the following examples:

In 2002, Shahram Massoudinia was convicted of fraud through the vehicle of a modelling agency.

Massoudinia and his associates enticed people to part with fees for the chance at nonexistent modeling jobs. Some individuals were convinced to pay approximately $850 for a modelling portfolio as a prerequisite to be considered for modelling jobs. Others were coerced into paying $5000 to be registered on a computer site to obtain exposure to potential clients. Approximately 1400 people were defrauded of an amount in excess of $2 million.[11]

In 2006, Carmen Fernandez, a freelance travel agent using offices in different travel agencies is alleged to have defrauded over 40 customers and several travel agencies in Montreal and Laval of hundreds of thousands of dollars. Apparently, she sold plane tickets to clients far in advance of their trip and once they paid she would book the tickets with the airline but sometime before departure she cancelled the tickets. Later she would buy the tickets

---

10. *Hodgkinson v. Simms*, [1994] 3 S.C.R. 377. For a summary of this case, see Chapter 22.
11. *R. v. Massoudinia*, (2002), 65 W.C.B. (2d) 765 (Ont. S.C.J.).

back at cheaper rates and keep the profit. The scheme did not always work, leaving some customers stranded.[12]

CRITICAL ANALYSIS: How can a businessperson/ principal manage the risk of an agent committing a fraud? How far should the law go in protecting a principal from the actions of an unscrupulous agent?

Duties of the Principal

A principal's duties usually are not as onerous as an agent's and normally are set out in the contract creating the agency relationship. Such contracts usually obligate the principal to

- pay the agent a specified fee or percentage for services rendered
- assist the agent in the manner described in the contract
- reimburse the agent for reasonable expenses associated with carrying out his agency duties
- indemnify against losses incurred in carrying out the agency business

In the example involving Lisa and her buying agent Leonard, it may be that Leonard has had to fly to Toronto to make the necessary purchases. In the absence of any agreement to the contrary, Lisa would be required to reimburse Leonard for his airfare. This is a cost that rightfully belongs to Lisa since Leonard incurred it on a buying trip she instigated and sent him on. Similarly, she has an obligation—either express or implied—to reimburse him for meals and hotel and other reasonable expenses associated with the buying trip.

Contract Liability in the Agency Relationship

Liability of the Principal to the Outsider

The most significant result of an agency relationship is that when an agent enters into a contract on behalf of a principal with a third party, it is the principal, not the agent, who ordinarily is liable on the contract. To a large extent, discussion of this point is simply the flip side of a discussion regarding an agent's actual and apparent authority. Put another way, the principal's liability to the third party depends on the nature of the agent's authority.

---

12. "On Your Side: Rogue Travel Agent—Part I" (8 May 2006) and "Rogue Travel Agent—Part II" (10 May 2006) at http:// montreal.ctv.ca/cfcf/news/oys&id=1134 (accessed 23 November 2006).

As we have already seen under the discussion of an agent's authority above, Lisa is liable on the ugly clothes contract—even though she does not much like the deal—because Leonard was acting within his actual authority. Leonard did exceed his actual authority on the second contract because it went over the monetary limit his principal had placed on him, but the doctrine of apparent authority likely applies. The outsider did not know about the limitation on Leonard's authority, so on this basis, Lisa is bound. She will not have an opportunity to renegotiate this contract in order to get a lower price.

Liability of the Agent to the Outsider

warranty of authority
A representation of authority by a person who purports to be an agent.

An agent who acts without authority and contracts with an outsider is liable to the third party for breach of **warranty of authority.** In this situation, there is no contract between either the principal and the outsider or the agent and the outsider.[13]

For example, Lisa would not be bound by a contract Leonard enters into on her behalf to purchase a private jet. She could adopt, that is, ratify, such a contract, but otherwise she is not bound because such a contract is not within Leonard's actual or apparent authority. Leonard may be sued by the vendor of the jet because he wrongly claimed to have the authority to act on Lisa's behalf in the purchase of a jet.

An agent may also be bound when he contracts on his own behalf to be a party to the contract along with his principal.[14]

For example, if Leonard negotiated the contract such that both he and his principal were ordering the clothes and promising to pay for them, then he has as much liability to the outsider as Lisa. They are both parties to the contract—Leonard is contracting on his own behalf as well as on Lisa's behalf.

Liability of an Undisclosed Principal

undisclosed principal
A principal whose identity is unknown to a third party, who has no knowledge that the agent is acting in an agency capacity.

An agent may incur liability when he contracts on behalf of an **undisclosed principal.** A principal is said to be "undisclosed" when the third party does not know that she is dealing with an agent at all and assumes that the party she is face to face with is acting only on his own behalf. From the perspective of the outsider, there is no principal waiting in the background.

When the agent is acting for an undisclosed principal, the general rule is that the principal is still liable on the contract so long as the agent is acting within his authority.[15] The agent has no liability, however.

For example, assume that in negotiations with outsiders Leonard represents himself neither as an agent nor as a principal and that he could be acting in either capacity. In such circumstances, Lisa will generally be liable on the contract, but not Leonard. This is a simple application of the general rule stated above.

The general rule, however, has been subject to qualification that may operate to render the agent liable on the contract in certain circumstances.[16] One such qualification relates to representations made by the agent.

Suppose that for the purposes of a buying trip to a small clothing manufacturer overseas, Lisa wishes to keep her identity a secret. She thinks that Leonard, her purchasing agent, will get a better price if the seller (the outsider) is unaware of her identity.[17]

---

13. *Supra* note 1 at 231–244.
14. F.M.B. Reynolds, *Bowstead & Reynolds on Agency*, 16th ed. (London: Sweet & Maxwell, 1996) at 552.
15. *Supra* note 1 at 253. This rule has been subject to heavy criticism as being inconsistent with the general principles of contract law.
16. *Supra* note 1 at 258–264.
17. This is a not uncommon practice in the real estate industry, particularly when a developer wishes to purchase several tracts of land.

If Leonard pretends to be the principal—representing to the outsider that he is actually the owner or proprietor of the clothing business—and does not disclose the existence of Lisa, his principal, then Leonard runs the risk of being personally liable on the contract that is concluded. For example, if the written contract expressly indicates that Leonard is the principal, the parol evidence rule[18] may operate to prevent the admission of evidence of an undisclosed principal.[19] In such circumstances, Leonard is liable.

A variation on the undisclosed principal is the unnamed principal.[20] If Leonard tells the seller that he is acting for a principal but that he is not at liberty to reveal that person's identity, Lisa will be liable on any contract he enters into with the seller. In such circumstances, Leonard himself has no liability on the contract because the outsider was fully aware of his status. The outsider did not know the identity of his principal but decided to enter into a contract anyway. If the outsider did not want to deal with an unnamed principal, the outsider could simply have refused to enter the contract in the first place.

Liability of the Agent to the Principal

When an agent exceeds his authority, the principal can sue the agent for breach of their contract—assuming that there is such a contract in place.

Because Leonard exceeded his authority on the second contract (involving the Montreal fashion house), Lisa could sue him for breach of their agency or employment agreement. It is unlikely that she could successfully sue him on the first contract for buying what she considered to be ugly clothes, because it seems in this particular instance that he and Lisa simply have a difference of opinion as to what will sell in her store.

Tort Liability in the Agency Relationship

As a general rule, an agent is personally liable for any torts that she commits. The fact that she may have been acting on behalf of another is no defence in a tort action.[21]

The principal is liable for any tort committed by the agent while the agent is acting within the scope of the agent's authority.[22] Put another way, a principal is vicariously liable for an agent's actions so long as the agent is acting within express, implied, or apparent authority.[23]

For example, assume that Leonard is given the responsibility for selling to discount houses Lisa's inventory of clothing from previous seasons. Suppose that Leonard represents to a discount house that some of this clothing is from a famous designer's latest collection and, based on this representation, the discount house purchases a large number of items. In this situation, Leonard has committed the tort of deceit by representing the clothing as new stock when in fact it is old stock. Leonard is personally liable for committing a tort. Lisa is also liable for Leonard's actions since they were committed within the scope of his authority.

---

18. The parol evidence rule is discussed in Chapter 7.
19. *Supra* note 1 at 258–263. The law is unsettled in this area: it is unclear when the law will permit evidence of an undisclosed principal.
20. *Supra* note 14 at 30. As Bowstead notes, terminology in this area is not consistently employed by the judiciary and legal writers.
21. *Supra* note 1 at 325.
22. *Supra* note 1 at 315.
23. The question of vicarious liability arising from agency principles overlaps with the application of the doctrine in relation to the acts of employees and independent contractors. For example, a principal is liable for the acts of an agent only if the agent was acting within his actual and apparent authority; however, if the agent has the status of an employee, the employer is liable if the act was committed in the course of employment. Therefore, whereas a principal may not be liable for the agent's acts because they were outside the agent's authority, the employer may be liable for the agent's acts if the agent was an employee acting within the scope of his employment. The liability of employers for the actions of employees and independent contractors is explored in Chapter 20.

FIGURE 13.4

Summary of Contract
Liability in Agency

(1)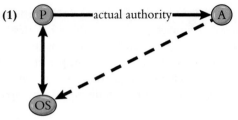

A acts within actual authority.
P is liable to outsider.

(2)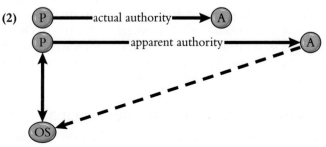

A exceeds actual authority but acts within apparent authority.
P is liable to OS unless OS knew or ought to have known of any
limitation on A's authority.
A is liable to P for breaching authority.

(3)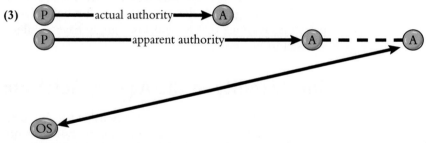

A exceeds both actual and apparent authority.
A is liable to OS for breach of warranty of authority.

(4)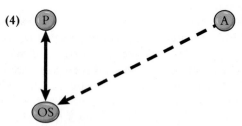

A acts without P's authority.
P is liable to OS if P adopts contract.

n the world of electronic communications, the use of electronic agents is widespread. Electronic agents are computer programs, or other electronic means, used to independently initiate an action or to respond to electronic messages or acts without review by an individual. Examples of e-agents include software that can search through many databases and retrieve relevant information for the user, and software that can make purchases and sales online. There has been considerable debate about the legal effect of using e-agents to transact business. For example: Is a contract formed by an e-agent binding on its principal? What is the extent of the e-agent's authority? Is the principal responsible if the software enters a contract contrary to the principal's intentions?

The common law does not have clear answers to these questions. Many jurisdictions, rather than waiting for court decisions to form a consistent and authoritative answer, have provided legislative responses.[24] In Ontario, for example, the *Electronic Commerce Act*[25] provides that a contract may be formed by the interaction of an electronic agent and an individual or by the interaction of electronic agents. The legislation also deals with errors made when transacting with electronic agents. It indicates that the electronic transaction will not have any legal effect when an individual makes a material error in electronic information provided that the electronic agent has not given the individual an opportunity to prevent or correct the error; on becoming aware of the error, the individual promptly notifies the other person of the error; and in the case where the individual receives consideration as a result of the error, either returns the consideration or deals with the consideration in the manner instructed by the other side. Where the individual receives no instruction from the other side, the transaction can still be avoided provided the individual deals with the consideration in a reasonable manner and does not benefit materially from it.

CRITICAL ANALYSIS: How does a principal's responsibility for the actions of an e-agent differ from the principal's responsibility for the actions of a human agent?

Termination of Agency Agreements

An agency agreement can come to an end in a number of ways:

- The parties may agree to bring their relationship to an end. For example, Lisa and Leonard may simply agree to end their relationship.
- One party may give notice of termination to the other.[26]
- An agency relationship can cease by operation of the law. Most commonly this occurs due to the death, dissolution (in the case of a corporate agent and/or principal), insanity, or bankruptcy of one of the parties.

When an agency agreement is terminated by the parties, the principal should give notice to third parties so that customers do not assume that the relationship is continuing. In the absence of such notice, the principal may face liability to outsiders, based on his agent's apparent authority.

---

24. See Chapter 6, note 18 for a complete listing of electronic commerce legislation.
25. S.O. 2000, c. 17, ss. 20–21.
26. As Leonard is Lisa's employee, the rules of notice in employment relationships are applicable. These rules are discussed in Chapter 20.

Business Law in Practice Revisited

1. What is the nature of the legal relationship between Lisa and Leonard?

Leonard is an employee of Lisa's business. In his position of marketing manager, he was granted power to make purchasing decisions on Lisa's behalf. Therefore, he is considered in law to be an agent, and the relationship between Lisa and Leonard comprises both employment and agency.

2. Is Lisa bound by the two contracts Leonard entered into during his Toronto buying trip?

Much of this chapter has been devoted to Lisa's liability on the unfortunate contracts Leonard made on her behalf. It has been emphasized that if Leonard makes poor or reckless purchase decisions, Lisa will normally be obligated to pay for the purchases. Agency law states that the principal, Lisa, is one party to the contract and that the other party is the outsider, the clothing manufacturer. The agent, Leonard, is merely the means by which the parties enter the contract. Lisa will not be liable for Leonard's purchases if the manufacturer knew or ought to have known that Leonard was not authorized to make the purchases he did. But a manufacturer is not expected to know or suspect that Leonard was limited to entering into contracts not exceeding $100 000. Lisa is bound, but she can hold Leonard liable for breaching his agency agreement in that he exceeded his authority. As noted, however, this will not relieve Lisa of her liability to the clothing manufacturer, and it is probably not an attractive course of action, as Leonard may not have the means of satisfying the debt. As well, suing one's agent can create a lot of adverse publicity.

3. How should Lisa have handled this agency relationship from the outset?

Lisa should have expressly granted Leonard the authority to enter contracts on her behalf either orally or in writing. The latter would have been the best course of action as it would have provided Leonard with proof of the relationship and clarified his authority (i.e., how much he can contract for), any limits on whom he can contract with, and so on. It also would have assisted Lisa if one day she was required to prove that Leonard exceeded his actual authority.

It is also incumbent on Lisa to monitor the activities of those who act on her behalf. Proper supervision may prevent an employee from acting in a manner that detracts from the achievement of business goals and objectives.

Chapter Summary

This chapter introduced one of the cornerstone relationships in business. Agency is a relationship that allows one person's actions to be attributable to another. In this way, agency permits one party to represent and bind another in contractual matters. Thus a business may use agents in many facets of its operations, such as buying, selling, leasing, and hiring. As a practical matter, without the advantage of agency relationships, business could not be conducted on any significant scale.

The agency relationship most commonly comes into existence when a principal grants authority to the agent to act on her behalf. The law, however, recognizes an agency relationship when the principal represents to another that she is represented by an agent—agency by estoppel—or when the principal adopts a contract made on her behalf by someone who is not her agent—agency by ratification. In this area, it is the substance of the relationship that is important, not what parties call their relationship. An agent's authority to act on behalf of a principal varies. An agent may have actual authority. This is the authority that he is actually given by the principal or that is implied from his position. Alternatively, an agent may have apparent authority. This is the authority that a third party would reasonably believe the agent to have based on the principal's representations. The scope of an agent's apparent authority is fact-specific and therefore varies with the circumstances.

An agent has both express and implied duties to his principal. Most importantly, an agent has a fiduciary duty to act in the best interests of the principal. The principal also has express and implied duties, particularly the duty to compensate the agent for services rendered and for costs associated with the agency relationship.

Agency operates in such a way that the principal is generally liable on contracts entered into by the agent on her behalf. A contract is formed between the principal and the outsider, and the agent drops out of the transaction. Though there are a number of potential problems, the agency relationship generally functions well and according to plan. However, it is possible that agency can operate in ways not desired. For example, the principal may be liable on contracts not desired, as when the agent negotiates a poor contract, or exceeds his actual authority but not his apparent authority. So too, a principal may be liable for torts committed by an agent. Thus, ironically, the same person who can help a business grow and prosper can lead that same enterprise to financial loss. The key point is that agency, like other aspects of a business, needs to be managed and monitored: businesspeople must choose an agent wisely, instruct him carefully, and review his work regularly.

Chapter Study

Key Terms and Concepts

actual authority (p. 294)

agency (p. 291)

agency by estoppel (p. 297)

agency by ratification (p. 300)

agent (p. 291)

apparent authority (p. 296)

fiduciary (p. 302)

fiduciary duty (p. 302)

law of agency (p. 293)

outsider (p. 292)

principal (p. 291)

undisclosed principal (p. 306)

warranty of authority (p. 306)

Questions for Review

1. What is agency? Give an example.

2. Why would a business use an agent to act on its behalf?

3. How is an agency relationship entered into?

4. What is the difference between the actual and apparent authority of an agent?

5. When will an agent have implied authority?

6. What is a power of attorney? What is the risk with using a power of attorney?

7. What is meant by agency by estoppel? How does agency by estoppel arise?

8. How is an agency by ratification created?

9. Is a real estate agent a typical agent? Explain.

10. What are the duties of the agent?

11. What are the duties of the principal?

12. Do all business advisors owe fiduciary duties? Explain.

13. When can an agent be personally liable on a contract entered into on behalf of a principal?

14. Describe how an agent can be liable to the principal.

15. When is a principal liable for torts committed by an agent? How can a principal reduce his liability for torts committed by an agent?

16. What is an undisclosed principal?

17. Is a contract formed by an electronic agent binding on a principal? Explain.

18. How may an agency relationship be terminated?

Questions for Critical Thinking

1. In the insurance industry, the agent acts primarily for the insurance company, which is the principal. Typically, the insurance agent also advises the client on the needed coverage and the meaning of the insurance policy. Do you see any potential problems with this situation?

2. Is it reasonable to hold principals responsible for contracts formed with only apparent authority? What are the tradeoffs?

3. In some real estate transactions, the agent advises both the vendor and the purchaser. Is this a violation of the real estate agent's duties? Why or why not?

4. The application of fiduciary duties to those who are brought within its ambit is to impose a high standard of morality. Is this to be applauded? Are there any concerns?

5. The agency relationship creates considerable risks for the principal. What is the nature of these risks in both contract and tort? How can these risks be managed? Does the agency relationship create risks for the agent? Explain.

Situations for Discussion

1. Kerry is interested in selling her convenience store for approximately $250 000 to $300 000. As Kerry is unfamiliar with the commercial real estate market in Red Deer, she engages a real estate agent, Patrick. The engagement is a standard listing agreement. Patrick shows the building to a young couple, Paul and Rick, who seem to be quite interested. In fact, they make an offer in writing to purchase the building for $250 000. They also indicate that they need a reply immediately. Patrick calls Kerry but is unable to reach her. Patrick is in a quandary, but knowing that Paul and Rick's offer is in Kerry's range, albeit at the bottom, Patrick accepts the offer on Kerry's behalf (he signs the written offer). Upon learning of Patrick's actions, Kerry is quite upset and wonders whether she must sell the building to Paul and Rick. Advise Kerry.

2. Mattie and Rajiv were interested in taking a dream vacation to celebrate their tenth wedding anniversary. They contacted Windemere Travel Agency and informed the proprietor of their needs—a seven-day, luxury Caribbean cruise with several stops at various resorts. The travel agent quoted a price of $1900 per person. Mattie and Rajiv paid the price in full. The cruise, however, turned out to be more of a nightmare than a dream—the ship was a refurbished oil tanker, it stopped at several resorts but only at night, and Mattie found a mouse in the bathroom. Unfortunately, Mattie and Rajiv were unsuccessful in obtaining a refund from the cruise line as it had gone out of business. Do they have any recourse against the travel agent?

3. Atlantic Life Ltd. is in the business of selling life insurance. The corporation hired Toby Ryan as

its representative in Newfoundland. Toby was provided with Atlantic Life business cards and brochures, and a company car with the Atlantic Life logo on it. A clause in the contract between the parties provided

> The representative will not without the prior approval of the Company incur any liability or debt on behalf of the Company, accept insurance or other risks, revive polices, waive forfeitures, extend the time of payment of any premium or waive premium payment in cash, or make, alter, or discharge any contract and will not make any expenditure on behalf of the Company.

Toby negotiated on behalf of Atlantic Life the sale of a life insurance policy to Sadie Clements, insuring her life for $500 000. Shortly thereafter, Sadie died and her beneficiaries claimed benefits under the policy. Atlantic Life refuses to pay on the basis that Toby did not obtain approval of Atlantic for the sale of the insurance policy.[27] Does Atlantic Life have to pay the benefits? If it does, how could it have prevented this situation?

4. Cesare Espinosa was an experienced and knowledgeable stock market investor who maintained a substantial retirement savings fund with Dominion Trust. The fund was managed by Scott, an employee of Milan, Fraser, & Reilly (MFR), a firm of stockbrokers. Cesare heard about a volatile and speculative stock called Bleakwater Resources, which was trading on the Vancouver Stock Exchange. On the morning of 8 February, he placed an order with Scott to purchase 13 000 shares for his RRSP account. At about 4:30 p.m. on the same day, he telephoned the offices of MFR to place an additional order for 11 000 shares of the same stock. Scott had left for the day, so the order was placed with another salesman, George. Cesare requested that the purchase take place "at the market price first thing in the morning." George undertook to do so. The next day, George arrived at the office at 7:00 a.m., but he did not place Cesare's order as he was concerned about the wisdom of the order. Instead he waited for Scott's arrival, which occurred between 8:30 and 9:00 a.m., at which time George referred the order to Scott. Trading in the shares was suspended at 8:45 a.m. that day and Cesare's order was never placed. When trading resumed the shares had more than doubled in price.[28] Does Cesare have an action against George or Scott? If so, on what basis? Would your answer be the same if, when trading resumed, the shares had dropped in price by half?

5. Mollie Morrow was a real estate agent working for Commercial Properties. She was approached by Shane Jacobs to find a commercial building in downtown Halifax. She did some investigating and found a suitable property owned by Haldane Properties (HP). She approached the owners about selling and they agreed to pay a commission of 2 percent if she acted as their agent in the sale of the building. After considerable negotiations, the sale was concluded for $6 000 000. Unknown to HP, Mollie had agreed to pay half of her commission to Shane. When HP learned about this it refused to pay the commission. Mollie argued that HP had received what it wanted out of the deal; she had made a sacrifice by giving up part of her commission, and her sacrifice ensured that the deal went through. In short, her actions helped, not harmed, HP. Is Mollie entitled to the commission?[29]

6. Hamilton Utility Inc. appointed Juan Abrams as one of its corporate officers. Juan rented cars from Quality Cars Ltd., a car rental business. The rental agreements named Juan as renter, and he signed the agreements describing himself as company secretary of Hamilton Utility. Juan, however, used the cars for personal purposes and not for company business. Hamilton refused to pay the charges as Juan had not been given any authority to enter contracts on its behalf.[30] Is Hamilton liable to pay the car rental charges?

27. Based on Schwartz v. Maritime Life Assurance Co. (1997), 149 Nfld. & P.E.I.R. 234 (Nfld. C.A.), leave to appeal to S.C.C. refused [1997] S.C.C.A. No. 362.
28. Based on Volkers v. Midland Doherty Ltd. et al. (1985), 17 D.L.R. (4th) 343 (B.C.C.A.).
29. Based on Ocean City Realty Ltd. v. A & M Holdings Ltd. et al. (1987), 36 D.L.R. (4th) 94 (B.C.C.A.).
30. Based on Panorama Developments (Guildford) Ltd. v. Fidelis Furnishing Fabrics Ltd., [1971] 2 Q.B. 711 (C.A.).

Explain. What would be the result if Hamilton appointed Juan to a secretarial position?

7. Adriana Santosh is in the business of selling antique furniture. As her company has increased significantly the Internet portion of the business, Adriana has determined that she does not need as much retail space as previously. She plans to sell her large downtown store and move to smaller rented premises. As Adriana is extremely busy, she is unable to do the selling herself and therefore she is considering engaging the services of a real estate agent. What are the advantages and disadvantages of using a real estate agent? What questions should Andrea ask a real estate agent before engaging his services? What legal risks are involved in using a real estate agent?

8. Ty Sharim has been employed as an agent for Farley's Game and Fishing Lodge Inc. for the past 10 years. Farley's runs an exclusive hunting and fishing camp in northern Ontario. Ty's contractual duties include advertising the camp and soliciting customers at fish and gun shows and conventions in North America and elsewhere. One weekend while on a fishing trip with his family, Ty came across a small fishing camp that was for sale. As Ty has always dreamed of owning and operating his own business, he is thinking of putting in an offer on the camp. Is Ty entitled to put in an offer to purchase the camp or must he inform Farley's of the camp? Would your answer differ if Ty terminated his relationship with Farley's before offering to buy the camp?

For more study tools, visit
http://www.businesslaw3e.nelson.com

Chapter

14

Objectives

After studying this chapter, you should have an understanding of

- the characteristics of the major forms of business organizations
- the advantages and disadvantages of the major forms of business organizations
- the legal consequences of a partnership
- methods of arranging business activity

Business Forms and Arrangements

Business Law in Practice

Adam Lane is young, energetic, smart, and largely broke. In fact, Adam has only two assets of any real value: a recently completed degree in Computer Science and a 1974 vintage Corvette worth over $15 000. The vehicle was a gift from his father. On the liability side, Adam has student loans totalling over $10 000.

Adam has spent the past few summers experimenting and thinks that he has come up with an improved voice-recognition system for computers. He wants to contract out the manufacture of his product and set up an organization for its distribution and sale. He already has a name in mind: "I-know-that-it's-you Enterprises," or IK Enterprises for short.

Adam's father, Cameron Lane, is retired and reasonably well off. He has $100 000 that he is willing to invest in IK Enterprises, but he does not wish to risk his position and that of Adam's young brother by having any greater commitment to the business.

Adam has also found Diane Levesque, a manufacturer's agent for many products, who is willing to advise Adam on setting up IK Enterprises and to assist in marketing the product. Diane is willing to invest $20 000 and to devote some of her time and expertise to the new business. The bank, under a young entrepreneurs' program, is also willing to lend some start-up capital.

1. What forms of business organization are available for carrying on Adam's business?
2. What are the major considerations in choosing a particular form?
3. Which form is best for Adam's business?

Forms of Business Organization

Choosing how to own a business is a critical decision because it determines in large part who

- is financially liable for the business
- shares in business profits and other assets
- makes and is accountable for management decisions

The Sole Proprietorship

sole proprietorship
A unincorporated business organization that has only one owner.

The **sole proprietorship** is the oldest form of business organization and the one most often used by small business. It is a particularly popular choice for the home-based enterprise. From a legal perspective, it also represents the simplest form of business organization because there is no legislation pertaining to the sole proprietorship as such. A discussion of the legal consequences of this form of business is really a discussion of the rights and liabilities of an individual.

Financial Liability

The financial consequences to Adam should he conduct his computer business as a sole proprietorship are both straightforward and significant: any obligation of the business is Adam's personal obligation. Consider the following examples:

- *The bank loan.* If Adam decides to borrow start-up capital from the bank, it is Adam who promises to repay the loan, not his business. This is because a sole proprietorship, unlike a corporation, is not legally capable of borrowing money on its own. Adam is the business. Adam is the debtor and is responsible for the debt.

Suppose that IK Enterprises, Adam's sole proprietorship, begins to falter and the loan cannot be repaid. The bank will take the appropriate legal steps—discussed in more detail in Chapter 26—to recover as much as it can on the loan. All of Adam's business and personal assets are subject to the debts of the business. Also, any judgment against him can be kept alive indefinitely unless he declares bankruptcy, in which case, most judgments against him will be discharged. However, Adam's personal credit rating will be adversely affected, now and in the future. This may make it next to impossible to ever start another venture that would depend on Adam's creditworthiness.

- *The breach of contract.* If at some point IK Enterprises supplies defective computers to a customer, Adam, not IK Enterprises, is in breach of contract. This is because, as noted above, IK Enterprises cannot enter into a contract. As in the preceding example, Adam is the one who will be sued, and it is Adam's assets that are at risk.

unlimited liability
Unrestricted legal responsibility for obligations.

In short, a sole proprietor has what is known in law as **unlimited liability.** Regardless of what the owner has invested in his business, his personal assets—and not just the business assets—may be seized to pay the outstanding debts of the business. Unfortunately, these debts can far exceed anything anticipated when the business was started.

Profit Sharing

The sole proprietor bears the risk of failure, but also enjoys this advantage: all the profits after taxes accrue to the sole proprietor alone. If IK Enterprises is a runaway success, Adam reaps all the benefits. The profit motive can be a strong incentive for the sole proprietor to seek to ensure the success of the business.

Decision Making

The sole proprietor, having no partners and no board of directors to report to, can make business decisions very quickly and independently. She has a lot of personal freedom to do exactly as she pleases concerning all aspects of the business, even if it means deciding to discontinue business activities altogether. Should the owner die, the business is terminated—in other words, the proprietorship has a limited life span.

There are, of course, disadvantages to working alone in this way: few people are good at everything, yet the sole proprietor is responsible for every aspect of the business, from buying and selling to financing and advertising. Another serious consideration is that the sole proprietor's absence through illness or incapacity can adversely affect the business because so much of the enterprise revolves around this one individual. Though the sole proprietor may hire employees, they have limited opportunities for advancement, since by definition a sole proprietorship is a one-person show. As a result, these workers may not be particularly motivated or able to provide a high level of commitment.

Sources of Capital

A major difficulty with "going it alone" is that the sole proprietor has limited access to capital. Since the proprietor has no business partners, he is limited to his own assets and to whatever credit he can draw on to finance the operation. Usually this is less than what would be available if more than one person was involved, as in a partnership, for example.

Taxation

Because a sole proprietorship is not a legal entity separate from the owner, there are no formal or specialized tax rules governing it. Profits and losses are simply reported on the owner's personal income tax return. This may be favourable or unfavourable depending on the taxpayer's circumstances, including whether the owner's marginal tax rate is higher or lower than the applicable corporate tax rate.

Transferability

A sole proprietorship cannot be transferred or sold to another because it has no legal status. There is, in effect, nothing to transfer. However, the assets associated with the proprietorship—such as inventory—are transferable.

Regulations

The legal requirements for establishing and conducting this form of business organization are minimal—one simply commences business activity. There is no general need to incur legal fees to create the business vehicle. In short, doing business through the sole proprietorship is simple and inexpensive.

This is not to say that sole proprietorships are unregulated. They are subject to the same general legislation as any other business form. One important requirement is the registration or licensing of the business. Requirements vary from province to province, but generally persons who offer specialized services to the public must be licensed to practise their particular skill. Thus, lawyers, doctors, dentists, and electricians, for example, are required to follow provincial legislation governing their activity before providing services. Some businesses, such as those involving interprovincial trucking, require a federal licence to operate. Other types of business, such as door-to-door selling and the transportation of goods, are subject to specialized rules. The fees associated with licensing and registration are generally not substantial.

In addition to the regulations put in place by the federal and provincial governments, municipalities often impose their own registration or licensing requirements. For example, taxi businesses frequently require municipal licences to operate within municipal boundaries.

A sole proprietor who wishes to use a name other than her own for conducting the business must register the name at the local registry office or other government office designated by the province, where such records are kept and made available to the public.[1] The objective is to enable a person who deals with such a business to determine the identity of the proprietor of the business. Failure to register may result in a fine or other penalty, and the inability to sue for an obligation incurred in connection with the business except with leave of the court.[2]

Aside from these requirements, the sole proprietor is subject to laws of general application. Local zoning bylaws may require sole proprietors to locate in certain areas, provincial tax laws may require them to obtain a permit to act as a collector of sales tax, and health legislation may require them to maintain a high degree of cleanliness where food service or processing is involved. As well, a sole proprietor

---

1. The use of trade or business names is discussed in Chapter 18.
2. See, for example, *Business Names Act*, R.S.O. 1990, c. B-17, s. 7.

who hires employees must comply with all applicable legislation, such as that regulating employment standards, employment insurance, workers' compensation, and occupational health and safety.

A sole proprietor (unlike a public corporation) is not required to publish the business's financial statements. Success or failure in the business is a private matter, restricted to the proprietor, the business's accountant, Canada Revenue Agency, and perhaps the local bank manager.

FIGURE 14.1

Pros and Cons of the Sole Proprietorship

Pros

Simplicity: There are few licensing and registration requirements. The sole proprietor just starts doing business and is free to discontinue business activities at any time.

Speed and independence: Since the sole proprietor has no partners and is not answerable to a board of directors, he can make decisions quickly and independently.

Profit motive: Any after-tax profit or other assets that accrue go entirely to the sole proprietor.

Lower costs: The fees for provincial and municipal licences are relatively small, varying according to the nature and size of the business and the municipality in which it is located. Generally, there is no need to incur legal fees.

Tax benefits: Profits and losses are reported on the owner's personal income tax return. This may be favourable or unfavourable depending on the taxpayer's circumstances.

Cons

Unlimited personal liability: The sole proprietor carries the risk of the business failing and losing both business and personal assets.

Working alone: The sole proprietor is responsible for all aspects of the business operation. Though a sole proprietor can hire employees, it is difficult to retain high-calibre people because of the limited opportunities available to them in a sole proprietorship.

Limited access to capital: The capital available to the business is limited to the assets of the proprietor and the extent of her credit.

Limited life span: The owner's death terminates the business. The proprietorship cannot be transferred.

Tax disadvantages: See tax benefits.

The Partnership

partnership
A business carried on by two or more persons with the intention of making a profit.

When two or more persons want to pool their resources and carry on business together, the most common option is to form a **partnership** or create a corporation.[3] A partnership is much like a sole proprietorship in that neither has a legal personality—or legal existence—separate from the people who comprise them. There are no special steps to create a partnership. It is simply the legal relationship that automatically arises when two or more people do business together with the objective of making a profit.

The rules governing partnerships come from three sources: partnership legislation (in place in every province), contract law, and agency law. Later in the chapter, these sources will be analyzed in some depth. What follows is a general account of the basic principles that govern partnerships.

---

3. There can be restrictions on professionals, such as accountants and lawyers, incorporating companies. See Chapter 22 for detail.

Financial Liability

If Adam, Cameron, and Diane decide to join forces and bring Adam's product to market through a partnership, each has unlimited liability for partnership debts and other obligations. Consider the following examples:

- *The bank loan.* If the partners borrow start-up money from the bank (say $100 000 plus interest) and fail to repay it, Cameron, Adam, and Diane are liable for the full amount outstanding. This is because—like a sole proprietorship but unlike a corporation—a partnership is not legally capable of borrowing money on its own. The partners are the partnership. The partners are the debtors and are responsible for the debt.

  A very important feature of partnership law is that each partner is fully responsible for all the debts and obligations of the partnership and not just for some appropriate proportion. Accordingly, the bank can proceed against the partner with the most assets—perhaps Adam's father, Cameron—and collect from that one individual the entire amount owing on the debt. In law, this is known as **joint liability.**[4] The liability is considered to be joint because responsibility is not in relation to the partner's share in the partnership; rather, each one of the partners has full and complete exposure on each and every obligation incurred. If the bank proceeds only against Cameron for repayment of the bank loan, however, Cameron is entitled to be reimbursed by his partners for their share of the debt. Of course, if the other partners have no assets, Cameron will end up bearing the partnership debts himself.

- *The breach of contract.* If the partnership supplies defective computers to a customer, each of the partners is liable for the entire amount of the damages. The contract is between the customer, on the one hand, and all the partners, on the other.

The key point from a liability perspective is that each partner's personal assets can be seized and sold through the judicial process if the partnership assets are insufficient to satisfy partnership obligations. This legal reality should give Adam's father, Cameron, particular cause for concern. Since Cameron wants to limit his financial

joint liability
Liability shared by two or more parties where each is personally liable for the full amount of the obligation.

---

4. See, for example, *Partnership Act*, R.S.N.B. 1990, c. P-4, s. 10: every partner in a firm is liable jointly with the other partners for all debts and obligations of the firm while he is a partner.

exposure to $100 000—in part because he has a young son whom he supports—Cameron will probably not find the partnership to be a feasible business vehicle through which to bring Adam's product to market. This is because a partnership, like a sole proprietorship, puts all of Cameron's assets at risk, not just his capital contribution. Adam and Diane also have cause for concern. Though they may have less at risk they still need to consider the impact of a judgment on their assets and their future.

Profit Sharing

It is the partners themselves who decide how profits and other firm assets are to be divided. If they fail to agree on this point, partnership legislation requires them to share profits equally.[5]

Adam, Cameron, and Diane may decide to divide the partnership into unequal interests because the contribution of each partner varies. Since Adam has come up with the product and presumably will be working full time at the business, the partners may decide that he should hold a majority interest in the firm, for example, 60 percent. Diane will be contributing her expertise as well as some cash, so she may end up with 30 percent. Since Cameron is unlikely to have much involvement in the day-to-day operations and primarily will be contributing capital, his interest in the firm may be set at 10 percent. The point is that the relationship among the partners themselves—including profit sharing—is something they are free to define in any way they see fit.

Decision Making

Because a partnership comprises two or more persons pooling their resources, the management base is potentially strong. Adam's product knowledge, Diane's marketing savvy, and Cameron's general life experience will all assist in making IK Enterprises a viable operation. If one of the partners becomes sick or otherwise unable to devote sufficient attention to the business, the other partners are in place to carry on.

The downside is that managing the business will require consultation among the partners, and they may not always achieve consensus. A dispute or disagreement between the partners can be extremely disruptive. Even though the partners may have agreed in advance—through a partnership agreement—on a method of dispute resolution, such clauses can be subject to varying interpretations and can be the source of ill feeling among the partners.

Just as there is the danger of disagreement, there is also the danger of divided authority, which may impede decision making. Although the partners may have determined that they will have authority in different areas, instances are bound to arise in which responsibility overlaps. This too can result in conflict and delayed decision making.

Sources of Capital

Because a partnership is composed of two or more persons, it provides more sources of capital than the sole proprietorship. The partnership looks to each partner for a capital contribution and can rely on the creditworthiness of each one to secure financing from other sources, including the bank.

---

5. *Ibid.* s.25(a)
   The interests of partners in the partnership property and their rights and duties in relation to the partnership shall be determined, subject to any agreement express or implied between the partners, by the following rules: all partners are entitled to share equally in the capital and profits of the business, and must contribute equally towards the losses whether of capital or otherwise sustained by the firm.

Taxation

The partnership is not a separate legal entity, and therefore any income from the partnership business is allocated to the partners—on the basis of their interest in the partnership—and they must, in turn, include it on their individual tax returns.[6]

Transferability

The partnership does not provide for the ready transfer of interest from one owner to another. Partners do not individually own or have a share in specific partnership property. Each partner has an interest in all partnership property, from the photocopier to the filing cabinets to its intellectual property.

Agency and the *Partnership Act*

Partnership law is based in large part on contract law, agency law, and provincial partnership legislation, known in every jurisdiction as the *Partnership Act*.[7] The legislation in place in the common law provinces provides mandatory rules with respect to

- when a partnership exists
- what the relationship of partners is to outsiders

These acts have optional rules (i.e., the rules are subject to an agreement to the contrary) with respect to

- the relationship of partners to one another
- how and why a partnership ends

Some of these partnership concepts have already been introduced to give a sketch of how partnerships operate relative to other business vehicles. The following section describes partnerships from a more technical and detailed perspective.

When a Partnership Exists   According to the *Partnership Act*, a partnership exists when two or more people "carry on business in common with a view towards profit." The definition excludes charitable and not-for-profit endeavours. It does not, however, exclude unprofitable ventures that otherwise meet the definition of partnership so long as an intention to make a profit is present.

The statutory definition of partnership covers people who expressly intend to be partners as well as people who may not necessarily intend to be partners but act as if they were. That is, a person who conducts himself as if he were a partner—by sharing in profits, by managing the business, by contributing capital to establish a business—is a partner in the eyes of the law. Such a person, therefore, has all the rights and liabilities of a partner.

The *Partnership Act* also sets out a number of circumstances that point toward there being a partnership but not conclusively so.[8] For example, if two or more persons own property together, this does not of itself make them partners. However, if in addition to owning property together, the persons share profits associated with that property and restrict their ability to sell unilaterally their interest in the property, a court is likely to conclude that a partnership exists.[9] This would likely

6. J. Anthony VanDuzer, *The Law of Partnerships and Corporations*, 2nd. ed. (Toronto: Irwin Law, 2003) at 28.
7. Legislation is virtually identical across the common law provinces.
8. *Supra* note 4, s. 3. The legislation provides that a number of situations do not by themselves create a partnership. A relationship is not necessarily a "partnership" in the following situations: the parties jointly own property; one party receives repayment of a debt out of profits; an employment contract where remuneration varies with profits; a loan where the lender's compensation is to be a share of profits; an annuity paid out of profits to a spouse or child of a deceased partner; and receipt of a share of profits of a business paid to a vendor as consideration for the sale of a business.
9. For a discussion of the difference between partnership and mere co-ownership, see *A.E. LePage Ltd. v. Kamex Developments Ltd.* (1977), 78 D.L.R. (3d) 223 (Ont. C.A.), aff'd (1979), 105 D.L.R. (3d) 84n (S.C.C.).

be the result even though the parties have indicated in their written agreement that their relationship is not a "partnership."[10] The court will look to the essence of the relationship rather than the labels used by the parties.

This means, for example, that if Cameron wants to take an active part in the management of the business and share in the profits yet simultaneously avoid the joint, unlimited personal liability that goes with partnership, he is unlikely to succeed. If the business runs into financial difficulties, creditors can come after Cameron for the liabilities, even if Cameron has a document—signed by Diane and Adam—stating that Cameron is not a partner. In classifying Cameron's status, what matters is what Cameron actually does in relation to the business, not what a document says.

The Relationship of Partners to One Another   If Adam, Cameron, and Diane become partners, the *Partnership Act* provides that they also become one another's agents as well as the agents of the firm in matters relating to the partnership's business. This is significant because it imports the law concerning agency discussed in Chapter 13. It also means that the partners owe fiduciary duties to one another, which require a partner to put the interests of her partners above her own interests.

Accordingly, Adam cannot set up a secret business that competes with the partnership he has formed with Diane and Cameron. He cannot tell a client of the firm to buy its computer equipment from him "on the side" and then proceed to pocket the profits, or use the firm photocopier at night to run a duplicating service without his partners' permission. In short, the law does not allow a partner to make personal profit from the partnership property, to compete against the partnership, or to use a partnership opportunity for exclusive personal gain. Adam is required by law to put the interests of the partnership ahead of his own.

Persons who wish to be associated in partnership should have a partnership agreement, preferably one drafted by a lawyer; Figure 14.2 summarizes the issues that the agreement should address. The partnership agreement provides the parties with significant freedom to define their relationship. For example, a partnership agreement can provide for the division of profits among Cameron, Adam, and Diane in any proportion they see fit. If there is no agreement, the *Partnership Act* will dictate that Cameron, Adam, and Diane will share in profits equally—a result that may not be wanted nor intended.

FIGURE 14.2	
Partnership Agreement Checklist	A partnership has been described as a "marriage without love" because many of the concerns that partners face are similar to the ones faced by spouses—sharing of work, financial matters, authority to make decisions, and resolution of disputes. And just as many marriages end in divorce, so too many partnerships fail. Just as a marriage contract cannot save a bad marriage, a partnership agreement cannot guarantee a successful partnership. An agreement can, however, help in avoiding costly litigation and personal animosity if a "divorce" proves necessary.

A partnership agreement should address the following issues:

Creation of the partnership—name and address of partners; partnership name; term of partnership, if any; description of firm's business

Capital contribution—description of contribution by each partner, how shortfalls are handled, how the accounts are managed

Decision making—description of the partners' duties, any limits on authority, dispute resolution mechanism

---

10. *Lansing Building Supply (Ontario) Ltd. v. Ierullo* (1989), 71 O.R. (2d) 173 (Dist. Ct.).

Profit distribution—description of how profits are to be shared, how and when they are to be distributed, rights of withdrawal

Changes to partnership—rules for changing the relationship, admission of new partners, retirement of partners, option to purchase partner's interest, valuation of interests

Dissolution of partnership—description of what events trigger dissolution, how it will be handled, valuation of assets

A partnership agreement should also be reviewed and updated periodically to reflect changes in circumstances.

As already noted, if the partners do not have a contract or if they have a contract that is silent on some points, the *Partnership Act* of the province in which the partners are residing will govern the relationship.

Business and Legislation

The *Partnership Act:* The Relations between Partners

All of the common law provinces have a *Partnership Act* modelled on the British act of the same name.

These acts are substantially similar from province to province and have been subject to little change since their original enactments.

The acts have both mandatory and optional provisions. The mandatory provisions relate to the relationship between partners and outsiders. The optional rules with respect to the relationship between partners can therefore be varied by agreement.

In each province, the *Partnership Act* provides for the following optional rules:

1. All partners are to share equally in the capital and profits of the business and must contribute equally to the losses.
2. Property acquired for the partnership shall be used exclusively for the partnership and not for the private purposes of individual partners. Property purchased with partnership money is deemed to be partnership property.
3. A partner shall be indemnified by the other partners for any liability incurred on behalf of the partnership. This means that all partners are liable for partnership liabilities and that a partner who pays a debt is entitled to reimbursement from her partners.
4. A payment made by a partner for the purposes of the partnership in excess of his agreed subscription shall earn interest.
5. Each partner may take part in the management of the business.
6. No partner is entitled to remuneration for acting in the partnership business.
7. No new member shall be admitted to the partnership without the consent of all the partners.
8. Disputes regarding the partnership business may be decided by a majority, but the nature of the partnership may not be changed without the consent of all the members.
9. Partnership books shall be kept at the partnership's place of business, and all partners shall have access to them.
10. No simple majority may expel any partner.

Source: *Partnership Act*, R.S.N.B. 1990, c. P-4.

Relationship of Partners to Outsiders While partners are free to enter into a partnership agreement in order to set out the rights and obligations between them, this will not modify the relationship between partners and outsiders, which is governed specifically by the *Partnership Act* and generally by partnership law, including agency law.

First and foremost, a partner is an agent of the firm. She acts for herself as well as for her partners, who from the perspective of the agency relationship are her principals. For this reason, the firm is responsible for contracts she enters into with actual or apparent authority. For example, assume that Diane purchases a BlackBerry to be used for partnership business and enters into a long-term contract for wireless communication services. Assume further that Cameron and Adam are appalled, since it is not clear that a BlackBerry is needed at this point, let alone for an extended period of time. They are still bound, however, because Diane—as a partner and therefore as their agent—has the apparent authority to enter into contracts for wireless communication access for the purpose of the partnership. Between the disappointed principals (Cameron and Adam) and the wireless communication company that had no idea that Diane was entering into a contract unpopular with her partners, the law protects the wireless communication company. This is because Diane's partners are in a better position to monitor and restrict her ability to do business on behalf of the firm, even to the point of voting her out of the partnership altogether. They must, therefore, absorb the risk of her "going astray."

Indeed, because the relationship between partners is based on agreement, Diane's authority to enter into contracts on behalf of the firm can be restricted. The parties can enter into an agreement whereby Diane promises not to enter into any long-term contract without first securing her partners' approval. Diane will presumably respect and abide by this restriction. However, should she enter into a contract that exceeds her actual authority, the firm will still be bound unless the outsider knows or should know that her authority has been limited in this way. The firm is obligated by virtue of the doctrine of apparent authority.

The *Partnership Act* and agency law also make partners responsible for one another's mistakes. For example, if Adam gives poor advice to a client as to its computer systems needs and is sued for the tort of negligence, all the partners, not just Adam, are liable for any damages that result. This is because Adam was acting in the course of firm business and incurred a liability by committing a tort. He and his partners have **joint and several liability.**[11] Each partner is individually as well as collectively responsible for the entire obligation. This means that the client can recover all of the damages from any partner or he can recover some of the damages from each. A partner who pays the debt may, however, have a right of contribution from the other partners.

joint and several liability
Individual and collective liability for a debt. Each liable party is individually responsible for the entire debt as well as being collectively liable for the entire debt.

---

11. See, for example, *Partnership Act*, R.S.N.B. 1990, c. P-4, s. 13, which provides that every partner is liable jointly with co-partners and also severally for wrongful acts or omissions of a partner acting within the course of employment. The differences between joint and joint and several liability are subtle. They mainly affect the procedures for maintaining the right to sue a partner who was not originally included in a legal action. Except to this extent, the differences simply do not matter. Regardless of whether liability is joint, or joint and several, partners are both individually and to the extent of the partnership assets, accountable to third parties.

CASE ▼

3464920 Canada Inc. v. Strother, (2005) 38 B.C.L.R. (4th) 159 (C.A.).

THE BUSINESS CONTEXT: A partnership is exposed to tremendous liability as a result of the actions of one partner. The following case explores the potential liability of a law firm for the actions of one lawyer.

FACTUAL BACKGROUND: In the early 1990s, Monarch Entertainment Inc. (a numbered company, 3464920 Canada Inc. at the time of the litigation) retained Davis & Company, a Vancouver-based law firm. Robert Strother, a partner specializing in taxation, was responsible for a crucial aspect of Monarch's business—setting up tax-sheltered syndication deals to finance film productions. In 1996, Strother and Monarch signed a written agreement that included an exclusivity clause prohibiting Strother from acting for Monarch's competitors. Near the end of 1997, the federal government implemented new rules that appeared to effectively shut down the tax shelters. Strother informed Monarch that he had no "technical fix" and, acting on this advice, Monarch abandoned its tax shelter business. The agreement prohibiting Strother from acting for competitors ended in December 1997; however, Strother and Davis continued to do legal work for Monarch throughout 1998. In early 1998, Strother was approached by a former employee of Monarch, Paul Darc, who presented "a way around" the new rules. Strother agreed to prepare a tax ruling request in return for a share in the profits of the venture (called Sentinel Hill). Strother did not inform Monarch of his new client nor did he inform Monarch that there might be a way around the new rules. Strother obtained a favourable tax ruling that allowed Sentinel Hill to sell tax-sheltered limited partnerships to finance film productions. In early 1999, Strother left Davis and joined Darc as shareholder of Sentinel Hill. The venture was extremely successful, and during the period from 1998 to June 2001, Strother earned more than $32 million from

it. When Monarch discovered the Sentinel Hill tax ruling it sued both Strother and Davis for breach of fiduciary duty. At trial, Strother and Davis were successful in arguing that any obligation to keep Monarch advised of tax shelters ended when the formal agreement ended near the end of 1997. Monarch appealed

THE LEGAL QUESTION: Had Strother breached his fiduciary obligations to Monarch by failing to advise Monarch of "the way around" the tax shelter rules? If so, was Davis & Company liable for Strother's actions? Additionally, was Davis required to refund legal fees earned from acting for Monarch and Sentinel Hill?

RESOLUTION: The Court of Appeal held that Strother was in breach of his fiduciary duty to Monarch. Strother's contractual duty to advise his client may have expired at the end of 1997 but his fiduciary duties went well beyond his contractual duties. In agreeing to work with Darc, a former executive of Monarch, Strother had created a duel conflict—between Monarch and the new client, and due to his personal interest in the new venture, between himself and Monarch. The duty not to place himself in a conflict of interest and the duty to disclose any personal interest are implied by law and are unlikely to be excluded or diminished by contract. In other words, it did not matter that the written agreement had expired by the time Strother had embarked on his venture with the former executive of Monarch; he still had fiduciary obligations. Strother was ordered to disgorge his estimated $32 million profit from his involvement with Sentinel Hill.

With regards to the liability of Davis,[12] the court considered whether Davis was jointly and severally liable with Strother for the $32 million profit that Strother received and whether Davis had to account for all the profits Davis received as a result of acting for Sentinel Hills. The court held that Davis was neither directly nor vicariously liable to account for Strother's $32 million in profits. Davis was not directly liable because it did not provide "knowing assistance" to Strother in the breaching of his duty to

---

12. *3464920 Canada Inc. v. Strother* (2005), 44 B.C.L.R. (4th) 275 (C.A.).

Monarch, nor was it reckless or willfully blind to his misconduct. Davis was unaware of Strother's secret dealings with Sentinel and when informed by Strother of his "potential" involvement with Sentinel Hill, Davis expressly forbade him to go into business with Sentinel Hill. Davis was not vicariously liable because Strother was not acting in the ordinary course of the firm's business or with the authority of his partners. He was on a frolic of his own—no part of Davis's ordinary business involved taking secret interests in clients. The court also noted that generally the equitable remedy of accounting or disgorgement is not ordered against an innocent person who has not received any of the profits resulting from the wrong.

With respect to the claim for the profits Davis received in the form of legal fees from Sentinel, Davis was ordered to disgorge to Monarch the profits it earned from acting for Sentinel Hill. It was also ordered to return to Monarch the fees Monarch paid to the firm during the time Davis acted for both

Monarch and Sentinel Hill. The court held that Davis was vicariously liable for Strother's breach of fiduciary duty not to place himself in a conflict of duty. Strother was in a conflict by advising two competing clients, Sentinel Hills and Monarch. Davis was liable because advising clients is in the firm's ordinary business and no knowledge or fault on Davis' part is required for vicarious liability to apply. Strother, Davis, and Monarch are appealing the decision.[13]

CRITICAL ANALYSIS: If Monarch is successful at the Supreme Court of Canada, Davis & Company partners will be liable for damages in excess of $30 million. These damages are likely outside of insurance coverage because B.C. Law Society's professional liability insurance policy excludes from coverage a claim in connection with any organization in which a lawyer has greater than a 10 percent ownership interest at the time of the error. How should partnerships like Davis & Company manage the risk of liability for the actions of one of their partners?

How and Why a Partnership Ends   The *Partnership Act* provides for the termination of a partnership under certain circumstances:

- if entered into for a fixed term, by the expiration of the term
- if entered into for a single venture or undertaking, by the termination of that venture or undertaking
- by any partner giving notice to the others of her intention to dissolve the partnership
- following the death, insanity, or bankruptcy of a partner

Nevertheless, these provisions may be varied by agreement.[14] For example, many partnership agreements do in fact provide for the continuation of the business by the remaining partners even if the particular partnership entity is dissolved. For example, large professional partnerships—such as accounting firms and law firms—have partners joining or leaving every year. Their carefully drafted agreements generally call for an immediate transfer of all assets and liabilities from the old partnership to the new one.

On dissolution of a partnership, partnership legislation provides a process for dealing with partnership property. It must be applied in payment of the debts and liabilities of the partnership first and then to payment of what is due the partners. In the event that the partnership property is insufficient to satisfy all of the firm's obligations, partners must individually contribute to the obligations in proportion to their entitlement to profits or in another agreed-upon proportion.

---

13. Leave to appeal to the Supreme Court of Canada granted 2005 CanLii 46890 (S.C.C.). The appeal was argued in October 2006 and judgment reserved.
14. See Figure 14.2, Partnership Agreement Checklist.

After all of the firm's debts are satisfied, any excess is applied, in the following order, to

1. repayment of loans made to the firm by partners
2. repayment of capital contributed by the partners
3. payment of any surplus to partners according to their respective rights to profits.[15]

Regulations

As with sole proprietorships, there are no legal requirements for the establishment and conduct of a partnership. The partners simply begin their business activity. While a lawyer may be required to assist in the preparation of a partnership agreement, doing business through a partnership is reasonably simple and inexpensive.

FIGURE 14.3
Pros and Cons of the Partnership

Pros

Simplicity: There are few licensing and registration requirements for partnerships.

Lower costs: The fees for provincial and municipal licences tend to be small. However, a lawyer may be required to assist in drafting the partnership agreement.

Greater access to capital: The capital available to the business includes the assets of each partner and the extent of each partner's credit.

Profit motive: Any after-tax profits or other assets accrue to the partners, according to their partnership interest.

Tax benefits: Profits and losses are reported on each partner's personal income tax return, according to that person's share in the partnership. This may be favourable or unfavourable, depending on the taxpayer's circumstances.

Cons

Unlimited personal liability: Each partner carries the entire risk of the business failing. If it does, both the partnership assets and each partner's personal assets are at risk.

Loss of speed and independence: The partners must work together, and a consensus is not always achievable.

Limitations on transferability: The partner's interest in the partnership is not freely transferable.

Profit sharing: The partners must share profits equally or according to their partnership agreement.

Tax disadvantages: See tax benefits.

Partnerships are bound by all rules of general application, including the obligation to comply with laws concerning licensing, employment, tax collection, and public health, for example. Additionally, most provinces require the filing of a declaration of partnership[16] that contains information on the partners, the partnership name, and the duration of the partnership. Failure to file a declaration is not fatal, but it can impede legal actions filed in the name of the partnership and can result in fines.[17]

---

15. These provisions may be varied by agreement.
16. Ontario, British Columbia, Alberta, and New Brunswick require filing a declaration only when the partnerships involve mining, trading, and manufacturing.
17. There are variations in this area from province to province.

The risks associated with the partnership form of doing business are not insignificant. First, each partner is the agent of the partnership, meaning that each of the partners may bind the partnership when acting in the usual course of the partnership business. Second, each partner is fully liable for partnership obligations, meaning that all his personal assets may be seized to satisfy them. In addition, a partner who leaves a partnership may be liable for partnership debts incurred after he leaves if creditors are unaware of the partner's departure. Partners have both legal and practical methods of addressing liability concerns. The partnership agreement may expressly limit and control a partner's ability to bind the partnership. For example, the agreement may provide that all expenditures above a certain amount require the approval of a majority of partners. Such a measure will not be effective against third parties who are unaware of the restrictions. It will, however, provide a basis for a contractual claim by the partners against the partner who exceeded his authority.[18]

From a practical perspective, partnership risks can also be reduced by

- choosing partners with care (partner only with people who can be trusted)
- educating partners on their authority and limits, and the consequences of exceeding them
- monitoring the activities of partners to help prevent partners from overreaching their authority or entering unwanted transactions
- notifying clients and customers of the departure of partners so that the partnership cannot be held liable for debts contracted by the departed partners
- insuring against liabilities that might result from a partner's wrongdoing

CRITICAL ANALYSIS: How do the partnership variations discussed below, reduce the risks associated with a general partnership?

Partnership Variations

There are two variations on the partnership: the limited partnership and the limited liability partnership.

Limited Partnership

limited partnership
A partnership in which the liability of some partners is limited to their capital contribution.

A **limited partnership** is a partnership in which at least one partner has unlimited liability while others have limited liability. General partners have unlimited liability whereas the limited partners have a liability limited to the amount that they have contributed to the partnership capital.

This vehicle has been used mostly as an investment device. Limited partners put money into a business, such as health care (Health First Doctors' Offices) or real estate (Journey's End motels), in return for tax breaks and profits. The general partner manages the investment for a fee and carries the responsibility—assuming that the limited partners have not made guarantees or commitments beyond their investment.

This type of business entity cannot be created informally. A limited partnership requires a written agreement that must be registered with the appropriate provincial body. Without this filing, the limited partnership does not exist. The registration of the agreement is also important because it provides public notice of the capital

---

18. *Supra* note 6 at 11.

contribution of the limited partners and identifies the general partners. This, in effect, allows members of the public to decide whether they want to do business with the limited partnership.

General partners have substantially the same rights and powers as partners in ordinary partnerships; limited partners have more narrowly defined rights. They have the right to share in profits and the right to have their contribution returned on dissolution, but they cannot take part in the management of the partnership. If they do, they lose their status of limited partners and become general partners. This is a significant consequence, since it puts all their assets, not just the amount of their capital contribution, at risk should the enterprise fail. Furthermore, what constitutes partaking in management is difficult to define and can be a contentious issue. In the end, the question is resolved by courts assessing the extent and the nature of the limited partner's involvement and deciding whether, on the balance, the limited partner should lose protected status.

Because Cameron wishes to protect his assets, he might want to suggest that Adam's product be marketed through a limited partnership. The advantage is that Cameron's losses as a limited partner will be restricted to his capital investment. For example, creditors will not be able to come after his personal assets. The disadvantage is that Cameron must not take part in management or he risks unlimited personal liability.

Limited Liability Partnership

limited liability partnership (LLP)
A partnership in which the partners have unlimited liability for their own malpractice but limited liability for other partners' malpractice.

A **limited liability partnership (LLP)** is a variation on the partnership form of business. It is designed to address concerns of professionals who are not permitted to use incorporation as a means of achieving limited liability.[19] Ontario,[20] Alberta,[21] Saskatchewan,[22] Manitoba,[23] Quebec,[24] Nova Scotia,[25] New Brunswick,[26] and British Columbia[27] have amended their partnership acts to allow for this variety of partnership.

The LLP is similar to a general partnership in that all partners have unlimited liability for the ordinary contract debts of the partnership. As well, partners in an LLP continue to have liability for negligence and malpractice attributable to their own actions. The LLP is different from an ordinary partnership in that a partner is provided a "liability shield" for claims that arise from the acts or omissions of her partners so long as she is 'innocent" or "uninvolved"[28] in their wrongful acts or omissions.[29] In short, an innocent partner's personal assets cannot be seized to satisfy these claims. That said, there are, however, substantial differences in the application of the liability shield. For example, in Ontario the shield is denied to a partner responsible for supervising the person who commits the negligent act or omission. In Alberta, the benefit of the liability shield is not automatically denied a supervisor; it is denied only if the supervisor has been negligent. Also, in Alberta, the benefit of the liability shield is denied to partners who knew about the wrongful acts and did nothing about them.

---

19. Alberta Law Reform Institute, *Limited Liability Partnerships*, Report 77 (Edmonton: The Alberta Law Reform Institute, 1999) at 5.
20. S.O. 1998, c. 2 amending *Partnerships Act*, R.S.O. 1990, c. P-5.
21. S.A. 1999, c. 27 amending *Partnership Act*, R.S.A. 1980, c. P-2.
22. *Partnership Amendment Act 2001*, S.S. 2001, c. 27.
23. *Partnership Amendment and Business Names Registration Act*, S.M. 2002, c. 30.
24. *An Act to Amend the Professional Code and Other Legislative Provisions as Regards the Carrying on of Professional Activities within a Partnership or Company*, S.Q. 2002, c. 35.
25. *Partnership Act*, R.S.N.S. c. 334, ss. 48–71.
26. *Partnership Act*, R.S.N.B. c. P-4, ss 46–54
27. *Partnership Act*, R.S. B. C. 1996, c. 348, ss. 94–129.
28. What constitutes involvement for purposes of liability varies in LLP legislation. A partner may be "involved" by having supervised the person who actually committed the wrongful act.
29. Saskatchewan adopts a different approach. Partners are not provided a liability shield but rather they are personally responsible for only any partnership obligation for which they would be liable if the partnership were a corporation of which they were directors.

The LLP may be used for the purpose of practising a profession (for example, accounting or law), provided the statute governing the profession expressly permits its members to practise using this vehicle. An LLP must include the words "limited liability partnership" or its abbreviation "LLP" in the partnership name. Also the legislation may require professionals to have liability insurance to help ensure victims will be compensated for losses from wrongful acts.

Business Application of the Law

Becoming a Limited Liability Partnership

Limited liability partnerships for eligible professions are permitted in most provinces and many large accounting and law firms—Torys LLP, Ogilvy Renault LLP, Deloitte LLP, Grant Thornton LLP, for example—have registered as limited liability partnerships. The procedure to change the status of a partnership from general to "limited liability" is straightforward and generally involves the following:

- preparation of a written agreement indicating that all partners agree to the change in status

- registration of a partnership name that includes the words "limited liability partnership" or the abbreviation LLP or L.L.P with the appropriate companies office

- confirmation of eligibility to practice as a LLP from the appropriate professional body

- certificate of insurance indicating that the partnership has liability insurance

- registration of the LLP agreement, confirmation of eligibility, and certificate of insurance with appropriate government office along with the payment of a registration fee

- notification to clients of LLP status (some provinces require notification in writing; others permit a notice in a newspaper)

CRITICAL ANALYSIS: What are the arguments for changing from a general partnership to a LLP? What are the arguments against changing from a general partnership to a LLP?

The Corporation

The corporation is the most important form of business organization today. Chapters 15 and 16 explore the corporation in detail, including its formation, operation, and termination. The purpose of this section is to provide a brief account of the corporation for the purpose of contrasting it with the other business vehicles already discussed.

Financial Liability

shareholder

A person who has an ownership interest in a corporation.

director

A person elected by shareholders to manage a corporation.

The corporation is the safest vehicle that Adam, Cameron, and Diane could choose to conduct their business because a corporation is a distinct legal entity in law and is therefore capable of assuming its own obligations. Adam, Cameron, and Diane can participate in the profits of the corporation as **shareholders** and manage its operations as **directors.**

Consider the following examples:

■ THE BANK LOAN. If Adam, Cameron, and Diane form a corporation, the corporation has the legal capacity to borrow the necessary start-up capital. This means that the corporation promises to repay the loan with interest, making the corporation, and no other entity, the debtor.

If the corporation cannot repay the loan, the bank will take the necessary steps to recover as much as it can from the corporation to make up the full amount owing. The bank will be in a position to seize anything owned by the corporation. However, the bank will not be able to seize assets belonging to Adam, Cameron, and Diane. Even though they have a close relationship to the corporation as its three shareholders, they did not promise to repay the loan. That commitment came from the corporation alone. Put another way, the corporation, not the shareholders, is the debtor.

There is an important proviso to this analysis, which concerns guarantees.[30] When a corporation does not have an established track record of creditworthiness and perhaps holds few assets, the bank will seek personal guarantees from those involved in the corporation, such as the shareholders. There is a very strong possibility that when Diane, Cameron, and Adam approach the bank for a loan to the corporation, the bank will agree only if the three provide personal guarantees. A personal guarantee means that if the corporation fails to meet its obligation to the bank, Diane, Cameron, and Adam will be held responsible for that default. Then, as with a partnership or sole proprietorship, all their personal assets will be at risk. At such a point, it becomes irrelevant that a corporation is a separate legal entity capable of assuming its own obligations. Diane, Cameron, and Adam would have no more protection than if they had proceeded by way of a partnership.

- **THE BREACH OF CONTRACT.** If the corporation supplies defective computers to a customer, it is the corporation and no other entity that is in breach of contract. It is the corporation that will be sued, and it is the corporate assets that are at risk.[31]

Again, recall the discussion of guarantees. Any entity that deals with a corporation may demand the personal guarantee of the corporation's shareholders or directors.

limited liability
Responsibility for obligations restricted to the amount of investment.

The key characteristic of a corporation is that it provides **limited liability** to its shareholders. That is, should the corporation's financial health take a bad turn, the shareholder's loss is limited to what she paid to purchase shares in the corporation. Unless, in addition, the shareholder provided a personal guarantee, she has absolutely no liability for the corporation's obligations, however they were incurred.[32]

Profit Sharing

Profits of the corporation are distributed to shareholders through dividends. That is, shareholders are paid a return on their investment in the corporation, but only if there is profit, and only if the directors declare a **dividend.**

dividend
A division of profits payable to shareholders.

The corporate form of business organization is inherently flexible from an investment perspective, because it permits varying degrees of ownership and various means for sharing profits.

Decision Making

The corporation is managed by a board of directors, which in turn is elected by the shareholders.

---

30. See Chapter 26 for a discussion of guarantees.
31. Of course, if an employee of the corporation misrepresented the product or committed a tort of some description, that employee would be liable. This is a matter distinct from the contractual liability of the corporation. See Chapter 16.
32. Only in rare situations, such as fraud on the creditors, will the courts hold the shareholders personally responsible for the corporation's actions. See Chapter 16.

In addition, officers—that is, high-ranking corporate employees—can be hired by the board to assist in running the corporation. This provides a broad management base that allows the corporation to benefit from specialized and top-level expertise. However, it can also result in layers of authority that can delay decision making.

Sources of Capital

A corporation can get its capital in two ways: it can borrow, or its directors can issue shares. The purchase price of the shares is an important and potentially large source of capital for the corporation. A share represents an equity position in the corporation and provides the shareholder with the chance of making a profit through the declaration of dividends, which it is hoped will be greater than the interest rate the shareholder would have received had he simply lent the money. The disadvantage is that if the corporation fails, the shareholder is left with nothing while the creditor technically retains the right to be repaid. However, if the corporation is insolvent, that right is of little value.

Because the principle of limited liability protects investors against unlimited losses, the corporation is well suited to raise large amounts of capital.

Corporations that offer their shares to the public must publish information concerning their finances; this makes the corporation subject to greater outside scrutiny than the partnership or sole proprietorship.

Taxation

Because it is a separate legal entity, a corporation pays its own taxes. In other words, the income of the corporation is subject to taxation quite apart from the taxation of its owners. A shareholder of a corporation will be taxed if she earns a salary from the corporation, receives a dividend from it, or realizes a capital gain from the sale of her shares. Advantages in the form of reduced or deferred taxes may sometimes be gained through the appropriate splitting of distributions to shareholders between dividend and salary payments. For example, Cameron could take a salary from the corporation and his son could receive income through dividends. This may produce a more favourable tax treatment than if Cameron took both a salary and dividend payments himself. The ultimate effect of this kind of income splitting depends on a variety of factors, including the corporate tax rate and the marginal tax rate of the shareholder and employee. It is significant that the partnership and sole proprietorship enjoy no such options, since all income from the business is taxed at personal rates.

Transferability

The fact that a corporation has a separate legal identity often allows for easy transference of an ownership interest represented by shares. A shareholder can sell or bequeath his shares with no interference from corporate creditors because the shareholder has no liability for corporate debts. The shares belong to him and he can do what he wants with them. Transferability is, however, subject to restrictions in the corporation's incorporating documents and may also be restricted by a shareholders' agreement.

Perpetual Existence

Because the corporation exists independently of its shareholders, the death or bankruptcy of one or more shareholders does not affect the existence of the corporation. The corporation continues in existence perpetually unless it is dissolved by order of a court, for failure to comply with statutory regulations, or through a voluntary surrender of its legal status to the government.

Regulations

Like sole proprietorships and partnerships, a corporation must comply with laws of general application.

Most significantly, however, the corporation comes into existence only if proper documents are submitted to the government and it issues, in return, a certificate of incorporation. Thus, it is almost always more expensive to organize a corporation than a sole proprietorship or partnership because there are legal bills and additional filing fees to pay. As well, there are extensive rules contained in corporations statutes that govern many corporate decisions and result in the need for considerable record keeping. These extra requirements and expenses, however, can be more than offset by the protection provided to investors by the principle of limited liability.

FIGURE 14.4

Pros and Cons of the Corporation

Pros

Limited liability: Because it is a separate legal entity, a corporation can assume its own liabilities. The shareholder stands to lose the amount he invested in the corporation, but no more.

Flexibility: A corporation permits differing degrees of ownership and sharing in profits.

Greater access to capital: Limited liability makes the corporation a very suitable vehicle through which to raise capital.

Continuous existence: The life span of a corporation is not tied to its shareholders.

Tax benefits: Though this is a fact-specific issue, a corporation can facilitate greater tax planning, for example, by permitting income splitting.

Transferability: Ownership in a corporation is more easily transferable through shares.

Potentially broad management base: A corporation is managed by directors and officers, who can provide a level of specialized expertise to the corporation.

Cons

Higher costs: Creating a corporation incurs filing fees and legal costs.

Public disclosure: When a corporation offers shares to the public, the corporation must comply with strict disclosure and reporting requirements.

Greater regulation: Corporation statutes govern many decisions, which limits management options and requires specific kinds of record keeping.

Dissolution: Ending a corporation's life can be complicated.

Tax disadvantages: A corporation may be subject to double taxation, depending on the circumstances. This is a fact-specific issue.

Possible loss of control: A corporation has diminished control because it issues shares with voting rights.

Potential bureaucracy: The many levels of authority in a corporation may impede decision making.

FIGURE 14.5

A Comparison of Major Forms of Organizations*

Characteristic	Sole Proprietorship	Partnership	Corporation
Creation	• at will of owner	• by agreement or conduct of the parties	• by incorporation documents
Duration	• limited by life of owner	• terminated by agreement, death	• perpetual unless dissolved
Liability of owners	• unlimited	• unlimited	• limited
Taxation	• net income taxed at personal rate	• net income taxed at personal rate	• income taxed to the corporation; dividends and salary taxed to shareholders
Transferability	• only assets may be transferred	• transferable by agreement	• transferable unless incorporating documents restrict transferability
Management	• owner manages	• all partners manage equally unless otherwise specified in agreement	• shareholders elect a board to manage the affairs of the corporation; officers can also be hired

These are the legal differences between the major business forms. In practice, however, there are ways of minimizing the consequences of these differences. Whether one form of business organization or another is chosen will depend on individual circumstances. As with all other legal concerns, legal, accounting, and management advice should be sought in order to make an informed decision.

Business Arrangements

The preceding sections introduced the basic forms of business organizations. Subject to some specialized exceptions, such as real estate investment trusts and mutual funds, every business will use one of these forms.

There are additional ways to carry on the business activity itself. These ways are not distinct business organizations but are, for the lack of a more accurate term, arrangements. These arrangements do not have any strict legal meaning as such; most commonly they refer to some sort of contractual commitment between two or more business organizations. These relationships are important from a legal perspective because they involve agency principles and fiduciary duties in addition to contractual obligations.

Adam, for example, may not be able to raise the capital necessary to manufacture and sell his product. He may then decide to license rights in his product or he may enter an arrangement with another business to sell his product. Adam's business may be very successful and he may want to expand his business. One option is to grow internally by opening new branches, expanding existing branches, and hiring new employees. He may, however, for many reasons decide to enter an arrangement with another entity. Adam may want to capitalize on the goodwill he has developed in his business, or another organization may more easily be able to penetrate a market, or he may simply feel that he does not have the time and expertise needed to handle an internal expansion. The following section explores the range of options open to entrepreneurs like Adam.

franchise
An agreement whereby an owner of a trademark or trade name permits another to sell a product or service under that trademark or name.

The Franchise

A **franchise** is a contractual arrangement between a manufacturer, wholesaler, or service organization (franchisor) and an independent business (franchisee), who buys the right to own and operate one or more units of the franchise system.

Franchise organizations are normally based on some unique product, service, or method of doing business; on a trade name or patent; or on goodwill that the franchisor has developed.

Almost every kind of business has been franchised—motels, fast food restaurants, dental centres, hair salons, maid services, and fitness centres, to name a few. Some familiar examples are Pizza Hut, 7-Eleven, McDonald's, Subway, Molly Maid, Magicuts, and Curves. Adam, too, could potentially franchise his business if it is successful.

Franchising involves a contract between the franchisor and the franchisee. Wide variations exist in franchise agreements, but generally they cover arrangements regarding such matters as how the business is to be run, where supplies may or must be purchased, royalty levels to be paid to the franchisor for sharing its business operation plan and other benefits, and charges for management, advertising, and other corporate services. The agreement negotiated depends on the relative bargaining power of the parties and the issues brought to the table. Usually, however, the franchisor, having a great deal more information about the business, is in the better position to negotiate an advantageous agreement or to insist on the use of a standard form contract.[33]

The Franchise Relationship

The relationship between a franchisor and a franchisee is one of contract. The contractual relationship is governed by the general principles of contract. In Alberta,[34] Ontario,[35] and Prince Edward Island,[36] the general principles are augmented by specific franchise legislation. The legislation is designed to provide protection for franchisees.

What legal factors are important to the success of a franchise?

---

33. See Chapter 5 for a discussion of the role of bargaining power and standard form contracts.
34. *Franchises Act*, R.S.A. 2000, c. F-23. Alberta's legislation was first enacted in 1971 and substantially revised in 1995.
35. *Arthur Wishart Act (Franchise Disclosure)*, 2000, S.O. 2000, c. 3.
36. *Franchises Act*, R.S.P.E.I 1998, c. F-14.1. The legislation was enacted in 2005 and partially proclaimed in force on 1 July 2006. The disclosure provisions came into force on 1 January 2007.

Business and Legislation

Prince Edward Island's Franchise Legislation

In 2005, Prince Edward Island, following the lead of Alberta and Ontario, became the third Canadian province to enact franchise legislation. New Brunswick has introduced a franchise bill that has passed first reading and is now subject to public consultation.[37] All four statutes are essentially the same but there are differences in some details. The basic elements of the PEI statute are a definition of franchise, disclosure requirements of the franchiser, a duty of good faith and fair dealing on all parties to the franchise agreement, and a right of association for the franchisee.

Definition of franchise: The definition of franchise is very broad and captures both the "business format" franchise such as fast food outlets and "business opportunities" arrangements such as vending machines. In short, the definition captures not only traditional franchise operations but also distributorships and other arrangements that have not been traditionally thought of as franchises. This means that many businesses may be operating a franchise system without realizing it.

Disclosure requirements: Franchisors are required to deliver a disclosure document to prospective franchisees 14 days prior to the franchisee entering into binding agreements or paying money.[38] The disclosure requirements set out in the regulations require the franchisor to disclose all material facts relating to the franchise. The disclosure document must contain (among other information) the business background of the franchisor, its finances, its bankruptcy and solvency history, the franchisee's expected costs of establishing the franchise and contact particulars for both current and former franchisees.

Franchisees have the right to rescind or cancel the franchise agreement within certain time periods if they do not receive a disclosure document or if they receive it late. In such cases, they are entitled to receive everything they paid for the franchise, as well as compensation for any losses incurred. In addition, the franchisee has a right of action for damages where it suffers a loss because of a misrepresentation contained in the disclosure document or as a result of a franchisor's failure to comply with its disclosure obligations.

Fair dealing and good faith: Parties to a franchise agreement have a duty of fair dealing in the performance and enforcement of the agreement. The duty of fair dealing includes a duty to act in good faith and in accordance with reasonable commercial standards. This means, in effect, that both the franchiser and the franchisee have at least the obligation to consider the interests of the other in making decisions and exercising discretion. The act also establishes a right to sue for the breach of the duty.

Right of association: Franchisees have the right to associate with one another and form or join an organization of franchisees. Franchisors may not interfere, either directly or indirectly, with the exercise of this right. The franchisee has a right of action for damages for contravention of this section.

CRITICAL ANALYSIS: Franchise legislation has substantially increased the duties and obligations of the franchiser and the remedies available to the franchisee. What does this mean from a practical perspective for the franchiser?

Source: Suzanne Rent, "Prince Edward Island and New Brunswick Create Franchise Legislation" *The Lawyer's Weekly* (3 February 2006) at 6.

The relationship between a franchisor and a franchisee does not normally create fiduciary obligations.[39] However, the legislation imposes on the parties a duty of good faith and fair dealing in the performance and enforcement of the franchise agreement. The courts have also adopted this concept at common law.

---

37. The Uniform Law Commission of Canada has also adopted similar model franchise legislation.
38. There are a number of exemptions from the disclosure requirements under the legislation. For example, there is an exemption from providing financial statements for larger franchisors.
39. *Jirna Limited v. Mister Donut of Canada Ltd.,* [1975] 1 S.C.R. 2.

CASE ▼

Shelanu Inc. v. Print Three Franchising Corporation (2003), 64 O.R. (3d) 533 (C.A.).

THE BUSINESS CONTEXT: Franchise legislation specifies that the parties to a franchise agreement owe each other a duty of fair dealing, which includes the duty to act in good faith and in accordance with reasonable commercial standards. The following case[40] confirms the applicability of the duty of fair dealing to franchise relationships at common law and explores the scope of that duty.

FACTUAL BACKGROUND: In 1987, BCD Print Inc, a corporation owned by Brian Deslauriers, purchased a print store franchise from Print Three Corporation. In 1989, Deslauriers and his wife purchased Shelanu Inc, which operated two Print Three stores. In 1990, Print Three set up a new business, Le Print Express, composed of small print outlets targeted at individuals and small businesses. Print Three franchises targeted a commercial and higher-volume clientele. In 1991, Shelanu, with the concurrence of Print Three, closed one of its stores. In 1995, Print Three and BCD orally agreed that BCD could close its store and combine its operations with the remaining Shelanu store (this would mean that by reporting its sales as a single franchise, Shelanu would be entitled to a higher royalty rebate). Also around this time a dispute arose between Print Three and some of its franchisees including Shelanu, about the expenditure of advertising fees on the Air Miles advertising program (some franchisees were opposed to spending all the advertising fees on a program where not all the benefits would be capable of being used for their businesses). The relationship between Print Three and Shelanu deteriorated, and Print Three denied the termination of the BCD store and continued to treat the operation as two stores for royalty purposes. Shelanu brought an action alleging that Print Three stores had failed to make royalty payments in accordance with the oral agreement,

had unilaterally changed the terms of the Air Miles program (rather than distributing unused Air Miles to the franchisees for their benefit, took control of Air Miles not distributed to customers), and had established another system of retail printing stores that competed with its existing franchises.

THE LEGAL QUESTION: Do the parties to a franchise agreement owe each other a duty of good faith? If so, has Print Three breached the duty?

RESOLUTION: The Court of Appeal upheld the trial court's recognition of the existence of a common law duty of good faith in franchise agreements. The court determined that a duty of good faith applies to franchise relationships because franchisees do not usually have equal bargaining power; franchise agreements are not freely negotiated but are drawn up by the franchisor and imposed on the franchisee, and the franchisor remains in a dominant position throughout the relationship. The court also opined that the franchise relationship is not a fiduciary relationship. The duty of good faith requires that a franchisor give due consideration to the franchise's interests in exercising its powers and discretions, but it is not required to favour a franchisee's interests over its own. The court upheld the trial judge's finding that there had been a breach of the duty of good faith with respect to the payment of royalty rebates and acting unreasonably with respect to the

What are some specific ways franchisors can comply with the duty of good faith?

---

40. This case was decided pursuant to the common law. The court of appeal held that Ontario's franchise legislation did not apply because conduct complained of occurred prior to the legislation coming into force. Also note that the summary below deals only with the good faith issue.

Joint Venture

joint venture

A grouping of two or more businesses to undertake a particular project.

A **joint venture** is an association of business entities—corporations, individuals, or partnerships—that unite for the purpose of carrying on a business venture. Normally the parties agree to share profits and losses and management of the project. The key feature of a joint venture is that it is usually limited to a specific project or to a specific period of time. For example, several oil and gas companies may join for offshore exploration in a certain region, or a steel fabricator may combine with a construction company to refurbish a nuclear plant. Adam could conceivably enter into a joint venture with another entity for purposes of marketing and selling his product to a particular event such as an international trade show.

The joint venture itself can take a variety of forms. The joint venture may be a partnership, in which case all the legal consequences associated with a partnership apply. It may also be what is known as an equity joint venture. This is when the parties incorporate a separate corporation for the project and each party holds shares in that corporation, in which case the consequences of incorporation apply. A joint venture also may be simply a contractual arrangement between the parties. In such a case, the contract may spell out the nature of the relationship between the parties. Also, the law can impose duties on the parties beyond those specified in the contract.[41] Most significantly, parties to a joint venture can be held to owe fiduciary duties to one another in relation to the activities of the joint venture.

Strategic Alliance

strategic alliance

An arrangement whereby two or more businesses agree to cooperate for some purpose

A **strategic alliance** is a cooperative arrangement among businesses. It is an arrangement that may involve joint research, technology sharing, or joint use of production, for example.[42] Toshiba, a Japanese electronics company, has alliances with many companies to develop new products, such as mobile telecommunication equipment and computer chips. Adam could form a strategic alliance with another entity to do joint research into applications of his voice-recognition product.

Like a joint venture, a strategic alliance does not have a precise legal meaning. The underlying relationship between the parties is normally contractual. The contract or a series of contracts will spell out the parties' rights and obligations including whether or not they are agents for each other. Whether the parties to a strategic alliance owe fiduciary obligations to each other is unclear.

---

41. *Supra* note 6 at 69.
42. The term "strategic alliance" is sometimes used to include joint ventures. There is little precision in terminology in this area. The key point is that terms usually describe a contractual arrangement between two or more parties.

Distributorship or Dealership

distributorship
A contractual relationship where one business agrees to sell another's products

A product or service **distributorship** is very much like a franchise. A contract is entered into whereby a manufacturer agrees to provide products and the distributor or dealer agrees to carry products or perform services prescribed by the manufacturer. This kind of arrangement is often encountered in the automotive and computer industries. Rather than selling his product himself, Adam could engage a distributor or dealer to sell his products.

The relationship between the parties is governed by the contract. There are no fiduciary obligations owed by the parties to each other beyond those spelled out in the contract. As well, a distributorship does not normally involve an agency relationship. In fact, the contract may specify that the distributorship is not an agency.

Sales Agency

sales agency
An agreement in which a manufacturer or distributor allows another to sell products on its behalf

A **sales agency** relationship is usually an arrangement whereby a manufacturer or distributor contracts with an agent to sell goods or services supplied by the manufacturer or distributor on a principal/agent basis.[43] The agent is not the actual vendor but acts on behalf of a principal, who is the owner of the goods or services. As this relationship is one of agency, fiduciary obligations are owed. This arrangement is often encountered in the travel and insurance industries.

International Perspective — Going Global

Strategic alliances are one of the leading business strategies of the 21st century. They take many forms: from simple market exchanges or cross-licensing agreements to complex cooperative-manufacturing arrangements or joint-equity ventures. Strategic alliances can help firms lower costs, exploit each other's specialized skills, fund costly research and development efforts, and expand into foreign markets. Using a strategic alliance to access a foreign market usually involves "partnering" with a "local" to take advantage of his familiarity with the social, cultural, legal, and other conditions in the market. There can also be a host of other advantages to this business arrangement including sharing costs and risks with the local partner, avoiding import restrictions and other trade barriers, and meeting the host country's requirements for local ownership.

CRITICAL ANALYSIS: What are the risks associated with using a strategic alliance to access a foreign market? Why would a country require that a foreign business have local participation? Can you think of any legal reasons?

Product Licensing

product licensing
An arrangement whereby the owner of a trademark or other proprietary right, grants to another the right to manufacture or distribute products associated with the trademark or other proprietary right

In this arrangement, the licensee is granted the right to manufacture and distribute products associated with the licensor's trademarks or other proprietary rights, usually within a defined geographic area. Licensing is common for many consumer goods such as clothing, sporting goods, and merchandise connected to the entertainment industry. Assuming Adam obtains rights such as a patent for his product, he could license these rights to another. Rather than doing the manufacturing and selling himself, he could license the rights in return for royalties. The relationship

---

43. See Chapter 13 for a discussion of the duties and liabilities of agents.

between the parties is contractual, and the agreement usually covers such matters as the granting of rights, the obligations of the parties, the term of the agreement, and fees and royalties. This arrangement is explored in more depth in Chapter 18.

Business Law in Practice Revisited

1. What forms of business organization are available for carrying on Adam's business?

Adam may carry on his business as a sole proprietorship, in partnership with others, or through a corporation.

2. What are the major considerations in choosing a particular form?

Adam's father, Cameron, is willing to invest in the business but is unwilling to accept risk beyond his investment. This consideration eliminates an ordinary partnership, as it would expose him to additional risk. A limited partnership is a possibility. However, Cameron would not be able to partake in the management of the organization. If he did, he could lose his limited liability status. As Adam is young and presumably inexperienced, he might want to be able to seek the assistance of his father. A sole proprietorship exposes only Adam to unlimited liability; however, if Cameron participates in profits and management, there is a risk of an "unintended" partnership. Thus, it would seem that the most viable alternative is a corporation with Cameron investing his money in shares. This alternative limits his exposure to risk and also allows for his potential participation in profits.

Diane is interested in taking a role in the management of the venture, as well as in investing a sum of money. These considerations could be accommodated within a partnership agreement, although it may be difficult to agree on the valuation of her time and expertise, as she will not be working full time on the project. As well, she may be averse to the risks associated with a partnership. The other option is a corporation with Diane investing in shares. This would allow her to participate in profits as a means of compensation for her services. A contractual arrangement to compensate her for her services may not be viable, as Adam probably does not have the means to pay her.

3. Which form is best for Adam's business?

For the reasons given above, a corporation may be the most appropriate, but the success of Adam's business is not dependent on the form chosen. Much more important is the viability of his idea and his ability to bring it to fruition.

Chapter Summary

Most businesses are carried on using one of the basic forms—sole proprietorship, partnership (or one of its variations), or corporation. These forms have varying characteristics, most notably with respect to the exposure to liability. Sole proprietorships and partnerships expose their owners to personal liability for the business obligations. A corporation, on the other hand, has the attraction of limited liability for the owners—their liability is limited to the amount of their investment. This characteristic, however, can be neutralized. For example, a sole proprietor can escape the effects of unlimited liability by transferring assets to a relative prior to commencing business. As well, the advantage of limited liability in the corporate form can become meaningless if creditors insist on a personal guarantee from the owners of the corporation.

Each form has other advantages and disadvantages. The form chosen for a business enterprise depends on an evaluation of numerous factors such as investors' aversion to risk, their desire to earn profits, and their wish to participate in decision making. In short, the best form for a particular situation depends on all the circumstances.

A partnership is the form most often found in the professions. This is due, in part, to prohibitions against some professionals incorporating. A partnership subjects the partners to unlimited liability. The other defining feature of a partnership is agency—a partner is an agent for other partners and for the partnership. The effects of agency between the partners can be modified by a partnership agreement; however, the effects of agency in relation to outsiders cannot, and are governed by the *Partnership Act*.

A business may also at some point enter into an arrangement with another entity for carrying out business activities. The various arrangements are all based on a contract negotiated between the parties. Regardless of the arrangement entered into, the business still needs to be carried on using one of the basic business forms.

It is important to remember that it is the viability of the business itself that is critical, not necessarily the form of the business or the particular arrangements made. Put another way, a business does not succeed because it chooses a franchise arrangement over a distributorship. The key to a successful business is having a solid business plan that is well executed.

Chapter Study

Key Terms and Concepts

director (p. 332)

distributorship (p. 341)

dividend (p. 333)

franchise (p. 336)

joint and several liability (p. 326)

joint liability (p. 321)

joint venture (p. 340)

limited liability (p. 333)

limited liability partnership (LLP) (p. 331)

limited partnership (p. 330)

partnership (p. 320)

product licensing (p. 341)

sales agency (p. 341)

shareholder (p. 332)

sole proprietorship (p. 317)

strategic alliance (p. 340)

unlimited liability (p. 318)

Questions for Review

1. Define sole proprietorship, partnership, and corporation.

2. What are the advantages and disadvantages of a sole proprietorship?

3. How is a sole proprietorship created?

4. What are the advantages and disadvantages of a partnership?

5. How can a partnership come into existence?

6. Does the sharing of profits result in the creation of a partnership? Explain.

7. How can a partnership come to an end?

8. How can the risks of the partnership form be managed?

9. What is the difference between a general and a limited partner?

10. Explain the difference between a limited partnership and a limited liability partnership.

11. What are the advantages and disadvantages of the corporate form?

12. How is a corporation created?

13. What is the difference between a business form and a business arrangement?

14. What is the basis of a franchise? What is the relationship between parties to a franchise agreement?

15. How does franchise legislation change the relationship between a franchiser and a franchisee?

16. Is a joint venture a partnership? Explain.

17. What is the difference between a joint venture and a strategic alliance?

18. Is a distributor an agent? Explain.

Questions for Critical Thinking

1. What kinds of business activities are particularly well suited to the following arrangements: franchise, joint venture, strategic alliance, distributorship, product licensing agreement, and sales agency? What are the legal considerations in entering into these arrangements?

2. Many people think of franchising as a quick and easy way to start their own business. Indeed, some buyers have experienced almost instant success, but far more have experienced dismal failure. It is estimated that about 20 percent of all franchises fail within the first three to five years. The key to success is often the choice of franchise and the franchise package, or contractual arrangement. What should the franchise contract contain? What issues should it address?

3. The limited liability partnership is a response to concerns about professionals' exposure to liability for their partners' malpractice. What is the nature of the liability created by the partnership form? How does the creation of an LLP address this liability concern? Is it appropriate that accountants and lawyers, for example, enjoy limited liability? Is there a downside for a law or accounting firm to converting to an LLP?

4. What are the circumstances in which a partnership may be found to exist? What steps can be taken to avoid a finding of partnership? How can the consequences of being found a partner be minimized?

5. In *Shelanu v. Three Print*, the Ontario Court of Appeal held that franchisors owe a duty of good faith to franchisees. What factors led the court to this conclusion? In what other contractual relationships might one party owe the other party a duty of good faith? What does "good faith" mean? How can franchisors comply with good faith obligations?

6. The three basic business forms are sole proprietorship, partnership, and corporation. How is each formed? How is each owned? How does each form allocate the risk associated with doing business?

Situations for Discussion

1. Michael Wright, Kyle Wright, and William Wright are farmers. Michael and Kyle are brothers and William is their father. All three farmers have cattle ranches and William has a grain operation. Each farmer keeps his own books of account, prepares his own income tax return, and maintains his own bank account. With regard to the cattle operations, each farmer has his own herd of cattle, which he individually markets. The cattle are fed and pastured together without regard to the source of the feed, and the farmers share machinery and labour. Some of the land is registered to the men individually and some is registered in the names of all three farmers. With regard to the grain operations, William is responsible for all aspects including crop rotation, seed selection, and fertilizer purchases. Michael and Kyle are not involved in the grain cultivation and do not receive any gross or net profit from the grain operation. They are, however, allowed to share in the crops by way of cattle feed.[44] Are Michael,

---

44. Based, in part, on *Redfern Farm Services Ltd. v. Wright*, 2006 MBQB 4 (CanLII).

Kyle, and William partners? What factors do the courts consider in determining whether a partnership exists? What are the consequences of a finding that there is a partnership relationship?

2. Edie, Alma, and Tim established a restaurant called EATs. Edie, a retired teacher, invested $20 000 in the venture, and Alma and Tim each invested $10 000. Edie, Alma, and Tim do not have a formal agreement concerning the allocation of responsibilities, but they each take turns doing the cooking. The serving and cleanup tasks are done by staff. One day, while Edie was doing the cooking, Juan got food poisoning from the food. Juan intends to sue EATS, Edie, Alma, and Tim for damages of $100 000. If Juan is successful, how will the damages be allocated among the parties? If the restaurant was incorporated under EATS Inc. and Edie owns 50 percent of the shares, Alma owns 25 percent, and Tim owns 25 percent, how would the damages be allocated? What do these two situations illustrate about risk?

3. Rocco wanted to start a magazine catering to the alternative music scene. He first incorporated a company called Onedge Magazine Inc. with himself as an employee. He then had Onedge enter into a limited partnership with him and several other individuals who were willing to finance the magazine. Rocco and the financiers were limited partners, and Onedge was the general partner. Klipper supplied printing services to the partnership for the production of the magazine but was not paid. He sued Rocco.[45] What factors determine the liability of Rocco? Are Rocco's actions, in arranging his business affairs, unethical?

4. Review *3464920 Canada Inc. v. Strother* on page 327. At the time of the dispute between Monarch, Strother and Davis & Company, Davis operated as a general partnership. It became possible for a British Columbia law firm to become a limited liability partnership (LLP) only in 2005. At that time Davis, along with many other B.C. firms, became an LLP. Assume that Davis was an LLP at the time of the dispute with Monarch. How would being a member of an LLP affect Strother's personal liability to Monarch? How would Davis being an LLP affect the liability of the other partners? How do you think the LLP structure affects the relationship between a law firm and its clients? How do you think the LLP structure affects the relationship between lawyers within a law firm?

5. Roj and Maki purchased a fast-food franchise located in a shopping mall. They signed a standard form contract and paid a $50 000 initiation fee. After they took possession, problems developed; sales were well below what Roj and Maki thought they would be and well below what the franchisor implied they would be.[46] Do they have any cause of action against the franchisor? What additional information would be useful? What are the legal risks associated with "purchasing" a franchise? How can the risks be managed?

6. Ken, a recent graduate of a professional accounting program, formed a partnership with a classmate, Lloyd, to provide various accounting services to small and medium-sized businesses. Lloyd made a serious error in the preparation and presentation of a cash budget to a client. Ken is wondering about his responsibility for Lloyd's mistakes.[47] In particular, if Ken compensates the client for all losses, can he claim reimbursement from Lloyd? Would the answer be the same if Ken and Lloyd had several other partners? How should losses between partners be dealt with? How should Ken manage the risks associated with the partnership form of carrying on a business?

7. Thomas, a young entrepreneur, started a construction business. Ari, who owned and operated an ethnic radio station, agreed to run some advertisements for him. Unfortunately, Thomas was unable to pay Ari for the services. In the hopes of making the business profitable so that

---

45. Based on *Haughton Graphic Ltd. v. Zivot* (1986), 33 B.L.R. 125 (Ont H.C.), aff'd (1988), 38 B.L.R. xxxii (Ont. C.A.), leave to appeal refused (1988), 38 B.L.R. xxxii (S.C.C.).
46. Based on *447927 Ontario Inc. v. Pizza Pizza Ltd.* (1987), 62 O.R. (2d) 114 (H.C.), aff'd by (1990), 72 O.R. (2d) 704 (C.A.).
47. Based, in part, on *MacDonald v. Schmidt*, [1992] B.C.J. No. 230 (S.C.) (QL).

he could get payment under the broadcasting contract, Ari, without remuneration, assisted Thomas in his business. In fact, Ari signed a contract with Lopez on behalf of Thomas for plumbing and heating supplies. When payment for the supplies was not forthcoming, Lopez sued Ari, claiming that Ari was a partner of Thomas and was therefore responsible for the debt. Ari claimed that when he signed he was acting as Thomas's agent.[48] What difference does it make whether Ari is considered to be Thomas's agent or his partner? What factors are important in determining the nature of a relationship between individuals?

8. Jillie is a young entrepreneur who has invented a skateboard that can be used on a variety of surfaces including gravel, pavement, snow, and ice. To take advantage of a government program to create jobs, she has established a manufacturing facility in Quebec. However, she wants to sell her product across Canada and in other countries such as Sweden and Finland that have climates similar to Canada's. Jillie has located Spencer, an experienced salesperson, to help her achieve her sales targets in Canada, but she is unsure about how to access foreign markets. How should Jillie structure her relationship with Spencer? What are the options? What are the advantages and disadvantages of each? How can Jillie establish a presence in countries such as Sweden and Finland?

For more study tools, visit
http://www.businesslaw3e.nelson.com

---

48. Based, in part, on *Lampert Plumbing (Danforth) Ltd. v. Agathos*, [1972] 3 O.R. 11 (Ont. Co. Ct.).

Chapter

15

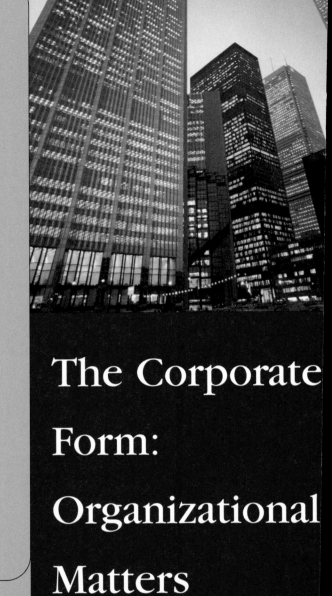

Objectives

After studying this chapter, you should have an understanding of

- a corporation as a legal person
- the distinction between federal and provincial incorporation
- the share structure of a corporation
- the selection of a corporation's name
- how a corporation is created
- how the corporation is financed
- how securities are regulated

The Corporate Form: Organizational Matters

Business Law in Practice

Adam (introduced in Chapter 14) is still young, energetic, and smart but not quite as broke. He has developed a prototype of his voice-recognition system for computers, and received glowing industry feedback at a recent trade show. Market studies have indicated that there is significant demand for a product such as his. Diane, who has been instrumental in assisting him in developing a business plan, has made a definite commitment to help develop a detailed marketing strategy. A lending institution has responded favourably to his business plan and has suggested that Adam incorporate a company. Adam thinks that the best approach is to start with a small local company. However, as the product has great national and international sales potential, he projects a fairly rapid expansion.

Adam has made an appointment with a lawyer to assist him with incorporating a company. He plans to hold half the shares in the company as he will be the manager of the business. Half of the shares will be held by Diane to compensate her for her advice and expertise in marketing. Adam's father, Cameron, is committed to investing $100 000 in the company. Adam wants Cameron to simply lend the money to the company as he thinks that this is the only way to protect Cameron from unlimited liability should the business venture fail.

The other matter he has been considering concerns financing—the company will need more than $100 000 for its initial operations. "Simple," says Adam. "If the bank will not lend me enough money, I will sell some shares to a bunch of friends."

1. How is a corporation formed, and what factors should Adam consider in forming a corporation?
2. Does Adam appear to understand the concept of limited liability adequately?
3. What other financing options are available, in addition to Cameron lending money to the corporation?
4. What factors should Adam consider in seeking to raise money by selling shares?

The Corporation Defined

The corporation[1] is the predominant business vehicle in modern commerce because it is a separate legal entity. For this reason, it is able to remedy many of the shortcomings associated with the other prevalent business forms—the sole proprietorship and the partnership.

The notion that the corporation possesses a legal identity separate and distinct from its owners has fundamental repercussions. It means that the corporation alone is responsible for its own debts and other liabilities. Should the corporation fail to make good on its obligations, the shareholders are not responsible for the default. The most that they stand to lose is the purchase price of their shares.

If Adam decides to run his computer business as a sole proprietorship, he is gambling his personal assets if the venture proves to be a financial disaster. Yet if he decides to run the identical business through a corporation, none of Adam's assets are at risk.

The law recognizes this different outcome as being perfectly legitimate and eminently just. As indicated in Chapter 14, the key question is this: Who has incurred the obligation in question? Liability falls on that entity—be it an individual or a corporation—and that entity alone. Put another way, the creditor must decide with whom she is doing business and live with the consequences of that decision.

---

1. In British Columbia, a corporation is usually called a "company." Although, strictly speaking, the terms are not synonymous, they are used interchangeably in this text.

The concept of a corporation being a separate legal entity is complex.[2] It was established in 1897 in a case that remains at the centre of modern corporations law.

Since *Salomon*, the separate legal existence of the corporation has not been seriously challenged. Corporations, with few exceptions, continue to be treated as entities separate from their shareholders. The cornerstone of corporations law—limited liability—is secure.

Landmark Case ▼

Salomon v. Salomon Ltd., [1897] A.C. 22 (H.L.)

THE HISTORICAL CONTEXT: When *Salomon* was decided, the corporate form was just coming into wider usage. At the time, it was unclear whether companies with few shareholders would be recognized as separate legal entities.

FACTUAL BACKGROUND: Aron Salomon carried on a profitable shoe manufacturing business for many years as a sole proprietor. He decided to form an incorporated company—Aron Salomon and Company, Limited—as the vehicle through which to run his business. The *Companies Act*, which set out the rules for creating a company, required that a company have a minimum of seven shareholders. Therefore, Aron took one share and members of his family took the remaining six shares. Aron became the managing director. Practically speaking, Aron Salomon and Company, Limited, was a "one-person company" since Aron entirely controlled the company. Put another way, the other participants in the company had no involvement in operations: any decision the company took was only because Aron wanted it to follow that particular course of action.

Next, Aron Salomon and Company, Limited, agreed to purchase the assets of Aron's sole proprietorship. As the corporation had little cash, Aron was issued 20 000 shares and a mortgage secured by the shoe business assets. In this way, Aron became a highly protected creditor of his own company.

The business suffered financial problems due to a series of strikes and the loss of government contracts. The company became insolvent, and a trustee was appointed to deal with its creditors and close down the business. Many creditors of Aron Salomon and Company, Limited, lined up for payment but there were insufficient assets to satisfy them. In response, the trustee in bankruptcy took the position that Aron was personally responsible for all his company's debts.

THE LEGAL QUESTION: Was Aron liable for the debts of Aron Salomon and Company, Limited? Was Aron a legitimate creditor of the company?

RESOLUTION: A corporation—large or small—is a separate legal entity and, as such, is totally responsible for its own obligations. Indeed, one of the main reasons for creating a company is to limit liability in the event of bankruptcy. The court rejected the argument that there was something essentially improper about an individual conducting his business through a one-person corporation to secure the protection of limited liability. If a number of persons can limit their liability in this way, then why shouldn't a single person be able to do the same thing? After all, it should not make any difference to a creditor whether one or several shareholders limit their liability.

The House of Lords also confirmed that there is nothing wrong with a shareholder being a creditor of the corporation, even when that shareholder essentially controls the company in question. Furthermore, the creditors had chosen to deal with Aron's company—not with Aron, the individual—and had chosen to do so on an unsecured basis. They, in turn, would have to live with the adverse outcome of that business decision.

CRITICAL ANALYSIS: Do you think that the court went too far in giving independent existence to the corporation, especially when the interests of Aron and his company were virtually identical? Should the shareholder of a one-person company be entitled to limited liability? How could the creditors, other than Aron, have better protected themselves in this situation?

---

2. Most of the distinguishing characteristics of a corporation—limited liability for shareholders, perpetual existence, separation of ownership and management, ease of transferring ownership, and separate taxation—are a consequence of a corporation being a legal entity distinct from its shareholders. The characteristics of a corporation are discussed in Chapter 14.

Stakeholders in the Corporation

stakeholder

One who has an interest in a corporation.

The corporation has a legal existence and, as such, is treated in law as a person. That said, the corporation is an artificial entity whose activities are controlled entirely by human beings. A corporation not only comes into being through the actions of humans, but also can make decisions, formulate policy, and enter contracts only through the actions of humans. These individuals, or groups of individuals, are often referred to as the internal **stakeholders** of the corporation. In short, internal stakeholders are those who have either a direct or indirect role in governing the corporation and determining its mission and how it will be achieved. Shareholders are those persons who have invested in the corporation by buying shares in return for a potential share of the corporate profits and other benefits. Shareholders do not have any direct authority to manage the corporation. However, they do have the power to elect the board of directors and therefore can have a strong influence on the direction of the corporation. The board of directors is charged with management functions—including policy development—and is answerable to the shareholders since, should it perform poorly, the board runs the risk of being voted out of office. Corporate officers, such as the president, secretary, and treasurer, are another important internal group. They are hired by the board of directors and are charged with managing the day-to-day operations of the corporation.

Not surprisingly, the internal stakeholders may come into conflict with one another, as well as with the corporation itself. The bulk of corporations law seeks to regulate the relationships among the corporation's internal stakeholders. Chapter 16 will provide a more detailed account of internal stakeholders. They are introduced here to establish some of the basic vocabulary associated with the corporate form, as well as to identify its central players.

The internal stakeholders are not the only stakeholders. The corporation has a tremendous impact on much of society. External stakeholders are people who have dealings with or are affected by the corporation but do not have an explicit role in governing the corporation. Examples are government, the general public, employees, customers, and creditors. These groups, although external in the sense that they are generally not involved in corporate governance, nonetheless have an interest in the corporation, and their interests receive recognition in some circumstances. The relationship between the corporation and its external stakeholders is explored briefly in Chapter 16.

Pre-Incorporation Issues

Assuming Adam decides to do business through a corporation, he must make a number of decisions prior to preparing and filing incorporation documents. He must decide

- whether to incorporate federally or provincially
- what type of shares will be available and to whom
- what to name the corporation

These decisions will be influenced by a host of factors such as the kind of business Adam intends to operate, where he intends to operate, how he intends to manage the corporation, how he wishes to accommodate future growth, and in the case of a corporate name, its availability.

Provincial and Federal Incorporation

Adam has the choice between incorporating federally and incorporating provincially. He has this choice because jurisdiction over the incorporation of companies is divided between the federal government and the provincial governments. Both levels of government have passed legislation that provides for the incorporation of companies. These acts embody different models or prototypes as to how the corporation comes into existence.[3] Although the way in which the corporation is created varies, the different methods of incorporation have much in common. All methods allow for the creation of an entity that is recognized as a legal person, is owned by shareholders who enjoy limited liability for the debts of the entity[4], and is managed by directors who owe fiduciary duties to the entity.

When, then, should a business incorporate federally, and when would it be best advised to incorporate provincially? There is no hard and fast answer to this question. Federally incorporated corporations have a right to carry on business in each province, whereas provincially incorporated corporations have the right to carry on business only in the province in which they are incorporated. This difference has little practical significance because each province has straightforward licensing procedures through which corporations incorporated in other provinces can do business in that province.[5]

For corporations that intend to operate in more than two provinces, federal incorporation may result in lower administrative costs. For corporations that intend to operate in only one or two provinces, provincial incorporation usually results in lower administrative costs.[6] Since Adam intends to operate nationally and even internationally, he should seriously consider incorporating under federal legislation.

Shares and Shareholders

share structure

The shares that a corporation is permitted to issue by its constitution.

As part of the preparation for incorporation, Adam must decide on a **share structure** for the corporation. This entails deciding on the class or classes of shares that the corporation will be authorized to issue, what rights and privileges attach to each class, and the number of each authorized for issuance. Adam must also consider how the shares will be available and to whom they will be available.

Classes of Shares

A share represents an ownership interest in the issuing corporation. It is, however, a unique kind of ownership interest. It does not give to the owner or holder any right to use the assets of the corporation or any right to directly control or manage the corporation. It does, however, give to the owner those rights that specifically attach to the share.

---

3. The different models currently in use are articles of incorporation, memorandum of association, and letters patent. The federal government, Alberta, Manitoba, New Brunswick, Newfoundland, Ontario, and Saskatchewan follow the articles of incorporation model. See *Canada Business Corporations Act*, R.S.C. 1985, c. C-44; *Business Corporations Act*, R.S.A. 2000, c. B-9; *Corporations Act*, R.S.M. 1987, C.C.S.M. c. C-225; *Business Corporations Act*, S.N.B. 1981, B-9.1; *Corporations Act*, R.S.N. 1990, c. C-36; *Business Corporations Act*, R.S.O. 1990, c. B.16; and *Business Corporations Act*, R.S.S. 1978, c. B-10. Nova Scotia follows the memorandum of association model. See *Companies Act*, R.S.N.S. 1989, c. 81. Prince Edward Island and Quebec follow the letters patent model. See *Companies Act*, R.S.P.E.I. 1988, c. C-14 and *Companies Act*, R.S.Q. 1977, c. C-38. British Columbia has features of both the articles of association and the memorandum of association models. See *Business Corporations Act*, S. B. C. 2002, c. 57.
4. Recent amendments to Alberta's *Business Corporations Act* provides for an unlimited liability corporation (ULC). ULCs are useful to American-based multinationals with operations in Canada because of the special treatment ULCs receive in the United States under the U.S. *Internal Revenue Code*. Nova Scotia also permits ULCs.
5. Peter Hogg, *Constitutional Law of Canada*, vol. 1, looseleaf (Scarborough: Carswell, 1997) at 23–27.
6. Kevin Patrick McGuinness, *The Law and Practice of Canadian Business Corporations* (Toronto: Butterworths, 1999) at 108–109.

A corporation may simply have one type or class of shares with all the basic shareholder rights attached to it. In this case, the share must include the right to

- vote for the election of directors
- receive dividends declared by the directors
- share in the proceeds on dissolution of the corporation, after the creditors have been paid

A one-person corporation with no plans or aspirations for growth may choose this option. However, to ensure that the corporation has the flexibility to meet future needs, it is prudent to establish different classes at the outset. Though different classes could be created when the need arises, this would require an amendment to the corporation's constitution—a potentially costly and complicated procedure.

There are many possibilities for creating shares with diverse rights (see Figure 15.1) so long as the basic rights mentioned above are distributed to one or more classes. For example, if Adam's father simply wants to be a passive investor in Adam's business, shares without voting rights could be created to meet his needs. If he wants some qualified assurance of the return of his share capital when and if IK Enterprises winds downs, then shares with preference rights on dissolution could be created. The possibilities are almost limitless; however, careful consideration must be given to how management and financial rights are distributed among classes of shares. These issues are explored further in Chapter 16.

Adam may limit the number of shares of each class that can be issued by stating a maximum number, or he can simply leave matters open-ended by indicating that the number is "unlimited."

FIGURE 15.1	
Creating Classes of Shares	A class of share may include a combination of various rights and privileges. Examples of typical rights that may attach to a class of shares include the following: • Voting rights: the right to vote for election of directors • Financial rights: the right to receive dividends when declared by directors or the right to receive fixed dividends on a regular basis • Preference rights: the right to receive dividends before dividends may be paid to any other class of shareholders and/or the right, on dissolution, to receive investment before any payments are made to any other class of shareholder • Cumulative rights: the right to have a dividend not paid in a particular year added to the amount payable the following year • Redemption rights: the right to have the corporation buy back the shares at a set price

widely held corporation
A corporation whose shares are normally traded on a stock exchange.

securities legislation
Laws designed to regulate transactions involving shares and bonds of a corporation.

closely held corporation
A corporation that does not sell its shares to the public.

Availability of Shares

A corporation may issue shares to the general public. This type of corporation is usually referred to as a **widely held** or public corporation.[7] A corporation that issues shares to the public is subject to regulation pursuant to the relevant **securities legislation** in those provinces in which the securities are issued or traded. Securities legislation, discussed in more detail below, imposes registration and disclosure requirements on the issuers of the shares.

A corporation that does not issue its shares to the general public is usually known as a **closely held** or private corporation.[8] The vast majority of Canadian corporations, including some very large enterprises, such as McCain's and Irving in

---

7. The term "widely held" is used interchangeably with "public" to denote a corporation that offers its shares for sale to the public. In some jurisdictions, the term "offering" or "reporting" is also used.
8. The term "closely held" is used interchangeably with "private" to denote a corporation that does not offer its shares for sale to the public. In some jurisdictions, the term "nonoffering" or "nonreporting" is also used.

New Brunswick, N.M. Paterson and Son Ltd. in Manitoba, and Holt Renfrew in Ontario, fall within this category. These corporations are generally exempt from most of the obligations of securities regulation so long as they meet the definition of a private corporation. For example, in Ontario, the *Securities Act*,[9] provides that a corporation qualifies as a private corporation if it has the following provisions in its incorporating documents:

■ a restriction on the transfer of shares

■ a limit (with certain exceptions) on the number of shareholders in the corporation to no more than 50

■ a prohibition on any invitation to the public to subscribe for the corporation's shares

An added advantage of private corporation status is the potential for a lower rate of income tax. The *Income Tax Act*[10] provides that a Canadian-controlled private corporation is entitled to a lower tax rate on its first $200 000 of business income earned in Canada in its fiscal year. In effect, a qualifying corporation pays about half the normal corporate income tax rate of approximately 50 percent on this income.

What are the advantages of being a private corporation as opposed to a public corporation such as CPR?

Business Application of the Law

Lord Black and Abuse of the Corporate Form

The legal woes of Conrad Black, the former newspaper baron, are numerous. In January 2004, Hollinger International announced a $US200 million lawsuit against Black, its former chairman of the board and chief executive officer, and David Radler, its former deputy chairman and chief operating officer, seeking the return of management fees and other payments. In September 2004, a group of Canadian investors launched a class-action lawsuit against Black and several of his associates, seeking over $4 billion in damages. In November 2004, the U.S. Securities Exchange Commission laid a civil fraud suit against Black, Radler, and Hollinger Inc. In March 2005, Hollinger Inc. and its subsidiary Domgroup sued Black, his private companies, and several associates for $635 million in damages. In December 2005, the U.S. Attorney's officer in

Chicago charged Black with mail fraud, wire fraud, racketeering, obstruction of justice, and money laundering. In August 2006, additional charges of tax evasion were added to the U.S. indictment. If convicted of all the criminal charges, Lord Black of Crossharbour faces more than 40 years in prison.

Allegations: Black stands accused of pillaging hundreds of millions of dollars from Hollinger International, violating his fiduciary obligations, and ignoring corporate governance principles. Among the many accusations, it is alleged that Black and other senior Hollinger International executives received $32.15 million in "non-compete" payments (payments received from the sale of some of Hollinger International's community newspapers and the sale of the *National Post* to CanWest Global, which should have gone to Hollinger International) that were not

---

9. R.S.O. 1990, c. S.5, ss. 1(1), 35 (2) (10), 73 (1) (a).
10. R.S.C. 1985, c. 1 (5th Supp.), s. 125.

authorized by the board or its audit committee; that Black received (through his holding company, Ravelston Inc.) millions in management fees that were not properly authorized; that he misled the directors of Hollinger International about his plans to sell control of Hollinger Inc. to Press Holding International owned by Britain's Barclay brothers; that he improperly used confidential corporate information from Hollinger International to advance his own personal interests in the proposed sale of his interest in Hollinger Inc. to the Barclays; that he diverted to himself a valuable opportunity presented to Hollinger International (the sale of the Telegraph Journal to the Barclays); that he took credit for charitable donations made by Hollinger International; and that he charged personal expenses to Hollinger International. In this regard, it is alleged that he charged the following (among other personal expenses) to the company: $530 000 for a 2001 flight on the corporate jet for a vacation to Bora Bora; $43 000 for the 60th birthday party of his wife, Barbara Amiel at a New York restaurant; $1.8 million in 2002 for nonbusiness flights on the corporate jets for himself and Radler; $1.4 million in staff expenses from 1997 to 2005 at his London, New York, and Florida homes; $1.5 million in renovations to a New York apartment on Park Avenue in order to house his servants; $25 000 for "summer drinks"; and various sums for Lady Black's handbags, jogging suit, exercise equipment, and a briefcase. In total, it is alleged that the aggregate funds taken by Black and his associates is over $400 million in the years 1997–2003, about 92 percent of Hollinger International's entire adjusted income for this period.

If the allegations are proven to be true, then the Hollinger scandal represents greed, deceit, and corruption on a scale seldom seen, and raises profound and serious questions about how Black was able to loot Hollinger International of millions. Some of the answers may lie in the corporate governance structure of Hollinger International.

Corporate Structure: Hollinger International (renamed Sun-Times Media group) is a Delaware public company whose media empire once included London's *Daily Telegraph, The Chicago Sun-Times, The Jerusalem Post,* Canada's *National Post,* and many smaller American and Canadian community newspapers. At the time of the alleged wrongdoings outlined above, Hollinger International was controlled by Hollinger Inc., a publicly traded holding company, which, in turn, was controlled by Ravelston Corp., Black's private holding company. Hollinger Inc. was able to control Hollinger International through what is known as a dual-class structure—different classes of shares have different voting rights. Hollinger Inc. owned all of Hollinger International's Class B shares, which gave it 30 percent of the equity but 73 percent of the votes. The multiple-voting share structure allowed Hollinger Inc. to control the fate of Hollinger International while holding a fraction of the equity. This structure has been a favourite of Canadian corporate empire builders and remains entrenched despite criticism from shareholder activists. The structure, in essence, allowed Black to call the shots and to select Hollinger International's board of directors. Indeed, the board was largely filled with prominent, outside directors, hand selected by Black and with whom he had a social, political, or business relationship. Apparently the "Black Board" functioned like a social club or public policy association, with extremely short meetings followed by a good lunch and a discussion of world affairs—actual operating results or corporate performance were rarely discussed. The board was often given false or misleading information but it did not do much on its own about excessive management fees and noncompete payments. It took no steps and asked no questions.

CRITICAL ANALYSIS: How did the share structure of the Hollinger companies contribute to the alleged abuse of the corporate form of carrying on business?

Source: Gordon A. Paris, Chairman, *Report of Investigation by the Special Committee of the Board of Directors of Hollinger International Inc.* (30 August 2004) at http://www.sec.gov/ Archives/edgar/data/868512/000095012304010413/y01437 exv99w2.htm (accessed 24 November 2006).

Lord and Lady Black

Who May Own Shares

A share is a piece of property and is freely transferable unless there is a restriction in place. In widely held corporations, shares are almost always freely transferable; otherwise the shares will not be accepted for listing on a stock exchange. In closely held corporations where shares are generally issued to family or friends, the shareholders have a strong interest in having control over who the other shareholders are. It is therefore common to have a provision in the incorporating documents that shares cannot be transferred without the agreement of the directors or a majority of the shareholders of the corporation. At the same time, shareholders require some flexibility in being able to transfer their shares; thus it is common to include "a right of first refusal" for directors or shareholders. When a right of first refusal is in place, it means that the shareholder wishing to sell must first offer her shares to the directors (or shareholders, as the case may be) at the same price she has negotiated with the outsider. This gives the insiders one last chance to acquire the shares for themselves instead of having to welcome a new investor to the company.

As an alternative to having a restriction in the corporation's constitution, the shareholders could have an agreement that covers transferring. Shareholders agreements are discussed in Chapter 16.

A Corporate Name

All jurisdictions require a company to be identified by a name or designated number. The selection and use of corporate names is subject to regulation by trademarks law,[11] torts law,[12] and corporations law.

The basic requirements for a name are that

- It must be distinctive (different from other existing names in the same field).
- It must not cause confusion with any existing name or trademark.
- It must include a legal element (e.g., Limited or Ltd., Incorporated or Inc., or Corporation or Corp. or the French equivalents). The purpose of the word is to distinguish a corporation from a partnership and a sole proprietorship and to signal to the public the fact of limited liability.
- It must not include any unacceptable terms (for example, it must not suggest a connection that does not exist, falsely describe the business, or be obscene or scandalous).

On choosing a name for their corporation, entrepreneurs like Adam are advised to be particularly careful. If the corporate registry inadvertently approves a name that is confusingly similar to the name of another business, Adam can be sued for trademark infringement and the tort of passing off.[13] He will be liable for any damages that the other business has suffered and, perhaps even more problematically, be ordered to change the name of his corporation.

This will require Adam to re-establish a corporate identity and reputation in the marketplace, as well as replace letterhead, invoices, business signs, and anything else bearing his former corporate name. This is obviously costly. *Paws Pet Food & Accessories Ltd. v. Paws & Shop Inc.* illustrates how such a dispute can arise.

---

11. See Chapter 18.
12. The tort of passing off.
13. This is because Adam would be representing to the public—either intentionally or not—that there is a relationship between his business and the other business when no such relationship exists.

CASE ▼

Paws Pet Food & Accessories Ltd. v. Paws & Shop Inc. (1992), 6 Alta. L.R. (3d) 22 (Q.B.)

THE BUSINESS CONTEXT: A name is an important and valuable asset to a business. It helps distinguish one business from another.

FACTUAL BACKGROUND: Paws Pet Food & Accessories Ltd. (Paws Pet Food) was incorporated in 1987 under the Alberta *Business Corporations Act*. Three years later, Paws & Shop Inc. (Paws & Shop) was created under the same piece of legislation. Both corporations operated in Calgary, and both were in the business of retailing pet food and accessories. Paws Pet Food took the position that the registrar should not have allowed the second company to incorporate under a name that was so confusingly similar to its own. It went to court for an order directing the second company to change its name.

THE LEGAL QUESTION: Is Paws & Shop Inc.—the second company—confusingly similar to Paws Pet Food & Accessories?

RESOLUTION: The court decided that the registrar had made an error in permitting the second corporation to incorporate under the name of Paws & Shop. There was evidence that customers of Paws Pet Food mistakenly believed that it was associated or affiliated with Paws & Shop. The registration of Paws & Shop was therefore contrary to the Alberta *Business Corporations Act* and related regulations because it was leading to public confusion. On this basis, Paws & Shop was forced to change its name.

CRITICAL ANALYSIS: This case illustrates that there is no inherent protection in the fact that the registrar has approved a corporate name for use. A judge can overrule the registrar and, furthermore, since the tort of passing off can be committed unintentionally, a company with a name that is confusingly similar to that of another company can end up paying damages even though the registrar had approved the name to begin with. Is this fair? Who should bear the risk of a mistake being made—the business itself or the taxpayers?

NUANS report
A document that shows the result of a search for business names.

Assuming that Adam wants to incorporate federally, he will have to send his proposed name—IK Enterprises Ltd.—to the federal corporate registry for approval. He will also have to have a Newly Upgraded Automated Name Search, or **NUANS report.** This document lists those business names and trademarks—if any—that are similar to the name being proposed. A NUANS report is prepared using a database containing existing and reserved business names, as well as trademarks. If some other business is using the name IK Enterprises Ltd. or a name similar to it—such as IK Investments Inc.—the NUANS report would presumably contain such information. Adam should avoid the name and come up with an alternative name for his fledgling business.

It is common for a company's legislation to permit a corporation be assigned a numbered name. Under the federal legislation, for example, the corporation can be issued a designating number, followed by the word "Canada" and then a legal element—such as "Limited" or "Incorporated." A numbered company is useful when a corporation must be created quickly, when the incorporators are having difficulty coming up with a suitable name, or when there is a wish to create a **shelf company.** Shelf companies are often incorporated by law firms for the future use of their clients. The company does not engage in any active business. It simply sits "on the shelf" until a firm's client needs it.

shelf company
A company that does not engage in active business.

The Process of Incorporation

All Canadian jurisdictions follow a similar procedure for the creation of a corporation, though precise requirements do vary. Assuming that Adam wants to incorporate federally, he must submit the following to the federal corporate registry in Ottawa:[14]

- articles of incorporation[15]
- notice of registered office
- notice of directors
- newly upgraded automated name search (NUANS) report
- the filing fee, payable to the Receiver General of Canada

articles of incorporation
The document that defines the basic characteristics of corporations incorporated in Newfoundland, New Brunswick, Ontario, Manitoba, Saskatchewan, Alberta, and the federal jurisdiction.

incorporator
The person who sets the incorporation process in motion.

The **articles of incorporation** set out the basic features of the corporation—name, place of the corporation's registered office, class and number of shares authorized to be issued, any restrictions on the transferring of shares, the number of directors, any restrictions on the business that can be carried on, and any other provisions that an **incorporator** requires to customize the corporation to meet his needs. For example, incorporators may include provisions that require directors to own at least one share in the corporation, provisions prescribing how shareholders will fill a vacancy in the board of directors, or provisions that limit the number of shareholders to a certain number. The name or names of the incorporators must also be included in the articles of incorporation.

The Notice of Registered Office form is very brief because it has only one purpose: to provide a public record of the corporation's official address. This is the address that those having dealings with the company can use to communicate with the corporation, particularly with respect to formal matters, including lawsuits.

The Notice of Directors form contains the names and residential addresses of the directors and must correspond with the number of directors given in the articles of incorporation.

The completed forms, along with the requisite fee, are then submitted to the appropriate government office—the Corporations Directorate of Industry Canada. If the forms are in order, the directorate will issue a "birth certificate" for the corporation, known as the "certificate of incorporation."

Provincial incorporation legislation has its own requirements, which are parallel but are not necessarily identical to the requirements and procedures under the *Canada Business Corporations Act*.

Organizing the Corporation

Following incorporation, the first directors will ordinarily undertake a number of tasks. Under federal legislation, for example, the directors are required to call an organizational meeting to

bylaws
Rules specifying day-to-day operating procedures of a corporation.

- make **bylaws**[16]
- adopt forms of share certificates and corporate records
- authorize the issue of shares and other securities

---

14. Federal incorporation is available online by accessing the Electronic Filing Centre on the Corporations Directorate's Strategis website at http://www.strategis.ic.gc.ca/corporations
15. The term "articles of incorporation" is also used in Alberta, Manitoba, New Brunswick, Newfoundland, Ontario, and Saskatchewan. The equivalent term in Nova Scotia is "memorandum of association"; in Prince Edward Island and Quebec, it is "letters patent"; and in British Columbia it is "notice of articles."
16. "Bylaws" is the term used in the articles of incorporation and letters patent jurisdiction. In Nova Scotia, articles of association—the very general equivalent of bylaws—is the term used and in British Columbia the term is articles.

- appoint officers
- appoint an auditor to hold office until the first annual meeting of shareholders
- make banking arrangements
- transact any other business[17]

Federal legislation also specifies that the directors named in the articles of incorporation hold office until the first meeting of the shareholders. That meeting must be called within 18 months of incorporation.[18] At that first meeting, shareholders elect the permanent directors, who hold office for the specified term.[19] The directors carry on the management of the corporation until the next annual meeting, at which time they report to the shareholders on the corporation's performance.

Business and Legislation
Incorporating in British Columbia

The new *British Columbia Business Corporations Act*[20] came into force in March 2004. The act replaces the *Company Act* and represents the first major reform of corporate legislation in B.C. in 30 years.

The act retains the contract model of incorporation (shareholders can specify the nature of their agreement with the corporation) rather than adopting the statutory model that is used in the *Canada Business Corporations Act (CBCA)* and in the companies legislation of most other provinces. The new act does, however, adopt many features of the *CBCA* while including features not found elsewhere.

The major changes embodied in the new act include the following:

- *Charter documents.* The memorandum and articles are replaced by notice of articles and articles (the CBCA uses articles of incorporation and bylaws). The notice of articles is the only document required to be filed in the office of the Registrar.

- *Share capital.* The authorized capital is now unlimited. The new act continues to allow both par value shares and shares without par value (the *CBCA* permits only shares without par value) but now par value in foreign currency is permitted.

- *Directors and officers.* There is now no residency requirement for directors (the CBCA requires 25 percent resident Canadians). Also a company is not required to have a president and secretary (matching the CBCA's requirements).

- *Directors' duties.* The duties of directors and the events that trigger liability are much the same as in the *CBCA*. However the solvency test for determining liability is simpler. Under the new act it means "the inability to pay debts as they become due in the usual course of business" (under the *CBCA* there are several definitions). Also now there is no requirement for court approval for directors' indemnification unless the action is by the company against the director or officer (this provision is the same under the *CBCA*)

- *Shareholders.* A company is expressly permitted to hold its own shares (under the CBCA this is prohibited with limited exceptions). Unlike its predecessor the new act recognizes unanimous shareholders' agreements (this is the same under the CBCA).

Companies governed by the former act had two years to complete a transition to the new act.

---

17. *Canada Business Corporations Act*, R.S.C. 1985, c. C-44, s.104.
18. *Ibid.* at s. 133(a).
19. *Ibid.* at s. 106(3).
20. S.B.C. 2002, c. 57.

Financing the Corporation

Adam needs to finance his company to have the funds to operate. He has two basic means of doing so: IK Enterprises Ltd. can issue shares (equity financing) or borrow money (debt financing).

Debt Financing

A corporation may raise money by borrowing. The company may obtain a loan from shareholders, family or friends of shareholders, lending institutions, or, in some cases, the government. If it is borrowing a substantial sum of money on a long-term basis the corporation may issue **bonds** or **debentures.** The terms "bond" and "debenture" are often used interchangeably and refer to a corporate IOU, which is either secured or unsecured. Note that the word "bond" is sometimes used to describe a secured debt, and debenture to refer to an unsecured debt,[21] but the only way to know what is actually involved is to read the debt instrument itself.

A bond or debenture does not represent any ownership interest in the corporation, and the holder does not have any right to participate in the management of the corporation.[22] However, these debts are often secured by a charge on the assets of the corporation. This means that if the debt is not repaid, the assets can be sold to repay the debt and the bondholder has a better chance of recovering his investment. Bonds and debentures—like shares—may have any number of features and are freely transferable, creating a secondary market for their purchase and sale.

The advantage of raising cash by issuing bonds is that Adam does not have to relinquish formal control. That is, he can raise money to run his operation without having to give management rights to his lenders. On the other hand, there is a requirement that the interest on the bonds be paid regardless of whether a profit is earned. In fact, if the interest is not paid on the debt, the corporation faces bankruptcy unless it can reach a new agreement with the bondholders.

Equity Financing

Shares are frequently used to raise money for the use of the corporation. This is done by issuing shares to investors in exchange for a purchase price.

Shares provide a flexible means of raising capital for a corporation because they can be created with different bundles of rights attached to them to appeal to different investors. Shares can be attractive to investors because, unlike debt where the return is usually limited to a fixed amount, shares provide an opportunity to benefit from the corporation's growth. If the corporation prospers, the value of the shares will increase. Shares are advantageous to the issuer in that the money raised by selling shares does not have to be repaid in the way a loan must. On the other hand, the sale of shares may mean the relinquishing of management rights. Although it is possible to raise capital through the sale of shares that do not have any voting rights attached, investors may be interested only in shares that give them a say in the control and operation of the corporation.

Shares and bonds represent two very different ways of raising money for corporate activities. There are, however, many combinations of these two types of **securities.** Much depends on the features that investors are interested in purchasing. Most businesses, particularly large ones, use some combination of these various methods of raising funds, maintaining a reasonable balance between them.

bond

A document evidencing a debt owed by the corporation, often used to refer to a secured debt.

debenture

A document evidencing a debt owed by the corporation, often used to refer to an unsecured debt.

securities

Shares and bonds issued by a corporation.

---

21. *Supra* note 6 at 462.
22. It is possible, however, for bondholders to obtain management rights if the company defaults on the loan. This depends on the terms of issuance.

conversion right
The right to convert one type of security into another type.

Furthermore, shares and bonds can come with **conversion rights.** A convertible bondholder, for example, is entitled to convert his debt interest into shares and thereby assume an equity position in the company instead of being a creditor.

FIGURE 15.2

Securities Compared

	Shareholder	Bondholder
Status of holder	Investor/owner	Investor/creditor
Participation in management	Elects directors (if voting rights); approves major activities	Does not participate (except in special circumstances)
Rights to income	Dividends, if declared	Interest payments
Security for the holder on insolvency of corporation	Entitled to share in proceeds after all creditors paid	Entitled to payment from proceeds before general creditors, if secured, and before shareholders

Ethical Considerations — Socially Responsible Investing

When making investment decisions most people simply use some measure of a business's profitability or its potential for profitability. There is, however, a small but growing segment of investors that also considers another factor—their conscience or values. Socially responsible investing (SRI), or ethical investing, integrates social and environmental values into the investment decision-making process. Factors that a socially responsible investor may consider in making investment decisions include the amount of money given to charity; support for the local community; record on the environment; treatment of employees, particularly members of minority groups and women; and involvement with military weapons or nuclear power.

CRITICAL ANALYSIS: How could corporations attract the socially responsible investor? Are there any risks associated with ignoring the socially responsible investor?

Does shareholder activism affect the price of shares?

The issuance of securities including bonds, debentures, and shares to the general public is governed by securities legislation. This means that the issuer must follow a complicated and potentially costly procedure. Securities legislation seeks to ensure that the potential purchasers know what they are getting into before they make any decision.

Securities Legislation

All provinces have enacted securities acts.[23] In very general terms, the aim of all securities legislation is to

- provide the mechanism for the transfer of securities
- ensure that all investors have the ability to access adequate information in order to make informed decisions
- ensure that the system is such that the public has confidence in the marketplace
- regulate those engaged in the trading of securities
- remove or punish those participants not complying with established rules

With these objectives at the forefront, all securities regimes have three basic requirements: registration, disclosure, and insider-trading restrictions.

Technology and the Law

The Regulation of Internet Securities Activities

The Internet has had a tremendous impact on the securities industry—it has spawned online brokerages, has emerged as the primary source of information for investors, and is the means by which businesses can distribute prospectuses, financial statements, news releases, and the like. The Internet is a valuable tool for the industry, but it also poses considerable challenges for regulators who seek to protect investors and the integrity of the capital markets. The global, invisible nature of the Internet increases the likelihood of online securities fraud. As scam artists can anonymously and cheaply communicate with a vast number of people from anywhere in the world, they can readily spread rumours that result in the manipulation of market prices, trade in securities without being registered to do so, and distribute securities in nonexistent entities. Scam artists have, of course, always perpetrated frauds; the Internet simply allows them to swindle a larger number of people. The challenge of combating online securities fraud is complicated by questions of jurisdiction. For example, does securities law apply to the Internet, or is the Internet immune from traditional law? Similarly, which country's securities laws apply to Internet activities that occur in more than one jurisdiction?

The notion that cyberspace is a separate jurisdiction and, therefore, not subject to regulation has been rejected by regulators and legal scholars around the world. Securities regulators have taken the position that both general securities laws and traditional principles of jurisdiction apply to Internet activities. They assert that they can regulate both Internet activity that originates within their jurisdiction, and also conduct that occurs outside their jurisdiction that is directed to persons within their jurisdiction or that has adverse effects within their jurisdiction. For example, the Alberta Securities Commission considered its jurisdiction over Internet securities activities in *Re World Stock Exchange*.[24] Two residents of Edmonton established the World Stock Exchange (WSE), an Internet-based stock exchange. They incorporated the WSE as a Cayman Island corporation, and operated the website from a server located in Antigua. Alberta companies were solicited to become listed on the exchange, and the WSE website was accessible to anyone who knew the domain name. The WSE and its principals were convicted of carrying on an exchange and trading in securities in Alberta without the necessary regulatory approvals. The Alberta Securities Commission held that Alberta law applied because the WSE and its principals were engaged in conduct that was directed at Albertans and that had unlawful consequences in Alberta.

---

23. The *Canada Business Corporations Act* also contains provisions that regulate securities that are issued or traded by *CBCA* corporations.
24. Alberta Securities Commission Decision, 15 February 2000.

CRITICAL ANALYSIS: What do you think is the rationale for regulating trade in securities? Do you think the rationale changes when the commercial activity is conducted over the Internet?

Sources: Michael Geist, *Internet Law in Canada*, 3rd ed. (North York, Ont.: Captus Press, 2002) at 790–802; and Brad Freedman, "Internet Presents Challenge to Securities Regulators" *The Lawyers Weekly* (9 February 2001) at 13.

Registration

Any company intending to sell securities to the public in a given province must be registered to do so with the relevant provincial securities commission. Furthermore, all persons engaged in advising on and selling securities to the public must be registered with the relevant securities commission. The definitions of those covered by the various statutes vary between provinces but generally extend to advisors, underwriters, dealers, salespeople, brokers, and securities issuers.

Disclosure

prospectus

The document a corporation must publish when offering securities to the public.

The company must comply with disclosure or **prospectus** provisions set forth in the securities legislation. With limited exceptions, this means that any sale or distribution of a security—in this case, meaning either debt (bonds) or equity (shares)—must be preceded by a prospectus that is accepted and approved by the appropriate securities commission. A prospectus is the statement by the issuing company of prescribed information. The list of information required to be in the prospectus is lengthy and ranges from financial information to biographical information about the directors. The overriding requirement is for "full, true, and plain" disclosure of all material facts, that is, facts that are likely to affect the price of the securities. The legislation assumes that prospective investors will rely on the prospectus in making investment decisions.

The issuer of securities has an obligation to continue to keep the public informed of its activities. In general terms, this means that it must notify the public of any material change in its affairs, first by issuing a press release and second by filing a report with the securities commission within ten days of the change. A material change is defined as one that is likely to have a significant effect on the market value of the securities and is not known to the public in general.

Business and Legislation — Ontario's *Securities Act* and Secondary Market Liability

Corporate scandals in the United States—Enron, WorldCom, Tyco—and in Canada—Bre-X, Livent, YBM Magnex—have caused a significant erosion of investor confidence. In an effort to restore and foster confidence in the integrity of the capital markets, Canada's legislators have undertaken significant corporate and securities law reform.

In Ontario, the *Securities Act*[25] has been amended to provide a new statutory right of action for misrepresentations contained in secondary market disclosures. The objective of this right of action is to create a meaningful civil remedy for secondary market investors and to facilitate class-action lawsuits.

---

25. R.S.O. 1990, c.S-5, Part XXIII.1, s.138.3 (1).

Prior to the amendments, the *Securities Act* provided only a statutory cause of action to investors who purchased securities in the primary market (i.e., purchased pursuant to a prospectus, offering memorandum or securities exchange takeover bid circular). Investors in the secondary market[26] (i.e., purchasing or selling from third parties) had to rely on a common law action for fraudulent or negligent misrepresentation. This meant that the secondary market purchasers had to establish that they relied on the defendants' misrepresentations in making their investment decisions. This requirement made it next to impossible to have a class action certified because of the individual issues of reliance. The amendments create the statutory cause of action "without regard to whether" the purchaser or seller relied on the alleged misrepresentation. In other words, the investor is deemed to have relied on the disclosures and does not have to prove that she relied detrimentally on the misrepresentation. This amendment facilitates the certification of class actions by removing the issue of proof of individual class member reliance.

The key provisions of the amendments are

Cause of action. Secondary market investors have a right to sue where they bought or sold securities during a period where there was an uncorrected misrepresentation made by or on behalf of an issuer in a document released by the company or in a public oral statement. The right to sue is also available where there was a failure to make timely disclosure of a material change in the issuer's business.

Defendants. The class of people that may be liable for a company's misrepresentation or failure to disclose is broad and includes the reporting issuer; its directors, officers, influential persons (including controlling shareholders, promoters, and insiders); and experts (including auditors and lawyers).

Defences. There are a number of defences available to defendants including reasonable investigation (defendant had conducted a reasonable investigation and had no reason to believe the document or oral

statement contained a misrepresentation), plaintiff's knowledge (defendant proves that the plaintiff knew there was a misrepresentation of failure to disclose at the relevant time), no involvement, and reasonable reliance on experts.

Damages. There is a complex formula for calculating damages but generally a person who is found liable will be responsible for the losses the investor suffers (the difference between the price paid or received for a security and the average price in the ten-day period following the disclosure or public correction). If more than one person is liable, each defendant will be responsible only for the proportionate share of damages that correspond to his responsibility unless he knowingly participated in the misrepresentation or failure to disclose. Also, liability for damage awards is capped except when a defendant knowingly participates in the misrepresentation or failure to disclose. Liability for individual defendants is the greater of $25 000 and 50% of their compensation from the issuer in the prior 12 months. The liability limits for corporate defendants are the greater of 5 percent of capitalization and $1 million.

CRITICAL ANALYSIS: How do the amendments enhance investor protection? Do the amendments do enough for investors?

---

26. It is estimated that secondary market trading accounts for more than 90 percent of all equity trading in Canada.

Insider-Trading Restrictions

insider trading
Transactions in securities of a corporation by or on behalf of an insider on the basis of relevant material information concerning the corporation not known to the general public.

insider
A person whose relationship with the issuer of securities is such that he is likely to have access to relevant material information concerning the issuer that is not known to the public.

tippee
A person who acquires material information about an issuer of securities from an insider.

The objective of **insider-trading** provisions is to ensure that trading in securities takes place only on the basis of information available to the public at large. Securities legislation achieves this aim in two primary ways: first, it requires **insiders** to report any trading that they have engaged in, and second, it prohibits trading by certain insiders—such as directors, senior officers, employees, and the corporation itself—on the basis of information not publicly available.

The reason insiders must report any trade is simple: if someone in this capacity is either buying or selling large blocks of securities, this is critical information for the investing public. Even small trades can be relevant. Insiders are prohibited not only from trading on material information not publicly disclosed but also from passing on this information to a third party or **tippee.** This person is similarly prohibited from trading on such information.

Those who engage in insider trading are subject to both criminal and civil liability under securities legislation and under corporations legislation.[27] In addition, the federal government has amended the *Criminal Code* to create improper insider trading and tipping offences. The insider trading offence carries a penalty of up to ten years in prison and the tipping offence is punishable by up to five years in prison.[28]

In considering whether to offer securities to the public through a stock exchange, Adam has a number of factors to consider. Although a means of obtaining funds from a wide group of investors, selling securities entails public disclosure of information that would otherwise not be known to competitors, and certainly requires costly compliance with regulations.[29]

Business Application of the Law

Insider-Trading Scandals in Canada

In the past several years, Canada has had its share of high profile insider-trading scandals. In 2000, Glen Harper, the President of Golden Rule Resources, was convicted in an Ontario court of insider trading. He sold approximately $3 million in Golden shares between 3 January and 6 May 1997. Evidence indicated that on 2 or 3 January 1997, Harper had received negative gold assay results from the company's mineral interests in Ghana. He received further negative assay results on 12 March. Neither set of results was disclosed to the public during the relevant time period. Harper was sentenced to one year in jail and was fined $4 million. The summary convictions appeal judge reduced the jail sentence to six months and the fine to $2 million.

The Court of Appeal[30] upheld the fine and the jail sentence, which is the longest sentence ever imposed in Canada for the offence of insider trading.

Also in 2000, the case against John Felderhof, the chief geologist of Bre-X Minerals, went to trial. Felderhof has pleaded not guilty to eight violations of the Ontario *Securities Act* including four based on insider trading. It is alleged that Felderhof sold $84 million of Bre-X stock in 1996 while having information about the company that had not been publicly disclosed. The nearly 3.6 million shares were sold seven months before the company's reported gold find was exposed as a fraud. The trial has been marred by numerous delays including a three and one-half year adjournment for an unsuccessful

---

27. *Supra* note 17 at s. 131(4). Note that under recent amendments the definition of insider has been expanded to catch more transactions.
28. *Criminal Code*, R.S.C., 1995, c. C-4, Part X, ss. 382.1 (1) (2).
29. Edmund M.A. Kwaw, *The Law of Corporate Finance in Canada* (Toronto: Butterworths, 1997) at 121–122.
30. *R. v. Harper* (2000), 232 D.L.R. (4th) 738 (Ont. C.A.).

attempt by the Ontario Securities Commission (OSC) to have the presiding judge removed from the trial.[31] Closing arguments were heard in August 2006 and a decision is expected in early 2007. Felderhof, who resides in Indonesia, made a court appearance in March 2005 but never testified in the case. If convicted, he faces penalties ranging from a fine of $1 million to imprisonment for two years, as well as financial penalties of up to three times any profits he earned on the insider trading.

In 2005, former RBC Dominion Securities Inc. investment banker Andrew Rankin was found guilty in Ontario provincial court of 10 counts of tipping a friend, Daniel Duic, about pending corporate deals. Duic used the tips to make a net profit of over $4.5 million in stock trades between February 2001 and February 2002. Insider-trading charges against Duic were dropped in return for his testimony against Rankin and the payment of a $3 million fine. Rankin was acquitted of ten counts of the more serious offence of insider trading because he was apparently not aware of his friend's deals and he did not directly profit from them. Rankin was sentenced to six months in jail. However, in November 2006, the Ontario Superior Court, citing contradictory evidence (inconsistencies in Duic' evidence) and errors by the trial judge, overturned Rankin's conviction and ordered a new trial.

CRITICAL ANALYSIS: There have been very few successful insider-trading prosecutions in Canada. What factors make prosecutions difficult? Why is improper insider trading considered to be more serious than tipping?

Defense lawyer Brian Greenspan and Andrew Rankin

Business Law in Practice Revisited

1. How is a corporation formed, and what factors should Adam consider in forming a corporation?

A corporation is formed by an incorporator or incorporators making an application to the appropriate government body. The choice of the corporate form requires the consideration of a number of issues, including the cost of incorporation and where the corporation will conduct its business. Adam wishes to start small but foresees rapid expansion nationally and internationally; thus a federal incorporation would probably be the logical choice.

Adam also needs to consider such factors as whether the name he has chosen is already in use, what sort of capital structure he will employ, and how the corporation will be capitalized. In particular, Adam needs to recognize that his proposed share structure—half the shares to himself and half to Diane—may result in shareholder deadlock.

2. Does Adam appear to understand the concept of limited liability adequately?

Adam appears to be under a misconception concerning the nature of limited liability. He suggests that Cameron lend the money to the company as this will protect him from unlimited liability. In fact, Cameron would be protected from

---

31. *R. v. Felderhof* (2003), 68 O.R. (3d) 481 (C.A.).

unlimited liability both as a creditor and as a shareholder. A shareholder is not, except in rare situations, responsible for the debts of the corporation beyond the original investment. Thus, whether Cameron invests in debt or shares has little effect on the liability issue.

3. What other options are available, in addition to Cameron lending money to the corporation?

Cameron could invest as a shareholder, but a loan would give him priority over shareholders in the event of dissolution; however, a loan provides little opportunity to participate in profits unless the interest rate is tied to the profitability of the corporation. Shares offer profit opportunities but have greater risks of loss of investment should the company fail. Cameron's investment—whether in shares or debt—can be tailored to address Cameron's desire to participate in profits while avoiding risk.

4. What factors should Adam consider in seeking to raise money by selling shares?

In attempting to raise money by issuing shares, Adam needs to consider a number of factors. Most importantly, both public and private sales involve a consideration from a financial perspective as to whether there is a market for the corporation's shares. As well, any issuance or sale of shares involves an assessment of the impact on the control of the corporation. Sales on the public market also involve requirements as specified by the relevant securities legislation. These requirements can be significant and costly.

Chapter Summary

The corporate form is prevalent and widespread. The characteristic that distinguishes it from the other basic forms for carrying on business is its separate legal status. This means that the owners are not liable for the debts and obligations of the corporation. It also means that those who are dealing with a corporation need to understand that the owner's risk is limited. Thus, if security is important, they should demand a personal guarantee.

A corporation may be incorporated federally or provincially. There are few distinct advantages of incorporating in one jurisdiction versus another. Prior to commencing the incorporation process, incorporators must decide on a share structure, that is, the classes and number of shares authorized for issuance. The share structure may be simple or complex depending on the needs of the investors.

The actual process of establishing a corporation is relatively simple, and essentially the same format is followed in all jurisdictions. It is a matter of completing and filing the correct forms with the appropriate government body. That said, the incorporation process is not without risks, such as the risk of choosing a name that is similar to that of another business. This risk can be substantially reduced by obtaining legal advice.

A corporation can be financed by equity or debt. Equity represents what the shareholders have invested in the corporation in return for shares. Debt consists of loans that have been made to the corporation. The issuance of shares and debt instruments such as bonds to the public is strictly regulated by securities laws.

Chapter Study

Key Terms and Concepts

articles of incorporation (p. 358)

bond (p. 360)

bylaws (p. 358)

closely held corporation (p. 353)

conversion right (p. 361)

debenture (p. 360)

incorporator (p. 358)

insider (p. 365)

insider trading (p. 365)

NUANS report (p. 357)

prospectus (p. 363)

securities (p. 360)

securities legislation (p. 353)

share structure (p. 352)

shelf company (p. 357)

stakeholder (p. 351)

tippee (p. 365)

widely held corporation (p. 353)

Questions for Review

1. What does limited liability mean?

2. Who are the corporation's internal stakeholders? Who are the corporation's external stakeholders?

3. When should a business incorporate federally, and when should it incorporate provincially?

4. What basic rights must attach to at least one class of shares?

5. A class of shares may include a combination of various rights and privileges. Name three examples of typical rights that may attach to a class of shares.

6. What is the difference between a widely held and a closely held corporation?

7. How can a corporation qualify as a private corporation in Ontario? What are the advantages of a corporation qualifying as a private corporation?

8. Are shares freely transferable? Explain.

9. What are the basic requirements for a corporate name?

10. What is a NUANS report, and what is its purpose?

11. What is a shelf company, and what is its purpose?

12. Describe the process for incorporating a company.

13. Compare shares to bonds. Which is the more advantageous method of raising money?

14. What are the objectives of securities legislation? How are the objectives achieved?

15. In Ontario, the *Securities Act* has been amended to provide a new statutory right of action for misrepresentations contained in secondary market disclosures. What is the difference between the primary market and the secondary market for securities? What is the new statutory right of action for purchasers in the secondary market? Explain.

16. What is meant by insider trading? insider? tippee?

17. Is all insider trading prohibited? Explain.

18. What is a prospectus? What is its purpose?

Questions for Critical Thinking

1. *Salomon v. Salomon* stands for the proposition that the corporation has a separate existence from its shareholders. This means that creditors of a corporation do not have recourse against the shareholders' assets. Is this fair? Is it fair that creditors of a sole proprietorship seek the sole proprietor's personal assets? What is the justification for the difference in treatment?

2. A stakeholder is defined as someone who has an interest in the corporation. The general public and government are considered to be external stakeholders. What is the general public's interest in a corporation? What is the government's interest in a corporation?

3. Dual-class share structures are prevalent in Canada. It is estimated that over 20 percent of the companies listed on the Toronto Stock exchange use some form of dual-class structure. For example, Magna International issues both Class A subordinate-voting shares and Class B shares. The Class B shares carry 500 votes for every Class A vote. This structure has allowed Frank Stronach to maintain control of Magna with just 3.4 percent of the company's equity. Why do you think dual-class structures have emerged in Canada? What are the advantages and disadvantages of dual-class structures? What can companies with dual-class share structures do to make themselves more accountable to minority shareholders?

4. Many private companies go public to raise capital; however, there also seems to be a trend in public companies going private.[32] What factors might cause a public company to go private?

5. Since 1935, various Royal Commissions, provincial securities regulators, academics, and industry groups have recommended the creation of a single securities regulator for all of Canada.[33] What are the arguments in favour of a single securities regulator? What are the arguments against a single regulator?

6. In March 2004, the Canadian Securities Administrators introduced National Instrument 51-102—*Continuous Disclosure Obligations*. It requires reporting issuers to file an annual information form (AIF) that discloses the social and environmental policies implemented by the issuer that are fundamental to the operations of the issuer. The Social Investment Organization (SIO), a national, nonprofit association for the socially responsible investment industry in Canada, has criticized the instrument for its failure to require issuers to disclose social and environmental risks such as union disputes, discrimination and harassment complaints, product quality and safety issues, human rights complaints, and emissions problems.[34] Should companies be required to disclose their social and environmental risks? Why or why not?

Situations for Discussion

1. Jemson and Smithson have established a corporation for the manufacture and distribution of laser instruments used in the health care industry. They need to raise about $500 000 in working capital to finance the acquisition of inventory. How could this be done? What would be the advantages and disadvantages of the different alternatives?

2. Steering Clear Ltd. is a manufacturer of an expensive automatic helmsman that is used to

---

32. Tom Strezos and Monty Bhardwaj "Companies Going Private, When Others Are Going Public" *The Lawyers Weekly* (28 January 2005) at 9.
33. Lori Andrea Stein "Panel Explores Possibility of Canadian Securities Regulator" *The Lawyer's Weekly* (27 January 2006) at 9.
34. Eugene Ellmen "Comments on Proposed National Instrument 51-102, Continuous Disclosure" *Social Investment Organization* (6 August 2003) at http://www.socialinvestment.ca/Policy&Advocacy/CSAComments803.doc (accessed 15 January 2007)

navigate ocean cruisers. Perry Jones ordered such a helmsman on behalf of a company called Cruisin' Ltd. The helmsman was supplied, but Cruisin' Ltd. did not pay its account. Because of this delinquency, Steering Clear Ltd. decided to investigate the background of Cruisin' Ltd. and discovered that it has a grand total of two issued shares—one held by Perry and the other by his wife. Perry has advised Steering Clear Ltd. that the debtor company has only $5 in the bank and may have to go out of business soon. Steering Clear Ltd. wants to sue Perry personally for the debt.[35] Will Steering Clear Ltd. be successful? On what basis? What is the largest obstacle facing Steering Clear Ltd.'s potential action against Perry? What should Steering Clear Ltd. have done differently from a business perspective?

3. Sophie Smith has an opportunity to open a designer shoe store in a new mall. She believes that the shoe store will be quite lucrative because of the mall's location adjacent to a condominium development catering to young professionals. To exploit favourable tax laws, Sophie has decided to incorporate a company, and to save money she is going to do it herself. She knows that she will need a name for her corporation. Some of names that she is considering are Shoe Store Inc., Princess Sophie's Shoes Ltd., Down Town Shoes Inc., Sophie Smith Ltd., Nu Shuz Inc., Sophie Smith Clothing and Apparel Inc. and, simply, Sophie's Shoes. Are there any problems with the names that Sophie is considering for her corporation? Explain. Assume that Sophie has XZONIC Shoes Inc. approved as the corporation's name. What rights does registration of a corporate name give Sophie?

4. Robert Merchant has been in the commercial real estate business for over 15 years. He wants to start his own real estate business under the name Merchant Commercial Real Estate Services Inc. He is well known in the industry and believes that by using his surname as the distinctive element in his corporate name, he will best be able to capitalize on the goodwill he has built up over the years. He expects, however, that a local competitor, Larry Wasyliw, would object since Mr. Wasyliw operates under the name and style of Merchant Realty Ltd. and has been doing so for a number of years.[36] Is it permissible for Mr. Merchant to incorporate under the name Merchant Commercial Real Estate? What are the objections to the name? What is the test that the court would apply in determining the permissibility of the proposed name?

5. Homer, Raddison, and Bloke are friends who wish to incorporate an enterprise to carry on a small-business consulting, bookkeeping, and accounting business. Homer and Raddison will each contribute $80 000 and Bloke will contribute $40 000 to the start-up costs of the venture. Homer has had some experience in running this type of business and wants a say in how the business is run. Raddison has no experience and is content to leave management decisions to the other two. Bloke has considerable experience and wants an equal voice in the corporation's affairs. Homer and Bloke are interested in the long-term growth of the business; however, Raddison is hoping to receive a regular return on his investment. What are the potential problems with the proposed venture? What share structure would you recommend to account for the contributions and interests of the three?

6. During the summer of 2000, Jesse Hogan used four e-mail accounts provided through three Internet service providers to send thousands of fraudulent e-mails and to post thousands of fraudulent chat room and bulletin board messages at various Internet sites (including Yahoo.com and SiliconInvestor.com). Using various nicknames and aliases (such as stockboy2002), he targeted five publicly traded companies whose shares were quoted on the NASD Over-the-Counter Bulletin Board. In a simple "pump-and-dump" scheme, he sent the e-mails and posted the messages intending to

35. Based on *Henry Browne & Sons Ltd. v. Smith*, [1964] 2 Lloyd's Rep. 477 (Q.B.).
36. Based on *Merchant Commercial Real Estate Services Inc. v. Alberta (Registrar of Corporations)* (1997), 199 A.R. 12 (Q.B.).

create the appearance of trading activity in the companies' shares and to cause the share prices to rise. Subsequently he bought and sold shares and earned thousands of dollars in profit from the artificially high prices caused by his misrepresentations. Hogan defended his conduct by arguing that Internet users have different expectations regarding the accuracy of Internet information, and that a different regulatory approach ought to apply to Internet securities activity. Hogan emphasized the warnings and disclaimers typically found on Internet message boards and chat rooms, argued that it was patently unreasonable for investors to base their decisions on information found on Internet message boards or chat rooms, and submitted that members of the "Internet subculture" are "technically savvy and understand how the game is played."[37] Do you agree with Hogan's arguments? Do you think different rules should apply to the Internet? Should there be a different regulatory approach toward the Internet?

7. In June 2003, Sam Waksal, the co-founder and former CEO of ImClone was sentenced to seven years in prison and fined $4 million on charges of insider trading. He was found guilty of leaking confidential information to family and friends in the days leading up the release of a federal ruling that rejected the company's Erbitux cancer drug. Among the friends said to have been tipped was Martha Stewart. She sold nearly 4000 shares on ImClone on the day prior to the regulator's announcement. The sale saved her about US$51 000. Stewart pleaded not guilty to charges of insider trading, conspiracy, obstruction of justice, and making false statements to investigators. She argued that she had an agreement with her stockbroker to sell the shares if the price went below $60. The prosecution said Stewart had misled investigators by saying she did not recall if her stockbroker called on the day she sold her shares. The presiding judge dropped the insider-trading charge and a jury convicted her of conspiracy, obstruction of justice, and making false statements to investigators. Stewart was sentenced to five months in prison, five months home arrest, two years probation and a fine of $30 000. In January 2006, a federal appeals court in New York upheld her conviction. Was Martha Stewart an insider in relation to ImClone? What are the problems with insider trading? Should insiders be prohibited from trading in shares? Why is difficult to prove improper insider trading?

8. Alimentation Couche-Tard Inc. is the Canadian leader in the convenience store industry. At 8:30 a.m. on Monday, October 6, 2003, Couche-Tard publicly announced a deal to purchase the 2013-store Circle K chain. Completion of the deal would make Couche-Tard the fourth largest convenience store operators in North America. When trading opened on the Toronto Stock Exchange at 9:30 a.m., the company's class B stock was up 40 cents at $17.50. The price steadily gained all day to close at $21, for a gain of $3.90. Within five minutes of the opening, Roger Longré, a Couche-Tard director bought 1500 shares and by 10:30 he bought a further 2500. At the end of the day, he had a one-day gain, on paper, of $11 372.[38] Did Longré breach any legal requirements? Did he breach any ethical requirements? Should insiders be prohibited from trading prior to earning announcements and after major announcements? Should insiders be required to clear all proposed trades in the company's securities with a designated in-house trading monitor?

For more study tools, visit
http://www.businesslaw3e.nelson.com

---

37. Based on *Re Hogan*, (2002), BCSECCOM 537.
38. "Insider Trading: A Special Report" *The Globe and Mail* (18 December 2003) at B6–B7.

Chapter

16

Objectives

After studying this chapter, you should have an understanding of

- the liabilities of a corporation
- the duties and liabilities of corporate directors and officers
- the rights and liabilities of shareholders and creditors
- how the corporation is terminated

The Corporate Form: Operational Matters

Business Law in Practice

IK Enterprises Ltd., incorporated under the *Canada Business Corporations Act*, has been in operation for a little over a year. Adam owns 50 percent of the common shares and Diane the remaining 50 percent. Adam's father, Cameron, was issued 100 preferred shares. Adam and Diane are directors and officers of the corporation and Cameron is an officer, although not a director. He is the president of the corporation.

The company has done reasonably well with the marketing and selling of its enhanced voice-recognition system for computers. Although demand was less than anticipated, sales exceeded $500 000 for the first year of operations. There is, however, a major problem confronting the company.

Diane has recently come across a software program that translates computer output into French, Spanish, and German, which she thinks would be quite compatible with the company's present product. She is interested in buying the rights to the translation product for IK Enterprises. Adam, however, is not interested in expansion and wants to concentrate on a limited product line. Diane is contemplating forming another company to exploit this opportunity if the disagreement between her and Adam cannot be resolved. Cameron does not want to get involved in the dispute at all because he has much more immediate concerns.

Cameron believes that IK Enterprises is plagued by lax standards in its day-to-day operations. From Cameron's perspective, this is what Adam and Diane should focus their attention on. For example, Cameron has discovered that IK Enterprises has not been deducting and remitting income tax on salary paid to certain employees. Cameron not only finds this unacceptable from an accounting perspective, but also worries about IK Enterprises' liability and fears that he may have personal liability for this "oversight."

1. Is IK Enterprises liable for the failure to deduct and remit income tax? Does Cameron, as an officer of IK Enterprises, have any personal liability for the failure to deduct and remit the taxes?
2. What obligations do Cameron, Diane, and Adam have as corporate officers and directors?
3. How can the disagreement between Adam and Diane be resolved?
4. Are there any problems with Diane forming her own company to take advantage of the translation product opportunity?
5. What are Cameron's rights as a shareholder if he does not like how Diane and Adam are managing the company?

Corporate Liability

A corporation is a legal person in the eyes of the law. The corollary is that the corporation is responsible for its own actions. The responsibility of the corporation is, however, complicated by the necessity of corporations acting through human agents. The law has developed rules regarding how a corporation can be said to have committed a tort, committed a crime or regulatory offence, or entered a contract. These rules are particularly important to stakeholders such as Cameron because they determine the legal consequences of corporate behaviour.

Liability in Tort

A corporation can experience two distinct kinds of liability in tort: primary liability and vicarious liability.

A corporation has primary liability for a tort when, in law, it is regarded as the entity that actually committed the tort in question. The idea of a corporation having primary liability is inherently problematic since a corporation, as noted above, can work only through human agents. How can a corporation commit a tort when it does not have a mind of its own and does not have a physical existence?

The courts have overcome this hurdle by developing what is known as the **identification theory** of corporate liability.[1] A corporation has liability—and could therefore be described as directly "at fault"—when the person committing the wrong was the corporation's "directing mind and will."

identification theory
A theory specifying that a corporation is liable when the person committing the wrong is the corporation's directing mind.

The theory seeks to determine which person or persons are the directing mind of the corporation. When that person (or persons) commits a tort related to the business enterprise, this conduct is identified with or attributed to the corporation itself. The liability of the corporation is thereby made direct—not vicarious—because in law, the conduct of the directing mind is the conduct of the corporation.

Generally, it is the highly placed corporate officers who are classified as "directing" minds while low-level employees are not. Whether a mid-range employee would be a directing mind is a more complicated and fact-specific inquiry. A corporation may have more than one directing mind. Each may be responsible for a different aspect of the corporation's business. For example, the vice president for marketing may be the corporation's directing mind in relation to the marketing function whereas the vice president for finance may be the directing mind in relation to finance.

A corporation has vicarious liability[2] when the tort has been committed by an agent or employee who is not a directing mind of the corporation. The law of vicarious liability does not distinguish between the natural employer/principal—that is, a living, breathing human being—and the artificial employer/principal—that is, a corporation. Instead, the same principle applies to both.

Liability in Contract

While there is no reason the identification theory could not be used as a way of assessing a corporation's liability in contract, the courts generally have not followed this approach. Instead, agency law largely determines when a corporation is liable on a contract and when it is not.

A corporation is bound by the actions of the agent only if the agent is acting within his actual or apparent authority. For example, if Diane were to enter a contract on behalf of IK Enterprises to purchase the rights to translation software, IK Enterprises would be bound to the contract so long as Diane had the actual or apparent authority to enter the contract. Historically, an agent's apparent authority could be limited by filing with the incorporation documents a specific limitation of the agent's authority. As these documents were publicly filed, outsiders were deemed to have notice of them and to have read their contents. This was known as the doctrine of constructive notice and produced commercial inconvenience, since the only way that an outsider could fully protect herself would be to go down to

---

1. *Lennard's Carrying Co. v. Asiatic Petroleum Co.*, [1915] A.C. 705.
2. Vicarious liability is discussed in Chapters 10 and 20.

the registry office and review what the company had filed there. The doctrine has been abolished,[3] meaning that outsiders can now generally rely on the apparent authority of agents. In such a case, the corporation would be liable on the contract.

To avoid personal liability, the person signing a document on behalf of a corporation should ensure that the document contains a clause clearly indicating that the person is signing on behalf of the corporation and is not signing in her personal capacity. This precaution is equally important in the case of pre-incorporation contracts.

Pre-incorporation contracts are contracts that have been entered into by the company's promoters[4] on behalf of the corporation before it has even been created. Such contracts are governed by federal and provincial corporate law statutes, which permit the company to adopt the contract—something that was impossible to do at common law. When adoption occurs, the corporation assumes liability on the contract. The promoter can avoid liability so long as the pre-incorporation contract expressly indicates that the promoter was acting on behalf of the corporation.[5] Pre-incorporation contracts can be problematic if they do not indicate clearly who is intended to be liable[6] and if the corporation fails to come into existence.

From a risk management perspective, people would probably do well to avoid pre-incorporation contracts altogether. Although such contracts are sometimes necessary in order to take advantage of a valuable business opportunity that just cannot wait, it is usually possible to find a corporate vehicle quickly—such as through the purchase of a shelf company. In this way the corporation is immediately in place and can enter the contemplated contract directly.

Criminal and Regulatory Liability

Criminal Liability

The criminal liability of a corporation poses the same conceptual problems as tort liability. As Baron Thurlow, L.C., observed in the 18th century, "Did you ever expect a corporation to have a conscience, when it has no soul to be damned and no body to be kicked?"

The judiciary solved this problem by adapting the identification theory to the criminal law scenario. The theory maintains that a corporation has committed a crime if the person who committed the crime was a directing mind of the corporation and he committed it in the course of his duties and did so mostly for the benefit of the corporation.[7] A directing mind of a corporation is an individual(s) who exercises decision-making authority in matters of corporate policy. This approach to corporate criminal liability has been augmented by amendments to the *Criminal Code*.[8] The following box explores the amendments.

---

3. See, for example, *Canada Business Corporations Act*, R.S.C. 1985, c. C-44, s. 17.
4. A promoter is someone who participates in setting up a corporation.
5. *Supra* note 3; see, for example, s. 14(4):
   Exemption from personal liability—If expressly so provided in the written contract, a person who purported to act in the name of or on behalf of the corporation before it came into existence is not . . . bound by the contract.
6. The legislative provisions protecting the promoter from personal liability have been strictly construed by the courts. For example, in *Landmark Inns of Canada Ltd. v. Horeak* (1982), 18 Sask. R. 30 (Q.B.), the court held that merely naming the yet-to-be incorporated corporation as a party to the contract was insufficient to relieve the promoter of personal liability. The contract must also contain an express provision that specifically relieves him of liability.
7. A corporation is not liable for an offence committed by a "directing mind" that is totally unrelated to her corporate position. For example, a corporation is not liable for a break and enter committed by the president on her way home from the office.
8. R.S.C. 1985 c. C-46.

On 9 May 1992, 26 miners died in an underground an explosion at the Westray coal mine in Plymouth, Nova Scotia. The public inquiry that followed the disaster found that the explosion could have been prevented if the mine's owners and managers had paid attention to repeated safety warnings. Despite this finding, no one was ever fined or imprisoned for the deaths of the miners. The public inquiry's findings also highlighted the difficulty in holding corporations criminally responsible. In response, the federal government passed Bill C-45, "*An Act to Amend the Criminal Code (Criminal Liability of Organizations).*[9] On 31 March 2004 the amendments were proclaimed in force. The most significant provisions are:

Liability for organizations. Criminal liability is extended to "organizations," which includes corporations, companies, partnerships, trade unions, and any association of persons created for a common purpose, has a structure and holds itself out as an association of persons. Prior to the amendments, the code narrowly defined the types of entities capable of being charged with an offence. Now, few public or private sector corporations or voluntary associations will be able to successfully argue that they do not fall within the definition of an "organization."

The type of individuals who may trigger an organization's criminal liability has been expanded. Prior to the amendments a corporation could be liable for a criminal offence only if the directing mind of the corporation committed the offence. The amendments expand the range of individuals whose actions can trigger liability of the corporation to senior officers. These are individuals who play an important role in the establishment of the organization's policies or are responsible for managing an important aspect of the organizations' activities. This prevents corporations from avoiding liability by suggesting that wrongdoers simply had a management function and did not set policy.

Elements of a crime. For offences that require intent,[10] an organization will be criminally liable if a senior officer, while acting in the scope of his or her authority and intending at least in part to benefit the organization, either actively engages in unsafe conduct, directs representatives[11] to do it, or knows about the unsafe conduct but does nothing or not enough to put a stop to it, and death or injury results. The effect of the changes is that it is no longer necessary that the intent and the guilty act of a criminal offence reside in the same person. Also, senior officers are now under a positive obligation to act when they have knowledge that an offence has been or will be committed; failure to act will result in corporate criminal liability.

For offences based on negligence,[12] an organization can be convicted if any representative providing services for the organization causes injury or death by unsafe conduct and the senior officer or officers in charge of the activities of the representative departs markedly from the reasonable standard of care necessary to prevent the incident. These changes broaden negligence offences by allowing the combined conduct of two individuals, who individually may not be acting in a manner that is careless or reckless, to constitute the necessary elements of the crime in order to hold the corporation responsible.

New legal duty. The amendments establish a new legal duty[13] for everyone who undertakes or has the authority to direct how another does work to take reasonable steps to prevent bodily harm to anyone arising from that work. This provision appears to expand the direct application of criminal punishment to individuals within the organization and encourages a proactive approach to occupational health and safety at all levels of the organization.

---

9. S.C. 2003, c.21, s.2.
10. Most crimes in the *Criminal Code* fall within this category; for example, fraud, theft, and bribery.
11. A representative includes everyone working or affiliated with an organization such as a director, partner, employee, agent, or contractor.
12. Examples of negligence-based crimes are storing a firearm in a careless manner, operating a motor vehicle in a manner dangerous to the public, and showing wanton and reckless disregard for the lives or safety of others.
13. See Chapter 20 for further discussion of the new health and safety crime.

Penalties. The amendments provide for stiffer penalties and corporate probation orders. A less serious summary conviction offence carries a fine up to $100 000 (an increase from $25 000) and fines for more serous indictable offences remain with no pre-scribed limits. The legislation also enumerates factors that the courts must consider when setting fines including moral blameworthiness (i.e., the economic advantage gained by the organization by committing the crime), public interest (i.e., the cost of investiga-tion and prosecution, the need to keep the organiza-tion in business), and the prospects of rehabilitation (remedial steps directed to preventing the likelihood of a subsequent offence). A corporate probation order may involve conditions such as providing resti-tution to victims, publishing the offence in the media, and implementing policies and procedures. Its purpose is to allow the court to oversee and reg-ulate an organization's efforts to reform.

CRITICAL ANALYSIS: What steps should corporations take to address the risks created by the amendments to the *Criminal Code?*

Westray Mine Memorial

Regulatory Offences

In addition to criminal liability under the *Criminal Code of Canada*, a corporation faces liability pursuant to a wide range of statutory enactments related to taxation, human rights, pay equity, employment standards, consumer protection, unfair or anticompetitive business practices, occupational health and safety, and environ-mental protection, to name a few. The relevant legislation often imposes penalties on the corporation, and sometimes even its directors and officers, including civil lia-bility for damages.

regulatory offence
An offence contrary to the public interest.

The offences alluded to above are known as **regulatory offences.** They have a criminal aspect because they involve forbidding some kind of conduct that is con-trary to the public interest, such as polluting streams, and providing a punishment for those who disobey.

Owing to the large number of regulatory offences affecting business, as well as the expense and public relations problems associated with their commission, corpo-rations have become increasingly concerned with assessing and managing their exposure. Although it is difficult to gauge the extent to which corporate liability in this area has increased, there have been dramatic examples of corporations being subjected to regulatory penalties. Consider, for example, the following:

- M/V Cala Palamos was fined $100 00 for discharging 4300 litres of waste oil into Halifax Harbour.[14]

- Mining giant Inco was fined $650 000 pursuant to Ontario's *Occupational Health and Safety Act* as a result of a mining death.[15]

---

14. Donalee Moulton, "Oil Spill Brings $100 000 Fine" *The Lawyers Weekly* (22 April 2003) at 3.
15. John Jaffey, "Inco Sudbury Mining Fatality Leads to Record $550 000 Fine" *The Lawyers Weekly* (5 October 2001) at 3.

- Union Carbide Canada Ltd. was fined $1.7 million after pleading guilty to conspiring to fix prices of compressed gases; Canadian Oxygen Ltd., which had a smaller share of the $200 million bulk gas market, received a fine of $700 000.[16]
- The owner of the *Baltic Confidence*, a bulk carrier, was fined $125 000 for discharging pollutants off Sable Island.[17]

IK Enterprises' operations may be affected by many legislative provisions. For example, the *Income Tax Act*[18] requires that every person paying salary, wages, or other remuneration withhold a prescribed amount of income tax. IK Enterprises is a person paying salary so it comes within the provisions of the legislation. Its failure to deduct and remit income taxes can trigger penalties including, for a first offence, a fine of 10 percent of the amount owing. Liability under this taxation legislation is strict[19] and defences are therefore rare.[20]

Directors and Officers

The directors, who are elected by shareholders, manage or supervise the management of the business and the affairs of the corporation.[21] In addition to this general authority, directors have specific powers and obligations set out in legislation. For example, directors can declare dividends, call shareholder meetings, adopt bylaws, and issue shares. Directors are, however, not usually in a position to carry out the actual management themselves; generally they are authorized to appoint officers to carry out many of their duties and exercise most of their powers.[22] This power of delegation does not, however, relieve the directors of ultimate responsibility for the management of the corporation.

Duties of Directors and Officers

In exercising their management function, directors and officers have obligations contained in two broad categories: a fiduciary duty and a duty of competence.

The Fiduciary Duty

This duty requires directors and officers to act honestly and in good faith with a view to the best interests of the corporation. They cannot allow themselves to favour one particular group of shareholders, for example, because their duty is not to that group but rather to the corporation as a whole. One of the central principles informing fiduciary duties in corporate law can be summarized as follows: directors and officers must not allow their personal interest to conflict with their duty to the corporation. Not surprisingly, then, the fiduciary principle arises in multiple circumstances, two of which are explored below.

---

16. *Calgary Herald* (7 September 1991) at F5.
17. Alison Auld, "Sea Pollution Draws Record $125 000 Fine" *The Edmonton Journal* (26 February 2002) at A9.
18. R.S.C. 1985, c. 1 (5th Supp.), s. 153(1).
19. The vast majority of regulatory offences are strict liability offences. This means that the accused may avoid liability if he can show that he acted with due diligence or took all reasonable care. Few offences impose absolute liability, that is, liability is imposed for doing the act, and it is not open to the accused to show he was without fault.
20. Vern Krishna, "Directors' Liability for Corporate Taxes" *The Lawyers Weekly* (14 July 2000) at 5.
21. This general power may be circumscribed by the bylaws or by a unanimous shareholder areement.
22. Note that some matters, such as declaring dividends and approving the annual financial statements, may not be delegated.

Corporate scandals such as Enron and WorldCom in the United States and Hollinger in Canada have shaken investor confidence in the competence and integrity of management. They have also prompted shareholders to demand better accountability from public companies. In response, the United States passed the *Sarbanes-Oxley Act* in 2002. The act introduced far-reaching provisions to strengthen accountability of corporate officers, improve corporate disclosure, enhance auditing standards, and limit conflicts of interests.

Following the American lead, Canada has also gradually introduced corporate and securities law reform. The Canadian Securities Administrators[23] have introduced a series of national policies including rules requiring CEO/CFO certification of annual and quarterly reports, rules relating to new standards and an expanded role for the audit committee, rules establishing the Canadian Public Accountability Board to oversee the auditing profession, and rules dealing with the disclosure by Canadian public corporations of their governance practices.[24]

Regulation of corporate governance is not new. In 1995, the Toronto Stock Exchange (TSE) commissioned a report to examine corporate governance in Canada.[25] Also known as the Dey Report, it made 14 recommendations for the reform of corporate governance in public companies. Included were recommendations that a majority of the board be composed of directors who were independent of management and free of any interest that could interfere with their ability to act in the best interests of the corporation; that every board adopt a structure such as having a chair who was independent of management, to allow the board to act independently of management; and that the audit committee comprise outside directors. The TSE adopted the non-mandatory best practices and required listed companies to annually disclose their practices for comparison with the TSE standards. Since then there have been other reports on corporate governance in Canada[26] and further amendments to the TSE guidelines. The Canadian Securities Administrators (CSA) rules are similar to the TSE guidelines. Effective 30 June 2005 the Canadian Securities Commissions adopted the CSA polices on corporate governance ("best practices")[27] and the disclosure of corporate governance practices.[28]

The corporate governance "best practices" include the following:

- that a board have a majority of *independent* directors, that the chair of the board be independent, and that independent directors hold regularly scheduled meetings

- that a board adopt a *written mandate* that explicitly acknowledges responsibility for the stewardship of the company. The written mandate should include expectations and responsibilities of directors and measures to receive feedback from shareholders

- that a board develop clear *position descriptions* for the chair of the board and all committee chairs

- that a board ensure that new directors undertake a comprehensive orientation and provide continuing board *education* for all board members

- that a board adopt a written *code of business conduct and ethics* and monitor compliance with that code

23. The Canadian Securities Administrators is a body composed of the 13 provincial and territorial securities regulators whose role is to coordinate and harmonize securities regulation policy across Canada.
24. The CSA rules are called multilateral instruments or MIs, and national instruments or NLs. These provisions have been adopted by all jurisdictions in Canada with the exception of British Columbia, which has not adopted the rules with respect to the CEO/CFO board certification and audit committees. Most provisions are now in force.
25. Peter Dey, *Where Were the Directors?: Guidelines for Improved Corporate Governance in Canada* (Toronto: Toronto Stock Exchange, 1994).
26. Guylaine Saucier, "Beyond Compliance: Building a Governance Culture" *Final Report of the Joint Committee on Corporate Governance* (Toronto: Toronto Stock Exchange, Canadian Venture Exchange, Canadian Institute of Chartered Accountants, 2001). For more information, see http://www.cica.ca/multimedia/Download_Library/Research_Guidance/Risk_Management_Governance/Governance_Eng_Nov 26.pdf (accessed 30 November 2006).
27. National Instrument 58-201 Corporate Governance Guidelines.
28. National Policy 58-101 *Disclosure of Corporate Governance Practices*

- that a board have *nominating and compensation committees*, both comprising independent directors, and both of whose written charters clearly set out the committee's purpose, responsibilities, operations, and member qualifications

- that each board and committee member be *regularly assessed* as to his effectiveness.

The corporate governance guidelines are not mandatory; rather, publicly traded companies are encouraged to consider them in developing their own corporate governance practices. However, companies are required to describe their adopted corporate governance practices and, where the adopted practice is different than the "best practice," explain how what is being done satisfies the objectives of the "best practice."

CRITICAL ANALYSIS: Are there any problems with having a majority of a board of directors composed of independent directors? Should good governance practices be mandated or can the market be relied on to impose good governance practices?

self-dealing contract
A contract in which a fiduciary has a conflict of interest.

The Self-Dealing Contract   To understand how a **self-dealing contract** works, assume the following scenario. IK Enterprises requires some office furniture, which Adam just so happens to be in a position to supply. He has several reasonably nice executive desks stored in his basement and is willing to sell them to the corporation. Adam is now in a conflict-of-interest situation.

As director of IK Enterprises Ltd., Adam is obligated to try to buy the furniture at as low a price as possible. As vendor of the furniture, however, Adam may be motivated by self-interest to sell the furniture at as high a price as possible. In this way, his duty to the corporation and his self-interest may collide because Adam is on both sides of the contract.

FIGURE 16.1

Self-Dealing Contract

Adam (the corporate director) ➡ buys from ➡ Adam (the individual)

In law, Adam is said to be in a self-dealing contract: he is dealing with himself in the purchase and sale of the office furniture.

Many jurisdictions have enacted procedures through which self-dealing contracts are permissible. The idea is to ensure that the corporation is not "ripped off" and, at the same time, to avoid a blanket prohibition on self-dealing contracts since some of them could be beneficial to the company. Under the *Canada Business Corporations Act*, for example, Adam's contract to sell furniture to his own company will be enforceable provided that

- Adam discloses the contract to the corporation in writing
- Adam does not participate in any vote of the directors approving the contract
- the contract is fair and reasonable to the corporation[29]

Failure to follow these statutory provisions gives the corporation the right to ask a court for a remedy, including that the contract be set aside or "cancelled" on any terms the court sees fit.

---

29. *Supra* note 3, s. 120.

Corporate Opportunities Another area in which conflicts of interest frequently arise concerns **corporate opportunities.** Directors and officers are often required to assess any number of projects in which their corporation could become involved. These projects are known in law as "corporate opportunities"—they are opportunities to do business that the company can pursue or decline. If the directors and officers were permitted to take up any of these opportunities for themselves, problems very much like the ones present in the self-dealing contract scenario would arise.

Assume that IK Enterprises has been approached by an Ontario company that is in the business of educating executives in the latest technology available for the workplace. That company would like to work with IK Enterprises to create a course on voice-recognition systems, the revenue potential of which appears to be very high. Adam is in a conflict-of-interest situation. As a director, he is required to assess the corporate opportunity on its own merits. As an individual, however, because he is interested in the contract for himself, he is motivated by self-interest. Put another way, if Adam were permitted to pursue the opportunity himself, he would be tempted—in his capacity as director—to turn down the project, not because it was in the best interests of the corporation to do so but because he wanted to present the course himself.

Landmark Case ▼

Canadian Aero Service Ltd. v. O'Malley,
[1974] S.C.R. 592

THE HISTORIAL CONTEXT: The Supreme Court's decision in this case is the leading analysis of the principles underlying the corporate opportunity doctrine in Canada. The case is also important because of the court's recognition that officers may owe fiduciary duties to the corporation and a director or officer may be precluded from appropriating a business opportunity even after she resigns.

FACTUAL BACKGROUND: On behalf of their company, Canadian Aero Service Ltd. (Canaero), the president and executive vice president had been negotiating to win an aerial mapping contract in Guyana. Subsequently, both officers left Canaero and set up their own company, Terra Surveys Limited. Terra began to pursue the very same line of work as Canaero and successfully bid on the aerial mapping contract in Guyana. Canaero brought an action against Terra and its former executives for improperly taking Canaero's corporate opportunity.

THE LEGAL QUESTION: Were the former executives in breach of their fiduciary duty to Canaero? Did the fact that the two had resigned and then, some time later, acquired the opportunity for themselves mean that there was no liability?

RESOLUTION: The former executives were held liable to account to Canaero for the profits they made under the contract. They had breached their fiduciary duties by taking something that belonged to the corporation. In determining whether the appropriation of an opportunity is a breach of fiduciary duty, the court suggested an examination of factors such as these:

- the position or office held by the directors and officers (the higher they are in the organization, the higher their duty)

- the nature of the corporate opportunity (how clearly was the opportunity identified by the corporation and how close was the corporation to acquiring the opportunity?)

- the director's or managerial officer's relation to the opportunity (was the opportunity one that the fiduciary worked on or had responsibility for?)

- the amount of knowledge the directors and officers possessed and the circumstances in which it was obtained

- the time between when the opportunity arose and when the officers took the opportunity for themselves

- the circumstances under which the employment relationship between the officers and the company terminated (was termination due to retirement, resignation, or discharge?)

Because the former officers violated their fiduciary duty, any profit gained—even if it was not at the expense of their former company—had to be given to the company. That they had resigned before pursuing the opportunity did not change the analysis.

CRITICAL ANALYSIS: When do you think a director of a corporation should be able to take advantage of a business opportunity? In other words, when is a business opportunity her own and when does it belong to the company she serves as director?

Ethical Considerations
Corporate Social Responsibility and Directors' Duties

Corporate Social Responsibility (CSR) is a term without a precise definition. It is used generally to encompass a business's policies and practices in relation to such issues as investment in community outreach, the creation and maintenance of employment, consumer protection, environmental sustainability and the like. In short, CSR is about companies moving beyond mere compliance with laws to integrating social responsibility into their decision-making processes. Examples of CSR responsibility are MAC cosmetics raising more than US$70 million for the fight against HIV/AIDS, CIBC sponsoring "The Run for the Cure" to help the battle against breast cancer, Home Depot ensuring that it uses wood products only from sustainable managed forests, and IBM Canada partnering with government to enhance Aboriginal economic opportunities.

The concept of CSR is underpinned by the notion that business is accountable to a wide range of stakeholders including employees, suppliers, customers, government, nongovernmental organizations, and the community. CSR, however, is not enshrined in the legal system. Corporate legislation gives little recognition to stakeholders such as employees and the community within which the business is located, who may have an interest in corporate decisions. For example, directors, who are charged with the responsibility of managing a corporation, have a duty to act honestly and in good faith with a view to the best interests of the corporation. This fiduciary duty is owed to the corporation—not to stakeholders. The Supreme Court of Canada in *Peoples Department Stores v. Wise*[30] stated, "At all times, directors and officers owe their fiduciary obligation to the corporation. The interests of the corporation are not to be confused with the interests of the creditors or those of any other stakeholders." The court also stated, "We accept as an accurate statement of the law that in determining whether they are acting with a view to the best interests of the corporation it may be legitimate, given all the circumstances of a given case, for the board of directors to consider *inter alia* the interests of shareholders, employees, suppliers, creditors, consumers, governments, and the environment." In essence, the court stated that directors *may* consider the interests of various stakeholders—but they are not bound to consider their interests.

CRITICAL ANALYSIS: Despite the lack of corporate legislation compelling directors to consider the interests of all stakeholders, CSR is becoming increasingly important to business. What factors are pushing business toward CSR? What can business gain from being socially responsible? What are the risks? Should government have a role in promoting CSR?

---

30. (2004), 244 DLR (4th) 564 (S.C.C.).

Given her fiduciary duty as director, Diane must proceed cautiously if she is still determined to pursue the translation product opportunity. Provided that Diane secures Adam's and Cameron's fully informed consent, perhaps in the form of a directors' resolution and a shareholders' resolution, there is no obvious legal impediment to her proceeding to develop the translation product. She is being above-board and acting fairly *vis-à-vis* IK Enterprises. Since IK Enterprises does not want to pursue the opportunity, it would be highly unlikely that a court would decide that Diane was in breach of her fiduciary duty to IK Enterprises by taking the opportunity for herself.

The Duty of Competence

This duty requires directors and officers to exercise the care, diligence, and skill that a reasonably prudent person would exercise in comparable circumstances. Put more informally, directors and officers must meet a general standard of competence.

At one time, directors had very minimal obligations to act with care in exercising their responsibilities. In *Re City Equitable Fire Insurance Co.*,[31] for example, the court held that "a director need not exhibit in the performance of his duties a greater degree of skill than may reasonably be expected from a person of his knowledge and experience." This meant that if the director were ill-informed and foolish, then little could be expected of her; she was required only to display the competence of an ill-informed and foolish person. The unfortunate outcome at common law was that the less qualified a director was for office, the less time and attention she devoted to her duties, and the greater the reliance she placed on others, the lower was the standard that she was required to meet in managing the business affairs of the company.

Recognizing that the common law standard of care was unduly low, legislatures have codified and upgraded what is expected of directors. The present standard contained in corporation legislation requires directors and officers to display the care, diligence, and skill that a reasonably prudent person would exercise in comparable circumstances. Recently the Supreme Court, in the following case, stated that this is an objective standard and while directors are not expected to be perfect, they are to act prudently and on a reasonably informed basis.

CASE ▼

Peoples Department Stores Inc. (Trustee of) v. Wise (2004), 244 DLR (4th) 564 (S.C.C.).

THE BUSINESS CONTEXT: The *Canada Business Corporations Act* imposes a duty on directors and officers to act honestly and in good faith with a view to the best interests of the corporation (the fiduciary duty) and to exercise the care, diligence, and skill that a reasonably prudent person would exercise in comparable circumstances (a duty of care).[32] There have been questions about whether the duties of directors

extend to creditors, particularly when the corporation is financially troubled. In this case, which is now Canada's leading case on directors' duties, the Supreme Court addresses this question.

FACTUAL BACKGROUND: Lionel, Ralph, and Harold Wise were majority shareholders and directors of Wise Stores Inc., a publicly traded company operating about 50 junior department stores in Quebec with annual sales of $100 million. In 1992, Wise Inc. acquired all of the shares of Peoples Department Stores Inc., from Marks & Spencer for $27 million. Peoples owned 81 stores and generated sales of $160 million annually. The Wise brothers became

---

31. [1925] 1 Ch. 407 at 428.
32. Most provincial corporate statutes provide for similar duties.

the sole directors of Peoples. The joint operation of Wise and Peoples did not function smoothly. In an effort to help the sagging fortunes of the companies, the Wise brothers implemented a joint inventory purchasing policy on the recommendation of the companies' vice-president of administration and finance. The result of the policy was that Peoples purchased and paid for most of Wise Inc.'s inventory, subject to reimbursement by Wise Inc. Peoples ended up extending large amounts of trade credit to Wise and by June 1994, Wise owed more than $18 million to Peoples. The financial situations of both companies continued to deteriorate and both ended up bankrupt in January 1995. After the sale of the assets and the payment of secured creditors, approximately $21.5 million in trade debt went unpaid. The Peoples' trustee in bankruptcy, representing the interests of the unpaid creditors, sued the Wise brothers, alleging that in implementing the joint inventory procurement program, they breached their duties as directors of Peoples.

THE LEGAL QUESTION: Did the Wise brothers as directors of Peoples owe duties to the creditors of Peoples? If so, did they breach these duties?

RESOLUTION: In a unanimous decision, the Supreme Court of Canada held that the Wise brothers did not owe a fiduciary duty to the creditors. While directors are entitled to have regard to the interests of various stakeholders—shareholders, employees, suppliers, creditors, consumers, government and the environment—they owe their fiduciary duty only to the corporation. The directors' fiduciary duty does not change when the corporation is in the "vicinity of insolvency." The court further noted that stakeholders, like creditors, have other avenues of potential relief. The creditors can use the oppression remedy to protect their interests from the prejudicial conduct of directors.

The Court also held that creditors can pursue an action based on breach of the duty of care as the identity of the beneficiaries of this duty was "more open ended" and "obviously" included creditors (this marks the first time that the Supreme Court has extended the duty of care beyond the corporation). The Court stated that the duty of care is to be judged objectively. In analyzing whether particular conduct met the standard of care, the Court will consider the factual circumstances as well as socioeconomic conditions. The Supreme Court (also for the first time) endorsed the "business judgment rule" in assessing whether directors have fulfilled the duty of care. The rule holds that the Court will not second-guess business judgments that are made honestly and on the basis of reasonable information. The Wise brothers did not breach their duty of care to creditors as the inventory policy was a reasonable effort to address inventory management problems.

CRITICAL ANALYSIS: Is the decision in *Peoples v. Wise* good news for directors of corporations? Is it good news for creditors?

Liabilities of Directors and Officers

Directors and officers are exposed to a broad range of liabilities relating to the business of the corporation, including liability for torts and contracts, and for statutory offences.

This section will discuss such liabilities in relation to directors, while recognizing that the same analysis usually also applies to officers.[33]

Liability in Tort and Contract

When a director is acting on behalf of a corporation and commits a tort, his actions may be attributed to the corporation itself by virtue of the identification theory. Similarly, when the director enters into a contract, as agent for his corporation, his actions make the corporation the other party to that contract and the director slips out of the equation altogether. There are times, however, when a director has personal liability for a tort he may have committed or a contract he may have entered into.

---

33. For example, particular legislation may impose liability on directors but not officers of the corporation.

Liability in Tort   Traditionally, courts have been reluctant to say that a director or officer is automatically liable just because he commits a tort on company time. The idea is to permit the director to conduct company business without risking personal, unlimited liability at every turn. Think of it this way: if Adam were personally liable for any tort he committed during the course of his business day, there would really be no benefit in incorporating IK Enterprises from his perspective as a director. His liability would be the same whether he was running his business through a corporation or as a sole proprietorship, and the principle in *Salomon v. Salomon* would fall by the wayside.

In line with this approach, some courts have ruled that directors are not personally liable provided that they were acting in furtherance of their duties to the corporation and their conduct was justifiable.[34] Nevertheless, recent case law from Ontario seems to take a step back from such a perspective. It appears to suggest that directors and officers will almost always be responsible for their own tortious conduct even if they were acting in the best interests of the corporation.[35] With this in mind, prudent directors will take care not to commit torts, and thereby avoid having to establish what the law concerning the matter is in their jurisdiction.

Most certainly, where the director's conduct is extreme, she will be found liable for committing a tort regardless of the approach taken by the court in question. For example, assume that Adam is meeting in his office with a customer who has not paid his bill to IK Enterprises Ltd. Things get a little out of hand and Adam bars the door for several hours, saying to the customer, "You're not getting out of here until you write a cheque for what you owe us." On these facts, Adam would face personal liability no matter what the legal test applied might be.

Liability in Contract   The director does not generally attract liability for the corporation's contracts—the principles of agency operate in such a way that the corporation is liable to the outsider and the director who has acted as agent for the corporation drops out of the transaction.

Nonetheless, a director faces personal liability on a contract if the facts indicate that the director intended to assume personal liability, as when

- the director contracts on his own behalf, as well as on behalf of the company
- the director guarantees the contractual performance of the company

Liability by Statute

In addition to the exposure that directors face for breaching their general management duties, dozens of pieces of legislation place obligations on them (see Figure 16.2 on page 387 for examples of the range of legislation affecting directors). These statutes impose potentially serious penalties for failure to comply, including fines of up to $1 million and imprisonment for up to two years.[36]

For example, the failure of IK Enterprises to withhold and remit income taxes can result in the directors being personally liable for the corporation's failure unless the directors can demonstrate that they acted in a reasonable and diligent manner.[37] Thus Adam and Diane, as directors of IK Enterprises, face personal liability for IK

---

34. *McFadden v. 481782 Ontario Ltd.* (1984), 47 O.R. (2d) 134 (H.C.).
35. See, for example, *ADGA Systems International Ltd. v. Valcom Ltd.* (1999), 43 O.R. (3d) 101 (C.A.), leave to appeal to S.C.C. refused, [1999] S.C.C.A. No. 124. Also see Edward M. Iacobucci, "Unfinished Business: An Analysis of Stones Unturned in *ADGA Systems International v. Valcom Ltd.*" (2001) 35 *Can. Bus. LJ.* 39–54; Janis Sarra, "The Corporate Veil Lifted: Director and Officer Liability to Third Parties" (2001) 35 *Can. Bus. LJ.* 55–71; and Christopher C. Nicholls, "Liability of Corporate Officers and Directors to Third Parties" (2001) 35 *Can. Bus. LJ.* 1–38.
36. See, for example, the federal *Hazardous Products Act*, R.S.C. 1985, c. H-3.
37. *Supra* note 18, s. 227.1 (1) (3).

Enterprises' failure. Interestingly the *Income Tax Act* does not impose personal liability on officers—like Cameron—for this particular failure. While Cameron owes duties as a corporate officer under the *Canada Business Corporations Act*, at common law, and under his employment contract, he does not have any direct personal liability for his company's failure to remit under the *Income Tax Act*. It is important to check the provisions of legislation to determine who may be potentially liable.

Unlike the *Income Tax Act*, environmental protection legislation imposes environmental liability on both directors and officers. *R. v. Bata* illustrates this liability.

CASE ▼

R. v. Bata Industries Ltd. (1992), 9 O.R. (3d) 329 (Prov. Div.), aff'd (1993), 14 O.R. (3d) 354 (Gen. Div.), varied (1995), 25 O.R. (3d) 321 (C.A.)

THE BUSINESS CONTEXT: Canadian environmental legislation often imposes liability directly on corporate directors and officers. These individuals may be liable for offences committed by the corporation if they participated in their commission or, as in the following case, they failed to take all reasonable care to prevent the corporation from committing the offence. *R. v. Bata* is the leading Ontario case dealing with the statutory responsibilities of directors and officers for the environmental conduct of their corporations.

FACTUAL BACKGROUND: Bata Industries manufactured shoes at a factory in Batawa, Ontario. The company was experiencing financial difficulties and in an effort to reduce costs, waste chemicals were stored on-site in drums rather than being disposed of properly. The storage containers were in poor condition and some of the chemical contents leaked into the soil. As a result, the corporation was charged with (and convicted of) offences under environmental protection legislation, and three of its directors were charged for failing to take all reasonable care to prevent discharge of contaminants into the environment.

THE LEGAL QUESTION: Were the directors liable for failing to take all reasonable care to prevent Bata from committing environmental offences?

RESOLUTION: The three directors charged were the chairman of the board, the company president, and the plant manager (who reported to the company president). The chairman, who visited the plant only once or twice a year and had no knowledge of the storage problems, was acquitted. It was established that he was aware of his environmental responsibilities, and had directed that a technical advisory circular addressing proper waste disposal be circulated to all his companies. Also, he had placed an experienced director on-site and was entitled to rely on that director to address environmental concerns. The court determined that the chairman had taken all reasonable care.

By way of contrast, the president visited the plant once a month, had personal knowledge of the storage problems, and yet took no steps to rectify them. It was insufficient to simply give verbal instructions to plant staff, who were overworked, without following up on the instructions to see that the problem was solved. He was found liable.

The plant manager also had a "hands-on" role. He had experience in production, the authority to act, and the knowledge that toxic chemicals were present on the site. As he was an on-site director, he had special responsibilities, including the duty of inspecting the site and ensuring the problems were rectified, that made him particularly vulnerable to prosecution. He too was found liable. In sum, the plant manager and the president had failed to take all reasonable care to prevent the discharge of contaminants.

CRITICAL ANALYSIS: What do you think the rationale is for prosecuting the directors personally, as well as prosecuting the corporation, for environmental offences?

FIGURE 16.2

Directors' Statutory Liabilities: A Sampling

Statutory Breach	Type of Statute	Nature of Penalty
Failure to pay employee wages	Federal and provincial incorporation statutes	Liability for wages
Directing, authorizing, or permitting the release of a toxic substance into the environment	Federal and provincial environmental protection statutes	Fines and/or imprisonment
Failure to remit required taxes	Provincial and federal revenue acts	Liability for amount outstanding and interest or penalties
Failure to maintain health and safety standards	Provincial workplace health and safety legislation	Fines and/or imprisonment
Insider trading—using confidential information in buying and selling shares	Provincial securities acts, federal and provincial incorporation statutes	Fines and/or imprisonment
Engaging in anticompetitive behaviour	Federal *Competition Act*	Criminal and civil liabilities
Paying a dividend when company is insolvent	Federal and provincial incorporation statutes	Personal repayment
Misrepresentation in a prospectus	Provincial securities legislation	Damages
Improperly transporting dangerous goods	Federal and provincial transportation of dangerous goods legislation	Fines and/or imprisonment

Avoiding Liability

Directors have onerous duties to the corporation, and no one should agree to become a director without a sound understanding of the obligations involved. Willingness, enthusiasm, and ability are not enough: "the job may well require a considerable and unforeseen time commitment with ultimately limited compensation and considerable exposure of one's own personal assets."[38] The exposure to risk suggests that a risk management plan as discussed in Chapter 3 is warranted. The basis for such a plan is provided in the following Business Application of the Law box.

---

38. David Ross, "Director's Obligations" in *Fiduciary Obligations—1995* (Vancouver: Continuing Legal Education Society of B.C., 1995) at 5.1.01.

irectors can reduce their exposure to personal liability by exercising care, diligence, and skill in the performance of their duties.

Directors can meet the statutory standard of care by being attentive, active, and informed. In this regard, directors should

- make all their decisions informed decisions

- do what is necessary to learn about matters affecting the company

- identify possible problems within the company

- stay apprised of and alert to the corporation's financial and other affairs

- regularly attend directors' meetings

- ensure that they receive reliable professional advice

Directors may also protect themselves by ensuring that an **indemnification** agreement with their company is in place. The purpose of such an agreement is to ensure that the corporation pays any costs or expenses that a director faces as a result of being sued because he is a director.

Directors should also ensure that the corporation carries adequate insurance. Directors' and officers' liability (D&O) insurance provides coverage to the director who has a judgment or other claim against him. Directors should carefully review the policy's exclusion clauses to ensure that maximum protection is provided.

Source: Johanne Ingram, "Directors' and Officers' Duties and Obligations," *Business Law: 31st Banff Refresher Course* (Edmonton: Legal Education Society of Alberta, 1998).

indemnification

The corporate practice of paying litigation expenses of officers and directors for lawsuits related to corporate affairs.

Shareholders and Creditors

Shareholders

A shareholder is someone who invests in a company by buying shares. As soon as IK Enterprises was created, for example, the company—through the directors—issued shares in the company to Adam, Cameron, and Diane. Another way of becoming a shareholder is by buying the shares from an existing shareholder or receiving the shares as a gift.

Regardless of how the shares are obtained, the shareholder has few responsibilities with respect to the corporation. Unlike directors and officers, the shareholder has no duty to act in the best interests of the corporation.[39] She can freely compete with the corporation in which she holds a share. She is not obligated to attend shareholder meetings, cast her vote, read the corporation's financial reports, or take any interest whatsoever in the progress of the corporation. And, of course, she is not generally liable for the debts and obligations of the corporation because of the principle in *Salomon*.

There are exceptions to this immunity, however, as the following section explores.

---

39. There is an exception in some jurisdictions where an obligation can be imposed on shareholders if they hold enough shares to be classified as insiders, in which case they must not use insider information to their own benefit.

Shareholder Liability

lifting the corporate veil
Determining that the corporation is not a separate legal entity from its shareholders.

Owners of the corporation are occasionally held responsible for debts and liabilities incurred by the corporation. In other words, the corporation is not considered a separate entity from its shareholders. This is known as piercing or **lifting the corporate veil.** Due to the *Salomon* principle, courts are generally reluctant to lift the corporate veil except when they are satisfied that a company is a "mere facade" concealing the true facts.[40] It must be shown that there is complete domination and control by the person or entity sought to be made liable, and that the corporate form must have been used as a shield for conduct akin to fraud that deprives claimants of their rights.[41]

For example, in *Big Bend Hotel Ltd. v. Security Mutual Casualty Co.*,[42] the court ignored the separate existence of the corporation when the corporation was being used to hide the identity of the person behind the corporation. Vincent Kumar purchased insurance for his company, Big Bend Ltd., which owned a hotel. The hotel burned down, but the insurance company refused to pay because Kumar had failed to disclose on the application for insurance that he had been president and sole shareholder of another corporation whose hotel had burned down less than three years earlier. The court held that the insurance company should be able to disregard the separate existence of the corporation and treat the policy as if it had been applied for by Kumar himself.

CASE ▼

LeCar GmbH v. Dusty Roads Holding Ltd. (2004), 222 N.S.R. (2d) 279 (N.S.S.C.).

THE BUSINESS CONTEXT: A corporation is an entity separate from its shareholders and the courts will not readily ignore the corporate form and hold shareholders liable for the conduct of the corporation. The most common basis for doing so is objectionable conduct amounting to fraud.

FACTUAL BACKGROUND: In 1995, LeCar GmbH, a German company that imported automobiles manufactured in other countries for sale in Germany entered into an agreement with Dusty Roads Holdings Inc., a company owned and operated by David Daley. LeCar wanted to acquire for resale in Germany new Mexican-built Volkswagen Golfs that could be sold at a lower price than comparable German-made models. Because there were obstacles to direct dealings between LeCar and Mexican interests and because Dusty Roads and Daley had contacts in Mexico who could supply the cars, a deal was made whereby Dusty Roads engaged a supplier in

Mexico to provide and ship vehicles to LeCar in Germany. The oral arrangements between the parties provided that LeCar would advise Dusty Roads of the number and model of cars it wanted and Daley would contact the supplier. LeCar paid the amount specified by Daley plus a $100.00 commission for each car for Dusty Roads. LeCar did not pay the Mexican supplier directly but transferred the money to Dusty Roads, which paid the Mexican supplier. When LeCar placed an order, it was expected to pay Dusty Roads 25 percent of the purchase price. A 1995 shipment of 105 cars went smoothly. A 1996 order for 176 cars was not completed. When only 121 cars were delivered, LeCar sued Dusty Roads and Daley for outstanding deposits and damages for failure to deliver. Daley claimed Dusty Roads was entitled to keep the deposits.

LEGAL QUESTION: Were Dusty Roads and Daley liable for breach of contract?

RESOLUTION: The court found that the deposits were refundable as there was no evidence that they were nonrefundable. The court also held that LeCar was entitled to recover damages from Dusty Roads for breach of contract. The key issue was whether

---

40. Kevin Patrick McGuiness, *The Law and Practice of Canadian Business Corporations* (Toronto: Butterworths, 1999) at 31–32 points out a number of other situations where the veil will be lifted, including when it is required by statute, contract, or other documents, and when it can be established that the company is the agent of its controllers or shareholders.
41. *Gregorio v. Intrans-Corp.* (1994), 18 O.R. (3d) 527 (C.A.).
42. (1980), 19 B.C.L.R. 102 (S.C.).

liability could be imposed on Daley. The court determined that a 25 percent deposit was not required by the Mexican supplier and Dusty Roads did not relay the entire deposit to the Mexican supplier. Dusty Roads was required only to relay a 20 percent deposit and it had retained the extra 5 percent to cover any deficiencies, expenses, or unpaid commissions. Daley also altered documents received from Mexico before relaying them to LeCar to remove references to 20 percent. The court held that Daley's conduct with reference to the "additional deposit" warranted piercing the corporate veil and imposing liability on him. He misrepresented the use of the additional deposit and deceived LeCar by inducing it

to provide an advance payment of 25 percent. Daley was therefore responsible for excess deposits on the entire order of 170 cars (US$87 000). The remaining damages (US$189 000) relating to the overpayment for undelivered cars was the responsibility of Dusty Roads, as these losses were not the result of any misconduct by Daley.

CRITICAL ANALYSIS: Despite the success of LeCar in having the court "pierce the corporate veil," courts are generally reluctant to do so. Can you think of situations where it would be appropriate to lift the corporate veil?

FIGURE 16.3

Summary of Liability for Corporate Conduct

	Liability in Tort Law	Liability in Contract Law	Liability in Criminal Law	Liability for Regulatory Offences
Corporation	Identification Theory: The corporation is liable when a directing mind commits the tort in the course of carrying out her duties. Vicarious Liability: A corporation is vicariously liable for the torts of employees (who are not directing minds) committed in the course of employment	Agency Theory: The corporation is liable so long as the agent was acting within actual or apparent authority	Identification Theory: The corporation is liable if a senior officer of the corporation committed the offence at least partially in the interests of the corporation. A senior officer is someone who plays an important role in the establishment of the corporation's policies or is responsible for managing an important aspect of the corporation's activities.	The legislation specifies liability but generally the corporation is liable when a person engages in the prohibited behaviour on behalf of the corporation
Directors/Officers	Law unclear and jurisdiction specific. While formerly liable only for more extreme conduct, possibly liable for virtually any tort committed in the course of carrying out duties.	Agency Theory: No liability unless intended to assume liability	Personally liable for the commission of criminal offences	Statutes may impose liability on directors, officers, or both for a corporation's conduct
Shareholders	Generally not liable for corporation's torts unless corporate veil lifted	Generally not liable for corporation's contracts unless corporate veil lifted	No liability for corporation's crimes	No liability imposed on shareholders by statute

Shareholder Rights

Shareholder rights fall into three broad categories: the right to vote, the right to information, and financial rights. How directors decide to allocate these rights when issuing different classes of shares is largely up to them, as there are few requirements in this area. One kind of share can have all three rights, while another kind of share may have only one of these rights. All that is normally required, in this regard, is that voting and financial rights referred to above be allocated to at least one class of shares; however, all those rights are not required to be attached to only one particular class.

The idea behind having different classes of shares is to permit different levels of participation in the corporation. As noted earlier, if Cameron does not want much of a role in the company, he may be content with nonvoting shares. These are often called **preferred shares.**[43] Voting shares are usually called **common shares.** Although nonvoting shares are normally called preferred and voting shares are normally called common, this is not always the case. The only way to know for certain what rights are attached to shares is to review the share certificate itself, as well as the articles of incorporation.

Right to Vote   Corporations legislation requires that there be at least one class of voting shareholders in a corporation. The most significant voting right traditionally attached to common shares is the right to vote for the board of directors. Note that the number of votes that a particular shareholder may cast depends on the number of shares he holds. If Adam holds 1000 common shares, he has 1000 votes. If he holds a majority of the shares, he will be in a position to elect at least a majority of the board of directors and therefore control the company.

As well, voting shareholders have the right to approve or disapprove of directors' actions since the last general meeting. This is because the right to vote brings with it other rights, including the right to

- hold a shareholder general meeting each year
- be given notice of the meeting
- attend the meeting
- ask questions
- introduce motions

A shareholder who cannot attend a meeting can exercise her voting power through a **proxy.** This means granting formal permission to someone else to vote her shares on her behalf. The use of a proxy is important, particularly in large corporations when there is a dispute between competing groups of shareholders. Whichever group does the best job of soliciting proxies is most likely to carry the day. Nonvoting shareholders—usually preferred shareholders—have the right to vote in certain specialized matters. Under the *Canada Business Corporations Act*, for example, Cameron—as the holder of preferred shares in IK Enterprises Ltd.— would have the right to vote on any proposal to sell all the corporation's assets.[44] The rationale is that even nonvoting shareholders should have a say when such a fundamental change in corporate direction is being put forward.

preferred share
A share or stock that has a preference in the distribution of dividends and the proceeds on dissolution.

common share
A share that generally has a right to vote, share in dividends, and share in proceeds on dissolution.

proxy
A person who is authorized to exercise a shareholder's voting rights.

---

43. They are called preferred shares because ordinarily the holders of preferred shares get priority—or have a "preference"—on taking a slice of the corporation's assets if it is liquidated.
44. *Supra* note 3, s. 189(3).

Right to Information

Shareholders have the right to certain fundamental information concerning the corporation. This includes the right to

- inspect the annual financial statement for the corporation
- apply to the court to have an inspector appointed to look into the affairs of the corporation if it can be shown that there is a serious concern about mismanagement
- inspect certain records, including minute books, the register of share transfers, incorporating documents, bylaws and special resolutions, and the registry of shareholders and directors
- know whether directors have been purchasing shares of the corporation. This is to permit shareholders to determine whether directors have been using confidential information to make personal profits.[45]

Financial Rights

Shareholders generally buy shares with the hope or expectation that the corporation will prosper and generate financial rewards, in terms of either capital gains or income for them. In this respect, one of the fundamental rights of the shareholder is the right to receive any dividend declared by the corporation. The shareholder has no right to have dividends just because the corporation has earned large profits, since the declaration of dividends is within the discretion of the board of directors. However, if the shareholders can show that the directors are abusing their discretion, they can consider bringing an oppression action, which is discussed later in this chapter.

Once dividends are declared, directors are bound to pay them in order of preference assigned to the classes of shares. As well, there cannot be any discrimination among shareholders belonging to the same class. If Diane and Cameron both own the same class of shares, it is illegal for the directors to declare that Diane gets a certain dividend but Cameron does not.

Shareholders have a right to share in the assets of a corporation on dissolution after creditors are paid. Again, the right is dependent on the priorities of each class of shares. Preferred shareholders are often given the right to be first in line for corporate assets once all the creditors have been paid.

Additionally, shareholders may have what are known as **pre-emptive rights.** When this right exists, it requires the corporation to offer existing shareholders the chance to purchase a new issue of shares before these shares are offered to outsiders. This gives existing shareholders a chance to maintain their level of control or power in the corporation. For example, assume that Adam has 1000 common shares in IK Enterprises Ltd., and, because of other entrepreneurial interests, he has unwisely resigned as a director in the company for the time being. Diane is the only corporate director left. Assume further that she resolves to issue 2000 common shares to Cameron. This issue would transform Adam's position from being an equal shareholder—with Diane—of common shares to being in the minority, but his pre-emptive right would allow him to maintain his proportional interest in the company if he could afford to purchase further shares.

pre-emptive right
A shareholder's right to maintain a proportionate share of ownership by purchasing a proportionate share of any new stock issue.

Shareholder Remedies

A shareholder, such as Cameron, who is dissatisfied with a corporation's performance or management has a number of remedies available to him.

---

45. See, for example, *Securities Act*, R.S.O. 1990, c. s-5, ss. 106–109.

Selling the Shares   Often the simplest and least costly remedy for a shareholder who is dissatisfied with the operation or performance of a corporation is to simply sell her shares. This, of course, is an easily viable remedy only in the widely held or public corporation, where shares are traded on the stock exchange and there are no restrictions on their transferability.

The situation is quite different in the closely held or private corporation. In this case, there are usually restrictions on the transference of shares and—even where the restrictions are minimal—it may be difficult to find someone willing to buy such shares. Historically, this reality put the minority shareholder in the unenviable position of having little input into the operation of the corporation and no easy way to extricate his investment. In response, both the common law and the legislatures developed a number of remedies to protect a minority shareholder from abuse by the majority. The most important are the appraisal remedy, the derivative action, and the oppression remedy.[46]

Exercising Dissent and Appraisal Rights   In situations where shareholders, by a two-thirds majority vote, approve a fundamental change to the corporation, a dissenting shareholder may elect to have her shares bought by the corporation.[47] This **dissent and appraisal right** is limited to specific actions such as changes to the restrictions on share transfers or restrictions on the business a corporation may carry on; the amalgamation or merger with another corporation; or the sale, lease, or exchange of substantially all of the corporation's assets. The procedure for obtaining the remedy is complex, and the dissenter must strictly follow the prescribed steps.

Bringing a Derivative Action   Because of their managerial control, directors are well placed to rob the very corporation that they are charged with serving. For example, they could take a corporate opportunity and develop it for their own personal gain, they could vote that the corporation sell corporate assets to one of them at a price ridiculously below market, or they could vote themselves outrageously high compensation packages. What can a minority shareholder do when the directors are breaching their duty to the corporation and causing it injury?

At common law, courts permitted minority shareholders to take action on behalf of the corporation against the directors, but the system was far from adequate. In response, corporate law statutes have created what is called the statutory **derivative action.**[48] This permits a shareholder to obtain leave from the court to bring an action on behalf of the corporation, where he can establish that

- directors will not bring an action
- he is acting in good faith
- it appears to be in the interests of the corporation that the action proceed

This action means that directors cannot treat the corporation as their own personal fiefdom with impunity. They owe strict duties to the corporation. Even if they breach those duties with the support of the majority of the shareholders, the minority has recourse to the courts and can secure any number of remedies on behalf of the corporation. By virtue of the derivative action, if the directors have stolen a corporate opportunity, they can be forced by the court to account for that profit. If they have disposed of corporate assets at below market value, the court can order them to account for the difference between what the asset is actually worth

dissent and appraisal right

The right of shareholders who dissent from certain fundamental changes to the corporation to have their shares purchased by the corporation at a fair price.

derivative action

A suit by a shareholder on behalf of the corporation to enforce a corporate cause of action.

---

46. Other remedies include winding up, which involves dissolution of the corporation and the return of surplus assets to the shareholders. The use of this remedy is therefore uncommon.
47. See, for example, *Canada Business Corporations Act, supra* note 3, s. 190(5).
48. For a discussion of the jurisdictions that provide for such an action, see Bruce Welling, *Corporate Law in Canada: The Governing Principles,* 2nd ed. (Toronto: Butterworths, 1991) at 525 and following.

and what was paid for it. If they have voted to overpay themselves, the court can order them to return their ill-gotten gains. The court even has the power to remove the directors from office and replace them. In fact, the legislation empowers the court to make any order it sees fit.

Bringing an Oppression Action   The most widely used remedy by shareholders in Canada is called the **oppression remedy.** A shareholder who has been treated unfairly or "oppressively" may apply to a court for relief. Conduct that the courts have found to be oppressive usually falls into the following categories.

- lack of a valid corporate purpose for the conduct
- transactions that are not at arm's length
- lack of good faith on the part of the directors of the corporation
- discrimination between shareholders with the effect of benefiting the majority shareholder to the exclusion or the detriment of the minority shareholder
- lack of adequate and proper disclosure of material information to minority shareholders
- a plan or design to eliminate minority shareholders[49]

The court is entitled to make such an order as it deems just and appropriate, including ordering the corporation to purchase the complainant's shares, ordering the improper conduct to cease, and, in extreme circumstances, ordering the company to be dissolved. The remedy is extremely flexible and has few attendant technicalities. Unlike a derivative action, which is brought on behalf of the corporation, the oppression remedy is a personal action, which can be brought by shareholders and specified stakeholders—security holders, creditors, directors, or officers.

CASE ▼

Pelley v. Pelley, [2003] 221 Nfld. & P.E.I.R. 1 (C.A.)

THE BUSINESS CONTEXT: The oppression remedy is one of the broadest and most flexible statutory remedies available. It allows the court to rectify situations involving oppression, unfair prejudice, or unfair disregard for the interests of shareholders, directors, officers, creditors, or security holders.

FACTUAL BACKGROUND: In 1974 Verdon Pelley started a small logging business. By 1976 he had also acquired, by Crown lease, lands from which he cut trees as part of his logging business and that he then cleared for a strawberry farm. In 1981, his younger brother Calvin returned to Newfoundland from the mainland and immediately started working with Verdon in the logging and strawberry business. Verdon paid Calvin a salary and in the off season Calvin applied for and received employment insurance (then unemployment insurance) benefits. Verdon and Calvin worked side by side in all aspects of the business except financial matters. Calvin deferred to Verdon in management matters relating to the business and concentrated on the more physical aspects of logging and strawberry farming. Verdon dealt with the bank and the government in applying for land and farm loans and grants, and in the purchase of equipment. All plans related to the acquisition of additional land to extend the strawberry operation and the purchase of any significant piece of equipment were discussed between Verdon

---

49. M. Patricia Richardson, *McCarthy, Tetrault: Directors' and Officers' Duties and Liabilities in Canada* (Toronto: Butterworths, 1997) at 78–79.

and Calvin and a joint decision was made, even though legal title to property and responsibility for loans were entirely in Verdon's name.

Around 1983 Joan started to work at the market operated by the farm. Verdon became romantically involved with her and they married in 1987. Joan worked in the farmer's market, which was housed in a building purchased by Verdon. The market, which sold not only strawberries but also vegetables, crafts, ice cream, and other confectionaries, grew into a significant part of the business. Eventually, the farm expanded into hay production, which was used to feed the farm's own livestock, with the excess being sold to other local farmers.

Following Joan's involvement with Verdon, Calvin became concerned about his position in the farm. In 1987, he approached Verdon to discuss what could be done to protect his interests. They agreed to incorporate a company called Pelley's Farm Limited with 39 common shares to Verdon, 39 to Calvin and 22 to their mother. She took no part in the farm operations and later transferred her shares equally to Verdon and Calvin. Verdon and Calvin also entered into a shareholders' agreement whereby certain decisions would require the consent of both and in the event of a deadlock in the day-to-day management, Verdon had the deciding vote.

Shortly after incorporation of the company, in 1988, the parties had a falling-out that they resolved, in May 1990, by Verdon agreeing to purchase Calvin's shares for the sum of $100 000, provided the company could generate sufficient profits and subject to certain other conditions. Calvin moved to the mainland for some time. No payments were made by Verdon to Calvin pursuant to the share purchase agreement. In 1992 there was reconciliation between the brothers. Calvin returned to the business, and upon his return, Verdon had Calvin execute a form of power of attorney giving Verdon the right to vote Calvin's shares in the company in any way he saw fit as if they were his own.

By 1997 the parties were at odds again and a solicitor, acting for Calvin, purported to invoke the "shotgun clause" in the shareholders' agreement that would result in one party purchasing the shares of the other party. After exchanges of correspondence between solicitors, the dispute remained without resolution. Calvin was removed as a director and removed from direct participation in the operations of the company.

Calvin commenced an action claiming oppression and Verdon counterclaimed. The trial judge found in favour of Calvin and ordered a number of remedies, including ordering Verdon to sell his shares in the company to Calvin. Verdon appealed.

THE LEGAL QUESTION: Did the actions of Verdon amount to oppression of Calvin? Did the actions of Calvin amount to oppression of Verdon? If so, what is the appropriate remedy?

RESOLUTION: The appeal court agreed with the conclusion of the trial judge that the actions of Verdon were oppressive of, unfairly prejudicial to, or unfairly disregarded the interests of Calvin as a shareholder and director. The court noted that a determination of whether conduct is oppressive or unfair must be done in the context of determining what the reasonable expectations of that person were according to the arrangements between the parties. The removal of Calvin as a director and his removal from any participation in the operations of the company was contrary to his expectation as an equal shareholder.

However, the appeal court disagreed with the trial court's remedy, ordering the sale of Verdon's shares to Calvin. Although a court has broad discretion to fashion a remedy that is appropriate, it does not have discretion to fashion *any* remedy. The court is to grant a remedy to rectify the matter complained of—not simply one that it thinks is appropriate.

Considering the history of the development of the business, the relative level of involvement of each of the brothers, and the level of legal obligation and responsibility each carried, the trial court's remedy does more than simply rectify oppression. The order requiring Verdon to sell his shares to Calvin is a remedy that gives to Calvin something that he never could have reasonably expected—full control and exclusive ownership of the entire business venture—and it gives him the means of taking virtually the entire fruits of Verdon's efforts away from him.

The court ordered Calvin to sell his shares to Verdon.

CRITICAL ANALYSIS: Many of the cases that apply the oppression remedy have unique, fact-driven conclusions since most of them stem from long, often bitter family disputes. How can a family business avoid the risk of long, costly disputes?

Like all litigation, however, the process in securing a shareholder remedy is time consuming, costly, and unpredictable. Furthermore, the courts historically have been less than enthusiastic about getting involved in the internal affairs of corporations. Put another way, it is often a heavy and onerous burden to convince the court that the majority is in the wrong and has been oppressive.

As a way of avoiding litigation, shareholders may decide to enter into an agreement at the very beginning of their association in order to deal with potentially contentious areas and to streamline the procedure leading to the resolution of any conflict. Depending on the jurisdiction, there are two possibilities in this regard: a shareholders' agreement and a unanimous shareholders' agreement, also called a USA. Of course, such agreements do not guarantee that litigation will be avoided, since the meaning and enforceability of these agreements can themselves become the subject matter of litigation.

Asserting a Remedy under Shareholders' Agreement or USA

Shareholders' agreements are common, particularly in small, closely held corporations. They serve a multitude of purposes, but in particular they allow shareholders to define their relationship in a manner that is different than that provided by the governing statute. Such agreements may address, for example, how the corporation is to be managed, shares will be transferred, and disputes will be resolved.

A **unanimous shareholders' agreement (USA)** is a specialized kind of shareholders' agreement among all shareholders that restricts, in whole or in part, the powers of the directors to manage the corporation. The purpose of a USA is to ensure that control over matters dealt with in the USA remains with the shareholders. When shareholders, through a USA, take management powers away from directors, those directors are relieved of their duties and liabilities to the same extent. This means that if the shareholders improperly manage the corporation, they may be successfully sued for negligence or breach of fiduciary duty, for example.

shareholders' agreement
An agreement that defines the relationship among people who have an ownership interest in a corporation.

unanimous shareholders' agreement (USA)
An agreement among all shareholders that restricts the powers of the directors to manage the corporation.

Business Application of the Law

Managing Risk through Shareholders' Agreements

A shareholders' agreement allows the shareholders to define their relationship, now and in the future. It should, as well, provide mechanisms and procedures that can be employed when the relationship encounters difficulties, and means for undoing the relationship if the need to do so arises. An agreement must be tailored to meet the requirements of the particular situation and should address the following issues:

1. *Management of the company.* Who will be responsible for management? What will their rights and obligations be? How will they be appointed or elected or hired? How will they be paid?

2. *Protection for the minority shareholder.* How will the minority be protected from domination by the majority? How will representation on the board of directors be achieved? How will fundamental issues, such as dividends, sale of assets, and the like, be handled?

3. *Control over who will be the other shareholders.* What are the qualifications needed for being a shareholder? What happens in the event of a shareholder's death, retirement, disability, or simple loss of interest in the company?

4. *Provision of a market for shares.*[50] What are the circumstances that require a shareholder to sell her shares? What happens if a shareholder dies? Who will buy the shares and for how much? How will the purchase be funded?

5. *Capital contribution.* What happens if the corporation needs more cash? Who will provide it and how much? How will payment be compelled?

6. *Buy-sell arrangements in the event of a dispute.* What (e.g., death, retirement, insolvency) triggers a sale? How will the shares be valued? What method will be chosen for their valuation (i.e., independent third party, formula, value fixed in advance and updated annually)?

7. *Mechanism for terminating the agreement.* How can the agreement be terminated? Can it be terminated on notice? How much notice?

CRITICAL ANALYSIS: How would a properly drafted shareholders' agreement have assisted the Pelley brothers in resolving their dispute?

Source: James W. Carr, "Shareholder Agreements" in *Advising the Business Client* (Edmonton: The Legal Education Society of Alberta, 1995) at 14–16.

The objective of a shareholders' agreement is to comprehensively set out—by agreement and in advance of any conflict—what the shareholders' expectations are, how the company is to be managed, and how disputes will be addressed. Shareholders' agreements seek to confront the reality that disagreements are inevitable and can be resolved according to mechanisms set up during the "honeymoon" phase of a business relationship.

Diane, Cameron, and Adam most definitely need a shareholders' agreement for the reasons given above.

Creditor Protection

A corporation is responsible for its own liabilities, including its debts. As such, the shareholders/owners may be tempted to strip the entity of its assets in an attempt to defeat creditors, but doing so would be illegal. For example, if IK Enterprises Ltd. falls on hard financial times, Adam cannot clean out all the computer inventory and bring it home with him to sell later. This is because the inventory belongs to the corporation, not to Adam, and the corporation's creditors have a prior claim on such property.

To help prevent abuses by shareholders, a number of legislative provisions have been enacted. For example, section 42 of the *Canada Business Corporations Act* forbids the corporation to pay a dividend to shareholders if doing so would jeopardize its ability to pay its own debts as they fall due (the liquidity test). The same section forbids such a dividend if that would make the company insolvent—that is, leave it without enough assets to cover its liabilities.[51] Directors who consent to a dividend under such circumstances are personally liable to restore to the corporation any amounts so paid.

---

50. Common mechanisms in shareholders agreements for selling shares include a right of first refusal and a shotgun clause. A right of first refusal involves a shareholder offering to sell shares to other shareholders; if they refuse to purchase, then, for a limited time, the shareholder may sell to someone else for the same price. A shotgun clause involves a shareholder offering to sell shares at a certain price to another shareholder who must either buy all the shares at that price or sell all his shares at the same price.

51. Insolvency is discussed in Chapter 27.

The Supreme Court of Canada has also indicated that duty of care imposed on directors by s. 122 (1) (b) of the *CBCA* is owed not just to the corporation but also to the creditors.[52] As well, the same court stated that creditors can avail themselves of the oppression remedy as a means of protecting themselves from the prejudicial conduct of directors.

Termination of the Corporation

When and if the time comes for IK Enterprises to shut down, it can be dissolved in several ways. In most jurisdictions, provisions in the companies act or a separate **winding up** act set out a process. The steps involved can be somewhat complicated, so in many instances it is more feasible simply to let the company lapse. This is particularly the case with a small, closely held corporation. The principals may simply neglect to file their annual report or follow other reporting requirements; this will ultimately result in the company being struck from the corporate register.

A court has the authority to order a company to be terminated when a shareholder has been wrongfully treated and this is the only way to do justice between the parties. As well, a corporation whose debts exceed its assets may eventually go bankrupt. The result of bankruptcy is usually the dissolution of the corporation.

winding up
The process of dissolving a corporation.

Business Law in Practice Revisited

1. Is IK Enterprises liable for the failure to deduct and remit income tax? Does Cameron, as an officer of IK Enterprises, have any personal liability for the failure to deduct and remit the taxes?

The *Income Tax Act* imposes liability on a person for failure to withhold and remit income taxes, and as IK Enterprises is considered to be a person, it is liable for this failure. Additionally, the act imposes liability on the directors of the corporation for the corporation's failure to withhold and remit taxes. Therefore, unless they have a valid defence, Adam and Diane are exposed to liability. The act, however, does not impose liability on officers; therefore, Cameron is not exposed to personal liability on this front.

2. What obligations do Cameron, Diane, and Adam have as corporate officers and directors?

As corporate officers and directors, Cameron, Adam, and Diane are obliged to competently manage the corporation and to act in the best interests of the corporation. This means, in effect, that they must not only apply their skills and knowledge to the operations of the corporation but also put the corporation's interests above their own personal interests.

3. How can the disagreement between Adam and Diane be resolved?

The dispute between Adam and Diane is problematic. Each owns 50 percent of the common shares of the corporation, and thus each has an equal voice in the management of the corporation. Their situation is the classic one of shareholder deadlock. In hindsight, the potential for deadlock should have been addressed in the decision to issue shares, or in a shareholders' agreement, or both. An agreement could have provided for a mechanism such as Cameron or an independent person

---

52. *Peoples Department Stores (Trustee of) v. Wise* (2004), 244 D.L.R. (4th) 564 (S.C.C.).

casting a deciding vote. In the absence of an agreement, the parties could still agree to pursue an alternative dispute resolution mechanism. If one party is unwilling, there is little that can be done to resolve the dispute, short of litigation.

4. Are there any problems with Diane forming her own company to take advantage of the translation product opportunity?

If Diane decides to incorporate a company to pursue the translation product opportunity, she needs to be mindful of her fiduciary obligations to IK Enterprises. The law is somewhat unclear as to when a director may pursue an opportunity that came to her as a result of her position as director. However, as the company has rejected the opportunity, it would seem that Diane in the circumstances (she was in favour of IK Enterprises pursuing the opportunity) is free to take it up on her own, particularly upon securing the informed consent of both Adam and Cameron.

5. What are Cameron's rights as a shareholder if he does not like how Diane and Adam are managing the company?

Cameron could simply sell his shares, if he is permitted to do so and if he can find a buyer. The companies legislation also provides for shareholder remedies; however, the remedies are not usually available simply because a shareholder dislikes how the corporation is being managed. There must be something more, such as oppressive conduct by the directors. Even if oppression can be proved, litigation can be costly and time consuming. Again, this issue should have been considered in advance, and a remedy or alternative course of action built into a shareholder agreement.

Chapter Summary

Of particular concern to anyone launching a corporation is the potential liability, both civil and criminal, that the corporation and its stakeholders are exposed to. A corporation, as a distinct legal entity, may be liable in tort, in contract, and for criminal and regulatory offences. Likewise, directors and officers also may be liable both in criminal and civil law for actions relating to the business of the corporation.

Directors and officers who are charged with the management of the corporation owe duties of competence and fiduciary duties to the corporation, and they may be liable to the corporation for breach of these duties.

Shareholders generally face few liabilities with respect to the actions of the corporation. There are, however, limited exceptions to this general rule—most importantly when the corporate form is being used to commit a fraud. Shareholders do, however, have certain statutory rights with respect to the operations of the corporation—the right to vote, the right to information, and financial rights. They also have remedies to enforce their rights. Shareholders can enter into agreements that define their relationships with one another, and that provide mechanisms for resolving disputes and means for protecting their interests.

Creditors have few rights, other than those specifically negotiated, and they have only limited statutory protection.

A corporation can enjoy perpetual existence; however, it can also be dissolved. The most common methods of dissolution are winding-up procedures and simply letting the corporation lapse.

Chapter Study

Key Terms and Concepts

common share (p. 391)

corporate opportunity (p. 381)

derivative action (p. 393)

dissent and appraisal right (p. 393)

identification theory (p. 374)

indemnification (p. 388)

lifting the corporate veil (p. 389)

oppression remedy (p. 394)

pre-emptive right (p. 392)

preferred share (p. 391)

proxy (p. 391)

regulatory offence (p. 377)

self-dealing contract (p. 380)

shareholders' agreement (p. 396)

unanimous shareholder agreement (USA)
  (p. 396)

winding up (p. 398)

Questions for Review

1. How can a corporation be liable in tort law? Explain.

2. How does a corporation enter a contract? Explain.

3. How is the criminal liability of a corporation determined?

4. When is a director personally liable for committing a tort?

5. To whom do directors owe duties?

6. What is a self-dealing contract?

7. What are the duties of directors? of officers?

8. Do directors owe duties to the corporation's creditors? Explain.

9. Is a director liable for a corporation's contracts? Explain.

10. How may a director avoid personal liability when carrying out her corporate duties?

11. What is meant by the term lifting the corporate veil? When will courts "lift the corporate veil?"

12. What three main rights do shareholders have?

13. What rights to dividends do shareholders have?

14. When is the dissent and appraisal remedy appropriate?

15. What is the difference between a derivative action and an oppression action?

16. When is a shareholder agreement appropriate? What issues should a shareholder's agreement address?

17. What protection do creditors have from shareholders stripping the corporation of its assets?

18. How is a corporation terminated?

Questions for Critical Thinking

1. What are the arguments for prosecuting, convicting, and punishing corporations? Does holding corporations criminally responsible serve any social purpose? What are the arguments against prosecuting, convicting, and punishing corporations?

2. The Canadian Democracy and Corporate Accountability Commission, an independent body designed to investigate corporate influence, issued its final report in January 2002. Among its 24 recommendations were that corporations laws should be amended to allow directors, at their discretion, to take into consideration the effect of their actions on the corporation's employees, customers, suppliers, and creditors; the effects of their actions on the community in which the corporation resides; as well as the long-term and short-term interests of the corporation and its shareholders.[53] What is the problem with directors owing duties to all stakeholders? Are stakeholders' interests accounted for in the existing Canadian law of directors' duties?

3. Directors are subject to more and more liabilities. Why do you think this has occurred? What are the problems associated with holding directors to higher standards? How can directors protect themselves in an increasingly litigious environment?

4. Directors face onerous environmental responsibilities. They are, however, usually entitled to argue that they took "all reasonable care." What factors should be considered in developing a risk management plan that addresses the environmental liabilities of directors?

5. Should a professional, such as a lawyer or chartered accountant, accept an invitation to act as a director for a corporate client? What are the advantages for the professional? What are the advantages for the corporation? What problems could arise?

6. Review the Business Application of the Law: Lord Black and Abuse of the Corporate Form on page 354 in Chapter 15. Should boards of directors contain mostly independent or outside directors? What are the advantages of outside or independent directors? What are the disadvantages of independent or outside directors?

Situations for Discussion

1. Ines held one-third of the shares in a corporation that operated a small retail business. She was also the manager of the one store that the corporation owned until the other directors voted to terminate her position. What courses of action are available to her?

2. Alicia, the president and CEO of a computer software company, broke into the offices of a competitor late one night in order to see what kinds of products they were in the process of designing. She was caught in the act by the police, who brought to her attention the following provision from the *Criminal Code*:

   s. 348 (1) Every one who

   breaks and enters a place with intent to commit an indictable offence therein … is guilty of an offence …

   Has Alicia's computer software company committed the crime of break and enter?

3. Lennie purchased a quantity of pressure-treated lumber from GoodWood Building Ltd.

(GoodWood) supplies last April. Lennie used the wood to build a deck around the front of his house. By the fall, however, he found that the wood was starting to rot and it appeared that the stain used to treat the wood was peeling away. When Lennie tried to contact GoodWood, he discovered that the store had closed and the company was insolvent. Lennie managed to locate the salesman who sold him the wood and he agreed that the wood appeared to be defective. He also told Lennie that the wood had been imported from Thailand so a lawsuit against the manufacturer would probably be long and expensive. He suggested that Lennie bring an action against the directors and shareholders of GoodWood. The shareholders and directors are Jim, Tim, and Tom. What are Lennie's chances of success against the shareholders and directors? Does your answer change if GoodWood is an unincorporated business in which Tim, Jim, and Tom are the owners and managers? What are Lennie's chances of success against them in this circumstance?

---

53. Canadian Democracy and Corporate Accountability Commission, *The New Balance Sheet: Corporate Profits and Responsibility in the 21st Century* (January 2002).

4. Ludmila is the president and CEO of a shoe manufacturing company that produces much of its product line in a low-wage country. Ludmila is concerned both that her company will become the subject of an international boycott for this reason and that she will not be maximizing shareholder return if she agrees to raise the wages of the company's offshore employees. Furthermore, in her view, the wages the company is paying those employees are competitive with the wages other companies are paying their workers in the same country. Does Ludmila's company have a social responsibility to pay its workers a higher wage?

5. Ryan and Sean are shareholders and directors of Springfield Meadows Ltd. (Springfield), a company that has developed land for a large trailer park. Springfield has 20 other shareholders. Ryan and Sean are approached by Louise, who wants to create a company whose business it will be to lease trailers. Ryan and Sean are interested in participating as directors and shareholders in this new company, since this would be a good way to fill up some of the vacant sites at Springfield's trailer park. The new company is a big success, and Sean and Ryan receive impressively high dividends on a regular basis. Eventually, the other shareholders in Springfield learn about Sean and Ryan's new company and sue them for breach of their fiduciary duty. The shareholders contend that Sean and Ryan should have developed the opportunity to get into the trailer-leasing business for the benefit of Springfield and should not have taken that opportunity for themselves. Are Sean and Ryan in breach of their duty to act in the best interest of Springfield?

6. Peter sold his barbershop business to Andy for $25 000. As part of the agreement of purchase and sale, Peter agreed to a restrictive covenant that prohibited him from providing barbering services in an area within a ten-mile radius of his former shop for a period of one year. Within a month of the sale, Peter incorporated a company and commenced cutting hair in violation of the restrictive covenant.[54] Can Andy do anything about this situation? Should he do anything?

7. Providence Realty Inc. owned a large piece of property suitable for development. It received an offer on its property from Botswell Street Developments Ltd., an active company with assets and favourable financial records. One month prior to the signing of the agreement of purchase and sale of Providence's property, the shareholders of Botswell Street Developments Ltd. changed the name of the corporation to Botswell Street Holdings Ltd. The same shareholders incorporated a shell company (a company without assets) and gave it the name Botswell Street Developments Ltd. The corporation that actually signed the deed was the newly incorporated shell company. It backed out of the deal, and Providence sued Botswell Street Developments Ltd. and its shareholders for breach of contract.[55] Are the shareholders of Botswell Street Developments Ltd. liable for the actions of Botswell Street Developments Ltd.? Explain.

8. Condelle Systems and Marcodious Ltd. were competitors in the security systems industry. For a number of years, Condelle had a substantial contract with Correctional Services of Canada for technical support and maintenance of security systems in federal prisons. On a call for tenders on renewal of the contract, Correctional Services required all tendering parties to submit a list of senior technicians and their qualifications.

Marcodious did not have any employees of this nature, so Belding, one of Marcodious's two directors, approached a number of Condelle's employees. He was able to convince them to allow their names to be put on Marcodious's tender and to agree to come to work for Marcodious if it was successful in getting the contract with Correctional Services. As it turned out, Marcodious was successful even though its tender contained the same names as Condelle's tender.[56] Does Condelle have a cause of action? On what basis? Against whom? What is the likely outcome?

For more study tools, visit
http://www.businesslaw3e.nelson.com

54. Based on *Gilford Motors Co. v. Horne*, [1933] Ch. 935 (C.A.).
55. Based, in part, on *B.G. Preeco I (Pac. Coast) Ltd. v. Bon Street Hldg Ltd.* (1989), 37 B.C.L.R. (2d) 258 (C.A.).
56. Based, in part, on *ADGA Systems International Ltd. v. Valcom Ltd.* (1999), 43 O.R. (3d) 101 (C.A.), leave to appeal to S.C.C. refused, [1999] S.C.C.A. No. 124.

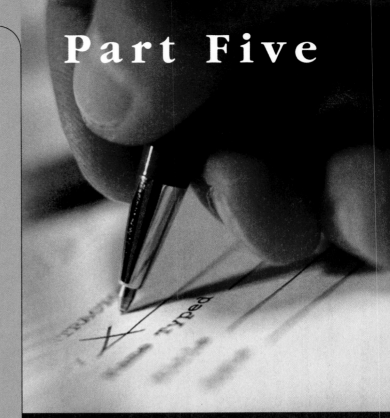

Part Five

PROPERTY CONSISTS OF RIGHTS AND INTERESTS IN anything of value that can be owned. The law of property provides for the protection of those rights and interests.

Real property refers to land and anything attached to it. All other forms of property are included under personal property, which consists of tangible and intangible items. Tangible personal property has a physical substance from which it derives its value. Examples are trucks and appliances, which are sometimes called goods or chattels. Intangible personal property derives its value from legal rights rather than its physical form. Examples are the right to enforce a contract and copyright in a published work. A business is likely to own an interest in many different forms of property that are important to its operation and value. An appreciation of the distinctions is useful for applying the rules that govern ownership and possession of the various forms and for understanding the legal options for using property and generating value from it.

Property

Chapter 17 Personal Property

Chapter 18 Intellectual Property

Chapter 19 Real Property

Chapter

17

Objectives

After studying this chapter, you should have an understanding of

- the different forms of property
- how ownership and possession of property are acquired
- the obligations and rights associated with property
- the nature of the bailment relationship
- various types of bailment for reward

Personal Property

Business Law in Practice

Safe With Us Ltd. (SWUL) operates a large warehouse facility in Moncton, New Brunswick, where it provides storage and safekeeping of customers' property. The customers are commercial enterprises and they store a wide variety of property with SWUL, including surplus equipment, inventory, and supplies; seasonal inventory and displays; and business records and files.

SWUL owns the land on which the warehouse facility is located. SWUL is situated in a suburban industrial park and has space for the warehouse, parking for customers and employees, and a vehicle garage. Because storage requirements vary according to customer need, the warehouse is divided into sections that can provide variations in storage conditions such as temperature and humidity. The building also contains extensive dividers, containers, and shelving. SWUL leases five delivery vehicles and three forklifts from local equipment dealers. Other property owned by SWUL includes accounts receivable, bank accounts, investments, and customer records. Of considerable value is the goodwill associated with the SWUL business name, which has been recognized and respected in the community for 30 years. The Safe With Us name and logo are registered trademarks.

A couple of problems have troubled SWUL management recently. Several customers have claimed that when their property was returned to them by SWUL it was damaged. One customer's documents had suffered water damage. Another customer complained of valuable equipment that was broken when returned. In addition, the vehicles leased by SWUL are requiring more frequent repairs.

1. What types of property are used in SWUL's business?
2. How did SWUL acquire these various items of property?
3. What are SWUL's rights in relation to its property?
4. What obligations does SWUL have in terms of its property?

The Context of Personal Property

Description

personal property
All property, other than land and what is attached to land, that can be identified by its mobility.

tangible property
Personal property, the value of which comes from its physical form.

intangible property
Personal property, the value of which comes from legal rights.

Real property (see Chapter 19) refers to land, whatever is permanently attached to it, and the associated legal rights. SWUL, as the owner of the land on which its business is located, also owns the building and any items such as light fixtures and the walls that divide the warehouse into sections. **Personal property** includes everything other than what is included under real property. Personal property falls into two major categories—tangible and intangible.

Tangible property refers to property that is concrete or material. In its business SWUL uses trucks, forklifts, furniture, office supplies, and other portable items that are not attached to land or a building. In law, these kinds of personal property are known as "chattels."

Intangible property derives its value from legal rights, rather than concrete, physical qualities. Examples of intangible property are insurance policies, accounts receivable, bank accounts, and customer records, as well as the various forms of intellectual property. For example, the value of the fire insurance that SWUL may have on its warehouse is not based on the piece of paper itself, which describes the terms of the insurance coverage. Rather, the value inherent in the fire insurance is the right that the policy creates, namely, the *right* to be compensated in the event that a fire destroys the warehouse. SWUL's registered trademarks are a form of intellectual property (see Chapter 18) protected by legislation. In law, these kinds of property are known as "choses in action." Seen in this light, intangible property is no less real or significant than tangible property—in fact, it drives much of our modern economy.

Acquisition of Ownership

Ownership of property is acquired by a business in a variety of ways:

- Land is acquired through purchase or lease.
- The ownership of goods is acquired by purchasing or manufacturing them.[1]
- Insurance coverage is bought by paying premiums and is described in the insurance policy, which gives the customer the right to recover losses in specified circumstances.[2]
- Accounts receivable are created by delivering goods or services to customers, who agree to pay at a later date. The supplier acquires the right to collect the accounts, which can be sold to other businesses.[3]
- Certain kinds of intellectual property, such as copyright, are owned as a result of being created. Ownership of other forms—such as a trademark—is established through simple use, or registration, or both. Intellectual property can also be bought from other owners.[4]

There is no comprehensive system for publicly registering title to personal property as there is with real property, although there are some specialized registries for items such as motor vehicles, patents, and trademarks. One reason for the difference concerns the mobility of personal property. There is little utility in having a provincial registration system for most personal property when goods are so easily transported to another province. In addition, the value of individual items of personal property may not justify the cost of administering a registration system or the cost to owners of registering.

Interests in chattels are registered, however, when that property is used as security in its purchase on credit or later as collateral for a loan. Registration is considered economical because it protects the creditor's rights to the pledged property.[5]

Possession without Ownership

One party may gain possession of the property of another, often with the intent that possession ultimately be returned to the owner. Such an arrangement involves possession without ownership. There are several examples in the SWUL scenario that are common in a business environment:

- SWUL has chosen to lease trucks and forklifts rather than buy them.
- SWUL's customers are using its facilities to store their property temporarily. There is no intention for SWUL to become the owner of the stored property.
- SWUL could lease its warehouse space from the owner of real property or in turn lease to another business a portion of the space that it owns.
- SWUL could grant a licence to a business in another location to use its name and logo.

---

1. See the sale of goods in Chapter 23. Ownership can also be created by gift or inheritance.
2. See Chapter 28.
3. Known as assignments of contractual rights (see Chapter 9).
4. See Chapter 18.
5. This system of registration is governed by legislation in each province and is discussed in Chapter 26.

What most often drives the temporary split of ownership and possession is that it meets the business needs of both parties in each situation. For instance, by leasing, SWUL gets the benefit of using vehicles and equipment without a large capital outlay. By storing equipment with SWUL, customers get the benefit of a valuable service without having to purchase or lease a building themselves for that purpose.

Obligations Arising from Ownership and Possession

The owner of property bears ultimate responsibility for its protection. The law requires that someone other than the owner who has possession of property must take reasonable care of it and pay applicable charges for use of the property. Similarly, when a business such as SWUL is providing a service to the owner, such as storage or repair, the service must be performed as agreed and reasonable care must be taken of the property until it is returned to the owner. This requirement to take reasonable care applies whether the arrangement is contractual or not:

- SWUL must take good care of the leased equipment.
- SWUL must return its customers' property in the same basic condition in which it was delivered.

If the chattels in SWUL's possession have been lost, damaged, mishandled, or exposed to water, smoke, fire, or any number of other hazards, SWUL is in breach of its obligation to take reasonable care. It will have to pay damages to the owners by way of compensation. Damages will be awarded in the amount necessary to restore the customer to the position it would have been in had the contract been properly performed.

Since the owner of property is the one who ordinarily bears the risk of loss from its damage or destruction, the owner may take steps to shift the risk to another business by such means as an insurance contract. When such a contract is in place, the insurance company agrees to reimburse the insured for its loss in return for payment of premiums.

Where property is in possession of someone who is not the owner, the question of who will purchase insurance should be addressed, since there is no utility in both parties insuring the same property. For example, SWUL and its customers should agree on which of them is responsible if a customer's property is damaged or lost while in SWUL's facilities. Whoever bears the risk of loss should place the insurance policy and keep it in good standing by paying the premiums. In the same manner, the lease agreement between SWUL and the equipment dealer should specify who is responsible for damage to the vehicles. That party, in turn, should insure the property.

Rights Arising from Ownership and Possession

The owner of property who is also in possession is entitled to deal with it essentially as she sees fit. Her options include

- selling the property and transferring ownership and possession to the buyer
- leasing the property to another business with the intent of regaining possession or selling it when the lease expires
- using the property as security for a loan, thereby giving the lender the right to seize or sell the property if the borrower defaults on the loan
- transferring possession of chattels to another business for storage, repair, or transport with the corresponding right to regain possession

The possessor of property has the right to keep the property for the period of time provided for in the agreement with the property's owner. For example, SWUL has possession of the trucks and forklifts for the duration of time set forth in the lease document. In terms of storage of customers' property, SWUL has the right to be paid the agreed storage charges and generally is not required to relinquish possession until those charges are paid.

Personal Property Issues

Many legal problems relating to tangible personal property arise from its basic nature. Goods or chattels are by definition portable and therefore more difficult to track than real estate. Proof of ownership and valuation can be a challenge, as the following Business Application of the Law demonstrates.

Business Application of the Law

Million Dollar Baseball

On 7 October 2001, at Pacific Bell Park in San Francisco, Barry Bonds hit his 73rd home run of the 2001 baseball season to break the single season home-run record. Alex Popov was a spectator in the right-field stands. When Bonds's home run sailed over the fence, the ball landed in Popov's glove. He was immediately hit from all sides by other spectators. The ball popped out of his glove and Popov was knocked down. When the scuffle ended, Patrick Hayashi had the ball. Popov had scratches, bruises, a bloody nose, and broken eye glasses. Popov sued Hayashi and the ball was held by the court pending the outcome of the litigation. While the lawsuit was underway, the ball could not be sold and Popov posted a bond in case the record was broken, with the result that the value of the ball would be much less than the current estimate of several million dollars.

The baseball itself gives no indication of its value or whose property it is. A normal baseball is worth less than $10. The Barry Bonds record ball is worth as much as someone is willing to pay. Difficult issues arise:

- how to prove that this ball is the real ball hit by Bonds

- how to ensure continuing authentication as the Bonds ball

- how to decide who has rights to the ball

Potential claimants included Hayashi, Popov, Barry Bonds, the pitcher, the team, the owners of the ballpark, and Major League Baseball.

There is no well-established set of rules to decide ownership of this sort of property, so many arguments can be made for resolving the dispute:

- Popov "caught" it, so he should get to keep it.

- Popov was assaulted by other spectators (including Hayashi), so they should not benefit from their criminal acts.

- Hayashi ended up with the ball. In a situation such as this, possession is the important factor.

- The rules of baseball should apply: the ball is not caught until the fielder or spectator with a glove has control.

- An umpire should decide after watching the replay.

- Use the common law that applies to hunting: the person whose harpoon first entered the whale or whose arrow first pierced the bird gets the carcass.

Judge McCarthy ultimately ruled that when the ball left the playing field, it became "intentionally abandoned property" and that the legal claims of Popov and Hayashi "are of equal quality and they are equally entitled to the ball. The ball must be sold and [the proceeds] divided equally between the parties."

Another dispute over ownership of a baseball resulted when Doug Mientkiewicz, a player for the Boston Red Sox, caught the ball in the play that ended the 2004 World Series. He kept the ball, claiming it was his. The Red Sox team also claimed ownership. The consensus was that a ball that does not leave the playing field is treated much differently from one that does. It belongs to the team because the player is an employee.

CRITICAL ANALYSIS: How do these examples help to resolve uncertainty about ownership and valuation?

Sources: Martin Fletcher, "Million Dollar Baseball" *The Times of London* (12 December 2001) at T2, 4; Larry Millson, "Bonds' HR Ball Cut in Half" *The Globe and Mail* (19 December 2002) at S1; and Paul Finkelman, "This One's for the Birds" *The New York Times* Online (12 January 2005).

Principles of Bailment

Overview

There are two key aspects of involvement with personal property—ownership and possession. Quite often the two aspects reside in the same party. For example, SWUL owns and possesses the dividers and containers in its warehouse. However, it is also common for one person to be in possession of property owned by someone else. For example, SWUL is only in possession of its leased equipment—the equipment is owned by the dealer. Similarly, it is only in possession of its customers' property, which it holds for safekeeping in exchange for a fee. The property that SWUL stores is owned by SWUL customers, who are entitled to retrieve their property at any time.

A **bailment** is a temporary transfer of possession of personal property from the owner, known as a **bailor,** to another party, known as a **bailee.** Ownership remains with the bailor. Possession, however, is transferred to the bailee. This is what distinguishes bailment from a contract of purchase and sale.

There are many examples of bailment in commercial transactions, including the following:

- the short-term rental of a vehicle[6]
- the long-term lease of a vehicle (e.g., SWUL's leases of trucks and forklifts)
- the delivery of property for repair
- the transport of property by a commercial carrier
- the storage of property in a warehouse (i.e., the main business of SWUL)
- the shipping of an envelope by courier

bailment
Temporary transfer of possession of personal property from one person to another.

bailor
The owner of property who transfers possession in a bailment.

bailee
The person who receives possession in a bailment.

---

6. See *Tilden Rent-A-Car Co. v. Clendenning* (1978), 83 D.L.R. (3d) 400 (Ont. C.A.) in Chapter 7.

Bailments are also common in the consumer context, as shown in these examples:

- renting DVDs
- leaving clothing at a dry-cleaning shop
- depositing cars at a garage for servicing
- storing furniture
- borrowing library books

Any transaction that meets the definition of bailment—whether commercial, consumer, or simply personal—is covered by the general discussion in this section. To identify the rights and obligations relating to bailments, two basic questions need to be answered:

Is Payment Involved?

Most commercial bailments are based on a contract requiring payment for the use of the property or as compensation for storage or another service. These are known as **bailments for value.**

bailment for value
Bailment involving payment for use of property or a service.

Possession of property may also be transferred without payment by virtue of a loan or a free service. This would occur when, for example, a prospective buyer tries out a vehicle for a few days or someone parks his car in his neighbour's garage for the winter. Because there is no compensation involved in such arrangements, such instances are known as **gratuitous bailment** in the sense of being free or "without reward."

gratuitous bailment
Bailment that involves no payment.

For Whose Benefit Is the Bailment?

The question of who benefits from a gratuitous bailment is particularly important, since the answer helps later in the chapter to determine the bailee's responsibility for the property. Gratuitous bailments can benefit the bailor or the bailee. When someone stores his car in his neighbour's garage for the winter at no charge, for example, the bailee—the person who owns the garage—derives no advantage from the relationship, while the bailor—the person who owns the car—now has protection for his vehicle from harsh weather. It is the bailor, therefore, who gains from the bailment.

Conversely, when a person borrows his neighbour's lawnmower, the owner of the lawnmower—the bailor—is simply doing a favour and does not derive any tangible benefit from the bailment. The borrower—the bailee—can now cut his grass without having to buy or lease a lawnmower from someone else and is therefore the party who profits from the relationship.

Bailments that benefit both the bailor and the bailee are most common in the commercial world and usually involve bailments for value—that is, bailments in which one of the parties is paid for the provision of a service or other benefit. For example, the owner of the vehicles and forklifts leased by SWUL benefits from the relationship since it is paid by SWUL. SWUL also benefits since it gains possession of delivery vehicles and forklifts. Similarly, SWUL benefits from storing the property of its customers since it is paid to provide the service. SWUL's customers benefit because their property is stored and protected by SWUL.

The Contract of Bailment

In bailments for value, the contract between the bailor and the bailee is central. The parties are free to negotiate the details of their own agreement. A contract for services will normally include a description of these aspects:

- the services to be provided by the bailee
- the price to be paid by the bailor and payment terms
- the extent to which the bailee is liable for damage or loss
- the remedies of the parties for failure to perform

In a storage contract, for example, the focus is on the bailee's liability for loss to the chattels in question and the bailee's remedies for collecting storage charges. Because a warehouse operator deals with the property of many customers in similar circumstances and is under pressure to keep prices competitive, a business such as SWUL is likely to have a standard form agreement that all customers are expected to sign. The main object from SWUL's perspective is to minimize its responsibility for damage caused to property in its possession in order to keep costs down. At the same time, it is important for SWUL to maintain a good reputation in the industry. Limiting liability through standard form agreements is common in the storage industry, as in the following clauses:

(a) The responsibility of a warehouseman in the absence of written provisions is the reasonable care and diligence required by the law.

(b) The warehouseman's liability on any one package is limited to $40 unless the holder has declared in writing a valuation in excess of $40 and paid the additional charge specified to cover warehouse liability.[7]

Who is responsible for property damaged during delivery? Who is responsible for damage to a leased truck?

---

7. *London Drugs Ltd. v. Kuehne & Nagel International Ltd.* (1992), 97 D.L.R. (4th) 261 (S.C.C.) in Chapter 9.

warehouseman
A bailee who stores personal property.

While clause (b) may seem unfair—after all, if the **warehouseman's** negligence causes more than $40 in damage, should it not have to pay the full tab? —its function is to signal which party should buy insurance on the item being stored, the bailor or the bailee. In this case, the onus is on the bailor (as the owner who is limited to a claim for $40) to purchase insurance, since the item being stored is likely worth much more than that amount.

The other focus of a bailment contract is on the remedies that the bailee can use to obtain payment from delinquent customers. For example, the contract may provide that SWUL is entitled to retain possession of the chattel until payment is received and may also give SWUL the right to sell the chattel, after the passage of a prescribed period of time, in order to apply the proceeds to the outstanding account. Of course, SWUL's prime interest is timely payment from customers. It is interested in the right to keep customers' property only as a backup remedy.

The terms of SWUL's bailment agreement for the leasing of vehicles are likely to be written by the owner of the vehicles, called the "lessor," who is interested in protecting its property while that property is in SWUL's possession. This is accomplished by inserting a clause in the contract making SWUL responsible for any damage and by imposing limits on the extent to which SWUL can use the vehicles (such as distance for the trucks and time for the forklifts). Again, insurance should be purchased to cover loss or damage, in this case by SWUL. The owner of the vehicles should consider making it a term of the contract that it be named in the insurance policy as the party who is paid in event of loss.

Liability of Bailees

Liability issues arise when some mishap occurs in relation to the property while it is in the possession of the bailee.[8] For example, the property of SWUL's customers might be lost, damaged, or destroyed while in SWUL's warehouse; employees might drop valuable equipment while moving it around; a forklift might run into items in its path; property could be stolen from the warehouse; there might be damage from water or a fire in the warehouse; if the property is perishable, it could spoil if not properly stored.[9]

Ideally, the contract between SWUL and its customers will specify the extent of SWUL's liability for these events. SWUL is likely to place significant limits on its legal liability through exclusion or limitation of liability clauses as described above. If there is no formal agreement, the common law rules of bailment will apply.

The obligations of bailees to care for the goods of their bailors have evolved through various stages. Initially, bailees were 100 percent liable for the return of bailed chattels as well as for any damage, whether the bailee caused the damage or not and even where the bailee exercised reasonable or even extreme diligence. There are still remnants of this strict regime. Common **carriers** such as railways, as well as **innkeepers,** are caught by this old law; however, statutes have lessened and in some instances displaced the strict obligations of the early common law.

carrier
A bailee who transports personal property.

innkeeper
Someone who offers lodging to the public.

Later, the burden of the bailee to care for the goods of the bailor was determined by the concept of "benefit of the relationship." If a bailment benefited the bailor exclusively, the bailee was required to exercise slight care and was liable only for "gross neglect." If the bailment benefited the bailee exclusively, the bailee was required to exercise great care and was liable for even "slight negligence." If there was reciprocal benefit, the bailee was required to exercise ordinary diligence and was liable for "ordinary neglect."

---

8. The work of Professor Moe Litman of the Faculty of Law, University of Alberta, in this section is gratefully acknowledged.
9. Note that bailees who are employers are vicariously liable for the acts of their employees committed in the course of their employment. See Chapter 20.

Today, bailees are expected to exercise reasonable care in all circumstances, which include

- **WHO BENEFITS FROM THE BAILMENT.** If the bailment is gratuitous and for the benefit of the bailor, the standard of care is very low. If the bailment is gratuitous and for the benefit of the bailee, the standard is very high.

- **THE NATURE AND VALUE OF THE PROPERTY.** The bailee's standard is higher for more valuable property and should be appropriate for the type of property. This means that the bailee must show greater care when storing perishables as opposed to commodities such as wood products.

- **WHETHER PAYMENT IS INVOLVED.** A bailee for reward must show greater care than a gratuitous bailee.

- **THE TERMS OF THE CONTRACT.** The contract may raise or lower the standard of care owed by the bailee.

- **THE LIMITS ON LIABILITY.** The contract may set the standard at ordinary care and diligence but limit the amount of damages for which the bailee may be held liable.

- **SPECIAL REGULATIONS FOR THE TYPE OF BAILMENT THAT MAY SET OUT THE STANDARD OF CARE.** Contracts to transport goods, for example, are subject to standard statutory terms.

- **SPECIAL CIRCUMSTANCES IN THE TRANSACTION.** Where the bailee is instructed by the bailor as to the value of the goods or special storage requirements, for example, this increases the standard of care that the bailee must meet.

- **THE EXPERTISE OF THE BAILEE.** A bailee who specializes in a certain type of bailment (such as storage) is expected to take greater care than an ordinary person.

Bailees may not escape their responsibilities by turning over a bailed chattel to employees. If the chattel is damaged, lost, or stolen as a result of employees' negligence, the employer as bailee is vicariously liable so long as the employees were acting within the ordinary course or scope of their employment, that is, the employees were engaged in the performance of their assigned duties. In addition, bailees are liable for the intentional wrongdoing of their employees. A bailee who entrusts bailed goods to an employee is personally (not vicariously) liable for the theft of the goods by the employee. Another basis of liability of a bailee for theft by an employee is the law of negligence. The employer has a duty to hire honest, responsible people. Accordingly, failure to engage in proper hiring practices may result in liability for the employer.

Liability of Bailors

In contractual bailments, bailors warrant that the goods used by their bailees are fit for the purpose for which they were bailed.[10] If the goods are unfit and a bailee is injured while using a bailed chattel, the bailor may be liable. For example, if a SWUL employee is hurt when the wheel falls off the forklift he is operating, the lessor will face liability.[11] This high obligation on the bailor can be reduced in the contract between the parties, however. In any event, insurance is likely to be in place to take care of the loss.

---

10. The work of Professor Moe Litman of the Faculty of Law, University of Alberta, in this section is gratefully acknowledged.
11. In *Matheson v. Watt* (1956), 19 W.W.R. (N.S.) 425 (B.C.C.A.), the owner of a roller-skating rink was held liable for injuries sustained by the plaintiff when a wheel came off the roller skate the plaintiff had leased from the rink. In this type of litigation, if a bailee establishes that goods were used in a reasonable manner, the onus then shifts to the bailor to prove that the defect could not have been prevented by reasonable care and skill from anyone in the distribution chain, beginning at the manufacturer and ending at the bailor. It is only when the defect is one that no one in this chain could reasonably have foreseen (a "latent defect") that the bailor escapes liability for injury to the bailee. From the perspective of a bailor, this warranty is extremely burdensome.

The standard of care of a bailor in a gratuitous bailment focuses on personal misconduct. Gratuitous bailors must exercise reasonable care to ensure that they are aware of defects and must inform their bailees of the existence of such defects.

Remedies

Remedies for failure to perform obligations arising in a bailment relationship arise in two contexts:

- When a bailee is attempting to recover a fee for services performed in relation to the property.
- When a bailor is trying to recover for damage done to the property while it was in the bailee's possession. This, in turn, usually involves two issues: First, has the bailee met the relevant standard of care and, second, does the agreement cancel or limit the bailee's liability? The following case illustrates these two issues.

CASE ▼

Punch v. Savoy's Jewellers Ltd. (1986), 33 B.L.R. 147 (Ont. C.A.)

THE BUSINESS CONTEXT: This case explores a claim for lost property in a bailment. It illustrates how a simple transaction such as the repair of a ring can become legally complicated when several businesses become involved and are later asked for compensation.

FACTUAL BACKGROUND: Punch owned a diamond ring for which the appraised value was $11 000. She took it to Savoy's in Sault Ste. Marie for repairs. Savoy's mailed it to Walker's in Toronto to have the repairs done. Savoy's followed normal practice by using registered mail and listing the value for insurance purposes as $100. By the time Walker's had completed the repairs, a postal strike was on. Walker's decided to use CN Rapidex (a courier service) to return the ring to Savoy's. CN's standard clause limited liability to $50 or the declared value if higher. Walker's declared the value to be $100. The ring was never delivered, and there seemed a strong possibility it had been stolen by the CN driver. Punch claimed compensation from Savoy's, Walker's, and CN. CN attempted to limit its liability to $100.

THE LEGAL QUESTION: Did the three defendants perform their obligations to Punch? What protection did CN's limitation clause provide to the three defendants?

RESOLUTION: Justice Cory summarized his ruling as follows:

Both Savoy and Walker are liable to Lenore Punch for breach of their duty as bailees. They breached this duty by failing to obtain instructions from the owner as to the means of carriage in light of the postal strike; by failure to give a proper evaluation of the ring to the carrier; and by failure to stipulate as a term of the carriage insurance coverage for the true value of the ring itself. CN also is liable to the owner for the unexplained loss of the ring. Savoy and Walker are to be indemnified by CN for any loss which they must make good to the owner.

The standard of care to which all the defendants were held as bailees for value was to "exercise due care for the safety of the article entrusted to [them] by taking such care of the goods as would a prudent man of his own possessions." Their actions were evaluated according to what someone in Punch's situation as owner would have done.

For a variety of reasons, CN's limitation clause did not protect it against anyone. Punch knew nothing about CN or the clause. Savoy's knew that CN was being engaged by Walker's, but knew nothing of the contract terms. Even Walker's, which made the contract with CN, was not affected because the clause did not specifically cover theft and because of the totally unexplained failure of CN to deliver the ring.

Business Application of the Law

Defining Liability in Contracts of Bailment

As demonstrated by the clauses limiting liability to $50 in the case above and $40 in the *London Drugs* case in Chapter 9, a key aspect of a bailment contract is often limitation of the liability that the common law rules of bailment create. The terms of these contracts are normally written by the businesses whose livelihood is based on the bailment relationship. For example, in a bailment for services such as the SWUL storage business, SWUL as bailee will create the standard form agreement. In a leasing contract, the lessor as bailor will write the contract. Of course, limitation clauses are found in a wide variety of commercial and consumer contracts beyond bailments (see the discussion in Chapters 7 and 9).

In the *London Drugs* case, the enforceability of the $40 clause between the customer and the warehouse company was not challenged. However, in the *Punch* case above, all parties challenged the applicability to them of CN's $50 clause. The court's refusal to apply the $50 limit to any of the parties involved indicates the vulnerability of such clauses and the various ways in which they can be challenged:

- Failure to bring the standard terms to the attention of the customer. See the *Tilden* case in Chapter 7 for an example.

- Failure of the language in the clause to exclude liability for the event that occurred. See the *Punch* case above concerning theft and the *Carling* case on page 420 for the meaning of "package."

- Serious defect affecting the formation or performance of the contract. See the *Hunter Engineering* case in Chapter 9.

Exemption and limitation clauses may also be regulated by statute:

- In the United Kingdom, a statute regulates contract terms that limit or exclude damages.[12] For example, bailees in rental agreements cannot exclude or restrict liability for failure of the goods to correspond with their description or in respect to their quality or fitness for a particular purpose. The statute requires that other terms limiting or excluding liability be "reasonable."

- New Brunswick consumer protection legislation[13] applies to consumer sales that include leases. Clauses that limit liability will not be enforced unless they are considered to be "fair and reasonable."

- Industry-specific legislation may set the terms. See the *Carling* case on page 420.

The courts are inclined to apply differing standards to commercial and consumer contracts. A business customer may be better presumed to understand contract terms and intend to be obligated than a consumer. Courts may also consider the contract price in relation to potential losses in deciding whether it is reasonable to enforce a limitation.[14]

CRITICAL ANALYSIS: Do these contract terms indicate that some businesses are exploiting customers who are less knowledgeable, less aware, or weaker, or do these clauses illustrate effective risk management? Are courts and legislatures injecting ethical standards into business by applying standards such as "unfair," "unreasonable," and "unconscionable"?

---

12. *Unfair Contract Terms Act, 1977* (U.K.), c. 50, ss. 1, 3.
13. *Consumer Product Warranty and Liability Act*, S.N.B. 1978, c. 18.1.
14. See *Fraser Jewelers (1982) Ltd. v. Dominion Electric Protection Co.* (1997), 148 D.L.R. (4th) 496 (Ont. C.A.)

Types of Bailment for Reward

The general principles of bailment described above differ to some extent when applied to the following types of bailment for reward. See Figure 17.2 at the end of the chapter for a summary of the following sections.

The Lease

There are important legal distinctions between buying and leasing property. The most obvious one is that a lessee of property is not the owner and has possession subject to any limitations in the lease. In addition, because a lease is not a sale, it is not covered by the large number of terms implied through legislation governing the sale of goods.[15] There is a common law–implied term that leased property will be reasonably fit for its intended use. For example, it would be implied that the fork-lifts leased by SWUL are suitable for the tasks normally performed with forklifts. The lessee must take reasonable care of the property while that property is in its possession and return it in the state that would be expected, subject to the normal wear and tear involved in its use. Of course, it is more prudent to address these issues of suitability, quality, and responsibility expressly in the lease agreement.

chattel lease

A contract where a lessee pays for the use of a lessor's tangible personal property.

There is no legislation dealing specifically with **chattel leases,** so the rules come mainly from the general law of contract. The parties negotiate their own agreement as they see fit. These are some of the issues addressed in a typical lease:

- the risk that the lessee will remove the property from the district or province
- limits on the use of the property by the lessee in terms of the type and extent of work done with the equipment
- suitability of the equipment for its intended or typical uses
- responsibility for maintenance
- responsibility for damage
- the state in which the property must be returned at the end of the lease
- the period of time for which the lease runs
- the amount and schedule of payments
- termination of the lease
- remedies for breach by either party

The short-term lease or rental of property is an attractive way for a business to acquire the use of equipment for a particular task or period of time. It makes little sense to purchase something that is not needed for a long period, unless, of course, the rental charges approach the cost of buying. At the end of a short-term rental, the property is returned to the owner (the lessor). This is known as an **operating lease.** Examples of this type of lease are the crane rental, which was the subject of the *D.J. Lowe* case[16] (see Chapter 6), and the car rental agreement discussed in the *Tilden* case[17] (see Chapter 7). Lowe needed the crane only for a few days. A customer normally rents a car for a short time, such as a day, a weekend, or a week.

operating lease

A lease where the property is returned to the lessor when the term is up.

Leasing is also a means to acquire property needed on a permanent basis and is an alternative to purchasing. For example, the trucks and forklifts leased by SWUL are needed as part of the ongoing operation, and SWUL has made the financial

---

15. See Chapter 23.
16. *Lowe (D.J.) (1980) Ltd. v. Upper Clements Family Theme Park Ltd.* (1990), 95 N.S.R. (2d) 397 (S.C.T.D.).
17. *Tilden Rent-A-Car Co. v. Clendenning* (1978), 83 D.L.R. (3d) 400 (Ont. C.A.).

FIGURE 17.1

Forms of a Chattel
Lease

A. Two-party leasing arrangement

Result: One contract—SWUL has remedies against the dealer for problems with the property.

B. Three-party leasing arrangement

Result: Two contracts—dealer sells to financier, who leases to SWUL. SWUL has no contract with the dealer.

decision to lease rather than buy. The lease is a means of financing SWUL's acquisition of the equipment, through payment of rent over a defined period of time. SWUL may lease the equipment directly from the dealer, in which case the dealer remains the owner and the lessor (see Figure 17.1 A). In a more complicated version of the transaction, the dealer sells the equipment to a financial company, that in turn leases it to SWUL (see Figure 17.1 B). Both variations are known as **financing leases,** but they involve quite different rights and obligations. A feature of both is the possibility that SWUL may buy the equipment at the end of the lease, rather than return it to the lessor.

The contractual arrangements are more complicated if the lessor is a financial company rather than the original owner. In such a transaction there are two contracts—one of sale between the dealer and the financier, and the other the lease between the financier and the lessee. The only parties to the contract for the purchase are the dealer and the financier. The dealer is not a party to the lease and therefore has no obligations to the lessee connected with it. If the lessee has relied on statements or assurances from the dealer in deciding to lease the property from the financier, it is difficult to hold the financier responsible for those statements.

SWUL should know who the lessor is and ensure that the lease adequately protects it if the arrangement fails to go as planned. For example, SWUL should ensure that its obligation to make payments is tied to the suitability and performance of the equipment. SWUL's current concern about increased repair costs may be addressed by the lease terms. This is normally the case if SWUL is leasing from the dealer, but if the lessor is a finance company, the lease will likely protect the financier from the normal rights that a buyer would have in a sale. Each type of transaction involves different risks to be managed.

financing lease

A lease that enables the lessee to finance the acquisition of tangible personal property.

Storage

This type of bailment forms the core of SWUL's business—storage of customers' property. Customers entrust their property to SWUL and have limited means for monitoring SWUL's treatment of their property. As a result, the law imposes a high level of accountability on SWUL for its treatment of customers' property. Of particular importance are any limits on what SWUL can do with the property in terms of the type of storage or the possibility of moving it to other locations. For example, SWUL must keep items that would be harmed by cold temperatures in adequately heated space. SWUL may need permission from customers to store property in any facilities other than its own. Customers expect their property to be returned in the same condition in which it was delivered, unlike in the case of SWUL's leased vehicles, where the intent is for SWUL to use them. If the property is lost, damaged, or destroyed, customers will look to SWUL for compensation. The main concern from SWUL's perspective is payment of the storage fees by customers and its ability to collect.

SWUL's general responsibility toward its customers' property is to treat it as a "skilled storekeeper" would deal with its own property.[18] This imposes a standard of reasonableness that includes responsibility for all foreseeable risks. Because the standard is high and the potential losses are high, SWUL is likely to limit its liability to its customers in its standard form agreements with them. A typical limitation clause is the one shown on page 411, where the contract limits the bailee's liability to $40.

The remedies of a storage bailee, known as a warehouseman, are contained in legislation in each province.[19] The bailee has a lien over the property until the owner pays the storage fees. This means that SWUL can keep its customers' property until payment is complete. If payment is not forthcoming, SWUL also has the right to sell the property in a public auction and apply the proceeds to the outstanding charges. Any surplus proceeds of the sale go to the owner. The legislation contains safeguards for the owner in that notice of the intended sale must be given and the bailee must deal with the property in a reasonable manner—for example, not sell valuable property for the amount of a relatively small storage bill.

These rights and responsibilities relating to a storage bailment apply only if the arrangement meets the definition of a bailment—there must be a transfer of possession and control from the owner to another person. Otherwise the responsibility for the property is much less and the remedies for collection are less effective. For example, leaving a vehicle in a parking lot and paying a parking fee does not amount to a bailment unless the keys are delivered to an attendant, thereby transferring control of the vehicle. If the owner keeps the keys, the parking lot is not in control of the vehicle and the transaction is likely one for the use of the parking space, with minimal responsibility for what is in the space.[20] Operators of parking space commonly issue tickets that are meant to define the relationship (use of space rather than bailment) and either exclude liability completely or limit it to a small amount. As with any standard form contract, the customer must receive adequate notice of onerous and unexpected terms.

Repairs

When the owner of property takes it to a repair shop, the main purpose of the transaction is the repairs. If the property is left at the shop, a storage bailment, which is incidental to the main purpose of the arrangement, is also created. At the appointed time for pickup, the owner—the bailor—expects to receive the property in a good state of repair and otherwise in the condition in which it was delivered. The bailee must provide reasonable safekeeping for the property and complete the repairs in a workmanlike manner, as a reasonably competent repairer of that sort of property would.

From a business perspective, it makes sense to agree on a price in advance, but if the parties do not agree on the price for storage and repairs at the outset, the repairer's compensation will be a reasonable amount for the service provided. The

---

18. See *Punch v. Savoy's Jewellers Ltd.* (1986), 33 B.L.R. 147 (Ont. C.A.).
19. See, for example, *Warehouse Lien Act*, R.S.B.C. 1996, c. 480; *Warehouser's Lien Act*, R.S.N. 1990, c. W-2; *Repair and Storage Liens Act*, R.S.O. 1990, c. R-25.
20. Bruce H. Ziff, *Principles of Property Law*, 3rd ed. (Toronto: Carswell, 2000) at 287.

lien

The right to retain possession of personal property until payment for service is received.

repairer cannot charge more than is reasonable, nor can the owner refuse to pay anything, just because no price was agreed in advance. An example of a repair bailment and the complications that can arise is found in the *Punch* case.

Most provinces have legislation[21] giving the bailee a **lien** against the property for the value of the repairs as long as the bailee has possession of the property. As with the storage situation, the bailee also has the right to sell the property (subject to procedural requirements) to recover the repair charges.

Transportation

Bailees who receive property and transport it according to the owner's instructions are called carriers. There are several categories of carriers, each with different obligations toward the property. The most relevant in business are common carriers—those who represent themselves to the public as carriers for reward, meaning they are prepared to transport any property for any owner so long as their facilities permit and they are paid for the service. Common carriers are held to a very high standard of care regarding the property they carry. If property is lost or damaged while in their possession, it is presumed that the carrier is liable. The owner is not required to prove fault by the carrier, mainly because it is difficult for the owner to know what happened to the property during the transport. Carriers are required to account for their treatment of the property and justify the application of one of the limited legal defences, which mainly relate to circumstances within the control of the owner or beyond the control of the carrier. For example, if the owner fails to pack fragile goods adequately or the goods are destroyed in a natural disaster, the carrier could be excused from liability.

As a result of this heavy responsibility based on legislation and the common law, carriers normally include provisions in their standard form agreements with customers that the carriers' liability will be severely limited should mishap occur with the property. These clauses typically limit liability to a low dollar amount. An example is the CN clause in the *Punch* case. Customers are protected by legislation covering each form of transport—rail, road, sea, and air. Clauses used in contracts on international or interprovincial routes must be approved by the Canadian Transport Commission. The case on the next page illustrates potential problems with the transport of goods.

Carriers do not have the same legislative remedies as those that repair or store property. Carriers have a common law lien against the property for transport charges, but enjoy no corresponding right to sell the property if the owner fails to pay.

Lodging

Those who offer lodging to the public are known as innkeepers. At common law, their responsibility for guests' property is similar to that of common carriers. They must take great care of guests' property and are responsible for loss or theft. There is an important practical distinction in the degree of control between carriers and innkeepers. Carriers have total control of the property when it is delivered for shipment, while guests share control over their property through their occupation of rooms.

---

21. See, for example, *Mechanics Lien Act*, R.S.N. 1990, c. M-3, R.S.N.S. 1989, c. 277; *Repairers' Lien Act*, R.S.B.C. 1996, c. 404; *Repair and Storage Liens Act*, R.S.O. 1990, c. R-25.

CASE ▼

Carling O'Keefe Breweries of Canada Ltd. v. CN Marine Inc. (1989), 104 N.R. 166 (F.C.A.)

THE BUSINESS CONTEXT: Deciding who is responsible for damaged goods and for how much requires a full investigation of the events that occurred and a detailed examination of the terms of the contract, any legislation, and applicable international rules.

FACTUAL BACKGROUND: Carling engaged CN to ship 4240 cases of beer from St. John's to Goose Bay. CN arranged shipping aboard a ship owned by Labrador Shipping. The beer was placed in three large containers and stowed on the deck of the ship with the edges of the containers protruding over the sides of the ship. The containers were washed overboard in heavy seas. Carling claimed the value of the beer ($32 000) from CN and the owners of the ship. The shipowners became insolvent, leaving CN as the defendant able to pay a judgment. CN argued that it was acting only as agent for the shipowners and therefore had no liability, and that in any event its liability should be limited to $500 per container (a total of $1500) by virtue of the applicable federal legislation.

THE LEGAL QUESTION: Did the contract relieve CN from liability as carrier and limit damages to $500 for each container? Did the $500 limit apply to each of the three large shipping containers or to each of the 4240 cases of beer?

RESOLUTION: The contract was governed by federal legislation (the *Carriage of Goods by Water Act*), which incorporated the *Hague Rules* (an international convention providing for standardized terms in such transactions). The *Hague Rules* prevented a carrier from avoiding liability for improper storage of goods but also limited claims to $500 "per package." The court found that CN was the carrier (not just the agent of the shipowners) because it had signed the contract in its personal capacity (becoming a "carrier" as defined in the *Hague Rules*) and because it had acted as a carrier in the loading and stowage of the cargo on board the vessel.

In terms of the number of "packages" on which Carling O'Keefe could recover up to $500, the court looked to the intention of the parties as revealed by the language of the documents, what they said, and what they did. The shipping documents listed 4240 packages. It was also noted that "it is common knowledge that beer is shipped in cases." On this basis, Carling recovered its full loss from CN.

CRITICAL ANALYSIS: Is the adoption of international rules an effective way to manage risk? How could CN have limited its liability to $1500 instead of $32 000? How could Carling control its risk?

Transportation of goods involves many parties, contracts, and risks. What are some potential legal problems arising from this scene?

Innkeepers are permitted by legislation[22] to limit their liability to a specific amount ($40 to $150, depending on the province) if they post the legislated limits in the establishment. Their protection is lost if the loss to property is due to a negligent or deliberate act of the innkeeper (or the inn's employees) or if the property has been deposited with the inn for safekeeping.

---

22. See, for example, *Innkeepers' Act*, R.S.O. 1990, c. I-7, R.S.N.S. 1989, c. 229; *Hotel Keepers Act*, R.S.M. 1987, c. H-150.

FIGURE 17.2

Summary of Bailment

Type of bailment	Lease	Storage	Repair	Transport	Lodging
Specialized designation for the bailor	Lessor	Customer	Customer	Shipper	Guest
Specialized designation for the bailee	Lessee	Warehouse	Repairer	Carrier	Innkeeper
Bailee's standard of care	Reasonable	Reasonable	Reasonable	High	High
Liability normally limited	Wear and tear	Contract	Contract	Contract	Legislation
Who gets paid for a service	Bailor	Bailee	Bailee	Bailee	Bailee
Remedies for nonpayment	Possession, damages	Lien, sale	Lien, sale	Lien	Lien
Applicable legislation?	No	Yes	Yes	No	Yes

Risk Management

The risks relating to personal property concern proof and protection of ownership, rights to possession, and the preservation of economic value. With tangible property, the major concern is with responsibility for loss or damage to the property. In bailments for value, an additional risk is the failure of the customer to pay for services such as storage or repair.

Businesses subject to these risks can use the risk management model to minimize their impact on the success of the business. For example, SWUL can decline to accept items for storage that are particularly susceptible to loss or unsuitable for SWUL's facilities, thereby avoiding such risks. SWUL will strive to reduce the remaining risks through well-developed and administered procedures within its storage facilities. In bailment transactions, the transfer of risk is prominent. Carefully negotiated contracts will indicate who bears the loss in a variety of circumstances. The contract will assign the loss and thereby indicate which party should seek to transfer its risk through appropriate insurance policies. As in most business situations, the risks that cannot be avoided, reduced, or transferred will be retained.

Business Law in Practice Revisited

1. What types of property are used in SWUL's business?

SWUL uses real property (its land, warehouse, and anything permanently attached to the land and warehouse), tangible personal property (shelving, dividers, vehicles, customers' property), and intangible personal property (trademarks, accounts receivable). A typical business would use a similar range of property, including examples of the major classifications of property.

2. How did SWUL acquire these various forms of property?

SWUL acquired its property by purchase (land, warehouse furnishings), lease (vehicles), bailment (customers' property), creation and use (business name), and dealing with customers (accounts receivable, customer records).

3. What are SWUL's rights in relation to its property?

SWUL's rights depend to a large extent on whether it is the owner or merely in possession of each type of property. For example, as owner of the land, SWUL has total control subject to any contracts or statutory restrictions (see Chapter 19). For property it does not own, but of which it has temporary possession, SWUL has more limited rights. For example, SWUL has the right (according to legislation) to hold customers' property until they pay the agreed storage fees. If customers don't pay, SWUL can sell their property at public auction to recover the outstanding fees.

4. What obligations does SWUL have in terms of its property?

For property it does not own, SWUL's obligations arise from the nature of the transactions involving the property and the terms of the applicable contracts and legislation. For example, SWUL has a duty to treat customers' property as a reasonably competent warehouse proprietor would treat its own property, subject to the protection for SWUL contained in its standard form customer contracts. If customers' stored documents suffer water damage, SWUL needs to improve its treatment of this type of property. This protection will relate to SWUL's conduct and its level of liability in dollar terms. In addition, SWUL must take reasonable care of the leased vehicles subject to normal wear and tear. The leases will likely set out SWUL's obligations, including responsibility for repairs, in considerable detail.

Chapter Summary

Property can be divided into real and personal. There are two categories of personal property: tangible, which includes goods or chattels, and intangible, which includes various contractual and statutory rights.

Ownership is acquired by purchase or manufacture (goods); creation, registration, or purchase (intellectual property); or trading (accounts receivable). Possession can be acquired along with ownership or through a bailment.

The owner of property has full responsibility for it and bears the risk of loss. The owner also has the right to deal with the property in whatever way he chooses.

A bailment is the temporary transfer of possession with no change in ownership. A commercial bailment (bailment for value) benefits both the bailor (owner) and bailee (possessor). Key issues in bailment are the standard of care that the bailee must observe in relation to the property and the remedies that the parties have for recovering fees. Standard form contracts are a common feature of bailments.

The most common types of bailments are leasing, storage, repairs, transportation, and lodging. Each has somewhat different rules for liability and remedies.

Chapter Study

Key Terms and Concepts

bailee (p. 409)

bailment (p. 409)

bailment for value (p. 410)

bailor (p. 409)

carrier (p. 412)

chattel lease (p. 416)

financing lease (p. 417)

gratuitous bailment (p. 410)

innkeeper (p. 412)

intangible property (p. 405)

lien (p. 419)

operating lease (p. 416)

personal property (p. 405)

tangible property (p. 405)

warehouseman (p. 412)

Questions for Review

1. How is personal property different from real property?

2. What are some examples of personal property?

3. How is tangible property different from intangible property?

4. Choose a business with which you are familiar and identify as many items of property as you can that are used in that business. Classify each item as real, tangible personal, or intangible personal.

5. Who bears the risk of loss to personal property?

6. How is ownership of personal property acquired?

7. What can the owner of personal property do with it?

8. When is the owner of personal property not in possession of it?

9. What is a bailment?

10. What are some examples of bailments?

11. Do commercial bailments work differently from consumer bailments?

12. How can a bailee for value collect fees?

13. What is the liability of a bailee for damage to the goods?

14. How can a bailee limit the liability for damage to the goods?

15. When are contractual limits on damages not enforced?

16. What are the major differences among the types of bailment for reward?

17. What role does insurance play in bailment?

18. What risks relate to personal property?

Questions for Critical Thinking

1. Personal property in the form of chattels is portable. Proving and tracking ownership and possession are challenging. Should we establish a comprehensive system of registering all chattels as we do for motor vehicles? How would such a system help in verifying and tracking? Would the benefits justify the expense?

2. Intangible personal property consists of legal rights, which may be contained in legal documents such as a lease or a loan agreement. Are these rights as difficult to control as chattels? Should those documents be available for examination in a public registry?

3. In the business you chose in Question for Review 4, what are the major risks involving its property? How can those risks be managed?

4. The standard of care in a bailment depends on the type of bailment and the particular circumstances of the transaction. Therefore, the obligations of the bailor and bailee may be difficult to define in a contract in advance of a dispute. Would legislation be an easier way to set the standard?

5. Bailments can be commercial (such as a forklift lease) or consumer (such as a video rental). Both are bailments for value and therefore governed by a contract. It could be argued that consumers accept whatever terms are offered while businesses are able to negotiate terms. Is this a valid argument? Is there a need for legislative intervention?

6. Commercial bailees generally try to minimize their liability in a standard form contract. They justify these low limits as a means of controlling risk and keeping their prices competitive. Is there a market opportunity for more generous liability terms? For example, could a storage business increase market share by accepting a greater risk of liability than its competitors and charging a higher price?

Situations for Discussion

1. ABC has a large fleet of company cars. The entire fleet is aging and needs replacement in the next couple of years. ABC has a long-standing relationship with a local dealer and has purchased vehicles there for many years. Clancy, the acquisitions manager of ABC, is considering the possibility of leasing rather than buying the new vehicles. One factor Clancy must consider is pressure on ABC's cash flow. In addition to the financial considerations, what are the legal issues relating to reliability and liability? What will determine whether Clancy should choose operating or financing leases?

2. Clancy is the acquisitions manager of ABC. He has an appointment at a local car dealer to explore the possibility of leasing some vehicles for ABC. Clancy parks his company car at the rear of the dealer's showroom and leaves his laptop computer in the back seat. When he returns to get his vehicle about an hour later, it is gone (and his computer with it). Has a bailment been created? Identify the potential bailor and bailee. What circumstances would determine the bailee's standard of care? How should Clancy, ABC, and the car dealer handle this situation?

3. Ying leased a machine to haul large logs in her lumbering business. The lease required Ying to keep the machine in good repair and fully insured, and to return it at the end of the lease in its original condition, subject to "normal wear and tear." The machine never worked very

well. Ying ran up large repair bills and began to suspect the machine was not heavy enough for the needs of her business. When she contacted the leasing company, she was reminded that the lessor had made no promises about performance of the equipment. Ying is thinking about stopping her lease payments and insurance premiums and leasing a heavier machine from another dealer. She needs that heavier machine to maintain profitable levels of production. What factors should she consider? What would you advise her to do?

4. Ying took her logging machine in for repairs. A week later she got a call from the shop to tell her that the machine was fixed and the bill was $4500. Ying had left strict instructions with the shop that she must approve all work before it was done. What rules of contract determine whether Ying is obligated to pay the bill? If she refuses, what are the shop's remedies? What safeguards and risks are involved in those remedies for Ying?

5. Roach owned a truck with a large crane attached. Roach took the truck to Vern's Auto to have the crane removed with the intention of mounting it on another vehicle in the future. Vern's allowed Roach to leave the crane in its yard, assuring him it would be safe. A few months later, Roach decided to sell the crane. When he went to get the crane, it was gone. Vern's had no idea what had happened to it, and because the company had charged nothing for storing it, were not interested in finding out.[23] Is Vern's responsible for the missing crane? What are the determining factors? What information is missing? What steps should Roach and Vern's have taken to safeguard the crane?

6. Seaway Distributors hired Chet's Transport to move a load of carrots from Boston to Newfoundland with instructions to keep the temperature of the carrots between 2 and 6 degrees Celsius. The carrots were five days late when delivered in Newfoundland, and when unloaded they were heating and beginning to spoil. They were sold at a loss of $5000. Seaway wants to recover its loss of $5000. Chet's is seeking the freight charges of $4000.[24] Evidence showed that the truck was at the proper temperature when it left Boston. What other evidence is important? Which company has the burden of proof? What should these companies do differently in future contracts?

7. Horst is a collector of hockey memorabilia. He is particularly interested in hockey sticks that are autographed by well-known players in the National Hockey League. When Horst checked on eBay, he found many autographed hockey sticks for sale, including several signed by his favourite players. He is prepared to pay the going rate, but wants to be sure that the autographs are authentic and that the current owners acquired the sticks legitimately. Horst has heard of organizations that purport to authenticate autographs, but has also heard of many "fake" autographs that were authenticated. What legal issues should Horst consider? How should he manage the risks facing him?

8. Canfor hired B.C. Rail to transport wood pulp from the interior of B.C. to a shipping terminal for eventual delivery to a customer in Scotland. The contract between Canfor and B.C. Rail specified that the rail cars would be clean and the pulp delivered free from contamination. Canfor insisted on wood-lined boxcars and also routinely inspected and swept out the cars before loading bales of pulp. When the pulp arrived in Scotland, it was contaminated with wood splinters and rejected by the customer. Canfor had to compensate its customer and pay for transporting the pulp back to B.C.[25] Can Canfor recover its losses from B.C. Rail? Explain.

For more study tools, visit
http://www.businesslaw3e.nelson.com

---

23. Based on *Lowe (D.J.) (1980) Ltd. v. Roach* (1994), 131 N.S.R. (2d) 268 (S.C.), aff'd (1995), 138 N.S.R. (2d) 79 (C.A.).
24. Based on *Chet's Transport Inc. v. Seaway Distributors Ltd.* (1987), 81 N.S.R. (2d) 299 (N.S.S.C.).
25. Based on *B.C. Rail Ltd. v. Canadian Forest Products Ltd.* (B.C.C.A., 7 July 2005) (31159).

Chapter

18

Objectives

After studying this chapter, you should have an understanding of

- the nature of intellectual property
- the rights that attach to intellectual property
- how intellectual property is acquired
- how to protect the intellectual property assets of an organization

Intellectual Property

Business Law in Practice

For the past 15 years, Chuck Morrow has owned and operated Chuck's Grill House in Burnaby, British Columbia. His restaurant offers a selection of beef dishes including prime rib, steaks, burgers, and ribs. The most popular dish on the menu is Chuck's BBQ Ribs. The ribs are cured and smoked using a secret method invented by Chuck, slow roasted and then finished on a grill. Recently, Chuck discovered that a new restaurant has opened in Vancouver featuring most of the same dishes as Chuck's Grill House including a dish called "Chucky's BBQ Ribs." Chuck wants to stop the new restaurant from selling "Chucky's BBQ ribs." Also, Chuck has developed a new and improved method of curing and smoking ribs using flavoured wood chips and he wants to protect it so that others cannot use it.

1. How can Chuck protect his new and improved method of curing and smoking ribs from being used by others?
2. How can Chuck prevent the new restaurant from selling "Chucky's BBQ Ribs?"

Introduction

intellectual property
The results of the creative process such as ideas, the expression of ideas, formulas, schemes, trademarks, and the like; also refers to the protection attached to ideas through patent, copyright, trademark, industrial design, and other similar laws.

Intellectual property is a term often used to describe the results of intellectual or creative processes.[1] Put another way, the term is used for describing ideas or ways of expressing ideas. Some common business examples of intellectual property are

- recipes and formulas for making products
- manufacturing processes
- methods of extracting minerals
- advertising jingles
- business and marketing plans
- the distinctive name given to a product or service

Chuck's name for his ribs and his method of curing and smoking are also examples.

The term "intellectual property"[2] is also used to describe the "bundle of rights" that people have regarding their ideas or the ways in which they are expressed. These rights are rewards or incentives for creating and developing ideas. There are differing rights in intellectual property as the law gives varying types of protection to its many forms. The main categories of intellectual property laws are patents, trademarks, copyrights, industrial designs, and confidential (business) information.[3] There are other laws, however, that provide protection for specific types of intellectual property. For example, there are laws that protect plant varieties,[4] integrated circuit topographies,[5] and personality rights.[6]

---

1. The suggestions of Professor Wayne Renke of the Faculty of Law, University of Alberta, and Professor Peter Lown, director of the Alberta Law Reform Institute, in reviewing an earlier draft of this chapter are gratefully acknowledged.
2. The term "intellectual property" is used to refer to both intangibles—such as ideas, their expression, formulas, schemes, trademarks and the like—and rights that may attach to these intangibles. However, not all intellectual property can be technically called "property," as the basis for protection is not always "property" principles but principles of contract and tort as well as specific statutory provisions.
3. The term "confidential information" includes a broad range of information, such as government secrets and private personal information. In this text, the term "confidential business information" is used to distinguish information of a commercial nature from other types of information.
4. *Plant Breeders' Rights Act*, S.C. 1990, c. 20. This act provides 18-year patent-like protection for distinct new plant varieties.
5. *Integrated Circuit Topography Act*, S.C. 1990, c. 37. This act provides ten-year protection for layout designs embedded in semiconductor chips or circuit boards (e.g., microchips).
6. Personality rights or the right not to have one's name or likeness appropriated for another's gain are protected under tort actions, trademark legislation, and privacy legislation, such as British Columbia's *Privacy Act*, R.S.B.C. 1996, c. 373.

Intellectual property is a necessary and critical asset in many industries, as illustrated in these examples:

- Patents protect inventions and are essential to businesses in the pharmaceutical, electronics, chemical, and manufacturing industries, as patents may be used to exclude others from using new technology.

- Industrial designs protect the appearance of useful articles against copying and are relevant to businesses that offer goods to consumers.

- Trademarks serve to distinguish the goods or services of one provider from those of another and are essential to all businesses that sell goods or services to the public.

- Copyright prevents the copying of certain works and is the basis for businesses involved in art, publishing, music, communications, and software, as copyright provides the basis for a saleable product.

- The law governing confidentiality is the means of protecting such information as marketing plans, customer lists, databases, and price lists, and is crucial to all businesses.[7]

Intellectual property offers both opportunities and challenges to business. Businesses can gain a competitive advantage by developing new products, innovative business methods, and creative brand names. Also, they can exploit these things by assigning or licensing their use to other businesses. However, the development of various technologies, such as photocopiers, tape recorders, video cameras, and computers, has made it easier for others to "take" intellectual property. In short, it is often difficult to police and protect intellectual property.[8]

This chapter explores the creation, acquisition, and protection of intellectual property.

Creation of Intellectual Property Rights

Chuck's intellectual property comprises methods for smoking and curing ribs, the name of his restaurant, a name for the ribs, and written materials such as menus, advertising brochures, marketing plans and the like. Various aspects of his intellectual property may qualify for protection under different legal regimes.

Patents

patent
A monopoly to make, use, or sell an invention.

Chuck's new and improved method for curing and smoking ribs may qualify for **patent** protection. A patent is a statutory right[9] that provides protection for inventions.

---

7. Sheldon Burshtein, "Executives Remain Unaware of the Value of Intellectual Property Assets" *The Lawyers Weekly* (27 June 1997) at 23.
8. For example, in recognition of the difficulties in policing copyright infringement of music, a levy on blank tapes has been introduced. See *Copyright Act*, R.S.C. 1985, c. C-42, as am. by S.C. 1997, c. 24, s. 50.
9. The federal government has jurisdiction to make laws concerning patents, copyrights, and trademarks. See *Constitution Act, 1867*, s. 91.

Patents Defined

The *Patent Act*[10] defines an invention as "any new and useful art, process, machine, manufacture or composition of matter or any new and useful improvement[11] in any art, process, machine, manufacture or composition of matter." The definition is very broad and encompasses a number of different kinds of inventions such as

- processes or methods (e.g., a pay-per-use billing system, a system for applying a selective herbicide to improve crop yield, a method of cleaning carpets)

- machines or apparatuses (e.g., computer hardware, a hay rake, a vacuum cleaner)

- products or compositions of matter (e.g., pharmaceuticals, chemical compounds, microorganisms)

Substances intended for food or medicine were not patentable until recently, although the processes for producing them were. The question of whether new life forms created as the result of genetic engineering should be patentable has been the subject of much controversy.

CASE ▼

Monsanto v. Schmeiser [2004]
1 S.C.R. 902

THE BUSINESS CONTEXT: In 2002, in *Harvard College v. Canada (Commissioner of Patents)*,[12] the Supreme Court of Canada held by a narrow 5 to 4 margin that higher life forms, including plants, are not patentable. Although the process for genetically modifying cells was held to be patentable, the end result, a mouse susceptible to cancer, was not. The decision was a large disappointment to many in the biotechnology industry as Canada's major trading partners, including the United States, Europe, Australia and Japan, permit such patents. The decision also created uncertainty as to the scope of protection afforded to biotechnology-related inventions.

FACTUAL BACKGROUND: Percy Schmeiser is a Saskatchewan farmer who grows canola. Monsanto is a multinational firm specializing in biotechnologies used in agriculture. In the 1990s, Monsanto introduced Roundup Ready Canola, a variety of canola containing genetically modified genes and cells patented by Monsanto. Roundup Ready

Canola is resistant to Roundup, a pesticide, which means that the canola plants can be sprayed with Roundup to kill weeds but not harm the crop. Monsanto licensed its Roundup Ready canola to farmers for a fee provided the farmers purchased the canola seeds from an authorized Monsanto agent.

Schmeiser did not purchase Roundup Ready canola seeds nor did he obtain a license from Monsanto. By chance, he discovered some Roundup Ready canola growing on his property. It is unclear how the canola got onto his property, but it is possible that the seeds blew there from a neighbour's land. Schmeiser collected and cultivated the seeds and most of his 1998 canola crop comprised Roundup Ready canola. Once his activities were detected, Monsanto sued him for patent infringement.

THE LEGAL QUESTION: Had Schmeiser, by collecting and planting the seeds and harvesting and selling the plants, infringed Monsanto's patents relating to genetically modified canola?

RESOLUTION: By a narrow 5 to 4 margin, the Supreme Court of Canada held that Monsanto's patents were valid and that Schmeiser had infringed them. Schmeiser had argued that he had not "used" the invention by growing canola plants because the

---

10. R.S.C. 1985, c. P-4, s. 2. The *Patent Act* was substantially amended in 1987, R.S.C. 1987, c. 33 (3d Supp.) and became effective 1 October 1989. Patents issued prior to this date remain subject to the earlier law. Substantial amendments, notably in respect to pharmaceuticals, were also effected by the *Intellectual Property Law Improvement Act*, S.C. 1993, c. 15.
11. Ninety percent of all patents are for improvements to existing patented inventions. See *Patent Guide*, Canadian Intellectual Property Office online at http://www.strategis.gc.ca
12. [2002] 4 S.C.R. 45.

plants are not covered by Monsanto's patents, only the plant cells containing the modified gene. The majority disagreed. The court held that the plants were composed of modified plant cells containing the modified genes, and therefore growing the modified plants constituted use of the invention. The majority used the following analogy: "if an infringing use were alleged in building a structure with patented Lego blocks, it would be no bar to a finding of infringement that only the blocks were used and not the whole structure." In essence, the Court confirmed the patentability of cells and genes, and held that the rights in patented genes and cells extend to plants containing them.

CRITICAL ANALYSIS: Are there any concerns with manipulating genes in order to obtain better weed control or higher yields? How does this decision support the Canadian biotechnology industry?

What are the benefits of granting patents for life forms?

Exclusions from Patent Protection

There are also exclusions or exceptions to what may be patented. The most common are the following:

■ THINGS THAT RECEIVE EXCLUSIVE PROTECTION UNDER OTHER AREAS OF THE LAW. For example, computer programs (i.e., software) are not patentable, as they receive protection under copyright law. They could, however, receive patent protection as part of a broader patent, as, for example, a computerized method of controlling the operation of a plant.[13]

■ THINGS THAT DO NOT MEET THE DEFINITION OF A PATENT. For example, scientific principles, natural phenomena, and abstract theorems are "discoveries" as opposed to inventions and are therefore not patentable. A practical application of a theory could, however, qualify for protection.

■ THINGS THAT ARE, FOR POLICY REASONS, NOT PATENTABLE. For example, methods of medical or surgical treatment, and illicit objects are not patentable. Also historically, business methods such as franchising arrangements, accounting methods, insurance schemes, tax loopholes and protocols for interacting with customers have not been patentable.[14] However, the Canadian Patent Office guidelines state business methods[15] are not automatically excluded from patent protection and a number of business methods patents have been issued in Canada. There is, however, no definitive legal decision on the validity of business methods patents.

---

13. David Vaver, *Intellectual Property Law* (Concord, ON: Irwin Law, 1997) at 129.
14. Business-methods patents are allowed in the United States. See *State Street Bank & Trust v. Signature Financial Group*, 149 F. 3d 1368 (Fed. Cir.1998).
15. *Manual of Patent Office Practice*, s. 12.04.04, at http://strategis.ic.gc.sc_mrksv/cipo/patents/mopop/mopop-e.html (accessed 1 December 2006).

The BlackBerry Litigation

Research In Motion Ltd. (RIM), located in Waterloo, Ontario, manufactures the BlackBerry, a handheld wireless e-mail device. From 2000 to 2006, RIM was engaged in a patent battle with NTP Ltd., the holder of several U.S. patents.

The dispute has its origins in 1995, when Thomas Campana Jr. was granted several U.S. patents for his idea to merge existing e-mail systems with radio-frequency wireless communications networks. The patents were transferred to NTP, a company formed by Campana and his patent lawyer to hold and lease the patents.

In January 2000, NTP gave RIM notice that RIM's products were infringing its patents and offered a license. When RIM refused, NTP filed a patent infringement suit in Virginia, alleging that RIM's BlackBerry device and associated services infringed several of its patents. In 2003, the District Court granted summary judgment of some claims to NTP, and submitted others to the jury. In November 2003, the jury found that RIM had infringed 14 claims in five NTP patents and awarded NTP approximately $23 million in damages. In a final judgment, the District Court increased the damages to $53.7 million and entered a permanent injunction against RIM. The effect of the injunction would be to disable service to the 3.2 million BlackBerry users in the United States. The injunction was stayed pending an appeal to the Federal Circuit on the basis of the District Court's claims interpretation and the applicability of the U.S. *Patents Act* to extraterritorial operations. In particular, RIM argued that because its relay server, through which all BlackBerry e-mails pass is in Waterloo, the U.S. patents laws do not apply. RIM's appeal was denied. On the extraterritoriality issue, the Court held that because RIM's customers were in the United States and the "the location of the beneficial use and function of the whole operable system is the United States," this satisfies the territoriality requirements. In short, a U.S. patent may be infringed even when one or more elements of the patented method or system are located outside the United States. In March 2005, RIM and NTP reached a US$450 million settlement but shortly thereafter the settlement collapsed. In January 2006, the Supreme Court of the United States refused to hear an appeal. In the meantime, the Patent and Trademark Office (PTO) took the unusual step of re-examining the validity of NTP's patents. As well, RIM started separate re-examination proceedings attacking NTP's patents. The validity of the NTP's patents remains unclear. The PTO has initially rejected the patents on a preliminary basis, but the re-examination process will probably remain pending for several years, and the final decision of the PTO is subject to appeals. In February 2006, the District Court indicated that it was prepared to issue its injunction. Faced with the shutdown of its system in the United States, RIM reached a settlement with NTP. It agreed to pay NTP US$612.5 million as a full and final settlement of the dispute. The settlement also included a perpetual, fully paid up license going forward.

CRITICAL ANALYSIS: Traditionally, it has been generally understood that patent rights are territorial in nature. However, with advances in communication technologies and the establishment of multijurisdictional operations, geographic boundaries for patent rights are difficult to define. What strategies should Canadian companies adopt to deal with what may be a more liberal interpretation of the territorial reach of patent rights?

Sources: *NTP Inc. v. Research in Motion Ltd., 392* F.3d 1336, (Fed. Cir. 2004); and Tai W. Nahm, "*NTP Inc. v. Research in Motion Ltd:* Extraterritorial Application of U.S. Patent Rights? A Caution for Canadian Technology" *Internet and E-commerce Law* (April 2005) at 12.

What are the legal problems with litigating a patent dispute?

Requirements for Patentability

Not all inventions, however wonderful, are patentable. A patent will be granted only for an invention that is new, useful, and unobvious.

New   The invention must be new or novel. An invention, however, need not be absolutely new.[16] It is "new" if it has not been disclosed publicly. This means that any public disclosure, public use, or sale of the invention prior to filing for a patent renders the invention "old" and unpatentable.[17] For example, displaying the new product at a trade show, distributing marketing brochures that describe or display the product, or advertising the product in a way that reveals the invention[18] is a disclosure and a bar to obtaining a patent.

There is, however, a one-year grace period. If the inventor or someone who derived knowledge from the inventor makes a disclosure within the year preceding the filing of the application, this will not operate as public disclosure. Chuck needs to determine whether his new and improved method of curing and smoking ribs has already been disclosed to the public in some manner. He can have a patent agent search relevant literature so that an opinion can be formed as to whether an invention is novel.

Useful   An invention must solve some practical problem and it must actually work—that is, do what it purports to do. An invention that does not work is useless and unpatentable. The invention must have industrial value, although it need not be commercially successful. The invention must have practical use as opposed to being a mere scientific curiosity. For example, a perpetual motion machine[19] lacks utility as it does not have a practical use.

Unobvious   The third requirement relates to "inventiveness." It means that there must be some ingenuity or inventive step involved in the invention. Changes to something that would be obvious to someone skilled in the art to which the invention pertains would not be patentable. For example, simply using a different material for making a product would not be patentable as it does not involve an inventive step.

The test is difficult to apply in practice as it involves ascertaining the state of the art or knowledge prior to the invention and analyzing whether the invention was merely the obvious, next step in the state of the knowledge or instead involves an inventive step.

The question of whether Chuck's new method is unobvious can be answered only by asking someone knowledgeable in the field of curing and smoking methods. The patent agent who searches the literature to determine whether an invention is novel will also express an opinion on whether the invention is obvious. Many methods of food preparation are not patentable because they are obvious and do not involve an inventive step.

16. *Supra* note 13 at 131.
17. Also of relevance to the issue of novelty are applications for patents filed in other countries. Canada is a signatory to both the *Paris Convention for the Protection of Industrial Property* and the *Patent Co-Operation Treaty*. An applicant, by filing in a member country, can claim this date in other countries so long as the corresponding applications are filed within one year. This means that the earlier date becomes the disclosure date for purposes of establishing novelty.
18. Ronald Dimock, *Canadian Marketing Law* (Toronto: Richard DeBoo, 1991) at 3–4.
19. *Supra* note 13 at 128.

Patent Protection and Application

Patent protection, unlike some other intellectual property rights, does not arise automatically. An application for a patent must be filed with the Canadian patent office.[20] Timing of the application is a critical concern because the patent regime is based on a first-to-file system.[21] This means, for example, that if more than one person has independently invented the same process, method, or machine, the patent office gives priority to the first person to file the application.

The inventor is generally the first owner of the invention and thus the person entitled to apply for a patent. The *Patent Act* does not contain specific provisions for the ownership of inventions created by employees in the course of employment; generally, however, an employee will be the owner unless (1) the employee was specifically hired to produce the invention and makes the invention in the course of employment or (2) there is an express or implied agreement that precludes the employee from claiming ownership of inventions relating to and developed in the course of employment.[22] This means that contracts with employees, as well as contracts with consultants, should consider the ownership of all intellectual property including inventions produced in the course of employment.

The preparation of a patent application is a highly complex matter and is normally done by a **patent agent,** who has particular expertise in this area. The application has two main parts: one part describes how the product is made or the best way to perform the process or method. This is known as the **specifications.** The other part is known as the **claims.**[23] These are the sequentially numbered, single-sentence definitions of the invention. This part in effect defines the exclusive rights enjoyed by the patent holder. In short, the specifications tell the reader how to put the invention into practice after the patent expires. The claims tell the reader what he cannot do prior to the expiry of the patent.

The application is examined[24] by the patent office to ensure that the invention has not already been invented and that the application complies with the *Patent Act*. If the application is successful, a patent is issued upon the payment of the required fee. The word "patented" and the patent number may be put on all manufactured goods. Marking is not mandatory, but it is legally useful as it notifies others of the existence of a right and reduces the number of "innocent" infringers. Often manufacturers will put the term "patent pending" or "patent applied for" on their products before the patent is issued. This warns others that a patent may eventually be issued for these products and they could be liable to pay damages for infringing the patent once the patent is granted. A patent gives the inventor the right to exclude others from making, selling, or using the invention to which the patent relates for a period of 20 years from the date of filing the application[25] so long as the appropriate maintenance fees[26] are paid.

patent agent

A professional trained in patent law and practice who can assist in the preparation of a patent application.

specifications

The description of an invention contained in a patent.

claims

The exclusive rights of the patent holder.

---

20. The Canadian Intellectual Property Office's database is online and can be accessed at http://www.strategis.ic.gc.ca/sc_mrksv/cipo/welcome/welcom-e.html
21. Until 1989, Canada's patent regime was based on a first-to-invent system.
22. *Supra* note 13 at 147–148.
23. The Supreme Court of Canada released three decisions at the end of 2000 on claims construction. The unanimous court endorsed an approach for interpreting and defining claims in patents. This approach is to be used in both cases involving the infringement of a claim and cases involving the validity of a claim. See *Free World Trust v. Elecrio Santé Inc.,* [2000] 2 S.C.R. 1024; *Whirlpool Corp. v. Maytag Corp.,* [2000] 2 S.C.R. 1116; *Whirlpool Corp. v. Camco Inc.,* [2000] 2 S.C.R. 1067.
24. *Supra* note 10 at s. 35(1). An application for a patent is not automatically examined. The applicant must specifically request that an examination be done. Requests must be made within five years of filing the application, or the application will be deemed abandoned. The delay for requesting an examination gives the applicant a period of time to test the market for the invention.
25. *Supra* note 10 at s. 45. Patent applications filed before 1 October 1989 carry a term of 17 years from the date the patent was granted. However, a recent amendment to the *Patent Act* extends the term of unexpired patents to 20 years. See *An Act to Amend the Patent Act,* S.C. 2001, c. 10. s. 1.
26. Annual maintenance fees vary depending on how long a patent has been issued and whether the holder of the patent is a small or large entity. The amount paid by a large entity is usually double that paid by a small entity.

Patents are national in nature in that they exist only in the country in which the applications are made and granted.[27] The rights under a Canadian patent do not apply elsewhere. For example, an owner of a Canadian patent cannot stop the use or sale of the invention in the United States, unless the owner also has a U.S. patent.

Chuck's new and improved method of smoking and curing ribs may qualify for patent protection if the method is considered to be new, useful, and unobvious. If it is patentable, he will need to apply for a patent and pay the requisite fee. The patent process requires him to disclose his discovery to the world; in return, he receives a monopoly over the invention for 20 years. The patent process is costly and time consuming, so Chuck needs to evaluate the costs and benefits of pursuing this route.

Industrial Designs

The *Industrial Design Act*[28] provides protection for the appearance of mass-produced (i.e., numbering more than 50) useful articles or objects.[29]

Industrial Designs Defined

The term **"industrial design"** is not defined in the act. An industrial design is usually taken to mean a feature of shape, configuration, pattern, or ornament, or any combination of these, that in a finished article appeals to and is judged solely by the eye.[30] Put another way, an industrial design protects the shapes or ornamental aspects of a product but does not protect the functional aspect.

Typical examples of industrial designs are the shape and ornamentations applied to toys, vehicles, furniture, and household utensils, and the patterns applied to wallpaper or fabric. Also, the electronic or computer-generated icons displayed on computer monitors, cellular telephones, radio pagers, home appliances, and the like may be registered as industrial designs.[31]

What features of consumer goods may be protected by industrial design legislation?

Requirements for Registration

To be registered, an industrial design must be original and novel. The originality standard is lower than the standard of inventiveness found in patents. A high degree of ingenuity or creativity is not necessary. The design may be entirely new, or it may be an old design that had not previously been applied for the purpose of ornamenting the article in question.

27. There is no such thing as an international patent. International treaties, however, have simplified the procedures for obtaining patents in different countries.
28. R.S.C. 1985, c. I-9.
29. Works that qualify as industrial designs may also qualify for protection under the *Copyright Act*. To address the overlap, copyright protection is not given to designs applied to useful articles that are produced in quantities of more than 50. See *Copyright Act*, R.S.C. 1985, c. C-42, s. 64(2), as am. by *An Act to Amend the Copyright Act and Other Acts in Consequence Thereof*, S.C. 1988, c. 65.
30. Martin P.J. Kratz, *Canada's Intellectual Property Law in a Nutshell* (Scarborough: Carswell, 1998) at 63.
31. Wing T. Yan, "Screen Display Icons Protectable as Industrial Designs", *The Lawyers Weekly* (17 November 2000) at 14.

An industrial design must be novel. Disclosure or use of the industrial design or of articles displaying, bearing, or embodying the industrial design is a bar to registration unless it was within the year prior to filing the application.[32]

Registration Process and Protection

As with patents, industrial design protection does not arise automatically. An application, usually drafted by a patent agent, must be submitted to the industrial design office.

The owner of the rights in the design is entitled to make the application. The designer is the owner unless the design was ordered and paid for by another. The application normally consists of a written description and a graphic depiction, photograph, or drawing. If the application meets the requirements of the act, a certificate of registration will be issued.

The registration gives the owner the exclusive right to make, import, or sell any article in respect to which the design is registered. As well, the owner of the design can stop competitors from manufacturing and selling a design that looks confusingly similar. An industrial design registration lasts for ten years.

It is not mandatory to mark the design to indicate that it is registered; however, doing so will enhance the owner's rights in a successful infringement action. If the product is marked, a court may award monetary damages for infringement. If there is no marking, the court is limited to awarding an injunction. The proper marking is

Ⓓ, name of the proprietor

Trademarks

Chuck's intellectual property also comprises the name of his product—Chuck's BBQ Ribs. This aspect of his intellectual property may qualify for protection under trademark law.

Trademark Defined

trademark
A word, symbol, design, or any combination of these used to distinguish the source of goods or services.

A **trademark**[33] is a word, symbol, design, or any combination of these used to distinguish a person's products or services from those of others. Its function is to indicate the source or origin of the goods or services.

Theoretically, a trademark could be anything, but it is usually one of the following:

- a word (e.g., Exxon, Xerox, Lego, Billabong)
- words (e.g., The Body Shop, The Pink Panter, Shake n' Bake)
- a slogan (e.g., "Just Do It," "Mr. Christie, You Make Good Cookies")
- a design (e.g., McDonald's golden arches, Disney's cartoon characters)
- a series of letters (e.g., ABC for laundry detergent, BMW for a car)
- numbers (e.g., 6/49 for lottery services, 900 service for telephone operations)
- a symbol (e.g., a series of Chinese characters, Nike's "swoosh")
- a **distinguishing guise** (e.g., Coca-Cola bottle, Perrier bottle)
- any combination of the above (e.g., London Fog with the depiction of Big Ben for clothing)

distinguishing guise
A shaping of wares or their container, or a mode of wrapping or packaging wares.

---

32. *Supra* note 13. International conventions also apply to the application for industrial designs. Foreign applications filed up to six months before the Canadian filing may have priority to obtain a patent.
33. In addition to the type of trademark used by a business to identify goods or services, another category of trademark is the certification mark. This mark is used to indicate that a product or service conforms to a particular standard. For example, "Wool Mark," which is a certification mark of the Wool Bureau of Canada, is used to identify garments made from pure wool. Also, the Canadian Standards Council uses "CSA Approved" to indicate products of a certain standard. Certification marks are not owned by producers; thus, they are not used to distinguish one producer from another. Instead, the mark certifies that a product meets a defined standard.

A colour is not registrable as a trademark but colour[34] (such as pink for insulation) may be claimed as part of a trademark. Smells or odours have not been registered as trademarks in Canada and sounds too are generally not registrable.[35]

Trade Names

Closely related to trademarks are **trade names,** which also receive protection under trademark law. A trade name is the name under which a business is carried on. It may be the name of a corporation, a partnership, or a sole proprietorship. An important connection between trade names and trademarks is that the adoption of a trademark may prevent the use of an identical or similar trade name, and vice versa—that is, the adoption of a trade name can prevent the adoption of a trademark. For example, Chuck's adoption of Chuck's Grill House as a trade name prevents others from using the name or a similar one as a trademark in the same line of business.

Common Law Trademarks

Trademarks may be registered or unregistered. If unregistered, they are often referred to as common law trademarks. Whether registered or unregistered, trademarks receive protection under both the common law and the *Trade-marks Act*.[36]

A common law trademark comes into existence when a business simply adopts and uses it. Chuck's adoption of Chuck's BBQ Ribs is an example of a common law trademark. Such a trademark is considered to be part of the goodwill of a company, and rights attach to it in much the same manner as they do to registered trademarks. Infringement of the trademark by a competitor using the same or similar trademark can be addressed through the tort of passing off.[37]

The rights that attach to common law trademarks, however, tend to be more restrictive, and there are certain advantages associated with registration. A common law trademark has rights only in the geographic areas in which it has been used and in areas in which the reputation of the owner has spread. For example, Chuck can prevent others from using his trademark or a similar one only in the areas to which his reputation has spread. A registered trademark enjoys protection throughout the country. Registration is also advantageous in that it creates a presumption of ownership and validity.

Requirements for Registration

To register a trademark, an applicant must demonstrate that he has title to the trademark (this requirement is sometimes simply referred to as use), that the trademark is distinctive or capable of becoming distinctive, and that the trademark is registrable.

---

34. *Supra* note 13 at 188–189. The validity of registering smells as trademarks is uncertain.
35. In 1989, Capital Records Inc. was able to register (No. 359,318) a sound mark for a series of musical notes but subsequent applications for sounds such as MGM's roaring lion and Yahoo's yodel have not been approved.
36. R.S.C. 1985, c. T-13.
37. The tort of passing off is discussed in Chapter 12.

The growth of electronic commerce and the use of the Internet have spawned new kinds of commercial disputes. One of the most prevalent involves disagreement over the right to domain names.

Domain names. A domain name is essentially an Internet address. It consists of two or more elements divided into a hierarchical field separated by a "dot." To the right of the dot is an abbreviation describing the root identifier or a top-level domain (TLD). A TLD is either generic such as .com, .org, or .net or country-specific such as .ca for Canada or .uk for the United Kingdom. To the left of the dot is the second-level domain, which is usually a business name, trademark, or other identifier. For example, in Nelson.com, "com" is the TLD and "Nelson" is the second-level domain. A domain name is a unique address, meaning that no two sites can have the same address on the Internet. A domain name can be a very valuable asset as it not only provides the owner with access to the Internet but also can serve as a tool for marketing the owner and the owner's business.

"Owning" a domain name. Generic domain names such as .com, .org, and .net are controlled by the Internet Corporation for Assigned Names and Numbers (ICANN), a U.S. nonprofit corporation.[38] ICANN-accredited registrars issue domain names for a fee. The system operates on a first-come, first-served basis—whoever is prepared to pay the very modest fee for a name is entitled to it. There are no limits on the number of generic domain names that a business or organization can own.

The country-specific domain names are assigned by national authorities. For example, in Canada, the Canadian Internet Registration Authority (CIRA)[39] is responsible for maintaining Canada's Internet domain names. Until recently, there were very restrictive rules on registering a .ca name. Applicants had to not only satisfy Canadian residency requirements but also show a correlation between the domain name applied for and their business name or trademarks. Also, a business or organization could register only one domain name. For these reasons,

relatively few .ca names have been registered. The rules changed as of November 2000. Although there are still residency requirements, .ca domain names are now issued on a first-come, first-served basis and there is no limit to the number that a business or organization can register.

Domain names and trademarks. The nature of the domain name system requires that each domain name be unique. Since most elements of the address are generic, the distinguishing feature is the second-level element—usually a trademark or business name. A business or organization that claims a certain domain name, say imperial.com, may come into conflict with other businesses that have legitimate claims to the same domain name. The nature of the domain name system, however, dictates that there can be only one imperial.com. This is different than in trademark law, where more than one entity may use the same trademarks so long as they are used for different products or services and create no likelihood of confusion. For example, "imperial" is used in relation to tobacco, margarine, and oil. Therefore, as two or more entities may both have legitimate rights to use the same trademark, a dispute may arise as to which entity should have the exclusive right to the trademark as part of its Internet address.

Other, less legitimate kinds of disputes occur when someone obtains an Internet domain name that includes a well-known trademark or trade name, and then uses it for a confusing commercial purpose. Also of great concern is the practice known as **"cyber-squatting."** This occurs when domain names are obtained for the purposes of reselling them for a profit, extorting money from the holder of famous trademarks, or preventing the competition from securing the most obvious domain names (i.e., a business obtains domain names that include its competitors' trademarks or trade names to prevent the competitors from obtaining them).

Dispute resolution. Disputes that arise due to the incompatibility between the domain name system and trademark principles can be settled through litigation using the general law on the adoption and

---

38. For more information see http://www.icann.org
39. For more information see http://www.cira.ca

use of trademarks in each jurisdiction. This process can be long and expensive and is complicated by questions of jurisdiction because, given the global nature of the Internet, it is not always clear where to bring an infringement action.

For some types of disputes such as cyber-squatting there are alternative dispute resolution mechanisms. ICANN offers an online dispute resolution mechanism for alleged bad-faith registration of a domain name. The Uniform Domain Resolution Policy[40] provides a quick and cheap process for resolving disputes. The policy provides that if the registration is "abusive," that is, the complainant has trademark rights in the name and the respondent has no legal interest in the name, the registrar can either disconnect the domain name or transfer the name to the complainant. CIRA also has a similar dispute resolution policy.

CRITICAL ANALYSIS: Should trademark registration confer automatic rights to a domain name? Why or why not? How can a business, short of litigation, protect its portfolio of trademarks from "cyber-squatters?"

domain name
The unique address of a website.

cyber-squatting
The bad-faith practice of registering trademarks or trade names of others as domain names for the purpose of selling the domain name to the rightful owner or preventing the rightful owner from obtaining the domain name.

Title: An applicant may register only a trademark that he owns. Ownership or title is not established by inventing or selecting a mark. It comes from

- use of the trademark
- filing an application to register a proposed trademark
- making it known in Canada

A trademark is deemed to be in "use" in Canada if the trademark is on the goods or the packaging at the time of any transfer in the ordinary course of business. With respect to services, a trademark is deemed to be in use if it is used or displayed in the performance or advertising of the services. If Chuck has used a mark in this manner, normally he has title to the mark and can apply to register it. A distinguishing guise is registrable only on this basis.

A trademark can be registered if it is not yet in use, as long as use commences before the registration is actually issued.

An application to register can be made on the basis that the mark, although not in use in Canada, is nonetheless well known in Canada. An applicant would need to demonstrate that the mark is, in fact, well known in Canada, that knowledge of the mark arose from advertisements that circulated in Canada, and that the applicant used the mark in another country.[41]

Distinctiveness: The second general requirement goes to the heart of trademark law. The mark must be distinctive—in other words, it must actually distinguish the goods or services in association with which it is used. Invented words like "Lego," "Exxon," and "Kodak" are distinctive and are ideal candidates, particularly with respect to applications based on proposed use. Other, more descriptive words, such as "pleasant," "sudsy," and "shiny" do not have the same quality of distinctiveness. They may gain this quality only through use in business and advertising.

Registrability: The *Trade-marks Act* specifies that a mark must be "registrable." To be registrable, the trademark must *not* be

- primarily the name or surname of an individual who is living or has died within the preceding 30 years (e.g., "Smith" or "Joe Enman")

---

40. The dispute resolution policy is available on the website.
41. The foreign country must have been a country that is a member of the *Paris Convention* or the World Trade Organization.

- descriptive[42] of the character or quality of the wares or services, or their place of origin (e.g., "sweet" for apples, "Ontario wines" for wines from Ontario, or "shredded wheat" for cereal[43])
- deceptively misdescriptive of the character or quality of the wares or services, or their place of origin (e.g., "sugar sweet" for candy artificially sweetened, "all-silk" for cotton blouses)
- the name in any language of any ware or service in connection with which it is used or proposed to be used (e.g., "avion" for airplanes, "wurst" for sausages)
- confusing with another registered trademark (e.g., "Mego" for children's plastic building blocks; "Devlon" for hair care products)
- an official[44] or prohibited[45] mark

Chuck's trademark "Chuck's BBQ Ribs" may be registrable depending on the above factors. A key concern will be whether the same or a similar trademark has been registered in relation to food products and whether the mark is considered sufficiently distinctive.

CASE ▼

Mattel v. 3894207 Canada Inc. 2006 SCC 22

THE BUSINESS CONTEXT: A famous trademark—such as COCA-COLA or WALT DISNEY—has the power to attract legions of consumers. The extent to which Canadian trademark law protects famous marks from use by others is unclear. The following case explores the scope of protection accorded to famous and well-known marks.[46]

FACTUAL BACKGROUND: In 1992, a Quebec restaurateur opened the first of four Montreal-area licensed BBQ restaurants named "Barbie's." When the restaurateur tried to register "BARBIE & Design" as a trademark for use across the country in the restaurant, takeout, catering, and banquet business, Mattel Inc., the maker of the Barbie doll, protested. Mattel had registered "BARBIE" and "BARBIE'S as trademarks in Canada for doll-related products more than 30 years previously. In 2002, the Trade-marks Opposition Board of the Canadian Intellectual

Property Office accepted the restaurant's argument that its use of "BARBIE" would not create consumer confusion with Mattel's dolls. Both the Federal Court and the Federal Court of Appeal upheld the Board's decision.

THE LEGAL QUESTION: Does the monopoly protection extended by the *Trade-mark Act* to Mattel's BARBIE trademark prevent others from registering similar marks in connection with non-doll-related goods and services?

RESOLUTION: Under the *Trade-mark Act,* registration of a trademark is not permissible if the trademark could reasonably be confused with a previously registered trademark. Mattel contended that allowing adult-oriented bars or grills to register "BARBIE" would create confusion in the minds of the public who might think that the restaurants are linked to the doll. The restaurant responded that most Canadians know that the term "Barbie" refers to the "Bar-B-Q" as in "throw some burgers on the barbie!" In a unanimous decision, the Supreme Court found that there was no likelihood of confusion in the marketplace between the doll and the restaurant. The Court's

---

42. Note that descriptive words can be used as part of a trademark so long as the applicant includes a disclaimer that he does not claim exclusive rights in the descriptive words.
43. *Canadian Shredded Wheat Co. Ltd. v. Kellogg Co. of Canada Ltd.* (1938), 55 R.P.C. 125 (P.C.).
44. Public authorities have the right to adopt an official mark and use that mark in respect of its wares or services. For example, The Official Island Store is an official mark of the Gateway Village Development Inc. of Prince Edward Island.
45. Prohibited marks include marks that are likely to be mistaken for symbols or emblems of government, royalty, the Armed Forces, the Royal Canadian Mounted Police, the Red Cross, the Red Crescent, or the United Nations; flags and symbols of other countries; and symbols of public institutions. Also prohibited are scandalous, immoral, and obscene words, and anything that suggests a connection with a living or recently deceased individual.
46. In a companion decision, *Veuve Clicquot Ponsardin v. Boutiques Cliquot Ltee,* 2006 SCC 23, the Supreme Court held that the French champagne maker Veuve Clicquot Ponsardin could not prevent the use of the mark Cliquot in relation to women's clothing shops in Quebec and Eastern Ontario.

decision was based upon the facts and evidence that included the absence of any instances of actual confusion. In other words, the evidence showed that Mattel's BARBIE mark was famous only when used in association with dolls and doll accessories.

Importantly, the Court went on to make it clear, however that a difference between goods or services associated with trademarks is only one factor to be considered in determining the likelihood of confusion. All surrounding circumstances, including the distinctiveness of the marks; the length of time the marks were used; the nature of the wares, services or businesses; the nature of the trade and the degree of resemblance must be considered and different factors will be given different weight in different situations. The court also suggested that some marks such as WALT DISNEY are so famous that they can transcend product lines. Thus, while fame does not by itself provide absolute protection for a trademark, it may in some instances result in the trademark having a broader scope of protection. The question of whether a famous mark is entitled to broader protection will depend on the facts.

CRITICAL ANALYSIS: Although Mattel lost its appeal, the very fact-driven nature of the decision leaves the door open to a different outcome for other well-known trademarks. Should the scope of protection afforded a trademark extend beyond the goods or services in relation to which it is registered? Would this provide too much protection to trademark owners?

How much protection should be given to famous trademarks?

Registration Process and Protection

The first person who uses or makes a trademark known in Canada is entitled to trademark registration. In the absence of use, the first to file a trademark application is entitled to registration.[47]

Prior to applying for registration a trademark agent usually does a search of the trademarks office[48] to ensure that the trademark or a similar one is not registered. Federal and provincial business name registries and other sources, such as trade journals, telephone directories, and specialty magazines, are also consulted to determine whether there are common law rights.

The application must comply with all the provisions of the act. In particular, applicants must provide a comprehensive list of products or services associated with the trademark. An examiner reviews the application, and if it is acceptable the trademarks office advertises the trademark in the trademark journal. Any interested members of the public can object to the registration on the grounds that they have a better title to the trademark than the applicant, that the trademark is not distinctive, or that the trademark does not meet the requirements of registrability. If, on the other hand, there is no opposition or the opposition is overcome, the registration will be issued on payment of the appropriate fee.

---

47. Canada is a signatory to the *Paris Convention*, which means that applicants from member countries have reciprocal rights with respect to filing in member countries. The date of filing in a convention country becomes the Canadian filing date, so long as the Canadian application is filed within six months of the date of the first filing in a convention country.
48. The Canadian Intellectual Property Office's trademark database is online and can be accessed at http://www.strategis.ic.gc.ca/sc_mrksv/cipo/welcome/welcom-e.html

A trademark registration gives the owner the exclusive right to use the trademark in association with the wares and services specified in the registration. It also provides a right to prevent others from using a confusingly similar trademark. A trademark owner should clearly indicate its ownership of a trademark with the following marks:

® for registered trademarks

™ for unregistered trademarks

Registration provides protection across Canada for a period of 15 years. The registration can be renewed for further 15-year terms as long as the renewal fee is paid and the trademark continues in use.

Copyright

Chuck's intellectual property may also include promotional brochures, business plans, menus, and other written material that qualifies for **copyright** protection.

Copyright is governed almost entirely by the *Copyright Act*.[49] Copyright is intended to provide a right of exploitation to authors of certain works. As its name suggests, copyright is intended to prevent the copying of works. In other words, subject to certain exemptions, only the author (or the owner of the copyright) has the right to copy a work. Others are not entitled to copy the work unless they fit within one of the exemptions or have the author's permission to make a copy. This "right to copy" or "copyright" however, does not protect the author's underlying ideas or facts. For example, no one has copyright in the life story of Ken Thomson or K.C. Irving, but once the story is written, copyright resides in the expression of the life story.

Copyright Defined

Copyright applies to both traditional and nontraditional works. Copyright applies to every original literary, dramatic, musical, and artistic work, such as the following:

- *literary works*—books, pamphlets, compilations, translations, and computer programs
- *dramatic works*—any piece for recitation, choreographic works, scenic arrangements, and cinematography productions, such as plays, operas, mime, films, videos, and screenplays
- *musical works*—any combination of melody and harmony, including sheet music
- *artistic work*—paintings, drawings, maps, charts, plans, photographs, engravings, sculptures, works of artistic craftsmanship, architectural works of art

In essence, copyright extends to almost anything written, composed, drawn, or shaped. Items not protected include facts, names, slogans, short phrases, and most titles. The examples of works included in each category are nonexhaustive, which means the categories can encompass new technologies and new forms of expression. Copyright also applies to nontraditional works such as sound recordings, performances, and broadcasts.[50]

There are many business examples of these various kinds of works. In fact, whole industries are founded on works of this nature, particularly the entertainment and publishing industries. Businesses that are not so directly affected still create many works that may attract copyright protection, such as advertising copy, photographs, manuals, memorandums, plans, sketches, and computer programs, to name a few common examples.

copyright

The right to prevent others from copying or modifying certain works.

---

49. R.S.C. 1985, c. C-42.
50. *Ibid*, s.15, s.18, s.21.

Requirements for Protection

To attract copyright protection, a work must meet requirements of originality and fixation.[51] Originality means that the work must "originate" from the author, not be copied from another, and involve the exercise of skill and judgment. In *CCH Canadian Ltd. v. Law Society of Upper Canada*,[52] the Supreme Court of Canada held that the headnotes (a short summary of a case and key words) of a legal decision are "original" works. However, the edited version of a court decision is not original because it involved only minor changes and additions—a mere mechanical exercise too trivial to warrant copyright protection.

A work must also meet the requirement of fixation,[53] that is, be expressed in some fixed form such as paper or diskette. Works such as speeches, luncheon addresses, and lectures that do not exist in a fixed form do not attract copyright. The fixation requirement exists to separate unprotectable ideas from protectable expression and to provide a means of comparison for judging whether copyright has been infringed.

Registration Process and Protection

Copyright protection arises automatically on the creation of a work. There is an optional registration process that has an evidentiary advantage in that registration provides a presumption of ownership. The owner of a copyright may mark a work; however, there is no requirement to do so to enforce copyright in Canada. The mark can, however, enhance international protection of the work. The following is the typical form of a copyright notice:

© year of publication; name of owner

Under the *Copyright Act*, the author[54] of a work is the copyright owner unless there is an agreement to the contrary. The major exception is for works created in the course of employment, in which case the employer is the owner. A further exception relates to photographs, engravings, and portraits that are ordered and paid for by another; in the absence of an agreement to the contrary, the customer is the first owner of the copyright.

Copyright protection is generally for the life of the author or composer plus 50 years.[55]

Rights under Copyright

Copyright gives certain rights to the owner of the copyright (the rights may vary somewhat depending on the type of work). These rights include

- *reproduction*—the right to reproduce the work or a substantial part of it in any material form
- *public performance*—the right to perform the work or a substantial part of it
- *publication*—the right, if the work is unpublished, to publish the work
- *translation*—the right to produce, reproduce, perform, or publish any translation of the work

---

51. The nationality requirement is no longer very important, as Canada has implemented the *Agreement on Trade-Related Aspects of Intellectual Property Rights* (TRIPS). This agreement means that virtually every work qualifies for protection, regardless of the author's nationality.
52. (2004), 236 DLR (4th) 395 (S.C.C.).
53. The fixation requirement is expressly found in the *Copyright Act* only for dramatic works and computer programs. The requirement in relation to other works has developed through the common law.
54. Copyright law recognizes the concept of joint authorship; however, the contribution of a copyrightable work to a project does not in and of itself create joint authorship. The parties must intend to be joint authors. See *Neudorf v. Nettwerk Productions*, [2000] 3 W.W.R. 522 (B.C.S.C.).
55. For some works, such as sound recordings, the term of protection is 50 years.

- *adaptation*—the right to convert works into other formats (e.g., a book into a movie)
- *mechanical reproduction*—the right to make sound recording or cinematographic recording
- *cinematographic presentation*—the right to reproduce, adapt, and publicly present the work by filming or videotaping
- *communication*—the right to communicate the work to the public by telecommunication
- *exhibition*—the right to present in public, for purposes other than sale or hire, an artistic work[56]
- *rental*—the right to rent out sound recordings and computer programs
- *authorization*—the right to "authorize" any of the other rights

Copyright is infringed when anyone does, without the consent of the owner, anything only the owner can do. This includes, for example, copying *all or a substantial part* of a work. The question of what is substantial is vexing. It is generally thought that *substantial* has both a qualitative and a quantitative aspect. The test seems to be whether the part that is taken is a key or distinctive part.[57]

It is also infringement for anyone to authorize doing anything that only the copyright owner is allowed to do. Authorization means to "sanction, approve and countenance".[58] A person does not, however, authorize infringement by merely providing the means that could be used to infringe copyright. For example, the provision of photocopiers does not constitute authorization of the use of the copiers to infringe copyright, particularly in the case where the provider has little control over the user.

The enforcement of rights has been problematic, particularly the collection of fees and royalties for the use of copyrighted works. These problems have been addressed by provisions in the *Copyright Act* for the establishment of collectives, which negotiate agreements with users on royalties and use. For example, Access Copyright, the Copyright Licensing Agency (formerly known as CanCopy), represents numerous publishers and authors, and negotiates agreements with institutions, such as universities, libraries, and copy shops, providing for the payment of royalties for photocopying from books. Similar collectives such as the Society of Composers, Authors, and Music Publishers of Canada (SOCAN) operate in the music industry.

Moral Rights

moral rights
The author's rights to have work properly attributed and not prejudicially modified or associated with products.

The author of a work has what are known as **moral rights.** Moral rights exist independently of copyright and provide authors with some control over how their works are used and exploited. Moral rights include the following:

- *Paternity.* The author has the right to be associated with the work as its author by name or under a pseudonym and the right to remain anonymous if reasonable in the circumstances.
- *Integrity.* The author has the right to object to dealings or uses of the work if they are prejudicial to the author's reputation or honour.
- *Association.* The author has the right to object to the work being used in association with a product, service, cause, or institution.

---

56. This applies only to works created after 7 June 1988, and does not apply to charts, maps, and plans.
57. *Supra* note 13 at 81–82.
58. *Supra* note 52.

CASE ▼

Snow v. The Eaton Centre Ltd. (1982), 70 C.P.R. (2d) 105 (Ont. H.C.)

THE BUSINESS CONTEXT: Many works that receive copyright protection are created for the purpose of making a profit through a sale. However, the sale of a work does not extinguish all of the author's or creator's rights.

FACTUAL BACKGROUND: Michael Snow created a sculpture of geese known as *Flight Stop*, which was sold to the owners of the Eaton Centre in Toronto. In connection with a Christmas display, the Eaton Centre attached red ribbons to the necks of the 60 geese forming the sculpture. Snow claimed that his naturalistic composition had been made to look ridiculous by the addition. In short, he alleged that his moral rights in the sculpture had been infringed.

THE LEGAL QUESTION: Were the acts of the Eaton Centre a distortion or modification of Snow's work that would be prejudicial to his honour and reputation?

RESOLUTION: The court held that the ribbons distorted and modified Snow's work and that Snow's concern that this was prejudicial to his honour and reputation was reasonable in the circumstances. The Eaton Centre was required to remove the ribbons.

CRITICAL ANALYSIS: Since the Eaton Centre paid for the sculpture, why should it not be able to do as it wants with the sculpture? Would the outcome have been the same if the sculpture had been sent to the dump or otherwise destroyed?

Michael Snow's Flight Stop

Exemptions

There are a large number of exceptions or defences under the *Copyright Act.* Many—among them the exemption for home copying;[59] the exemption for libraries, museums, and archives; the exemption for people with disabilities; and the exemption for educational institutions—apply to specific situations and have little business application. The exemptions that are particularly relevant to business are the following:

fair dealing
A defence to copyright infringement that permits the copying of works for limited purposes.

- *Fair dealing.* The **fair dealing** exemption permits the copying of works for the purposes of private study, research, criticism, or review. The copying must be for one of the enumerated purposes. In *CCH Canadian Ltd. v. Law Society of Upper Canada,*[60] the Supreme Court ruled that research must be given a large and liberal interpretation and not be limited to noncommercial or private research. The dealing must also be fair. In assessing whether the dealing is fair, the following factors are considered:

  - the purposes of the dealing

  - the character of the dealing

  - the amount of the dealing

  - alternatives to the dealing

---

59. *Supra* note 50, s. 80 exempts the copying of musical works by an individual for private use from copyright infringement. In return, copyright collectives can collect levies on blank audio media in order to compensate the rights holders.
60. *Supra* note 52.

- the nature of the work

- the effect of the dealing on the work

- *Computer software.* The exemption relating to computer programs is quite specific. It permits the owner of the program to make a copy for adaptation for use on another computer and a copy for backup purposes.

Technology and the Law | Music Swapping on the Internet

Swapping music over the Internet is a common practice. The Canadian Recording Industry Association (CRIA) estimates that the practice cost the industry $541 million in lost music sales from 1991 to 2005.[61] The recording industry has attempted to stem the distribution of copyrighted music by establishing commercial download services (e.g., PureTracks, iTunes), educating the public on copyright, using technological deception to prevent copying, lobbying government for changes to the law,[62] and suing "swappers" and Internet service providers (ISPs). The law, however, is unclear on whether, and to what extent, music swapping on the Internet infringes the *Copyright Act*.

Applicable Copyright Principles

The *Copyright Act* provides that copyright exists in musical works, the performance of musical works, and sound recordings (e.g., compact disc, tapes etc.). The owner of the copyright has certain exclusive rights including

- the right to reproduce the work in whole or part;

- the right to communicate the work to the public by telecommunication; and

- the right to "authorize" others to do the foregoing.[63]

These provisions are qualified in two important ways. First, a person whose only act is to provide the means of communication necessary for another person to communicate a work to the public by telecommunication does not infringe copyright.[64] Second, it is not an infringement to reproduce a sound recording on an audio recording medium for the *private use* of the person who makes the copy,[65] so long as the person does not distribute the work or communicate the work to the public by telecommunications. This exemption is coupled with a levy on blank audio recording media as a means of compensating performers.

Music Swapping

Most of the music sharing that goes on over the Internet uses a peer-to-peer (P2P) network, a system that allows individuals to share files directly from their computers. The system involves "uploaders"— persons who make music files available over the Internet, "downloaders"— persons who use software to locate music files and copy them onto the hard drives of their personal computers or MP3 players and software companies, and providers of P2P software (e.g., KaZaA, Grokster) that set up the actual Internet connection through which a music file is transmitted.[66]

Liability Issues

The Software Companies

The question with respect to the liability of the software company hinges on the meaning of the communication exemption outlined above. There is not a case that directly deals with this issue. In a related case,[67] the music industry brought action against several Internet service providers (ISPs) to

---

61. Kevin Restivo, *The Financial Post* (3 March 06) FP5.
62. In 2005, the federal government introduced Bill C-60, an act to amend the *Copyright Act*. The amendments were intended to strengthen copyright protection of works in an online environment and clarify ISP liability. The bill died with the change in government in 2006.
63. *Supra* note 49, ss. 3 (1) (a) and (f).
64. *Supra* note 49, s. 2.4 (1) (b).
65. *Supra* note 49, s. 80.
66. Timothy Squire, "Swapping Music over the Internet: The Canadian Debate", *Internet and E-Commerce Law*,4:9 (November 2003) at 68.
67. *Society of Composers, Authors and Music Publishers of Canada v. Canadian Association of Internet Providers*, [2004] 2. S.C.R. 427.

recover royalties related to the downloading of music by ISP clients. The Supreme Court of Canada ruled that when ISPs act in a conduit function, they are protected from liability by the communication exemption. In other words, when ISPs act only as "intermediaries," they are not responsible for what their customers do on the Internet. The reasoning in this decision may be applicable to software companies that provide the means for swapping music.

Uploaders

An uploader places copyrighted music into "shared" folders in her computer, which can then be accessed by others connected to the same P2P network. The question whether this act amounts to infringement of copyright has not been directly addressed by Canadian courts. The argument of the uploaders is that there is no infringement because they do not copy and they do not do anything to initiate the copying of their files by downloaders. The music industry argues that uploaders "authorize" reproduction because they make their music available, and they expect or intend that their files will be copied by others. Uploaders counter that making music files available is like providing a photocopy machine in a room full of copyrighted material; the provider of the photocopier is not generally liable for the authorizing infringement. So too, the uploader should not be liable for authorizing the downloader's infringement.

Downloaders

A person who downloads swapped music files over the Internet is copying the work and therefore is *prima facie* infringing copyright. The downloaders argue that their infringement is covered by the private-use exemption. The music industry argues that the private-use exemption was not meant to apply to downloading onto the hard drive of a computer or a MP3 player. In support of their argument, they cite *Canadian Private Copying Collective v. Canadian Storage Media Alliance*,[68] where the Federal Court of Appeal ruled that MP3 players do not constitute blank recording media as defined under the *Copyright Act*. The implication is that when a person downloads onto a MP3 player, the private-use exemption does not protect against infringement.

In 2004, in an effort to clarify some of the issues surrounding music swapping on the Internet, a group of recording companies represented by CRIA sued 29 unnamed file sharers for copyright infringement.[69] In *BMG Canada v. Doe*,[70] the music industry alleged that the unnamed defendants were responsible for the unauthorized downloading of thousands of songs. At the onset, BMG brought a motion to compel five ISPs to produce the actual names and addresses of those individuals who were swapping music over their Internet sites. The Federal Court of Appeal, citing privacy concerns and evidentiary problems, denied their motion.[71] The court did, however, outline the test that the recording industry would have to meet in order to get the identities of the alleged infringers of copyright. It is expected that CRIA will continue to pursue music file sharers.

CRITICAL ANALYSIS: Do you agree with the recording industry's strategy of suing individual users? Should ISPs be required to reveal the names of their customers?

Confidential Business Information

confidential business information
Information that provides a business advantage as a result of the fact that it is kept secret.

The law of confidential information may protect Chuck's method of curing and smoking ribs.

There is no specific statutory protection for **confidential business information**[72] and therefore no statutory definition for the term. Generally, however, the term refers to information that is used in a business or commercial context and is private or secret.

---

68. [2005] 2 F.C.R. 654, leave to appeal refused [2005] S.C.C.A. No. 70 and [2005] S.C.C.A. No. 74.
69. In 2003, members of the Recording Industry Association of America (RIAA) launched lawsuits against 261 individuals who had been distributing substantial amounts of copyrighted music via peer-to-peer networks.
70. [2005] 4 F.C.R. 81 (C.A.).
71. In the United States the *Digital Millennium Copyright Act*, 112 Stat. 2860 (1998) provides a process whereby ISPs are required to disclose the identity of their customers.
72. The term "trade secret" is also sometimes used either interchangeably with "confidential business information" or as a subset of "confidential information." The terms are used interchangeably in this text.

The general categories of business information that is used or capable of use in business are these:

- strategic business information (e.g., customer lists, price lists, bookkeeping methods, presentation programs, advertising campaigns)
- products (e.g., recipes, formulas)
- compilations (e.g., databases)
- technological secrets (e.g., scientific processes, know-how)

Requirements for Protection

A key requirement for protection is the secrecy or confidentiality of the information. A number of factors are considered in ascertaining whether the information is "confidential":

- *Economic value as a result of not being generally known.* The information must have some commercial value to the company or its competitors. An indication of the commercial value of the information may be the efforts by others to obtain it. The value of the information derives in large measure from the fact that it is not known by some or is not generally known.
- *Subject to efforts to keep it secret.* There must be efforts to keep the information secret. Thus, if a company is careless about information or fails to take steps to protect the confidentiality of information, the information may indeed lose its status of "confidential."
- *Not generally known in the industry.* Information does not have to be absolutely confidential; it can be a compilation of readily available information from various sources. As well, information can be known by some and still maintain its status. In this regard, the extent to which the information is known within the company, as well as outside the company, is relevant.

Process and Scope of Protection

Confidential business information may be protected forever so long as the information is not disclosed to the general public. Recipes for well-known products such as Coca-Cola Classic, Hostess Twinkies, Mrs. Field's Chocolate Chip Cookies, Listerine, and Kentucky Fried Chicken have been "secret" for many years. So too, Chuck could keep his method of curing and smoking a secret for years. There are no application procedures for protection. Information receives protection through claims for breach of express terms, for breach of confidence, or through implied obligations.

Parties may have express obligations to keep information confidential. Nondisclosure agreements require recipients of information to respect its confidentiality by agreeing not to discuss, disclose, or use it. Employees are often required by the terms of their employment contracts to keep certain information confidential.

In the absence of an express provision regarding confidence, an obligation of confidence may be implied in a contract or arise by virtue of a fiduciary relationship. This is the case in the employment context, particularly in industries in which there is a lot of confidential information and the importance of confidentiality is stressed.

Finally, an obligation of confidence can exist when information was conveyed in circumstances suggesting a relationship of confidence. The following case is a leading decision on receipt of confidential information in circumstances of confidentiality.

Landmark Case ▼

LAC Minerals Ltd. v. International Corona Resources Ltd. (1989), 61 D.L.R. (4th) 14 (S.C.C.)

THE HISTORICAL CONTEXT: In the negotiations preceding a contract, the parties may divulge a great deal of information, some of which is sensitive and confidential. This is often necessary in order to reach contractual consensus. This case explores the obligations of recipient of the information to the revealer of the information, in the absence of a contract of confidentiality.

FACTUAL BACKGROUND: Corona was the owner of a group of mining claims that it was exploring. Being a junior company, it was eager to attract investors and had publicized certain information about its property. LAC Minerals, a major mining corporation, became interested, and a site visit was arranged. The LAC geologists were shown core samples and sections, and the parties discussed the geology of Corona's site, as well as the property to the west known as the Williams property. Another meeting was held a couple of days later in Toronto, during which it was again mentioned that Corona was attempting to purchase the Williams property. No mention was made of confidentiality. Following this meeting, there were further discussions and an exchange of joint venture ideas, as well as a full presentation by Corona of its results and its interest in the Williams property. A short time after these meetings, negotiations between LAC and Corona broke down. Subsequently, LAC made an offer to purchase the Williams property. The offer was accepted, and LAC proceeded to develop the property on its own. It turned out to be the biggest gold mine in Canada, and LAC made huge profits. Corona sued for breach of confidence and breach of fiduciary duty.

THE LEGAL QUESTION: Was LAC liable for breach of confidence or fiduciary duty?

RESOLUTION: The Supreme Court of Canada unanimously found LAC liable on the grounds of breach of confidence. The court confirmed that there are three elements that must be established to impose liability on this ground:

- The information conveyed was confidential.

- It was communicated in circumstances in which a duty of confidence arises.

- It was misused by the party to whom it was communicated.

Although some of the information conveyed by Corona was not confidential, clearly most of it was, and LAC used it to acquire the Williams property. The court said the information was communicated with the mutual understanding that the parties were working toward a joint venture or some other arrangement. A reasonable person in the position of LAC would know that the information was being given in confidence. LAC used the information to its gain and at the expense of Corona. Although the court did not go so far as to find a breach of a fiduciary duty, there was a violation of confidence.

CRITICAL ANALYSIS: What is the importance of this case for business? How can a business determine whether information is confidential? Would it have been easier for Corona simply to have had LAC sign an express confidentiality agreement at the outset?

Limitations on Protection

Confidential business information loses the protection of the law when the information is no longer secret either because the information has been divulged or because the information has been discovered by independent development through using publicly available information or by reverse engineering (i.e., finding the secret or confidential information by examining or dissecting a product). Chuck takes a risk that the method for curing and smoking will become known either through independent development or through someone telling others the recipe.

Information is also no longer confidential when it becomes part of the employee's personal knowledge, skill, or expertise (i.e., trade information). In distinguishing between information that is "confidential" and trade information, the courts attempt to strike a balance between the employee's right to use the skills, knowledge, and experience gained during the course of employment and the employer's right to protect its information.

Physique Health Club Ltd. v. Carlsen
(1996), 141 D.L.R. (4th) 64 (Alta. C.A.),
leave to appeal dismissed, [1997] S.C.C.
No. 40.

THE BUSINESS CONTEXT: It is not uncommon for employees, after gaining knowledge and experience, to leave their employer to start their own business. When the employee engages in a business in the same industry as the former employer and uses the same general know-how and customer connections, the question is often whether the employee has used that which legitimately belongs to the employer.

FACTUAL BACKGROUND: Glenn Carlsen worked at Physique Health Club as its manager from November 1987 until March 1992, when he left following a pay dispute with the owner, his uncle. A few weeks later, he opened his own store just 18 blocks from his uncle's site. He sold the same exercise equipment to the same market and featured an almost identical sign. His business was instantly successful, and had a serious impact on Physique's operations. Physique sued.

THE LEGAL QUESTION: Did Carlsen breach his fiduciary duty to his former employer? Did Carlsen use confidential information in the operation of his business?

RESOLUTION: Physique argued that pricing policies, marketing techniques, and store layout, although not confidential on their own, eventually take on an economic value that makes them confidential. Carlsen agreed that he was a better businessperson as a result of running his uncle's store but argued that that was the result of his own hard work and initiative. He also said that if general knowledge about a store's operations were confidential, employees would never be able to leave and start their own businesses. The trial judge agreed but added that the right of an employer to protect his investment takes precedence over the rights of employees who want to start their own businesses.

The Court of Appeal, however, was not of the same opinion. General knowledge about a business is not confidential. As there was no suggestion that Carlsen took customer lists or acquired any special or unique knowledge that belonged to Physique, he was not liable for breach of confidence. Carlsen had not breached any fiduciary duty as he did not actively solicit specific customers of his former employer, nor did he take a maturing business opportunity from Physique.

CRITICAL ANALYSIS: What is the distinction between confidential business information and trade information? How could the uncle have protected his business from competition from his nephew?

FIGURE 18.2

A Comparison of Major Forms of Intellectual Property

	Patents	Industrial designs	Trademarks	Copyrights	Confidential business information[1]
Subject matter	Inventions	Shape, configuration, pattern, ornamentation	Word, symbol, design	Literary, dramatic, musical, and artistic works, sound recordings, performances, broadcasts	Business information (e.g., technology, product recipes, databases)
Requirements	New, useful, unobvious	Original, novel	Title, distinctiveness, registrable	Original, fixed	Economic value, efforts to keep secret, generally not known
Protects against	Use, sale, manufacture	Use, sale, manufacture	Use	Copying, modifying	Disclosure, use

Term of protection	20 years	10 years	15 + 15 + 15 + years	Life + 50 years	Indefinite (until disclosure)
First owner[2]	Inventor	Designer	First person to use or apply	Author	Creator
Application process	Mandatory	Mandatory	Mandatory[3]	Optional	Not applicable
Example	Microwave oven	Design on the out- side of oven	Name of the oven	User's manual	Ideas for improvement

1. The term "confidential business information" is used interchangeably with "trade secrets."
2. Ownership rights are subject to contracts that may specify other owners. This is particularly the case in employment.
3. Registration is required for protection under the *Trade-marks Act*. Unregistered trademarks receive protection under the common law.

Acquisition and Protection of Intellectual Property

Intellectual property rights can be extremely valuable to a business. Intellectual property is often created within the business in much the same manner as Chuck created his methods of curing and smoking and his choosing his names. The process of doing so can be time consuming and costly. This suggests that an effective intellectual property program should be put in place to ensure that intellectual assets are valid, enforceable, and effectively exploited. Such a program should include identification of all intellectual property assets; the determination of the nature, scope and validity of the assets; and the evaluation of any potential risks and opportunities.

Assignments and Licences

assignment
The transfer of rights by an assignor to an assignee.

licence
Consent given by the owner of rights to someone to do something that only the owner can do.

Although intellectual property may be created in-house, it is also possible to purchase or receive an **assignment** of intellectual property rights or to receive a **licence** to use the intellectual property. By the same token, it is possible for a business to exploit its rights by assigning them or licensing their use. An assignment involves a change of ownership from the assignor to the assignee. As a general rule, all intellectual property rights are assignable in whole or in part. An exception to the general rule is that moral rights cannot be assigned, although they may be waived.

A business may also obtain a licence to use another's intellectual property. A licence is consent or permission to use the right on the terms specified in the licence. All intellectual property rights are capable of being licensed. The process of getting an assignment or licence of intellectual property is not always easy. The process is often complicated by technological developments. Consider, for example, multimedia works that integrate text, graphics, still images, sounds, music, animation, or video and with which the user can interact. The product involves various forms of media working together and may rely on literally thousands of sources, including copyrighted text, images, and music, for its content. The developer of the multimedia work has to ensure that all the relevant rights to these copyrighted works have been obtained, either through ownership or some form of licence or other permission.

Intellectual rights are often subject to compulsory licensing. For example, the patent office may order a patent holder to grant a licence if the exclusive rights under the patent are deemed to be "abused." Examples of abuses are refusal by the patent holder to grant a licence on reasonable terms, thereby prejudicing trade or industry, and failure by the patent holder to meet local demand for a patented article.

Protection of Intellectual Property

Intellectual property is an asset in the same manner as other business assets. Just as an organization takes measures to protect its buildings, land, equipment, and personnel, so too must it take steps to protect its intellectual property. It is not sufficient for Chuck to simply "create" intellectual property rights. His rights require continuous monitoring and protection.

Use

Intellectual property rights are subject to loss if they are not properly used and maintained, as is shown in the following examples:

- A patent may be considered abused if, among other things, insufficient quantities of the patented item are produced to meet demand in Canada. As a result, a licence to use the patent may be granted to another, or the patent may even be revoked.

- Industrial design rights may be substantially reduced if the goods are not properly marked. A defence of innocent infringement is available unless proper notice (i.e., Ⓓ) is used on articles or their containers. The defence has the effect of limiting the owner's remedy for infringement to injunctive relief.

- A trademark can be subject to attacks for nonuse or abandonment if it is not used continuously in association with the goods or services for which it is registered. A trademark may also be lost if it loses its distinctiveness, as when it slips into everyday usage. For example, nylon, kleenex, zipper, escalator, cellophane, and dry ice, once trademarks, lost their distinctiveness and thus their status as trademarks by falling into everyday usage and becoming generic terms.

- Confidential business information is lost once it is disclosed. A business needs to be particularly vigilant in protecting confidential business information. A business can implement a program for maintaining security that includes restricting access to confidential information, implementing physical security measures (e.g., labelling documents "secret" or "confidential," locking areas where the information is kept, and changing computer passwords), and using confidentiality agreements that require others to maintain confidences.

Business Application of the Law

Corporate Espionage at Coca-Cola

In July 2006, three people including an employee of Coca-Cola Co. were charged with stealing confidential information, including a sample of a new drink from Coca-Cola. It is alleged that a person identifying himself as "Dirk" wrote PepsiCo claiming to be a high-level employee with Coca-Cola. He asked for $10 000 for trade secrets and $75 000 for a new product sample. Pepsi informed Coke, which contacted the FBI. An undercover agent paid $30 000 for the documents marked "classified and confidential," and the sample. He promised the balance after the sample was tested. The agent offered Dirk $1.5 million for other trade secrets. The suspects were arrested on the day that the exchange was to occur. The information and sample came from an executive assistant to a high-level Coke executive at the company's Atlanta headquarters. Video surveillance showed her at her desk going through multiple files and stuffing documents into her bags.

CRITICAL ANALYSIS: Was the information that is alleged to have been stolen from Coke "confidential business information"? What steps should companies like Coca-Cola take to protect confidential business information?

Source: Kathleen Day "3 Accused in Theft of Coke Secrets" *The Washington Post* (6 July 2006) at D01.

Litigation

At some point it may be necessary to engage in litigation in order to protect intellectual property rights. Intellectual property litigation is complex and expensive, often requiring the services of experts.

In many intellectual property infringement cases, it is common for the plaintiff to seek an injunction before trial to prevent the infringer from continuing to damage the business of the plaintiff. An injunction is granted if the applicant can demonstrate that there is a serious issue to be tried, irreparable harm may be caused, and the balance of convenience favours the applicant. In addition, because infringers may flee and destroy evidence, the law provides for the seizure of property before judgment. An **Anton Pillar order** allows the plaintiff to access the defendant's premises to inspect and seize evidence of infringement.

The most common intellectual property actions are as follows:

- *Patent infringement.* Infringement is not defined in the *Patent Act*, but it is generally taken to mean an unlicensed intrusion on the patent holder's rights (i.e., making, selling, using, or constructing something that comes within the scope of the patent claims). There is no requirement to show that the infringer intended to infringe on the patent, nor is it a requirement that the infringer's action come within the precise language of the claims. So long as the infringer is taking the substance of the invention, that will suffice. A successful action for patent infringement may result in the infringer having to pay damages or turn profits over to the patent holder, also known as the patentee. The patentee may also be entitled to an injunction prior to trial or after trial to prevent further infringement and a "delivering-up" of the infringing product.

- *Copyright infringement.* Copyright is infringed whenever anyone, without the consent of the owner of the copyright, does anything that only the owner has the right to do. As noted above, this could involve various activities—copying, publishing, performing, translating, and the like. The copyright owner has a full range of remedies. An owner may also elect statutory damages of up to $20 000 instead of damages and profits. As well, the infringer is subject to criminal sanctions of fines up to $1 million and/or five years in jail.

- *Industrial design infringement.* The *Industrial Design Act* prohibits anyone from applying a registered industrial design to the ornamentation of any article without the permission of the owner. The prohibition also includes applying a confusingly similar design. The traditional remedies for infringement are an injunction to restrain further use of the design, damages, and an accounting of profits made by the defendant in using the design. The act also provides for nominal criminal sanctions.

- *Trademark infringement.* Infringement of trademark is protected by both the *Trade-marks Act* and the tort of passing off. The action can be brought against a trader who misrepresents the source of goods or services so as to deceive the public. This may be done by using the same or a similar trademark. Remedies for trademark infringement include injunctions, damages or an accounting of profits, and the destruction or delivery of the offending goods or the means to produce them as well as criminal sanctions.

- *Confidential business information.* There is no statutory cause of action related to the misappropriation of confidential business information. There are, however, common law actions for breach of express and implied terms and breach of confidence, as discussed above. It must be shown that the information was confidential, that the information was disclosed under circumstances of confidence, and that the recipient misused the information to the detriment of the owner. Remedies available include injunctions, damages, and an accounting and/or a declaration of the entitlement to the information.

Anton Pillar order
A pretrial order allowing the seizure of material, including material that infringes intellectual property rights.

t is difficult to protect intellectual property in a domestic setting; however, it is even more difficult to protect it in an international setting as, unlike tangible property, intellectual property is not bound by borders or geography. Protection is not just a question of designing and implementing rules for protection. There are very different perspectives on whether intellectual property should receive protection. Developing countries have little incentive to provide protection, as they need intellectual property in order to grow and prosper. Developed countries have a somewhat different perspective, as they consider intellectual property a valuable investment and worthy of protection.

Canada is a signatory to a number of treaties that give a measure of international protection to intellectual property rights. The major international conventions are these:

- *Paris Convention for the Protection of Industrial Property.* This convention provides national treatment and foreign filing priorities for patents, trademarks, and industrial designs.

- *Patent Co-operation Treaty.* This treaty is designed to facilitate the acquisition of patent protection in multiple countries around the world. Benefits are available only to nationals of contracting states.

- *Berne Convention.* This convention, which applies to literary and artistic works, provides for automatic copyright protection to nationals of member states without any requirement for formalities.

- *Universal Copyright Convention.* This convention provides national treatment for foreign copyrighted works provided the copyright symbol, the name of the copyright owner, and the date of publication are on the work.

- *Agreement on Trade-Related Aspects of Intellectual Property* (TRIPS). This is an agreement of the World Trade Organization (WTO) that establishes certain minimum standards of intellectual property protection for patents, trademarks, and copyrights. The agreement provides that a country should treat foreign nationals no less favourably than its own nationals with respect to intellectual property rights. Developing countries have a transition period for implementing it.

Canada has also signed but not yet ratified two Internet treaties: the *World Intellectual Property Organization's Copyright Treaty* (WCT) and *Performances and Phonograms Treaty* (WPPT). Both treaties respond to challenges posed by digital technology and are designed to update the Berne and Rome conventions.

The broad intent of the international agreements is to provide protection for foreign intellectual property. For example, works that have copyright protection in Canada have protection in countries that are signatories to the Berne Convention. By the same token, an author who is a citizen of a convention country receives copyright protection in Canada.

CRITICAL ANALYSIS: What is the justification for providing protection for foreign intellectual property? When intellectual property protection is extended in this manner, whose interests are curtailed?

Business Law in Practice Revisited

1. How can Chuck protect his new and improved method of curing and smoking ribs from being used by others?

Chuck has two options available for protecting his method. The method may be patentable if he can demonstrate that it is new, useful, and unobvious. Although there are methods of food preparation that are patented (e.g., a process for making a ketchup substitute, a method of making a deep-dish pizza crust and a microwavable sponge cake, to name a few examples), many methods are not patented because they are not new and they are obvious. In addition, the high cost of patenting can be prohibitive for a relatively low-priced item and patent protection is limited to 20 years.

A second and probably more viable choice for Chuck is to keep his new method a trade secret. This is the choice of many makers of well-known products, such as McDonald's secret sauce, Coca-Cola, and Listerine. The advantages are that secrecy does not cost anything in terms of filing fees, and secrecy can last forever. The disadvantages are that the owner must be vigilant in guarding the secret and once the secret is public (either through disclosure or independent discovery) anyone can use it.

2. How can Chuck prevent the new restaurant from selling "Chucky's BBQ Ribs?"

Although Chuck does not have a registered trademark in "Chuck's BBQ Ribs," he has a common law trademark. Such a trademark is considered to be part of the goodwill of Chuck's business and he can prevent a competitor from using the same or a similar trademark through an action based on the tort of passing off. So long as the competitor's trademark is the same or confusingly similar to Chuck's and Chuck's reputation has spread to the area in which the competitor is operating, Chuck should not have a problem in preventing the new restaurant from selling ribs called "Chucky's BBQ Ribs."

Chuck may also consider registering his trademark to obtain national protection. To do so he must meet requirements of use, distinctiveness, and registrability. Chuck has used the trademark in relation to his ribs and although the name is not particularly distinctive, it may have gained the quality through use in his business and advertising. Chuck will have to determine whether the trademark is registrable; in particular whether the name might be confused with another registered trademark in the same line of business.

Chapter Summary

The term "intellectual property" is used to describe the results of an intellectual or creative process. The term is also used to describe the rights people have or acquire in ideas and in the ways they express those ideas. The main categories of intellectual property rights are patents, industrial designs, trademarks, copyrights, and confidential information. The rights that attach to each category vary but generally encompass the right to use and the right to exclude others from using.

There is considerable overlap between the various categories of intellectual property. It is possible for more than one area of intellectual property law to protect different aspects of a single product or process. As well, there may be alternatives for protecting a single product. For example, an invention may qualify for patent protection, or the invention can be kept secret through the mechanism of a trade secret. Patent protection provides a monopoly for a period of time, but the price of the monopoly is the requirement to disclose the invention. A trade secret is just that—a secret! Once disclosure occurs, there is no protection. The ornamentation of a product subject to patent protection may receive industrial design protection.

Businesses acquire intellectual property in a number of ways. A lot of intellectual property is created in-house by employees, but it can also be bought or acquired through a licensing agreement.

Intellectual property, like other business assets, must be protected. An effective intellectual property policy should encompass its acquisition and proper use. Failure to acquire and maintain intellectual property rights may result in missed opportunities and losses for the business. In some cases, intellectual property rights ultimately may need to be protected by bringing legal action against infringers.

Chapter Study

Key Terms and Concepts

Anton Pillar order (p. 452)

assignment (p. 450)

claims (p. 433)

confidential business information (p. 446)

copyright (p. 441)

cyber-squatting (p. 438)

distinguishing guise (p. 435)

domain name (p. 438)

fair dealing (p. 444)

industrial design (p. 434)

intellectual property (p. 427)

licence (p. 450)

moral rights (p. 443)

patent (p. 428)

patent agent (p. 433)

specifications (p. 433)

trade name (p. 436)

trademark (p. 435)

Questions for Review

1. What is intellectual property?

2. What are the major forms of intellectual property rights?

3. What is a patent? Give an example.

4. Are life forms patentable in Canada? Explain.

5. Are computer programs patentable in Canada? Explain.

6. What are the three requirements for patentability?

7. What is the difference between specifications and claims in a patent application?

8. How long does patent protection last?

9. What is an industrial design? What are the requirements for industrial design registration? How long does an industrial design registration last?

10. What is the advantage of marking an industrial design to indicate that the design is registered?

11. What is the purpose of a trademark?

12. What is the relationship between trademarks and trade names?

13. Must trademarks be registered to receive legal protection? Explain.

14. What is meant by the term "cyber-squatting?"

15. Who owns the copyright in a book? How long does copyright last?

16. What are the moral rights of an author? Give an example.

17. One of the exemption under the *Copyright Act* is fair dealing. What is fair dealing?

18. What are the requirements for the protection of confidential business information?

19. What is the difference between an intellectual property assignment and a licence?

20. Give an example of how intellectual property rights may be lost if they are not properly used.

Questions for Critical Thinking

1. In some instances, intellectual property rights give a monopoly over certain technologies. What is the justification for the monopoly? Do you think intellectual property rights should be strictly enforced in all countries including developing countries?

2. The Internet has revolutionized the distribution of music and raised a host of copyright issues. Canadian law does not yet squarely address these issues, particularly the legality of trading copyrighted music over computer networks. The music industry, however, argues that peer-to-peer file sharing is costing the industry millions of dollars in lost sales. Should the *Copyright Act* be amended to address the concerns of the music interest? For example, should it be illegal to put copyrighted material into the shared directories of file-sharing systems? Should it be illegal to bypass copy-protection mechanisms in copyrighted material?

3. A trademark may be lost if it is not properly used. How should a trademark be properly used? What are the critical elements of a trademark-use policy for employees?

4. In the United States, the U.S. Patent Office allows patents for all manner of business methods including, for example, a patent for Amazon's 1-Click method for purchasing goods on the Internet with a single click of the mouse; Priceline's name-your-own price reverse auction process; and Mattel's system that allows its customers to order personalized toys. Business-method patents have been criticized because they tend to cover subject matter that is old or obvious. What are other criticisms of allowing patents for business methods? What are the advantages of business-methods patents?

5. A patent troll is a person or company that holds patents for the sole purpose of extracting licence revenue or suing infringers. The troll does not make, use, or sell new products or technologies, but waits until a company has invested in, developed, and commercialized an idea and then it pounces—offering a licence in return for cash (see the BlackBerry litigation on page 431). The target company is often left with only two options: pay up or litigate.[73] How can companies manage the risk posed by patent trolls?

Situations for Discussion

1. Meredith opened a restaurant called Checkers in St. John's, Newfoundland. After about six months, she received a phone call informing her that "Checkers" is the name of a restaurant in Vancouver, British Columbia, and that she must immediately cease using the same name. Must she comply? Why or why not? How can Meredith obtain rights to the name?

2. Hannah attended a seminar put on by the local chamber of commerce on how to successfully market a home-based business. At the seminar, she received a number of printed handouts from the facilitator. Hannah wants to use portions of the material in her business. Is she entitled to do so? Explain.

3. Anne recently returned from a holiday in Ottawa. While there, she visited the National Gallery and was most impressed by a landscape painting by one of the Group of Seven artists. Anne believes that the scene depicted in the painting would provide a wonderful design for her housewares business. She would like to use

---

73. Sarah Chapin Columbia and Stacy L. Blasberg, "Beware Patent Trolls", *Risk Management Magazine* (April 2006) at 22–27.

it for wallpaper, dishes, and other bric-a-brac. Does her plan have any implications in terms of intellectual property? Explain.

4. Daniel is a carpenter who has designed a unique doghouse. He has sold a few houses at a local craft show and is now in full production to keep up with demand. Another business has copied Daniel's design and is selling a doghouse very much like Daniel's. Can Daniel do anything to prevent the competitor from selling doghouses that are almost identical to his? Should he pursue any action?

5. Mechanical engineer Vladislav Ircha was hired by Seanix Technology Inc. in March 1995 to design chassis and cases for computers. For the first few months, Ircha spent most of his time meeting with a subcontractor who was developing a case for Seanix's newest motherboard. Ircha soon realized, however, that the subcontractor's design was flawed, so he began working on a design of his own. Lacking proper design facilities at Seanix's office, he did most of the work at home, and was able to produce a completed mockup of a new "swing-out" case in early 1996. Ircha's design was so impressive that the president of Seanix offered him a 30 percent salary increase and a bonus for a European vacation. Ircha, however, refused the president's offer, left the company, and claimed rights in the case. Seanix brought action for rights in the case. What legal issue(s) must be resolved?[74] Outline the law that governs them. How could Seanix have prevented this dispute?

6. Coco Sharpe is a software developer specializing in online games and puzzles. He has developed a revolutionary, new poker game aimed at enhancing the skills of would-be poker players. Coco believes that he can make a lot of money selling the game online. Coco calls his game COCO CARDSHARP and he has received a registered trademark for the name. However, when Coco applies to register the domain name, he discovers that www.COCOCARDSHARP.com is registered to Janet Rollins.

When contacted by Coco, Janet claims that she knows nothing about Coco's game but that she is willing to sell the rights in the domain name to Coca for $50 000. What are Coco's options? How should Coco attempt to settle the dispute with Janet? What are the advantages and disadvantages of pursuing online dispute resolution? What are the advantages and disadvantages of pursuing litigation?

7. Inspector Clouseau is the bumbling Parisian detective in the *Pink Panther* movies that starred the late Peter Sellers. Despite his bungling, Clouseau always solved the crime. In the inaugural film, Clouseau was called on to investigate the theft of a fabulous gemstone with one small flaw. When held to the light, the gemstone resembled a pink panther. Hence the name.

The name Pink Panther lives on, not only in films but also in a cartoon series and in the movie's theme music, which won an Academy Award for Henry Mancini. A cosmetics company that operates beauty salons wants to use the name Pink Panther Beauty Corp. in its business. United Artists, the producer of the films, objects.[75] Is the cosmetics company permitted to use the name? Why or why not?

8. Alice Taxin is the president of Taxin & Company Engineering, a small consulting firm specializing in the design of cooling systems for manufacturing plants. Alice recently discovered that a former employee, Jill Jacobs, has been passing on tender documents and customer information to her new employer, a competitor of Taxin Engineering. Is the information that Jill passed on to Taxin Engineering's competitor confidential business information? Explain. Does Taxin Engineering have any remedies against Jill for passing on the information? What steps can companies like Taxin Engineering take to protect sensitive information?

For more study tools, visit
http://www.businesslaw3e.nelson.com

74. Based, in part, on *Seanix Technology Inc. v. Ircha* (1998), 78 C.P.R. (3d) 443 (B.C.S.C.).
75. Based, in part, on *United Artists Pictures Inc. v. Pink Panther Beauty Corp.* (1998), 225 N.R. 82 (Fed.C.A.), leave to appeal granted (1998), 235 N.R. 399 (S.C.C.).

Chapter

19

Objectives

After studying this chapter, you should have an understanding of

- the nature and ownership of real property
- the various ways to acquire and transfer ownership
- how a mortgage works
- the rights and duties of landlords and tenants

Real Property

Business Law in Practice

Universal Furniture Ltd. (Universal), located in Halifax, Nova Scotia, manufactures and sells custom-made furniture. The consistently high quality of Universal's products has earned it a reputation beyond Nova Scotia so that orders are now coming from several other provinces, as well as from the state of Maine. Universal's website is also attracting interest, which may result in the need for warehouse space to accommodate online orders. Universal's current facility, which is leased, is not large enough to accommodate its growing business. The current lease expires within the next year and management is contemplating a move from the current isolated location to an industrial mall.

As a result of these factors, Universal has several business decisions to make that have significant legal consequences. The first is an investment matter regarding several options as to how expansion will proceed. Universal could lease a larger space and remain a tenant. The company could purchase land with an existing building suitable for current and future needs. Another option is to buy land on which to construct a building. A related matter concerns size. Universal could acquire space just adequate for its immediate needs or large enough to allow for future growth. Extra space would require another decision about its use until it was needed by Universal. A final matter is the need for financing if Universal decides to buy or build. The real estate market is booming and Universal's cash flow is tight.

1. What are the legal features of the various real estate options available to Universal?
2. What factors should Universal consider in deciding how to expand?
3. How could Universal use a mortgage to finance the expansion?

Ownership

real property
Land or real estate, including buildings, fixtures, and the associated legal rights.

The legal concept of **real property** refers to land or real estate.[1] When people own real property, they own a defined piece of land that includes not only the surface of the land but also everything above and below it—expressed in law as "the earth beneath and the air above." In practice, however, these broad ownership rights are limited by legal rules facilitating air travel, mining, and oil and gas production, to name a few examples. The term "real estate" also includes structures on the land, such as fences and buildings, as well as anything attached to those structures. Items so attached are known as **fixtures** and include heating ducts, lights, and plumbing—any item attached to the land through screws, nails, bolts, or similar means.[2]

fixtures
Tangible personal property that is attached to land, buildings, or other fixtures.

Land has always been a valuable commodity, and therefore the rules governing real property have deep historical roots. The value of land results from two key attributes. First, land is permanent and immovable, so it is easier to track and control than other, more portable forms of property, such as cars and furniture. Second, although land can be adapted for different purposes, the total quantity is finite. The value is determined by the market for a particular type and location of land.

Real property is largely governed by common law, and, traditionally, the law is devoted to protecting rights to property, such as determining who owns the same piece of land when more than one person is making a claim. Nowadays, however, public policy—in the areas of conservation and environmental protection, for example—means that statute law is an increasingly significant factor.

---

1. Bruce H. Ziff, *Principles of Property Law*, 3rd ed. (Toronto: Carswell, 2000) at 85.
2. Henry Campbell Black, *Black's Law Dictionary*, 6th ed. (St. Paul, MN: West, 1990) at 638.

Interests in Land

The highest and most comprehensive level of ownership of land possible under our system of law is known as a **fee simple**.[3] An owner in fee simple essentially owns the land (subject to the limits described below) and can dispose of it in any way she sees fit. Ownership of land need not, however, be concentrated in one person or remain with that person in an uninterrupted fashion. In fact, ownership of land is easily divisible.

Division of Ownership

One piece of land can be owned by several people at once. For instance, if Universal cannot afford a building on its own, it may strike an arrangement with one or more of its shareholders so that they buy the building and split the cost. The co-owners have an undivided interest in the entire building. Each owns a portion of the whole, but their respective shares cannot be singled out or identified in any distinct way.

Though Universal and its shareholders are the owners of the real estate, they are called tenants in this context. In ordinary usage, a tenant generally refers to someone who leases space rather than owns it outright; however, the legal use of the word "tenant" is much broader and includes someone who has any kind of right or title in land.

In the time leading up to purchase, Universal and its shareholders can negotiate either **tenancy in common** or joint tenancy. If they choose to be tenants in common, they each have an undivided interest in the land, meaning they can deal with their own interest in any way they see fit and without having to consult the other co-owners.[4] In a related fashion, if one of the tenants in common dies—a shareholder, in our example—his undivided interest in the real estate forms part of his personal estate and goes to his heirs.[5]

A **joint tenancy** is also a form of undivided co-ownership but is distinguished by the right of survivorship. Should one of the joint tenants die, his undivided interest goes directly and automatically to the other joint tenants.[6] The heirs of the deceased shareholder would have no claim on the land co-owned with Universal. Both forms of co-ownership require cooperation among the owners in order to use or sell the property.

Division of Ownership in Time

Ownership in land can also be divided in time. The most common example is a lease. If Universal buys a building that has more space than Universal needs at the moment, it may decide to find a tenant to use the extra space for a time. Through the mechanism of a lease, the owner—or landlord—gives a tenant possession of the building (or a portion thereof, depending on the agreement) for a period of time in exchange for rent. When the lease terminates at the end of the defined period, the landlord resumes control.

---

3. *Supra* note 1 at 148.
4. The parties can, of course, enter into a contract whereby they agree not to deal with their respective interests freely but to offer the other a right of first refusal, for example.
5. Corporations do not die, but they do wind up. If Universal winds up, its half-interest forms part of the assets used to pay out creditors and shareholders. To facilitate liquidation, the shareholder may offer to buy the land outright or the co-owners may decide to sell. Alternatively, if the shareholder is uncooperative, Universal can seek an order of partition and sale. This would permit the real estate to be sold and the proceeds to be divided between the owners.
6. Most married couples own property as joint tenants because of this right of survivorship.

Limits on Ownership

There are numerous restrictions on land use imposed by statute law and common law, including the following:

- Municipal governments have the authority to control land use through planning schemes and zoning regulations. For example, if an area of a town is zoned for residential use, it is normally not available for commercial development.

- Environmental regulations affect the use of land by limiting or prohibiting the discharge of harmful substances.

- The common law of nuisance limits any use of land that unduly interferes with other owners' enjoyment of their land. A landowner who produces smoke or noise is subject to being sued for the tort of nuisance.[7]

- Many government agencies have the authority to expropriate land for particular purposes. For example, if a new highway is to be built, the government can assume ownership of the portions of land along the route after providing compensation to the owners according to specified procedures.

- In a similar fashion, government agencies can make use of privately owned land for a particular purpose, such as a pipeline.

- Ownership of land in a foreign country can be limited by that country's governmental policy. For example, foreign governments may nationalize whole industries without compensation to landowners from other countries. Foreign governments may also impose limits on the quantity of land that can be owned by nonresidents.

Other limits on ownership result from contracts made by the landowner. In short, the landowner has the option to "sell" part or all of his rights to the land in exchange for a payment of money or other benefit. For example, the landowner may do the following:

easement
The right to use the land of another for a particular purpose only.

- Grant an adjoining landowner the right to use a portion of his land for a particular purpose. For example, a landowner may give a neighbour the right to drive across his land to access her own. In law, this is known as an **easement.**

- Grant a lease to a tenant, thereby giving the tenant the right to occupy the land for the specified period in exchange for rent.

- Grant an oil, gas, or mineral lease to occupy a portion of the land, access that portion, and remove materials.[8]

- Grant a mortgage on the land as security for a loan. This makes ownership subject to repayment according to the agreed terms of the loan. The right of the lender to be repaid takes priority, and the "owner" then holds the land "subject to the mortgage."

restrictive covenant
A restriction on the use of land as specified in the title document.

- Make the land subject to **restrictive covenants.** Covenants are legally enforceable promises contained in the document transferring ownership. For example, title documents to lots of land in a housing development may contain covenants that prohibit or restrict certain activities (such as cutting trees or erecting storage sheds) for the purpose of preserving the character of the development and thereby enhancing its value.

---

7. See Chapter 12.
8. The law governing oil, gas, and mineral rights is complex. For example, in Alberta the government owns the rights and negotiates the leases.

These various limits on ownership create a significant risk for businesspeople. Anyone contemplating the acquisition of any interest in land needs to do a thorough investigation of potential restrictions that could affect the rights to the particular piece of land. Otherwise, a buyer may end up owning land that cannot be used for its intended purpose.

Registration of Ownership

The provinces have constitutional jurisdiction over property rights.[9] A key aspect of this jurisdiction is the documentation and recording of interests in land. The value of land justifies a system in which those with an ownership interest are able to record or register their interests in a public fashion. The purposes of this type of system are twofold: first, to enable owners to give notice of the land they own and the extent of their ownership; and second, to enable anyone contemplating the acquisition of an interest in land to investigate the state of ownership in order to verify its status.

Because of the provincial control, the systems of registration vary from province to province, though there are only two general types.

A Registry System

The **registry system,** which originated in the eastern provinces,[10] provides the facilities for recording documents and the maintenance of the registrations. The public has access to the records and can examine or search the records to evaluate the state of ownership of a particular piece of land. This process is known as "searching the title." The main purpose of the search is to verify the seller's ownership by investigating the "chain of title" to confirm that no one has a conflicting claim to all or part of the land in question. Also required is an evaluation of the results of the search to decide whether the title is "clear" or not. If there are title defects, the parties will seek to fix those defects. For example, if Universal has negotiated to purchase property for its expansion, but a search reveals that there is an unregistered title document (known as a deed) in the chain, it may be possible to register the missing deed and perfect the registered record—cure the defect in the current owner's registration. If the defect cannot be cured, Universal may still decide to proceed with the deal but extract a price concession from the vendor. For example, if the search reveals a small encroachment on the property by an adjoining owner, Universal may decide to proceed with the transaction at a reduced purchase price.

The administrators of a registry system take no responsibility for the validity of the documents that are filed and express no opinion on the state of the title of a particular piece of property. Lawyers retained by the buyer of property are responsible for the search and the evaluation of the results. Law clerks or **paralegals** retained by the lawyer may do the actual search.

The Land Titles System

The other system, the one in place in the Western provinces,[11] is the **land titles system.** The administrators of this system assume a much more active role in that they evaluate each document presented for registration and maintain a record of the documents relating to each piece of property. They are also responsible for the accuracy of the information they provide, and they maintain an insurance fund to

---

9. *Constitution Act, 1982*, s. 92(13): "property and civil rights in the province."
10. Nova Scotia, New Brunswick, Prince Edward Island, Newfoundland, and parts of Ontario and Manitoba.
11. Saskatchewan, Alberta, British Columbia, and parts of Manitoba and Ontario.

compensate those who suffer loss because of their errors. When someone wishes to know the state of the title to a piece of land, she need only consult the certificate of title and is not ordinarily required to do an historical search. The certificate contains a legal description of the property and identifies the nature of and owners of the various interests in the land. Because the certificate itself is authoritative proof of title, there is less potential for competing claims. The greater certainty and reliability of the land titles system has caused several provinces that use the registry system, such as Ontario, New Brunswick, and Nova Scotia, to begin the transition toward using the land titles system.

The sequence of registration is crucial to both systems. If there are conflicting claims to the same piece of land, the person who registered his interest first has priority, regardless of which transaction was completed first. So long as the one who registers first has no knowledge of the earlier transaction and has paid valuable consideration for the land in question, that person's interest in and claim to the land is fully protected. The party who registers second has no claim to the land but may have actions against those who assisted in the failed transaction or who made representations concerning the status of title.

Technology and the Law
B
Electronic Registration and Interests in Land

The development of technology has huge potential for increased efficiency and accessibility in the registration of interests in land. All provinces, whether operating under the registry or land titles systems, are aggressively using technology to improve their systems of land registration.

There are several technology-based improvements that are being implemented to varying degrees in all provinces:

- *Creation of a central database in the province:* a vast improvement over a system where each county or district has its own separate registry of records.

- *Improved access:* the central database can be accessed from any of the county or district offices and even remotely from law offices and other locations with access to the system.

- *Conversion of paper records to electronic records:* the savings in storage costs are huge.

- *Electronic filing of title documents:* instantaneous updating of records is assured.

- *Electronic searching of records:* access is available from anywhere in the province, elimi- nating the need for visiting the record offices.

Nova Scotia provides an example of the combination of two conversions—from registry to land titles and from paper to electronic. Each lot of land in the province is in the process of being assigned a parcel identifier number. The title for each parcel will eventually be certified and registered under the new system, eliminating the existing need for an historical search every time the parcel is transferred. As a second stage, interested parties will be able to file documents and conduct searches online. Also planned is the centralization of many registries and government offices with records relevant to the transfer of land in business.

There are some real and potential drawbacks to these major conversions. The cost of converting existing paper records to an electronic database is enormous, resulting in conversion over several years. There is a need for appropriate software for accessing and using the electronic systems. These systems are subject to the usual weaknesses of electronic databases—ensuring adequate capacity; controlling access; protection from viruses, crashes, and hacking; and the need for adequate backups.

CRITICAL ANALYSIS: The cost of converting a paper-based system to an electronic database is significant. An electronic system is in many ways more vulnerable than a paper system. What advantages compensate for these weaknesses?

Sources: Paula Kulig, "The Virtual Landscape" *The National* (May 1999) at 21; Donalee Moulton, "P.E.I. Land Registry Fully Online" *The Lawyers Weekly* (22 March 2002) at 2; Donalee Moulton, "Nova Scotia Modernizes Its Land Registry System" *The Lawyers Weekly* (24 May 2002) at 11; and Dave Bilinsky, "Land Registration Systems in Throes of Change Across Canada" *The Lawyers Weekly* (19 March 2004) at 9.

Acquisition of Ownership

There are several ways to acquire an interest in land. Universal can buy land with a building already in place, or it can buy land on which to build its own structure. Either purchase is likely to require financing, probably in the form of a loan from a financial institution secured by a mortgage on the property being purchased. If the space acquired exceeds current needs, Universal may lease the extra space to a tenant, thereby relinquishing possession during the period of the lease. As an alternative to buying, Universal can lease larger premises as a tenant. By doing so, Universal gains possession of the land for the term of the lease, but acquires no permanent ownership of the property.

The Purchasing Transaction

Buying land is a buyer-beware situation, expressed in law as *caveat emptor*. It is up to the buyer (also known as the purchaser) to investigate and evaluate the property both in financial and legal terms. The risks are significant and require careful management. The seller (known as the vendor) must not mislead the buyer but generally is under no obligation to disclose information about the property, even when that information might cause the buyer to hesitate. There are legal and ethical complications to this general rule, as the following Ethical Considerations box shows.

Ethical Considerations

What Should the Owner Tell the Buyer?

Buying and selling land involves negotiating the optimum deal for buyer and seller. Each has the obligation to ensure that the contract contains the terms essential to her. The seller must not mislead the buyer, but is generally not required to disclose negative aspects of the land. How does the rule work in practice? In legal language, "misleading" means misrepresentation, whether innocent or fraudulent (see Chapter 8). Misrepresentations may be oral or written false statements, but may also take the form of active attempts to hide defects in the property being sold. Silence and half-truths that imply something other than the truth may also be misrepresentation. There is a positive duty to disclose significant latent defects (not easily visible) that are known to the seller, especially if the defects cause the property to be dangerous or uninhabitable. Where there is a misrepresentation, the seller cannot justify it by claiming that the buyer could have discovered the truth through investigation.

In land cases, fraud has concerned issues such as misrepresenting:

- revenue potential
- uses permitted by zoning regulations
- whether there is permission to subdivide
- adequacy of water supply

One case concerned the purchase of a house that was infested by termites. The owners bought the house unaware of the termites, but knew of the problem when they listed it for sale two years later. They said nothing to the buyers about termites and in fact their son stated that any repairs had been done because of water damage. The court found that when the property was transferred, it was so badly infested as to be uninhabitable and dangerous. The termites were a defect not easily visible to an untrained eye, and therefore a latent defect that had to be disclosed by the owners because they were well aware of it. Their failure to disclose was equivalent to an intention to deceive. Combined with their active concealment of the problem, they had committed fraud, to which the "buyer-beware" defence did not apply.

An important development is the use of a Property Condition Disclosure Statement, which requires the seller to provide detailed information on many aspects of the property. This statement can then be incorporated into the agreement of purchase and sale and thereby eliminate much of the uncertainty surrounding potential defects.

CRITICAL ANALYSIS: Should the owner of property seek legal advice on which negative aspects of the land must be disclosed to potential buyers? Alternatively, should landowners in good conscience provide full disclosure of all aspects of the land that they know about? How should the buyer manage this risk?

Sources: Paul M. Perell, *Remedies and the Sale of Land* (Toronto: Butterworths, 1988) at 88–91; *Jung v. Ip*, [1988] O.J. No. 1038 (D.C.); and Shannon O'Byrne, "Culpable Silence: Liability for Non-Disclosure in the Contractual Arena" (1998) 30 *Can. Bus. L.J.* 239.

If Universal decides to purchase, the first step is to identify a property that appears to be appropriate in terms of price, size, location, and suitability for Universal's manufacturing and sales operations. Universal should have its legal advisor involved from the outset to identify, among other matters, the contractual significance of communication and documents used by Universal and the current owner. The technical nature of real estate transactions makes the use of professional advice a practical necessity.

Participants in the Transaction

The main participants in a real estate transaction are the buyer and the seller. In a commercial deal, such as the one Universal is contemplating, the parties to the contract of purchase and sale are likely to be corporations. Individuals from both corporations will be chosen to coordinate the deal and conclude the contract. In addition, each party may have a real estate agent, a property appraiser, a land surveyor, an engineer, and a lawyer providing expert advice and guidance. The seller, for example, will likely have engaged a real estate agent to find suitable buyers. For its part, Universal might engage an agent to identify suitable properties. The lawyers on both sides will advise on the main agreement between the buyer and the seller. Appraisers may be hired to formally value the property, based on the structure and the current market. Surveyors may be retained to determine the physical boundaries of the property. Engineers may be retained to provide an expert report on the structural integrity of the building in question. Consultants may be involved to check for any environmental hazards.

From a legal point of view, Universal's transaction is a complicated set of contracts revolving around the main contract for the transfer and sale of the property. Universal must decide which professionals it requires and be clear regarding what services and advice each will provide. For example, a lawyer will normally do the investigation of title but is likely not in a position to place a value on the land.

Traditionally, lawyers have accepted responsibility for evaluating the reliability of the title of property their clients are buying. This is especially the case in registry systems, under which the lawyer searches the title and gives an opinion on its validity. Lawyers have professional liability insurance that compensates clients if lawyers are negligent in providing advice on title to property. In fact, a significant portion of claims made against lawyers arise from such situations. The cost of this insurance is reflected in the fees charged to clients in property transactions.

Title insurance is also growing in importance in real estate transactions. It originated in the United States but is gaining popularity in Canada. The use of title insurance diverts much of the responsibility, work, and related fees from lawyers. Insurance companies offer protection to property buyers against problems with the title to the property such as boundary encroachments, zoning problems, survey defects, liens, and fraudulent transfers or mortgages. The premium charged is significantly less than the fee charged by lawyers. However, there is some concern for the integrity of land registration systems if property can be transferred and title documents registered without full investigation of title and the resulting repair of defects that thorough searches reveal. A title search is preventive in that it identifies problems before the transaction closes. Title insurance provides compensation if a problem is discovered later, but it may not result in the repair of the problem with the registered title. Real estate lawyers across the country are struggling with this development, which may displace or complement their services in real estate transactions.

In addition to the buyer, the seller, and professionals, others are less directly involved, as illustrated in the following examples:

- If the property is currently occupied by tenants, Universal's ownership may be subject to the rights of those tenants, depending on the jurisdiction involved and the length of the lease.

- If the property is currently mortgaged, that obligation must be discharged by the vendor, assumed by the purchaser, or otherwise addressed in the financial adjustments between the parties.

- If Universal needs a loan to finance its purchase, the bank or some other lender must be brought into the transaction. Universal will be required to grant the bank a mortgage on the property for the amount borrowed plus interest.

Stages in the Transaction

There are three stages in the transaction resulting in the transfer of the land to Universal: the agreement of purchase and sale, the investigation, and the closing.

Agreement of Purchase and Sale

Of prime importance is the agreement of purchase and sale between Universal and the seller. Though the content of this agreement is entirely as negotiated between the parties, normal elements would include provision for Universal to conduct a full investigation of the property, the opportunity to bring matters of concern to the seller, time for Universal to arrange its financing, and a specific date for the conclusion (closing) of the transaction. This agreement can also be made conditional, for example, "subject to a satisfactory engineer's report" or "subject to financing." If Universal makes good-faith efforts to secure financing but is unable to find a willing lender, it can terminate the agreement with the vendor because the condition of being able to secure financing has not been fulfilled.[12]

---

12. For discussion of conditions precedent and conditional agreements, see Chapter 7.

What stages of a real estate transaction have occurred before this sign appeared?

Universal's agreement with the seller is the main contract and therefore must contain all requirements or terms of importance to Universal (see the *Hayward* case below). As with any contract, once this one is signed, it is difficult to change without the agreement of both parties.[13] An important legal requirement that affects this contract is that it must be in writing and signed by the parties.[14] This eliminates attempts to incorporate into the agreement items that may have been discussed but on which no formal agreement has been reached.

The contents of the agreement of purchase and sale depend on the nature of the property and the value of the transaction. The basic terms are these:

- the precise names of the parties
- precise identification and description of the property, including reference to the registered title and sufficient detail so as to leave no doubt as to location, size, and boundaries
- the purchase price, deposit, and method of payment
- a statement of any conditions on which the agreement depends
- a list and description of exactly what is included in the price (e.g., equipment, fixtures)
- the date for closing and a list of what each party must deliver on that date
- a statement of who is responsible for what during the period between signing and closing

CASE ▼

Hayward v. Mellick (1984), 26 B.L.R. 156 (Ont. C.A.)

THE BUSINESS CONTEXT: The agreement between the buyer and the seller should include all terms and conditions that are important to them. A buyer should not rely on information outside the contract, even if the information comes from the seller or an agent. If the information is important, it should be included as an express term of the contract.

FACTUAL BACKGROUND: The Mellicks owned a farm that the Haywards were interested in buying. During negotiations, the Mellicks' agent told the Haywards that the farm contained a total of 94 acres, with 65 acres under cultivation, and Mellick confirmed the statement. The offer to buy described the farm as containing 94 acres but made no mention of acres under cultivation. The agreement contained a clause indicating that there were no conditions, representations, or agreements other than those expressly contained in the offer. The deal closed, and several months later, the Haywards discovered that there were only 51.7 acres of land under cultivation.

---

13. See the law of mistake in Chapter 8.
14. See the discussion of the *Statute of Frauds* in Chapter 8.

Normally, Universal would submit an offer to buy, and the seller would accept it or respond to it with a counteroffer, which Universal would then accept or vary, and so on until they both agreed unconditionally on all the terms. Only then would a contract exist.[15]

The Investigation

The second stage consists of the investigation by the buyer and the seller's response to any problems the buyer may raise.

The buyer must thoroughly investigate all aspects of the property during the search period allowed in the contract. Normally, Universal's lawyer will conduct various searches on Universal's behalf. These searches are described below.

title search
Investigation of the registered ownership of land in a registry system.

Title to the Property: Since this property is located in Nova Scotia, a **title search** in the local registry of deeds[16] may be needed. If this property has not been converted to the new system, the search normally goes back 40 years to ensure clear title. Any problems that can be fixed, such as an unregistered deed, will be remedied. If there is a more serious problem (e.g., someone else owns part of the land), Universal will have the option to pull out of the deal. The search will also reveal registered restrictions on use of the land such as restricted covenants or easements. If the land has previously been converted to the new system in Nova Scotia or if it were located in a land titles province, the search will not be necessary; Universal can rely on the certificate of title from the land titles office.

Legal Claims against the Seller: Searches should be done to establish what legal claims exist against the seller of the property in question. For example, judgments registered against the seller are valid for a number of years; the exact duration varies from jurisdiction to jurisdiction. Such a judgment can form the basis of a claim against any land owned by the seller—a matter that a prospective purchaser would

---

15. See Chapter 6.
16. *Registry Act*, R.S.O. 1990, c. R-20; R.S.N.S. 1989, c. 392. See also *Land Registration Act*, S. N. S. 2001, c. 6.

want to know about. Universal would not want to own a piece of land subject to such a claim because it would have less than clear title.

Verification of Boundaries: Universal will retain a surveyor to confirm that the boundaries described in the registered title fit the physical boundaries of the land. For example, if the title provides for 1000 metres of road frontage but the surveyor finds only 800 metres, there is a problem.

Physical Examination: Universal must confirm that the property is in the state it is expecting according to the agreement. If there are tenants in possession, Universal must confirm the space occupied by those tenants. Universal must also confirm the building's structural integrity, as provided for in the engineer's report. Excessive dampness and mould are also significant defects.

Environmental Audit: Universal must ensure that there are no lingering or hidden environmental hazards. For example, if the property was used at some time as a gas station, Universal must ensure that there is no leaked fuel in the ground, or abandoned underground tanks that might leak (see the Environmental Perspective below).

Taxes: Universal must be sure that the municipal property taxes and any other local charges related to the property are paid up to date. If they are not, they will be deducted from the total due to the seller at closing.

Local Bylaws: Universal must verify that the property can be used for its desired purpose. If buying land on which to build or using an existing building for a new purpose, Universal must be especially careful that the zoning regulations permit that activity.

- Any problems revealed by the various searches and investigations will be addressed according to the terms of the agreement. They will be fixed, or result in the renegotiation of the agreement or its termination.

Environmental Perspective
Responsibility for Contaminated Land

The permanence of land facilitates the tracking of ownership because land cannot be moved or hidden. One of the negative features of this permanence concerns the long-term effects of commercial activities that may be harmful to the land itself and the surrounding community. In terms of pollution to the ground from toxic substances or leakage of safe substances (such as gasoline), the legal issues concern liability for cleanup and for resulting harm to the environment and public health.

Scientific advances have altered the public view of some activities. Commercial activities that were acceptable even ten years ago may not be any longer. The difficult issue is how to allocate responsibility for the harm already caused. There is a huge risk in buying property with a long history of use for industrial purposes (i.e., how should such "tainted" property be valued, and should the buyer purchase it or not?). A purchaser could face a large bill to clean up contamination caused by previous owners.

Liability for contaminated land has become such a barrier to development that all three levels of government are taking measures to encourage redevelopment of brownfields, the term for "abandoned, idle or under-utilized industrial or commercial facilities where expansion or redevelopment is complicated by real or perceived environmental contamination." For example, Ontario legislation provides limited immunity from regulatory control after a site has been restored to specific standards. Municipalities are considering property tax relief for redevelopers. Environmental insurance is also available in such situations.

In the absence of these initiatives, the "polluter pays" principle is well established. The Supreme Court[17] recently confirmed the right of a provincial regulatory authority to order further cleanup of a contaminated site that had been sold, cleaned up, and developed, only to exhibit subsequent effects of the earlier pollution. The broad social issue is how to balance the need to encourage development and commercial activity with the need to control and prohibit dangerous activities.

CRITICAL ANALYSIS: Who should bear the cost of environmental protection: the businesses that generate profits or the public sector? What are the risks in encouraging redevelopment of land that may be contaminated?

Source: Dan Kirby, Shari Elliott, and Kate Dobson, "Insurance Is a Risk Management Tool for Brownfields" *The Lawyers Weekly* (5 October 2001) at 10.

The Closing

closing

The final stage of a real estate transaction when final documentation and payment are exchanged.

The third stage, the **closing,** occurs after all price adjustments have been made. At this point final payment is made and a formal transfer of ownership occurs.

If any difficulties found during the various searches can be remedied and Universal is able to get its mortgage, the closing will proceed after the price is adjusted for such items as prepaid taxes (added to the price) or rent already received from tenants (deducted). Universal will then make the final payment, and the seller will deliver the title document along with keys and other means of access to the property. Universal will then immediately register its title at the local registry office to ensure that no competing claims intervene to disrupt its ownership. If electronic registration is available, this risk is eliminated. At the moment of closing, Universal becomes responsible for the property. Universal must therefore arrange for insurance coverage to be transferred at that time as well.

FIGURE 19.1

Summary of a Real
Estate Transaction

Seller	Buyer
• decides to sell a piece of land	• decides to buy land
• determines the value of the land, possibly through a professional appraisal	• engages an agent to find suitable land
• engages a real estate agent to find a buyer and signs a listing agreement	• engages an appraiser to value the seller's land
• engages a lawyer to advise on the legal requirements	• engages a lawyer to advise on the legal requirements
• engages a surveyor to confirm boundaries	

Seller and Buyer
• negotiate, possibly with the assistance of their agents and their lawyers
• reach agreement on all terms and conclude a formal written agreement

---

17. *Imperial Oil Ltd. v. Quebec (Minister of the Environment),* [2003] 2 S.C.R. 624.

Seller	Buyer
• addresses any problems discovered through the buyer's investigation	• investigates all aspects of the property, including the seller's title and any outstanding claims • confirms the boundaries of the land by retaining a land surveyor • arranges for financing • has an engineer assess the structural soundness of the building • has a consultant investigate environmental soundness

Seller and Buyer (and/or their lawyers)	
• attend the closing	

Seller	Buyer
• delivers the title document • delivers the keys to the property	• makes final payment • registers the title document • arranges for insurance • moves in

Incomplete Transactions

A deal may fall through for a number of reasons, some of which the agreement will anticipate. For example, if there is a title problem that cannot be fixed or the buyer is unable to arrange financing pursuant to a conditional agreement, the buyer normally has the right to bow out of the deal. In other situations, the buyer or the seller may find a better deal and simply refuse to complete the transaction as required by the agreement. Refusal to complete for a reason not contemplated by the agreement is a breach of contract and entitles the party not in breach to a remedy. If the buyer backs out, for example, the seller must try to mitigate by finding a replacement buyer. In such circumstances, the seller may experience costs in finding a new buyer and may, in fact, end up selling the property for less than the defaulting buyer had agreed to. In such circumstances, the seller is entitled to recover the difference between these two prices from the defaulting buyer by way of damages for breach of contract. For example, if the defaulting buyer had agreed to buy the property for $200 000 and the seller is able to find a buyer for the property for only $150 000, the defaulting buyer is liable to pay damages to the seller in the amount of $50 000.

If the seller refuses to complete, the buyer is entitled to the extra expense in acquiring a similar property. If monetary compensation is not adequate, the buyer can claim for specific performance—a special remedy for situations in which the subject of the contract is unique and the buyer cannot be compensated with anything less than the property itself.[18] In contrast, if the contract involves the purchase of goods, such as a computer, or services, such as office renovations, and the supplier fails to deliver, the customer can find another source and be fully compensated by an award for the extra cost. The following case illustrates the remedies for breach of an agreement for the sale of land.

---

18. See Chapter 9.

Landmark Case ▼

Semelhago v. Paramedevan (1996), 197 N.R. 379 (S.C.C.)

THE BUSINESS CONTEXT: In this case, the Supreme Court of Canada dealt with damages for failure to complete a sale and challenged the traditional wisdom that breach of contract by the seller of land automatically entitles the buyer to specific performance.

FACTUAL BACKGROUND: Paramedevan agreed to sell land to Semelhago for $205 000 and later backed out. Semelhago sued for breach of contract, initially seeking an order for specific performance, but later chose to accept damages instead. By the time the trial took place, the market value of the property had increased to $325 000. Land owned by Semelhago at the time of contract had also increased in value from $190 000 to $300 000. Since Semelhago kept his existing property, he enjoyed the benefit of the increase in value.

THE LEGAL QUESTION: Should Semelhago's damages be based on the value of the property on the date of the breach of contract or the value on the date of the trial? Should the increase in the value of Semelhago's property be deducted from the damage award? Could Paramedevan have insisted on specific performance of the contract?

RESOLUTION: Justice Sopinka dealt with the amount of damages that would replace specific performance:

> The difference between the contract price and the value "given close to trial" as found by the trial judge is $120 000. I would not deduct from this amount the increase in value of the [buyer's] residence which he retained when the deal did not close. If the [buyer] had received a decree of specific performance, he would have had the property contracted for and retained the amount of the rise in value of his own property. Damages are to be substituted for the decree of specific performance.

The buyer ultimately recovered $120 000 less deductions for certain financing charges that he saved by remaining in his original property.

The court also discussed the right to specific performance:

> While at one time the common law regarded every piece of real estate to be unique, with the progress of modern real estate development this is no longer the case. Residential, business and industrial properties are all mass produced much in the same way as other consumer products. If a deal falls through for one property, another is frequently, though not always, readily available.

CRITICAL ANALYSIS: The Supreme Court of Canada said in this case that land is not automatically considered to be unique. The buyer must prove this fact in order to secure an order for specific performance. What are the features of a piece of commercial real estate that might make it unique?

The Real Estate Mortgage

How a Mortgage Works

If Universal requires financing to purchase the land, it may borrow or seek further investment in the company. In this chapter, a mortgage on the land itself is discussed.[19] Universal will approach potential lenders, usually banks or other financial institutions but possibly private lenders. Assuming that Universal has a good working relationship with its own bank and is creditworthy, the bank is likely to be the lender, provided that the parties can agree on such matters as the rate of interest and a repayment schedule.

---

19. See corporate financing in Chapter 15 and personal property security in Chapter 26.

A mortgage transaction has two aspects. First, a **mortgage** is a contract for the extension of credit and is a debt owed by Universal to its bank. The lender advances the principal sum to the borrower, who promises to repay the principal plus interest over the specified period. Second, the mortgage transaction also involves the bank taking a security interest in the land purchased by Universal. To attain this security protection, the bank must register the mortgage document, thereby giving notice to all creditors of Universal—as well as anyone considering purchasing the property from Universal—that the bank has first claim against the land. Registration gives the bank secured status, which will protect its claim against the land even if the borrower becomes bankrupt.

Any claims already registered against the land have priority over the new mortgage and will affect the bank's decision to grant the loan. The bank's mortgage does not forbid Universal from attempting to borrow more money in future using this land as security, but those subsequent lenders will be aware that the already registered mortgage forms a prior claim. There is no legal limit to the number of mortgages against a property, but lenders' security is subject to those who have previously registered mortgages. Each subsequent mortgage against the same land involves significantly greater risk for the lender.

Under the land titles system, registration of the mortgage creates a legal charge on the land. In short, the registered mortgage amounts to a claim—or lien—on the land until repayment is complete. In provinces under the registry system, in contrast, the mortgage actually transfers ownership of the land to the lender for the duration of the lending period. The bank becomes the legal owner, but Universal remains the equitable owner. This means that Universal has the **equity of redemption**—the right to have legal ownership restored to it upon repayment.

Although the effect of the mortgage on ownership varies according to the land registration system in place in the particular province, the practical effect on the use of the land is the same. Universal is the borrower, known as the **mortgagor.** Universal remains the occupier of the land, so there is no apparent change in control of the land. The bank as the lender is known as the **mortgagee.** As long as Universal makes the required payments on the loan, the bank is content to allow Universal to carry on normal business activities on the land.

equity of redemption
The right to regain legal title to mortgaged land upon repayment of the debt.

mortgagor
The party who borrows the money and signs the mortgage promising to repay the loan.

mortgagee
The party who lends the money and receives the signed mortgage as security for repayment.

Terms of the Mortgage

The focus of the mortgage is on preserving the value of the land in question. This protection is achieved by preventing the borrower from doing anything with the land that would lower its value and by giving the lender maximum flexibility in dealing with the borrower. For example, if the mortgagor does not adequately insure the property, the mortgagee (the bank) has the right to secure proper insurance and hold the borrower responsible for the cost.

The bank will not grant the loan unless it is confident of Universal's ability to repay. As a precaution, however, the amount of the loan is likely to be less than the current value of the land, for two reasons. First, the mortgage is a long-term arrangement, so the bank will consider the possibility of developments in Universal's business or the market that might diminish the value of the security. Second, if Universal defaults and the bank needs to use the security to recover its money, it is unlikely that the land will produce its full market value in a quick sale. A serious drop in the market could result in negative equity for the owner—that is, the amount owed on the mortgage could be more than the value of the property.

The mortgage document is normally prepared by the lender. Though each bank has its own standard form of mortgage, all of them include the following as basic terms:

- amount of the loan (known as the principal)
- interest rate
- date of renegotiation of the interest rate
- period of repayment over which the loan is amortized
- schedule of payments
- provision for payment of property taxes
- provision for full insurance coverage on the property, with the proceeds to be paid directly to the lender
- borrower's obligation to keep the property in a good state of repair and refrain from any activity that would decrease its value
- complete legal description of the land
- provision for early repayment (possible penalty)
- acceleration clause, which provides that on default of payment by the borrower, the whole amount of the loan becomes due
- remedies of the lender on default
- discharge (release) of the mortgage at the end of the term when the full loan is repaid

Of particular interest are the clauses dealing with taxes and insurance. The bank needs to be sure the taxes are paid because the appropriate municipal or provincial authorities have the right to sell the property to recover any unpaid taxes levied against the property. The land would then be owned by the purchaser at the tax sale and would not be available to the bank.

The bank's interest in insurance is twofold. First, the bank needs full coverage on the property so that if a fire occurs, the proceeds from the insurance will essentially replace the portion of the security destroyed by the fire. In addition, the bank needs direct access to those insurance proceeds. If paid to the borrower as the insured party, the money is more difficult for the bank to recover than the property would have been before the fire. As a result, the mortgage will contain a term assigning the insurance proceeds to the lender.

Life of a Mortgage

If the mortgage transaction proceeds as intended by both the borrower and the lender, the borrower will repay the loan as the mortgage requires and the lender's claim or charge against the land will cease. The lender will provide a document to release, or discharge, the mortgage. When this document is registered, it provides public notice that the borrower's obligations have been satisfied. However, since a mortgage is a long-term arrangement, many events can occur that result in some change to the liability, such as the following:

- Universal may choose to pay off the mortgage before it is due. The mortgagee will likely anticipate this possibility in the mortgage document and require Universal to pay a "penalty" or extra charge. This is to compensate the bank for interest it loses until it finds another borrower for the money lent to Universal.
- If Universal buys more land than it needs for its operation, it may choose to sell some of the excess. Since the mortgage forms a claim on all the land, Universal

needs to negotiate with the bank for a release of the piece to be sold. Only when this partial release is registered can Universal transfer clear title to that piece.

- Universal may need to renegotiate the mortgage for further financing. If the value of the land is well above the amount of the outstanding loan, the land could be used as security for an additional amount. This is a separate issue from the periodic renegotiation of the interest rate on the original loan. For example, the repayment period for the loan may be amortized—or spread out—over 25 years, with the interest rate adjusted every five years.

- Corporate takeover or reorganization may change the identity of the bank. The lending bank would assign all of its outstanding mortgages to the new entity. Universal must then make its payments to the new entity.

- Universal may decide to sell the land. This requires that Universal pay out the mortgage fully or negotiate with the buyer to take over or "assume" the mortgage if the terms are attractive. For example, if Universal has a lower interest rate than the current market rate, the lower rate could be used as a selling point by Universal. This "assumption" requires the agreement of the bank and likely entails a significant risk for Universal. When a mortgage is assumed, the original borrower—Universal—remains liable for payment. Hence, if the new buyer defaults under the terms of the mortgage, the bank can claim the balance owing from Universal.[20]

- Universal's business may suffer to the point where cash flow no longer allows for payments to the bank. This is the situation that the bank most fears and that the mortgage is primarily designed to address. Mortgagee's remedies are discussed below.

Mortgagee's Remedies

The bank is likely to give Universal some leeway in payment, especially if the bank is hopeful that Universal's business may recover. If this fails, the bank will proceed to exercise its legal remedies pursuant to the mortgage and applicable legislation. The rights of the lender and the procedures to be followed vary from province to province,[21] but all involve a combination of four remedies—suing the borrower, taking possession of the land, selling the land or having it sold, and **foreclosure.**

Foreclosure refers to the lender's right to terminate the borrower's interest in the property. It is the end of the process that allows the lender to realize the value of the land by selling it directly or through a court-supervised sale. Whichever procedure applies, the objective is to allow the lender to maximize the proceeds from the property to be applied against the outstanding loan. Most provinces[22] also permit the lender to proceed against the borrower for the shortfall—known as the **deficiency**—between the outstanding amount and the proceeds from sale of the property.

At any point before the foreclosure process is complete, the borrower is able to repay the loan and regain ownership of the land (assuming of course that another source of financing becomes available). If Universal cannot repay the loan, it loses the land and may be left owing a substantial debt. The bank is left with a bad debt

foreclosure
The mortgagee's remedy to terminate the mortgagor's interest in the land.

deficiency
The shortfall between the outstanding mortgage balance and the proceeds from sale of the land.

---

20. However, see *Citadel General Assurance Co. v. Iaboni* (2004), 241 D.L.R. (4th) 128 (Ont. C.A.) where the original mortgagors were not held responsible after they had sold their equity of redemption and the mortgage had been renewed without notice to them.
21. Sale by the court is preferred in Alberta, Saskatchewan, and part of Manitoba and is the only remedy in Nova Scotia. Otherwise, foreclosure by the mortgagee is allowed.
22. In Alberta, Saskatchewan, and British Columbia, the mortgagee cannot sue individual borrowers and can sue only corporations that have waived their statutory protection.

and the knowledge that the decision to lend the money was flawed. If there is more than one mortgage registered against the land, the remedies of the various mortgagees are more complicated. What remains clear is that each mortgagee's rights and remedies are determined in strict order of registration of the mortgages. As a result, mortgagees beyond the first are likely to recover less than those that registered ahead of them.

The Real Estate Lease

The Landlord-Tenant Relationship

Universal is currently in a landlord–tenant relationship because it is leasing its space. Universal is the **tenant.** The owner of the building that Universal occupies is the **landlord.** One of the options Universal is considering is whether to buy or build larger premises and lease the unneeded portion. If it proceeds on this basis, Universal will become an owner and landlord, and enter into a lease with someone else as tenant.

A **lease** is a contract between a landlord and a tenant. It records the rights and obligations of both parties. It is also an interest in land. Leases are of two general types—commercial and residential. The two types are significantly different in terms of the ability of the parties to negotiate their own terms, the rights and obligations in the lease, remedies, and enforcement mechanisms.

Residential leases are heavily regulated by provincial legislation[23] that

- prescribes the form and content of the lease
- limits the amount of security deposits that can be required of residential tenants
- defines the rights and obligations of the landlord and tenant
- requires the landlord to maintain the premises
- provides remedies for breach of the terms of the lease
- provides the procedures for resolving disputes

Commercial leases are relatively unregulated. The terms are negotiated solely by the landlord and tenant. They are free to agree on the format and content of the lease. If Universal were the owner of an apartment complex and an office building, the apartment lease would be under the residential regime and the office lease governed by commercial rules. The discussion that follows is geared mainly to commercial situations.

A lease is a means of dividing ownership of property for a time. Its key feature is the idea of **exclusive possession,** which means the tenant has a high level of control and responsibility over the premises during the term of the lease. This concept of exclusive possession is doubly important because first, it is the main factor in deciding whether a lease has been created to begin with and, second, it is the major consequence of the creation of a lease. For example, a five-year lease means that the tenant has the right to occupy and control the property for the full five years and cannot be legally evicted from the land unless the lease is violated by that tenant in a major way. If Universal, as landlord, enters into a long-term lease with a tenant and later wrongfully terminates that lease, Universal is in breach of contract and must pay damages to the tenant. Universal may also be subject to an order for specific performance or an injunction preventing the eviction of the tenant.

tenant
The party in possession of land that is leased.

landlord
The owner of land who grants possession to the tenant.

lease
A contract that transfers possession of land from the landlord to the tenant in exchange for the payment of rent; also refers to the tenant's interest in land.

exclusive possession
The tenant's right to control land during the term of a lease.

---

23. See, for example, *Residential Tenancies Act*, R.S.N.S. 1989, c. 401; *Residential Tenancies Act, 2006*, S.O. 2006, c. 17; R.S.M. 1987, c. L-70.

As with any contract, the parties need to appreciate the point at which they have achieved sufficient consensus to form a legal relationship. Each party wants terms acceptable to it and wants to obligate the other party to them. At the same time, the parties want to avoid unintentional obligations. An offer to lease or an agreement to lease becomes enforceable only if it contains all the key terms listed below and has been accepted by the other party.

In a commercial context, a number of factors will determine the lease content, including the relative bargaining positions of the parties and the nature of the market for the property in question. If suitable space is scarce, the landlord has the advantage and can largely dictate terms, especially the amount of rent. If there is a glut of property and the tenant is in no hurry to move from its current premises, the tenant may be able to negotiate concessions from the landlord.

Terms of the Lease

The complexity of the lease depends on the value, nature, and size of the property. A lease for an office tower is lengthy and complicated because there are many issues to address and a great deal is at stake. Conversely, a lease of a garage to store surplus equipment could be quite simple.

These are some basic terms in every commercial lease:

- identification of the parties
- description of the premises
- permitted alteration of the space by the tenant and what happens to the alteration when the lease ends
- ownership of improvements to the space
- calculation of rent (i.e., per square foot and/or based on sales)
- responsibility for repairs and maintenance to the leased space and any common areas

Parties in a commercial lease are free to negotiate their terms. What are some key terms in the lease of this building?

- security and damage deposits
- permitted uses of the space by the tenant
- limits on the landlord's ability to lease other space to the tenant's competitors
- time period of the lease
- provisions for renegotiation or renewal
- remedies for either party if the other fails to comply with the lease
- what happens in case of fire that damages the leased property and adjacent property owned by the landlord or others
- protection of the landlord in the event of the tenant's bankruptcy

Rights and Obligations

The rights and obligations contained in a commercial lease are formally known as covenants and consist largely of whatever the parties negotiate in the lease. Commercial leases vary significantly and must be reviewed closely in order to establish the rights and obligations of the parties. However, some covenants arise from the tenant's exclusive possession and corresponding responsibility:

- The tenant is responsible for repairs unless the lease imposes some obligation on the landlord.
- The tenant is entitled to exclusive and quiet possession of the premises for the full term. In return, the tenant must pay rent and observe the terms of the lease.
- The tenant cannot withhold rent, even if the landlord fails to meet a requirement in the lease. The tenant's remedy is to claim compensation from the landlord while continuing to pay rent.
- The tenant cannot terminate the lease and move out unless the landlord's breach of the lease has made the premises uninhabitable for normal purposes.
- Ordinarily, the tenant can assign the lease or sublet the property to another tenant. Assigning the lease transfers full rights for the remainder of the term. A sublease, in contrast, is an arrangement whereby the tenant permits someone else to occupy the leased premises for part of the time remaining in the lease. The original tenant remains fully liable under the lease but has rights against the subtenant—should the subtenant fail to pay the subrent, for example. It is common for the lease to require the landlord's consent for both of these arrangements. Such leases normally also provide that the landlord's consent may not be unreasonably withheld.[24]

The landlord's basic obligations are to refrain from interfering with the tenant's use or enjoyment of the property and to provide any benefits or services promised in the lease. The landlord's goal is that the tenant pay rent, use the premises for acceptable purposes, and cause no damage to the property. The major risk for landlords is that the tenants may get into financial difficulties. Thus, remedies for landlords focus on collecting unpaid rent and evicting tenants for defaulting on payment or for other serious breaches. Unlike the usual contract situation, a commercial landlord has no obligation to mitigate damages if the tenant abandons the premises. Commercial landlords also have the remedy of **distress:** if a landlord follows proper procedures, she can seize the property of the tenant located in the leased premises, sell the property, and apply the proceeds to the unpaid rent.[25] The following case deals with a dispute about the terms of a commercial lease.

distress
The right of a commercial landlord to seize the tenant's personal property for nonpayment of rent.

---

24. *Supra* note 1 at 265.
25. *Supra* note 1 at 272.

How can shopping mall leases deal with potential competition among tenants?

CASE ▼

Goodman Rosen Inc. v. Sobeys Groups Inc., 2003 N.S.C.A. 87

THE BUSINESS CONTEXT: This case illustrates the importance of the terms of a commercial lease, especially regarding the permitted activities of a tenant over the period of a long-term lease.

FACTUAL BACKGROUND: Sobeys signed a 25-year lease for space in a shopping mall in which to operate a supermarket. A clause in the lease stated, "… the Lessee shall use the Leased premises only for the purposes of the business of the retail sale of a complete line of food products, as well as general retail merchandising, as carried on by the rest of the majority of its stores." The lease also contained a covenant by the landlord not to permit any part of the mall to be used for the purpose of carrying on the business of the sale of food in any form. This noncompetition covenant was a fundamental term of the lease that, if breached, would entitle Sobeys to terminate the lease. Shortly after Sobeys opened its store in the mall, Shoppers Drug Mart leased space for 20 years

in which to operate a pharmacy. Shortly before the expiry of its lease, Sobeys opened a pharmacy within its supermarket as part of a corporate strategy to include a pharmacy in all of its stores. The landlord claimed that Sobeys' pharmacy was a violation of the lease and demanded that it be closed.

THE LEGAL QUESTION: Does the Sobeys' pharmacy violate the lease? If so, what remedy is available to the landlord?

RESOLUTION: The court interpreted the clause in question to allow the retail sale of goods, but not the sale of services. The professional services offered by a pharmacy are outside the meaning of "general retail merchandising." The court also found that pharmacies were not yet part of the majority of Sobeys stores and therefore not permitted on that basis. The court granted an injunction to the landlord ordering Sobeys to cease the operation of its pharmacy.

CRITICAL ANALYSIS: How can the language of a long-term lease provide for developments in retail operations? What is likely to happen at the end of the Sobeys lease?

Termination of the Lease

The parties may be able to terminate their relationship if the terms of the lease are not followed. Normally, the lease runs its natural course and ends when the agreed period for the tenant's occupation expires.

There are two types of leases in terms of time. One identifies the exact duration of the lease. If Universal's lease of its current space was for a fixed term of five years, which is about to expire, the lease will automatically end on the specified date. Neither party is required to give any notice, and neither party has any obligations to negotiate a renewal or extension. Therefore the landlord should realize that Universal is free to move, and Universal should realize that it has no right to stay beyond the specified date.

periodic tenancy
A lease that is automatically renewed unless one party gives proper notice to terminate.

The other type is known as a **periodic tenancy** and automatically renews itself unless one party gives the required notice before the current term expires. For example, if Universal has a lease from year to year, that lease will automatically be renewed for another full year unless either Universal or the landlord gives sufficient notice (likely about three months).

Which type of tenancy has been created depends on the actions and agreement of the parties. If they have not clearly indicated their intentions in the lease, a court will classify the lease based on their actions and other circumstances of the case. To avoid uncertainty, the parties should deal with termination in detail in the lease so that there is no doubt about the length, renewals, or the need for notice to terminate.

A lease as an interest in land is, in theory, not affected by the sale of the property by the landlord. The tenant is entitled to stay until the end of the lease with the new owner as landlord. However, long-term leases must be registered in some provinces, and in any event should be registered to give those investigating title clear notice of their existence.

Upon securing a new location, Universal's ability to terminate its current lease will depend on its terms and Universal's ability to negotiate with the landlord. If Universal chooses to lease a larger space (rather than buy), it needs to weigh the stability of a longer-term lease with the need to keep its expansion options open through a short-term arrangement. If Universal buys or builds a structure and leases part of it to a tenant, Universal should consider finding a tenant who is prepared to enter a periodic tenancy from month to month. This would permit Universal to regain full possession of the premises when the need arises. The disadvantage is that this may make the property less attractive to tenants unless their needs are short-term ones as well.

Disposition of Property

The owner of the fee simple in real property has total control over the disposition of ownership in that property. The options are as follows:

- Use the land as security for a loan by granting a mortgage. The owner remains in possession of the land and retains control, subject to the obligation to repay the debt and abide by the terms of the mortgage.

- Lease all or part of the land to tenants. The owner gives up possession for a defined period of time but retains ownership. At the end of the lease, possession reverts to the owner.

- Transfer the land to family or others by gift or through a will on death. There are various legal options available to the owner in terms of dividing ownership (such as a joint tenancy).
- Sell all or part of the land. This results in a complete transfer of the fee simple in the portion of land sold. Full ownership rights are transferred to the purchaser, who becomes the registered owner.

Risk Management

The major risk relating to real property is the complexity of the law. This chapter avoids many of the complexities that are beyond the scope of a basic text such as this one and provides an overview of the key aspects of the law. A businessperson entering a transaction to buy, lease, or mortgage land needs to obtain competent legal advice to guide her through the complications and ensure that her interests are adequately protected. Real property is largely a buyer-beware proposition in that those involved are expected to do their own thorough investigations before committing to a real estate transaction. Risk reduction is crucial.

Key commitments relate to contracts for the purchase or sale of land, the lease, or the mortgage. The language is inevitably complex and it is crucial for those involved to understand the language in some detail as well as the broader implications of the transactions. A buyer of land must ensure that the agreement contains all terms of importance. A landlord and tenant need to understand the degree of control that the lease provides for the tenant. One who signs a mortgage should understand the far-reaching rights enjoyed by the lender in the event of default.

In many situations, the bargaining power of the businessperson may be limited by financial need, the challenge of dealing with large institutions, or the fluctuations of the market. The ability to avoid, reduce, or transfer risk may be limited. What cannot be bargained can always be understood with the help of expert advice.

Business Law in Practice Revisited

1. What are the legal features of the various real estate options available to Universal?

A lease provides control of land for a limited period but is not ownership. It requires no purchase financing. Buying or building to meet current needs provides ownership and control, but requires financing and involves the expense and responsibility of ownership. Buying or building to provide for expansion involves the largest investment and is the most complicated. Universal will be owner of the entire property and landlord of the leased portion.

2. What factors should Universal consider in deciding how to expand?

Universal must consider the limits on ownership of land (such as zoning regulations) and the liability it entails (such as environmental damage). There is the financial risk in becoming a mortgagor (borrower) that the business will not produce sufficient income to pay the mortgagee (lender) and the mortgaged property could be lost. The temporary nature of a lease means that as tenant, Universal has no rights beyond the agreed term of its current lease. If Universal becomes a landlord of part of its new premises, it has no right to end the lease simply because it requires the leased space sooner than expected.

Of considerable importance to Universal's decision are the nonlegal factors such as its projected need for space, its financial stability, and the markets for real estate and Universal's products.

3. How could Universal use a mortgage to finance the expansion?

Universal can borrow on the security of the land under consideration for purchase. If a building is in place, the value of the land may be adequate security for a mortgage. If Universal buys vacant land on which to build, it is likely that additional assets will be required as security and shareholders may be called on to provide additional security from their personal assets.

Universal must be confident of its ability to make the mortgage payments. Default gives the lender significant rights in relation to the land.

Chapter Summary

Real property is permanent and immoveable, and the total quantity is fixed. The focus of the law is on the land itself rather than the buildings or fixtures attached to it. Ownership is called the fee simple and includes everything on, above, and below the land, subject to a wide variety of limits on use. The owner of land can transfer and divide ownership in a number of ways. Registration of any interest in land is required to preserve priority over other claimants. There are two systems of registration—registry and land titles—although most provinces are moving toward an electronic land titles system. The most common ways to acquire ownership are to purchase the fee simple through a real estate transaction or to become a tenant through a lease. In buying land, there is considerable risk involved, which can be managed through investigation of all aspects of the land.

A mortgage is security for a loan that emphasizes the preservation of the value of the property. A mortgage gives the lender the right to sell the land or have it sold if the loan is not repaid.

The landlord transfers to the tenant the right of exclusive possession of the land for the term of the lease. In return, the landlord is entitled to rent and has the right to regain possession at the end of the lease or earlier if the tenant defaults. The lease will end when a specified term expires or when one party gives the required notice to the other.

The holder of the fee simple can dispose of her interest as she chooses: lease the land temporarily, sell it, or give it away while she is alive or in her will upon death.

Chapter Study

Key Terms and Concepts

closing (p. 470)

deficiency (p. 475)

distress (p. 478)

easement (p. 461)

equity of redemption (p. 473)

exclusive possession (p. 476)

fee simple (p. 460)

fixtures (p. 459)

foreclosure (p. 475)

joint tenancy (p. 460)

landlord (p. 476)

land titles system (p. 462)

lease (p. 476)

mortgage (p. 473)

mortgagee (p. 473)

mortgagor (p. 473)

paralegal (p. 462)

periodic tenancy (p. 480)

real property (p. 459)

registry system (p. 462)

restrictive covenant (p. 461)

tenancy in common (p. 460)

tenant (p. 476)

title search (p. 468)

Questions for Review

1. What are the unique features of land as a form of property?

2. What is a fee simple?

3. What are the limits on an owner's use of his land?

4. How does a joint tenancy operate?

5. How can ownership of land be divided by time?

6. What is the purpose of registering title to land?

7. What are the two systems of land registration in Canada and how do they work?

8. What are the benefits of an electronic registration system?

9. What are the three stages in a transaction for the purchase and sale of land?

10. What should a buyer of land investigate?

11. What is clear title?

12. What happens at the closing of a property transaction?

13. What are the key features of a mortgage?

14. What are a lender's remedies if the borrower fails to make mortgage payments?

15. What are the essential terms in a lease?

16. What is the remedy of distress?

17. What is a periodic tenancy?

18. How can the owner of land dispose of his interest?

Questions for Critical Thinking

1. Land registration determines property rights strictly according to the order of registration, unless there has been fraudulent activity. Should the system allow for late registration in exceptional circumstances, such as when a buyer either fails to consult a lawyer or the lawyer neglects to register the documents? Can you think of other exceptional circumstances?

2. Title insurance companies provide their services at a lower cost than lawyers charge to represent clients on property transactions. Lawyers argue that clients are not fully covered by title insurance and the integrity of the registration system may suffer. Could the opposition of lawyers to title insurance be an attempt to protect their income? Which is more important, an accurate land registry or cheaper property transactions?

3. Real property law originated as a means of protecting rights to private property when land comprised the bulk of large estates. In today's society, other assets such as intellectual property have greatly increased in importance. Should protection of rights still be the prime purpose of property law, or are there more important public concerns?

4. In most cases, a lender has more expertise and experience in credit transactions. Do the rules of contracts and mortgages allow the mortgagee (lender) too much protection at the expense of the mortgagor (borrower)? Should the lender bear some responsibility for a decision to lend that turns out to be a bad one?

5. Residential tenancies are much more heavily regulated than commercial tenancies, largely to protect residential tenants from being exploited by landlords. Are residential tenancies too heavily regulated? Should commercial tenancies be more closely regulated? Should the market be the regulator?

6. There are many professional groups involved in real estate transactions. Their fees contribute to the high cost of transferring land. Are real estate transactions unduly complicated by the involvement of so many participants? Could such transactions be simplified?

Situations for Discussion

1. Janus owns a farm on the route for a new natural gas pipeline. He has been notified that the pipeline developer has the right to come onto his property to lay the pipe and to visit in future for pipeline maintenance. Janus thinks natural gas is a dangerous substance and sees the pipeline as a hazard for his farm and family. He is strongly opposed to the pipeline being anywhere near his farm. Is the pipeline a justified imposition on landowners such as Janus along its route? Should Janus be able to refuse permission to use his land? Should he be able to claim increased compensation for the use of his land because of his opposition to natural gas?

2. Campbell's business is in financial difficulty. Technology is advancing quicker than Campbell can move. She is faced with a gradual reduction in business operations and a related need for less space. She has 20 years left in the lease of her business premises, but cannot afford to pay the monthly rent. How should Campbell approach her landlord? What are her legal options? Is the situation different if Campbell owns her business premises subject to a mortgage on which she cannot make the payments? How should she approach her banker? What are her legal options?

3. Bayshore Trust granted a loan to Assam based on a mortgage for $210 000 with interest at 14 percent for a one-year term. The monthly payment was $2540. At the end of the term, Bayshore renewed the mortgage for another year at 14.5 percent. During that year, Assam defaulted and Bayshore sued Assam, who argued that Bayshore induced him into a state of financial disaster by granting a mortgage with monthly payments he could not possibly make. Assam alleged that Bayshore should never have lent him such a large sum of money. At the time of the mortgage, Assam's annual income was $28 000. He had vague plans to lease rooms in the property (which he never did).[26] Who should decide whether a lender such as Assam can make payments on a loan? Should Bayshore be required to do anything more than protect its own interest in the mortgage?

4. Jeanette bought a strip mall development with a 25 percent cash payment and a 75 percent mortgage. The total price was $400 000, and her monthly mortgage payment was $3000. Traffic past the mall did not meet the expected volume. Jeanette's major tenant defaulted on its lease and left. Jeanette sued for unpaid rent, but the lawsuit is dragging on. She was unable to keep up her payments on the mortgage, and the bank foreclosed. The mall was eventually sold for $200 000. Because the outstanding balance on the mortgage was $280 000, the bank is now suing Jeanette for the $80 000 shortfall plus its legal expenses. Jeanette believes that the property was worth much more than $200 000 and wants to attack the bank's conduct of the sale and avoid the claim against her. Has the bank acted properly? Could Jeanette have decreased her risk?

5. Hugh is interested in buying a property formerly used as a building supply outlet. When he investigates the land, he discovers that the adjacent property contains a former auto service centre with underground gasoline tanks. What is the risk to Hugh in buying the building supply land? How can he determine the extent of the risk? How should he deal with it?

6. Bresson bought a piece of land for commercial development for $3 million. He was assured that it contained an unlimited supply of water from an existing well. When construction began, it was discovered that the water was unusable due to a large cavity in the well and that half of the land was a bog covered with fill and unsuitable for building.[27] What investigation should Bresson have done before the deal closed? What can he do now? Was the seller obligated to disclose the state of the land?

7. Kelly was a major tenant in a commercial mall owned by Highway Properties (HP). The lease applied to space "to be used for [a] grocery store and super market" for 15 years. There was prescribed annual rent, payable monthly, with additional rent based on a formula. Kelly agreed to pay rent, taxes, and maintenance costs; to pay into a mall promotion fund; and not to do anything detrimental to insurance coverage. There were clauses dealing with renewal and repairs. The landlord (HP) promised quiet enjoyment. The lease permitted HP to resume possession after the rent was in arrears for 15 days by giving 15 days' notice. Kelly also agreed to carry on its business continuously for the term of the lease. The lease was signed on August 19, 2005. By the following February, there were only five other tenants in the mall. The Kelly store closed on March 24. HP commenced action against Kelly in July for failure to pay rent and for letting its premises "go dark." In September, HP resumed possession.[28] What damages have been suffered by HP? Are they limited to losses as of the date of termination of the lease, or do they include prospective damages for Kelly's failure to carry on business for the full term of the lease?

8. Greenwood rented office space to Evergreen for five years with an option for renewal of three or five years. In the second year of the lease,

---

26. Based on *Bayshore Trust Co. v. Assam*, [1992] O.J. No. 715 (Gen. Div.).
27. Based on *Bresson v. Ward* (1987), 79 N.S.R. (2d) 156 (Cty. Ct.); *Edwards v. Boulderwood Development* (1984), 64 N.S.R. (2d) 395 (C.A.).
28. Based on *Highway Properties Ltd. v. Kelly, Douglas & Co. Ltd.* (1971), 17 D.L.R. (3d) 710 (S.C.C.).

Greenwood informed Evergreen that it could not comply with its obligations under the lease beyond the end of the current year; Greenwood planned to demolish the building and erect a 21-storey office tower. Greenwood offered Evergreen preferential treatment in the new building when it was completed. Evergreen refused to move, claiming that the current building had architectural value and should be preserved. The lease did not include clauses dealing with demolition or the landlord's right to resume possession during the term of the lease.[29] How does this situation illustrate rights of ownership and landlord–tenant relations? How could the dispute be resolved?

For more study tools, visit
http://www.businesslaw3e.nelson.com

---

29. Based on *IBI Leaseholds Ltd. v. Evergreen Building Ltd.* (BCCA, Nov. 29, 2005), leave to appeal to S.C.C. granted 22 June 2006.

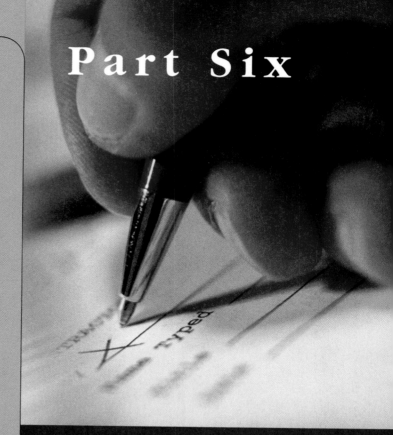

EMPLOYMENT AND PROFESSIONAL RELATIONSHIPS are essential components of business. Without the skills, knowledge, and experience of others, businesses would be unable to function and compete effectively. Most businesses require a wide range of services, including managerial, clerical, administrative, and professional services, which they acquire by hiring employees or by contracting for the services as needed.

The employment of others, whether through the employment relationship or through an independent service contract, has been affected by significant social change: the entry of women in large numbers into the workforce; recognition of the disadvantaged position of minorities; great awareness of the needs of people with disabilities; heightened public concern for the fair treatment of workers; adaptation to technological developments; and concern for job security. Not surprisingly, there has been much legal intervention to address these developments. In addition to the common law, a vast array of federal and provincial legislation affects all aspects of employment.

Employment and Professional Relationships

Chapter 20 The Employment Relationship

Chapter 21 Terminating the Employment Relationship

Chapter 22 Professional Services

Chapter

20

Objectives

After studying this chapter, you should have an understanding of

- the basic elements of the employment relationship
- the ways in which the law affects recruitment practices
- the content of a typical employment contract
- the legal issues relating to the terms and conditions of employment

The Employment Relationship

Business Law in Practice

Hiram Dupuis owns and operates an independent, weekly newspaper in southern Ontario. The newspaper has a circulation of 250 000 and focuses on mainly community news and human interest stories.

Several months ago Hiram engaged the services of Jeong Nash to write a column as well as feature stories on the local sports scene. Hiram refers to all of the reporters as independent contractors and permits them to accept writing assignments from other newspapers so long as they do not conflict with obligations to Hiram's newspaper. Hiram pays Jeong on the basis of a fee per word published as well as a base monthly salary of $3000. Hiram provides Jeong with office space and a computer and gives Jeong the freedom to pursue whatever stories she likes so long as they have a sports angle.

Recently Hiram learned that Jeong sent an e-mail message to a local sports celebrity requesting an interview. When the hockey player declined the request, Jeong sent him a nasty reply. In addition, Jeong posted possibly defamatory remarks about the hockey player on a website dedicated to hockey.

1. Is Jeong an employee or an independent contractor?
2. Why is the distinction between an employee and an independent contractor important?
3. Is Hiram responsible for Jeong's conduct?

Employment Law

The employment relationship is a critical component of business activity. Engaging the services of others provides the means by which a business can carry out its mission. Employment, however, is much more than an engine of business. It is a relationship that provides a livelihood for a large proportion of society. Given the importance of this relationship to both the employer and the employee, it is not surprising that there is a vast body of law regulating employment.

Employment law in all the Canadian jurisdictions, with the exception of Quebec, is rooted in the traditions of the English common law, with an overlay of legislation. Both the federal and provincial governments have jurisdiction to pass employment legislation, and both levels have been active in this area.

The federal government has jurisdiction to make laws affecting employees of the federal government and federally regulated industries, such as the banking, airline, broadcasting, railway, and shipping industries. It is estimated that about 10 percent of all employees are subject to federal regulation. The provincial governments have jurisdiction to make laws affecting all other employees, including provincial employees. For example, as the newspaper industry is not federally regulated, employees of newspapers come under provincial jurisdiction. An employee is subject to either federal or provincial jurisdiction, and it is not unusual for employees working in close proximity to be subject to different employment legislation.

Both levels of government have enacted human rights legislation and an array of employee welfare legislation, such as employment standards, occupational health and safety standards, and workers' compensation. In addition to legislation of general application, governments have passed legislation that affects employees in specific jobs. Public sector employees, such as police officers, teachers, medical personnel, and civil servants, are commonly affected by specific legislation.

Employees may also be unionized, in which case labour relations legislation is applicable to the employment relationship. The federal government and all of the provinces have enacted labour or industrial relations statutes that facilitate the unionization process.

This chapter focuses on laws that affect the employment process in the private, nonunionized sector, as the majority of employees fall within this category. At the end of the chapter, a note is provided on differences in the union environment.

The Employment Relationship

employment relationship
A contractual relationship whereby an employer provides remuneration to an employee in exchange for work or services.

The **employment relationship** involves a contract whereby one party, the employer, provides remuneration to another, the employee, in return for work or services.[1] Not everyone who works for another or provides services to another is an employee, however. In some situations, those who provide services are considered agents[2] or **independent contractors.** Usually, doctors and lawyers, for example, provide services in the capacity of independent contractors, rather than as employees of their patients/clients.

independent contractor
A person who is in a working relationship that does not meet the criteria of employment.

With the advent of "downsizing" and "right-sizing," people who traditionally worked as employees are increasingly working as independent contractors. The benefits for independent contractors are tax savings, flexibility, and independence in arranging a work schedule. An employer may prefer to engage independent contractors because the relationship offers simplicity and fewer financial and legal obligations.

Employee versus Independent Contractor

The distinction between an employee and an independent contractor is not always readily apparent. It is common to think of independent contractors as being short term and temporary, while employees are long term and permanent. In practice, this might be the case, but it is not a distinction based in law. Historically, the courts have used a variety of tests to distinguish between the two relationships, including the following:

- THE DEGREE OF CONTROL EXERCISED OVER THE INDIVIDUAL BY THE EMPLOYER. The more direction and supervision provided by the employer, the more likely that the relationship is employment. As Hiram exercises little control over how Jeong carries out her work, and permits her to pursue other assignments, this is indicative of an employer and independent contractor relationship.

- THE OWNERSHIP OF TOOLS, CHANCE OF PROFIT, AND THE RISK OF LOSS FROM PERFORMANCE OF THE REQUESTED SERVICE.[3] Sharing profits and losses and the ownership of tools is indicative of an independent contractor. On this basis, it appears as if Jeong is an employee because she does not own her own tools or share in the profits or losses of the business.

- THE DEGREE OF INTEGRATION. The nature of the work being performed is considered in relation to the business itself. The question is whether the work being performed is "integral" to the business, or is "adjunct" to the normal work of the business.[4] The more the work is integrated into the company's activities, the more likely it is that the individual is an employee. For example, Jeong's work is integral to the operation of a newspaper, therefore on this factor, she appears to be an employee.

1. The historical terms for employer and employee are "master" and "servant."
2. The law affecting agents is discussed in Chapter 13.
3. *Montreal (City of) v. Montreal Locomotive Works Ltd.* (1947), 1 D.L.R. 161 (P.C.).
4. *Co-operators Insurance Association v. Kearney* (1964), 48 D.L.R. (2d) 1 (S.C.C.).

The Supreme Court of Canada in the following case has indicated that there is no one conclusive test that can be universally applied. The nature of a relationship is a question of fact and will vary with the situation.

CASE ▼

671122 Ontario Ltd. v. Sagaz Industries Canada, Inc. (2001), 18 B.L.R. (3d) 159 (S.C.C.).

THE BUSINESS CONTEXT: Changes in the workplace—corporate restructuring, globalization, and employee mobilization—have resulted in a shift away from traditional employment relationships. However, as relationships have grown more flexible, they have also grown more complex, and the question of whether a relationship is that of an employer and employee or that of an employer and independent contractor is receiving increased attention.

FACTUAL BACKGROUND: A design company sold seat covers to Canadian Tire. However, it lost its contract with Canadian Tire to Sagaz because of the actions of American Independent Marketing (AIM), hired by Sagaz to assist in securing Canadian Tire business. AIM and its employee bribed an employee of Canadian Tire in order to induce Canadian Tire to buy from Sagaz. As a result, the design company lost a substantial amount of money and went into steep decline.

THE LEGAL QUESTION: Was Sagaz vicariously liable for the bribery scheme perpetrated by AIM?

RESOLUTION: Vicarious liability is a theory that holds one person responsible for the misconduct of another because of the relationship between them. The most common relationship that attracts vicarious liability is the relationship between employers and employees. The relationship between employers and independent contractors, subject to limited exceptions, does not give rise to a claim for vicarious liability.

There is no one conclusive test that can be universally applied to determine whether a person is an employee or an independent contractor. What must always occur is a search for the total relationship of the parties. The central question is whether the person who has been engaged to perform the services is performing them as a person in business on his own account.

The contract designated AIM as an "independent contractor" but this classification is not always determinative for the purposes of vicarious liability. However, as AIM was in business on its own account, it is an independent contractor. This conclusion is supported by the following factors: AIM paid all of its own costs of conducting its business; AIM was free to carry on other activities and to represent other suppliers; Sagaz did not specify how much time AIM was to devote to representing Sagaz; AIM worked on commission on the sales of Sagaz's products; and AIM controlled how the work was to be done.

CRITICAL ANALYSIS: The determination of whether a worker is an employee or an independent contractor is critical as employee status is the gateway to most employment protection under both the common law and employment-related legislation. What factors indicate the presence of an employer and employee relationship?

Implications of an Employment Relationship

Employees have certain statutory rights and benefits, such as paid holidays and paid overtime, that are not conferred on independent contractors. Employers have certain obligations with respect to employees, namely deduction of income taxes and employment insurance premiums, the payment of Canada (or Québec) Pension Plan premiums, the provision of paid vacations, and the like, which they do not have with respect to independent contractors. The consequences of incorrectly characterizing a work relationship as an independent contractor arrangement can include retroactive responsibility for paying benefits as well as liability for penalties and interest charges.

Establishing the employment relationship is important to certain legal principles. For example, an employee can initiate an action for wrongful dismissal, but this avenue is not available to an independent contractor. An employer is responsible for the tort of an employee committed in the ordinary course of employment, whereas an employer is not usually responsible for the torts of an independent contractor committed in the course of carrying out the contract.[5] An independent contractor, however, may be an agent for the employer, in which case the employer can be vicariously liable for the acts of the agent under traditional agency principles.

Risks in Hiring

The hiring of workers is critical to business. Hiring well can be a boon to a business, and hiring poorly can result in low productivity and possibly a costly termination. From a business perspective, hiring the candidate who is best suited for the job results in the optimal use of resources. From a legal perspective, hiring well can reduce the risks associated with the employment relationship, in particular those associated with vicarious liability and negligent hiring.

Vicarious Liability

As previously stated, an employer is liable for the torts of an employee committed in the ordinary course or scope of employment. An employee's wrongful conduct is within the ordinary course or scope of employment if authorized by the employer. Thus, an employer is liable when an employee commits a wrong while carrying out assigned duties or authorized tasks. An employee's wrongful act is also within the ordinary course or scope of employment if it is an unauthorized mode of doing something that is authorized by the employer. Because the distinction between an unauthorized "mode" of performing an authorized act and an entirely independent act is difficult to discern, particularly in the case of intentional torts, the courts will consider whether the tortious conduct of the employee is significantly related or connected to conduct authorized by the employer. In other words, the employer will be vicariously liable if there is a significant connection between the wrongful acts of the employee and the creation or enhancement of the risk of the wrongful act by the employer. For example, when Jeong posted the possibly defamatory statement on the website, she was not carrying out assigned duties or authorized tasks; therefore, her employer will be liable for her acts only if there is a significant connection between her possibly wrongful conduct and the creation or enhancement of the risk of the wrongful conduct by the employer. Although the possibly defamatory statements are connected to conduct authorized by the employer—Jeong was authorized by her employer to write feature stories on the local sports scene—it is entirely possible that Jeong acted outside the employment relationship in that she was responding in a personal capacity to a perceived affront. An employer is not responsible for wrongs that occur completely outside the employment relationship.

As noted in Chapter 10, the justifications for holding employers responsible for their employees' actions include

- Employers have the ability to control employees and therefore should be liable for the employee's conduct.

- Employers benefit from the work of the employees and therefore should be responsible for liability incurred by employees.

---

5. The distinction between an employee and independent contractor for purposes of vicarious liability is increasingly being called into question. For example, in *Thiessen v. Mutual Life Assurance* (2002), 219 D.L.R. (4th) 98 (B.C.C.A.), leave to appeal to S.C.C. refused, [2002] S.C.C.A. No. 454, the B.C. Court of Appeal imposed vicarious liability on an insurance company for the misconduct of a sales representative who was characterized as an independent contractor, not an employee.

- Employers are usually in a better position than employees to pay damages. Imposing liability on employers helps ensure that an innocent victim is compensated.
- Employers have an incentive to try to prevent torts from occurring in the first place.

The imposition of vicarious liability does not relieve the employee of liability. Both the employer and employee may be liable to the plaintiff. The employee may also be liable to the employer for breach of the employment contract; however, it is rare for an employee to pursue an action against an employee because of the inability of the employee to pay damages and the negative publicity associated with a legal action.

Negligent Hiring

Another potential risk for employers in the hiring process is in the area of "negligent hiring." An employer has a duty to use skill and care in hiring employees (the extent of the duty will vary according to the position the candidate is to fill).[6] Therefore, if an employee injures another employee or causes harm to a third party, there may be an action against the employer for being negligent in having hired that employee. This action differs from vicarious liability, which holds the employee strictly liable for the actions of the employee as long as the actions are sufficiently related to the employment. With vicarious liability, there is no requirement to prove that the employer was at fault. Negligent hiring, on the other hand, requires the plaintiff to prove that the employer was careless in, for example, hiring, training, or supervising.

The Hiring Process

The hiring process involves a number of steps. In hiring employees, employers would normally

- develop job descriptions
- advertise the positions
- have candidates complete an application form or submit a résumé
- short-list candidates
- check backgrounds or references
- interview selected applicants

All aspects of employment are affected by human rights legislation, and in some cases by employment equity legislation. The legislation may affect the kind of advertising done, the form the application takes, the questions that are asked in the interview, and the decision of whom will ultimately be hired.

Human Rights Requirements

Human Rights Commission

An administrative body that oversees the implementation and enforcement of human rights legislation.

The federal, provincial, and territorial governments have enacted human rights legislation[7] whose objective is to provide equal access to employment opportunities for all. To this end, discrimination in employment is prohibited. The acts also provide for the establishment of **Human Rights Commissions,** which are charged with administering the legislation and investigating and hearing complaints.

---

6. Stacey Ball, *Canadian Employment Law*, looseleaf (Aurora: Canada Law Book, 2006) at 20.66.1.
7. See, for example, *Canadian Human Rights Act*, R.S.C. 1985, c. H-6.

Prohibited Grounds of Discrimination

Human rights legislation does not prohibit all discrimination in employment, but only discrimination on certain prohibited grounds. There are variations from jurisdiction to jurisdiction as to what are prohibited grounds, but generally these grounds are similar (see Figure 20.1).

If a particular ground of discrimination is not included in the human rights legislation, the exclusion may be challenged as a violation of the equality provisions of the *Canadian Charter of Rights and Freedoms*. If the challenge is successful, the courts may "read in" the ground. For example, alcohol dependency is included in physical disability; pregnancy[8] and sexual orientation[9] are included in sex.

FIGURE 20.1

Prohibited Grounds of Discrimination

The following are prohibited grounds of discrimination under all Canadian legislation:

☒ marital status

☒ race

☒ colour

☒ physical or mental disability

☒ religion or creed

☒ sex

☒ age

Examples of other common grounds that are expressly included in some jurisdictions are national or ethnic origin, family status, social condition, sexual orientation, criminal record, ancestry, place of origin, language and linguistic origin, and political beliefs.

Business Application of the Law

Ending Mandatory Retirement

Mandatory retirement has existed in Canada since the 1950s. Although forced retirement at a particular age is discrimination on the basis of age, the practice has been defended on the basis that it is a reasonable limit on the equality rights of older persons—usually because of the importance of giving younger workers job opportunities. However, with slow population growth and an aging workforce, it is increasingly recognized that older workers are an important source of labour. As well, there is an increased sensitivity to the fact that productivity does not necessarily decline with age.

The provisions covering mandatory retirement vary from jurisdiction to jurisdiction. Quebec abolished mandatory retirement in 1982. Alberta, Manitoba, Prince Edward Island, Yukon, the Northwest Territories, and Nunavut have also abolished mandatory retirement. Exceptions are permitted for *bona fide* occupational requirements. Ontario is the most recent province to abolish mandatory retirement. The legislation, *Ending*

---

8. See Ball, *supra* note 6 at 33.62.
9. For example, in Newfoundland, sexual orientation was "read in" in *Newfoundland (Human Rights Commission) v. Newfoundland (Minister of Employment and Labour Relations)* (1995), 127 D.L.R. (4th) 694 (Nfld. S.C.T.D.). The Supreme Court of Canada decided, in *Vriend v. Alberta*, [1998] 1 S.C.R. 493, that sexual orientation is a prohibited ground of discrimination in all jurisdictions.

Mandatory Retirement Statute Law Amendment Act, 2005[10] took effect December 2006.

Both the legislatures of New Brunswick and Nova Scotia have introduced bills eliminating mandatory retirement. Although British Columbia, Saskatchewan, Newfoundland, and the federal jurisdiction permit mandatory retirement the trend is toward eliminating mandatory retirement. It is also noteworthy that the United States has abolished this practice.

CRITICAL ANALYSIS: Is ending mandatory retirement good for business? What are the advantages and disadvantages of mandatory retirement policies?

Source: Clarence L. Bennet, "Mandatory Retirement Still Remains in Atlantic Canada," *The Lawyers Weekly* (4 November 2005) at 16; and Morton G. Mitchnick, "What Are the Real Effects of Ontario's End to Mandatory Retirement?" *The Lawyers Weekly* (19 May 2006) at 10.

Discrimination Defined

discrimination
Treating someone differently on the basis of a prohibited ground.

The human rights acts prohibit **discrimination** but do not define the term.[11] The usual meaning is to treat someone differently on the basis of a prohibited ground. For example, to post an advertisement that says "Wanted: Malaysian workers for Malaysian restaurant" would be an act of discrimination because it discriminates on the basis of race. On the other hand, it is not discrimination to require job applicants to meet certain educational or training requirements.

adverse effects discrimination
Discrimination that occurs as a result of a rule that appears neutral but in its effects is discriminatory.

systemic discrimination
Discrimination that results from the combined effects of many rules, practices, and policies.

Not only is direct or explicit discrimination prohibited, but **adverse effects** and **systemic discrimination** are also prohibited. Adverse discrimination involves the application of a rule that appears to be neutral but has discriminatory effects.[12] For example, a rule that requires all workers to wear hard hats or to work every second Saturday appears to be neutral, but its effect may be to discriminate against those whose religion requires them to wear a turban or to refrain from work on Saturdays. Systemic discrimination refers to the combined effects of many rules, practices, and policies that lead to a discriminatory outcome.[13] For example, if a workforce is overwhelmingly dominated by male workers, this may mean that there is systemic discrimination.

Defences to Discrimination

bona fide **occupational requirement (BFOR)**
A defence that excuses discrimination on a prohibited ground when it is done in good faith and for a legitimate business reason.

There are situations where it is permissible to discriminate on one of the prohibited grounds. The most common defence to an allegation of discrimination is a *bona fide* **occupation requirement (BFOR);** other defences include approved affirmative action or equity plans, and group insurance and pension plans. A BFOR is a discriminatory practice that is justified on the basis that it was adopted in good faith and for a legitimate business purpose. For example, a requirement that a person have a valid driver's licence discriminates against some persons with physical disabilities, but a valid driver's licence is a BFOR for the job of truck driver. Similarly, the requirement of wearing a hard hat discriminates against those whose religion requires them to wear a turban, but the hard hat requirement may be a BFOR for those working in construction. BFORs have been subject to much controversy, as there is little consensus on what constitute legitimate, meaningful qualifications or requirements for job applicants. The Supreme Court of Canada in *Meiorin* set out a three-step test for determining whether a discriminatory standard qualifies as a BFOR.

---

10. S. O. 2005, c. 29.
11. Only the Manitoba and Quebec acts offer statutory definitions of discrimination.
12. *Ontario (Human Rights Commission) v. Simpson-Sears Ltd.* (1985), 23 D.L.R. (4th) 321 (S.C.C.).
13. *Action Travail des Femmes v. C.N.R. Co.* (1987), 40 D.L.R. (4th) 193 (S.C.C.) sub nom. *Canadian National Railway Co. v. Canada (Canadian Human Rights Commission)* (1985), 20 D.L.R. (4th) 668 (F.C.A.).

CASE ▼

British Columbia (Public Service Employee Relations Commission) v. BCGSEU (the Meiorin case), [1999] 3 S.C.R. 3

THE BUSINESS CONTEXT: Employers often implement physical performance standards or requirements for particular jobs. Standards are easy to apply and appear to be an objective or neutral basis for evaluating employees.

FACTUAL BACKGROUND: The province of British Columbia established a number of fitness standards for forest firefighters. Among the standards, which included sit-up, pull-up, and push-up components, was an aerobic standard. The aerobic standard required a firefighter to run 2.5 kilometres in 11 minutes. Tawney Meiorin, a three-year veteran of the service, was terminated from her job because she could not meet the standard. She needed an extra 49.4 seconds. Meiorin complained to the B.C. Human Rights Commission.

THE LEGAL QUESTION: Did the aerobic standard discriminate on the basis of sex?

RESOLUTION: The court held that the standard on its face was discriminatory, owing to physiological differences between males and females. Most women have a lower aerobic capacity than most men and cannot increase their aerobic capacity enough with training to meet the aerobic standard.

To justify the standard as a BFOR, the employer would have to show that

- the standard was adopted for a purpose rationally connected to the performance of the job;

- the standard was adopted in an honest and good-faith belief that it was necessary to fulfill a legitimate, work-related purpose; and

- the standard was reasonably necessary to the accomplishment of that purpose. To show that a standard was reasonably necessary, it must be demonstrated that it is impossible to accommodate individuals affected by the discriminatory standard without imposing undue hardship upon the employer.

Applying the approach, the court concluded that passing the aerobic standard was not reasonably necessary to the safe and efficient operation of the work of a forest firefighter. The government had not established that it would experience undue hardship if a different standard were used. In other words, the employer failed to establish that the aerobic standard was reasonably necessary to identify those who are unable to perform the tasks of a forest firefighter safely and efficiently.

CRITICAL ANALYSIS: The onus of proving that a standard, requirement, or qualification is a BFOR lies with the employer. What issues will the employer have to address in order to establish a BFOR?

Tawney Meiorin with lawyer John Brewin

duty to accommodate
The duty of an employer to modify work rules, practices, and requirements to meet the needs of individuals who would otherwise be subjected to unlawful discrimination.

The test in *Meiorin* incorporates a **duty to accommodate** the special needs of those who are negatively affected by a requirement, up to the point of undue hardship for the employer. This means, in effect, that employers when designing standards, requirements, and the like must consider the need for individual accommodation. This approach to accommodation has been confirmed and expanded on by the Supreme Court of Canada.[14]

---

14. *British Columbia (Superintendent of Motor Vehicles) v. British Columbia (Council of Human Rights),* [1999] 3 S.C.R. 868.

However, it remains an open question as to what constitutes undue hardship and how far an employer must go to accommodate special needs. Factors such as the size of the organization, its financial resources, the nature of operations, the cost of the accommodation measures, the risk the accommodation measures will pose to the health and safety of the employee and his colleagues and the public, the effect of the accommodation measure on other employees and the productivity of the organization have all been taken into consideration by courts in assessing the scope of the employer's duty.[15]

Penalties

Failure to avoid or eliminate discriminatory practices can result in a complaint to the Human Rights Commission. This, in turn, can result in a board of inquiry investigating the complaint. If the board finds the complaint to be valid, it can order that the employer stop its practices, hire a particular individual, pay monetary compensation, write a letter of apology, reinstate an employee, or institute an affirmative action plan. Regardless of the outcome, a complaint may result in unwelcome publicity, expenditures of time and money to answer the complaint, and an unsettled work environment. To reduce the risk of a human rights complaint, an employer needs to review all aspects of the employment process. The following box provides some examples of ways to reduce the risks.

Business Application of the Law

Avoiding Discrimination in Hiring Practices

A human rights complaint can be a costly and embarrassing situation for a company. Each step of the hiring process should be reviewed to ensure that the company is not discriminating.

JOB DESCRIPTION

Do develop a list of job-related duties and responsibilities.

Don't describe job openings in terms of prohibited grounds (e.g., busboy, hostess, policeman, waitress).

ADVERTISEMENTS

Do advertise for qualifications related to ability to do the job.

Don't advertise for qualifications unrelated to ability to do the job (e.g., single, Canadian-born, young, tall, slim).

APPLICATION FORMS

Do solicit information that is related to the applicant's ability to do the job.

Don't ask for information that suggests prohibited grounds are being considered; for example, age, sex, photograph, or title (Miss, Ms., Mr., Mrs.).

INTERVIEW

Do ask questions related to the applicant's suitability for the job.

Don't ask questions related to prohibited grounds (e.g., Are you planning to start a family? Do you have any physical disabilities (unless the requirement to not have the disability is a *bona fide* occupational requirement)? Have you ever been treated for a mental illness? How old are you? What church do you attend? What is your mother tongue? Have you ever received income assistance?).

An employer should provide human rights training for supervisors and other employees and also develop policies prohibiting discrimination. Employees need to be made aware of the policies.

CRITICAL ANALYSIS: Why should employers be so constrained in the hiring process?

Source: "Pre-Employment Enquiries," *The New Brunswick Human Rights Commission*, at http://www.gnb.ca/hrc-cdp/e/inquire.htm#questions (accessed 2 December 2006).

---

15. Ontario's *Human Rights Code*, R.S.O. 1990, c. H-19, s. 7(2) restricts the criteria to the cost, outside sources of funding, and health and safety requirements.

Employment Equity

employment equity legislation
Laws designed to improve the status of certain designated groups.

Employment equity may also affect hiring decisions. Employment equity attempts to achieve equality in the workplace by giving underrepresented groups special consideration in hiring. Human rights legislation prohibits discrimination; **employment equity legislation** requires employers to take positive steps to make the workplace more equitable.

The federal *Employment Equity Act*[16] targets the underrepresentation of women, Aboriginal peoples, people with disabilities, and visible minorities in the workforce. The act, which is administered by the Canadian Human Rights Commission,[17] applies to businesses that have 100 or more employees and that are under the regulation of the federal government. It requires employers to

- consult with employee representatives regarding the implementation of employment equity
- identify and eliminate barriers to the employment of the designated groups
- institute policies and practices and make reasonable efforts at accommodation to ensure that the designated groups have a degree of representation in the portion of the workforce from which the employer can reasonably be expected to draw employees
- prepare a plan that sets out the goals to be achieved and a timetable for implementation

There has been much debate about whether such programs are a form of reverse discrimination. The equality provisions of the *Charter of Rights and Freedoms* specifically permit such programs; however, the programs are not insulated from claims of discrimination. The Supreme Court of Canada has stressed that government programs targeted at disadvantaged groups are not immune from challenges of being "underinclusive" or claims that they contravene the right of equality.[18]

None of the provincial jurisdictions has legislation in this area.[19] However, many employers have their own voluntary employment equity programs. As well, the federal government has a nonlegislated federal contractors program. This program seeks to ensure that all contractors that have 100 or more employees and are bidding on federal contracts worth more than $200 000 achieve and maintain a fair and representative workforce.

Formation of the Employment Contract

During the negotiations leading to an offer of employment, a lot of information is exchanged. In many cases disputes have arisen upon termination, based on representations in the negotiations leading up to the offer. There may have been pre-hiring promises, or representations made concerning the nature of the employment that did not materialize. On termination, the employee may be able to allege breach of oral promises, as *Queen v. Cognos* illustrates.

---

16. *Employment Equity Act*, S.C. 1995, c. 44.
17. The Canadian Human Rights Commission was given the role of enforcing the legislation in 1996. Information on the Employment Equity Branch of the Commission can be obtained at http://www.chrc-ccdp.ca
18. *Lovelace v. Ontario*, [2000] 1 S.C.R. 950.
19. The only provincial government to pass legislation in this area was Ontario. However, its legislation, passed in 1993 by an NDP government, was repealed in 1996 after the Progressive Conservative Party took power.

Offer of Employment

After employers have recruited job applicants, interviewed them, and checked their references, the next step is usually an offer of employment. The offer normally comes from the employer to the employee, but there is no legal requirement that it must.

CASE ▼

Queen v. Cognos Inc. (1993), 99 D.L.R. (4th) 626 (S.C.C.)

THE BUSINESS CONTEXT: A company seeking to attract the most qualified candidate may sometimes oversell itself or the job. Promises and representations are often freely made.

FACTUAL BACKGROUND: Douglas Queen was hired by Cognos to help develop an accounting software package. Queen was told by an employee of Cognos that the project would run for a number of years and would be well funded. Based on these representations and a signed employment contract, Queen quit a secure job in Calgary and moved to Ottawa. About two weeks later, the company shifted funding into a different product. Queen was kept on for 18 months, during which time he had a number of fill-in jobs. After being dismissed, he brought an action against Cognos for negligent misrepresentation. He claimed that he would not have accepted the position had it not been for the representations about the scope and viability of the job.

THE LEGAL QUESTION: Does an interviewer owe a duty of care to a prospective employee?

RESOLUTION: The Supreme Court of Canada held that an interviewer has a duty to take reasonable care to avoid making misleading statements. Here, the interviewer failed by misrepresenting the security of the job. Although the contract Queen signed had a disclaimer that allowed the company to reassign or dismiss him, the disclaimer did not save the company from liability for making false promises about the job. Cognos was required to pay damages for Queen's loss of income, loss on the sale of his house in Calgary and the purchase of his house in Ottawa, emotional stress, and expenses incurred in finding a new job.

CRITICAL ANALYSIS: False promises or misunderstandings in the recruitment process can be devastating for the employee and costly for the employer. What steps can an employee take to protect himself? What steps can an employer take to protect itself?

Like offers in other types of contracts, the offer must be reasonably certain to constitute an "offer" in law. Thus, the statement, "We would like you to work for us" is not considered an offer, as it does not define the job, remuneration, or any of the other terms of employment. The offer, however, need not be in a particular form or in writing. As long as the statements are reasonably complete and certain, casual comments may be considered offers. Once made, the offer is capable of acceptance until it is terminated. Therefore, an offer of employment made to two candidates could result in two acceptances and two employment contracts for the one job. Offers should have time limits so that there are no problems with ascertaining when the offer expires.

Prior to making an offer, the employer should determine whether the candidate has any obligations to her most recent employer. These obligations may impede her ability to perform the job and could result in legal action against the new employer, such as in the following ways:

- **INDUCING BREACH OF CONTRACT.** If the newly hired employee breaks an existing employment contract in order to accept an offer, the former employer may sue the new employer for the tort of "inducing a breach of contract."[20]

---

20. The tort of inducing breach of contract is discussed in Chapter 12.

- **RESTRICTIVE COVENANTS.** It is also not uncommon for employment contracts to contain restrictive covenants limiting the former employee's ability to compete against the former employer. The contract may seek to restrict the solicitation of customers and employees or the use of confidential information, for example. These restrictions are particularly common in industries in which businesses are highly dependent on customer contacts or skilled employees, and there is a lot of confidential information and trade secrets.[21]

- **FIDUCIARY OBLIGATIONS.** A potential employee may also be considered to be in a "fiduciary" relationship with his former employer. Whether or not an employee is a fiduciary will be determined by the position held by the employee, the employee's duties and responsibilities, the nature of the business, and the organizational structure. Generally, only senior employees are considered to be in this relationship, but there does appear to be support for broadening the scope of the definition to include any "key" employee.[22] A finding of a fiduciary relationship may mean that such employees are prohibited from soliciting customers from their former employer and from taking advantage of business opportunities discovered through the former employer.[23]

Ethical Considerations

When Employees Leave

In January 2005, the Canadian Imperial Bank of Commerce (CIBC) launched a lawsuit against a number of its former employees and Genuity Capital Markets. CIBC is seeking damages in excess of $10 million. CIBC alleges a variety of transgressions including the theft of client information and the solicitation of its employees. CIBC alleges that the former CEO of CIBC World Markets (CIBC terminated the CEO in February 2004) and others set up a competitor, Genuity Capital, while still employed with CIBC. In less than a year, a total of over 20 senior employees of CIBC left to join Genuity. The allegations are supported by copies of numerous BlackBerry messages exchanged by the defendants in the summer of 2004. Since CIBC filed its suit, the defendants have counterclaimed for $14 million, alleging that the bank breached the privacy of the defendants by going through their e-mail. Further, the former CEO has stated that he was not restricted by any agreement from competing with CIBC.

CRITICAL ANALYSIS: Assuming that the former CEO was not restricted by any agreement from competing with CIBC, does that exonerate him from liability?

What can companies like CIBC do to avoid similar situations? What steps can an employer take to minimize the risks associated with the loss of employees and intellectual assets such as client lists, business strategies and the like?

Source: Andrew Willis, "CIBC sues 6 former Employees" *The Globe and Mail* (6 January 2005) at B1; and Marjo Johne, "How to Cover your Assets" (August 2005) at http://www.e2rsolutions.com/05%2008%20The%20Bay%20Street%20Bull.pdf (accessed 2 December 2006).

What obligations do departing employees owe to their ex-employers?

21. The enforceability of restrictive covenants in contracts is discussed in Chapter 8.
22. See *Canadian Aero Service Ltd. v. O'Malley*, [1974] 1 S.C.R. 592.
23. Confidential business information is discussed in Chapter 18.

The Employment Contract

fixed- or definite-term contract

A contract for a specified period of time, which automatically ends on the expiry date.

indefinite-term contract

A contract for no fixed period, which can end on giving reasonable notice.

The employment relationship is contractual. The contract may be for a specified period of time, in which case the contract is known as a **fixed- or definite-term contract.** The contract, however, need not specify any period of time. Contracts such as these are known as **indefinite-term contracts.** The distinction is particularly important with respect to termination.[24] Historically, most employment contracts were indefinite, but term contracts are becoming more common. The contract may be oral or in writing,[25] but most commonly it is written.

Express and Implied Terms

Whether it is oral or in writing, the contract may include express terms and implied terms.[26] Express terms are those that have been actually agreed upon by the parties. They are included in the contract or incorporated by reference. Benefits packages, job descriptions, and company rules and policies are often in separate documents and included by reference. Implied terms are those that have not been specifically agreed upon by the parties but are what the courts believe the parties would have agreed to, had they sat down and negotiated the point. Employment is an area where traditionally there have been a great many implied terms. For example, if the parties do not specify the duration of the contract, it is implied that the contract is for an indefinite period of time. Therefore, the contract does not come to an end until one of the parties gives notice of termination. This term leads to another implied term that the notice of termination must be reasonable.[27]

Content of the Contract

Most employers and employees now see the need to introduce certainty into the employment relationship by putting their relationship into writing.

Besides the advantage of certainty, a written employment contract offers other advantages, including a forum for negotiating terms and conditions that are tailored to the situation—notice periods, restrictive covenants, and limitation of precontractual promises, to name a few (see Figure 20.2). Written terms will override terms that are implied at law.

FIGURE 20.2

Essential Content of an Employment Contract

An employment contract should contain the following information:

- ✔ names of the parties
- ✔ date on which the contract begins
- ✔ position and description of the work to be performed
- ✔ compensation (i.e., salary, wages, bonuses)
- ✔ benefits (i.e., vacation, vacation pay, health and dental plans, pensions, etc.)
- ✔ probation period, if any
- ✔ duration of the contract, if any

---

24. For example, if an employee's contract is classified as indefinite term, the employee is entitled to the common law protection of reasonable notice of termination. By contrast, if the contract is classified as fixed term, then the contract ends when the fixed term expires without the requirement of notice.
25. Writing requirements are discussed in Chapter 8.
26. Implied terms in contracts are discussed in Chapter 7.
27. Notice and termination are discussed in Chapter 21.

- ✓ evaluation and discipline procedures

- ✓ company policies or reference to employee policy manual

- ✓ termination provisions (i.e., cause for dismissal, notice of termination, severance package)

- ✓ recital of management rights (i.e., employer has a right to make changes to job duties and responsibilities)

- ✓ confidentiality clause, if appropriate

- ✓ ownership of intellectual property, if appropriate

- ✓ restrictive covenants, if any

- ✓ "entire agreement" clause (i.e., the written contract contains the whole agreement)

Written employment contracts provide a mechanism for employers to address concerns about employees leaving. Although employers cannot prevent their employees from leaving, they can negotiate for reasonable terms in the contract that prohibit the employees from working for competitors for a period of time or from revealing confidential information. More important is providing favourable working conditions so that employees are disinclined to leave.

Terms and Conditions

The ability of an employer and an employee to negotiate their contract has been abrogated to some extent by legislation designed to protect the employee. The terms of the employment contract are affected by legislation, and so are the conditions of employment.

Employee Welfare Issues

Employment Standards

employment standards legislation
Laws that specify minimum standards in the workplace.

All the provinces and territories, as well as the federal government, have **employment standards legislation** (also sometimes called labour standards legislation) that sets out minimum standards in the workplace. This legislation has often been referred to as the collective agreement for nonunionized employees. An employer may provide greater benefits than those provided for in the legislation but not lesser. In short, any contractual provisions that provide lesser benefits than those set out in the legislation are not enforceable.

There are variations in the legislation from jurisdiction to jurisdiction. Most, however, cover the same general categories of benefits. A sampling of typical standards follows:

- ▪ HOURS OF WORK AND OVERTIME. Hours of work that an employee can be asked to work vary from 40 to 48. Overtime is usually paid at 1.5 times the employee's regular wages. In some provinces it is paid at 1.5 times the minimum wage.

- ▪ MINIMUM WAGE. The minimum wage is usually set on an hourly basis. For example, in New Brunswick,[28] the minimum wage is $7.00 per hour.

---

28. N.B. Reg. 2006-40.

- **VACATIONS AND VACATION PAY.** The length of paid vacation that an employee is entitled to usually depends on the amount of service. For example, in Alberta,[29] an employee is entitled to two weeks after one year of employment, and three weeks after five years.

- **TERMINATION AND SEVERANCE.** The legislation normally provides for notice and severance pay. For example, in British Columbia,[30] an employee is entitled to one week's notice after three months, two weeks after 12 months, three weeks after three years, and one additional week for each additional year of employment, to a maximum of eight weeks.

- **STATUTORY (PAID) HOLIDAYS.** Every jurisdiction requires that employers pay employees for specific public holidays. For example, in Newfoundland,[31] employees are entitled to New Year's Day, Good Friday, Canada Day, Labour Day, Christmas Day, and Remembrance Day.

- **BEREAVEMENT AND SICK LEAVE.** All jurisdictions have provisions for leaves, either paid or unpaid for various reasons. For example, the federal jurisdiction[32] provides for 12 weeks of sick leave after three months of employment.

- **MATERNITY AND PARENTAL LEAVE.** Every jurisdiction provides for pregnancy leave after a minimum amount of service. For example, in Manitoba,[33] an eligible person is entitled to 17 weeks' maternity leave after seven months of service. Most provinces provide parental leave for eligible persons.

Other typical standards include equal pay for equal work, prohibitions against sexual harassment, prohibitions against the employment of children, and various leave provisions such as court and family emergency.

Certain employees, such as doctors, lawyers, farmers, domestic workers, construction workers, and information technology professionals, may not be covered by the legislation or may be exempt from certain provisions, such as hours of work, minimum wages, and overtime pay.

The legislation also provides a mechanism for enforcing employment standards. In Ontario, for example, employment standards officers, employed by the Employment Standards Branch, investigate complaints, carry on general investigations, and, when necessary, issue orders requiring compliance with provisions of the *Employment Standards Act*.

Safety and Compensation

Workers' compensation legislation is designed to address accidents and injuries in the workplace. It provides for a type of no-fault insurance scheme. Employers are required to pay into a fund, and workers who have job-related injuries, accidents, or illnesses are compensated from the fund, regardless of fault. Compensation covers lost wages, medical aid, and rehabilitation. The scheme prevents a civil suit by the employee against the employer relating to a workplace injury or accident. Not all employees, accidents, or illnesses are covered by the legislation, however. Illness must be job related, which is not always easy to determine, particularly as the causes of many illnesses are unclear and the illnesses themselves can take decades to develop.

All jurisdictions have enacted comprehensive occupational health and safety legislation that generally applies to all sectors of the economy. In addition to general provisions, there are industry-specific provisions and hazard-oriented provisions. The

---

29. *Employment Standards Code*, R.S.A. 2000, c. E-9, s. 34.
30. *Employment Standards Act*, R.S.B.C. 1996, c. 113, ss. 63 (3).
31. *Labour Standards Act*, R.S.N. 1990, c. L-2, s. 14(1).
32. *Canada Labour Code*, R.S.C. 1985, c. L-2, s. 239(1).
33. *The Employment Standards Code*, R.S.M. 1987, c. E-110, ss. 53, 54(1), 58(1).

purpose of the legislation is to protect workers in the workplace by giving them a right to participate in safety issues, a right to know about hazards in the workplace, and a right to refuse to work in unsafe conditions.

Also, the *Criminal Code of Canada*[34] has been amended to impose a new legal duty on organizations and individuals to protect the health and safety of workers.[35]

Business Application of the Law

Criminal Liability for Health and Safety Violations

In August 2004, 68-year-old Domenico Fantini, a supervisor at a construction site in King Township, Ontario, became the first person charged under amendments to the *Criminal Code* that created a new legal duty on all organizations and their representatives to take every reasonable step to protect workers. Fantini was charged with criminal negligence causing death after the driver of a mini-excavator was fatally crushed while working in an unsupported trench on a project to install weeping tiles in the basement walls of a house. The criminal charge against Fantini was withdrawn after he pleaded guilty to three occupational health and safety offences (failing to ensure that a worker did not enter an excavation that was not properly shored

or sloped, failing to ensure that a worker was wearing protective headgear, and failing to ensure the worker was wearing protective footwear). He was also assessed a $50 000 fine.

CRITICAL ANALYSIS: The withdrawal of the criminal charge has created uncertainty about the extent to which the amendments will be applied and enforced. Why do you think the criminal charges were withdrawn? How should employers respond to the risks imposed by the criminalization of careless conduct that causes injury or death?

Source: "Criminalizing the Careless Employer" *The Canadian Lawyer* (2005 July) at 38.

Employee Economic Safety

Two legislative schemes in the area of employee economic safety are employment insurance and the Canada and Quebec pension plans.

The *Employment Insurance Act*[36] is federal legislation that applies to both the federally and provincially regulated sectors. The basic concept of employment insurance is that the employer and employee contribute to a fund that provides insurance against loss of income. The plan provides benefits for unemployment, maternity and parental leave,[37] and sickness, as well as some retirement benefits. A limited number of employees are not covered by the scheme. The most common exclusions are casual workers, some part-time workers, and those employed in agriculture.

The *Canada* (and Quebec) *Pension Plan*[38] is an insurance plan designed to provide pensions or financial assistance in the case of retirement, disability, or death. Both the employer and the employee contribute to the plan.

---

34. R.S.C. 1985, c. C-46, s. 217.1 provides; "Everyone who undertakes, or has the authority, to direct how another person does work or performs a task is under a legal duty to take reasonable steps to prevent bodily harm to that person, or any other person, arising from that work or task."
35. See also c. 16 (Business and Legislation: Extending criminal Liability) for a discussion of the amendments.
36. S.C. 1996, c. 23. The act was formerly known as the *Unemployment Insurance Act* but was renamed in 1996 as part of a general reform package. It covers provincial sectors as a result of a specific amendment to the Constitution.
37. The act was amended in 2000 to provide up to 50 weeks of insurable benefits for employees on pregnancy and parental leave.
38. R.S.C. 1985, c. C-8.

Workplace Discrimination

Discrimination on certain grounds is prohibited in all aspects of employment, including promotions and terminations. One aspect of discrimination that has received a great deal of attention is workplace harassment, including sexual and racial harassment that occurs in the workplace.

Workplace Harassment

An anti-harassment policy addresses inappropriate behaviour in the workplace. What should the policy contain?

Human rights legislation, in both the federal and provincial jurisdictions, prohibits harassment. For example, the *Canadian Human Rights Act* section 14(1)[39] provides "It is a discriminatory practice ... (c) in matters related to employment, to harass an individual on a prohibited ground of discrimination." In addition, employment standards legislation often protects employees from harassment, particularly sexual harassment, and the *Criminal Code* protects people from physical and sexual assault.

Harassment is defined as any unwanted physical or verbal behaviour that offends or humiliates the victim and detrimentally affects the work environment or leads to adverse job-related consequences for the victim. Such conduct can take many forms including threats; intimidation; verbal abuse; unwelcome remarks or jokes about race, religion, sex, disability, or age; the display of sexist, racist, or other offensive pictures; sexually suggestive remarks or gestures; unnecessary physical contact, such as touching, patting, pinching, or punching; and physical assault including sexual assault.[40]

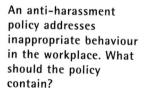

Business and Legislation — Bullying at Work

Complaints of psychological harassment, hostile work environment and bullying are becoming commonplace in the workplace.[41] Typical bullying behaviour involves teasing, swearing or yelling, calling names, criticizing and threatening. For the most part, Canadian legislation does not specifically address these complaints.

Quebec has become the first North American jurisdiction to adopt specific statutory provisions aimed at preventing psychological harassment in the workplace. Effective 1 June 2004 amendments to the province's labour standard legislation[42] provide that employees have a right to work in an environment free from psychological harassment. Psychological harassment is defined broadly as "any vexatious behaviour in the form of repeated and hostile or unwanted conduct, verbal comments, actions or gestures, that affects an employee's dignity or psychological or physical integrity and that results in a harmful work environment for the employee." Employers have an obligation to take steps to prevent psychological harassment and to put a stop to such behaviour when it occurs. In

---

39. *Supra* note 7.
40. See the Canadian Human Rights Commission website at http://www.chrc-ccdp.ca
41. Jim Middlemiss, "Hostile Workplace Claims Rise" *The Edmonton Journal* (28 July 2004) at F5. See also Raymond T. Lee, "Dealing with Workplace Harassment and Bullying: Some Recommendations for Employment Standards of Manitoba" at http://www.gov.mb.ca/labour/standards/pdf/submission/lee.pdf
42. *An Act Respecting Labour Standards*, R.S.Q. c. N-1.1, ss. 81.18–81.20.

order to meet their obligation, employers must implement harassment policies that include mechanisms to prevent harassment, an investigation process for cases where it is alleged, and sanctions or remedial guidelines. Employees who are victims of psychological harassment have the responsibility to file a complaint in writing to the Labour Standards Commission within 90 days of the last incident. The Labour Standards Commission investigates the complaint and if it is justified the complaint is referred to the Labour Relations Commission, which has the power to "render any decision it considers appropriate." For example, employers may be ordered to reimburse the employee for lost wages, pay punitive damages, or pay for the cost of any psychological support needed by the employee. The decision of the Labour Relations Commission is subject to a limited right of appeal.

CRITICAL ANALYSIS: How is workplace bullying or psychological harassment addressed in the other provinces? What are the advantages and disadvantages of legislation that specifically addresses workplace bullying?

Sources: Annie Berthiaume and Karina Desmarais, "Quebec First in North America to Forbid 'Psychological Harassment'" *The Lawyers Weekly* (17 October 2003) at 9; Nick Craine, "Taking Aim at Workplace Bullies" *Canadian Lawyer* (July 2005) at 4.

The prohibition against harassment extends not only to employers but also to their employees. The employer is vicariously liable for any violations of human rights legislation committed by its employees.[43] Several jurisdictions modify this position by providing for a due diligence defence. For example, the Manitoba legislation[44] provides that an employer is responsible for any act of harassment committed by an employee or an agent of the employer in the course of employment unless it is established that the employer did not consent to the act and took all reasonable steps to prevent the act from being committed and, subsequently, took all reasonable steps to mitigate or avoid its consequences.

In order to fulfill their responsibilities under human rights legislation, it is incumbent on employers to develop and implement a workplace harassment policy. Although employers may still be liable for harassment, whether they knew of it or not, the penalties will be less or nonexistent for employers that not only respond quickly and effectively to instances of harassment but also take action to prevent the wrongful conduct from occurring in the first place.

Pay Equity

Discrimination in pay scales between males and females has led to legislation designed to ensure that female and male employees receive the same compensation for performing the same or substantially similar work. All jurisdictions provide for some type of equal pay in their human rights legislation.[45] In addition, some jurisdictions have equality of pay provisions in their employment standards law and some have enacted specific **pay equity** statutes.[46]

pay equity
Provisions designed to ensure that female and male employees receive the same compensation for performing similar or substantially similar work.

Pay equity provisions are designed to redress systemic discrimination in compensation for work performed. They require an employer to evaluate the work performed by employees in order to divide the workforce into job classes. The classes can then be considered to determine whether they are male or female dominated. Employers must then value each of the job classes in terms of duties, responsibilities, and required

---

43. *Robichaud v. The Queen* (1987), 40 D.L.R. (4th) 577 (S.C.C.). The decision makes it clear that subject to statutory provisions to the contrary, vicarious liability applies to human rights law.
44. *Human Rights Code*, S.M. 1987–88, c. 45, s. 10.
45. For example, the *Canadian Human Rights Act*, s. 11 specifies that it is discriminatory to establish or maintain different wage rates for men and women doing work of equal value in the same establishment.
46. The provinces of Manitoba, New Brunswick, Nova Scotia, Prince Edward Island, Ontario, and Quebec have specific pay equity legislation. Ontario and Quebec are the only provinces in which the legislation applies to the private sector. The other provinces limit the legislation's application to the public sector. See *Pay Equity Act*, R.S.O. 1990, c. P-7 and *Pay Equity Act*, R.S.Q. c. E-12.001.

qualifications; compare like classes; and then endeavour to compensate each female job class with a wage rate comparable to the male job class performing work of equal value. This procedure, however, has been difficult to administer and apply.[47]

Business and Legislation — Pay Equity in the Federal Sector

Pay equity has been the law in the federal jurisdiction since 1978. Section 11 of the *Canadian Human Rights Act* (CHRA) specifies that it is discriminatory to establish or maintain different wage rates for men and women doing work of equal value in the same establishment. Since its enactment, the Canadian Human Rights Commission has dealt with more than 400 pay equity complaints. A majority of the complaints have been dismissed, while others have been resolved through negotiated settlements. However, some have resulted in long and protracted litigation. For example, a complaint against the Federal Treasury Board took 15 years to resolve and a complaint against Bell Canada took more than 14 years to resolve.

The Canadian Human Rights Commission has indicated the current system has proven ineffective in large pay equity cases. The problems identified include

- Allegations of human rights violations tend, by their very nature, to generate a defensive reaction and lead to litigation and delays.

- The complaint-based approach produces uneven implementation, since employers not targeted by complaints often choose to keep a low profile and refrain from taking initiatives on pay equity.

- The significant knowledge and resources it takes to mount a major pay equity complaint has meant that people performing female-dominated work in nonunionized, federally regulated sectors have benefited little from pay equity provisions.

- The haphazard application of pay equity can lead to competitive disadvantages in that an employer who implements pay equity may be the only player in the industry to pay the price of correcting wage discrimination.

- The standards and concepts used in the legislation tend to be vague and ambiguous, leading to countless days spent on their meaning. For example, pay equity complaints against Air Canada and Canadian Airlines have been held up for over 15 years because of the meaning of "establishment." The airlines have argued that flight attendants, ground crews, and cockpit crews each work in a different establishment. The Supreme Court of Canada[48] recently ruled that the workers belong to the same establishment for wage comparison purposes. The case was remitted back to the Human Rights Commission to continue its investigation.

CRITICAL ANALYSIS: How could the current system for implementing pay equity in the federal sector be improved?

Source: *Special Report to Parliament*, Canadian Human Rights Commission website at http://www.chrc-ccdp.ca (accessed 30 November 2006).

---

47. In 1999, the Government of Canada established a Pay Equity Task Force to review the federal legislation. In 2004, the Task Force recommended that the government adopt stand-alone proactive pay equity legislation "Pay Equity: A New Approach to a Fundamental Right," *Pay Equity Task Force, Final Report,* 2004.
48. *Canada (Human Rights Commission) v. Canadian Airlines International Ltd.,* 2006 SCC 1.

Drug and Alcohol Testing

Employers have a legitimate interest in having a safe workplace. Sometimes they have attempted to achieve this goal through drug and alcohol testing of their employees. Such testing, however, is contentious as it is *prima facie* discriminatory. Employers can nevertheless justify discriminatory rules if they can meet the three-part test in *Meiorin*. As illustrated by the decision in *Entrop v. Imperial Oil Limited*, below, alcohol and drug testing is permissible only in limited circumstances.

CASE ▼

Entrop v. Imperial Oil Limited (2000), 189 D.L.R. (4th) 14 (Ont. C.A.)

THE BUSINESS CONTEXT: Following incidents such as the *Exxon Valdez* oil spill in Alaska, in which alcohol and drugs were thought to be contributing factors, companies became concerned that substance abuse threatened the safety of their employees, the public, and the environment. As a result, some workplaces introduced comprehensive drug and alcohol policies.

FACTUAL BACKGROUND: In 1991, Imperial Oil Limited, at the request of its major shareholder, Exxon Corp., instituted an alcohol and drug policy. The key aspects of the policy for employees in safety-sensitive positions were no presence in the body of drugs nor a blood-alcohol level exceeding 0.04 percent, unannounced random drug and alcohol testing, automatic dismissal for a positive test, mandatory disclosure of a current or past substance abuse problem, and reassignment to another position for disclosure of an abuse problem.

Martin Entrop, who worked for Imperial Oil at its Sarnia Refinery for over 17 years, was a senior control board operator, a position that was classified as safety-sensitive. In accordance with the provisions of the alcohol and drug policy, he notified management that he had previously been an alcoholic but that he had been sober continuously for the past seven years. Imperial immediately reassigned him to a non-safety-sensitive position at the same rate of pay. Entrop filed a complaint with the Ontario Human Rights Commission alleging that he had been discriminated against.

THE LEGAL QUESTION: Does Imperial Oil's drug and alcohol policy discriminate on the basis of a handicap or perceived handicap (i.e., alcohol or drug dependency)?

RESOLUTION: The Court of Appeal concluded that the policy is discriminatory. The Ontario *Human Rights Code* guarantees every person a right to equal treatment with respect to employment without discrimination because of a handicap. Substance abuse or perceived substance abuse is a handicap. Persons testing positive on an alcohol or drug test (i.e., substance abusers or perceived substance abusers) are adversely affected by the policy.

The court applied the test developed by the Supreme Court of Canada in *Meiorin* to determine whether the drug and alcohol policy could be justified as a BFOR. The court concluded that the purpose of the policy—to minimize the risk of impaired performance due to substance use in order to ensure a safe, healthy, and productive workplace—was rationally connected to the performance of work at Imperial Oil's two refineries. The court also found that the company had developed and implemented the policy honestly and in good faith. It had consulted widely with employees and experts and had assembled one of Canada's most comprehensive databases on workplace alcohol and drug use.

The third step in the test focused on the means used by Imperial Oil to accomplish its purpose. Imperial Oil had to show that the alcohol and drug testing are reasonably necessary to identify those persons who cannot perform work safely at the refineries because they are impaired by drugs or alcohol and that it cannot accommodate individual capabilities and differences without undue hardship. The court noted that there is a critical difference between alcohol and drug tests. Alcohol tests can test whether a person is actually impaired at the time the test is administered whereas a drug test can detect only past drug use. In other words, an alcohol test can tell whether a person is fit to do his job but a drug test cannot tell whether a person is impaired and unable to do his job now, or in the future. With this distinction in mind, the court concluded that random alcohol testing of employees in safety-sensitive positions was permissible; however, pre-employment or random drug testing for employees in safety-sensitive (or other) positions could not be justified as the tests cannot measure present or future impairment on the job. The court also concluded that Imperial's sanction for a positive test by an employee in a safety-sensitive position—dismissal—was not sufficiently sensitive to individual capabilities.

CRITICAL ANALYSIS: On the basis of this decision, what sort of drug and alcohol testing might not offend human rights legislation? What methods, other than drug and alcohol testing, could companies employ in dealing with employee impairment?

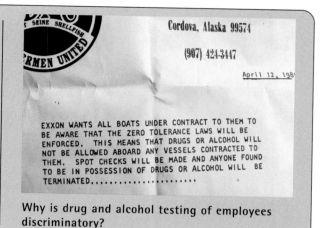

Cordova, Alaska 99574

(907) 424-3447

April 12, 198?

EXXON WANTS ALL BOATS UNDER CONTRACT TO THEM TO BE AWARE THAT THE ZERO TOLERANCE LAWS WILL BE ENFORCED. THIS MEANS THAT DRUGS OR ALCOHOL WILL NOT BE ALLOWED ABOARD ANY VESSELS CONTRACTED TO THEM. SPOT CHECKS WILL BE MADE AND ANYONE FOUND TO BE IN POSSESSION OF DRUGS OR ALCOHOL WILL BE TERMINATED.....................

Why is drug and alcohol testing of employees discriminatory?

Workplace Privacy

Privacy, particularly since technological developments have made it easier to "watch" or monitor employees, has become a real concern in the workplace. Issues centre on collecting and disseminating information about employees, watching and searching employees, and monitoring employees' electronic communications.

Collection and Dissemination of Information

Employers have the ability to collect and store, in hard copy or electronically, a great deal of employee data—performance reviews, work activity reports, medical records, disciplinary reports, credit ratings, and letters of recommendation. Employees, however, have rights to control the collection and use of information.

A wide array of legislation in the public sector, at both the federal and provincial levels, gives individuals the right to control personal information. For example, the federal *Privacy Act*[49] regulates the collection and use of personal information held by the federal government. The act gives individuals the right to see information and to request corrections if it is inaccurate. Similar provincial legislation applies to information held by provincial governments.[50] The *Personal Information and Electronic Documents Act*[51] (PIPEDA) extends these rights to the private sector. PIPEDA applies to employee information in federal works, undertakings, and businesses. PIPEDA does not, however, apply to employee information in the provincial private sector. This information is regulated by similar provincial legislation. To date, Quebec,[52] Alberta[53] and British Columbia[54] have enacted similar legislation.

The basic principle of PIPEDA and its provincial counterparts is that personal information should not be collected, used, or disclosed without the prior knowledge and consent of the individual concerned. PIPEDA defines "personal information" as information about an identifiable individual, but does not include the name, title, business address, or telephone number of an employee of an organization. Therefore, to collect all other types of employee information the employer

---

49. R.S.C. 1985, c. P-21.
50. Only Prince Edward Island and Newfoundland do not have legislation controlling personal information collected by their governments.
51. S.C. 2000, c. 4.
52. *Act Respecting the Protection of Personal Information in the Private Sector*, RSQ, cP-39.1.
53. *Personal Information Protection Act*, S.A. 2003, c.P-6.5.
54. *Personal Information Protection Act*, S.B.C. 2003, c.63.

requires the consent of the employee. The Alberta and British Columbia legislation contain an exception. For example, the Alberta legislation allows employers to access the personal information reasonably necessary to administer the employment relationship without obtaining consent.

To meet their obligations under PIPEDA and similar provincial legislation, employers are required to

- identify and document the limited purposes for which personal information is collected, prior to collecting the information
- communicate the identified purposes to the individual prior to obtaining the individual's consent
- collect, use, and disclose the personal information only for the identified purposes
- obtain the express consent of individuals for "sensitive" information such as health records and financial information (implied consent may be sufficient for less sensitive information)
- maintain responsibility for personal information under its possession or custody
- designate a personal information supervisor
- maintain the accuracy of personal information held by the organization
- retain information only as long as required for the purposes identified
- adopt security safeguards to protect personal information from loss and unauthorized use
- provide access and the right to amend inaccurate information to each individual

Penalties for breach of the act include making public an organization's personal information policies, fines ranging from $10 000 to $100 000, and court orders to correct practices and to pay damages to the complainant.

Surveillance and Searches

The surveillance of employees with video cameras or closed-circuit television is sometimes used to prevent, detect, or investigate fraud, theft, and harassment. The appropriateness of surveillance has been challenged pursuant to PIPEDA.

CASE ▼

Eastmond v. Canadian Pacific Railway
(2004), 254 F.T.R. 169 (Fed. Ct.)

THE BUSINESS CONTEXT: The use of surveillance equipment in the workplace is a contentious issue as it is difficult to find the correct balance between the employer's security interests and the employee's privacy interests. This case represents the court's first consideration of this debate pursuant to PIPEDA.

FACTUAL BACKGROUND: Erwin Eastmond, an unionized employee at Canadian Pacific Railway, complained to the Federal Privacy Commissioner regarding CPR's installation of six digital recording surveillance cameras focused on door entrances and exits. Eastmond complained that the installation was unacceptable because they were installed without union consent, there was no security problem that justified this invasion of privacy, and they could be used to monitor employees' work performance. CPR responded that the installation was necessary to reduce vandalism and deter theft, to reduce its potential liability for property damage, and to provide security for staff. In support, CPR cited two incidents of vandalism and two incidents in which female employees had reported feeling vulnerable. The Commissioner investigated the complaint and recommended that CPR remove the cameras. The complainant applied to the Federal Court for an ordering confirming the Commissioner's decision

Intrusive searches of employees or their belongings are carefully scrutinized by the courts. An employer would need to have some particularly compelling reasons, such as bomb threats being issued or thefts occurring, to undertake such practices. Additionally, the employer would need to demonstrate that all other alternatives for dealing with the threats had been exhausted. Employees should be informed in advance of any policy in this regard, and any searches would need to be conducted in a systematic and nonarbitrary manner; otherwise, the employer may be vulnerable to charges of discrimination.

Monitoring of Communications

Many employees, particularly those who work in an office, have access to e-mail and the Internet, as well as traditional means of communication—telephone and facsimile. Employers have a legitimate interest in ensuring that employees are not spending excessive amounts of time on personal communication and are using company equipment for legitimate uses. Employees, on the other hand, have a legitimate expectation that their private and personal communications will not be monitored or intercepted. Currently, there is no comprehensive law in Canada prohibiting the ability of employers to monitor an employee's e-mail and Internet activities.

The *Criminal Code*[55] provides that it is an offence to intercept a private communication. The section, however, does not apply to communications that are not private or to interception that is consented to by one of the parties. A communication is private if the parties have an expectation that it will not be intercepted. There is judicial authority for the notion that e-mail via the Internet ought to carry a reasonable expectation of privacy, although it is not to be accorded the same level of privacy protection as first-class mail.[56] However, the manner in which the technology is managed may serve to diminish the user's expectation of privacy. For

---

55. R.S.C. 1985, c. C-46, s. 184.
56. See: *R.* v. *Weir,* [1988] A.J. No. 155 (Alta. Q. B.).

example, a comprehensive technology-use policy, which addresses the employer's monitoring activities, may make it clear that an employee has no reasonable expectation of privacy in the use of the employer's communication tools.

The PIPEDA and provincial privacy legislation may affect the employer's ability to monitor electronic communications. Although the legislation does not expressly address this issue, it requires that all organizations, including businesses, in order to collect, use, and retain personal information get the consent of the individual concerned. This suggests that in order to monitor and view the content of communications, employers will require the consent of employees. Presumably, an employer could require such consent as a condition of employment.

The Union Context

Discussion in this chapter, thus far, has focused on the hiring and employment of nonunionized employees. It has also focused on private as opposed to public sector employees, as there is often specific legislation that affects their employment.

In a unionized environment, many of the same employment issues that arise in a nonunionized environment are also relevant—recruiting, terms, and conditions of employment, and so on. However, negotiating and entering an employment contract is a much different process.

Both the federal and provincial governments have enacted labour or industrial relations legislation that guarantees the right of employees to join trade unions. The acts apply to most employees, but certain employees—namely, managers and those in specific occupations, such as domestic workers and farmhands—are excluded. The legislative enactments provide for a **certification** process, by which the union is recognized as the bargaining agent for a group of employees. An employer, however, can voluntarily recognize the union as the bargaining agent for the employees without a certification process. The certification process is basically a method by which the **Labour Relations Board** approves the union as the employees' representative, upon the union being able to show that a majority of the employees in the bargaining unit want the union to represent them.

The legislation provides a mechanism known as **collective bargaining,** by which the parties enter a collective agreement or contract. The contract applies to all employees in the bargaining unit, regardless of whether they voted for the union representation. The union and the employer have a duty to bargain in good faith—that is, they must make a substantive effort to negotiate the agreement. The collective agreement, like an individual employment contract, sets out the terms and conditions of employment. The two types of contracts cover many of the same issues, such as wages, benefits, and the like, but a **collective agreement** is usually far more comprehensive. As well, a union bargaining on behalf of many employees generally has far more bargaining power than a single individual negotiating with an employer (although some highly skilled or specialized employees do have a lot of individual bargaining power). During the term of the collective agreement, there can be no legal strikes by the employees or lockouts by the employer.

In return, the legislation provides a process involving grievance and arbitration procedures for resolving disputes. These procedures are discussed in Chapter 21.

Business Law in Practice Revisited

1. Is Jeong an employee or an independent contractor?

The distinction between an employee and an independent contractor is not always readily apparent. The label that the parties apply to their relationship is not conclusive as the nature of the relationship is a question of fact. The courts have developed

certification
The process by which a union is recognized as a bargaining agent for a group of employees.

Labour Relations Board
A body that administers labour relations legislation.

collective bargaining
A mechanism by which parties enter a collective agreement or contract.

collective agreement
The employment agreement reached between the union and employer setting out the bargaining unit employees' terms and conditions of employment.

a number of tests to make the determination. Some factors, such as the lack of control, suggest that Jeong is an independent contractor. Other factors, such as the employer providing a computer, the method of payment, and the degree of integration, suggest that Jeong is an employee. In the final analysis, as Jeong does not appear to be in business for herself, it is likely that the courts will consider her an employee.

2. Why is the distinction between an employee and an independent contractor important?

The distinction is important because an employer is responsible for torts committed by an employee in the course of employment whereas the employer is not generally responsible for the torts of an independent contractor. In addition, the distinction is critical because common law, as well as statutory rights and obligations, in most cases apply only to employees and not to independent contractors.

3. Is Hiram responsible for Jeong's conduct?

Assuming that Jeong is an employee, then Hiram is responsible for the torts committed by Jeong in the course of employment. Hiram is not responsible for the torts committed by Jeong outside the course of her employment. Although the posting of the possibly defamatory statement on the hockey website is related to her work, it is likely that her actions will be considered to be outside the scope of employment because it appears that she was responding in a personal capacity to a perceived affront. Assuming this is the case, Hiram is not responsible.

Chapter Summary

The employment relationship is one of the most fundamental relationships in business. The cornerstone of this relationship is a contract, either individual or collective, whereby one party provides services to another in return for remuneration. However, not everyone who provides services to another through a contract is an "employee." The distinction is crucial because common law, as well as statutory rights and obligations, in most cases applies only to employees and not to independent contractors.

The hiring process has a number of phases—advertising, application submission, interviewing, and reference checking. Legal issues such as discrimination and employment equity apply to each of these steps and provide the opportunity for potential liability for the unwary employer. Most of the costly mistakes made by employers who end up the subject of a human rights investigation or the recipient of a wrongful dismissal suit can be avoided. Organizations need to be proactive by designing and implementing policies, practices, and procedures to address the legal issues at all stages of the employment relationship.

A well-drafted employment contract sets out the terms and conditions of employment. It describes the employment relationship and at a minimum sets out the job to be performed and the remuneration to be provided. The employment contract can be advantageous for both the employer and employee, as it contributes to certainty and clarity in the relationship.

The ability to freely negotiate an employment contract has been somewhat curtailed by a host of legislation designed to protect employees. This protection is provided not only with respect to the terms of employment, such as wages, vacation, and hours of work, but also with respect to the conditions of employment. There is a vast array of legislation affecting employee welfare, discrimination in the workplace, and privacy.

When a union is in place, negotiating and entering into an employment contract takes place through a process known as collective bargaining. The collective agreement that emerges from negotiations applies to all employees, regardless of whether they voted for union representation.

Chapter Study

Key Terms and Concepts

adverse effects discrimination (p. 495)

bona fide occupational requirement (BFOR) (p. 495)

certification (p. 512)

collective agreement (p. 512)

collective bargaining (p. 512)

discrimination (p. 495)

duty to accommodate (p. 496)

employment equity legislation (p. 498)

employment relationship (p. 490)

employment standards legislation (p. 502)

fixed- or definite-term contract (p. 501)

Human Rights Commission (p. 493)

indefinite-term contract (p. 501)

independent contractor (p. 490)

Labour Relations Board (p. 512)

pay equity (p. 506)

systemic discrimination (p. 495)

Questions for Review

1. Which level of government has jurisdiction to make laws in the area of employment?

2. What are the tests for determining the difference between an employee and an independent contractor? Why is it important to distinguish between an employee and an independent contractor?

3. Define vicarious liability and negligent hiring. How do they differ?

4. The human rights acts attempt to prohibit discrimination in employment. What is meant by "discrimination"?

5. What is the difference between systemic and adverse effects discrimination?

6. What is a *bona fide* occupational requirement? Give an example.

7. What is the "duty to accommodate"?

8. What is the purpose of the federal *Employment Equity Act?*

9. Do employees have fiduciary obligations? Explain.

10. Do employment contracts need to be in writing to be enforceable? What are the advantages of a written employment contract? Can you think of any disadvantages?

11. What is the purpose of employment standards legislation? Give an example of an employment standard.

12. Explain how the freedom to contract in employment has been affected by legislation, and give examples.

13. What is the purpose of workers' compensation legislation?

14. Would displaying a picture of a nude person be an example of sexual harassment in the workplace? Explain.

15. What is the purpose of pay equity?

16. Is alcohol and drug testing in the workplace permissible? Explain.

17. Do employees have a right to privacy? Explain.

18. Describe how unionized employees enter into employment contracts.

Questions for Critical Thinking

1. It has long been recognized that addiction to alcohol and drugs are disabilities under human rights legislation. Should addiction to nicotine also be recognized as a disability? How would such a finding affect an employer's ability to regulate the workplace?

2. An advertisement that reads "Wanted: Vietnamese waiters for a Vietnamese restaurant" is discriminatory. On what basis does the advertisement discriminate? Could or should ethnicity qualify as a *bona fide* occupational requirement? Would it make any difference where the restaurant was located?

3. The distinction between an independent contractor and an employee is not always clear. What steps can an employer, who wishes to engage independent contractors, take to ensure that its workers will be classified as independent contractors? What are the risks associated with having "independent contractors" classified as employees?

4. Many employers require employees to sign agreements that contain nonsolicitation clauses, confidentiality clauses, and noncompetition clauses.[57] What are the risks for employees of signing or not signing these agreements?

5. Mandatory drug testing in the workplace is a contentious issue. In the limited circumstances in which testing is justified, employees who test positive must be accommodated to the point of undue hardship. What is "accommodation"? What is "undue hardship"? When would an employer be relieved of the duty to accommodate the individual needs of the alcohol- or drug-dependent employee?

6. In the wake of evolving methods of communication (e-mailing, Blackberry messaging, and blogging) and methods of surveillance (closed-circuit cameras and software for monitoring Internet and e-mail use) privacy in the workplace is an area of growing contention. On one side is the employer's right to monitor its workforce and on the other is the employee's right of privacy with respect to technology use. One of the ways to strike an appropriate balance between these competing interests is a computer-use policy. What are the benefits of such a policy? What should such a policy contain?

---

57. Kevin Marron, "To Sign or Not to Sign?" *The Globe and Mail* (21 July 2004) at C1.

Situations for Discussion

1. In 1991, Cindy Choung became British Columbia's first accredited Chinese-language court interpreter. Interpreters are called by court services (a branch of the government) when needed and are selected from a list in rotation. They are paid an hourly rate, plus expenses. All travel arrangements are made by and paid for by court services. There is no guarantee of a minimum amount of work, and there is no prohibition against working for other agencies. Court services makes no deductions for income tax, employment insurance, or pension plans. A code of professional conduct implemented by court services governs how interpreters are to translate and to dress in court. It also sets out rules of confidentiality and prohibits interpreters from assigning their work to another interpreter.

   In 1994 the court services' executive director received complaints about Cindy's work and decided to remove her name from the list of interpreters. Cindy is considering bringing an action for wrongful dismissal.[58] Is she entitled to bring such an action? What does she need to prove? Explain.

2. Jan Delaney was hired by Tulay Cosmetics and Skin-Care Products Ltd. as a sales consultant and technical trainer. This position involved selling and providing information seminars to other salespersons on Tulay's skin-care products. When hired, Jan signed an employment contract that contained a two-year nonsolicitation covenant.

   The relationship between Jan and Tulay eventually deteriorated, and Jan subsequently secured a similar position with a competitor. Tulay brought an action for an injunction to restrain Jan from working for the competitor.[59] What factors would the court consider in deciding whether to grant an injunction? What additional information would be helpful?

3. Pierre Légère was a marketing representative for Compu-plus, a consulting firm that provided computer services to various government departments in New Brunswick. As a marketing representative, he developed contacts within government and among independent contractors who were retained to provide the computer services on a contract basis. Pierre, without giving any notice, left Compu-plus and joined a competitor that had actively pursued him and had offered substantially more money. Compu-plus is concerned about the impact that Pierre's defection will have on its business.[60] What should Compu-plus do? What potential actions does it have? What factors should Compu-plus consider before it proceeds?

4. a. Bill Reyno owns and operates a bottle-recycling plant. He has recently experienced a rash of thefts and break-ins and wants to hire a night watchman or security guard. Bill wants someone large and feisty in case there are any problems. What steps should Bill take in hiring someone to fill the position?

   b. Jon Blondin applied for the position. When he showed up for the interview, he seemed to be a little "unstable." In fact, Bill thought he might have been drinking, but he was not sure. Other than this concern, Jon seemed to be perfect for the job. Bill would like Jon to take a drug and alcohol test. Is it permissible for Bill to make this request?

5. Jodene recently got a job with a company that sells herbal medicines and related products. There are two aspects to her job: part of the time she is located in a small booth in a mall, and part of the time she demonstrates and sells products at home parties. In both situations she is paid by commission. One day, on her way from the mall to a home party, she accidentally

---

58. Based on *Truong v. British Columbia* (1999), 178 D.L.R. (4th) 644 (B.C.C.A.).
59. Based on *Phytoderm v. Urwin*, [1999] O.J. No. 383 (Ont. Gen. Div.).
60. Based on *MacDonald v. Klein*, [1998] O.J. No. 4922 (Ont. Gen. Div.).

ran over a very valuable dog. Assuming that Jodene was negligent, who is liable to pay for the dog? Assuming the company is liable, how can it avoid liability in future?

6. Jennifer Moxley is a recent university graduate employed in the human resources department of a medium-sized firm in the textile industry. This is Jennifer's first full-time position. The company has a very small HR department. In fact, there is only Jennifer and her manager, who has other responsibilities in the company. Jennifer's manager is away at a convention and the following situation has arisen:

The company is in the process of hiring a new employee for the design department. One of the vice presidents has given her the résumé of a person who went to school with his daughter, with the following comment: "Don't bother wasting time checking this kid's background—I can vouch for him." On examining the résumé, Jennifer finds that the person has no previous full- or part-time employment, that he graduated with distinction from a computer design course at a well-known institution, that he has listed the vice president as his only reference, and that he has done volunteer work at the Pilgrim House Retreat. Advise Jennifer.

7. Abigail Fletcher worked as a marketing analyst in the soft drinks division of Food Group International. The vice president of sales and marketing for her division touched her inappropriately and said, "Are you wearing shorter skirts yet, Abigail, because it would make your job a whole lot easier."

Is the employer, Food Group International responsible for the actions of the vice president of marketing and sales? Explain.

What steps should Food Group take to deal with workplace harassment? Why is it important to take steps to deal with workplace harassment?

8. In May 2006, WestJet Airlines apologized to rival Air Canada and agreed to pay it $5.5 million for investigation and legal fees plus donate $10 million to children's charities to settle a lawsuit. In 2004, Air Canada sued WestJet and several of its executives, in Ontario Superior Court, for $220 million. It was alleged a former Air Canada employee, now employed by WestJet, passed on confidential, proprietary information to WestJet.

Apparently the former Air Canada employee, who continued to have access to an Air Canada website for the limited purpose of booking personal travel, gave his password to a WestJet executive. Apparently WestJet accessed Air Canada's website approximately a quarter of a million times and created automated technology to download and analyze passenger load and booking information. By obtaining this confidential information, Air Canada claimed WestJet was able to compile computer-generated reports for its own strategic planning, routing, and pricing decisions. WestJet countered with accusations that Air Canada hired private investigators to sift through an executive's garbage then had a U.S. firm digitally reconstruct shredded documents.[61]

What obligations did WestJet have to Air Canada as a result of the decision to hire one of its former employees? Were WestJet's actions wrong or were they just taking advantage of lax security?

For more study tools, visit
http://www.businesslaw3e.nelson.com

---

61. Craig Wong, "WestJet Accused of Spying" *The Globe and Mail* (7 April 2004) at G1; Richard Blackwell, "Dogfight Ends, War Continues" *The Globe and Mail* (30 May 2006) at B1.

Chapter

21

Objectives

After studying this chapter, you should have an understanding of

- how the employment relationship ends
- the differences among dismissals for just cause, dismissals with notice, constructive dismissals, and wrongful dismissals
- the issues arising from a wrongful dismissal suit
- the components of a termination settlement

Terminating the Employment Relationship

Business Law in Practice

Hiram Dupuis, the owner and operator of an independent newspaper in southern, Ontario is reviewing his options in light of a dramatic drop in circulation. In recent years, the newspaper industry has changed significantly due the merger of several large dailies and the advent of online sources of news. Hiram believes that there is still a role for the weekly community newspaper, but in order to survive he will have to downsize his workforce. He has come to the conclusion that Jeong Nash will have to go. Jeong, a staff reporter, is 32 years old and has been with the newspaper for a couple of years, but her stories are often controversial and Hiram has had to defend her on a couple of occasions. Most recently, she wrote a story about an aging basketball player that has upset a number of advertisers, and they are threatening to take their business elsewhere.

The other change that Hiram is contemplating is the merger of two of the newspapers' departments—Community Homes and Gardens, and Living in our Community. The managers of the departments are 58-year-old Stella Blanchard, who has been with the newspaper for 25 years, and 37-year-old Josiah Rutgers, who has been with the newspaper for 5 years. As Stella is the older, more senior employee, Hiram wants to make her the manager of the new department. Josiah will retain his title and the same salary. The only difference is that after the merger, he will report to Stella rather than to Hiram. The restructuring of the newspaper will give Hiram an opportunity to terminate the general manager, 56-year-old Levi Cameron. Although he has been with the newspaper for 15 years, he has, over the years, committed a number of infractions. He often tells off-colour jokes and sometimes makes comments about the appearance and dress of female colleagues. Most recently Hiram discovered inappropriate content on Levi's computer.

1. Is Hiram justified in terminating Jeong Nash and Levi Cameron?
2. Is Hiram entitled to change Josiah Rutgers's position?
3. What course of action would you advise Hiram to pursue?

Ending the Relationship

In many instances, the employment relationship ends in an amicable fashion. An employee resigns to pursue other interests, retires, or simply leaves at the end of a fixed-term employment contract.

The employment relationship can also come to an end through less pleasant means, as when the employer

- summarily dismisses, or fires, an employee
- gives the employee notice of termination
- acts in such a manner that the employment relationship becomes untenable

It is an implied term of an employment contract that an employer may terminate the employment relationship without any notice if there is "just cause." This implied term is subject to collective agreements and individual employment contracts, which may specify the terms for ending the employment relationship. The term is also subject to legislation that may give to certain employees, such as teachers, police officers, and firefighters, special rights in the case of dismissal.

It is also an implied term that an employer may terminate the employment contract by giving the employee reasonable notice of the termination. In this case the employer is not required to have a reason or cause for the termination. The implied term is also subject to collective agreements and individual employment contracts that provide for notice periods and rights on dismissal. As well, provincial and federal employment standards legislation provides for notice periods and procedures on dismissal. The periods of notice provided by the legislation are only minimum periods, and often employees are entitled to more notice.

This area of the law has become increasingly important for employers, owing to the courts' recognition of the importance of work in people's lives. It has been the subject of much litigation over the last couple of decades and thus has seen profound changes.

Dismissals for Just Cause

just cause

Employee conduct that amounts to a fundamental breach of the employment contract.

When there is **just cause,** an employer may dismiss an employee without notice. Just cause for dismissal means, in effect, that the employee has breached a fundamental term of the employment contract.

Just cause exists when the employee is guilty of one or more of the following:

- serious misconduct
- habitual neglect of duty
- incompetence
- conduct incompatible with duties or prejudicial to the employer's business
- willful disobedience in a matter of substance[1]

The grounds for dismissal with cause are easy to articulate but difficult to apply in practice because whether an employee's conduct justifies dismissal is a question of fact that requires an assessment of the context and circumstances of the conduct. It is impossible to specify all of the conduct that may constitute just cause; however, it is possible to make some general comments about the various categories.

Is "goofing off" at work just cause for dismissal?

---

1. *R. v. Arthur, Ex parte Port Arthur Shipbuilding Co.* (1967), 62 D.L.R. (2d) 342 (Ont. C.A.), reversed on other grounds, *Port Arthur Shipbuilding Co. v. Arthurs,* [1969] S.C.R. 85 (S.C.C.).

Serious Misconduct

A minor infraction by an employee is insufficient to justify dismissal, although the cumulative effect of many minor instances may be sufficient. The cumulative effect must be such that there is a serious impact on the employment relationship. For example, Levi's telling of an off-colour joke would not be sufficient grounds for dismissal. However, if the telling of the joke is combined with a number of other incidents, such as making inappropriate comments and having inappropriate content on his computer, then the cumulative effect of the incidents may be considered **serious misconduct.**

If Hiram wants to terminate on the basis of an accumulation of a number of minor incidents, he has a duty to warn the employee and give an opportunity to improve performance. This duty is particularly important in situations where there is a **progressive discipline policy** in place. This is a system whereby the employer applies discipline for relatively minor infractions on a progressive basis. Each step in the progression carries a more serious penalty, until the last step—dismissal—is reached. The warning may be oral[2] or in writing and should be clear and understood by the employee. The employee should be advised not just about the unacceptable conduct, but also about the consequences of failure to improve.

A single act of misconduct can justify dismissal if it is sufficiently serious. For example, a single act of dishonesty can be sufficient grounds for dismissal, as when an employee steals a large sum of money from the employer. However, an act of dishonesty, in and of itself, is not necessarily sufficient to warrant just cause for dismissal. The nature and context of any dishonesty must be considered.[3] Other examples of conduct that may constitute serious misconduct include lying to an employer, forging signatures and documents, and cheating. What constitutes serious misconduct may also be affected by workforce policies. For example, having an affair with a coworker does not constitute just cause for dismissal unless the employer can prove that the conduct negatively affected the business or the employer has a policy against office romance.

An important principle with respect to any of the grounds for dismissal is **condonation.** Condonation occurs when an employer indicates through words or actions that behaviour constituting grounds for dismissal is being overlooked. For example, an employer who is aware of the harassing activities of an employee and who ignores or tolerates the activities will have difficulty arguing just cause for termination. Condonation occurs only if the employer is fully aware of the wrongful behaviour.

serious misconduct
Intentional, harmful conduct of the employee that permits the employer to dismiss without notice.

progressive discipline policy
A system that follows a sequence of employee discipline from less to more severe punishment.

condonation
Employer behaviour that indicates to the employee that misconduct is being overlooked.

Business Application of the Law

Personal Use of the Employer's Property

The introduction of technologies such as fax machines, e-mail, and the Internet into the workplace has greatly increased the possibility of employees using company property for personal use. It is a new spin on the old nuisance of employees making personal phone calls at work—but with greatly magnified consequences. Use of the technologies by employees ranges from occasional online shopping ventures to hours spent surfing on the Net and the use of a company computer to run a personal business.

CRITICAL ANALYSIS: Should excessive Internet use be grounds for dismissal? Under what circumstances? Other than to prevent lost productivity, why would an employer want to control an employee's Internet use?

---

2. Warnings, especially oral warnings, need to be documented so that an employer can establish that the duty to warn was fulfilled.
3. *McKinley v. BC Tel*, [2001] 2 S.C.R. 161.

Habitual Neglect of Duty

habitual neglect of duty
Persistent failure to perform employment duties.

An employee may be terminated with cause for chronic absenteeism and lateness that are considered **habitual neglect of duty.** The absenteeism must be without the employer's permission or authorization and be more than an occasional absence. Important to this ground is whether warnings were issued, whether there was any excuse for the absence, and whether the absence occurred at a critical time for the employer.

It is more difficult to establish lateness than absenteeism as grounds for dismissal. The courts will consider whether the employee had a valid excuse, whether there were warnings concerning lateness, and whether the time was ever made up, as well as related factors.

Incompetence

incompetence
Lack of ability, knowledge, or qualification to perform employment obligations.

To dismiss on the ground of **incompetence,** the employer must be more than merely dissatisfied with an employee's work. There must be actual incompetence. The substandard level of performance must be evident after the employee has been given a warning and an opportunity to improve. An employer must establish fair and reasonable performance standards against which to measure performance. An employee can raise a number of issues to explain poor performance—inadequate training, insufficient volume of business, inexperience, and condonation of performance problems.

A single act of incompetence is rarely grounds for dismissal, unless it shows a complete lack of skills that an employee claimed to have possessed.

Conduct Incompatible

conduct incompatible
Personal behaviour that is irreconcilable with employment duties or prejudicial to the employer's business.

An employer may be justified in terminating with cause for **conduct incompatible** with the employee's duties or prejudicial to the employer's business—for example, accepting lavish and inappropriate gifts from the employer's clients. The conduct complained of is not limited to conduct on the job—it can also apply to conduct outside working hours. For example, a school board was justified in dismissing a school superintendent who was convicted of a petty fraud outside the performance of his duties.[4]

Closely related to incompatible conduct is the ground for dismissal related to an employee's conflict of interest. For example, if an employee were to run a business that was in direct competition with the employer's business, that could be a breach of the employee's duty of loyalty and good faith to the employer.[5]

Willful Disobedience

willful disobedience
Deliberate failure to carry out lawful and reasonable orders.

An employer is entitled to expect an employee to carry out lawful and reasonable orders. Failure to do so is considered **willful disobedience.** A single act of disobedience would not ordinarily constitute grounds for dismissal, unless that act was very serious, such as not attending an important meeting or refusing to follow important safety rules. To rely on this ground, the employer would have to establish that the instructions or directions given to the employee were unambiguous and that the employee had no reasonable excuse for disobeying. Less serious instances of disobedience may justify dismissal when combined with other types of misconduct, such as insolence and insubordination.

---

4. *Cherniwchan v. Two Hills (County No. 21)* (1982), 21 Alta. L.R. (2d) 353 (Q.B.).
5. Stacey Ball, *Canadian Employment Law*, looseleaf (Aurora: Canada Law Book, 2006) at 11–24.

An employer is entitled to expect an employee to carry out orders without extended debate and with respect. Whether an employer is justified in terminating an employee who fails to meet this standard depends on a number of factors, such as whether the employee was provoked, whether the employee was upset, and whether it was a moment of temporary anger.

Other Causes

In addition to the grounds discussed thus far, there can be other bases for termination without notice. Most may fit within the general category of misconduct; examples include harassment, including sexual harassment; disruption of corporate culture; consumption of alcohol or drugs in the workplace; and drug abuse. However, each situation needs to be analyzed on its facts and examined in relation to whether the

- conduct was a single act
- conduct was condoned in some manner
- employee had a disability
- employee had been warned about conduct and the consequences of failure to improve

CASE ▼

McKinley v. BC Tel, [2001] 2 S.C.R. 161

THE BUSINESS CONTEXT: Employers often argue that a single act of dishonest conduct by an employee gives rise to just cause for dismissal. Employees contend that any act, including dishonesty, should be judged on its context and its entirety.

FACTUAL BACKGROUND: Martin McKinley, 48, was a chartered accountant who worked 17 years for BC Tel. He held various positions with the company, and in 1991 was promoted to controller. In May 1993, he began to experience high blood pressure, and in May of the following year, on the advice of his physician, he took a leave of absence. By July, his supervisor raised the issue of termination. McKinley indicated that he wished to return to work in a position that carried less responsibility. However, alternative positions were never offered to him, and in August his employment was terminated. BC Tel claimed that it had just cause to dismiss McKinley as he had been dishonest about his medical condition and treatments available for it. He had failed to clearly disclose that his doctor told him he could return to work if he took beta blockers, a medication with various side effects.

THE LEGAL QUESTION: Does an employee's dishonest conduct, in and of itself, give rise to just cause for dismissal?

RESOLUTION: The court noted that there were two approaches that have been adopted in various Canadian jurisdictions. One approach dictates that any dishonesty by an employee, however minor, is automatically considered just cause for dismissal. The other approach requires a determination of whether the nature and degree of the dishonesty warrants dismissal in the context of the entire employment relationship. The court adopted the "contextual" approach, and restored the trial court's finding that McKinley had been wrongly dismissed. In other words, McKinley's conduct did not merit just cause for dismissal. The court did note, however, that in cases involving serious fraud, theft, or misappropriation, either approach would ultimately lead to a finding of just cause.

The court also went on to say that although less serious dishonesty may not merit firing without notice, "that is not to say that there cannot be lesser sanctions for less serious conduct. For example, an employer may be justified in docking an employee's pay for any loss incurred by a minor misuse of company property." The court indicated that was one of several disciplinary measures that an employer may take in these circumstances.

CRITICAL ANALYSIS: Given that not all dishonesty is just cause, how big a lie must an employee tell before he can be fired for just cause? For example, could an employer fire an employee who told his boss that he had a headache and then went to the mall to shop?

Non-Cause and Near Cause

There are many potential reasons or situations that may constitute just cause for dismissal. However, it is important to note that what might seem to be a good reason for terminating an employee is not necessarily just cause. For example, the newspaper has suffered economic setbacks, and although this is a good reason to scale back its workforce, it is not "just cause" for termination. Similarly, Jeong is a difficult employee, but although this may be a good reason to terminate her employment, again, it is not "just cause."

reasonable notice

A period of time for an employee to find alternative employment prior to dismissal.

In the absence of just cause, the employer who wishes to terminate employees is required to give notice or pay in lieu of notice. The period of notice will either be the term agreed upon in the employment contract or **reasonable notice.** What constitutes "reasonable" notice is to be determined in relation to factors such as age, length of service, availability of employment, and the status of the employee.

In some situations, an employer may have an employee who is neither particularly good nor bad. Is an employer entitled to give the "so-so" employee a lesser period of notice? In *Dowling v. Halifax (City of),*[6] a long-service stationary engineer who would have been entitled to about 24 months' notice on termination, had the notice period reduced to six months by the employer because of inappropriate conduct—favouring one contractor over another and making work difficult for the competing contractor. The Supreme Court flatly refused to accept any argument by the employer that the reduction was justified because of near cause and sent the matter back to the trial judge for an assessment of reasonable notice. Thus, either an employer has just cause to dismiss an employee and the employee is not entitled to any notice, or the employer does not have just cause to dismiss and the employee is entitled to the full period of reasonable notice. There is no halfway position.

However, the Supreme Court of Canada in *McKinley* indicates that conduct that does not merit dismissal without notice can be addressed by lesser sanctions. The court gives the example of an employer docking an employee's pay for dishonest conduct that does not warrant firing. This approach may open the door to employers giving forms of discipline such as suspensions for "near cause" conduct.

Risks in Just Cause Dismissals

Since an employee is not entitled to any compensation when dismissed for cause, the employee is more likely to bring a suit against the employer. An employer should carefully consider all of the potential costs of dismissing for cause and consider a termination settlement.

An employer who determines that dismissal for cause is justified can reduce the risks considerably by ensuring that sound policies and procedures for dismissal with just cause are established and practised.

---

6. [1998] 1 S.C.R. 22.

Dismissal with Notice

An employee who has been hired for an indefinite period of time may be dismissed at any time and without cause as long as the employer gives notice of the termination (or pay in lieu of notice).[7] While indefinite-term employment contracts are the norm in most industries, many individuals do work for fixed periods of time.[8] For those employees, their contracts end without any notice when the term expires. Termination of a fixed-term contract prior to its expiry is a breach of contract.

The period of notice required to terminate an indefinite-term employment contract would be either the period agreed upon in the employment contract, the period specified in employment standards legislation, or reasonable notice. In many cases the parties do not agree in the employment contract on a period of notice, and even in cases when they do, the courts do not always uphold the provisions. This is particularly the case when the agreed-upon notice is considerably less than what would be implied by the courts as reasonable notice. The courts may justify ignoring the contractual provisions on the basis that the circumstances of the employment contract have changed or that the contract was unfair and unconscionable. It is therefore often the case that employees are entitled to reasonable notice, despite the contractual terms that provide for lesser periods of notice. The period of notice provided in employment standards legislation is a minimum period only.[9] Many employees are entitled to considerably more than the statutory period of notice. As Hiram is unlikely to establish just cause for terminating Jeong and possibly Levi, the better course of action is to give reasonable notice.

Reasonable Notice Periods

In theory, notice is a period of time to enable the soon-to-be terminated employee to find alternative employment. In determining how much notice, the primary factors to be considered are those set out in *Bardal v. Globe & Mail Ltd.*[10]

- character of employment
- length of service
- age
- availability of similar employment

Character of Employment

This factor refers to whether the employee was at a high-status position in the organization. Generally, a senior, high-level, or management employee is entitled to more notice than a junior, nonmanagement employee. For example, Levi occupies a higher position at the newspaper than Jeong, so on this basis Levi is entitled to more notice than Jeong. The rationale behind this factor is the assumption that it takes a higher-level employee a longer period of time to find alternative employment than it does a lower-level employee. In recent years, however, this distinction has been called into

---

7. Note that employers cannot give effective notice or payment in lieu of notice to someone who is unable to work, since an employee who is disabled or on pregnancy or parental leave cannot take advantage of the notice period to look for other work.
8. Note that a series of fixed-term contracts may be interpreted as a contract for an indefinite term. For example, in *Ceccol v. Ontario Gymnastic Federation* (2001), 204 D.L.R. (4th) 688 (Ont. C.A.), the Ontario Court of Appeal held that a series of 15 one-year contracts was an indefinite-term contract and therefore the employee was entitled to reasonable notice of termination.
9. Typically, employment standards legislation provides one week of notice for each year of service up to a maximum of eight weeks, whereas reasonable notice for middle-level employees is on average more like one month of notice for each year of service up to a maximum of 24 months.
10. (1960), 24 D.L.R. (2d) 140 (Ont. H.C.). These factors were endorsed by the Supreme Court of Canada in *Machtinger v. HOJ Industries Ltd.*, [1992] 1 S.C.R. 986.

question. Mr. Justice McPherson in *Cronk v. Canadian General Insurance*[11] noted that those who are better educated or professionally trained are more likely to obtain other employment after dismissal than individuals with fewer skills. His decision to grant a 55-year-old clerical worker with 35 years experience 20 months reasonable notice, however, was reduced to 12 months on appeal.[12] Nevertheless, the case is important because it signals a willingness on the part of the judiciary to re-examine the notice factors. Also the court of appeal decision in *Cronk* has been severely criticized as being repugnant to modern social values in contemporary Canada, and subsequent courts have taken a narrow approach to the decision in order not to reduce notice periods. These cases have held that all of factors in Bardol must be appropriately weighted, and an inappropriate weight should not be given to "character of employment."[13]

Length of Service

A longer-term employee is entitled to more notice than a shorter-term employee. On this basis Levi, with 15 years' service, is entitled to more notice than Jeong, with a mere two years' service. The rationale is that a long-serving employee does not have the same degree or breadth of experience as an employee who has had several shorter-term jobs. In essence, a long-serving employee has a smaller range of comparable re-employment prospects.

Reasonable notice is not calculated by a rule of thumb of one month of notice for every year of service.[14] Short-term employees, in particular, have often received notice periods well above the one-month per year of service benchmark.

Why are older employees generally entitled to more notice than younger employees?

Age

Older employees, particularly those over 50 years of age, are entitled to more notice than younger employees because they have more difficulty finding employment. Many employers are unwilling to hire older persons. Levi, at 56 years of age, is entitled to more notice than 32-year-old Jeong.

Younger employees in their 20s and 30s are generally entitled only to short periods of notice despite high rates of unemployment among youth.

Availability of Similar Employment

The more employment opportunities available, the shorter the period of notice to which the employee will be entitled. The availability of employment opportunities may be gauged by expert opinion of job openings, advertisements, and other indicators of market conditions. From a practical perspective, the availability of job opportunities will be affected by an employee's experience, training, and qualifications.

Developments in Notice

Although the factors in *Bardal v. Globe & Mail* remain of prime importance in determining reasonable notice, they are not an exhaustive list. Other factors that tend to lengthen notice are

- a high degree of specialization
- inducement to join an organization

11. (1994), 19 O.R. (3d) 515 (Gen Div.).
12. *Cronk v. Canadian General Insurance* (1995), 25 O.R. (3d) 505 (C.A.).
13. *Supra* note 5 at. 9–22.1.
14. *Supra* note 5 at 9–15.

- company policy
- custom and industry practice
- personal characteristics
- economic climate[15]

Risks in Dismissal with Notice

The calculation of reasonable notice is a task fraught with uncertainty. Although the factors used in the calculation are well known, the weight to be given to each is uncertain, other than each factor must be appropriately weighted. Most courts list the factors and then state a period of notice without indicating whether one factor has been given more weight than another. Notice periods have generally increased, and there have even been a couple of cases where the notice period has exceeded two years.[16] This development suggests that there is not a general cap on notice, although in most provinces it is recognized that the maximum range for reasonable notice is between 18 and 24 months.[17]

How much notice would Levi and Jeong be entitled to? Levi is a 56-year-old management employee with 15 years' experience and unknown employment opportunities. He would be entitled to approximately 16 to 18 months notice. Jeong is a 32-year-old staff reporter with two years' experience and unknown employment opportunities. She would probably be entitled to notice of one to two months.

Ethical Considerations

Competing for Employees

In some industries, competition is fierce for employees with certain skills, qualifications, and experience. Employers go to great lengths to entice a prospective employee to join their organization. Employers often succeed in hiring employees away from competitors by promising security, bonuses, stock options, and a host of other benefits. There is no guarantee, however, that the employment relationship will be a mutually profitable one, and sometimes it may be necessary to terminate the employment of the very person the employer went to great lengths to hire.

CRITICAL ANALYSIS: What role, if any, should the "enticement" of the employee have in the dismissal process? Should it lengthen the notice period? By how much? Should inducement as a factor in notice be discounted after a period of years?

Constructive Dismissal

An employer has no entitlement to make a fundamental change to the employment contract without the employee's consent. The employee may accept the change and create a new employment contract or refuse to accept the change, quit, and sue for

---

15. See generally Ellen Mole, *The Wrongful Dismissal Handbook*, 2nd ed. (Toronto: Butterworths, 1997) at 170–196.
16. See, for example, *Dey v. Valley Forest Products Ltd.* (1995), 162 N.B.R. (2d) 207 (C.A.), where the court awarded 28 months; *Donovan v. N.B. Publishing* (1996), 184 N.B.R. (2d) 40 (N.B.C.A.), where the court awarded 28 months; and *Selick v. 149244 Canada Inc.*, (1994), 15 C.C.E.L. (2d) 176 (O.C.A.), where an elderly employee was awarded three years' notice.
17. *Supre* note 5 at 9-11-9-12.

constructive dismissal
Employer conduct that amounts to a breach of a fundamental term of the employment contract.

fundamental term
A term that is considered to be essential to the contract.

what is called **constructive dismissal.** The dismissal is not express—the employer has not said to the employee, "You're fired"—but changing a key aspect of the employment contract may be equivalent to dismissal.

Fundamental Changes

For constructive dismissal to arise, the employer must make a significant change to a **fundamental term** of the contract, without the employee's consent. A minor change will not generally trigger a constructive dismissal, although the cumulative effect of many minor changes may do so. As well, the employment contract may reserve for the employer the right to make certain unilateral changes without triggering a constructive dismissal. For example, geographical transfers are often provided for in the contract.

Generally, the changes that are considered to be fundamental are adverse changes to salary/benefits, job function, responsibility, and the power/reporting structures, although other changes may be considered fundamental depending on the circumstances. It is negative changes that trigger constructive dismissal, as employees normally readily accept positive changes. Hiram's contemplated merger of two departments with the result that Josiah reports to Stella rather than Hiram may trigger a constructive dismissal. Even though Josiah may have the same job title and may be earning the same money, changing the reporting structure is, in effect, a demotion.

CASE ▼

Farber v. Royal Trust Co., [1997] 1 S.C.R. 846

THE BUSINESS CONTEXT: In the 1980s, it was common to see whole industries restructure and downsize. Many employees lost their jobs; others saw their jobs changed.

FACTUAL BACKGROUND: In June 1984, as part of a major restructuring of its real estate arm in Quebec, Royal Trust decided to eliminate all but one of its regional manager positions.[18] At the time, David Farber, age 44, was the highly regarded regional manager for Western Quebec. He had been with the company for 18 years and had received many promotions. As regional manager, he supervised 400 real estate agents and administered 21 offices, whose real estate sales exceeded $16 million in 1983. He had a base salary of $48 800, but with commissions and benefits, his earnings were $150 000 in 1983.

Royal Trust offered him the manager's job at one of the company's least profitable branches in Quebec—a position he had been promoted from eight years previously. The branch employed 20 real estate agents and had sales of $616 000 in 1983. As well, the company proposed to eliminate his base salary and to pay him by commission only. Farber estimated that his income would be reduced by half. He tried to negotiate with the company, but to no avail. He was told to appear at the new branch on a certain date; if he did not, he would be deemed to have resigned. Farber did not show up for work and sued.

THE LEGAL QUESTION: Had Farber been constructively dismissed from his job?

RESOLUTION: Farber lost both at trial and on appeal largely owing to the admission of evidence showing that sales at the new branch were very good in 1984 and that Farber would have earned about the same as he had earned in 1983. The trial judge, in particular, thought that Royal Trust's offer was reasonable and adequate, both in terms of money and prestige, and that Farber should have accepted it.

---

18. Although this case arose in Quebec and was decided pursuant to the civil law, the court noted that the doctrine of constructive dismissal, a creature of the common law, is now also part of the civil law. The case therefore has application to Canadian jurisdictions outside Quebec.

The Supreme Court of Canada overturned the decision and awarded Farber damages equivalent to one year's pay. The court held that where an employer decides unilaterally to make substantial changes to the essential terms of an employee's contract and the employee does not agree to the changes and leaves her job, the employee has not resigned, but has been dismissed. This is a constructive dismissal. The test for determining whether a substantial change is made is an objective one; the basic question is whether at the time of the change the reasonable person would believe that essential terms of the employment contract were being changed. Subsequent evidence of what actually happened is irrelevant—the critical time for assessment is the time the changes were made. The change to

Farber's employment was substantial, since it amounted to a demotion with less income.

The court also noted that an employer can make changes to an employee's position, but the extent of the changes depends on what the parties agreed to at the time of entering into the contract. Constructive dismissal does not have to involve bad faith on the part of the employer. There need be no intent on the employer's part to force the employee out. In other words, sound business reasons for making changes are not a defence in a constructive dismissal suit.

CRITICAL ANALYSIS: Do you think the doctrine of constructive dismissal unduly affects a company's ability to manage its affairs?

"Bad" Behaviour

Although most constructive dismissal cases involve demotions and pay cuts, the doctrine is not limited to these kinds of factors. Unacceptable or unethical practices by an employer may amount to constructive dismissal. For example, the B.C. Supreme Court awarded constructive dismissal damages to an employee who quit when he discovered that his boss was sending out fraudulent bills.[19] Humiliating or abusive behaviour, such as shouting and swearing, and threats of dismissal can also constitute constructive dismissal.[20]

In *Shah v. Xerox Canada Ltd.*,[21] the Ontario Court of Appeal upheld an employee's claim of constructive dismissal where the employer's conduct, which included unjustified criticisms and unfair performance appraisals, created intolerable working conditions. The court indicated that it is unnecessary that an employee establish that the employer breached a specific term of the employment contract. It is sufficient that the employee prove a poisoned or intolerable work environment.

Risks in Constructive Dismissal

A change in a fundamental term of an employment contract can trigger constructive dismissal. Before making changes that affect an employee's job, employers need to consider the nature of the change, whether the change is likely to be acceptable to the employee, why the change is being made, and whether there are any contractual provisions that permit the contemplated changes. An employer could also provide a "try-out" period where the employee can assess the changes prior to being required to accept them. These actions can help minimize the risk of triggering a constructive dismissal. Employers should also have procedures and systems in place for dealing with incidents or complaints of "bad" behaviour.

---

19. *Nethery v. Lindsey Morden Claim Services Ltd.* (1999), 127 B.C.A.C. 237 (B.C.C.A.).
20. See *Lloyd v. Imperial Parking Ltd.* (1996), 25 C.C.E.L. (2d) 97 (Alta. Q.B.).
21. (2000), 49 C.C.E.L. (2d) 166 (Ont. C.A.).

The term "whistleblowers" is often used to describe employees who "blow the whistle" or report wrongdoing involving their employers. Employees such as Lynn Brewer and Sherron Watkins, who disclosed the accounting irregularities and fraud at Enron, are sometimes greeted as heroes; often, however, they are viewed as rats or cranks and subjected to acts of retaliation and termination from their employment.

Take, for example, Linda Merk, the office manager and bookkeeper for Iron Workers Local 771 in Regina, Saskatchewan. She complained of irregular payment practices by two supervisors, the local's president and the business manager. She alleged that they misused a union credit card and were triple-claiming some expenses. She reported the wrongdoing to her direct supervisor, then to the board of trustees that reviews the monthly bills, then to the auditor who did the annual statement of the union, and then to the director of the international union. She was fired.

Merk invoked s. 74 of Saskatchewan's *Labour Standards Act* [22] which states, in part, that "no employer shall discharge or threaten to discharge an employee because the employee has reported or proposed to report to a lawful authority any activity that is likely to result in an offence ...." She won the first successful private prosecution under a whistleblower law in Canada. However, the union was later acquitted by a split Saskatchewan Court of Appeal. It held that the law did not protect her because she complained to her bosses, who were not a "lawful authority." The Supreme Court of Canada disagreed, stating that

"[T]he plain meaning of 'lawful authority' includes those who exercise authority in both the private and public interest." This includes individuals within the employer organization who exercise lawful authority over the employees complained about or over the activity that may result in an offense. Merk was ultimately reinstated to her job and awarded $250 000 in compensation. The union was fined $2000 for a first offence under the legislation.

The *Merk* decision has had a significant impact on whistleblowing legislation. Saskatchewan has acted to strengthen its legislation by broadening the definition of "lawful authority" and by allowing the director of labour standards to investigate and issue decisions respecting an employee's complaint of wrongful dismissal resulting from reporting wrongdoing. Also the Gomery Commission report referred to the *Merk* decision has called for amendments to the federal whistleblowing legislation to beef up the protection afforded to whistleblowers.

CRITICAL ANALYSIS: Does whistleblowing by an employee conflict with the employee's duty of loyalty and good faith to the employer? How should an employee's duty of loyalty and good faith be reconciled with the public's interest in exposing corporate wrongdoing? How can employees be encouraged to disclose corporate wrongdoing?

Source: *Merk v. International Assn. of Bridge, Structural, Ornamental and Reinforcing Iron Workers, Local 771*, [2005] 3 S.C.R. 425; and Deanna Driver, "Whistleblower Reinstated to Her Job in Saskatchewan" *The Lawyers Weekly*, (24 February 2006) at 1.

Wrongful Dismissal Suit

A wrongful dismissal suit may arise in several situations, for instance when an employee has been dismissed for cause and the employee claims there was no just cause, or when an employee is given notice of dismissal and the employee claims the notice was inadequate. Wrongful dismissal can also arise from a constructive dismissal. An employee is not obligated to go to a court to claim wrongful dismissal; she may proceed by making a claim to an employment standards tribunal. This action would limit an employee's compensation to an amount equivalent to the

22. Only Saskatchewan and New Brunswick have general legislative protection for good faith whistleblowing employees.

statutory period of notice. It is the route most often used by low-level employees, as they are often entitled to no more than the statutory notice and this method is considerably less expensive.

Specific performance or reinstatement is rarely an option in the nonunionized sector.[23] The common law does not provide for this remedy, on the rationale that after a termination the employment relationship is usually irreparably damaged.

CASE ▼

Wallace v. United Grain Growers, [1997] 3 S.C.R. 701

THE BUSINESS CONTEXT: Termination of employment can be a traumatic event for the employee. When such an event is handled in bad faith, it can be especially devastating.

FACTUAL BACKGROUND: Jack Wallace, age 59, had been a marketing manager for United Grain Growers for 14 years when he was terminated without explanation. Prior to his employment with United, he had worked for a competitor for 25 years. When he was originally approached by United, he was disinclined to leave his stable job. However, he was assured that if he performed satisfactorily he could work until retirement. In fact, he was United's top sales representative in each year prior to his abrupt termination. He sued for wrongful dismissal, whereupon the company alleged that it had cause to fire him. The company claimed that he was insubordinate and failed to carry out his duties. This allegation was abandoned at trial. The termination of employment and the allegations of cause created emotional difficulties for Wallace. He was forced to seek psychiatric help, was unable to find another job, and eventually declared bankruptcy.

THE LEGAL QUESTION: How much notice was Wallace entitled to?

RESOLUTION: The Supreme Court awarded Wallace 24 months' notice—14 months for reasonable notice based on age, length of service, and limited prospects for re-employment, and another 10 months for United's bad-faith conduct in the manner of dismissal.

The court stated that the end of the employment relationship is a very traumatic time for an employee—a time when the employee is most vulnerable and in need of protection. To ensure that the employee receives protection, employers ought to be held to an obligation of good faith and fair dealing in the manner of the dismissal. Mr. Justice Iacobucci wrote:

> The obligation of good faith and fair dealing is incapable of precise definition. However, at a minimum, I believe that in the course of dismissal employers ought to be candid, reasonable, honest and forthright with their employees and should refrain from engaging in conduct which is unfair or in bad faith by being for example, untruthful, misleading or unduly insensitive.

The court found several examples of bad faith on the part of United—the abrupt manner of dismissal after complimenting him on his work only days before; unfounded allegations of cause, which were maintained until the day of the trial; and the conscious decision of United to play "hardball" with Wallace. The finding of bad faith extended the notice period. The extension compensated for intangible injuries such as humiliation, embarrassment, and loss of self-esteem as well as tangible injuries to the employee's prospects for future employment.

CRITICAL ANALYSIS: The Supreme Court decision requires an employer to pay extra damages when unfounded allegations are made in the termination process or the employer otherwise treats the dismissed employee in a reprehensible fashion. Should employees be required to pay damages when they make unfounded, damaging, or irresponsible claims in the termination process?

---

23. Human rights legislation, however, provides for reinstatement.

Manner of Dismissal

An employer who conducts a dismissal "in bad faith" may be vulnerable to additional damages beyond those required for reasonable notice. This circumstance has become known as the *Wallace* factor.

The *Wallace* decision introduced the standard of good faith and fair dealing into the workplace. In addition to the instance of alleging cause when there is none, the Supreme Court gave several examples of bad faith:

- refusing to provide a deserved letter of reference
- terminating while on disability leave
- failing to communicate a termination decision in a timely manner
- communicating false allegations to potential employers

Since *Wallace* the courts have found a breach of the duty of good faith and fair dealing in numerous circumstances—failing to conduct a proper investigation prior to dismissal, neglecting to give an employee an opportunity to explain her version of events, conducting the termination insensitively, withholding statutory severance unless the employee signs a release, being insensitive in timing the termination, escorting an employee out the door, and making it difficult for an employee to find new employment.[24] Also, *Wallace* damages are not limited to acts of the employer at the time of termination but may also involve pre- and post-termination conduct.[25]

The *Wallace* factor can increase considerably the notice period in appropriate cases. Although it is difficult to estimate exactly how many months of notice is added for bad faith conduct, generally the range is from one to six months.[26]

Wrongful Dismissal Damages

Once a court determines how many months' notice a successful claimant is entitled to, the general approach is to multiply this number by the salary and the benefits that the employee was entitled to for each month. In addition, the claimant may be entitled to other special damages for out-of-pocket losses associated with the termination. From the total, a deduction is made for any money earned (income from a new job) or received (employment insurance) during the notice period. As well, a deduction can be made for a failure to mitigate damages by promptly seeking replacement employment. Figure 21.1 illustrates a typical damage award in a successful wrongful dismissal case.

FIGURE 21.1

A Sample Damage Award for Wrongful Dismissal

Purchasing Manager, 29 years of service, annual salary of $80 000

Salary: ($6666.67 × 24 months' notice)	$160 000
Bad faith dismissal: ($6666.67 × 3 months' notice)	$20 000
Loss bonus entitlement:	$47 800
Fringe benefits: ($96.24 × 27 months)	$2 598.48
Total damages:	$230 398.48

Source: *Mitchell v. Westbourne Supply Alberta,* [2000] 2 C.C.E.L. (3d) 87 (Alta. Q. B.).

A claimant may also be entitled to other types of damages, such as aggravated and punitive damages. These will be awarded only where the damages arise from a separate, actionable wrong, such as deceit, breach of fiduciary duty, abuse of power, or defamation. These damages are generally awarded only in very exceptional circumstances.

---

24. Bill Rogers, "The 'Wallace Factor': Where's the Top?" *The Lawyers Weekly* (2 April 1999) at 7.
25. *Supra* note 5 at 22.42.
26. *Supra* note 5 at 9-78–9-80.

THE BUSINESS CONTEXT: When an employee carries a white cane wears a hearing aide, or sits in a wheelchair, an employer's duty to accommodate is obvious. When an employee has a "hidden" disability—depression, mental illness, chronic fatigue syndrome—the employer has no less an obligation to accommodate.

FACTUAL BACKGROUND: Kevin Keays began working at Honda's Alliston, Ontario, assembly plant in 1986. After 20 months on the production line, he moved to the Quality Engineering Department, where he became a specialist in implementing design changes in cars. His health deteriorated, and in 1996 he began receiving disability payments. Two years later the payments were terminated when the insurance company concluded that his claim could not be supported by "objective medical evidence." He returned to work, although his doctor had diagnosed him as suffering from chronic fatigue syndrome. Keays continued to experience work absences, and when he complained that a disability caused his absences, Honda put him on a program that required him to produce a doctor's note every time he was absent. When Keays's absences exceeded his doctor's estimates, he was directed to the company doctor who expressed reservations about his condition and suggested that he be sent back to the production line. When Honda subsequently requested him to see an independent medical specialist, Keays refused unless the purpose of the second medical assessment was clearly stated. The company refused and terminated Keays for insubordination. Keays was advised of his termination by a coworker who phoned him at home to tell him that his dismissal had been announced to the department.

THE LEGAL QUESTION: Was Keays wrongfully terminated from his employment?

RESOLUTION: The trial court found that Honda's request for Keays to see the independent medical specialist was not made in good faith but was made as a prelude to terminating him to avoid having to accommodate his disability. Keays, because of previous difficulties with his employer over his absences, had a reasonable basis for believing that Honda would continue to refuse to recognize the legitimacy of his disability. Therefore, Keays had good cause for his failure to follow the employer's direction. Honda's reaction to Keays's alleged insubordination was disproportionate. It was not just cause for dismissing Keays. The court awarded Keays 15 months notice for his almost 14 years of service, 9 months notice for the egregious bad faith displayed by Honda in the manner of dismissal, and $500 000 punitive damages on the basis that Honda had committed acts of discrimination and harassment in relation to Keays's attempts to resolve his accommodation difficulties.

In a 2-1 decision, the Court of Appeal upheld the trial court's decision, but reduced the punitive damages to $100 000 on the basis that the trial judge relied on findings of fact that were not supported by the evidence and because the award did not meet the requirement of proportionality. In particular, the appeal court stated that the trial judge's finding that Honda's outrageous conduct had persisted over a period of five years was a gross distortion of the circumstances. The misconduct for which Honda was responsible took place over a seven-month period. Also, while the appeal court acknowledged the gravity of some of the conduct of Honda, it could not be characterized as "malicious."

CRITICAL ANALYSIS: Although the Court of Appeal reduced the punitive damages award by 80 percent, it still stands as the largest punitive damages award in a wrongful dismissal case in Canada. Do you think the award is still disproportionate to the loss or damage? What message does this case send to employers?

Duty to Mitigate

Employees who have been terminated or constructively dismissed have a duty to mitigate their damages. This is not a duty that is unique to employment law. As pointed out in Chapter 9, this duty arises on the breach of most contracts.

The duty requires that an employee take reasonable steps to find comparable employment. What is required of an employee depends on the nature of the job, on the job market, and on the way that a job would normally be obtained in that market (e.g., by searching newspaper advertisements, registering at a human resource centre, searching the Internet, or engaging the services of an employment agency).

The duty requires the employee to look for comparable or similar employment. It does not require an employee to take or look for a lower-level job. Nor does it require an employee to take a lower position with the same employer, since working at the same place after a dismissal may be untenable.[27]

Terminated employees have a duty to mitigate their damages. What does this duty entail?

Whether the duty to mitigate requires an employee to move to look for employment depends on a host of factors, including age of employee, family situation, attachment to the community, prospects of employment in the present area, and the housing market. A failure to mitigate will result in a deduction from the damage award. The amount of the reduction varies and depends on the circumstances.

Business Application of the Law

Dealing with Wrongful Dismissal Suits

1. Review the claim carefully. Is it a claim you want to defend? Make sure you have not overlooked anything that could negatively affect your position.
2. Choose the right lawyer. Find a lawyer who specializes in employment law and who has the same philosophy as your organization on how such matters should be handled.
3. Ask for a legal opinion early on. It is better to be informed of a weak position at the beginning than to find out at trial.
4. Provide all relevant information and documentation to your lawyer, as your case will be only as good as the facts.
5. Never allege cause when none exists—just cause is difficult to defend, it usually means a lengthy trial, and if it is unsuccessfully argued it could cost you a lot of money.
6. Investigate even after termination. Evidence of improper conduct by the employee may come to light later, and this evidence may be used to strengthen your case.
7. Avoid defamatory statements, as they may lead to an action for defamation.
8. Consider providing a reference letter even if you have alleged cause. An accurate, factual reference will not automatically undermine your allegation of cause, but failure to provide a letter may increase the damages if the employee succeeds in a wrongful dismissal suit.
9. Always consider whether an offer to settle should be made, as a settlement may avoid further time and costs.
10. Consider mediation. Generally, neither party fares as well as it would like to, but the downside is never as bad either.

Source: Malcolm MacKillop, "Ten Ways to Deal with a Wrongful Dismissal Suit" The Globe and Mail (8 April 1997) at B13.

---

27. See *Farquhar v. Butler Bros. Supplies Ltd.* (1988), 23 B.C.L.R. (2d) 89 (C.A.).

Developments in Wrongful Dismissal Suits

In addition to wrongful dismissal suits, some employees have turned to other avenues to procure relief. In some situations the dismissed employee can sue for defamation. The advantage of this route is that damages for defamation are usually significantly higher than those for breach of the employment contract, as the amount of damages is not limited by the notice period. As well, the courts are more willing to award punitive damages pursuant to a defamation claim. A further claim that can be made by an employee is intentional infliction of mental suffering.[28]

Regardless of the action taken by a dismissed employee, litigation is an expensive process. It is a particularly expensive proposition in cases where an employee may not be entitled to a large sum of money in compensation if successful, even though there is legitimate cause of action. However, the availability of contingency fee arrangements, the class-action suit, and alternative dispute mechanisms is changing these dynamics somewhat and making it feasible for a group of ill-treated employees to pursue small claims.

Business Application of the Law | Class-Action Suits and ADR

Silicorp Limited is a large convenience store chain based in Ontario and operating under the names Mac's Milk and Mike's Mart. In 1996 it acquired the 530 stores of the Becker Milk Co., a rival. Consequently, Silicorp closed 30 stores and dismissed 90 redundant employees.

A former Becker's manager, Sherrie Gagne, initiated a class-action suit claiming that Silicorp had delayed payments of termination pay provided for under the *Employment Standards Act* (ESA), and had not provided reasonable notice as required under the common law. On behalf of all former employees dismissed in Ontario, she sought compensatory damages of $11 million, punitive damages of $1 million, and injunctive relief compelling payment of benefits required by the ESA.

Silicorp quickly opted to settle the suit, and the parties entered into a settlement agreement, which was approved by a Justice of the Ontario Court (General Division). Certification of the action as a class-action suit was granted by consent. It was the first mass class-action lawsuit for wrongful dismissal anywhere in Canada, and both parties claimed victory.

The settlement provided for the determination of individual claims for compensatory damages through a comprehensive ADR procedure. Silicorp agreed to pay ESA entitlements and party costs. The claim for punitive damages was dismissed. Within five months, most of the claims had been settled—half by mediation and half by arbitration. This was breathtaking speed, compared with litigation. Most employees received considerably more than the employment standards minimums. In total, the 60-plus members of the class-action suit recovered over $2 million in damages.

CRITICAL ANALYSIS: Why do you think both parties claimed victory?

Source: Jeff Burtt, "Class Action, ADR Give Downsized Workers Speedy Remedy" *The Lawyers Weekly* (8 October 1998) at 8.

Termination Settlements

The costs associated with a wrongful dismissal suit can be high. Therefore, it may be incumbent on an employer to offer a termination settlement or severance package rather than dismiss for just cause.

---

28. The Ontario Court of Appeal has awarded damages for such a claim in the employment context. See *Prinzo v. Baycrest Center for Geriatric Care*, (2002). 60 O.R. (3d) 474 (C.A.).

Negotiation of the Settlement

severance pay

An amount owed to a terminated employee under employment standards legislation.

The package offered should contain all monies due to the employee at the time of termination including statutory entitlements such as **severance pay.** The package may also include other items such as pension benefits, medical or dental coverage, disability insurance, tax-sheltered income, stock options, and financial or career counselling. An employer should also consider providing a factual letter of reference to assist the employee. An employee should be given a period of time (one to two weeks) to consider the termination settlement and should be encouraged to seek independent advice on the fairness of the offer.

The termination settlement may help the departed employee feel better about the termination. A fair offer and settlement may also help keep remaining employees motivated. A fair settlement may ultimately avoid a lawsuit and be less costly in the long run. It also helps maintain a positive corporate image.

The Release

release

A written or oral statement discharging another from an existing duty.

When an employee accepts a termination package, it is customary to have the employee sign a **release.** The release normally indicates that the employee has been dismissed and paid a sum of money in return for giving up any right of action against the employer. The release form may include a stipulation that the employee will not pursue an action for wrongful dismissal, as well as a statement that the employee has not been discriminated against and therefore will not pursue a claim under human rights legislation. It may also contain provisions to keep the settlement confidential and restrictions preventing the employee from competing against the former employer.

A release will normally be binding on the employee, provided that the settlement was fair and reasonable, the release was clear and unambiguous, and the employee had ample time to consider the package and obtain independent advice. On the other hand, a release will likely be unenforceable if the termination package was "unconscionable" and the employee did not obtain independent advice.

The Union Context

The provisions of a collective agreement will vary depending on the nature of the industry involved and the issues the parties bring to the negotiating table. The agreement will provide for a process for settling disputes arising from the agreement. This procedure is usually the only route a unionized employee has to challenge an employer's dismissal decision.[29] The final step in the procedure is arbitration, which is binding on the parties. Unlike the situation in the nonunionized sector, courts do not make the final decision.

In addition, most agreements will have specific provisions relating to termination.

Grievance and Arbitration

grievance process

A procedure for resolving disputes contained in union contracts.

Regardless of the individual content of collective agreements, disputes about their interpretation, administration, or application are required to be submitted to a **grievance process.** The grievance procedure will vary widely from organization to organization. Some procedures involve only a couple of steps; others have several. All usually have time limits attached to the steps, and most begin with an informal consultation. The final step in almost all jurisdictions is third-party binding arbitration.[30] This step arises when the dispute cannot be resolved by less formal means and all the other steps in the grievance process have failed.

---

29. The existence of a collective agreement that applies to an employee and provides for final settlement of disputes bars a wrongful dismissal action. *Supra* note 15 at 128.
30. Saskatchewan is the exception.

The arbitration itself usually involves either a single arbitrator or a three-person panel, which conducts a hearing of the grievance and renders a decision. The arbitrator may dismiss the grievance; order compensation for breach of the collective agreement; order reinstatement of the employee without loss of seniority and with back wages and benefits; or, in most jurisdictions, fashion a remedy somewhere between dismissal and full reinstatement. The arbitration award can be filed with the court and enforced in the same manner as a judicial decision.

Seniority

Most collective agreements contain an extensive clause dealing with seniority (the length of time the employee has been with the company). These clauses usually provide that an employer cannot promote, demote, transfer, lay off (usually defined as temporary suspension of the employment relationship), or recall without giving some consideration to the seniority of the employee. These clauses do not, however, affect the employer's ability to terminate the employment relationship (usually referred to as "discharge" in labour law).

Discipline and Discharge

The general rule in the union context is that an employer may not discipline or discharge an employee without justification or just cause.

The discipline and discharge of employees is the largest category of grievances carried to arbitration. In assessing whether the penalty imposed by the employer was appropriate in the circumstances, the arbitrator will look for evidence of progressive discipline. In other words, discipline should progress from warnings to suspensions and only finally to discharge. In upholding a particular penalty imposed by an employer, the arbitrator will consider many factors, including the following:

- the record and service of the employee
- provocation
- any special economic hardship imposed on the employee by the penalty
- the seriousness of the offence
- premeditation
- uniform enforcement of policies and rules
- circumstances negating intent
- condonation

The arbitrator has the authority to mitigate or soften the severity of the penalty imposed by the employer. In other words, the arbitrator may substitute his judgment for that of management (unless the collective agreement mandates a specific penalty for the infraction).

Business Law in Practice Revisited

1. Is Hiram justified in terminating Jeong Nash and Levi Cameron?

A dramatic drop in circulation that results in a genuine lack of work is a good reason for terminating employees, but it is not legal or just cause, which deprives employees of reasonable notice. Jeong's controversial stories do not amount to incompetence or misconduct, particularly in view of Hiram's apparent condonation. The cumulative effect of Levi's infractions—off-colour jokes, sexist comments, and inappropriate material on his computer—may constitute misconduct. However, prior to dismissal, the employer must consider the following questions: Was Levi's behaviour contrary to a company policy? Was Levi aware of the company policy? Was Levi given a warning about his behaviour? Did he understand that failure to improve could lead to termination? That said, a single incidence of bad conduct may be sufficient grounds for dismissal without notice. For example, if Levi downloaded truly offensive material onto his work computer, that could amount to grounds for dismissal.

2. Is Hiram entitled to change Josiah Rutgers's position?

The merger of two departments resulting in a change to the reporting structure may trigger a constructive dismissal. Although Josiah would receive the same pay and have the same title, reporting to Stella rather than Hiram is an obvious demotion. Hiram may want to consider whether Josiah is likely to accept the change and whether there are sufficient benefits to the change that, in the overall context, he will not view the change negatively. Also, Hiram may want to offer Josiah a period of time to try out the change to see if he likes it. An employer is entitled to make some changes without triggering a dismissal; Hiram should check Josiah's employment contract to see what is permissible.

3. What course of action would you advise Hiram to pursue?

As it is highly unlikely that Hiram has grounds to dismiss Jeong and, possibly, Levi, he needs to consider what a reasonable settlement would be. Levi is an older, long-serving, high-level employee, so he is probably entitled to notice somewhere in the 16- to 18-month range. For Jeong, a younger, shorter-term, low-level employee, reasonable notice would probably be somewhere in the one- to two-month range. The amount of notice for both employees is affected in either direction by the availability of alternative employment. Hiram should seek legal advice on this issue, as this area of the law is somewhat unpredictable and subject to rapid change.

Hiram should know that the proposed change in Josiah's position may trigger a constructive dismissal. He needs to consider whether Josiah is likely to view the change negatively. If he does he needs to reconsider the change or terminate Josiah with reasonable notice. As a younger, short-term, middle-level employee, he is likely entitled to notice in the 2- to 4-month range depending, again, on alternative employment opportunities.

Hiram should carefully choose the manner of dismissal. The predicted range of notice for the employees could be severely affected by any bad-faith conduct on his part, such as alleging cause when there is none, escorting the employee out the door, refusing to provide a fair reference, or otherwise acting in bad faith.

Chapter Summary

Employment ends when an employee resigns or retires, or when the employer dismisses, gives notice, or otherwise terminates the relationship. An employer may, subject to contractual provisions, summarily terminate an employee if just cause exists. What constitutes just cause is a question of fact, but it must involve a situation where the employee has breached a fundamental term of the employment contract. In the absence of just cause, an employer must give notice (or pay in lieu) of termination. Notice is either what is specified in the employment contract or reasonable notice. The latter is determined by reference to the employee's age, position within the organization, and length of service, and by the availability of alternative employment. When the employer breaches a fundamental term of the employment contract (i.e., demotes or cuts pay), the employee may treat the breach as a constructive dismissal. The termination of employment by the employer is often a traumatic event in the life of the employee. Courts have increasingly put an onus on the employer to act fairly and decently toward the terminated employee. In the event of a successful wrongful dismissal suit, an employer may be required to compensate for unfair and harsh conduct in the termination process. Wrongful dismissal suits can be costly, time consuming, and embarrassing. An employer may want to reduce the risks by considering a termination settlement that provides a measure of compensation to an employee. It may be much cheaper in the long run.

Chapter Study

Key Terms and Concepts

condonation (p. 521)

conduct incompatible (p. 522)

constructive dismissal (p. 528)

fundamental term (p. 528)

grievance process (p. 536)

habitual neglect of duty (p. 522)

incompetence (p. 522)

just cause (p. 520)

progressive discipline policy (p. 521)

reasonable notice (p. 524)

release (p. 536)

serious misconduct (p. 521)

severance pay (p. 536)

willful disobedience (p. 522)

Questions for Review

1. In what circumstances may an employee be terminated?

2. What is meant by "just cause"?

3. What is a progressive discipline policy? How does a progressive discipline policy affect the termination of employees?

4. When does incompetence amount to just cause for dismissal?

5. An employer may dismiss an employee for cause when the employee's conduct is prejudicial to the employer's business. Give an example of conduct that is prejudicial to the employer's business.

6. In the absence of just cause, how much notice of termination must an employee be given?

7. In the absence of just cause, how much notice must a superior performing employee be given?

8. How is reasonable notice calculated?

9. In the calculation of reasonable notice, which factor is the most important? Explain.

10. In general, a longer-term employee is entitled to more notice than a shorter-term employee. What is the rationale for this distinction?

11. What is constructive dismissal? Give an example.

12. How can a wrongful dismissal suit arise? Name three ways.

13. Why is the manner of termination important?

14. When is a successful litigant entitled to punitive damages? Explain.

15. What is the duty to mitigate? When does it arise?

16. What should a termination settlement contain?

17. How does the process for termination differ between the union and nonunion sectors?

18. What is the grievance process? When is it used?

Questions for Critical Thinking

1. Some lower courts have suggested that there are or should be caps on notice periods—12 months for low-level employees and 24 months for high-level employees. What are the advantages and disadvantages of caps?

2. Cleo was fired shortly after a leak from her company resulted in sensitive information being aired on a radio news show. A search of company phone records revealed that Cleo had made a call to the radio station.[31] Do you think she has an action for wrongful dismissal?

3. Are superior employees entitled to more notice than mediocre ones? Should they be? Should there be less notice for mediocre employees (as in near cause)? What would be the problems with such a system?

4. The rationale for not awarding specific performance or reinstatement in wrongful dismissal cases is that the employment relationship may be irreparably damaged. How would you argue against this rationale?

5. An employer who breaches the duty of good faith and fair dealing when terminating an employment relationship is required to pay *Wallace* damages. Should every wrongful dismissal case result in an award of *Wallace* damages? What should happen if the employee's allegation of bad faith was frivolous and unfounded?

6. It is not uncommon for a prospective employee to set out his qualifications and past experience in a favourable light when applying for a position with a new company. Do you think that overstating qualifications when applying for work should constitute just cause for dismissal?

Situations for Discussion

1. The Consumers' Association of Canada had been without an executive director for a number of months when it hired David Simpson in 1989. Over the next couple of years, Simpson received positive evaluations on his performance, particularly in respect to securing maximum potential funding from the federal government. In 1992, the board of directors received several complaints about Simpson's inappropriate conduct—he had invited his staff to his cottage, stripped down, and gone skinny-dipping; he invited staff members to a strip club; he had an affair with a subordinate; and on another occasion, he jumped naked into a hot tub, joining others who were partially dressed.[32] Is the board of directors justified in dismissing Simpson? Explain.

2. Ramone Johnson, age 34, was fired from her job as assistant spa manager at the luxurious Ocean Pointe Resort Hotel in Victoria after five years'

---

31. "Cleo Makes an Unfortunate Call" *The Globe and Mail* (11 August 1998) at B15.
32. Based on *Simpson v. Consumers' Assn. of Canada* (2001), 209 D.L.R. (4th) 213 (Ont. C.A.).

employment. She had returned from maternity leave just one month prior to her termination. At that time she found that her duties had been taken over by other employees. The hotel manager offered Ramone five weeks' statutory severance pay on the condition that she sign a release protecting the hotel from any further action. She signed the release but now feels "exploited."[33] What should she do?

3. William A. Campbell worked for Hong Kong–based Wellfund Audio-Visual Ltd. at a salary of $8000 a month. He had been with the company for only eight months when he was terminated. The company claimed that he was dismissed for financial irregularities, but the real reason was that he had refused to cooperate when asked to create reasons for terminating the company's controller. When Campbell refused to cooperate, Wellfund executives began harassing and threatening him. He took a six-week leave for stress and on his return was fired.

At the time of his termination, Campbell's health had deteriorated from stress caused by the harassment. As well, a genetic predisposition to migraine headaches had been exacerbated. Following his termination, he suffered nightmares, panic attacks, paranoia, depression, and other anxiety-related disorders. He was unable to work for two years after his termination, and at one point he had to go on social assistance to support himself and his family. Campbell successfully sued Wellfund for wrongful dismissal.[34] What factors would the courts consider in an award of damages?

4. Randal Martin joined International Maple Leaf Springs Water Corp. of Vancouver, B.C., in July 1994. He was hired to assist with the construction of a bottling plant at a spring near Chilliwack, B.C., and to develop markets in North America and Asia. He had been running a similar operation in Saskatchewan but left on the assurance that the B.C. company was viable and

would be able to finance the new plant and fund the marketing initiatives. By March 1995, Martin had settled contracts with six companies and was close to three more, including a major deal with an American brewery that wanted to use its own brand name on Maple Leaf's products.

In April 1995, the company fired Martin, accusing him of dishonesty and of coming to work drunk. Maple Leaf alleged that Martin was dishonest in registering trade names belonging to the company. Martin had registered trade names personally, as the company did not have the funds to do this itself. The president of Maple Leaf knew about Martin registering the trade names and knew that the trade names would be transferred to the company as soon as Martin was repaid. There was no evidence of Martin's coming to work drunk. Martin successfully sued for wrongful dismissal.[35] What would be reasonable notice in this situation? What factors would the courts consider in awarding a period of notice?

5. Clyde Peters worked as a senior systems analyst for 17 years at NJ Industries. He had a good work record and a positive image throughout the company. Recently, he came under the supervision of the new controller, John Baxter, who quickly found himself dissatisfied with Peters's performance. Baxter believes that Peters failed to properly implement the company's new computerized financial system. As well, he feels that Peters has failed to design a strategic plan for his department.

These two matters have caused considerable problems between the two. Baxter is considering recommending Peters's termination.[36] How should the problem be resolved? Do grounds for termination exist?

6. Zizel Utility has reason to believe that one of its long-term trusted employees has been defrauding the company. Joe Plates, the supervisor of the accounts receivables department, has

---

33. Based on *Stolle v. Daishin pan (Canada) Inc.* (1998),37 C.C.E.L. (2d) 18 (B.C.S.C.).
34. Based on *Campbell v. Wellfund Audio-Visual Ltd.* (1995), 14 C.C.E.L. (2d) 240 (B.C.S.C.).
35. Based on *Martin v. International Maple Leaf Springs Water Corp.* (1998), 38 C.C.E.L. (2d) 128 (B.C.S.C.).
36. Based on *Russell v. Nova Scotia Power* (1996), 150 N.S.R. (2d) 271 (S.C.).

worked for Zizel for 17 years and has an excellent work record. While Joe was on holidays, his replacement discovered a fraud. A review of the bank statements indicate that $14 000 is missing from one of Zizel's bank accounts. As Joe is in charge of depositing customer payments, it is probable that he has taken the money. What are Zizel's options in dealing with the alleged fraud? What are the risks associated with each option?

7. Philip Kelly was a materials manager for Linamar Corporation. He supervised approximately 10 to 12 employees, some reporting to him directly and some indirectly. He was required to instruct his staff on a regular basis and had disciplinary authority over them. In addition, he was a member of the plant operating committee, which was a management committee. As such, he was regularly involved with management issues with his peers and other divisions of the company. In addition to his responsibilities within the company, Kelly was also responsible for contact with suppliers and customers of the company. He had worked at five different divisions of the company and was well known throughout the organization.

On 21 January 2003, Kelly was charged with possession of child pornography as a result of an investigation into a Texas child porn ring. By that time, he had been an employee with the company for 14 years, had a good employment record, and was earning $64 000 per year. Two days later Linamar dismissed Kelly for cause.[37] Does Linamar have just cause for dismissal?

Who has the onus to prove just cause? What is the standard of proof? What factors will the court consider in determining whether just cause exists?

8. Terry Schimp, 25, worked as a bartender for RCR Catering and Pubs. Although he was occasionally tardy, sometimes missed a staff meeting, and a few times was short on his cash, he was considered a productive employee. At the end of a private function that RCR was catering, one of Schimp's supervisors noticed an open water bottle on his bar. He took a drink and discovered that it was vodka, not water. Suspecting that Schimp had stolen the vodka, the supervisor immediately fired Schimp. He was escorted off the premises in front of about 50 other staff members, and he was banned for six months from returning to the hotel premises where RCR's offices were located. Schimp was extremely upset, but within a month he was able to get a new job with the same hourly rate of pay, only without tips. He sued for wrongful dismissal. At trial he was awarded $30 000 in damages. On appeal the damages were reduced to $10 000, of which approximately $7000 was compensation for the humiliation and degradation he suffered.[38] Aside from the damage award, what costs did RCR incur as a result of this situation? How should RCR have acted differently?

For more study tools, visit
http://www.businesslaw3e.nelson.com

---

37. Based on *Kelly v. Linamar Corporation*, [2005] O.J. No. 4899.
38. Based on *Schimp v. RCR Catering Ltd.* (2004), 221 N.S.R. (2d) 379 (C.A.).

Chapter

22

Objectives

After studying this chapter, you should have an understanding of

- how business uses the services of professionals
- the legal responsibilities of professionals to their clients and others who rely on their work
- the role of professional bodies

Professional Services

Business Law in Practice

Ted Dalmo is the CEO of Dalmo Technology Ltd. (DT), a well-established business supplying components to large telecommunications companies. Early in 2005, Ted and his management team (which included chief financial officer, Sandra Roberts, a professional accountant) decided to explore a major expansion of the business, in order to take advantage of the current revival in the industry. DT engaged its accounting firm, Asher & Breem, to do a feasibility study of the expansion plans. Asher & Breem had performed DT's audit for several years, but this was its first consulting engagement with Dalmo. Ted indicated to the firm that the projected profitability of the expanded business would need to be favourable in order to attract lenders and investors.

Asher & Breem's report indicated that based on DT's plans and projections, the expansion should produce sufficient cash flow to repay lenders and generate profits for a healthy return on equity for investors. DT was able to borrow from the Provincial Bank and sell shares in the company to a group of local investors. A few months after the expansion got under way, one of DT's major customers ran into financial difficulty, putting DT's revenue projections in jeopardy. In addition, when Asher & Breem did its next audit, it was revealed that revenue was inflated because of premature recognition of revenue from sales. The bank and the investors became nervous and began to exert pressure on Ted for better financial performance. Ted met with Sandra and told her that to survive the current crisis and keep the business going, the company would continue to recognize revenue as soon as possible and that Sandra as the CFO should seek additional means of improving the bottom line.

Meanwhile, to allay its fears about DT's profit picture, Provincial Bank insisted that DT have another audit conducted by a different accounting firm. Sandra was concerned that Ted's demands were dangerous. In her opinion, current practices at DT were pushing the limit of what is acceptable under generally accepted accounting principles. She was reluctant to explore further changes in reporting practices for the sole reason of improving DT's bottom line. Sandra consulted Bill Caton, DT's in-house legal counsel, regarding her legal and ethical position. To receive an independent opinion, Bill engaged DT's outside law firm, Holland & Hart. The firm advised Bill and Sandra to leave it to the auditors. DT continued to operate and its situation worsened. Within a year, the company was bankrupt.

1. Did the professionals fulfill their obligations to DT?
2. Did the professionals act consistently with their obligations to their professional bodies?
3. Can creditors and investors in DT recover their losses from the professionals?

Businesses and Professional Services

This chapter balances two different perspectives of professionals and business. The main focus is for students going into business careers to understand the professions and the various duties of their members. This enables businesspeople to structure their relationships with professionals and develop realistic expectations of professional services. The other focus is for students who will become members of professions and therefore need some understanding of the workings of professional bodies. Knowledge of these workings is also useful for business clients who engage professionals in order to maximize the utility of their services and manage their related risks.

Relationships and Obligations

professional

Someone engaged in an occupation requiring the exercise of special knowledge, education, and skill.

Businesses depend on **professional** services, which can be either supplied in-house or contracted out to private firms. Most mid- or large-sized businesses have professionals on staff. For example, DT employs a professional accountant, Sandra, as its CFO, and a practising lawyer, Bill, as in-house legal counsel. Other professional services, such as those of an engineer or architect, are hired on an *ad hoc* or project basis.

Whether the professional is an employee or an independent supplier of a service, that person owes responsibilities to the business. Professionals who are employees are governed by the basic principles of employment law. Relationships with external professional service providers are defined by contract law. In addition, the professional–client relationship is a special relationship of trust and loyalty that goes beyond the protection normally provided by contract. Professionals are held to higher standards than other service providers.

The legal or ethical obligations these professionals owe the business vary according to the capacity in which they are hired. For example, some professionals may move into purely managerial functions, and the individual will become non-practising with the relevant professional body.

Other employees choose to retain their professional status and are hired in this capacity. Corporate counsel are practising members of the provincial bar and are hired for their professional expertise. The chief financial officer, for example, may hold one or more of the three professional accounting designations and be a member of the relevant provincial body.

In principle, the legal obligations of employed professionals are the same as those working in private practices outside the firm. They are in a fiduciary relationship with their employer, where there exist elements of trust, confidence, and reliance on the professionals' skill, knowledge, and advice. They can be liable for negligence and their employers can be vicariously liable.

Ethical Obligations

Also significant to the employer are professionals' ethical obligations. Managers value the services of, for example, in-house lawyers, because of the independence and ethical training they bring to the task. Professionals retaining membership in the profession continue to be bound by the rules of professional conduct and codes of ethics of their professional bodies. These obligations bring a level of independence that distinguishes a professional employee from a manager. Both owe ethical obligations to their employers, but professionals have additional obligations imposed by their governing bodies.

Ethical conflicts or dilemmas tend to arise when the business is under stress. Ted pressured Sandra to adopt aggressive accounting practices that she believed were counter to her professional obligations. The motive appeared honourable—to "save the company." However, the accounting profession had good reasons for establishing the rules governing Sandra. If she violates these rules, she is breaching her own professional responsibilities and risking sanction (up to and including removal from the profession). Moreover, she will be placing DT at further risk, since outsiders reviewing the conduct will hold DT responsible for any harm that results.

Hiring Professionals In-House

Deciding whether to acquire professional services on a contract basis from outside firms or to hire full-time professionals as employees is difficult. If the cost of external professional services for a business becomes significant, the business will likely consider the employment option. It is important that this decision be approached systematically and that all costs, quantitative and qualitative, be incorporated in the analysis. What level of experience is required of an in-house professional? Is there a need for specialization, and will there still be a need to hire externally from time to time, and if so at what cost? In-house professionals should provide enhanced value through their knowledge of the organization, their skill in managing external services, and their ability to contribute to risk management programs. DT has at some point decided to hire an accountant as CFO and a lawyer as counsel. However, outside services are still required, such as the audit from Asher & Breem and independent legal opinions from Holland & Hart. DT should regularly evaluate the cost-effectiveness of these arrangements.

Responsibilities of Professionals to Clients and Others Who Rely on Their Work

Professionals owe a range of responsibilities to their clients, many of which are identical to those of all service providers. The accounting firm, Asher & Breem, and the law firm, Holland & Hart, owe contractual responsibilities to DT. Likewise, professionals owe tort duties; in particular, those arising from negligence. Finally, beyond contract and tort duties, professionals owe fiduciary responsibilities to their clients.

Responsibilities in Contract

Professional responsibilities in any given engagement are defined, in part, by contract. The nature of the service to be provided, the timeliness of the delivery of the service, and the way in which that service will be billed are established by the terms of the contract between the professional and the client. The legal rules governing the contract are those described in Part Two of this text.

In practice, contractual terms are often determined by the professional, and only a well-prepared user might think to negotiate additional or alternative provisions. Clients are often unaware of provisions in the contract dealing with how work will be billed and how and when **retainers** will be required. Clients should treat their contracts with professionals in the same careful and questioning manner as other contracts for goods and services.

retainer
An advance payment requested by a professional from a client to fund services to be provided to the client.

Both professional and client must comply with the terms of the contract negotiated. The most contentious issues in practice tend to be those relating to quality of service and the fee. If a client is dissatisfied, most professional associations have mechanisms for providing advice and investigating fee and quality-of-service disputes. Lawyer–client bills are subject to special provisions.[1] Clients may submit lawyers' bills to taxing officers for review. The officer determines whether the sum charged was fair and reasonable in the circumstances.

---

1. For example, *Legal Profession Act*, R.S.B.C. 1998, c. 9, ss. 78–83.

rior to engaging a professional's services, a client needs to address the key terms of the contract. Of particular importance are the following:

- How will fees be charged—by the hour, as a flat fee for the particular task, as a percentage of the value of the transaction, or on a contingency-fee basis?[2] Although the flat-fee and percentage approaches appear more certain, the client must be satisfied that the charges are appropriate for the nature of the service. Hourly rates can, with proper monitoring, provide control over costs. Professionals generally are receptive to alternative fee structures and terms of payment that fit the client's business structure and practices.

- What expertise is required for the work? Does the professional fully understand the client's business needs? The professional should inform the client if expertise should be sought from another source.

- Do both parties understand the nature of the work to be performed and the likely results? Are the client's expectations appropriate and reflected in the agreement?

- When is the project to be completed? How will the changes to the schedule be addressed?

- How frequently will the professional contact the client? The relationship should provide for reasonable consultation and input from the client.

- How will disputes about the engagement be handled? The agreement should contain a process acceptable to both parties.

- How will risk be allocated? The agreement should provide for unforeseen developments during the course of the contract.

If a contract price is not stated, the principle of *quantum meruit* applies—the professional provides an appropriate level of service, and the client pays a reasonable amount for that service. For small tasks performed by a familiar service provider, this situation is satisfactory because fee disputes are unlikely and there is little at risk. However, for larger engagements or contracts with a new service provider, such an arrangement leaves too many issues unresolved.

CRITICAL ANALYSIS: What are the risks if a professional service contract is not in place?

Fiduciary Responsibilities

The word "fiduciary" was introduced in Chapters 13, 14, 16, and 20. Agents owe fiduciary responsibilities to their principals; directors owe fiduciary responsibilities to the corporation; partners owe fiduciary responsibilities to one another; and senior or key employees owe fiduciary responsibilities to their employers. The essence of the professional–client relationship is also fiduciary. Professionals act in a fiduciary capacity and are deemed by law to owe duties of loyalty, trust, and confidence that go beyond those contractual or tort responsibilities owed by the nonprofessional service provider.[3]

---

2. See Chapter 4.
3. *Hodgkinson v. Simms*, [1994] 3 S.C.R. 377.

A fiduciary must act primarily in the interest of the person to whom a responsibility is owed. This is a broad and overriding concept captured by the notions of loyalty and trust. It is also expressed in terms of specific obligations. The professional as fiduciary must

- avoid any conflict of interest between the client's affairs and those of the professional or the firm
- refrain from using the relationship for personal profit beyond charging a reasonable fee for services provided
- follow the client's instructions
- disclose all relevant information to the client
- act honestly, in good faith, and with due care
- maintain confidentiality of client information

The fiduciary must comply with the *spirit* of the obligation and not merely the letter. The case below illustrates the fiduciary obligation. See also the *Strother* case in Chapter 14.

CASE ▼

Hodgkinson v. Simms, [1994]
3 S.C.R. 377

THE BUSINESS CONTEXT: Professionals sometimes blur their professional and business activities, raising questions of where the boundaries of the fiduciary obligations begin and end.

FACTUAL BACKGROUND: In 1980 Hodgkinson hired Simms, a chartered accountant, for independent advice about tax shelters. Simms recommended investment in multi-unit residential buildings (MURBs). Their relationship and Hodgkinson's confidence in Simms were such that Hodgkinson did not ask many questions regarding the investments. He trusted Simms to do the necessary analysis and believed that if Simms recommended a project, it was a good investment. Hodgkinson made substantial investments in four MURBs recommended by Simms. In 1981 the real estate market in British Columbia collapsed, and Hodgkinson lost most of his investment. His claim against Simms was based on breach of fiduciary duty. Specifically, by not advising Hodgkinson that he had a personal stake in the MURBs (the developers were also Simms's clients and, in addition to fees, Simms received a bonus for MURBs sold), Simms failed to provide the independent advice for which he was hired and thus breached his fiduciary duties to Hodgkinson.

THE LEGAL QUESTION: Did Simms owe a fiduciary responsibility to Hodgkinson and, if so, did his actions amount to a violation of that responsibility?

RESOLUTION: Justice La Forest examined the nature of the relationship between Simms and Hodgkinson and found that a fiduciary duty was owed, based on "the elements of trust and confidence and reliance on skill and knowledge and advice." He also discussed the relationship between fiduciary responsibilities and the rules of the respective professions, stating that the rules of the accounting profession of which Simms was a member required that "all real and apparent conflicts of interest be fully disclosed to clients, particularly in the area of tax-related investment advice. The basis of this requirement is the maintenance of the independence and honesty which is the linchpin of the profession's credibility with the public."

Therefore, the fiduciary duties imposed by courts should be at least as stringent as those of a self-regulating profession. Simms had been in a clear conflict of interest. The court accepted Hodgkinson's evidence that he never would have purchased the MURBs had he been aware of Simms's interest in selling them. The breach of fiduciary obligation was deemed to be so serious that the court was prepared to place all risk of market failure on Simms.

The fiduciary obligation to give independent advice free from self-interest has a distinct meaning in the case of the audit. The auditor, besides acting without self-interest, must also act independently of any interest of the company, since she is fulfilling a public function—namely, providing assurance to shareholders (and, indirectly, to the financial markets, in the case of publicly listed companies) that the financial statements have been prepared according to established guidelines. Audit firms are prohibited from involvement in their clients' business and are increasingly reluctant to provide services other than the audit to their audit clients.[4]

duty of confidentiality
The obligation of a professional not to disclose any information provided by the client without the client's consent.

Professionals must maintain client **confidentiality** because of both fiduciary principles and professional rules of conduct.[5] For example, a rule of conduct for professional engineers is the following:

> 4.10 Engineers shall not disclose information concerning the business affairs or technical processes of clients or employers without their consent.[6]

privilege
The professional's right not to divulge a client's confidential information to third parties.

Related to confidentiality is the concept of professional-client **privilege.** When Bill seeks legal advice on behalf of DT, Holland & Hart must not divulge the contents of that consultation to others. The basis for this principle is the overriding need of clients in specific circumstances to be able to put their entire trust in their professional advisor. The only advice to which privilege attaches is legal advice.

What questions about the soundness of the engineering design arise from a construction disaster?

---

4. Gordon Pitts, "Stick-handling Past the Scandals" *The Globe and Mail* (27 June 2005) at B16.
5. In very limited circumstances, confidentiality must be violated, such as when a patient tells her doctor that she plans to seriously harm herself or others.
6. *Association of Professional Engineers and Geoscientists of New Brunswick, By-laws and Code of Ethics 2005, Section 2, Code of Ethics,* at http://www.apegnb.ca/e/013/By-Laws-Ethics-06-01-25.pdf

Privilege may extend to the advice given by other professionals only when they prepare documentation at a lawyer's request and solely as part of the lawyer's advice to the client.

Responsibilities in Tort

General Responsibility

Professionals have duties in tort equivalent to those of other service providers. While they can be responsible for a range of torts, negligence is most common. The professional must perform the services in accordance with the standards of the reasonably competent member of that profession.

Professional liability for negligence was introduced in Chapter 11. In order for a professional to be liable for negligence, the basic elements of a negligence action must be present:

- The professional owes the claimant a duty of care.
- The professional has breached the standard of care.
- The professional's conduct has caused the claimant's loss.
- The claimant's loss is not too remote from the professional's actions.

In the context of professional services, these basic elements involve particular challenges:

- To whom does a professional's duty of care extend? Who can claim compensation? Is the duty limited to clients or does it extend to others who might rely on the professional's work such as lenders, investors, or the general public?
- What performance standards must professionals meet? Who determines the level of expertise required in a particular situation?
- For what types of losses should claimants be able to seek compensation? Personal physical injuries are the most straightforward. Damage to property and pure economic loss are more challenging.

The most difficult cases are those in which professionals give careless advice—make misrepresentations—with negative economic consequences for claimants who are third parties (not clients). For example, the auditors, Asher & Breem, have produced reports on which DT's bank and investors may have relied. Those users will claim compensation for their losses resulting from DT's bankruptcy. Why should this be any different from any other form of negligence liability? What is the difference between a negligently prepared appraisal or audit and a negligently manufactured widget? In cases of professional negligence, there is a risk of imposing liability "in an indeterminate amount for an indeterminate time to an indeterminate class."[7]

The remainder of this section will focus on this difficult category of professional responsibility.

Responsibility to Third Parties

Traditionally, courts have denied the claims of third parties (i.e., nonclients) who have relied on a professional's negligent misstatements. Underlying these decisions has been the public policy concern of maintaining the economic viability of those professions in the business of giving advice. For example, while a property appraiser

---

7. This remains the best-known statement of this problem and comes from a U.S. case: *Ultramares Corp. v. Touche* (1931), 255 N.Y. 170 (C.A.).

can manage the risk exposure to the client, extending such risk to all subsequent purchasers of property may be economically oppressive. If all existing and potential investors could sue for negligence as a result of depending on a negligently prepared audit opinion for a public company, the delivery of audit services might no longer be economically feasible. Nonetheless, denying claims against the professionals in such situations does not necessarily leave the user without remedy. The purchaser of contaminated land can sue the vendor. Audit failures typically are uncovered because of some significant failure in the company itself. Shareholders can pursue their rights in company law and also sue the directors. The professions have been attractive targets for plaintiffs principally because they have the "deep pockets" otherwise lacking in these contexts. In the event of business failures, they may be the only persons left with the economic resources to meet claims.

The potential for third-party claims for economic loss resulting from negligent misrepresentations was first recognized in Britain in 1964[8] and in Canada in the case below.

CASE ▼

Haig v. Bamford (1976), 72 D.L.R. (3d) 68 (S.C.C.)

THE BUSINESS CONTEXT: An audit is normally conducted because legislation requires it. However, businesses not requiring an audit by statute may still seek one in order to provide information to third parties such as lenders.

FACTUAL BACKGROUND: A mill-work business required additional funding. The Saskatchewan Economic Development Corporation (Sedco) agreed to provide a portion of the funding on the following conditions: that the business provide satisfactory audited financial statements and that it acquire additional equity capital from a further investor or investors. The business approached R.L. Bamford & Co., an accounting firm, and asked it to prepare the audited statements. It was made known to the firm that these statements would be shown to potential investors. Haig invested on the basis of favourable audited statements. In fact, the business's

bookkeeper had made an error in crediting a sum to revenue that should have been shown as a liability, and the accountants failed to spot the error. The business failed, and Haig lost his investment.

THE LEGAL QUESTION: Should Haig, a third party, be allowed to recover his loss because he lent money based on a negligently prepared audit?

RESOLUTION: The Supreme Court found that the accountants had not performed a competent audit. In determining whether a duty of care was owed to the third party, it applied a test appropriate for the particular circumstances: a duty of care is owed where the defendant had "actual knowledge of the limited class that will use and rely on the statement."

In this case, the careful wording of the test was important. The accountants knew the statements would be shown to a small group of investors but did not know their names. Knowledge of the actual identity of the users was unnecessary. It was sufficient that Haig was a member of the limited class.

CRITICAL ANALYSIS: Does the test in this case establish a reasonable scope for the duty of care? How does the test fit with foreseeability?

From the auditor's perspective of risk management, imposing liability in a *Haig v. Bamford* context did not extend liability beyond that of most other providers of goods and services. The existence of the limited group of third parties who might use the audit opinion was known at the time of the engagement.

---

8. *Hedley Byrne & Co. v. Heller & Partners*, [1964] A.C. 465 (H.L.). In fact, an exclusion clause protected the Heller Bank.

The difficult question remaining after *Haig v. Bamford* was whether liability should extend beyond this relatively narrow scope. Of critical importance was the question of whether liability would also exist in situations where third parties were neither known nor limited in number. Specifically, would a court apply the general foreseeability test from *Donoghue v. Stevenson*[9] in cases of negligent misrepresentation resulting in economic loss? In the context of auditing, would investors in a public company be entitled to make claims if the audit opinion they relied on for their investment decision was negligently prepared?

For many years, these issues were widely debated in Canada and elsewhere[10] and eventually addressed by the Supreme Court of Canada in *Hercules Managements Ltd. v. Ernst & Young*.[11] This case is summarized and discussed in detail under "Negligent Misstatement" in Chapter 11. Readers should consult that material before proceeding further in this chapter. In the case, shareholder investors in a company brought action against the auditing firm Ernst & Young based on inaccurate financial statements produced as the result of an incompetent audit. To decide whether the auditors owed the investors a duty of care, the court applied the two-step test and found that in the case of an audit, it is reasonably foreseeable that a large number of persons will use and rely on the statements. Applying the first stage of the test, a duty of care exists. However, in applying the second step and evaluating possible policy considerations, the court examined the limited purpose of the audited financial statements as set out in the relevant legislation—"to assist the collectivity of shareholders of the audited companies in their task of overseeing management."

Because the shareholders were using the audited statements for investment decisions and not the statutory purpose of the audit, they were owed no duty of care. The court held that to decide otherwise "would be to expose auditors to the possibility of indeterminate liability, since such a finding would imply that auditors owe a duty of care to any known class of potential plaintiffs regardless of the purpose to which they put the auditors' reports." The only remedy investor plaintiffs have is the indirect right to bring a derivative action on behalf of the company (see Chapter 16).

This issue of third-party liability for negligently uttered words remains contentious, particularly in the context of the audit. The *Hercules* decision, while popular with the public accounting profession, is controversial among the business community. Regulatory changes in reaction to the Enron debacle have focused to a large extent on the audit function. They are discussed at the end of this chapter.

In the Business Law in Practice scenario, DT, Provincial Bank, and the investors may now consider suing Asher & Breem and Holland & Hart for negligence:

■ Both firms owe their client (DT) a duty of care using the two-step test.

■ The firms owe Provincial Bank and the investors, third-party claimants, a duty only under certain circumstances. The key remains whether any policy considerations exist that would limit the duty of care as defined by foreseeability. Such considerations would prevent liability extending to third-party investors relying on a negligently prepared audit where that audit was mandated by law. In contrast, when DT approached Asher & Breem for a feasibility study, the firm knew that financiers would see and rely on their report. If the work is negligently done, the firm likely owes a duty of care to those who lent or invested based upon it. The liability is not unlimited—it is exactly as described at the

9.   [1932] A.C. 562 (H.L.) in Chapter 11.
10. In a further case, the Supreme Court of Canada referred to the requirement of a "special relationship" between plaintiff and defendant: *Queen v. Cognos Inc.* (1993), 99 D.L.R. (4th) 626 (S.C.C.). See Chapter 20 for a summary of this case.
11. [1997] 2 S.C.R. 165.

time Asher & Breem accepted the engagement. The law firm, on the other hand, is unlikely to be held responsible to anyone other than its client. There was no indication that anyone other than DT and those acting on its behalf would rely on the law firm's opinion.

- The claimants must prove that the firms breached their standard of care. Professional testimony as to generally accepted auditing standards and standards of competency in the legal profession will be crucial in resolving this issue.

- The claimants must be able to establish the requisite causation and lack of remoteness of damage. Did the claimants, for example, actually use the consulting report, the audited financial statements, and the legal opinion? If so, did they rely on them to make their decision, and did that reliance cause the loss?

- The principles of contributory negligence also apply. If users ignored cautions or other significant advice, they may be partially responsible for their loss.

Business Application of the Law — Liability of Accounting Firms

Accounting firms and auditors, in particular, have long been subject to claims for compensation by clients and investors who allege they have suffered loss due to negligent work by members of the firm. These claims have normally been considered on a case-by-case basis. *Haig v. Bamford* and *Hercules Management* are two examples presented earlier in this chapter. Auditors were responsible in one case but not the other. The prevention of such claims is a key part of risk management by the firms. The rise of class actions by investors against auditors and directors of companies has raised the stakes, but normally no single case threatens the survival of the firm.

The Enron affair was a disaster on many fronts, but particularly for the entire accounting profession. Prior to the Enron collapse in 2002, Arthur Andersen was one of the Big Five firms in the profession and the firm providing auditing and consulting services to Enron. In the flurry of investigations after the collapse, the firm was charged with the criminal offence of obstruction of justice based on alleged concealment and destruction of key documents. A jury found Arthur Andersen guilty. The firm's reputation was destroyed and it dissolved, leaving only four key firms in the profession. In 2005, the conviction was overturned by the U.S. Supreme Court based on the trial judge's failure to require the jury to find a dishonest motive or conscious wrongdoing before

convicting. Long before this decision, the damage was done—the firm was destroyed as the result of difficulties with one client.

The potential disappearance of another major firm was recently avoided in another case, involving KPMG. In 1997 the firm began offering clients what became "questionable" tax shelters. Over the next seven years, four shelters produced $11 billion in "losses" that saved clients $2.5 billion in taxes and generated $124 million in fees for KPMG. The firm came under increasing scrutiny by law enforcement authorities and in 2005 agreed to a settlement to forestall criminal charges that could have consigned the firm to the same fate as Arthur Andersen. The shelters were never judged to be improper, but the firm acknowledged wrongdoing, agreed to pay $456 million, accepted an outside monitor of its operations, and accepted restrictions on its tax practice. Since the settlement, 17 former executives and partners have been charged with conspiracy and tax evasion. The firm has survived.

CRITICAL ANALYSIS: How does the risk of litigation affect the viability of professional firms?

Sources: Kurt Eichenwald, "Reversal of Andersen Conviction Not a Declaration of Innocence" *The New York Times* (1 June 2005); and Jonathan D. Glater, "Settlement Seen on Tax Shelters by Audit Firm" *The New York Times* (27 August 2005) at http://www.nytimes.com (accessed 23 October 2006).

Professionals' Risk Management Practices

How professionals manage risk exposure arising from their responsibilities has a direct impact on the businesses that hire them. Clients need to be aware of the risk management strategies of professionals and plan their affairs accordingly. Three ways in which professionals can manage risk are through contracts, incorporation or limited liability partnerships, and insurance.

Professional Service Contracts

As discussed previously, these contracts are a vehicle for defining the parameters of the work that professionals are engaged to do. Both parties benefit from a clear and careful agreement that includes all essential terms.

Incorporation and Limited Liability Partnerships

Historically, businesses have managed risk through corporations with limited liability for shareholders, while professional service providers have been required to assume liability personally. There are now other models for managing professional liability.

Some professions may incorporate. Generally, professions may incorporate only if they are specifically permitted to do so by the legislation governing the particular profession in that province.[12]

Even where incorporation exists, it typically does not protect the professional from the liability of greatest concern—namely, personal liability for negligence. For example, where accountants have been able to incorporate, the act establishing the right to practise specifies that the personal liability of the accountant for negligence will not be affected by the limited liability of the shareholders, directors, or officers of the corporation.[13]

From the client's perspective, the individual professional generally remains personally liable for negligent work, and the assets of the professional organization (the corporation) can be accessed.

Partnerships may register as limited liability partnerships (LLPs) (see Chapter 14). The impetus for allowing this business form came from the large professional partnerships that considered it unfair that a partner in Vancouver should be responsible for the negligence of a partner in Ontario. LLPs have been introduced by amendments to the provincial partnership acts. Whether or not individual professions allow members to form LLPs is determined by the provincial legislation governing that profession.[14]

LLPs protect individual partners from personal responsibility arising from negligence claims that are brought against the partnership in general or other partners in the firm. Individual partners remain liable for their own negligence. Likewise, the firm itself retains liability, and firm assets (and insurance) can be used to compensate for losses.

From the perspective of the client or user who is suing, the concern is whether there will be compensation, which in turn depends on the availability of insurance.

Insurance

Errors and omissions insurance is described in Chapter 28. It is a condition of practice in most professions that members carry this professional liability insurance. For the client/user, guarantees of insurance coverage are essential. Insurance coverage,

---

12. For example, *Business Corporations Act*, S.N.B. 1981, c. B-9.1, s. 13(3)(d); *Business Corporations Act*, R.S.O. 1990, c. B-16, s. 3(1).
13. For example, *Public Accountants Act*, R.S.N.S. 1989, c. 369, s. 22A(2).
14. For example, *Partnerships Act*, R.S.O. 1990, c. P-5, s. 10(2) (Ontario) and *Partnership Act*, R.S.A. 2000, c. P-3 (Alberta). See also the *Law Society Act*, R.S.O. 1990, c. L-8 as am. by S.O. 1998, c. 2.

however, has an important consequence for claimants. Professional insurers, such as the Canadian Medical Protection Association, are highly specialized and expert at defending claims. If the loss is significant, the user should not contemplate litigation without hiring a lawyer who has the necessary expertise. Where contingency fees are unavailable, the cost associated with hiring such lawyers can effectively prevent many claimants from pursuing litigation.

Governance Structures of Professions

Legislation

Professions are "self-regulating"—that is, there are provincial statutes that establish the rights of the professions to self-governance. The acts create the governing body for the profession and specify when individuals may represent themselves as being qualified to practise in that province. The legislation gives autonomy and sometimes a monopoly over specific activities to professional bodies sanctioned by the legislation. For example, the *Legal Profession Act*,[15] which governs the practice of law in British Columbia,

- provides a very detailed definition of the "practice of law"
- defines members of the Law Society as those barristers and solicitors who hold a practising certificate for the current year
- states that only members of the Law Society in good standing are allowed to engage in the practice of law
- recognizes that the society is governed by elected members of the profession (benchers)
- states that the benchers govern and administer the affairs of the society, including determining whether or not a person is a member in good standing of the society, and establishing and maintaining a system of legal education and training

Each profession is governed by similar legislation in each province. The provincial professional associations are often linked to federal associations.

The organization of the accounting profession in Canada is more complex than others, since there are three professional accounting bodies: the Certified General Accountants Association of Canada (CGA—Canada), the Canadian Institute of Chartered Accountants (CICA), and Certified Management Accountants of Canada (CMA—Canada). Historically, the key distinction between the associations has been the right to perform the audit as defined by provincial legislation. In recent years, this distinction has been largely removed in most provinces. For example, Ontario legislation creates a mechanism whereby members of all three accounting bodies can apply for an audit licence if they meet new internationally recognized standards.[16]

In the DT organization, Sandra Roberts is described simply as a "professional accountant." In practice, she could be a member of any one of the three professional accounting bodies.

Professional Practice

From a business perspective, the licensing of professionals may seem an issue of little relevance. However, any business operating across several provinces, like DT, may need to seek advice in different jurisdictions. Business has recently been assisted by the removal of many of the interprovincial barriers to professional practice that

---

15. S.B.C. 1998, c. 9.
16. *Public Accounting Act, 2004*, S.O. 2004, c.8, as am. by S.O. 2006, c. 19, Sched. B, s. 16.

once existed. Professionals must belong to provincial societies or associations in order to practise within the particular province. They attain the right to practise in different provinces by demonstrating familiarity with local legislation and rules. All professions have firms that operate nationally, with practitioners in different provinces. If DT is sued in another province, for example, Ted can employ the services of a regional or national law firm, or he can ask his existing firm, Holland & Hart, to hire a local firm in the other jurisdiction on DT's behalf.

Professional firms are finding means of organizing themselves to better meet the needs of clients. Some firms operate internationally. While accounting firms (now often known as "professional service firms") were the leaders in international practice, other professions are increasingly moving in the same direction.

multidisciplinary practice (MDP)

A firm of professionals that offers the services of several different professionals within one practice.

Some firms have combined the services of different types of professionals within one practice, in what is known as a **multidisciplinary practice (MDP).** There are concerns about MDPs related to conflicts of interest. Can the long-established and well-crafted standards of each profession be maintained in a merged practice? Recent events such as the collapse of Enron have highlighted these concerns about potential conflicts and created considerable pressure on regulators and professionals to unbundle professional services. The current trend appears to be toward a return to traditional boundaries between the professions.

MDPs are only one example of significant change in the delivery of professional services. In the United States, for example, major corporations such as American Express and H&R Block are creating nationwide one-stop financial and professional service firms. There are collectives of law firms that are expanding rapidly in the United States and in Canada. Some are linked to the concept of pre-paying for services (a form of insurance). From the client's perspective, many of these changes offer increased convenience and better service.

Disciplining Professionals

Each profession in Canada has established rules of professional conduct or codes of ethics that prescribe acceptable behaviour. Each has established mechanisms for enforcing those rules and disciplining any member who violates them.

Professional rules and codes are critical for the protection of the client. Most professional associations or societies now have materials (usually on websites) outlining the processes for users to follow if they have a complaint. In the disciplinary process itself, clients (complainants) are, however, only witnesses and observers. For damages or other compensation, the client must sue the professional involved. Depending on the nature of the claim, the professional may have insurance to draw upon. The legal profession also has an indemnification or assurance fund to compensate clients whose money has been stolen by members of the profession, usually from funds held in trust.

To be effective, the investigatory and disciplinary process must protect the rights of complainants and professionals. Any investigation is a serious matter for the professional, who must respond and who will usually need legal representation. If the process proceeds and the professional is found to have violated the rules, the consequences can extend to withdrawal of the right to practise. Although the disciplinary process is formal, there may be alternative dispute resolution options to resolve complaints before formal hearings are held.[17]

---

17. "Reviewing the Conduct of Lawyers" *The Law Society of Alberta* (18 August 2004) at http://www.lawsocietyalberta.com/ LSA_Archives/index.cfm?page=arclawyerconduct.cfm; Nicky Brink, "Use of ADR Processes by the Law Society of Alberta" *The Canadian Bar Association Newsletter* (2002) at http://www.cba.org/CBA/newsletters/adr%2D2002/ad2.aspx; see also Chapter 4, this text.

The fallout from the collapse of Enron and Arthur Andersen LLP and the involvement of Enron's primary outside counsel, Vinson & Elkins, have highlighted several areas of concern:

- The accounting and law firms had internal conflicts of interest. Arthur Andersen had provided consulting advice and auditing services relating to questionable accounting practices. Vinson & Elkins had designed business structures for Enron and also provided legal opinions on the legality of those structures.

- Both firms were dependent on Enron as a major client, so their ability and willingness to give objective advice (perhaps unfavourable to management) was suspect.

- Former members of Arthur Andersen were employees of Enron, creating possible conflict with their former colleagues.

- Even in ordinary circumstances, professionals employed outside private practice are faced with ethical dilemmas. For example, the *Management Accountants Handbook*[18] provides guidance as to how to handle any conflicts that might arise from various ethical standards—legal, societal, professional, personal, and business:

    Where there is a clear conflict between stated organization ethics and The Society of Management Accountants' *Code of Ethics*, the member's choice is clear, resign from the Society, or resign from the organization.

Although Enron has been the focus of much attention, there are many other examples of suspect financial results leading to lost confidence in management, the corporation, auditors, and the entire system of corporate governance. Perhaps the most prominent Canadian example is Nortel whose financial results are under scrutiny all the way back to 1999. The company is facing class action suits and criminal and regulatory investigations in Canada and the United States.

Regulators have tended to focus on auditors and senior managers of companies in their aggressive reaction to this serious lack of confidence:

- In the United States, the *Sarbanes-Oxley Act of 2002* established the Public Company Accounting Oversight Board to set auditing standards and oversee the accounting profession, in particular the audit of public companies. Auditors must assess the internal controls of their clients and report any material weaknesses. Senior management must certify the audit results.

- In Canada, the accounting profession has established the Canadian Public Accountability Board with authority to oversee auditing firms by periodic inspections dealing with particular audit files, training programs in the firms, standards for accepting new clients, and employee compensation. The Board is financed by public audit firms that are required to register as members.

Since the imposition of these new regulatory regimes, there has been a backlash. The changes have been criticized for the level of intervention and detail, and the ensuing cost to companies of compliance. It is suggested that this encourages clients and auditors to seek legitimate means of circumventing the regulations. There is also concern that fewer accounting firms will be willing to perform audits of public companies.

CRITICAL ANALYSIS: It has been suggested that it is impossible to regulate trust; that public confidence can be restored only by developing social and professional norms through a principles-based regulatory framework where business and the professions are encouraged to demonstrate their commitment to high standards. Can business and the professions develop their own solutions or is more legislation inevitable?

---

18. Society of Management Accountants of Ontario, *Management Accountants Handbook* (Toronto: The Society, 1992) 5400 at 5-12.

Sources: John Saunders, "Accountants Propose Tougher Standards" *The Globe and Mail* (6 September 2002) at B1; Sheldon Gordon, "The Enron Effect" *The National* (May 2002) at 14; Beppi Crosariol, "New Rules Chase Public Auditors Out the Door" *The Globe and Mail* (9 August 2004) at B11; Karen Howlett, "Critics Point Fingers at Board and Auditors" *The Globe and Mail* (13 January 2005) at B7; and Stephen Labaton, "Four Years Later, Enron's Shadow Lingers as Change Comes Slowly" *The New York Times* (5 January 2006) at http://www.nytimes.com (accessed 23 October 2006).

Business Law in Practice Revisited

1. Did the professionals fulfill their obligations to DT?

DT is concerned with the quality of accounting and legal services received from employees—Sandra Roberts and Bill Caton—and the firms they have retained—Asher & Breem and Holland & Hart. The obligations of Sandra and Bill to DT are largely a function of their employment—to perform their defined duties according to defined or reasonable standards. The outside firms have obligations to DT based on contract, tort, and fiduciary relationships. Contractual obligations are found in the express terms of the contract or implied as obligations to provide the services requested to the standard of a reasonably competent professional. The duties of the firms in tort are similarly based. Fiduciary obligations relate to the avoidance of conflicts of interest and placing DT's interests first. Both firms must provide DT with sound independent advice in the form of an audit or legal opinion. Neither should be based on what is in the business interest of the firm. In the new professional environment, Asher & Breem should have given serious consideration to the advisability of doing a feasibility study for its audit client, DT.

2. Did the professionals act consistently with their obligations to their professional bodies?

The accountants and lawyers must act in accordance with the professional and ethical standards of their professional bodies. They cannot put their firm's interest first. The in-house professionals must avoid conflicts between their professional and ethical duties and the wishes of their employer. Sandra is facing the classic conflict between ethical obligations owed to the employer and to the profession, as well as possible conflicts with her own personal values. In terms of ethical obligations owed to the employer and those owed to the profession, the latter must prevail, even if that calls for her to quit her position with DT. In practice, she must explain to Ted the reasons for the audit itself and the rules the company must follow in presenting its financial information. There may be legitimate alternatives she can present to Ted that at least partially meet his objectives. However, under no circumstances can Sandra engage in any practices that violate the rules of professional conduct. To do so not only would be ethically wrong, but also expose Roberts to the risk of professional discipline and create serious risk for herself, the company, and Ted.

3. Can creditors and investors in DT recover their losses from the professionals?

Provincial Bank and the investors can sue only for negligence, and their principal obstacle will be establishing that a duty of care was owed to them. The difficulty will not be in terms of establishing that the bank and investors were foreseeable users of the consulting report and audited financial statements. Rather, Provincial Bank and the investors must establish that no policy considerations exist that might limit this duty. This issue will depend on the stated purpose of the consulting and the audit. In this situation, the audit was not mandated by legislation, and therefore it is not relevant to apply that aspect of the *Hercules* case. Determining the stated purpose will call for an interpretation of what Ted told Asher & Breem at the time the engagement contracts for consulting and auditing were formed. Since Asher & Breem was told that its consulting report would be important for financing purposes, the limited group of third-party users would be owed a duty of care. If Ted failed to be this explicit, then a court, applying a policy analysis, would not likely find that a duty of care was owed.

Claimants will need to prove the other elements of negligence. The standard of care issues are equivalent to those in DT's claims. More critical will be the need to prove that claimants did indeed use the reports for the described purposes and that this reliance caused their loss. Since the financiers had no other known source of information about the financial state of DT, these last issues in this particular case should be reasonably easy to prove. If the claim is successful, damages will include the amount lost on the loan and the investments.

The law firm, on the other hand, is unlikely to suffer any third-party liability. Its opinion was provided only to DT and not relied upon by any third parties.

Chapter Summary

Professionals owe a range of duties to their clients. Professionals are governed by contract and tort law. They must deliver services as contracted for and in accordance with the requisite professional expertise. If they are negligent in performing their responsibilities, they will likely be responsible for damages. In addition, professionals may be in a fiduciary relationship with their clients if the elements of trust and confidence and reliance on skill and knowledge and advice are present. Because of inherent vulnerability or dependency, the client is owed this duty of loyalty and trust. Professionals also owe duties to those who are not clients, but who rely on their work and advice. Whether a duty is owed in a particular situation depends on foreseeability and the need to impose reasonable limits on potential liability.

Professional service providers manage risk for the same reasons as businesses in general, but without the same freedom of choice. From the client's perspective, insurance is critical, and many professions make such coverage obligatory. Professionals can consider organizing their practices as limited liability partnerships or corporations, although other trends have greater immediate impact for clients. In particular, new forms of practice, such as national and international firms and multidisciplinary practices, offer benefits for users.

The professions are governed by legislation that establishes them as self-regulating entities. The professions create codes of conduct or rules of practice. These determine the standards that their members must meet, and provide a measure of the expected standard of care in contracts, torts, and fiduciary obligations.

Most professions have created dispute resolution services or complaint procedures to assist clients. They also maintain a discipline process that provides assurance to users that professionals violating professional rules will be disciplined, up to and including removal from membership.

The challenge facing clients and professionals is to ensure that the individual professionals continue to comply with the ethical obligations of their profession, despite increasing pressures, both from their own members and from clients, to become more "business minded."

Chapter Study

Key Terms and Concepts

duty of confidentiality (p. 549)

multidisciplinary practice (p. 556)

privilege (p. 549)

professional (p. 545)

retainer (p. 546)

Questions for Review

1. Who is a professional?
2. What is the meaning of "fiduciary" in the context of professional–client relationships?
3. How may professionals be in a conflict of interest?
4. What should a professional services contract contain?
5. What are the options for setting professional fees?
6. What is a retainer?
7. What is the basis for determining the cost of professional services if there is no formal contractual term addressing the issue?
8. What are the three types of professional responsibility?
9. What was the basic attribute of negligence actions against accountants that traditionally protected them from third-party claims?
10. How did the Supreme Court of Canada define the duty of care for negligently uttered statements in the *Hercules* decision?
11. What is the meaning of a self-regulating profession?
12. In the basic contract between the accounting firm and the client, for which services can liability be excluded and for which ones can it not?
13. During a disciplinary process, why is it important to protect the rights of the professional against whom a complaint has been made?
14. What are LLPs?
15. What law establishes who can be a member of a particular profession?
16. If a conflict between a professional's ethical obligations to the profession and those to the client cannot be resolved, what must the professional do?
17. What is a professional's duty of confidentiality?
18. Why did Arthur Andersen dissolve as an accounting firm and KPMG survive?

Questions for Critical Thinking

1. The following is an example of the standard unqualified auditor's report:

   > To the Shareholders of ABC Ltd.
   >
   > We have audited the balance sheet of ABC Ltd. as at X date, and the statements of income, retained earnings, and cash flows for the year then ended. These financial statements are the responsibility of the company's management. Our responsibility is to express an opinion on these financial statements based on our audit.
   >
   > We conducted our audit in accordance with generally accepted auditing standards. Those standards require that we plan and perform an audit to obtain reasonable assurance whether the financial statements are free of material misstatement. An audit includes examining, on a test basis, evidence supporting the amounts and disclosures in the financial statements. An audit also includes assessing the accounting principles used and significant estimates made by management, as well as evaluating the overall financial statement presentation.
   >
   > In our opinion, these financial statements present fairly, in all material respects, the financial position of the company as at X date, and that the results of its operations and cash flows for the year then ended are in accordance with generally accepted accounting principles.
   >
   > EFG,
   >
   > Chartered Accountants[19]

   There are many standard practices auditors follow. For example, auditors are not responsible for detecting management fraud unless they ignore "red flags" warning them of improper activities. They may test on a sampling basis. Do you think that the report they issue could be written in such a way as to make it clearer to users the extent of their responsibilities?

2. If you are the manager in an organization responsible for finalizing contracts with professional service providers, what are the pros and cons of having the professional charge on an hourly basis versus a per-job basis? What protections might you build into the contract?

3. The *Hercules* decision was heavily criticized by some members of the business press, but was also received with great relief by public accountants. Did the Supreme Court of Canada define the purpose of the audit too narrowly? Will cases like Enron tend to broaden the purpose and the resulting duty of care in the long term?

4. Professionals are gradually receiving more flexibility in organizing their practices and protecting their personal assets through options such as LLPs and incorporation. What are the pros and cons of these developments for clients, professionals, and the public?

5. Most professionals are required to maintain a minimum level of liability insurance in the event that claims are brought against them by those who rely on their advice. However, the cost of this insurance is passed on to clients through the fees they pay for services received. Does this system encourage professional responsibility? Is there a more effective method?

6. Professional organizations are authorized by legislation to regulate their own members in terms of permission to practice, setting standards, and imposing discipline. Can the public expect to receive fair treatment from professional organizations that have a vested interest in protecting their own members?

---

19. Adapted from a standard audit report presented in A.J. Arens, J.K. Loebbecke, & W.M. Lemon et al., *Auditing*, 8th Can. ed. (Scarborough: Prentice Hall, 1999) at 36.

Situations for Discussion

1. Lan had, over the years of running her small business, acquired sizable savings. She wanted to get the best return on this money and discussed this with her lawyer, Harvey. He advised her that this was an excellent time to get into real estate; he had many clients who required financing. Lan could provide either first or second mortgages, depending on her desired level of risk and return. Harvey said he had some clients involved in a large townhouse development. Lan trusted him implicitly, as he had been her lawyer since she had first started her business. Thus, she lent the bulk of her savings—$200 000—as a second mortgage, which would earn interest at 19 percent per annum over five years.

   Within eight months the real estate market collapsed. The mortgagees defaulted on payment, and once the first mortgage holders had foreclosed, there was nothing left for Lan. When she complained to Harvey, he said that investments of any sort carry inherent risk. His personal investment company, for example, had been one of the partners in the townhouse development, and he too had lost his entire investment.

   Lan is shattered by Harvey's lack of concern and seeks advice about what she can do to recoup her losses. Discuss Lan's options.

2. Good Property engaged the services of a professional real estate appraisal firm, McGee and McGee, prior to purchasing a large tract of property on the outskirts of town. When Dan, the CFO of Good Property, first discussed the appraisal with Andy McGee, he said the appraisal was required by 10 January. Andy said this was impossible owing to other commitments and proposed 26 January. It was agreed that Andy would be the appraiser. Dan said he would get back to Andy about the date.

   The project was more complex than either Good Property or the appraisers expected. The local Water Conservation Authority was about to issue a report that seriously affected the land, so Andy waited for it. The appraisal was not handed to Good Property until 29 January. By this time, another purchaser had acquired the property. When Dan was handed the sizable invoice for the work, he claimed that Andy had breached the contract by finishing the work late, and he had therefore lost out on being able to buy the land. Furthermore, the invoice was far more than he expected to pay. How are these matters likely to be resolved? What arguments can Good Property and McGee raise?

3. Assume that in Situation 2 above the appraisal was completed on time and without dispute. Good Properties acquired the land. Some months later, the Water Conservation Authority published its report, which seriously affected the value of the land. On closer inspection, it turned out that McGee made a basic mistake in failing to discover the Authority's work. What rights does Good Property have against McGee?

4. Phelps Development (PD) proposed a new property development that would require major debt financing. It contacted its bank and several venture capital firms, and was advised that it must first present audited financial statements. Phelps, the CEO of PD, approached its accounting firm and told the partner, Kaur, of PD's plans and why it needed an audit. Kaur accepted the engagement.

   The audit was completed and Phelps showed it to several interested parties, including Money Lenders (ML). ML had heard about PD's proposals and was anxious to join this venture, since it already had several other successful interests in the vicinity. ML provided $500 000 debt financing. Eight months later, PD faced a serious cash crisis and was unable to meet its debts as they fell due. ML's loan was not repaid. On closer examination, it turned out that the audited financial statements included a serious material misstatement: liabilities were understated by $250 000.

ML is now attempting to recover its loss. Since PD is unable to pay, it seeks compensation from the accounting firm and Kaur as the individual partner responsible for the audit. Present arguments for both parties.

5. Big Cleanups was a public company that had developed products used to address environmental cleanups. Its market performance attracted considerable investor attention. One particular investor, Max Find, acquired a significant holding in Big Cleanups over a five-year period. He tracked all performance announcements closely and increased his holdings with each favourable announcement.

   In the past year there were rumours of some underlying problems with Big Cleanups's technology. Max therefore paid particularly close attention to the most recent annual report. Surprisingly, the report indicated further strong performance and Max, on the basis of the report, increased his holdings in Big Cleanups.

   Some months later, the third-quarter results for Big Cleanups were published. They showed unexpected losses, and the share price precipitously declined. The auditor withdrew the audited statements and later issued new statements, which showed a large loss.

   Max claims that his losses are due to the allegedly misleading audit report. If he had known the true state of affairs he would have reduced, not increased, his holdings in the company. The auditor claims that the audit was prepared according to generally accepted principles and that the firm was not responsible for this turn of events.

   Outline the primary arguments for Max and the auditors.

6. Yul is a CGA working as comptroller for Jones Manufacturing. He is concerned about the cash flow position of the company. There have been large orders, but Andrew (the CEO) has insisted on an aggressive pricing policy, and prices charged do not cover costs.

   Yul approaches Andrew with his concerns, but Andrew will not listen. Andrew is a high-profile member of the local community; the success of the company means that it can hire a large number of people in this economically depressed area, and it is inconceivable to him that booming sales could translate into losses. Yul tries another approach. He explains that the auditors will be coming soon and, if he doesn't expose the current position, they will uncover it anyway. Andrew tells him that he understands, but that he wants Yul to do whatever it takes to get through this audit. Afterward, prices can be raised, since by then the company will be in a strong position in the marketplace and this temporary hurdle will have been overcome.

   Yul is trying to devise a strategy to reconcile his professional responsibilities and the survival of this company. It would be devastating to see the company close if he is unable to find a way of presenting the information to satisfy the auditors.

   Discuss the pressures Yul faces. What should he do now?

7. Environmental Consultants Ltd. (ECL) was hired by Crass Developments Ltd. (CD) to evaluate a prospective development site for signs of pollution. The site had previously been used for a variety of industrial purposes, but was then vacant. CD was considering a number of possible sites and wanted to choose the one with the lowest environmental risk. At the time, ECL had plenty of work and wished to complete the evaluation for CD as quickly as possible. The senior partner at ECL assigned two junior employees to the CD job—one with two years experience and the other just recently hired. They did a site inspection and conducted a few soil tests that were appropriate for a "clean" site, but not one that had been used previously. They produced a positive report. The senior partner was out of the office for a few days, so the report was sent to CD without his approval. CD bought the land; a year later, signs of pollution began to emerge and CD was responsible for an expensive cleanup effort. To what degree are ECL and the three employees responsible for CD's cleanup costs?

8. The B.C. government (BC) embarked on an ambitious building program to replace 50 aging schools. In an attempt to lower construction

costs, the government decided to build a few variations of the same model. BC hired ABC Architects to design the basic model and variations, DEF Engineering to oversee the construction, and GHI Construction to actually do the building. The project took three years to complete. Five years later, serious problems began to emerge in the schools. Cracks appeared in the walls, many of the windows leaked, and mould was found in the walls. What responsibility do the architects, engineers, and builders have for these problems? What forms of risk management are relevant?

For more study tools, visit
http://www.businesslaw3e.nelson.com

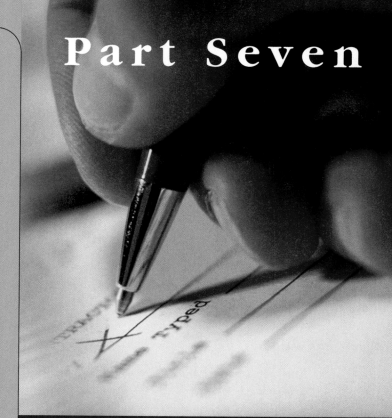

Part Seven

WHAT IS THE ROLE OF LAW IN THE MARKETING process? The law can be seen as a set of barriers for creative activity, but its objective is fairness. The law seeks to ensure that customers' needs are met and that transactions are conducted according to terms that are generally fair to both parties. Marketing law is the regulatory tool that requires fair competition and ensures that all market participants operate according to the same principles.

Chapter 23 begins with presentation of the contract of sale. The remainder of the two chapters deals with the four components of marketing strategy, commonly called the marketing mix—product, promotion, price, and place or distribution—along with management of the legal risks in marketing.

Sales and Marketing

Chapter 23 Sales and Marketing: The Contract, Product, and Promotion

Chapter 24 Sales and Marketing: Price, Distribution, and Risk Management

Chapter

23

Objectives

After studying this chapter, you should have an understanding of

- the scope of marketing law
- the rights and obligations in a contract of sale
- the legal obligations associated with the product component of marketing
- the legal obligations associated with the promotion component of marketing

Sales and Marketing: The Contract, Product, and Promotion

Business Law in Practice

Pacific Play Centres Inc. (PPC), based in Prince George, British Columbia, specializes in children's play equipment for parks and schools. PPC's current products are made from metal and plastic for durability, but the company is developing a new product—smaller equipment sets made from wood and designed for residential backyards. Lisa Patel, the CEO of PPC, believes there is demand for a wood product for home purchases. She thinks that upscale homeowners and parents are more interested in a natural-looking alternative in their backyards than the greater durability of metal or plastic.

Lisa intends to promote, distribute, and sell the new products nationally. The equipment will be sold partially assembled and will be boxed with pictures of the product on the outside. Assembly instructions and all required parts will be included in the packaging. Initially, products will be designed for relatively young children (under the age of eight), although the strategy is to have equipment grow with the children, with add-ons becoming available over time. The marketing theme will stress the environmental friendliness of the product, the creativity of the design, and safety. Promotion will be primarily through in-store displays and print media, with a special focus on advertising in parenting magazines.

The premium pricing will reflect the strategy of selling to affluent parents who are eager to ensure that their children have access to products that maximize play value. The products will be sold through national hardware and toy retail chains, and directly by PPC on the Internet.

Lisa is aware that her company is moving into a new market and that there are many regulations and general legal concerns she will need to address. Since small children use playground equipment, safety is a major consideration. Lisa understands that risk management is critical in this business.

1. How does the law affect PPC's marketing strategy?
2. What are the key aspects of PPC's contracts with its customers?
3. What impact does the law have on PPC's product?
4. What impact does the law have on the promotion of PPC's product?

What Is Marketing Law?

Marketing practices, like other aspects of business, are directed and influenced by laws and regulations. The fundamental laws affecting the marketing process are the common law principles explained in Parts Two and Three of this text. Marketing is also regulated by all three levels of government: federal, provincial, and municipal. The main objectives of these laws are

- to protect consumers from physical harm
- to foster fair competition
- to protect consumers from unfair selling practices

These objectives give rise to laws regulating a multitude of issues, including implied conditions and warranties for the sale of goods and services, product safety standards, disclosure on packaging, standards for honest promotion, anticompetitive practices, and distribution of products.

If a business sells its products internationally, the marketing practices of that business are subject to the laws and regulations of other countries as well.

marketing law
All areas of law that influence and direct the creation, promotion, pricing, and distribution of goods, services, or ideas.

Marketing law is presented here in terms of the basic four "Ps" of the marketing mix: product, promotion, price, and place or distribution. This chapter considers the product and promotion components of the marketing mix, and Chapter 24 addresses price, place, and risk management.

Traditional business law topics falling under the marketing function of business include the contract of sale and many pieces of federal and provincial legislation relating to competition and consumer protection. The key aspects of the rules governing contracts of sale are presented in a separate section directly below. The various legislative provisions are considered over the two chapters where appropriate in terms of the four aspects of the marketing function.

Contract of Sale

There are several key aspects of the contract of sale that are the focus of legal rules and therefore worthy of particular attention—the terms of the contract relating to the product, remedies for breach of those terms, the transfer of ownership of the goods, and the principles relating to delivery of the goods.[1]

Terms Relating to the Product

When customers make a purchase, they have expectations concerning the product's attributes and characteristics. Purchasers of PPC's outdoor play equipment will assume, for example, that the material used to build the equipment is sound and that children will enjoy playing on it.

Whether such expectations are protected from a legal perspective is an entirely different matter. The foundation of the common law concerning the product—such as playground equipment or the provision of a service—is contained in the Latin phrase **caveat emptor.** *Caveat emptor* means "let the buyer beware" or "let the buyer take care." The common law requires prospective purchasers to take care of themselves, to be aware of what they are purchasing, and to make appropriate investigations before buying. If the purchaser wants the product to exhibit certain characteristics, the common law requires that expectation to be contained in the contract. Otherwise, the purchaser can be left without a remedy if the product should prove to be deficient.[2]

caveat emptor
Let the buyer beware or let the buyer take care.

Because an unwavering application of the doctrine of *caveat emptor* can produce unfair results, as early as the 19th century judges began to create principles that would provide a measure of protection for the purchaser of goods. This development is discussed below.

Sale of Goods Legislation in Canada

The law governing the sale of goods is a specialized branch of contract law. This means that it is governed by legislation and, where the legislation is not relevant, by the common law rules of contract.

---

1. The assistance of Dion Legge (LL.B.), now a lawyer with MacLeod Dixon LLP, in researching and writing an earlier draft of this section of the book is gratefully acknowledged.
2. See Chapter 8 for a discussion of the law concerning mistake as well as negligent and fraudulent misrepresentation.

Beginning in the 1800s, English judges generated the basic principles that inform the modern law concerning the sale of goods. "Goods" in this context refers to personal property in its tangible form such as dishes, furniture, and anything of substance that is portable. Hence, all items of merchandise would be included. "Goods" also would encompass property that is attached to land but can be severed, such as crops. The various kinds of personal property are discussed in Chapter 17.

In response to the harshness of *caveat emptor*, judges began to evolve common law rules that, among other matters, implied specific terms into contracts for the sale of goods, whether the parties had expressly agreed to those terms or not. On this basis, a reasonably predictable set of exceptions to the doctrine of *caveat emptor* was established. For example, at common law, a contract for the sale of goods ordinarily is understood to contain a term that the item sold is fit—or appropriate—for the purpose sold and is of merchantable—or reasonable—quality.

In 1893, the English Parliament enacted the *Sale of Goods Act*,[3] an influential piece of legislation based on such common law principles. In this way, the act summarizes—rather than reforms—the case law of the time.

This historic legislation protected buyers because, echoing the common law, it implied a set of terms into a sales transaction unless this would be contrary to the parties' intentions. For example, the legislation provided that the contract contained a term that the seller had the right to sell the item in question and that the item was merchantable and fit for its intended or usual purpose. The legislation also provided remedies to the buyer should these statutory terms be breached. Of course, terms prescribed by the statute were in addition to any express terms or representations made by the seller at the time of contracting.

England's 1893 *Sale of Goods Act* forms the cornerstone of modern sale of goods legislation everywhere in Canada except Quebec.[4]

Source: M.G. Bridge, *Sale of Goods* (Toronto: Butterworths, 1988) at 1-5. See too M.G. Bridge, *The Sale of Goods* (Oxford: Clarendon Press, 1997).

Sale of goods legislation applies only to the sale of *goods*. Under the legislation, "goods" generally means what it meant at common law: personal property in its tangible, portable form as well as items attached to land that can be severed. "Goods" includes the playground equipment retailed by PPC but does not apply to the sale of land or the provision of services, for example. Sale of goods legislation implies terms into a contract for the sale of goods and classifies them and provides remedies to the purchaser based on how the breached term has been classified.

Unless the parties expressly agree to the contrary or are otherwise able to exclude the operation of the *Sale of Goods Act*, a number of terms are automatically implied into their contract. In addition to implying terms, the legislation classifies them as either conditions or warranties. This common law distinction, along with innominate terms that cannot be easily classified, was discussed in Chapter 9. Conditions are terms that are important or essential to the purpose of the contract. Though warranties are classically understood as being minor or collateral terms, they can also be very important. In this area of law, they are best understood as terms that are not conditions.

---

3. *Sale of Goods Act, 1893*, (56 & 57 Vict.) c. 71(a). The act has been repealed and replaced by the *Sale of Goods Act, 1979* (U.K.), c. 54.
4. For example, *Sale of Goods Act*, R.S.O. 1990, c. S.1 (Ontario); *Sale of Goods Act*, R.S.A. 2000, c. S-2 (Alberta). Articles 1726-1731 of Quebec's *Civil Code* contain warranties implied in sales transactions.

The conditions and warranties that the legislation implies into a sales transaction are as follows:

Conditions

- that the seller has the right to sell the goods
- that the goods will be reasonably fit for the intended purpose where the buyer, expressly or by implication, makes it known what the intended purpose of the goods will be, in such a way as to show that he is relying on the skill and judgment of the seller. Note that a buyer does not have to make his intended purpose known when goods are used for their ordinary purpose
- that the goods will be of merchantable quality, where the goods are bought by description. Merchantable quality means that the goods are of reasonable quality considering the price paid. The essence of a sale by description is the *reliance* by the buyer on some description by the seller and, accordingly, there may be reliance even where the buyer has seen or inspected the goods.
- that, where the goods are sold by sample, the goods will correspond to the sample and that the buyer will have a reasonable opportunity to compare the goods with the sample
- that, where goods are sold by description, the goods will correspond with the description

Warranties

- that the buyer will have and enjoy quiet possession of the goods, which generally means that third parties will not claim rights against them
- that the goods are free from liens and encumbrances in favour of third parties that were not declared or known to the buyer at the time the contract was made

In order to understand how the act might apply to business transactions, consider the following problems that PPC might encounter concerning its online ordering system.

EXAMPLE 1 An institutional customer relied on one of PPC's online advisors in order to purchase, over a six-month period, equipment suitable for older children. When the customer received its first shipment, it discovered that the recommended equipment was so small and low to the ground that it could provide entertainment only for children under five.

Sale of Goods Act Violation: PPC has violated a condition implied by the *Sale of Goods Act*, namely that the goods are suitable for the purpose sold. The scenario fits all the requirements of the section in question: the customer made its purpose known by telling the PPC advisor that the equipment was for older children. The customer relied on PPC's advice in selecting the product. The product proved unsuitable for this purpose since it is geared toward significantly younger children.

EXAMPLE 2 A retail customer purchased an expensive play set on PPC's website. Within one year, the equipment was falling apart.

Sale of Goods Act Violation: Since the play equipment has been sold by description and is not of reasonable quality, PPC has violated the condition of merchantability implied by the *Sale of Goods Act*.

Remedies

Classification of the relevant term of the contract is essential to determining the remedy that a court is entitled to give the disappointed purchaser. As already discussed in Chapter 9, breach of a condition—whether in a sale of goods contract or not—may give the innocent party the right not only to damages but also to reject the goods and treat the contract as ended. This is known as the right of repudiation and means that the balance of the contract and further obligations under it can be dismissed, if the nondefaulting party so chooses. For example, the institutional customer that received play equipment which was not suitable for the purpose sold is not obligated to accept further shipments from PPC. The customer can bring its contract with PPC to an end, return the equipment, and find another supplier.

When a warranty is breached, by way of contrast, the sale of goods legislation permits the buyer to maintain an action for damages or ask the court to reduce the purchase price due to the breach.

The buyer cannot return the goods and is obligated to continue with the contract in question and comply with any outstanding terms. If the buyer refuses to perform after breach of warranty, the buyer will also be in breach of contract.

Limitations of Sale of Goods Legislation

While sale of goods legislation provides helpful inroads on the doctrine of *caveat emptor*, it does have its limitations. For example, the legislation

- generally applies only to sales of goods, not land or services
- requires that there be privity of contract between the customer and the "offending" party; breach of warranties by the manufacturer, for example, are not covered
- permits contracting out of the implied terms
- does not address precontractual representations made by the vendor[5]

All provinces have recognized the need to address these limitations as they affect consumers. This recognition arises from the assumption that consumers are at a disadvantage compared to businesses and therefore require legislative protection. The concept of protecting the consumer implicitly assumes that the commercial purchaser is better able to take care of itself and does not require any kind of special safeguards.

Consumer Protection Legislation

All provinces have supplemented the traditional *Sale of Goods Act* with legislation that effectively prevents the express exclusion of implied conditions and warranties in consumer transactions. Generally, these statutes apply only when goods are purchased for personal use. The adopted approach in some provinces[6] has been to imply certain conditions and warranties similar to those contained in the *Sale of Goods Act*

---

5. These, and other deficiencies, are discussed in D. Young & B. Fraser, *Canadian Advertising and Marketing Law*, vol. 1 (Toronto: Carswell, 1990) at 4-29 and following.
6. *Consumer Protection Act*, R.S.M 1987, c. C-200, s. 58 (Manitoba); *Consumer Protection Act*, R.S.N.S. 1989, c. 92, ss. 26, 28 (Nova Scotia); *Consumer Protection Act*, R.S.N.W.T. 1988, c. C-17, s. 70 (Northwest Territories); *Consumer Protection Act*, R.S.Y. 2002, c. 40, s. 58 (Yukon).

into all retail sales of consumer products and to prevent their exclusion. Others[7] have adopted an approach that prevents the exclusion of the *Sale of Goods Act* conditions and warranties in consumer transactions.

All provinces[8] have gone further and enacted broader consumer protection legislation. Ontario has most recently enacted a comprehensive act that consolidates several existing pieces of legislation and addresses consumer rights, unfair trade practices, consumer agreements (including online agreements), credit agreements and leases, along with remedies and enforcement. While there are some differences in the approach in the various provinces, overall the statutes are quite similar. As a starting point, this model of legislation has a broader scope in that it applies to all forms of transactions for consumer products, not just sales. Protected transactions include contracts of lease, conditional sales, and contracts for services, or for labour and materials, if supplied with a consumer product. It is also no longer possible to exclude the operation of the implied warranties. In many provinces, privity of contract cannot be raised as a defence against the ultimate consumer.

The legislation also eliminates the sometimes artificial distinction between warranties and conditions by implying warranties into protected transactions and providing specific remedies in the event of a breach of an implied warranty. The remedies available generally depend on the seriousness of the breach. Under the New Brunswick statute, for example, if the problem is relatively minor and repairable, the onus is typically upon the consumer to attempt to have the problem corrected and to allow the party at fault a reasonable time to correct the defect. If that does not occur, there is an entitlement to compensation. If the problem is major or more serious, the consumer is entitled to end the contract and receive compensation where relevant. In either case, the onus is on the consumer to act quickly. The act also permits recovery of any reasonably foreseeable damages.

While the implied warranties under the legislation are similar to those provided for under sale of goods statutes, greater protection is afforded to consumers by virtue of

- stronger warranties with respect to quality and fitness for purpose
- a warranty of durability to ensure that the goods are merchantable and fit for a reasonable amount of time. What is reasonable depends, generally, on the nature of the goods, the intended purpose, and the price paid
- a warranty of reasonably acceptable quality of services
- a provision that makes all representations designed to induce a consumer into a transaction, whether written, oral, or otherwise, into express warranties given by the seller to the buyer

Are these imposed provisions unfair to a manufacturer, distributor, or retailer? As the following case illustrates, judges apply the provisions of such legislation in a pragmatic way and tend to recognize that such legislation is endeavouring to balance consumer expectations with practical business concerns.

---

7. *Sale of Goods Act*, R.S.B.C. 1996, c. 410, s. 20 (British Columbia).
8. *Consumer Protection Act*, S.S. 1996, c. C-30.1, ss. 39–75 (Saskatchewan); *Consumer Product Warranty and Liability Act*, S.N.B. 1978, c. C-18.1 (New Brunswick); *Consumer Protection Act, 2002*, S.O. 2002, Sched. A, c. 30 (Ontario).

How well does the law protect buyers of used cars?

CASE ▼

Grabka v. Regina Motor Products (1970) Ltd., [1997] S.J. No. 770 (Prov. Ct.)

THE BUSINESS CONTEXT: Those engaged in selling goods secondhand have unique problems in terms of disclosing quality and durability of goods. Where do the seller's responsibilities for disclosure end and the purchaser's responsibilities for discovery begin?

FACTUAL BACKGROUND: Grabka bought an 11-year-old car "wholesale" and "as is." He had ample opportunity to inspect it. Within a short time, there were problems with the car that required costly repairs.

THE LEGAL QUESTION: Regarding secondhand cars sold "as is," how far do the seller's obligations related to "acceptable quality" and "durability" extend?

RESOLUTION: The court held that the obligations of the seller should be determined by the factual context. Here, it was relevant that the purchaser knew the vehicle was 11 years old with over 170 000 kilometres on the odometer (the expert testimony was that automatic transmissions in cars of this type and year commonly wear out around that time or even

earlier); that the vehicle had the appearance of not being well maintained; that it was only recently received by the seller as a trade-in; and that it was being "wholesaled" to the buyer, suggesting that this was a discount price. Furthermore, the purchaser had ample opportunity to investigate the vehicle prior to purchase and have it professionally examined. For these reasons, it was found not only that the vehicle was of acceptable quality as defined by the legislation, but also that the period of durability for which the purchaser was entitled to expect a warranty to cover his vehicle was something less than the relevant period in this case (3800 kilometres). The judge made the following general comment:

> Buyers acquiring high kilometrage older model vehicles for modest prices are engaged in a somewhat risky activity. It is to be expected that such vehicles will at any time require major and costly repairs. Such buyers must expect that the risk for such repairs will remain with retail sellers under those circumstances for a short period of time only.

CRITICAL ANALYSIS: Did the court strike a fair balance between the rights of the dealer and the purchaser in this case?

Transfer of Title

The concept of ownership of personal property in the form of goods is discussed in detail in Chapter 17. Ownership entails control of the property, but also the risk of loss from damage or destruction. Transfer of title or ownership of goods from the seller to the buyer is fundamental to the sales transaction and has an impact on a number of business concerns, especially the transfer of risk. Consider these examples:

■ If a truckload of goods is destroyed by fire in mid-delivery, who owns them and who bears the loss if they are destroyed?

■ If goods are to be paid for within 30 days of sale, does the 30 days begin upon delivery of the goods or at some earlier point?

■ Who owns a completed custom-built machine that has yet to be delivered?

At the heart of the transfer of title issue is the notion that possession and ownership of goods can be held by different parties. Possessing goods without owning them (i.e., without having title) confers certain obligations and rights, which were discussed in Chapter 17. Ownership confers additional rights.

The best way for parties to ensure clarity is to write the contract in a way that specifies when and how ownership moves from the seller to the buyer. If they fail to do so, there are statutory provisions that resolve the issue.

International Perspective

Contracts for the International Sale of Goods

In 1980 the United Nations Commission on International Trade Law (UNCITRAL) produced a treaty, the *Convention on the International Sale of Goods* (CISG). The treaty went into force in 1988 and has been ratified by more than 30 countries, including Canada and the United States. The goal of the convention is to create a uniform body of international commercial law. The CISG applies to business-to-business contracts for the sale of goods. The convention automatically applies to the contract if the parties are from ratifying countries, unless they contracted out of its provisions. It does not apply to contracts for services and technology, leases and licences, or goods bought for personal, family, or household use.

The convention provides a uniform set of rules for forming contracts and establishes the obligations of the buyer and seller. It addresses such issues as the requirement of writing; acceptance; implied terms; performance of the contract, including the buyer's and seller's obligations; and breach of contract. However, some reservations have been expressed in a recent article:

… while the CISG was enacted with the laudable goal of promoting uniformity in international transactions, the opposite may be occurring. At least in North America, the CISG may be a trap for the unwary—a set of only partially tested and poorly understood rules which courts neither uniformly nor predictably apply.

CRITICAL ANALYSIS: The CISG is a compromise agreed to by many nations and encompassing aspects of many different legal systems. Questions may have different answers under the convention than under domestic law. How useful is this convention to Canadian business?

Sources: *United Nations Convention on Contracts for the International Sale of Goods*, 1980 (CISG) at http://www.cisg .law.pace.edu/cisg/text/treaty.html; and Benjamin M. Zuffranieri, Jr. and Joshua I. Feinstein, "UN Sale of Goods Convention May Be Trap for the Unwary" *The Lawyers Weekly* (12 December 2003) at 11.

The provincial sale of goods acts set out a series of rules[9] that determine when title changes in the absence of terms in a contract. The rules are stated below, along with an example of each. In broad terms, the acts address two contrasting sets of circumstances. In most contracts for sale, goods are already in existence and can be clearly identified when the contract is formed (Rules 1 through 4 below). These are known as **specific goods.** However, sometimes goods either are yet to be set aside and identified as being the subject of the contract or have not yet been produced. In this scenario, described in Rule 5, goods are said to be **unascertained.**

specific goods
Goods that are identified and agreed on at the time a contract of sale is made.

unascertained goods
Goods not yet set aside and identifiable as the subject of the contract at the time the contract is formed.

Rule 1

Where there is an unconditional contract for the sale of specific goods in a deliverable state, the property in the goods passes to the buyer when the contract is made, and it is immaterial whether the time of payment or the time of delivery or both is postponed.

Example: Pacific Play Centres has an inventory surplus at the end of its prime season and offers special discounts off wholesale prices. ABC Discounter goes to PPC's warehouse, orders, and pays on the spot for all the remaining equipment, which is immediately set aside in the loading dock for pickup the next day. There is a major fire at the warehouse that night, and all the equipment is destroyed. The destroyed goods belonged to ABC. Title shifted when the contract was made, since the goods were ready for delivery at that time.

Rule 2

Where there is a contract for the sale of specific goods and the seller is bound to do something to the goods for the purpose of putting them in a deliverable state, the property does not pass until the thing is done and the buyer has received notice.

Example: XYZ Discounter places an order for play centres at the spring trade show in Toronto. The sale specifies that PPC will pack the equipment in boxes carrying the XYZ name and logo. In this case, XYZ does not become owner of (acquire title to) these goods until PPC has notified it that the goods have been packed in the appropriate boxes. If the warehouse burns either before the goods are packed in the XYZ boxes or before XYZ is told the goods are ready, PPC remains the owner and incurs the loss. Title does not change until the goods have been put in a deliverable state and XYZ has been notified.

Rule 3

Where there is a contract for the sale of specific goods in a deliverable state but the seller is bound to weigh, measure, test, or do some other act or thing with reference to the goods for the purpose of ascertaining their price, the property does not pass until such act or thing is done and the buyer has received notice.

Example: PPC buys the plastic components for its equipment offshore. Since quality is important, the contract specifies that the plastic must be tested for strength before shipping. The plastic components have already been manufactured but have not been tested. The manufacturer decides to fill another customer's order with the

---

9. For example, *Sale of Goods Act*, R.S.O. 1990, c. S-1, s. 19.

components made for PPC. Until the goods have been tested, title has not passed. There is an act or event that must take place as a condition of the agreement for sale, and until that act or event has taken place, PPC does not acquire title.

Rule 4

Where goods are delivered to the buyer on approval or on "sale or return" or other similar terms, the property passes to the buyer

    (a) when she signifies her approval or acceptance to the seller or does any other act adopting the transaction

    (b) if she does not signify her approval or acceptance to the seller but retains the goods without giving notice of rejection; if a time has been fixed for the return of the goods, on the expiration of such time, and if no time has been fixed, on the expiration of a reasonable time.

Example: PPC has a standing contract with ABC Discounter that it will ship out play sets at specified times and in set quantities to the ABC warehouse, and that ABC can return these goods if they are not sold. PPC ships 50 play sets to the ABC Discounter's warehouse in compliance with this agreement. After three weeks, there is severe water damage in the ABC warehouse and the sets in storage are destroyed. ABC did not signify acceptance and there is no fixed time for return. Therefore, title will change after a reasonable time, which will depend on the circumstances and prior practices between PPC and ABC.

Rule 5

Where there is a contract for the sale of unascertained or future goods by description and goods of that description and in a deliverable state are unconditionally appropriated to the contract, either by the seller with the assent of the buyer, or by the buyer with the assent of the seller, the property passes to the buyer, and such assent may be express or implied and may be given either before or after the appropriation is made.

Example: XYZ places an order with PPC for 50 play sets. The operator of the forklift truck in the PPC warehouse accidentally drops some boxes that could have been sent to XYZ. Since the order is generic or unascertained (there is no way of knowing which boxes in the warehouse will be used to fill XYZ's order), title changes only when the goods are unconditionally appropriated to the contract. Here, title has not shifted, as boxes for XYZ are still mixed in with general inventory. If, however, the forklift had dropped XYZ's order as it was loading it onto the truck or the truck was involved in an accident en route to XYZ and the order destroyed, XYZ would have title and incur the risk.

Although the *Sale of Goods Act* rules are important, they are complex. In practice, it is always preferable to avoid the rules by drafting contracts that set out clearly when title and the corresponding risk shift from the seller to the buyer.

The rules determining when title to goods shifts also affect the damages the seller is entitled to in the event of breach by the buyer. For example, if the buyer commits breach by cancelling an order, the seller is entitled to damages for breach. If title has not shifted according to these rules, the seller still owns the goods. The seller is therefore entitled to the normal measure of **damages for nonacceptance,**

damages for nonacceptance
Damages to which a seller is entitled if a buyer refuses to accept goods prior to the title shifting.

recognizing that the seller has an obligation to mitigate the loss. If title has shifted, the buyer owns the goods and must pay the full amount of its obligation under the contract. The seller's claim is known as **action for the price.**

Delivery of Goods

It is beyond the scope of this text to address specialized laws affecting the transportation of goods. More general principles applying to carriers are discussed in Chapter 17.

Business has developed standardized terms that describe documentation in particular types of contracts. For illustration of these terms, assume that PPC contracts to sell $10 000 worth of play sets to Lumiere, a Montreal-based retailer, and the goods will be shipped through a carrier called Custom Trucking.

Bill of Lading: The **bill of lading,** generically known as a "shipping document," is the contract between the seller (PPC) and the carrier (Custom Trucking). It specifies to whom the goods must be delivered and provides evidence that the goods have been transferred from the seller to the carrier.

The time it takes for goods to reach their destination can be significant, particularly in foreign trade. What happens when, one day after shipping, PPC learns that Lumiere is insolvent? At this time, PPC has the right to exercise **stoppage in transitu.** It can direct the carrier to return the goods, even though title may have moved to Lumiere. Provided Custom Trucking receives this direction before it has delivered the goods to Lumiere, it must return them (at PPC's expense) to PPC.

Cost, Insurance, and Freight: The initials **c.i.f.** stand for "cost, insurance, freight." In a c.i.f. contract, the seller is responsible for arranging the insurance (in the buyer's name) and shipping. The purchase price includes the cost of the goods, insurance, and shipping. The seller must deliver the goods to the carrier and send copies of all documentation and a full statement of costs to the buyer. If the contract

**What are the legal
issues created by the
shipping of goods?**

between PPC and Lumiere is "c.i.f. Montreal," PPC must arrange shipping and insurance and will not have fulfilled its contractual obligations to deliver to Lumiere until it has transferred the goods to the shipper and provided Lumiere with all necessary documentation.

f.o.b.

A contractual term whereby the buyer specifies the type of transportation and the seller arranges that transportation and delivery of goods to the shipper at the buyer's expense.

Free on Board: The initials **f.o.b.** stand for "free on board." In an f.o.b. contract, the buyer specifies the type of transportation to be used, and the seller arranges this and delivers the goods to that shipper. The seller's responsibilities are over when the goods are delivered to the shipper. The seller incurs the cost of delivering the goods to the shipper, and generally the buyer pays for shipping and insurance. So if the contract is "f.o.b. Mississauga," Lumiere will advise how the goods are to be transported, and PPC will arrange for that transportation and ensure that the goods are delivered to the relevant carrier.

c.o.d.

A contractual term requiring the purchaser to pay the shipper cash on delivery of goods.

Cash on Delivery: A **c.o.d.** or "cash on delivery" contract was once common with consumer orders, particularly before credit cards. The purchaser is obliged to pay for the goods upon delivery.

In international trade it is important that shipping terms be standardized to ensure that there is a common understanding between jurisdictions. The International Chamber of Commerce has published a set of definitions for trade terms, known as INCOTERMS. These definitions do not have the force of law but are often adopted by contracting parties. They may differ from the terms outlined above. Businesspeople need to be familiar with the appropriate terms applying to their specific transaction.[10]

The Product

Basic Principles

Traditionally, the word "product" implied tangible goods, and this was the focus of early regulation. Today, the word and the regulations that apply to it are far broader in scope. A product is anything a business sells. It may be goods, services, or ideas.

PPC is developing a product that involves inherent and practically unavoidable risks that are obvious and legally acceptable. Children may fall off even the best-designed climbing frames and break limbs. However, provided the climbing frame is properly built and not dangerously high, PPC is unlikely to have any legal responsibility for such unfortunate incidents.

In essence, doing the right thing in terms of safe product design coincides with what the law demands from business enterprises. PPC is required by the law of negligence to avoid causing harm that is reasonably foreseeable. PPC is required by contract law to supply a safe product. PPC is also required to meet regulatory standards designed to protect the public, over and above what the common law requires. In addition, businesses follow voluntary industry codes. Regulatory standards, in relation to product design, manufacture, and packaging and labelling, are discussed below.

---

10. International Chamber of Commerce, *INCOTERMS 2000* (Incoterms 2000, Publication 560).

Design and Manufacture

Governments, through legislation, impose minimum standards for many goods and services where they consider it to be in the public interest to reduce the risk of harm. Governments also establish standards for product design and patent protection. For example, if another person or company has registered a particular industrial design, PPC cannot produce or sell playground equipment based on that design unless PPC obtains explicit permission in a licence from the registered owner.

In addition, organizations such as the Canadian Standards Association develop voluntary guidelines for use by both producers and users of goods. Guidelines are developed with the assistance of a broad range of experts, including representatives from industry.[11] These guidelines may be adopted by regulators as mandatory standards, and they will typically represent the measure of the standard of care for tort liability.

All businesses should be familiar with voluntary guidelines that apply to their goods and services and must become familiar with the mandatory standards in their field of operation. For example

- Some industries must comply with specific legislation. *The Motor Vehicle Safety Act* "... regulate[s] the manufacture and importation of motor vehicles and motor vehicle equipment to reduce the risk of death, injury and damage to property and the environment."[12]

- Importers, advertisers, and vendors of certain products are subject to specific legislative requirements such as the *Hazardous Products Act* (HPA).[13]

- The sale or distribution of some products or substances is prohibited. For example, if PPC sold painted playground equipment, the paint could not contain lead. If goods are inherently dangerous and have no overriding value, they are banned by the HPA.

What legal challenges are presented by the design of this product?

---

11. The *Standards Council of Canada Act*, R.S.C. 1985, c. S-16, s. 3 creates a Standards Council, which, in turn, accredits bodies, including the Canadian Standards Association, that create different standards. The Canadian Standards Association also provides testing and certification of products under its brand name CSA International. The international standards-setting body is the International Organization for Standardization (ISO).
12. S.C. 1993, c. 16.
13. R.S.C. 1985, c. H-3.

Producers of goods and services may consider both regulations and voluntary guidelines to be impediments to their right to develop an effective marketing mix. It is more useful, however, to view them as the collective opinion of specialists in risk assessment. For example, the voluntary standards on Children's Playspaces and Equipment[14] developed by the Canadian Standards Association represent the consensus of qualified experts, including industry participants, as to what is reasonable to maintain child safety. Viewed in this light, they are a valuable resource for producers like PPC. Ignoring the standards would seriously compromise PPC's marketplace reputation and significantly increase its exposure to legal liability.

Product attributes and characteristics were addressed in the previous section dealing with the contract of sale.

Packaging and Labelling

Marketing concerns the design of product packaging as well as creation of the product itself. While package design is used to attract customers, it must also comply with laws concerning safety and honesty. Part Three of this text considers the impact of tort law on product packaging. When designing packaging and drafting the label contents, the law of negligence is of primary concern.

Labelling and packaging legislation complements common law. Its focus is the imposition of standards in order to prevent harm. Trademark law (see Chapter 18) also affects package design. Most packaging and labelling legislation is federal and therefore applies throughout the country.[15] Some legislation is industry specific—for example, the *Food and Drugs Act*[16] (food, drugs, cosmetics, and other therapeutic devices), the *Textile Labelling Act*,[17] and the *Tobacco Act*.[18] Other legislation regulates consumer products generally.

Labelling of Prepackaged Goods

The *Consumer Packaging and Labelling Act* (CPLA)[19] sets out minimum packaging and labelling requirements for almost all prepackaged goods sold in Canada, other than drugs, cosmetics, and medical devices. The act encourages fair competition between manufacturers and other sellers by ensuring that consumers can compare the price and quantity of products. It is enforced by the federal department Industry Canada.

The CPLA requires manufacturers to

- provide the consumer with certain essential information, specifically, the generic description, net quantity, and identity of manufacturer or importer
- eliminate any misleading information about the nature or quantity of the product that might flow either from statements made on the container or from the shape or size of the container. For example, imported goods cannot be labelled "Made in Canada."

---

14. Canadian Standards Association International, *A Guideline on Children's Playspaces and Equipment*, Doc. No. CSA Z614-98 (Toronto: CSA International, 1998).
15. The principal exception to this is the Quebec language legislation, most importantly that found in section 51 of the *Charter of the French Language*, R.S.Q. c. C-11. Otherwise, provincial legislation tends to apply to specialized industries such as alcohol, milk, and margarine.
16. R.S.C. 1985, c. F-27. See also Andrew C. McLachlin, "Companies Should Review Food Labels Before Regulations Come Into Force" *The Lawyers Weekly* (22 July 2005) at 14.
17. R.S.C. 1985, c. T-10. The voluntary Canadian Care Labelling Program was devised under the direction of National Standards of Canada; see *Guide to the Canadian Care Labelling Program* (Fair Business Practices Branch, Competition Bureau, 9 March 2000).
18. S.C. 1997, c. 13.
19. R.S.C. 1985, c. C-38.

The regulations are intended to provide customers with the product information required to make purchasing decisions. PPC proposes to sell its playground equipment partially assembled, in boxes. If PPC prints only its name and a graphic on the packaging, purchasers will not know how big the equipment is, whether all the parts are included and holes predrilled, whether the wood requires a sealant, and whom should be contacted if there are any questions or parts are missing. Failure to provide this information may confuse consumers and may also violate the CPLA.

Much of the information required by law must be disclosed in both French and English. In addition, the regulations can be very specific. For example, wrapping paper and tinfoil (bi-dimensional products) must be described in appropriate units—square metres, or dimensions of roll, ply, and the number of perforated individual units for paper towels. All information must be prominently and clearly presented. Without this information, the prospective purchaser would have to guess about the quantity being purchased, and a manufacturer might be tempted to make the product look bigger than it is.

Product Warnings

Some products are inherently hazardous, and there is a need both to warn of hazards and to provide critical information about what to do if the product causes harm to the user.

The HPA provides at least 23 identified categories of "restricted" products—products that must be labelled in a specific manner or meet certain standards to be sold legally in Canada.[20] About half of these are chemicals (for example, household cleaners) or petroleum distillates. The rest of these "restricted" products include a wide range of goods, such as pressurized metal cans, flammable carpets, baby cribs and car seats, tents, cigarette lighters, and children's sleepwear.

Warnings must be clear and in the prescribed form, including first aid and related information. Also, the packaging itself must be "child resistant," where relevant, and meet specific standards in this regard.

What aspects of this product warning are required by law?

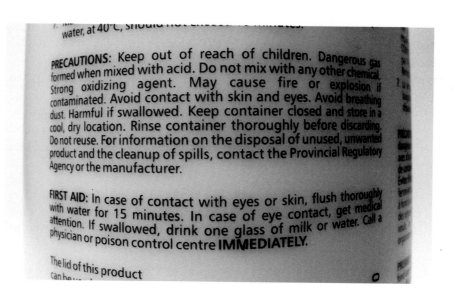

---

20. These restricted products are set out in the *Hazardous Products Act, supra* note 13, Sch. 1, part 2.

Promotion

A leading marketing text defines promotion as the "communications link between buyers and sellers [with the] function of informing, persuading, and influencing a consumer's purchase decision."[21] Influencing the consumer is achieved through an optimal mix of the key elements of promotion—namely, advertising, public relations, personal selling, and sales promotion.

Industry Standards and Legislation

For both business and consumers, promotion is the most visible component of the marketing mix. As with design and production, promotion is governed by both voluntary industry standards and legislation. The most important voluntary standards are those of Advertising Standards Canada (ASC), an organization established by the advertising community to promote public confidence in its products and services, and those of the Canadian Broadcast Standards Council (CBSC), a council supported by the Canadian Association of Broadcasters (CAB) with the approval of the Canadian Radio-television and Telecommunications Commission (CRTC).

The ASC addresses advertising in general and has a detailed code of industry guidelines. It provides a mechanism for public complaints concerning violations of that code, as well as business-to-business complaints. Complaints are investigated and, if found to be valid, result in a finding that the advertiser should change or remove the offending promotion. Since this is a voluntary process, enforcement relies on moral suasion. However, findings are publicized, and members of the advertising community can ill afford to ignore a ruling made against them by their peers.

The CBSC has an equivalent code of ethics and complaints process, related specifically to promotion in broadcast media. In addition, it has developed more specialized codes, such as those related to sexual stereotyping and violence. The promotion of goods is also regulated by legislation.

Misleading Advertising

false or misleading advertising
Promotional statements that either are false or have the ability to mislead a consumer as to their truth.

The most important provision relating to **false or misleading advertising** is found in the federal *Competition Act*.[22] The act defines false or misleading advertising as arising where

> A person . . . who, for the purpose of promoting, directly or indirectly, the supply or use of a product or for the purpose of promoting, directly or indirectly, any business interest, by any means whatever,
>
> (a) makes a representation to the public that is false or misleading in a material respect . . .

This provision is stated in broad terms so as to capture not only those who deliberately make false statements, but also those who push the limits of truth—intentionally or otherwise—in the impressions given to buyers.

---

21. L.E. Boone, D.L. Kurtz, H.F. MacKenzie, and K. Snow, *Contemporary Marketing*, 1st Can. ed. (Toronto: Nelson, 2007) at 53.
22. R.S.C. 1985, c. C-34. Other legislation tends to focus on specific issues. For example, *the Consumer Packaging and Labelling Act, supra* note 19, prohibits misleading advertising, specifically in the context of prepackaged goods; it would be misleading to describe the product box as "full" or "large" if this is not the case.

Falsity is judged by an objective test. Whether or not a statement is misleading is measured by the impression that might be formed by the average member of the group of persons to whom the statement is directed. What is important is the impression created by the advertisement in its entirety, including illustrations and disclaimers. The misrepresentation must be "material"—that is, it must apply to statements that entice prospective purchasers to the place of business or that influence the customer's decision to purchase the particular item. For example, a fitness company recently admitted that by failing to disclose additional mandatory fees in its advertising of membership offers in newspapers, billboards, and storefront signs, it had led consumers to believe that the price of memberships was significantly less than the actual price.[23]

The following overview and introduction to the *Competition Act* relates to many of the anticompetitive activities discussed in these two chapters, including misleading advertising.

Business and Legislation — The *Competition Act*

The federal *Competition Act* has its origins in antitrust legislation passed first in Canada in 1889.[24] While it retains a critical role in proscribing behaviour that manipulates a competitive market (see Chapter 24), today it also plays an important part in regulating activities that improperly benefit one producer over another through misleading or unfair practices affecting consumers.

The Commissioner of Competition, an independent official, is responsible for enforcing and administering the act, and in particular, for the conduct of examinations and inquiries under the act. For administrative purposes, the commissioner is the head of the Competition Bureau, which is part of Industry Canada. The commissioner publishes an annual report that describes the bureau's activities (for the year ending 31 March 2005, see http://www.competitionbureau.gc.ca/internet/index.cfm?itemID=2097&lg=e) The commissioner is also responsible for administering and enforcing the *Consumer Packaging and Labelling Act,* the *Textile Labelling Act,* and the *Precious Metals Marking Act.*[25]

Provisions in the *Competition Act* are either criminal or civil in nature. Criminal matters are called **prohibited offences** and are considered by legislators to be of a more serious nature than civil **reviewable matters.** Prohibited offences include materially false or misleading representations made knowingly or recklessly, deceptive telemarketing, double ticketing, and pyramid selling. Under the criminal regime, alleged offences are investigated by the bureau, and evidence obtained in criminal matters can, at any stage of an inquiry, be referred by the commissioner to the attorney general of Canada, who will, in turn, decide whether to proceed to prosecution, as is the normal practice with criminal matters.

The civil regime for reviewable matters is applied to a number of deceptive marketing practices proscribed under the *Competition Act,* including misleading advertising, bait-and-switch selling, misleading performance claims, and misleading price offers. This process was developed to address concerns about the time and difficulty of proving criminal cases. The primary purpose of the civil

---

23. "Competition Bureau Reaches Settlement with Goodlife Fitness Clubs in Advertising Case" online at http://www.competitionbureau.gc.ca/internet/index.cfm?itemID=195&lg=e (9 February 2005).
24. *Act for the Prevention and Suppression of Combinations Formed in the Restraint of Trade,* S.C. 1889, c. 41.
25. R.S.C. 1985, c. P-19.

CHAPTER 23 SALES AND MARKETING: THE CONTRACT, PRODUCT, AND PROMOTION •

regime is to stop the misleading activity. The Competition Bureau will typically seek an order prohibiting the use of the deceptive practice. Persons found responsible for deceptive practices may also be ordered to publish an information notice and may be ordered to pay an administrative penalty. Any violation of an order may itself be a criminal offence. While the penalties are not as severe as in the criminal provisions, the cases are far easier to prove since proof of intent is not necessary.

The prohibited and reviewable offences listed above are discussed in detail later in this chapter and the next.

Sources: *Competition Act*, R.S.C. 1985, c. C-34; and the Competition Bureau website at http://www.competitionbureau.gc.ca

---

prohibited offences
Offences under the *Competition Act* that are criminal in nature.

reviewable matters
Offences under the *Competition Act* that are assessed according to a civil burden of proof and resolved by voluntary agreement or by order of the Competition Tribunal.

due diligence
A defence based on adopting reasonable steps to avoid the violation of a legal duty.

Complaints and Defences

If a business is suspected of false or misleading advertising of goods or services, officers of the Competition Bureau will conduct an investigation. If the misrepresentation is sufficiently serious, criminal charges under the *Competition Act* may be laid, in which case the prosecutor will need to prove that the misrepresentation was made "knowingly and recklessly." More frequently, a complaint of false or misleading advertising will be pursued through the civil regime, which can be swift, particularly where there is a risk of immediate harm, and can result in an order to halt the deceptive practice and/or an administrative penalty.

Section 36 of the *Competition Act* allows for civil actions to be brought by individuals or commercial complainants who are seriously concerned about the actions of competitors, particularly in the context of comparative advertising. Since stopping the advertising campaign is of primary importance, the complainant may seek an injunction, as well as pursue claims for damages if the loss is quantifiable. The *Mead Johnson Canada* case, discussed in Chapter 12, was the first case in which an injunction under section 36 was allowed.

The best defence to allegations of misleading advertising is that the elements of the offence have not been proven.

All reviewable matters have an additional defence, namely that of **due diligence:**

... consideration of what a reasonable man would have done in the circumstances. The defence will be available if the accused reasonably believed in a mistaken set of facts which, if true, would render the act or omission innocent, or if he took all reasonable steps to avoid the particular event.[26]

Since this is a defence, the onus is on the accused to demonstrate due diligence. Consider the following examples of the application of due diligence in the context of potentially misleading representations:

Example 1: PPC imports some products from overseas. It is advised by the exporter that the goods meet Canadian Standards Association standards, and thus, PPC makes this statement in its promotional materials. In fact, the goods meet some lesser standards, and there has been no attempt by the exporter or PPC to establish

---

26. *R. v. Sault Ste. Marie (City)*, [1978] 2 S.C.R. 1299 at para. 60. Note that inclusive language has only more recently become part of the common law.

that Canadian standards have been met. PPC will fail to prove due diligence. As a seller in Canada, PPC should have exercised reasonable care; failing to make any checks is inadequate.

Example 2: PPC publishes and distributes the *PPC Children's Play Catalogue*, a biannual publication. The catalogue lists 250 items, and it is found to have a high incidence of errors in their descriptions. PPC's defence is that it spot checks every tenth product listed for accuracy.

The sampling is unlikely to be considered adequate for this type of catalogue. "Reasonableness" may not involve the checking of each individual description, but it certainly involves more than one in ten.

The Competition Bureau will be influenced by whether or not the advertiser has sought to correct errors. Speedy retraction may also be evidence of due diligence. The advertiser should retract an error quickly and in a manner consistent with the original advertisement. A pattern of similar errors corrected repeatedly, however, may suggest both a cynical marketing strategy and a lack of due diligence.

The retailer using materials provided by the producer (or another party in the distribution chain) does not face liability unless it has transformed the representation made by the manufacturer into its own advertisement and promoted the product itself.

Performance Claims

Statements about the performance of a product or service may fall within the general provisions described earlier under misleading advertising.

The *Competition Act* also has a specific provision directed to performance claims. It is reviewable conduct to make a representation about the quality of a product that is not based on an "adequate and proper test."[27] Statements such as "the PPC climber develops your child's gross motor skills better than any other play equipment on the market" and "PPC's environmentally friendly harvesting of woods enhances regeneration of local forests" must be neither false nor misleading. PPC must also establish that before making these claims there was appropriate testing of their accuracy, and that the testing met the state of the art in scientific tests or consumer analysis.

Performance claims are one of the most frequent sources of complaint to the Competition Bureau. The following feature highlights several recent cases.

Business Application of the Law

Unjustified Performance Claims

Performance-enhancing products are common, but the manufacturer cannot make claims about their effectiveness without proof of their truth. Three recent cases have involved claims relating to fuel-saving devices, health benefits of tanning, and weight loss.

---

27. *Supra* note 22, s. 74.01(1)(b).

Econoco Inc. marketed the Econopro as a device to save fuel and reduce emissions, and claimed that it produces fuel savings of 10 percent or more; completely eliminates gas engine emissions; and improves engine performance. The Competition Bureau applied for an order to prohibit the company and its directors from making such claims that are not based on adequate and credible tests. The company and directors consented to comply. They also agreed to inform consumers and pay an administrative penalty.

Fabutan Sun Tan Studios claimed that moderate indoor tanning is a treatment for vitamin D deficiency and seasonal affective disorder; stimulates metabolism; and prevents or reduces the risk of cancer, heart disease, osteoporosis, and sunburn. The bureau filed an application for an order to cease such representations. The application was later resolved by agreement when Fabutan consented to ensure that any messages connecting tanning to health benefits be accompanied by specific warnings and statements, and be justified by scientific evidence. Fabutan also agreed to maintain a corporate compliance program, post a notice on its website, and pay an administrative penalty of $62 500.

A chain of weight loss clinics marketed a weight loss device and natural products based on claims that they would produce weight loss in specific areas, induce the effects of liposuction without surgery, help dissolve fat, enable weight loss of nine pounds in seven days, and burn off fat during the night. The bureau claimed that people would be led to believe that there were easy solutions to excess weight and that the claims were not supported by credible studies. The bureau sought an order that the company cease making the unsupported claims. The tribunal issued a ten-year prohibition order against the company and its president and imposed administrative penalties against both.

CRITICAL ANALYSIS: Why are sellers tempted to make claims that they cannot support?

Sources: "Competition Bureau Obtains Agreement to Stop Marketing of Econopro, a Bogus Fuel Saving Device" (28 September 2006) at http://www.competitionbureau. gc.ca/internet/index.cfm?itemID=2203&lg=e (accessed 24 October 2006); "Fabutan Agrees to Stop Promoting Unproven Health Benefits of Indoor Tanning" (27 February 2006) at http://www.competitionbureau.gc.ca/internet/ index.cfm?itemID=2027&lg=e (accessed 24 October 2006); and "Tribunal Decision Follows Competition Bureau Investigation Into Bogus Claims" (25 September 2006) at http://www.competitionbureau.gc.ca/internet/ index.cfm?itemID=2192&lg=e (accessed 24 October 2006).

Tests and Testimonials

Advertisers often promote products and services either by presenting supportive test results or by using the assurances of convincing spokespersons, real or hypothetical. Tests must be carried out prior to the promotion. If conducted by a third party, there must be permission to draw from the tests or they must already be in the public domain.

PPC may claim to have tested its products on a sample of nursery schools in the Prince George area. Provided PPC quotes accurately from these tests and they are fairly presented, this is in compliance with the act. Alternatively, suppose *Consumer Reports* or *Today's Parent* has published surveys of different play equipment, and PPC wishes to quote from these surveys in promotional material. If copyright approval is required and received, and the quotes are accurately represented, this form of promotion is acceptable.

PPC may also wish to use testimonials, for example, from a child care professional, an expert in child development, or a parent. These testimonials will be acceptable provided they are accurately stated and current, and provided the persons providing the testimonials have actually used or evaluated the product. Using a well-known personality to provide the desired testimonial will attract close scrutiny. If, however, PPC is using an actor to represent, say, a hypothetical parent, the statements will be measured by the provisions for false and misleading advertising in general.

Promotion through Selling Practices

Promotion is more than advertising. Where promotional practices are unfair to consumers, specific legislative provisions have evolved to regulate or prohibit them.

Bait and Switch

An unscrupulous promotional practice is **bait and switch.** The product is advertised at a very low price (the bait) but the supply is insufficient to meet expected demand. When consumers take the bait, they are informed that this product is "not in stock," "of poor quality," or "inferior to Product B." They are then persuaded to purchase the higher-priced Product B (the switch). It is, of course, Product B that the promoter intended to sell all along, usually because it has better profit margins.

Unfair Practices

Provinces have legislated to address selling practices that generally can be described as unfair, usually because they prey on ill-informed consumers.[28] The word "unfair" typically arises in the context of unequal bargaining power.

Unfair practices arise, for example, when the business intentionally

- targets customers with "physical infirmity, ignorance, illiteracy, inability to understand the language or the agreement, or other similar factors" and who are therefore unable to understand the serious nature of the agreement
- sells at a price that "grossly exceeds the price at which similar goods or services are readily available to like consumers"
- engages in a calculated and cynical marketing scheme that is "subjecting the consumer to undue pressure to enter into the transaction"
- persuades a customer to buy where there "is no reasonable probability of payment of the obligation in full by the consumer"
- imposes terms and conditions "of the proposed transaction [which] are so adverse to the consumer as to be inequitable"

Should a vendor's actions be unfair, the consumer is typically entitled to rescission or to a return of money paid. The relevant government agency may also choose to prosecute the seller when a complaint is made.

Business Law in Practice Revisited

1. How does the law affect PPC's marketing strategy?

PPC's marketing strategy covers the four aspects of the marketing mix: the product, its promotion, its retail price, and the way it reaches the consumer (distribution or place). Even though the industry in which PPC operates is not highly regulated, both common law and statute law affect every aspect of the marketing mix.

---

bait and switch
Advertising a product at a very low price to attract customers, then encouraging them to accept another product that is more expensive.

unfair practices
Illegal business practices that exploit the unequal bargaining position of consumers.

---

28. For example, *Business Practices and Consumer Protection Act*, S.B.C. 2004, c. 2 (British Columbia); *Trade Practices Act*, R.S.N. 1990, c. T-7 (Newfoundland); *Consumer Protection Act, 2002*, S.O. 2002, Sched. A, c. 30 (Ontario); *Business Practices Act*, R.S.P.E.I. 1988, c. B-7 (Prince Edward Island); *Consumer Protection Act*, R.S.Q. c. P-40.1 (Quebec).

PPC is selling to children, so safety is paramount. In practice, it must comply with the Canadian Standards Association safety standards, and these also provide guidance for the minimum standard of care in tort and contract. The goods are sold boxed and therefore must comply with the *Consumer Packaging and Labelling Act* (CPLA). PPC is promoting mainly through the print media and in-store displays. It must be familiar with the provisions related to false and misleading advertising and to tests and testimonials in the *Competition Act*. Any claims of environmental benefits must be supported by evidence.

2. What are the key aspects of PPC's contracts with its customers?

The producer must meet the terms of its contract; otherwise, the purchasers may claim that a breach has occurred. Statute law—for example, the *Sale of Goods Act*—imposes some conditions and warranties concerning the quality of the product. PPC should be aware of how the implied conditions and warranties of the sale of goods acts affect its contractual obligations. In particular, the goods must match the description PPC provides on the box and be of merchantable quality. Additionally, the goods must be fit for the purpose for which they are sold. PPC will also need to comply with the requirements of provincial legislation that supplements the *Sale of Goods Act* for consumer sales. In addition, PPC must be aware of terms relating to the transfer of title and delivery of goods.

3. What impact does the law have on PPC's product?

The federal CPLA will govern how PPC packages the goods by providing minimum disclosure requirements. Since this is a national marketing campaign, information must be in both official languages. Under tort law, and the law of negligence and product liability in particular, PPC should take steps to avoid any reasonably foreseeable harm to users of its products that might arise from design, manufacture, and packaging. It should limit any potential liability through warnings. PPC must also consider the full range of voluntary guidelines that affect the products, since these, in practice, will define the standard of care in negligence.

4. What impact does the law have on the promotion of PPC's product?

Promotion of the product introduces additional requirements, most found in the federal *Competition Act*, although compliance with provincial legislation will also be required where applicable. Representations must be neither false nor misleading, and will be evaluated in their entirety. Where the due diligence defence applies, PPC must establish both that it had a reasonable belief in the accuracy of any representations and that it took reasonable steps to avoid any inaccuracies. PPC must be careful if it makes claims about the performance capabilities of its products. All such claims must be backed by prior and fully supportive testing. If PPC uses testimonials, these must be given by real people who are familiar with the products, or by people identified as actors. Tests must be current, used with permission if appropriate, and accurately stated. Any environmental claims must be justified.

Chapter Summary

Compliance with the relevant laws coincides, for the most part, with good marketing practice. Providing reliable and safe products and ensuring that consumers are accurately and fully informed goes a long way toward achieving the key feature of effective marketing policy—namely, meeting customer expectations.

Inevitably, however, some market participants disregard these basic principles and attempt to profit at the customers' expense. If there were no regulations in place, such practices would clearly place "good" producers at a distinct disadvantage. Legislation is therefore intended to ensure fair competition.

All sellers must be aware of the implied conditions and warranties of the sale of goods acts and other consumer protection legislation. The rules for establishing when title to goods shifts are set out in the sale of goods acts unless otherwise provided by contract. Sellers require knowledge of the meaning of a series of standard terms used in shipping of goods, such as c.i.f. and f.o.b.

Two parts of the marketing mix that are affected by the law are product and promotion. Regulation relating to the product component addresses the product (or service) itself and its packaging and labelling. The producer must be familiar with voluntary and statutory guidelines for product design and standards. Product labelling regulation is important where the customer cannot see the goods and there are explicit requirements for disclosure. In promoting goods, the most important regulation is the false and misleading advertising provision of the *Competition Act*. More specific legislative provisions also apply—for example, to tests and testimonials, and performance. Finally, close attention will be paid to any practices that induce purchases through unfair or improper means. Here, both provincial and federal legislation applies.

Chapter Study

Key Terms and Concepts

action for the price (p. 577)

bait and switch (p. 587)

bill of lading (p. 577)

c.i.f. (p. 577)

c.o.d. (p. 578)

caveat emptor (p. 568)

damages for nonacceptance (p. 576)

due diligence (p. 584)

f.o.b. (p. 578)

false or misleading advertising (p. 582)

marketing law (p. 568)

prohibited offences (p. 584)

reviewable matters (p. 584)

specific goods (p. 575)

stoppage in transitu (p. 577)

unascertained goods (p. 575)

unfair practices (p. 587)

Questions for Review

1. What is the relationship between voluntary standards such as those created by the Canadian Standards Association and common law obligations in tort and contract?

2. What are the two different ways the *Hazardous Products Act* regulates inherently dangerous products?

3. What is the origin of sale of goods legislation?

4. What is the primary difference between an implied condition and a warranty in the *Sale of Goods Act*?

5. Give one example of a condition implied by the *Sale of Goods Act* into a contract of sale.

6. Give one example of a way in which *Sale of Goods Act* provisions have been adapted to consumer contracts of sale.

7. What are "specific" goods?

8. What rules decide when title to goods passes from the seller to the buyer?

9. What is a bill of lading?

10. What broad problem does the *Consumer Packaging and Labelling Act* address?

11. What are the two approaches to enforcement in the *Competition Act*?

12. What are the critical differences between the two approaches in question 11 above?

13. What is misleading advertising?

14. How could an advertising company defend itself from an accusation of misleading advertising related to a campaign it worked on?

15. What is the due diligence defence?

16. What are the rights of a corporation to enforce the misleading advertising provisions of the *Competition Act* against a competitor?

17. If a company is investigated for an improper performance claim about its products, what is its best defence?

18. Explain the selling practice known as bait and switch.

Questions for Critical Thinking

1. If consumer protection legislation equates to good marketing practices, why have legislators gone to such lengths to pass legislation? Would basic market forces not sort these issues out without state intervention?

2. To what potential tort liability is PPC exposed relating to its products?

3. The standards relating to children's playground equipment are controversial. Some see them as being too cautious and as imposing undue burdens on service providers such as parks and schools that might have to replace all equipment. Why has this controversy arisen? What interests need to be balanced?

4. Compare the details of the regulations in the *Consumer Packaging and Labelling Act* relating to disclosure for prepackaged goods with some of the conditions or warranties that are provided by the *Sale of Goods Act*. Why is it necessary to provide this extent of detail in the CPLA?

5. Why does the *Competition Act* focus on regulating the behaviour of business rather than providing remedies directly to consumers? Does provincial legislation serve consumers more effectively?

6. Compare the criminal and civil regimes relating to deceptive marketing practices in the *Competition Act*. What are the advantages of the civil regime?

Situations for Discussion

1. The Best Foods Supermarket (BFS) chain is seeking to gain a marketing edge over its principal competitors by adopting a "green" approach to encourage consumers to believe that it is socially responsible. BFS wants to reduce its dependency on plastic containers for produce and delicatessen goods. The marketing team has devised packaging for delicatessen and produce, whereby a fibre product (made out of recycled materials) will replace the standard plastic containers. The marketing team is now finalizing the following theme for the advertising campaign.

   The wording "Best Foods goods are always packaged to please Mother Nature because we care about the future for your children and ours" will appear on all ads.

   What message is Best Foods selling? Does the message comply with the provisions of the *Competition Act*? What evidence should Best Foods have available to defend any complaints about the campaign?

2. Hammer and Nails Hardware, a nationwide chain, has devised a new product line. It has discerned a growing niche in the market among new home owners, whom it describes as typically young and not having much in the way of know-how or basic tools and equipment, and older "empty nesters," who are moving into

apartments or condominiums from a home. It has devised a "We meet all your basic … needs" campaign that prepackages home repair and paint and wallpapering products. It intends to introduce a series of ten different lines over a six-month period. They will be boxed in an attractive, consistent style of cardboard packaging that includes "how-to" books. The packages will include the basic items needed for particular household tasks.

Focus on the provisions of the *Consumer Packaging and Labelling Act* and the *Competition Act*. How will these two pieces of legislation affect the Hammer and Nails campaign? What must it do in order to comply with these provisions and avoid creating inflated expectations from customers?

3. Outdoor World sells new and used snowmobiles. It makes most of its money from new products and attempts to move secondhand ones quickly, particularly since the season is short and it does not want to be caught with extensive storage costs throughout the summer. Each January it has a major "blowout" sale that is heavily promoted and provides genuine savings.

Morley is in the market for a used snowmobile. He tells the salesperson he wants a basic machine, "no hassles," and as good a deal as he can get. The salesperson shows him three; he starts each one and says that they are roughly equivalent. Morley takes a quick look and picks one basically on colour, since he knows little about snowmobiles. The listed price was $3500, but because Outdoors is anxious to clear the line and Morley is extremely price-sensitive, he is able to bargain down the price to $2000.

Two days later there is a good snowfall and Morley takes the machine out for a run. Five kilometers from home, the snowmobile splutters to a stop. Morley cannot get the machine started. In the end, a friend rescues him, and Morley gets the machine towed straight back to Outdoor World.

What are Morley's rights under the common law? Do the *Sale of Goods Act* warranties and conditions help? Do Morley's rights vary according to the province the sale occurred in?

4. Huge Electronics sells a full range of home entertainment systems. Recently, it has extended its product line into computers. It sells "packages" that are put together by major manufacturers and designed to meet basic consumer needs. The systems are such that the basic package does most things needed by the average user, but provides the seller with little markup. It is with the middle- and high-priced lines that Huge makes its money.

Huge salespeople work on commission. The incentive scheme is consistent with profit margins, so there is a far greater commission "reward" for selling higher-priced computer packages. Huge does not carry extensive stock in the low price range because of the low profit margin. However, these products are an important part of its advertising campaign, as the low prices get the customers in the door. Huge ensures that its low-price-range computers are priced sufficiently lower than those of its competitors in order to be attractive. Once consumers are in the store, they are encouraged to buy a system that "better meets their needs," and this pitch often works.

The Competition Bureau has received complaints about Huge's marketing practices and is now investigating. What is the problem with this marketing strategy? Can Huge defend this practice? How might Huge avoid this problem?

5. Softest Diapers is one of two leading producers of diapers for infants. It has spent several years researching and testing a new brand of superabsorbent diaper. It is now devising an advertising campaign that will make direct comparison with its competitor's products. The marketing team has spent months comparing the two lines of products and genuinely believes that the new Softest diapers absorb significantly more moisture than do the equivalently priced products of the competitor. The team has asked the scientists to confirm their results, and after several months of testing, the scientists report that there is, on average, a 10 percent increase in absorbency.

The campaign is an immediate success. The competitor, recognizing the threat, immediately seeks an injunction to stop this campaign under the provisions of section 36 of the *Competition Act*. What provisions of the act and what arguments will the competitor rely upon? What will Softest use in its defence? What are the possible outcomes?

6. Acme Face Creams produces high-priced night creams. The creams consist primarily of natural substances, but one ingredient can result in an allergic reaction in a small minority of users. The product must be packaged in glass, as its properties can become unstable when in contact with plastic. Designers have created a smoky (opaque) navy blue pot with a plastic rim inside the lid.

   What must Acme consider in designing its labels for this product? What should the labels show?

7. In 1996, Shawna and Jim bought a new Dodge truck from Dodge City Auto. The truck was manufactured by Chrysler Canada. When the truck was a year old and had traveled 30 000 kilometres, it burst into flames and was destroyed. When Shawna approached the dealer and the manufacturer, they refused to assist her in any way and referred her to her insurance company as her only remedy. Shawna later learned that two other 1996 Dodge trucks self-incinerated in her province. She also learned that the cause of the fires was a defective daytime running light module, of which Chrysler was aware.[29] Comment on Shawna's remedies arising from her purchase of the truck. How would you evaluate Chrysler's marketing strategy relating to its product?

8. Trans fats are found in snack food, fast food, and processed food. They are significantly unhealthy, contributing to increases in obesity, heart disease, diabetes, and Alzheimer's disease. However, trans fats extend the shelf life of food, make food taste and look better, and make food cheaper. Now that trans fats have been identified as a serious health problem, how should they be handled—through labelling regulations, limits on quantity, or an outright ban? Should consumers be left to take care of themselves through consumer buying choices? Could consumers successfully sue manufacturers that use trans fats?

For more study tools, visit
http://www.businesslaw3e.nelson.com

---

29. Based on *Prebushewski v. Dodge City Auto* (1984) Ltd., 2005 SCC 28.

Chapter

24

Objectives

After studying this chapter, you should have an understanding of

- the legal obligations associated with the price component of marketing
- the legal obligations associated with the distribution (place) component of marketing
- the role of risk management and corporate compliance in marketing

Sales and Marketing: Price, Distribution, and Risk Management

Business Law in Practice

Pacific Play Centres Inc. (PPC), introduced in the previous chapter, is continuing to develop its marketing strategy for its new line of wooden backyard play centres for children. The preliminary marketing plan included a premium pricing strategy of selling to affluent parents who want attractive and high-quality play equipment for their children. The plan also included distribution through national hardware and toy retail chains, and directly by PPC online. Steve Martin, the head of sales, has

questions and concerns about several aspects of pricing and distribution of the new product line. Some retailers are engaging in aggressive competitive practices, and he is worried that PPC is being challenged to cross the line of legality in what it does. In particular, there is a new market participant insisting on preferential terms that would give it a distinct advantage over other competitors. Its most recent demand has been for a higher discount and longer payment terms.

To support the premium pricing strategy, Steve is exploring ways of discouraging distributors and retailers from selling PPC products at discount prices. He is anxious to stop the product line being used as a loss leader and proposes to place a "recommended retail price" sticker on the packaging. Steve thinks that arranging for exclusive dealerships in different regions of the country might be the best way to promote the high-quality image of the new products. Steve is interested in promoting and selling the new products through PPC's website, but he wants to proceed cautiously. In general, Steve and Lisa Patel, the CEO, wish to develop and implement a marketing plan that avoids unnecessary legal risks.

1. How does the law affect PPC's pricing strategy?
2. How does the law affect PPC's distribution strategy?
3. How can PPC effectively manage its exposure to legal risk in the context of marketing?

What are the legal pitfalls with sale prices?

Price

Generally, price is freely negotiated when forming a contract, although prices in a few industries in Canada continue to be regulated by government agencies or are subject to regulatory bodies that set prices between producers/growers and users—for example, utilities and agricultural marketing boards. For the most part, the legal regulation of price is directed against pricing practices that will create an unfair or uneven playing field between market participants, thus destroying competition, or treat consumer purchasers unfairly. Regulations aim to protect the right to negotiate prices.

In reviewing the relevant issues surrounding pricing, it is useful to separate pricing between producer and seller from pricing between seller (including, at times, producer) and consumer. Furthermore, it will continue to be important, when discussing provisions found in the *Competition Act*,[1] to remember the distinction between prohibited offences and reviewable matters explained in Chapter 23. In broad terms, prohibited offences, which are criminal in nature, are more serious, are referred to the attorney general for prosecution, and are more difficult to prove because of the higher burden of proof necessitated by the more serious consequences of a guilty verdict. Reviewable matters are civil in nature, and if not resolved by voluntary agreement, may result in a remedial order from a judge or the Competition Tribunal.

Pricing Practices between Producer and Commercial Purchaser

The federal *Competition Act* prohibits unfair pricing practices, including those involving the producer and its (commercial) purchaser. An important policy objective of the legislation is to create a level playing field with respect to channel power—that is, the respective powers members of the marketing or distribution channel may exert over one another. The act seeks to ensure that commercial customers are not subject to unfair differential treatment that could seriously reduce competition in the marketplace.

The *Competition Act* defines many pricing practices as criminal in nature.

Pricing Conspiracies

An obvious way for business to manipulate a market is through conspiring with direct competitors to control prices. For example, assume there are only three suppliers of the wood that PPC requires for its play sets. PPC observes that all three suppliers quote equivalent prices for equivalent orders. Each supplier likely faces similar costs, and all three may have similar profit expectations. It could also be the case, however, that this is part of a conspiracy to control the cost of wood to major producers such as PPC. If this can be proven, the wood suppliers will be guilty of a criminal offence under section 45 of the *Competition Act*, a broad provision that addresses more than pricing conspiracies. It proscribes the practices that were the original focus of antitrust legislation in Canada and elsewhere. The pricing conspiracy offence is defined in these terms:

> Every one who conspires, combines, agrees or arranges with another person
> . . . to prevent, limit or lessen, unduly, the manufacture or production of a
> product or to enhance unreasonably the price thereof, or . . . to otherwise
> restrain or injure competition unduly, is guilty of an indictable offence and
> liable to imprisonment for a term not exceeding five years or to a fine not
> exceeding ten million dollars or to both.

For a criminal offence to be proven, it must be established not only that there was an agreement or a conspiracy to set prices, but also that the agreement unduly lessened competition. This latter requirement relates to the market structure (factors such as number of competitors and barriers to entry) and the behaviour of the parties (implementation of their agreement combined with market power).[2]

---

1. R.S.C. 1985, c. C-34.
2. *R. v. Nova Scotia Pharmaceutical Society et al.*, [1992] 2 S.C.R. 606.

Convictions under section 45 are common, mostly as a consequence of guilty pleas. Fines can be heavy, as in the following examples:

- Following the exposure of the international conspiracy by Archer Daniels Midland and others to fix prices and allocate markets for lysine and citric acid, fines of $17 570 000 and $9 575 000, respectively, were levied following guilty pleas.[3]

- Eight firms were fined a total of $3.875 million for a conspiracy to fix prices and allocate market shares for vitamin B sold in bulk. In addition, a senior executive was fined $150 000 for his role in multiple conspiracies.[4]

- Three firms admitted to conspiring to avoid competing with each other in the market for carbonless sheets in Ontario and Quebec. Carbonless sheets are used by commercial printers in the production of forms and receipts. Each company was fined $12.5 million, record amounts for domestic conspiracies. The companies were also prohibited from similar conduct in future and required to provide continuing proof of compliance. They are required to educate senior personnel about competition rules and actually remove some key personnel from their positions in the paper merchant business.[5]

If the conspiracy is considered sufficiently serious, violators can be incarcerated. Jail sentences of up to one year have been imposed.[6]

Bid Rigging

Bid rigging is a specialized form of conspiracy by producers/suppliers to manipulate a market through price. **Bid rigging** occurs when suppliers conspire to "fix" the bidding process in a manner that suits their collective needs or wishes. It is a serious criminal offence, since it attacks the heart of the competitive process. Penalties include fines and/or imprisonment. Bid rigging can take many forms such as agreements to submit bids on a rotating basis or to split a market geographically.

Bid-rigging prosecutions are not uncommon. For example, suppliers of bulk compressed gases to hospitals and medical centres across Canada pleaded guilty to controlling the selling price of gases for many years through bid rigging.[7] The Competition Bureau reports fines for bid-rigging offences totalling approximately $9 million since 1980.[8]

Price Discrimination

Price discrimination[9] is the practice where a seller provides different pricing terms and conditions to competing customers for equivalent volume sales at an equivalent time. This situation may arise either because a producer, unsolicited, offers discriminatory prices, or, more commonly, because the producer responds to a customer's pressure tactics. The producer may see this as the only way of maintaining its position in the market.

---

3. Harry Chandler, Deputy Commissioner of Competition, Criminal Matters, and Robert Jackson, *Beyond Merriment and Diversion: The Treatment of Conspiracies under Canada's* Competition Act (Toronto: Competition Bureau, 25 May 2000).
4. "Competition Bureau Investigation Leads to over $4-Million in Fines for International Bulk Vitamin Conspiracies" (16 October 2002) at http://www.competitionbureau.gc.ca/internet/index.cfm?itemID=456&lg=e (accessed October 29, 2006).
5. "Competition Bureau Investigation Leads to Record Fine in Domestic Conspiracy" (9 January 2006) at http://www.competitionbureau.gc.ca/internet/index.cfm?itemID=2018&lg=e (accessed 12 December 2006).
6. *Supra* note 3 (*Sherbrooke Driving Schools* case 1996 and 1997; *Chlorine Chloride* case 1999).
7. *North York Branson Hospital v. Praxair Canada Inc.* (1998), 84 C.P.R. (3d) 12 (Ont. Ct. Gen. Div.).
8. *Supra* note 3.
9. *Supra* note 1, s. 50(1)(a). See also Director of Investigation and Research, Bureau of Competition Policy, Consumer and Corporate Affairs Canada, *Price Discrimination Enforcement Guidelines* (Hull, Que.: 17 August 1992) at http://www.competitionbureau.gc.ca/internet/index.cfm?itemID=1810&lg=e (accessed 29 October 2006).

For example, ABC Discounter has a strategy of attaining rapid market penetration in Canada by taking market share away from XYZ Discounter, an established player in the market. It has identified certain products that it will discount and is applying pressure to manufacturers to sell to it at significantly lower prices and allow longer payment terms than they would to XYZ. PPC, believing it has little choice, is prepared to accommodate ABC.

Price discrimination is a criminal offence under the *Competition Act*, since it can destroy or restrict competition. In practice, convictions have been rare under this provision because of the difficulty of meeting the criminal burden of proof. Nonetheless, the bureau reports many requests for advice and interpretation and considers this to be evidence of the business community's desire to comply with the law.

Differential discounts are legal provided it can be shown that customers who were prepared to purchase under equivalent conditions were offered the same terms. Any differences must be a direct reflection of cost differentials, say, in terms of volume or delivery. It should be noted that in cases of price discrimination, the buyer is considered as culpable as the seller. If PPC bends to ABC's demands, both risk prosecution if XYZ becomes aware of PPC's actions and reports them to the Competition Bureau.

Predatory Pricing

predatory pricing
The offence of setting unreasonably low prices to eliminate competition.

Predatory pricing[10] occurs when the seller sets prices unreasonably low with the intent of driving out its competition. This offence can be committed at different levels of the distribution chain.

Predatory pricing is a criminal offence under the *Competition Act*. To attain a conviction, it must be shown that prices are unreasonably low and that they effectively reduced competition. Because of this burden of proof, relatively few charges have ever been brought. As an alternative to criminal prosecution, the Competition Bureau can refer complaints under the reviewable anticompetitive behaviour provisions to the Competition Tribunal. The tribunal applies the civil burden of proof and has the authority to make orders preventing or stopping the particular behaviour. Should such orders be ignored, penalties could be imposed. Today, the threat of the civil regime may well lead to a voluntary agreement between the offending party and the bureau.

The Competition Bureau uses a two-step approach to evaluate predatory pricing practices:

1. Does the alleged predator have the ability unilaterally to affect industry pricing?
2. Will that dominant position or power be used to recoup the losses incurred during the period of predatory pricing, once the competitor is gone?

What amounts to "unreasonably low prices" and predatory effect is seldom clear-cut. Most intervention by the Competition Bureau follows complaints made by competitors or concerned suppliers, such as PPC. ABC Discounting may be committing the offence of predatory pricing if it can be shown that ABC's dominant position will affect pricing and that, if the practice reduces competition, ABC will likely recoup losses by subsequently raising prices.

In 2002, the bureau released new enforcement guidelines[11] for unreasonably low pricing policies, described as policies of selling below cost in order to either deter entry into a market or force competitors out of a market. The changes include

---

10. *Supra* note 1, s. 50(1)(c). See also Director of Investigation and Research, Bureau of Competition Policy, Consumer and Corporate Affairs Canada, *Predatory Pricing Enforcement Guidelines* (Hull, Que.: 17 August 1992) at http://www.competitionbureau.gc.ca/internet/index.cfm?itemID=1746&lg=e (accessed 29 October 2006).
11. Online at http://www.competitionbureau.gc.ca/internet/index.cfm?itemID=1727&lg=e.

more emphasis on the duration, frequency, depth, and pattern of low-pricing behaviour and less reliance on the ability to recoup losses, and a new basis for analyzing costs and revenues.

Price Maintenance

The producer can commit the criminal offence known as **price maintenance** by attempting to drive upward the final retail price at which its goods are sold to the public. The producer might commit this offence by exerting pressure on the retailer or placing notice on the goods themselves.

For example, because of its increasing concern that widely advertised low prices for its products will damage product image, PPC may instruct sales staff to advise retailers to cease dropping prices, and to monitor their compliance. PPC might also print on the packaging the "recommended retail price" and refuse to sell to any retailer selling below this price.

Two aspects of this strategy are illegal: the attempt to influence the final retail price upward and the recriminations against noncompliant retailers. Both attempt to prevent competition and to discipline the marketplace. PPC can use the words "recommended retail price," provided this statement determines only maximum and not minimum prices.

There are some circumstances that justify this practice. PPC can refuse to sell to retailers that are selling at unreasonably low prices, provided it can show that the retailers were using its products in any of the following ways:

- as loss leaders (typically, below cost price)
- for bait-and-switch selling
- in misleading advertising
- in sales where they fail to provide a reasonable level of service

Two examples[12] illustrate the range of outcomes that may result from the investigation of price maintenance by the Competition Bureau:

- Toyota Canada Inc. agreed to amend its sales, promotion, training, and monitoring practices for its Access Toyota Program in response to allegations that it prohibited dealers from selling vehicles below its specified "Access/Drive-Away Prices." Toyota also agreed to make donations totalling $2.3 million to several charities. Richard Taylor, deputy commissioner of competition, said, "Toyota fully cooperated with the Bureau's investigation and its willingness to address the Bureau's concerns . . . without costly litigation for taxpayers, was an important factor in settling this case."

- Labatt Brewing Company Ltd. was fined $250 000 after pleading guilty to price maintenance attempts on discount beer sold by nine independent retailers in Quebec. Labatt's attempts affected the price of discount beer manufactured by Labatt's and some competitors. Denyse MacKenzie, senior deputy commissioner of competition, said, "In order to safeguard the competitive process and ensure that consumers benefit from the lowest possible prices for goods and services, the Competition Bureau will continue to fully enforce the price maintenance provision of the *Competition Act*."

---

12. "Competition Bureau Settles Price Maintenance and Misleading Advertising Case Regarding the Access Toyota Program" (28 March 2003) at http://www.competitionbureau.gc.ca/internet/index.cfm?itemID=300&lg=e (accessed 29 October 2006); "Labatt Pleads Guilty and Pays $250,000 Fine Following a Competition Bureau Investigation" (23 November 2006) at http://www.competitionbureau.gc.ca/internet/index.cfm?itemID=2003&lg=e (accessed 29 October 2006).

Successful criminal prosecutions under trade practices legislation often depend on the willingness of members of offending businesses to come forward with evidence of criminal activity and testify in court. The standard term for such people is "whistle blowers," since they are reporting information about improper practices that is secret and would otherwise remain unknown.

Whistle blowing, however, involves risk and uncertainty. Employers may go to extraordinary lengths to suppress information and effect retribution. It is also necessary to separate genuine whistle blowing from attempts by disaffected employees to gain revenge.

Regulators such as the Competition Bureau, which rely on whistle blowers, must screen information carefully. When there is substance to the accusations, regulators have entered into informal arrangements or plea bargains whereby, for example, if the whistle blower was a participant in a conspiracy or other criminal offence, lesser charges will be brought against the informer or a lesser penalty will be sought. For individuals who are not the subject of prosecution themselves, this arrangement is ineffective. Moreover, it is no protection against, for example, dismissal from employment, though the employee can sue for wrongful dismissal if discharged without just cause or reasonable notice (see Chapter 21).

Section 66 of the *Competition Act* now provides basic protection for these individuals. The act protects the confidentiality for whistle blowers (employees and independent contractors) who supply information. Should they be required to testify, this confidentiality cannot be maintained; however, simply providing the evidence at the investigative stage often leads to a guilty plea. The act also provides protection from reprisals, such as dismissal or other adverse employment-related action, against any employee who supplies evidence acting in good faith. It is an offence for an employer to violate this provision.

CRITICAL ANALYSIS: Are whistle blowers adequately protected? Why are the words "in good faith" used in section 66?

Pricing Practices between Seller and Consumer

The main protection for consumers is through the civil and criminal misleading advertising provisions that are considered under "Promotion" in Chapter 23. This section addresses more specific provisions.

Sale or Bargain Prices

It is a reviewable offence for the seller to state that a price is less than the ordinary price ("on sale," "reduced," "clearance") when it is not.[13] An advertiser may legitimately claim a price to be the ordinary price if

> . . . [it] reflects the price at which suppliers generally in the relevant market area have either

- sold a substantial volume of the product within a reasonable period of time before or after making the representation (volume test) or
- offered the product for sale in good faith for a substantial period of time recently before or immediately after making the representation (time test).

---

13. *Supra* note 1, ss. 74.01(2), 74.01(3), and 74.1(1); Director of Investigation and Research, Bureau of Competition Policy, Consumer and Corporate Affairs Canada, *Ordinary Price Claims, Information Bulletin* (Hull, Que.: Competition Bureau, 22 September 1999) at http://www.competitionbureau.gc.ca/internet/index.cfm?itemID=1227&lg=e (accessed 29 October 2006).

Both the volume test and the time test are applied according to specific guidelines established by the Competition Bureau. Any review by the Competition Bureau requires the supply of extensive sales data for the entire relevant market. Placing a restriction to the promise in small print on the advertisement is no protection if the overall impression remains misleading.

When does stating that prices are "subject to error" protect the advertiser? Generally, such a clause provides protection only in the context of catalogue sales, since catalogues are not printed regularly and some protection is reasonable for the seller. Because this is a reviewable offence, the due diligence defence applies, and the promoter should always correct errors quickly and in a manner consistent with the original promotion.

Complaints regarding inflated "regular" prices have been common in recent years and have generated activity at the bureau. The following case is the first contested proceeding.

CASE ▼

Canada (Commissioner of Competition) v. Sears Canada Inc. [2005] C.C.T.D. No. 1 (Trib. Dec. No. CT2002/004/158b)

THE BUSINESS CONTEXT: Consumers are attracted by bargains. Retailers may be tempted to make their bargains appear as attractive as possible as they compete for consumer sales. The challenge for retailers is to fairly present the bargain price in comparison with the regular or ordinary price.

FACTUAL BACKGROUND: In 1999 Sears advertised five lines of all-season tires. The ads contained claims such as "save 40%" and "1/2 price" and drew comparisons between Sears' ordinary prices and its sale prices. During a lengthy investigation and hearing, Sears admitted that it failed to meet the volume test.

THE LEGAL QUESTION: Did Sears satisfy the time test in terms of good faith and substantial period of time?

RESOLUTION: The Tribunal concluded that good faith should be determined on a subjective basis— did Sears truly believe that its ordinary prices were genuine and *bona fide* prices, set with the expectation that the market would validate the prices as ordinary? Sears' claims of good faith were rejected based on its admission that it expected only 5–10 percent of the tires to be sold at the ordinary price; Sears' ordinary price was not competitive in the market; and Sears could not track the number of tires sold at the ordinary price. In terms of

substantial period of time, the tribunal concluded that if a product is on sale more than half the time, then it has not been offered at its ordinary price for a substantial period of time.

Following the Tribunal's decision, Sears reached a settlement with the bureau regarding penalty. Sears agreed to pay $100 000 as an administrative penalty and $387 000 toward the bureau's legal costs.

CRITICAL ANALYSIS: In other recent cases, prominent retailers such as Forzani Group (Sport Chek), Suzy Shier, and Grafton-Fraser (Jack Fraser Menswear, Tip Top Tailors) have agreed to pay substantial penalties (some in excess of $1 million). Will these high profile cases alter the behaviour of retailers? Will consumers have greater confidence in advertised bargain prices?

What must this retailer ensure to avoid complaints about this sale?

Double Ticketing

double ticketing

The offence of failing to sell at the lower of the two prices appearing on a product.

Sellers can commit pricing offences in their direct contact with the customer. For example, if there are two or more prices on goods, the product must be sold at the lower of those prices. To do otherwise amounts to the criminal offence of **double ticketing.** Obligations extend to in-store promotions and displays, as well as prices listed in store computers. If consumers intentionally move the goods (or change pricing labels), they are committing fraud.

The Competition Bureau is particularly concerned about differentials between prices posted on store shelves and those stored in automatic price-scanning systems, since it is easy for customers to fail to notice an increased price at the checkout.

Business Application of the Law

Scanner Price Accuracy Voluntary Code

In 2002, several Canadian retail associations launched this code to demonstrate their commitment to accurate scanner pricing. The associations involved are the Retail Council of Canada, the Canadian Association of Chain Drug Stores, the Canadian Association of Independent Grocers, and the Canadian Council of Grocery Distributors. The code acknowledges that incorrect prices can harm customer relations and attract legal sanctions. Its purposes are to demonstrate retailer commitment to scanner accuracy, provide retailers with a national framework, and provide a mechanism for consumer complaints. The code has been endorsed by the Competition Bureau. Over 5000 retailers are voluntary participants.

Key aspects of the code are

- The Item Free Scanner Policy, which states that for claims that a scanned price exceeds the advertised or display price, the customer is entitled to the product free of charge where the correct price is less than $10 and to the correct price less $10 where it exceeds $10.

- Retailers should correct errors as quickly as possible.

- Retailers must establish appropriate internal policies, procedures, and training programs.

- Clear and legible labels must be affixed to the shelf next to the product.

- Clear and complete receipts must be provided to customers.

- A Scanner Price Accuracy Committee is established to oversee the code.

- There is a multistep consumer complaint process that culminates in arbitration.

There has been some criticism of the absence of accountability in the code. There is no effective way to discipline retailers that fail to follow the code and no independent review of how the code is working.

CRITICAL ANALYSIS: Do voluntary codes such as this one provide helpful strength to the provisions of the *Competition Act*? Can voluntary codes replace regulation and enforcement?

Scanning Code of Practice

If the scanned price of a non-price ticketed item is higher than the shelf price or any other displayed price, the customer is entitled to receive the first item free, up to a $10 maximum. If a Code of Practice problem cannot be resolved at the store level, please call 1-866-499-4599 to register your complaint.

Code de procédure d'application pour le balayage électronique

Si le prix d'un produit non étiqueté lu par balayage est plus élevé que le prix affiché en magasin ou tout autre prix affiché, le client obtiendra le premier article gratuitement, jusqu'à un maximum de 10 $. Si un problème concernant le Code de procédure d'application pour le balayage électronique ne peut être réglé en magasin, vous pouvez appeler au numéro 1-866-499-4599 afin d'y soumettre votre plainte.

Canada

Source: Competition Bureau, "Consumers to Be Compensated for Overcharged Scanned Purchases" (11 June 2002) at http://www.competitionbureau.gc.ca/internet/index.cfm?itemID=415&lg=e (accessed 29 October 2006).

Distribution (Place)

Distribution is defined in a leading marketing text as "the movement of goods and services from producers to customers."[14] Distribution includes the process of ensuring that goods get into the customers' hands—that is, shipping and transportation. Distribution decisions also determine whether goods will be sold by retailers, wholesalers, door-to-door salespeople, or e-commerce vendors. How corporations are structured, including merger decisions resulting in horizontal or vertical integration, is part of the broad notion of distribution. The material in this section is therefore presented under three broad headings—organization structure, including mergers, acquisitions, takeovers, and multilevel marketing; discriminatory distribution practices such as refusal to deal and tied selling; and the various forms of direct marketing.

The contract of sale involves several distribution issues, in particular the transfer of title and delivery of goods. These issues are discussed in detail as part of the "Contract of Sale" section at the beginning of Chapter 23. That material should be reviewed at this point.

Organizational Structure

Typically, businesses are free to structure themselves in the manner they consider most effective for organizing their distribution channels to market their products. However, if competition is adversely affected, particularly through mergers, acquisitions, or takeovers, regulators may step in.

Mergers, Acquisitions, and Takeovers

In Canada it is recognized that there is a fine line between allowing business to expand through merger, acquisition, or takeover in order to operate profitably in what is a relatively small market, and avoiding the negative consequences of what might through these processes become harmful, monopolistic behaviour.

The *Competition Act* sets out the conditions under which the bureau can seek an order ending a proposed or actual merger. A merger is the union of two or more companies to form one larger company. The critical question in each case is whether a merger or proposed merger prevents or lessens, or is likely to prevent or lessen, competition substantially. What is considered "substantial" by the bureau is described in its guidelines as the result of material increase in prices that is not likely to be offset by increased competition.

The *Competition Act* recognizes the complexity of examining mergers and has a notification requirement for large proposed mergers. The businesses proposing the merger must notify the director of their intentions prior to the merger; within a specified time, they will be provided with a determination as to whether the director considers that the merger will substantially prevent or lessen competition. The director will then decide whether the merger can proceed as notified, only on specified conditions, or not at all.

multilevel marketing
A scheme for distributing products or services that involves participants recruiting others to become involved in distribution.

Multilevel and Pyramid Selling[15]

Multilevel marketing plans arise through what are known as distributorships. Income is earned through commissions to distributors, and fees are paid upward to those creating the schemes.

---

14. L.E. Boone, D.L. Kurtz, H.F. MacKenzie, and K. Snow, *Contemporary Marketing*, 1st Can. ed. (Toronto: Nelson, 2007) at 428.
15. *Supra* note 1, ss. 55, 55.1. Also *Franchises Act*, R.S.A. 2000, c. F-23 (Alberta); *Pyramid Franchises Act*, R.S.S. 1978, c. P-50 (Saskatchewan); *Criminal Code of Canada*, R.S.C. 1985, c. C-46, s. 206(1)(e).

Multilevel marketing or selling is not always illegal. The legitimacy of the activity will be determined by such factors as whether there is a genuine selling opportunity for those buying distributorships in the plan and whether there is a realistic opportunity for distributorships to expand. If a genuine business activity is not obvious, the multilevel selling scheme is likely illegal. Such schemes are unstable, and inevitably those joining at the late stages receive little or no value as the scheme collapses for lack of new participants.

Legal multilevel selling schemes are the subject of regulation, in particular, relating to disclosure. There must be "fair, reasonable and timely disclosure" of earnings or expected earnings.

Pyramid selling is the form of multilevel marketing that is illegal. It is a criminal act under the provisions of the *Competition Act* if

pyramid selling

An illegal form of multilevel selling under the *Competition Act*.

- participants pay money for the right to receive compensation for recruiting new participants;

- a participant is required to buy a specific quantity of products, other than at cost price for the purpose of advertising, before the participant is allowed to join the plan or advance within the plan;

- participants are knowingly sold commercially unreasonable quantities of the product or products (this practice is called inventory loading); or

- participants are not allowed to return products on reasonable commercial terms.[16]

For businesses, it is essential that any multilevel marketing scheme avoid violation of the provisions of the *Competition Act*. The very term "pyramid selling" carries serious negative connotations. Even an accusation that this is the basis of the distribution scheme will damage the reputation of a business.

Complaints tend to focus on inadequate disclosure. For example, the bureau recently investigated a company operating a multilevel marketing plan known as the Cocooning Club to promote and sell computer software on nutrition and other subjects. The investigation found that the company and participants in the plan made representations on a website and a television infomercial that exaggerated income expectations without disclosing the income of a typical participant in the plan. The company was fined $75 000 and its vice president given a conditional jail sentence.[17]

Discriminatory Distribution Practices

Producers may discriminate unfairly between customers through distribution policies as well as pricing practices. The consequence in either case is the same: the practice reduces or eliminates competition.

Many practices that discriminate in this way are reviewable matters. The Competition Bureau will investigate the activity and, if it believes an offence is being committed, seek a remedial order. These offences are best illustrated through practical examples.

- PPC's playground slides have become one of the dominant brands. All major discount retailers are using these as a means of attracting customers. XYZ finds that PPC will not supply it with the slides, even though XYZ is willing and

---

16. Director of Investigation and Research, Bureau of Competition Policy, Consumer and Corporate Affairs Canada, *Pyramid Selling and Multi-level Marketing Schemes* (Hull, Que.: Competition Bureau, 2 June 1999) at http://www.competitionbureau .gc.ca/internet/index.cfm?itemID=1278&lg=e (accessed 29 October 2006).
17. "Multi-level Marketing Firm Pleads Guilty to Misleading Participants" (11 March 2005) at http://www.competitionbureau .gc.ca/internet/index.cfm?itemID=2003&lg=e (accessed 12 December 2006).

able to meet the same conditions of sale as ABC. This practice likely falls within the definition of **refusal to deal** and will be reviewable provided that it is "substantially" affecting XYZ, that XYZ is willing to meet the usual trade terms offered to ABC, and that PPC has an adequate supply of the slides that it refuses to provide.

■ PPC tells its distributors that it will continue to supply them with PPC equipment only if they buy from no other suppliers of play equipment. If this practice lessens competition substantially, it falls within the definition of **exclusive dealing** and is therefore reviewable.

■ PPC advises XYZ that it will supply the "hottest" play set product of the spring season only if XYZ also buys a number of less popular products and refrains from buying from any competitor. This practice may be **tied selling** and is reviewable provided, again, that the action lessens competition substantially.

■ PPC considers (1) dropping prices significantly to prevent Western Playgrounds Ltd., a major competitor, from expanding in the market and (2) buying D & E Hardware Chain, Western's major customer, in order to squeeze Western out of the market. These practices may be reviewable as **anticompetitive behaviour.**

Direct Marketing

Direct marketing is "a broad concept that includes direct mail, direct selling, direct-response retailing, and automatic merchandising; [any] direct communications, other than personal sales contacts, between buyer and seller, designed to generate sales, information requests, or store or website visits."[18]

Regulators traditionally focused on door-to-door sellers, but over time, began to look for ways to protect consumers from intrusion by other means. The *Competition Act* now addresses telemarketing specifically. Online shopping is regulated by more general provisions in the *Competition Act*, such as those related to promotion and pricing, and a variety of provincial legislation.

Regulation in the area of **door-to-door selling** focuses on protecting consumers from untoward pressure and on allowing them the chance for second thought and the opportunity to cancel the sale. This form of selling is regulated under provincial consumer protection legislation that typically requires

■ those selling door-to-door to be licensed

■ contracts in excess of a certain dollar figure to be in writing and to disclose specific matters

■ consumers who sign a contract to be allowed a "cooling-off" period[19] during which they may cancel the contract

Marketers typically define **telemarketing** as including both inbound sales calls, where the retailer advertises a product and makes it available through telephone orders, and outbound calls, where the focus is on unsolicited calls to consumers in their homes. The regulations apply to any "interactive telephone communication" but do not extend to fax, Internet communications, or automated, prerecorded messages. Regulation is similar to what governs door-to-door sellers. It protects the consumer from high-pressure tactics. Basic information about the vendor and the product must be disclosed, and deceptive practices are defined as offences. For

---

18. *Supra* note 14 at 477.
19. For example, *Fair Trading Act*, R.S.A. 2000, c. F-2; *Direct Sellers' Regulation Act*, R.S.N.S. 1989, c. 129. In Alberta and Nova Scotia, the cooling-off period is ten days.

What are the legal parameters of telemarketing?

example,[20] several Montreal companies were fined $300 000, prohibited from engaging in similar activities for ten years, and required to contribute $180 000 to a remediation program. The telemarketing companies had misrepresented the purpose of their calls, provided false information about prior relationships, failed to disclose restrictions on the return of goods, and failed to disclose the continuing nature of customer agreements.

In another case,[21] 11 individuals were charged for their roles in a prize pitch scam that targeted consumers in Australia over a five-week period. Consumers were informed that they had won valuable prizes, but were required to buy promotional items in order to claim their prizes. Consumers were misled and deceived about the quantity and value of the prizes. Penalties included conditional jail sentences, probation, fines, and community service.

Online Retailing

Internet selling is the fastest-growing area of retailing. Regulation is moving beyond the general marketing practice provisions in the *Competition Act* and provincial consumer protection provisions that affect all sales of goods and services. Marketers and their industry organizations are instituting means—often through contract law—of gaining the trust of prospective purchasers. For example, sellers may guarantee that consumers can return goods at no cost if the goods do not meet expectations.

---

20. "Montreal Telemarketing Companies Plead Guilty for Deceptive Telemarketing Activities" (19 June 2002) at http://www .competitionbureau.gc.ca/internet/index.cfm?itemID=417&lg=e (accessed 29 October 2006).
21. "Competition Bureau Investigation into Deceptive Telemarketing Operation Concludes" (20 June 2005) at http://www .competitionbureau.gc.ca/internet/index.cfm?itemID=1869&lg=e (accessed 12 December 2006).

There is some reluctance by consumers to buy through e-commerce because of the following concerns:

- *Identity of the business.* Websites come and go, and the location of the vendor is often unknown. Consumers tend to favour well-known brands and companies at the expense of smaller, less-familiar businesses.

- *Privacy and personal information.* Private information supplied by consumers may become a resource that other marketers use and abuse.

- *Security.* How effective are the current encryption devices in protecting personal and financial information, especially credit card information? Is there risk of identity theft?

- *Applicability of existing laws.* What happens if something goes wrong? Which laws apply? Will there be any available redress?

The Internet has created new opportunities for fraud. The challenge is to apply existing and necessary new law without stifling the commercial opportunities of the Internet. Governments and business are addressing these issues through various means, including

- *Encouraging the establishment of principles for protecting e-commerce customers.* Such principles are established by both industry groups and governments. For example, a group of interested parties (industry groups, consumers, and government) has created the *Canadian Code of Practice for Consumer Protection in Electronic Commerce*, which sets out good business practices for merchants conducting online commercial activities. The Canadian Marketing Association has amended its codes of ethics and standards of practice to address issues of consumer consent and the Canadian Association of Internet Providers (CAIP) has a new voluntary code of conduct. There already are third-party seal programs, such as the CA WebTrust program created by the Canadian Institute of Chartered Accountants and the American Institute of Public Accountants.

- *Applying provisions of the* Competition Act. The *Competition Act* provisions concerning anticompetitive practices already apply to websites, cybermalls, electronic bulletin boards where advertisements may be posted, banner ads in browser programs and search engines, and the use of e-mail. Section 52(1) of the *Competition Act*, which refers to representations, applies to third parties such as web page designers, proprietors of cybermalls, proprietors of electronic bulletin boards, and Internet service providers. In criminal prosecutions, it must be proven that these third parties acted "knowingly or willfully." Otherwise, the bureau would rely on civil orders or on the other forms of compliance already available. The bureau has issued an *Information Bulletin on the Application of the* Competition Act *to Representations on the Internet*[22] and has initiated Project FairWeb, an Internet surveillance and enforcement program to combat misleading and deceptive advertising on the Internet.

- *Enacting privacy legislation.* As outlined in Chapter 20 on employment and Chapter 26 on credit, the federal government has passed the *Personal Information Protection and Electronic Documents Act*, which requires all organizations to obtain consent for the collection, use, or disclosure of personal information. The act required provincial equivalents by 2004 and requires marketers to obtain consent for the use or disclosure of personal information for any purpose, including direct or targeted marketing or even market research.

---

22. Competition Bureau (18 February 2003) at http://www.competitionbureau.gc.ca/internet/index.cfm?itemID=1213&lg=e (accessed 29 October 2006).

- *Encouraging international cooperation.* There is a strong need for international cooperation, particularly between enforcement agencies on issues relating to cross-border jurisdiction. The Competition Bureau has participated in international Internet sweeps targeting bogus product claims and other scams.

- *Updated consumer protection legislation.* All provinces have endorsed the Internet Sales Contract Harmonization Template. For example, Ontario's new *Consumer Protection Act* has special provisions for Internet agreements that require disclosure of specified information about the goods or services, dispute resolution limits, full disclosure of contract terms, an express opportunity to accept or decline the contract, a copy of the contract in written or electronic form, the right to cancel the contract within a specified time, and the right to refunds from sellers and credit card companies.

As discussed in Chapter 6, a major concern relating to e-business is the dramatic increase in spam—bulk, unsolicited, "junk" e-mail. Several American jurisdictions have legislation directed at spam. In Canada, ways to deal with spam are under study.

Sources: N. Ladouceur, "Calibrating the Electronic Scales: Tipping the Balance in Favour of a Vigorous and Competitive Electronic Market for Consumers" (Address to the Canadian/United States Law Institute, The Impact of Technological Change in the Canada/United States Context, 16–18 April 1999); "New Electronic Commerce Principles to Protect Consumers" at http://www.ic.gc.ca/cmb/welcomeic.nsf/cdd9dc973c4bf6bc852564ca006418a0/85256779007b79ee852568240065f6f2!OpenDocument (accessed 28 October 2006); Patrick Allossery, "A Bill That Goes Way Too Far" *National Post* (25 February 2002) at FP6; Robin Harvey, "Minister Wants More Consumer Protection" *Toronto Star* (1 March 2002) at http://www.torontostar.com (accessed 28 October 2006); *Consumer Measures Committee, Internet Sales Contract Harmonization Template,*(29 May 2001) at http://strategis.ic.gc.ca/epic/internet/inoca-bc.nsf/en/ca01642e.html (accessed 28 October 2006); and Eva Chan, "*Consumer Protection Act* Creates a Major Increase in Consumer Rights" *The Lawyers Weekly* (2 June 2006) at 9.

Risk Management in Marketing

Risk management in marketing requires consideration of the four-step risk management model presented in Chapter 3 and the business risks discussed in contracts and torts in Parts Two and Three of this text. The products and services must perform as intended, the design of any products must be fundamentally sound and address all reasonably foreseeable risks, and promises must not exceed what it is possible to deliver.

The following figure is a compilation of the issues and concerns addressed in these two marketing chapters that may create risks requiring management.

FIGURE 24.1

Sources of Legal Risks in Marketing

The Contract of Sale

- Terms: express and implied
- Contracting out of express terms vs. implied terms
- Commercial vs. consumer sales
- Transfer of title rules
- Delivery terms

Product

- Design
- Quality
- Packaging
- Labelling
- Warnings

Promotion

- False, misleading, or deceptive advertising or claims
- Environmental claims
- Performance claims
- Tests and testimonials
- Selling practices such as bait and switch

Price

- Conspiracies to fix prices or rig bids
- Discriminatory practices
- Attempts to control retail prices (price maintenance)
- Unreasonably low or predatory prices
- Misleading sale prices
- Double ticketing and inaccurate price scanning

Distribution

- Mergers, acquisitions, and takeovers
- Multilevel selling
- Discrimination through exclusive dealing or tied selling
- Deceptive telemarketing
- Disclosure of terms and cancellation for online sales

Here are the basic practices that a business such as PPC should adopt in order to minimize its risk exposure

- PPC must establish a climate in which maximizing safety of the product is considered paramount. For any business producing goods or services for children, this is especially important. Even one preventable injury can destroy the viability of the product line. Product designers must be familiar with all relevant design regulations. Senior management should support this approach to design, even when faced with competing demands for resources or pressure for sales and profits.

- The organization should acquire, through its trade association and specialized professional advisors such as lawyers and industrial engineers, the knowledge of what standards must be met for both the production and the labelling of the goods. If goods or services are unsuitable for the very young, this information must be effectively communicated on product labelling, and all promotions must be consistent with this message. If the goods come partially assembled, as is the case with PPC, information must be provided so that prospective purchasers can visualize the assembled product.

- PPC should follow the basic guidelines for promotion—that is, ensure that statements and promises are both honest and clear. Those responsible for advertising must be well versed in the properties of the product or service. They should understand what it can and cannot deliver. Those directly responsible for creating in-store promotions and for explaining products or services to customers must be well educated in the qualities of a product, even when they are not the producer's employees.

■ PPC must recognize that it cannot use pricing policies to manipulate the market or try to drive out competitors. Manufacturers such as PPC are not permitted to dictate the retail prices for sales to the consumer. Apart from these limitations, PPC can charge its customers whatever prices it wishes, so long as all customers in the same market are treated the same.

■ In terms of distribution, PPC must avoid structuring distribution channels or making agreements with competitors or distributors that substantially interfere with competition. What is most efficient and profitable for PPC may not be acceptable under competition law. Since PPC has chosen to engage in direct marketing through the Internet, the prime considerations are ensuring clear disclosure to buyers and refraining from pressure selling.

■ Guidelines for sales and shipping staff should set out all pricing and distribution practices that PPC might be tempted or pressured to participate in and all those that are prohibited. Both the nature of the practices and the penalties imposed for engaging in them should be described. A clear protocol must be established for decision making and for addressing questionable practices. The Competition Bureau has an Immunity Program to encourage early and complete cooperation regarding any questionable activities.

■ Since much of the regulation of marketing activities is found in the *Competition Act*, Lisa and Steve can turn to the compliance program materials provided by the Competition Bureau for guidance. The goal of the bureau is compliance before harm. It promotes a sequence of enforcement activities known as the "Conformity Continuum"; thus, it has devised guidelines[23] for a credible and effective corporate compliance program, including the involvement and support of senior management; development of relevant policies and procedures; ongoing education of management and employees; monitoring, auditing, and reporting mechanisms; and internal disciplinary procedures.

■ PPC should also provide information about all aspects of shipping the goods. It will have standard practices that transfer title or risk. Employees should know the significance of these practices to the risk of the business. Also, basic shipping terminology should be defined so that employees understand the implications of contractual terms.

■ PPC should establish an informed and properly responsive customer relations process. This is the primary line of communication between the producer and the customer. It can ward off serious problems, reassure customers, and reduce the potential for subsequent complaints and claims. It can also be an early warning system of the need to reconsider design or production techniques.

■ Since no organization can prevent all untoward events, PPC must have adequate insurance coverage to address expected risk. It must have access to professional advisors who understand the business, including specialized insurance brokers and lawyers.

---

23. *Corporate Compliance Programs, Industry Canada* (Hull, Que.: Competition Bureau, 3 July 1997), at http://www.competitionbureau.gc.ca/internet/index.cfm?itemID=1638&lg=e, currently under review. See also Conformity Continuum Information Bulletin at http://www.competitionbureau.gc.ca/internet/index.cfm?itemID=2018&lg=e (accessed 12 December 2006).

Business Law in Practice Revisited

1. How does the law affect PPC's pricing strategy?

Generally, the law requires PPC to treat all of its customers in a similar fashion when they are purchasing under similar conditions. PPC has good reason to be concerned about the practices that retailers are pressuring it to partake in, since these practices may violate the provisions of the *Competition Act* and PPC may well be the subject of an investigation. If the retailer insists that PPC sell to the competitor under less favourable purchasing terms, PPC may be subject to investigation for the offence of price discrimination. The fact that PPC is being pressured to partake in such illegal schemes will provide no defence. PPC has limited rights to control the final price at which its goods are sold. Directives can be only toward providing a maximum selling price, not a minimum. The exception is where PPC seeks to prevent a retailer, for example, from using its products as loss leaders or engaging in improper activity such as bait-and-switch selling.

2. How does the law affect PPC's distribution strategy?

PPC is selling to an increasingly competitive retail market and is finding its margins under attack. Under these conditions, PPC is considering imposing terms on customers that may violate the law. It cannot, for example, insist that customers purchase less-popular goods along with popular items, and it must not differentiate between comparable customers that are willing and able to purchase under similar conditions. If a dominant retailer insists that PPC stop selling to a major competitor, PPC may be the subject of investigation for refusing to deal. PPC is entitled to refuse to deal with retailers that might harm the reputation of the company or its products through their selling practices. If the retailer fails to support the product or promote it fairly, PPC can discontinue supplying.

3. How can PPC effectively manage its exposure to legal risk in the context of marketing?

PPC is making and selling goods that have significant legal risk exposure, as they are designed for children. Any untoward event has the potential of destroying market confidence in the products. PPC must ensure that it maintains a "safety-first" strategy, with all employees buying into this fundamental notion. Likewise, all promotion must be truthful. Maximizing safety and honesty will minimize risk. Using all the resources provided by the relevant federal and provincial governments, Advertising Standards Canada, and the Canadian Standards Association will also assist. Guidelines for sales and shipping staff can clarify PPC's policies and indicate practices that are illegal. Finally, PPC should ensure that it has full insurance coverage.

Chapter Summary

Price and distribution are two of the four components of the marketing mix. Price includes more than the provisions designed to protect consumers. There is also strong public interest in ensuring that businesses compete fairly. If unfair practices are permitted, honest businesses will find themselves at a competitive disadvantage or will be squeezed out of the marketplace. While it is perhaps a common perception that anything goes in competition between businesses, the regulations outlined in this chapter related to business-to-business dealings show that this assumption is incorrect. Laws have evolved to address some of the issues that are of particular concern to Canadians, given the size of this country and its relatively small population. Businesses may have to become dominant in the marketplace to achieve economies of scale. Nonetheless, such market dominance cannot be allowed to lead to unfair or discriminatory practices.

The word "distribution" covers a range of activities and practices. Distribution practices that discriminate between customers and thereby substantially reduce competition are reviewable by the Competition Bureau. Direct-marketing practices are regulated both provincially and federally. Risk management in marketing entails paying close attention to all aspects of a marketing plan to identify risks relating to the business and its customers. A plan should set clear guidelines for staff and ensure awareness of marketing activities that are not permitted. A corporate compliance program is a critical factor in any investigation by the Competition Bureau. More importantly, it positions the business so that compliance with all legislation is a fundamental principle by which it operates.

Chapter Study

Key Terms and Concepts

anticompetitive behaviour (p. 605)

bid rigging (p. 597)

door-to-door selling (p. 605)

double ticketing (p. 602)

exclusive dealing (p. 605)

multilevel marketing (p. 603)

predatory pricing (p. 598)

price discrimination (p. 597)

price maintenance (p. 599)

pyramid selling (p. 604)

refusal to deal (p. 605)

telemarketing (p. 605)

tied selling (p. 605)

Questions for Review

1. Who decides the price in a commercial sale?

2. What are two important facts that must be proven in order to establish illegal price discrimination?

3. What is a conspiracy to fix prices?

4. What is predatory pricing?

5. Under what conditions is it acceptable to state "recommended retail price" on a product?

6. What are two situations where it is legitimate for a seller to refuse to supply to a retailer?

7. What is bid rigging?

8. What is the meaning of "ordinary price" in evaluating the promotion of goods?

9. How did Sears' tire advertising break the law?

10. What is double ticketing?

11. What is the difference between legal multilevel selling and pyramid selling?

12. What must be disclosed to potential participants in a multilevel marketing plan?

13. How are door-to-door sellers regulated?

14. What are two primary concerns of consumers buying online?

15. What are key features of legislation governing online contracts?

16. What is a corporate compliance program in relation to marketing regulations?

17. How does a business seek immunity from prosecution for violating competition law?

18. Why is whistle blowing to be encouraged?

Questions for Critical Thinking

1. The prohibition of various unfair pricing practices by the *Competition Act* is intended to promote a level playing field and prevent pricing policies that limit competition. Why are market forces not able to eliminate unfair competitors? Why are customers not able to distinguish the fair competitors from the unscrupulous?

2. A manufacturer that wishes to market a product at a premium price is prohibited from attempting to influence the resale price of its product by distributors. How then can manufacturers protect the premium image of their products and discourage discount prices?

3. The regulation of mergers must reach a balance between promoting competition while allowing participants in an industry to cooperate or join together in order to become more efficient. In the final analysis, which side of the argument should rule?

4. Internet shopping opens up a broad range of risks to consumers. What recommendations would you have for federal and provincial governments moving to regulate in this area to enhance consumer confidence?

5. Canadian car drivers are often disgruntled when gasoline prices change. It seems that whether the price goes up or down, every gas station in town adjusts its price at the same time. Is this an indication of a price conspiracy by the oil companies? What market factors are relevant?

6. Assume you are a relatively new marketing manager in a fast-moving consumer products business. You are concerned because the firm encourages managers to operate quickly, independently, and aggressively. You are aware of the advisability of a risk management plan or a corporate compliance program under the *Competition Act*. How could you persuade management to adopt this approach given the existing corporate culture?

Situations for Discussion

1. Mega Goods Inc. is a major discount retailer operating throughout Canada. The Home Co-op is also a nationwide chain, but it is a cooperative buying group of smaller retailers that band together in order to achieve buying power. Both retailers buy large volumes of plastic food containers from the major manufacturer (PFC Inc.) in the market. The product line is an important customer draw and is often used in special promotions.

Mega Goods is eager to increase its market share, particularly with the entry of a multinational, U.S.–based discounter into the Canadian market. It decides to attempt to eliminate the direct competition from the Co-op in smaller centres. Mega Goods approaches PFC and requests changed conditions of purchase. Specifically, it asks for a significant drop in price in return for a reduced payment period. This change will place it at a distinct advantage over the Co-op, as the Co-op cannot pay quickly because of its membership structure. Mega Goods intends to approach all other major suppliers if this proposal works.

PFC management is quite concerned, as the Co-op is a long-standing customer. Would supplying on Mega Goods's terms be legal? Is it a wise business practice?

2. There are three major suppliers of highly specialized industrial chemicals in Canada. They have all operated for many years and respect each other and the quality of their products. They recognize that the market, while profitable, is finite, and that for each to survive, none can assume a greater market portion than currently held. For many years, it has been accepted that when calls for supplies are made by various industries, Company A will respond for Western Canada, Company B for Ontario, and Company C for Quebec and the Maritimes.

Recently, purchasers from these suppliers have been questioning why, of all supplies purchased, these chemicals are subject to the least price fluctuation. Word is getting back to the three suppliers that questions are being asked. Do they have any reason to be concerned? Is this the only way all three can survive?

3. John Smith is a sales supervisor with Company A in Situation 2 above. He has been aware for some time of the market-sharing arrangement by the three companies. He is not a contented employee, having been overlooked for promotions for many years. He has heard rumours of a reorganization in Company A that involves downsizing in the sales department.

John fears that his job is in jeopardy and decides to take action of his own. He knows that no one will ever know the whole story about the arrangements between the three chemical suppliers unless an insider tells. He is unsure how to use this inside information and what protection he might receive if he releases what he knows outside Company A.

What are John's options? Will he be protected if his disclosure damages Company A?

4. Textiles Inc. is a major chain of fabric sellers. In this market, there are a few high-end sellers of fashion designer fabrics, some small independents, and three chains, with Textiles being the largest and most profitable. Textiles thrives on its ability to attract customers, often through discount pricing.

Every few weeks Textiles has a major promotion, with certain materials being sold at a reduced cost. The business sells both regular fabrics and fashion fabrics. Textiles tends to discount the regular fabrics to get purchasers in the door, who are then inevitably drawn to the attractively arranged, high-markup fashion fabrics with sample clothing and patterns prominently displayed. After a while, even though advertisements state that fabric prices are reduced by 30 percent and even 50 percent, regular customers have become so accustomed to these reductions that they seldom expect to pay the full price.

These practices are attracting the attention of competitors, which have notified the Competition Bureau. Why is the bureau likely to be interested in Textiles's pricing practices?

5. Air Canada's dominance of the domestic Canadian airline market has been challenged by smaller regional carriers such as WestJet and CanJet. The regionals can operate more efficiently in their smaller markets and offer sharply lower fares than Air Canada over the same routes. Air Canada has tried two policies to combat this competition. One was to meet or undercut all regional fares in order to eliminate the regionals' price advantage. The other was to break off several regional airlines from Air Canada itself in order to compete with the regionals in their own territory. Are these Air Canada strategies permissible under marketing law? Are there other ways for Air Canada to protect its market share?

6. Partridge developed a marketing plan that involved the purchase and sale of travel vouchers. The travel vouchers had little value for sale purposes, but could be redeemed. A person purchased a packet of travel vouchers for $500 but knew that the broker selling it had paid only $62.50. The participant purchased the packet not to acquire and use the vouchers, but only to become a seller of packets and benefit from the markup when selling to new participants. Partridge discussed the scheme with several acquaintances who thought it was a good idea if enough participants became involved.[24] Is this a legitimate multilevel selling venture or a pyramid scheme prohibited by law? How can Partridge find out if his plan is legitimate?

7. The Rolling Stones produced a new four-disc DVD called *Four Flicks*. TGA Entertainment, the Stones' management company, made an agreement with Future Shop granting FS the exclusive right to sell the DVD set to consumers. In return, the Stones received a larger portion of profits from the DVD than they would have through normal distribution. The music retailer HMV Canada anticipates huge demand for the DVD and wants to be able to sell it through its outlets. TGA refuses to sell to HMV because of the agreement with FS.[25] Is this agreement valid under marketing law? Explain.

8. Merck & Co. is the fourth largest pharmaceutical company in the world. It developed and tested an effective painkiller called Vioxx that was particularly helpful to those suffering from arthritis. The drug was approved by the regulatory authorities and put on the market in 1999. Over the next five years it was taken by 20 million patients, generating $2.5 billion in sales and 11 percent of Merck's revenue each year. In 2004, a report was released indicating an elevated risk of heart attack and stroke among those who took Vioxx for 18 months or longer. Merck decided to withdraw Vioxx from the market. Since then, Merck has been named as defendant in over 16 000 lawsuits involving Vioxx. So far, Merck has won four cases, lost five and paid $350 million in damages. Meanwhile, Merck's competitors continue to sell similar drugs with severe warnings on the packages regarding possible health risks.[26] Should Merck have put Vioxx on the market? Should it have been withdrawn from the market in 2004? How should Merck deal with the pending litigation? What broader marketing law and consumer protection issues does this situation raise?

For more study tools, visit
http://www.businesslaw3e.nelson.com

---

24. Based on *R. v. Partridge* (1996), 32 W.C.B. (2d) 259 (Sask. C.A.)
25. The Canadian Press, "Music Retailers Seek Satisfaction" *The Chronicle Herald* (14 November 2003) at C2.
26. Based in part on Alex Berenson, "Maker of Vioxx Says Some Suits May Be Settled" *The New York Times* (26 August 2005) at http://www.nytimes.com (accessed 29 October 2006).

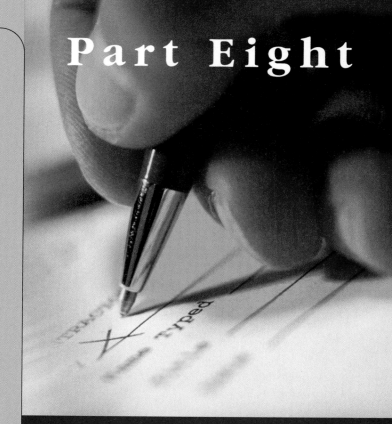

Part Eight

THE DECISIONS RELATED TO FINANCING A BUSINESS range from paying a supplier to financing an expansion of operations and dealing with financial difficulties. Virtually all financial aspects of starting, operating, and terminating a business have legal implications. As with other sectors of a business, an understanding of the legal aspects of finance can be used to structure activities in a way that minimizes unfavourable legal consequences.

Part Eight presents the various aspects of financing a business not simply as a list of legal topics, but rather as a businessperson might encounter them. The major chapter topics are dealing with banks, obtaining credit, and coping with business failure.

Financing the Business

Chapter 25 Business and Banking

Chapter 26 The Legal Aspects of Credit

Chapter 27 Bankruptcy and Insolvency

Chapter

25

Objectives

After studying this chapter, you should have an understanding of

- the relationship between a business and its bank
- the legal framework of negotiable instruments
- the rights and obligations of those connected with negotiable instruments
- the legal challenges involved in electronic banking

Business and Banking

Business Law in Practice

Bill Ikeda and Martha Wong are a married couple who operate a building supply outlet in Timmins, Ontario. They also sell hardware, plumbing, and electrical supplies. Their customers are retail and commercial. They operate the business through a corporation, Hometown Hardware Ltd. (Hometown). Bill is the CEO and majority owner. He conducts most of the business apart from the operation of the store. Martha is the vice president and owns the remaining shares. She manages the store. The business has dealt with the local branch of the same bank for many years—the Full Service Bank (FSB). Both Bill and Martha have signing authority.

Bill and Martha have recently begun to reconsider their relationship with FSB. The branch has a new manager. There have been other personnel changes, so that Hometown's accounts and loans are now handled by unfamiliar employees who seem uninterested in Hometown's business and have recently been unhelpful. Bill is also not sure that he has the appropriate types of accounts. He is concerned about high service fees on his accounts and rising interest rates on his loans. He wonders whether he should consider moving his business to another bank. Martha has been advised by business acquaintances that much of Hometown's banking can be done more easily and cheaper online.

Bill is also concerned about the growing number of cheques being returned to him by the bank because customers have insufficient funds in their accounts to cover them. He currently accepts payment by cash, cheque, debit card, and credit cards. Hometown also extends credit to some commercial customers. Bill is interested in the cost and risk of these various payment options.

1. What do Bill and Martha need to know about the legal aspects of the relationship between their business and a bank?
2. What are the risks and benefits of using cheques to pay bills and allowing customers to pay by cheque?
3. What are the added risks and benefits to doing banking electronically?

When operating a building supply store, what financial decisions with legal consequences must the owners make?

The Banking Relationship

In its simplest form, the relationship between a business and its bank consists of one bank account into which the business deposits its cash receipts from customers and from which it makes payments to suppliers, employees, government, and owners. As a result of regulatory changes and decisions by banks to broaden their range of services, the relationship now can be much more comprehensive. Banks have become financial marketplaces, offering services in cash management, investment advice and brokerage, and business financing. Therefore, it is a challenge for someone in Bill's position to decide what banking services he needs, which services he can afford, and who will do the best job of providing them.

Regulation of Banks

Traditionally, the Canadian financial services industry had four distinct sectors: banks, trust companies, stockbrokers, and insurance companies. To ensure stability within each sector and to avoid conflicts of interest resulting from institutions providing services from several sectors, each was separately regulated, and institutions in one sector were prohibited from conducting business beyond that sector.

The internationalization of the financial services industry in the 1980s placed pressure on governments to deregulate and relax the strict separation of the four sectors. In 1987, Canadian legislation was reviewed and revised to allow banks to go beyond traditional banking and participate in other sectors in their branches or through subsidiary firms. The most recent legislation[1] further blurs the distinctions between different types of financial institutions by allowing greater structural flexibility. Among many other changes, it also provides for liberalized ownership rules for banks. The financial sector legislation must be reviewed every five years, although the next review is now scheduled for 2007.

Banks are under federal jurisdiction and are regulated through the federal *Bank Act*.[2] The main purposes of the act are to ensure the stability and liquidity of banks and to identify and regulate the types of business they are permitted to conduct. The relationship between a bank and its individual customers is not a primary concern of the act. The terms and conditions of that relationship are, instead, found primarily in the agreements made between the bank and its customers, which are influenced by banking practice and common law rules. Contract law is the prime source of guidance in interpreting and enforcing the rights and obligations of the parties in this relationship.

Banks are increasingly offering international banking services, such as letters of credit, cross-border transfers, and accounts in different currencies. These services are governed largely by voluntary rules created by international bodies, such as the Bank for International Settlements and the International Chamber of Commerce. Parties involved in international transactions frequently incorporate these rules into their agreements.

The Bank–Customer Agreement

banking agreement
A contract that specifies the rights and obligations of a bank and a customer.

The purpose of the **banking agreement** is twofold:

- to specify who has the authority to issue instructions to the bank on behalf of the customer
- to allocate the risk of loss resulting from problems with verifying the customer's authority and carrying out the customer's instructions

---

1. *Financial Consumer Agency of Canada Act*, S.C. 2001, c. 9.
2. S.C. 1991, c. 46, as am. by S.C. 1998, c. 30.

The customer designates those with authority to issue instructions to the bank through such means as signing cheques. At this time in Hometown, Bill and Martha are the only persons with that authority.

The second focus of the banking agreement—namely, the allocation of loss—is of greater significance. Bill must be cautious in his dealings because the bank–customer agreement is drafted by the bank to limit its duties and liabilities. For example, a verification clause commonly found in banking agreements gives the customer 30 days to detect and report any unauthorized payments that the bank makes from the customer's account. Beyond that period, the customer absorbs the loss. Normally, the bank also has flexibility in dealing with all of the customer's accounts. For example, the bank can transfer funds from an account with a positive balance to one that is overdrawn.

The key document involved in opening a bank account is the operation of account agreement, which includes provisions dealing with issues such as

- the bank's ability to apply charges to the customer's accounts (commonly known as service charges)
- arrangements concerning the issue of cheques and instructions for payment by the customer
- confirmations and stop payments on cheques
- release of information by the bank about the customer

Duties of the Bank and the Customer

The common law and banking practice imply additional duties on both parties to the banking contract. For example, the bank must

money laundering
The false reporting of income from criminal activity as income from legitimate business.

- honour cheques and repay deposits
- collect cheques for the customer
- provide account information to the customer on a regular basis
- maintain secrecy of the customer's affairs[3]

Business Application of the Law

Client Information and Money Laundering

The bank's duty to maintain secrecy of customer information is subject to the law concerning money laundering—that is, the false reporting of income obtained through criminal activity as income gained through legitimate business enterprises. Since 1991, banks have been urged to verify the identity of individual and corporate customers and the validity of their business activities, and to determine the source of transfers exceeding $10 000.[4]

New legislation was passed in 2000[5] to enable Canada to meet its international obligations in combating **money laundering.** The legislation created a mandatory reporting system in which banks, trust companies, insurance companies, and professionals must report to a new independent body—the Financial Transactions and Reports Analysis Centre (FINTRAC)—suspicious financial transactions and large cross-border currency transfers. Suspicious

---

3. Alison R. Manzer and Jordan S. Bernamoff, *The Corporate Counsel Guide to Banking and Credit Relationships* (Aurora, ON: Canada Law Book, 1999) at 14.
4. *Proceeds of Crime (Money Laundering) Act*, S.C. 1991, c. 26.
5. *Proceeds of Crime (Money Laundering) and Terrorist Financing Act*, S.C. 2000, c. 17.

transactions are not defined in the act, but FIN-TRAC provides guidelines under headings such as "economic purpose" of the transaction. For example, if a transaction seems to be inconsistent with the client's apparent financial standing or usual pattern of activities, does not appear to be driven by normal commercial considerations, or is unnecessarily complex for its stated purpose, it should be considered suspicious.

FINTRAC is responsible for managing the information reported by the various organizations affected by the act and deciding which transactions to refer to law enforcement agencies for investigation.

Subsequent regulatory changes have tightened the reporting requirements, but the effectiveness of the entire regime has been questioned. Lawyers are exempt from reporting due to lawyer–client confidentiality. Enforcement has been low key and it is suspected that money launderers are engaging in "smurfing"—organizing their transactions at amounts below the reportable threshold.

CRITICAL ANALYSIS: To what extent should the confidentiality of individual client accounts be compromised to combat money laundering by a minority of clients? How is the effectiveness of this regime measured? Is the regulatory burden justified?

Source: Eric Reguly, "Money Laundering Watchdog Should Have More of a Bite" *The Globe and Mail* (12 July 2005) at B2.

Customers also have implied duties to the bank. They must

- take reasonable steps to provide documentation as to who is authorized to give instructions to the bank, in order to prevent fraud and forgery
- keep authorizations current
- notify the bank of any suspected problems
- provide safeguards for electronic communications (including telephone, fax, and computer)[6]

As long as Bill and Martha are the only ones with signing authority at the bank, authorization should not be a problem. When they reach the point at which they need to share that responsibility, they must make the terms of the arrangement clear to the persons receiving the authority and to the bank. Bill must also familiarize himself with the practices of his bank related to authorization by phone, fax, or computer if he chooses to use them.

The Bank–Customer Relationship

Standard banking documents are designed to protect the bank, not the customer. Large customers may have some bargaining power, but small businesses such as Hometown have very little. Understanding the terms and conditions in the agreement will enable Bill to identify risks arising from the banking aspects of his business. He can then establish practices to avoid incidents resulting in loss for which the banking agreement would make him responsible.

The legal nature of the relationship is clear. In terms of the customer's money on deposit with the bank, the relationship is that of the bank as debtor and the customer as creditor. Normally, the bank is not obligated to give advice or to look out for the best interest of the customer, unless, for example, the bank provides services

---

6. *Supra* note 3 at 15.

such as financial advice, which are outside the normal scope of traditional banking services. In that situation a fiduciary relationship may exist, and the bank has several additional onerous duties, including

- to provide advice with care and skill
- to disclose any actual or potential conflicts of interest
- to consider the interests of the customer ahead of those of the bank[7]

For example, if Bill has sought and received advice from his banker as to the amount and structure of the financing he needs for Hometown, he can expect to receive competent advice from the bank and should be encouraged to seek an independent opinion before agreeing to a financing arrangement operating heavily in the bank's favour.

The practical advice for customers is to appreciate the basic nature of the relationship and to understand that banks generally have no obligation to look beyond their own self-interest. However, banks are under considerable pressure to deal fairly with customers and to refrain from strict enforcement of agreements that are onerous for their customers. For example, the risk of diminished customer service was a key factor in the 1998 ruling by the Competition Bureau against proposed mergers by the major banks.[8] Since then, the financial services legislation[9] established the Financial Consumer Agency of Canada (FCAC)[10] to protect and educate consumers through the monitoring of institutions' business practices regarding such matters as account fees and credit card rates. In addition, the financial services industry in cooperation with the federal government has created the Centre for the Financial Services OmbudsNetwork (CFSON)[11] to provide a one-stop complaint procedure covering brokers, banks, insurance companies, and sellers of mutual funds in order to ensure fair and impartial complaint resolution for consumers.

Negotiable Instruments

cheque
A written order to a bank to pay money to a specified person.

promissory note
A written promise to another person to pay a specified amount.

bill of exchange
A written order to a person to pay a specified amount to another person.

negotiable instrument
A written contract containing an unconditional promise or order to pay a specific sum on demand or on a specified date to a specific person or bearer.

When Bill pays an account with one of his suppliers, he has several options. He can use cash, with the inconvenience and risk of having adequate cash on hand to pay bills. Other options are to pay by **cheque** (a written order to his bank) or by electronic funds transfer (a paperless transaction). The rules for cheques are well defined and are part of the law of negotiable instruments. Electronic transfers are a more recent development and create special legal challenges, which are considered later in the chapter.

A cheque is the most common example of a negotiable instrument, but the rules also apply to other documents, such as promissory notes and bills of exchange. A **promissory note** is a written promise by one person to pay a specified amount on a certain date or on demand to another person. A **bill of exchange** is an order to someone else to pay funds to another person. A cheque is a special type of bill of exchange, which is payable on demand and where the party instructed to pay is a bank. These instruments are federally regulated by the *Bills of Exchange Act*.[12] The rules in this legislation focus on the attributes and transferability of pieces of paper called **negotiable instruments.** The development of electronic transfers without paper undermines the utility of the existing rules for resolving disputes in that context.

---

7. *Supra* note 3 at 36.
8. See various documents, including bank merger guidelines and letters from the bureau to the banks, at the Competition Bureau website http://www.competition.ic.gc.ca
9. *Supra* note 1.
10. See www.fcac-acfc.gc.ca
11. "Government Supports Financial Sector Ombudservice," Department of Finance, http://www.fin.gc.ca; http://www.cba.ca
12. R.S.C. 1985, c. B-4.

There are several technical requirements for an instrument (a document) to become negotiable or transferable without the need to investigate its validity through reference to the circumstances of its creation or other documents. The essence of the requirements is that the instrument must be a self-contained obligation. It must be in written form and signed by the person making the promise or authorizing the payment. It must specify an amount of money to be paid on a specified date or on demand, and the obligation must be unconditional. For example, if a promise is made to pay "the balance due" on a construction contract, the promise cannot be a negotiable instrument because the balance can be determined only by consulting the original contract and investigating the work done and payments already made. A negotiable instrument must be for a specific sum without conditions. When Bill issues a cheque (on behalf of Hometown) to a supplier of goods or services, he gives a written order to his bank to pay a specified sum to the supplier. The cheque is a negotiable instrument.

As indicated in Figure 25.1, Bill is the creator of the instrument. The supplier is the payee (the business entitled to payment). Bill is formally known as the drawer because he is ordering his bank to pay the supplier. The bank, as the recipient of Bill's instructions, is known as the drawee.

Bill's instructions to his bank in the form of a cheque and the bank's actions to carry out his instructions by paying money from the Hometown account to the designated supplier are at the centre of the bank–customer relationship. The written agreement will address these transactions in some detail, but a number of duties are imposed on the two parties through the common law. For example, the customer must keep adequate funds in his accounts to pay any cheques that are issued, and must provide clear and unambiguous instructions to the bank concerning payment. The bank must take reasonable care in honouring instructions to pay out the money, provided there are sufficient funds in the customer's account.[13]

Bill's supplier will likely take the cheque to its bank for deposit. Through the centralized clearing process, the cheque will find its way from the supplier's bank to Hometown's bank, and the specified sum will be taken from Hometown's account.

FIGURE 25.1

An Annotated Cheque

---

13. *Supra* note 3 at 30.

Hometown (Creator and Drawer) issues cheque to Supplier (Payee).
Supplier deposits cheque in its bank.

Supplier's bank places funds in Supplier's account.

Through the cheque-clearing process, the cheque moves from the
Supplier's bank to Hometown's bank (Drawee).

Hometown's bank removes funds from his account and transfers to
the Supplier's bank.

Supplier's bank recovers its funds.

As long as there are adequate funds in Hometown's account and there is no defect in the cheque, it will proceed smoothly through the steps. If Bill accepts cheques as payment from his customers, the customer is the drawer and Hometown is the payee, in relation to the steps in Figure 25.2. The following sections describe the potential problems and risks for the participants if difficulties arise in the circulation or cashing of the cheque.

Implications of Creating a Cheque

When Bill chooses to pay a supplier by cheque, he is discharging a debt that Hometown owes as debtor to the supplier as creditor. That debt has arisen through the contract between Hometown and the supplier for the provision of goods or services. Assuming that Bill buys his building supplies from a number of distributors, he will have regular payment obligations arising from his contractual arrangements with those distributors. If he encounters problems with the supplies, he will have a valid complaint against the supplier (subject to their contract). He can pursue that complaint as he would any breach of contract.

However, his claim on the contract is a totally different matter from his obligation to pay the cheque. By issuing the cheque, he has made an unconditional promise to pay the specified sum not just to the supplier, but potentially to anyone (known as a **holder**) who presents the cheque to Hometown's bank for payment. The special status of the cheque and the holder are confirmed by legislation[14] that deliberately places the holder in a strong position in terms of collecting on the cheque. If the holder has acted in good faith (meaning she has no reason to doubt the validity of the cheque), that person acquires the status of a **holder in due course.** There are limited arguments (for example, a forged signature or an alteration of the cheque) that Bill can use to justify refusing payment to a holder in due course. The rights of such a holder are not affected by any terms of Bill's contract with the supplier. Bill must allow his bank to pay out the cheque, and he must then seek compensation separately from the supplier.

holder
A person who has possession of a negotiable instrument.

holder in due course
A holder in good faith without notice of defects who acquires greater rights than the parties who dealt directly with each other as the drawer and drawee.

---

14. *Bills of Exchange Act, supra* note 12, s. 55.

A cheque involves a radically different situation from an ordinary assignment of contractual rights, where there can be any number of defences against paying. For example, if Hometown owes money to a distributor, that distributor can assign the right to collect to someone else (known as an assignee). In the absence of a negotiable instrument, the assignee's right to collect from Hometown is subject to any problems with the contract between Hometown and the distributor. Thus, if Bill has a valid reason for refusing to pay the distributor's claim, he can use the same reason to avoid paying the assignee. In law, this idea is captured in the expression "an assignee can have no better rights than the assignor."[15]

This important distinction between an assignment and a negotiable instrument is illustrated by the former practice in some consumer sales (in which the buyer is the final user of the goods for a noncommercial purpose) where the separation of obligations arising from the negotiable instrument and the contract of sale was abused. If a consumer bought something on credit and signed a negotiable instrument such as a promissory note in favour of the seller, that seller could sell the note to another party (such as a finance company). The legal result of the transfer of the note was that the financier became a holder in due course. The buyer's obligation to pay the financier was then nearly absolute and independent of problems with the quality and performance of the purchased goods. Such problems could be pursued against the seller based on the contract of sale, but they did not affect the consumer's continuing obligation to make payments to the holder of the note. These rules enabled collusion between unscrupulous sellers and financiers to sell substandard goods to consumers and require them to make all payments, even when the goods were defective or worthless.

The law was amended[16] to classify these promissory notes arising from consumer credit sales as **consumer notes.** The holder of a consumer note is not accorded the special status of a holder in due course and is subject to claims arising from the original contract of sale. The consumer's obligation to pay the note is subject to remedies against the seller if the goods are defective.

A cheque normally follows a relatively short route, as shown in Figure 25.2, but it may also be transferred many times. Eventually, it is presented by a holder to the maker's bank for payment. The transfer process is known as **negotiation**—hence the name of the instrument. However, negotiation in this context has a distinct meaning from its more common use as a process for resolving disputes. All that is needed for the negotiation of an instrument is for the current holder to **endorse,** or sign, the instrument over to a new holder, who then becomes entitled to either present the instrument for payment or transfer it to yet another holder.

consumer note

A negotiable instrument signed by a consumer to buy on credit.

negotiation

The process of transferring negotiable instruments from one person to another.

endorsement

The process of signing a negotiable instrument to enable negotiation.

FIGURE 25.3

Comparison of Payment and Collection Arrangements

Type of arrangement	Parties involved	Enforcement rights
Contract	Buyer (debtor) Seller (creditor)	Seller can collect subject to performance of its obligations.
Assignment of contractual right	Debtor Creditor (assignor) Assignee	Assignee's right to collect is subject to the debtor's obligation to pay the assignor.
Negotiable instrument (i.e., a cheque)	Drawer (debtor) Payee (creditor) Holder	Holder in due course's right to collect is not tied to the original contract.
Consumer note	Consumer Seller Financier	Financier does not have the status of a holder in due course—consumer's obligation depends on the original contract.

15. See Chapter 9 for a more complete discussion of assignments.
16. *Supra* note 12, s. 191.

The essential point for the creator of a cheque is that the cheque is a self-contained obligation, the validity of which does not depend on any circumstances outside the cheque. The creator has issued instructions to the bank to pay the designated payee or a holder in due course. As long as the cheque contains the necessary endorsements (signatures) to confirm the holder's right to possession of the cheque, the bank will pay it. Despite the strong position of a holder in due course, there are certain risks, described below.

Implications of Accepting a Cheque

The major risk involved in accepting a cheque relates to the financial health of the maker, rather than any legal rules. The strong and secure legal position of a holder in due course is of no value if the drawer's account does not contain enough money to cover the cheque when it is presented for payment. The likelihood of that happening is the key consideration in Bill's decision whether to accept any payments by cheque from customers. Deciding to accept cheques is equivalent to extending credit, since there are several days between handing over goods and receiving payment from a cheque.

In major transactions, the method of payment that overcomes the above risk is the certified cheque. **Certification** is a process in which the drawer (or sometimes the payee) takes the cheque to the drawer's bank and has the bank certify it for payment. The bank immediately removes the money from the customer's account and holds it in reserve until the cheque is presented for payment. This process removes the risk of there being insufficient funds in the drawer's account when the cheque is cashed.

Certification usually prevents the drawer from putting a **stop payment** on the cheque. A stop payment means that the drawer (as the bank's customer) countermands (or cancels) its instructions to pay the cheque and orders the bank to refuse payment when the cheque is presented. These instructions can be issued at any time before a cheque has been charged against the drawer's account. However, the bank will likely require the customer's agreement that the bank will not be responsible if the cheque is cashed accidentally, despite the stop payment order. The drawer of a cheque may also postdate it, which makes it payable on the future specified date and not on the date of creation. Since the bank must follow the drawer's instructions, it cannot cash the cheque until that future date.

Despite the secure position of holders in due course, those who are called upon to accept the transfer of a cheque may be reluctant to do so without verification of the various endorsements on the cheque and some means of recovering funds advanced on a cheque that turns out to be invalid. Thus, banks are reluctant to cash cheques for anyone who is not a customer of that bank and who does not hold a significant balance on account. If the cheque comes back to the bank owing to a lack of funds in the drawer's account, the amount can be deducted from the customer's account (likely in accordance with the bank–customer agreement). The bank, therefore, will not suffer the ultimate loss on the cheque. If the bank cashes a cheque for someone who is not a customer, it will be more difficult to recover the funds if the cheque turns out to be worthless. If Bill accepts cheques from customers in his store, he runs the risk that his bank will deduct the value of worthless cheques from his account.

Although a bank or anyone else who gives money in return for a cheque runs the risk that the drawer is not able or obligated to honour it, anyone who has endorsed the cheque is potentially liable for the amount. This liability is a significant risk for anyone who endorses a negotiable instrument.

certification
The process whereby a bank guarantees payment of a cheque.

stop payment
The process whereby the person who writes a cheque orders the bank not to pay the holder who presents it for payment.

A bank's responsibility to carry out the instructions of its customers includes verifying a customer's signature on a cheque. The bank and its customers both have obligations when forgery is involved. The bank has a duty to detect unauthorized instructions (such as a forged signature), and customers must take reasonable steps to prevent forgeries and immediately report any potential problems to the bank. If a bank is left with liability for a forged cheque, it can look to prior endorsers of the cheque to recover its money. Therefore, anyone accepting a cheque should verify the authenticity of the endorsements on it.

Those in possession of cheques should take steps to safeguard them and transfer them by endorsing in a way that minimizes the risk that others may illegally obtain and cash them. Simply signing a cheque on the back is known as an **endorsement in blank.** This means that the signatures are complete and that anyone who acquires the cheque can cash it (subject to a bank's willingness to do so). Holders should therefore take care with the form of endorsements. Businesses commonly endorse cheques "for deposit only." These are known as **restrictive endorsements** and mean that the cheques can be deposited only in the account of that business. Restrictive endorsements stop the circulation of cheques and remove the risk of anyone else acquiring and cashing them. If Bill accepts cheques from customers, he should routinely endorse them in this manner as soon as possible. If a cheque received by a payee is to be transferred to someone other than a bank, it is wise to endorse it directly to that person (for example, "Pay to Desmond Chu/signed Bill Ikeda"). This is known as a **special endorsement;** it ensures that only the designated person is able to deal with the cheque further.

endorsement in blank
Signing a cheque without any special instructions.

restrictive endorsement
Signing a cheque for deposit only to a particular bank account.

special endorsement
Signing a cheque and making it payable to a specific person.

CASE ▼

Canadian Pacific Hotels Ltd. v. Bank of Montreal (1987), 40 D.L.R. (4th) 385 (S.C.C.)

THE BUSINESS CONTEXT: There are situations where the bank fails to detect forged signatures and the customer does not immediately notice that the forged cheques have been cashed from its account. In these cases, the courts will look to the bank–customer agreement. If there is none, the common law rules apply.

FACTUAL BACKGROUND: Sands was the accountant for a business unit of Canadian Pacific (CP). He forged the signatures on a number of cheques payable from the CP account to companies he controlled. CP eventually discovered the forgeries. There was no verification agreement between CP and the bank, which would have made CP responsible for unauthorized cheques if not detected and reported by CP within a specified period. CP sued to recover its money from the bank.

THE LEGAL QUESTION: Was the customer, CP, responsible for detecting the forgeries?

RESOLUTION: The Supreme Court of Canada found that CP was not responsible. Justice LeDain ruled that

> ... a customer of a bank does not, in the absence of a verification agreement, owe a duty to the bank to examine his bank statements and vouchers with reasonable care and to report any discrepancies within a reasonable time, nor does a customer, "sophisticated" or otherwise, owe a duty to its bank to maintain an adequate system of internal accounting controls for the prevention and minimization of loss through forgery.

Justice LaForest suggested a broader basis for the decision as

> ... the necessity for clear rules of general application. In the case of forged cheques the rule was clear. The banker was supposed to know his customer's signature and the liability was his if he honoured a cheque on which his customer's signature had been forged.

Those accepting cheques should realize that there are financial and legal reasons collection may be a problem. Apart from a certified cheque, there is no guaranteed payment. Bill must understand that if a customer's cheque is returned to him by Hometown's bank because of insufficient funds in the customer's account, he will recover the funds only if he can collect from the customer. If the customer cannot be located or is unable to pay the amount, Bill will ultimately bear the loss. However, if he can locate the customer, the cheque is valuable evidence of the customer's contractual obligation.

A negotiable instrument has a life of its own, quite separate from the contract that produced it. Liability for payment is independent of the original debtor–creditor relationship. The purpose of the rules is to produce convenience and dependability with the negotiable instruments in the commercial environment. The tradeoff is that a relatively small but still significant number of the instruments must be honoured by makers in situations where there is a good reason for liability to be borne by another party such as someone who breached the originating contract through failure to deliver goods or services.

Commercial and consumer transactions are increasingly being conducted online. The volume of cheques is declining. Even traditional paper cheques are sometimes converted to digital images for processing. In practical and legal terms, the focus is shifting to electronic banking.

Electronic Banking

electronic banking
Financial transactions through the use of computers, telephones, or other electronic means.

Electronic banking includes a growing range and variety of transactions that previously required formal documentation. A wide variety of technological developments are changing the ways that business deals with banks, customers, and other businesses. Banks are encouraging customers to conduct their banking business through ATMs or online, rather than through traditional in-person transactions in bank branches. These methods can be more convenient for customers and significantly less expensive for the banks. Some new banks have no physical branches at all and conduct all their business as virtual banks in cyberspace.

There are several legal issues arising from electronic transactions. Existing laws relating to negotiable instruments apply only to documented or paper transactions. Electronic storage means that data are subject to system crashes or hackers. Fraud has become a significant concern. In particular, identity theft has become a serious issue. The Internet has increased the possibility of obtaining others' personal information to use for fraudulent credit cards or loans to the extent that one's entire financial situation is compromised. A common method for initiating identity theft is through "phishing," in which con artists send e-mail messages that appear to be from reputable companies such as banks, directing recipients to websites that appear genuine, where victims are urged to disclose personal information in order to verify

---

17. *Supra* note 3 at 15.

their accounts and ensure their continued access. The information is then used to steal funds from the accounts. This fraudulent activity has recently migrated to the telephone in the form of "voice phishing."[18]

The basis of the well-established and comprehensive set of rules governing negotiable instruments is the instrument itself—the piece of paper. The information it contains and where it goes are the key features of any dispute. Electronic transfers present several challenges in relation to this set of rules. First, since there is no key piece of paper that circulates through the system, there is no paper trail in the event of a dispute. Second, electronic transfers are instantaneous, so there is no opportunity to change the instructions for payment (for example, by issuing a stop payment). There is no need for the certification process because the transfer is unlikely to be effective unless the account from which the transfer is made has sufficient funds. Electronic deposits may result in problems if no one verifies the validity of the instruments being deposited. For example, if there is a serious defect in a cheque deposited electronically, the amount will initially be added to the customer's balance, but it will be deducted later when the defect is discovered. By this time, the customer may have already used the money.

There is a tradeoff between increased efficiency and the absence of rules. Electronic transfers are cheap and efficient. The absence of paper is a distinct advantage. There is no need to track or store the documents. Instructions can be issued by the customer to the bank instantly, and the funds are transferred to the recipient immediately. However, safeguarding the authority for such transfers becomes a major challenge for customers. Rather than verifying signatures on cheques, banks are looking for the necessary authorization codes in electronic messages. If the codes are there, the bank will have no reason to question the authority. The methods and potential for forgery and fraud are changed and expanded.

What rules govern ATM transactions?

18. Craig Wong, "Fraudsters Take New Tack" *The Chronicle Herald* (8 September 2006) at C3.

Another potential problem for customers is the occasional transmission failure or system crash. As business comes to rely increasingly on instant payments, possibly at the last minute, the potential loss from a failed or delayed transfer is significant. Banks may be tempted to limit their liability in such cases through their agreements with customers, but may be more interested in reassuring customers by assuming responsibility themselves.

Most of the legal uncertainty surrounding electronic banking is the result of the irrelevance of existing legislation to a paperless environment. The process and timing of electronic transactions do not fit with existing rules related to risk allocation for authentication, verification, and finalization of payments.[19]

The gap in the rules governing electronic banking is being filled in two ways. First, banking contracts now include provisions for the risks of electronic transactions that specify the customer's duties to report problems to the bank and the bank's responsibility for electronic failures. In addition, customers may be required by agreement to choose personal identification numbers (PINs) that are not obvious (such as birthdays) and to safeguard those PINs from unauthorized use. If they fail to meet these requirements, customers may be liable for any losses that result. Banks are also placing daily and weekly monetary limits on transactions in order to control the losses in the event of fraud. Second, there is also greater reliance on international rules, such as the UNCITRAL *Model Law for International Credit Transfers*,[20] since electronic transfers are completed as easily across the world as within the local community. If the sending and receiving banks are in different countries, these international rules deal with the obligations of the parties, timing for payment, consequences for technical problems, and liability and damages.

Technology and the Law — Electronic Payments Systems

Customers are offered a range of electronic options by the traditional banks. Some examples are automatic payments from chequing accounts, direct deposit of cheques, automatic teller machines (ATMs), payment by telephone or computer, and point-of-sale transfers with debit cards. Credit card transactions are now processed electronically as well. They involve two contracts—one between the card issuer and the user, and the second between the credit card company and the merchant.

Automatic teller machines are available for deposits, withdrawals, transfers between accounts, and bill payments. Telephone banking and online banking can be used for everything other than cash transactions, including applications for mortgages and loans.

There are many models for cashless transactions. Debit cards allow buyers to purchase goods and services and to transfer payment directly from a bank account to the seller. Money cards carry a computer chip that enables virtual money to be loaded on the card and transferred directly from the card to the seller. Electronic money or digital cash takes no physical form, but instead is loaded onto computer hard drives or electronic wallets, enabling payment to be made as easily as sending e-mail. "Smart cards" can now combine all of the above features. They enable payments for small transactions that may be impractical for credit cards by simply waving a card at a reader. They contain large memory for managing information concerning the holder's personal and financial affairs. Encryption features can generate a

19. *Supra* note 3 at 41.
20. "UNCITRAL Model Law on International Credit Transfers" (1993), 32 I.L.M. 587.

different identification number every time the card is used, greatly increasing security in relation to magnetic strips.

In addition, cellphones can now be used for wireless payments.

Payments can also be made through secure online commercial intermediaries such as PayPal.

CRITICAL ANALYSIS: There is already a wide variety of electronic payment mechanisms with new ones under continual development. Are there significant risks (legal and otherwise) with these methods? Are the risks outweighed by the low cost, convenience, and customer demand? Can the developers of such methods stay far enough ahead of those who seek to breach security?

Sources: Simon Avery, "Smart Cards to Make Credit, Debit Dealings Easier—and Safer" *The Globe and Mail* (11 October 2005) at B9; and Michael Ryval, "PayPal Clicks with Entrepreneurs" *The Globe and Mail* (11 April 2006) at B8.

Although fraud and data security breaches are matters of concern, there is little evidence yet of significant legal problems arising from electronic transfers. Business customers of banks are interested in security, convenience, and low costs in terms of banking services. As long as banks can demonstrate to customers that their needs are being met without significant risks, the volume of electronic banking is likely to grow. In legal terms, electronic banking is an expansion of the tradeoff that makes negotiable instruments work. The convenience and volume of electronic transactions outweigh the occasional injustice resulting from a defective transaction. Tracing the cause of an electronic loss may be difficult. Someone must bear that loss, but in terms of the public good, the reliability and convenience of the transfer system may be more important than identifying the one responsible.

Bill needs to ask the relevant questions of his bank related to the risks and to what happens if, for example, an electronic transfer simply does not happen or the bank transfers funds without proper authorization. He needs to ensure that the bank has anticipated potential problems and has a reasonable way of dealing with them. In risk management terms, he needs to evaluate the risk against the potential benefits of electronic banking.

Do the same rules apply to various payment choices?

Methods of Payment

The factors in Bill's decision as to the methods of payment he will accept from his customers relate to marketing and finance, as well as to legal risks. He must be responsive to the needs and demands of his customers and sensitive to the cost of various payment options. This is especially true in light of his concern about "bad" cheques.

Regarding debit cards and credit cards, Bill needs to understand the implications of the agreements he has with those service providers. By accepting the cards, Bill will pay a portion of the proceeds of those sales to the card providers. In return, he gets immediate payment for debit card sales and a guarantee of payment on credit card sales, as long as he complies with the requirements in his agreements, such as verification of signatures.

The possibility of extending credit to customers is the subject of Chapter 26.

FIGURE 25.4

Comparative Risks of Methods of Accepting Payment

Form of payment	Nature of payment	Risk for person accepting payment
Cash	Immediate	The money may be counterfeit or the proceeds of a crime.
Cheque	Deposited	There may be insufficient funds in the account on which the cheque was drawn; the cheque may be forged.
Credit card	Guaranteed	Risk is borne largely by the card provider.
Debit card	Immediate transfer	Risk is borne largely by the payments system.
Credit	Payment at a later date	The debtor may be unable or unwilling to pay.

Business Law in Practice Revisited

1. What do Bill and Martha need to know about the legal aspects of the relationship between their business and a bank?

They need to appreciate that their basic relationship with the bank is one in which the bank must safeguard their money and follow their payment instructions but is otherwise not responsible for their interests, unless the bank is engaged to provide expert advice. Bill and Martha need to appreciate the importance of the contract with the bank and become familiar with its basic rights and obligations. Bill and Martha should understand that the contract is written largely to protect the bank and that their bargaining power is limited. They should, however, seek a level of service and comfort that meets their needs and allays their concerns with their current bank.

2. What are the risks and benefits of using cheques to pay bills and allowing customers to pay by cheque?

The risk of paying by cheque is that Bill cannot avoid his obligation to honour the cheque (apart from stopping payment) if he has a problem with the goods or services for which he paid using the cheque. The risk of allowing customers to pay by cheque is that they may have insufficient funds in their accounts, they may be engaged in fraud or forgery, they might issue a stop payment, or there may be a technical defect in the cheque.

The legal benefits of paying by cheque are the relative security compared with cash, the paper trail provided by the cheque, and the ability to issue a stop payment before the cheque is cashed. Accepting payments by cheque is more risky than taking only cash, but it is safer than credit. As the holder of a cheque, Bill has an instrument in his possession that provides proof of his right to collect.

3. What are the added risks and benefits to doing banking electronically?

If Bill engages in electronic banking, it will likely be cheaper and faster, but he risks having transmission problems, he cannot easily cancel e-transactions because they are instantaneous, and he is left with no paper trail to follow the transaction. Bill needs to thoroughly discuss these risks with his bank so that he feels comfortable with his banking arrangements. He should not simply sign whatever documents the bank requests and hope for the best. Since Bill accepts payments by credit card and debit card, he needs to negotiate with the providers of those services and be prepared to pay their fees. Such arrangements are not part of his package of banking services.

Chapter Summary

Customers should be wary of their relationship with their banks, not because banks attempt to take advantage of them, but because the relationship is a contractual one. The rights and obligations are found in the contract, and because the banks write the contracts, the language tends to favour the banks' interests more than those of the customers. The chief effect of a banking contract is to transfer risk from the bank to the customer. If the customer appreciates this reality, the level of disappointment, frustration, and financial loss is likely to be less than if her expectations of the bank are unrealistic.

The established system for negotiable instruments focuses on the commercial convenience of instruments circulating freely, with little need for the various holders to be concerned about their validity so long as the requirements for negotiability are met. It is a paper-based system that places prime importance on the piece of paper and the secure status of those in possession of it.

The primary right is the ability of a holder in due course to collect from the creator of the instrument—the person whose promise to pay originated the transaction. The main obligation is that of the creator or drawer of the instrument to pay regardless of events that preceded or followed the creation of the instrument.

The instantaneous nature of electronic transactions greatly improves efficiency, but it also makes the transfers irrevocable. The absence of paper and the inapplicability of the rules that govern paper transactions create major challenges for security and liability.

Chapter Study

Key Terms and Concepts

banking agreement (p. 620)

bill of exchange (p. 623)

certification (p. 627)

cheque (p. 623)

consumer note (p. 626)

electronic banking (p. 629)

endorsement (p. 626)

endorsement in blank (p. 628)

holder (p. 625)

holder in due course (p. 625)

money laundering (p. 621)

negotiable instrument (p. 623)

negotiation (p. 626)

promissory note (p. 623)

restrictive endorsement (p. 628)

special endorsement (p. 628)

stop payment (p. 627)

Questions for Review

1. What is the basic nature of the bank–customer relationship?

2. How are banks regulated?

3. Why are mergers of Canadian banks so controversial?

4. What are the key issues addressed in a banking contract?

5. What are the key duties of the customer and the bank?

6. What are the requirements for an instrument to be negotiable?

7. Why is the volume of cheques declining?

8. Why are electronic transfers not subject to the same regulations as paper transactions?

9. When a business issues a cheque to a supplier, who is the drawer, the drawee, and the payee of the cheque?

10. Who bears the loss for a forged cheque if the forger has disappeared?

11. What are the key risks for a business in creating cheques for suppliers and accepting cheques from customers?

12. Why is the holder in due course in a stronger position to collect on a negotiable instrument than the assignee is to collect a debt?

13. What are the banks' obligations regarding suspected money laundering?

14. What is "smurfing"?

15. What are the benefits of electronic banking?

16. What are the legal uncertainties in electronic banking?

17. How do smart cards work?

18. What is "phishing"?

Questions for Critical Thinking

1. In normal banking relationships, customers are expected to take care of themselves and to negotiate and be aware of their rights and obligations. Is this a reasonable expectation in view of the size and level of expertise of the banks? Should banks have an obligation to look after their customers?

2. Banking contracts are in theory negotiated by customers and the banks. In practice, the terms are largely dictated by the banks and found in standard form agreements that are not open to negotiation. Should banking contracts be regulated to ensure a basic level of fairness for customers?

3. Electronic banking presents a regulatory challenge in that paper-based rules do not work and the nature of electronic transactions produces a new set of potential problems. What are some of those problems? Are the regulations likely to be outpaced by developments in technology?

4. The divisions among the four types of financial services (banks, trust companies, insurance companies, investment brokers) have been relaxed. Now, banks are able to provide all four types of services in some form. Who benefits most from this relaxation—clients or banks?

5. Considering the number of negotiable instruments and electronic transfers, there are relatively few legal disputes arising from them. Does that mean the system is working well? What criteria might be used to measure the effectiveness of the system?

6. Electronic transactions can result in the creation and combination of databases containing sensitive business and personal information. Those who provide this information are naturally concerned about its security and their privacy. One way to deal with such concerns is to enable anonymous transactions through such means as encryption, which in turn creates concern for illicit activities such as money laundering. Which is more important—providing security or preventing fraud or crime?

Situations for Discussion

1. Paul, a bookkeeper employed by Harvey's Car Lot, forged Harvey's signature on a number of cheques over the course of a year. The cheques were made payable to fictitious payees. Paul deposited the cheques in his account at Y Bank. He forged the endorsement on some and was able to deposit the rest with no endorsement. Y Bank accepted them all, as did Z Bank when they came to be deducted from the account that Harvey maintains there. Paul was able to conceal his fraudulent transactions in the course of his work. The fraud was not discovered for more than a year, when Harvey hired a new audit firm that detected the fraud in a random check. Meanwhile, Paul has left Harvey's and left town.[21] Who should bear the loss from Paul's fraud—Y Bank, Z Bank, or Harvey? What practices should Harvey put in place to prevent future fraud?

2. Ken needed $50 000 to start his video rental business. He sought advice from W Bank. Pamela is the loans officer at the bank and suggested a working capital loan on certain specified terms. She assured Ken that there should be no problem being approved if he decided to

---

21. Based on *Boma Manufacturing Ltd. v. CIBC* (1996), 203 N.R. 321 (S.C.C.).

apply for a loan. The approval process took longer than normal, but Ken went ahead and signed a lease for space for his shop and a three-year video rental contract with a distributor. Eventually, W Bank rejected Ken's application. Based on recent experience, the bank decided that video rental shops are too risky and hardly ever last beyond six months. Ken was unable to arrange alternative financing in time and suffered a large loss in his business.[22] Is this a typical banking relationship where Ken must look out for himself, or does the bank have some responsibility for his plight? What should Ken and the bank have done differently?

3. Ratty Publications wrote a cheque payable to LePage on its account at CIBC in payment for the first month's rent on an office lease. Ratty changed its mind about the lease and instructed CIBC to stop payment on the cheque. The following day, LePage got the cheque certified at another branch of CIBC and deposited the cheque in its account at TD Bank. When TD presented the cheque to CIBC for payment, CIBC refused to honour it.[23] Which prevails— the stop payment or the certification? Does the validity of the cheque depend on the lease agreement between Ratty and LePage? Which of the four parties should bear the loss?

4. Harvey's Car Lot bought a used car from Luke. When Luke delivered the car, Harvey gave him a cheque for $5000. Luke cashed the cheque immediately. When Harvey put the car in the garage, he discovered that the bottom was severely rusted and the engine was shot.[24] What can Harvey do about the cheque? How should Harvey change his purchasing practices? How would the outcome be different if instead of giving Luke a cheque, Harvey had promised to pay Luke when Harvey resold the car?

5. Ravanello is a computer hacker. He is motivated primarily by the challenge of breaking systems, but he figures he might as well make some money at the same time. After many months of dedicated effort, he penetrated the electronic customer files of EZ Bank. Not wanting to appear greedy or be caught, Ravenello devised a system to skim $10 from random accounts every month. He began to accumulate money in his account faster than he could spend it. It was nine months before a customer of EZ convinced the bank that his account was short by three $10 withdrawals and the bank was able to trace the reason. What does this scenario reveal about the perils of electronic banking? Do you think this scenario could really happen? Is such a risk likely to be prevented by banking practices, contracts, or the law? Who is responsible for the losses?

6. Rubin and Russell were partners in RRP Associates. They did their personal and business banking with Colossal Bank, where they arranged their accounts so that transfers from one to the other could be made by either partner online, by phone, or in person. Although the business prospered, Rubin and Russell had difficulty working together. Following a serious disagreement, Russell went online and transferred $50 000 from the RRP account to his personal account. When Rubin discovered this transaction, he complained to the bank and was told that the transfer was done in accordance with the agreement between RRP and the bank. How can partners best balance the risks arising from banking arrangements with the need for convenient banking? What action can Rubin take now?

7. Fraser had an agreement with ABC Bank that any overdrafts in his chequing account would be automatically covered by a cash advance charged to his credit card. On such advances, Fraser was charged interest immediately. Over a year, Fraser experienced 20 overdrafts totalling almost $4000. The bank made 20 deposits to Fraser's chequing account, but mistakenly charged the cash advances to the credit card of Bush, another customer of the bank. Fraser and Bush both did their banking online. It was a year before Bush

22. Based on *Royal Bank of Canada v. Woloszyn* (1998), 170 N.S.R. (2d) 122 (S.C.).
23. Based on *A.E. Lepage Real Estate Services Ltd. v. Rattray Publications* (1994), 21 O.R. (3d) 164 (C.A.).
24. Based on *William Ciurluini v. Royal Bank of Canada* (1972), 26 D.L.R. (3d) 552 (Ont. H.C.).

noticed the mistakes and brought them to the bank's attention. After much discussion, the bank reluctantly refunded Bush and then sought payment from Fraser.[25] Fraser claimed that too much time had passed and he had no obligation to pay the money. The bank nevertheless charged the entire amount to his credit card. Who is responsible for the bank's error?

8. Michael lives in Surrey, British Columbia. He has been employed by the municipal government as an information officer for 25 years and has recently taken early retirement. He has saved some money and needs an activity to keep him occupied. Michael has a passion for the movies and is frustrated by the limited selection of video rentals available from the large outlets in his area. He has decided to open a small video rental shop to cater to specialty tastes not served by the existing outlets. Michael has no experience in running a business. One of the many challenges he faces is the need to establish banking arrangements. He knows he needs a bank account for making deposits and writing cheques, but he is unsure of what other banking services he may need or whom to ask for advice. Michael has heard that banks provide a variety of services, including insurance, investment advice, and help for small business. He has some interest in computers and knows that banks are heavily involved in technology. He has heard of packages of electronic banking services developed especially to assist small businesses like his. Michael also needs to decide how to accept payments from customers—whether to accept cheques, credit cards, or debit cards—and how to make payments to suppliers. How would you advise Michael about his banking needs?

For more study tools, visit
http://www.businesslaw3e.nelson.com

---

25. Based on *Bank of Nova Scotia v. Fraser* (2002) NSSC 197.

Chapter

26

Objectives

After studying this chapter, you should have an understanding of

- the legal significance of credit transactions in business
- the difference between secured and unsecured creditors
- the ways that lenders and borrowers are protected
- the implications of guaranteeing a debt

The Legal Aspects of Credit

Business Law in Practice

Hometown Ltd. (HT) and its owners, Bill Ikeda and Martha Wong, were introduced in Chapter 25. They operate a building supply outlet in Timmins, Ontario. Bill has become concerned about rumours that a big box store will soon be arriving in Timmins. A major international hardware and building supply chain is planning to open a large outlet in a new shopping complex on the edge of town. Bill is worried about the impact on HT and has decided that the only way he can remain competitive is to expand his outlet to offer a broader range of supplies. He is confident that his customers will remain loyal to HT if they can obtain the same range of products from HT as will be available from the new competitor.

In order to finance the planned expansion, Bill figures that he needs $400 000. Two of his business acquaintances who are now retired are keen to invest in HT. Bill and Martha have decided to sell each of these friends shares in HT worth $100 000. Bill and Martha hope to borrow the remaining $200 000. They have recently changed banks and are encouraged by the reception they have received.

1. What are potential lenders likely to require from HT before granting the loan and during the repayment period?
2. What are the risks for the business in borrowing $200 000?
3. Is there potential personal liability for Bill, Martha, and the two new shareholders?

Overview of Credit

A business participates in an array of transactions on a daily basis that involve credit. Some credit arrangements are formal and deliberate, with carefully negotiated terms, while others are an incidental feature of routine transactions. A business like HT is involved in numerous credit transactions—some as a borrower (debtor), and others as a lender (creditor). When HT orders lumber from suppliers, the shipment is delivered with an invoice, likely requiring payment within 30 days. When HT fills orders for its commercial customers, they are expected to pay on a similar basis. Retail customers are likely expected to pay immediately.

These examples illustrate what is known as **unsecured credit.** HT's suppliers have a contractual right to payment from HT for goods delivered, and HT has a similar right to collect from its customers. In the majority of these transactions, payment is made within the designated period and collection remedies are not needed. HT will have no trouble receiving orders on credit from suppliers

What legal risks arise in financing the expansion of a business?

unsecured creditor
A creditor with no security interest in the debtor's property.

it has dealt with before. HT will not hesitate to fill customer orders in advance of actual payment if those customers have paid as expected in the past. The unsecured element of these transactions becomes obvious if a debtor fails to pay what is due. The creditor then has a contractual right to collect and may sue the debtor for payment, but the creditor has no security interest in the debtor's assets to recover payment. A judgment obtained against the debtor is satisfied from its general financial resources. If the debtor is financially healthy, the creditor is likely to receive payment. When the debtor is in financial difficulty and is unable to respond to claims from many creditors, the lack of security becomes a problem. These arrangements are more uncertain if the parties have not dealt with each other before, especially if the supplier and the customer are located in different countries. The following International Perspective box reviews an example of such dealings.

Credit arrangements outside normal business activities tend to be more formal and provide more security to the lender. Borrowing a large amount of money to purchase a major asset or to finance an expansion, as HT is planning to do, is an example of a credit transaction in which the rights and obligations of the parties are carefully negotiated. When HT approaches a bank or another potential lender to request a loan of $200 000, the lender will require extensive documentation, such as a business plan and cash-flow projections. The lender will then consider two major criteria in evaluating the loan application. First, the lender will focus on HT's financial health—in particular, the likelihood that the expansion plans will succeed and that HT will be able to repay the loan within the period that the lender considers reasonable. This evaluation of risk will determine whether the lender grants the loan and, if so, on what terms (i.e., the interest rate will reflect the risk). Second, the lender will investigate the security HT can provide for repayment. Even healthy borrowers can get into financial difficulty and become unable to make loan payments as planned. A lender wants security, or **collateral,** to back up the borrower's promise to pay. The lender therefore carefully examines the borrower's assets (such as land, buildings, inventory, accounts receivable, and intellectual property) in terms of their current value and any other claims from existing creditors. For example, HT may own the land and building on which its business is located, but if the property is already mortgaged to another lender, its utility as security for a new loan is limited.

If the creditor approves the application for a loan, the resulting arrangement is a credit agreement (a contract). The lender agrees to lend the money based on the terms of the agreement, which essentially require the borrower to repay the loan on a specified schedule and provide security in the event of **default.** The security may be specific assets or blanket coverage of all assets, and it may include assets that the borrower acquires in the future. The lender may officially register its claim against the borrower's assets and acquire priority over other creditors with subsequent claims. If the debtor defaults, the creditor can take action to have the assets seized and sold to satisfy the unpaid debt. As extra security, the lender may also seek assurance from persons other than those borrowing the money. In the HT situation, the lender may call upon Bill and Martha, and even the new shareholders, to give their personal guarantees for repayment of the loan by HT.

The result of this system of credit granting is that the lender can extract whatever promises of security it deems necessary to protect its loan. Borrowers can shop around for better terms or less restrictive lending conditions, but ultimately they must meet a lender's requirements in order to get the loan.

collateral
Security for a borrower's promise to repay a loan.

default
Failure to make required payments on a loan.

Canadian companies import products from countries around the world to sell in Canada. For example, an international trade relationship might originate with a visit by representatives of the Canadian government and importers to a country that is identified as a potential source of trade. Assume that Star Clothing, based in Toronto, participates in such a trip to China and identifies two manufacturers that could supply high-quality clothing at a lower cost than suppliers in Canada can. Representatives of Star communicate with their counterparts in the two Chinese companies and choose one of them (Beijing Clothing) as the best prospect. Star and Beijing eventually negotiate a contract worth $25 000 for clothing to be delivered in time for the spring fashion season in Canada. The contract includes quantity, price, and delivery date, and it specifies who is responsible for insurance and freight.

Since these companies are dealing with each other for the first time, they are sensitive to the risks involved. Beijing wants payment as soon as possible, ideally before shipment, to finance the production of the clothing. There is a large risk for Beijing if it ships the clothing to Canada with no means of ensuring payment. Beijing appreciates the difficulties involved in suing a Canadian company to recover payment, so it is unwilling to transfer title to the clothing before being paid and wishes to receive payment through its own bank in China.

On the other side of the transaction, Star is reluctant to pay for the clothing until it has received the agreed quality and quantity of clothing at the agreed time and place. Star is unwilling to pay before the clothing is manufactured and shipped and insists on at least receiving the title documents before making payment. Star knows that suing a Chinese company for breach of contract is difficult.

The services of international bankers and letters of credit are a common means of distributing these risks and dealing with the challenges of distance, unfamiliarity of the parties, and different legal rules and enforcement mechanisms. A **letter of credit** is a written promise made by the importer's bank (on the importer's instructions) and given to the exporter's bank to make payment to the exporter when specified conditions are met. These conditions relate to the exporter's delivery of documents, such as an invoice, shipping receipt, proof of insurance, and customs declaration. Although these documents are often presented and payment is made to the seller well before the importer receives the goods, the importer has considerable assurance that the goods will arrive.

CRITICAL ANALYSIS: Is the letter of credit a device that could be used to manage risk in domestic as well as international transactions? Can it take the place of reputation and experience in commercial dealings?

Source: Mary Jo Nicholson, *Legal Aspects of International Business* (Scarborough: Prentice Hall, 1997) at 190.

---

letter of credit
A written promise by a buyer's bank to a seller's bank to pay the seller when specified conditions are met.

consumer debt
A loan to an individual for a noncommercial purpose.

Regulation of Credit

Government intervention in the system of credit is mainly through provincial consumer protection legislation, which applies to transactions that lead to **consumer debt,** where the borrower is a consumer rather than a business. Its main purpose is to protect the consumer from the potentially unfair bargaining advantage that lenders enjoy. Those with blemished credit records are especially vulnerable, and their need for credit may be greater than those on more solid footing. Consumers must take the initiative to enforce the legislation by filing complaints or taking legal action, so if they are unaware of legislative rights or process, the protection is of little practical utility. This is a problem that governments seek to address by providing consumer information and counselling (for example, in Nova Scotia through Service Nova Scotia and Municipal Relations).

Within each province, the forms of protection are often scattered throughout a number of statutes but are united by the theme of seeking to regulate the provision of credit in the areas of licensing, permitted activities, and terms of credit.

A review of the various consumer credit regulations illustrates that

- there are specific rules a business must follow when it extends credit to consumers (otherwise, it risks any number of penalties, including the credit being declared unenforceable, licence suspension or revocation, and fines)
- these same rules function as a guide that businesses can use to protect themselves and to ensure good customer relations

The particular aspects of consumer credit that are subject to regulation include the following:

credit bureau
An agency that compiles credit information on borrowers.

- **Credit bureaus** provide a service to lenders by compiling credit information on consumers and reporting on their credit history. Lenders use this information to evaluate requests for loans. There are licensing systems to ensure the respectability of credit bureaus, and regulations to ensure the accuracy of the information that is compiled. Consumers have access to their files and the opportunity to correct any errors.[1]

- Lenders are specifically prohibited from making misleading statements in the application and negotiation process. These regulations bolster contract law protection against misrepresentation.

- In order to protect the consumer from those who would provide credit at exorbitant rates, the *Criminal Code*[2] prohibits lending at a rate of interest above 60 percent on an annual basis. Provincial legislation enables the courts to reopen transactions where "the cost of the loan is excessive and the transaction is harsh and unconscionable"[3] and regulates business practices (including credit transactions) by prohibiting, for example, transactions where there is "no reasonable probability of making payment in full" or where there is no substantial benefit to the consumer.[4]

- To prevent hidden charges by the lender and to better enable the borrower to appreciate the cost of the transaction, legislation[5] requires disclosure of the true cost of lending in terms of (1) the amount borrowed, the amount of interest, any other charges such as registration fees or insurance, and the total balance payable, and (2) the annual rate of interest (as a percentage) and the period over which the rate applies. Governments are adopting a template for the harmonization of cost of credit disclosure rules that includes a common terminology, expanded disclosure procedure, and new rules for advertising disclosure. For example, Ontario has recently included this template in its new consumer protection legislation.[6]

- The remedies that a borrower can seek where a lender has failed to observe the regulations include filing a complaint against the lender with a regulatory body (which can lead to fines, licence suspension or revocation, and orders prohibiting further violations), or applying to the courts to have the terms of the loan adjusted, or in some situations claiming damages.

---

1. See, for example, *Consumer Reporting Act*, R.S.O. 1990, c. C-33, s. 280.
2. R.S.C. 1985, c. C-46, s. 347.
3. *Unconscionable Transactions Relief Act*, R.S.N.S. 1989, c. 481, s. 3.
4. *Consumer Protection Act, 2002*, S.O. 2002, Sched. A, c. 30, s.15. See Chapter 24.
5. *Business Practices and Consumer Protection Act*, S.B.C. 2004, c. 2.
6. *Supra*, note 4, Part VII.

- Collection agencies provide a service to lenders who have difficulty recovering loans. These agencies are subject to a licensing scheme and cannot harass, threaten, or exert undue pressure on defaulting borrowers. They are also prohibited from contacting anyone other than the borrower (such as a family member or business associates), even when the debtor is bankrupt or deceased.[7] Agencies that go beyond the allowed means of collection risk revocation of their operating licence.

How can payday loans be regulated?

Ethical Considerations

The Payday Loans Dilemma

There has been considerable publicity in recent years surrounding what have come to be called payday loans. These are loans usually granted for a short period of time by a storefront operation for the purpose of tiding the borrower over until payday. The concern focuses on the actual cost of these loans, which can amount to 1000 percent when the nominal interest rate is calculated on an annual basis and various fees, commissions, and penalties are added. For example, a plaintiff in a class-action suit borrowed $300 on 19 March, rolled it over five times and repaid it in full on 11 July. He paid the principal of $300 plus $470 in broker fees, $40 in interest, and $22 in transaction fees.

There is concern that borrowers are being exploited by the lenders, both in terms of the cost of

credit and their lack of awareness of the actual cost. On the other hand, it is argued that these borrowers are not well served by banks and are attracted to payday lenders by their location, hours of business, and accessibility.

There are many different approaches to this dilemma

- Lenders could be prosecuted under the *Criminal Code* since the actual cost of these loans is well in excess of the permitted 60 percent annual maximum.

- The industry could be made exempt from the criminal provisions and regulated in a noncriminal fashion.

---

7. *Collection Agencies Act*, R.S.O. 1990, c. C-14.

- The federal government could delegate its authority over interest rates to the provinces for regulation under consumer protection legislation.

- Participants in the industry could be subjected to a licensing regime.

- The practice of payday loans could be banned outright.

- The industry could be left to regulate itself through industry associations and voluntary codes of conduct.

- Consumers could be left to protect themselves through individual contract disputes or class-action claims.

CRITICAL ANALYSIS: Which option or combination of options is likely to be most effective?

Sources: The Canadian Press, "Payday Loan Regulation May Fall to Provinces" *The Edmonton Journal* (25 April 2006) at F9; and Rita Trichur, "Ottawa Urged to Introduce Payday Loan Law this Fall" *The Chronicle Herald* (27 September 2006) at D3.

A major concern for consumers who apply for credit is the protection of the personal information they are required to provide in their applications to lenders. Canada's privacy law now addresses this concern.

Business and Legislation
Privacy Legislation and Credit Transactions

Public institutions in Canada have been subject to rules protecting citizens' privacy for some time. The *Personal Information Protection and Electronic Documents Act*[8] (PIPEDA) is Canada's major initiative in privacy law. It applies to the public and private sectors. The law came into force for federally regulated organizations on 1 January 2001, and for those regulated provincially on 1 January 2004, unless provinces have adopted a compatible regime. So far, Quebec, Alberta, and British Columbia have done so. The law's two chief purposes are to increase confidence in online activity, especially e-business, and to address international concerns about Canada's protection of data. The privacy portion of the act is meant to achieve a balance between the rights of individuals to protect their information and the need for organizations to collect and use the information.

The act applies to every organization that collects, uses, or discloses personal information in the course of commercial activities. The basic obligation imposed on organizations is to comply with the following principles:

- to be accountable for information under their control

- to identify the purposes for which information is collected

- to confine collection, use, disclosure, and retention to the identified purposes

- to obtain the consent of the owner for any collection, use, or disclosure

- to ensure the accuracy and security of the information

- to be open about their policies and practices

- to allow the owners access to their information and the ability to challenge the organization's compliance with the code

Organizations that are subject to this regime are expected to have privacy policies in place to comply with the specified principles. These policies form part of an organization's privacy compliance infrastructure, which should also include periodic compliance audits.

---

8. S.C. 2000, c. 5. See the background papers of the federal government Task Force on Electronic Commerce at http://e-com.ic.gc.ca. The Privacy Commissioner's website is at http://www.privcom.gc.ca

Individuals who suspect that their personal information is not being managed in accordance with the principles can first complain to the organization that is accountable and then to the federal privacy commissioner who has authority to investigate, engage in mediation or conciliation, and make findings and recommendations to resolve the complaint. Here are some examples of complaints relating to credit information:

- *Bank's notification to customers triggers* Patriot Act *concerns.* A Canadian bank sent notification to its credit card customers amending its cardholder agreement. The notification referred to the use of a U.S. service provider and the possibility that personal information of Canadian cardholders could be accessed by U.S. regulatory agencies. A number of customers complained that they were being required to consent to the disclosure of their information to U.S. authorities as a condition of service; they could not opt out; and the bank was not properly safeguarding their personal information. The assistant privacy commissioner found that the Canadian law did not prohibit the use of foreign service providers and therefore could not prevent the application of foreign law to personal information of Canadians. Canadian law does require that organizations be transparent about their information-handling practices and ensure to the extent possible a level of protection comparable to that in Canada. Under the terms of the bank's cardholder agreement, customers were not permitted to opt out of such practices.

- *Faxes misdirected to a U.S. company.* Over a three-year period, a Canadian bank sent faxes containing personal information of customers to the wrong fax numbers, most notably to a scrap yard in Virginia. The recipients notified the bank immediately and were asked to shred the faxes. The misdirected transmissions continued. The commissioner found that the bank's privacy policy was ineffective. The misdirected faxes were not recognized as a privacy problem, and bank staff were inadequately trained. The bank was further criticized for failing to notify customers until the story became public and failing to retrieve the misdirected information. The bank eventually took a number of measures to identify privacy problems and implement solutions to enhance safeguards.

- *Bank's refusal to release a complainant's credit score.* The bank refused because the score was based on a unique scoring model that it developed and customized to suit its strategic business priorities. Revealing it would disclose confidential commercial information, which is exempt from the requirements of the act. The commissioner found that "personal information" includes information collected from individuals and information internally generated by the bank. However, there was evidence that the internal credit-scoring models developed by individual banks are closely guarded from competitors, and therefore protected confidential information. The bank was not required to disclose the complainant's score, but the complainant was entitled to a full and satisfactory explanation in understandable terms for any decision the bank made in her regard.

CRITICAL ANALYSIS: PIPEDA is currently under review. How can the awareness and effectiveness of this legislative regime be evaluated?

Source: Privacy Commissioner's website at http://www.privcom.gc.ca.

The Credit Agreement

The aspects of credit that are regulated in relation to consumer loans are left to the parties to negotiate in the commercial context. Both lender and borrower must look after their own interests. The process of applying for a loan and formulating the terms of credit is much the same as for the negotiation of any other contract. HT's need for $200 000 is major in terms of its expansion plans, but it is a routine transaction for a large commercial lender. The lender has the advantage in bargaining power. When HT applies for the loan, the lender will demand whatever information it deems necessary in order to assess the risk and determine how much, if anything, it is prepared to lend to HT and on what basis. If the lender decides to grant the loan, it will offer terms to HT in the form of a **letter of commitment,** which sets out in detail the basic terms dealing with

letter of commitment
A document that is provided by a bank to a borrower and sets out the terms of a loan.

- amount of the loan
- interest
- repayment terms
- renewal
- security
- requirements for maintenance of the borrower's financial position
- events that constitute default
- lender's remedies

This letter may be the actual agreement (if the borrower agrees), or it may lead to other formal documentation. HT can try to negotiate adjustments in those terms, but ultimately, if HT wants the loan, it must meet the lender's terms or seek another lender (whose terms are likely to be similar).

Security

The two major elements of the credit agreement are the borrower's promise to repay the loan and the lender's collateral or security if the borrower fails to repay. Security for the loan can be any interest in property that is of value to the lender, namely

- *Real property.* This is accomplished through a mortgage, as discussed in Chapter 19.
- *All forms of personal property.* For example, if HT borrows in order to buy a new piece of equipment, the security for the loan may be the equipment itself. HT may finance its working capital by assigning accounts receivable (book debts) to the bank.

general security agreement
A loan contract that includes all of the assets of a business as collateral.

In HT's current application for expansion funds, the lender will likely require broader security in the form of a **general security agreement,** which will include several different types of security on assets currently held by HT, as well as other assets acquired during the term of the loan. HT is free to carry on business and use its assets as long as it makes the required payments on the loan. If HT defaults on the loan, the creditor's security interest attaches to the assets covered by the agreement and held by HT at the time of default.

Assets used as security can be classified in terms of whether or not they are meant to be retained in the business by the debtor. For example, if HT buys equipment for use in the business over the course of its useful life, it is available as security for a substantial length of time. Other assets, such as inventory and accounts receivable, are meant to circulate through the business on a regular basis. The security is the value of those assets at any given time. The loan agreement will require the borrower to maintain certain levels of those assets. However, it is understood and expected that the business will regularly be selling inventory and buying more, and that it will be collecting accounts from customers while delivering more orders on credit. In addition, the agreement will require the borrower to submit financial reports to the lender at specified intervals and maintain a specified debt-equity ratio.

Security may also consist of assets to be produced in the future. For example, a manufacturer may need financing in order to convert raw materials into finished goods. The federal *Bank Act*[9] enables the finished goods to be the security for the loan. As the goods are manufactured, the bank gains priority over the inventory against other creditors.

HT should appreciate the implications of the credit agreement—in particular, the degree of control over its assets that the lender will acquire should HT default. HT's ability to repay depends on the success of the expanded business, so it is not surprising that the lender wants considerable control over the business and its assets.

Lenders demand as much security as possible, to the extent that its current value may exceed the extent of the lender's risk. One reason for this demand for extensive security is the uncertain value of the assets. If HT borrows money to buy one piece of equipment and defaults on the loan, the lender's security is a used piece of equipment. The lender knows that the proceeds from a quick sale of the asset are likely to be much less than its value to HT in its ongoing business. Similarly, if HT gives a general security agreement, the value of all of HT's assets in the event of the business failing is much less than it appears at the time a financially healthy HT receives the loan. Credit insurance is available to lenders as an additional source of protection against the risk of uncollectible accounts.

Environmental Perspective — Credit and Environmental Risk

The value of land as security for credit depends on a variety of factors, including the health of the real estate market and the nature of the specific piece of land. Lenders want to minimize the risk of the land being worth less than the outstanding loan should the borrower default. Financial institutions engaged in commercial lending with real property as security generally require environmental assurance as part of the credit documentation. This assurance consists of representations and warranties by the borrower regarding the environmental status of the property, supplemented by surveys and questionnaires in the standard form of the particular lender. In addition, lenders may require more detailed environmental reviews and investigations from the borrower.

These reviews may be in two stages. The first stage identifies clearly visible contamination resulting from current or past use of the property. It consists of

- review of the borrower's records concerning such things as site history and documented contamination

- site visits

- inventory of hazardous materials

- interviews with site personnel and others involved with the borrower's use of the property

The results of the first stage of investigation may cause the lender to require a secondary report, either to eliminate questions raised by the environmental

---

9. *Bank Act*, S.C. 1991, c. 46, s. 427.

consultant or to address possible contamination. The second stage involves more intensive investigation, such as taking core samples, sampling underground water, and reviewing surrounding properties. This stage may help eliminate concerns raised by the consultants in the first stage, particularly with regard to adjoining properties, but it may also identify contamination leading to potential environmental liability.

CRITICAL ANALYSIS: Are these extensive environmental reviews a reasonable part of the credit application process? Are they more appropriate for certain types of land?

Source: Alison R. Manzer and Jordan S. Bernamoff, *The Corporate Counsel Guide to Banking and Credit Relationships* (Aurora: Canada Law Book, 1999) at 70.

What environmental hazards could affect the value of the security interest in this property?

Priority among Creditors

For security to be of value as collateral, the lender must be confident of its claim to the assets in the event of default. When considering the loan application, the lender needs a means of verifying ownership of the assets being offered as possible collateral and of determining whether the assets already form security for a loan. Assets that are free and clear—or otherwise unencumbered—are most attractive as security. Assets already used as security for debt may be considered if they are worth more than the existing debt. Once the loan is granted, the lender needs a means of informing existing and future creditors and potential purchasers of the assets that it has a claim against the property. If the borrower seeks additional financing, potential creditors need an accurate picture of the borrower's assets as security.

All provinces have two systems in place to provide creditors with priority over others regarding their security for loans. The system in place for real property was discussed in Chapter 19. The system for the other form of property—personal property—takes the form of personal property security legislation. All provinces have one statute[10] that applies to all forms of personal property security arrangements. These comprehensive provincial statutes have several common features:

registration
The process of recording a security interest in a public registry system.

financing statement
The document registered as evidence of a security interest in personal property.

after-acquired property
Assets acquired by a debtor after giving a security interest.

- There is one set of **registration** rules in each province for all arrangements using personal property as security.

- The creditor registers a **financing statement,** which identifies the debtor and the property that is security for the loan. Designated items must be registered by serial number. Other security is described by item or kind, or by including all present and **after-acquired property** (property acquired after the agreement was signed).

- Financing statements are maintained in a central computerized registry, which is public.

---

10. See, for example, *Personal Property Security Act*, R.S.O. 1990, c. P-10 and S.N.S. 1995–96, c. 13.

- Anyone interested in the degree of encumbrance of the assets of a business or an individual need conduct only one search within the province in order to discover all registered claims against the assets of that business or person. Serial numbered items can be searched by that number.
- Anyone who discovers a relevant registered financing statement can obtain from the creditor the full details as contained in the written security agreement.
- In the event of conflicting claims for the same assets, priority goes to the creditor who registered the financing statement first.
- The priority of registration is subject to the limitation that specific security agreements (e.g, HT's purchase of a piece of equipment) have priority over clauses in general security agreements that apply to after-acquired property.

These centralized and uniform systems are a vast improvement over the earlier patchwork of different statutes and rules within each province. However, they do not remove inconsistencies among provinces or address the practical problem that personal property is portable and may easily be moved beyond the ambit of a single province's registration system. The result for corporations doing business in several provinces is major inconvenience and expense stemming from the need to comply with many different sets of rules.

The system does provide creditors with a considerable level of protection, however. They have a means of informing the borrower's other creditors what their security is. Credit agreements are public knowledge. Any subsequent credit arrangements are subject to those registered commitments. The same assets can provide security for more than one credit arrangement, but the claims of competing lenders are subject to priority according to the order of registration of their agreements. All registered interests have priority over those that are not registered.

Remedies

A creditor's remedies in the event of the borrower's failure to pay are largely determined by the status of the creditor. The major distinction in status is between secured and unsecured creditors. Unsecured or general creditors have the right to sue the debtor for unpaid debts and at the end of that process achieve a judgment against any assets of the debtor that are not already claimed by **secured creditors** with a registered claim against all or a portion of the debtor's assets. Secured creditors have the remedies enjoyed by unsecured creditors, but in addition they have first claim against the assets covered by their security agreement with the debtor. These secured assets are unavailable for the claims of unsecured creditors, even if the debtor becomes bankrupt. As a result, when assets are distributed in a bankruptcy, secured creditors recover a higher portion of what they are owed than unsecured creditors do (see Chapter 27).

Lenders' Remedies

If the borrower defaults on the loan, secured lenders have a variety of remedies from two sources: the credit agreement and the legislation under which the agreement is registered.

Credit agreements normally permit the lender to call the entire loan based on default of one payment, through what is known as an **acceleration clause.** The default accelerates the time when the entire debt is due to the date of the default, thereby giving the debtor an incentive to make timely payments. The lender can enter the borrower's premises and seize the secured assets. The lender can then

secured creditor
A lender who through a registered security interest has the right to seize and sell specific assets of a borrower to collect a debt.

acceleration clause
A term of a loan agreement that makes the entire loan due if one payment is missed.

proceed to collect on the collateral (such as accounts receivable) or sell or otherwise dispose of it (in the case of inventory or equipment, for example) in order to generate funds to cover the unpaid balance.

At this point, the lender's evaluation of the security at the time the loan was granted is tested. If the lender valued the security conservatively and granted credit for less than the full value, the recovery on default should be complete. But if the lender took a less cautious approach (by overvaluing the security or lending its full value) or if the market for the type of security has suffered, the proceeds of sale may be inadequate. The lender then has an action (as a general creditor) against the borrower for the shortfall or **deficiency** in what is owed and shares the remaining unsecured assets with all general creditors. If the sale of the security generates funds in excess of those needed to repay the loan, the excess must be paid to the borrower for the benefit of other creditors.

Legislation generally confirms and supplements the contractual remedies, enabling the creditor to begin legal action for arrears, retain or take possession of collateral, and appoint a receiver or manager if there is a general security agreement in place.[11]

deficiency
The shortfall if secured assets are sold for less than the amount of the outstanding loan.

Limits on Lenders' Remedies

Creditors may be prohibited from seizing assets that provide security for their purchase if the debtor has already made payments equal to two-thirds of the loan.[12] In some provinces[13] the lender is limited to the proceeds from the seized assets and is therefore unable to sue the debtor for any deficiency between the outstanding balance and the proceeds from the seized assets. In all provinces, the creditor must deal with assets in a commercially reasonable manner.[14] This means taking reasonable steps to realize as much from the seized assets as possible. Creditors are not expected to retain assets until the ideal buyer can be found because the courts recognize that creditors are in the lending business—they are not dealers in a wide variety of vehicles, equipment, and other assets. Creditors must avoid conflicts of interest created by buying assets themselves or selling to related businesses at a price less than fair market value.

receiver
A person appointed by the secured creditor to seize the assets and realize the debt.

The major restraint on creditors' remedies is the requirement to give the debtor reasonable notice before calling a loan, appointing a **receiver,** and seizing assets. This notice is especially important in situations where a general security agreement gives the creditor first claim over the bulk of the debtor's assets and allows the creditor to appoint a receiver in the event of default. Receivers essentially control the business and can exclude the debtor from making decisions. Nevertheless, the debtor is anxious to salvage the business, perhaps by refinancing and generating revenue to pay creditors and carry on business. However, the creditor has already made the decision to call the loan and has the primary objective of redeeming sufficient assets to clear the loan. The survival of the business is secondary to the creditor. The following case illustrates the difficulty involved in these default situations.

---

11. See, for example, *Personal Property Security Act*, R.S.O. 1990, c. P-10.
12. This limitation applies, for example, in New Brunswick, Nova Scotia, and Ontario.
13. This limitation applies, for example, in British Columbia and Alberta.
14. For example, *Personal Property Security Act*, S.N.S. 1995–96, c. 13 s. 66(2).

CASE ▼

Murano v. Bank of Montreal (1995), 20 B.L.R. (2d) 61 (Ont. Gen. Div.), varied (1998), 41 B.L.R. (2d) 10 (Ont. C.A.)

THE BUSINESS CONTEXT: A creditor with a general security agreement has considerable power that can threaten the survival of the business. As a result, the courts have developed the requirement of notice to provide an opportunity for the debtor to raise funds from other sources to pay the loan. Creditors are reluctant to give such notice, as they are fearful that valuable assets may disappear during the notice period.

FACTUAL BACKGROUND: Murano owned and operated a chain of video rental stores called the Hilton division. He also owned five "Top 30" video stores and had plans to open 70 more. He had also agreed to buy 52 stores in the Bandito Video chain. When one of the Hilton stores changed locations, the bank immediately demanded payment of its loans on the basis of terms in the credit agreement and appointed a receiver for the Hilton division two hours later. Murano was not told of the bank's reasons for its actions. The bank told other lenders, business associates of Murano, and suppliers that it acted because of Murano's dishonest activities related to his desperate financial situation. Murano claimed that the bank's actions destroyed the Hilton division and prevented the Top 30 and Bandito projects from proceeding. In addition, Murano could not maintain payments on several real estate loans or refinance his business operations. The bank's actions caused the real estate lenders to seize those assets and sell them at distressed prices. The bank defended its conduct on the basis that Murano's businesses were a highly leveraged "house of cards" waiting to fall.

THE LEGAL QUESTION: Was the bank justified in acting as quickly as it did? If not, what losses did the bank cause to Murano?

RESOLUTION: A creditor must give a debtor reasonable notice that repayment of a loan is required, even where the loan is payable on demand. The length of notice depends on the circumstances in each case, including the amount of the loan, the risk to the creditor, the length of the relationship between debtor and creditor, the character and reputation of the debtor, and the potential for the debtor to quickly raise the funds to pay the loan.

The bank did not give Murano reasonable notice of its intentions. There were no special circumstances beyond the normal fears of all lenders that the borrower may default. There was no indication that Murano planned to disappear with his assets. The bank used the move of the one Hilton store as a pretext for acting quickly. The bank's disclosure of information about Murano to others was unnecessary to protect the bank or the public and was therefore a breach of the bank's duty of confidentiality in relation to its customer's affairs.

The court awarded Murano a total of $3.77 million in damages, including $1.55 million for the loss on the Hilton division, and $1 million for each of the Top 30 and Bandito transactions.

CRITICAL ANALYSIS: Does this case interfere too much with the bank's ability to protect its security? Did the court go too far in holding the bank responsible for a borrower's losses on business deals?

Borrowers' Remedies

The borrower has the basic right to limit the lender to the remedies permitted by legislation and defined by the agreement. Therefore, the borrower can best protect its interest by trying to negotiate flexible terms when the business is relatively prosperous. If the borrower later has financial difficulties, the lender will quickly focus on damage control and be less inclined to be flexible.

On an ongoing basis, the borrower is entitled to an accounting of the state of the loan, mainly in terms of the outstanding balance. If default occurs, the borrower has several rights in relation to the lender's seizure and sale of assets. The borrower is entitled to prescribed or reasonable notice of seizure and sale in order to be able to monitor the process and know when an infusion of funds could halt the collection process and enable the borrower to carry on. The borrower can challenge a sale that is improperly conducted or that produces unreasonably low proceeds, known as an **improvident sale,** and recover surplus proceeds from a sale of assets, or any property seized but not sold to satisfy the debt.[15]

Since businesses in financial difficulty are not in a position to engage in expensive litigation over credit disputes with their banks, they may consider instead the complaint resolution procedure in each of the major banks. These procedures relate to the *Model Code for Bank Relations with Small- and Medium-Sized Businesses* established by the Canadian Bankers Association. If a bank's procedure fails to satisfactorily resolve the complaint, the business is referred to the Ombudsman for Banking Services and Investments (OBSI).[16]

These rights and remedies available to the borrower relate to credit agreements with particular creditors. If the borrower is in serious financial difficulty, there are broader remedies available to facilitate the refinancing of businesses that are in trouble but that have potential for recovery (see Chapter 27).

Personal Guarantees

If HT's bank grants the loan for expansion, it is highly likely that one of the requirements will be personal guarantees of the loan from at least some of the shareholders. These guarantees provide more collateral for the loan to HT because the personal assets of the shareholders will be available to the bank if HT defaults. The bank's rights against HT are found in the credit agreement and the legislation and are limited to assets owned by HT. Potential claims against the shareholders personally are defined by the contracts of guarantee they sign with the bank and are likely unlimited in terms of which of their assets the bank can pursue as an unsecured creditor.

improvident sale
A sale of the borrower's assets by the lender for less than fair market value.

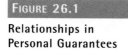
Figure 26.1

Relationships in Personal Guarantees

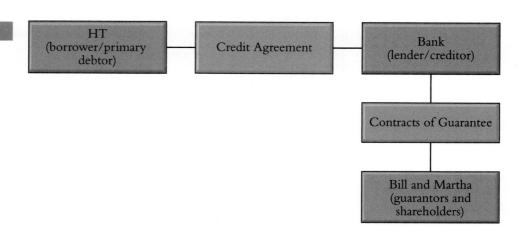

---

15. Alison R. Manzer & Jordan S. Bernamoff, *The Corporate Counsel Guide to Banking and Credit Relationships* (Aurora: Canada Law Book, 1999) at 65.
16. Canadian Bankers Association at http://www.cba.ca.

guarantee

A conditional promise to pay a debt to a creditor if the debtor defaults.

guarantor

A person who signs a guarantee.

A **guarantee** is a contract between the bank as creditor and the shareholders as **guarantors.** Therefore, the terms and conditions are those contained in the guarantee agreement. Any arrangements between the guarantors and the debtor (HT) do not affect the rights of the bank. The essence of the guarantee is a promise by those who sign it to repay the debtor's loan if the debtor defaults. Their promises are conditional or secondary to the primary obligation of the debtor. Bill, Martha, and the others may also be called upon to cosign HT's loans, but only then will they become primarily liable for repayment along with HT.

The implications for shareholders (or others) who sign personal guarantees are significant. They lose their limited liability protection to the extent of their promises to the bank by putting their personal assets at risk. As officers of HT, Bill and Martha sign many documents on behalf of HT, but the guarantees create personal obligations.

Another major danger of guarantees is their continuing nature. They often include the total debt owed to the bank at any given time. When the initial loan is granted, the guarantors are confident in HT's future and comfortable with the amount of the loan. As time passes, the amount of credit may increase, and HT's financial health may deteriorate. Meanwhile, the bank holds the guarantees. If financial disaster strikes and the bank proceeds on the guarantees, the guarantors will view their commitment and risk much differently than they did when they signed several years earlier. In a typical disaster situation, where the sums owed by the corporate debtor are substantial, the guarantors may be unable to respond to the bank's demands on the guarantees and be forced into personal bankruptcy.

The Guarantee Agreement

A guarantee is one of the few contracts that must be in written form and signed by the guarantor in order to be enforceable.[17] A written record is important because the guarantee has major implications for the individuals who sign, and it may be in force for a long period.

A guarantee is not normally an independently negotiated arrangement, but one requirement in a larger credit arrangement. The lender requires that guarantees be provided on the lender's standard form, which is designed to maximize the lender's ability to obligate the guarantors—by severely limiting ways for the guarantors to avoid liability—and to give the lender maximum flexibility in dealing with the debtor. The guarantors may be compelled to sign in order for the loan to be granted, but they need to make this commitment in a deliberate rather than casual manner. In the HT situation, guarantees from the shareholders will be a condition for the loan to HT, so they need to consider this as an important factor in their decision to seek debt financing.

The following are some typical terms in a contract of guarantee:

- All guarantors are liable for the full amount; thus, if Bill and Martha sign a guarantee for the $200 000 loan, they are each 100 percent liable for that full amount. The bank can recover the total amount of the loan from either one of them because the guarantors are jointly liable.

- The guarantee normally applies to all credit extended to the debtor while the guarantee is in force. If the shareholders wish to limit their liability to $200 000, they must negotiate this term with the bank and ensure that the contract they sign states that limit in clear terms.

---

17. Manitoba is the exception. The writing requirement is in place in all other provinces, generally in the *Statute of Frauds.*

- Guarantees are normally in force for an unlimited period. Those who sign must realize the risk this term entails and try to negotiate either a time limit or a clause that allows them to terminate their obligations by giving notice to the bank.

- Guarantees normally exclude any terms, conditions, statements, or representations that are not in the agreement. Guarantors should not sign based on any assurances or assumptions that are not expressly stated in the document.

- A standard guarantee ordinarily provides that the creditor is authorized to deal with the debtor and the terms of credit without affecting the guarantors' liability (for example, by increasing the amount of the loan). This is a direct reversal of the common law rule that ends the guarantee if the terms of the debt are changed without the guarantors' consent.

Avoiding Guarantor Obligations

By the time a bank takes action to enforce a guarantee, the debtor's situation is hopeless, and there is no benefit for the guarantors in making payments because the business is failing. However, when and if the guarantors do make payments on behalf of the primary debtor, they have a right of **subrogation** against the debtor. This means that if HT defaults on its loan and the shareholders are required to pay through their guarantees, they have the right to recover their money from HT. However, if HT were able to repay the guarantors, it is unlikely the default would have occurred in the first place.

Guarantors have some common law defences. For example, the guarantors' obligation is limited to the terms of the debt they guaranteed. If the terms of that loan are changed in any way that increases the risk to the guarantors, the agreement is terminated unless the guarantors have agreed to the changes. Changes having this effect include increasing the amount of the loan or the rate of interest, extending the time for payment, or altering the collateral the debtor has provided for the loan. However, these and other defences are often eliminated by the words of modern guarantees that specifically prevent the guarantor from using the common law defences to payment.

A defence available to some guarantors is their lack of understanding of the terms of the contract and their risk. If the signors are individuals who are not directly involved in the debtor's business or in the particular credit transaction, they should obtain independent advice before signing. Spouses or other relatives of the shareholders with little or no involvement in HT may sign under pressure from family and friends. Without independent advice, they may make commitments that they fail to understand and may as a result be relieved of their obligations. Bill, Martha, and likely the new shareholders are directly involved in the HT business, so this defence is not available to them. They are presumed to know the implications of HT's loan request and how their guarantees affect that arrangement. Bank personnel may also make assumptions about the willingness and level of knowledge of the prospective guarantors. Subject to the various exceptional possibilities for avoiding contractual obligations (see Chapter 8), guarantors have little chance to escape liability if the debtor defaults.

The written guarantee will normally take precedence over reassurances or other statements that contradict or modify its terms. However, the courts tend to study the written terms carefully since they give the creditor considerable power over the guarantor. The following case illustrates this judicial approach.

subrogation

The right of a guarantor to recover from the debtor any payments made to the creditor.

CASE ▼

Manulife Bank of Canada v. Conlin
(1996), 203 N.R. 81 (S.C.C.)

THE BUSINESS CONTEXT: Although the terms of guarantees tend to favour the creditor over the guarantor and the chances of a guarantor avoiding liability are slim, the courts closely scrutinize the terms and hold the guarantor responsible only to the extent that the terms clearly indicate.

FACTUAL BACKGROUND: In 1987 Dina Conlin signed a three-year mortgage on an apartment building in favour of Manulife in the amount of $275 000 at 11.5 percent interest. Her husband, John Conlin, signed the mortgage as guarantor. The guarantee clause of the mortgage stated that the guarantor was obligated despite "the giving of time for payment . . . or the varying of the terms of payment . . . or the rate of interest." It also stated that the guarantor's liability was continuous and that he was liable until payment in full by the borrower. Another clause of the mortgage provided for renewal by agreement in writing. The Conlins separated in 1989, and the next year the mortgage was renewed at 13 percent interest. Only Dina signed the renewal agreement. John was not notified, even though the agreement provided space for a guarantor's signature. In 1992 Dina defaulted, and Manulife foreclosed and sued John on his 1987 guarantee.

THE LEGAL QUESTION: Was John Conlin obligated to guarantee the renewed mortgage?

RESOLUTION: Despite the language of the agreement, the Supreme Court of Canada released John from his obligations after applying the following sequence of rules:

- Any material alteration of the contract of debt will change the terms upon which the guarantor was to be liable and will result in a change in the guarantor's risk.

- A guarantor will be released from liability when the creditor and the debtor agree to a material alteration of the terms of the contract of debt without the consent of the guarantor (the common law rule).

- The guarantor and the creditor can agree to opt out of this rule in their contract.

- Where the creditor argues that the guarantee agreement provides a blanket authorization to make material alterations to the contract of debt, the wording must be clear that such a right was intended.

- If there is doubt or ambiguity about the meaning of the clauses in the agreement, they must be resolved in favour of the guarantor.

- When the guarantee clause is interpreted, it must be considered in the context of the entire transaction, including the terms and arrangements for the renewal agreement.

CRITICAL ANALYSIS: Does the courts' scrutiny of the terms of standard form guarantees provide adequate protection for guarantors? What risk management action by the bank and the banking industry is likely to result from a decision like this?

Apart from the requirement that guarantees be in writing, the only regulation of guarantees in Canada is a statute in Alberta.[18] It provides that for any guarantee to be valid in that province, it must be certified by a notary public that the guarantors were aware of the contents of the guarantee and understood them. The statute places no limits on the content of the guarantee, so creditors can make the terms as restrictive as they like without affecting the validity of the guarantee.

It has been argued that guarantee terms are inherently so one-sided that banks should be strongly encouraged or forced to change the language.

---

18. *Guarantees Acknowledgment Act*, R.S.A. 2000, c. G-11.

ecause the language of guarantees is dictated by banks, it includes broad terms intended to give the banks maximum discretion in dealing with the borrower, the security for the borrower's loan, and the terms of the lending agreement without affecting the guarantors' liability to the bank. For example, common terms are "the bank may deal with the security as it sees fit" and "the bank may vary the terms of the loan as it sees fit." Banks maintain that these clauses allow them to release other guarantors or sell security in any way they choose (the security clause) or to raise interest rates or lend more money (the terms of the loan). Guarantors who wish to challenge the banks' interpretation of such language can do so in the courts, as Mr. Conlin did in the case above. However, courts have differing views and apply different sets of values in these cases. Some take a straightforward approach and rely primarily on the written terms. For example, in a recent case, the judge considered a standard form of guarantee containing complex language and concluded

> I am in agreement with counsel for [the bank] that the exemption clause is clear. The guarantors have contracted out of any potential defence relating to the way the bank dealt with its client's credit facility.

Others take a more contextual approach and question whether the meaning of the language would be plain and obvious to guarantors or whether the language is specific and clear enough for guarantors to understand that the contract gives the bank such wide powers.

Jan Weir is a civil litigation lawyer who sees the law of guarantees as a real concern for those in small business who are required to sign such agreements. These people understand interest rates and repayment terms, but not the language of standard form agreements and its consequences: "It would probably take a law professor with a large magnifying glass several hours to review and explain the usual bank guarantee form to a layperson."

He further argues that there is no real competition among banks relating to these terms and therefore no real equality of bargaining power between banks and guarantors: "In my view, the banks have used a statutorily sanctioned monopoly position to use one-sided agreements that often deprive unsuspecting and unrepresented small businesspeople of protections and fair principles that judges have developed."

Weir suggests that we need small business lobby groups to develop fair standard form guarantees.

CRITICAL ANALYSIS: Do you agree with Weir's analysis? Is it ethical for banks to impose these one-sided terms on small businesspeople?

Sources: Jan Weir, "Banks vs. Small Business: An Unequal Match" *The Lawyers Weekly* (9 February 2001) at 9; and *Royal Bank of Canada v. Speight*, 2006 NSSC 151.

Business Law in Practice Revisited

1. What are potential lenders likely to require from HT before granting the loan and during the repayment period?

Before the loan is granted, HT will be asked to provide detailed financial statements and a business plan for the expansion. Lenders will also require HT to pledge assets of sufficient worth to cover the loan. During the repayment period, HT will be required to maintain minimum levels of accounts receivable and inventory, to stay within a specified debt-equity ratio, and to report to the bank at specified intervals. HT will also need the lender's permission to deal with secured assets.

2. What are the risks for the business in borrowing $200 000?

The major risk is the possibility that the business will be less profitable than planned and that cash flow problems will result in default on the loan payments. Default will lead to loss of assets to the lender and possibly the end of the business. If HT fails to repay, the secured assets can be seized and sold by the lender, and probably the lender will have the power to appoint a receiver to assume control of the business. Only if HT can refinance will it be able to recover and carry on.

3. Is there potential personal liability for Bill, Martha, and the two new shareholders?

Bill and Martha will likely be required to personally guarantee the loan to HT. The new shareholders could also be asked to sign. If HT defaults, their personal assets are available to the lender. They lose their limited liability protection to the extent of this loan, as defined by the terms of the written guarantee.

Chapter Summary

Credit transactions are an important and normal part of every business. A business can be a debtor or a creditor, depending on the transaction. Some arrangements are continuous and revolving, such as with a customer and supplier. Others are major individual transactions and involve a formal credit agreement specifying the rights and obligations of the borrower and the lender. Unsecured creditors have equal claim against the assets of the borrowing business. They can sue and obtain a judgment and apply that against the debtor's unsecured assets. If a business is involved in significant debt financing, most of its assets will be covered by credit agreements, which secured creditors will register to obtain priority over unsecured creditors. If the business defaults, secured creditors have first claim over the assets covered by their registered agreements.

Lenders are protected by the contracts that borrowers sign and by the legislation that provides for security through registration. Unsecured creditors have the right to litigate their claims.

Borrowers are also protected through their agreements with creditors and legislation. Lenders can exercise only the rights provided by contract and legislation and must act reasonably in doing so.

Guarantors place their personal assets at risk when they sign a guarantee. They should be aware of the onerous terms in most guarantees and ensure that they limit their exposure to the extent possible in the standard form agreements.

Chapter Study

Key Terms and Concepts

acceleration clause (p. 650)

after-acquired property (p. 649)

collateral (p. 641)

consumer debt (p. 642)

credit bureau (p. 643)

default (p. 641)

deficiency (p. 651)

financing statement (p. 649)

general security agreement (p. 647)

guarantee (p. 654)

guarantor (p. 654)

improvident sale (p. 653)

letter of commitment (p. 647)

letter of credit (p. 642)

receiver (p. 651)

registration (p. 649)

secured creditor (p. 650)

subrogation (p. 655)

unsecured creditor (p. 640)

Questions for Review

1. What are some examples of credit transactions?

2. What are the privacy principles in the federal legislation?

3. What are the rights of an unsecured creditor?

4. What are the two key aspects of a secured credit agreement?

5. What are the disclosure requirements for a consumer loan?

6. What is a criminal rate of interest?

7. Do you think payday loans should be regulated?

8. What is a general security agreement?

9. What is the role of a financing statement in personal property security registration?

10. What is a financing statement?

11. What are the practical differences between real and personal property in terms of registering security interests?

12. What are the common features of personal property registration rules in the various provinces?

13. What is the role of a receiver appointed by a creditor?

14. What is an improvident sale?

15. What is a deficiency in a credit transaction?

16. Who are the parties in a contract of guarantee?

17. Who writes the language in most guarantees?

18. How does a guarantee affect the limited liability of a shareholder of a corporation?

Questions for Critical Thinking

1. When a business fails, most of the assets are claimed by secured creditors. Other creditors receive very little, and the shareholders are left with nothing. Is the protection accorded to secured creditors justified?

2. There is a complex web of rules governing consumer credit. Should commercial credit be regulated the way consumer credit is now or left to the lender and borrower to arrange?

3. The registration systems used by secured creditors give priority to the creditors who register first, regardless of when the credit agreement was finalized. Should a creditor's reason for failing to register on time be considered in determining the priority of the creditors? If so, what reasons might be acceptable?

4. Creditors holding general security agreements are required to give the borrower a reasonable period of time to refinance the loan before appointing a receiver to take over the business. How should a secured creditor decide how much time to give a debtor?

5. The Canadian Constitution gives the provinces control over property and civil rights, which includes the registration of property as security for credit. Do the benefits to the provinces of autonomy outweigh the burden on business of dealing with so many sets of rules?

6. In light of this chapter, what factors would you advise Bill and Martha to consider in financing their expansion? Did they make the right decision in selling shares? When they borrow, how should they try to structure the terms of the loan to minimize the risk to the corporation and themselves?

Situations for Discussion

1. Careful Bank made a loan to Sampson and took his truck as security in a credit agreement. The bank filed a financing statement in Ontario. Sampson took the truck to Manitoba and used it as a trade-in on a new one. The truck dealer knew Sampson was not from Manitoba but never asked where exactly he was from. The bank discovered Sampson's move and registered a financing statement in Manitoba. When Sampson defaulted on his loan, the bank seized the truck from the dealer's lot.[19] Who is entitled to the truck—the dealer or the bank? What should each have done differently? How likely is it that the bank could trace the truck in circumstances such as these? To complicate matters, the bank sold the truck without informing Sampson of the time and place of the sale. The sale proceeds were not enough to pay the balance on the loan, so the bank is now suing Sampson for the shortfall.[20] On what basis can Sampson challenge the bank's actions and defend the claims against him? How important are the terms of the security agreement and the applicable laws?

2. The Weiss Brothers operated a successful business in Montreal for 30 years. They bought a bankrupt hardware business in Ottawa, even though they had no experience in Ottawa or in selling hardware. Their bank, Toronto Dominion, got nervous about their financial stability and suggested they seek financing elsewhere. They contacted a former employee of TD who was then with Aetna Financial Services and negotiated a new credit arrangement with

---

19. Based on *Westman Equipment Corp. v. Royal Bank of Canada* (1982), 19 B.L.R. 56 (Man. Co. Ct.).
20. Based on *Royal Bank of Canada v. Segreto Construction Ltd.* (1988), 38 B.L.R. 134 (Ont. C.A.).

Aetna, consisting of a line of credit up to $1 million with conditions attached related to accounts receivable and inventory. Security for the loan was a general security agreement, pledge of accounts receivable, mortgage on land, and guarantees by the Weiss brothers. Six months later, the brothers defaulted on their loan. Aetna demanded payment in full and appointed a receiver, who seized all the assets three hours later.[21] What can the Weiss Brothers do now to save the business and their personal assets? What could they have done to prevent this disaster? How should they have analyzed the risk before buying the hardware business?

3. Dave and Betty Wilder arranged a loan for their company, Wilder Enterprises Ltd., and personally guaranteed the loan. Janson was the manager of their bank branch and told them that he thought he could get authorization from his regional office for a fixed term at a fixed rate of interest. However, the loan documents showed a loan repayable on demand with a floating interest rate. When the company experienced financial difficulty, the Wilders negotiated an arrangement whereby the bank increased its credit to the company, agreed to honour the company's cheques, and agreed to refrain from demanding payment for a specified time. In return, the Wilders gave more security. Without warning, the bank stopped honouring cheques and appointed a receiver. Wilder Enterprises went bankrupt, and the bank called the guarantees, all of which permitted the bank to "deal with the customer as the bank may see fit."[22] Will the Wilders be obligated on their guarantees? How sympathetic are the courts likely to be? Could the Wilders have structured their affairs differently to avoid high personal risk for the escalating debts of their failing business?

4. Kyle owned and operated a retail sporting goods shop. A new ski resort was built in the area and, to take advantage of increased activity, Kyle decided to expand his shop. He borrowed money from his bank, which took a security interest in his present inventory and any after-acquired inventory as collateral for the loan. A year later an avalanche destroyed the ski lodge. Kyle's business suffered, and he was left with double the inventory he had when he obtained the loan. When he defaulted on his payments, the bank seized all of his inventory. Kyle claims the bank is entitled only to the value of the inventory at the time of the loan. How much inventory can the bank claim? Could Kyle have negotiated better terms in the beginning?

5. Excel is a new business engaged in manufacturing and selling ski equipment to large retail stores, as well as to smaller sports shops. Excel has been unable to get customers to pay before or at the time of delivery, so most sales are now made on credit. Customers have 30 days to pay for the equipment they buy from Excel. If payment is not made within 30 days, Excel wants to be able to repossess the equipment. What criteria should Excel use in evaluating customers' applications for credit? What credit terms should Excel demand from customers? What about the payments due for equipment already sold to the retailers' customers?

6. Kings Tire Shop agreed to buy a vacant building-supply outlet to expand its tire business. To finance the purchase, Kings negotiated a loan from its bank, with the land and building as security. As part of the loan documentation, the bank required a report stating that the property was not environmentally contaminated in any way. Kings engaged a local environmental consulting firm to investigate and prepare the report for the bank. The firm gave the property a clean bill of health, and the loan was granted. Two years later, it was discovered that the adjacent property, which was formerly a gas station, had seriously contaminated the soil, and pollution was leaching into the soil of Kings' property. The cleanup cost is significant, and Kings cannot afford it. As a result, Kings' property is seriously devalued and the bank is concerned about the value of its security, especially since Kings'

---

21. Based on *Kavcar Investments v. Aetna Financial Services* (1989), 62 D.L.R. (4th) 277 (Ont. C.A.).
22. Based on *Bank of Montreal v. Wilder* (1986), 32 D.L.R. (4th) 9 (S.C.C.).

business is not doing well. Who is responsible for this environmental damage? What are the bank's options? What are Kings' options?

7. New Solutions Financial (NSF) lent Transport Express (TE), a transport trucking company, $500 000 under a commercial lending agreement. The interest rate was 4 percent per month calculated daily and payable monthly. This arrangement produced an effective annual rate of 60.1 percent. Other clauses in the agreement specified other charges, including legal fees, monitoring fee, a standby fee, royalty payments, and a commitment fee totalling 30.8 percent for a total effective annual rate of 90.9 percent. TE found the terms of the agreement too onerous and refused to make the agreed payments.[23] Is this agreement enforceable? Should a commercial arrangement like this be treated differently from a payday loan?

8. RST Ltd. is an independent printing company in a medium-sized town in Saskatchewan. It was established 15 years ago by Ron, Sandra, and Tara, who each own one-third of the shares in the company. Last year, RST revenues were $4 million, mainly from local contracts for such items as customized office stationery, business cards, advertising posters, calendars, and entertainment programs. Because the business is prospering, the owners are planning to expand their printing and sales space. They know that significant financing is required for the expanded facilities and the increased business. The current financial structure of RST is 60 percent owners' equity and 40 percent debt. Rather than sell shares to other investors, the owners are prepared to put more equity into the business by purchasing additional shares in order to maintain their debt/equity ratio. The expansion project will cost $1 million, so they need to borrow $400 000. Do you agree with the owners' financing decisions? What are the risks?

For more study tools, visit
http://www.businesslaw3e.nelson.com

23. Based on *Transport North American Express Inc. v. New Solutions Financial Corp.*, [2004] 1 S.C.R. 249.

Chapter

27

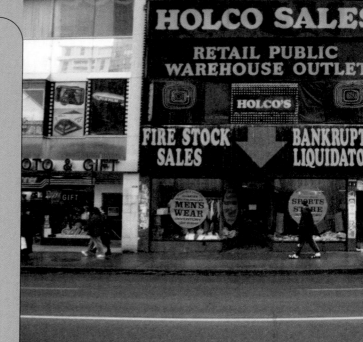

Objectives

After studying this chapter, you should have an understanding of
- the legal aspects of business failure
- the rights and obligations of debtors and creditors when a business fails
- the stages in the bankruptcy process

Bankruptcy and Insolvency

Business Law in Practice

Hometown Hardware Ltd. (HT) and its owners, Bill Ikeda and Martha Wong, were introduced in Chapters 25 and 26. They have successfully operated a building supply outlet in Timmins, Ontario, for the past 35 years. Eighteen months ago, Bill and Martha became concerned about the imminent arrival of a major international hardware supply chain in a new shopping area on the outskirts of town. They decided to expand their operation in order to respond to this competitive threat. To finance the expansion, they sold $200 000 worth of shares in HT and were able to borrow $200 000 from their bank. The loan was secured by a mortgage for $100 000 on HT's land and buildings, a line of credit for $100 000 secured by inventory and accounts receivable, and personal guarantees signed by Bill and Martha. The expansion strategy failed. HT has experienced a 30 percent drop in sales to consumers and local tradespersons. Bill does not expect this decline to abate.

When the chain first opened in Timmins, Bill reacted with a costly promotional campaign. To cover this extra expense, Bill borrowed $10 000 from his brother, George. More recently, he was under pressure from a major supplier, Good Lumber Ltd. (GL), to pay his overdue account. Bill sold land that the company owned adjacent to the store. With the proceeds, Bill paid $20 000 to GL and repaid George.

Bill wants to keep his business running as long as possible, but fears that the store may no longer be viable and is wondering whether he should try to preserve, sell, or close it. The company owns the property (subject to a mortgage) on which the business is located and leases several vehicles and pieces of machinery. Bill hopes to continue to draw his regular salary from the business; pay Martha as the store manager; and make regular payments to the bank on the mortgage and line of credit, to the lessors of the equipment he is using, and to his regular suppliers. He is concerned about the guarantees that he and Martha have signed for the bank relating to the corporation's loans. He is also late in remitting employee deductions for income tax and pensions to the government.

1. What choices does HT have in dealing with this financial crisis?
2. What rights do HT's creditors have?
3. What will happen to HT, its owners, its creditors, Bill, and Martha if bankruptcy occurs?

Business Failure

Business failure is often overlooked in the study of business, which emphasizes success and entrepreneurship in new ventures. Even when the economy booms, many new businesses fail or falter because of poor management or lack of adequate financing. When an industry or the overall economy experiences a downturn, even healthy businesses may run into difficulty. HT is caught in a changing market in which downtown business is threatened by the big-box retailers. Whether these threats bring the business to an end or result in major reorganization, they affect many people in addition to the business owners. HT must deal with cash flow problems, persistent and competing creditors, and possible legal action. If HT fails, customers, suppliers, and employees will be harmed, and the business district in downtown Timmins will suffer. How the law addresses the respective interests of creditors and what it allows in terms of reorganization are critical for a wide section of the local community—business and otherwise.

In order to ensure that both the business in difficulty and its creditors are treated fairly, a body of law, generically called insolvency law, has evolved. In addition to negotiated agreements between debtor and creditor and informal arrangements, the law provides several options for debtors and creditors as well as a framework for the ultimate financial failure—bankruptcy.[1]

Debtor Options

If a business such as HT is no longer able to cope with a specific debt or its obligations in general, there are several possibilities to be explored—ranging from informal negotiations to bankruptcy.

Informal Steps

Before contemplating bankruptcy, many in the position of HT, Bill, and Martha may first attempt to solve their financial distress by way of a negotiated settlement. If Bill can convince his creditors that the business can be salvaged, they may be willing to make concessions in terms of payment. He can deal with creditors individually or as a group. A settlement can be more or less formal, depending on the circumstances. Creditors may agree to meet with the debtor and, possibly using the services of a professional facilitator (an accountant, a lawyer, or a debt counsellor), reach an agreement that is acceptable to all and either allows the business to continue operating or to terminate without expensive legal proceedings.

The key to negotiated settlements is ensuring that all creditors agree to the arrangement. They will agree if they see the settlement has the potential to produce greater payments than legal proceedings would. One of the dangers is that some creditors will attempt to push through an agreement that is unfair to others or that simply ignores them. The value of using a facilitator with appropriate expertise is that he is trained to identify these risks. Furthermore, the parties collectively may not recognize alternatives that would result in greater returns overall. A skilled facilitator will direct attention to these choices.

In hopeless cases, negotiations may not be a viable option or fail after a reasonable attempt. Creditors may recognize that it is not worth their time to pursue their claims. It is then up to the debtor to seek remedies through insolvency law in order to bring closure to her obligations.

Proceedings before Bankruptcy

If informal negotiations fail to produce a settlement with HT's creditors and pressure continues from those creditors, Bill will likely explore more formal proceedings. He should seek advice from a lawyer or accountant with insolvency expertise and will eventually need a **trustee in bankruptcy** who has legal authority to administer legal proceedings.

Trustees are practising professionals who choose their cases. The trustee's decision will be based on two factors: Is there any conflict of interest (perhaps a creditor is an existing client), and does the client have sufficient assets in the estate to pay for the trustee's services? If debtors cannot find a trustee willing to accept the appointment—a relatively common occurrence—their only recourse may be some form of debt counselling service.

trustee in bankruptcy
The officer assigned legal responsibility for administering the affairs of bankrupt corporations or individuals.

---

1. Governed by the *Bankruptcy and Insolvency Act*, R.S.C. 1985, c. B-3.

estate

The collective term for the assets of the insolvent or bankrupt.

At the first meeting of the trustee and debtor, the trustee outlines the nature of the services offered. The trustee also begins assessing the **estate** and prepares a preliminary statement of assets and obligations. Often, this assessment calls for an untangling of business from personal affairs. In HT's case, the pending bankruptcy is that of Hometown Hardware Ltd., since it owns the business and assets, although it is possible that Bill and Martha may also become bankrupt.

Following consultation with Bill, the trustee will prepare a statement such as the one shown in Figure 27.1.

FIGURE 27.1

Preliminary Statement of Assets and Liabilities for Hometown Hardware Ltd.

Assets* at estimated cash value

Cash	$ 1 000
Accounts receivable	11 000
Inventory of plumbing supplies	27 000
Land and Building	105 000
Equipment	30 000
	$ 174 000

Liabilities

Unremitted payroll deductions (due to Canada Revenue Agency)	$ 24 000
Accounts payable to suppliers	87 000
Mortgage on land and building	97 000
Line of credit at bank (secured by inventory and accounts receivable)	85 000
Salaries due to employees	17 000
	$ 310 000

* Leased property is not an asset of the estate but will revert to the lessors upon default.

insolvency

The inability to meet financial obligations as they become due or having insufficient assets to meet obligations.

From this initial assessment, it is obvious that HT is **insolvent**—that is, it

- owes more than $1000, and
- is unable to meet financial obligations as they fall due, or
- has ceased paying obligations as they fall due, or
- has insufficient assets to meet obligations[2]

proposal

A contractual agreement between the debtor and creditors that allows an insolvent debtor to reorganize and continue in business.

If Bill wants to keep the business going, he should make a **proposal** to his creditors.

Proposals are contractual arrangements for the payment of debts between the debtor and creditors that allow the business to continue. With a proposal, the business is allowed some breathing room to reorganize. If successful, the debtor will benefit and creditors will receive a greater portion of their debts than they would if the business ceased. An alternative to a proposal is an arrangement under the *Companies' Creditors Arrangement Act*[3] (*CCAA*) which is used for corporations that have debts over $5 million and have considerable impact on the broader business community. Both procedures enable the debtor to seek bankruptcy protection while the proposal is under development. This prevents creditors from pursuing their normal legal remedies during the reorganization period.

---

2. *Ibid.* s. 2(1).
3. R.S.C. 1985, c. C-36.

While the goal of a proposal is to allow the business to continue, this can occur only if recovery is feasible and creditors agree to such an arrangement. A proposal is designed to achieve three purposes:

- to reduce the amount to be paid to creditors while the debtor retains assets to carry on business
- to extend the time for payment of claims
- to arrange for the trustee to control assets for the benefit of the creditors for the period of the proposal

Because of the risk of proposals being used as delaying tactics, they operate under rigid time lines. The proposals are contracts between debtor and creditors, and, as such, there is a wide variety of forms they might take, provided certain basic obligations are met—for example, employees are paid as they would be under bankruptcy. For approval purposes, creditors are divided into classes with common interests. Within each class, a majority of creditors who hold two-thirds of the debt in that class must approve the proposal. If any class does not approve, there is a deemed **assignment in bankruptcy** by the debtor. If the proposal is approved by creditors, it must then be approved by the court. The business will continue to function in accordance with the terms of the proposal and under the supervision of the trustee. All creditors, including those who voted against the terms of the proposal, are bound. New debts are not covered by the proposal and typically must be paid in full. Any default on the proposal terms can lead to bankruptcy.

assignment in bankruptcy
The debtor's voluntary assignment to the trustee in bankruptcy of legal title to the debtor's property for the benefit of creditors.

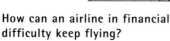

How can an airline in financial difficulty keep flying?

In recent years, there have been many high-profile cases where corporations have sought protection from their creditors and an opportunity to re-organize the business to ensure its long term survival. These attempted re-organizations proceed quite differently in terms of duration, the interests of stakeholders, and degree of success. What follows are brief accounts of three Canadian companies, all of whom applied for protection under the CCAA.

Air Canada applied for protection on 1 April 2003, and successfully emerged on 30 September 2004, when its re-organization plan received almost unanimous approval by creditors. Total debts were $13 billion at the time of filing. The plan provided creditors with 7.6–10.5 percent of their claims (depending on their priority) paid with shares in the re-organized company. There was considerable strife during the 18 months involving unions, lessors of airplanes, key suppliers, and new investors. The plan provided for a drastically reduced cost structure and a shifting of focus to international air routes. Air Canada continued normal operations throughout the re-organization period.

Jetsgo was a much smaller Canadian airline. On 11 March 2005, Jetsgo ceased operations without warning. As a result, 29 planes were grounded, 17 000 passengers were stranded in airports, 1200 employees lost their jobs, and the company left outstanding debts of $108 million. Jetsgo initially received protection from creditors for 30 days. This was extended for a further 30 days, during which the owner submitted a plan to revive the airline as a summer charter service with eight leased planes. One key creditor with effective veto over any re-organization plan effectively scuttled it. There were also safety and regulatory concerns. The company voluntarily filed for bankruptcy on 13 May 2005.

Stelco is a steel maker based in Hamilton, Ontario. The company lost $500 million in 2003 and sought protection in January 2004, owing a total of $660 million. Over the next two years, the price of steel fluctuated, initially producing a significant profit and igniting several takeover attempts. There were protracted and difficult negotiations and conflict with bondholders, unions, two levels of government, and financiers. There was litigation regarding membership on the board of directors. A key issue was a large unfunded pension liability. Agreement by government to extend the period for funding this deficit was key to the re-organization. The plan involved splitting the company into nine separate business units. It was approved by creditors holding 78 percent of the debt. They received new debt plus cash or shares in the restructured company.

CRITICAL ANALYSIS: How would you judge the bankruptcy protection process from these three examples? Are the interests of stakeholders, including the public, adequately protected?

Sources: Paul Veiira, "Creditors Give Strong Backing to 'New' Air Canada" *Financial Post* (18 August 2004) at FP1; Brent Jang, "Jetsgo Packs Its Bags; Scraps Comeback" *The Globe and Mail* (14 May 2005) at B5; and Beth Marlin, "Reconstructing the Stelco Restructuring" *Law Times* (5 December 2005) at 9.

Bankruptcy

If the proposal option does not work, HT can attempt to carry on, cease business, or make an assignment in bankruptcy, which means that the debtor voluntarily assigns "all his property for the general benefit of his creditors"[4] to the trustee in bankruptcy. The assignment transfers all legal responsibility for assets and liabilities from the debtor to the appointed trustee. The debtor now is **bankrupt,** which is a distinct legal status from the financial difficulty of insolvency. The bankruptcy process is discussed in detail after a review of creditors' options.

bankrupt
The legal status that results when an assignment in bankruptcy is made or a receiving order is issued (also used to describe a debtor who is bankrupt).

Creditor Options

A creditor whose payments from HT are overdue has several options. The creditor should first try to determine the extent of HT's financial health—is this a temporary lapse or an indication of serious difficulty? Are other creditors owed substantial amounts as well? This information will help the creditor decide whether to continue doing business with HT and create additional debt or to cease trading and focus on recovering what is already owed. There is a difficult tradeoff between taking legal action before HT has a chance to recover and letting matters go on too long.

4. *Supra* note 1, s. 49(1).

A supplier can exert pressure on HT: "pay us now or we'll stop supplying and sue you." This was the threat made by Good Lumber. A lender such as a bank can threaten to enforce its legal rights such as calling a demand loan. Creditors can engage in negotiations on their own or with other creditors to alter payment terms with the object of allowing HT some breathing space, while obtaining firm commitments from HT. These negotiations may also be initiated by HT and take the form of a formal proposal. Each creditor must then decide whether the proposed arrangement is likely to produce greater recovery of debts in the long run than exercising legal remedies.

Creditors may take formal action:

- any creditor can sue based on its debt
- a secured creditor can take private action against specific assets
- creditors may petition the debtor into bankruptcy

Action Taken by Secured Creditors against Specific Assets

This is the most common action taken by secured creditors (see Chapter 26), since what happens to the balance of the estate is of no concern to them, unless the value of their security does not cover money owed. The secured creditor is essentially enforcing the terms of the credit agreement.

The contract may entitle the creditor to appoint a receiver for the purpose of seizing the assets and paying the debt. The receiver owes a fiduciary obligation not only to the secured creditor but also to all others with an interest in the insolvent's estate to make reasonable efforts to get the best price when selling the debtor's assets.

Petitioning the Debtor into Bankruptcy

If other options fail or a creditor decides that HT's situation is hopeless, one or more creditors can petition HT into bankruptcy by meeting the conditions required by legislation. Creditors initiate action by filing a **petition,** which is a statement of what is owed and to whom. In order for the creditors' action to proceed, the debtor must owe at least $1000 and have committed an **act of bankruptcy.**[5]

petition
The statement filed by the creditor(s) claiming that the debtor owes at least $1000, has committed an act of bankruptcy, and should therefore be declared bankrupt.

act of bankruptcy
One of specified acts that the debtor must commit before creditors can petition the debtor into bankruptcy.

FIGURE 27.2

Acts of Bankruptcy

A debtor who does one of the following commits an act of bankruptcy:

✓ makes an assignment to the trustee

✓ makes a fraudulent transfer of property of any kind

✓ makes a fraudulent preference

✓ tries physically to avoid creditors, for example, by leaving Canada or moving to another location and failing to notify creditors

✓ permits the sheriff to execute an order against (seize) property when there is insufficient value in the property to pay the debt

✓ advises creditors that she is insolvent or cannot pay any debts

✓ attempts to deceive creditors by disposing of property in any way

✓ advises creditors that he has suspended payment on debts

✓ defaults on an approved proposal

✓ stops meeting liabilities as they fall due

5. *Supra* note 1, s. 43(1).

receiving order

The court order following a creditor's petition that formally declares the debtor to be bankrupt and transfers legal control of the estate to the trustee.

Creditors of the HT estate will have no difficulty meeting these formal requirements. Bill and HT have likely engaged in several of the activities listed above, and the company owes more than $1000.

The petition is filed in the bankruptcy court and, if approved, the court issues a **receiving order.** This is the equivalent of the assignment in bankruptcy. The debtor becomes bankrupt, and responsibility for the estate is taken out of the hands of the debtor and given to a trustee. The steps that follow are the same whether bankruptcy has occurred through an assignment by the debtor or a petition by the creditors.

B Business and Legislation — Origins and Purposes of Bankruptcy Legislation

The most famous observer of the miseries of insolvency was Charles Dickens. In the early 19th century, debtors' prisons still existed in most countries. The dubious logic of imprisoning a person for failing to pay creditors was not lost on Dickens, whose own father was imprisoned in the Marshalsea Prison when Charles was 12.

Dickens's writings made a powerful impact on the reading public throughout the English-speaking world. The desperate plight of the debtor was, however, only one concern. In Dickens's novels, not all creditors were sleazy and undeserving. For every miserable debtor there are several equally miserable and worthy creditors who may themselves be pushed into insolvency by this failure to pay. Moreover, some debtors may have less than honourable intentions, and even the honest may be inclined to favour one creditor over another when money gets tight.

Largely as a result of Dickens's writings, bankruptcy legislation was introduced in England and elsewhere. The purposes of the legislation are confirmed in the Canadian version:

- to provide a means for honest but unfortunate debtors to get beyond their insolvent position and be free from debts

- to establish priorities between creditors

- to impose punishment in the case of debtors who commit bankruptcy offences

A fourth purpose arises from the commercial environment:

- to ensure, if possible, that potentially viable businesses are reorganized so they can continue operating for the benefit of creditors

Marshalsea Prison, the debtors' prison where Dickens's father was incarcerated.

Bankruptcy

Administration of Bankruptcy

The administrative structure and rules for dealing with bankrupt estates are found in the *Bankruptcy and Insolvency Act.*[6]

The *Bankruptcy and Insolvency Act* is federal legislation that falls within the mandate of Industry Canada. As federal legislation, it provides a uniform set of rules across the country. The administrative process resembles a pyramid, with the superintendent

---

6. *Supra* note 1, s. 43(1).

of bankruptcy having overriding supervisory authority. The country is divided into manageable-sized units or bankruptcy districts, with at least one official receiver in each district. This administrative official is legally responsible for all aspects of the bankrupt's estate upon the making of the bankruptcy order. The official receiver transfers responsibility for the administration of the estate to the trustee.

The trustee must be licensed by the superintendent of bankruptcy in order to practise. The professional body to which most trustees belong is the Chartered Insolvency Practitioners Association (CIPA). A certified insolvency practitioner (member of CIPA) must hold a CA, CGA, or CMA designation or be employed by a corporate trustee (generally a part or an affiliate of a public accounting practice). Candidates for CIP take a three-year course culminating in rigorous written and oral qualifying exams. Trustees must comply with the Code of Conduct as set out in the *Bankruptcy and Insolvency General Rules*.[7]

Insolvency practitioners are more than trustess and liquidators. They need to be knowledgeable in business and know how to assist insolvent debtors to preserve their businesses. The practice requires people who cope well with risk and uncertainty, are organized and good managers, and operate well under pressure. They must enjoy negotiations and being in the midst of controversy since insolvency, by definition, involves a scarcity of assets with competing interests to be resolved. Most major assignments involve many other disciplines such as tax, mergers and acquisitions consulting, and operations consulting. Cross-border issues are common and are usually substantial.[8]

inspector
A person appointed by creditors to act on their behalf and supervise the actions of the trustee.

Creditors appoint **inspectors** to act on their behalf and supervise the actions of the trustee.[9] In practice, an inspector is usually an employee or officer of one of the major creditors—for example, the controller or production manager—with knowledge of the debtor and the debt. While inspectors have fiduciary obligations to all creditors, they tend to focus on the interests of the creditor with which they are associated.

Protection of Assets

Following an assignment in bankruptcy or a receiving order, the trustee gives public notice of the bankruptcy as a first step in order to identify and protect assets and to identify all liabilities. Typically, the trustee will

- change the locks on the business premises and secure storage facilities
- post notices on the doors of the business
- conduct a detailed examination of assets
- prepare the appropriate statements
- ensure that assets are adequately protected, including arranging insurance
- establish the appropriate books and accounts for handling the estate finances
- sell any perishable goods immediately

Only in exceptional circumstances does the trustee continue running the business.

Protection of assets calls for a review not only of assets existing at the time of bankruptcy, but also of what has happened to assets prior to bankruptcy. If the debtor made payments to creditors in the ordinary course of business, they will not be challenged. However, if payments were made to favour one creditor over

---

7. C.R.C., c. 368, ss. 34–53.
8. Based on comments from Bill Goss, former insolvency practitioner with Ernst & Young Inc.
9. *Supra* note 1, s. 116. The trustee must post a bond representing the estimated value of the assets in the estate. The security is almost always in the form of a bond with a guarantee company (s.16).

another, the primary purpose of the act—namely, ensuring that creditors are treated equitably and according to the priorities of the act—will have been defeated. Payments prior to bankruptcy fall within three categories: fraudulent preferences, reviewable transactions, and settlements and fraudulent conveyances.

Fraudulent Preferences: Any payment made within three months of bankruptcy that favours one creditor over others is deemed by the *Bankruptcy and Insolvency Act* to be a **fraudulent preference** and, as such, is void. The key to this provision is that the bankrupt has been preferring, or favouring, one or more creditors to the detriment of the others. Not all creditors have been treated fairly, and therefore the trustee can insist (through court order if necessary) that the transaction be reversed and the assets returned to the estate. In evaluating whether there was intention to prefer, it is irrelevant that Bill acted with good intentions in paying GL while other suppliers were not paid. If, however, the payment was made in the ordinary course of business, or if the debtor genuinely believed that making this payment would allow the business to continue, it may be allowed to stand.

In the HT example, the payment to GL was made within three months of bankruptcy and likely after the corporation became insolvent. HT gave GL priority over other creditors. The payment was a fraudulent preference, and GL will need to repay the money and join other unsecured creditors to claim its debt. Provided the salaries paid to Bill and Martha were genuine payments for services given, they will not be categorized as fraudulent preferences and will not be recoverable. The payments to trade creditors in the relevant period were likely made in the normal course of business and, as such, would not be subject to challenge.

Reviewable Transactions: Debtors in financial trouble are often tempted to repay close relatives before other creditors. Such action defeats the purpose of bankruptcy. A **reviewable transaction** is a payment made to a person related to the bankrupt within one year of the bankruptcy order and with the intention of giving this person priority over at least one other creditor. If the bankrupt is a corporation, a related person is any person who is a blood relative (or relative by marriage or adoption) of a person with a controlling interest in the corporation. In the HT case, George's blood relationship with Bill makes him a related person. Since payment to George was within the year preceding bankruptcy and was intended to give him priority over other creditors, provided the business was insolvent at the time, the payment will be recoverable and George, like GL, will become an unsecured creditor.

Settlements and Fraudulent Conveyances: These transactions are between the debtor and someone who is not a creditor. Perhaps Bill, recognizing the predicament of the business, transferred valuable assets to his children for $1 six months before the bankruptcy. Such an action violates the intent of the *Bankruptcy and Insolvency Act*. It is categorized as a **settlement** under the act, and the transfer is void if it was within one year of the bankruptcy or within five years of the bankruptcy and it can be shown that the debtor at that time was unable to pay his debts without the relevant property.

The most important exception to this provision is if the transfer was made in good faith and for valuable consideration. The transfer of assets by Bill to his family for $1 would undoubtedly be a settlement and therefore void. Provincial fraudulent conveyances acts complement the federal legislation and affect conveyances of real or personal property made with the intent to defeat, hinder, delay, or defraud

fraudulent preference
A payment made by an insolvent debtor within three months of bankruptcy with a view to favouring one creditor over others.

reviewable transaction
A payment made to a person related to the bankrupt within one year of the bankruptcy order with the intention of giving the related person priority over at least one other creditor.

settlement
A sale that can be declared void because it was not made in good faith or for valuable consideration.

creditors.[10] If the transfer was for valuable consideration, it is necessary to prove fraud on the part of both parties in order to void it. If the transfer was not for good consideration, it is necessary only to show fraud on the part of the debtor making the transfer. The sale by HT of its adjacent piece of land will be examined as being a possible settlement. However, if the vendor and purchaser can show good faith and prove that the sale was for valuable consideration (a reasonable price), the transaction will not be void as a fraudulent conveyance.

International Perspective — International Insolvencies

In 1997 the *Bankruptcy and Insolvency Act* was amended to introduce Part XIII, dealing with international insolvencies. Generally, these provisions address two questions: What happens when a Canadian bankrupt has assets in a foreign jurisdiction? And what happens when a foreign creditor wishes to seize assets that are located in Canada pursuant to a foreign order? There are a number of important public interests at stake. Given the importance of international trade to the Canadian economy, it is critical that participants both in Canada and abroad feel confident that the bankruptcy laws of all countries will be respected and, in the event of a bankruptcy order being made, that assets will be accessible, wherever they are located. Furthermore, it would be offensive if a Canadian bankrupt could shield assets from Canadian creditors by ensuring that they are located outside the jurisdiction. It is also important that only foreign orders that generally equate to similar provisions in Canadian law be capable of execution in Canada.

Sections 267–275 of the *Bankruptcy and Insolvency Act* provide for these concerns. Generally, a foreign creditor can gain access to a debtor's assets located in Canada pursuant to a foreign order. Furthermore, Canadian creditors can gain access to assets located outside the jurisdiction. Section 18.6 of the CCAA also provides for recognition of foreign insolvency proceedings. Note, however, that such actions are also subject to international treaties. Should a Canadian bankrupt have assets in a foreign country where reciprocity does not exist, and should that same bankrupt choose to relocate to that country, Canadian creditors will likely have no chance of recovery.

Canadian insolvency law is undergoing major review and revision. Bill C-55[11] has received legislative approval, but may be subject to change before proclamation into law. The bill would repeal current insolvency provisions of both the BIA and CCAA and replace them with a modified version of the *UNCITRAL Model Law on Cross-Border Insolvency*. This incorporation would provide a complete code for the recognition of foreign insolvency proceedings, in line with international standards.

CRITICAL ANALYSIS: In practice, to what extent might these provisions be avoided by debtors who are determined to keep their assets from bankruptcy authorities?

Identification of Debts

proof of claim
A formal notice provided by the creditor to the trustee of the amount owed and the nature of the debt.

Creditors find out about the bankruptcy through formal notice. Details are provided at the first meeting of creditors, held usually at the office of the official receiver for business bankruptcies or at the office of the trustee for personal bankruptcies.

Each creditor must file a **proof of claim** as formal notice of the amount owed. Filing this document entitles the creditor to participate in the creditors' meetings through voting and, ultimately, to receive a proportion of whatever money is

---

10. *Fraudulent Conveyances Act*, R.S.O. 1990, c. F-29, s. 2.
11. Received Royal Assent 28 November 2005; (to be proclaimed).

available for distribution. The trustee examines each proof of claim or security, and either accepts or rejects the validity of the claim. The trustee rejects security and priority of payment if there is inadequate evidence either of the debt itself or of its secured status.

Some claimants have superior status. Canada Revenue Agency (CRA) is in a unique position in the case of unremitted payroll deductions. These debts are considered not to be part of the estate and as such will be payable ahead of all creditors, including those who are secured.[12] Suppliers are given special protection under the act. They are allowed to recover any goods shipped in the past 30 days, provided the debtor is now bankrupt and the goods are in the same condition as when shipped.[13]

Distribution to Creditors

The trustee must establish priorities for payment according to the three broad categories of creditors: secured, preferred, and unsecured. The implications of creditors being secured and unsecured were described in Chapter 26. Secured creditors have a security interest in particular assets. In the HT estate, the bank holding the mortgage and the line of credit is a secured creditor. The bank also holds personal guarantees from Bill and Martha, and it is these guarantees that may push them into personal bankruptcy.

preferred creditors
Certain unsecured creditors who are given priority over the other unsecured creditors in the legislation.

Preferred creditors exhibit characteristics both of the secured and unsecured creditors. They are paid after secured creditors and before unsecured creditors and in strict order of priority, as set out in section 136 of the *Bankruptcy and Insolvency Act*. Those on the list of preferred creditors reflect the value that society has placed on the debts incurred. Included are

- funeral expenses
- trustee fees and expenses
- wages (limited to $2000 for each employee over the previous six months)[14]
- municipal taxes
- arrears of rent

Preferred creditors are paid a reasonable amount for the services they have provided according to their order of priority, if the money is available. HT has at least two preferred creditors: the trustee and the unpaid employees.

Unsecured creditors have no claim to specific assets. They share proportionately the assets that remain after secured creditors have seized those to which they are entitled and preferred creditors have been paid. HT has several unsecured creditors—suppliers, the bank (if secured assets are worth less than the outstanding debt), and employees. In addition, if the trustee recovers the payments made to GL and George, they become unsecured creditors. Each will receive the same portion of outstanding debt. For example, in the final distribution of HT assets, suppliers are owed $80 000 (see Figure 27.3). The amount available on distribution for unsecured creditors is 18.129 cents on the dollar (total remaining assets over total unsecured debts). Thus, suppliers will receive in total $80 000 × 0.18129 = $14 503 (see Figure 27.4).

---

12. The provision for source deductions is somewhat complex. The *Bankruptcy and Insolvency Act* recognizes "trusts" as exempt property (s. 67). Source deductions fall within this definition by s. 227 of the *Income Tax Act*, R.S.C. 1985, c. 1 (5th Supp.) and the equivalent provincial legislation. As exempt property, they are not considered part of the estate and are payable immediately to Canada Revenue Agency.
13. *Supra* note 1, s. 81.1.
14. Bill C-55, *supra* note 11, would create the Wage Earner Protection Program, a new type of super priority allowing employees to be paid from a government fund that would then have a subrogated claim against the estate.

FIGURE 27.3

Revised Statement of Assets and Liabilities for Hometown Hardware Ltd.

Assets at estimated cash value	
Cash	$ 31 000*
Accounts receivable	11 000
Inventory	20 000**
Land and building	105 000
Equipment	30 000
Cash available for distribution	$197 000

Liabilities at estimated cash value	
CRA payroll deductions	$ 24 000
Mortgage on land and building	97 000
Trustee's fees and expenses	4 000
Preferred part of salaries due	10 000***
Accounts payable to suppliers	80 000
Salaries due to employees	7 000
Amounts owed GL	20 000
Amounts owed George	10 000
Line of credit at bank	85 000****
	$337 000

* Includes original balance ($1000) plus monies recovered from George and GL ($10 000 + $20 000).

** Portion ($7000) of original was taken back by suppliers (reducing accounts payable from $87 000 to $80 000).

*** Five employees were owed a total of $17 000. Each employee has a preferred claim of $2000, while the remainder of $7000 is unsecured.

**** Since Bill and Martha Ikeda have provided personal guarantees for the line of credit, they will be personally liable for any outstanding balance, after distribution.

FIGURE 27.4

Final Distribution of Assets of Hometown Hardware Ltd. by Class of Creditor

Schedule 1: Distribution of cash to secured and preferred creditors

Opening balance available	$197 000
Pay CRA the payroll deductions	24 000
	173 000
Secured creditors	
Pay mortgage on land and building	97 000
Pay bank from inventory and accounts receivable	31 000
	$ 45 000
Preferred creditors	
Trustee's fees and expenses	$ 4 000
Pay preferred part of salaries due	10 000
Balance available for unsecured creditors	$ 31 000

Schedule 2: Distribution of cash to unsecured creditors

Balance available for unsecured creditors	$ 31 000
Balance due to unsecured creditors:	
Accounts payable to suppliers	80 000
Salaries due to employees	7 000
Amounts owed George	10 000
Amounts owed GL	20 000
Line of credit at bank	54 000
	$171 000

Proportion of amount to be paid per dollar of unsecured debt: $31\,000/171\,000 = .18129$

Payments to unsecured creditors (rounded)	
Accounts payable to suppliers	$ 14 503
Salaries due to employees	1269
Payment to George	1813
Payment to GL	3626
Line of credit at bank	9 789
Total payments to unsecured creditors	$ 31 000
Balance	0

Bill and Martha Ikeda personally owe the bank the unpaid balance of the line of credit since they have guaranteed the debt: ($85 000 – (31 000 + 9789) = $44 211).

Discharge

discharge of bankruptcy
The formal order releasing the debtor from bankrupt status and from most remaining debts.

The **discharge of bankruptcy** formally releases the honest but unfortunate debtor from most remaining liabilities. While the discharge is not a right, it comes automatically for first-time individual bankrupts nine months following the commencement of bankruptcy, provided it is not opposed by the superintendent, trustee, or creditors. Bill and Martha may benefit from this process. A discharge is not available to a corporation (such as HT), unless debts have been paid in full.

The discharge will be opposed, for example, if a bankruptcy offence has been committed (see below), where there is evidence of extravagance prior to the bankruptcy, or where the unsecured creditors will receive less than 50 cents on each dollar owed. In the HT case, there will be no discharge of the corporation, since its debts cannot be paid in full.

Personal Bankruptcy

Personal bankruptcies affect businesses mainly in the sense that they will be unable to collect money owed to them by bankrupt individuals. Otherwise, a personal bankruptcy may arise in situations where the "owner" of the business—whether a sole proprietor, partner, or director/officer of a corporation—has been obliged to provide a personal guarantee or cosign for debts of that business and has insufficient assets to meet the obligation. Bill and Martha have personally guaranteed the line of credit for the business, and may have insufficient personal assets to pay the bank the amount owing after the distribution of HT's assets.

The legislation provides a streamlined process for small consumer estates. For example, any estate with debts (other than those secured by the family residence) under $75 000 may fall within the provisions for Consumer Proposals.[15] This approach is becoming popular and effective to prevent personal bankruptcy while providing payments to creditors. Likewise, in certain provinces[16] there is provision for "orderly payment of debts." In all other situations, the general bankruptcy provisions of the act apply up to and including discharge. In all of these processes, debtors are entitled to retain sufficient assets to support themselves and their families. There are a number of statutes containing exemptions with respect to the seizing of assets to satisfy court orders. For example, all provinces have the equivalent of Ontario's

---

15. *Supra* note 1, ss. 66.11–66.4.
16. *Supra* note 1, s. 217 (Manitoba and Alberta); *Bankruptcy and Insolvency General Rules*, C.R.C. 1978, c. 368, ss. 34–53 (British Columbia, Saskatchewan, Northwest Territories, Nova Scotia, and Prince Edward Island).

Execution Act, which provides exemptions for items such as tools of the trade up to $2000, necessary wearing apparel up to $1000, and household furniture and utensils up to $2000.[17]

Not all liabilities are released by the discharge. Fines, penalties, alimony or support payments, and student loans are among the liabilities that survive the discharge. These exemptions serve the public interest. Allowing a debtor to avoid liability for debts arising, for example, out of fraudulent acts by declaring bankruptcy and subsequently receiving a discharge would defeat the purpose of the original penalty. However, the provision that bars graduates from being discharged from their student loans for ten years after graduation is controversial.

Bankruptcy Offences

bankruptcy offences
Criminal acts defined by the *Bankruptcy and Insolvency Act* and committed by a participant in the bankruptcy and insolvency process.

For the *Bankruptcy and Insolvency Act* to be respected, it must also provide penalties for those who violate its provisions. These violations are known as **bankruptcy offences.** They are criminal acts and can be committed by any of the key participants, including debtors, creditors, and trustees.

To ensure that the bankrupt knows what she can and cannot do, the trustee is obliged to give specific notice of what constitutes an offence. In general, offences occur if bankrupts are not truthful in any declaration made or if they attempt to dispose of property or otherwise defeat the purposes of the act. For example, if Bill acted fraudulently when disposing of the land before bankruptcy, a bankruptcy offence has been committed.

Creditors commit bankruptcy offences if they, for example, make false claims. Inspectors commit offences if they accept payments over and above their entitlement provided for in the act. Finally, trustees may commit offences by violating specific duties established in the legislation or acting in a conflict of interest.

The following case deals with business and personal bankruptcy, discharge, and the examination of the debtors' affairs.

CASE ▼

Bankruptcies of Southwick-Trask and Trask, 2003 NSSC 160

THE BUSINESS CONTEXT: Personal bankruptcy of those involved in a business can follow the insolvency of that business. The individuals are eligible for discharge of the unpaid debts at the end of the process, but the discharge may be conditional. Those conditions can be a matter of dispute between the individuals, creditors, and trustee.

FACTUAL BACKGROUND: Trask (T) was president, CEO, director and shareholder of RDI Group, a company that operated call centres in Halifax for 15 years and employed up to 150 people. Southwick-Trask (ST) was married to T. She was a director of RDI and operated her own business in strategic management consulting. In 2001, a large account receivable of RDI fell past due and had to be written off. This resulted in the insolvency of RDI. At the time, RDI owed TD Bank $525 000 on a revolving line of credit secured by accounts receivable and guaranteed by T and ST. They attempted to negotiate a settlement with the bank and presented a proposal, but the attempts were unsuccessful. The bank petitioned both T and ST into bankruptcy. At the time, their total debt was in excess of $2 million, of which $573 000 was owed to the bank. The trustee recommended they be discharged, subject to

---

17. R.S.O. 1990, c. E-24, s. 2.

payments of \$18 000 by T and \$36 000 by ST. T and ST disputed the amount of these payments.

THE LEGAL QUESTION: Are S and ST eligible for discharge from bankruptcy and, if so, on what terms?

RESOLUTION: The judge found that the bankruptcies of S and ST resulted from misfortune in business. He reviewed general principles:

> The act permits an honest debtor, who has been unfortunate in business to secure a discharge so that he or she can make a fresh start and resume his or her place in the business community. The conditional discharge, which is most frequently a result of proving that the value of assets was less than half the liabilities, may also address the purpose of fair distribution. Aside from cases where the conduct of the bankrupt has been reprehensible, setting a condition for discharge requires a balance of

rehabilitating the bankrupt and providing the creditors with some dividend.

The judge went on to consider specific factors—RRSPs held by the couple, transfers of their residence and cottage to a family trust, debts for income tax, T's earning capacity, ST's drawings from her business, and household expenses.

Based on the cause of the bankruptcies (misfortune in business), the significant value of assets in the estate, and the absence of any misconduct, the judge ordered that T be discharged without condition and that ST be discharged subject to the payment of \$750 per month for 24 months or an equivalent lump-sum payment.

CRITICAL ANALYSIS: Does this case preserve the integrity of the bankruptcy regime? Did the court adequately balance the interests of the debtor, creditors, and the public?

Managing Legal Risks in Financing a Business

There are significant legal risks in all aspects of financing a business. In banking, there is the formality of the relationship with the bank—based mainly on complex agreements written to favour the bank's rights over those of the customer. There is the complex set of rules governing paper-based negotiable instruments, but a much less predictable legal regime governing electronic transactions.

In credit arrangements, there is the practical necessity of granting lenders the terms and conditions that they require in order to accept the risk of lending money to a business. Lenders manage their risks through collateral and agreements that give them often overwhelming control of the borrower's assets and business affairs. Personal guarantees expose individuals to considerable risk arising from the business whose obligations they guarantee.

Insolvency law creates a key risk that those operating a business may carry on beyond the point of insolvency and expose themselves to findings of acts of bankruptcy, reviewable transactions, preferences, and even bankruptcy offences.

Most of these risks cannot be avoided in the operation of a business. They can be reduced and perhaps transferred through careful review of financing contracts and expert advice. Such actions will create valuable awareness of the consequences of their business decisions on the part of those who are subject to such contracts.

Business Law in Practice Revisited

1. What choices does HT have in dealing with this financial crisis?

HT has several options that may be affected by how its creditors choose to exercise their options. The company can seek a voluntary negotiated settlement with creditors in order to continue the business or bring it to an end. It can seek bankruptcy protection and make a proposal to creditors that would allow the business to continue under conditions that meet both creditors' and debtors' needs and wishes. The last resort is to make an assignment in bankruptcy.

2. What rights do HT's creditors have?

Creditors can exert pressure on HT in an attempt to be paid what they are owed. They can exercise their contractual rights by calling loans and seizing any security they have for their debts. They can take action to recover the amount owed and refuse to do further business with HT. Creditors can also engage in negotiations with HT that might result in a successful proposal. Ultimately, creditors can petition HT into bankruptcy by meeting the fairly minimal requirements.

3. What will happen to HT, its creditors, its owners, Bill, and Martha if bankruptcy occurs?

The court order that creates the bankruptcy will transfer control of all of HT's assets to the trustee, whose function is to protect those assets and gather in any others that may have been lost through reviewable transactions. The trustee then distributes the proceeds to secured, preferred, and unsecured creditors according to their legislative and contractual priorities. Any unpaid debts that Bill and Martha have guaranteed will become their personal responsibility and may result in their personal bankruptcies. Corporations are never discharged from their unpaid debts, but individuals such as Bill and Martha may be discharged if their conduct meets the requirements.

Chapter Summary

The provisions of the *Bankruptcy and Insolvency Act* and related legislation are complex and arise generally under circumstances of great business and personal turmoil. The role of skilled experts with ethical obligations is critical to the fair distribution of assets. Even with the best of motives, debtors like HT (through Bill) may treat the rights of creditors in an arbitrary and unfair manner. The provisions of the act provide for certainty and equity.

The key feature of the law providing for business failure is that the owners of the business have two alternatives: they can have the business continue in a reorganized fashion, or they can bring it to an end. In either case, the law provides the process for ensuring that the rights and obligations of both creditors and debtor are met. Furthermore, while understanding the basic steps in the process is important, in practice specialized professionals will provide the appropriate guidance.

When there are secured assets, the most common consequence of a failure to pay a debt as it falls due is the secured creditor enforcing the credit agreement directly.

If a debtor's position is indeed hopeless, there is little point in spending good money attempting to recover what is not there. In practice, creditors usually resort to the proceedings provided for under the *Bankruptcy and Insolvency Act* only when they are seeking to reverse priorities or defeat other claims. Otherwise, the most they might do is participate if someone else bears the cost of initiating the process. Likewise, for businesses organized in the corporate form, under which there is no personal liability for the "owners" other than the loss of investment in the corporation, owners simply abandon the corporation. Secured creditors will take the assets in which they hold a security interest. For other creditors, there is generally little left over. When bankruptcy does occur, the legislation provides a comprehensive framework for all participants.

Chapter Study

Key Terms and Concepts

act of bankruptcy (p. 669)

assignment in bankruptcy (p. 667)

bankrupt (p. 668)

bankruptcy offences (p. 677)

discharge of bankruptcy (p. 676)

estate (p. 666)

fraudulent preference (p. 672)

insolvency (p. 666)

inspector (p. 671)

petition (p. 669)

preferred creditors (p. 674)

proof of claim (p. 673)

proposal (p. 666)

receiving order (p. 670)

reviewable transaction (p. 672)

settlement (p. 672)

trustee in bankruptcy (p. 665)

Questions for Review

1. How can negotiated settlements be used when a business is in financial difficulty?

2. What is the difference between insolvency and bankruptcy?

3. What are the purposes of bankruptcy legislation?

4. What is the difference between an assignment in bankruptcy and a petition into bankruptcy?

5. What are two examples of an act of bankruptcy?

6. What is a fraudulent preference?

7. Who investigates preferences and reviewable transactions?

8. What are two key purposes of the initial meeting of creditors?

9. Who are preferred creditors?

10. How are preferred creditors treated differently from secured and unsecured creditors?

11. How are employees protected in the bankruptcy of their employer?

12. Under what circumstances will a bankrupt likely not be discharged automatically from bankruptcy?

13. What is a conditional discharge?

14. What debts are not released in a discharge?

15. What is the purpose of a proposal?

16. When might a proposal not be approved by the court?

17. What happens if unsecured creditors do not vote to approve a proposal?

18. What is one bankruptcy offence that may be committed by a debtor?

Questions for Critical Thinking

1. Business decisions made prior to bankruptcy can be challenged by the trustee if they are found to be fraudulent preferences, reviewable transactions, or settlements. What is the rationale for giving the trustee this authority? How does it relate to the purposes of bankruptcy legislation?

2. Current bankruptcy law bars graduates from being discharged from their outstanding student loans for ten years after the completion of their studies. This ten-year prohibition is being challenged as unfair differential treatment of a specific source of debt that prevents an individual's personal circumstances and conduct from being considered in bankruptcy decisions. Defenders of the prohibition maintain that it is designed to protect the integrity of the student loan system and prevent easy abandonment of such obligations. Should the period of ten years be shortened? Should the ban be completely removed?

3. A debtor who is in financial difficulty has a number of options ranging from informal negotiations to bankruptcy. What factors should the debtor consider in developing a strategy to deal with financial difficulty?

4. Proposals are an important part of the bankruptcy and insolvency legislation. However, despite the controls that exist, they can have the effect of delaying legal actions by creditors to protect their interests. Does the potential benefit of proposals in salvaging troubled businesses outweigh the potential losses to creditors?

5. The category of preferred creditors is not found in the bankruptcy legislation of many countries. Canadian law provides specific but limited protection for those in this category. What is the rationale for this protection? Is it worth the deprivation caused to those creditors who are not preferred?

6. Recent bankruptcies in the news have involved senior executives receiving large salary increases and benefits such as stock options during the period of their corporation's financial decline. Should the creditors (through the trustee) be able to recover such amounts for the estate? Does current law facilitate such recovery?

Situations for Discussion

1. Before creditors can petition a debtor into bankruptcy, they must be able to show that at least one of the ten acts of bankruptcy has been committed by the debtor. Review the events in the HT situation and identify any possible acts of bankruptcy. Do the ten types have a common theme? Should it be obvious to a debtor such as HT that such conduct is inadvisable? When the debtor has committed an act of bankruptcy, at what point should the creditors act upon it?

2. Ontario Realty (OR) is a major property developer based in Toronto. It is in the business of building office towers and other commercial premises. In the past year, the Ontario economy has suffered a serious downturn and commercial properties have been particularly hard hit. OR now finds itself with several major city sites for which there is little chance of development until the economy recovers. OR's debts are now $150 million, and its assets at today's values are worth $80 million. Interest rates are slowly but steadily rising. Two banks hold security for 90 percent of the debt. The balance of the debt is unsecured. The company is unable to make regular payments on its loans.

John, the CEO of the company, has weathered this kind of crisis before. He is convinced that a recovery should begin within a year. His discussions with the two major creditors suggest that only one would be prepared to negotiate a more favourable payment scheme until the market recovers. John seeks advice from an insolvency practitioner about the pros and cons of making a proposal.

What advice is John likely to receive? What factors will the creditors consider in responding to OR's situation?

3. Designer Shirts is a supplier to Classic Stores (CS), a major national retail outlet. There are rumours that CS is in trouble, but the company has been in trouble before and has managed to recover. Industry analysts say that there is too much at stake to allow the company to fail. Furthermore, this is a troubled industry, and if all suppliers believed everything they heard about their customers, they would never make a sale.

CS has recently made an announcement about an infusion of cash from a major investor. On the basis of this news, Designer agrees to make deliveries, although it insists on a shorter payment period than normal. Designer makes the first delivery of summer stock at the end of March. It receives its payment within the specified 20 days. It then makes a second delivery, but this time payment is not forthcoming at 20 days. Based on further promises that the payment will be made "within two days," Designer makes a third shipment. Within ten days there is an announcement that CS has filed for bankruptcy protection. Designer has never received payment for either the second or third shipment and is owed $1.5 million.

What are Designer's rights and prospects? Could Designer have better managed its risk in this situation?

4. Mary is the owner-operator of an incorporated consulting practice that owns the building in which it is located. Mary lives above the offices and rents the apartment from the company. There are five employees working in the business, two of whom are her cousins. The business has a line of credit with a local bank.

The business rents office equipment and vehicles for Mary and the office manager.

Mary has developed the business successfully, but in recent years poor health has limited the number of hours she can devote to the business. She is reluctant to lay off any employees, so has switched those actively engaged in projects to a "commission" basis of payment, allowing her to keep paying the office staff. She has negotiated an extension of the payment schedule with the bank and is meeting payments. She is anxious about the building, as this remains her only security for retirement. Her lawyer has for many years been encouraging her to buy the building from the company, and finally she does this. Six months later she suffers a stroke and is unable to work. There is no income for wages, but her two cousins keep the office open for two months out of loyalty. The business is then forced into bankruptcy.

Could Mary have structured her affairs differently to have protected herself and her employees and avoided bankruptcy? What will happen to the building?

5. Kim owns a family business that is experiencing serious difficulties because of changing economic circumstances. It operates as a sole proprietorship and has borrowed from a number of sources (originally commercial, but lately from friends and family) over the last three years to keep the business afloat. There are three employees, without whose services Kim could no longer run the business. He is beginning to feel overwhelmed and needs some basic advice as to what he can and cannot do. For example, should he create a corporation and sell the business assets to that corporation? Should he consolidate his loans and pay off as many as he can now by extending his borrowing with the bank? Who should get paid first? He remembers a business acquaintance who found herself in difficulty when her business failed. Many payments she had made to relatives were reclaimed. Clearly, she had done something wrong, but what was it? Consider yourself Kim's advisor. Outline some basic guidelines he should follow.

6. The Great Big Bank has recently conducted a review of its small business loan failure rates and is concerned about the results. There is strong evidence that failures are increasing disproportionately to loans made, and that amounts recovered are decreasing. Interviews of local loans managers suggest a good deal of confusion about how to assess risk, when the bank should call a loan, and what mechanism best meets the bank's needs after the loan has been called. On the strength of this information, the bank is redesigning its basic training manual. The primary focus now is on the section entitled "The loan has gone bad. Now what do you do?" Develop guidelines that would offer practical advice and basic information for loans officers to act upon. Identify their options and the circumstances under which each might be appropriate.

7. Gaklis was the principal officer and shareholder of Christy Crops Ltd. He controlled the company and made all major decisions. The company had financial difficulty and was placed in receivership. Gaklis had guaranteed substantial debts of the company and was unable to respond to demands for payment. He was petitioned into bankruptcy and eventually applied for discharge. The trustee and the creditors opposed his application based on his conduct: Gaklis had disposed of land belonging to the company. He had given a security interest for $60 000 on an airplane and transferred ownership to his father. He failed to cooperate with the trustee by refusing to disclose particulars of bank accounts and insurance policies.[18]

Should Gaklis be discharged from bankruptcy and released from his unpaid debts?

8. Gregor Grant was the president and sole shareholder of Grant's Contracting Ltd. The company was petitioned into bankruptcy. In the course of investigating the company's affairs in the period before the petition, the trustee discovered that a cheque received in payment from a supplier had not been deposited in the company's account, but had been diverted to another company owned by Gregor's brother, Harper. Harper had kept some of the money for himself and returned the remainder in smaller amounts to Gregor.[19] What, if anything, can the trustee do about this transaction? What could be the impact on the two companies, the two brothers, and the customer who sent the cheque?

For more study tools, visit
http://www.businesslaw3e.nelson.com

---

18. Based on *Re Gaklis* (1984), 62 N.S.R. (2d) 52 (S.C.T.D.).
19. Based on *Grant Bros. Contracting Ltd. v. Grant*, 2005 NSSC 358.

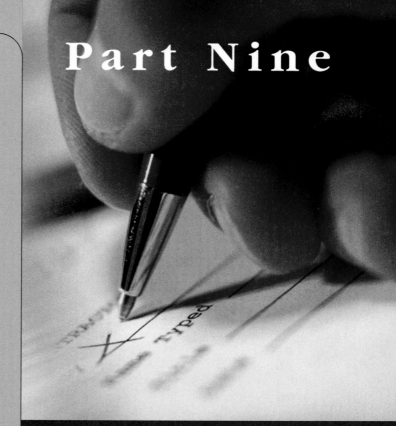

Part Nine

RISK MANAGEMENT IS THE PROCESS OF ESTABLISHING and maintaining procedures for identifying and reducing, avoiding, or retaining the consequences of risks. Throughout the preceding chapters, the focus has been on identifying legal risks and the means for minimizing them through risk reduction strategies.

This part of the text explores the transference of risk through the use of various insurance products. It explores the general principles of a contract of insurance and discusses how insurance can protect against contractual, tortious, environmental, other business, and legal risks.

Transference of Risk

Chapter 28 Insurance

Chapter

28

Objectives

After studying this chapter, you should have an understanding of

- the role of insurance in risk management
- the nature of an insurance contract, including the rights and obligations of the insurer and the insured
- the various kinds of insurance

Insurance

Business Law in Practice

Wire Experts and Company Ltd. (WEC) is a small business owned and operated by three shareholders. It is in the business of producing wires used to manufacture tires. It buys metal, formulates the alloys, extrudes the necessary wires, and then sells them to tire manufacturers both in Canada and abroad. The manufacture of the wire creates some contaminant waste products that require special storage and disposal. WEC's business office is on the first floor of its manufacturing plant. Suppliers, sales personnel, and representatives of various purchasers are frequent visitors. WEC also owns several trucks, which its delivery personnel use to deliver wires to customers.

As there are considerable risks associated with its business, WEC has purchased a full range of insurance products including comprehensive general liability, automobile, property, occupier's liability, errors and omissions, directors and officers, and business interruption.

In 2005, WEC moved its operations to Alberta to be closer to its customer base. WEC closed its manufacturing plant in New Brunswick and opened a new facility in Red Deer. Three months later, the vacant plant was destroyed by fire. WEC brought a claim under its fire insurance policy. The insurance company denied the claim on the basis that WEC failed to inform it that the plant was vacant. Furthermore, the insurance company alleged that the fire was suspicious and that perhaps WEC was involved in the plant's destruction.

1. Was WEC under a duty to disclose the plant's vacancy to the insurance company? If so, what is the effect of a failure to disclose?
2. What risk does the insurance company run by making allegations of arson?

Introduction

A cornerstone of an effective risk management program is insurance coverage. As discussed in Chapter 3, insurance is the primary means of transferring the risk of various kinds of losses. It permits a business to shift the risk, because through an **insurance policy,** the **insurer** promises to compensate the person (known as the **insured**) should the contemplated loss actually occur. The insurer provides this protection in exchange for payment, known as an insurance **premium,** from the insured.

Insurance is not, however, a panacea for all risks, as insurance can be costly and is not always available (or available only at an exorbitant cost). For example, in the wake of the scandals at Enron and WorldCom, directors' and officers' liability insurance premiums have skyrocketed; for many public companies, the premiums have tripled.[1] For some companies, this has meant that the insurance is so expensive that it is essentially unobtainable. It is also important to remember that insurance does not prevent a loss from occurring, nor does it prevent the potential adverse publicity associated with a loss.

insurance policy
A contract of insurance.

insurer
A company that sells insurance coverage.

insured
One who buys insurance coverage.

premium
The price paid for insurance coverage.

FIGURE 28.1

The Insurance Relationship

INSURER
(provides protection against a specified loss)

INSURED
(purchases protection against a specified loss)

---

1. Janet McFarland, "The Soaring Cost of a Boardroom Safety Net" *The Globe and Mail* (23 February 2006) at B12.

An insurance policy is a contract. By the terms of the contract, the parties agree to what kind of loss is covered, in what amount, under what circumstances, and at what cost. Insurance policies are also regulated by legislation in each of the provinces.

Insurance legislation serves a number of significant purposes, including the following:

- mandating the terms that must be found in insurance contracts
- regulating the insurance industry generally by setting out licensing requirements for insurance companies, insurance brokers, and insurance adjusters
- putting in place a system for monitoring insurance companies, particularly with respect to their financial operation

The main goal of insurance legislation is to protect the public from unscrupulous, financially unstable, and otherwise problematic insurance companies. It also provides working rules that create stability within the industry at large.

The three basic kinds of insurance are as follows:

- *Life and disability insurance* provides payments on the death or disability of the insured.
- *Property insurance (also known as fire insurance)* provides payment when property of the insured is damaged or destroyed through accidents. It also can cover the costs of machine breakdown.
- *Liability insurance (also known as casualty insurance)* provides payment in circumstances where the insured is held legally responsible for causing loss or damage to another, known as the third party.[2]

With the exception of life insurance contracts, insurance policies can be written so that the insured pays a **deductible.** This means that the insured is responsible for the first part of the loss, and the insurer has liability for the balance. Agreeing to a deductible generally reduces the premiums that the insured must pay for the coverage. For example, WEC agreed to a $100 deductible for windshield replacement on its delivery trucks. If a WEC vehicle windshield requires replacement and the cost is $600, WEC's insurers will pay $500. The $100 deductible is WEC's responsibility, and to that extent, WEC is self-insured.

deductible
The part of a loss for which the insured is responsible.

The Insurance Contract

Duty to Disclose

duty to disclose
The obligation of the insured to provide to the insurer all information that relates to the risk being insured.

Insurance contracts are of a special nature. They are known as contracts of utmost good faith. A key consequence is that the insured has a **duty to disclose** to the insurer all information relevant to the risk; if she fails in that duty, the insurer may choose not to honour the policy. For example, assume that WEC wants to change insurers in an effort to save on premiums. Max, one of WEC's employees, fills in an application for fire insurance. In response to the question, "Have you ever experienced a fire?" Max writes, "Yes"—in 2001. Max does not mention that WEC also had a fire in 2000, because he is convinced that WEC will end up paying an outrageously high premium. Max has failed to disclose a fact that is germane to the insurer's decision to insure, and to what the premiums should be in

---

2. The person who is injured or otherwise suffers loss is the third party in relation to the contract of insurance. In the contract of insurance, the insurer and insured are the first and second parties.

light of the risk. For this reason, if WEC tries to claim for fire loss should another fire occur at the plant, the insurer could refuse to honour the policy based on Max's nondisclosure.[3]

An insurance company can deny coverage for nondisclosure even if the loss has nothing to do with the matter that was left undisclosed. For example, since WEC has failed to disclose a previous fire loss, the insurer can deny a vandalism claim that WEC might make some time in the future.

The law places a duty of disclosure on the insured for a straightforward reason: the insurer has to be in a position to fully assess the risk against which the insured wants protection. The only way the insurer can properly assess risk is if the insured is candid and forthcoming. In short, the insured is usually in the best position to provide the insurer with the information needed.

The duty to disclose is not all encompassing, however. The law expects the insurer to be "worldly wise" and to show "personal judgment."[4] For this reason, there is no onus on the insured to inform the insurer of matters "not personal to the applicant."[5] For example, assume that in the application for fire insurance Max notes that some welding occurs on the premises, but he does not go on to observe that welding causes sparks, which, in turn, can cause a fire. This is not a failure to disclose—after all, the insurer is expected to be worldly wise. That said, the insured is much better to err on the side of disclosure, since a miscalculation on the insured's part can lead to the policy being void.

A duty to disclose exists not just at the time of applying for the insurance—it is an ongoing duty. The insurer must be notified about any change material to the risk. For example, if WEC decides to stop producing wire and turn its attention instead to manufacturing plastic cable, the insurer should be advised, in writing, of this change. In the same vein, when WEC leaves a building vacant, the insurer should be contacted so that necessary adjustments to the policy can be made.

When does an insured have a duty to disclose?

3.   *Insurance*, 19 C.E.D. (West 3rd) para. 332.
4.   C. Brown & J. Menezes, *Insurance Law in Canada*, 2nd ed. (Scarborough: Carswell, 1991) at 88–89.
5.   *Ibid.* at 89.

CASE ▼

Marche v. Halifax Insurance Co., [2005] 1 S.C.R. 47.

THE BUSINESS CONTEXT: The duty of an insured to report material changes to the risk in a fire insurance policy is currently prescribed by statutory conditions in all Canadian common law provinces. This case concerns the ability of an insurance company to deny coverage on the basis of the insured's alleged breach of the statutory condition requiring an insured to report a material change.[6]

FACTUAL BACKGROUND: Theresa March and Gary Fitzgerald (the insureds) purchased a house, converted it into apartments, and insured it under a fire insurance policy issued by the Halifax Insurance Co. In September 1998, the insureds left Cape Breton Island to find work in British Columbia. The house remained vacant from September to early December when Danny, a brother of one of the insured's, moved in. Danny fell behind in the rent but refused to vacate the premises. In an effort to induce Danny to move out, the insureds had the water and electrical power disconnected. On 7 February 1999, the house was destroyed by fire. At this time, Danny's possessions were still in the house.

Halifax denied liability on the grounds that the insureds had failed to notify Halifax of the vacancy between September and December 1998. The insurer alleged that this was a breach of Statutory Condition 4 of Part VII of Nova Scotia's *Insurance Act* that provides, in part, "Any change material to the risk and within the control and knowledge of the insured shall avoid the contract as to the part affected thereby, unless the change is promptly notified in writing to the insurer...."

The insured argued that, if their failure to report the vacancy constituted a breach, they should be relieved from the consequences of the breach by s. 171(b) of the *Insurance Act* that provides in part, "Where a contract ... contains any stipulation, condition or warranty that is or may be material to the risk ... the exclusion, stipulation, condition or warranty shall not be binding on the insured if it is held to be unjust or unreasonable...."

THE LEGAL QUESTION: Does s.171 (b) of the Nova Scotia *Insurance Act* apply to statutory conditions? Was there a breach of Statutory Condition 4?

RESOLUTION: The Supreme Court of Canada held that s. 171(b) applies to both contractual and statutory conditions. In coming to this conclusion, the majority rejected the notion that statutory conditions by definition cannot be unnecessary or unjust. The Court noted that as the purpose of s. 171(b) is to provide relief from unjust or unreasonable insurance policy conditions, it should be given a broad interpretation. The word "condition" in s. 171 (b) is not qualified by a restrictive adjective and further, a reading of the entire act does not support the contention that "condition" in s.171 (b) refers only to contractual conditions. The Court stated that s.171 (b) authorizes the Court to not only relieve against conditions that are *prima facie* unjust but also to relieve against conditions that in their application lead to unjust or unreasonable results.

The Court noted that while the insured had failed to report the vacancy, it is unclear whether the failure constituted a breach of Statutory Condition 4 as the vacancy had been rectified prior to the loss occurring. In any event, if the insureds were in breach, s. 171(b) should be applied to relieve the insureds from the consequences of this breach. It would be unjust to void the insurance policy when the vacancy had been rectified prior to the loss occurring and was not causally related to the loss.

CRITICAL ANALYSIS: The Court rejected the insurance company's attempt to deny coverage based on an alleged breach of Statutory Condition 4. What is the uncertainty created by the decision for insurers?

---

6. See also: *Royal Bank of Canada v. State Farm Fire and Casualty Co.,* [2005] 1 S.C.R. 779. This case deals with the statutory condition requiring reporting of a material change in relation to an insurance policy's standard mortgage clause.

Insurable Interest

insurable interest

A financial stake in what is being insured.

The special nature of the insurance contract also means that its validity is contingent on the insured having an insurable interest in the thing insured.[7] The test for whether the insured has an **insurable interest** is whether he benefits from its existence and would be prejudiced from its destruction.[8] The rationale behind this rule is that allowing people to insure property they have no real interest in may, for example, lead them to intentionally destroy the property in order to make an insurance claim. If WEC's bank holds a mortgage on the WEC production plant, it can purchase insurance on the plant because the bank has an insurable interest in property that is being used as security for a loan. The bank benefits from the continued existence of the plant and would be prejudiced by its destruction. Once the mortgage is paid off, the insurable interest of the bank no longer exists, and the bank cannot file a claim.

Business Application of the Law

Dealing with Your Insurance Company

Though some litigation over insurance policies can be extraordinarily complex, many problems arise because the insured has failed to keep its insurance company properly informed. There are three simple but productive steps a business can take to avoid coverage problems.

- *Review.* The business should review with its insurance broker the extent and nature of its insurance coverage at least once a year. This review forces the business to assess any number of matters, including what new property it has acquired and new business activity in which it might want to engage. It allows the broker to assess the existing policies for comprehensiveness and suggest alterations or additions to those policies. The broker then takes the matter to the insurance company so that the necessary adjustments can be made.

- *Report.* The business should report to the insurer any changes material to the risk, ideally before these changes even happen. For example, if a businessperson has decided to close down her operation for a month because of health problems, she must advise the insurer that the premises

will be vacant for that period of time or risk being uninsured in the event of a fire. This is because most fire insurance policies will exclude coverage when the insured building has been left vacant for more than 30 consecutive days and a loss occurs. Likewise, if the business is acquiring a new piece of equipment, it should notify its insurer immediately. This is because the existing policy for property coverage may not include the equipment in question at all or not in the amount necessary to replace or repair the equipment, should that become necessary.

- *Alert.* When an incident occurs that will lead the insured to make a claim on its policy, the insured must immediately notify the insurer. However, it is advisable for the insured to alert the insurer as soon as anything happens that may result in the insured making a claim on the policy sometime down the road. For example, if a customer slips and falls in the business premises but seems to be OK and leaves without complaint, it would still be prudent for the insured to notify the insurer.

---

7. *Supra* note 4 at 65. Note that the ordinary insurable interest test is typically altered by statute for life insurance. In life insurance, the statutes generally provide that certain dependants have an insurable interest in the life insured, as does anyone else who gets the written consent of the person whose life is being insured.
8. *Lucena v. Craufurd* (1806), 2 B. & P. (N.R). 269 at 301 (H.L.). Discussed in Brown & Menezes, *supra* note 4 at 66–67.

That way, if the customer returns several months later, and alleges that the fall has caused him serious back and jaw injuries, the insured is in good shape from a coverage perspective. He has already alerted the insurance company and has in no way prejudiced the insurer's right to make a proper investigation of the accident itself.

It takes time for a business to keep its insurer and broker properly informed, but this time is well spent. It leads to the best outcome for everyone and means that when the insured does make a claim, the matter stands the greatest chance of being handled without controversy.

CRITICAL ANALYSIS: Why does an insured often fail to keep its insurer properly informed?

Source: James McGinnis, partner at the Edmonton law firm of Parlee McLaws.

Indemnity

indemnity
The obligation on the insurer to make good the loss.

With the exception of life insurance contracts, insurance contracts are contracts of **indemnity.** This means that the insured is not supposed to profit from the happening of the insured-against event, but at most will come out even. For example, if WEC insured its manufacturing plant against the risk of fire with two different insurance companies, WEC, in the event of a loss, is entitled to collect only the amount of the loss. WEC cannot collect the loss from both insurance companies. However, WEC would be entitled to select the policy under which it will claim indemnity (subject to any conditions to the contrary). The insurer, in turn, would be entitled to contribution from the other insurer on a prorated basis.

Some policies, such as fire insurance policies, require the insured to have coverage for a specified minimum portion of the value of the property in order to fully recover from the insurer in the event of a fire. This requirement takes the form of a co-insurance clause, which is intended to discourage the insured from insuring the property for less than its value on the gamble that any loss is likely to be less than total. If such a clause is in place, and the insured carries less insurance then the amount specified in the clause, the insurer will pay only a specified portion of the loss, and the insured must absorb the remainder. In essence, the insured becomes a co-insurer for the amount of the deficiency

FIGURE 28.2
Example of the Application of a Co-insurance Clause

Building value	$500 000
Actual insurance coverage	$300 000
Amount of loss	$100 000
Co-insurance clause	80%

$$\frac{\text{Amount of insurance coverage purchased}}{\text{Minimum required under co-insurance clause}} \times \text{Actual loss} = \text{Insurer's liability}^{(1)}$$

$$\frac{\$300\,000}{(\$500\,000 \times 80\%)} \times \$100\,000 = \$75\,000 \text{ (amount the insurer must pay)}$$

(1) *Subject to policy limits*

Subrogation

subrogation
The right of the insurer to recover the amount paid on a claim from a third party that caused the loss.

The insurer also has what is called a right of **subrogation.** This right means that when an insurer compensates the insured, it has the right to sue a third party—the wrongdoer—who caused the loss and to recover from that party what it has already paid out to its insured. In this sense, the right of subrogation permits the insurer to "step into the shoes" of the insured and sue the wrongdoer. Because of the insurer's right of subrogation, WEC must act carefully in the face of a loss. For example, it should not admit liability for any accident that has occurred, since doing so might wrongly and unfairly jeopardize any defence to any future action the insurer might commence against the wrongdoer. Instead, WEC should immediately contact its insurer, as well as legal counsel, for advice on how to proceed.

The Policy

rider

A clause altering or adding coverage to a standard insurance policy.

Insurance contracts are particularly technical documents. Their content is settled to some extent by legislation, which requires standard form policies for some types of insurance. Changes in standard policy terms take the form of riders and endorsements. A **rider** adds to or alters the standard coverage and is part of the policy from the outset. An endorsement is an alteration to the coverage at some point during the time in which the policy is in force. Policies generally contain a number of exclusion clauses that exclude coverage for certain situations, occurrences, or persons for which there would otherwise be protection. For example, the standard fire policy excludes coverage when the insured building has been left unoccupied for more than 30 consecutive days. If a loss occurs after this point, the policy does not cover it. Other common exclusions in property insurance include damage caused by wear and tear or mould, and vandalism or malicious acts caused by the insured.

Business Application of the Law

Marijuana "Grow-ops"

The use of residential dwellings for marijuana "grow operations" is a problem in many parts of Canada. First emerging as a trend in British Columbia more than 10 years ago, it is estimated that there are up to 50 000 residential grow operations in Canada at any one time. Growing marijuana can be an extremely lucrative business—a crop that costs between $2000 and $5000 to grow can be sold for $50 000 only 90 days later.

In many instances a rented house is converted to a hot house to cultivate the plants. The conversion usually involves ripping out walls, carpets, and fixtures; rerouting wiring; installing additional heating units; and bringing in soil, fertilizer, and liquid nitrogen. The consequent damage to the house can be devastating—a compromised electrical system, structural damage, condensation and mould—damage that can amount to a repair bill of tens of thousands of dollars. And it is unlikely that the damage is covered under the homeowner's insurance policy. This is because it is common practice in the insurance industry to include a clause that excludes damages that results from illegal activity, whether the homeowner is aware of the illegal activity or not, and a clause that specifically excludes damages that arises from marijuana growing operations.

CRITICAL ANALYSIS: How can a business that rents out real estate manage the risk posed by marijuana grow operations? What steps should the business take prior to renting out its property? What steps should the business take after the property has been rented out?

Sources: D. Carlson, "Combat Zone: As Marijuana 'Grow Ops' Mushroom, Insurers Struggle to Fight the New Perils of Pot," *Canadian Insurance,* (December 2004) at 28; and J. Gadd, "Marijuana 'Grow Ops' Spark Insurance Fears: Landlords Worried Insurers Won't Cover Damage Done to Residential Rental Units," *The Globe and Mail, (*16 January 2004) at G4 at http://www.theglobeandmail.com

Is damage caused by growing marijuana an insurable risk?

Insurance Products

Insurance is broadly divisible into three categories—life, property, and liability. However, there are many specialized insurance policies or products available to meet the risk management needs of business. In order to secure optimal coverage, a businessperson should assess the business operation and identify the kinds of legal risks it may encounter. For example, in its business, WEC faces a number of possible kinds of liabilities and losses, including the following:

- INJURY AND PROPERTY DAMAGE related to the operation of WEC's delivery trucks. If WEC's delivery personnel drive negligently, they may be involved in traffic accidents that cause injury to other people, as well as property damage to other vehicles. Additionally, such negligence may cause injury to the WEC drivers themselves and damage to WEC vehicles.

- PERSONAL INJURY to suppliers, sales personnel, and purchasers who visit the manufacturing plant floor. Since WEC's business office is located in its manufacturing plant, many people who are not directly involved in production may visit the plant on business. Injuries—from tripping on a carpet to being burned by the extrusion process—can be the result. As well, WEC employees who work in the manufacturing process and elsewhere face the risk of being hurt on the job.

- FINANCIAL LOSS AND INJURY to others caused by defective wire that WEC produced. If WEC delivers defective wires that are later incorporated into tires produced by WEC customers, those tires may fail while being used or repaired, causing both physical injury and financial loss to those involved.

- FINANCIAL LOSS AND INJURY caused by employees giving negligent advice to WEC customers concerning their wire needs. If an employee provides bad advice to WEC customers, they may end up with wire that is not appropriate for its intended use. This problem, in turn, may lead to physical injury and financial loss to WEC customers and to the ultimate consumers of the tires produced by WEC customers.

■ INJURY AND PROPERTY DAMAGE caused by a fire or other disaster in the manufacturing plant. If WEC experiences a fire in its plant, there can be a significant financial loss, since the building, as well as the equipment and machinery, will have to be repaired or replaced before company operations can resume.

■ LOSS OF PROFIT owing to business interruption as a result of a fire or other causes of a plant shutdown. In the event of a fire or other disaster, WEC may have to suspend business operations while it rebuilds. This loss of profit could cripple the company financially and even cause its demise.

■ ENVIRONMENTAL DAMAGE caused by improper storage or disposal of waste products. Environmental protection legislation in all jurisdictions prohibits businesses from discharging or spilling contaminants into the environment. Legislation may also permit the government to order the party responsible to clean up or otherwise repair the environmental damage that the contaminant caused. This cleanup can be costly for the company involved. As well, WEC can face civil actions by those who are injured or who suffer loss because WEC has improperly stored or disposed of its waste products. Since WEC produces fabricated metal products—a process that is likely to have significant environmental implications[9]—it needs to pay particular attention to this kind of potentially catastrophic liability.

■ DEATH of one of the shareholders in WEC. Should one of the WEC shareholders die, the others will likely want to buy out that person's shares. Financing the buyout will be a challenge for WEC.

In order to address these risks, WEC has in place the following policies.

Auto Insurance

An automobile owner is required by law to have insurance for liability arising from its ownership, use, and operation. While each jurisdiction has its own scheme in place, a common aim of these schemes is to ensure that owners are financially responsible for the liabilities that arise through use of their vehicles. Most people do not have the assets on hand to pay off a large judgment against them; insurance provides the funds to fulfill that financial responsibility, should it arise.

There are several types of auto insurance coverage. In Alberta, for example, the Standard Automobile Policy provides the insured with coverage against liability for the injury or death of someone else (third-party liability) caused by the operation of the insured vehicle. It also provides benefits to the insured for injury or death caused by an accident arising from the use or operation of the insured automobile, as well as compensation for loss or damage to the insured automobile itself. The latter is known as collision coverage.

Some people decide not to get collision coverage because the car itself is not worth very much. Purchasing third-party liability insurance, however, is not an option, but is required by law. Since a car accident causing paraplegia, for example, can result in millions of dollars of damages, owners should not be content with purchasing the minimum amount required by law. The minimum amount is simply

---

9. D. Belcher, "A Canadian Banker's Perspective on Proactive Due Diligence," at "Appendix A: Examples of Industries Likely to Have Significant Environmental Concerns," in *Managing Environmental Liability: A Practical Approach for Lenders* (Mississauga: Insight Press, 1991).

not enough to cover a catastrophic accident. If there is a deficiency between the amount of insurance coverage and the actual damages sustained by the plaintiff, the insured will be personally responsible for the difference.

Each province specifies through legislation the minimum amount of coverage an owner must obtain for third-party liability. In Ontario, for example, the statutory minimum is $200 000.[10] Since this amount is insufficient to pay damages to another who has been seriously injured, the owner should purchase additional coverage.

What are the advantages and disadvantages of no-fault automobile insurance systems?

Business Application of the Law

No-Fault Insurance Systems

Insurance systems vary significantly from province to province. A major distinguishing feature is the extent to which they rely on either a tort-based liability system or a no-fault system for compensating claims for bodily injury or death. A "no-fault" system involves the diminution of the ability to sue a tort-feasor for compensation. In this system, the emphasis is on providing accident benefits without regard to the victim's fault. This is a marked departure from the traditional tort system with its emphasis on fault-based liability.

Quebec was the first Canadian jurisdiction to adopt a no-fault system. Automobile accident victims have lost the right to sue in return for a form of income replacement benefit, medical and funeral expenses, and a modest award for pain and suffering depending on the extent of the injury. Manitoba has adopted no-fault legislation similar to Quebec's. Manitoba has eliminated all tort actions for bodily injury or death resulting from automobile accidents. Effective 1 January 2003, Saskatchewan consumers can choose between no-fault (or tort–restricted) auto insurance and a tort option. The tort option provides reduced accident benefits, but claimants can sue to recover general damages for their noneconomic losses. The no-fault option eliminates the right to sue

---

10. *Insurance Act*, R.S.O. 1990, c. I.8, s. 251(1) provides: "Every contract evidenced by a motor vehicle liability policy insures, in respect of any one accident, to the limit of at least $200,000 exclusive of interest and costs, against liability resulting from bodily injury to or the death of one or more persons and loss of or damage to property."

to recover damages for pain and suffering. In 1990, Ontario adopted a threshold no-fault scheme that limits claims by imposing a standard of severity of injury to be met before a plaintiff is entitled to sue for general damages. Since 1990, various changes have been made to the system including legislation defining the elements of the threshold test, but its effect remains essentially the same—automobile accident victims have severe restrictions on their ability to sue.

In the other provinces and territories, the automobile insurance systems are based on the tort-liability model. In Newfoundland, accident benefits under automobile policies are optional. As a result, some accident victims have no choice but to rely on tort law for recovery of their bodily injury or death claims. New Brunswick and British Columbia have undergone significant reforms to their tort-based models that have enhanced the level of accident benefits that claimants are entitled to receive. Also in New Brunswick and in Nova Scotia and Alberta, legislation has been passed to cap awards for pain and suffering related to minor injuries. The cap in Nova Scotia and New Brunswick is $2500 and in Alberta the cap is $4000.

CRITICAL ANALYSIS: What is the purpose of "pain and suffering" caps for minor injuries? Do you see any problems with imposing caps?

Source: C. Brown, J. Menezes & Cassels, Brock & Blackwell, *Insurance Law in Canada Vol. 2*, looseleaf (Scarborough: Carswell, 2005) at 17.1(i)–17.2(a).

Employees injured in car accidents on the job may have coverage through workers' compensation legislation. Under such legislation—which is in place in every Canadian province—participating employers pay premiums into a fund administered by a tribunal. Employees who are injured in the workplace or who suffer from a disease as a result, for example, of exposure to a pollutant in the workplace can then make a claim for benefits from this fund. When an employer participates in a workers' compensation board (WCB) plan, payment from the fund is the only compensation the employee is entitled to receive. Legislation prevents the employee from suing the employer, though there may be a right to sue others who are not participants in the workers' compensation scheme.[11]

CASE ▼

David Polowin Real Estate Ltd. v. Dominion of Canada General Ins. Co. (2005), 76 O.R. (3d) 161 (Ont. C.A.), leave to appeal to S.C.C. dismissed 26 January 2006.

THE BUSINESS CONTEXT: Each year over 99 000 vehicles are written off in Canada. In such cases, it is widespread industry practice for the insurer to pay the insured the actual cash value of the vehicle minus the deductible specified in the insurance policy. It is also common for the insurer to take possession of the wrecked vehicle and sell it for salvage.

FACTUAL BACKGROUND: In 1999, McNaughton Automotive Ltd. commenced a proposed class proceeding against Co-operators General Insurance Co, challenging the Ontario insurance practice of applying policy deductibles in total loss cases. In 2001, the Ontario Court of Appeal[12] held that the insurance industry's practice was in violation of mandatory statutory condition 6(7) that provided in part, "if the insurer exercises the option to replace the automobile or pays the actual cash value of the automobile, the salvage, if any, shall vest in the insurer." The court held that for the salvage to vest

---

11. M. Faieta *et al., Environmental Harm: Civil Actions and Compensation* (Toronto: Butterworths, 1996) at 405.
12. *McNaughton Automotive Ltd. v. Co-Operators Insurance Co.* (2001), 54 O.R. (3d) 704 (Ont. C.A.), leave to appeal to S.C.C. dismissed 7 March 2002.

in the insurer, the insurer must pay the "actual cash value," not the actual cash value minus a deductible. Following the release of the Court of Appeal's decision over 30 proposed class proceedings were commenced in Ontario, Alberta, and British Columbia against insurers from across Canada including one by David Polowin Real Estate and 7 other insureds against Dominion of Canada General Insurance Company and 7 other insurers. In 2003, the Ontario legislature amended the statutory conditions to expressly authorize the insurer in total loss cases to take title to the vehicle and apply a deductible. The legislature did not make the amendments retroactive.

Dominion of Canada General Insurance Company and the other insurers brought motions for summary judgment seeking dismissal of the proposed class proceedings brought against them by David Polowin Real Estate and the other insureds. In support of their motions, the insurers filed extensive statutory interpretation evidence relating to the legislative history of statutory condition 6(7). The motions judge dismissed the summary judgment motion on the basis that it was not open for a lower court to depart from *McNaughton*. The insurers appealed the dismissal and the Chief Judge of Ontario ordered a special five-member panel of the Court of Appeal to consider whether to override *McNaughton*.

THE LEGAL QUESTION: Did the Court of Appeal in *McNaughton* misinterpret statutory condition 6(7)? If so, should the Court of Appeal decision in *McNaughton* be overruled?

RESOLUTION: The court reviewed the legislative history of the statutory condition, noting that much of this material was not before the Court of Appeal in *McNaughton*. The court held that taking into consideration the basic purpose of the statutory condition, its mandatory inclusion in the standard automobile policy, the wording of the policy, and the important role of deductibles in the automobile insurance regime, the *McNaughton* decision misinterpreted Statutory Condition 6(7.) The court noted that the insured's position does not produce sensible results. For example, if two people buy identical cars and one

insures with a high deductible for a lower premium and the other opts for a lower deductible at a higher premium and both cars are damaged beyond repair each insured would receive the same amount—the actual cash value of the car—without any reduction for the deductible. This makes little sense because the insured who has agreed to a high deductible in exchange for a lower premium would receive the same as the insured who paid a higher premium with a lower deductible.

The court concluded that there were seven justifications for overruling *McNaughton*:

- The courts in Alberta and British Columbia have questioned the reasoning in the *McNaughton* decision, raising concerns about consistency in the interpretation of automobile insurance regimes across Canada;

- The interpretation of statutory conditions in *McNaughton* may be wrongly applied in other contexts.

- Although *stare decisis* generally promotes the value of certainty, that value has limited application on the question in this appeal because the insureds have not governed their conduct on the basis of *McNaughton*.

- *McNaughton* was a relatively recent decision.

- The court in this case has the benefit of the legislative history, which was not available to the court in *McNaughton*.

- A substantial amount of money was at stake.

- The court should not be less willing to depart from its own decisions because the Supreme Court of Canada can correct the error.

CRITICAL ANALYSIS: The Court specified that the substantial amount of money at stake was a relevant consideration in its decision to overturn *McNaughton*. How is the amount of money at issue a relevant consideration in overturning a decision? What do you think is the most compelling reason for overturning a decision?

Occupiers' Liability Insurance

WEC, as a building owner and occupier, is liable for injuries suffered to people on its premises if the injuries are due to WEC's failure to ensure that the premises are safe. WEC's occupiers' liability insurance will compensate WEC if unsafe conditions cause injury to someone else—for example, a visitor to its plant floor. Although WEC has a program in place to prevent such accidents, the insurance will fill the gap when and if the system fails.

Comprehensive General Liability Insurance

The purpose of comprehensive general liability insurance (also known as CGL insurance) is to compensate enterprises like WEC, in a comprehensive way, for any liabilities they incur during the course of their business. For example, an important general risk faced by WEC is that its wires will fail in use and lead to some kind of loss. WEC's CGL insurance will respond by compensating WEC for property damages, personal injury, loss of profit, and related losses suffered by a third party when WEC is legally responsible for such losses.[13] The CGL does not respond, however, to losses directly suffered by WEC itself. For this latter type of loss, WEC would need warranty insurance. The following examples reveal the important difference between these two kinds of insurance:

Example 1: WEC produces wire that is seriously defective. When the customer incorporates that wire into its tire-manufacturing process, the tires fail and must be discarded. The customer loses about $50 000 in materials, time, and profit—all of which is attributable to WEC's defective product. WEC's CGL insurance policy will cover this loss.

Example 2: WEC produces wire that the customer notices is defective as soon as WEC attempts to deliver the shipment. Accordingly, the customer refuses to accept delivery, and WEC loses $50 000 in revenue. CGL insurance does not cover this loss because it is not a loss sustained by a WEC customer or other third party—it is a loss suffered directly by WEC itself. For coverage in this situation, WEC would need a warranty policy. Because its cost is so high, WEC has not purchased warranty insurance. From a business perspective, WEC has determined that it is better off establishing an effective quality assurance and testing program, thereby dealing with such risks in-house rather than looking to an insurance company for coverage.

---

13. Note that coverage generally extends only to unintentional torts, rather than intentional acts.

The so-called Year Two Thousand (Y2K) computer problem resulted from the fact that computers were not initially programmed to recognize dates beyond 31 December 1999. Experts warned that the computer technologies on which the world relied for critical services could fail at midnight on New Year's Eve 1999/2000. To ensure that computers would continue to function in the year 2000, companies upgraded their computer systems to avert disaster. Canadian Pacific Railway Company upgraded its system and attempted to claim the costs of upgrading under its all-risks insurance policy. Its insurance company denied the claim. In the subsequent litigation, Alberta's Court of Queen's Bench[14] held that expenses incurred in rectifying the Y2K problem did not fall in the coverage provided by CPR's insurance policy. The court stated that the loss claimed by CPR was not a fortuitous loss. In other words, the loss was entirely certain and predictable—therefore, it was not a risk insured against. Second, the court held that even if the loss claimed was fortuitous, it was excluded under the policy as it was caused by inherent vice. CPR's policy contained exclusion for inherent vices, which are conditions "inherent in the property insured which causes it to be damaged when it is exposed to normal conditions." The Y2K problem was the result of neither a faulty design nor a design defect; rather it was the result of "planned obsolescence." Finally the Court held that CPR was not eligible for reimbursement under the sue and labour provisions of its policy. Sue and labour clauses permit the insured to be reimbursed for expenses it incurs to prevent or mitigate a loss. As the Y2K problem was not a covered loss, the sue and labour clause did not apply to afford coverage for the expenses.

CRITICAL ANALYSIS: The CPR case illustrates one kind of risk associated with computer technology. It also highlights the limited coverage insurers may provide for the risk of computer failure. What is the nature of the computer technology or cyber risks faced by business today? How can these risks be managed? What is the role of insurance in managing these risks?

How can a business manage the risk of the loss of electronic data following a computer crash?

Errors and Omissions Insurance

When WEC's engineers provide professional engineering advice to WEC customers, they are promising that they meet the standard of the reasonably competent person engaged in such activity.[15] Although this implied promise does not amount to a guarantee of perfection, they will be responsible for losses resulting from negligent advice. Through errors and omissions insurance (also known as E&O insurance), the insurer promises to pay on the engineers' behalf all the sums they are legally obligated to pay as damages resulting from the performance of their professional services.

14. *American Home Assurance C. v. Canadian Pacific Railway,* [2004] 44 Alta. L.R. (4th) 389.
15. K.G. Neilson, "Suing the Insurer: Construction Related Insurance" in *Suing the Insurer* (Edmonton: Legal Education Society of Alberta, 1982) at 51.

Investigation costs and legal expenses will also be covered by the policy.[16] Like all insurance policies, the engineers' coverage is subject to a number of conditions, such as the requirement that they give immediate notice to the insurer of a claim or potential claim. This notice allows the insurance company to carry out an investigation and otherwise gather facts associated with the alleged negligence.[17] Failure to give prompt notice or to comply with any other condition can result in the insurance company successfully denying coverage.

Corporate directors and officers also face liability for their errors and omissions related to operating their company. As discussed in Chapter 16, this risk can be insured against through directors' and officers' liability (D&O) insurance.

Property Insurance

WEC has insured its manufacturing plant and equipment in order to fund any rebuilding or replacement that a fire or other disaster might occasion. One of the key choices WEC made was whether to insure for the replacement value of its property or for the property's actual cash value.

If WEC had chosen the second option, it would receive from the insurance company only the value of the property at the time it was destroyed; that is, not enough to purchase a replacement. WEC chose the first option; therefore, it will receive a higher level of compensation from the insurer—and also pay a higher premium—but the insurer has the right to require WEC to actually rebuild or otherwise replace its property before it will pay out on the claim. WEC also chose coverage for a number of losses including loss caused by fire, falling aircraft, earthquake, hail, water damage, malicious damage, smoke damage, and impact by vehicles.[18] Not surprisingly, the more perils WEC insured against, the higher the premiums.

Business Application of the Law

Commercial and Personal Insurance

Business owners must be careful to distinguish between personal risks and business risks, since this distinction determines the kind of policy they should purchase in the first place. Sometimes the distinction is easy to make, as many kinds of insurance, such as credit insurance, are primarily business related. At other times, the distinction is more problematic, since some kinds of insurance relate to both home and business matters, such as fire, automobile, accident and sickness, third-party liability, and even life insurance.

Insurers distinguish between personal and commercial risks, as reflected in premiums and the language of policies. Failure to properly distinguish may result in the wrong type of policy being purchased

and serious difficulties when making claims. The difficulties depend on the type of insurance.

Accident and sickness insurance is relatively straightforward. Although the nature of the risk is the same in both individual and commercial contexts, the packaging and nature of the contracts are different. Individuals negotiate the terms of their own policy with an insurer. Commercial insurance is provided through group contracts, which are master contracts between the insurer and an employer or organization. Individuals are entitled to coverage through their membership in the group.

The distinction in fire and liability insurance is crucial because of the policies themselves. Coverage as part of a tenant's or homeowner's package will

---

16. *Ibid.* at 52.
17. *Ibid.* at 54.
18. *Supra* note 4 at 182.

normally exclude buildings used for commercial purposes and liability to third parties arising from professional or business activities.

Insurers selling automobile insurance policies must provide the coverage required by the applicable legislation, but they are permitted to exclude coverage for commercial activities (such as renting the vehicle or using it as a taxi) if the coverage is for private use of the vehicle.

Those buying insurance need to clarify their needs and activities with the insurer so that they acquire the appropriate type of policy with the particular coverage that their activities warrant.

CRITICAL ANALYSIS: Why do insurers distinguish between personal and business risks?

Source: C. Brown & J. Menezes, *Insurance Law in Canada*, 2nd ed. (Scarborough: Carswell, 1991) at 16–17.

Business Interruption Loss Insurance

This kind of coverage—often contained in what is called an "all-risk" policy—provides WEC with financial compensation should it have to cease or reduce operations owing to a fire or another cause of damage to its plant. The insurer is required to compensate for loss of profits to the extent of the limits of the policy.

CASE ▼

Triple Five Corp. v. Simcoe & Erie Group (1994), 159 A.R. 1 (Q.B.), aff'd [1997] 5 W.W.R. 1 (C.A.), leave to appeal to S.C.C. denied, [1997] S.C.C.A. No. 263

THE BUSINESS CONTEXT: The precise language of a policy is more important than what it is called or what the insured thinks is covered. This case illustrates that all-risk policies do not necessarily cover all possibilities.

FACTUAL BACKGROUND: Triple Five Corp. owned and operated West Edmonton Mall, a large shopping centre located in Western Canada. One of the features of the mall was an amusement park, and more specifically, a roller coaster. A terrible accident resulted in one of the cars of the roller coaster flipping off the tracks and causing the death of two people. The claims regarding these fatalities were settled out of court. What was litigated, however, was whether Triple Five was entitled to compensation for loss of profit and other expenses that resulted from the roller coaster being out of commission for some time after the accident.

THE LEGAL QUESTION: Is Triple Five's insurer liable to pay Triple Five for its business interruption losses?

RESOLUTION: The court ruled against Triple Five, and this outcome was affirmed on appeal. The fact that Triple Five lost profits because the roller coaster was out of commission for a period of time was not enough for its claim to be successful. Triple Five also had to prove that the cause of the accident itself fell within the terms of the policy. After hearing complicated expert evidence, the court ruled that the accident was caused by a design error. Since Triple Five had purchased insurance only to cover accidents external to the roller coaster itself—as opposed to something inherent or internal to the roller coaster—its loss was not insured.

CRITICAL ANALYSIS: Triple Five suffered a loss in gross revenues because the roller coaster was defectively designed. Would it therefore be able to sue the manufacturer of the roller coaster for breach of contract and perhaps for negligence?

Environmental Impairment Insurance

WEC not only may face substantial fines for failing to comply with environmental protection legislation and for any cleanup costs associated with a spill or other accident, but also can be sued by its neighbours for polluting the soil or ground water. Furthermore, if a subsequent owner of WEC's plant can trace pollutants back to WEC, WEC has civil liability for the cleanup and other associated costs, even though it no longer owns the land.

This liability explains why environmental impairment liability policies are very expensive and difficult to obtain.[19] A more viable—though not foolproof—alternative is for WEC to ensure that it has an operational management policy in place to prevent such accidents from happening in the first place.[20]

Key-Person Life Insurance

The partners in a firm or the shareholders of a small corporation likely wish their business to continue to be operated by the surviving owners if one of them dies. Their partnership agreement or shareholders' agreement will specify that the surviving owners have the right to buy the shares of the deceased owner. The effective exercise of that right requires a means of valuing the business and the shares of the deceased, as well as a means of financing the purchase of the shares by the survivors. Insurance on the lives of the owners is a means of financing the buyout. The owners need to agree on a method of evaluating the business when the insurance is purchased and at the time of death. They must then agree on how much insurance to purchase on the life of each key person. Key factors in this decision are the age of the key people, the extent of their ownership, and the payment method each prefers for their survivors.

The amount of life insurance purchased by the business for each key person will depend on the affordability of the premium, which will be higher for older owners. Because of their age or medical condition, key people may find that insurance is unobtainable. The owners must also decide whether to purchase enough coverage to provide a lump sum large enough to buy the share of the deceased outright, or whether the insurance will provide a portion of the buyout price, with the remainder paid to the heirs by the business over a period of time.

Since WEC is owned by three shareholders it would be prudent for there to be life insurance policies on each one of them. However, as this proved to be uneconomic for some of the shareholders, an agreement between them addresses how the deceased's shares will be purchased.

It may also be prudent for the main stakeholders in WEC to secure disability insurance so that if one of them is unable to work—owing to serious illness, for example—insurance will fund at least part of that person's salary or other remuneration.

Remedies of the Insured

Against the Broker

It was crucial for WEC to establish a solid working relationship with an **insurance broker** in order to secure proper advice as to what kind of insurance it required. The term "insurance broker" refers to the middle person between the insurance

insurance broker
One who provides advice and assistance to the insured in acquiring insurance.

---

19. G.J. Mannina, "Lender Liability—How to Minimize Environmental Risks" in *Managing Environmental Liability: A Practical Approach for Lenders* (Mississauga: Insight Press, 1991) at 28–29.
20. See Chapter 3.

companies and the insured. As the party who sought insurance, WEC needed the assistance of the broker in reviewing its business operations, assessing the risks it faces, and understanding the coverages available and the policy costs. If WEC did not spend sufficient time with the broker or chose a broker who was simply not up to the job, WEC may have ended up with the wrong coverage—or not enough coverage—and face a loss against which it has not been properly insured.

Should WEC face such a situation, it may have an action against its broker for negligence. If WEC is successful in its action, the broker will be required to reimburse WEC for any of its underinsured or uninsured losses or liabilities.

The term "**insurance agent**" usually refers to someone who acts on behalf of an insurer to sell insurance. An agent acting in that capacity is primarily obligated to the insurer as principal, and not to the third-party insured.

insurance agent
One who acts for an insurance company in selling insurance.

Against the Insurance Company

insurance adjuster
One who investigates and evaluates insurance claims.

When an insured makes a claim under its policy, an **insurance adjuster** will likely investigate the events and evaluate the loss. On the adjuster's advice, the insurer will offer to settle the claim. There may be disagreements between the insured and the insurer as to the nature or amount of coverage. Should they be unable to resolve these differences, the insured may have to sue the insurer for breach of contract. The claim will be that the insurer has failed to honour its obligations under the policy. This is what Triple Five (the owner of West Edmonton Mall) did when it sued its insurer for failure to pay out under its all-risks loss policy.

In addition to the obligations specified in the insurance policy, an insurer owes the insured a duty of good faith including a duty to deal with an insured's claim in good faith. Factors considered in determining whether an insurer has fulfilled its obligation to act in good faith include whether the insurer carried out an adequate investigation of a claim, whether the insurer properly evaluated the claim, whether the insurer fairly interpreted the policy, and whether the insurer handled and paid the claim in a timely manner.[21] When the duty of good faith has been breached the court may award punitive damages as was done in *Whiten v. Pilot Insurance Co.*

CASE ▼

Whiten v. Pilot Insurance Co. (2002), 209 D.L.R. (4th) 257 (S.C.C.)

THE BUSINESS CONTEXT: An insurer's bad faith conduct—alleging fraud when none exists or refusing to pay out under a policy, for example—can have a devastating effect on the insured. This kind of reprehensible conduct by the insurer can be addressed by an award of punitive damages. Prior to this decision, the highest punitive damage award handed down by a Canadian court against an insurance company had been $15 000.

FACTUAL BACKGROUND: In January 1994, the Whitens' family home burned down in the middle of the night, destroying all their possessions and three family cats. Knowing that the family was in poor financial shape, the insurer, Pilot Insurance, made a single $5000 payment for living expenses and covered the rent on a cottage for a couple of months. Pilot then cut off the rent without telling the family, and thereafter pursued a confrontational policy that ultimately led to a protracted trial. Pilot maintained that the Whitens had burned down the house, even though it had opinions from its adjuster, its expert engineer, an investigative agency retained by it, and the fire chief that the fire was accidental. After receiving a strong recommendation from its adjuster

---

21. *Adams v. Confederation Life Insurance*, [1994] 6 W.W.R. 662 (Alta Q.B.).

that the claim be paid, Pilot replaced the adjuster. Counsel for Pilot pressured its experts to provide opinions supporting an arson defence, deliberately withheld relevant information from the experts, and provided them with misleading information to obtain opinions favourable to an arson theory. Pilot's position was wholly discredited at trial. The jury awarded compensatory damages and $1 million in punitive damages. The majority of the court of appeal allowed the appeal in part and reduced the punitive damages award to $100 000.

THE LEGAL QUESTION: Should the jury's punitive damages award be restored?

RESOLUTION: The court held that although the jury's award of punitive damages was high, it was reasonable. Pilot's conduct had been exceptionally reprehensible. Its actions, which continued for over two years, were designed to force the Whitens to make an unfair settlement for less than what they were entitled to receive. The jury believed that Pilot knew its allegations of arson were not sustainable and yet it persisted. Insurance contracts are purchased for peace of mind. The more devastating the loss, the more that the insured is at the financial mercy of the insurer, and the more difficult it may be to challenge a wrongful refusal to pay.

The jury decided that a strong message of denunciation, retribution, and deterrence needed to be sent to Pilot. The obligation of good-faith dealing requires that the insurer must respect the insured's vulnerability and reliance on the insurer. It was this relationship that was outrageously exploited by Pilot.

An award of punitive damages in a contract case is permissible if there is a separate actionable wrong. In addition to the contractual requirement to pay the claim, Pilot was under an obligation to deal with the insured in good faith. The breach of this separate obligation supports a claim for the punitive damages. The award of $1 million in punitive damages was more than the court would have awarded but was still within the high end of the range where juries are free to make their assessment.

CRITICAL ANALYSIS: The Insurance Council of Canada was an intervenor at the Supreme Court. It submitted that there should be a judicially imposed cap of $25 000 on punitive damages awards. What are the arguments for such a cap? What are the arguments against such a cap?

Courts across Canada have followed the lead of *Whiten* in awarding punitive damages where bad faith on the part of the insurer has been found. However, uncertainty remains with respect to when an insurer's conduct crosses the line between *bona fide* due diligence and bad faith as well as to the range of circumstances in which awards might be granted.[22] The Supreme Court,[23] however, has stated that punitive damages will be awarded only in exceptional cases and courts must exercise restraint in this regard. It is only where there is overwhelmingly inadequate handling of the claim or the introduction of improper considerations into the claims process that a conclusion of bad faith might be warranted. For example, the denial of a claim that is ultimately successful is not, in itself, an act of bad faith. Similarly, a refusal to pay a claim does not amount to a breach of good faith so long as the denial of coverage is based on a reasonable interpretation of the insurer's rights and obligations under the policy. However, a standard practice of refusing or delaying claims on the basis of their amount regardless of the terms of the policy is bad faith. Also, making allegations of fraud and arson when there is no factual basis for the allegations would also probably amount to bad faith and result in punitive damages.

---

22. R. Beamish, "How Have Bad Faith Claims Affected Insurer/Insured Relations?" *The Lawyers Weekly* (12 August 2005) at 13.
23. *Sun Life Assurance Company of Canada v. Fidler* [2006] 2 S.C.R.

Business Law in Practice Revisited

1. Was WEC under a duty to disclose the plant's vacancy to the insurance company? If so, what is the effect of a failure to disclose?

A contract of insurance is a contract of good faith. This means that the insured has a duty to disclose all material facts to the insurer concerning the subject matter to be insured. Good faith on the part of the applicant is necessary for insurance firms to effectively assess risks and set premiums. The duty to disclose not only arises at the time of applying for insurance but also is a continuing obligation of disclosure. Leaving a building vacant for a period of time, particularly in excess of 30 days, would constitute a breach of the obligation to disclose. The effect of the breach would make the insurance contract null and void with respect to the loss suffered by WEC. In addition, it is probable that WEC's insurance policy contains a clause excluding coverage when the insured building has been left vacant for more than 30 consecutive days.

2. What risk does the insurance company run by making allegations of arson?

The insurer has a duty to deal with an insured's claim in good faith. An insurer's duty to act in good faith developed as a counterweight to the immense power that an insurer has over the insured during the claims process. An insurer may be in breach of its duty of good faith if it does not properly investigate a claim, does not properly evaluate the claim, and does not handle the claim in a timely manner, for example. Making unfounded allegations of fraud and arson is a breach of the duty of good faith and could result in an award of punitive damages if the dispute between WEC and the insurer ends up in litigation.

Chapter Summary

Insurance is one of the simplest and most cost-effective ways of managing risk in a business environment. It permits the business to shift such risks as fire, automobile accidents, and liability for defective products onto an insurance company in exchange for the payment of premiums by the business.

An insurance contract is a contract of utmost good faith. This means that the insured must make full disclosure at the time of applying for insurance, as well as during the life of the policy. Failure to do so may permit the insurer to deny coverage when a loss has occurred.

The insured must have an insurable interest in the item insured to prevent moral hazards. The test for insurable interest is whether the insured benefits from the existence of the thing insured and would be prejudiced from its destruction.

Insurance contracts are not intended to improve the position of the insured should the loss occur. Rather, they are contracts of indemnity and are intended to compensate the insured only up to the amount of the loss suffered.

When the insurer pays out under an insurance policy, it has the right of subrogation. This right permits the insurer to sue the wrongdoer as if it were the party that had been directly injured or otherwise sustained the loss.

A business needs to communicate effectively with its insurance broker, as well as its insurance company, in order to assess the kinds of risks its operation faces and the types of insurance coverage that can be purchased to address those risks. Though insurance policies can take a variety of forms, there are three basic kinds: life and disability insurance; property insurance; and liability insurance. More specific insurance policies are simply a variation on one of these types.

Insurance policies are technically worded and often contain exclusion clauses. These clauses identify circumstances or events for which coverage is denied. They may also identify people for whom coverage is denied.

If the insured ends up with insurance of the wrong type or in an inadequate amount, it may have an action against its broker for breach of contract and/or negligence. If the insurance company wrongly refuses to honour the policy, the insured may have to sue the insurer to obtain compensation for its losses.

Chapter Study

Key Terms and Concepts

deductible (p. 688)

duty to disclose (p. 688)

indemnity (p. 692)

insurable interest (p. 691)

insurance adjuster (p. 704)

insurance agent (p. 704)

insurance broker (p. 703)

insurance policy (p. 687)

insured (p. 687)

insurer (p. 687)

premium (p. 687)

rider (p. 693)

subrogation (p. 692)

Questions for Review

1. What is the purpose of an insurance contract?

2. What is a premium?

3. Every province has enacted insurance legislation. What are the purposes of insurance legislation?

4. What are the three main types of insurance?

5. What is a deductible? What effect does it have on insurance premiums?

6. What does it mean to say that an insured has a duty to disclose? What happens if the insured fails in this duty?

7. What is an insurable interest? Why is it important?

8. Why are contracts of insurance known as contracts of indemnity?

9. What is a coinsurance clause? What is its purpose?

10. What is the right of subrogation? When does the right of subrogation arise?

11. What is the difference between a rider and an endorsement in an insurance policy?

12. How do "no-fault" liability systems differ from tort-based liability systems?

13. Describe comprehensive general liability insurance. How does it differ from warranty insurance?

14. What is the purpose of errors and omissions insurance?

15. When should a business consider buying key-person life insurance?

16. What does an insurance broker do?

17. What is the purpose of an insurance adjuster?

18. Does the insurer have a duty of good faith? Explain.

Questions for Critical Thinking

1. A manufacturing business is in the process of applying for property insurance. What kind of information must the business disclose to the insurance company? Why can insurance companies deny coverage on the basis of nondisclosure or misrepresentation of information?

2. How much does it take to establish an insurable interest? For example, does an employer have an insurable interest in an employee's life? A retired executive's life? Does a creditor have an insurable interest in a debtor's life? The owner of property has an insurable interest in the property. Do mortgagees and lien holders have an insurable interest in property? Does a tenant have an insurable interest in the landlord's property? Does a thief have an insurable interest in stolen property?

3. The insurance industry has introduced a number of new insurance products aimed at reducing the risk of costly lawsuits. Lawsuit insurance, like other types of insurance, transfers some of the risks and uncertainties associated with litigation from the business to the insurance company. When should a business purchase this type of insurance? What factors should be considered in the purchase decision? Do you think this type of insurance is more important in some industries than in others?

4. Fraudulent insurance claims are a problem faced by the insurance industry. Common examples involve inflated property values, exaggerated personal injuries, arson and other deliberate acts of sabotage, and "insider theft." Insurance companies are entitled to question the authenticity of all claims. How far should the insurance company be able to go in obtaining evidence of fraud? On what basis should the insurance company be entitled to deny a claim? For example, should an unusual pattern of claims be a basis for denial?

5. In *Whiten v. Pilot,* the court upheld an award of punitive damages against an insurer for breach of the insurer's duty of good faith. Should the courts award punitive damages against claimants who make fraudulent insurance claims? For example, there have been instances where a group of individuals have conspired to stage motor vehicle accidents and then submitted false property damage and personal injury claims.[24] What factors should the courts consider in awarding damages for insurance fraud?

Situations for Discussion

1. Asbestos Inc. is a company involved in the mining and selling of asbestos and the manufacture and selling of asbestos products. Insurance Inc. issued Asbestos a comprehensive general liability policy providing insurance against various risks, including product liability. Insurance Inc. wishes to rescind the policy on the basis that Asbestos failed to disclose material facts relating to the health risks associated with the inhalation of asbestos fibres. Did Asbestos have a duty to disclose that there were health risks associated with the use of asbestos?[25]

---

24. See, for example, *Insurance Corp. of British Columbia v. Hoang,* (2002), 42 C.C.L.I. (3d) 235 (B.C.S.C.).
25. Based on *Canadian Indemnity Co. v. Canadian Johns-Mansville Co.,* [1990] 2 S.C.R. 549.

2. Marcus Bains has decided to open a health club in a strip mall. Marcus knows that there are legal risks associated with operating this business and he is investigating insurance coverage. What questions should Marcus ask his insurance representative? Suppose that rather than opening the health club in a strip mall, Marcus decides to open it in the large garage attached to his house. What questions should Marcus ask his insurance representative in this scenario?

3. Dorothy is a sole proprietor who recently incorporated her business in order to take the benefits of limited liability. As part of this change, she transferred all her business assets over to her corporation, Dorothy Ltd. Unfortunately, she forgot to change her insurance policies to name the company as the new insured. The property remains insured in Dorothy's name. Soon after the transfer, there was a break-in at Dorothy Ltd.'s corporate offices, and much of the company's expensive computer equipment was stolen. Dorothy made a claim on her policy, but the insurance company took the position that she did not have an insurable interest in the corporate property.[26]

   Explain why the insurance company refused Dorothy's claim. What can she do now? What arguments can she make in support of her claim? What practical advice would Dorothy now give to other small business owners?

4. Tanic leased office space from Landrum. A term of the lease required Landrum to fully insure the property against loss caused by fire. An employee of Tanic left a coffeemaker turned on over the weekend. This caused a fire that resulted in serious damage to Tanic's furniture, computers, and business records.[27]

   Can Tanic claim under Landrum's policy? Is Tanic an insured party? If the insurer pays the claim, does it have a right of subrogation against the employee who caused the fire? What other arrangements could Tanic and Landrum have made for insurance coverage?

5. Claudine Gagotta was the assistant manager of Toggles Company Limited when it purchased life insurance on her life. Several years later Claudine left the employ of Toggles and started a competing business. Toggles continued to maintain the policy and pay the premiums.[28] Does Claudine have any grounds to challenge the continuation of the policy by Toggles?

6. On 12 April 2001, portions of Toronto's Skydome's retractable roof collided when it was being opened. Pieces of the roof fell onto the playing field, making the Skydome unsafe for use. The regularly scheduled Major League Baseball game between the Toronto Blue Jays and the Kansas City Royals was postponed. The Blue Jays sued Sportsco, the owner/operator of the Skydome, for damages in the amount of $1 000 000, alleging a loss of revenues from the loss of use of the building on 12 April 2001. Sportsco made a claim under its Comprehensive General Liability Policy with ING Insurance for a defence to the Blue Jays' claims. ING denied coverage and brought an application seeking a declaration that it did not owe Sportsco a defence (Note: an insurer has a duty to defend the insured when allegations fall within the coverage of the policy).[29] Who has the onus of proving whether a claim falls within an insurance policy? On what basis may an insurance company like ING Insurance deny coverage to an insured?

7. Greenhouses Inc. owns and operates a greenhouse in rural Nova Scotia. On a busy Saturday in early spring a customer, Xavier Donnelly, tripped over some bags of potting soil and fell onto a table where large plants and shrubs are repotted. Xavier suffered a severe gash to his right arm and a large bruise on his forehead. The way in which accidents and other incidents are handled can have a significant impact on the ultimate cost of a claim. How should the employees of Greenhouse handle Xavier's accident? Outline the steps that they should take in this situation.

---

26. Based on *Kosmopoulos v. Constitution Insurance Co. of Canada,* [1987] 1 S.C.R. 2.
27. Based on *T. Eaton Co. v. Smith* (1977), 92 D.L.R. (3d) 425 (S.C.C.).
28. Based on *Chantiam v. Packall Packaging Inc. et al.* (1998), 159 D.L.R. (4th) 517 (Ont. C.A.).
29. Based on *ING Insurance Co. of Canada v. Sportsco International L.P.,* [2004] O.J. No. 2254 (Ont. Sup. Ct.).

8. In 1999, John Jacks signed a long-term car lease agreement, which was assigned by the dealership to GMAC Leaseco. On the same day, Jacks contacted a representative of the Wawanesa Mutual Insurance Company to insure the vehicle. The representative asked Jacks a few questions related to driving. In particular, the representative asked Jacks how many accidents he had had in the previous six years, whether he had ever been convicted of impaired driving, and whether his driver's license had ever been revoked or suspended.

In 2002 Jacks had an accident and his car was destroyed. In response to his claim for compensation, Wawanesa conducted an investigation and discovered that the insured had been convicted of several crimes between 1980 and 1991 including break and enter, theft, possession of property obtained by crime, abetting in fraud, identity theft, fraud, and possession of drugs. Wawanesa refused to pay compensation on the basis that Jacks had failed in his duty to inform.[30] What is the purpose of the insured's duty to disclose? What is the content of the duty to disclose? Who has the onus of proving whether the duty to disclose has been fulfilled? Did Jacks fulfill the duty to disclose? Discuss.

For more study tools, visit
http://www.businesslaw3e.nelson.com

---

30. Based on *Compagnie mutuelle d'assurances Wawanesa v. GMAC location ltée.* [2005] R.R.A. 25 (Que. C.A.).

Glossary

acceleration clause A term of a loan agreement that makes the entire loan due if one payment is missed.

acceptance An unqualified willingness to enter into a contract on the terms in the offer.

act of bankruptcy One of specified acts that the debtor must commit before creditors can petition the debtor into bankruptcy.

action for the price The seller's claim when title to the goods has shifted to the buyer.

actual authority The power of an agent that derives from either express or implied agreement.

administrative law Rules created and applied by those having governmental powers.

adverse effects discrimination Discrimination that occurs as a result of a rule that appears neutral but in its effects is discriminatory.

after-acquired property Assets acquired by a debtor after giving a security interest.

age of majority The age at which a person becomes an adult for legal purposes.

agency A relationship that exists when one party represents another party in the formation of legal relations.

agency by estoppel An agency relationship created when the principal acts such that third parties reasonably conclude that an agency relationship exists.

agency by ratification An agency relationship created when one party adopts a contract entered into on his behalf by another who at the time acted without authority.

agent A person who is authorized to act on behalf of another.

aggravated damages Compensation for intangible injuries such as distress and humiliation caused by the defendant's reprehensible conduct.

alternative dispute resolution (ADR) A range of options for resolving disputes as an alternative to litigation.

anticipatory breach Breach that occurs before the date for performance.

anticompetitive behaviour Conduct that restricts competition and is reviewable under the *Competition Act*.

Anton Pillar order A pretrial order allowing the seizure of material, including material that infringes intellectual property rights.

apparent authority The power that an agent appears to have to an outsider because of conduct or statements of the principal.

appeal The process of arguing to a higher court that a court decision is wrong.

appellant The party who begins or files an appeal.

arbitration A process through which a neutral party makes a decision (usually binding) that resolves a dispute.

arbitrator A person who listens to both sides of a dispute and makes a ruling that is usually binding on the parties.

articles of incorporation The document that defines the basic characteristics of corporations incorporated in Newfoundland, New Brunswick, Ontario, Manitoba, Saskatchewan, Alberta, and the federal jurisdiction.

assault The threat of imminent physical harm.

assignment The transfer of rights by an assignor to an assignee.

assignment in bankruptcy The debtor's voluntary assignment to the trustee in bankruptcy of legal title to the debtor's property for the benefit of creditors.

bailee The person who receives possession in a bailment.

bailment Temporary transfer of possession of personal property from one person to another.

bailment for value Bailment involving payment for use of property or a service.

bailor The owner of property who transfers possession in a bailment.

bait and switch Advertising a product at a very low price to attract customers, then encouraging them to accept another product that is more expensive.

balance of probabilities Proof that there is a better than 50 percent chance that the circumstances of the contract are as the plaintiff contends.

banking agreement A contract that specifies the rights and obligations of a bank and a customer.

bankrupt The legal status that results when an assignment in bankruptcy is made or a receiving order is issued (also used to describe a debtor who is bankrupt).

bankruptcy offences Criminal acts defined by the *Bankruptcy and Insolvency Act* and committed by a participant in the bankruptcy and insolvency process.

battery Intentional infliction of harmful or offensive physical contact.

bid rigging Conspiring to fix the bidding process to suit the collective needs of those submitting bids.

bill Proposed legislation.

bill of exchange A written order to a person to pay a specified amount to another person.

bill of lading A shipping document that serves as a contract between the seller and the carrier.

binding Final and enforceable in the courts.

***bona fide* occupational requirement (BFOR)** A defence that excuses discrimination on a prohibited ground when it is done in good faith and for a legitimate business reason.

bond A document evidencing a debt owed by the corporation, often used to refer to a secured debt.

breach of contract Failure to comply with a contractual promise.

burden of proof The obligation of the plaintiff to prove its case.

business ethics Moral principles and values that seek to determine right and wrong in the business world.

business law A set of established rules governing commercial relationships, including the enforcement of rights.

bylaw A law made by the municipal level of government; also rules specifying day-to-day operating procedures of a corporation.

c.i.f. A contractual term making the seller responsible for insurance and shipping.

c.o.d. A contractual term requiring the purchaser to pay the shipper cash on delivery of goods.

Cabinet A body composed of all ministers heading government departments, as well as the prime minister or premier.

Canadian Charter of Rights and Freedoms A guarantee of specific rights and freedoms enshrined in the Constitution and enforceable by the judiciary.

Canadian legal system The machinery that comprises and governs the legislative, executive, and judicial branches of government.

carrier A bailee who transports personal property.

causation The relationship that exists between the defendant's conduct and the plaintiff's loss or injury.

caveat emptor Let the buyer beware or let the buyer take care.

certification The process by which a union is recognized as a bargaining agent for a group of employees; also the process whereby a bank guarantees payment of a cheque.

chattel lease A contract where a lessee pays for the use of a lessor's tangible personal property.

cheque A written order to a bank to pay money to a specified person.

Civil Code of Québec The rules of private law that govern Québec.

claim The formal document that initiates litigation by setting out the plaintiff's allegations against the defendant.

claims The exclusive rights of the patent holder.

class action A lawsuit launched by one person who represents a larger group whose members have similar claims against the same defendant.

closely held corporation A corporation that does not sell its shares to the public.

closing The final stage of a real estate transaction when final documentation and payment are exchanged.

collateral Security for a borrower's promise to repay a loan.

collective agreement The employment agreement reached between the union and employer setting out the bargaining unit employees' terms and conditions of employment.

collective bargaining A mechanism by which parties enter a collective agreement or contract.

common law Rules that are formulated in judgments.

common share A share that generally has a right to vote, share in dividends, and share in proceeds on dissolution.

concurrent jurisdiction Jurisdiction that is shared between levels of government.

condition An important term that, if breached, gives the innocent party the right to terminate the contract and claim damages.

condition precedent An event or circumstance that, until it occurs, suspends the parties' obligation to perform their contractual obligations.

condition subsequent An event or circumstance that, when it occurs, brings an existing contract to an end.

condonation Employer behaviour that indicates to the employee that misconduct is being overlooked.

conduct incompatible   Personal behaviour that is irreconcilable with employment duties or prejudicial to the employer's business.

confidential business information   Information that provides a business advantage as a result of the fact that it is kept secret.

consideration   The price paid for a promise.

constitutional conventions   Important rules that are not enforceable by a court of law but that practically determine or constrain how a given power is exercised.

constitutional law   The supreme law of Canada that constrains and controls how the branches of government exercise power.

constructive dismissal   Employer conduct that amounts to a breach of a fundamental term of the employment contract.

consumer debt   A loan to an individual for a noncommercial purpose.

consumer note   A negotiable instrument signed by a consumer to buy on credit.

contingency fee   A fee based on a percentage of the judgment awarded and paid by the client to the lawyer only if the action is successful.

contract   An agreement between two parties that is enforceable in a court of law.

contract law   Rules that make agreements binding and therefore facilitate planning and the enforcement of expectations.

contractual entrant   Any person who has paid (contracted) for the right to enter the premises.

contractual *quantum meruit*   Awarding one party a reasonable sum for the goods or services provided under a contract.

contributory negligence   A defence claiming that the plaintiff is at least partially responsible for the harm that has occurred.

conversion right   The right to convert one type of security into another type.

copyright   The right to prevent others from copying or modifying certain works.

corporate opportunity   A business opportunity in which the corporation has an interest.

costs   Legal expenses that a judge orders the loser to pay the winner.

counterclaim   A claim by the defendant against the plaintiff.

counteroffer   The rejection of one offer and proposal of a new one.

credit bureau   An agency that compiles credit information on borrowers.

cyber-squatting   The bad-faith practice of registering trademarks or trade names of others as domain names for the purpose of selling the domain name to the rightful owner or preventing the rightful owner from obtaining the domain name.

damages   Monetary compensation for breach of contract or other actionable wrong.

damages for nonacceptance   Damages to which a seller is entitled if a buyer refuses to accept goods prior to the title shifting.

data or screen scraping   Gathering and assembling information from other Internet websites.

debenture   A document evidencing a debt owed by the corporation, often used to refer to an unsecured debt.

deceit or fraud   A false representation intentionally or recklessly made by one person to another that causes damage.

decision   The judgment of the court that specifies which party is successful and why.

deductible   The part of a loss for which the insured is responsible.

defamation   The public utterance of a false statement of fact or opinion that harms another's reputation.

default   Failure to make required payments on a loan.

defence   The defendant's formal response to the plaintiff's allegations.

defendant   The party being sued.

deficiency   The shortfall between the outstanding mortgage balance and the proceeds from sale of the land; also the shortfall if secured assets are sold for less than the amount of the outstanding loan.

derivative action   A suit by a shareholder on behalf of the corporation to enforce a corporate cause of action.

director   A person elected by shareholders to manage a corporation.

discharge of bankruptcy   The formal order releasing the debtor from bankrupt status and from most remaining debts.

discovery   The process of disclosing evidence to support the claims in a lawsuit.

discrimination   Treating someone differently on the basis of a prohibited ground.

dissent and appraisal right   The right of shareholders who dissent from certain fundamental changes to the corporation to have their shares purchased by the corporation at a fair price.

distinguishing guise   A shaping of wares or their container, or a mode of wrapping or packaging wares.

distress   The right of a commercial landlord to seize the tenant's personal property for nonpayment of rent.

distributorship   A contractual relationship where one business agrees to sell another's products

dividend   A division of profits payable to shareholders.

domain name   The unique address of a website.

domestic law   The internal law of a given country, which includes both statute and common law.

door-to-door selling   The act of selling in person directly to a customer's residence.

double ticketing   The offence of failing to sell at the lower of the two prices appearing on a product.

due diligence   A defence based on adopting reasonable steps to avoid the violation of a legal duty.

duress   The threat of physical or economic harm that results in a contract.

duty of care   The responsibility owed to avoid carelessness that causes harm to others.

duty of confidentiality   The obligation of a professional not to disclose any information provided by the client without the client's consent.

duty to accommodate   The duty of an employer to modify work rules, practices, and requirements to meet the needs of individuals who would otherwise be subjected to unlawful discrimination.

duty to disclose   The obligation of the insured to provide to the insurer all information that relates to the risk being insured.

duty to mitigate   The obligation to take reasonable steps to minimize the losses resulting from a breach of contract or other wrong.

easement   The right to use the land of another for a particular purpose only.

electronic banking   Financial transactions through the use of computers, telephones, or other electronic means.

employment equity legislation   Laws designed to improve the status of certain designated groups.

employment relationship   A contractual relationship whereby an employer provides remuneration to an employee in exchange for work or services.

employment standards legislation   Laws that specify minimum standards in the workplace.

endorsement   The process of signing a negotiable instrument to enable negotiation; also written evidence of a change to an existing insurance policy.

endorsement in blank   Signing a cheque without any special instructions.

entire contract clause   A term in a contract in which the parties agree that their contract is complete as written.

equality of bargaining power   The legal assumption that parties to a contract are able to look out for their own interests.

equity   Rules that focus on what would be fair given the specific circumstances of the case, as opposed to what the strict rules of common law might dictate.

equity of redemption   The right to regain legal title to mortgaged land upon repayment of the debt.

estate   The collective term for the assets of the insolvent or bankrupt.

evidence   Proof presented in court to support a claim.

exclusive dealing   Conduct that is reviewable under the *Competition Act* because the seller agrees to sell to the purchaser only if the purchaser buys from it exclusively.

exclusive jurisdiction   Jurisdiction that one level of government holds entirely on its own and not on a shared basis with another level.

exclusive possession   The tenant's right to control land during the term of a lease.

exemption clause   A term of a contract that identifies events causing loss for which there is no liability.

express term   A provision of a contract that states a promise explicitly.

f.o.b.   A contractual term whereby the buyer specifies the type of transportation and the seller arranges that transportation and delivery of goods to the shipper at the buyer's expense.

fair dealing   A defence to copyright infringement that permits the copying of works for limited purposes.

false imprisonment   Unlawful detention or physical restraint or coercion by psychological means.

false or misleading advertising   Promotional statements that either are false or have the ability to mislead a consumer as to their truth.

Federal Court of Canada   The court that deals with some types of litigation involving the federal government.

fee simple   The legal interest in real property that is closest to full ownership.

fiduciary duty   A duty imposed on a person who has a special relationship of trust with another.

fiduciary   A person who has a duty of good faith toward another because of their relationship.

financing lease   A lease that enables the lessee to finance the acquisition of tangible personal property.

financing statement   The document registered as evidence of a security interest in personal property.

fixed- or definite-term contract   A contract for a specified period of time, which automatically ends on the expiry date.

fixtures   Tangible personal property that is attached to land, buildings, or other fixtures.

foreclosure   The mortgagee's remedy to terminate the mortgagor's interest in the land.

formal executive   The branch of government responsible for the ceremonial features of government.

franchise An agreement whereby an owner of a trademark or trade name permits another to sell a product or service under that trademark or name.

fraudulent preference A payment made by an insolvent debtor within three months of bankruptcy with a view to favouring one creditor over others.

frustration Termination of a contract by an unexpected event or change that makes performance functionally impossible or illegal.

fundamental breach A breach of contract that affects the foundation of the contract.

fundamental term A term that is considered to be essential to the contract.

general security agreement A loan contract that includes all of the assets of a business as collateral.

government policy The central ideas or principles that guide government in its work, including the kind of laws it passes.

gratuitous bailment Bailment that involves no payment.

gratuitous promise A promise for which no consideration is given.

grievance process A procedure for resolving disputes contained in union contracts.

guarantee A promise to pay the debt of someone else, should that person default on the obligation.

guarantor A person who signs a guarantee.

habitual neglect of duty Persistent failure to perform employment duties.

holder A person who has possession of a negotiable instrument.

holder in due course A holder in good faith without notice of defects who acquires greater rights than the parties who dealt directly with each other as the drawer and drawee.

Human Rights Commission An administrative body that oversees the implementation and enforcement of human rights legislation.

identification theory A theory specifying that a corporation is liable when the person committing the wrong is the corporation's directing mind.

illegal contract A contract that cannot be enforced because it is contrary to legislation or public policy.

implied term A provision that is not expressly included in a contract but that is necessary to give effect to the parties' intention.

improvident sale A sale of the borrower's assets by the lender for less than fair market value.

incompetence Lack of ability, knowledge, or qualification to perform employment obligations.

incorporator The person who sets the incorporation process in motion.

indefinite-term contract A contract for no fixed period, which can end on giving reasonable notice.

indemnification The corporate practice of paying litigation expenses of officers and directors for lawsuits related to corporate affairs.

indemnity The obligation on the insurer to make good the loss.

independent contractor A person who is in a working relationship that does not meet the criteria of employment.

industrial design The visual features of shape, configuration, pattern, ornamentation, or any combination of these applied to a finished article of manufacture.

inferior court A court with limited financial jurisdiction whose judges are appointed by the provincial government.

injurious or malicious falsehood The utterance of a false statement about another's goods or services that is harmful to the reputation of those goods or services.

innkeeper Someone who offers lodging to the public.

innominate term A term that cannot easily be classified as either a condition or a warranty.

insider A person whose relationship with the issuer of securities is such that he is likely to have access to relevant material information concerning the issuer that is not known to the public.

insider trading Transactions in securities of a corporation by or on behalf of an insider on the basis of relevant material information concerning the issuer not known to the general public.

insolvency The inability to meet financial obligations as they become due or having insufficient assets to meet obligations.

inspector A person appointed by creditors to act on their behalf and supervise the actions of the trustee.

insurable interest A financial stake in what is being insured.

insurance adjuster One who investigates and evaluates insurance claims.

insurance agent One who acts for an insurance company in selling insurance.

insurance broker One who provides advice and assistance to the insured in acquiring insurance.

insurance policy A contract of insurance.

insured One who buys insurance coverage.

insurer A company that sells insurance coverage.

intangible property Personal property, the value of which comes from legal rights.

intellectual property The results of the creative process such as ideas, the expression of ideas, formulas, schemes, trademarks, and the like; also refers to the protection attached to ideas through patent, copyright, trademark, industrial design, and other similar laws.

intentional tort A harmful act that is committed on purpose.

interference with contractual relations Incitement to break the contractual obligations of another.

interlocutory injunction An order to refrain from doing something for a limited period of time.

international law Law that governs relations between states and other entities with international legal status.

invitation to treat An expression of willingness to do business.

invitee Any person who comes onto the property to provide the occupier with a benefit.

joint and several liability Individual and collective liability for a debt. Each liable party is individually responsible for the entire debt as well as being collectively liable for the entire debt.

joint liability Liability shared by two or more parties where each is personally liable for the full amount of the obligation.

joint tenancy Co-ownership whereby the survivor inherits the undivided interest of the deceased.

joint tort-feasors Two or more persons whom a court has held to be jointly responsible for the plaintiff's loss or injuries.

joint venture A grouping of two or more businesses to undertake a particular project.

judges Those appointed by federal and provincial governments to adjudicate on a variety of disputes, as well as to preside over criminal proceedings.

judgment debtor The party ordered by the court to pay a specified amount to the winner of a lawsuit.

judiciary A collective reference to judges.

jurisdiction The power that a given level of government has to enact laws.

just cause Employee conduct that amounts to a fundamental breach of the employment contract.

Labour Relations Board A body that administers labour relations legislation.

land titles system The system of land registration whereby the administrators guarantee the title to land.

landlord The owner of land who grants possession to the tenant.

lapse The expiration of an offer after a specified or reasonable period.

law The set of rules and principles guiding conduct in society.

law firm A partnership formed by lawyers.

law of agency The law governing the relationship where one party, the agent, acts on behalf of another, the principal.

lawyer A person who is legally qualified to practise law.

lease A contract that transfers possession of land from the landlord to the tenant in exchange for the payment of rent; also refers to the tenant's interest in land.

legal capacity The ability to make binding contracts.

legal risk A business risk with legal implications.

legal risk management plan A comprehensive action plan for dealing with the legal risks involved in operating a business.

legislative branch The branch of government that creates statute law.

letter of commitment A document that is provided by a bank to a borrower and sets out the terms of a loan.

letter of credit A written promise by a buyer's bank to a seller's bank to pay the seller when specified conditions are met.

liability Legal responsibility for the event or loss that has occurred.

liberalism A political philosophy that elevates individual freedom and autonomy as its key organizing value.

licence Consent given by the owner of rights to someone to do something that only the owner can do.

licensee Any person whose presence is not a benefit to the occupier but to which the occupier has no objection.

lien The right to retain possession of personal property until payment for service is received.

lifting the corporate veil Determining that the corporation is not a separate legal entity from its shareholders.

limitation of liability clause A term of a contract that limits liability for breach to something less than would otherwise be recoverable.

limitation period The time period specified by legislation for commencing legal action.

limited liability Responsibility for obligations restricted to the amount of investment.

limited liability partnership (LLP) A partnership in which the partners have unlimited liability for their own malpractice but limited liability for other partners' malpractice.

limited partnership A partnership in which the liability of some partners is limited to their capital contribution.

liquidated damages clause A term of a contract that specifies how much one party must pay the other in the event of breach.

litigation The process involved when one person sues another.

marketing law All areas of law that influence and direct the creation, promotion, pricing, and distribution of goods, services, or ideas.

mediation A process through which the parties to a dispute endeavour to reach a resolution with the assistance of a neutral person.

mediator A person who helps the parties to a dispute reach a compromise.

misrepresentation A false statement of fact that causes someone to enter a contract.

mistake An error made by one or both parties that seriously undermines a contract.

money laundering The false reporting of income from criminal activity as income from legitimate business.

moral rights The author's rights to have work properly attributed and not prejudicially modified or associated with products.

mortgage A credit arrangement where title to land is security for the loan.

mortgagee The party who lends the money and receives the signed mortgage as security for repayment.

mortgagor The party who borrows the money and signs the mortgage promising to repay the loan.

multidisciplinary practice (MDP) A firm of professionals that offers the services of several different professionals within one practice.

multilevel marketing A scheme for distributing products or services that involves participants recruiting others to become involved in distribution.

negligence Unreasonable conduct, including a careless act or omission, that causes harm to another.

negligent misstatement or negligent misrepresentation An incorrect statement made carelessly.

negotiable instrument A written contract containing an unconditional promise or order to pay a specific sum on demand or on a specified date to a specific person or bearer.

negotiation A process of deliberation and discussion used to reach a mutually acceptable resolution to a dispute; also the process of transferring negotiable instruments from one person to another.

neighbour Anyone who might reasonably be affected by another's conduct.

nonpecuniary damages Compensation for pain and suffering, loss of enjoyment of life, and loss of life expectancy.

novation The substitution of parties in a contract or the replacement of one contract with another.

NUANS report A document that shows the result of a search for business names.

nuisance Any activity on an occupier's property that unreasonably and substantially interferes with the neighbour's rights to enjoyment of her property.

objective standard test The test based on how a "reasonable person" would view the matter.

occupier Any person with a legal right to occupy premises.

offer A promise to perform specified acts on certain terms.

offeree The person to whom an offer is made.

offeror The person who makes an offer.

operating lease A lease where the property is returned to the lessor when the term is up.

oppression remedy A statutory remedy available to shareholders and other stakeholders to protect their corporate interests.

option agreement An agreement where, in exchange for payment, an offeror is obligated to keep an offer open for a specified time.

outsider The party with whom the agent does business on behalf of the principal.

paralegal One who performs legal work under the supervision of a practising lawyer.

paramountcy A doctrine that provides that federal laws prevail when there are conflicting or inconsistent federal and provincial laws.

parol evidence rule A rule that limits the evidence a party can introduce concerning the contents of the contract.

partnership A business carried on by two or more persons with the intention of making a profit.

passing off Presenting another's goods or services as one's own.

patent A monopoly to make, use, or sell an invention.

patent agent A professional trained in patent law and practice who can assist in the preparation of a patent application.

pay equity Provisions designed to ensure that female and male employees receive the same compensation for performing similar or substantially similar work.

pecuniary damages Compensation for out-of-pocket expenses, loss of future income, and cost of future care.

periodic tenancy A lease that is automatically renewed unless one party gives proper notice to terminate.

personal property All property, other than land and what is attached to land, that can be identified by its mobility.

petition The statement filed by the creditors claiming that the debtor owes at least $1000, has committed an act of bankruptcy, and should therefore be declared bankrupt.

plaintiff The party that initiates a lawsuit against another party.

pleadings The formal documents concerning the basis for a lawsuit.

political executive The branch of government responsible for day-to-day operations, including formulating and executing government policy, as well as administering all departments of government.

precedent An earlier case used to resolve a current case because of its similarity.

predatory pricing The offence of setting unreasonably low prices to eliminate competition.

pre-emptive right A shareholder's right to maintain a proportionate share of ownership by purchasing a proportionate share of any new stock issue.

pre-existing legal duty A legal obligation that a person already owes.

preferred creditors Certain unsecured creditors who are given priority over the other unsecured creditors in the legislation.

preferred share A share or stock that has a preference in the distribution of dividends and the proceeds on dissolution.

premium The price paid for insurance coverage.

price discrimination The offence of failing to provide similar pricing terms and conditions to competing wholesalers or retailers for equivalent volume sales at an equivalent time.

price maintenance The offence of attempting to drive the final retail price of goods upward and imposing recriminations upon noncompliant retailers.

prima facie At first sight or on first appearances.

principal A person who has permitted another to act on her behalf.

private law Areas of law that concern dealings between persons.

privilege The professional's right not to divulge a client's confidential information to third parties.

procedural law The law governing the procedure to enforce rights, duties, and liabilities.

product liability Liability relating to the design, manufacture, or sale of the product.

product licensing An arrangement whereby the owner of a trademark or other proprietary right grants to another the right to manufacture or distribute products associated with the trademark or other proprietary right.

professional Someone engaged in an occupation requiring the exercise of special knowledge, education, and skill.

progressive discipline policy A system that follows a sequence of employee discipline from less to more severe punishment.

prohibited offences Offences under the *Competition Act* that are criminal in nature.

promissory estoppel A doctrine whereby someone who relies on a gratuitous promise may be able to enforce it.

promissory note A written promise to another person to pay a specified amount.

proof of claim A formal notice provided by the creditor to the trustee of the amount owed and the nature of the debt.

proposal A contractual agreement between the debtor and creditors that allows an insolvent debtor to reorganize and continue in business.

prospectus The document a corporation must publish when offering securities to the public.

proxy A person who is authorized to exercise a shareholder's voting rights.

public law Areas of the law that relate to or regulate the relationship between persons and government at all levels.

public policy The community's common sense and common conscience.

punitive damages An award to the plaintiff to punish the defendant for malicious, oppressive, and high-handed conduct.

pure economic loss Financial loss that results from a negligent act where there has been no accompanying property or personal injury damage to the person claiming the loss.

pyramid selling An illegal form of multilevel selling under the *Competition Act*.

qualified privilege A defence to defamation based on the defamatory statement being relevant, without malice, and communicated only to a party who has a legitimate interest in receiving it.

ratify To authorize or approve.

real property Land or real estate, including buildings, fixtures, and the associated legal rights.

reasonable care The care a reasonable person would exhibit in a similar situation.

reasonable notice A period of time for an employee to find alternative employment prior to dismissal.

reasonable person The standard used to judge whether a person's conduct in a particular situation is negligent.

rebuttable presumption A legal presumption in favour of one party that the other side can seek to rebut or dislodge by leading evidence to the contrary.

receiver A person appointed by the secured creditor to seize the assets and realize the debt.

receiving order The court order following a creditor's petition that formally declares the debtor to be bankrupt and transfers legal control of the estate to the trustee.

refusal to deal Conduct that is reviewable under the *Competition Act* because the seller refuses to sell to a purchaser on the same terms as offered to the purchaser's competitors.

registration The process of recording a security interest in a public registry system.

registry system The system of land registration whereby the records are available to be examined and evaluated by interested parties.

regulations Rules created by the political executive that have the force of law.

regulatory offence An offence contrary to the public interest.

rejection The refusal to accept an offer.

release A written or oral statement discharging another from an existing duty.

remoteness of damage   The absence of a sufficiently close relationship between the defendant's action and the plaintiff's loss.

rescission   The remedy that results in the parties being returned to their precontractual positions.

respondent   The party against whom an appeal is filed.

restitutionary *quantum meruit*   An amount that is reasonable given the benefit the plaintiff has conferred.

restrictive covenant   A restriction on the use of land as specified in the title document.

restrictive endorsement   Signing a cheque for deposit only to a particular bank account.

retainer   An advance payment requested by a professional from a client to fund services to be provided to the client.

reviewable matters   Offences under the *Competition Act* that are assessed according to a civil burden of proof and resolved by voluntary agreement or by order of the Competition Tribunal.

reviewable transaction   A payment made to a person related to the bankrupt within one year of the bankruptcy order with the intention of giving the related person priority over at least one other creditor.

revocation   The withdrawal of an offer.

rider   A clause altering or adding coverage to a standard insurance policy.

risk avoidance   The decision to cease a business activity because the legal risk is too great.

risk reduction   Implementation of practices in a business to lower the probability of loss and its severity.

risk retention   The decision to absorb the loss if a legal risk materializes.

risk transference   The decision to shift the risk to someone else through a contract.

royal prerogative   Historical rights and privileges of the Crown, including the right to conduct foreign affairs and to declare war.

rules of construction   Guiding principles for interpreting or "constructing" the terms of a contract.

sales agency   An agreement in which a manufacturer or distributor allows another to sell products on its behalf

secured creditor   A lender who through a registered security interest has the right to seize and sell specific assets of a borrower to collect a debt.

securities   Shares and bonds issued by a corporation.

securities legislation   Laws designed to regulate transactions involving shares and bonds of a corporation.

self-dealing contract   A contract in which a fiduciary has a conflict of interest.

serious misconduct   Intentional, harmful conduct of the employee that permits the employer to dismiss without notice.

settlement   A sale that can be declared void because it was not made in good faith or for valuable consideration.

severance pay   An amount owed to a terminated employee under employment standards legislation.

share structure   The shares that a corporation is permitted to issue by its constitution.

shareholder   A person who has an ownership interest in a corporation.

shareholder agreement   An agreement that defines the relationship among people who have an ownership interest in a corporation.

shelf company   A company that does not engage in active business.

small claims court   A court that deals with claims up to a specified amount.

sole proprietorship   A unincorporated business organization that has only one owner.

spam   Unsolicited email advertising a product or service.

special endorsement   Signing a cheque and making it payable to a specific person.

specific goods   Goods that are identified and agreed on at the time a contract of sale is made.

specifications   The description of an invention contained in a patent.

stakeholder   One who has an interest in a corporation.

statement of claim   A document setting out the basis for a legal complaint.

statute law   Formal, written laws created or enacted by the legislative branch of government.

stop payment   The process whereby the person who writes a cheque orders the bank not to pay the holder who presents it for payment.

stoppage in transitu   The right of a seller to demand that goods be returned by a shipper to the seller, provided the buyer is insolvent.

strategic alliance   An arrangement whereby two or more businesses agree to cooperate for some purpose.

strict liability   The principle that liability will be imposed irrespective of proof of negligence.

subrogation   The right of a guarantor to recover from the debtor any payments made to the creditor; also the right of the insurer to recover the amount paid on a claim from a third party that caused the loss.

substantive law   Law that defines rights, duties, and liabilities.

superior court   A court with unlimited financial jurisdiction whose judges are appointed by the federal government.

Supreme Court of Canada   The final court for appeals in the country.

systemic discrimination Discrimination that results from the combined effects of many rules, practices, and policies.

tangible property Personal property, the value of which comes from its physical form.

telemarketing The use of telephone to communicate product and organizational information to customers.

tenancy in common Co-ownership whereby each owner of an undivided interest can dispose of that interest.

tenant The party in possession of land that is leased.

thin skull rule The principle that a defendant is liable for the full extent of a plaintiff's loss even where a prior vulnerability makes the harm more serious than it otherwise might be.

third party One who is not a party to an agreement.

tied selling Conduct that is reviewable under the *Competition Act* because the seller will sell to the purchaser only if the purchaser buys other, less desirable goods as well.

tippee A person who acquires material information about an issuer of securities from an insider.

title search Investigation of the registered ownership of land in a registry system.

tort A harm caused by one person to another, other than through breach of contract, and for which the law provides a remedy.

tort-feasor Person who commits a tort.

trade name The name under which a sole proprietorship, a partnership, or a corporation does business.

trademark A word, symbol, design, or any combination of these used to distinguish the source of goods or services.

treaty An agreement between two or more states that is governed by international law.

trespass The act of coming onto another's property without the occupier's express or implied consent.

trespass to land Interference with someone's possession of land.

trespasser Any person who is not invited onto the property and whose presence is either unknown to the occupier or is objected to by the occupier.

trial A formal hearing before a judge that results in a binding decision.

trustee in bankruptcy The officer assigned legal responsibility for administering the affairs of bankrupt corporations or individuals.

unanimous shareholder agreement (USA) An agreement among all shareholders that restricts the powers of the directors to manage the corporation.

unascertained goods Goods not yet set aside and identifiable as the subject of the contract at the time the contract is formed.

unconscionable contract An unfair contract formed when one party takes advantage of the weakness of another.

undisclosed principal A principal whose identity is unknown to a third party, who has no knowledge that the agent is acting in an agency capacity.

undue influence Unfair manipulation that compromises someone's free will.

unfair practices Illegal business practices that exploit the unequal bargaining position of consumers.

unjust enrichment Occurs when one party has undeservedly or unjustly secured a benefit at the other party's expense.

unlimited liability Unrestricted legal responsibility for obligations.

unsecured creditor A creditor with no security interest in the debtor's property.

vicarious liability The liability that an employer has for the tortious acts of an employee committed in the ordinary course or scope of employment.

vicarious performance Performance of contractual obligations through others.

void contract A contract involving a defect so substantial that it is of no force or effect.

voidable contract A contract that in certain circumstances an aggrieved party can choose to keep in force or bring to an end.

voluntary assumption of risk The defence that no liability exists as the plaintiff agreed to accept the risk inherent in the activity.

warehouseman A bailee who stores personal property.

warranty A minor term that, if breached, gives the innocent party the right to claim damages only.

warranty of authority A representation of authority by a person who purports to be an agent.

widely held corporation A corporation whose shares are normally traded on a stock exchange.

willful disobedience Deliberate failure to carry out lawful and reasonable orders.

winding up The process of dissolving a corporation.

workers' compensation legislation Legislation that provides no-fault compensation for injured employees in lieu of their right to sue in tort.

Copyright Acknowledgments

Index

Note: Boldface page locators indicate terms that are defined in the text.

Acceleration clause, **650**
Acceptance, **120**
    communication of, 120–26
    electronics and, 125–26
Accounting firms, liability of, 553
Act of bankruptcy, **669**
Administrative law, **39**
    tribunals, 40
Adverse effects of discrimination, **495**
Advertisements
    and offer, 114**n**
Advertising, *see also* Promotion; Sales and
    marketing
    bait and switch selling, 114**n**
    false, **582**–83
    misleading, **582**–83
After-acquired property, **649**
Age of majority, **168**
Agency, **291**
    by agreement, 293–94
    and authority, *see* Authority
    banking, **620**
    creation of, 293–300
    defined, 292–93
    disputes applicable to, 80
    duties in agent-principal relationship,
      301–305
    duties of principal, 305
    by estoppel, **297**–98
    fiduciary duty, **302**–303
    as fiduciary relationship, 302
    general security agreement and,
      647–48
    guarantee and, 654–55
    law of, **293**
    nature of, 291–92
    and outsider, **292**
    and power of attorney, 295
    of professionals and fiduciaries,
      303–304
    ratification creating, 300
    termination, 310

    tort liability and, 307
    warranty of authority, **306**
Agency by estoppel, **297**–98
Agency by ratification, **300**
Agent(s), **291**
    authority of, *see* Authority
    for both vendor and purchaser, 303
    duties, 301–307
    electronic, 309
    fiduciary breach vs. non-breach, 303
    insurance agent as fiduciary, 301
    real estate, 299–300
    warranty of authority, **306**
Aggravated damages, **233**
Agreement(s), *see also* Contract(s)
    banking, **620**–21
    click-wrap, 157
    collective, **512**
    conditional, 151–53
    condition precedent, **152**
    condition subsequent, 151
    contractual *quantum meruit*, **145**
    electronic evidence, 149
    entire contract clause, **146**
    express terms, **141**–42
    general security, **647**–48
    guarantee, **654**–55
    implied terms, **142**–46
    indemnification, re director's
      liability, 388
    legal doctrine of frustration and, 150
    limitation of liability clause and,
      153–**54**
    liquidated damages clause and, **158**
    non-disclosure, 447
    option, **119**
    partnership, 324–25
    plain meaning rule, 142
    of purchase and sale, 466–68
    rules of construction and, **141**
    and *Sale of Goods Act*, 145–**46**
    shareholders,' **396**
    shrink-wrap, 156–57
    terms of, 141–58
    to terminate contract, 196–97
    unanimous shareholders', **396**–97

Agreement of purchase and sale, 466–68
Alternative dispute resolution (ADR),
    77–82
    and contract, 80
    defined, **77**
    and international transactions, 81
    mediation, **78**, 80
    mediator, 78
    practitioners, **79**
    qualifications, 79
    sources, 80–82
    types of disputes and, 80
Anticipatory breach, **206**
Anticompetitive behaviour, **605**
Apparent authority, **296**
Appeals(s), **88**–89
    appellant, 89
    to provincial court of appeal, 89
    to Supreme Court of Canada, 89
Appellant, **89**
Arbitration, **8**
Arbitrator, **78**
Articles of incorporation, **358**
Assault, **224**, 275–76
Assignment, **197**, **450**
Assignment in bankruptcy, **667**
Assignment of contract, 197–98
    steps in, 198
ATM transactions, rules, *see* Electronic
    banking
Authority, 294–96
    actual, 294–95
    apparent, 296
    express and implied, 294–95
    warranty of, **306**

Bailee, **409**–12
    carrier, **412**
    liability of, 412–13
    warehouseman, **412**
Bailment, **409**–21
    and chattel lease, **416**
    financing lease, 417
    gratuitous, **410**
    innkeepers, **412**, 420
    lease and, 416–17

liability per contract, 415
liability and, 411–14
lien, **419**
and lodging, 419–20
and operating lease, **416**
remedies and, 414, 418–19
repairs and, 418–19
for reward, 416–19
storage, 417–18
table summarizing, 421
and transportation, 419
for value, **410**
Bailor, **409**–12
Balance of probabilities, **200**
Banking
    agreement, **620**–21
    business relationship to, 620–23
    cheques and, 625–29
    customer information and money
      laundering, 621–22
    customers, relationship with, 622–23
    duties of bank, and customers, 621–22
    electronic, **629**–32. See also
      Electronic banking
    ethical considerations and, standard
      form guarantees, 657
    methods of payment, 633
    negotiable instruments, **623**–29
    regulation of banks, 620
    risks, and payment methods, 633
Bankrupt, **668**
    estate, **666**
Bankruptcy, **668**
    act of, **669**
    administration of, 670–76
    assignment in, **667**
    creditor options and, 668–70
    debts, identification of, 673–74
    discharge of, **676**
    distribution to creditors, 674–76
    fraudulent preference, **672**
    inspector, **671**
    personal, 676–77
    petitioning debtor into, 669–70
    preferred creditors, **674**
    proceedings before, 665–67
    proof of claim and, **673**
    protection of assets, 671–73
    receiving order, **670**
    reviewable transactions, **672**
    settlements and fraudulent
      conveyances, 672–73
    trustee in, **665**
Bankruptcy offences, **677**
Battery, **224,** 275–76
Bid rigging, **597**
Bill, **34**
Bill of exchange, **623**
Bill of lading, **577**
Binding decision, **78**

Bluffing, ethical considerations
    and, 102–103
Bona fide occupation requirement
    (BFOR), **495**
Bond, **360**
Breach of contract, **6,** 203–12
    anticipatory breach, **206**
    condition, **203**
    corporations and, 333
    damages and, **206**–10
    duty to mitigate damages, **209**–10
    equitable remedies, 210–11
    ethical considerations and, 205
    exemption clause, 203–204
    fundamental breach, **203**
    innominate term and, **203**
    limitation of liability clause, 203–204
    pecuniary vs. non-pecuniary dam-
      ages, 206–207
    remedies for, 206–15
    restitutionary *quantum meruit*, **211**
    restitutionary remedies, 211
    risk management and, 212
    and termination, 203–206
    unjust enrichment and, **211**
    warranty and, **203**
Burden of proof, **87**
Business
    administrative bodies affecting, 41
    bankruptcy protection and corporate
      re-organization, 667–68
    banks and, client formation and
      money laundering, 621–22
    bullying at work legislation and,
      505–506
    business-to-business torts, 276–81
    commercial and personal insurance
      and, 701–702
    and *Competition Act*, overview, 583–84
    confidential information and
      corporate espionage, 451
    constitutional challenges by, 33
    credit, *see* Credit
    criminal liability re health/
      safety violations, 504
    directors avoiding personal
      liability, 388
    discrimination and hiring
      practices, 497
    dismissal and class actions, ADR
      use, 535
    failure of, *see* Business failure
    insurance, interruption loss, 702
    insurance and marijuana
      "grow-ops," 693–94
    insurance company and, dealing
      with, 691–92
    liability of accounting firms, 553
    mandatory retirement and, 494

    no fault insurance systems and,
      696–97
    organization, forms of, 317–26
    origins/purposes of bankruptcy
      legislation and, 670
    and *Partnership Act*, 325,
    pay equity in federal sector and, 507
    personal use of employer's
      property, 521
    power of attorney and agency
      and, 295
    privacy protection legislation and, 282
    products and unjustified
      performance claims, 585–86
    and professional services, *see*
      Professional services
    sale of goods legislation, and, 572
    scanners, price accuracy,
      self-regulation and 602
    sole proprietorships and, **317**
    unfair practice, 174–75
Business arrangements, 336–42
    distributor/dealership, **341**
    franchise, **336**–37
    joint venture, **340**
    product licensing, 341–42
    sales agency, **341**
    strategic alliance, **340**
Business ethics, **11**
    and the law, 11–12
Business failure
    and bankruptcy, 664–65
    creditor options and, 668–70
    debtor options and, 665–67
    secured creditors' action vs. specific
      assets, 669
Business law, **4**
Business operations
    torts rising from, 274–82
Bylaws, **26, 358**–59
    change, 72
    fines and penalties, 26
    municipal government, 26

Cabinet, **29**
    regulation-making power, 29
Canadian Charter of Rights and Freedoms,
    20, 22, **30**–34
    constitutional challenges to, 33
    equality provisions of, 30
    freedom of expression and, 20, 31, 32
    oppressive government conduct
      and, 31
    override of, notwithstanding
      provision, 32
    protected speech and, 22
    restraint on government action if
      discrimination, 34

Capital sources
    corporations and, 334
    partnerships and, 322
    sole proprietorships and, 318
Care
    duty of, 242
    future, 232
    reasonable, **241**
Carrier, **412**
    re bailment, 419
Causation, **246**
Caveat emptor, **568**
Certification, **512**, **627**
*Charter of Rights and Freedoms, see Canadian
    Charter of Rights and Freedoms*
Chattel lease, **416**
Cheque, **623**–29
    accepting a, 627–29
    certification of, **627**
    consumer note, **626**
    creating a, 625–27
    endorsement and, **626**
    endorsement in blank, **628**
    holder, **625**
    holder in due course, **625**
    negotiation of, **626**
    restrictive endorsement, **628**
    special endorsement, 628
    stop payment, **627**
C.i.f., **577**
Civil Code, see Quebec Civil Code
Civil court, *see* Small claims court
Civil law
    Civil Code of Quebec, **39**
    common law vs., 38–39
Claim(s), **85**
    counter-, 85
    creditors and, 673
    defendant's failure to respond to, 85
    delivery of, 85
    inventions and, 433
    judgment and, 85
    notice of, 85
    performance, 585–86
    small, court, 29
    statement of, **21**
Class-action(s) (suit), 83, **84**
    ADR and dismissal, 535
    in the United States, 91
Clip-wrap, 157
Closely held corporation, **353**
C.o.d., **578**
Collateral, **641**
Collective agreement, **512**
Collective bargaining, **512**
Commercial disputes
    courts dealing with, 30
Commercial expression, 22
    whether "protected speech" under
        the Charter, 22

Commercial litigation, *see* Litigation
    process
Common law, **36**
Common share, **391**
Communications, re employees and
    Criminal Code, 511
Company, *see also* Corporation(s);
    Director(s)
    shelf-, **357**
Competition laws
    complaints, defences and, 584–85
    mergers, acquisitions, takeovers
        and, 603
    performance claims and, 585–86
Competition Tribunal, 584
Concurrent jurisdiction, 24
Condition, **203**
Condition precedent, **152**
Condition subsequent, 151
Condonation, **521**
Conduct incompatible, **522**
Confidential business information, **446**–49
    limitations on protection, 448
    money laundering and, 621–22
    non-disclosure agreement, 447
    obligation of confidence, implied, 447
    process and scope of protection, 447
    receipt of, and confidence obliga-
        tion, *Lac Minerals* case, 448
    requirements for protection, **447**
    vs. trade information, 449
    trade secret, 446n
Consideration, 127–29
    promises enforceable without, 127–32
Constitution Act, 1867, 22
    federal vs. provincial powers, 28
Constitution, Canadian, 22–27
    judicial decisions, 22
Constitutional challenges by business, 33
Constitutional conventions, **23**
Constitutional law, **21**
    chart-summary, 40
Constructive dismissal, 527, **528**–29
    "bad" behaviour by employer, 529
    fundamental term change, 529
    risks of, 529
Consumer debt, **642**
Consumer note, **626**
Consumer protection legislation, 174–75,
    571–72
Consumer, regulation and credit, 643–44
Contingency fee, **89**–90
    and United States litigation, 90
Contract law, **7**, 38
Contract(s), **99**, *see also* Agreement(s);
    Breach of Contract
    agreement to terminate, 196–97
    assignment, **197**–98
    breach of contract and termination,
        203–206

bribes, 182
capacity to contract, *see* Legal capacity
communication between parties, 102
condition, **203**
contrary to public policy, **182**
corporate liability, 374–75
duress and enforceability, 170
electronics and, *see* Technology
enforcing, 200–12
entire contract clause and, **146**
and equal bargaining power, **104**
exclusion/exemption clause and,
    203–204
express terms in, 141–46
fixed-/definite term-, **501**
force majeure clauses and, 200
fundamental breach, **203**–04
guarantee, **184**
illegal contract, **181**
implied terms in, **142**–46
improvident bargain, 173
independent legal advice, 172
innominate term, **203**
intention to, 132–33
internet contracts, 186–87
land, dealing with, 185
liability and, *see* Liability
liability clause and, 153–54
liquidated damages clause, **158**
minors and, 168–69
misrepresentation and, 175–77
mistake, **178**–80
for necessaries, 168
novation, **196**
objective standard test and, **103**
offer, **113**–20
ordinary commercial pressure vs.
    duress, 170
performance by others, 196
performing the, 105–107, 195–96
pre-incorporation, 375
privity of, 201–202
professional services and, 546, 547
proving on balance of probabilities,
    200–201
ratification and minors, 169
remoteness test for damage, 206–207
reputation management re
    performance, 106
risk management and professional
    services, 554
of sale, 568–78
for sale of goods, 186. *See also* Sale of
    goods; Sales and marketing
"seeing the big picture," 105–106
self-dealing, **380**
signature requirements, **184**
standard form, 104
Statute of Frauds and, 183–86
termination of, 195–200, 203–206

terms of, 141–58
and tort law, 234
unconscionable, **172**–75
undue influence and
    enforceability, **170**
unenforceable, 167–75
unequal relationships and, 168–75
variation of, 129
void, **167**
voidable, **167**
warranty, **203**
writing of, 183–84
Contracts of guarantee, 184
Contracts for necessaries, **168**
Contracts not to be performed within a
    year, 184
Contractual entrant, **268**
Contractual *quantum meruit*, **145**
Contractual rights, transfer of, 198
Contractual terms, *see* Term(s)
Contributory negligence, **248**
    defences to negligence action
      and, 248
    liability and, 230
Conversion right, **361**
Convictions, criminal law and, 225
Copyright(s), **441**–43
    "author" and, 441, 442
    collectives for enforcement and, 443
    exemptions/defences, 444–45
    fair dealing and, **444**–45
    fees and royalties, 443
    infringement of, 443
    Internet music swapping and, 445–46
    ownership and, 442
    moral rights and, **443**
    notice, 442
    registration process and, 442
    requirements for protection, 442
    rights under, 442–43
    SOCAN, 443
    software and, 441, 445
    term of protection, 442
    and "work," 441
    works of art and, 441
Copyright Licensing Agency, 443
Corporate indemnification, **388**
Corporate opportunity, **381**
Corporation(s), 332–36
    articles of, **358**
    bond, **360**
    bylaws and, **358**–59
    certificate of incorporation, 335
    closely held, **353**
    conversion right, **361**
    corporate forum, abuse of, Lord
      Black and, 354–55
    creditor protection and, 397–98
    criminal liability, 375–77
    debt financing and, 360

decision making and, 333–34
defined, 349–50
director(s), **332**
directors and officers, 378–88
directors'/officers' liability,
    see Director(s)
disclosure and, 363–64
equity financing, 360–61
federal vs. provincial, 352
financing, 360–64
financial liability, 332–333
governance, reforms, 379–80
identification theory, **374**
incorporation process and, 358–59
incorporator, **358**
indemnification and directors, 388
insider trading and, 365–66
liability and, 373–78
liability "lifting the corporate
    veil," **389**
limited liability, **333**
minority shareholders and derivative
    action remedy, **393**
mergers, acquisitions, takeovers and,
    competition rules, 603
name of, 356–57
NUANS report re name and, 357
officers and, *see* Director(s)
organizing, 358–59
perpetual existence and, 335
pre-incorporation issues, 351, **352**
profit sharing and, 333
profits and dividend(s), 333
pros and cons of, 335
public vs. private, 354
registration, 363
regulations and, 335
regulatory offence(s), **377**–78
securities legislation and, 351, **353,**
    360–61, 362–65
as separate legal entity, 350
share(s) 352–53, 356
shareholder, **332**
shareholder's liability, 388–90
and shareholder's rights, 391–92
share ownership, 356
sources of capital and, 334
stakeholders and, **351**
taxes and, 334–35
termination of, *see* Winding-up
transferability and, 334
widely held, **353**
winding-up, **398**
Costs
    monetary award, 87
    partial recovery of expense only, 87
    solicitor and client costs, **88**
    at trial, **87**
Counterclaim, **85**
Counteroffer, **119**

Courts, system of, in Canada, 29–30
    Federal Court of Canada, **30**
    inferior courts, 29–30
    judgment of, *see* Decision
    language and, 136
    lawsuits/litigation and, 82–89
    small claims court, **29**
    superior courts, 29
    Supreme Court of Canada, **30**
Credit, 640–52
    agreement, 646–47
    borrower's remedies and, 643–44
    and collateral, **641**
    collection agencies, 644
    consumer credit regulations
      and, 643–44
    consumer debt and, **642**
    default, **641**
    environment risk and, 648–49
    lender's remedies and, 650–51
    letter of, **642**
    priority among creditors, 649–50
    regulation of, 642–46
    risk, re international trade, 642
    security and, 647–48
    transactions and privacy, 645–46
    unsecured, 640
Credit bureau, **643**
Creditor protection, and corporations/
    directors/shareholders, 397–98
Creditor(s)
    and personal property security
      system, 649–50
    priority among, 649–50
    secured, **650**
    unsecured, 640
Criminal law, **38**
    "accused" in, 225
    actions and, 225–26
    burden of proof in, 226
    civil law vs., 226
    "complainant" in, 225
    convictions and, 225
    "defendant" in, 225
    tort law and, 225–27
    victims and, 225n
Criminal sanctions, 5
Customer(s)
    bank agreement with, **620**–23
    delinquent, 73
    dissatisfied, 73, 75–76
    duties of, with banks, 621–22
    relationship with banks, 622–23
    torts and, 274–80
Cyber-squatting, **498**

Damages
    aggravated, **233**
    breach of contract and, **206**–10
    cost of future care, 232

insurance and, 695–96
loss of future income, 232
pecuniary vs. non-pecuniary,
206–207, 231–**32**
punitive, **233**
pure economic loss, **247**
recovery of non-pecuniary, 207–208
remoteness and, 206–207
remoteness of, **257**
special, 232
thin skull rule and, 247
tort law and, 231–34
Damages for nonacceptance, 576–77
Data or screen scraping, **158**
Dealership, **341**
Debenture, **360**
Deceit, **221, 276**
Decision, **87**
appeal from, 88–89
binding, 78
factual findings and, 87
as judgment of court, 87
legal rules and, 87
and orders against a party, 87
Decision making
corporations and, 333–34
partnerships and, 320–22
sole proprietorships and, 318
Deductible, **688**
Defamation, **278**–79, 280
Default, **641**
Defence, **85**
and counterclaim, **85**
Defendant, **84**
Deficiency, **475, 651**
Derivative action, 393
Direct marketing 605–606, 607
online marketing, 606–607
telemarketing, **605**
Director(s), **332,** 377–88
avoiding liability, 387–88
conflict of interest, 380, 381
contract liability, 383–84
corporate opportunities and, 381
duties of, 378–84
duty of competence, 383
fiduciary duty of, 378–83
indemnification and liability, 388
liability, 384–88
self-dealing contracts and, **380**
statutory liabilities, 385–87
tort liability, 384–85
Discharge of bankruptcy, **676**
Discovery, **85**–86
and documents, 86
and electronic data, 86
purpose of, 86
time frame of, 86
Discrimination, 494, 495–97
adverse effects of, **495**

bona fide occupation requirement
(BFOR), **495**–96
defences to, 495–97
distribution practices and, 604–606
duty to accommodate, **496**
hiring practices and, 497
Meiorin case and, 496–97
systemic, **495**
workplace, 505
Dismissal
age and, 526
"bad" behaviour and, 529
character of employment and, 525–26
constructive, 527, **528**–29
duty to mitigate, 533–34
good faith obligation, *Wallace* case, 531
for just cause, **520**–24
length of service, and notice, 526
manner of, good faith/fair
dealing, 532
for non-cause or near cause, 524
with notice, 525–27
reasonable notice, **524**
reasonable notice period, factors,
525–27
severance package and, 535–36
similar employment availability
and, 526
wrongful, damages and, 532–34
wrongful suits, 530–35
Dispute resolution, 8
arbitration, **8**
alternative methods for, *see* Alternative
dispute resolution (ADR)
domain name, trademark dispute
and, 437–38
forms of, 91
litigation process and, 82–89
mechanisms for, 8
mediation, **8**
Dissent and appraisal right of
shareholders, **393**
Distinguishing guise, **435**
Distress, 82–4
Distribution
anticompetitive behaviour, **605**
direct marketing and, 604–606
discriminatory practices, 604–606
door-to-door selling, **605**
exclusive selling, **605**
mergers, acquisitions and takeovers
and, 603
multilevel marketing, **603**–604
online retailing, sales and, 606,
607–608
organization and, 603
pyramidal selling, **604**
refusal to deal, **605**
technology, online sales, 607
telemarketing and, **605**

tied selling, **605**
Distributor/dealership, **341**
Domain name, **438**
Domestic law, **37**
Door-to-door selling, **605**
Double ticketing, **602**
Drug testing, 508
Due diligence, **584**–85
Duress, **170**
Duty to accommodate, **496**
Duty of care, **242**–45
prima-facie, **243**
Duty of competence, director's, 383
Duty of confidentiality, **549**
Duty to disclose, **688**–89
Duty to mitigate, **209**

Easement, **461**
E-commerce
online sales and, 607–608
Electronic banking, 629–32
debit card, 633
failures in system and, 631
personal indentification number
(PIN), 631, 633
risks and loss, 632, 633
rules governing, 631
technology, electronic payments
systems, 631–32
E-mail
addresses as personal information, 115n
mass, *see* Spam
monitoring of, employment and,
511–12
Employee(s)
competing for, 499–500, 527
dismissal of, *see* Dismissal
and fiduciary obligations, 500
independent contractor vs., 490–91
restrictive covenants and, 500
rights of, 491, 493–97, 502–505
welfare issues and, 502–504
Employer(s)
alcohol-related liability and, 254
criminal liability for health/safety
violations, 504
workplace harassment policy and, 506
Employment, 489–512
bona fide occupation requirement
(BFOR), **495**
Canada Pension Plan, and, 504
collective agreement, **512**
collective bargaining, **512**
communications monitoring, 511–12
compensation and, 503–504
contract, content of, 501–502
contract, formation of, 498–500
contract, terms and conditions,
501–512
discrimination and, 494, 495–97

drug and alcohol testing, 508
duty to accommodate, 496–97
employee information and, 509–10
employee vs. independent
    contractor, test, 490–91
Employment Insurance Act, 504
equity legislation, **498**
fixed- (or definite) term contract
    of, **501**
grievance, arbitration and, 536–37
habitual neglect of duty and, **522**
harassment and, 505–506
hiring process and, **493**–98
hiring risks and, 492–93
human rights requirements, 493–98
incompetence and, 522
information, collection and
    dissemination, 509–10
Labour Relations Board, and, **512**
monitoring communications, 511–12
negligent hiring, 493
offer of, 499–500
pay equity and, **506**–507
penalties for discriminatory hiring
    practices, 497
privacy of employees, 509–12
privacy obligations, legislation
    and, 510
relationship, 491–93
safety and, 503–504
severance, and negotiation, 535
severance package, **535**
standards legislation, **502**–503
surveillance and searches, 510–11
terminating, 519–29
termination settlements, 535–36
union context of, 512
union, and discipline/discharge, 537
union, and seniority, 537
union, and termination, 536–37
and vicarious liability, **227**, 492–93
Workers' compensation legislation
    and, 503–504
workplace discrimination/
    harassment, 505–506
and wrongful dismissal, *see* Dismissal
Employment equity legislation, **498**
Employment relationship, implications of,
    491–92
Employment standards legislation,
    502–503
Endorsement, **626**
    special, **628**
Endorsement in blank, **628**
Entire contract clause, **146**
Environment
    contaminated land, 469–70
    credit and environmental risk, 648–49
Equitable remedies, 210–11
    interlocutory injunction, **211**

injunction, 210–11
    specific performance, 210
Equity financing, 360–61
Equity, **37**
    of redemption, **473**
    remedies, 37
    rules of, **37**
    wages and pay-, 498
Estate, **666**
Estoppel
    agency by, **297**–98
    promissory, **130**–31
Ethical considerations
    bankruptcy, 665–67
    banks' standard form guarantees
        and, 657
    bluffing and contract, 102–103
    breach of contract, 205
    business failure, 664–65
    competing for employees, 500, 527
    contracts of bailment, liability
        and, 412–14
    departing employee and, 500
    directors' duties, 382
    disciplining professionals, 526, 527
    employment standards, 505–506
    gas tanks, 56
    socially responsible investing, 361
    spamming, 115
    payday loans, 644–45
    whistleblowers and the law, 530
    whistleblower protection, re trade
        practices, 600
Ethics, business, 11
Evidence
    parole evidence rule, **147**–49
    rules re, 87
    at trial, 87
Exclusive jurisdiction, 24
Exclusive possession, **426**
Exclusive selling, **605**
Exemplary damages, *see* Punitive damages

Fair dealing, **444**–45
False imprisonment, **274**
False/misleading advertising, **582**–83
Federal Court of Canada, **30**
Fiduciary, **302**
    insurance agent as, 301
Fiduciary duty, **302**–304
    employment and, 500
    professional services and, 547–50
Financing lease, **417**
Financing statement, **649**
Fixed-/(or definite) term contract, **501**
F.o.b., **578**
Fixtures, **459**
Force majeure, 200
Foreclosure, **475**–76
Formal executive, **28**

Franchise, **336**
Fraud, 221
Fraudulent conveyances and
    settlements, 672–73
Fraudulent misrepresentation, 276
Fraudulent preference, **672**
Freedoms, *See also Canadian Charter of
    Rights and Freedoms*
    fundamental, 30
Frustration, contract and, 150
    force majeure clause, 200
Frustration of contract, **198**–200
Fundamental breach, **203**
Fundamental term, 528

General security agreement, **647**–48
Global business, *See* International business
Goods and services, *see also* Pricing;
    Product(s); Professional services
    advertising of, *see* Promotion
Governance
    corporate reforms, 379–80
    professions and, 555
Government, 21–22
    executive branch, 21, 28–29
    federal, law-making powers, 24
    formal executive, **28**
    judicial branch, 21–22, 29–30. *See
        also* Judiciary
    legislative branch, 21
    municipal, *see* Municipal government
    political executive, **28**
    provincial, law-making powers, 24
Government policy, **21**
Gratuitous bailment, **410**
Grievance process, **536**
Guarantee(s), **654**
    agreement, 654–55
    credit/loans and, 653–56
    personal, 653–57
Guarantor, **654**
    obligations, avoiding, 655–56
    subrogation and, **655**

Habitual neglect of duty, **522**
Harassment, workplace, 505–506
Holder, **625**
Holder in due course, **625**
Human rights, *see also Canadian Charter of
    Rights and Freedoms*
    hiring process and, 493–97
    laws about, 4
Human Rights Commission, **493**

Identification theory, **374**
Illegal contracts, **181**
Implied term(s)
    business efficiency doctrine, 143
    good faith and, 143–44

trade custom and, 144
    statutory requirement and, 145
Imprisonment, false, **274**–75
Improvident bargain, 173
Improvident sale, **653**
Income, future, 232
Incompetence, **522**
Incorporation, articles of, **358**
Incorporator, 358
Indefinite term contract, **501**
Indemnification, **388**
Indemnity, **692**
    and fire insurance policy, **692**
Independent contractor, **490**
Industrial designs, 434–35
    defined, 434
    infringement of, 435
    and proper marking, 435
    protection, 435
    registration process, 435
Inferior courts, **29**
    provincially appointed judges, 29
Information
    banks and, 621–22
    confidential, *see* Confidential business
        information
    employment and, 509–510
    shareholders' right to, **392**
Infringement
    actions re intellectual property, 452
    compulsory licensing, 450
    confidential business information,
        see Confidential busines
        information
Injunction, 37
    and breach of contract, 210–11
Injurious/malicious falsehood, **281**
Innkeeper(s), **412**
Innocent misrepresentation, 176
Insanity, *see also* Mental incapacity
    offer and, 120
Insider, **365**
Insider trading, **365**–66
Insolvency, **666.** *See also* Bankruptcy
    international business and, 673
Inspector, **671**
Insurable interest, **691**
Insurance, 687–703. *See also* Insurance
    contract; Risk retention
    auto, 695–97
    business interruption loss, 702
    claims processing and bad faith,
        704–705
    commercial and personal, 701–702
    comprehensive general liability, 699
    damages, injury and, 695–96
    environmental impairment, 703
    errors and omissions, 700–701
    exclusion clauses and, 693
    insured's remedies vs. broker, 703–704

insured's remedies vs. insurance
    company, 704–705
    key-person life, 703
    kinds of, 688, 694
    liability (casualty), 688
    life and disability, 688
    no-fault systems and, 696–97
    occupiers' liability, 699
    property, 688, 701
    risk management and, 694–95
    workers' compensation coverage, 697
Insurance adjuster, **704**
Insurance agent, **704**
Insurance broker, **703**
Insurance contract, 688–89, 691, 692,
    693, 694
    as contract of indemnity, 692
    duty to disclose and, **688**–89
    insurable interest and, 691
    as the policy, 693
    rider and, **693**
Insurance policy, **687,** 693
Insurance products, 694–97, 699–703
Insured, **687**
Insurer, **687**
    claims processing, bad faith and
        Whiten case, 704–705
    subrogation, right of, **692**–93
Intangible property, **405**
Intellectual property (IP), **427**–53
    acquisition and protection of, 450–53
    Anton Pillar order, **452**
    compulsory licensing, 450
    copyright, *see* Copyright
    forms of, 428
    industrial design(s), 434–35
    and licenses, **450**
    litigation and, 452
    patent(s), *see* Patents
    protection of, 451–53
    rights and, 428–44
    trademarks, *see* Trademark(s)
    treaties/conventions and, 453
    "use" requirement, 451
Interference with contractual
    relations, **278**
Interlocutory injunction, **211**
International law, **37**
International tort, **224**
Internet, *see* Technology
Invitation to treat, **113**
    advertisements as, 114
    human rights legislation and, 114**n**
    subjective intent irrelevant, 113
Invitee, **268**

Joint and several liability, 326
Joint liability, **321**
Joint tenancy, 460
Joint tort-feasors, **229**

Joint venture, **340**
Judges, 29. *See also* Courts; Judiciary
Judgment, *see* Decision(s)
Judgment debtor, **88**
Judgment enforcement, 88
    against losing party's assets, 88
Judiciary, **29**
    adjudication power, **29**
    judges, **29**
    and system of courts, 29–30
Jurisdiction, law-making, **23**–24
    exclusive, **24**
    federal powers, s.91, *Constitution Act,*
        1867, 24
    provincial powers, s.92, *Constitution*
        Act, 1867, 24
Just cause, **520**

Labour Relations Board, **512**
Land, *see* Real property
Land titles system, **462**–63
Landlord, **476**
    –tenant relationship, 476–77
Language, contracts and, 141
Lapse of offer,
    expiry date, 119
    after reasonable period of time, **119**
Law, **4**
    administrative, **39,** 40
    agency, **293**
    by-, *see* Bylaw(s)
    civil, *see* Civil law
    common, *see* Common law
    constitutional, **21**
    contract, 38
    criminal, **38**
    domestic, **37**
    employment, 489–90
    employment equity
        legislation, 498
    employment standards legislation,
        502–503
    international, **37**
    marketing, 567, **568,** 569–72
    private, **38**
    procedural, **37**
    public, **38**
    rules and principles of, 4–8
    securities, *see* Securities legislation
    sources of, 36–37
    statute, **23**
    substantive, **37**
    tax, 38
    tort, 221–23
Law firm, **64**
Lawyer, **64**
Lawsuit(s), *see also* Litigation process
    appeals, **88**–89
    appellant, **89**
    class-action suits, 83

decision and, 88
defendant, 84
discovery and, 85–86
enforcement, 88
formal stages of, 84–86
plaintiff, 84
pleadings and, 85
respondent, **89**
trial and, 87
Lease(s), **476**–81
bailment and, 416–17
chattel, **416**
distress remedy, 478
exclusive possession, **476**
periodic tenancy, 480
real property and, 476–78, 480–81
rights and obligations, 478
tenant, **476**
termination of, 480
terms of, commercial, 477–78
Legal capacity, **168**–70
common law provinces, 169
Infants Act, (B.C.), 169
mental incapacity, 169
Legal costs, *see* Costs
Legal risk management plan, **11, 50**–60
devising a plan, 54–57
evaluating risks, 52–53
identifying risks, 50–52
implementing a, 57–60
insurance, *see* Insurance
law firm, 64
lawyer, 64
legal services and, 63–65
risk prevention failure and, 62–63
Legal system, Canadian, **21**–22
Legislation
bankruptcy, business, 470
consumer protection, 571–72
employment equity, **498**
privacy, **282**
professions, governance structures
and, 555
sale of goods, 568–71
Legislative branch, **23**
federal,
House of Commons, 23
Parliament, 23
Senate, 23
House of Assembly (Nova Scotia), 23
Legislative Assembly, 23
provincial, 23
Letter of commitment, **647**
Letter of credit, **642**
Liability, **8**
accounting firms and, 553
agent to outsiders, 306
agent to principal, **307**
agent's tort liability, 307

bailment, *see* Bailment
contract, in agency relationship, 308
contractual terms and, **153–54**
and contributory negligence, 230
and corporate conduct, 390
corporations and, 373–78
corporations and criminal liability,
375–77
criminal, violations of health/safety
laws, 504
directors, avoiding personal, 388
directors, officers and, 384–86
directors, statutory-, 385–87
joint, **321**
joint and several, **326**
joint tort-feasors and, **229**
"lifting the corporate veil" and, **389**
limitation of liability clause, **154**
limited liability partnership (LLP) and,
occupiers', 267–69
partners and, 321–22, 325–26
primary, tort, 227
principal and, 305–307
product, 251–52
shareholder, 388–90
sole proprietorships and, 317–18
tort, 227
tort, agency relationships and, 307
undisclosed principal, **306**–307
unlimited, **318**
vicarious, **227,** 229
Libel, 279
Liberalism, **21**
and constitutional law, 21
political philosophy, 21
Licence, **268, 450**
Licensee, **268**
Lien, **419**
Limitation period, **84**
Limited liability, 333
Limited liability partnership (LLP), **331**–32
Limited partnership, **330**
Liquidated damages clause, **158**
Litigation, **7.** *See also* Lawsuit(s); Litigation
process
and BlackBerry patents, 431
contingency fees and, 89–90
and intellectual property, 452
Litigation process, 82–89. *See also*
Lawsuit(s)
Loan(s)
borrower's remedies and, 652–53
collateral and, **641**
default on, **641**
and general security agreement, **647**
lender's remedies, 650–51
personal guarantees and, 653–57
and security for, 647–48

Marketing law, **568**
advertising, *see* Advertising;
Promotion; Sales and marketing
Mediation, **8**
Mediator, **78**
Mental incapacity, *see* Legal capacity
Minors, contract enforceability
and, 168–69
Misrepresentation, 175, **176**–77
actionable, 176–77
and deceit, **276**
innocent, 176
negligent, *see* Negligent misstatement
remedies for, 176–77
rescission as remedy, **176**
Mistake(s), **178**–80
Money laundering, and banks, 621–22
Moral rights, **443**
Mortgage(s), **473**
deficiency, on foreclosure, **475**–76
equity of redemption, 473
foreclosure, **475**–76
life of, 474–75
terms of, 473–74
Mortgagee, **473**
remedies of, 475–76
Mortgagor, **473**
Municipal government, 28
bylaws and, **26**
city councils, 23
Multidisciplinary practice (MDP), **556**
Multilevel marketing, **603**–604

Necessaries, 168
Negligence, **222**
alcohol, service of, 252
causation, 246
contributory, **230**
contributory negligence defence, **248**
duty of care, **242**
law of, 241–42
misrepresentation, *see*
Misrepresentation; Negligent
misstatement
neighbour, **242**
prima facie duty of care, **243**
reasonable care, **241**
reasonable person standard of
care, **245**
remoteness of damage, **247**
standard of care, 245
strict liability and, 256
thin skull rule, **247**
voluntary assumption of risk, **248**
Negligence action
defences to, 248–49
steps to, 242–43
Negligent misstatement, **249**–50
and professional, **250**–51
and third party, **250**–51

Negotiable instrument, **623**–29
Negotiation, 74–77, **626**
    alternative dispute resolution and, 77
    defined, **75**
    ethical considerations and, 102
    failure of, 76–77
    insurers and, 75
    process, 75
    rules governing, 75
    by senior management, 76
Non-competition claims, enforceability,
    182–83
No fault insurance, and business, 696–97
Non-pecuniary damages, **232**
NUANS report, 357
Nuisance, 271–73

Objective standard test, **103**
Occupier, **267**
Occupiers' liability, 267–73
    at common law, 267–69
    contracted entrant, **268**
    ethical considerations and, 270–71
    insurance, 699
    invitee, **268**
    legislation, 269
    license, **268**
    nuisance and, **273**–73
    trespasser, **268**
    statutory, 269
Offer, **113**
    acceptance, **120**–25
    advertisements and, 114
    certainty of, 113
    communication of acceptance, 120–24
    counter-, **119**
    counteroffer, effect of, 119
    deadlines and, 118–19
    death and insanity of offeror, 120
    electronics and, 125–26
    goods display, not an offer, 114
    vs. invitation to treat, 113–14
    lapse of, 119
    offeree, **116**
    offeror, **116**
    option agreement, **119**
    rejection of, effect, 119
    revocation of, **118**
    termination of, 116–20
    unqualified acceptance of, 120
Offeree, **116**
Offeror, **116**
Officers (corporate), *see* Director(s)
Operating lease, **416**
Oppression remedy, **394**
Option agreement, **119**
Outsider(s), **292**
Ownership, *see* Personal property

Paralegal, **462**
Paramountcy, doctrine of, **25**–26
    and inoperative provincial law, 25
    non-applicability of, 25
Parole evidence rule, **147**–49
    limitations on operation, 148
Partner(s)
    and joint liability, **321**
Partnership, **320**–32
    agency, 323
    agency, *Partnership Act* and, 323–29
    agreement checklist, 324–25
    capital sources and, 323
    decision making, 320–32
    ending, dissolution of, 328–29
    existence of, 323–24
    liability, 321–22, 325–26
    liability shield of LLP, 331
    limited, **330**
    limited liability partnership, **331**–32
    partners relationship, 324
    and *Partnership Act*, 323–26, 328–29
    profit sharing, 322
    pros and cons of, 329
    regulations, 329
    relations of partnership, 324
    relations of partners to
        outsiders, 325–26
    risk management, 330
    source of capital, 322
    taxes and, 323, 329
    transferability, 323
Partnership agreement checklist, 324–25
Patent agent, **433**
Patent protection, 430, 433
Patents, **428**–29
    applications and, 433–34
    business methods and, 429
    claims, **433**
    defined, 429
    inventions and, 429
    of life forms, 429–30
    patentability, requirements for, 432
    protection, exclusion from, 430
    revocation and "use," 451
    specifications, **433**
Pay equity, **506**–507
Pecuniary damages, **232**
Periodic tenancy, **480**
Personal care power of attorney, 295
Personal guarantees, 653–57
Personal property, **405**–21
description of, 405
    bailment, *see* Bailment
    intangible property, **405**
    leases and, *see* Lease(s)
    obligations and, 407
    ownership and, 406–408
    possession and, 406–408

    rights and, 407–408
    tangible property, **405**
Petition into bankruptcy, **669**
PIPEDA legislation, *see* Privacy
Pistol duel, 9
Plaintiff, **84**
Pleadings, 85
    service of, 85
Political executive, **28**
Power of attorney,
    general, 295
    for personal care, 295
    specific, 295
Practice, professional, *see* Professional
    services
Precedent, **36**
    rules governing application, 36
Predatory pricing, **598**–99
Pre-emptive right, **392**
Preferred creditors, **674**
Preferred share, **391**
Premium, **687**
Price discrimination, 597–98
Price maintenance, **599**
Pricing
    bargain prices, 600–601
    bid rigging and, **597**
    conspiracies, 596–97
    double ticketing, **602**
    ethical considerations, whistleblower
        protection, 600
    multilevel marketing, **603**–604
    practices, 596–602
    predatory, **598**
    price discrimination and, **597**–98
    price maintenance and, **599**
    sales and bargains, 600–601
    scanners, retailers' code, 602
    seller's practices, and consumers,
        600–602
Principal, **291**
    -agency relationships, 292
    duties of, re agent, 305
    -outsider relationship, 292
    liability of, to outsider, 305
    undisclosed, liability of, **306**
Privacy
    credit transactions, legislation and,
        645–46
    employer's obligations, PIPEDA
        legislation, 509–12
    and workplace, 509, 510, 512
Private law, **38**
Privilege, **549**
    qualified, **279**
Privity of contract, 201–202
Procedural law, **37**
Product(s), 578–82, *see also* Promotion
    caveat emptor, **568**

complaints and defences,
    re *Competition Act*, 584–85
complaints and defences, re mis-
    leading advertising, 584–85
defamation and, **281**
design and manufacture of, 579–80
labelling and, 580–81
liability; *see* Product liability
packaging and, 580
performance claims and, *Competition
    Act*, 585–86
prepackaged goods, labeling of,
    580–81
prohibited offences, and promotion
    of, **584**
promotion, *see* Promotion
sales and marketing, principles, 578
sale and terms relating to, 568
tests and testimonials, 586–87
unfair practices, **587**
warnings, 581
Product liability, **251**
    and negligence, 251–52
Product licensing, **341–42**
Professional, **250,** 545
Professional services
    businesses and, 544–47
    confidentiality, duty of, **549**
    disciplining professionals, 556
    ethical considerations and, 557
    ethical obligations and 544, 545, 557
    fiduciary duties, 547–50
    governance structures and, 555
    hiring, in-house, 545–46
    incorporation and, 554
    insurance and, 554
    limited liability partnerships (LLPs)
        and, 554
    multidisciplinary practice (MDP)
        and, **556**
    privilege and, **549**
    professional practice and, 555–56
    relationships and obligations, 545
    responsibilities to clients, 546–50
    responsibilities in contract, 546–47
    responsibility to third parties, 550–53
    responsibility in tort, 550–53
    and retainer, **546**
    risk management and, 554–55
Professions, *see* Professional services
Progressive discipline policy, **521**
Promise(s)
    enforceable without consideration,
        129–30
    gratuitous, 127
Promise under seal, 129–30
Promissory estoppel, **130–31**
Promissory note, 623
Promotion, 582–87
    advertising, false or misleading,
        582–85

bait and switch, and, **587**
Competition Act, overview, 583–84
due diligence and, **584**
industry standards, legislation
    and, 582
selling practices, 587
tests and testimonials, 586–87
unfair practices, 587
Proof, burden of, **87**
Proof of claim, **673**
Proposal, **666**
Prospectus, **363**
Proxy, **391**
Public law, **38**
    administrative court and, 38
    constitutional law, 38
    criminal law, 38
    tax court and, 38
Public policy, **182**
Punitive damages, **233–34**
    exemplary damages, **233**
    U.S. vs. Canadian, 233–34
Pure economic loss, **247**
Pyramid selling, **604**

Qualified privilege, **279**
Quantum meruit, 37
    contractual, **145**
    restitutionary, **211**
Québec Civil Code, **39**

Ratification, agency creation by, 300
Real estate agents, 299–300
Real estate, *see* Real property
Real property, **459**–81
    acquisition of ownership, 464–71
    agreement of purchase and sale,
        466–67
    buyers and sellers, 465–66
    division of ownership and, 460
    easement, **451**
    environmental, contaminated land,
        469–70
    fixtures, **459**
    incomplete transactions of, 471
    interests in land and, 460
    investigation of title to, 468–69
    joint tenancy, **460**
    landlord–tenant relationship, 476–77
    land titles system, **462–63**
    lease and time division of, 460
    leases and, **476–81**
    mortgages, 472–76
    ownership, 455–61
    ownership limits, 461–62
    purchasing transaction and, 464–68
    real estate transaction and, 470–71
    registration of ownership and, 462–63
    registry system, **462**
    restrictions, *see* Ownership limits

restrictive covenants, **461**
stages in land transactions, 466–71
title search, **468**
Reasonable care, **241**
Reasonable notice, **524**
Reasonable notice period, dismissal,
    524–27
Reasonable person, **245**
Receiver, **651**
Receiving order, **670**
Rectification, 37
Refusal to deal, **605**
Registration, re security interest, **649**
Registry system, **462**
Regulation of banking, 620
Regulations, **29**
    cabinet, made by, 29
    consumer credit and, 643–44
    corporations and, 335
    by lieutenant governor in council, 29
    by governor general in council, 29
    partnerships and, 329
    sole proprietorships and, 305
Regulatory offence(s), **377–78**
Remedies
    breach of contract and, 206–15
    equitable, 210–11
    insured's vs. insurance broker, 703–704
    insured's vs. insurance company,
        704–705
    loans and, 650–53
    for misrepresentation, 176–77
    restitutionary, 211
    shareholder(s)', 392–94, 396
    torts and, 231–34
Remoteness of damage, **247**
    foreseeable loss requirement, 247
    thin skull rule, 247
Reputation management, 106
Rescission, 37
    equitable remedies and, 194
Respondent, **89**
Restitutionary remedies, 211
Restrictive covenant, **461–62**
Restrictive endorsement, **628**
Retainer, **546**
Reviewable matters, **584**
Reviewable transaction, 672
Rider, **693**
Risk(s), *see also* Risk Management; Legal
    risk management plan
    contract formation and managing, 151
    in just cause dismissals, 524
    legal, in marketing, 608–609
    management by shareholders'
        agreement, 396–97
    practices to minimize re marketing,
        609–610
    and real property, 481
    tort risk, managing, 234
    voluntary assumption of, **248**

Risk avoidance, **54**
Risk management, *see also* Risk(s)
    breach of contract and, 212
    and commercial torts, 282–83
    contract unenforceability, 187
    personal property, 421
    and professional services, 554
    retail theft and fraud, 275
    service of alcohol and, 254
Risk prevention failure, 62–63
Risk reduction, **54**
Risk retention, **55–56**
Risk transference, **55**
Royal prerogative, **36**
Rules of construction, **141**
    plain meaning rule, 142

Sale of goods, *see also* Pricing; Sales and
    marketing
    bill of lading, **577**
    c.i.f., **577**
    c.o.d., **578**
    conditions, 570
    contracts for, 186
    f.o.b., **578**
    legislation re, 568–71
    nonacceptance, damages for, **576–77**
    remedies, 571
    specific goods, **575**
    stoppage in transitu, **577**
    title transfer and, rules about, 574–78
    unascertained goods, **575**
    warranties and, 570
Sales agency, **341**
Sales and marketing
    contract of sale, 568–71
    delivery of goods, 577–78
    distribution, *see* Distribution
    marketing law and, 567–68
    multilevel marketing, *see*
        Distribution; Pricing
    pricing, *see* Pricing
    product and, *see* Product(s); Promotion
    sale of goods, *see* Pricing; Sale
        of goods
    transfer of title in goods, *see* Sale
        of goods
Secured creditor, 650
    action vs. specific assets, 669
Securities, *see also* Bond; Share(s)
    disclosure, 363
    insider trading, 365–66
    Internet and, 362
    legislation, 362
    prospectus and, **363**
    regulators and, 363
    secondary market liability, 363–64
    registration, 363
Securities legislation, 326
Self-dealing contract, **380**

Selling practices, 587
Serious misconduct, **521**
Settlement, **672**
    negotiated vs. lawsuit, 84–85
    package, and release, **536**
Severance package, 535
Severance pay, **536**
Share(s), 352–54, 356, 391, 392
    availability of, 353–54
    classes of, 352–53
    common, **391**
    insider trading of, **365**
    ownership of, 356
    preferred, **391**
    and pre-emptive rights, **392**
    securities legislation and, **353**
Shareholder(s), **332**
    common share, **391**
    derivative action and, **393**
    dissent and appraisal right and, **393**
    information rights and, **392**
    liability and, 388–90
    liability, and lifting the corporate veil
        doctrine, 389
    oppression remedy and, **394**
    pre-emptive right and, 392
    preferred shares and, **391**
    proxy and, **391**
    remedies, 392–394, 396
    rights of, 391–92
    voting rights of, 391
Shareholders' agreement, **396**
    unanimous (USA), 396–97
Shelf company, **357**
Small claims court, 29
    monetary limit, 29
Sole proprietorship, **317–320**
    capital sources and, 318
    decision making, 318
    financial liability of, 317–18
    name of, 319
    profit sharing and, 318
    pros and cons of, 320
    regulations and, 319
    taxes and, 319
    transferability and, 319
    unlimited liability, **318**
Solicitor and client costs, **88**
Sources of law, 36–37
    common law, **36**
    precedent, **36**
    equity, **37**
    royal prerogative, **37**
Spam, 3
    Internet and, 115–16
Special damages, 232
Special endorsement, **628**
Specific goods, **575**
Specifications, **433**
Specific performance, 37, 210

Stakeholder(s), **351**
Standard form contract(s), 154–55
    inequality of bargaining power, 104
Standard of care
    reasonable person, and
        negligence, 245
Statement of claim, **21**
Statute law, **23**
    federal vs. provincial, 23–24
    and jurisdiction, **23**
Statute of Frauds, 183–86
Stop payment, **627**
Stoppage in transitu, **577**
Strategic alliance, **340**
Strict liability, **256**
    international EU trading partners
        and, 256
Subrogation, **655, 692–93**
Substantive law, **37**
Superior court, **29**
    federally appointed judges and, 29
    monetary jurisdiction, 29
    and procedure, 29
Supreme Court of Canada, **30**
Systemic discrimination, **495**

Tangible property, **405**
Taxes
    corporations and, 334–35
    partnerships and, 323, 329
    property, 436
    sole proprietorship and, 319–320
Technology
    browse-wrap agreement and, 157–58
    click-wrap agreement and, 157
    defamation on the Internet, 280–81
    domain name and trademark dispute,
        437–38
    and downloaders, 446
    electronic agents, 309
    electronic cash, payments systems
        and, 631–32
    electronic land registration, 463–64
    electronic signatures for contracts,
        184–85
    Internet music swapping, 445–446
    Internet securities activity, regulation
        of, 363
    online sales, 607–608
    Ontario *Electronic Commerce Act*
        and, 309
    shrink-wrap agreement and, 156–57
    and uploaders, 446
    Y2K problem and insurance, 700
Telemarketing, **605**
Tenant, **476**
Term(s)
    condition precedent, **152**
    condition subsequent, **151**
    contracts and, 141–58

express, **141**–42
implied, **143**–44
liquidated damages clause, **158**
risk management and contract,
150–52
Termination of contracts, 195–200
by agreement, 196–97
by breach of contract, 203–06
by frustration, **198**–200
and frustration of contractual rights,
197–98
by performance, 195–96
by transfer of contractual rights,
197–98
Third parties, 250
professional services and, 550–53
Tied selling, **605**
Tort(s), **221**. *see also* Tort law
assault, **224**
assault and battery, 275–76
battery, **224**
business to business, 276–81
and business operations, 274–82
as civil action vs. criminal
prosecution, 227
contract and, 234
corporate liability, 374
criminal law and, 225
customers and, 274–80
deceit, **276**
defamation, 278–79, 280
injurious falsehood, **281**
interference with contractual relations, **278**
liability, agency and, 307
negligence, *see* Negligence
nuisance, **271**, 273
passing off, 276–77
professional responsibility in, 550–53
and property use, 267–73
Trademarks Act and passing off, 277
trespass, 273–74
trespass to land, **221**
Tort-feasor, **222**
Tort law, 38, 221–23, *see also* Tort(s)
actions and, 225–26
actions and deceit, **221**
balance of probabilities proof, **226**
burden of proof, 226

damages in, 231–34
employment and, 227, 229
fraud, **221**
intentional tort, **224**
joint tort-feasors, **229**
liability, 227
negligence, **222**
tort-feasor, **222**
workers' compensation legislation
and, **230**
Tort risk
managing, 234
vicarious liability doctrine, 234
Trademark(s), 435–36, 438–39, 440–41
and abandonment, 451
common law and, 436
and cyber-squatting, **438**
defined, 435–36
and descriptive words, 438–39
disclaimer and descriptive
words, 439n
distinctiveness and, 438
distinguishing guise, **435**
international rights, *Paris
Convention*, 440n
marking for a registered, 441
marking for unregistered marks, 441
ownership rules, 438
period of protection, 441
prohibited, 439n
protection and, 440–41
registrability and, 438–39
registration process and protection,
440–41
unregistered, 441
"use" in Canada, 438
"use" rules, 438
Trade name, **436**
Trade secret, 446n
Transfer of contractual rights, 197–98
Transportation, 419. S*ee also* Bailment
Treaty, **28**
as international law, 28
ratifying, **28**
Trespass, 273–74
Trespasser, **268**
Trespass to land, **221**

Trial, **87**
burden of proof and plaintiff, **87**
costs, **87**
decision after, 87
evidence, **87**
submissions by parties, 87
Trial by ordeal, 9
Tribunals, 40
Trustee in bankruptcy, **665**

Unanimous shareholders' agreement
(USA), 396–97
Unascertained goods, **575**
Unconscionable contract, 172–75
Undisclosed principal, **306**
Undue influence, **170**–71
Unfair practices, 174–75, **587**
Union(s)
certification, 512
collective agreement, **512**
collective bargaining, 512
grievance and arbitration re termina-
tion, **536**–37
labour relations board and, **512**
Unjust enrichment, **211**
Unlimited liability, **318**
Unsecured creditor, **640**

Vicarious liability, **227,** 229
off-duty tort, 228
significant connection test, 227, 229
Vicarious performance, **196**
Void contract, **167**
Voidable contract, **167**
Volenti non fit injuria,
see Voluntary assumption of risk
Voluntary assumption of risk, **248**

Warehouseman, **412**
Warranty, **203**
Widely held corporation, **353**
Willful disobedience, **522**–23
Winding up, **398**
Workers' compensation legislation, **230**
Workers' compensation coverage, 503, 697
Workplace privacy, *see* Privacy
Wrongful dismissal, *see* Dismissal